Street by Street

HERTFORDSHIRE

PLUS BARNET, CHALFONT ST PETER, HARLOW, LUTON, STANSTED AIRPORT, WALTHAM ABBEY

Enlarged Areas Hemel Hempstead, St Albans, Stevenage, Watford

C000130403

Ist edition May 2001

© Automobile Association Developments Limited 2001

This product includes map data licensed from Ordnance Survey® with the permission of the Controller of Her Majesty's Stationery Office. © Crown copyright 2000. All rights reserved. Licence No: 399221.

All rights reserved. No part of this publication may be reproduced, stored in a retrieval system, or transmitted in any form or by any means– electronic, mechanical, photocopying, recording or otherwise – unless the permission of the publisher has been given beforehand.

Published by AA Publishing (a trading name of Automobile Association Developments Limited, whose registered office is Norfolk House, Priestley Road, Basingstoke, Hampshire, RG24 9NY. Registered number 1878835).

Mapping produced by the Cartographic Department of The Automobile Association.

A CIP Catalogue record for this book is available from the British Library.

Printed by G. Canale & C. S.P.A., Torino, Italy

The contents of this atlas are believed to be correct at the time of the latest revision. However, the publishers cannot be held responsible for loss occasioned to any person acting or refraining from action as a result of any material in this atlas, nor for any errors, omissions or changes in such material. The publishers would welcome information to correct any errors or omissions and to keep this atlas up to date. Please write to Publishing, The Automobile Association, Fanum House, Basing View, Basingstoke, Hampshire, RG21 4EA.

Ref: MX116

Key to map pages	ii-iii
Key to map symbols	iv-1
Enlarged scale pages	2-13
Street by Street	14-207
Index – towns & villages	208
Index – streets	209-235
Index – featured places	235-240

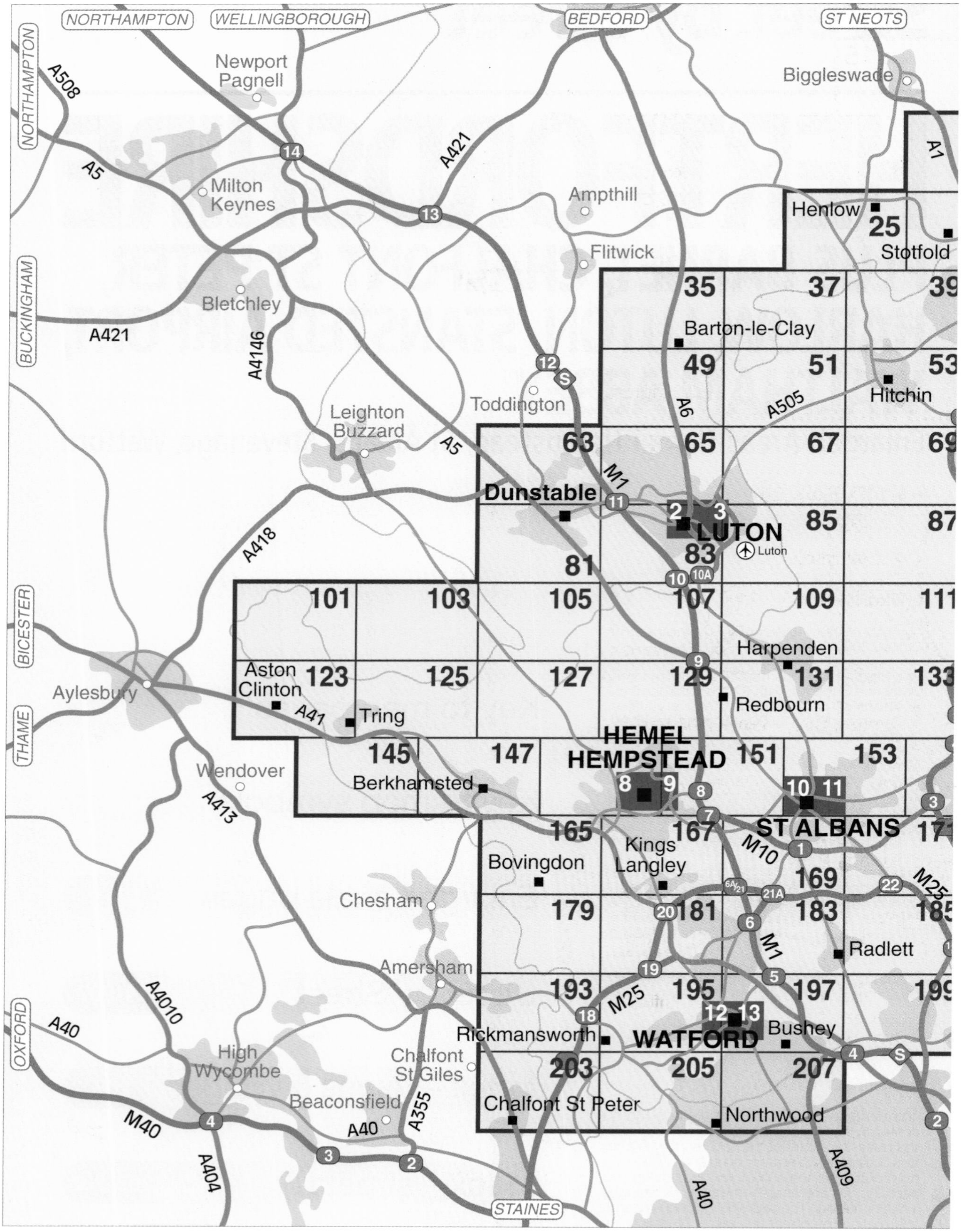

NORTHAMPTON WELLINGBOROUGH BEDFORD ST NEOTS

NORTHAMPTON
A508
A5
Newport Pagnell
14
A421
Milton Keynes
13
Bletchley
A421
A4146
BUCKINGHAM
A418
BICESTER
Aylesbury
THAME
A413
Wendover
A4010
OXFORD
A40
M40
4
High Wycombe
Beaconsfield
A404
A40
3
2
A355
Chalfont St Giles

Ampthill
Flitwick
Leighton Buzzard
A5
12 S
Toddington
Dunstable
M1
11
A418
Aston Clinton
A41
Tring
145
Berkhamsted
147
Bovingdon
Chesham
Amersham
Rickmansworth
193
M25
18
195
Chalfont St Peter
203
205
STAINES

Biggleswade
A1
Henlow
25
Stotfold
35 37 39
Barton-le-Clay
49 51 53
A6 A505 Hitchin
63 65 67 69
2 3 LUTON 85 87
83
✈ Luton
10 10A
101 103 105 107 109 111
Harpenden
9
123 125 127 129 131 133
Redbourn
HEMEL HEMPSTEAD 151 153
8 9 8 10 11
7 ST ALBANS 17
165 167 M10 1
Kings Langley 169
179 20 181 6A/21 183 185
6 21A
19 M1 Radlett
5
12 13 197 199
WATFORD Bushey 4 S
207
Northwood 2
A40 A409

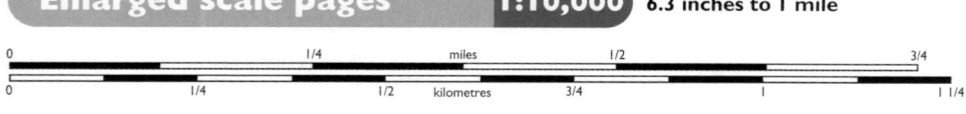

0   1/4   miles   1/2   3/4
0   1/4   1/2   kilometres   3/4   1   1 1/4

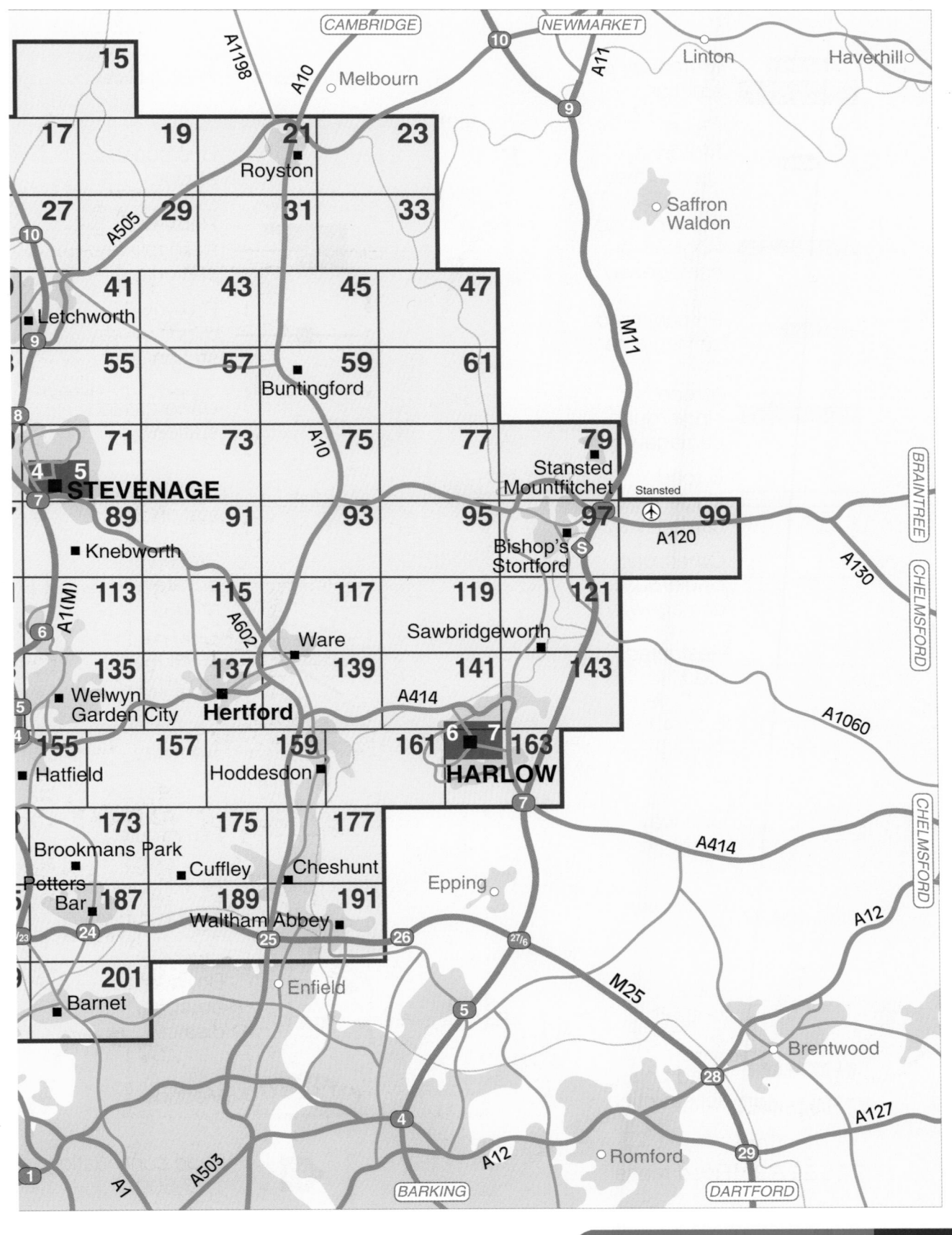

3.6 inches to 1 mile   **Scale of main map pages   1:17,500**

Symbol	Description	Symbol	Description
Junction 9	Motorway & junction	P+🚌	Park & Ride
Services	Motorway service area	🚌	Bus/coach station
	Primary road single/dual carriageway		Railway & main railway station
Services	Primary road service area		Railway & minor railway station
	A road single/dual carriageway	⊖	Underground station
	B road single/dual carriageway	⊖	Light railway & station
	Other road single/dual carriageway	+++++++++++	Preserved private railway
	Restricted road	LC	Level crossing
	Private road	•–•–•–•–	Tramway
← ←	One way street	------------	Ferry route
	Pedestrian street	....	Airport runway
	Track/ footpath	–·–·–·–·–	Boundaries- borough/ district
■■■■■■■■ ■■■■■■■■	Road under construction	\\\\\\|||///	Mounds
[= = = = ={	Road tunnel	**93**	Page continuation 1:17,500
P	Parking	**7**	Page continuation to enlarged scale 1:10,000

	River/canal lake, pier			Toilet with disabled facilities
	Aqueduct lock, weir			Petrol station
465 ▲ Winter Hill	Peak (with height in metres)		PH	Public house
	Beach		PO	Post Office
	Coniferous woodland			Public library
	Broadleaved woodland		*i*	Tourist Information Centre
	Mixed woodland			Castle
	Park			Historic house/ building
	Cemetery		Wakehurst Place NT	National Trust property
	Built-up area		M	Museum/ art gallery
	Featured building		†	Church/chapel
	City wall			Country park
A&E	Accident & Emergency hospital			Theatre/ performing arts
	Toilet			Cinema

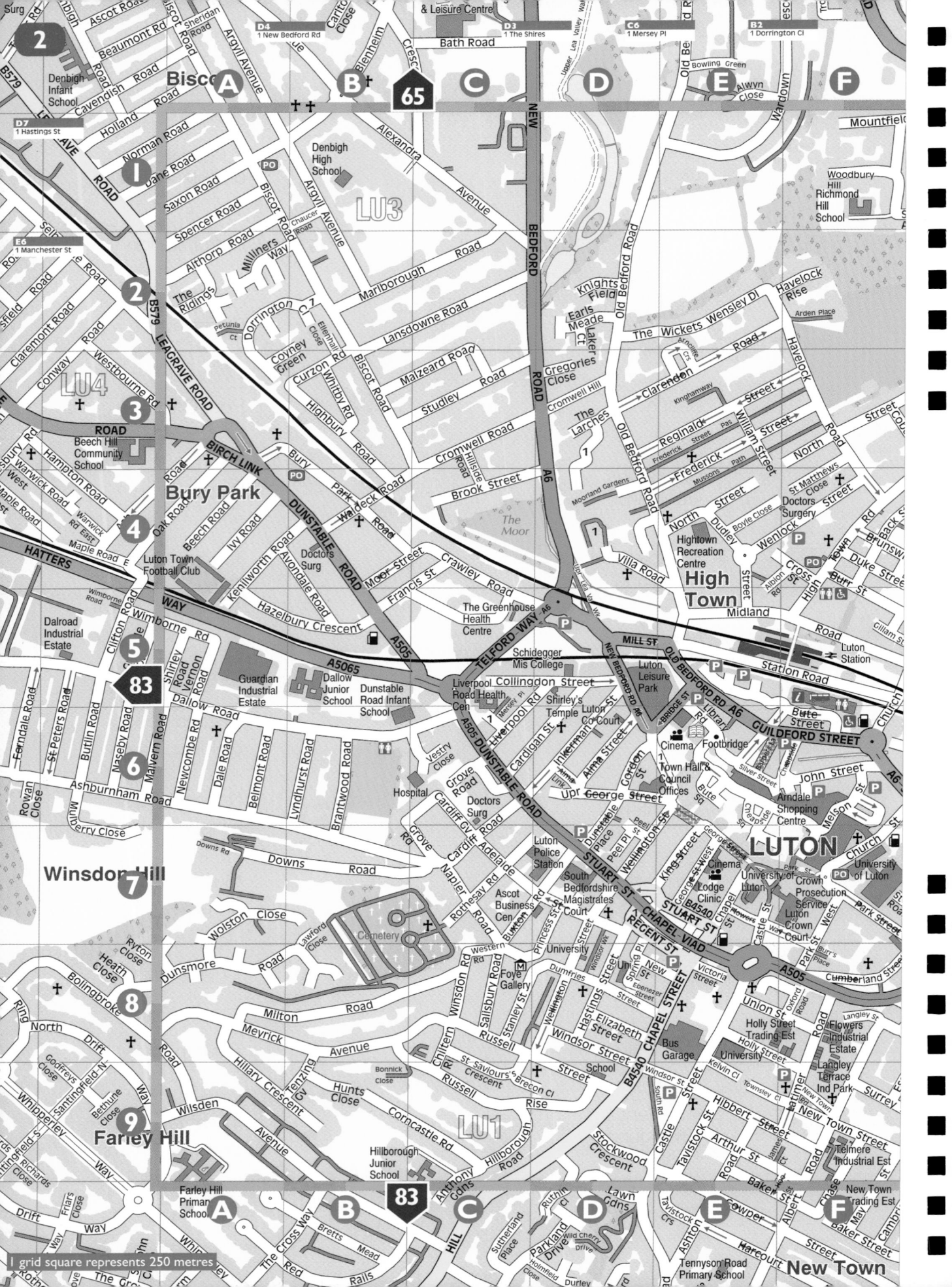

2
65
83
83
A
B
C
D
E
F
1
2
3
4
5
6
7
8
9
D4 1 New Bedford Rd
D3 1 The Shires
C6 1 Mersey Pl
B2 1 Dorrington Cl
D7 1 Hastings St
E6 1 Manchester St
Bath Road
& Leisure Centre
Ascot Road
Beaumont Rd
Sheridan Road
Biscot Road
Argyll Avenue
Carlton Close
Blenheim Crescent
Denbigh Infant School
Cavendish Road
Holland Road
Norman Road
Dane Road
Saxon Road
Spencer Road
Althorp Road
Milliners Way
Chaucer Road
Denbigh High School
Alexandra Avenue
LU3
Marlborough Road
Lansdowne Road
The Ridings
Petunia Ct
Dorrington Cl
Ellenhall Close
Coyney Green
Curzon Rd
Whitby Rd
Biscot Road
Malzeard Road
Studley Road
Highbury Road
Cromwell Road
Gregories Close
Cromwell Hill
Brook Street
Hillside Road
The Moor
NEW BEDFORD ROAD
A6
Upper Lea Valley Walk
Old Bedford Road
Bowling Green
Alwyn Close
Wardown
Mountfield
Woodbury Hill
Richmond Hill School
Havelock Rise
Arden Place
Knights Field
Earls Meade
Laker Ct
The Wickets
Wensley Dl
Arncliffe Crs
Clarendon Road
Kinghamway
Street
Havelock Road
The Larches
Reginald Street
Frederick Street
Frederick Pas
William Street
Mussons Path
North Street
Moorland Gardens
St Matthews Close
Doctors Surgery
Dudley Street
Boyle Close
Wenlock Street
Hightown Recreation Centre
High Town
Villa Road
Upr Lea Va Wk
Cross St
Albion Rd
High Town Rd
Burr St
Duke Street
Brunswick
Back St
Midland Road
Luton Station
Station Road
Gillam St
Mill St
Old Bedford Rd A6
Luton Leisure Park
Guildford Street
Bute Street
Church
Library Rd
Bridge St
Footbridge
Cinema
Town Hall & Council Offices
Silver Street
Cheapside
John Street
Arndale Shopping Centre
Melson St
Bute Sq
LUTON
University of Luton
Crown Prosecution Service
Luton Crown Court
Park St West
Park Street
Cumberland Street
A505
Chapel Viad
Stuart St
Regent St
B4540
Chapel Street
George Street
King Street
George St West
Lodge Clinic
Wellington St
Peel Pl
Dunstable Place
Upr George Street
Gordon St
Alma Street
Inkerman Street
Alma Link
Cardigan St
Liverpool Rd
Luton Co Court
Shirley's Temple
Collingdon Street
Schidegger Mis College
Telford Way
The Greenhouse Health Centre
Liverpool Road Health Cen
Mersey Pl
Dunstable Road
Luton Police Station
South Bedfordshire Magistrates Court
Ascot Business Cen
Buxton Rd
Princess St
University
Windsor Wk
Spring Pl
New St
Ebenezer Street
Dumfries Street
Hastings Street
Elizabeth Street
Windsor Street
Wellington St
School
Bus Garage
Victoria Street
Union St
Oxford Road
Holly Street Trading Est
Holly Street
Langley St
Flowers Industrial Estate
Langley Terrace Ind Park
Kelvin Cl
Townsley Cl
Latimer Rd
Hibbert Street
New Town Street
Surrey St
Telmere Industrial Est
Arthur St
Tavistock St
Castle Street
James St
Baker St
Chase St
New Town Trading Est
Cowper St
Albert Rd
Baker Street
Cambridge
Harcourt Street
Tennyson Road Primary School
New Town
Tavistock Crs
Ashton Rd
Lawn Gdns
Ruthin Cl
Parkland Drive
Wild Cherry Drive
Holmfield Close
Durley
Sutherland Place
Hill
Anthony Gdns
Hillborough Road
Hillborough Junior School
LU1
Stockwood Crescent
Concastle Rd
Rise
Brecon Cl
St Saviour's Crescent
Russell Street
Chiltern Rd
Salisbury Road
Winsdon Rd
Stanley St
Foyer Gallery
Western Rd
Rothesay Road
Napier Rd
Adelaide
Cardiff Road
Cardiff Gv
Grove Road
Grove Rd
Doctors Surg
Hospital
Vestry Close
Brantwood Road
Lyndhurst Road
Belmont Road
Dale Road
Newcombe Rd
Dallow Road
Dallow Junior School
Dunstable Road Infant School
Guardian Industrial Estate
Shirley Road
Vernon Road
Hazelbury Crescent
Francis St
Moor Street
Crawley Road
Waldeck Road
Bury Park Road
Avondale Road
Kenilworth Road
Doctors Surg
A505
A5065
Hatters Way
Birch Link
Dunstable Road
Ivy Road
Beech Road
Oak Road
Bury Park
Luton Town Football Club
Wimborne Road
Wimborne Rd
Clifton Road
Dalroad Industrial Estate
Maple Road
Warwick Rd East
Warwick Road
Hampton Road
Beech Hill Community School
Road
LU4
Westbourne Rd
Conway Road
Claremont Road
B579
Leagrave Road
Malvern Road
Naseby Road
Butlin Road
St Peters Road
Ferndale Road
Rowan Close
Mulberry Close
Ashburnham Road
Downs Rd
Downs Road
Winsdon Hill
Wolston Close
Lawford Close
Cemetery
Dunsmore Road
Ryton Close
Heath Close
Bolingbroke Road
Milton Road
Meyrick Avenue
Hillary Crescent
Tenzing Gv
Hunts Close
Bonnick Close
Wilsden Avenue
Farley Hill
Farley Hill Primary School
Whipperley Way
Whipperley Ring
North Drift Way
Godfreys Close
Santingfield N
Bethune Close
Richards Close
Friars Close
Drift Way
The Cross Way
Bretts Mead
Red Rails
1 grid square represents 250 metres

G4 1 Welbeck Rd
J6 1 Hart Hill La
K1 1 Turners Rd South
66
84
Luton Co-operative Sports Club
Moreton Park Industrial Est
Moreton Park Ind. Estate
Ramridge Junior School
Ramridge Infant School
Hart Hill
LU2
The Business Centre
Oxen Industrial Estate
Infant School
Hart Hill Junior School
Abbeygate Business Cen
Wenlock C of E School
Crawley Green Primary School
Cemetery
Windmill Trading Estate
Recreation Ground
Park Town
Luton Airport Parkway Station
Barratt
School
Vauxhall Way
A505
Hitchin Road
Crawley Green Road
Kimpton Road
Windmill Rd
Gipsy Lane
Crescent Road
Hart Lane
Abbots Wood Road
Turners Road
Hartsfield Road
Somerset Avenue
Saywell Road
Eaton Valley Road
Devon Road
Airport Way
Park Street
Osborne Road
River Lea or Lee

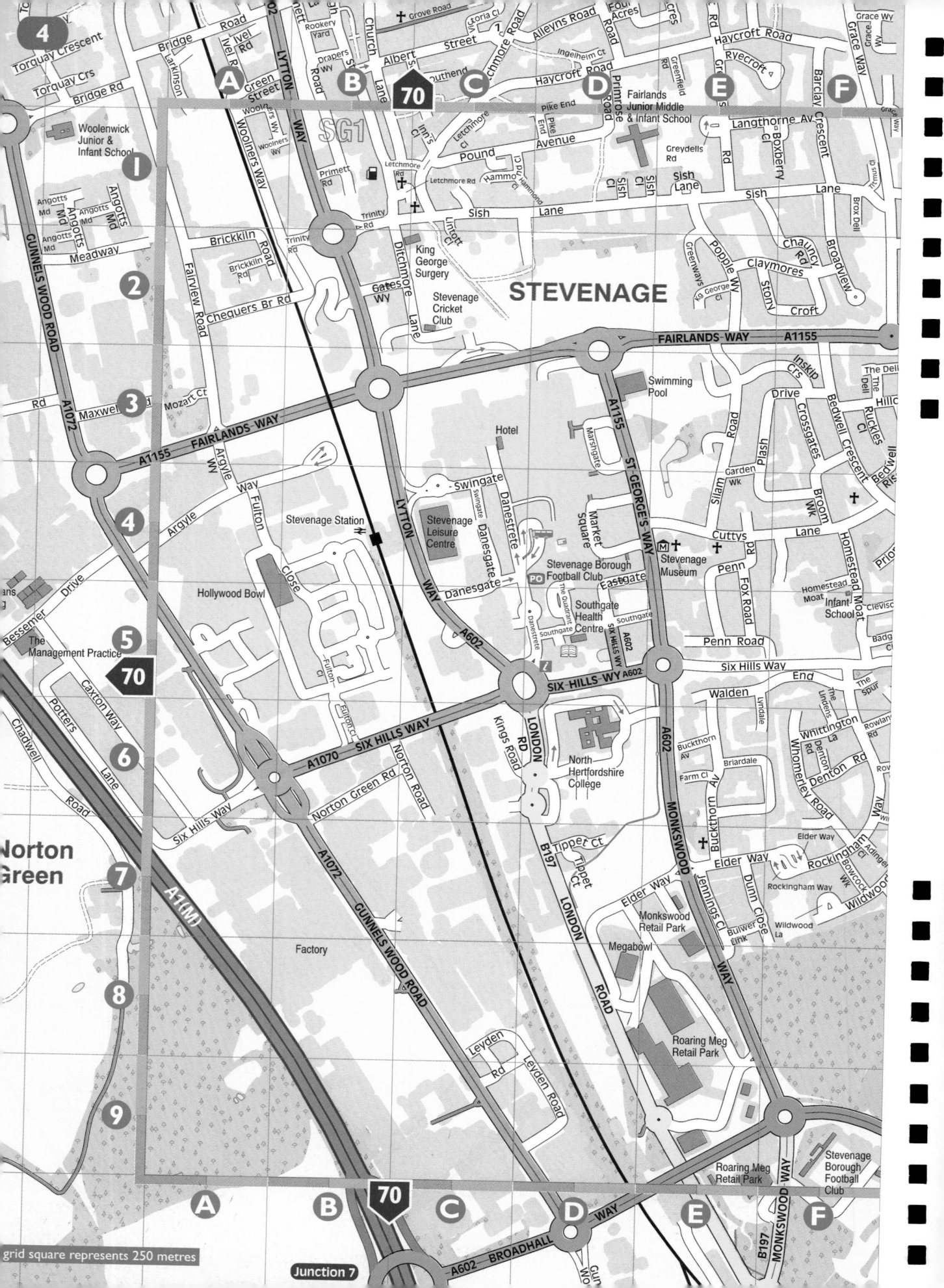
STEVENAGE
SG1
70
A
B
C
D
E
F
1
2
3
4
5
6
7
8
9
Norton Green
FAIRLANDS WAY A1155
LYTTON WAY
GUNNELS WOOD ROAD
A1072
SIX HILLS WAY
A1070
ST GEORGE'S WAY
MONKSWOOD WAY
A602
LONDON ROAD
B197
A1(M)
BROADHALL WAY
Junction 7
Stevenage Station
Stevenage Leisure Centre
Hollywood Bowl
Swimming Pool
Hotel
Stevenage Borough Football Club
Stevenage Museum
Southgate Health Centre
North Hertfordshire College
Monkswood Retail Park
Megabowl
Roaring Meg Retail Park
Factory
King George Surgery
Stevenage Cricket Club
Fairlands Junior Middle & Infant School
Woolenwick Junior & Infant School
Homestead Moat Infant School
The Management Practice
Stevenage Borough Football Club
grid square represents 250 metres

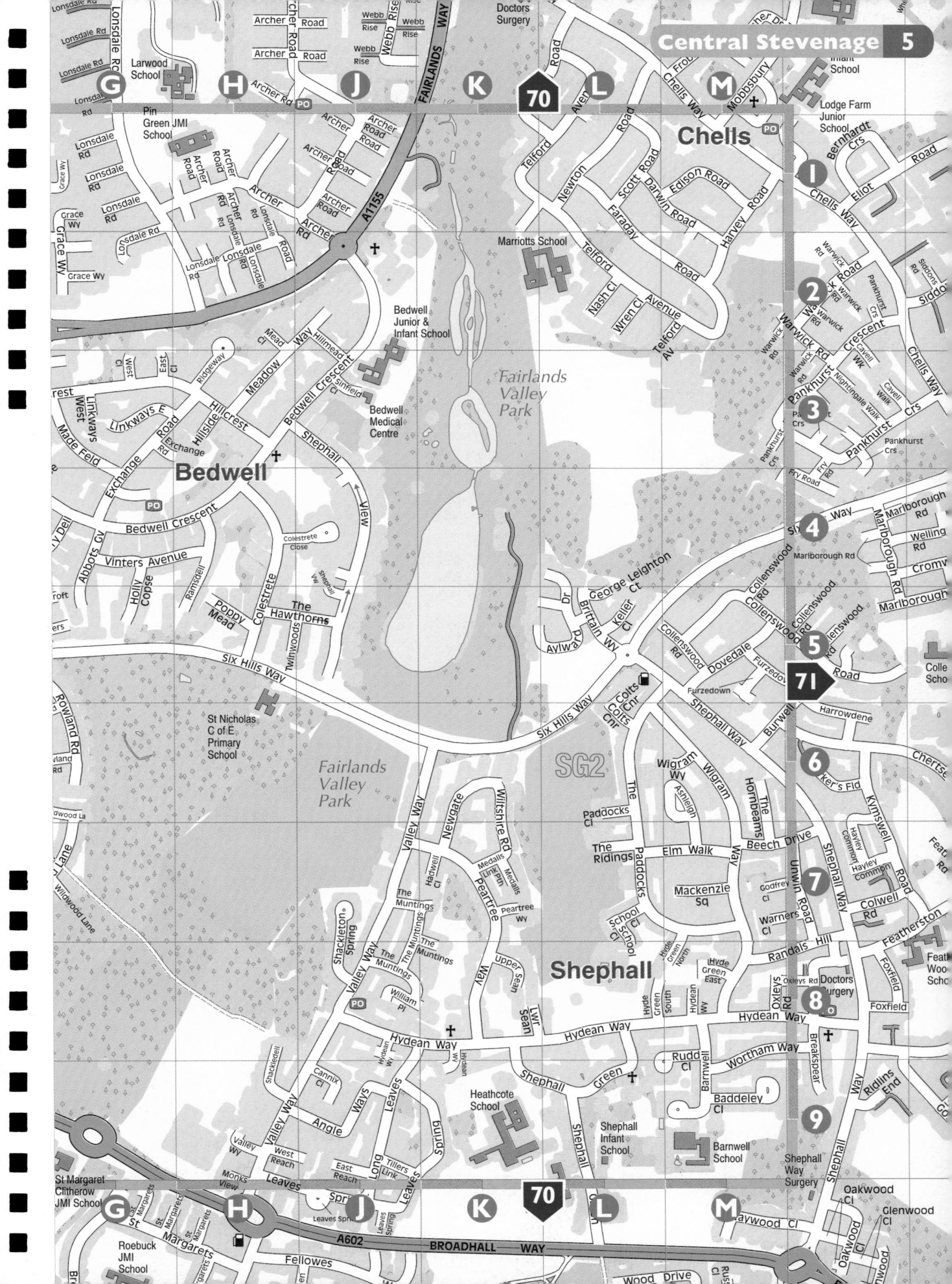
Chells
Bedwell
Shephall
Fairlands Valley Park
Fairlands Valley Park
SG2
FAIRLANDS WAY
A1155
A602
BROADHALL WAY
70
71
70
Doctors Surgery
Larwood School
Pin Green JMI School
Lodge Farm Junior School
Infant School
Marriotts School
Bedwell Junior & Infant School
Bedwell Medical Centre
St Nicholas C of E Primary School
Heathcote School
Shephall Infant School
Barnwell School
Shephall Way Surgery
Doctors Surgery
St Margaret Clitherow JMI School
Roebuck JMI School
Lonsdale Rd
Lonsdale Road
Archer Road
Archer Rd
Webb Rise
Grace Wy
Grace Way
Mobbsbury
Chells Way
Telford Avenue
Telford Av
Newton Road
Scott Road
Darwin Road
Edison Road
Faraday Road
Harvey Road
Nash Cl
Wren Cl
Bernhardt Crs
Eliot Road
Warwick Road
Warwick Rd
Pankhurst Crescent
Pankhurst Crs
Cavell Wk
Cavell Walk
Nightingale Walk
Fry Road
Fry Rd
Marlborough Rd
Welling Rd
Six Hills Way
Collenswood Rd
Collenswood Road
George Leighton Ct
Brittain Wy
Keller Cl
Aylward Dr
Dovedale
Furzedown
Shephall Way
Burwell Road
Harrowdene
Colts Cnr
Mead Cl
Meadow Way
Hillmead
Ridgeway
West Cl
East Cl
Linkways West
Linkways E
Hillside
Hillcrest
Exchange Road
Exchange Rd
Bedwell Crescent
Sinfield Cl
Shephall View
Made Feld
Abbots Gv
Vinters Avenue
Holly Copse
Ramsdell
Colestrete
Colestrete Close
Poppy Mead
The Hawthorns
Twinwoods
Rowland Rd
Wildwood Lane
Valley Way
Newgate
Wiltshire Rd
Medalls Link
Medalls Path
Peartree Way
Peartree Wy
Hadwell Cl
The Muntings
Shackleton Spring
William Pl
Upper Sean
Lwr Sean
Hydean Way
Hydean Wy
Wigram Wy
Wigram Way
Ashleigh
The Hornbeams
The Paddocks
Paddocks Cl
The Ridings
Elm Walk
Beech Drive
Mackenzie Sq
School Cl
Hyde Green North
Hyde Green East
Hyde Green South
Unwin Road
Godfrey Cl
Warners Cl
Randals Hill
Oxleys Rd
Foxfield
Kymswell Road
Hayley Common
Colwell Rd
Featherston
Rudd Cl
Barnwell
Wortham Way
Baddeley Cl
Breakspear
Ridlins End
Shephall Green
Shackledell
Cannix Cl
Angle Ways
Long Leaves
Tillers Link
East Reach
West Reach
Valley Wy
Monks View
Leaves Spring
St Margarets
Fellowes
Haywood Cl
Oakwood Cl
Glenwood Cl
Oakwood Drive
Wood Drive
PO
G
H
J
K
L
M
1
2
3
4
5
6
7
8
9

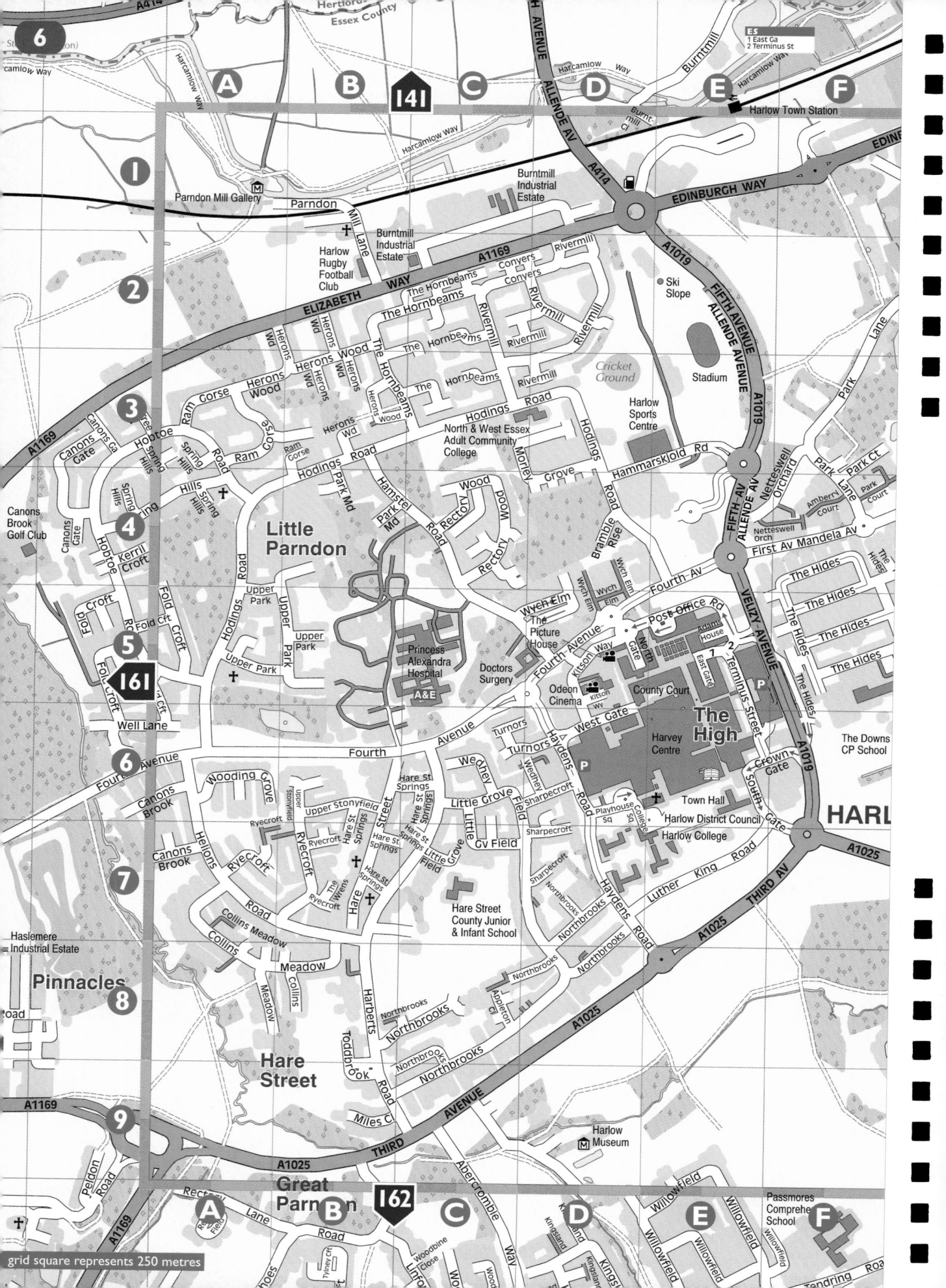
6
141
161
162
A B C D E F
1 2 3 4 5 6 7 8 9
Harlow Town Station
Parndon Mill Gallery
Burntmill Industrial Estate
Harlow Rugby Football Club
Ski Slope
Stadium
Cricket Ground
Harlow Sports Centre
North & West Essex Adult Community College
Canons Brook Golf Club
Little Parndon
Princess Alexandra Hospital
A&E
Doctors Surgery
The Picture House
Odeon Cinema
County Court
The High
Harvey Centre
Town Hall
Harlow District Council
Harlow College
The Downs CP School
HARL
Hare Street County Junior & Infant School
Haslemere Industrial Estate
Pinnacles
Hare Street
Harlow Museum
Great Parndon
Passmores Comprehe School
ELIZABETH WAY
EDINBURGH WAY
FIFTH AVENUE
ALLENDE AVENUE
VELIZY AVENUE
THIRD AVENUE
Fourth Avenue
A1169
A1019
A1025
A414
E5
1 East Ga
2 Terminus St
grid square represents 250 metres

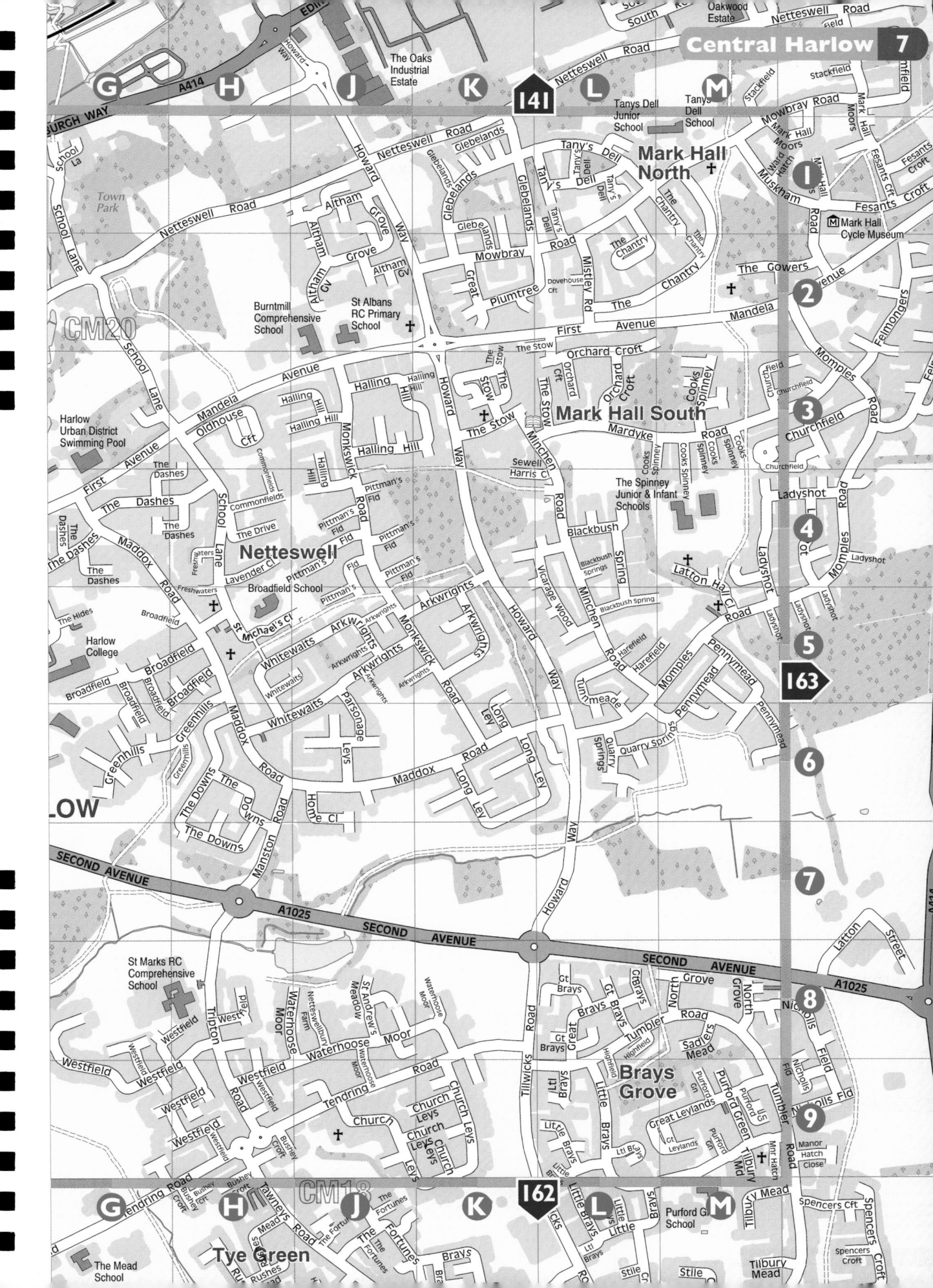
The Oaks Industrial Estate
Oakwood Estate
Netteswell Road
Mowbray Road
Tanys Dell Junior School
Tanys Dell School
Mark Hall North
Mark Hall Cycle Museum
Town Park
Burntmill Comprehensive School
St Albans RC Primary School
CM20
First Avenue
Mandela Avenue
Mark Hall South
Harlow Urban District Swimming Pool
The Spinney Junior & Infant Schools
Netteswell
Broadfield School
Harlow College
Howard Way
Second Avenue
A1025
A414
St Marks RC Comprehensive School
Brays Grove
CM18
Tye Green
The Mead School
Purford Green School
141
163
162
G
H
J
K
L
M
1
2
3
4
5
6
7
8
9

149

Grovehill

E1
1 Cwmbran Ct

B5
1 Andrews Cl
2 Mead Temple

A   B   C   D   E   F

Piccotts End Lane

Trevalga
Penrose
Cla
Turnpike
Square

Tremaine Grove

Camborne Drive

PO

Grove Medical Centre

Stevenage
Road

Aycliffe Drive Primary School

Hunting Gate

Aycliffe Drive

Kilbride Cl
Runcorn Cts

Hatfield Cts

1
7

Bracknell Pl

Crawley   Drive   A414

1

2

End

Marlborough

Severnmead

Brambling
Lapwing Cl
Rise

Wathins Cl

Wyn Ct
Peerlee Ct

Pennine

A4147

Wharfedale

Sleddale

The Hammond Junior Mixed Infant School

Hemel Hempstead Rugby League Club

3

Bathurst   Road

PO

Lonsdale

Ribblesdale
Way

Teesdale

Cambrian

Quantocks

Chevlots

Saturn Rd
Tethys
Rd
Tritan Rd

Hyperion Rd
Callisto
Ct
Europa
Rd
Ganymede

Fletcher Way

Mendip

Chilterns

Malvern Way

Hildalgo Court

PO

Highfield Surgery

Drive

47

Piccotts End

4

Fletcher Way

Wheatfield

Sharpcroft

Berefield
The Bounce

Broadcroft
Boxhill

Townsend

Layhill

Paston

Road

Bowmans Ct
Tybleden

Allandale
Road

Cattsdell

Bellgate JMI School

Solway

Jupiter

Highfield

Apollo Way

Uranus Road

Triton Way

Pallas Road

Jupiter Drive JMI School

Larchwo

ebridge Lane

Church

Smithfield

Street

2
7

Allandale

Taverners

Mercers

Gt. Heart

Randalls Ride

Drive

Neptune

Pluto Rise

Achilles Cl

Queensway

Highfield

Nicholas Way

The Apple Orch

The Graz

149

High

Chapel
Rd
Sunmead

Chapel Cottages

Street

Bowyers

Union Gn

Grover Cl
Clarendon Cl

Bayle Ct
Bayle Lane

Thumpers

Nicky Line

Bohemia

Woodhall
Lane

B487

Berry mead

Tannsfield Dr

Tannsmore Cl

Orchard
Cl

Ellingham

6

Austins Pl

St Mary's Road

Herbert Street

Street

Figtree
Heather Wy

Garland Ct

Ltl
Mimms

Slippers Hl

Mimms

Long

Little   Road

Rice Cl

Hobletts

Adeyfield Gardens

St
George

St

Community Mental Health Centre

QUEENSWAY

B487

Towers Road

Springfield

Ellen Close

Great

Road

7

West Herts College

Alexandra Road

Christchurch Road

Adeyfield Road

Westview

Normandy

St
Paul's
St

Downside
Road

Nicky Line

Manley Rd

Hardy
Road

Coral Gdns

Commons
La

Trebellan Dr

Laurel Cl

Longlands

Hammer Lane

The Queen's

8

Marlowes Health Centre
Civic Centre & Dacorum Borough Counsil

Broad St

East St
Road

Midland

Fernville La

Crescent Rd

Adeyfield   Road

Mountfield   Road

Seymour Crs

Quendell Wk

Chalfdell
Rd

Eastbrook Way

Broadfield

Road

Old   House   Road

9

Fernville Surgery
Beta Health Clinic

Alexandra Road

The Sidings

Mayflower Avenue

Concorde Dr

Hillfield Ct

Bencroft Rd

The Holt

Broadfield Infant School

Broadfield Junior School

Sawyers

The Driftway

Way

Sawyers Wy

Hertfordshire Country Constabulary

combe Street

Wa

Marlowes

Hillfield   Road

Scriveners

HEMEL HEMPSTEAD

Newfield

Longla

P

LEIGHTON BUZZARD ROAD

Bus Station

PO

Walnut Grove

Wod Farm Road

Acr

Windmill   Road

Windmill Road

A B C D E F

Bridge St

Maynard Road

Hemel Hempstead General Hospital A&E

149

Turners

Toms Croft

Furtherground

The Chase

White

Hart

ROAD

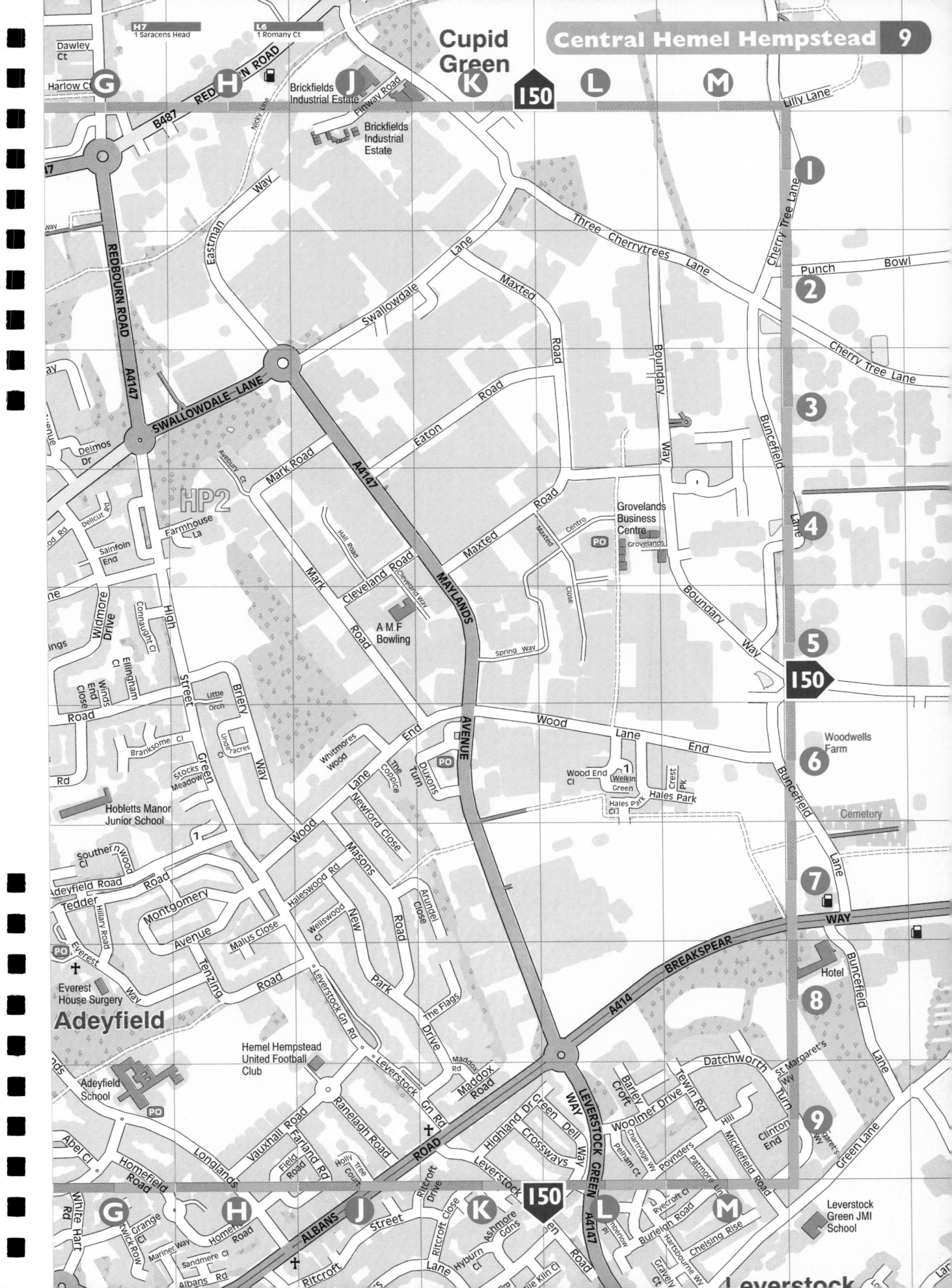
H7 1 Saracens Head
L6 1 Romany Ct
Cupid Green
150
Dawley Ct
Harlow Ct
REDBOURN ROAD
B487
Brickfields Industrial Estate
Finway Road
Brickfields Industrial Estate
Nicky Line
Lilly Lane
Eastman Way
Three Cherrytrees Lane
Cherry Tree Lane
Punch Bowl
Cherry Tree Lane
REDBOURN ROAD
A4147
Swallowdale Lane
Maxted Road
Boundary Way
SWALLOWDALE LANE
Eaton Road
Buncefield Lane
Deimos Dr
Mark Road
A4147
Avebury Ct
HP2
Dellcut Rd
Farmhouse La
Sainfoin End
Hall Road
Maxted Road
Grovelands Business Centre
Centro
Maxted Close
PO
Grovelands
Mark Road
Cleveland Road
Cleveland Way
MAYLANDS
AMF Bowling
Widmore Drive
Connaught Cl
High Street
Ellingham Cl
Boundary Way
Spring Way
Winds End Close
Little Orch
Briery Way
150
Road
Wood Lane End
Woodwells Farm
Branksome Cl
Underacres Cl
Whitmores Wood
The Coppice
Duxons Turn
AVENUE
PO
Stocks Meadow
Green
Wood End Cl
Welkin Green
Crest Pk
Hales Park
Hales Park Cl
Buncefield Lane
Rd
Hobletts Manor Junior School
Newford Close
Cemetery
Wood Lane
Southern Wood Cl
Masons Road
Adeyfield Road
Tedder Road
Haleswood Rd
Arundel Close
Montgomery Avenue
Hillary Road
Wellswood Cl
New Park Road
BREAKSPEAR WAY
A414
Malus Close
Hotel
Buncefield Lane
PO
Everest Way
Tenzing Road
Leverstock Gn Rd
Everest House Surgery
The Flags
Drive
Adeyfield
Hemel Hempstead United Football Club
Maddox Rd
Maddox Road
Datchworth
St Margaret's Wy
Leverstock Green Rd
LEVERSTOCK GREEN WAY
Barley Croft
Tewin Rd
Adeyfield School
PO
Ranelagh Road
Highland Dr
Green Dell Way
Woolmer Drive
Hill
Turn
Clinton End
Abel Cl
Vauxhall Road
Farland Rd
Crossways
Chartridge Wy
Pelham Ct
Poynders
Patmore Ln
Micklefield Road
Green Lane
Longlands
Field Road
Holly Tree Court
ROAD
Leverstock
Homefield Road
Ritcroft Drive
150
A4147
Leverstock Green JMI School
White Hart Rd
Grange Cl
Homefield Road
ALBANS
Street
Ritcroft Close
Ashmore Gdns
Rycroft Cl
Burleigh Road
Hartsbourne Wy
Chelsing Rise
Mariner Way
Sandmere Cl
Albans Rd
Ritcroft
Lane
Hyburn Cl
Kiln Cl
Road
Gravely Ct
Leverstock
G H J K L M
1 2 3 4 5 6 7 8 9

Batchwood Golf Club
Batchwood Hall
152
151
169
Townsend
St Albans City Hospital
Kingsbury Watermill Museum & Waffle House
St Michaels C of E JMI Sch
Verulamium Museum
St Albans School
Abbey Gate Cathedral
Abbey C of E JMI School
Westminster Lodge Sports Centre
St Albans Abbey Station
St Columbas College
Prae Wood JMI School
Batchwood School
Garden Fields JMI School
St Albans Music Sch
Aboyne Lodge Sch
Russell Clnc
Doctors Surg
Lodge Surg
St Albans Principal Health Cen
The Maltings Surgery
Police Station
Crown Prosec Service
Maltings Arts Theatre
Shen Nong Chinese Medical Centre
The Lake
AL3
VERULAM ROAD
FOLLY LANE A4147
CATHERINE ST
CHEQUER STREET
HIGH ST A5183
HOLYWELL HILL
A4147 HEMEL HEMPSTEAD ROAD
BLUEHOUSE HILL HEMEL HEMPSTEAD ROAD
A5183
Ver-Colne Valley Walk
River Ver
E6 1 Waddington Rd
D1 1 Batchwood Dr
grid square represents 250 metres

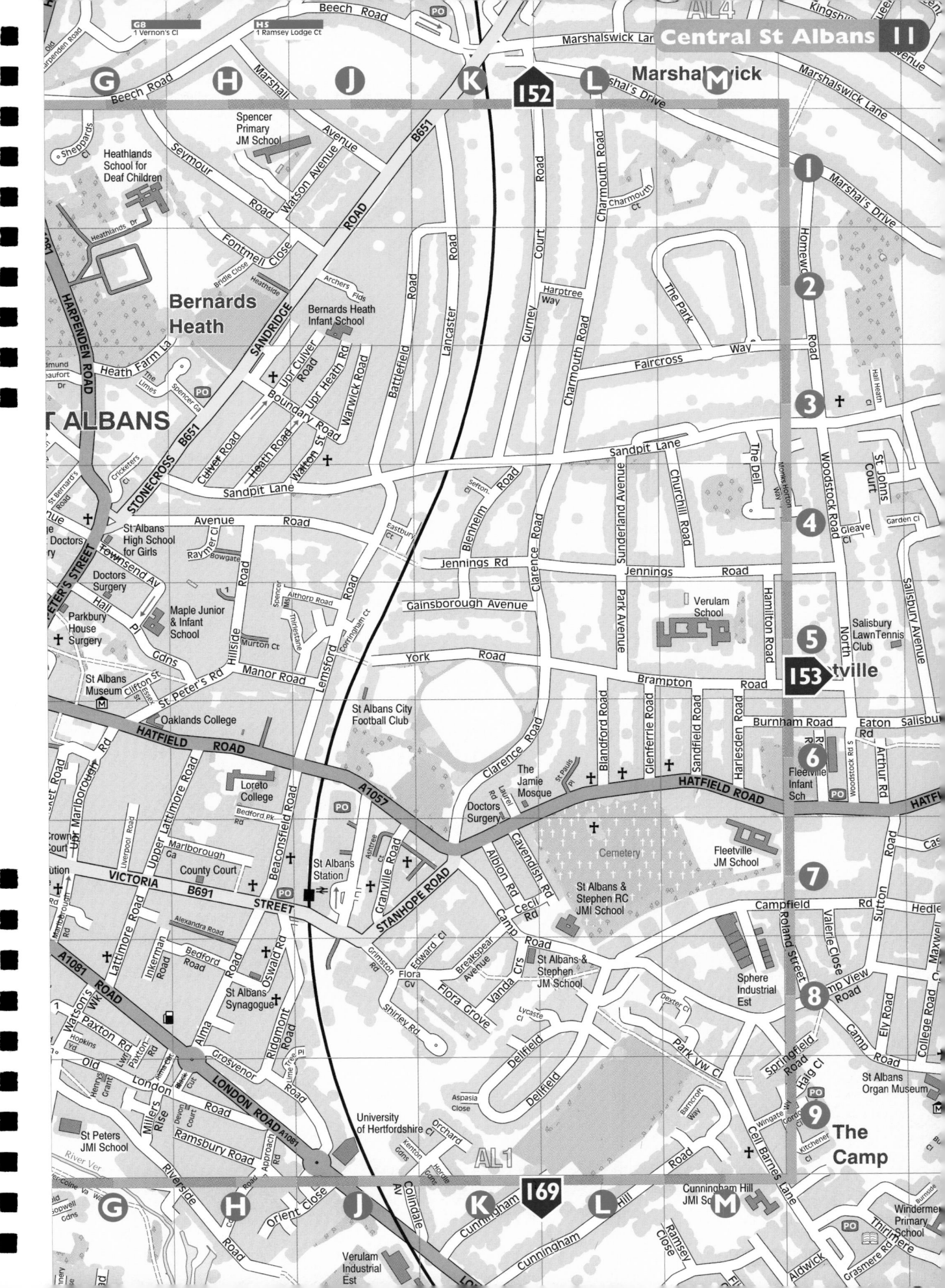

GB
1 Vernon's Cl

H5
1 Ramsey Lodge Ct

BEECH ROAD

G **H** **J** **K** **152** **L** **M**

Marshalswick Lane

Marshalswick Lane

Marshalswick

Spencer Primary JM School

Heathlands School for Deaf Children

Shepherds Cl

SEYMOUR ROAD

WATSON AVENUE

AVENUE

SANDRIDGE ROAD

B651

Marshal's Drive

Charmouth Road

Charmouth Ct

Marshal's Drive

I

Homewood Road

2

The Park

Hall Heath

Heathlands Dr

Bernards Heath

HARPENDEN ROAD

A1081

Heath Farm La

Edmund Beaufort Dr

The Limes

Spencer Ga

PO

Bridle Close

Heathside

Upr Culver Road

Bernards Heath Infant School

Archers Flds

Boundary Road

Upr Heath Rd

Warwick Road

BATTLEFIELD ROAD

LANCASTER ROAD

GURNEY ROAD

Harptree Way

Faircross Way

CHARMOUTH ROAD

3

The Dell

Monks Horton Way

WOODSTOCK ROAD

St Johns Court

Gleave Cl

Garden Cl

ST ALBANS

B651

STONECROSS

St Bernard's Road

Cricketer's Cl

Culver Road

Heath Road

Watton St

Sandpit Lane

Sefton Cl

Blenheim Road

Sandpit Lane

Sunderland Avenue

Churchill Road

The Dell

4

Salisbury Avenue

North

College Doctors Surgery

Townsend Av

AVENUE

ROAD

Raymer Cl

Bowgate

Althorp Road

Eastbury Ct

Jennings Rd

CLARENCE ROAD

Jennings Road

Park Avenue

Verulam School

Hamilton Road

Salisbury Lawn Tennis Club

St Albans High School for Girls

Doctors Surgery

Parkbury House Surgery

St Albans Museum

M

Oaklands College

Maple Junior & Infant School

Clifton St

Essex St

St Peter's Rd

Hillside

Spencer Mws

Thristestane

Corringham Ct

Murton Ct

LEMSFORD ROAD

Manor Road

Gainsborough Avenue

YORK ROAD

St Albans City Football Club

CLARENCE ROAD

Blandford Road

Glenferrie Road

Sandfield Road

Harlesden Road

Brampton Road

153 **Fleetville**

5

Burnham Road

Eaton Salisbury

HATFIELD ROAD

A1057

Marlborough Road

Liverpool Road

Upper Lattimore Road

Beaconsfield Road

Loreto College

Bedford Pk Rd

PO

Ashtree

Granville Road

The Jamie Mosque

St Pauls Pl

Laurel Rd

Doctors Surgery

Woodstock Rd S

Fleetville Infant Sch

PO

6

Arthur Rd

HATFIELD ROAD

HATFI

Crown Court

VICTORIA STREET

B691

Lattimore Road

Inkerman Road

County Court

Alexandra Road

PO

Bedford Road

St Albans Station

Astree

STANHOPE ROAD

Albion Rd

Cavendish Rd

Cecil Rd

Cemetery

Fleetville JM School

St Albans & Stephen RC JMI School

Campfield Road

7

Sutton Road

Hedle

A1081 ROAD

Watson's Wk

Paxton Rd

Alma Road

Ridgmont Road

St Albans Synagogue

Oswald Rd

Grimston Rd

Edward Cl

Flora Gv

Breakspear Avenue

Vanda Crs

Camp Road

St Albans & Stephen JM School

Lycaste Cl

Dexter Cl

Sphere Industrial Est

Roland Street

Camp View Road

Valerie Close

Ely Road

8

Camp Road

College Road

Cas

Hopkins Yd

Henry Grant Ct

Old London Road

Grosvenor Road

Shirley Rd

Flora Grove

Delifield

Delifield

Park Vw Cl

Springfield Road

Haig Cl

PO

St Albans Organ Museum

9

The Camp

St Peters JMI School

River Ver

Millers Rise

Devon Court

Lime Tree Pl

LONDON ROAD

A1081

RIVERSIDE ROAD

Ramsbury Road

APPROACH ROAD

University of Hertfordshire

Orchard Cl

Kenton Gdns

Horde Gdns

Collindale Av

AL1

Aspasia Close

Barncroft Way

Wingate Rd

Kitchener Cl

Cell Barnes Lane

Cunningham Hill JMI Sc

Windermere Primary School

Thirlmere

Grasmere Rd

Aldwick

Burnside

G **H** **J** **K** **169** **L** **M**

Orient Close

Cunningham Hill

Cunningham

Verulam Industrial Est

Ramsey Close

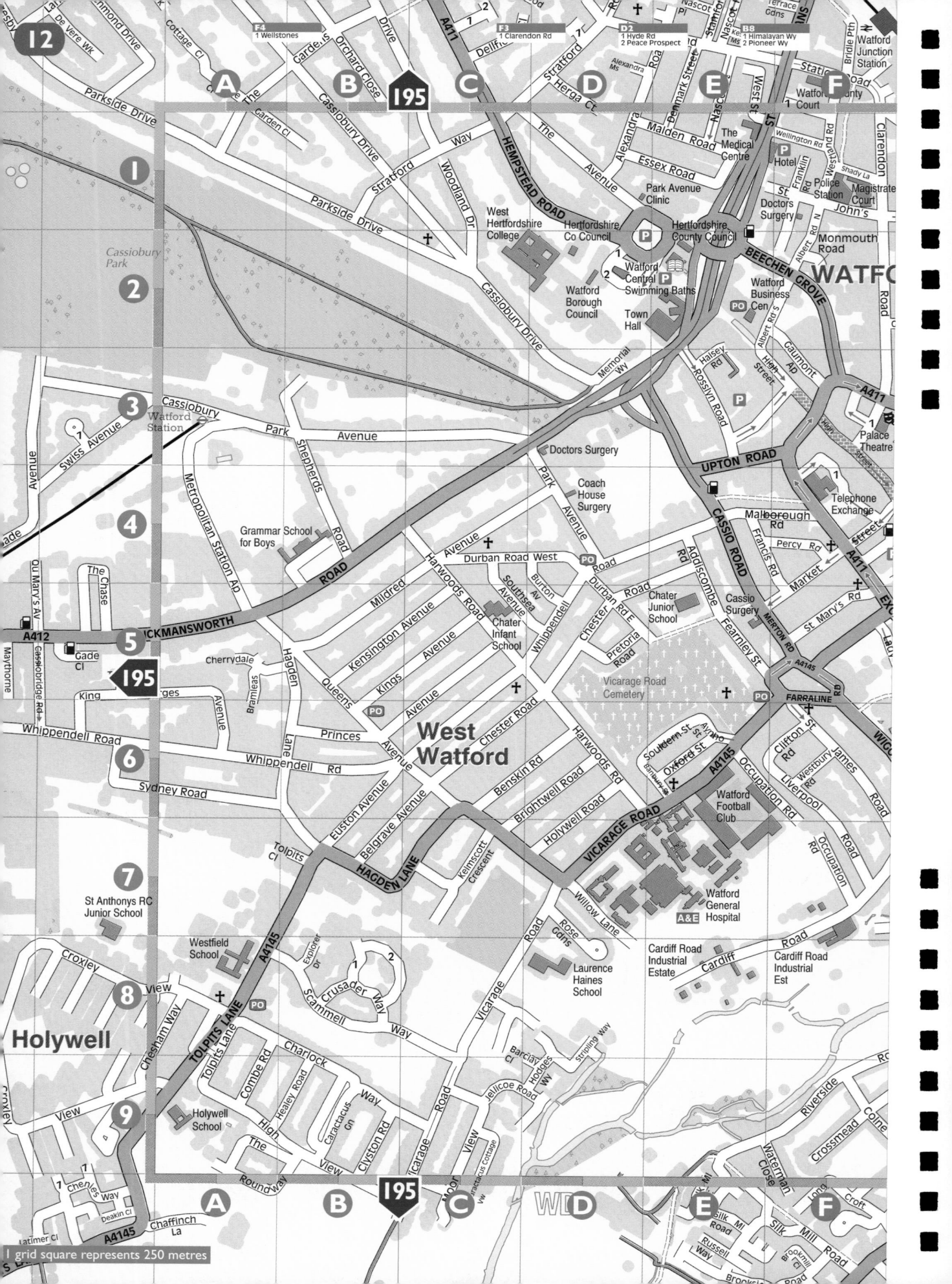

F4 1 Wellstones
F3 1 Clarendon Rd
D2 1 Hyde Rd 2 Peace Prospect
B8 1 Himalayan Wy 2 Pioneer Wy
195
A
B
C
D
E
F
1
2
3
4
5
6
7
8
9
De Vere Wk
Cottage Cl
Parkside Drive
The Gardens
Garden Cl
Orchard Close
Cassiobury Drive
Drive
A411
Delfield
Stratford Way
Woodland Dr
Herga Ct
Hempstead Road
The Avenue
Alexandra Road
Alexandra Ms
Malden Road
Essex Road
Denmark Street
Nascot Pl
Nascot St
West St
Station Road
Watford Junction Station
Bridle Path
Watford County Court
The Medical Centre
Wellington Rd
Hotel
Franklin Rd
Westland Rd
Shady La
Clarendon Road
Police Station
Magistrates Court
St John's Rd
Doctors Surgery
Park Avenue Clinic
West Hertfordshire College
Hertfordshire Co Council
Hertfordshire County Council
Albert Rd N
Monmouth Road
Beechen Grove
WATFO
Watford Central Swimming Baths
Watford Borough Council
Town Hall
Watford Business Cen
Albert Rd S
Gaumont Ap
High Street
Halsey Rd
Rosslyn Road
Memorial Wy
Cassiobury Park
Cassiobury Park Avenue
Watford Station
Swiss Avenue
Avenue
Shepherds Road
Metropolitan Station Ap
Doctors Surgery
Park Avenue
Coach House Surgery
Upton Road
A411
Palace Theatre
Telephone Exchange
Grammar School for Boys
Rickmansworth Road
Durban Road West
Durban Road
Cassio Road
Marlborough Rd
Francis Rd
Percy Rd
Market Street
The Chase
Our Mary's Av
A412
Gade Cl
Maythorne
Cassiobridge Rd
Mildred Avenue
Harwoods Road
Southsea Avenue
Burton Av
Whippendell
Chester Road
Durban Rd E
Addiscombe Rd
Chater Junior School
Cassio Surgery
Merton Rd
St Mary's Rd
Kensington Avenue
Kings Avenue
Chater Infant School
Pretoria Road
Fearnley St
Vicarage Road Cemetery
A4145
Farraline Rd
Cherrydale
Bramleas
Hagden Lane
King Georges Avenue
Queens Avenue
Whippendell Road
Princes Avenue
Whippendell Rd
Sydney Road
West Watford
Chester Road
Benskin Rd
Harwoods Rd
Brightwell Road
Holywell Road
Souldern St
Aynho St
Oxford St
Banbury St
Occupation Rd
Clifton Rd
Westbury Rd
James Road
Liverpool Road
Euston Avenue
Belgrave Avenue
Tolpits Cl
Hagden Lane
Keimscott Crescent
Vicarage Road
Watford Football Club
Occupation Road
Watford General Hospital
A&E
Willow Lane
St Anthonys RC Junior School
Westfield School
Explorer Dr
Crusader Way
Scammell Way
Rose Gdns
Laurence Haines School
Cardiff Road Industrial Estate
Cardiff Road
Cardiff Road Industrial Est
Croxley View
Holywell
Chesham Way
Tolpits Lane
Tolpits Lane
Combe Rd
Charlock Way
Healey Road
Caractacus Gn
Clyston Rd
Vicarage Road
Moor View
Caractacus Cottage Vw
Barclay Cl
Hodges Wy
Stripling Way
Jellicoe Road
Riverside Road
Crossmead
Colne
Holywell School
The High View
Round Way
Waterman Close
Silk Mill Road
Silk Mill Road
Long Croft
Russell Way
Brookmill Cl
Chenies Way
Deakin Cl
Chaffinch La
Latimer Cl
A4145
WD
1 grid square represents 250 metres

G1 1 Orphanage Rd
G5 1 Cambridge Rd 2 Kings Cl
G6 1 Roberts Rd
H2 1 Ottoman Ter 2 Pankhurst Pl
H3 1 Queen's Pl
H5 1 Chapmans Yd 2 Woodmans Yd
J1 1 Bevan House 2 Mandela Pl
L5 1 Hastings Wy
196
Park Avenue
Doctors Surgery
Link Road
Stephenson Way
Golf Course
West Herts College
Indoor Market
Harlequin Shopping Centre
Central Primary School
Watford High Street Station
Watford Museum
Watford Springs Pool
Grammar School for Girls
Superstore
Pump House Theatre
Field Junior School
Gazelda Industrial Estate
Watford Arches Retail Park
Colne Bridge Retail Park
Fisher Industrial Est
Hamilton Street
Chinese Medical Cen Watford
Waterfields Way
Bushey Hall Road
Aldenham Road
Chalk Hill
London Road
Oxhey Infant School
Bushey Manor School
Health Centre
Sacred Heart Junior Middle & Infant School
Bushey Station
Pinner Road
Deacons Hill Road
Oxhey
River Colne
Bromet School
Hollybush Close
WD2

A B C D E F

1

Dunton Fen

Sutton Road

2

Eyeworth

Sutton Road

High Street

3

4

Cambridge Road

Newton

5

Greenfield Way

Kings Pond Close

Lees Close

Boot Lane

Horseshoe

Magdalene Close

Dunton Primary School

PO

Dunton

Church Street

High Street

Chapel Street

Hallside

Springfield

Fox Close

Biggleswade Road

6

Millow Hall Farm

Millow

7

Millowbury Farm

8

Dunton Lodge Farm

A B C 17 D E F

Havan Farm

grid square represents 500 metres

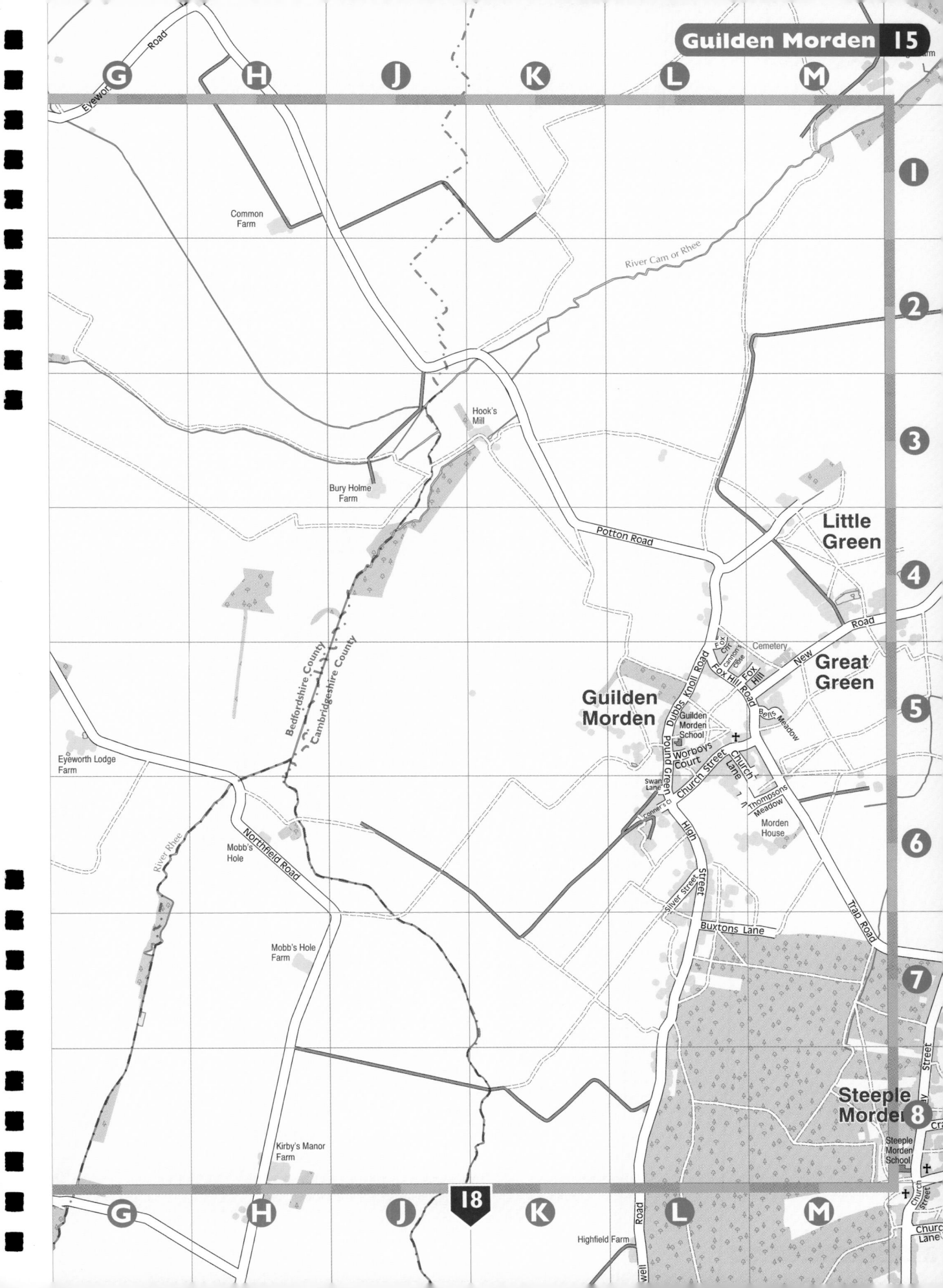

G H J K L M

I
2
3
4
5
6
7
8

Eyewort Road

Common Farm

River Cam or Rhee

Hook's Mill

Bury Holme Farm

Potton Road

Little Green

Cemetery

Fox Hill

Carlton's Close

Fox Hill

New Road

Great Green

Bedfordshire County

Cambridgeshire County

Eyeworth Lodge Farm

Guilden Morden

Dubbs Knoll Road

Guilden Morden School

Ben's Meadow

Pound Green

Worboys Court

Church Lane

Church Street

River Rhee

Swan Lane

Thompsons Meadow

Morden House

Conner's Cl

Northfield Road

Mobb's Hole

High Street

Silver Street

Buxtons Lane

Mobb's Hole Farm

Trap Road

Steeple Morden

Steeple Morden School

Kirby's Manor Farm

G H J K L M

18

Highfield Farm

well Road

Church Lane

A B C D E F

1

2

3

4

5

6

7

8

A B C D E F

LONDON ROAD

A1(T)

A1(T)

A1(T)

Farm

Newspring Farm

Bleack Hall

Manor Farm

Edworth Road

Edworth Road

Hill Farm

Astwick

Astwick Road

Mill Lane

Taylor's Road

Bedfordshire
Hertfordshire

1 grid square represents 500 metres

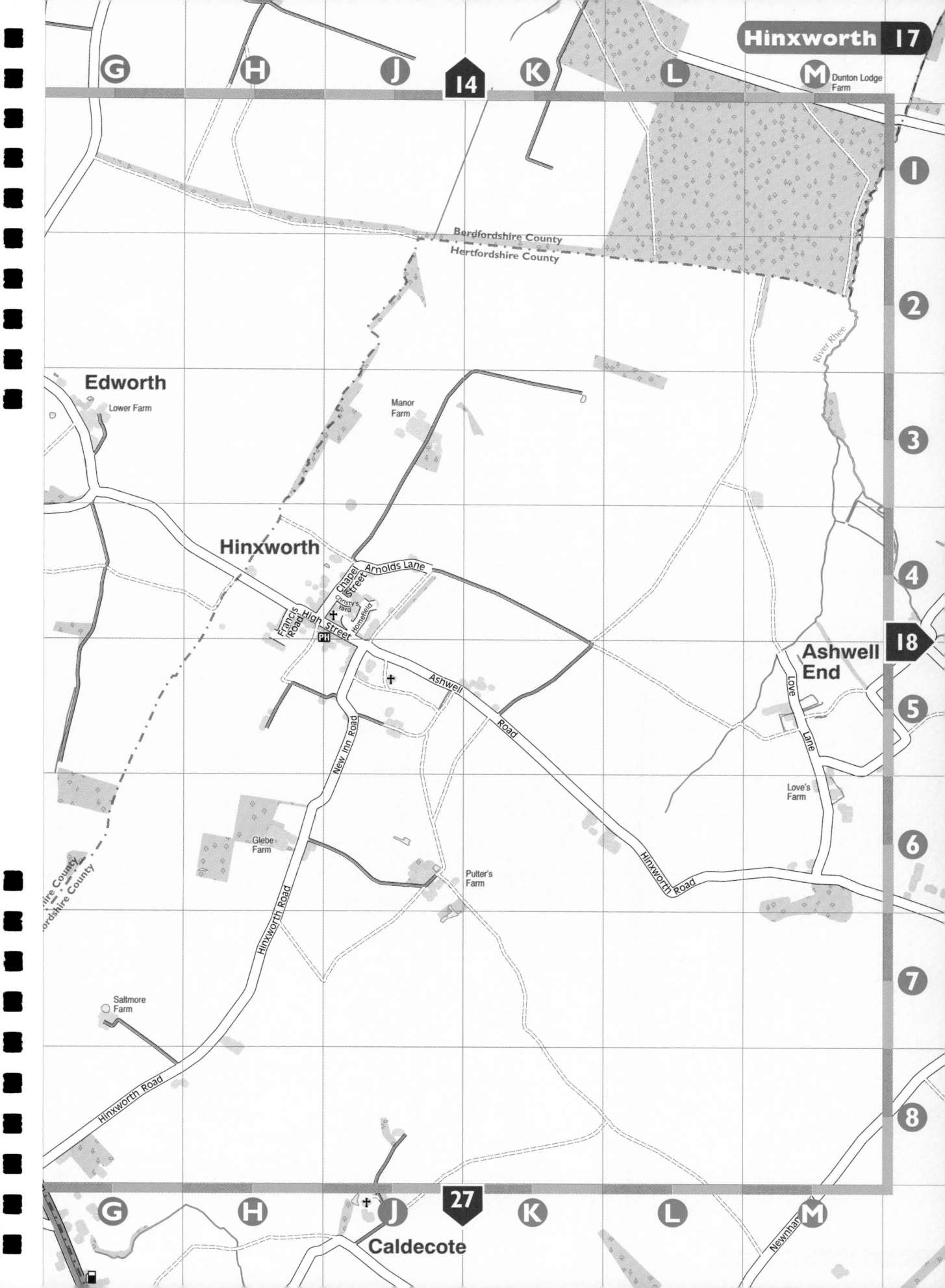

G H J 14 K L M Dunton Lodge Farm

I

Berdfordshire County
Hertfordshire County

River Rhee

2

Edworth

Lower Farm

Manor Farm

3

Hinxworth

Arnolds Lane
Chapel Street

4

Christy's Yard
Francis Road
High Street
Homefield
PH

18

Ashwell End

Ashwell Road

Love Lane

5

Love's Farm

New Inn Road

6

Glebe Farm

Pulter's Farm

Hinxworth Road

7

shire County
rdshire County

Saltmore Farm

8

Hinxworth Road

G H J 27 K L M

Newnham

Caldecote

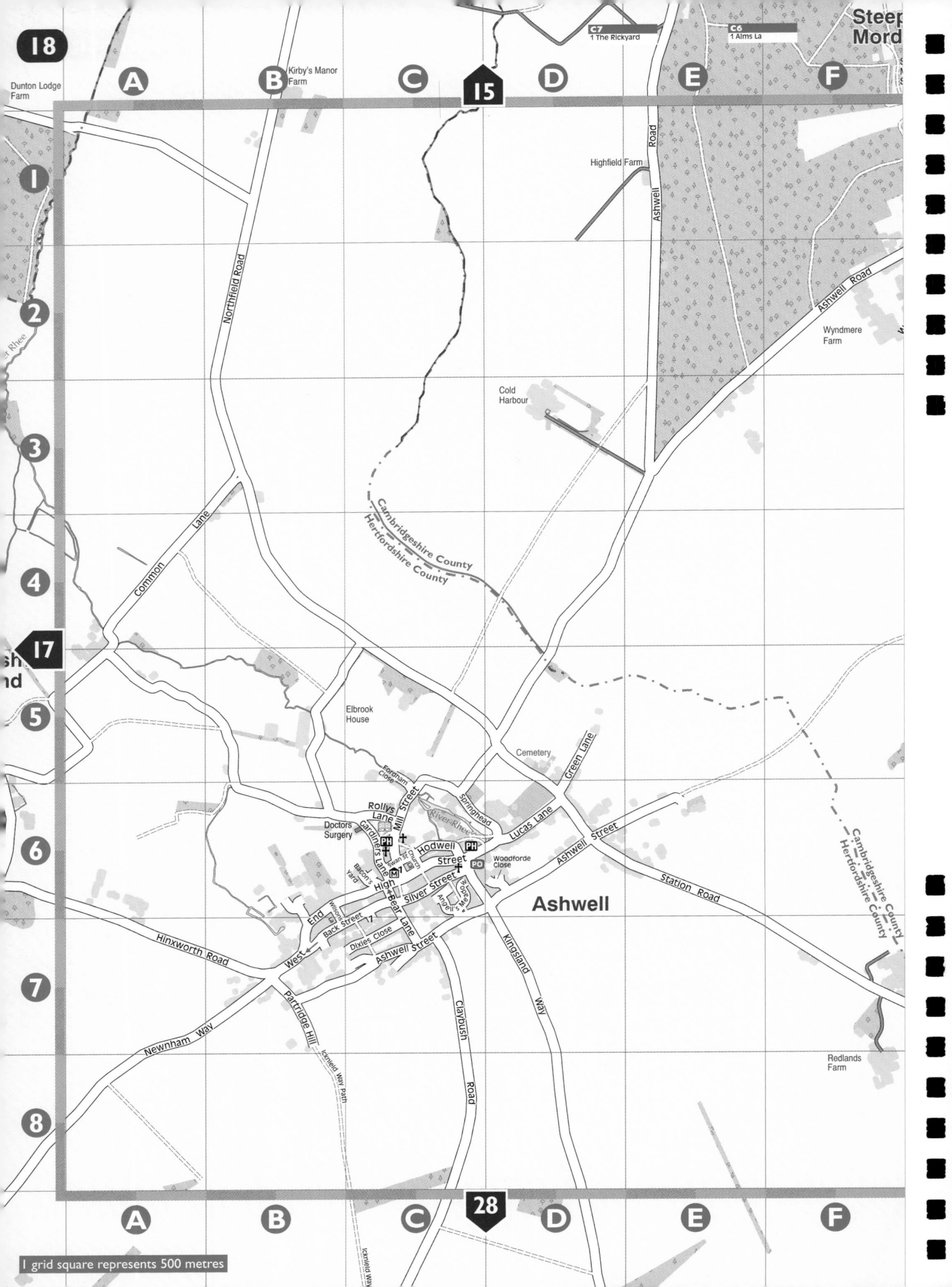

A B C D E F

Dunton Lodge
Farm

Kirby's Manor
Farm

C7
1 The Rickyard

C6
1 Alms La

Steep
Mord

15

Highfield Farm

Ashwell Road

Wyndmere
Farm

I1

2

River Rhee

3

Northfield Road

Common Lane

Cold
Harbour

Ashwell Road

17

Cambridgeshire County
Hertfordshire County

4

5

Elbrook
House

Cemetery

Green Lane

Cambridgeshire County
Hertfordshire County

6

Fordham Close

Rollys Lane

Mill Street

Springhead

River Rhee

Lucas Lane

Doctors
Surgery

Gardiner's Lane

PH

Hodwell
Street

PH

PO

Woodforde
Close

Ashwell Street

Bacon's
Yard

High
End

Back Street

Bear Lane

Silver Street

Angell's

Church
Me...

Ashwell

Station Road

Hinxworth Road

West
End

Dixies Close

Ashwell Street

Kingsland Way

7

Partridge Hill

Claybush Road

Redlands
Farm

Newnham Way

Icknield Way Path

8

A B C D E F

28

Meeting Lane

G

Hay

Craft Way

Steeple
Morden
School

1 Cherry Tree Cl

M1

Jubilee End

Cheyney
Close

Street

H

J

K

L

Litlington

M

Anvil Avenue

Cockhall Cl

Cockhall La

Royston

I

PO

Church Farm
Lane

Church
Street

The Green

Litlington

Road

Litlington

2

Church

South Street

**Morden
Green**

Icknield Way Path

3

Station Road

Westbrook Close

**Gatley
End**

Icknield Way Path

4

High Farm

Icknield Way Path

Morden
Grange
Farm

20

5

Station Road

*Morden
Grange
Plantation*

6

BALDOCK

7

Cheyneys
Lodge

Chain Walk

Cambridgeshire County

Hertfordshire County

Lower
Coombe Farm

8

Station Road

Chain

Walk

A505

Chain

Walk

Station

Ashwell &
Morden Station

G

H

J

29

K

L

M

Odsey

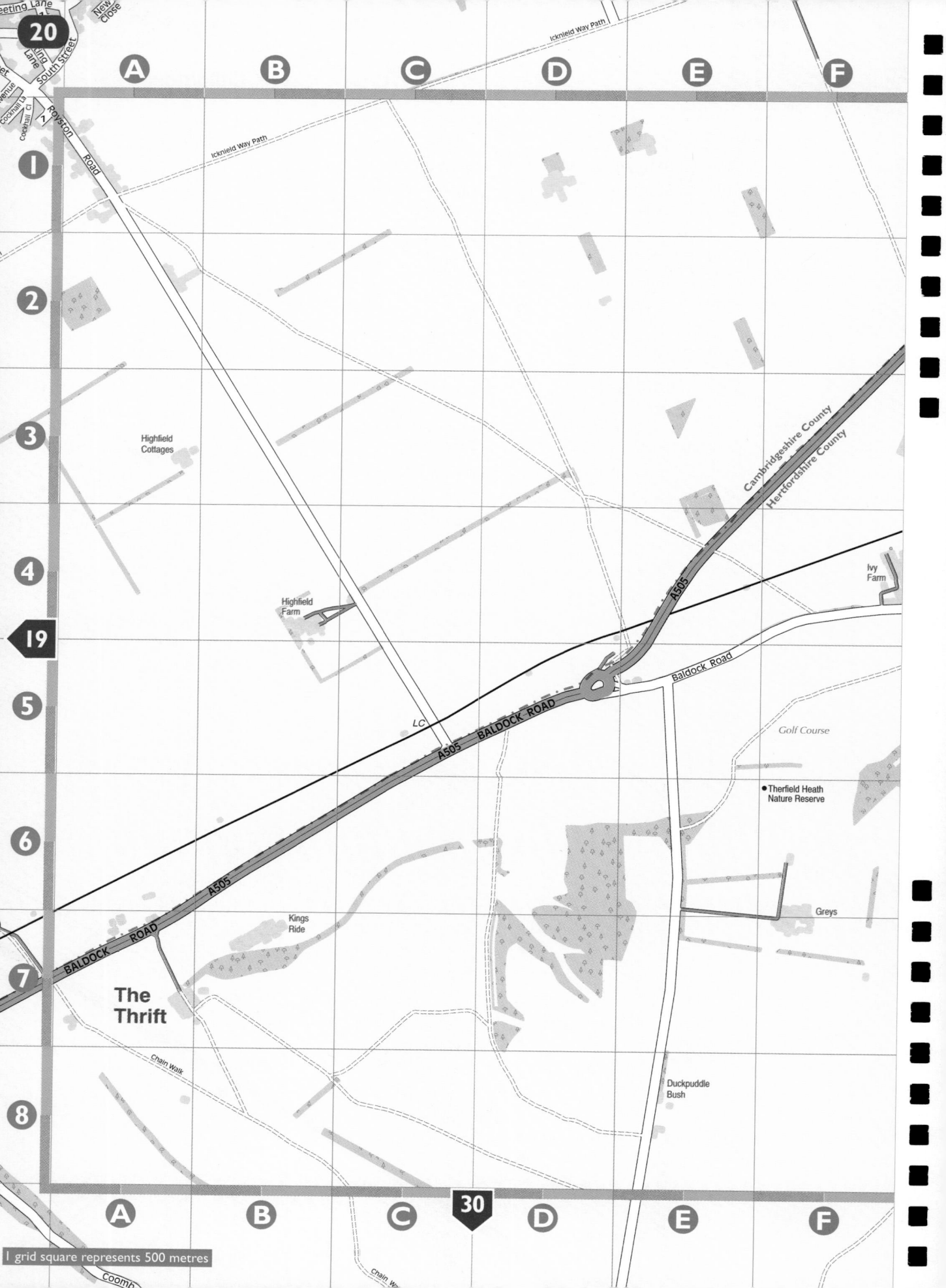

A B C D E F

Icknield Way Path

1

Royston Road

Icknield Way Path

2

3 Highfield Cottages

Cambridgeshire County

Hertfordshire County

4 Highfield Farm

Ivy Farm

A505

Baldock Road

5 LC A505 BALDOCK ROAD

Golf Course

Therfield Heath Nature Reserve

6 A505

Greys

7 BALDOCK ROAD

Kings Ride

The Thrift

Chain Walk

Duckpuddle Bush

8

A B C D E F

1 grid square represents 500 metres

Coomh

Chain Wa

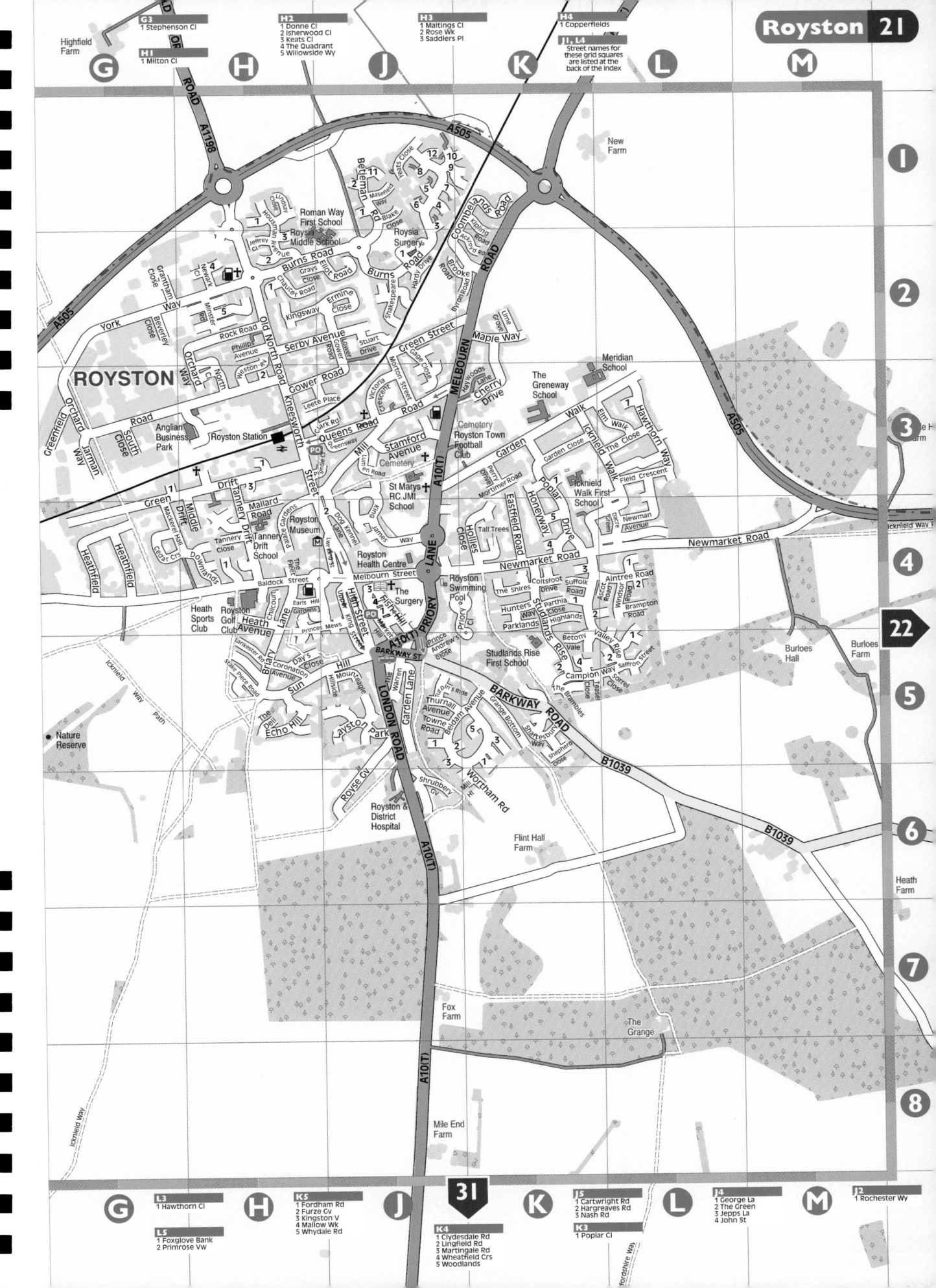

Highfield Farm

G · H · J · K · L · M

I · 2 · 3 · 4 · 22 · 5 · 6 · 7 · 8

ROYSTON

A505
A1198
A505
A10(T)
A10(T)

ROAD
COOMBELANDS ROAD
MELBOURN ROAD
MELBOURN LANE
PRIORY LANE
LONDON ROAD
BARKWAY ROAD
NEWMARKET ROAD
B1039
B1039

Highfield Farm
New Farm
Meridian School
The Greneway School
Royston Town Football Club
Royston Station
Anglian Business Park
Roman Way First School
Royston Middle School
Roysia Surgery
Royston Museum
Royston Health Centre
Royston Swimming Pool
Heath Sports Club
Royston Golf Club
St Marys RC JMI School
Icknield Walk First School
Studlands Rise First School
Royston & District Hospital
Nature Reserve
Burloes Hall
Burloes Farm
Heath Farm
Fox Farm
Mile End Farm
Flint Hall Farm
The Grange

A   B   C   D   E   F

NEW ROAD

A505

Dancey's Farm

Goffers Knoll

1

2

Heath Farm

A505

Icknield Way Path

North Hall Farm

A505

3

Hyde Hill Farm

Noon's Folly Farm

Icknield Way Path

Icknield Way Path

Cambridgeshire County

Hertfordshire County

A505

Icknield Way Path

B1368

BARLEY ROAD

4

21

Farm

5

Lowerfield

6

B1039

Heath Farm

B1039

B1368

7

ROYSTON RD

CAMBRIDGE ROAD

B1368

Bakers Lane

8

The Surgery

HIGH STREET

PICKNAGE ROAD

B1039

CHISHILL

Barley

Hanaper Dr

Barley Vp School

PH

Church End

Shaftenhoe

A   B   C   32   D   E   F

Newsells Farm

LONDON ROAD

Church End

1 grid square represents 500 metres

G   H   J   K   L   M

I

2

3

4

5

6

7

8

K8
1 Plaistow Wy
Bridge...

Heydon
Grange

Heydon
Grange
Golf Club

New Road

Icknield Way Path

Icknield Way Path

New
Buildings
Farm

Icknield Way Path

Heydon

Flowhere
High Road
Close

He

Ha

Woodgreen
Animal Shelter

Chishill Road

New Road

The Pudgell

Road

Reeves
Pightle

Great Chishill

Cambridgeshire County

Hertfordshire County

ROAD

B1039   BARLEY   ROAD

Chishill
Windmill

Heydon

B1039

May Street   Maltings
Lane

Cots
Croft

HALL LANE

Waller's
Close

Th
Ha

G   H   J   K   L   M

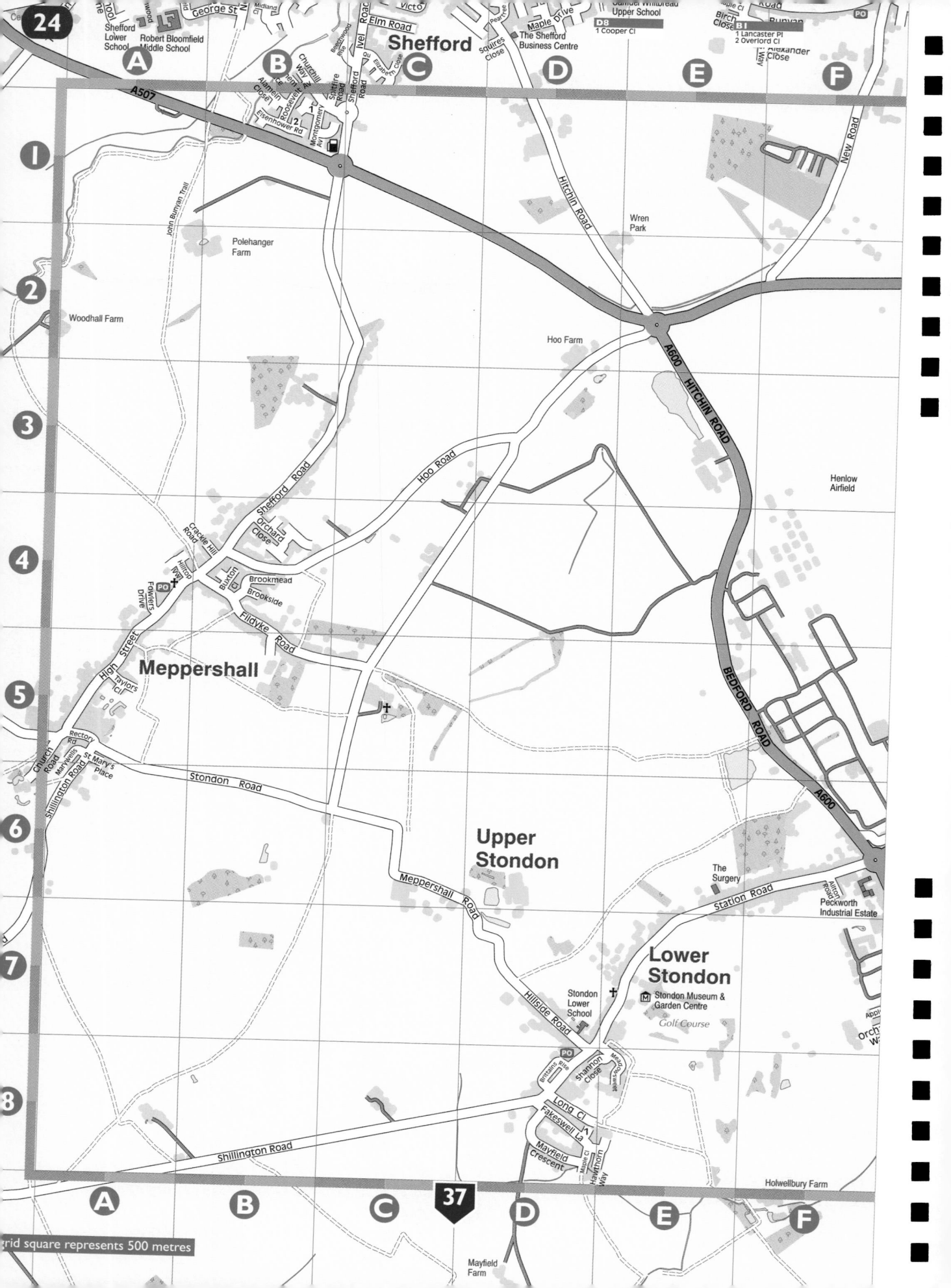

Shefford
Shefford Lower School
Robert Bloomfield Middle School
George St
Elm Road
Maple Drive
The Shefford Business Centre
Squires Close
Upper School
D8 1 Cooper Cl
B1 1 Lancaster Pl 2 Overlord Cl
Alexander Close
Churchill Way
Roosevelt Av
Alamein Close
Eisenhower Rd
Montgomery Av
Spitfire Road
Shefford Road
A507
John Bunyan Trail
Polehanger Farm
Hitchin Road
Wren Park
New Road
Woodhall Farm
Hoo Farm
A600
HITCHIN ROAD
Hoo Road
Shefford Road
Henlow Airfield
Crackle Hill Road
Orchard Close
Hilltop Way
Buxton Cl
Brookmead
Brookside
Fowlers Drive
Fildyke Road
High Street
Meppershall
Taylors Cl
BEDFORD ROAD
Rectory Rd
Church Road
Marywells
St Mary's Place
Shillington Road
Stondon Road
Upper Stondon
Meppershall Road
The Surgery
Station Road
Alltop Road
Peckworth Industrial Estate
Lower Stondon
Stondon Lower School
Stondon Museum & Garden Centre
Golf Course
Hillside Road
Brittains Rise
Shannon Close
Meadowsweet
Long Cl
Fakeswell La
Mayfield Crescent
Maple Cl
Hawthorn Way
Shillington Road
Holwellbury Farm
Mayfield Farm
A B C D E F
1 2 3 4 5 6 7 8
grid square represents 500 metres

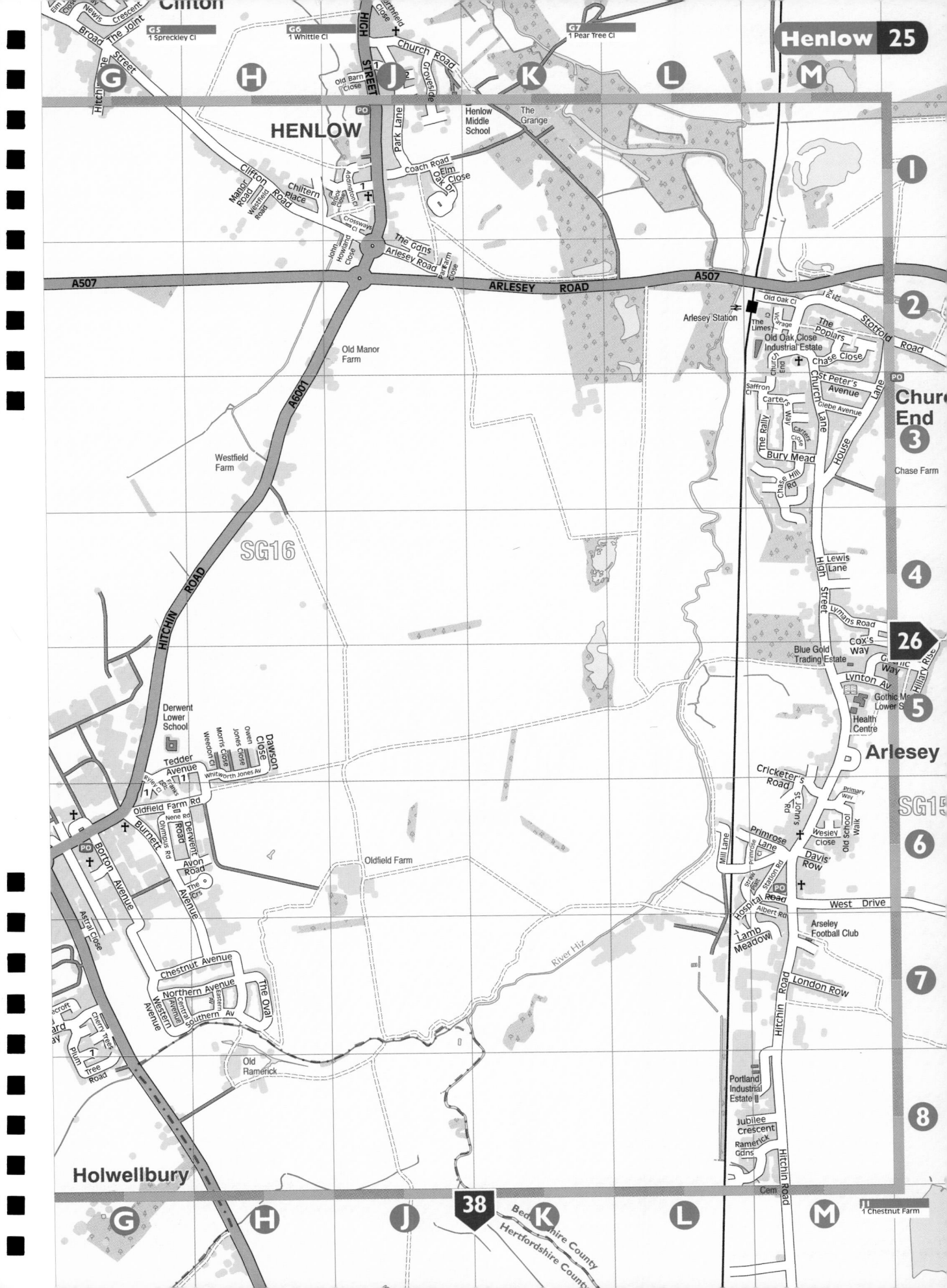

HENLOW
Clifton
Henlow Middle School
The Grange
Old Manor Farm
Westfield Farm
SG16
Derwent Lower School
Oldfield Farm
Old Ramerick
Holwellbury
Arlesey Station
Old Oak Close Industrial Estate
Church End
Chase Farm
Blue Gold Trading Estate
Health Centre
Arlesey
SG15
Arseley Football Club
Portland Industrial Estate
River Hiz
A507
ARLESEY ROAD
HITCHIN ROAD
A6001
HIGH STREET
Church Road
Park Lane
Coach Road
Stotfold Road
High Street
Hitchin Road
West Drive
London Row
Bedfordshire County
Hertfordshire County
G5 1 Sprecklev Cl
G6 1 Whittle Cl
G7 1 Pear Tree Cl
J1 1 Chestnut Farm
26
38

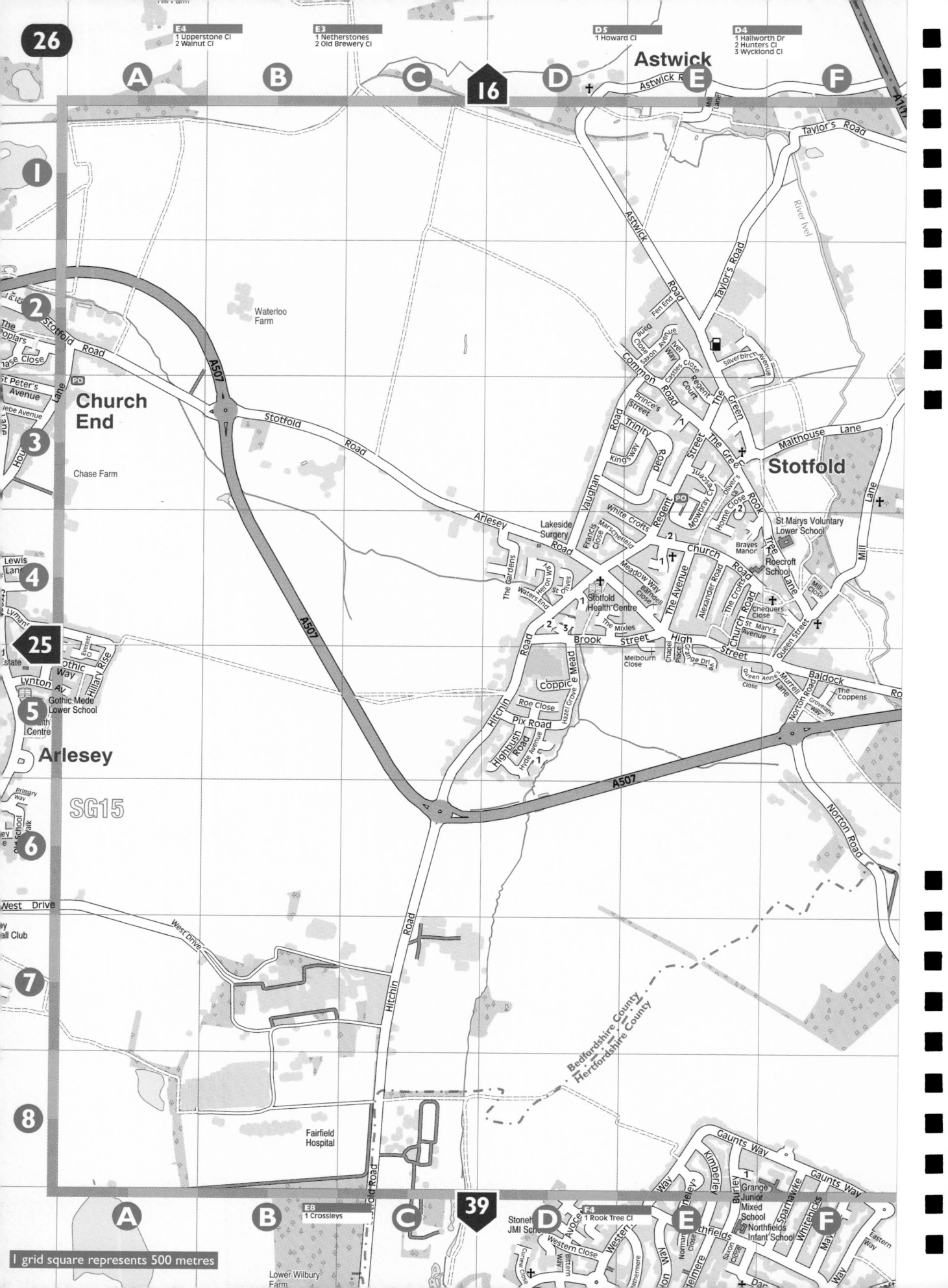
E4
1 Upperstone Cl
2 Walnut Cl
E3
1 Netherstones
2 Old Brewery Cl
D5
1 Howard Cl
D4
1 Hallworth Dr
2 Hunters Cl
3 Wycklond Cl
Astwick
A
B
C
16
D
E
F
Astwick Road
Mill Lane
Taylor's Road
A1(T)
1
River Ivel
Astwick Road
Taylor's Road
2
Waterloo Farm
Fen End
Dane Close
Saxon Avenue
Ivel Way
Silverbirch Avenue
Common Road
Castles Close
Regent Court
The Green
The Poplars
Stotfold Road
Chase Close
St Peter's Avenue
Glebe Avenue
Lane
A507
Church End
Prince's Street
Vaughan Road
Trinity Road
Kingsway
Malthouse Lane
Stotfold Road
3
Chase Farm
Regent Street
The Green
Crescent
Mowbray Crescent
Olivers
Home Close
Rook Tree Lane
Stotfold
Mill Lane
White Crofts
Marschefield
Francis Close
Arlesey Road
Lakeside Surgery
St Marys Voluntary Lower School
Brayes Manor
Church Road
Roecroft School
The Gardens
Heron Way
St Olives
Waters End
Meadow Way
Barndell Close
The Avenue
Alexander Road
The Crofts
Church Road
Mill Close
Lewis Lane
4
Stotfold Health Centre
Chequers Close
St Mary's Avenue
Queen Street
Lymans
A507
Brook Street
The Mixies
High Street
25
Estate
Everest Cl
Gothic Way
Hillary Rise
Lynton Av
Melbourn Close
Chapel Place
Grange Drive
Queen Anne Close
Murrell Lane
Baldock Road
Coppice Mead
Hitchin Road
Norton Road
The Coppens
Groveland Way
Gothic Mede Lower School
5
Health Centre
Roe Close
Pix Road
Hazel Grove
Highbush Road
Hyde Avenue
Arlesey
Primary Way
A507
SG15
Old School Walk
6
Norton Road
West Drive
Club
West Drive
Hitchin Road
7
Bedfordshire County
Hertfordshire County
8
Fairfield Hospital
Gaunts Way
Kimberley
Burley
Grange Junior Mixed School
Sparhawke
Gaunts Way
Whitehicks
A
B
E8
1 Crossleys
C
Old Road
39
D
F4
1 Rook Tree Cl
E
F
Stoneh JMI School
Avocet
Western Close
Western
Northfields
Northfields Infant School
Normandy Close
Saxon Close
Eastern Way
Curlew Close
Bittern Way
Way
Lower Wilbury Farm

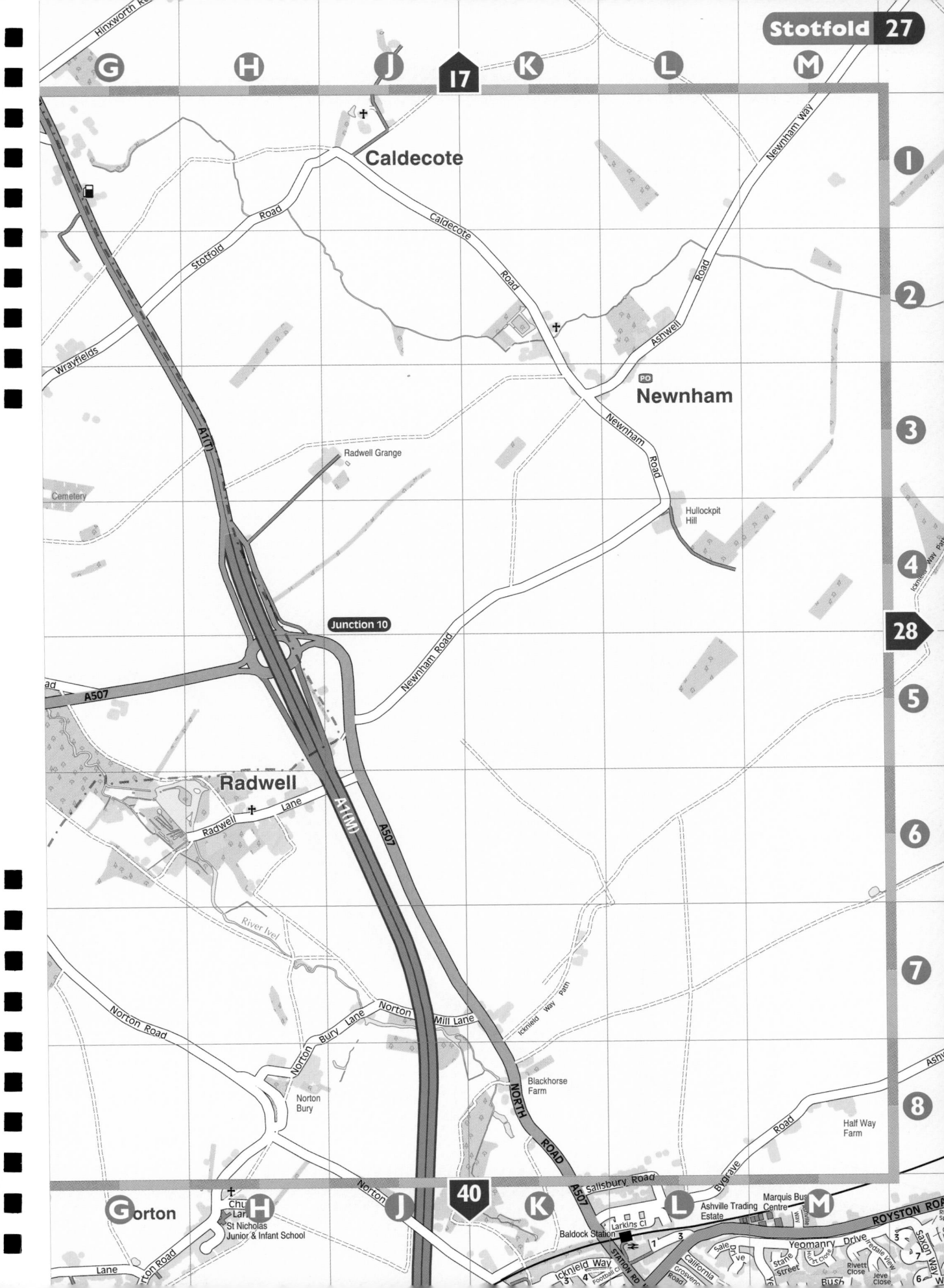

Stotfold 27
G
H
J
17
K
L
M
Hinxworth Road
Caldecote
Caldecote Road
Stotfold Road
Wrayfields
Newnham Way
Ashwell Road
PO
Newnham
Newnham Road
Radwell Grange
Cemetery
Hullockpit Hill
A1(T)
Junction 10
A507
Newnham Road
Icknield Way Path
28
Radwell
Radwell Lane
A1(M)
A507
River Ivel
Norton Road
Norton Bury Lane
Norton Mill Lane
Icknield Way Path
Blackhorse Farm
Norton Bury
NORTH ROAD
Bygrave Road
Half Way Farm
1
2
3
4
5
6
7
8
40
Gorton
St Nicholas Junior & Infant School
Norton Road
Lane
Salisbury Road
A507
Ashville Trading Estate
Marquis Business Centre
ROYSTON ROAD
Larkins Cl
Baldock Station
STATION RD
Icknield Way
Football Cl
Grosvenor Road
California
Yeomanry Drive
Stane Street
Rivett Close
Jeve Close
Saxon Way
Bush

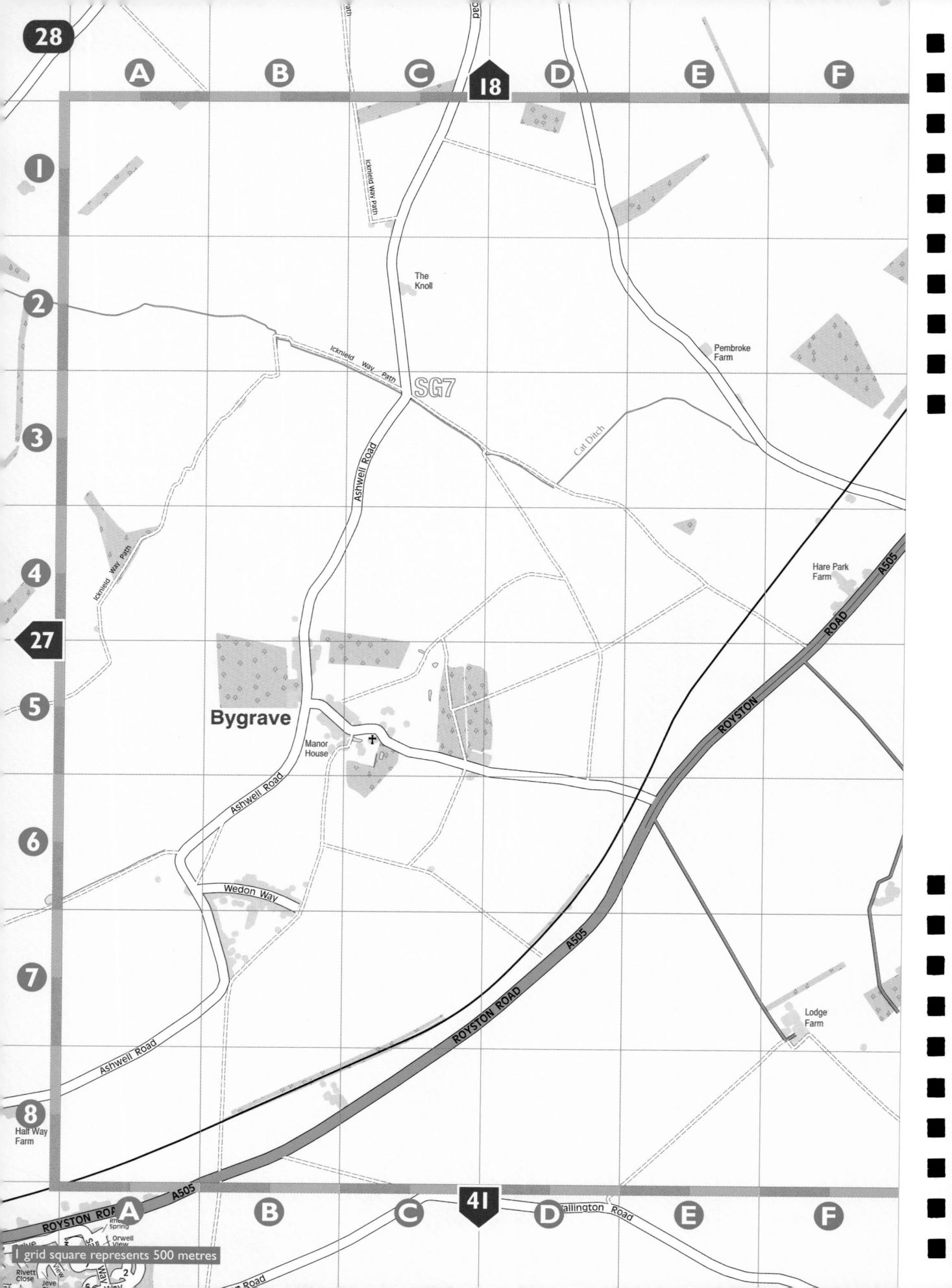
18
27
41
A
B
C
D
E
F
1
2
3
4
5
6
7
8
Icknield Way Path
The Knoll
Icknield Way Path
SG7
Pembroke Farm
Cat Ditch
Ashwell Road
Icknield Way Path
Hare Park Farm
A505
ROAD
ROYSTON
Bygrave
Manor House
Ashwell Road
Wedon Way
A505
ROYSTON ROAD
Lodge Farm
Ashwell Road
Half Way Farm
ROYSTON ROAD
A505
Wallington Road
Orwell View
Rivett Close
1 grid square represents 500 metres

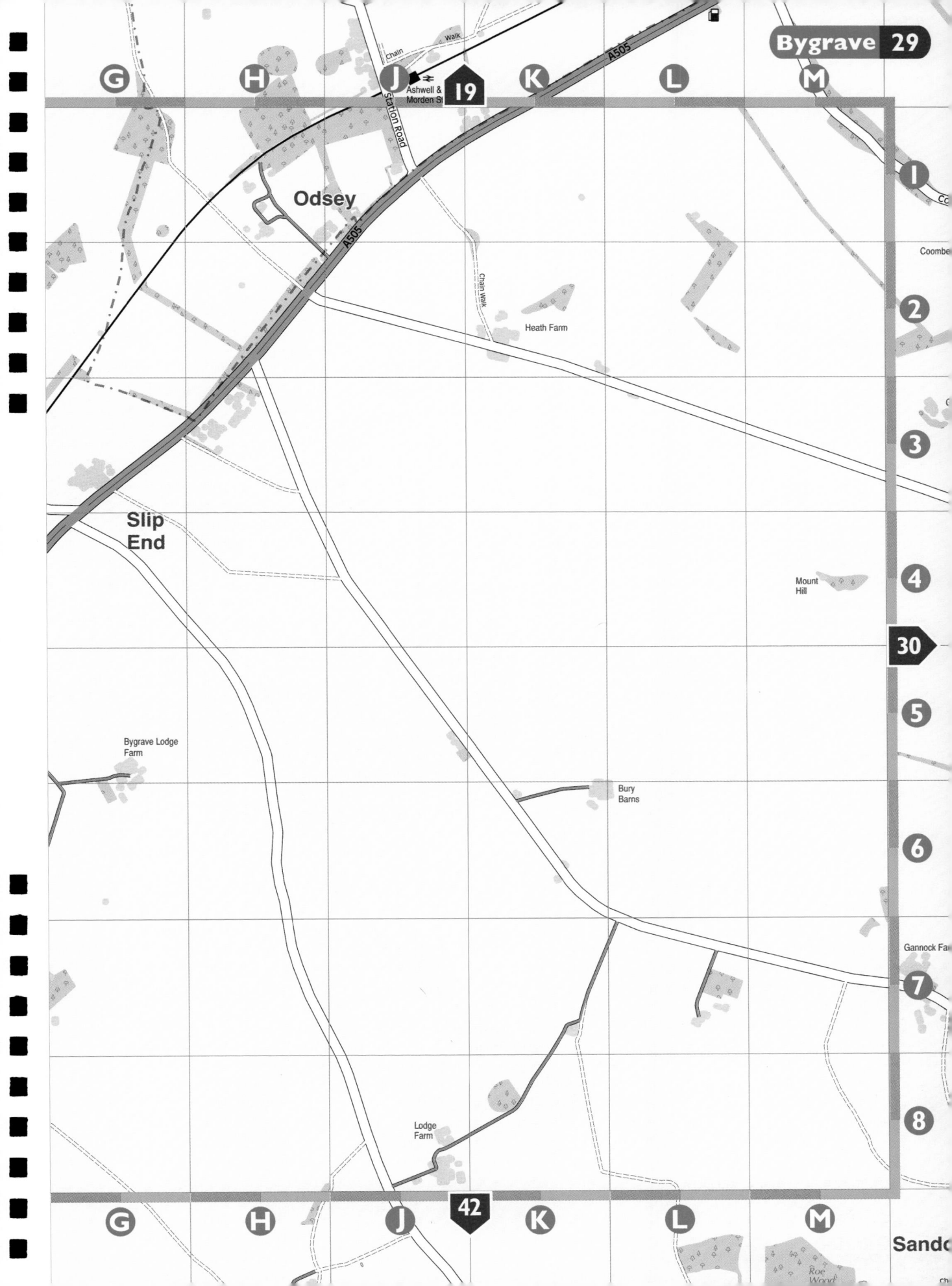

Odsey

Slip
End

Bygrave Lodge
Farm

Heath Farm

Chain Walk

Mount
Hill

Bury
Barns

Lodge
Farm

Station Road

Ashwell &
Morden St

A505

Coombe

Gannock Fa

Roe
Wood

Sand

G H J K L M

19

42

30

I
2
3
4
5
6
7
8

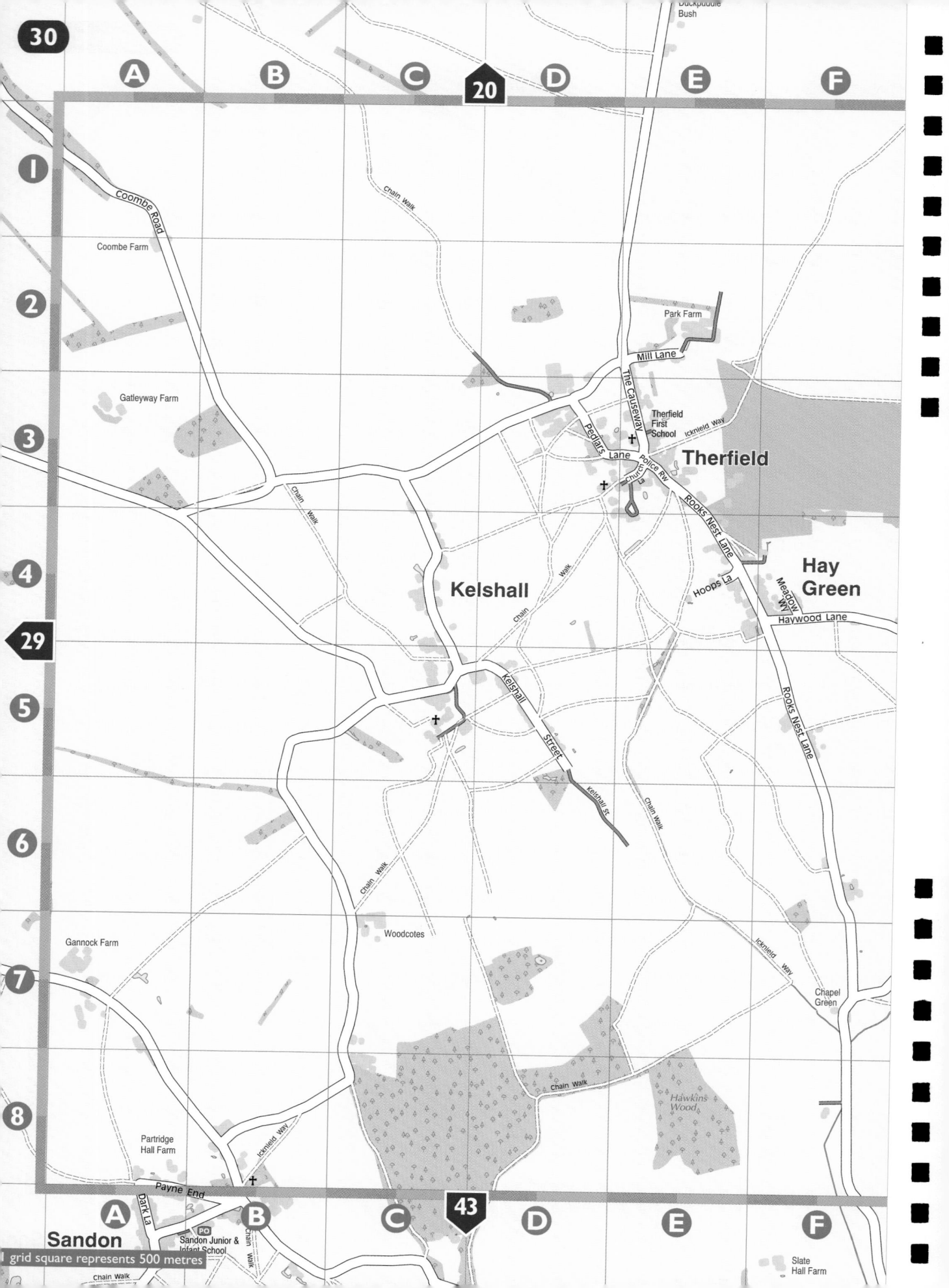

Ⓐ   Ⓑ   Ⓒ   **20**   Ⓓ   Ⓔ   Ⓕ

Duckpuddle Bush

Ⓘ

Coombe Road

Coombe Farm

2

Park Farm

Mill Lane

Gatleyway Farm

The Causeway

Therfield First School

Icknield Way

3

Chain Walk

Pedlars Lane

Police Rw

Church La

Therfield

Rooks Nest Lane

4

Walk

Hoops La

Meadow Wy

Hay Green

Kelshall

Chain

Haywood Lane

29

5

Kelshall Street

Kelshall St

Chain Walk

Rooks Nest Lane

6

Chain Walk

Woodcotes

Icknield Way

Gannock Farm

7

Chapel Green

Partridge Hall Farm

Icknield Way

Chain Walk

Hawkins Wood

8

Payne End

Sandon Ⓐ   Dark La   Ⓑ   Chain Walk   Ⓒ   **43**   Ⓓ   Ⓔ   Ⓕ

PO Sandon Junior & Infant School

grid square represents 500 metres

Chain Walk

Slate Hall Farm

G H J K L M

21

I
2
3
4

Mile End
Farm

A10(T)

Hertfordshire Way

Hatchpen

A10(T)

Ickfield Way

Reed End

Hertfordshire Way

The Joint

32

5

Brickyard La
Willow Cl
Blacksmith's Lane
Jackson's Lane
Reed First
School
Crown
Lane

Church

High Street

Wisbridge
Farm

Lane

Driftway

Reed

Dane
End

Dane
End

Reed Hall

Grannock
Green

6

7

8

G H J K L M

44

A   B   C   22   D   E   F

The Surgery
1 Greenbury Cl

Barle

CHISHILL

HIGH STRE
High St
PO

Hanaper Dr
7 PH
Barley Vp
School

Church
School End
Puddinge Lane
Lane
Churchfield

Shaftenhoe
End

1

LONDON ROAD

The
Mt

Smith's End Lane

**Smith's
End**

2

CAMBRIDGE

ROAD

Newsells
Farm

Bogmoor
Road

3

Newsells

CAMBRIDGE

B1368

Barkway
Hill

Newsells
Park

BARKWAY HILL

4

31

Walk
Wood

Royston

CAMBRIDGE ROAD

B1368

5

Windmill Ci
Road
Periwinkle
Cl

Cokenach

6

Hertfordshire Way

Barkway

Elms Farm

Church
Lane
HIGH STREET

Barkway Va
First School

Burrs
La

Earl's
Wood

7

B1368

Ash
Mt
Townsend

Gas Lane

Hertfordshire Way

Nuthampstead
Bury

Hertfordshire Way

Bell Farm

8

B1368

Nuthampstead Road

Barkway
Park
Golf Club

A   B   LONDON R   C   45   D   E   F

Barkway
Equestrian
Centre

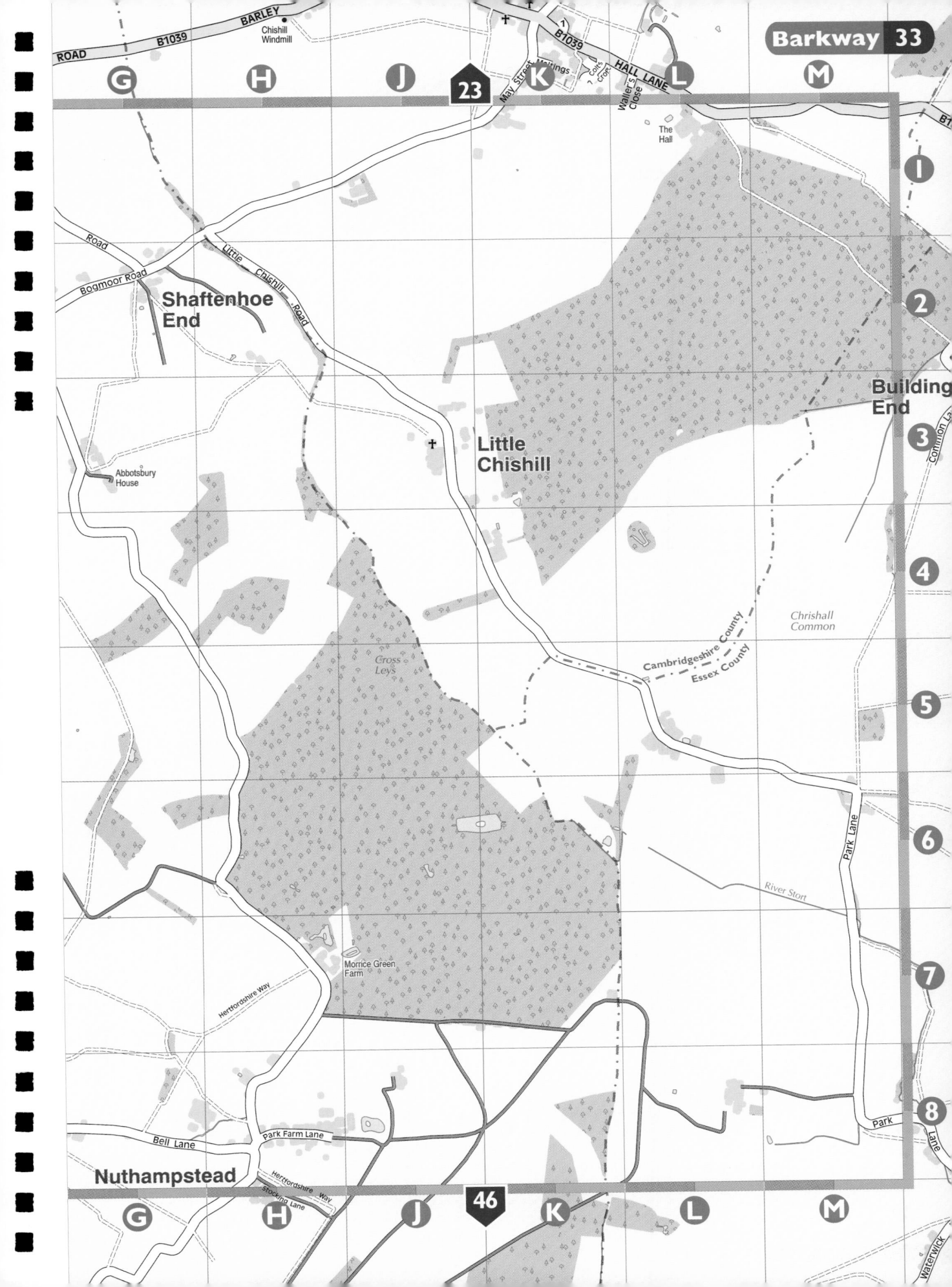

ROAD
BARLEY
B1039
B1039
HALL LANE

Chishill
Windmill

May Street Maltings

Waller's Close

Car's Croft

The Hall

G H J 23 K L M

1

Little Chishill Road

Bogmoor Road

Shaftenhoe End

2

Building End

Common La.

3

Abbotsbury House

Little Chishill

4

Chrishall Common

Cross Leys

Cambridgeshire County
Essex County

5

6

River Stort

Park Lane

Morrice Green Farm

Hertfordshire Way

7

Bell Lane

Park Farm Lane

8

Park Lane

Waterwick

Nuthampstead

Hertfordshire Way

Stocking Lane

G H J 46 K L M

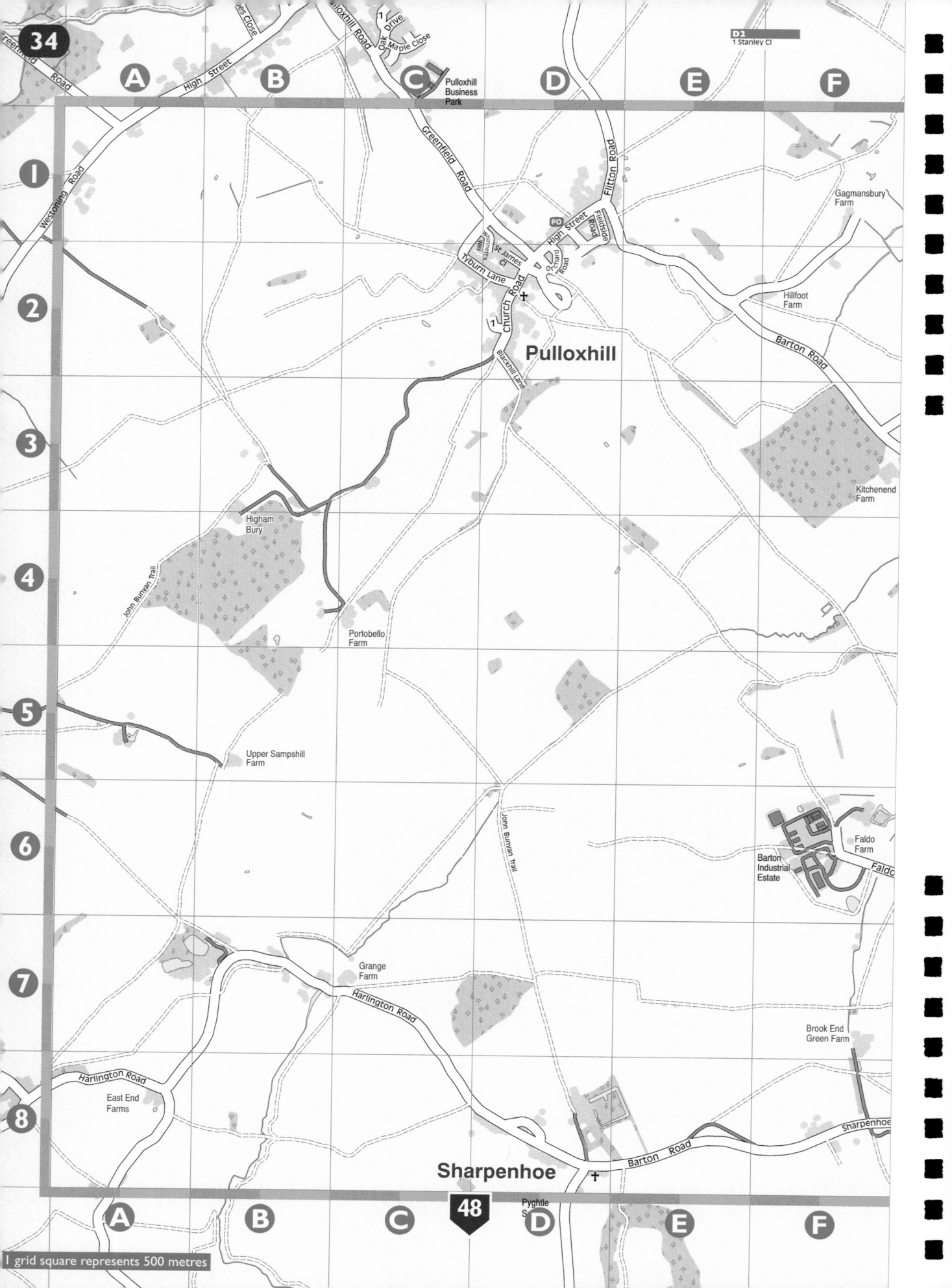

A   High Street   B   C   Pulloxhill Business Park   D   E   F

1   Pulloxhill Road   Oak Drive   Maple Close

D2
1 Stanley Cl

Greenfield Road

Westoning Road

Filton Road

Gagmansbury Farm

1

PO

High Street

Fieldside Road

St James Cl

Winners Way

Orchard Road

Hillfoot Farm

Tyburn Lane

Barton Road

2

Church Road

7

Blackhill Lane

Pulloxhill

3

Kitchenend Farm

Higham Bury

John Bunyan Trail

4

Portobello Farm

5

Upper Sampshill Farm

John Bunyan Trail

Barton Industrial Estate

Faldo Farm

6

Faldo

Grange Farm

7

Harlington Road

Brook End Green Farm

Harlington Road

East End Farms

8

Sharpenhoe

Barton Road

Sharpenhoe

A   B   C   Pyghtle S   D   E   F

1 grid square represents 500 metres

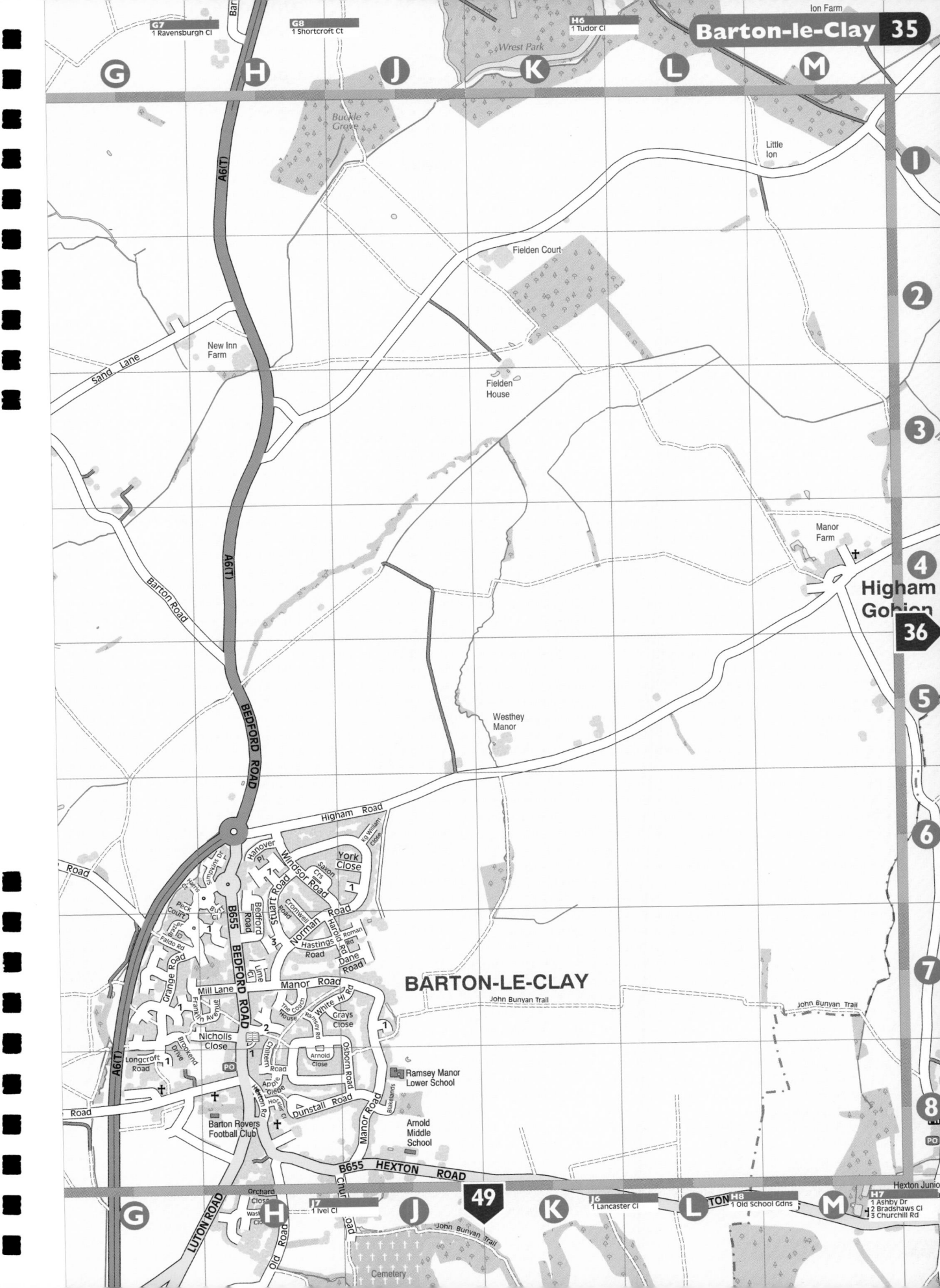

G7
1 Ravensburgh Cl

G8
1 Shortcroft Ct

H6
1 Tudor Cl

Ion Farm

G H J K L M

Wrest Park

Little
Ion

Fielden Court

Buckle
Grove

New Inn
Farm

Sand Lane

Fielden
House

2

3

Manor
Farm

4

**Higham
Gobion**

36

Westhey
Manor

5

6

A6(T)

Barton Road

BEDFORD ROAD

Higham Road

K9 William
Close

Hanover
Pl

Windsor Road

York
Close

Saxon
Ct

1

Road

Henry Road

Smokins Dr

Peck
Court

B655

Bedford
Road

Cromwell
Road

Norman
Road

Hastings
Road

Roman
Road

Dane
Road

7

John Bunyan Trail

John Bunyan Trail

Faldo Rd

Grange Road

BEDFORD ROAD

Mill Lane

Lime Lane

Manor Road

White Hl Rd

Grays
Close

1

BARTON-LE-CLAY

Franklin Avenue

The Coach
House

Ramsey Rd

Nicholls
Close

Chiltern
Road

Arnold
Close

Osborn Road

2

Longcroft
Road

Brookend
Drive

1

PO

Apple
Glebe

Blakelands

Ramsey Manor
Lower School

A6(T)

Road

Hexton Rd

Hook La

Dunstall Road

Manor Road

Arnold
Middle
School

8

PO

Barton Rovers
Football Club

B655 HEXTON ROAD

Hexton Junior

Luton Road

Orchard
Close

Wast
Cl

J7
1 Ivel Cl

Churchill Road

Old
Road

49

John Bunyan Trail

J6
1 Lancaster Cl

TON

H8
1 Old School Gdns

H7
1 Ashby Dr
2 Bradshaws Cl
3 Churchill Rd

Cemetery

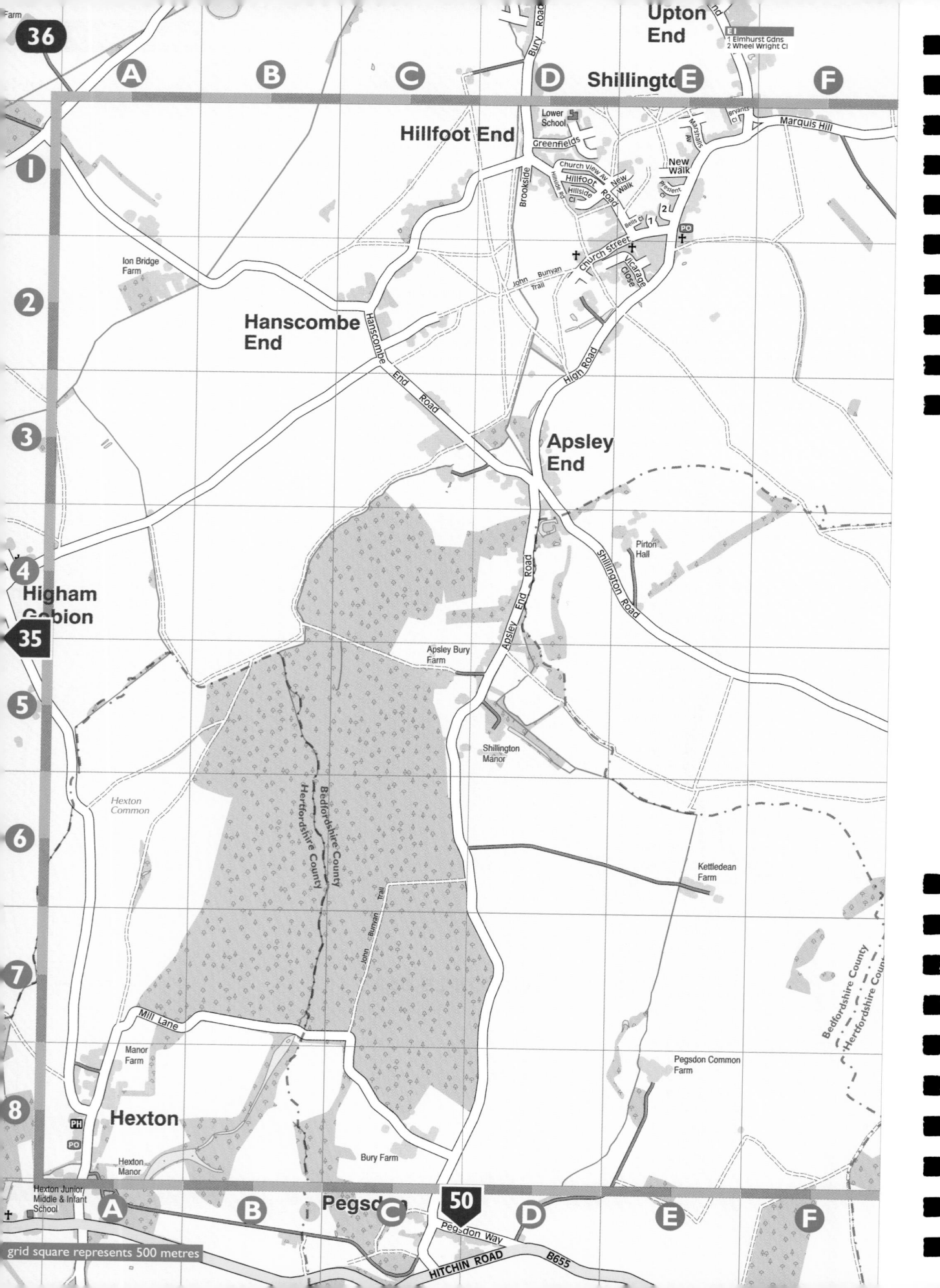

36
Upton End
E1
1 Elmhurst Gdns
2 Wheel Wright Cl
Shillington
Bury Road
Hillfoot End
Lower School
Greenfields
Church View Av
Hillfoot Road
Hillside Rd
Hillside Cl
New Walk
Brookside
Marshalls Av
Bryants Cl
Marquis Hill
Present Cl
Bells Cl
PO
Church Street
Vicarage Close
John Bunyan Trail
Ion Bridge Farm
Hanscombe End
Hanscombe End Road
High Road
Apsley End
Apsley End Road
Shillington Road
Pirton Hall
Higham Gobion
35
Apsley Bury Farm
Shillington Manor
Hexton Common
Bedfordshire County
Hertfordshire County
Kettledean Farm
Mill Lane
Manor Farm
Pegsdon Common Farm
Hexton
PH
PO
Hexton Manor
Bury Farm
Hexton Junior Middle & Infant School
Pegsdon
50
Pegsdon Way
HITCHIN ROAD
B655
grid square represents 500 metres
A B C D E F
1 2 3 4 5 6 7 8

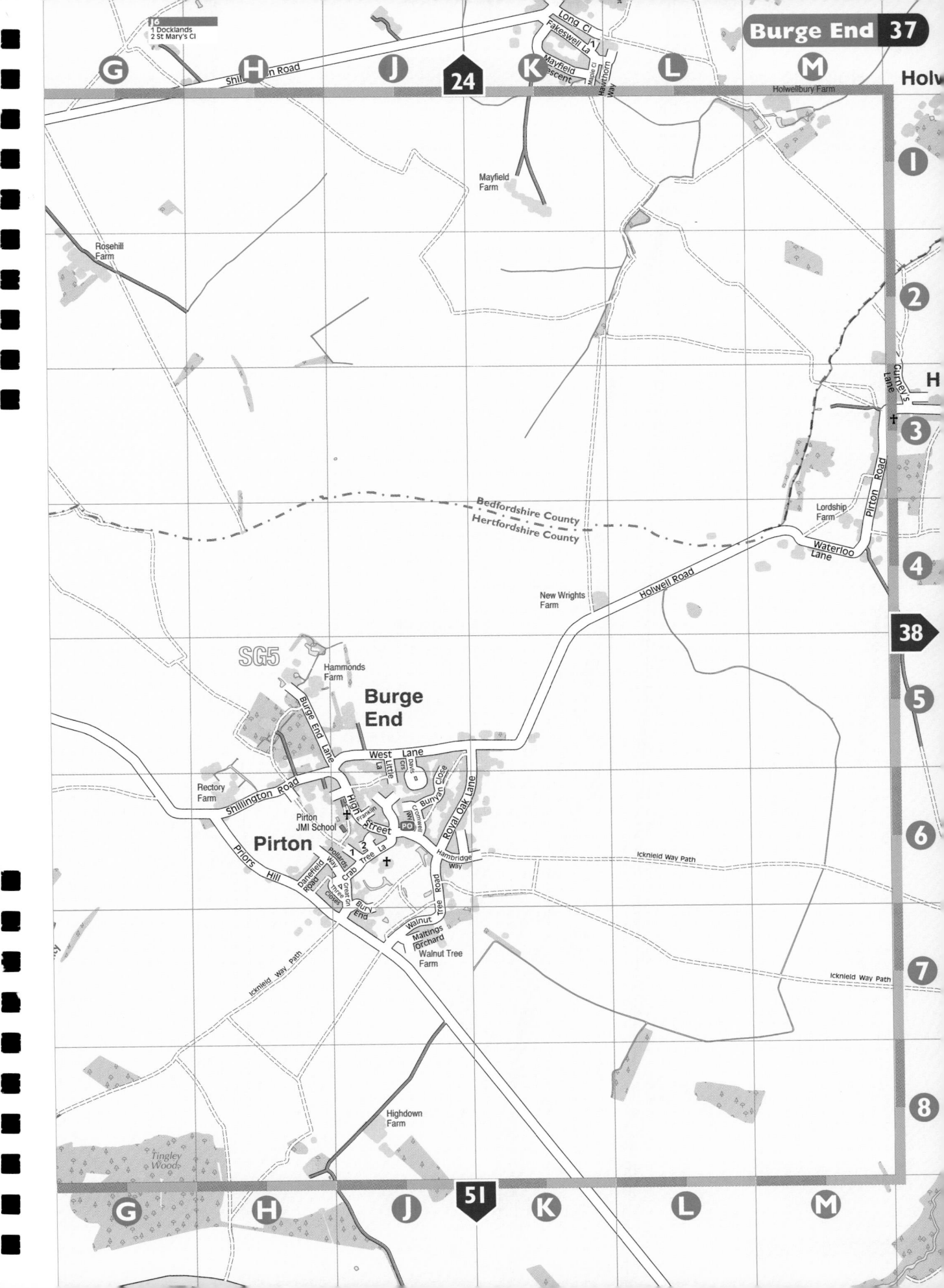

J6
1 Docklands
2 St Mary's Cl
Shillington Road
Long Cl
Fakeswell La
Mayfield Crescent
Maple Cl
Hawthorn Way
24
G
H
J
K
L
M
Holwellbury Farm
Holw
Mayfield Farm
Rosehill Farm
Gurney's Lane
H
Bedfordshire County
Hertfordshire County
Lordship Farm
Pirton Road
Waterloo Lane
Holwell Road
New Wrights Farm
38
SG5
Hammonds Farm
Burge End
Burge End Lane
West Lane
Little La
Crs
Davis
Bunyan Close
Cromwell Way
Royal Oak Lane
Rectory Farm
Shillington Road
High Street
Franklin
PO
Pirton JMI School
Pirton
Pollards Way
Crab Tree La
Hambridge Way
Icknield Way Path
Priors Hill
Danefield Road
Great Gn
Three Closes
Bury End
Walnut Tree Road
Maltings Orchard
Walnut Tree Farm
Icknield Way Path
Icknield Way Path
Highdown Farm
Tingley Wood
51
G
H
J
K
L
M
1
2
3
4
5
6
7
8

Holwellbury
Holwell
Gurney's Lane
Holwell Road
Meadow Farm
Rand's Meadow
Pirton Road
Ashcroft Farm
A600
BEDFORD ROAD
New Ramerwick Farm
Bedfordshire County
Hertfordshire County
Pestol Farm
Wilbury Farm
Hitchin Road
Arlesey Road
Snailswell
Snailswell Lane
Abbis Orchard
Longmeadow Drive
Cadwell
Icknield Way Path
Lower Green
Claymore Dr
Pound Farm
Ickleford
Witter Av
River Court
Chambers La
Wyatt Close
Greenfield Av
Walnut Way
Cedar Av
Icknield Close
St Katharines Close
Ryder Avenue
Turnpike Lane
Lodge Ct
Manor Close
Duncots Cl
Laurel Wy
Knowl Piece
Hillgate
Hunting Gate
Wallace Way
Bilton Road
Westmill Lane
River Oughton
Bessemer Close
Willow Tree Way
Cadwell Lane
Hillfield Avenue
Girdle Road
Burford Way
Portman Close
Priory School
Truemans Road
Mulberry Wy
Beechwood Cl
Times Close
Bedford Rd
Shepherds Mead
The Mead
Strathmore Infant School
Lammas Mead
Bury Mead Road
Heathfield Road
Millstream Close
Woolgrove
Swinburne Av
Westmill Road
River Mead
Milestone Rd
Seebohm Close
Westmill
Nature Reserve
John Barker Place
Bingen Road
Mattocke Road
Freemans Close
Wellingham Avenue
Bowyer's Close
Bearton Green
Old Hale Way
Brampton Park Road
Wilton Road
Strathmore Avenue
Whitehurst
Balmoral Road
Stormont Road
Bearton
HITCHIN
River Purwell
Walsworth
Algrey Trading
Ramerick Gdns
Crescent
Industrial Estate
Cem
E5 1 The Poplars
D6 1 Greenfield La
25
37
52
A
B
C
D
E
F
1
2
3
4
5
6
7
8
1 grid square represents 500 metres

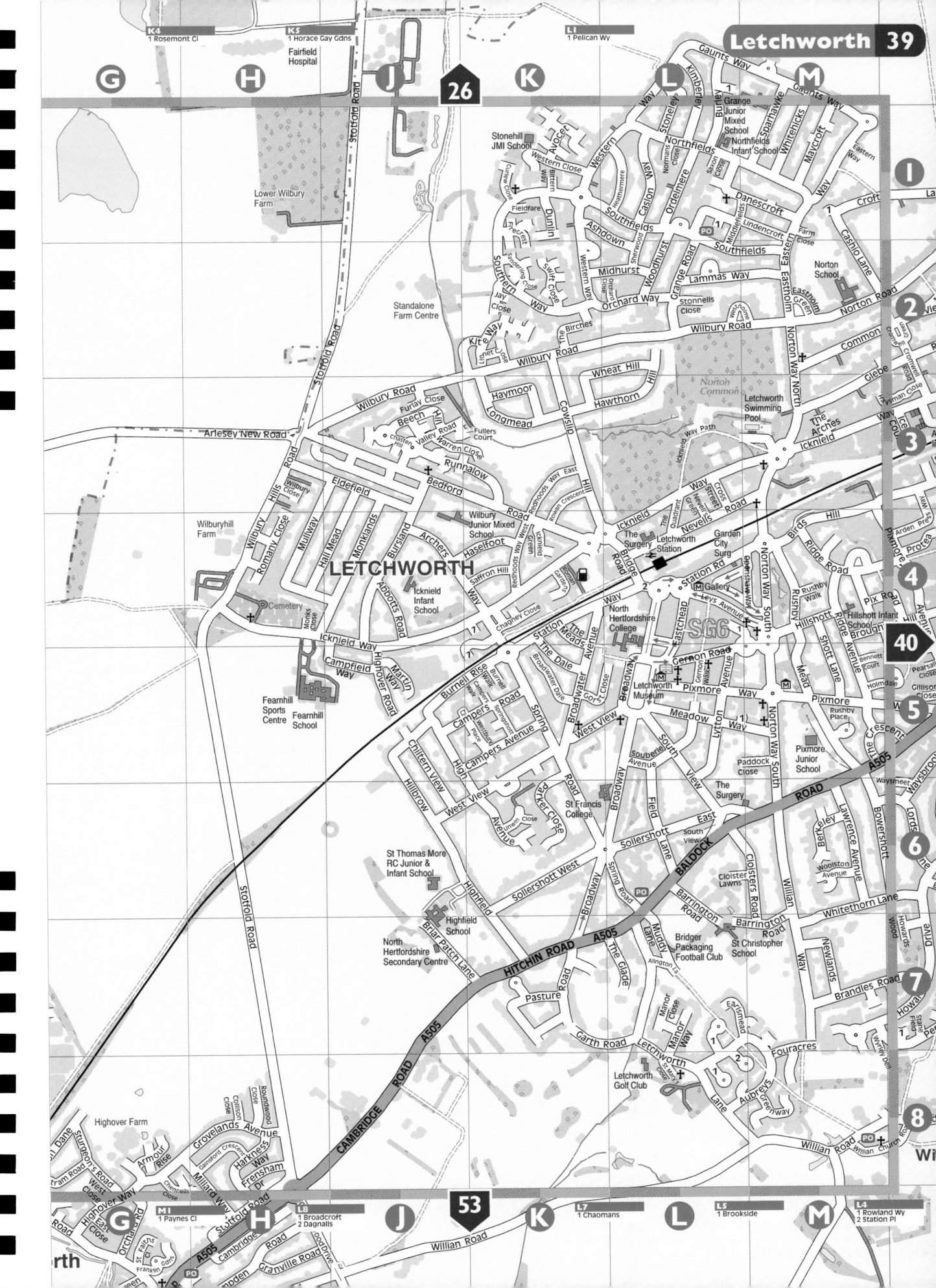
K4 1 Rosemont Cl
K5 1 Horace Gay Gdns
L1 1 Pelican Wy
Fairfield Hospital
G
H
J
26
K
L
M
Stotfold Road
Lower Wilbury Farm
Standalone Farm Centre
Stonehill JMI School
Western Close
Avocet
Bittern Way
Curlew Close
Fieldfare
Dunlin
Firecrest
Sanderling Close
Swift Close
Southern Way
Jay Close
Kite Way
Linnet Close
Gaunts Way
Kimberley
Stoneley
Burley
Grange Junior Mixed School
Northfields Infant School
Sparhawke
Whitehicks
Maycroft
Eastern Way
Northfields
Normans Close
Saxon Close
Western Way
Heathermere
Casion Way
Ordelmere
Danescroft
Southfields
Ashdown
Sherwood
Middlefields
Lindencroft
Farm Close
Cashio Lane
Croft
Midhurst
Woodhurst
Grange Road
Lammas Way
Orchard Close
Orchard Way
Stonnells Close
Eastern Way
Eastholm
Eastholm Green
Norton School
Norton Road
Wilbury Road
The Birches
Westholme
Norton Way North
Common
Cromwell Green
Cromwell Road
Glebe
Wheat Hill
Haymoor
Hawthorn Hill
Longmead
Cowslip Hill
Norton Common
Letchworth Swimming Pool
Icknield Way Path
Heysman Close
The Arches
Icknield Way
Wilbury Road
Furlay Close
Beech Hill
Chasten Hill
Valley Road
Warren Close
Fullers Court
Runnalow
Arlesey New Road
Bedford Road
Redhoods Way East
Rowan Crescent
Hill
Icknield Way
The Quadrant
Nevells Green
Cross Street
Nevells Road
Wilbury Hills Road
Wilbury Close
Eldefield
Wilburyhill Farm
Romany Close
Mullway
Hall Mead
Monklands
Bursland
Archers Way
Wilbury Junior Mixed School
Haselfoot
Icknield Green
Redhoods Way West
The Surgery
Letchworth Station
Garden City Surg
Bridge Road
Birds Hill
Ridge Road
Arden Press Way
Pixmore
Protea
LETCHWORTH
Saffron Hill
Roman Gardens
Station Rd
Openshaw Way
Rushby Walk
Pix Road
Avenue
Cemetery
Monks Close
Abbotts Road
Icknield Infant School
Gallery
Leys Avenue
Norton Way South
Rushby Mead
Hillshott
Hillshott Infant School
Brough
Chagney Close
Station Way
North Hertfordshire College
SG6
Eastcheap
Ridge Avenue
Shott Lane
Bennett Court
40
Icknield Way
Campfield Way
Highover Road
Martin Way
Fearnhill Sports Centre
Fearnhill School
The Meads
Avenue
The Dale
Broadwater Dale
Broadwater Avenue
Gernon Road
Gernon Walk
Letchworth Museum
Pixmore Way
Pixmore
Holmdale
Pearsall Close
Gillison Close
Burnell Rise
Burnell Walk
Campers Walk
Springshott
Campers Road
Spring Road
Gorst Close
Broadway
West View
Meadow Way
Lytton Avenue
Rushby Place
The Crescent
Campers Avenue
Westbury Place
Chiltern View
Hillbrow
High Avenue
West View
Souberie Avenue
South View
Paddock Close
Pixmore Junior School
A505
Waysmeet
Waysbrook
Lords
Unwin Close
Parker Close
St Francis College
Broadway
Field Lane
The Surgery
Norton Way South
ROAD
Berkeley
Lawrence Avenue
Bowershott
East
South View
Sollershott East
Sollershott
BALDOCK
Wooiston Avenue
Cloister Lawns
Cloisters Road
Willian Way
St Thomas More RC Junior & Infant School
Sollershott West
Spring Road
Highfield
PO
Barrington Road
Whitethorn Lane
Howards Wood
Drive
Highfield School
Briar Patch Lane
Broadway
Muddy Lane
Bridger Packaging Football Club
St Christopher School
North Hertfordshire Secondary Centre
HITCHIN ROAD
The Glade
Allington La
Newlands Way
Brandles Road
Howard
Pasture Road
Manor Close
Manor Way
Earlsmead
Stane Field
Garth Road
Letchworth Lane
Fouracres
Wyrley Dell
St Mary's Close
Letchworth Golf Club
Aubreys
Greenway
CAMBRIDGE ROAD
A505
Highover Farm
Sturgeon's Road
Collison Close
Close
Roundwood Close
Grovelands Avenue
Armour Rise
Gainsford Crescent
Harkness Way
Frensham Dr
Willian Road
Willian Church Road
PO
Highover Way
West Close
Chennells Close
Millard Way
Stotfold Road
Orchard Rd
Easy Close
Road
M1 1 Paynes Cl
L8 1 Broadcroft 2 Dagnalls
53
L7 1 Chaomans
L5 1 Brookside
L4 1 Rowland Wy 2 Station Pl
Willian Road
Cambridge Road
Granville Road
St Faiths Cl
Franklin Gdns
I
2
3
4
5
6
7
8

D3
1 Park Crs
2 Park Gdns
D4
1 Willian Wy
D2
1 Bell Rw
2 The Gardens
3 Saddlers Cl
4 Sun St
B7
1 Chalk Fld
2 Ennismore Cl
3 Rudham Gv
D1
Street names for this grid square are listed at the back of the index
A6
1 Howard Ga
A7
1 Thristers Cl
Blackhorse Farm
Half Way Farm
27
Norton
Church Lane
St Nicholas Junior & Infant School
Norton Road
Croft Lane
Cashio Lane
Common View
Glebe Road
North Avenue
Talbot Way
Cade Close
Kristiansand Way
Green Lane
Blackhorse Road
Flint Road
Knap Close
Works Road
Pyms Close
Hampden Close
Pascal Way
Tabbs Close
Cromwell Road
Pysman Close
Shaftesbury Industrial Centre
Saunders Close
Green Lane Industrial Estate
Ascot Industrial Estate
Iceni Court
Diamond Industrial Centre
Winton Close
Hadrian Way
Lacre Way
Jubilee Road
Jubilee Trading Estate
Fourth Avenue
Third Avenue
Campus Five
Woodside Ind Park
Arden Press Way
Protea Way
Pixmore Avenue
Amor Way
Letchworth Business Centre
Dunhams Lane
Second Avenue
Fifth Avenue
Sixth Avenue
One Avenue
Pix Road
Hillshott Infant
Jackman's Place
North Hertfordshire Leisure Centre
School Walk
Bidwell Close
Pearsall Close
Holmdale
Gillison Close
Letchworth Garden City Football Club
A505 BALDOCK ROAD
BALDOCK ROAD
A505
The Crescent
Schoolfields
Quinn Way
Webb Close
Radburn Way
Bayworth
Chatterton
Radburn JMI School
Woolgrove School
Waysbrook
Waysmeet
LETCHWORTH GATE
Denby
Goldon
Kyrkeby
Newells
Pryor Way
Quills
Maddles
Oakhill
Baldock Lane
Lannock
Parkfield
Jarden
Lordship Lane
Bowershott
Radburn Way
Rundells
Swanstand
Lannock JMI School
Townley
Yardley
Vincent
Bell Acre Gardens
Bell Acres
Howards Wood Drive
Ashbourne Cl
A6141 LETCHWORTH GATE
Whitechurch Gardens
Alban Road
Crabtree Dell
Blackmore
Creamery Court
Dents Close
Rookes Close
Olden Mead
Milne Close
Kestrel Walk
Stane Field
Penn Way
Pear Tree Dell
Netley Dell
Lapwing Dell
Larthing Drive
Whitethorn Lane
Baldock Lane
Willian Church Road
Willian
A1(M)
Junction 9
A6141
B197
Lannock Hill
Norton Road
NORTH ROAD
A507
Salisbury Road
Bygrave
Ashville Trading Estate
Marquis Business Centre
Larkins Cl
Baldock Station
STATION RD
Icknield Way
Football Cl
Orchard Road
Church Street
Pond Lane
The Sycamores
Cemetery
Coachman's Lane
Hopewell Road
Pepys Way
Avon Cresent
West Avenue
HITCHIN STREET
WHITEHORSE STREET
HIGH STREET
LETCHWORTH ROAD
Simpson Drive
Thurnall Close
Park Street
Knights Templar School
Brandles Close School
Weston Way
Mansfield Road
Park Drive
Holroyd Crescent
Baldock Health Cen
Chilvers Bank
The Glade
The Leas
The Close
Hill Top
The Rise
The Rowans
Alder Close
The Spinney
Bondor Business Cen
St Mary's Way
The Dell
St Marys Junior & Infant School
Nightingale Way
Mons Avenue
LONDON ROAD
London Road
Ashton's Lane
Baldock Industrial Estate
Hillcrest
Baldock Lane
Chalk Hills
Hatch Lane
Beechwood Close
Chiltern Road
Woodland Way
Pryor Road
Page Close
Ivel Way
Byrd Walk
Turpin's Way
Anchor Road
Icknield Way Path
Baldock
CLOTHALL ROAD
California
Grosvenor Road
Hartsfield Junior Middle & Infant School
Yeomanry Drive
Stane Street
Wynn Close
Bush Spring
Mercia Road
Westell Close
Wallington Road
Sale Drive
Rivett Close
Jeve Close
Hurst Close
Pembroke Road
Pinnocks Lane
Roman Lane
South Road
Walnut Avenue
Laxton Gardens
Limekiln La
Penfold Cl
School
The Orchard
Tene
A6141
A505
39
54
E1
1 Bramley Cl
2 Grosvenor Rd W
3 Icknield Wy East
E2
1 Elm Pk
2 Riddell Gdns
3 The Twitchell
E3
1 Elmwood Av
2 Providence Wy
3 South Cl
E4
1 Clare Crs
2 Templar Av
F1
1 Downlands
F2
1 Weavers Wy
Lannock Manor Farm
1 grid square represents 500 metres

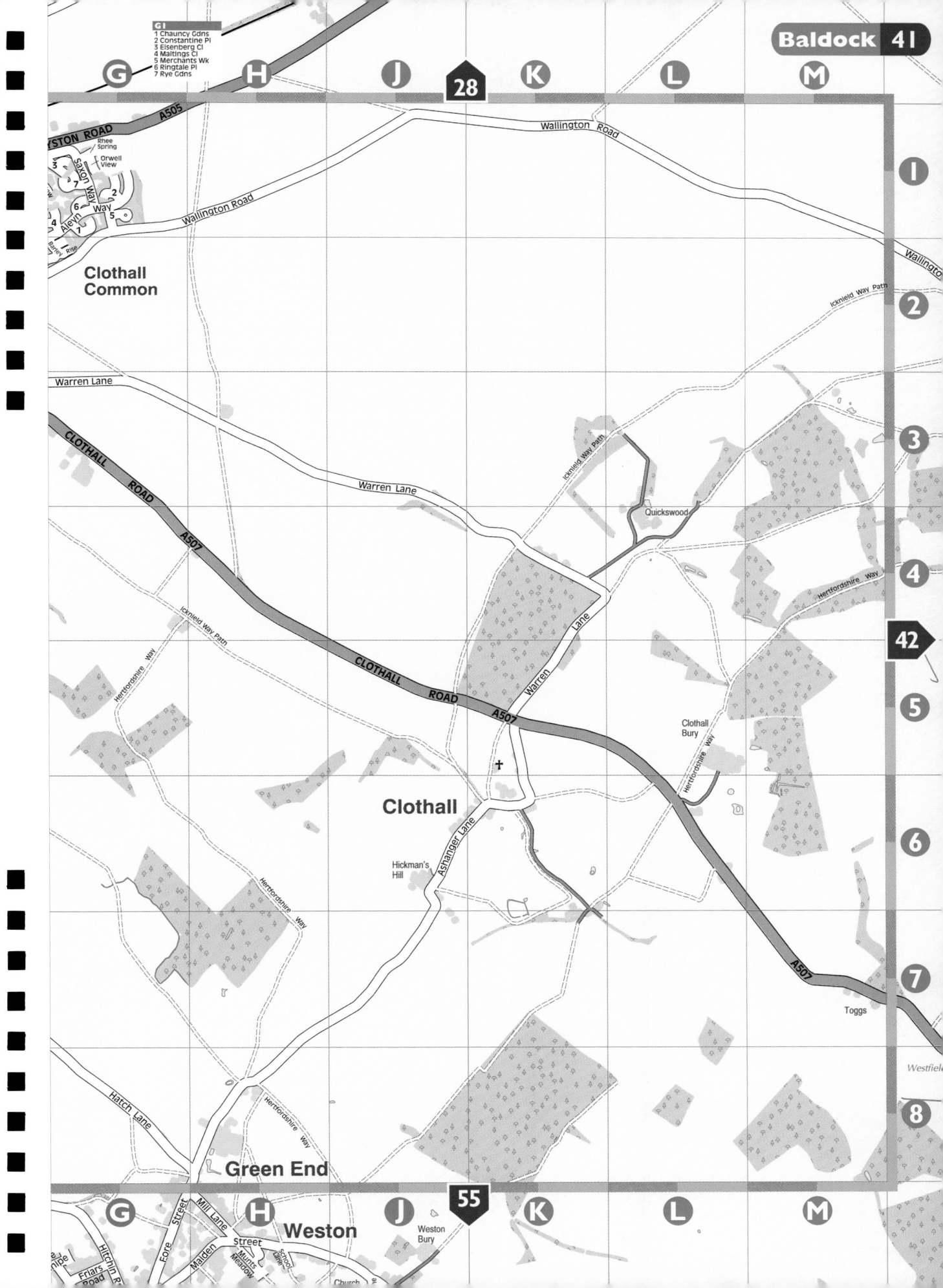

G1
1 Chauncy Gdns
2 Constantine Pl
3 Eisenberg Cl
4 Maltings Cl
5 Merchants Wk
6 Ringtale Pl
7 Rye Gdns

G · H · J · 28 · K · L · M

YSTON ROAD · A505

Rhee Spring

Orwell View

Saxon Way · Aleyn Way

Barley Rise

Wallington Road

Wallington Road

Clothall Common

Warren Lane

CLOTHALL ROAD · A507

Warren Lane

Icknield Way Path

Hertfordshire Way

CLOTHALL ROAD A507

Clothall

Hickman's Hill

Ashanger Lane

Warren Lane

Icknield Way Path

Quickswood

Hertfordshire Way

Clothall Bury

Hertfordshire Way

A507

Toggs

Westfield

Hertfordshire Way

Hatch Lane

Green End

Hertfordshire Way

G · H · J · 55 · K · L · M

Weston

Fore Street · Mill Lane · Maiden Street

Weston Bury

Hitchin Road · Friars Road · Munts Meadow · School Lane · Church St

I · 2 · 3 · 4 · 42 · 5 · 6 · 7 · 8

Wallington

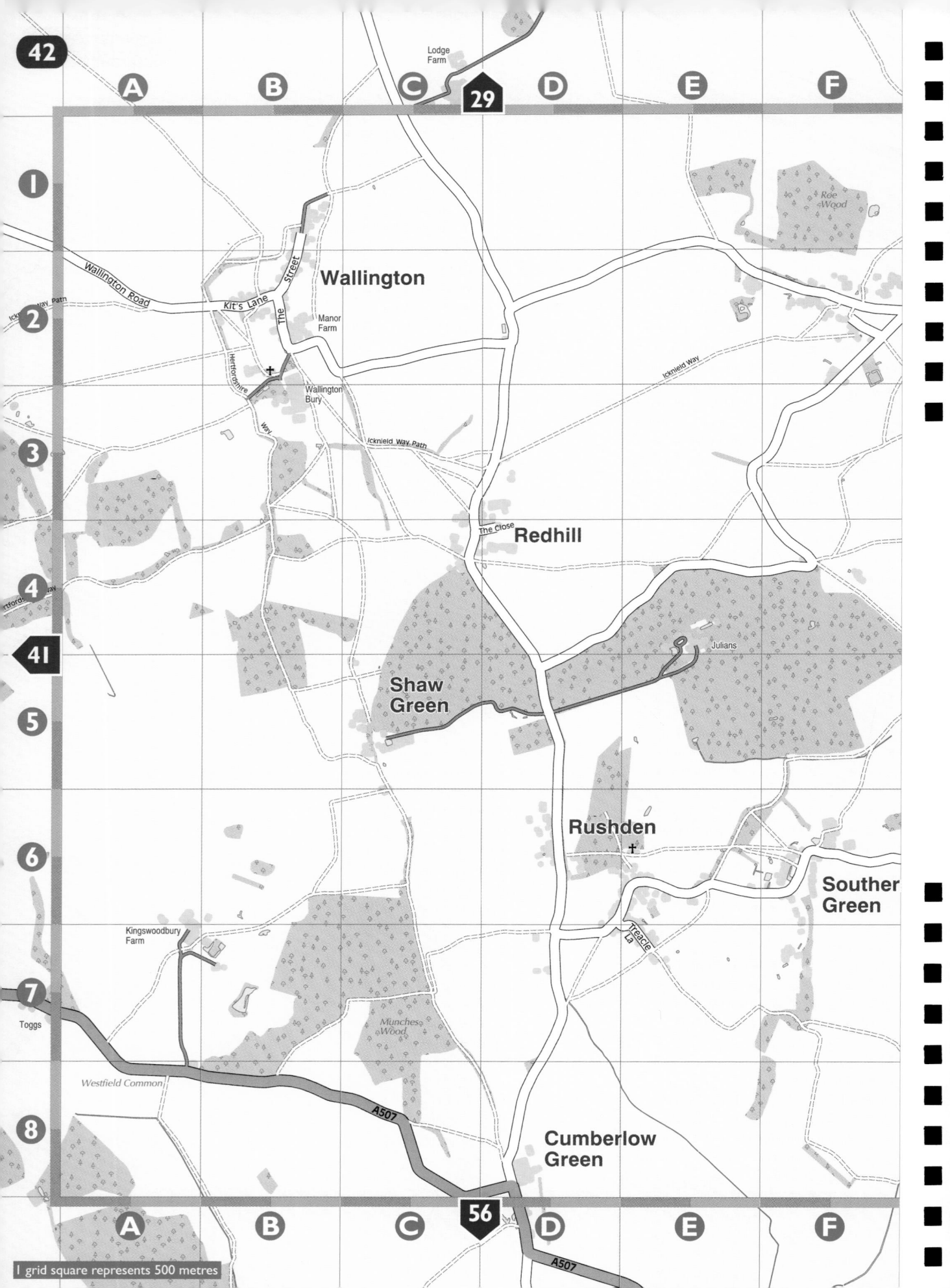

A B C 29 D E F

1

Roe
Wood

Wallington Road

Icknield Way Path

Kit's Lane

2

The Street

Wallington

Manor
Farm

Hertfordshire

Wallington
Bury

Icknield Way Path

Icknield Way

3

The Close Redhill

Hertfords Way

4

41

Julians

Shaw
Green

5

Rushden

6

Souther
Green

Kingswoodbury
Farm

Treacle La

7

Toggs

Munches
Wood

Westfield Common

A507

8

Cumberlow
Green

A B C 56 D A507 E F

I grid square represents 500 metres

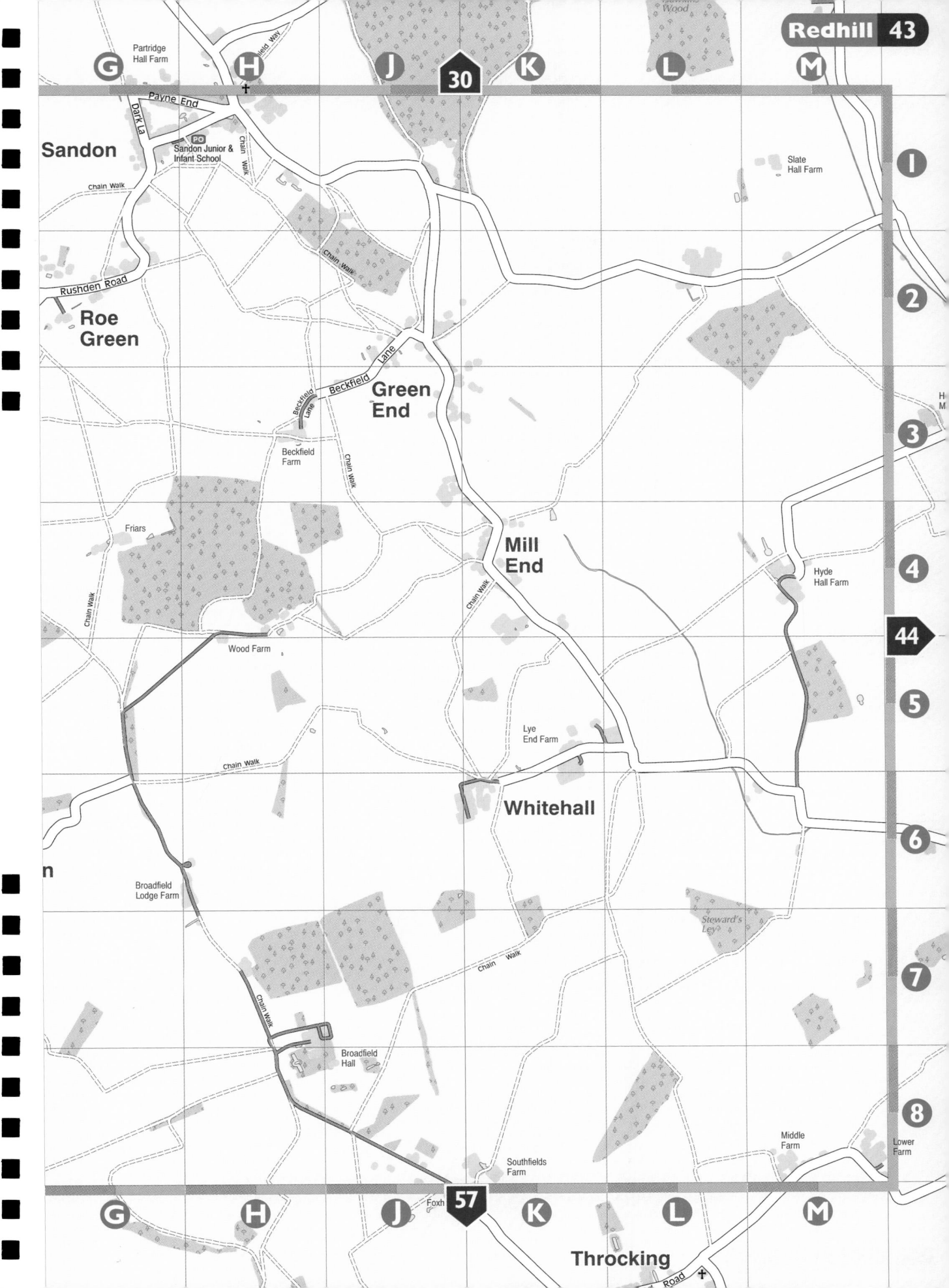

Partridge Hall Farm
Payne End
Dark La
Sandon
PO
Sandon Junior & Infant School
Chain Walk
Rushden Road
Roe Green
Slate Hall Farm
Beckfield Lane
Green End
Beckfield Farm
Friars
Mill End
Hyde Hall Farm
Wood Farm
Lye End Farm
Whitehall
Broadfield Lodge Farm
Steward's Ley
Broadfield Hall
Southfields Farm
Middle Farm
Lower Farm
Throcking
Road
30
44
57
G
H
J
K
L
M
1
2
3
4
5
6
7
8

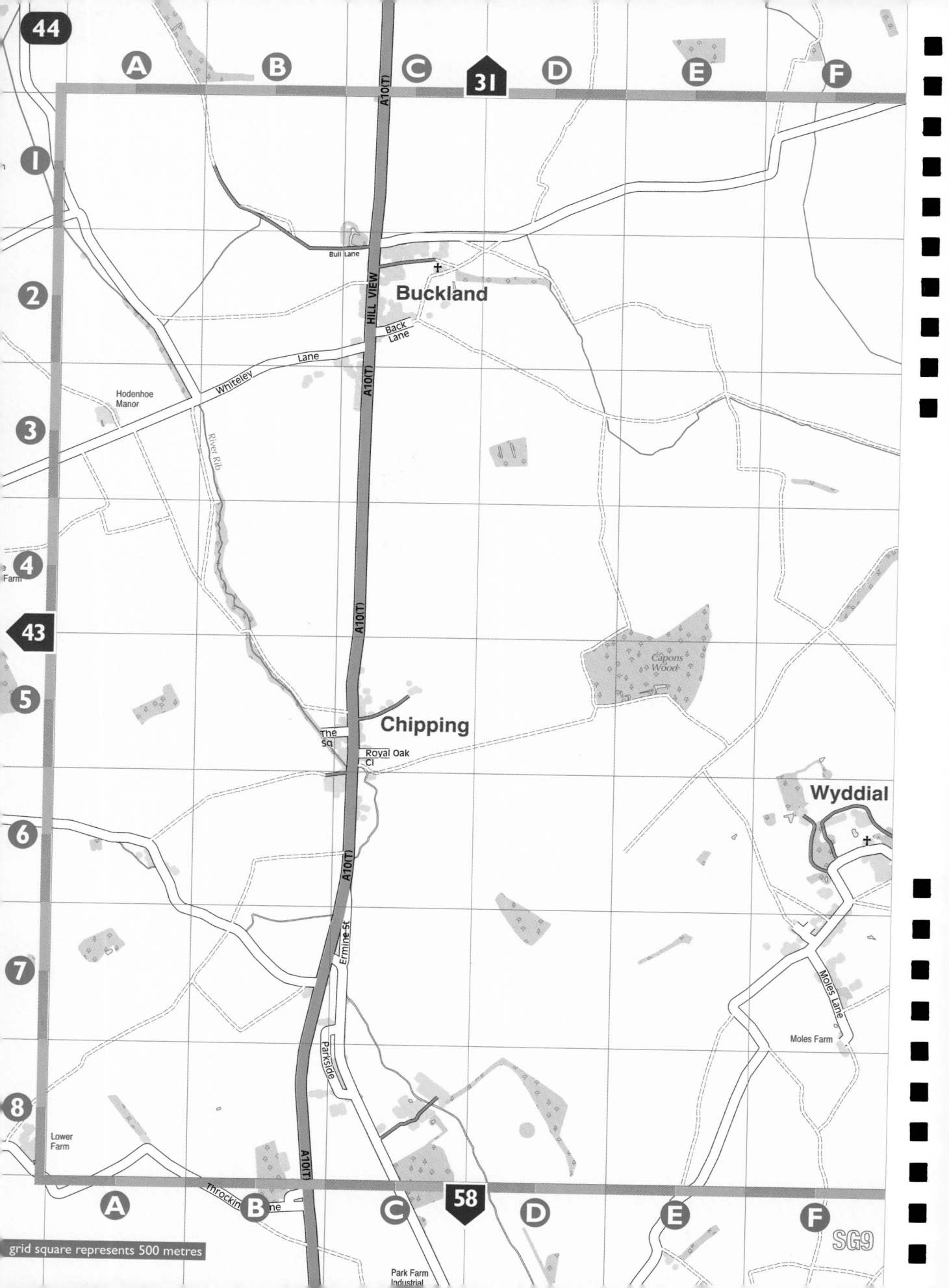

44

Ⓐ 　Ⓑ　 A10(T) 　Ⓒ　**31**　Ⓓ　Ⓔ　Ⓕ

Ⓘ

Bull Lane

HILL VIEW

†

Buckland

Back Lane

Ⓩ 2

Whiteley Lane

Hodenhoe Manor

River Rib

Ⓩ 3

A10(T)

Ⓩ 4

Farm

◄ **43**

Capons Wood

Ⓩ 5

The Sq

Royal Oak Cl

Chipping

Wyddial

†

Ⓩ 6

A10(T)

Ermine St

Moles Lane

Ⓩ 7

Moles Farm

Parkside

Ⓩ 8

Lower Farm

A10(T)

Ⓐ 　Throcking Lane Ⓑ　Ⓒ　◆ **58**　Ⓓ　Ⓔ　Ⓕ

SG9

grid square represents 500 metres

Park Farm Industrial

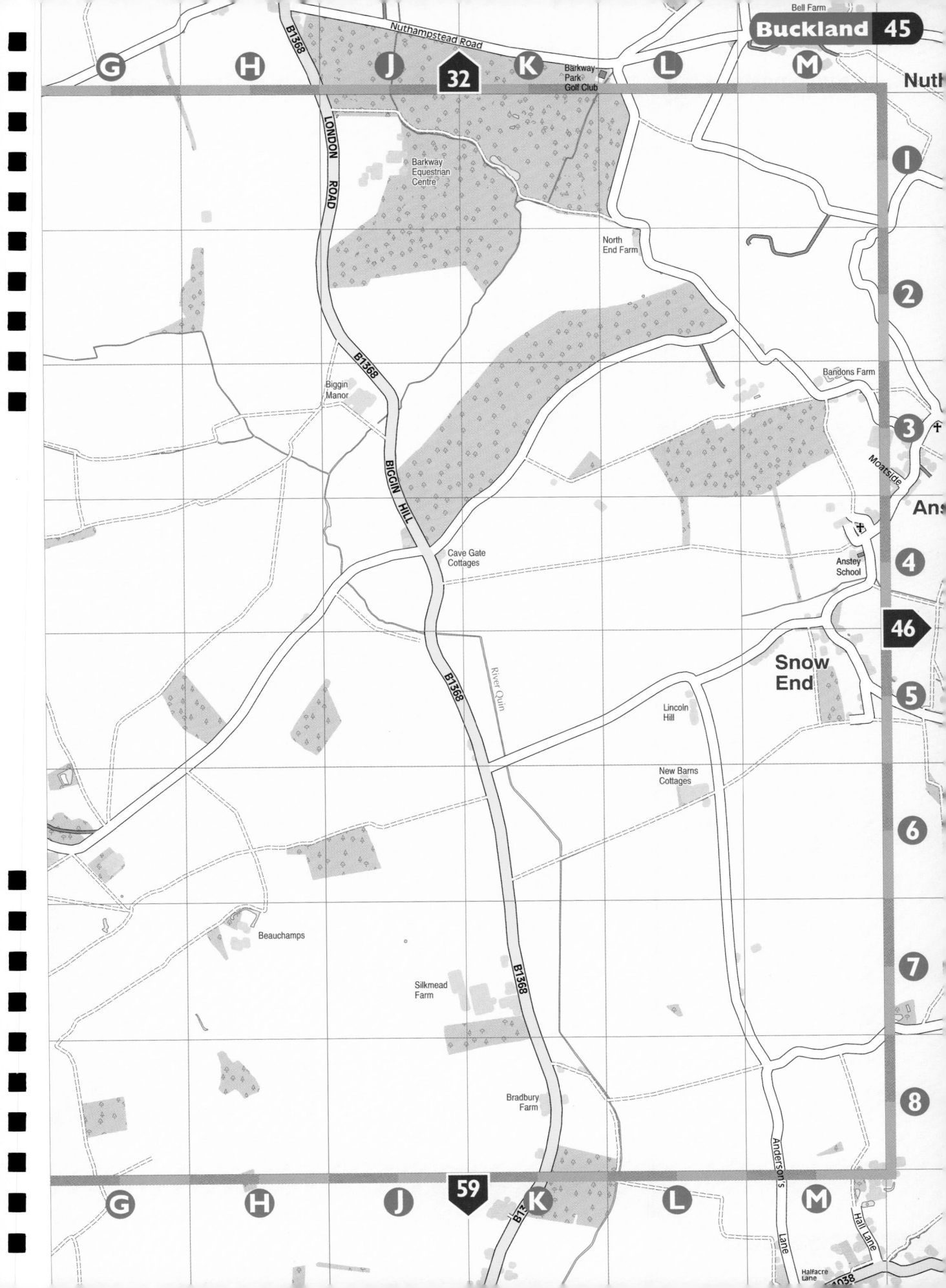

Bell Farm

Nuthampstead Road

Nuth

G   H   J   **32**   K   L   M

Barkway-
Park
Golf Club

1

Barkway
Equestrian
Centre

North
End Farm

2

Bandons Farm

LONDON ROAD

B1368

Biggin
Manor

BIGGIN HILL

3

Moatside

Ans

Cave Gate
Cottages

Anstey
School

4

46

River Quin

B1368

Snow
End

5

Lincoln
Hill

New Barns
Cottages

6

Beauchamps

7

Silkmead
Farm

B1368

Bradbury
Farm

Anderson's Lane

8

G   H   J   **59**   K   B1368   L   M

Hall Lane

Halfacre
Lane

46
33
45
60
A
B
C
D
E
F
1
2
3
4
5
6
7
8
Bell Lane
Park Farm Lane
Nutnampstead
Hertfordshire Way
Stocking Lane
Park
Scales Park
River Stort
Hertfordshire Way
Bandons Farm
Cheapside
Moatside
Anstey
Lower Green
Hertfordshire Way
Wood Lane
Mill Lane
Meesden
Coltsfoot
Anstey Bury
Hertfordshire Way
Puttock's End
Cole Green Farm
Brick House Farm
Brent Pelham
PUMP
B1038
Borley Green Cottage
B1038
CONDUIT LANE
Hall
The Causew
1 grid square represents 500 metres

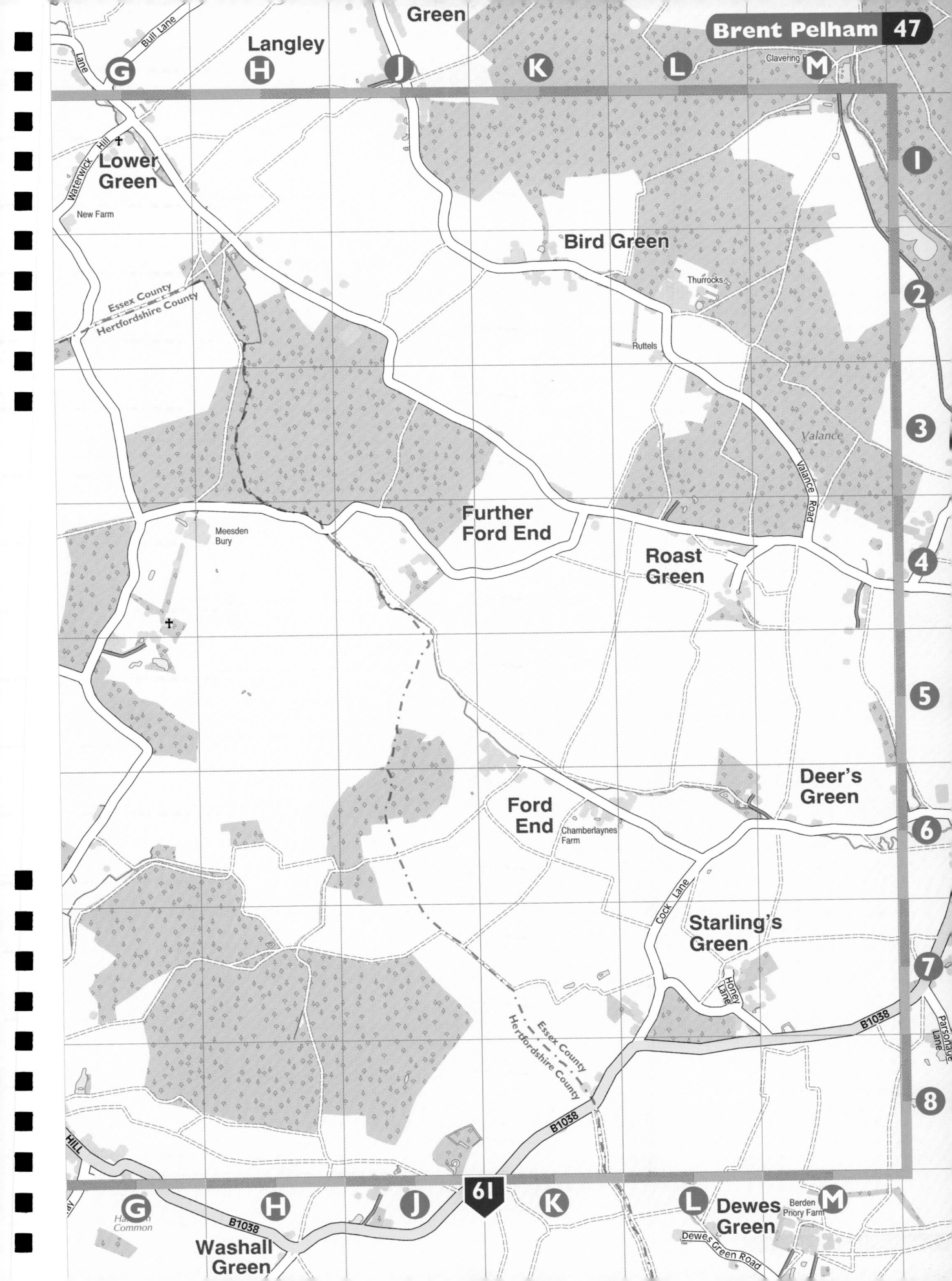

Green

Langley

G H J K L M

1

Waterwick Hill

Lower Green

New Farm

Bird Green

Thurrocks

2

Essex County

Hertfordshire County

Ruttels

3

Valance

Meesden Bury

Further Ford End

Valance Road

Roast Green

4

5

Deer's Green

Ford End

Chamberlaynes Farm

6

Cock Lane

Starling's Green

7

Honey Lane

Essex County

Hertfordshire County

B1038

Parsonage Lane

8

HILL

Hazel Common

G H J K L M

61

B1038

Dewes Green

Berden Priory Farm

Washall Green

Dewes Green Road

Clavering

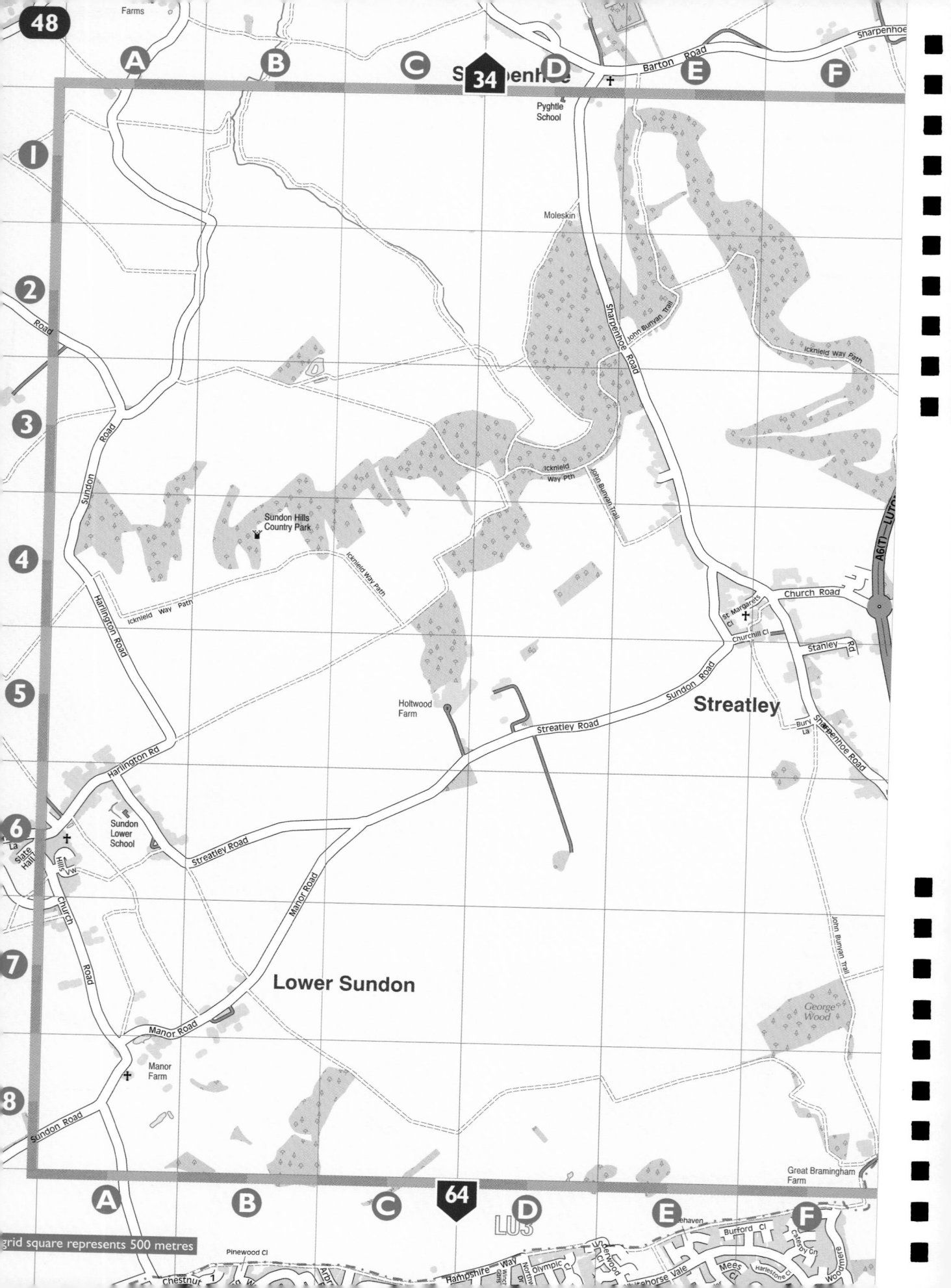

48

A B C **34** D E F

Farms

Sharpenhoe

Sharpenhoe Road

Barton Road

Pyghtle School

1

Moleskin

Sharpenhoe Road

John Bunyan Trail

2

Road

Sundon Road

Icknield Way Path

John Bunyan Trail

3

Icknield Way Pth

Sundon Hills Country Park

4

Icknield Way Path

Icknield Way Path

Harlington Road

St Margarets Cl

Church Road

A6(T) LUTON

Churchill Cl

Stanley Rd

5

Holtwood Farm

Streatley Road

Sundon Road

Streatley

Bury La

Sharpenhoe Road

Harlington Rd

6

La Slate Hall

Hills Vw

Sundon Lower School

Streatley Road

Streatley Road

Manor Road

7

Church Road

Lower Sundon

George Wood

John Bunyan Trail

8

Manor Road

Manor Farm

Sundon Road

A B C **64** D E F

LU3

Sharpenhoe

Burford Cl

Cheksby Gn

Mees

Woodmere

Harlestone Cl

grid square represents 500 metres

Pinewood Cl

Chestnut

Hampshire Way

Olympic

Northv

Charehorse Vale

G H J K L M

35

Road
Barton Rovers
Football Club
Dunstall Road
Manor Road
Arnold
Middle
School
B655 HEXTON ROAD
BARTON RD B655

Orchard
Close
Washbrook
Close
Luton Road
Church Road
Old Road

Hexton Junior
Middle & Infant
School

I

John Bunyan Trail
Cemetery

A6(T)

2

Ravensburgh
Castle

Jeremiah's
Tree

3

Bartonhill
Cutting

Fairy
Hole

John Bunyan Trail

4

50

John Bunyan Trail
Barton
Hill Farm

Luton Road A6(T)

5

Mortgrove
Farm

Sharpenhoe
Rd
Icknield Way Path
John Bunyan Trail

Hexton

Hertfordshire County
Bedfordshire County

6

Lille
Farm

Barton

Icknield Way Path

7

New
Farm

Road

8

Hertfordshire
Bedfordshire Co

John Bunyan Trail

Hayton
Cl
Skelton Cl
Quantock Rise
John Bunyan Trail
Turnpike Dr
Turnpike
Dr
South Bedfordshire
Golf Club

65

G H J K L M

Launton Cl
Charndon
Cl
Edgcott
Milburn Cl
Holford Wy
Elvington Gdns
Danvers
Barton Road
Turnpike Dr
Cardinal

Icknield Way

50

PH
PO

Hexton

A   Hexton
     Manor

B   Bury   C   36   D   E   F

Hexton Junior
Middle & Infant
School

Pegsdon

Pegsdon Way

1   HITCHIN ROAD   B655

Icknield Way Path

2

The Meg

3   Gravel
        Hill

Bedfordshire County
Hertfordshire County

Icknield Way Path

4   **Little
                                                         Offley**

49

Icknield Way Path

5 Mortgrove
       Farm

                                            Lilley
                                            Hoo

Hexton Road

6

Lilley Manor
Farm

John Bunyan Trail

Pond Farm

Lilley Hoo
Farm

7

Ward's
Farm

Hexton Road

Ward's Wood

John Bunyan Trail

Rectory

Gn
Acres

Lilleyhoo Lane

Luton Road

8   Hertfordshire County
        Bedfordshire County

John Bunyan Trail

East Street

Rueley Dell
Road

The Baulk

Hollybush Hill

Lilley

A   B   C **66** D   E   F
                    West Street

Lilley
Wood

Lilley Bottom

1 grid square represents 500 metres

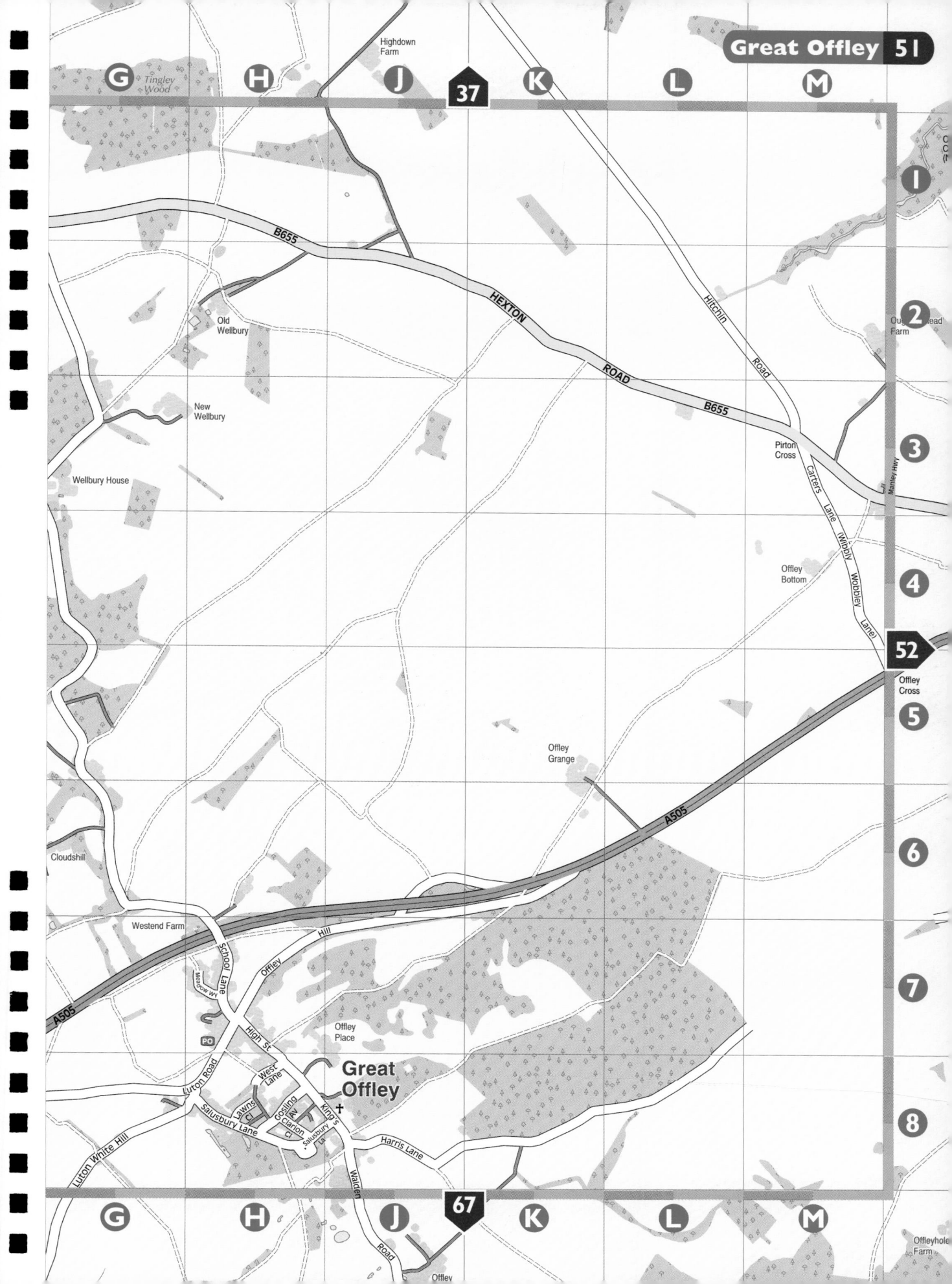

G H J **37** K L M

Highdown Farm

Tingley Wood

1

B655

2 Oug... Head Farm

HEXTON

Old Wellbury

ROAD
B655

Hitchin Manley Hwy

New Wellbury

Pirton Cross

3

Wellbury House

Carters Lane (Wibbly Wobbley Lane)

Offley Bottom

4

52

Offley Cross

5

Offley Grange

Cloudshill

A505

6

Westend Farm

Hill

Offley

School Lane

Meadow Wy

A505

Offley Place

7

PO

High St

Luton Road

West Lane

Lawns Cl

Great Offley

Gosling Wy

Clarton Cl

King's

Salusbury La

Salusbury Lane

Luton White Hill

Harris Lane

8

Walden Road

G H J **67** K L M

Offleyhol... Farm

Offley

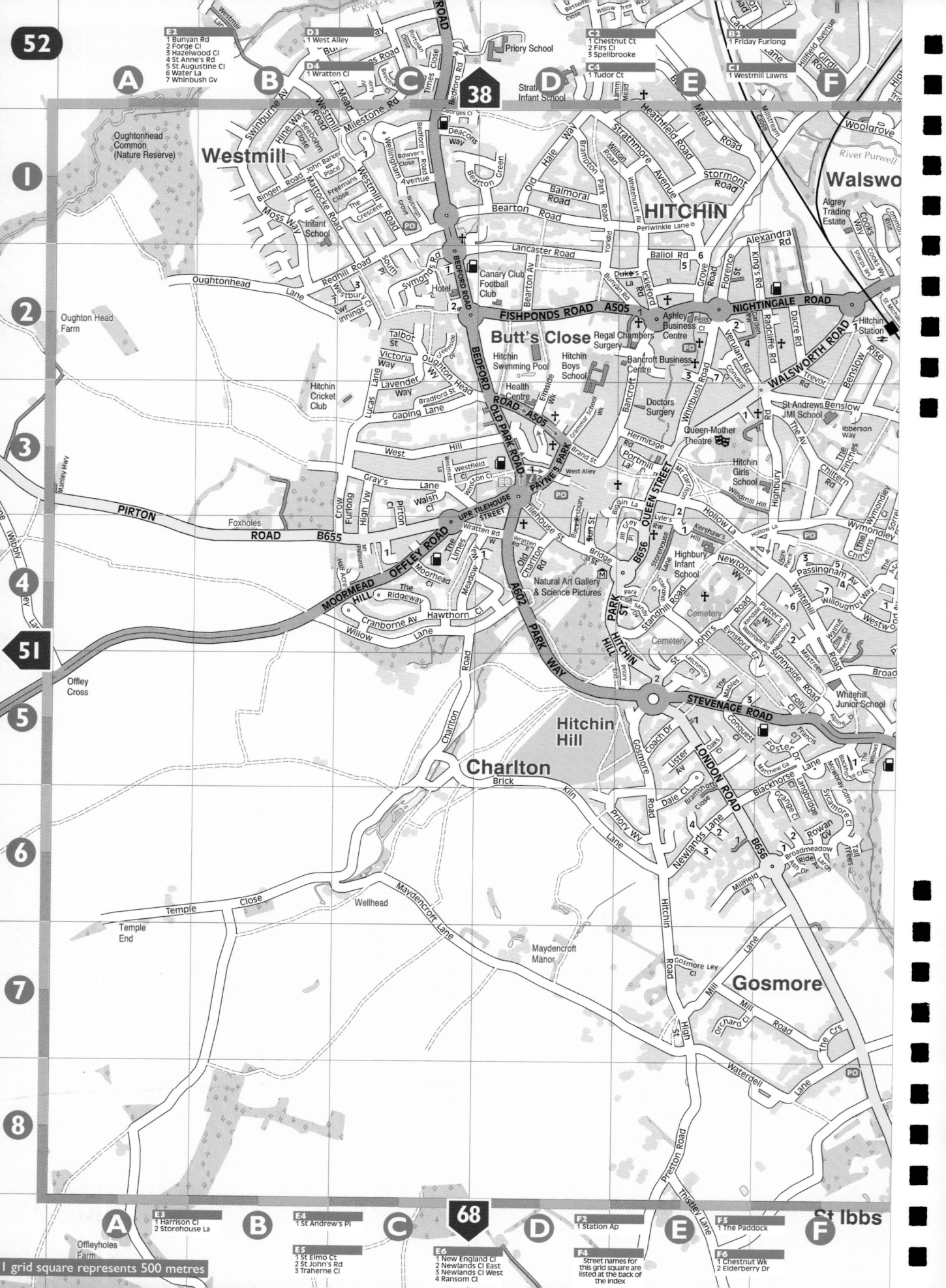

52
E2
1 Bunyan Rd
2 Forge Cl
3 Hazelwood Cl
4 St Anne's Rd
5 St Augustine Cl
6 Water La
7 Whinbush Gv
D3
1 West Alley
D4
1 Wratten Cl
C2
1 Chestnut Ct
2 Firs Cl
3 Spellbrooke
C4
1 Tudor Ct
B2
1 Friday Furlong
C1
1 Westmill Lawns
38
A
B
C
D
E
F
Priory School
Strathmore Infant School
Oughtonhead Common (Nature Reserve)
Westmill
HITCHIN
Walsworth
Algrey Trading Estate
River Purwell
Woolgrove
Westmill Road
Milestone Rd
Swinburne Av
Hine Way
Seebohm Close
John Barker Place
Bingen Road
Mattocke Road
Freemans Close
Moss Way
Infant School
The Crescent
Wellingham Avenue
Bowyer's Close
Nuttleigh Grove
Bedford Road
Deacons Way
Georges Cl
Bearton Green
Bearton Road
Old Hale Way
Balmoral Road
Brampton Park Road
Wilton Road
Strathmore Avenue
Heathfield Road
Mead Road
Stormont Road
Whitehurst Av
Periwinkle Lane
Lancaster Road
York Rd
Baliol Rd
Alexandra Rd
King's Rd
Florence St
Grove Road
Cooks Way
Common Rise
Oughtonhead Lane
Redhill Road
Westbury Cl
Lwr Innings
Symonds Rd
Hotel
Canary Club Football Club
Bearton Av
Duke's La
Bunyan Rd
Icklefort Rd
FISHPONDS ROAD A505
NIGHTINGALE ROAD
Hitchin Station
Oughton Head Farm
Butt's Close
Regal Chambers Surgery
Ashley Business Centre
Fells Cl
Garden Rw
Radcliffe Rd
Dacre Rd
WALSWORTH ROAD
Talbot St
Victoria Way
Lavender Way
Oughton Head Wy
Greenside Dr
Bradford St
Gaping Lane
Lucas Lane
Hitchin Cricket Club
Hitchin Swimming Pool
Hitchin Boys School
Health Centre
Elmside Wk
Grammar School Wk
Bancroft Business Centre
Bancroft
Doctors Surgery
Whinbush Road
Verulam Rd
Convent Cl
Trevor Rd
Benslow Rise
St Andrews JMI School
Benslow Lane
Ibberson Way
The Av
Queen Mother Theatre
Hermitage Rd
Portmill La
Hitchin Girls School
Windmill Hill
Highbury
Chiltern Rd
The Finches
Wymondley Rd
West Hill
Westfield Cl
Gray's Lane
Winston Cl
Walsh Cl
Pirton Cl
High Vw
Furlong
Crow Furlong
Manley Hwy
PIRTON ROAD B655
Foxholes
UPR TILEHOUSE STREET
Tilehouse St
Wratten Rd W
Bucklersbury
Sun St
West Alley
Brand St
PAYNE'S PARK
OLD PARK ROAD
BEDFORD ROAD
A505
QUEEN STREET
Mt Garrison
Hollow La
Biggin La
Lyle's Rw
Kershaw's Hill
Jill Grey Pl
B656
Storehouse Lane
Highbury Infant School
Newtons Wy
Acre Piece
Passingham Av
Willoughby Way
Whitehill Rd
Westwood
Sorrell
The Chilterns
OFFLEY ROAD
MOORHEAD HILL
Mt Pleasant
Half Acre
The Limes
Moorhead Cl
Meadow Way
The Ridgeway
Cranborne Av
Hawthorn Cl
Willow Lane
Old Charlton Rd
Bridge St
Natural Art Gallery & Science Pictures
PARK ST
Park Gdns
Sandy
Standhill Road
Cemetery
John's St
Eynsford Ct
Kendale
Putter's Wy
Waltham Rd
Wedmore
Sunnyside Road
Walnut Rd
Beeches
Maytrees
Broad
Whitehill Junior School
A602 PARK WAY
HITCHIN HILL
Hill End
Priory
Latchmore Cl
The Maples
Folly Cl
Conquest Cl
Alpine Cl
STEVENAGE ROAD
Francis
Foster Dr
Matthew Ga
Blackhorse Cl
Blackhorse Lane
McMorray Gdns
The Willows
Offley Cross
51
Charlton
Charlton Road
Hitchin Hill
Brick Kiln Lane
Gosmore Road
Coach Dr
Lister Av
Oaks Cl
LONDON ROAD
Dale Cl
Bramshott Close
Newlands Lane
Priory Wy
Langbridge
Grange Cl
Sycamore Cl
Rowan Gv
Tall Trees
Broadmeadow Ride
Ash Dr
Larch Av
Millfield La
B656
Temple Close
Temple End
Wellhead
Maydencroft Lane
Maydencroft Manor
Hitchin Road
Gosmore Ley Cl
Gosmore
Mill Lane
Mill Road
Orchard Cl
High St
The Crs
Waterdell Lane
Preston Road
Thistley Lane
St Ibbs
Offleyholes Farm
68
E3
1 Harrison Cl
2 Storehouse La
E4
1 St Andrew's Pl
E5
1 St Elmo Ct
2 St John's Rd
3 Traherne Cl
E6
1 New England Cl
2 Newlands Cl East
3 Newlands Cl West
4 Ransom Cl
F2
1 Station Ap
F4
Street names for this grid square are listed at the back of the index
F5
1 The Paddock
F6
1 Chestnut Wk
2 Elderberry Dr
1 grid square represents 500 metres
1
2
3
4
5
6
7
8

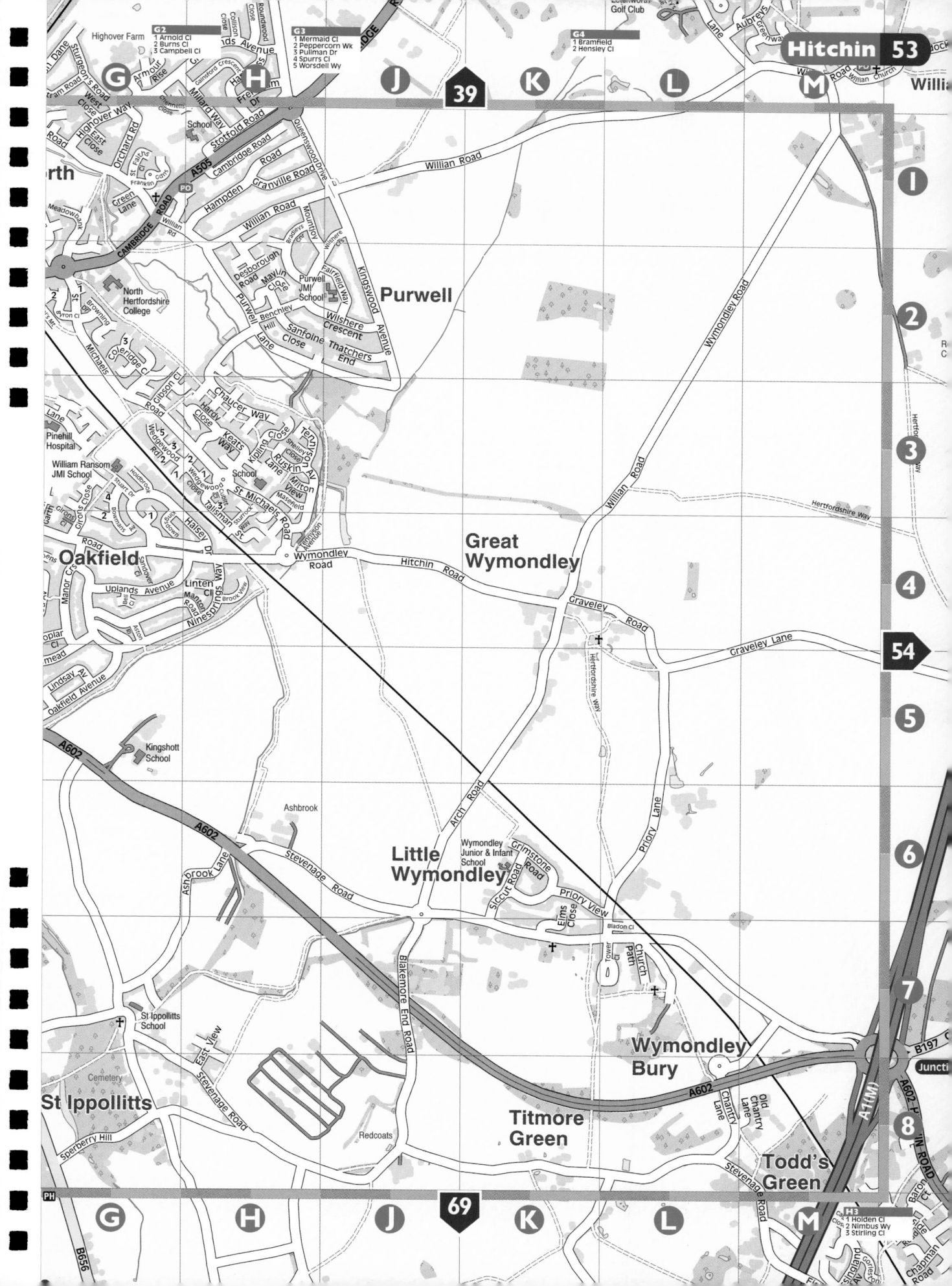
G2
1 Arnold Cl
2 Burns Cl
3 Campbell Cl
G3
1 Mermaid Cl
2 Peppercorn Wk
3 Pullman Dr
4 Spurrs Cl
5 Worsdell Wy
G4
1 Bramfield
2 Hensley Cl
H3
1 Holden Cl
2 Nimbus Wy
3 Stirling Cl
39
69
54
G
H
J
K
L
M
1
2
3
4
5
6
7
8
Highover Farm
Purwell
Great Wymondley
Little Wymondley
Oakfield
St Ippollitts
Titmore Green
Wymondley Bury
Todd's Green
Willian Road
Wymondley Road
Hitchin Road
Graveley Road
Graveley Lane
Priory Lane
Arch Road
Stevenage Road
Blakemore End Road
Hertfordshire Way
A505
A602
A1(M)
B197
B656
Cambridge Road
Stotfold Road
Cambridge Road
Queenswood Drive
Kingswood Avenue
Granville Road
Hampden Road
Purwell Lane
Wilshere Crescent
Thatchers End
Sanfoine Close
Desborough Road
Maylin Close
Fairfield Way
Purwell JMI School
North Hertfordshire College
Pinehill Hospital
William Ransom JMI School
Kingshott School
Wymondley Junior & Infant School
St Ippollitts School
Cemetery
Ashbrook
Ashbrook Lane
Redcoats
Chaucer Way
Keats Way
Kipling Close
Tennyson Av
Ruskin Lane
Milton View
St Michaels Road
Gibson Cl
Coleridge Cl
Uplands Avenue
Ninesprings Way
Linten Cl
Manton Road
Oakfield Avenue
Lindsay Av
Manor Crs
Halsey Dr
Grimstone Road
Siccut Road
Priory View
Elms Close
Bladon Cl
Tower Cl
Church Path
Chantry Lane
Old Chantry Lane
East View
Sperberry Hill
Highover Way
Orchard Rd
Millard Way
Green Lane
Willian Rd
Wedgewood Rd
Talisman St
Girons Close
Stuart Dr
Sandover Cl
Aston Cl
Bell Cl
Brook View
Chapman Road
Singland Av

54
Baldock Lane
Willian Church Road
A
B
C
D
E
F
40
B197
A614
E8
1 Middlesboro' Cl
2 Newcastle Cl
D8
1 Gloucester Cl
Lannock Manor Farm
Roxley Court
Hertfordshire Way
Jack's Hill
How Wood
A1(M)
53
Graveley
High Street
Church Lane
Oak Lane
Turf Common La
Milksey Lane
Ashwell Close
Ashwell Common
Pondside
Graveley Junior Mixed School
Doctors Surgery
Manor Farm
Chesfield Park
Weston Road
Great Ashby Way
Tamar Close
Wansbeck Close
Manchester Road
Old Bourne Way
St Davids Cl
St Andrews Drive
Graveley Road
B197
Junction 8
A602 Hitchin Road
North Road
Lister Hospital
A&E
Lister Close
Granby Road
Underwood Road
Chouler Gardens
The Brambles
Daltry Road
Daltry Close
Turner Close
Thurlow Close
Arnold Close
Chancellors Road
Rook's Nest
Islington Way
Iona Close
Lancaster Cl
Guildford Close
Canterbury Way
Canterbury Way Surgery
St Nicholas Health Cen
Ripon Road
Leys Primary School
Salisbury Road
Winchester Close
St Nicholas
70
Coreys Mill Lane
Ingleside
Caister Close
Foster Close
Boswell Gardens
Woodfield Road
Morgan Cl
Mathews Close
The Bury
Cemetery
Weston Road
St Albans Drive
York Road
Durham Rd
The Giles Infant & Junior School
Rectory Lane
Tudor Close
Whitney
The Old Walled Garden
1
2
3
4
5
6
7
8
1 grid square represents 500 metres

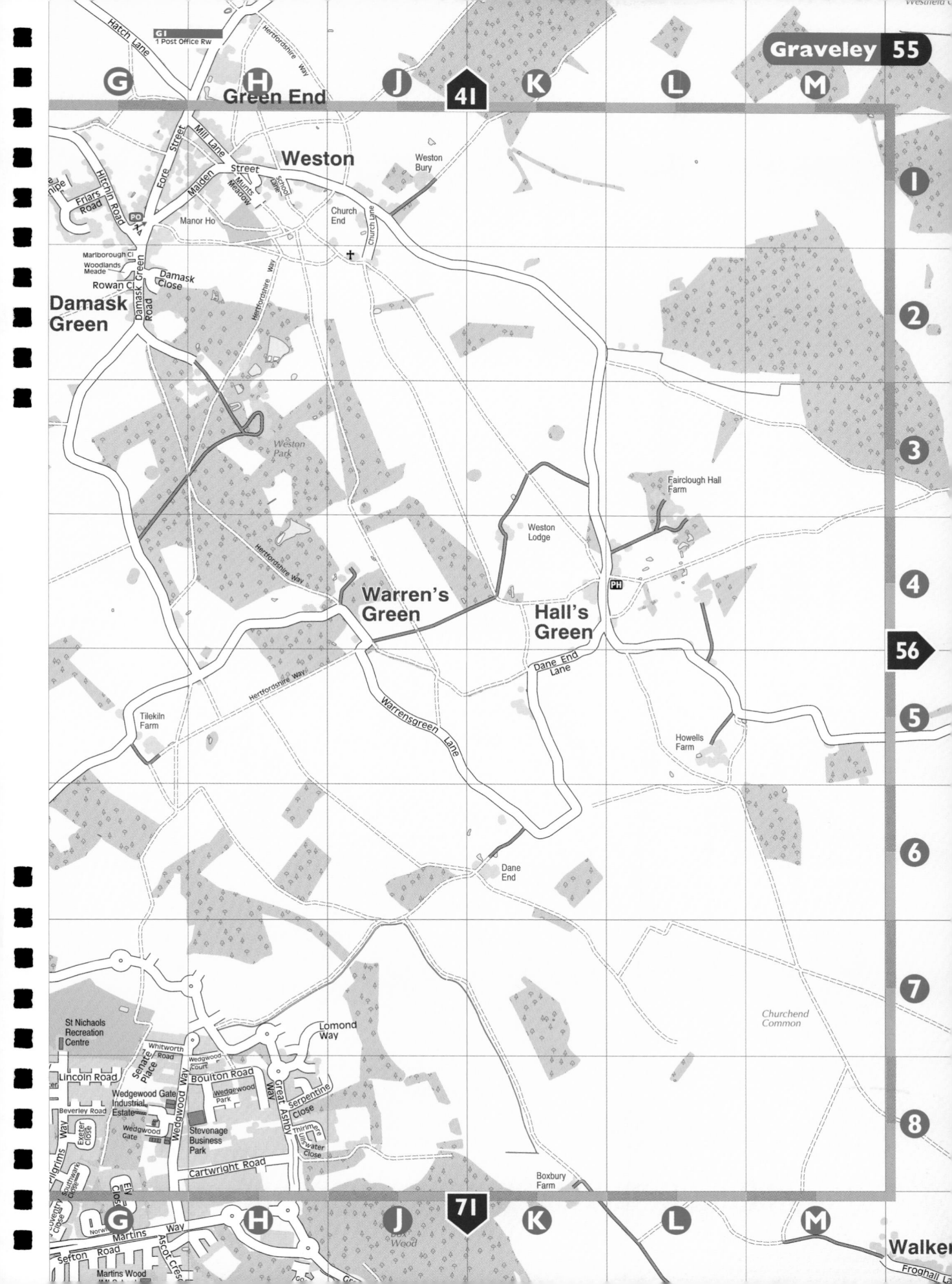
G1
1 Post Office Rw
Hatch Lane
Hertfordshire Way
G
H
J
41
K
L
M
Green End
Mill Lane
Fore Street
Weston
Weston Bury
Hitchin Road
Friars Road
Maiden Street
Munts Meadow
School Lane
Church End
Church Lane
Manor Ho
Marlborough Cl
Woodlands Meade
Rowan Cl
Damask Green Road
Damask Close
Damask Green
Hertfordshire Way
Weston Park
Fairclough Hall Farm
Weston Lodge
Hertfordshire Way
Warren's Green
Hall's Green
PH
Dane End Lane
Hertfordshire Way
Warrensgreen Lane
Tilekiln Farm
Howells Farm
Dane End
Churchend Common
St Nichols Recreation Centre
Lomond Way
Whitworth Road
Senate Place
Wedgwood Court
Lincoln Road
Boulton Road
Wedgewood Park
Great Ashby Way
Serpentine Close
Wedgewood Gate Industrial Estate
Beverley Road
Wedgwood Way
Wedgwood Gate
Exeter Close
Stevenage Business Park
Thirlmere
Ullswater Close
Pilgrims Way
Southwark Close
Cartwright Road
Ely Close
Boxbury Farm
Coventry Close
71
Martins Way
Sefton Road
Ascot Cres
Martins Wood
Box Wood
Walker
Froghall La
I
2
3
4
56
5
6
7
8

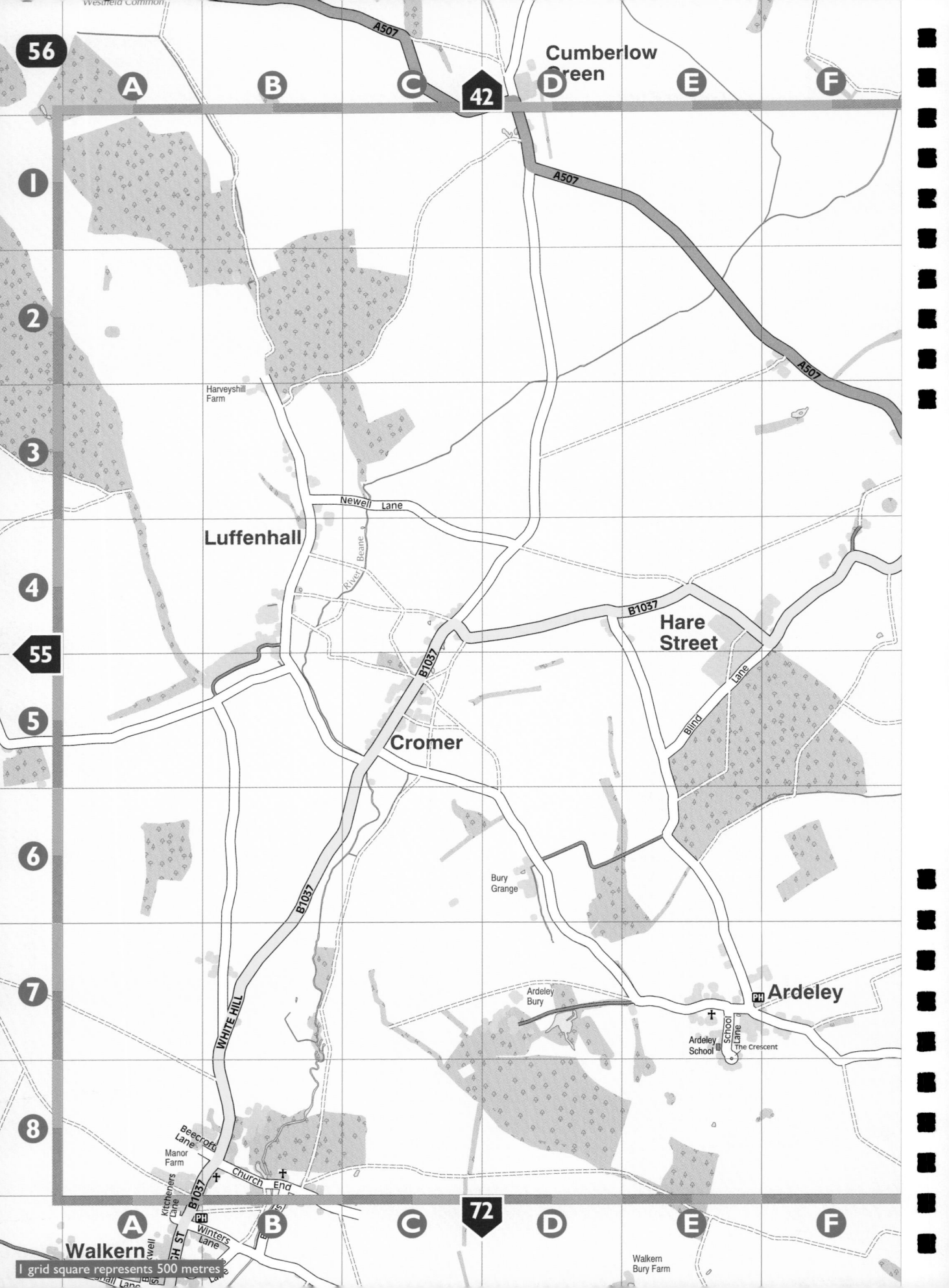

56

Ⓐ   Ⓑ   Ⓒ   **42**   Ⓓ   Ⓔ   Ⓕ

A507

Westfield Common

Cumberlow Green

A507

A507

1

2

Harveyshill Farm

3

Newell Lane

Luffenhall

River Beane

4

B1037

B1037

Hare Street

55

Blind Lane

School Lane

5

Cromer

6

Bury Grange

B1037

7

WHITE HILL

Ardeley Bury

Ardeley Bury

PH **Ardeley**

Ardeley School

The Crescent

8

Beecroft Lane

Manor Farm

Church End

Kitcheners Lane

B1037

PH

Winters Lane

Ⓐ   Ⓑ   Ⓒ   **72**   Ⓓ   Ⓔ   Ⓕ

Walkern

Walkern Bury Farm

1 grid square represents 500 metres

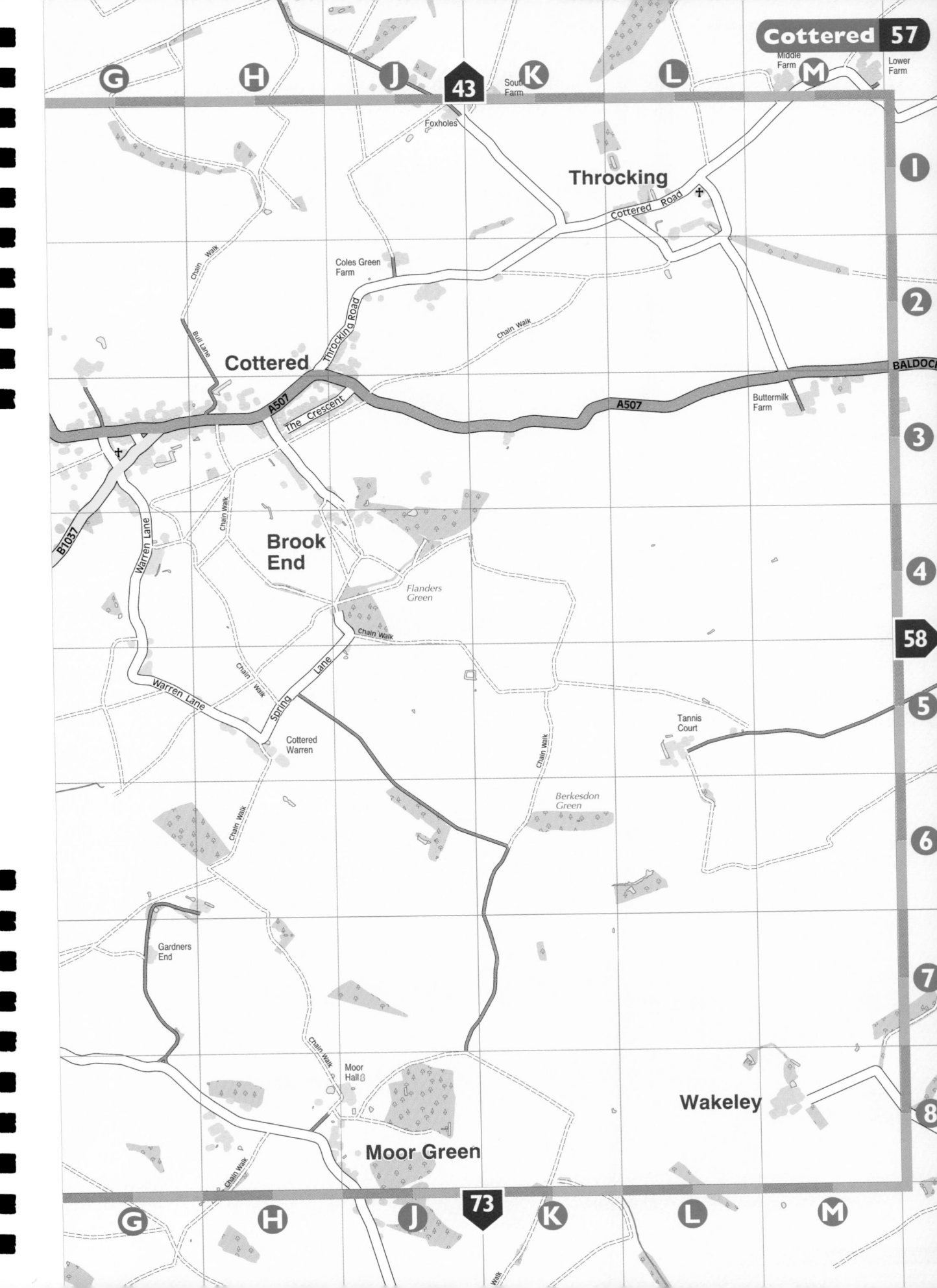

G H J 43 K L M

1

Throcking

2

BALDOCK

Cottered Road

South Farm

Foxholes

Middle Farm

Lower Farm

Coles Green Farm

Chain Walk

Chain Walk

Cottered

Throcking Road

A507

The Crescent

A507

Buttermilk Farm

3

Bull Lane

B1037

Warren Lane

Chain Walk

Brook End

Flanders Green

4

58

Chain Walk

Chain Walk

Spring Lane

Warren Lane

Cottered Warren

Tannis Court

5

Chain Walk

Berkesdon Green

6

Chain Walk

Gardners End

7

Chain Walk

Moor Hall

Wakeley

8

Chain Walk

Moor Green

G H J 73 K L M

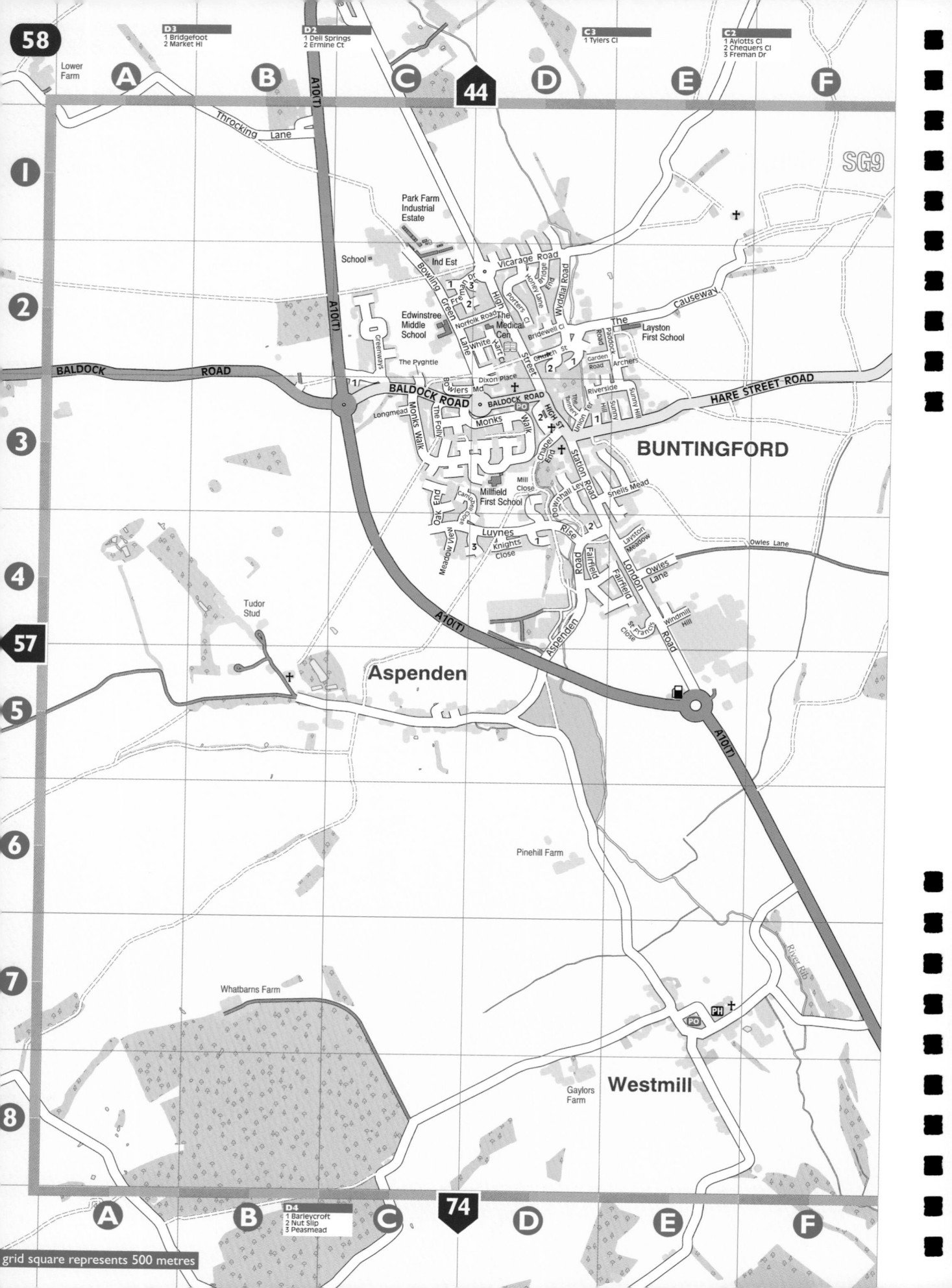

D3
1 Bridgefoot
2 Market Hl

D2
1 Dell Springs
2 Ermine Ct

C3
1 Tylers Cl

C2
1 Aylotts Cl
2 Chequers Cl
3 Freman Dr

A   B   A10(T)   C   44   D   E   F

SG9

Lower Farm

Throcking Lane

I

Park Farm Industrial Estate

School   Ind Est

Bowling Green Lane

A10(T)

Vicarage Road

Honey Lane   Bridge End   Wyddial Road

2

Edwinstree Middle School

Greenways

The Pyghtle

Norfolk Road   High Street

White Hart Cl   The Medical Cen

Bridewell Cl

Porters   Church St

The   Layston First School

Baldoock   Archers   Causeway

The

BALDOCK   ROAD

Bowlers   Dixon Place   Md

Garden Road

Riverside

Sunny Hill

HARE STREET ROAD

3

Longmead   Monks Walk   The Folly   **BALDOCK ROAD**   PO   Monks   Walk

High St   Sunny Hill

Timber   **BUNTINGFORD**

Mill Close   Chapel End   Station Road

Millfield First School   Bowhall Ley Road   Snells Mead

Park End   Campbell Rd   Luynes   Knights Close

4

Meadow View   Fairfield Rise   Fairfield   Layston Meadow

London Road   Owles Lane   Owles Lane

Tudor Stud

57

Aspenden   Rise   Aspenden Road   St Ends Close   Windmill Hill

5

A10(T)

6

Pinehill Farm

7

Whatbarns Farm

River Rib

PO   PH

8

Gaylors Farm   **Westmill**

A   B   **D4** 1 Barleycroft 2 Nut Slip 3 Peasmead   C   74   D   E   F

grid square represents 500 metres

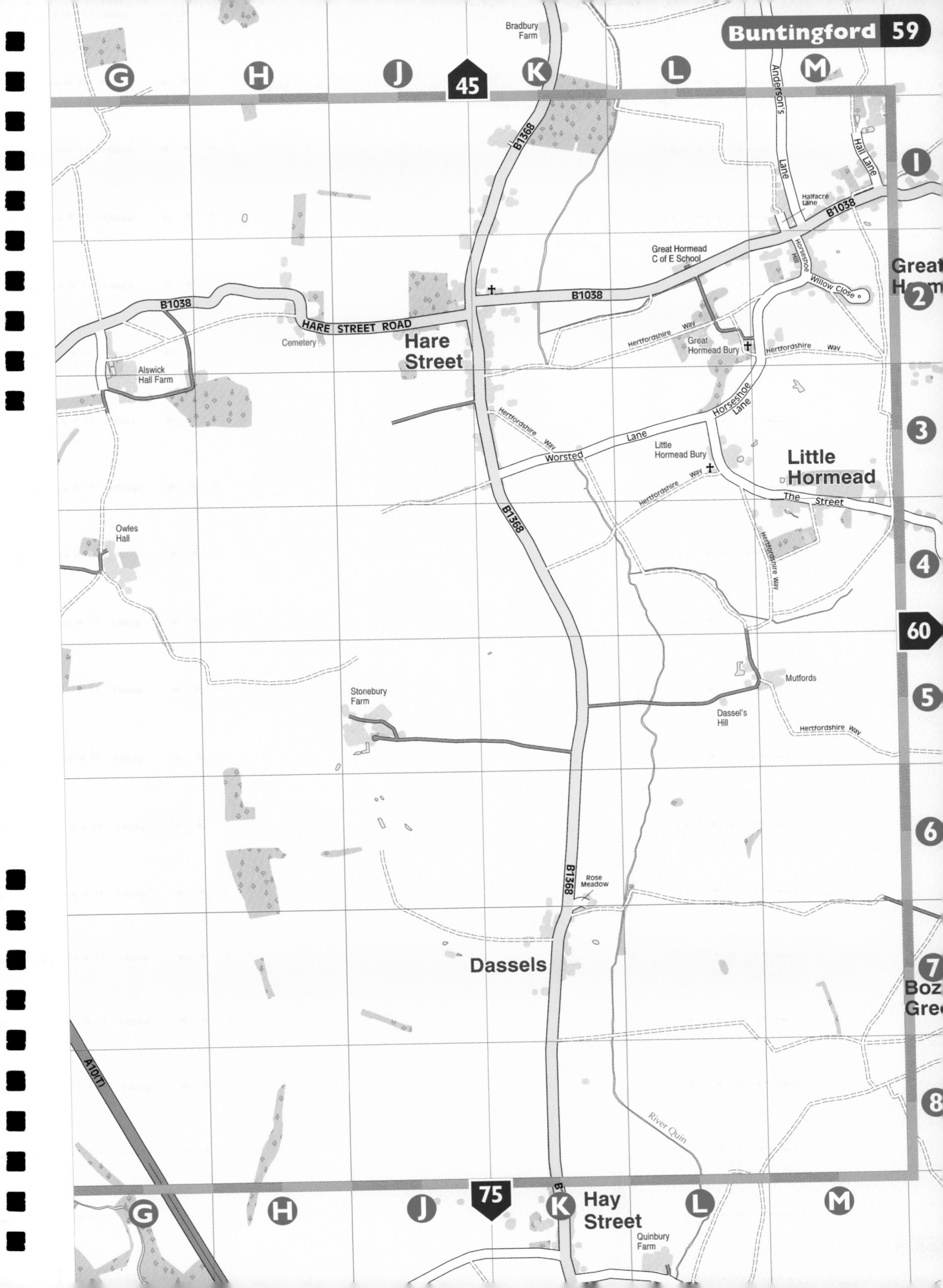
Bradbury Farm
G
H
J
45
K
L
M
Anderson's Lane
Hall Lane
Halfacre Lane
B1038
B1368
Great Hormead C of E School
Horseshoe Hill
Willow Close
Great
B1038
HARE STREET ROAD
Cemetery
Hare Street
Alswick Hall Farm
Hertfordshire Way
Great Hormead Bury
Horseshoe Lane
Worsted Lane
Little Hormead Bury
Little Hormead
The Street
Owles Hall
B1368
60
Mutfords
Dassel's Hill
Stonebury Farm
Rose Meadow
Dassels
A10(T)
River Quin
75
Hay Street
Quinbury Farm
1
2
3
4
5
6
7
8

Brent Pelham

A B C **46** D E F

PUMP

Borley Green
Cottage

B1038

CONDUIT LANE

B1038

1038

I

Ha

**Great
Hormead**

2

Whitebarns Lane

Whitebarns

3

Great
Hormead
Park

4

59

The Street

5

Whitebarns Lane

**Furne
Pelha**

The

PO

6

Furneux Pelham
C of E
School

The
Street

Hertfordshire Way

The Causeway

7

**Bozen
Green**

Hertfordshire Way

**Patient
End**

8

A B C **76** D E F

Causeway

grid square represents 500 metres

The Causeway

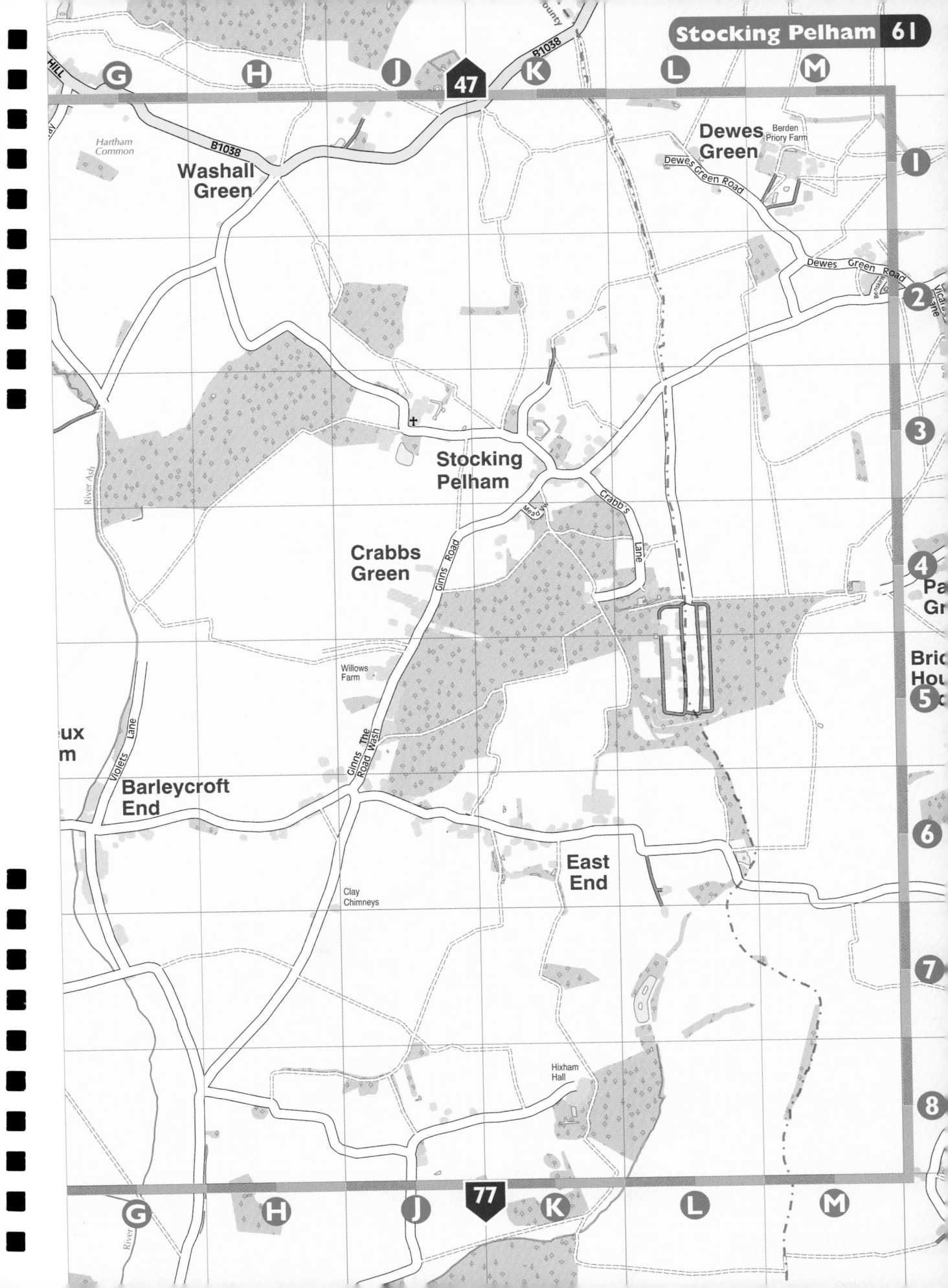

G H J K L M

Hartham
Common

B1038

47

Washall
Green

Dewes
Green

Berden
Priory Farm

Dewes Green Road

I

Dewes Green Road

2

River Ash

3

+

Stocking
Pelham

4

Pa
Gr

Crabbs
Green

Ginns Road

Mead W

Crabb's Lane

Bri
Hou

5

Willows
Farm

Ginns The
Road Wash

Violets Lane

6

ux
m

Barleycroft
End

Clay
Chimneys

East
End

7

Hixham
Hall

8

River

G H J K L M

77

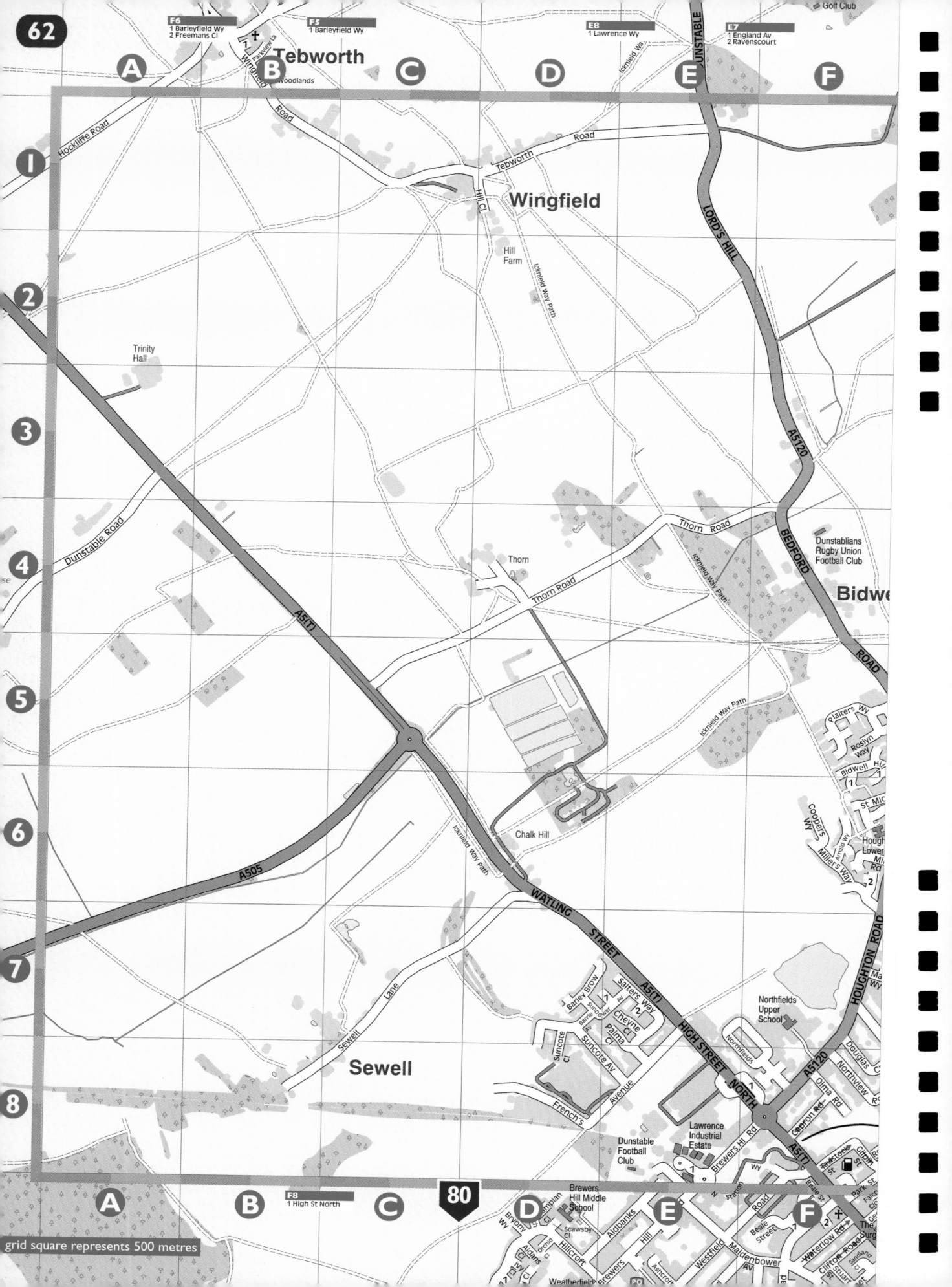

F6
1 Barleyfield Wy
2 Freemans Ci

F5
1 Barleyfield Wy

E8
1 Lawrence Wy

E7
1 England Av
2 Ravenscourt

A B C D E F

Tebworth

Hockliffe Road

Parkview La

Woodlands

1

Tebworth Road

Road

Wingfield

Hill Cl

Hill Farm

Ickneild Way Path

2

Trinity Hall

DUNSTABLE

LORD'S HILL

3

Dunstable Road

A5(T)

A5120

4

Thorn

Thorn Road

Thorn Road

Ickneild Way Path

BEDFORD

Dunstablians Rugby Union Football Club

Bidwe

ROAD

5

Ickneild Way Path

Plaiters Wy

Roslyn Way

Bidwell

St Mic

6

A505

Chalk Hill

Ickneild Way Path

Coopers Wy

Arnold Wy

Hough Lower Mi Rd

Miller's Way

7

Sewell Lane

Barley Brow

Salters Way

Suncote

Cheyne Cl

Palma Cl

Suncote Av

Suncote Cl

WATLING STREET

A5(T)

Northfields

HIGH STREET NORTH

Northfields Upper School

HOUGHTON ROAD

A5120

Douglas Cl

Northview Ro

8

Sewell

French's

Avenue

Lawrence Industrial Estate

Dunstable Football Club

Brewers Hl Rd

Olma Rd

Canon Rd

A5(T)

grid square represents 500 metres

A

B
F8
1 High St North

C

D

Brewers Hill Middle School

Scawsby

Aldbanks

Hillcroft

Brewers Hill

E

Westfield Rd

Maidenbower

F

Beale Street

Park St

Waterlow Rd

Clifton Rd

Golf Club

G5
1 Angels La
2 Beech Tree Wy
3 Church End
4 Harrington Hts
5 Peel St
6 Thorn View Rd

G7
1 Blackburn Rd

H4
1 Hayley Ct

J6
1 Drury Ci
2 Hammersmith Ci
3 Park Rd North
4 St Andrews La

J5
1 Gainsborough Dr
2 Keaton Ci

Chalton

Chalton Primary School

The La

Chalton Hts

Grove Farm

Sundon Road

Chalton Cross Farm

M1

Sundon Road

Luton Bedfordshire County

Camford Way

Sund Busin Park

North Luton Industrial Est

Ribocon Wy

Bay Cl

by Ri

Ladymi

Coverdale

64

Thornhill Lower School

Thornbury Court

Grove Rd

Yew St

Thornhill Cl

Hillborough Crescent

Eddiwick Av

Kent Road

Sundon Road

Kings Houghton Middle School

Kingsland Community College

Houghton Park Rd

Gold Crest
Fld Fare Gn

Kestrel Way

Cotsfoot Green

Ravenhill Way

Swan

Tithe Farm

Leaf Rd

Black Thorn Rd

Sycamore Road

Recreation Rd

Elm Pk Dr

Enfield Cl

Parkside Drive

Trident Drive

Hawthorn Park Lower School

Newbury Rd

Dolphin Drive

Conquest Rd

Cumbria Cl

Parkside Drive

Fenwick Rd

Blaydon
Blunham Rd
Blaze
Peregrine Rd
Lapwing
Linnet
Swallow
Finch Cl

Roydon Cl

Junior School

Tithe Farm Lower School

Dell Rd

Ash Rd
Longf

Meadow

Leaf Rd

Alsop Cl

Leaflields

Easthill Road

Sundon Road

Westminster

Chelsea Gdns

Bromley Gardens

Turner

Constable

Nash Cl

Henley Rd
Rochdale
Cli

Pastures Wy

Thresher

Paddock

Feldring

Sussex

Oakfield

Southfield Junior & Infant School

Parkside

Lower School

Hammersmith Gdns

Broomsbury Gdns

Lowry Drive

Stubbs

Bridgeman

Windsor Dr

Houghton Regis

Doctors Surgery

Radnor Rd
St Kilda Rd

Chantry Junior & Infant School

Lensey Fm Clinic

Pastures

Primary School

Houghton Regis Medical Cen

Crossways

Parkside Cl

Kingsland Drive

Beadlow Road

Trefoil
Clover

Sefton

Junior School

Hill Side

Camp Dr

Drum Cl

East End

The Green

Woodlands Av

Haiiey's Wy

Copperfields

Tudor Dr
Tennyson
Dr

Windsor

Wheatfield

Binder

Landrace Road

Haymaket Rd

Reaper

Thatch

Tomlinson

PO

Drayton Rd

Angus

Clydesdale Rd

Friesian Way

Suffolk

St Michaels Av

HIGH STREET

Houghton Regis Health Cen

PO

Clarkes Wy

High Whitehouse

Park

North

Milton Wy

Dr

Tennyson Av

Longbrooke

Regis Road

Marlin Rd

Cedar

Hoppy

Thurlow

Brunel

Friesian Way

Carfax

Belsize Rd

Kirkwood Road

Rodney

Leagrave

High School House

Lewsey Farm

Junior School

Baldoc

Abercorn

Ramsey

Guernsey

Minorca
Leghorn Wy

Hereford Rd

Queen St

The Lindens

Manor Park

Cemetery

Dunstable Road

Ivinghoe Business Cen

Foster Avenue

Arenson Wy

Boscombe Road

Porz Avenue

Humphrys Road

Lovett Way

Yerev Rd

Apex Business Cen

Houghton Hall

Windsor Road North

Humphrys Road

Wilbury Drive

Mill Vale School

Markham Crs

Ambhurst Rd

Braintree Cl

Bracknell

Halyard High School

Emerald Rd

Jilliter Road

Chapter House Road

Macaulay

Poets

Browning

Cloisters

Shenley Rd

Byron Rd

Crabtree

G X Superbowl

Dunstable

Chiltern Park

Chiltern Park Industrial Est

Holmwood Close

Goldstone Crs

Rideway

Hadrian Lower School

Hadrian

Duncombe Drive

Holliwick Rd

Lockington Crs

Katherine Drive

Pynders

Carterways

Walgrave Road

Linden

Gorham

Wingate Rd

Calcutt

St Christophers Lower School

Highfields Cl

Cresta

Evelyn Rd

Stadium Industrial Est

Ashton C of E Middle School

81

Hillcrest School

Chiltern Park Industrial Estate

Western Way

The Crest

Luton Road

A505

PO

The Retreat

Dale

G

M7
1 Harvest Cl
2 Orpington Cl

M8
1 Poets Gn
2 Vespers Cl

H

M5
1 Partridge Cl

M6
1 Eagle Cl
2 Goshawk Cl
3 Sparrow Cl

J

K

L7
1 Albermarle Cl
2 Aldenham Cl
3 Raglan Cl

L8
1 Thornbury

L

K7
1 Lollard Cl
2 Nettle Cl

M

K6
1 St James Cl
2 Shepherd Rd

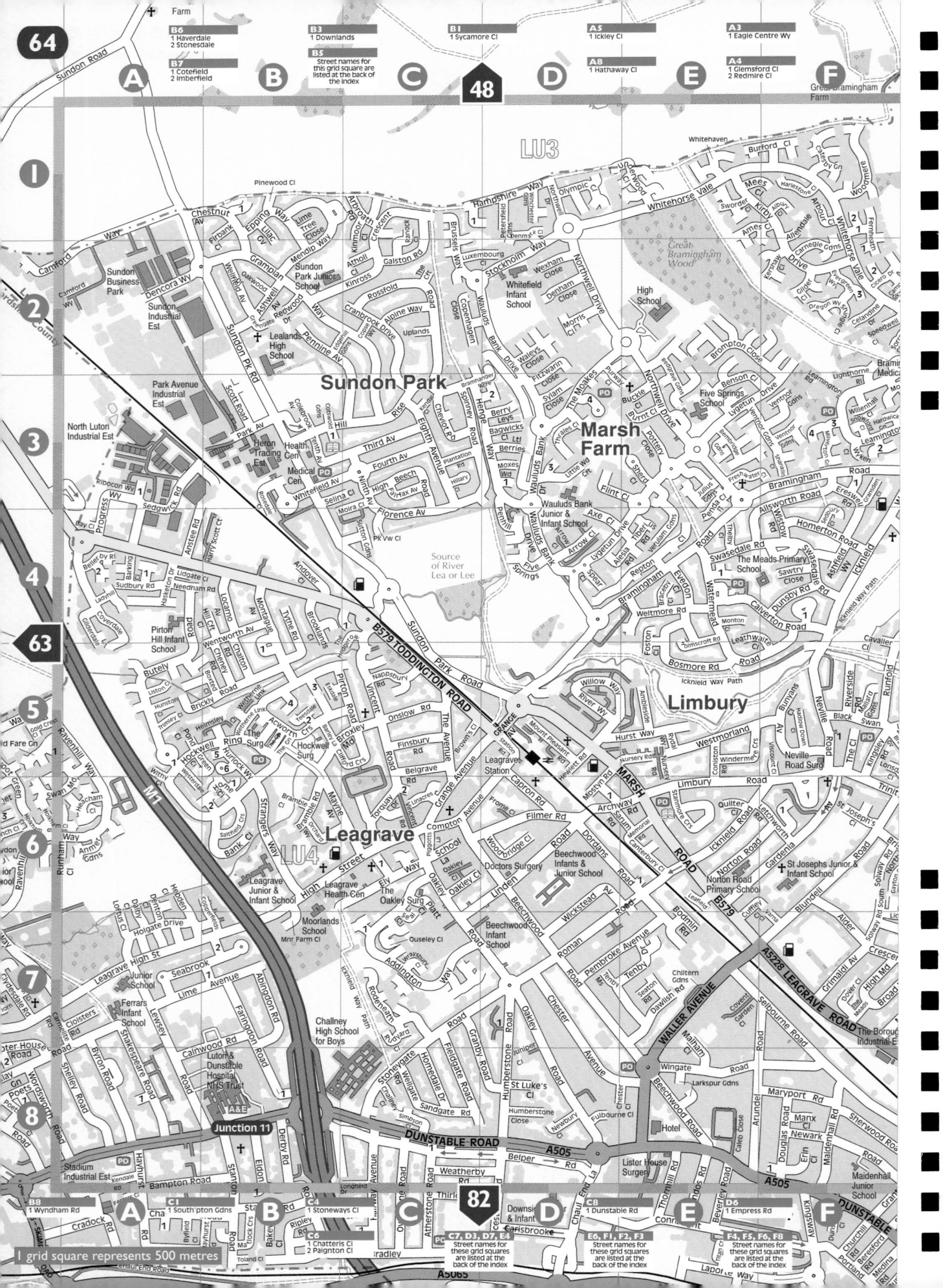
B6
1 Haverdale
2 Stonesdale
B7
1 Cotefield
2 Imberfield
B3
1 Downlands
B5
Street names for this grid square are listed at the back of the index
B1
1 Sycamore Cl
A5
1 Ickley Cl
A8
1 Hathaway Cl
A3
1 Eagle Centre Wy
A4
1 Glemsford Cl
2 Redmire Cl
48
LU3
Sundon Park
Marsh Farm
Limbury
Leagrave
LU4
Great Bramingham Wood
Source of River Lea or Lee
Sundon Business Park
Sundon Industrial Est
Park Avenue Industrial Est
North Luton Industrial Est
Heron Trading Est
Lealands High School
Sundon Park Junior School
Whitefield Infant School
High School
Five Springs School
Wauluds Bank Junior & Infant School
The Meads Primary School
Pirton Hill Infant School
Leagrave Station
Leagrave Junior & Infant School
Leagrave Health Cen
Moorlands School
Beechwood Infants & Junior School
Beechwood Infant School
Norton Road Primary School
St Josephs Junior & Infant School
Junior School
Ferrars Infant School
Challney High School for Boys
Luton & Dunstable Hospital NHS Trust
Junction 11
Stadium Industrial Est
Lister House Surgery
Maidenhall Junior School
Hotel
M1
B579 TODDINGTON ROAD
A5228 LEAGRAVE ROAD
DUNSTABLE ROAD
A505
A5065
WALLER AVENUE
63
82
B8
1 Wyndham Rd
C1
1 South'pton Gdns
C4
1 Stoneways Cl
C6
1 Chatteris Cl
2 Paignton Cl
C7, D3, D7, E4
Street names for these grid squares are listed at the back of the index
C8
1 Dunstable Rd
E6, F1, F2, F3
Street names for these grid squares are listed at the back of the index
D6
1 Empress Rd
F4, F5, F6, F8
Street names for these grid squares are listed at the back of the index
1 grid square represents 500 metres

G1
1 Balmore Wd
2 Gatehill Gdns

G3
1 The Crest
2 Sandalwood Cl

G4
1 The Kipling
2 St Olam's Cl
3 Waterslade Gn

G5
1 Belvedere Rd
2 Fenwick Cl

G6
1 Ellerdine Cl

H1
1 Spurcroft

49

John Bunyan Trail

South Bedfordshire
Golf Club

Icknield Way Path

Cardinal
Newman RC
School

Sunshine Riding
School

Bramingham
Business
Park

Barnfield
Coll

Wardown Park
Museum

Warden Hill Infant
School

Junior School

Whitehill
Farm

Butterfield
Green

Bedfordshire County
Luton

66

Icknield
High School

Barnfield
College

Medical
Centre

Bushmead
Infant
School

Stopsley
Common

Stopsley
Infant
School

Doctors
Surgery

6

Stopsley

Luton
Sixth Form
College

Bradgers

Honeygate

Stopsley High School
& Community College

Sacred Heart
RC Junior &
Infant School

7

William Austin
Junior School

Doctor
Surg

Infant
School

Graham
Gdns

Priory
Gdns

Westbury
Gdns

Greenhill
Gdns

A5228 MONTROSE AVENUE

A5228 STOCKINGSTONE ROAD

Wardown Swimming
& Leisure Centre

Luton Co-operative
Sports Club

Moreton Park
Industrial
Estate

8

VAUXHALL

Biscot

Round
Green

Denbigh
Infant
School

Denbigh
High School

Wardown

Mountfield
Rd

Woodbury
H1
Richmond
Hill School

Ramridge
Junior
School

2

3

Hart
Hill

G
L7
1 Felstead Cl

H
K4
1 Haycroft

K5
1 Edkins Cl
2 Pytchley Cl
3 Temple Cl

M6
1 Charmbury Ri

J
Knights
Fld
Earls
Mead
K3
1 Wiseman Cl

K

J3, J4
Street names for
these grid squares
are listed at the
back of the index

L

H4
1 Duncombe Cl
2 Markfield Cl
3 Wycliffe Cl

H8
1 Chaucer Rd
2 Sheridan Rd

M
H2
1 Lancaster Av
2 Warden Hill Cl

H5
1 Sheringham Cl
2 Wickmere Cl

A   B   C   50 y   D   E   F

65

I
2
3
4
5
6
7
8

A   B   C   84   D   E   F

C6
1 Amberley Cl
2 Middleton Rd
3 Pevensey Cl

B6
1 Balcombe Cl
2 Field End Cl

B7
1 Cowdray Cl
2 Keymer Cl

A7
1 Croft Rd
2 Rickyard Cl
3 The Severalls

B5
1 Boxgrove Cl

A6
1 Collingtree
2 Elderberry Cl

Luton Road

C7
1 Bolney Gn
2 Plumpton Cl

C8
1 Brierley Cl
2 Brimfield Cl
3 Sussex Pl
4 Waddesdon Cl
5 Whitechurch Cl

D8
1 Beanley Cl
2 Berrow Cl
3 Branton Cl
4 Manning Pl
5 Renshaw Cl
6 Trescott Cl

E8
1 Greenriggs
2 Lennox Gn
3 Reedsdale
4 Thaxted Cl

Lilley Wood
Lilley Bottom
Dog Kennel Farm
Luton White Hill
Lilley Bottom
Chalk Hill
Offley Chase
Putteridge Bury
University of Luton
Mangrove Green
Cockernhoe
Chalk Hill
Brickkiln Wood

Bedfordshire County
Whitehill Farm
Bedfordshire County Luton
Cem and Crematorium
Manor Farm
Putteridge High School & Community College
Putteridge Junior & Infant School
Recreation Centre
Doctors Surgery
Doctors Surg
Someries Junior School
Someries Infant School
Slaughter's Wood
Ramridge Junior School
Infant School
Moreton Park Industrial Est
Ashcroft High School
Wigmore Primary School

Topsley
LU2
VAUXHALL WAY

1 grid square represents 500 metres

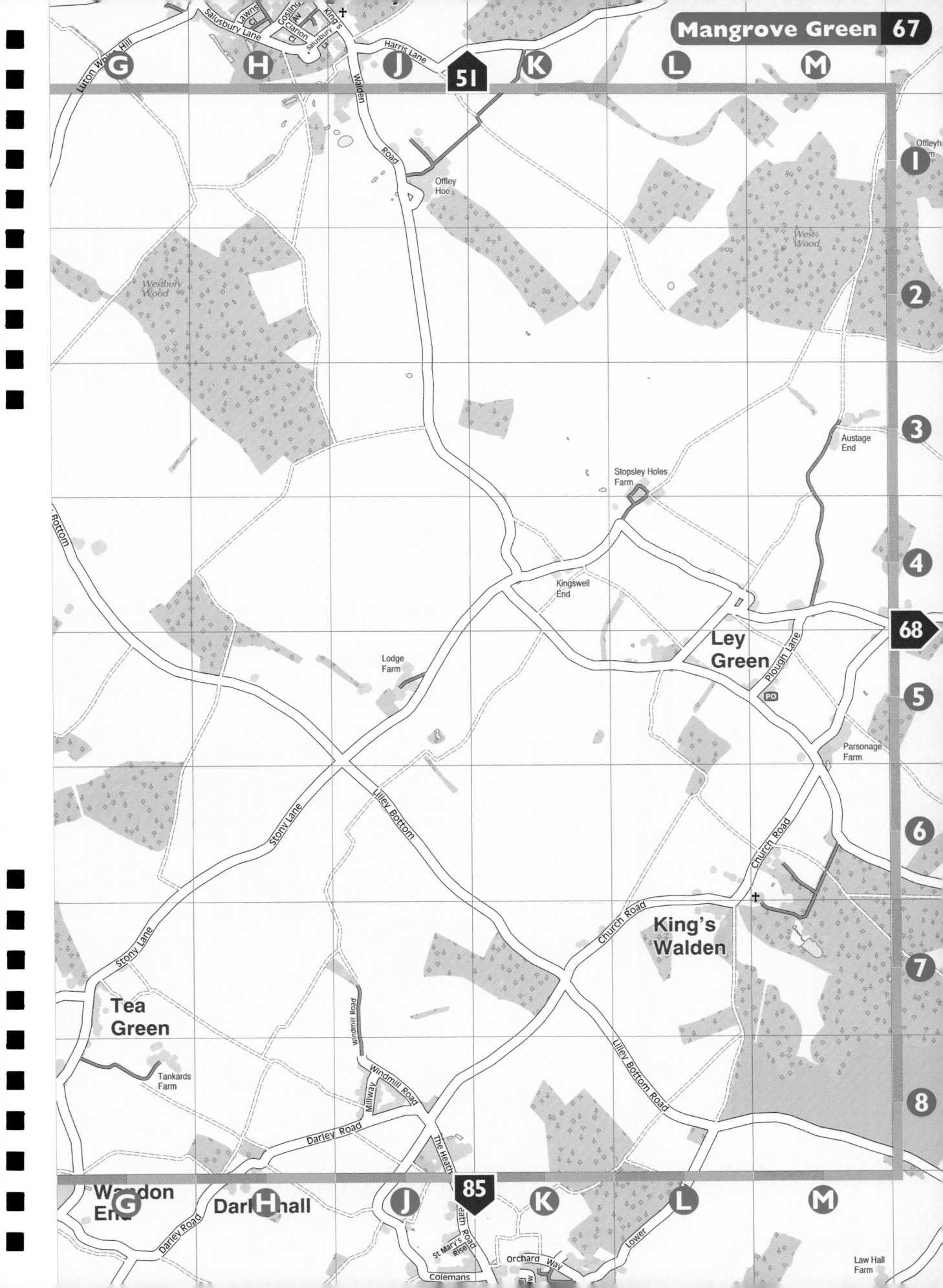

G H J 51 K L M

I

2

3

Offleyh

Offley Hoo

West Wood

Austage End

Stopsley Holes Farm

4

Kingswell End

68

Ley Green

PO

5

Parsonage Farm

Lodge Farm

6

Church Road

King's Walden

Stony Lane

Lilley Bottom

7

Tea Green

Windmill Road

Tankards Farm

Lilley Bottom Road

8

Stony Lane

Millway

Windmill Road

Darley Road

The Heath

Wandon End

Dar hall

Darley Road

J 85 K L M

St Mary's Rise

eath Road

Orchard Way

Colemans

Lower

Law Hall Farm

A B C **52** D E F

St Ibbs

I

Offleyholes
Farm

Littl
Alm

2

Tatmore
Place

3

Al te
End

Woman's Lane

Castle
Farm

Wain
Wood

Preston Road

4

Dead Lane

Chequers Lane

Templars La

The Princess
Helena
College

Preston

Butchers Lane

Church Lane

Back Lane

Poynders
End

67

School Lane

Temple
Dinsley

Lilley Bottom Road

5

Parsonage
Farm

Prestonhill
Farm

Lady
Grove

6

Hitch
Wood

Whitehall
Farm

7

SG4

Frogmore

8

Stagenhoe

A B **86** C D E F

St
W

Law Hall
Farm

B651

1 grid square represents 500 metres

St Ippollitts
Titmore Green
Redcoats
Tod Green
Stevenage Road
Sperberry Hill
Fishers Green
Symonds Green
The Symonds Green Health Centre
A1(M)
Hertfordshire Way
Chapelfoot
Almshoe Bury
White Lane
LONDON ROAD
B656
B651
Hill End Farm
Rush Green
Dyes Lane
Dyes Farm
Shepherds Lane
Kitching Lane
Meadway
Redcar Drive
Rutherford Close
Crompton Road
Cavendish Road
Hyatt Trading Estate
Babbage Road
Clovelly Way
GUNNELS WOOD ROAD
Shilley Green Farm
Langley Lane
Langleyhill Farm
Easthall
Village St
Homefield Lane
Langley
Paul's
53
70
87

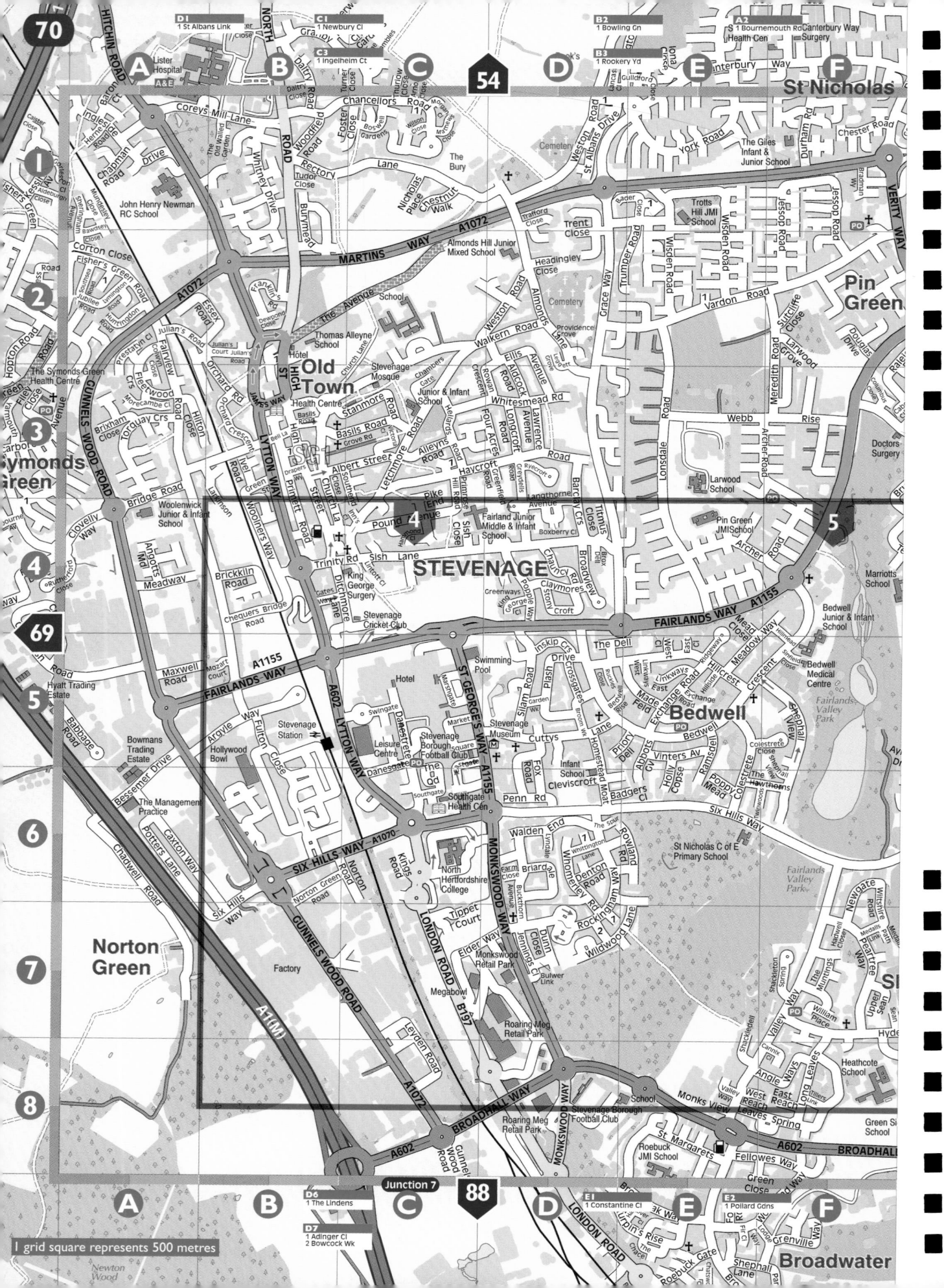
D1 1 St Albans Link
C1 1 Newbury Cl
C3 1 Ingelheim Ct
B2 1 Bowling Gn
B3 1 Rookery Yd
A2 1 Bournemouth Rd
54
St Nicholas
Lister Hospital
A&E
Coreys Mill Lane
Chancellors Road
Rectory Lane
The Bury
Canterbury Way Surgery
Health Cen
Canterbury Way
York Road
Chester Road
The Giles Infant & Junior School
Cemetery
Weston Road
St Albans Drive
John Henry Newman RC School
Chestnut Walk
Nicholas Place
Buryhead
MARTINS WAY A1072
Almonds Hill Junior Mixed School
Trent Close
Headingley Close
Trumper Road
Wisden Road
Trotts Hill JMI School
Jessop Road
VERITY WAY
Corton Close
Fisher's Green Road
Vardon Road
Pin Green
Sutcliffe Close
Thomas Alleyne School
The Avenue
School
Walkern Road
Providence Grove
Larwood Grove
Meredith Road
Douglas Drive
The Symonds Green Health Centre
Old Town
Stevenage Mosque
Health Centre
Chambers Gate
Junior & Infant School
Whitesmead Rd
Webb Rise
Doctors Surgery
Symonds Green
Basils Road
Albert Street
Lerchmore Road
Alleyns Road
Haycroft Road
Lonsdale Road
Larwood School
Bridge Road
Woolenwick Junior & Infant School
Pound Avenue
Fairland Junior Middle & Infant School
Pin Green JMI School
Archer Road
Clovelly Way
Trinity Rd
Sish Lane
STEVENAGE
King George Surgery
Marriotts School
Brickkiln Road
Meadway
Chequers Bridge Road
Stevenage Cricket Club
FAIRLANDS WAY A1155
Bedwell Junior & Infant School
69
Maxwell Road
Hyatt Trading Estate
FAIRLANDS WAY
A1155
Swimming Pool
Hotel
The Dell
Meadow Way
Bedwell Medical Centre
Fairlands Valley Park
Stevenage Station
Argyle Way
Bowmans Trading Estate
Hollywood Bowl
Leisure Centre
Stevenage Borough Football Club
Stevenage Museum
Cuttys
Bedwell
Exchange Road
Vinters Av
Shephall View
Danesgate
Southgate Health Cen
Penn Rd
Cleviscroft
Badgers Cl
The Hawthorns
Six Hills Way
The Management Practice
Caxton Way
Potters Lane
SIX HILLS WAY A1070
St Nicholas C of E Primary School
North Hertfordshire College
Tippet Court
Chadwell Road
MONKSWOOD WAY
LONDON ROAD
GUNNELS WOOD ROAD
Norton Green
Factory
Elder Way
Monkswood Retail Park
Bulwer Link
Wildwood Lane
Megabowl
A1(M)
Roaring Meg Retail Park
Leyden Road
Heathcote School
BROADHALL WAY
Monks View
Roaring Meg Retail Park
Stevenage Borough Football Club
Roebuck JMI School
St Margarets
Fellowes Way
Green Close
Green Si School
A602 BROADHALL
A602
Junction 7
88
D6 1 The Lindens
D7 1 Adinger Cl 2 Bowcock Wk
E1 1 Constantine Cl
E2 1 Pollard Gdns
Broadwater
Grenville Way
Shephall Lane
Roebuck Gate
1 grid square represents 500 metres
Newton Wood

G7 1 Hyde Gn East
H2 1 Aintree Wy 2 Chells La 3 Hadrians Wk
H3 1 Cornfields
G
H
J
K
L
M
55
Boxbury Farm
Box Wood
Walkern
Moors Ley
STEVENAGE ROAD B1037
1
2
3
4
5
6
7
8
72
Industrial Estate
Beverley Road
Stevenage Business Park
Cartwright
Martins Way
Sefton Road
Ascot Crescent
Martins Wood JMI School
Lingfield Road
Gresley Way
Trajan Gate
Valerian Way
Mildmay Road
Round Diamond School
Sandown Road
Julia Gate
Apollo Way
Augustus Gate
Ayr Close
Pacatian Way
Alexander Gate
Emperors Gate
Fortuna Cl
A1155
FAIRLANDS WAY B1037
The Pastures
Boxfield Gn
Crescent
Dryden
Knights Templars Gn
The Hedgerows
Uplands
Stanley Road
Fawcett Road
Livingstone Link
Marlowe Close
Byron Close
Keats Close
Crescent
Kings Walden Ri
Montfitchet Wk
Hayfield
Grass Meadows
Cook Road
Drakes Drive
Wheatlands
Chells Lane
Harvest Lane
The White Way
Hunters Close
Chalkdown
Nobel Secondary School
Junior School
Lodge Farm Infant School
Conifer Walk
Downlands
Chells Way
Frobisher Dr
Mobbsbury Way
Beane Avenue
Chells
Newton Road
Scott Road
Darwin Rd
Edison Road
Harvey Road
Faraday Road
Avenue
Nash Close
Wren Close
Telford Avenue
Elliot Road
Beale Close
Anderson Road
Warwick Road
Siddons Road
Ferrier Road
Beane Walk
Gresley Way
Lanterns Lane
Cavell Walk
Nightingale Walk
Pankhurst Crs
Flinders Cl
Christie Road
Fry Road
Barham Road
Aston End
Holders Lane
George Leighton Court
Britain Way
Keller Cl
Wellington Road
Marlborough Road
Cromwell Road
Jackdaw Close
Tatlers Lane
Watercress Cl
Walnut Tree Cl
Coopers Close
Milestone Cl
Edmonds Drive
Carters Cl
Parishes Mead
Lime Cl
Short Lane
Long Lane
Collenswood Road
Dovedale
Furzedown
Collenswood School
Redwing Close
Harrowdene
Bunyan Rd
Shephall Way
Colts Cnr
Wigram Way
SG2
Ashleigh
Chertsey Rise
Parker's Field
Kymswell Rd
Sparrow Drive
Magpie Crescent
Shearwater
The Lawns
Poplars
Brookfield Lane
Aston End Road
Walkern Road
High Wood
Benington Road
Paddocks Close
The Ridings
Elm Wk
Beech Dr
Unwin Road
Hornbeam
Hayley Common
Mackenzie Square
Godfrey Close
Warren Close
Colwell Rd
Featherston Rd
Fallowfield
Blackberry Mead
Cotney Crt
Skylark Cnr
Fieldfare
Bareleigh
School Close
Paddocks
Shephall
Randals Hill
Doctors Surg
Foxfield
Featherstone Wood Primary School
Rise
Sheepcroft H
Minsden Rd
Lapwing Ri
Arundel Close
St Marys School
Lower Dean Way
Rudd Cl
Barnwell
Wortham Way
Breakspear
Bandley
Harefield
Barleycroft
Osprey Cdns
Bittern Cl
Mallard Road
Kestrel Cl
Falcon Cl
Kingfisher Ri
School La
Brook Ri
Wrights Orch
Aston
Baddeley Close
Ridlins End
Conville
Leslie Cl
Sisson Cl
Crescent
Woodcock Road
Gresley Way
Barnwell School
Shephall Infant School
Shephall Way Surgery
Shephall Green
Taywood Close
Oakwood Close
Glenwood Close
Dene Lane
St Marys Close
Garden Fld
New Pk La
Benington Road
Yeomans Drive
Stringers Lane
Holbrook Farm
WAY
Wood Dr
Russell Close
Lane
89
Manor View
Green Acres
Longfields
A602
Vallansgate
Rockwood Dr
Park View
Oakfields
Lismore
Oakfields Close
Raban Close
Broadwater La
Burydale Junior Mixed School
Long Meadow Infant & Junior School
J7 1 Campkin Mead
Broadwater
Long Ridge
J5 1 Magellan Cl 2 Speke Cl
J3 1 The Spinney
J2 1 Hedgerow Cl
River Beane

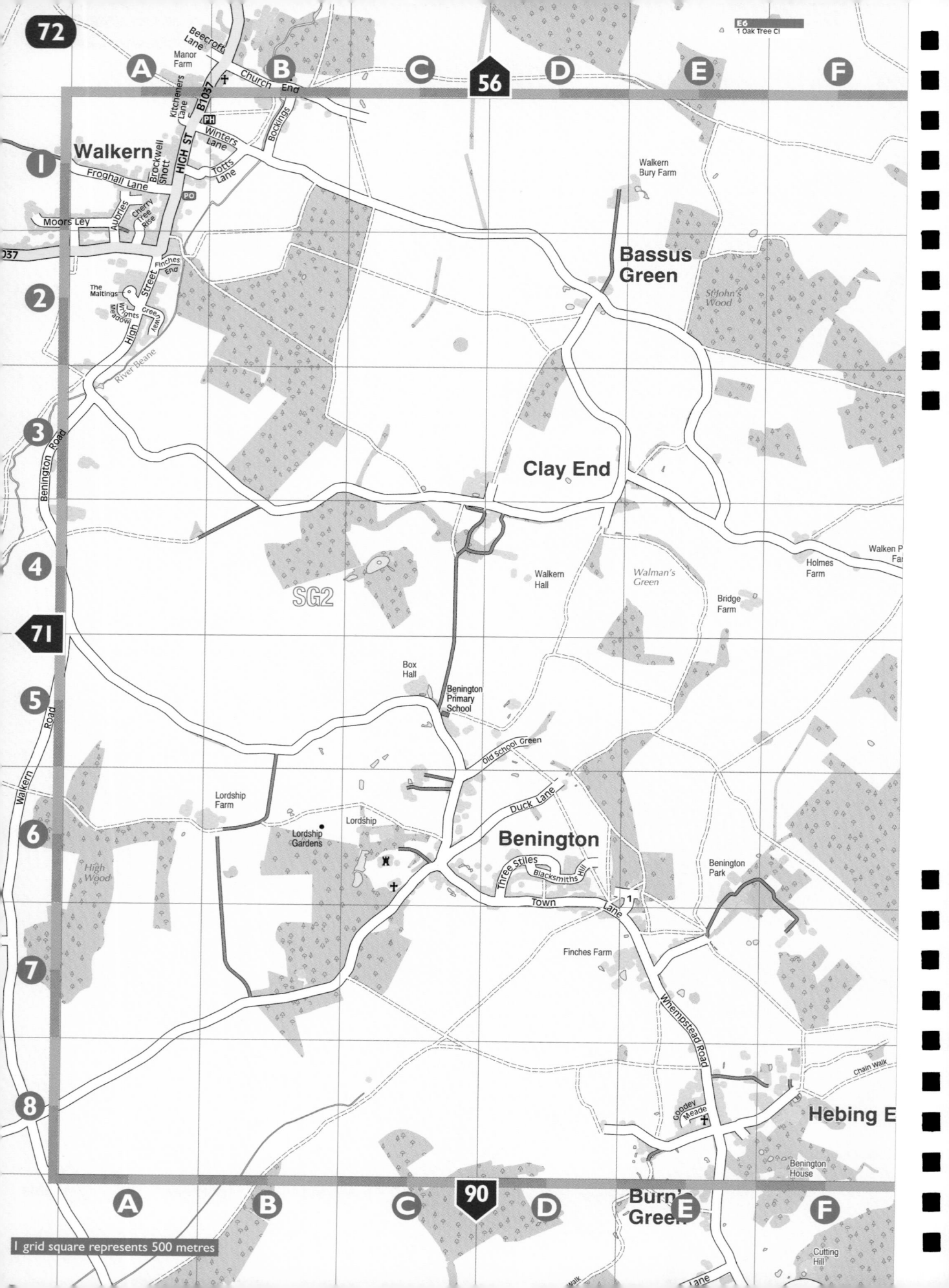
E6
1 Oak Tree Cl
A
B
C
56
D
E
F
Manor Farm
Beecroft Lane
Church End
Kitcheners Lane
B1037
PH
Bockings
Winters Lane
Walkern
Brockwell Shott
HIGH ST
Froghall Lane
Totts Lane
PO
Aubries
Cherry Tree Rise
Moors Ley
Finches End
The Maltings
Street
Wrights Meadow
Greenway
High
River Beane
Benington Road
Walkern Bury Farm
Bassus Green
St John's Wood
Clay End
Walkern Hall
Walman's Green
Holmes Farm
Bridge Farm
SG2
71
Box Hall
Benington Primary School
Old School Green
Walkern Road
Lordship Farm
Lordship
Lordship Gardens
Duck Lane
Benington
Three Stiles
Blacksmiths Hill
Town
Lane
High Wood
Benington Park
Finches Farm
Whempstead Road
Chain Walk
Goodey Meade
Hebing E
Benington House
90
Burn's Green
Cutting Hill
1
2
3
4
5
6
7
8
1 grid square represents 500 metres

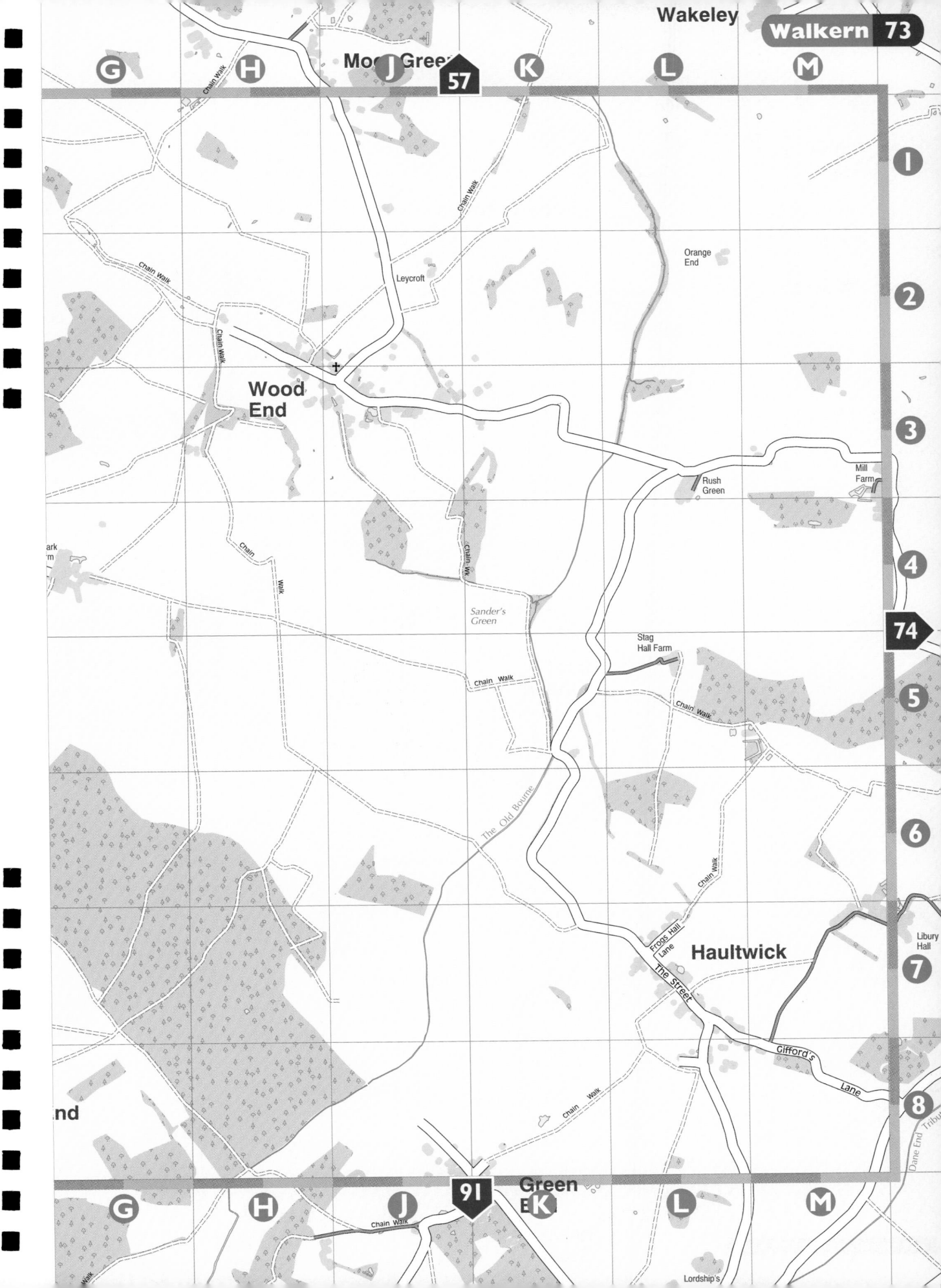

Wakeley

G   H   Moor Green   J   57   K   L   M

Chain Walk

Leycroft

Orange
End

Chain Walk

Chain Walk

†

Wood
End

Rush
Green

Mill
Farm

...ark
...m

Chain

Walk

Sander's
Green

Chain Wk.

Stag
Hall Farm

74

Chain Walk

Chain   Walk

5

The Old Bourne

Chain   Walk

6

Chain Walk

Frogs Hall
Lane

Libury
Hall

Haultwick

7

The Street

Gifford's

Lane

Dane End Tribut...

8

...nd

G   H   J   91   Green   K   L   M
E

Chain Walk

Lordship's

I
2
3
4
5
6
7
8

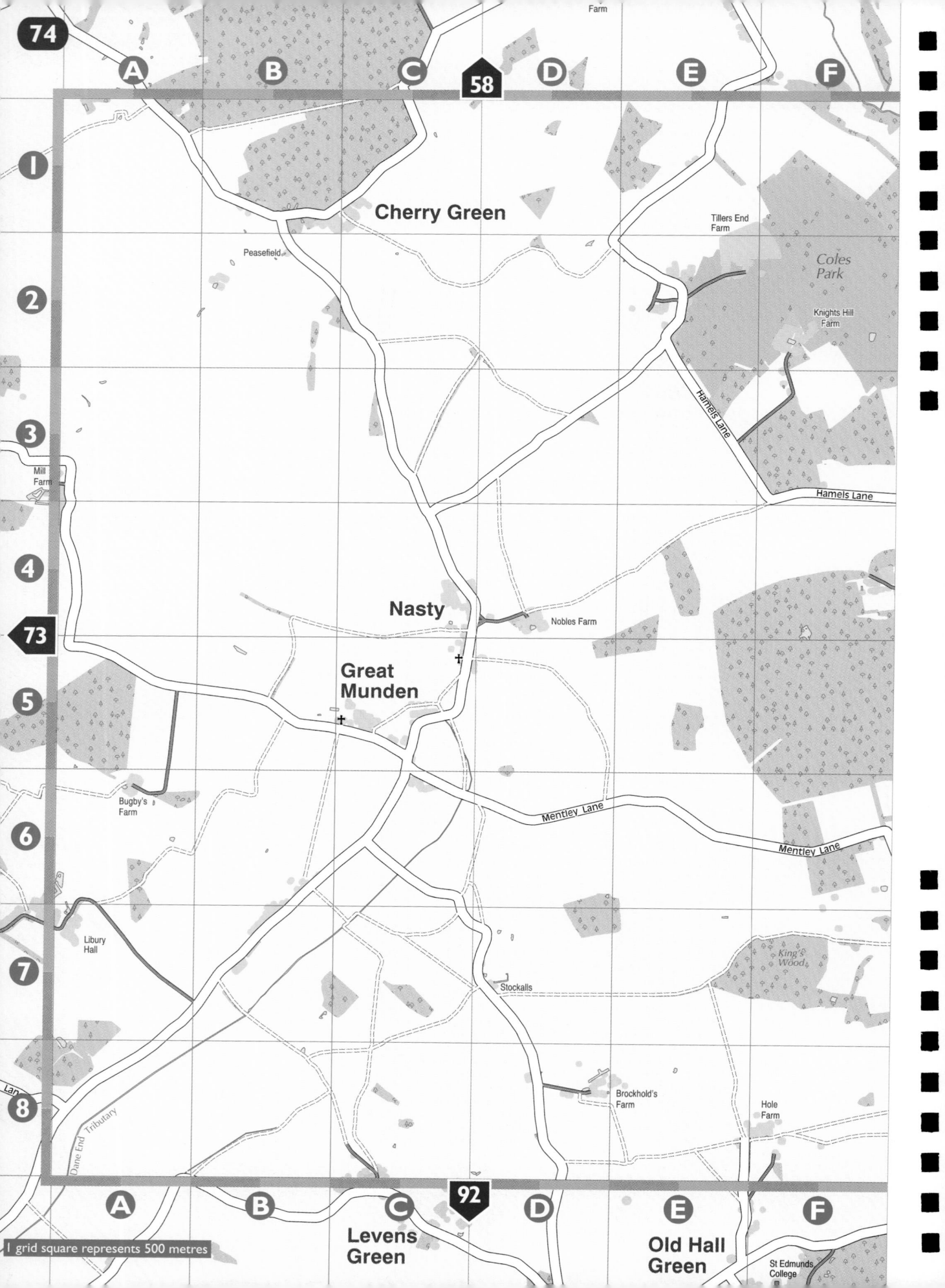

74

A   B   C   **58**   D   E   F

I

Cherry Green

Peasefield

Tillers End
Farm

*Coles
Park*

2

Knights Hill
Farm

Hamels Lane

3

Mill
Farm

Hamels Lane

4

Nasty

Nobles Farm

73

**Great
Munden**

5

Bugby's
Farm

King's
Wood

6

Mentley Lane

Mentley Lane

Libury
Hall

7

Stockalls

8

Brockhold's
Farm

Hole
Farm

Dane End Tributary

Lan

A   B   C   **92**   D   E   F

**Levens
Green**

**Old Hall
Green**

St Edmunds
College

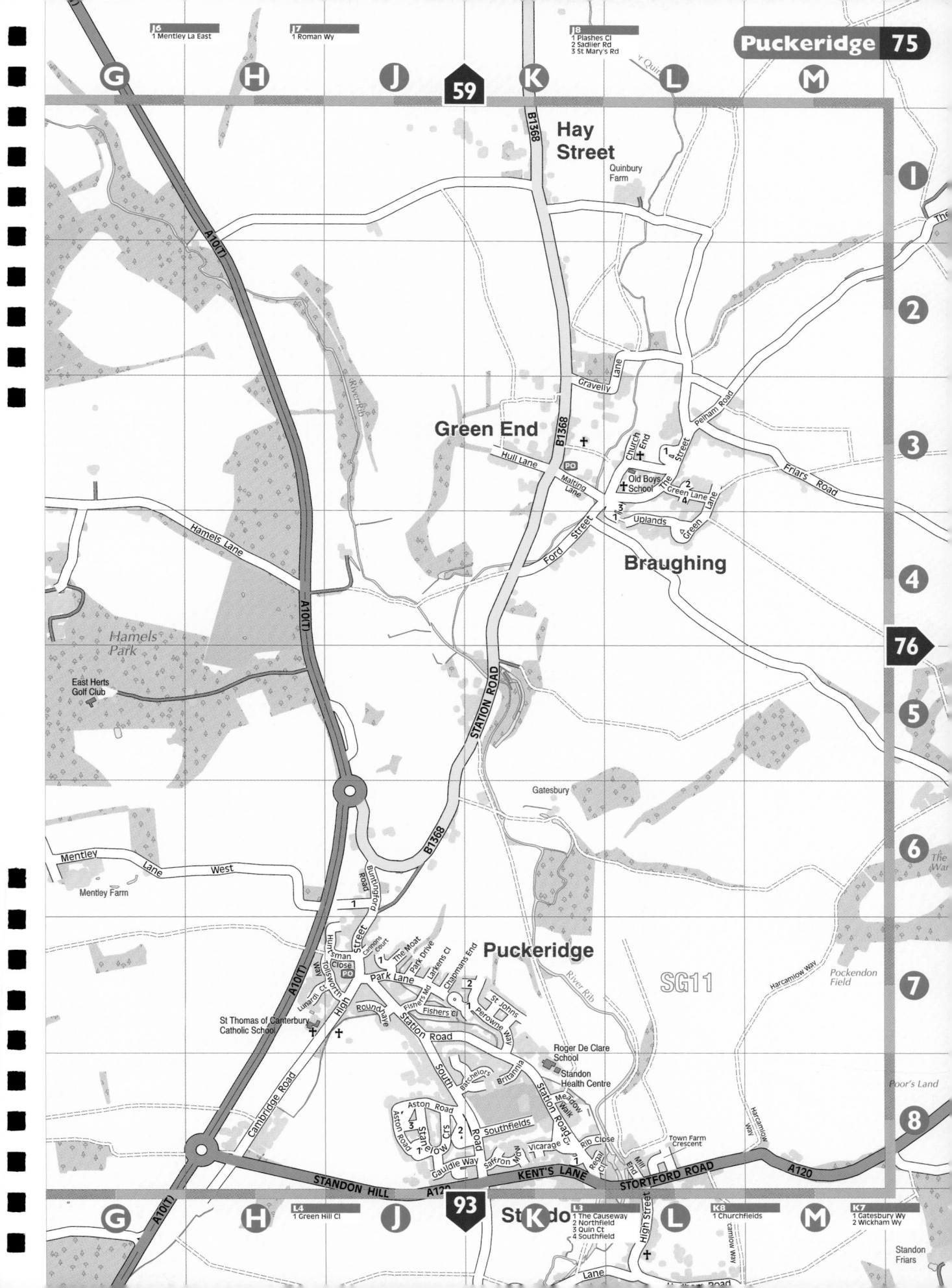

G H J 59 K L M

J6
1 Mentley La East

J7
1 Roman Wy

J8
1 Plashes Cl
2 Sadlier Rd
3 St Mary's Rd

I

Hay
Street

Quinbury
Farm

2

River Rib

3

Gravelly Lane

Green End

Hull Lane

PO

Malding
Lane

Braughing

Church
End

Old Boys
School

Green Lane

Uplands

Pelham Road

Friars Road

4

76

Hamels Lane

Ford Street

B1368

5

Hamels
Park

East Herts
Golf Club

STATION ROAD

Gatesbury

6

The
War

Mentley Lane West

Mentley Farm

B1368

Buntingford Road

1

Puckeridge

The Moat

Park Drive

Larkens End

Chapmans End

River Rib

SG11

Harcamlow Way

Pockendon
Field

7

Huntsman
Way

Tollsworth
Close

PO

Park Lane

Fishers Md

Fishers Cl

St Johns

Perowne Way

Roger De Clare
School

Standon
Health Centre

Poor's Land

St Thomas of Canterbury
Catholic School

High Street

Roundacre

Station Road

South Meadow Walk

Batchelor's

Britannia

Station Road

Rib Close

8

Aston Road

Aston Road

Stanlow Crs

2

Southfields

Vicarage

Regal

Town Farm
Crescent

Harcamlow Way

Gauldie Way

Saffron

Kent's Lane

Mill Terrace

High Street

STANDON HILL

A120

STORTFORD ROAD

A120

Standon
Friars

G H 93 K Stndo L M

L4
1 Green Hill Cl

L3
1 The Causeway
2 Northfield
3 Quin Ct
4 Southfield

K8
1 Churchfields

K7
1 Gatesbury Wy
2 Wickham Wy

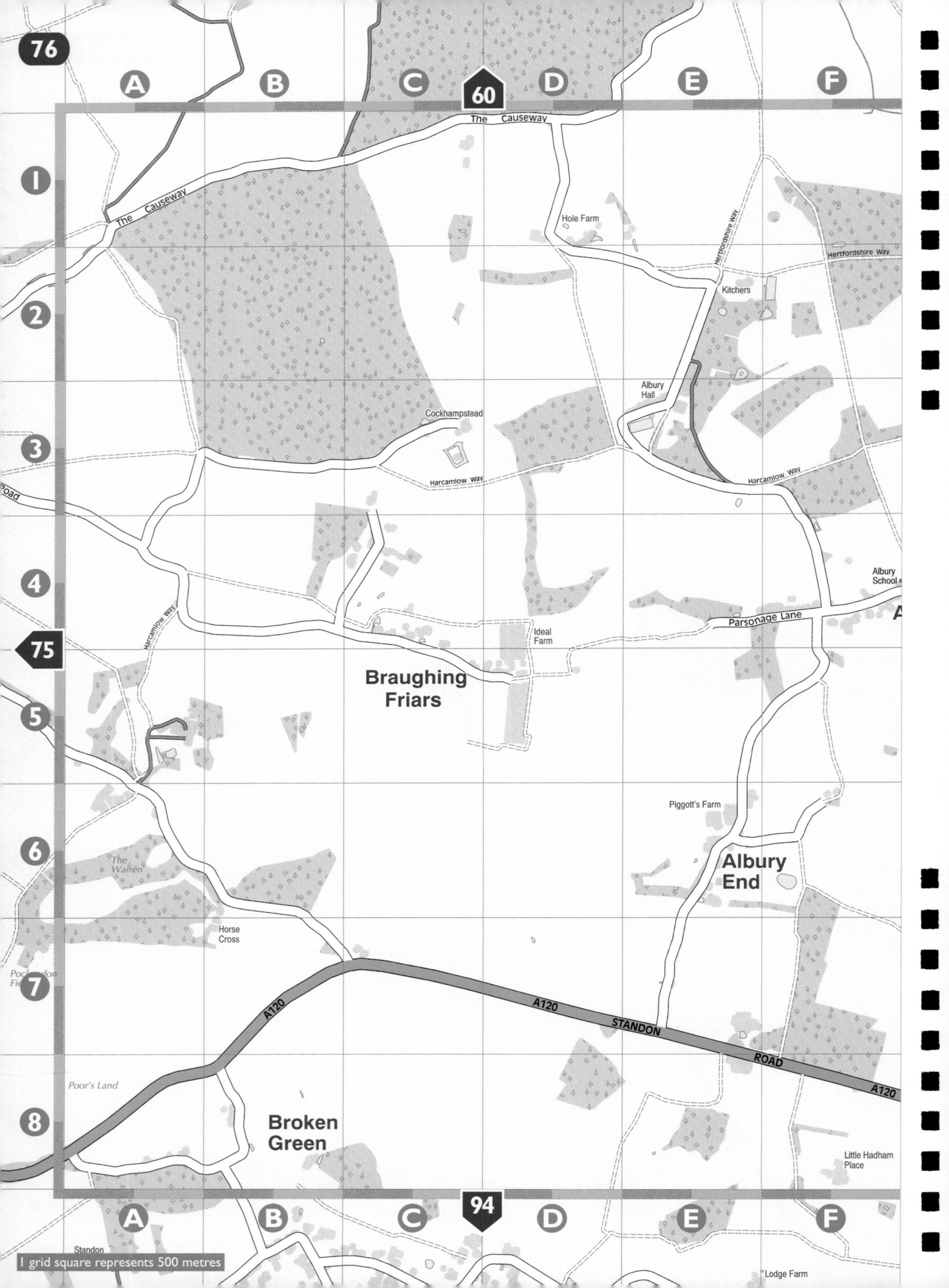

A   B   C   60   D   E   F

The   Causeway

1

The Causeway

Hole Farm

Hertfordshire Way

Hertfordshire Way

Kitchers

2

Albury
Hall

3

Cockhampstead

Harcamlow Way

Harcamlow Way

Albury
School

4

Road

Parsonage Lane

Albury

Harcamlow Way

Ideal
Farm

**Braughing
Friars**

5

Piggott's Farm

The
Warren

6

**Albury
End**

Horse
Cross

Pool...don
Fie...

7

A120   A120   STANDON   ROAD   A120

Poor's Land

8

**Broken
Green**

Little Hadham
Place

A   B   C   94   D   E   F

Standon

Lodge Farm

I grid square represents 500 metres

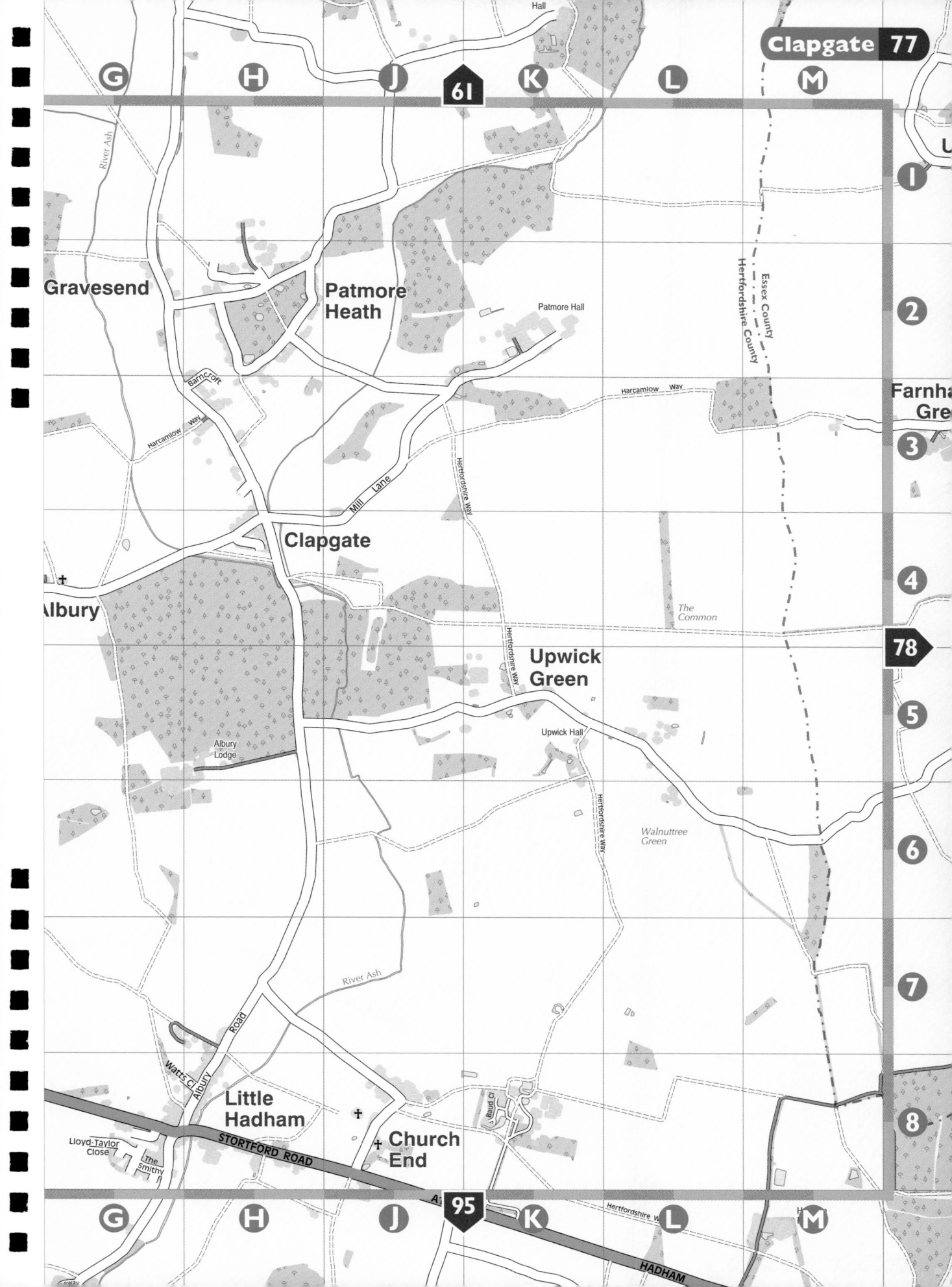
G
H
J
61
K
L
M
Hall
River Ash
Gravesend
Patmore Heath
Patmore Hall
Essex County
Hertfordshire County
Barncroft
Harcamlow Way
Harcamlow Way
Farnha
Gre
Mill Lane
Hertfordshire Way
Clapgate
Albury
The Common
78
Upwick Green
Upwick Hall
Albury Lodge
Walnuttree Green
River Ash
Road
Watts Cl
Albury
Little Hadham
Church End
Lloyd-Taylor Close
The Smithy
STORTFORD ROAD
95
Hertfordshire W
HADHAM
I
2
3
4
5
6
7
8

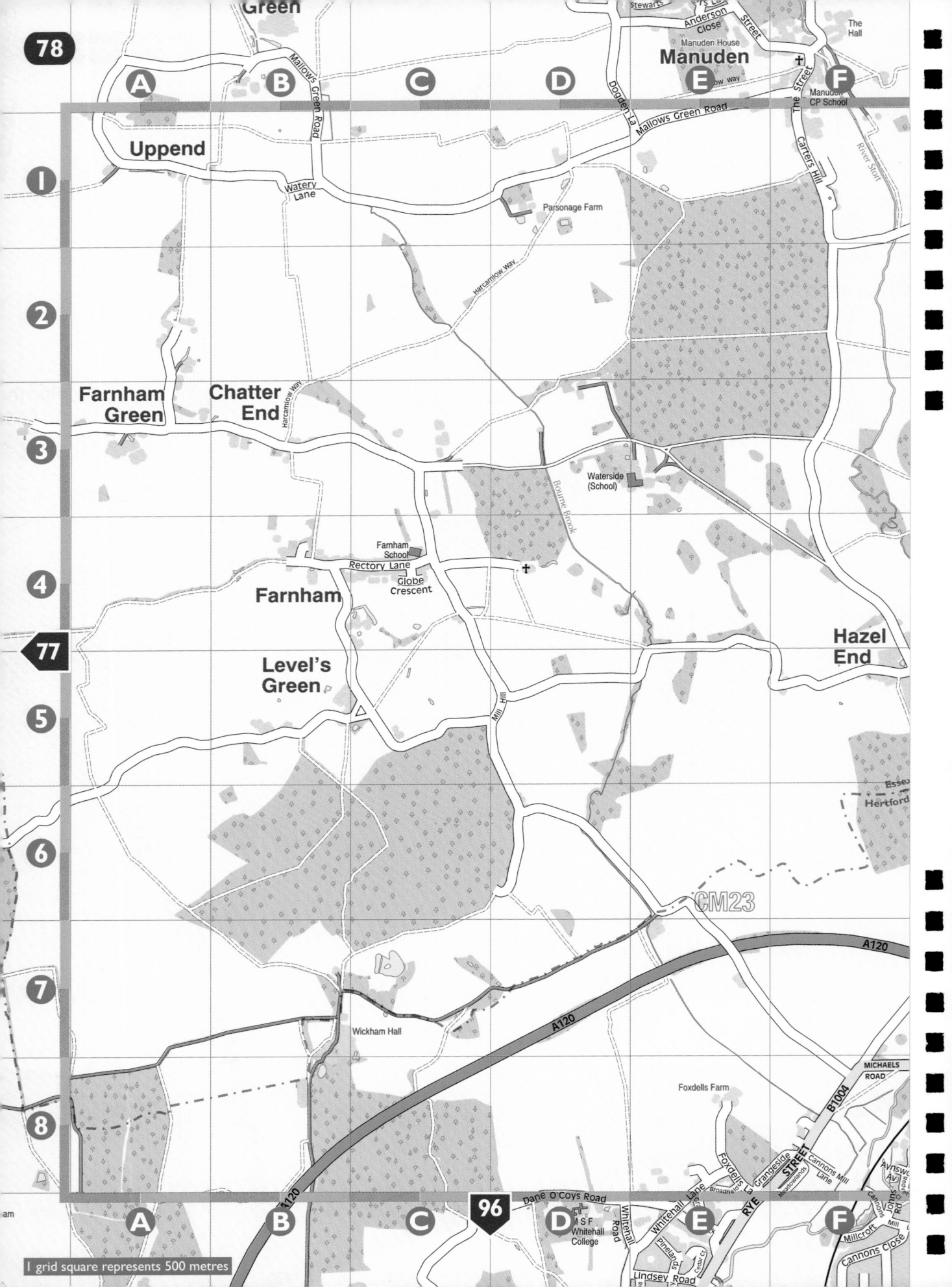

Green

Manuden

Manuden House

The Hall

Uppend

Mallows Green Road

Mallows Green Road

Dogden La

The Street

Carters Hill

River Stort

Manuden CP School

Anderson Close

1

Watery Lane

Parsonage Farm

Harcamlow Way

2

Farnham Green

Chatter End

Harcamlow Way

3

Bourne Brook

Waterside (School)

Farnham School

Rectory Lane

Globe Crescent

4

Farnham

77

Level's Green

Mill Hill

Hazel End

5

Essex
Hertford

6

CM23

A120

7

A120

Wickham Hall

Foxdells Farm

MICHAELS ROAD

B1004

8

Dane O'Coys Road

96

MSF Whitehall College

Whitehall Road

STREET

RYE

Cannons Mill Lane

Foxdells La

Grangeside

Whitehall Lane

Broadfields

Meadowlands

AVNSWO
AV

Millcroft

Cannons Close

Lindsey Road

Pinelands

1 grid square represents 500 metres

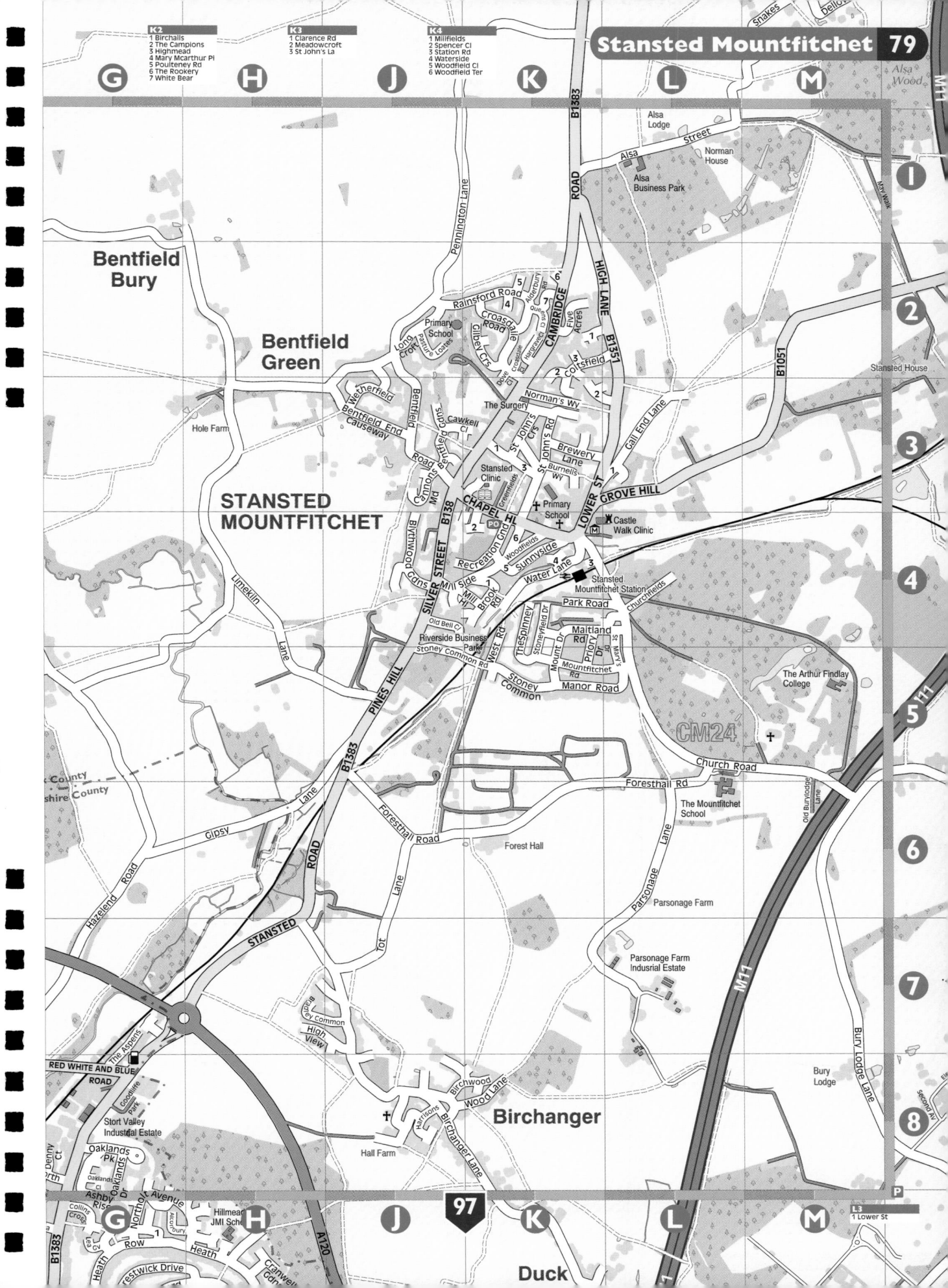
K2
1 Birchalls
2 The Campions
3 Highmead
4 Mary Mcarthur Pl
5 Poulteney Rd
6 The Rookery
7 White Bear
K3
1 Clarence Rd
2 Meadowcroft
3 St John's La
K4
1 Millfields
2 Spencer Cl
3 Station Rd
4 Waterside
5 Woodfield Cl
6 Woodfield Ter
G
H
J
K
L
M
1
2
3
4
5
6
7
8
Alsa Wood
M11
Alsa Lodge
Alsa Street
Norman House
Alsa Business Park
May Walk
B1383
CAMBRIDGE ROAD
Pennington Lane
Bentfield Bury
Bentfield Green
HIGH LANE
B1351
Rainsford Road
Alderbury Rd
Croasdaile Road
Gilbey Crs
Primary School
Long Croft
Pasture
Loates
Five Acres
Coltsfield
Stansted House
B1051
Wetherfield
Bentfield End Causeway
Bentfield
The Surgery
Norman's Wy
Cawkell Cl
St John's Crs
St John's Rd
Brewery Lane
Burnells Wy
Gall End Lane
Hole Farm
Bentfield Gdns
Cannons Md
Stansted Clinic
Greenfields
GROVE HILL
LOWER ST
STANSTED MOUNTFITCHET
Blythwood Gdns
B138
CHAPEL HL
Primary School
Castle
Walk Clinic
Recreation Gnd
Woodfields
Sunnyside
Water Lane
Stansted Mountfitchet Station
Churchfields
SILVER STREET
Mill Side
Mill Hl
Brook Rd
Limekiln Lane
Park Road
Maitland Rd
Old Bell Cl
Riverside Business Park
The Spinney
Stoneyfield Dr
Mount Dr
Priory Dr
St Mary's
Stoney Common Rd
West Rd
Mountfitchet Rd
Stoney Common
Manor Road
The Arthur Findlay College
PINES HILL
CM24
Church Road
Foresthall Rd
The Mountfitchet School
Old Burylodge Lane
Gipsy Lane
Foresthall Road
Forest Hall
Hazelend Road
ROAD
Tot Lane
Parsonage Lane
Parsonage Farm
STANSTED
Parsonage Farm Indusrial Estate
Bradley Common
High View
RED WHITE AND BLUE ROAD
The Aspens
Goodliffe Park
Birchwood
Wood Lane
Bury Lodge Lane
Bury Lodge
Second Av
Stort Valley Industrial Estate
Harrisons
Birchanger Lane
Birchanger
Hall Farm
Oaklands Pk
Oaklands Dr
Denny Ct
Northolt Avenue
Ashby Rise
Collins Cross
Row
Heath
Hillmead JMI Sch
A120
B1383
Trestwick Drive
Cranwell
97
L3
1 Lower St
Duck

Sewell

62

104

Totternhoe

Church End

Church
Gn

Totternhoe Lower
School

The
Ride

Ellesmere
Cl

Brightwell Av

Well

Head
Road

Church
Road

Road

Nature
Reserve

Castle Hill Road

Park Av

Totternhoe
Football
Club

Dunstable Town Cricket
Club

Furlong
Lane

Dunstable
Road

Road

Well
Head

Doolittle
Mill

Springfield
Rd

Bottom
Dr

Manton Rd

B489

Tring
Road

Icknield Way
Farm

Harling Road

Harling Rd

Valance-end
Farm

Way

Dagnall
Road

B4540

B4506

Harvey Rd

Marina
Dr

Gardners
Cl

Beacon Avenue

Coombe Dr

Coombe Dr

The Avenue

Totternhoe Road

Lancot Av

Oakwell Cl

Lancot Drive

Lancot
Lower
School

Spinney Crs

Icknield Way

Icknield Way Path

Icknield Way

Icknield Way

Tring Road

B489

Royce Gr

Westdown Gdns

Whipsnade Road

B4541

Five
Knolls

Icknield Way Path

Dunstable
Downs
Golf Club

Icknield Way Path

Dunstable Downs
Country Park

Dunstable
Downs

LU6

Chute
Farm

Tree
Cathedral

B4547

Beecroft

Brewers
Hill Middle
School

Brewers
Hill

Campian
Cl

Bryony
Wy

Cusworth
Cl

Greenfield Cl

Aldens

Hillcroft

Orchard
Cl

Scawsby
Cl

Weatherfield
School

Beecroft
School

Saxon
Cl

Norman
Cl

Weatherby

Cookfield

Drovers

Bunhill

Pascomb
Rd

PO

Aldbanks

Westfield

Ashcroft

Maidenbower
Av

Brewers Hill Rd

Hill
Road

Loring
Road

Beech Gn

Beecroft
Way

Worthington
Rd

Chiltern

Hambling
Pl

Franklin
Rd

Benning Av

Leighton

West Parade

Union

Princes St

Sundon

West Street

West-Street

Meadway

Westdown
Gdns

Spoondell

Spoondell

Hurlock Cl

Ulverston Rd

Bowland Crs

Buttercup

Caneswode

Q'
Sc

B489

Long
Meadow

Kirby Rd

Doctors
Surg

Cemetery

Carracre

Station
Road

Waterlow Rd

Clifton
Rd

Stuart
Street

Victoria
Street

Chadwell

Capron Rd

Olma Rd

View Rd

Park St

Falcon

Beale St

Rotherwood Cl

Lawrence
Industrial
Estate

Dunstable
Football
Club

1 Aynscombe Cl

E2

D1
1 Rotherwood Cl

F2
1 Nursery Cl

F1
1 Cross St North
2 Stewart Clark Ct

F4
1 Morland Cl

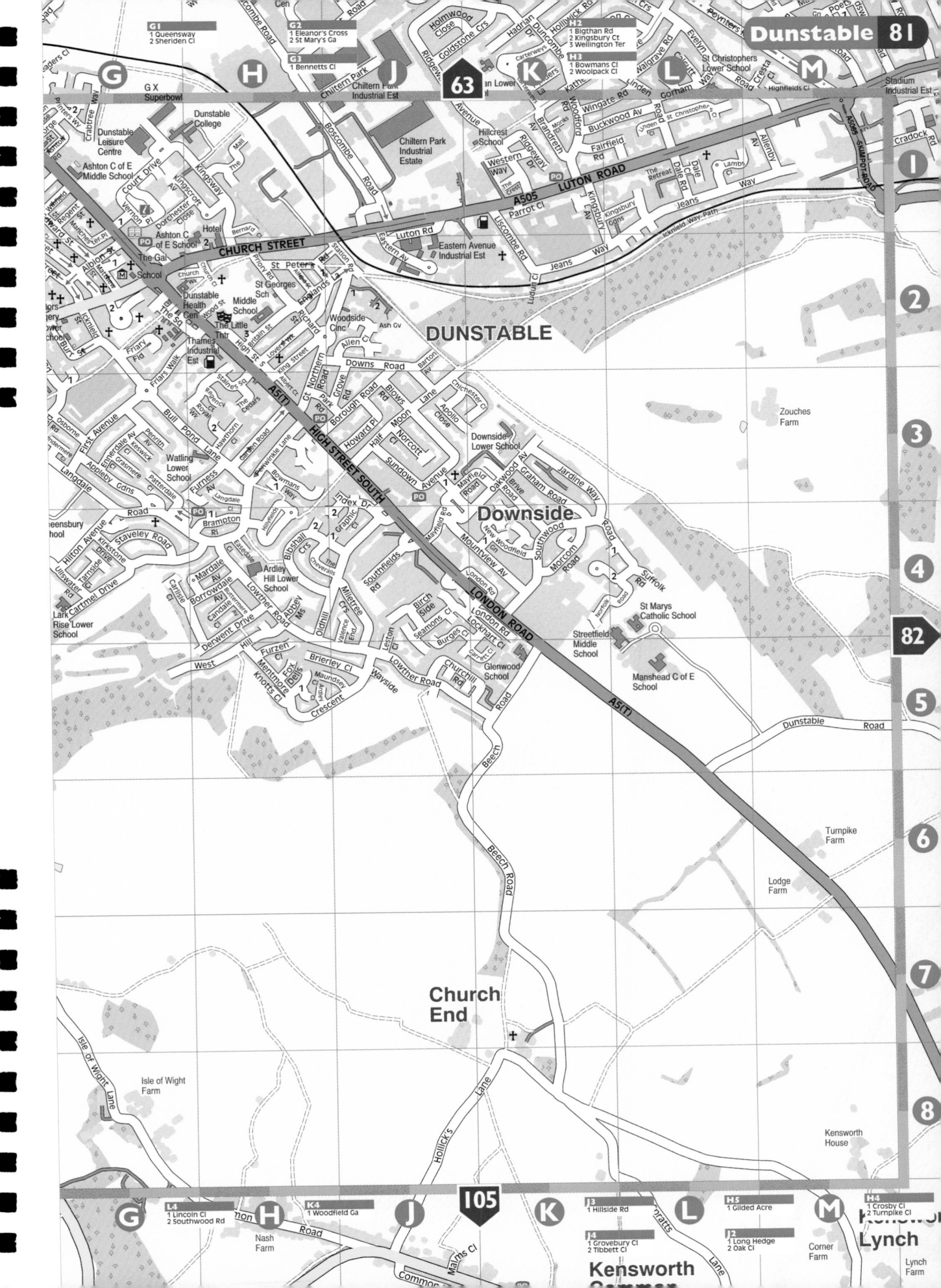
G1
1 Queensway
2 Sheriden Cl
G2
1 Eleanor's Cross
2 St Mary's Ga
G3
1 Bennetts Cl
H2
1 Bigthan Rd
2 Kingsbury Ct
3 Wellington Ter
H3
1 Bowmans Cl
2 Woolpack Cl
63
DUNSTABLE
Downside
Church End
Chiltern Park Industrial Estate
Dunstable College
Dunstable Leisure Centre
Ashton C of E Middle School
Eastern Avenue Industrial Est
Hillcrest School
St Christophers Lower School
Stadium Industrial Est
LUTON ROAD
CHURCH STREET
HIGH STREET SOUTH
LONDON ROAD
A5(T)
A505
Downside Lower School
Watling Lower School
Ardley Hill Lower School
Lark Rise Lower School
St Marys Catholic School
Streetfield Middle School
Manshead C of E School
Glenwood School
Zouches Farm
Turnpike Farm
Lodge Farm
Isle of Wight Farm
Kensworth House
Beech Road
Hollick's Lane
Isle of Wight Lane
Dunstable Road
82
105
L4
1 Lincoln Cl
2 Southwood Rd
K4
1 Woodfield Ga
J3
1 Hillside Rd
J4
1 Grovebury Cl
2 Tibbett Cl
H5
1 Glided Acre
J2
1 Long Hedge
2 Oak Cl
H4
1 Crosby Cl
2 Turnpike Cl
Nash Farm
Corner Farm
Lynch Farm
Kensworth
Lynch

Junction 11
DUNSTABLE ROAD
64
81
106
Stadium Industrial Est
Bampton Road
Cradock Rd
Charlwood Road
Staveley Rd
Bakewell Cl
Ripley Rd
Halfway Avenue
Overstone Road
Atherstone Road
Thirlestone Rd
Leicester Road
Bradley Road
Downside Junior & Infant School
Carisbrooke Rd
Chaul End La
Connaught Road
Thornhill Rd
Chandos Rd
Beverley Road
Kingsway
Maidenhall Junior School
A505
A5065
Chaul End Road
Cosgrove Way
HATTERS WAY
Bilton Way
Dallow Road
Foxdell Junior School
Firbank Industrial Estate
Kingsway Industrial Est
Kent Road
Summerfield Road
Foxdell Infant School
Runley Road
LUTON
M1
Chaul End
Bedfordshire County
Griffin Golf Club
Castle Croft Road
Whipperley Infant School
Cades Close
Chaul End Road
Inions Farm
Manor Farm
Luton Road
Folly Lane
Chaul End Rd
Caddington
Bury Farm
Meadow Way
Hyde Road
Caddington Surgery
Heathfield Lower School
Willow Field School
Manor Road
The Cresent
Five Oaks
Five Oaks School
Dunstable Road
Hawthorn Crs
Mancroft Road
Crosslands
Culworth Cl
Edgecote Close
Adstone Rd
Fairgreen Road
Ledwell Rd
Millfield Way
Littlegreen Lane
Manor Road
Caddington Sports Club
Millfield Lane
Woodside
Cotswold Business Park
Pipers Lane
Woodside Road
Aley Green
Elaine Gdns
Kensworth Lynch
Lynch Farm
Cemetery
Lower Farm
A5(T)
grid square represents 500 metres

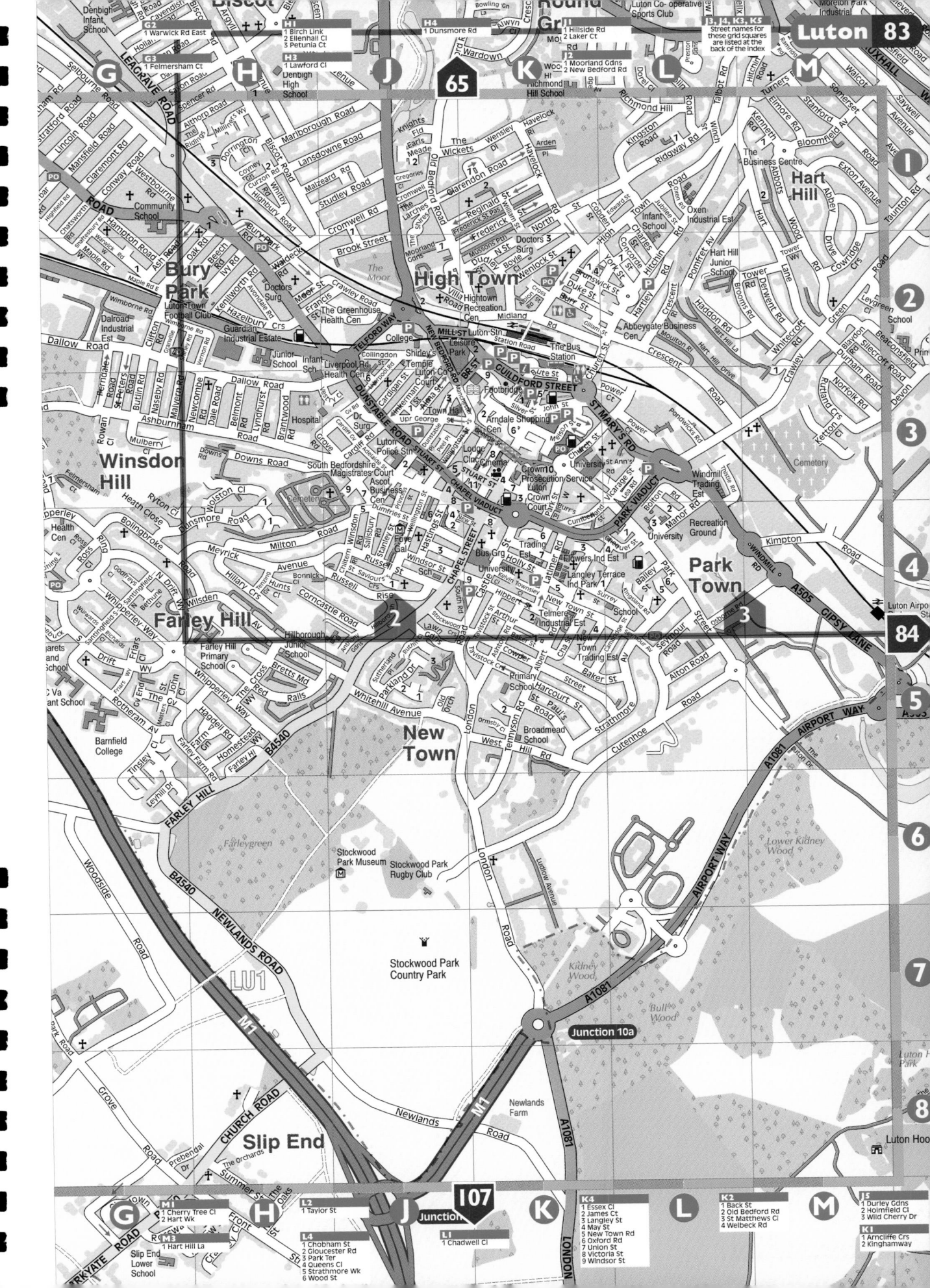

Luton 83
G2
1 Warwick Rd East
G3
1 Felmersham Ct
H1
1 Birch Link
2 Ellenhall Cl
3 Petunia Ct
H3
1 Lawford Cl
H4
1 Dunsmore Rd
J1
1 Hillside Rd
2 Laker Ct
J2
1 Moorland Gdns
2 New Bedford Rd
J3, J4, K3, K5
Street names for these grid squares are listed at the back of the index
65
84
107
2
3
Bury Park
High Town
Hart Hill
Winsdon Hill
Farley Hill
Park Town
New Town
Slip End
LU1
Junction 10a
Luton Stn
Stockwood Park Country Park
Stockwood Park Museum
Stockwood Park Rugby Club
Luton Town Football Club
Arndale Shopping Cen
Luton Airport
Farleygreen
Kidney Wood
Bull Wood
Lower Kidney Wood
Newlands Farm
Barnfield College
DUNSTABLE ROAD
LEAGRAVE ROAD
NEWLANDS ROAD
FARLEY HILL
CHURCH ROAD
AIRPORT WAY
GIPSY LANE
PARK VIADUCT
CHAPEL VIADUCT
ST MARY'S RD
GUILDFORD STREET
TELFORD WAY
London Road
M1
A1081
A505
B4540
M1
1 Cherry Tree Cl
2 Hart Wk
M3
1 Hart Hill La
L2
1 Taylor St
L4
1 Chobham St
2 Gloucester Rd
3 Park Ter
4 Queens Cl
5 Strathmore Wk
6 Wood St
L1
1 Chadwell Cl
K4
1 Essex Cl
2 James Ct
3 Langley St
4 May St
5 New Town Rd
6 Oxford Rd
7 Union St
8 Victoria St
9 Windsor St
K2
1 Back St
2 Old Bedford Rd
3 St Matthews Cl
4 Welbeck Rd
J5
1 Durley Gdns
2 Holmfield Cl
3 Wild Cherry Dr
K1
1 Arncliffe Crs
2 Kinghamway

66

A B C D E F

CI
1 Alderton Cl
2 Barnston Cl
3 Chelsworth Cl
4 Friston Gn
5 Hickling Cl
6 Melford Cl
7 Mutford Cft
8 Pinford Dell

DI
1 Ardleigh Gn
2 Baylam Dell
3 Nayland Cl
4 Radstone Pl
5 Tanfield Gn

BI
1 Nethercott Cl

AI
1 Highover Cl

Ashcroft High

Summers Rd

Barford Rd

VAUXHALL

WAY

A505

VAUXHALL WAY

Walcot

Somerset

Sarwell

Avenue

Crawley

Cowridge Crs

Taunton Rd

PO

Buchanan Drive

Eaton Valley Road

Devon

Eaton Valley Road

Fermor

Brendon Drive

Hollybush Road

Porlock Drive

Polzeath Cl

Lyneham Rd

High Ridg

High Road

Overfield

Lalleford

Holtsmere

Newnham

Mossbank Av

Gresham

Rowelfield

Chertsey

Eaton Green Road

Raynham Wy

Lindsey Cl

Barrowby

Eaton

Green

Road

Mossbank

Minstow

Mauldon

President Wy

Prince Wy

Airport App Rd

London Luton Airport

Eaton Green Rd

Heaton Dell

Laxton Rd

Colwell Rise

Corbridge Dr

Hedley

Lesbury Ct

Weldon

Paddons Wy

The Dell

Wbrook

Martlhouse Cl

Ennismore

School

Beaconsfield

Blaydon

Gayland Av

Primary School

Devon

Harrowden Rd

Norfolk Rd

Durham Road

Silecroft Road

Road

Evergreen

Prospect Wy

Provost Way

Percival

London Luton Airport

London Luton Airport

Airport Way

Prentice Way

Proctor Wy

Airport Way

83

Luton Airport Parkway Station

3

A505

Barrati Ind Park

Upper Lea Valley Walk

Airport Way

LOWER HARPENDEN ROAD

Lea

Valley

Walk

Somerie's

Someries

Luton

Bedfordshire County

Chiltern Hall

Dane Street Farm

Hertfordshire County

Bedfordshire County

Someries Castle

Copt Hall

Bush Pasture

George Wood

Chiltern Green

Luton Hoo Park

River Lea or Lee

The

Luton

Luton Hoo

A B C D E F

EI
1 Whittingham Cl

108

I 2 3 4 5 6 7 8

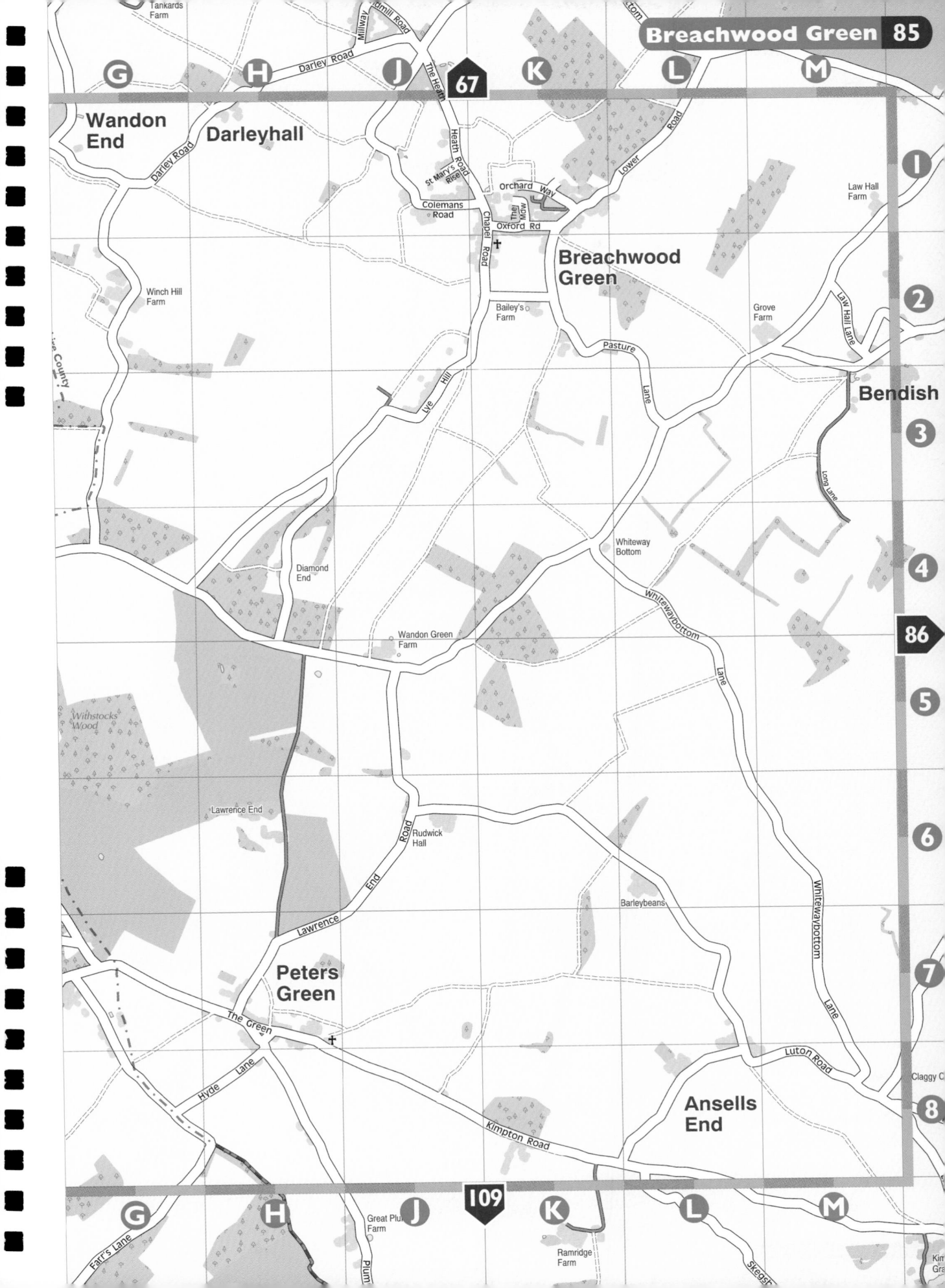

G H Darley Road J **67** K L M

I

Tankards Farm

Millwell

Millmill Road

Darley Road

The Heath

Heath Road

Rice

St Mary's Road

Colemans Road

Orchard Way

The Hollow

Oxford Rd

Chapel Road

Wandon End

Darleyhall

Winch Hill Farm

Lye County

Lye Hill

Breachwood Green

Bailey's Farm

Law Hall Farm

Law Hall Lane

2

Grove Farm

Pasture Lane

Bendish

3

Long Lane

Whiteway Bottom

Whitewaybottom

4

86

Diamond End

Wandon Green Farm

Lane

5

Withstocks Wood

Lawrence End

Road End

Rudwick Hall

Lawrence End

Whitewaybottom

6

Barleybeans

Lane

7

Peters Green

The Green

Hyde Lane

Farr's Lane

Kimpton Road

Ansells End

Luton Road

Claggy C

8

G H Great Plum Farm J **109** K L M

Plum

Ramridge Farm

Kim Gra

Skesh

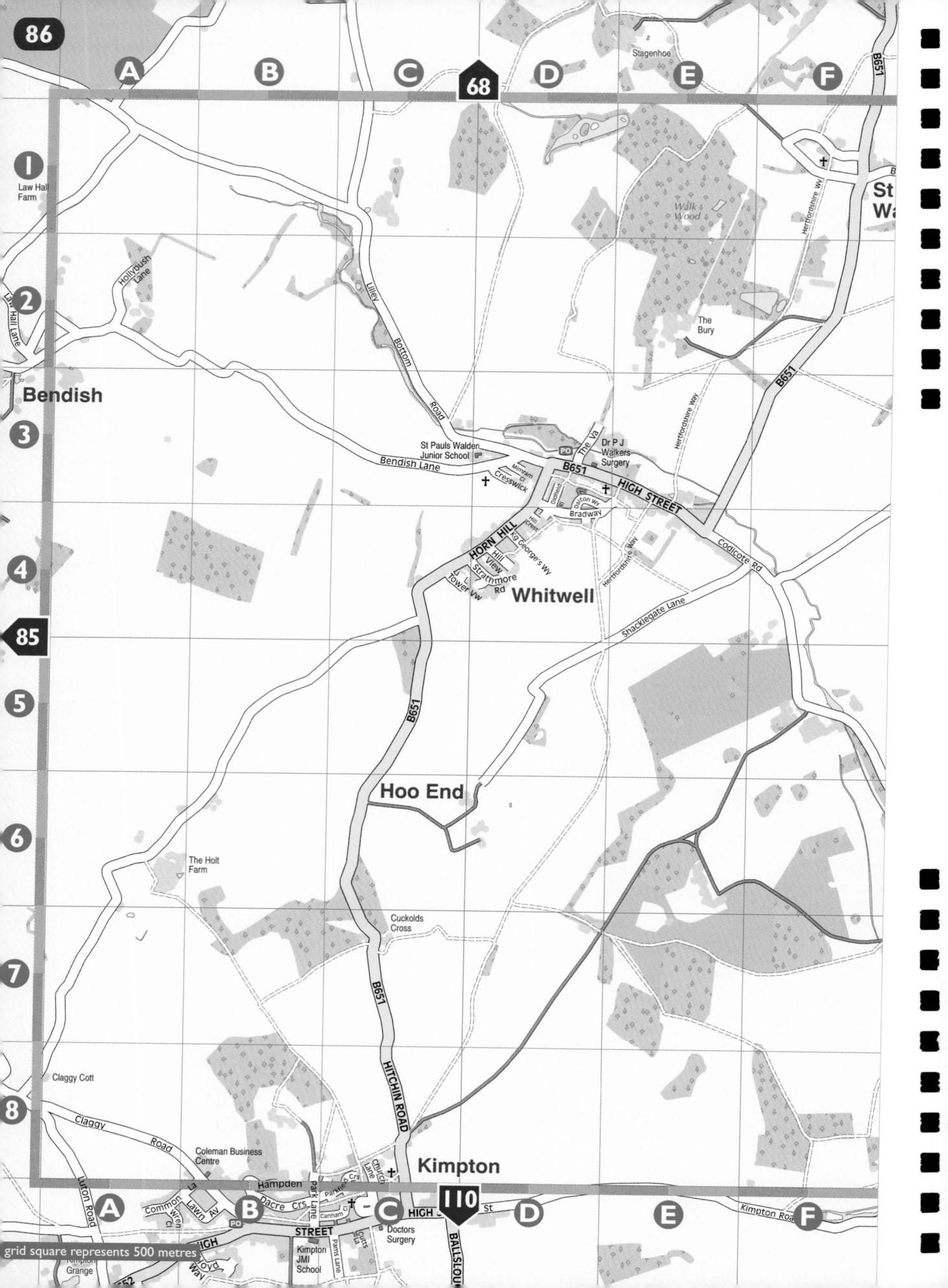

A B C D E F

68

I

Law Hall Farm

St
Wa

2

Law Hall Lane

Hollybush Lane

Lilley

Bottom Road

Walk Wood

The Bury

B651

Hertfordshire Wy

Bendish

3

St Pauls Walden Junior School

Bendish Lane

Cresswick

The Va

PO

Dr P J Walkers Surgery

B651

HIGH STREET

Mimram Cl

Glebe

Buxton Wy

Bradway

Codicote Rd

HORN HILL

Hill View

Hill View

Strathmore Rd

Tower Vw

Kg George's Wy

Whitwell

Hertfordshire Way

Shacklegate Lane

4

85

5

B651

Hoo End

6

The Holt Farm

Cuckolds Cross

7

B651

HITCHIN ROAD

Claggy Cott

8

Claggy Road

Luton Road

Coleman Business Centre

Church Lane

Kimpton

110

A B C D E F

Hampden

Common Wren La

Lawn Av

Dacre Crs

Park Lane

Parkers Crs

Canham

Pams Lane

HIGH STREET

Doctors Surgery

HIGH St

BALLSLOUGH

Kimpton Road

Lloyd Way

Kimpton JMI School

IGH

grid square represents 500 metres

Stagenhoe

Grange

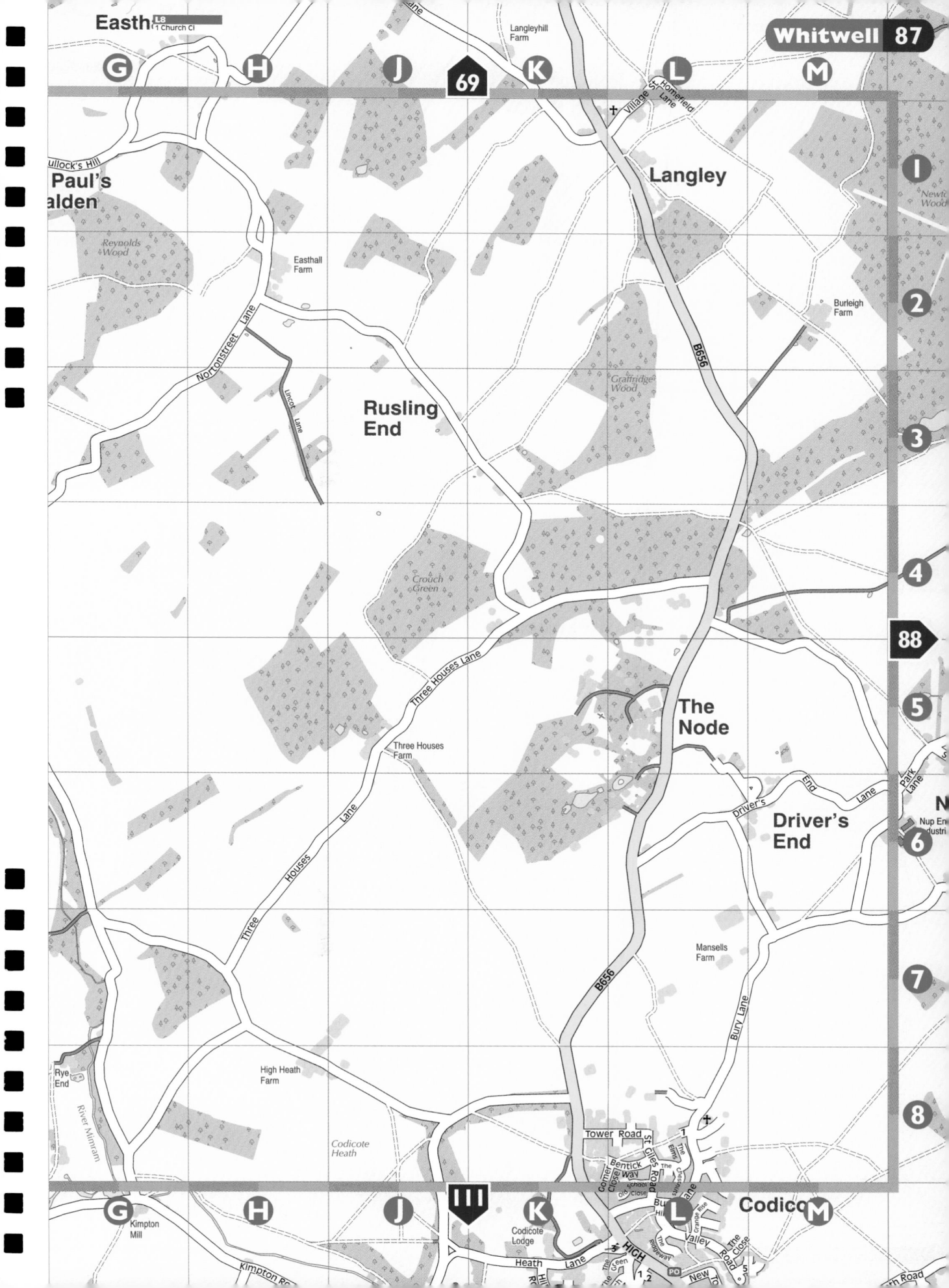
Easth
L8
1 Church Cl
Langleyhill Farm
G
H
J
69
K
L
M
Village St
Homefield Lane
Bullock's Hill
Langley
Paul's
alden
Reynolds Wood
Easthall Farm
Burleigh Farm
Nortonstreet Lane
Lincot Lane
B656
Graffridge Wood
Rusling End
Crouch Green
Three Houses Lane
88
The Node
Three Houses Farm
Driver's End Lane
Driver's End
Park Lane
Nup End Industri
Mansells Farm
Bury Lane
Rye End
High Heath Farm
River Mimram
Codicote Heath
Tower Road
St Giles Road
Bentick Way
Gomer Close
Old School Close
The Elms
The Chestnuts
Bury Lane
Grange Rise
Valley Road
The Close
The Ridgeway
Heath Lane
HIGH
New
PO
Codico
Kimpton Mill
Codicote Lodge
Kimpton Ro
111
1
2
3
4
5
6
7
8

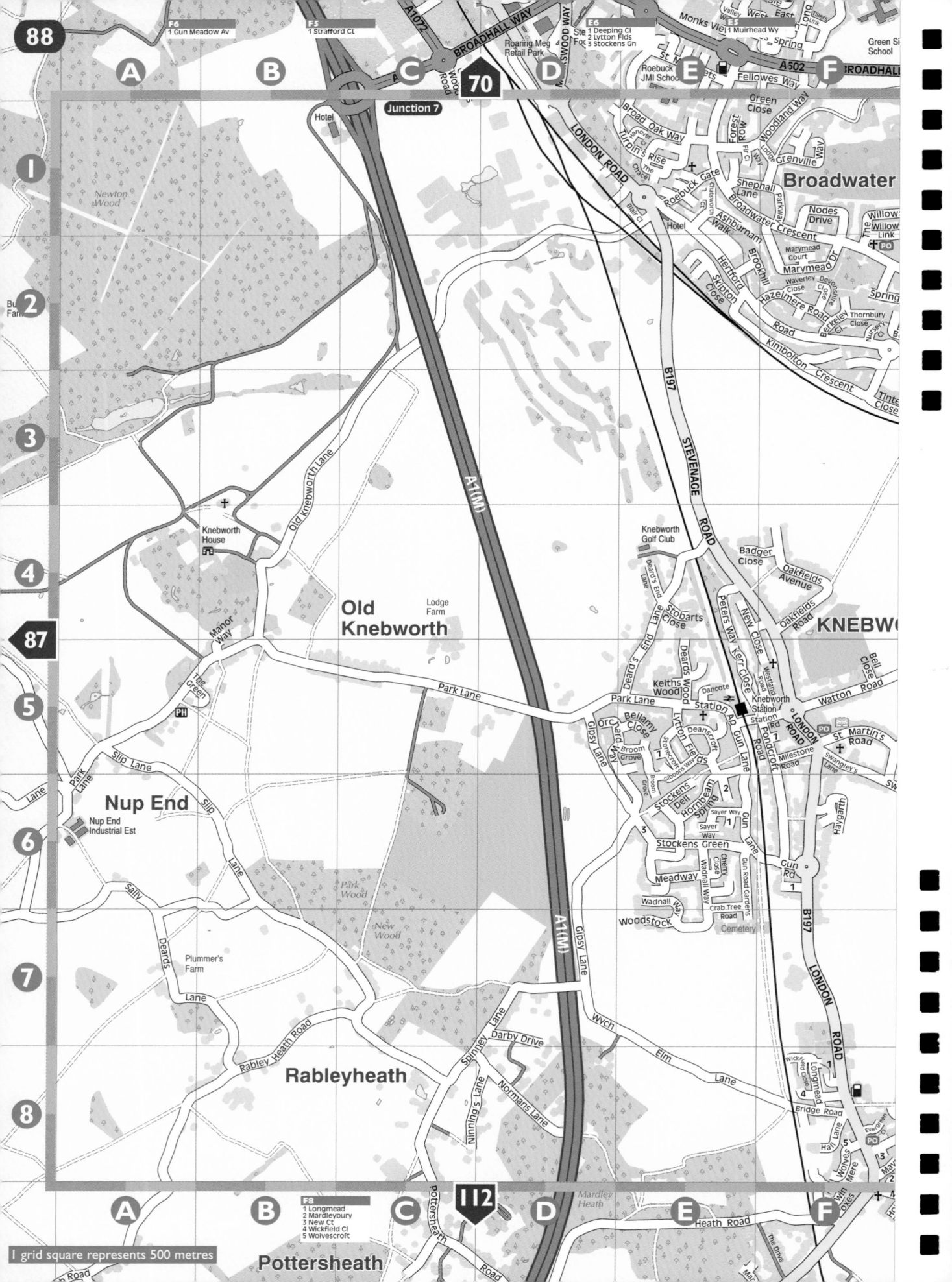
F6
1 Gun Meadow Av
F5
1 Strafford Ct
E6
1 Deeping Cl
2 Lytton Flds
3 Stockens Gn
E5
1 Muirhead Wy
70
87
112
Junction 7
Broadwater
Old Knebworth
Nup End
Rableyheath
Pottersheath
KNEBWO
Knebworth House
Knebworth Golf Club
Knebworth Station
Newton Wood
Park Wood
New Wood
Lodge Farm
Plummer's Farm
Nup End Industrial Est
Roaring Meg Retail Park
Roebuck JMI School
Green Si School
Hotel
Cemetery
A1(M)
B197
A602
A1072
BROADHALL WAY
LONDON ROAD
STEVENAGE ROAD
Park Lane
Old Knebworth Lane
Manor Way
Slip Lane
Deards Lane
Rabley Heath Road
Gipsy Lane
Wych Elm Lane
Spinney Lane
Darby Drive
Ninning's Lane
Normans Lane
Heath Road
Watton Road
Bridge Road
F8
1 Longmead
2 Mardleybury
3 New Ct
4 Wickfield Cl
5 Wolvescroft
1 grid square represents 500 metres

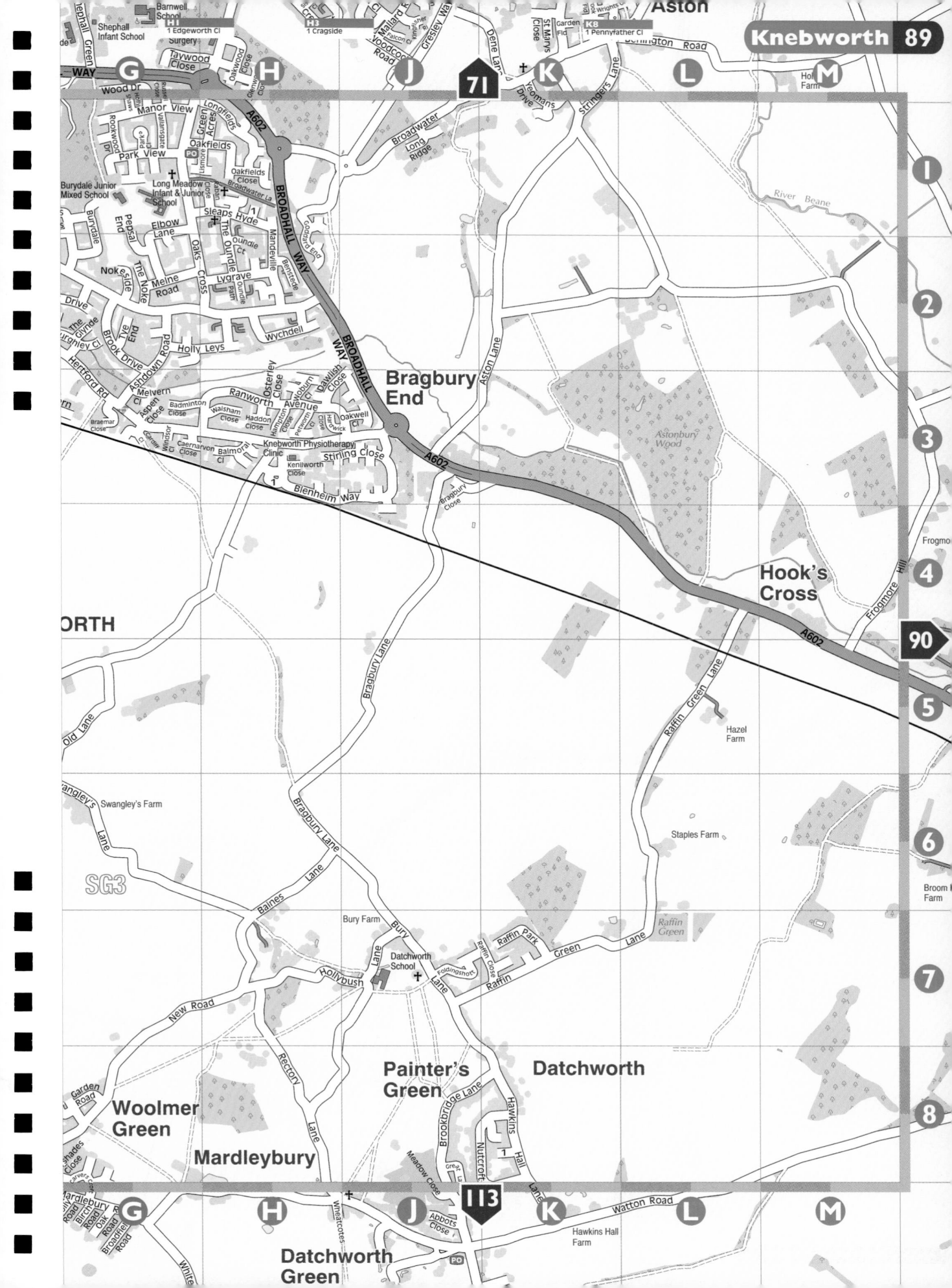

Aston
Bragbury End
Hook's Cross
Astonbury Wood
Datchworth
Painter's Green
Woolmer Green
Mardleybury
Datchworth Green
SG3
A602
BROADHALL WAY
Aston Lane
Bragbury Lane
Raffin Green Lane
Baines Lane
Hollybush Lane
New Road
Rectory Lane
Brookbridge Lane
Hawkins Hall Lane
Watton Road
Frogmore Hill
Stringers Lane
Swangley's Lane
Old Lane
Hertford Rd
Swangley's Farm
Bury Farm
Datchworth School
Staples Farm
Hazel Farm
Hawkins Hall Farm
Broom Farm
Raffin Green
River Beane
Knebworth Physiotherapy Clinic
Long Meadow Infant & Junior School
Burydale Junior Mixed School
Shephall Infant School
Barnwell School
H1 1 Edgeworth Cl
H3 1 Cragside
K8 1 Pennyfather Cl
71
90
113

C7 1 Great Innings S
C6 1 The Beaneside
Goodey Meade
Hebing E
A
B
C
72
D
E
F
Benington House
Burn's Green
Cutting Hill
Chain Walk
High Elms Lane
Idle Hill
White Hall
Chapel Farm
Gregory's Farm
Chain Walk
Leatherfield Common
Chain Walk
Mill
Frogmore
Walkern Road
Arbury Wood
Frogmore Hall
Frogmore Hill
89
Walkern Road
Blue Hill
Mill Lane
Bromley Common
A602
A602
Chain Walk
River Beane
Beane Road
Walkern Road
Laminas Road
Motts Close
High Street
Watton at Stone
Chain Walk
Broom Hall Farm
Great Innings North
The Surgery
Hazeldell
Hazeldell
Moorymead Close
Hockerhill
PH
High Street
Rivershill
PO
Bardolphs
Watton at Stone Station
Station Road
Glebe Close
Rectory La
School Lane
The Club House
Watton House
WARE ROAD
Watton Road
Ware Road
A119
114
Watkins Hall Farm
Chain
Home Farm
1 grid square represents 500 metres

K3
1 Whiteley Cl
L3
1 Windy Ri
73
Green End
Chain Walk
Lordship's Farm
Little Munden JMI School
Church Lane
Windmills
Gladstone Rd
Kingsfield Road
Founceley Av
Easington Road
Kennedy Rd
Road
PO
Dane End
Whitehill Farm
Munden
Pearman Drive
Comb's Wood
Whempstead Road
The Old Bourne
Whempstead
Whempstead Lane
Lane
Brookfield Common
Cock's Wood
Lodge Farm
92
Lowgate Lane
Sacombe Hill Farm
Sacombe Green Road
Marshall's Lane
Sacombe
Pound
Sacombe
A602
Heath Mount School
Woodhall Park
Sacombebury Farm
Sacombe House
The Clumps
115
Chain Walk
G
H
J
K
L
M
1
2
3
4
5
6
7
8

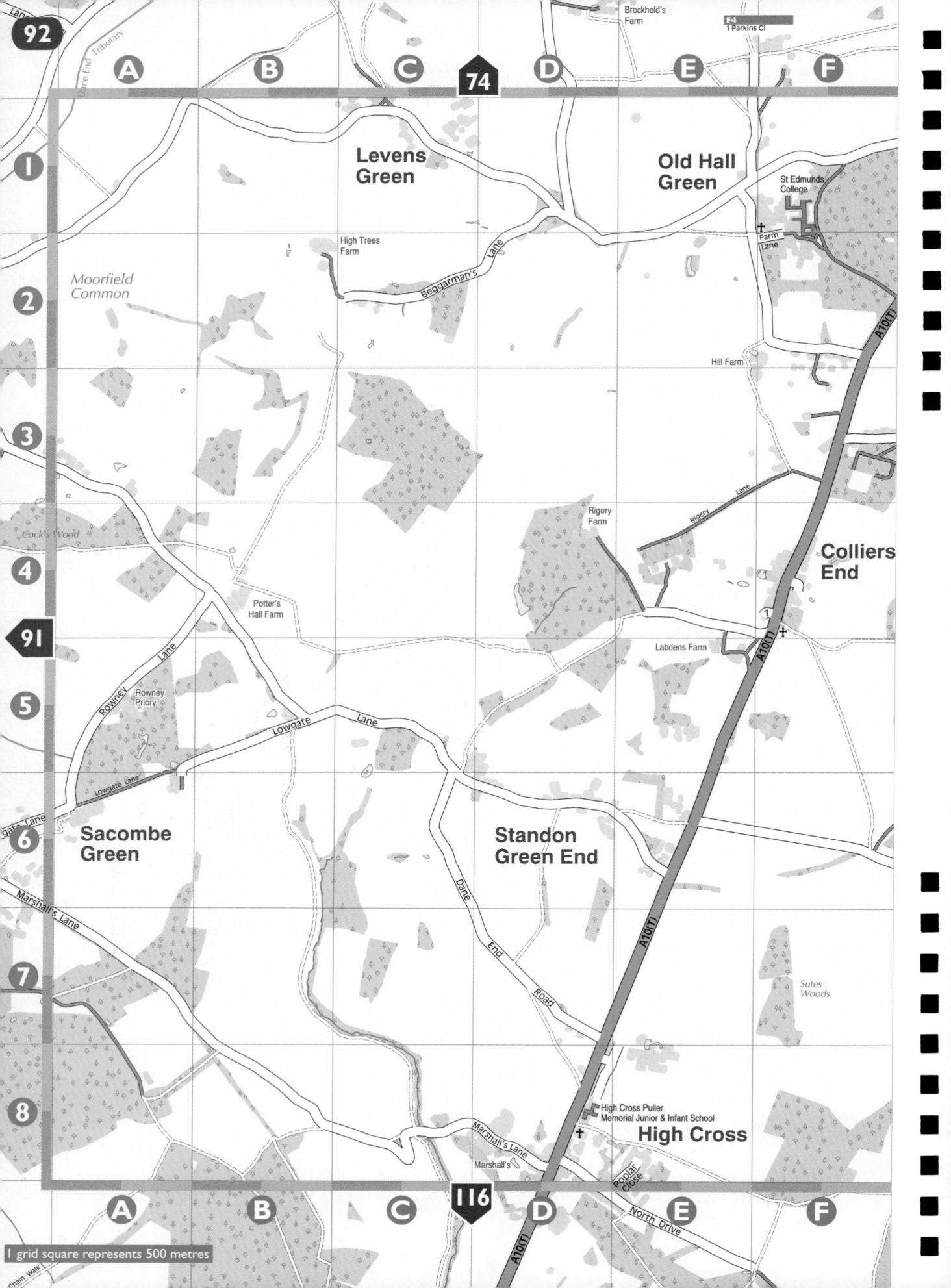

A   B   C   74   D   E   F

I
Levens
Green
Old Hall
Green
St Edmunds
College

2
Moorfield
Common
High Trees
Farm
Beggarman's Lane
Farm Lane
Hill Farm

3
Cock's Wood
Rigery Farm
Rigery Lane

4
Potter's
Hall Farm
Colliers
End
Labdens Farm

91

5
Rowney
Lane
Rowney
Priory
Lowgate   Lane

6
Lowgate Lane
Sacombe
Green
Standon
Green End

Marshall's Lane

7
Dane
End
Road
Sutes
Woods

8
High Cross Puller
Memorial Junior & Infant School
Marshall's Lane
High Cross
Marshall's

A   B   C   116   D   Poplar Close   E   North Drive   F

F4
1 Parkins Cl
Brockhold's
Farm

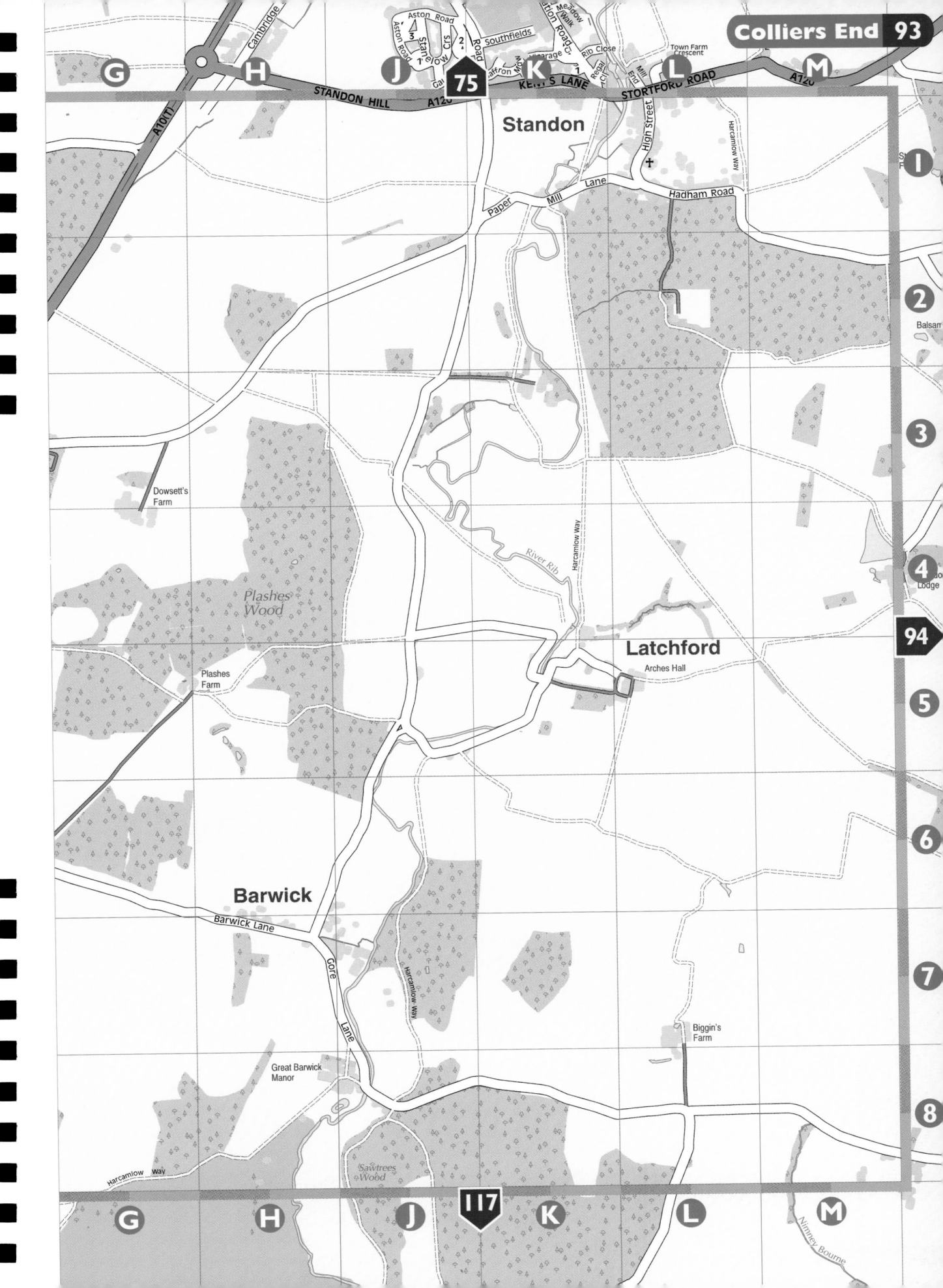
Standon
Latchford
Barwick
Plashes Wood
Sawtrees Wood
Dowsett's Farm
Plashes Farm
Arches Hall
Biggin's Farm
Great Barwick Manor
River Rib
Harcamlow Way
Nimney Bourne
STANDON HILL
A120
A10(T)
KENT'S LANE
STORTFORD ROAD
Paper Mill Lane
Hadham Road
High Street
Barwick Lane
Gore Lane
Aston Road
Southfields
Stanelow Crs
Meadow Walk
Rib Close
Town Farm Crescent
Mill End
Regal Cl
Vicarage Cl
Saffron Mdw
Cambridge
Lodge
Balsam
75
94
117
G
H
J
K
L
M
1
2
3
4
5
6
7
8

Broken Green

76

A B C D E F Little Hadham Place

I Standon Friars

Wellpond Green

Lodge Farm

Home Farm

Chapel Lane

Ford Field

2 Balsams

Westland Green

New Road

Bromley

Bromley Hall

Westfield Bury

3

Bridgefoot

River Ash

4 Standon Lodge

93

Lordship Farm

5

Chaldean Farm

6 New Barns

New Barns Lane

Winding Hill

B1004

7 Brand's Farm

Much Hadham

HIGH STREET

Church Lane

Hertfordshire Way

Moor Place

Hadham Cross

TOWER HILL

Oudle Lane

The Barn School

Health Centre

Walnut Close

Ash Meadow

Danebric

8

Kettle Green Road

Malting Lane

PO

Broadfield Way

Stans

Broadfield

B1004

WIDFORD

SG10

A B C D E F

118

id square represents 500 metres

Kettle Green

Windmill Way

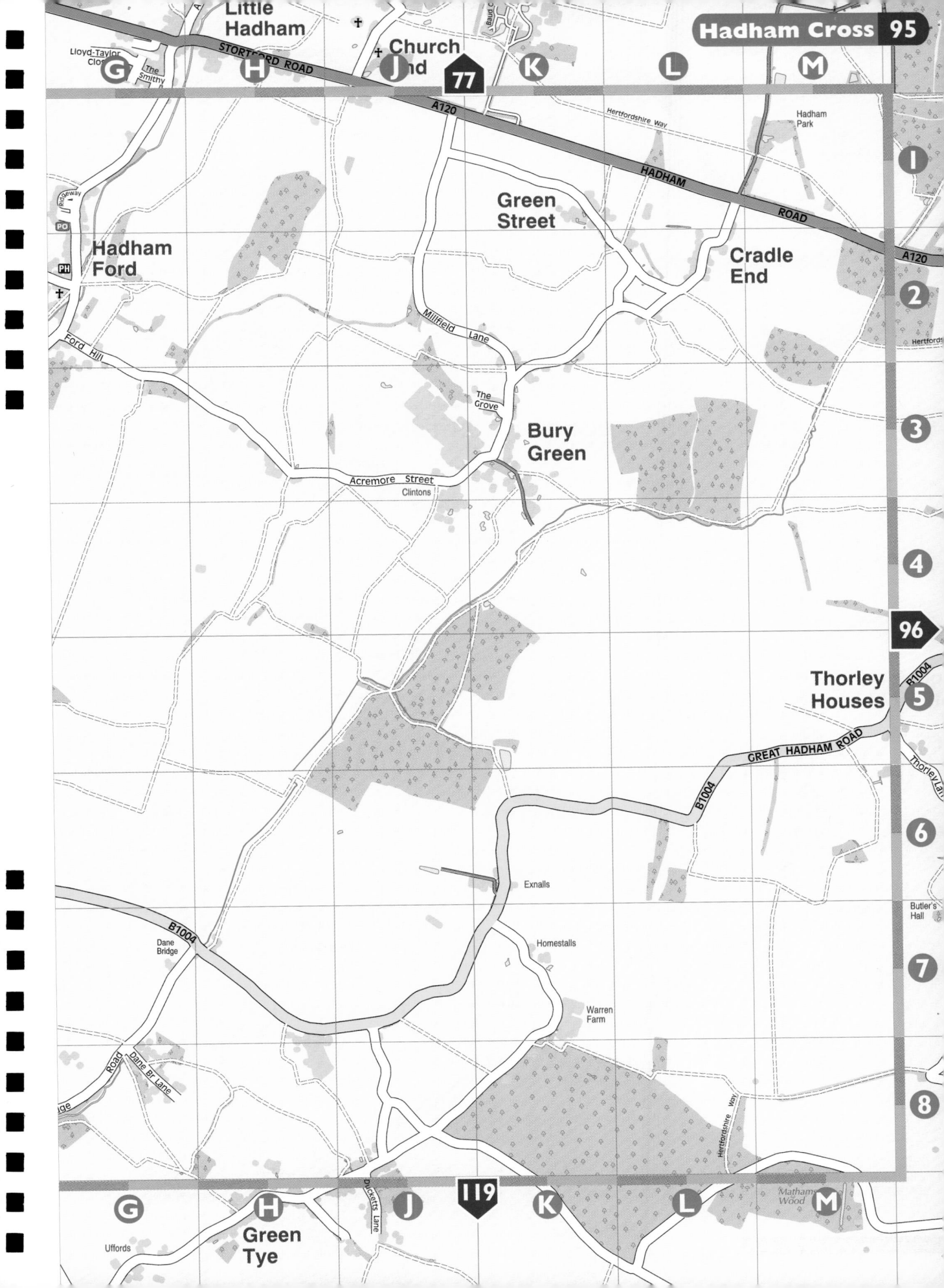

Little
Hadham
STORTFORD ROAD
Church
J nd
77
G
H
J
K
L
M

A120

Lloyd-Taylor
Close
The
Smithy

Hadham Park

Green
Street

HADHAM ROAD

I

A120

RIDGEWAY

PO

Hadham
Ford

PH

Cradle
End

2

Hertfords

Millfield Lane

Ford Hill

The
Grove

Bury
Green

3

Acremore Street
Clintons

4

96

Thorley
Houses

B1004

5

GREAT HADHAM ROAD

B1004

Thorley Lan

6

Exnalls

Butler's
Hall

B1004

Dane
Bridge

Homestalls

7

Warren
Farm

Ufforge
Road

Dane Br Lane

Hertfordshire Way

8

Mathams
Wood

G
H
J
119
K
L
M

Uffords

Green
Tye

Duckets Lane

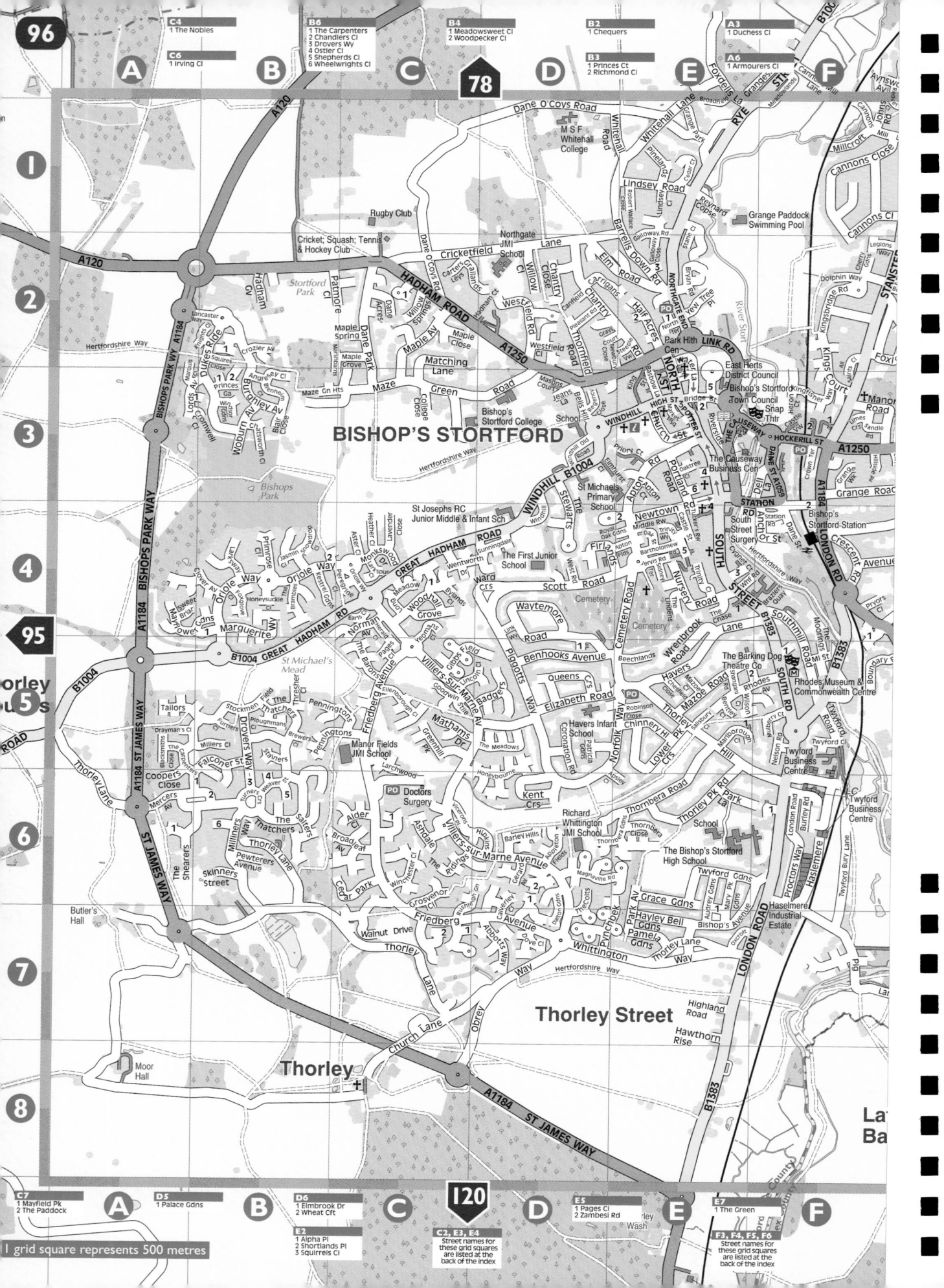

78

95

120

BISHOP'S STORTFORD

Thorley Street

Thorley

1 grid square represents 500 metres

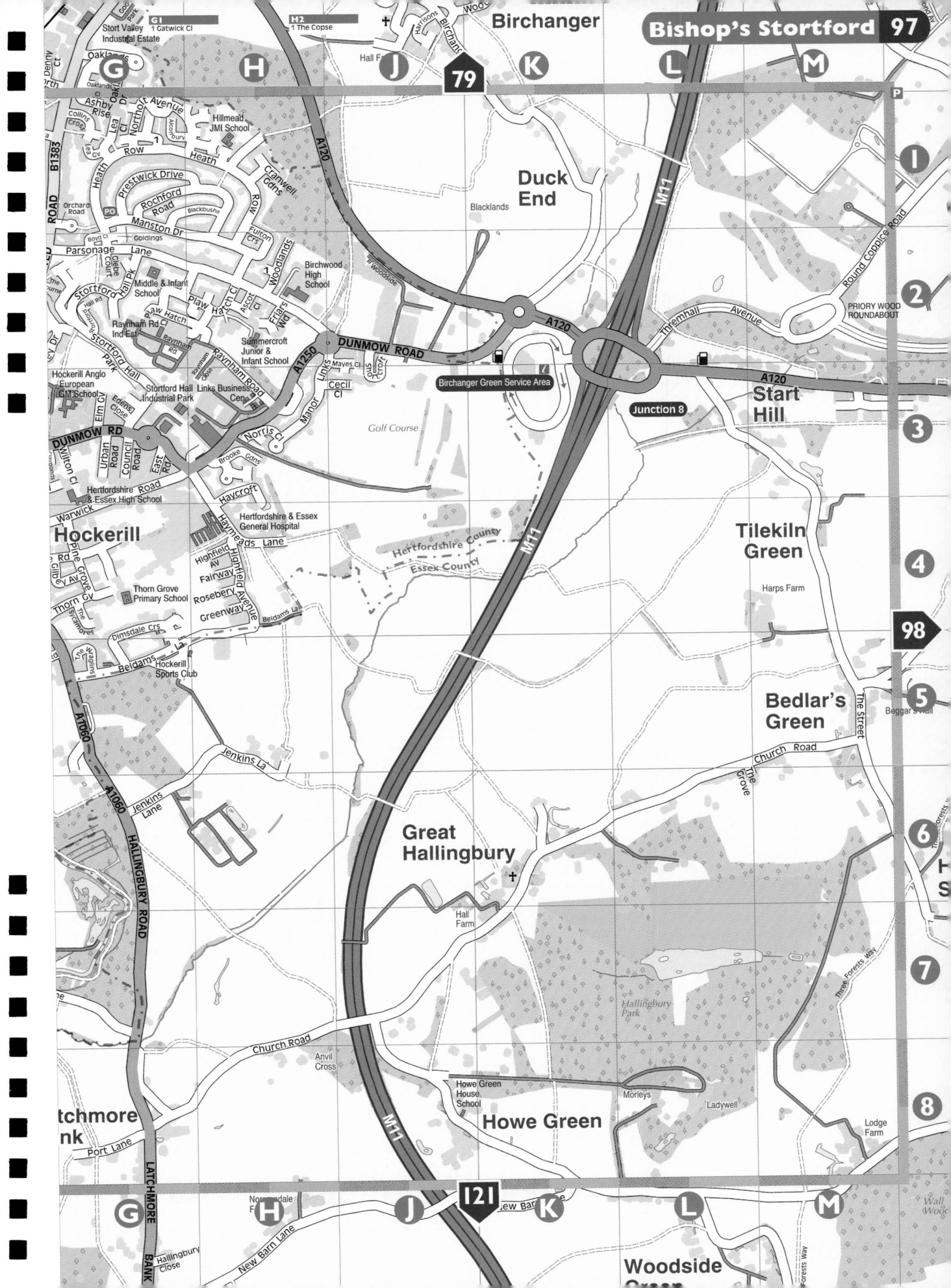
G1 1 Gatwick Cl
H2 1 The Copse
Stort Valley Industrial Estate
Birchanger
79
Duck End
Blacklands
Hillmead JMI School
Prestwick Drive
Rochford Road
Manston Dr
Parsonage Lane
Middle & Infant School
Birchwood High School
Raynham Rd Cl Ind Est
Summercroft Junior & Infant School
DUNMOW ROAD
A120
A1250
Threemhall Avenue
PRIORY WOOD ROUNDABOUT
Round Coppice Road
Birchanger Green Service Area
Junction 8
Start Hill
Hockerill Anglo European GM School
Stortford Hall Industrial Park
Links Business Cen.
DUNMOW RD
Golf Course
Hertfordshire Road
Hertfordshire & Essex High School
Haycroft
Hertfordshire & Essex General Hospital
Haymeads Lane
Hockerill
Hertfordshire County
Essex County
M11
Tilekiln Green
Harps Farm
Thorn Grove Primary School
Greenway
Beldams Lane
Dimsdale Crs
Hockerill Sports Club
98
Bedlar's Green
The Street
Church Road
Jenkins La
Jenkins Lane
A1060
HALLINGBURY ROAD
Great Hallingbury
Hall Farm
Three Forests Way
Hallingbury Park
Church Road
Anvil Cross
Howe Green House School
Morleys
Ladywell
Howe Green
Lodge Farm
Port Lane
LATCHMORE BANK
121
New Barn Lane
Hallingbury Close
Woodside
G H J K L M
1 2 3 4 5 6 7 8

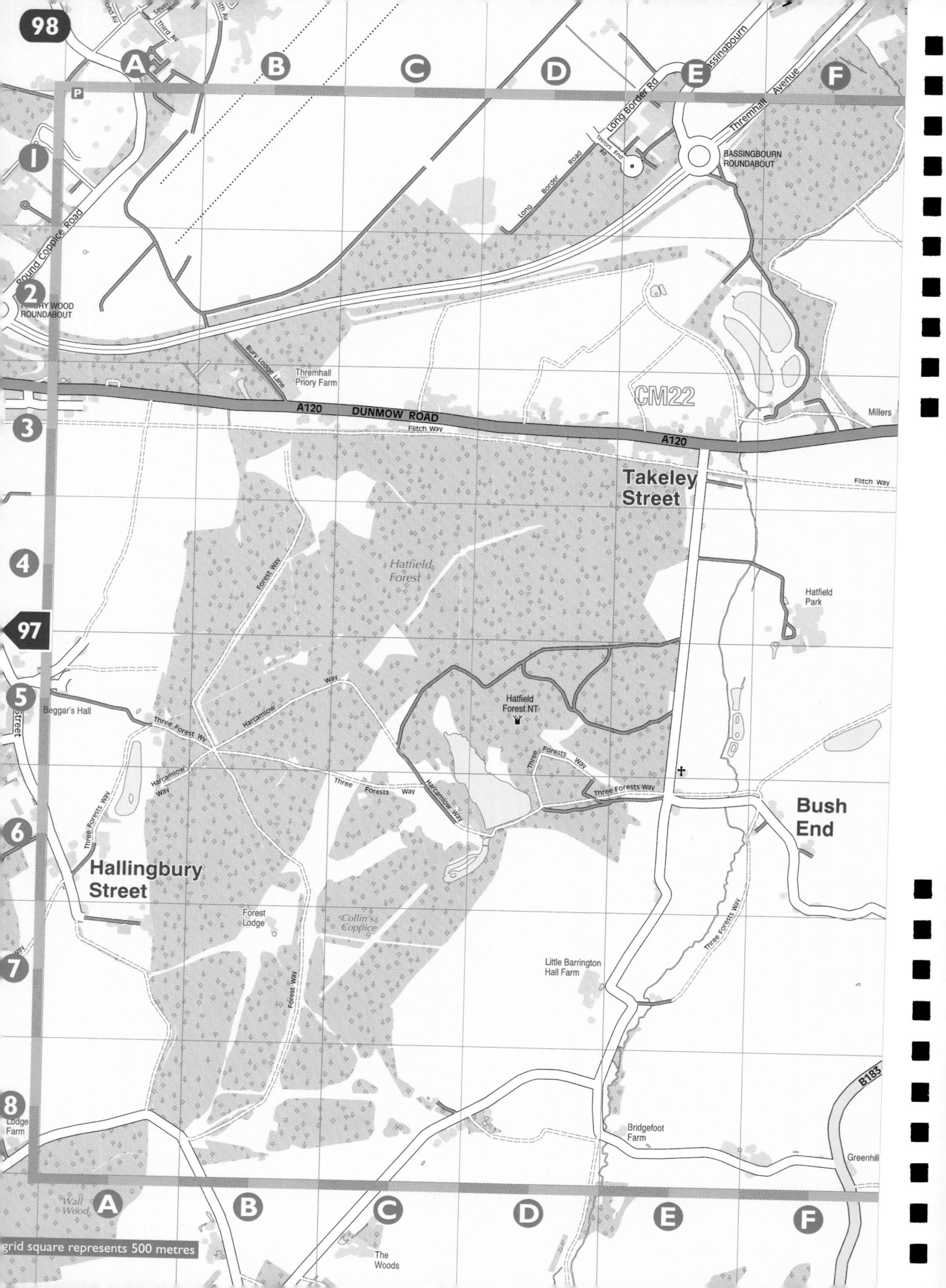

I

2

3

4

97

5

6

7

8

A
B
C
D
E
F

PRIORY WOOD
ROUNDABOUT

Pound Coppice Road

Bury Lodge Lane

Bassingbourn

Thremhall Avenue

Long Border Rd

Long Border Road

Tawney's End Rd

BASSINGBOURN
ROUNDABOUT

Thremhall
Priory Farm

CM22

A120   DUNMOW ROAD

Flitch Way

A120

Millers

Takeley
Street

Flitch Way

Hatfield
Forest

Forest Way

Hatfield
Park

Hatfield
Forest NT

Way

Harcamlow

Three Forest Wy

Beggar's Hall

Street

Three Forests Way

Harcamlow
Way

Three   Forests   Way

Harcamlow Way

Three   Forests   Way

Three Forests Way

Bush
End

Hallingbury
Street

Forest
Lodge

Collin's
Coppice

Forest Way

Little Barrington
Hall Farm

Three Forests Way

Way

Lodge
Farm

Bridgefoot
Farm

B183

Greenhill

Wall
Wood

A
B
C
D
E
F

The
Woods

grid square represents 500 metres

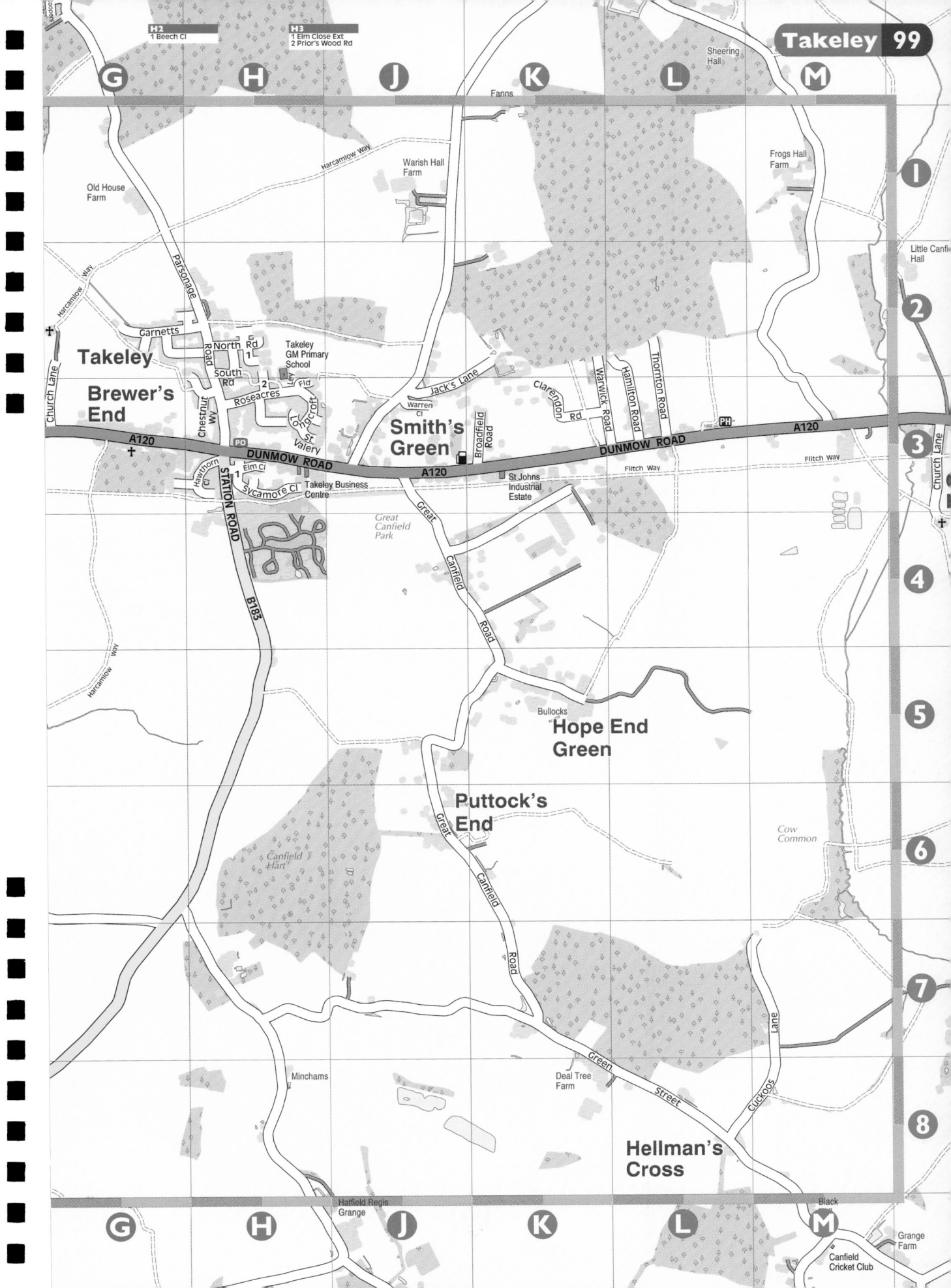
H2
1 Beech Cl
H3
1 Elm Close Ext
2 Prior's Wood Rd
G
H
J
K
L
M
Sheering Hall
Fanns
Warish Hall Farm
Frogs Hall Farm
Harcamlow Way
Old House Farm
Little Canfi Hall
Parsonage
Garnetts
Takeley
North Rd
Road
Takeley GM Primary School
South Rd
Roseacres
Fld
Longcroft
St Valery
Church Lane
Brewer's End
Chestnut Wy
Jack's Lane
Warren Cl
Smith's Green
Broadfield Road
Clarendon Rd
Warwick Road
Hamilton Road
Thornton Road
PH
A120
DUNMOW ROAD
PO
Hawthorn Cl
Elm Cl
Sycamore Cl
Takeley Business Centre
St Johns Industrial Estate
Flitch Way
STATION ROAD
B183
Great Canfield Park
Great Canfield Road
Bullocks
Hope End Green
Puttock's End
Cow Common
Canfield Hart
Minchams
Deal Tree Farm
Green Street
Cuckoos Lane
Hellman's Cross
Hatfield Regis Grange
Black
Grange Farm
Canfield Cricket Club
2
3
4
5
6
7
8

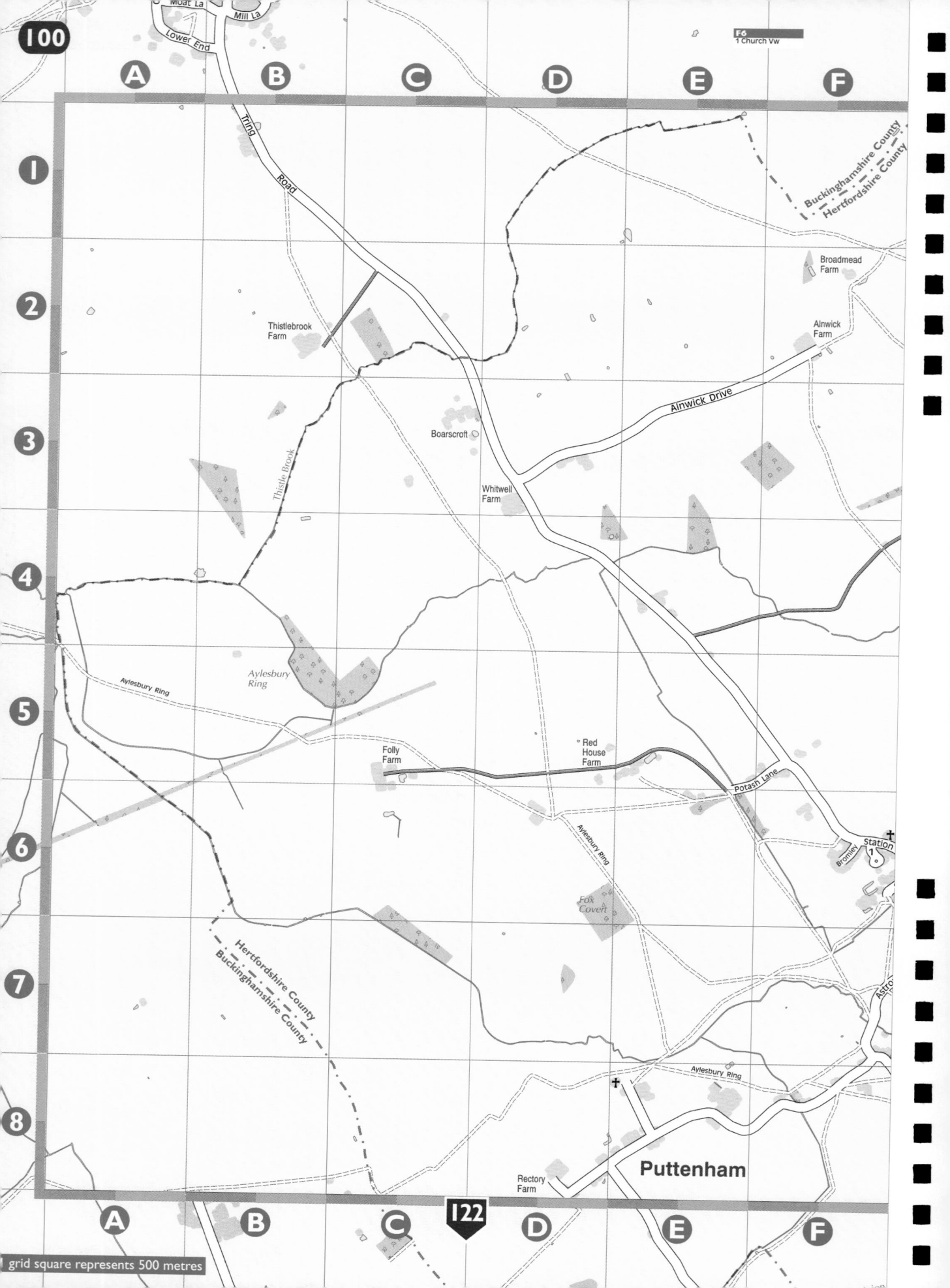

F6
1 Church Vw

Tring Road

Lower End
Moat La
Mill La

Thistlebrook
Farm

Thistle Brook

Broadmead
Farm

Alnwick
Farm

Alnwick Drive

Boarscroft

Buckinghamshire County
Hertfordshire County

Whitwell
Farm

Aylesbury Ring

Aylesbury
Ring

Folly
Farm

Red
House
Farm

Potash Lane

Station
1

Bromley

Aylesbury Ring

Fox
Covert

Hertfordshire County
Buckinghamshire County

Astro

Aylesbury Ring

Rectory
Farm

Puttenham

A B C D E F

grid square represents 500 metres

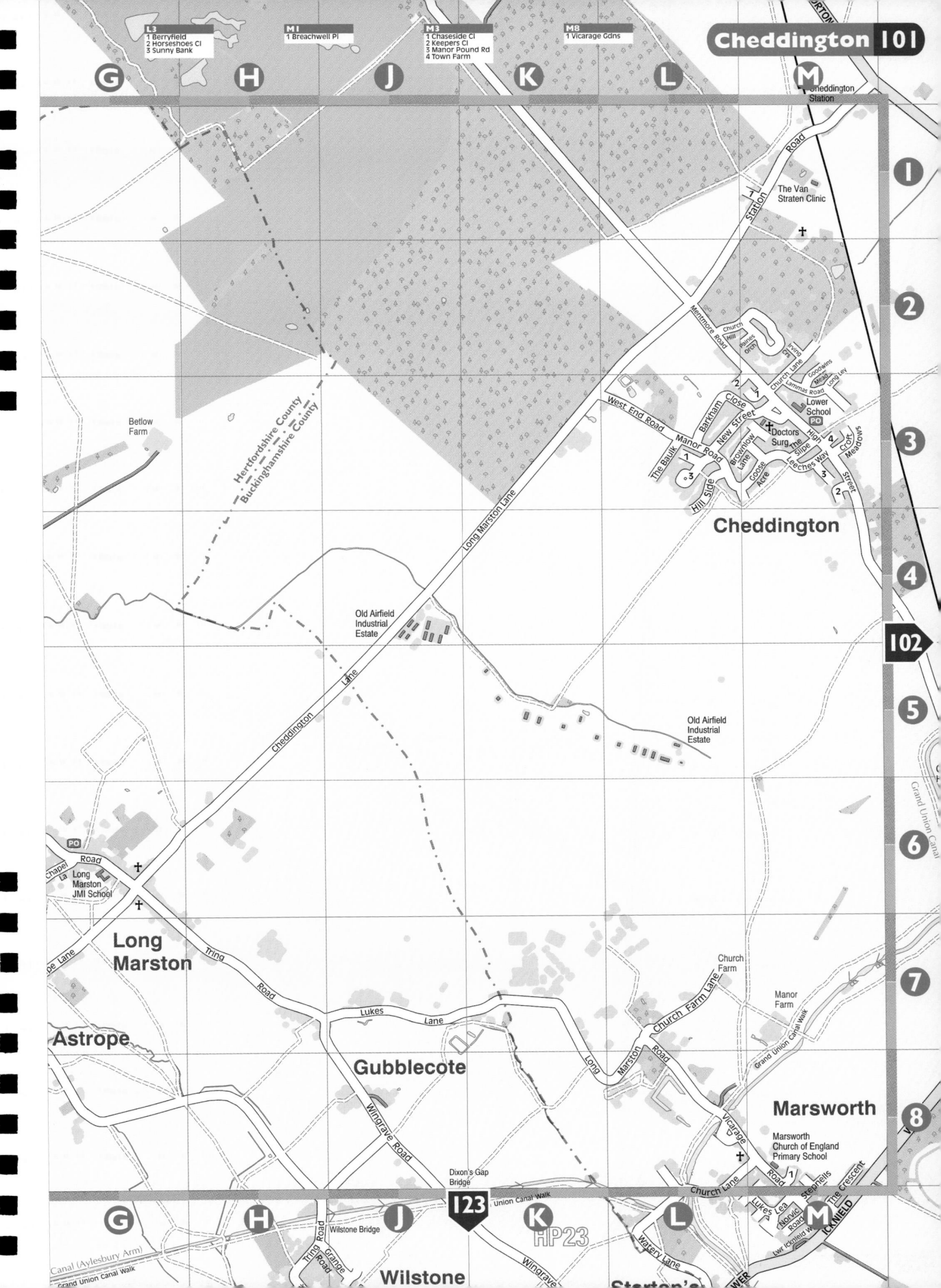

L3
1 Berryfield
2 Horseshoes Cl
3 Sunny Bank

M1
1 Breachwell Pl

M3
1 Chaseside Cl
2 Keepers Cl
3 Manor Pound Rd
4 Town Farm

M8
1 Vicarage Gdns

G H J K L M

Cheddington
Station

The Van
Straten Clinic

Menmore Road

Church
Hill

Paines
orch

Church Lane

Lammas Road

Goodwins
Mead

Long Ley

West End Road

Lower
School
PO

Barkham
Close

New Street

The Slade

High

Crok
Meadows

Doctors
Surg

Brownlow
Lane

Leeches Way

Manor Road

The Bauk

Gorse
Acre

Street

Hill Side

Cheddington

Betlow
Farm

Hertfordshire County
Buckinghamshire County

Long Marston Lane

Old Airfield
Industrial
Estate

102

Old Airfield
Industrial
Estate

Cheddington Lane

Grand Union Canal

PO

Chapel
La

Road

Long
Marston
JMI School

**Long
Marston**

Tring
Road

Lukes   Lane

Church
Farm

Manor
Farm

Grand Union Canal Walk

Astrope

Gubblecote

Long
Marston
Road

Church Farm Lane

Marsworth

Wingrave Road

Dixon's Gap
Bridge

Vicarage
Road

Marsworth
Church of England
Primary School

Church Lane

123
Union Canal Walk

G H J K L M

Canal (Aylesbury Arm)

Grand Union Canal Walk

Wilstone Bridge

HP23

Tring
Road

Grange
Road

Wingrave

Watery Lane

Stepnells

The Crescent

ICKNIELD

Lukes Lea

Icknield W

Lwr Icknield W

Wilstone

Sterton's

I
2
3
4
5
6
7
8

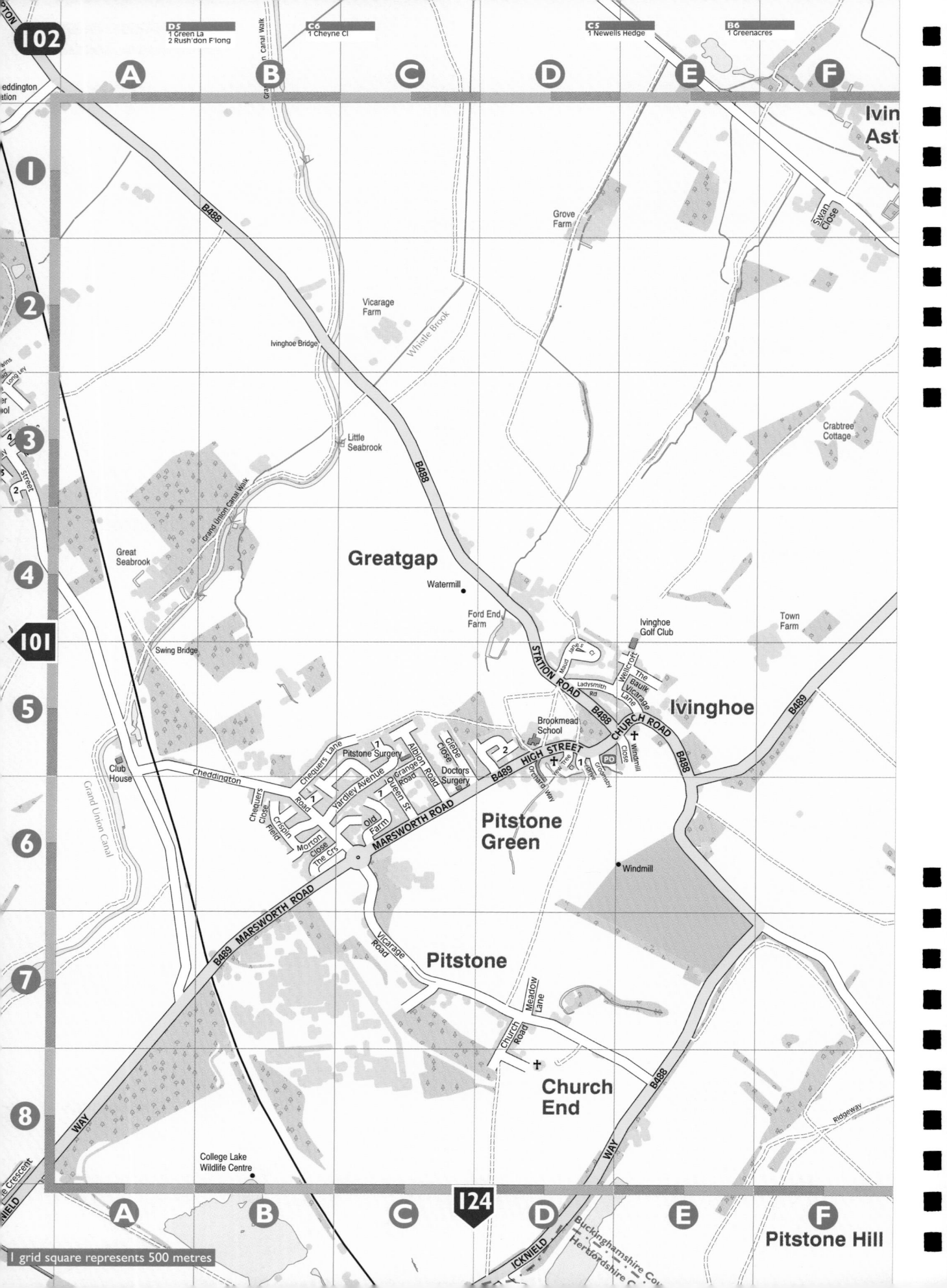

A   B   C   D   E   F

D5
1 Green La
2 Rush'don F'long

C6
1 Cheyne Cl

C5
1 Newells Hedge

B6
1 Greenacres

Ivin
Ast

eddington
tation

B488

I

2

wins
ng Ley
er
ol

3
4
5
2
Street
2

Vicarage
Farm

Whistle Brook

Grove
Farm

Swan
Close

Ivinghoe Bridge

Little
Seabrook

B488

Crabtree
Cottage

Great
Seabrook

Grand Union Canal Walk

Greatgap

Watermill

4

101

Ford End
Farm

Ivinghoe
Golf Club

Town
Farm

Swing Bridge

STATION ROAD

The
Baulk

Vicarage
Lane

Ivinghoe

B489

Club
House

Cheddington

Chequers Lane

Pitstone Surgery

Brookmead
School

Ladysmith Rd

Welcroft

B488

CHURCH ROAD

B488

5

Chequers
Close

Chequers
Field

Crispin

Yardley Avenue

Albion Road

Grange
Road

Queen St

Clebe
Close

2

Doctors
Surgery

HIGH STREET

B489

Orchard Way

1

PO

Groomsby

Windmill
Close

Grand Union Canal

WAY

Morton
Close

The Crs

Old
Farm

MARSWORTH ROAD

Pitstone
Green

6

B469   MARSWORTH ROAD

Vicarage
Road

Pitstone

Windmill

7

Meadow
Lane

Church
Road

B488

Church
End

8

WAY

College Lake
Wildlife Centre

Ridgeway

Crescent

FIELD

A   B   C   124   D   E   F

ICKNIELD

Buckinghamshire Co.
Hertfordshire C

Pitstone Hill

G
H
J
K
L
M
ghoe
on
A4146
LEIGHTON ROAD
Ivinghoe Way
ICKNIELD
1
Coombe Bottom
Pine Road
B489
Stet
2
Two Ridges Link
TRING ROAD
RAF Edlesborough
Coombe Hole
3
B489
A4146
MAIN ROAD
Chiltern Farm
Collyers
Two Ridges Link
Hill Fort
Ridgeway
4
Fairview Farm
104
Icknield Way
5
Hog Hall Lane
Ward's Coombe
Icknield Way
Icknield Way
6
Icknield Way
Ward's Hurst Farm
7
Ringshall Coppice
Icknield Way
Clipper Down
8
Down Farm
Beacon Road
Ivinghoe Common
Hall F
125
Icknield Way
Deer Le
Swimmi
Pool
Duncombe

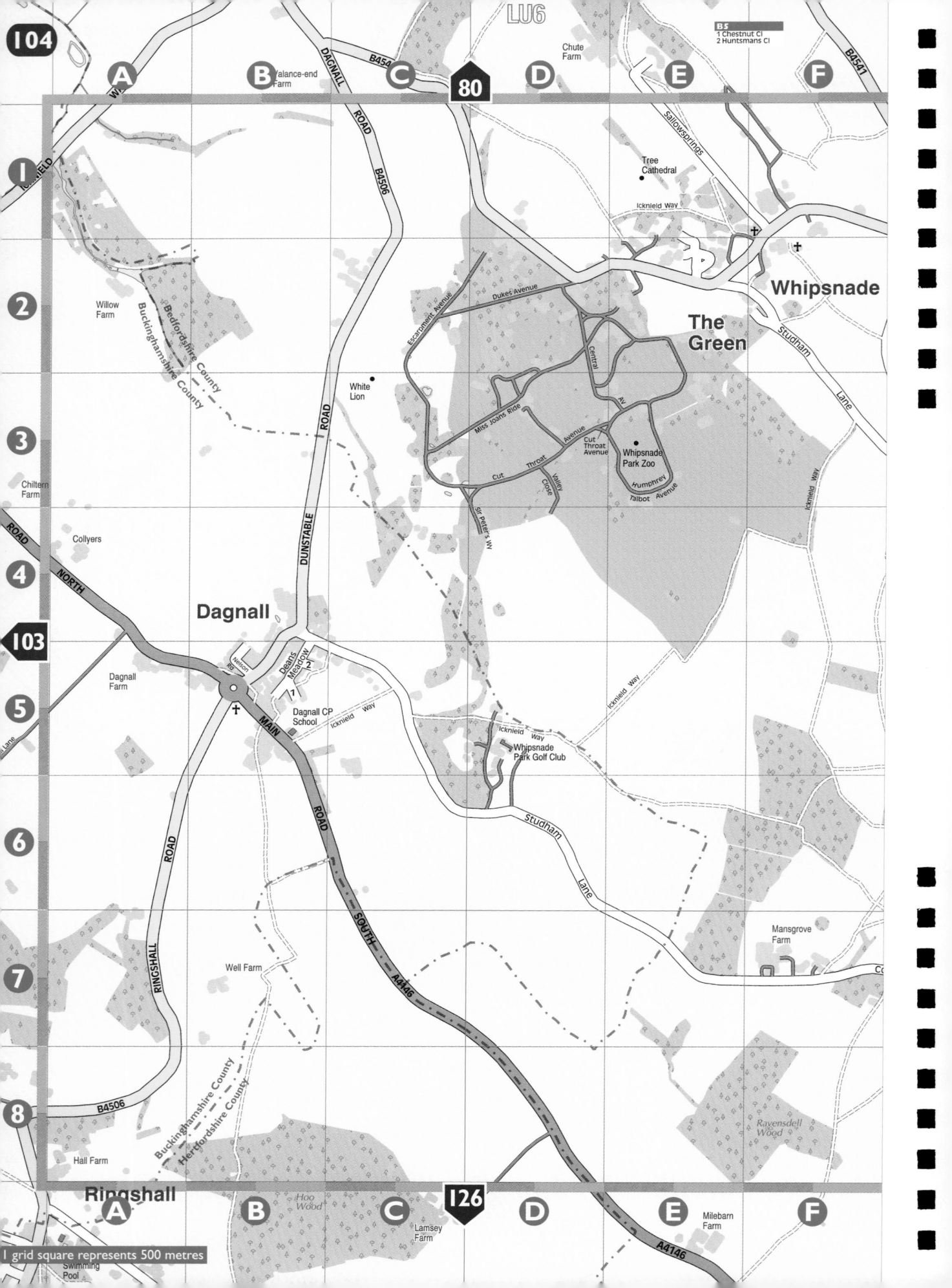

104
LU6
B5
1 Chestnut Cl
2 Huntsmans Cl
Chute Farm
Valance-end Farm
DAGNALL ROAD
B4506
B454
B4541
80
Sallowsprings
Tree Cathedral
Icknield Way
Whipsnade
The Green
Studham Lane
Dukes Avenue
Escarpment Avenue
Central Av
White Lion
Miss Joans Ride
Cut Throat Avenue
Whipsnade Park Zoo
Humphrey Talbot Avenue
Valley Close
Sir Peter's Wy
Willow Farm
Bedfordshire County
Buckinghamshire County
Chiltern Farm
Collyers
NORTH ROAD
DUNSTABLE ROAD
Dagnall
103
Dagnall Farm
Nelson Rd
Deans Meadow
Dagnall CP School
MAIN ROAD SOUTH
A4146
Whipsnade Park Golf Club
RINGSHALL ROAD
Well Farm
Mansgrove Farm
Ravensdell Wood
B4506
Hertfordshire County
Hall Farm
Ringshall
Hoo Wood
Lamsey Farm
126
Milebarn Farm
Swimming Pool
1 grid square represents 500 metres

G   H   J   K   L   M

81

I

Kensworth
Lynch

Lynch
Farm

Corner
Farm

Kensworth
se

Common   Road

Nash
Farm

Spratts   Lane

Common Road

PO

Malms Cl

Kensworth
Common

2

B4540

Whipsnade
Heath

Dove
House
La

Poplar Road

Maple Wy

Russell
Cl

Baker's La

Plewes
Cl

Elmside
Green
La

1

Ridgeway

COMMON   ROAD

Wick
Hill

The
Chilterns

Kensworth
Lower
School

Hall   Road

B4540   LYNCH

HILL

Clay

House

Dove

Lane

Buckwood Lane

Bedfordshire County

Hertfordshire County

3

Woodland

Rise

Oakway

Holywell   Road

Holywell
Cl

Holywell
Rd

Holywell

Oldhill
Wood

Byslips Road

Dedmansey
Wood

Buckwood Road

Buckwood
Stubs

4

106

5

Dunstable Road

Studham

Manor
Farm

Swanells Wood

Southern
Wy

PO

Kensworth Road

Hill
Farm

Byslips

Byslips Road

Roe End Lane

6

Roe

Church

Church
Rd

Valley
Close

Studham
VC Lower
School

Valley Road

ommon Road

Bury
Farm

Byslips Road

Clement's End

7

8

Long
Wood

Clements End Road

echwood Park
reparatory
School

G   H   J   K   L   M

127

Bellingdon

Kensworth Lynch
Lynch Farm
LYNCH HILL
Red Cow Farm
Millfield Farm
Cotswold Business Park
Aley Green
Pipers Lane
Hill Farm
Caddington Common
Cemetery
Mancroft Road
Woodside Road
Elaine Gdns
Lower Farm
Woodside Farm & Wildfowl Park
Woodside
D5
1 Summer Wk
2 Sursham Ct
3 William St
C4
1 Old Vic'age Gdns
LUTON ROAD B4540
Caddington Hall
Markyate Cell
A5(T)
fordshire County
fordshire County
Church End
Cemetery
Park View Dr
Grange Cl
Markyate Primary School
Cavendish Road
Cowper Road
Cowper Court
Cowper Rise
Becks Cl
Wesley Rd
Albert St
High Street
Roman Way
The Ridings
Hicks Road
Windmill Road
Markyate
Sharose Court
Sebright Rd
Parkfield Road
Park Cl
Corner Wood
The Coppins
Pickford Road
Cleveland Rd
George St
King St
The Long Meadow
London Road
Farrer Top
High View
Dammersey Cl
Green Lane
Rainbow Hall Farm
Cheverells Cl
Sebright School
Cheverell's Green
Roe End
Cheverells
Friendless Lane
Cotton Spring Farm
Valleybottom Farm
Valley Lane
Mill Lane
105
82
128

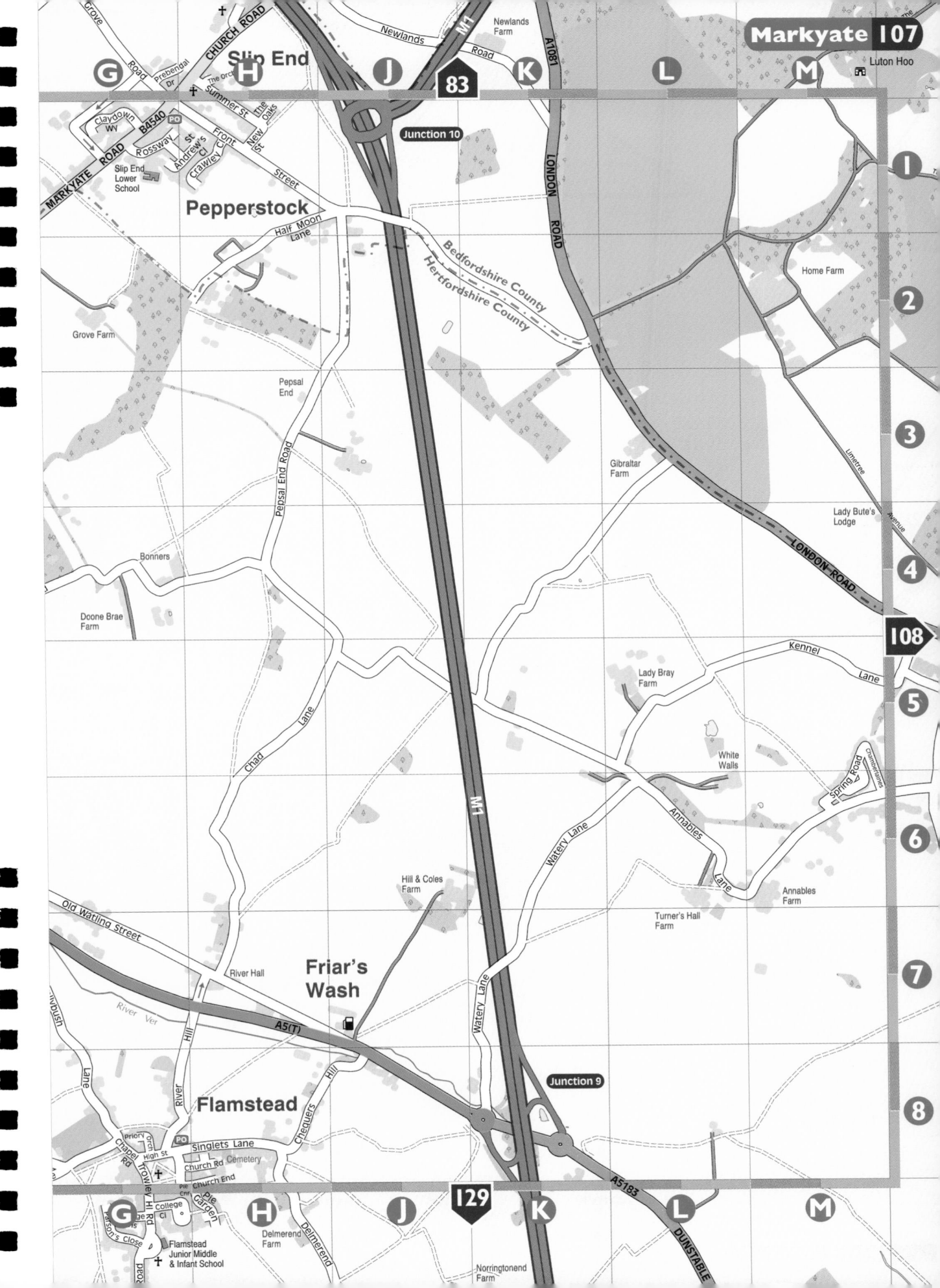
Slip End
Pepperstock
Friar's Wash
Flamstead
Junction 10
Junction 9
M1
A1081
A5(T)
A5183
LONDON ROAD
MARKYATE ROAD
CHURCH ROAD
B4540
Newlands Road
Newlands Farm
Luton Hoo
Bedfordshire County
Hertfordshire County
Half Moon Lane
Pepsal End Road
Pepsal End
Grove Farm
Grove Road
Prebendal Dr
Summer St
The Oaks
Front Street
New St
Claydown Wy
Rossway
St Andrew's Cl
Crawley Cl
Slip End Lower School
Home Farm
Gibraltar Farm
Limetree Avenue
Lady Bute's Lodge
Bonners
Doone Brae Farm
Kennel Lane
Lady Bray Farm
White Walls
Spring Road
Chamberlaines
Chad Lane
Annables Lane
Annables Farm
Watery Lane
Hill & Coles Farm
Turner's Hall Farm
Old Watling Street
River Hall
River Ver
River Hill
Chequers Hill
Singlets Lane
Cemetery
Church Rd
Church End
Priory Orch
High St
Chapel Rd
Trowley Hl Rd
College Cl
Pie Garden
Pie Cnr
Parson's Close
Flamstead Junior Middle & Infant School
Delmerend Farm
Delmerend Lane
Norringtonend Farm
DUNSTABLE
83
108
129
G H J K L M
1 2 3 4 5 6 7 8

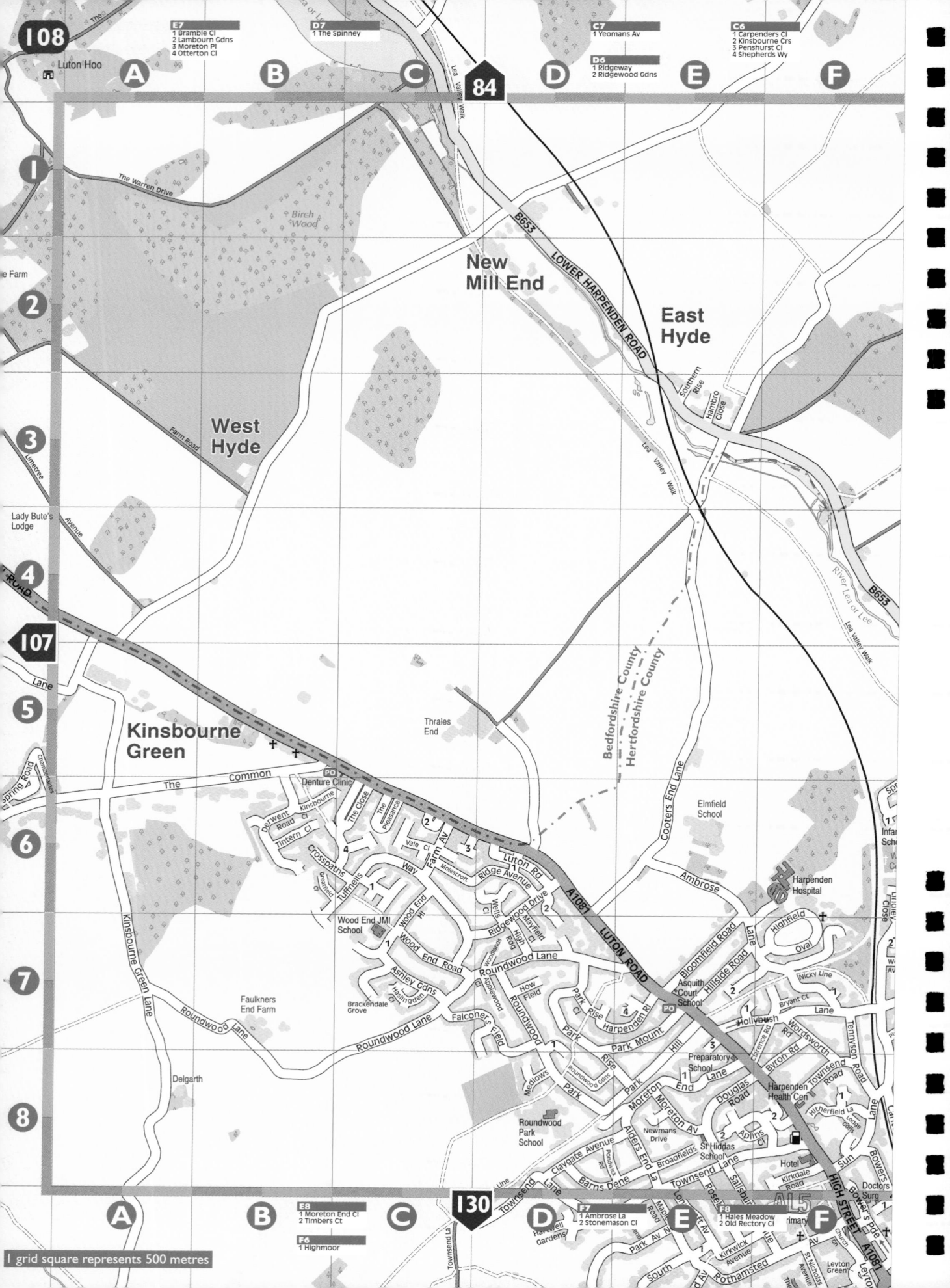

Luton Hoo

84

107

130

E7
1 Bramble Cl
2 Lambourn Gdns
3 Moreton Pl
4 Otterton Cl

D7
1 The Spinney

C7
1 Yeomans Av

D6
1 Ridgeway
2 Ridgewood Gdns

C6
1 Carpenders Cl
2 Kinsbourne Crs
3 Penshurst Cl
4 Shepherds Wy

A B C D E F

1 2 3 4 5 6 7 8

The Warren Drive

Birch Wood

New Mill End

East Hyde

West Hyde

B653

LOWER HARPENDEN ROAD

Southern Rise

Hambro Close

Lea Valley Walk

River Lea or Lee

B653

Lady Bute's Lodge

Limetree Avenue

ROAD

Lane

Kinsbourne Green

Thrales End

Bedfordshire County

Hertfordshire County

Cooters End Lane

Elmfield School

Harpenden Hospital

The Common

Denture Clinic

Derwent Road

Kinsbourne

Tintern Cl

Crosspaths

Greenfield

Tuffnells

The Close

The Pleasance

Vale Cl

Way

Farm Av

Molescroft

Ridge Avenue

Luton Rd

Ambrose

Bloomfield Road

Hillside Road

Highfield Oval

Wood End JMI School

Wood End Pl

Wood End Road

Ashley Gdns

Haslingden

Brackendale Grove

Ridgewood Drive

Mayfield

High

Ridge

Woodside

Appenwood

Roundwood Lane

How Field

A1081

LUTON ROAD

Asquith Court School

Nicky Line

Wicky Line

Bryant Ct

Lane

Wordsworth Road

Tennyson Road

Faulkners End Farm

Kinsbourne Green Lane

Roundwood Lane

Roundwood Lane

Falconers Field

Roundwood

Park Rise

Harpenden Rd

Park Rise

Park Mount

Hollybush

Park Rise

Hill

Preparatory School Lane

Clarence Rd

Byron Rd

Delgarth

Meadows

Park

Roundwood Gdns

Moreton

Moreton Av

Park Rise

Moreton End Lane

Douglas Road

Harpenden Health Cen

Townsend Road

Hitherfield La

Roundwood Park School

Newmans Drive

Claygate Avenue

Algers End

Potswick

Broadfields

St Hiddas School

Aplins

Hotel

Kirkdale Road

Salisbury

Sun

Bowers Pde

High Street

Doctors Surg

A5

A1081

Barns Dene

Townsend Lane

Rosery

Rothamsted

Leyton Green

E8
1 Moreton End Cl
2 Timbers Ct

F8
1 Highmoor

F7
1 Ambrose La
2 Stonemason Cl

C6
1 Hales Meadow
2 Old Rectory Cl

A B C D E F

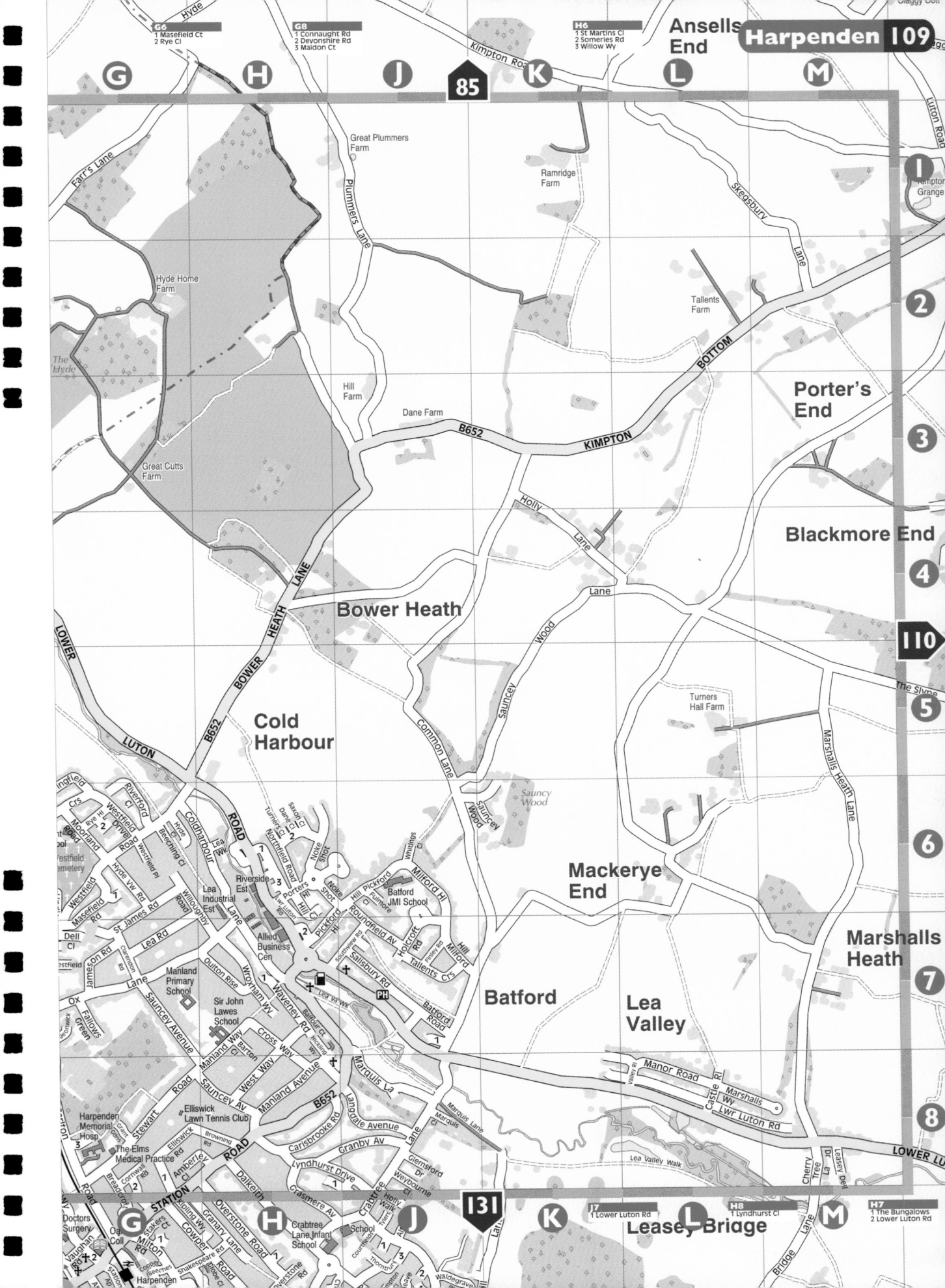

G6
1 Masefield Ct
2 Rye Cl
G8
1 Connaught Rd
2 Devonshire Rd
3 Maldon Ct
H6
1 St Martins Cl
2 Someries Rd
3 Willow Wy
Ansells End
85
Great Plummers Farm
Ramridge Farm
Hyde Home Farm
Tallents Farm
Hill Farm
Dane Farm
Porter's End
Great Cutts Farm
KIMPTON BOTTOM
B652
Blackmore End
Bower Heath
BOWER HEATH LANE
110
Turners Hall Farm
Cold Harbour
LOWER LUTON ROAD
Saunce Wood
Mackerye End
Marshalls Heath
Batford
Lea Valley
Manor Road
Lwr Luton Rd
Lea Valley Walk
LOWER LUTON ROAD
131
J7
1 Lower Luton Rd
H8
1 Lyndhurst Cl
H7
1 The Bungalows
2 Lower Luton Rd
Leasey Bridge
Harpenden Memorial Hosp
The Elms Medical Practice
Manland Primary School
Sir John Lawes School
Elliswick Lawn Tennis Club
Batford JMI School
Allied Business Cen
Lea Industrial Est
Riverside Est
Crabtree Lane Infant School
STATION ROAD
Harpenden

110
Claggy Road
Coleman B Centre
Kimpton
86
A
B
C
D
E
F
Hampden
Dacre Crs
Common La
Lawn Av
Wren Cl
Park Lane
Parkfield Crs
Church Lane
Canham Cl
HIGH ST
High St
Kimpton Road
Luton Road
HIGH STREET
Doctors Surgery
Kimpton JMI School
Pams Lane
Curtis La
BALLSLOUGH HILL
Kimpton Grange
B652
Lloyd Way
Cooper's Hill
Cooper's Close
Hall Lane
Kimpton Hall Farm
B651
Abbotshay
Prior's Wood
Lime Avenue
The Dr
Beech Way
Beech Wy
Bibbs Hall Lane
Blackmore Way
The Paddocks
Brownfield Wy
Kimpton Road
Bibbsworth Hall Farm
Shaw's Corner (Edwardian Hall NT)
109
Broadway
The
Firs Dr
Dale Av
Burton Cl
The Slype
Lamer House
Bride Hall
Bride Hall Lane
Gustard Wood
LAMER LANE
Mid Herts Golf Club
Marshalls Heath
Delaport
Lamer Farm
Codicote Road
The Folly
Folly Fields
Rose Lane
Sheepcote Lane
LOWER LUTON ROAD
B653
Garden Ct
132
CORY-WRIGHT
Lea Valley Walk
Kingfisher Cl
STATION RD
Mount Rd
Meads La
Ash Gv
Wheathampstead
1 grid square represents 500 metres
1
2
3
4
5
6
7
8

Codicote

G H J K L M

87

1 I

2

3

4

112

5

6

7

8

L1
1 Baker's La
2 Farriers Cl
3 Heath La
4 Mayflower Cl
5 The Paddocks

L2
1 The Opening
2 Poynders Mdw
3 Valley Rd South
4 Winch Cl

Codicote Heath

River Mimram

Kimpton Mill

Kimpton Road

Tanyard Lane

Codicote Bottom

Tower Road

Coomer Close
Bentick Way
St Giles Road
school
Old Close

Bury
Hillside
Grange Rise
Valley Road
The Close

Codicote Lodge

Heath Lane
Hill Road
Meadow Way

Codicote Junior & Infant School

The Green
The Arch

HIGH STREET

New Town

The Ridgeway
PO

St Albans Road

Cowards Lane

The Riddy

Dark Lane

The Birches

Rabley Heath Road

Sisservernes Farm

B656

CODICOTE

Rollswood Road

The Limes

Wistow House Clinic

Oakhill Drive

Fulling

Kimpton R

WELWY

Linces Farm

River Mimram

Mead Lane

Lord Lane

PH

Ayot St Lawrence

Hill Farm

Hill Farm Lane

Codicote Road

Ryefield Farm

Ayot St Peter Road

Ayot Bury

Codicote Road

Ayot St Peter

Ayot Place

Ayot Greenway

Ayot St Peter Road

Whitehill Farm

White Hill

Wilga Road
Wilshere Road
Haworth Rise

Queen Victoria Memorial Hospital

White Hill

The Fryth

Homerswood Lane

DIGSWELL

Ayot Little Green Lane

Waterer

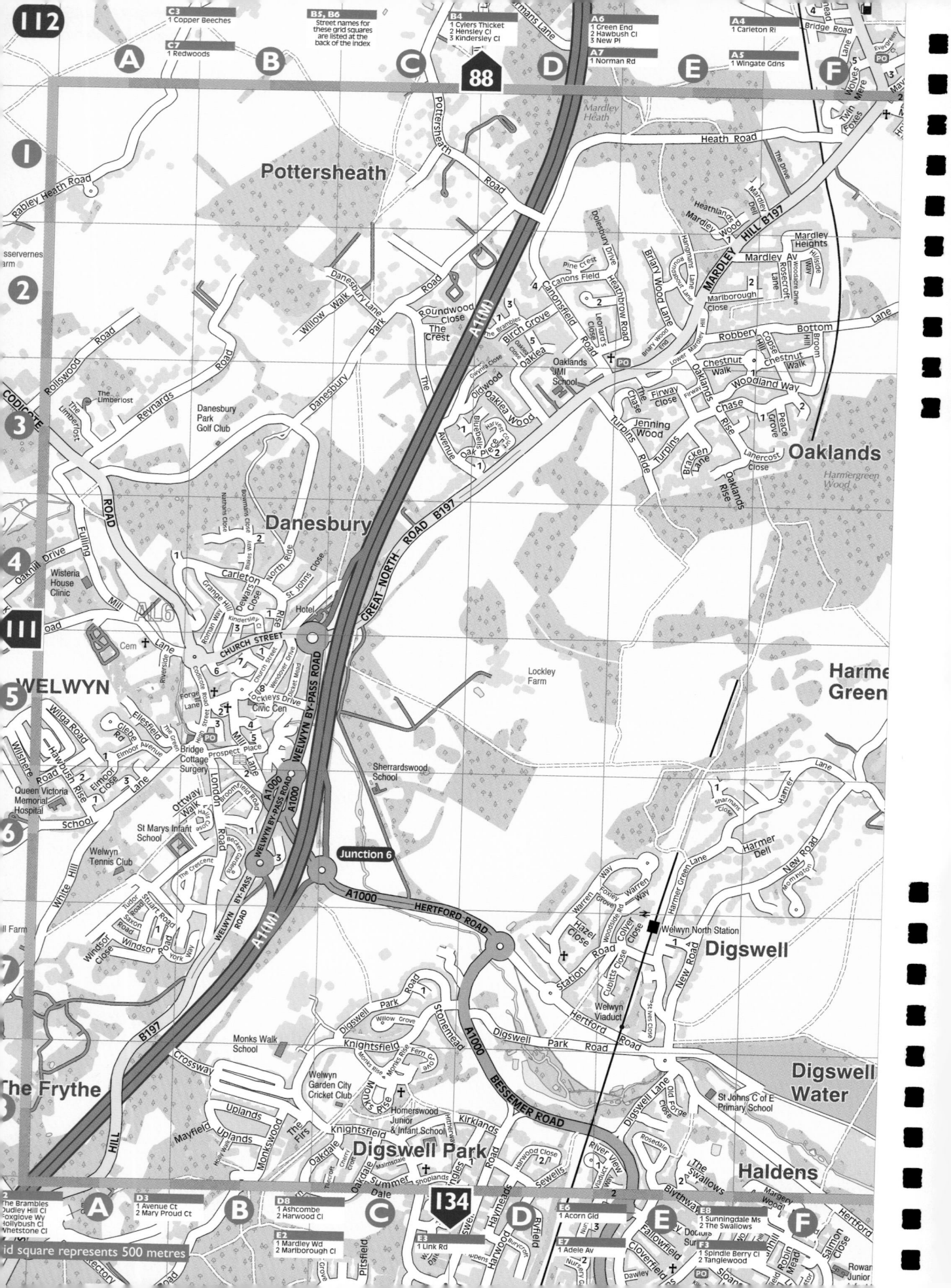

C3 1 Copper Beeches
C7 1 Redwoods
B5, B6 Street names for these grid squares are listed at the back of the index
B4 1 Cylers Thicket 2 Hensley Cl 3 Kindersley Cl
A6 1 Green End 2 Hawbush Cl 3 New Pl
A7 1 Norman Rd
A4 1 Carleton Ri
A5 1 Wingate Gdns
88
Pottersheath
Mardley Heath
Heath Road
Rabley Heath Road
Danesbury
Danesbury Park Golf Club
Oaklands
Harmergreen Wood
WELWYN
AL6
CODICOTE
A1(M)
GREAT NORTH ROAD B197
MARDLEY HILL B197
WELWYN BY-PASS ROAD
CHURCH STREET
Lockley Farm
Sherrardswood School
Junction 6
A1000 HERTFORD ROAD
Welwyn North Station
Digswell
Welwyn Viaduct
Digswell Water
St Johns C of E Primary School
Haldens
Monks Walk School
Welwyn Garden City Cricket Club
Homerswood Junior & Infant School
Digswell Park
BESSEMER ROAD
The Frythe
Queen Victoria Memorial Hospital
St Marys Infant School
Welwyn Tennis Club
Wisteria House Clinic
Bridge Cottage Surgery
Civic Cen
Oaklands JMI School
Harmer Green
134
D3 1 Avenue Ct 2 Mary Proud Ct
D8 1 Ashcombe 2 Harwood Cl
E2 1 Mardley Wd 2 Marlborough Cl
E3 1 Link Rd
E6 1 Acorn Gld
E7 1 Adele Av
E8 1 Sunningdale Ms 2 The Swallows
F3 1 Spindle Berry Cl 2 Tanglewood
1 grid square represents 500 metres

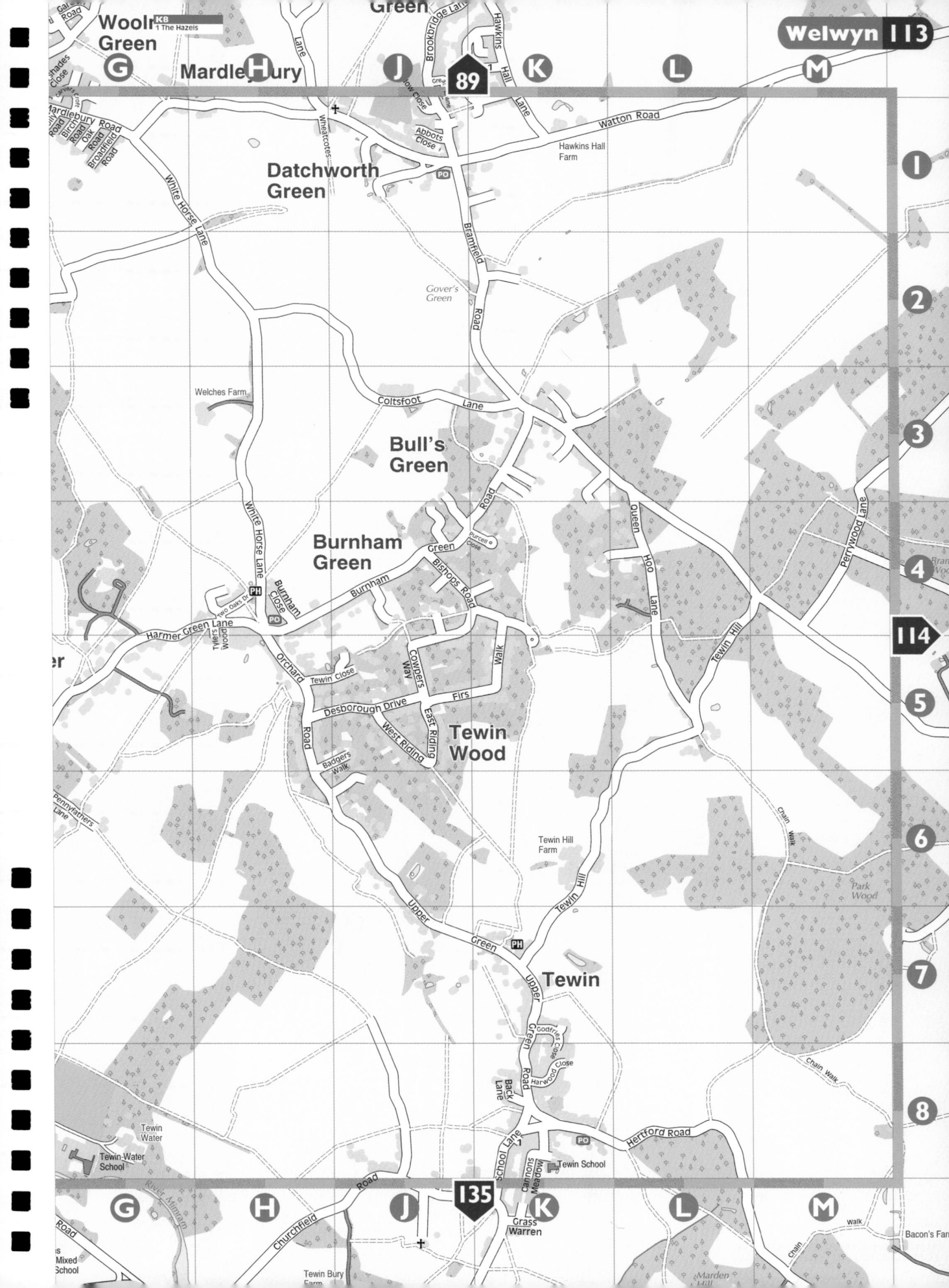
Woolmer Green
K8 1 The Hazels
Mardley Hury
89
Datchworth Green
Mardlebury Road
Birch Road
Oak Road
Broadfield Road
White Horse Lane
Wheatcotes
Abbots Close
Watton Road
Hawkins Hall Farm
Hawkins Hall Lane
Brookbridge Lane
Bramfield Road
Gover's Green
Coltsfoot Lane
Welches Farm
Bull's Green
Burnham Green
Burnham Green
Purcell Close
Bishops Road
Burnham Close
Two Oaks Dr
Harmer Green Lane
Tylers Wood
Orchard Road
Tewin Close
Cowpers Way
Walk
Firs
Desborough Drive
East Riding
West Riding
Tewin Wood
Badgers Walk
Queen Hoo Lane
Perrywood Lane
Tewin Hill
114
Pennyfathers Lane
Tewin Hill Farm
Chain Walk
Park Wood
Upper Green Road
Tewin
Godfries Close
Harwood Close
Back Lane
Hertford Road
School Lane
Cannons Meadow
Tewin School
Tewin Water
Tewin-Water School
River Mimram
Churchfield Road
135
Grass Warren
Tewin Bury Farm
Marden Hill
Bacon's Farm
G H J K L M
1 2 3 4 5 6 7 8

A B C **90** D E F

1

2

3

4

5

6

7

8

A B **136** C D E F

Watkins Hall Farm

Perrywood Lane

Perrywood Farm

Chain Wk

Chain Walk

Great Gobions Farm

Stapleford

Bramfield Woods

Chain Walk

Chain Walk

Row Wood

SG14

Winding Shott

Turners Close

Well Green

Bramfield House

Priest Wood

Park Wood

Bury Lane

PO

Bramfield

Chain Walk

Holly Grove Road

Main Road

Main Road

Bramfield Place Farm

Tattle

Westend

Bacon's Farm

walk

Home Farm

A119

Patchendon Farm

HIGH ROAD A119

Clusterboits

Church Lane

PO

River Beane

Hertfordshire Way

A119

Waterford Hall Farm

Bramfield Lane

Barley Cft

Vicarage

HIGH ROAD

Hertfordshire Way

Waterford

Timber Orchard

Goldings Lane

A119

Goldings

NORTH

1 grid square represents 500 metres

School
Woodhall Park
K6
1 Crouchfield La
G
H
J
91
K
L
The Clumps
M
1
Chain Walk
Burrs Green Farm
A602
WARE ROAD
Bengeo Temple Farm
Lane
Hertfordshire Way
Temple
2
Hertfordsh
3
Tonwell
The Orch
Temple Lane
Chappell Ct
Tonwell School
Ware
Bourne Honour
Road
Barleycroft
Southend Farm
Hertfordshire Way
Hertfordshire Way
Hertfordshire Way
Stony Hills
Stonyhills
ANCHOR
4
Paynes Hall
116
Chapmore End
WADESMILL ROAD
WESTMILL
5
ROAD
Sacombe Road
Bullsmill
B158
1
Westmill Farm
Rickneys
6
A602
Gentlemens Field
7
A10(T)
Lane
Waterford Common
The Hyde
Rendlesha
8
Ware Park Farm
WADESMILL ROAD
Trapstyle Road
Park Road
The Orch
Sacombe
G
H
J
137
K
L
M
The Wick
Road
A10

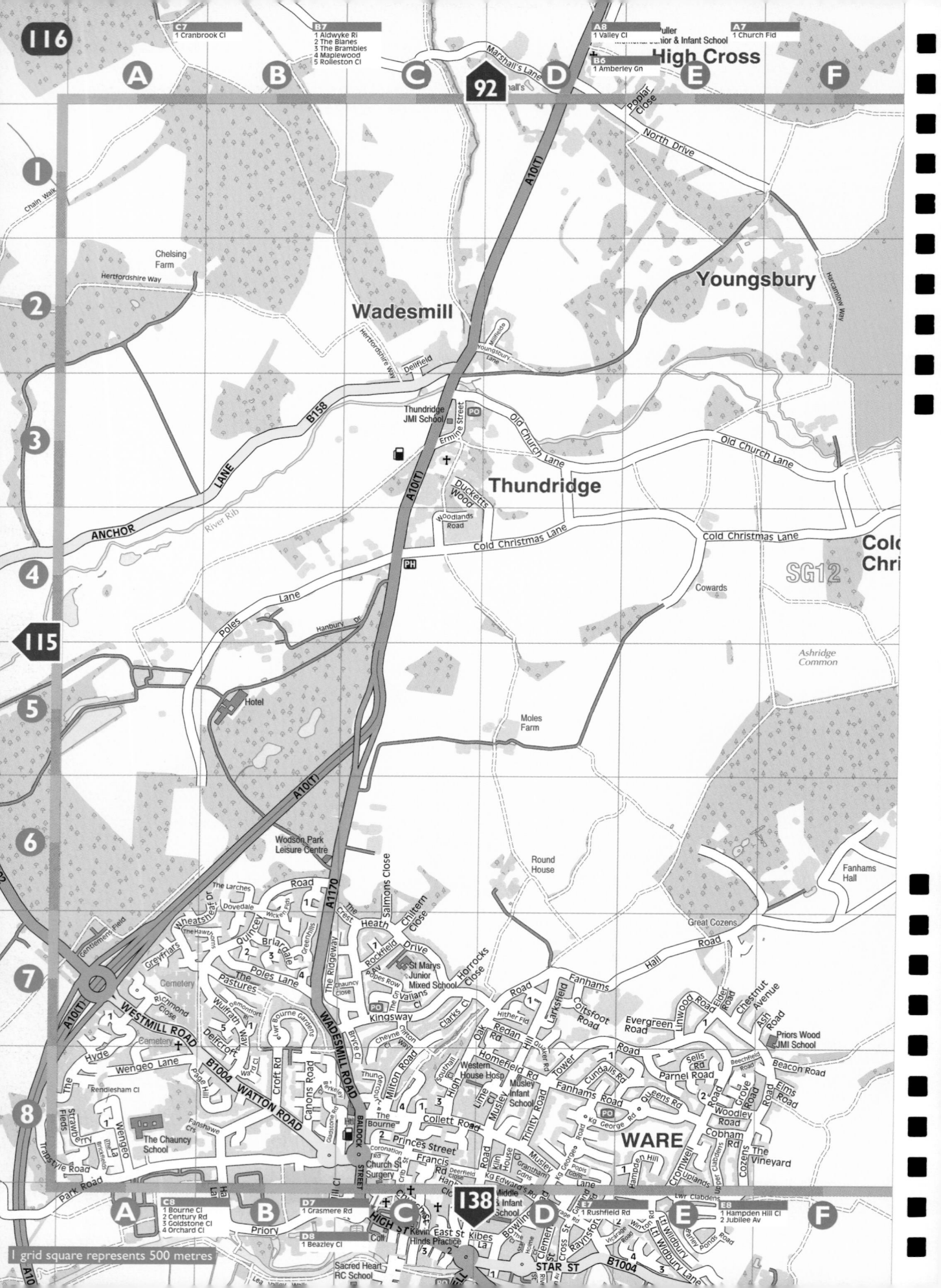

A   B   C   92   D   E   F

C7
1 Cranbrook Cl

B7
1 Aldwyke Ri
2 The Blanes
3 The Brambles
4 Maplewood
5 Rolleston Cl

A8
1 Valley Cl

B6
1 Amberley Gn

A7
1 Church Fld

Fuller
Memorial Junior & Infant School

Marshall's Lane

High Cross

Poplar Close

North Drive

Hartcanlow Way

Youngsbury

Chelsing Farm

Hertfordshire Way

1

2

Wadesmill

Minehele

Youngsbury Lane

B158

Hertfordshire Way

Dellfield

Thundridge JMI School

PO

Ermine Street

Old Church Lane

Old Church Lane

3

Thundridge

Ducketts Wood

Woodlands Road

Cold Christmas Lane

Cold Christmas Lane

Cold Christmas

SG12

River Rib

ANCHOR LANE

A10(T)

PH

4

Poles Lane

Hanbury Dr

Cowards

115

Ashridge Common

5

Hotel

Moles Farm

A10(T)

Wodson Park Leisure Centre

Round House

6

Great Cozens

Fanhams Hall

Hall Road

The Larches

Dovedale

Road

A1170

Salmons Close

Chiltern Close

The Crest

Heath

Wheatsheaf Dr

Quickley

Briardale

Greenhill

Rockfield Drive

St Marys Junior Mixed School

Horrocks Close

Fanhams Road

Chestnut Avenue

7

Greyfriars

The Hawth

Cemetery

The Pastures

Poles Lane

The Ridgeway

Chauncy Close

Popes Row

S Vallans Cl

Clarks Cl

Larksfield Road

Cotsfoot Road

Evergreen Road

Linwood Road

Elder Road

Ash Road

Priors Wood JMI School

Gentlemans Field

Richmond Close

Wulfrun Way

Delfcroft

Lwr Bourne Gardens

Genmonton Way

Kingsway

PO

Cheyne Orton Way

Hither Fld

Oak Rd

Redan Rd

Tower

Sells Rd

Beechfield Road

Beacon Road

A10(T)

WESTMILL ROAD

Cemetery

The Hyde

Wengeo Lane

Croft Rd

Canons Road

Bryce La

Berkeley Ct

Milton Road

Southall

Western House Hosp

Homefield Rd

Musley Infant School

Cundalls Rd

Parnel Road

Grove Road

Elms Road

8

Tradstyle Road

Strawberry Fields

Wengeo La

Rendlesham Cl

Page Hill

B1004 WATTON ROAD

Gladstone Rd

Baldock Street

Fanshawe

The Chauncy School

Coronation Crs

The Bourne

Princes Street

Collett Road

Francis Rd

Church St

Crib St

High

Musley Lane

Trinity Road

Kg Edwards Rd

Popis

Cobham Road

Woodley Road

Cozens Rd

The Vineyard

WARE

Cromwell Rd

Cozens Hill

Uplands

Hampden Hill

PO

Kg George Rd

Lwr Clabdens

A   B   138   C   D   E   F

C8
1 Bourne Cl
2 Century Rd
3 Goldstone Cl
4 Orchard Cl

D7
1 Grasmere Rd

D8
1 Beazley Cl

B7
1 Rushfield Rd

E8
1 Hampden Hill Cl
2 Jubilee Av

Priory

HIGH ST

Kevin East St Hinds Practice

Kibes La

STAR ST

Clement St

Bowling

Raynsford

Vicarage

Ltl Widbury

Ltl Widbury Lane

B1004

Sacred Heart RC School

A10

Lea Valley

1 grid square represents 500 metres

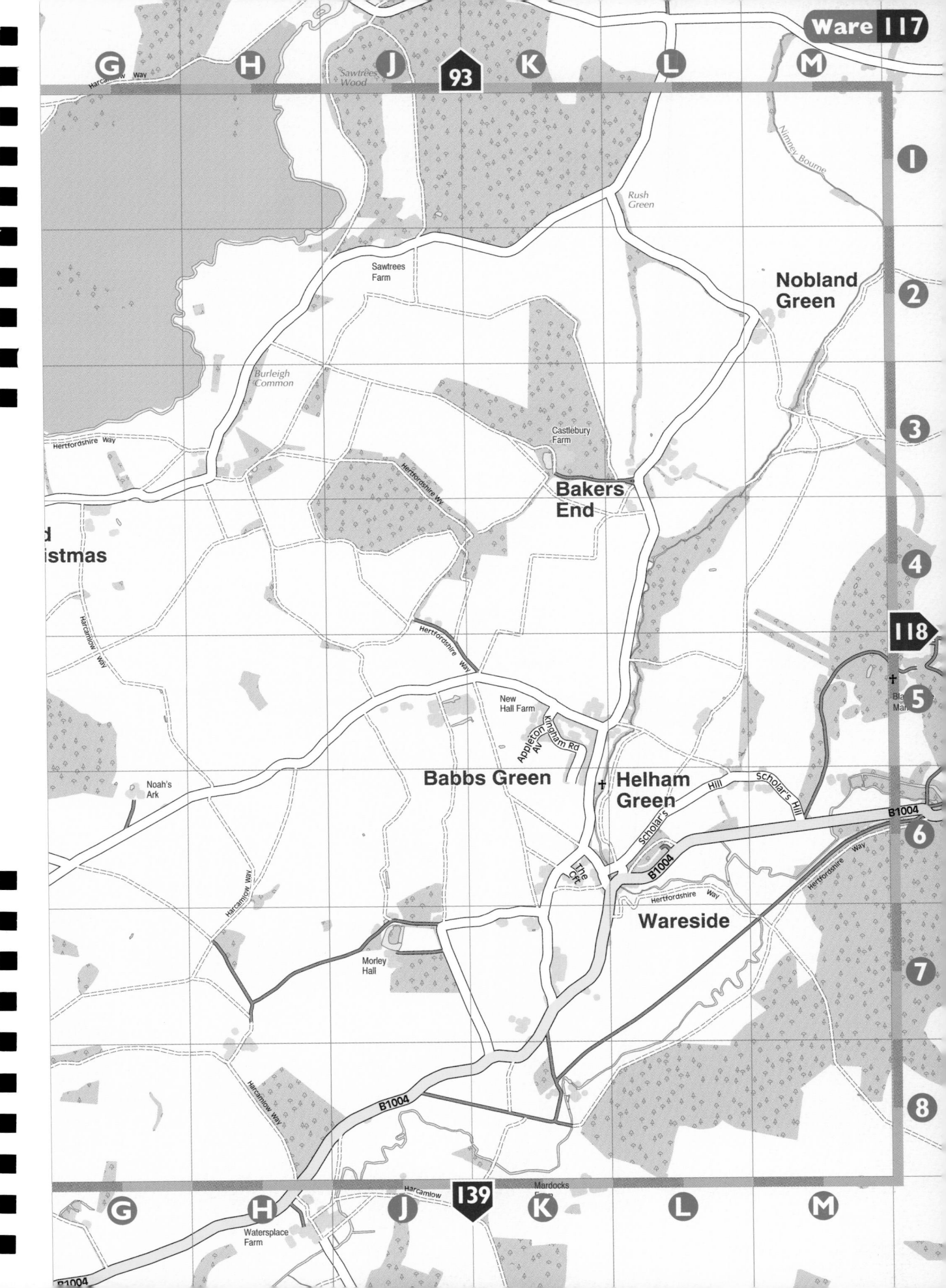

G H J **93** K L M

I
2
3
4
118
5
6
7
8

Nobland Green

Nimney Bourne

Rush Green

Sawtrees Wood

Sawtrees Farm

Burleigh Common

Hertfordshire Way

Castlebury Farm

Bakers End

Hertfordshire Wy

Hertfordshire Way

…istmas

Harcamlow Way

New Hall Farm

Appleton Av

Kingham Rd

Babbs Green **Helham Green**

Scholar's Hill

Scholar's Hill

B1004

Noah's Ark

The Cr…

B1004

Wareside

Hertfordshire Way

Harcamlow Way

Morley Hall

Harcamlow Way

B1004

G H J **139** K L M

Harcamlow

Mardocks

Watersplace Farm

B1004

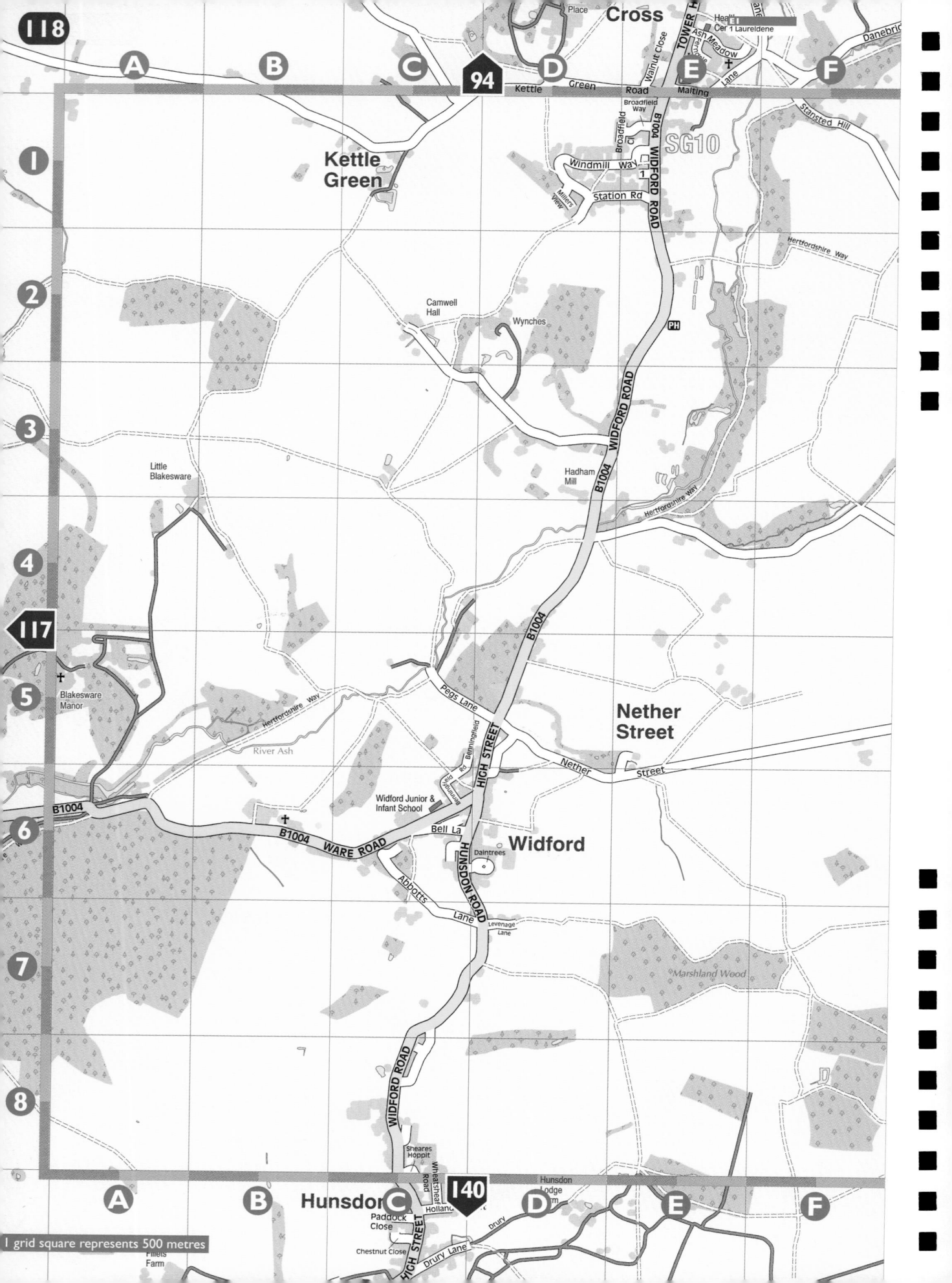

Cross
Place
Kettle Green Road
Malting
Walnut Close
TOWER H
Ash Meadow
Laureldene
Broadfield Way
Broadfield Cl
SG10
Stansted Hill
Kettle Green
Windmill Way
Millers View
Station Rd
B1004 WIDFORD ROAD
Hertfordshire Way
Camwell Hall
Wynches
PH
Little Blakesware
Hadham Mill
B1004
Blakesware Manor
Pegs Lane
Nether Street
River Ash
Bemingfield
HIGH STREET
Nether Street
Widford Junior & Infant School
B1004 WARE ROAD
Bell La
Widford
Daintrees
HUNSDON ROAD
Abbotts Lane
Levenage Lane
Marshland Wood
WIDFORD ROAD
Sheares Hoppit
Wheatsheaf Road
Hunsdon Lodge
Hunsdon
Holland
Paddock Close
Chestnut Close
Drury Lane
Fillets Farm
A
B
C
D
E
F
1
2
3
4
5
6
7
8
94
117
140

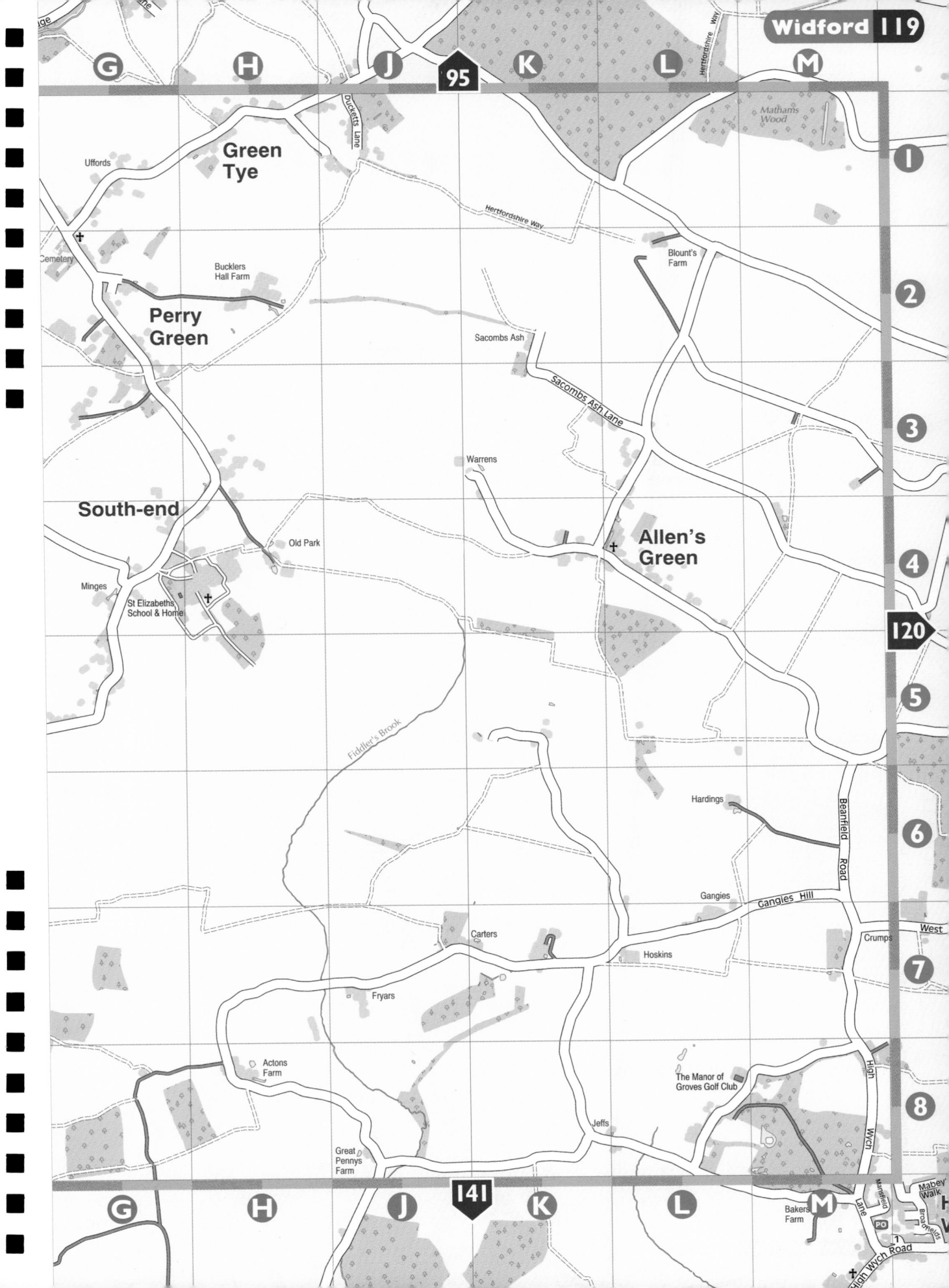

G   H   J   **95**   K   L   M

I

2

3

4

120

5

6

7

8

G   H   J   **141**   K   L   M

Green Tye

Uffords

Cemetery

Perry Green

Bucklers Hall Farm

South-end

Minges

St Elizabeths School & Home

Old Park

Ducketts Lane

Hertfordshire Way

Blount's Farm

Sacombs Ash

Sacombs Ash Lane

Warrens

Allen's Green

Fiddler's Brook

Hardings

Beanfield Road

Gangies   Gangies Hill

West

Crumps

Carters

Hoskins

Fryars

Actons Farm

The Manor of Groves Golf Club

Jeffs

Great Pennys Farm

High Wych Lane

Bakers Farm

Mansfield Lane

Broadfields

Mabey Walk

PO

High Wych Road

Mathams Wood

Hertfordshire Way

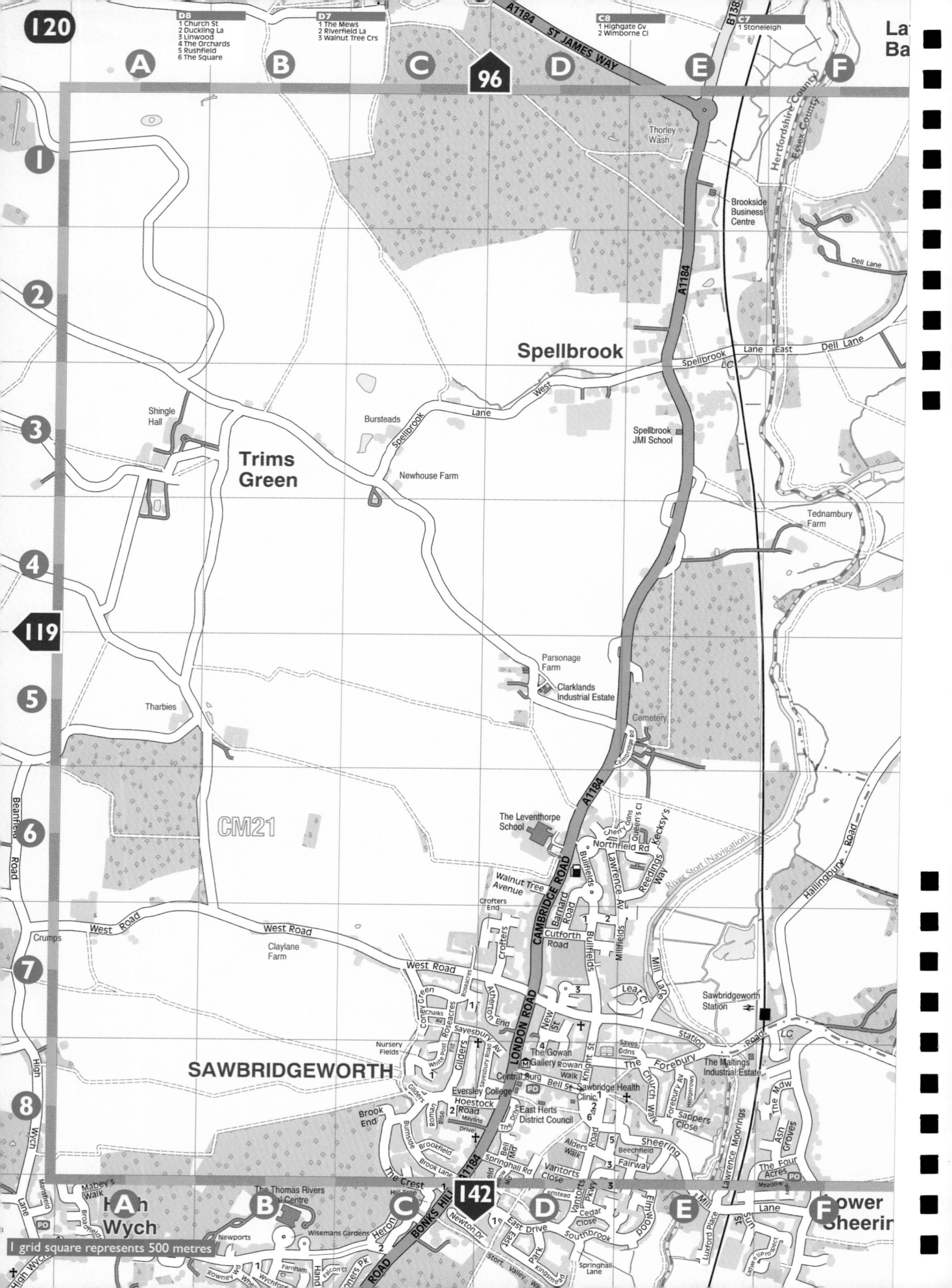
D8
1 Church St
2 Duckling La
3 Linwood
4 The Orchards
5 Rushfield
6 The Square
D7
1 The Mews
2 Riverfield La
3 Walnut Tree Crs
C8
1 Highgate Gv
2 Wimborne Cl
C7
1 Stoneleigh
96
119
142
A1184 ST JAMES WAY
B1383
Thorley Wash
Hertfordshire County
Essex County
Brookside Business Centre
Dell Lane
Spellbrook
Spellbrook Lane East
Spellbrook Lane West
Shingle Hall
Bursteads
Spellbrook JMI School
Trims Green
Newhouse Farm
Tednambury Farm
Parsonage Farm
Clarklands Industrial Estate
Tharbies
Cemetery
Cambridge Rd
The Leventhorpe School
CM21
Beanfield Road
Northfield Rd
Queen's Cl
Kecksy's
Cherry Gdns
Bullfields
Lawrence Av
Reedings Way
River Stort (Navigation)
Hallingbury Road
Walnut Tree Avenue
CAMBRIDGE ROAD
Crofters End
Barnard Road
Cutforth Road
Crofters
Millfields
Mill Lane
West Road
Crumps
Claylane Farm
Lear Cl
Sawbridgeworth Station
Coney Green
Roseacres
Atherton End
LONDON ROAD
New St
Station Road
Chalks Av
Sayesbury Av
Sayesbury Road
Nursery Fields
White Post Fld
Gilders
Sayes Gdns
The Gowan Gallery
Rowan Walk
Knight St
The Forebury
The Maltings Industrial Estate
SAWBRIDGEWORTH
Central Surg
Bell St
Sawbridge Health Clinic
The Church Walk
Forebury Av
Hedgerows
Eversley College
Hoestock Road
Roman Rise
Maylins Drive
East Herts District Council
The Drive
Sappers Close
Brook End
Burnside
Brookfield
Brook Lane
Bell Md
Springhall Rd
Alders Walk
Beechfield
Sheering
Fairway
Lawrence Moorings
The Mdw
Ash Groves
The Four Acres
Vantorts Close
The Crest
High Wych Lane
Mabey's Walk
Mansfield
Broadfield
High Wych
The Thomas Rivers Medical Centre
Wisemans Gardens
Newports
Heron
BONKS HILL
Newton Dr
East Drive
East Park
Vantorts Pkwy
Cedar Close
Southbrook
Elmwood
Mill
Luxford Place
Lane
Meadow
Lower Sheering
Rowney Wd
Farnham Cl
Falcon Cl
Stort Valley Way
Kingsmead
Springhall Lane
1 grid square represents 500 metres

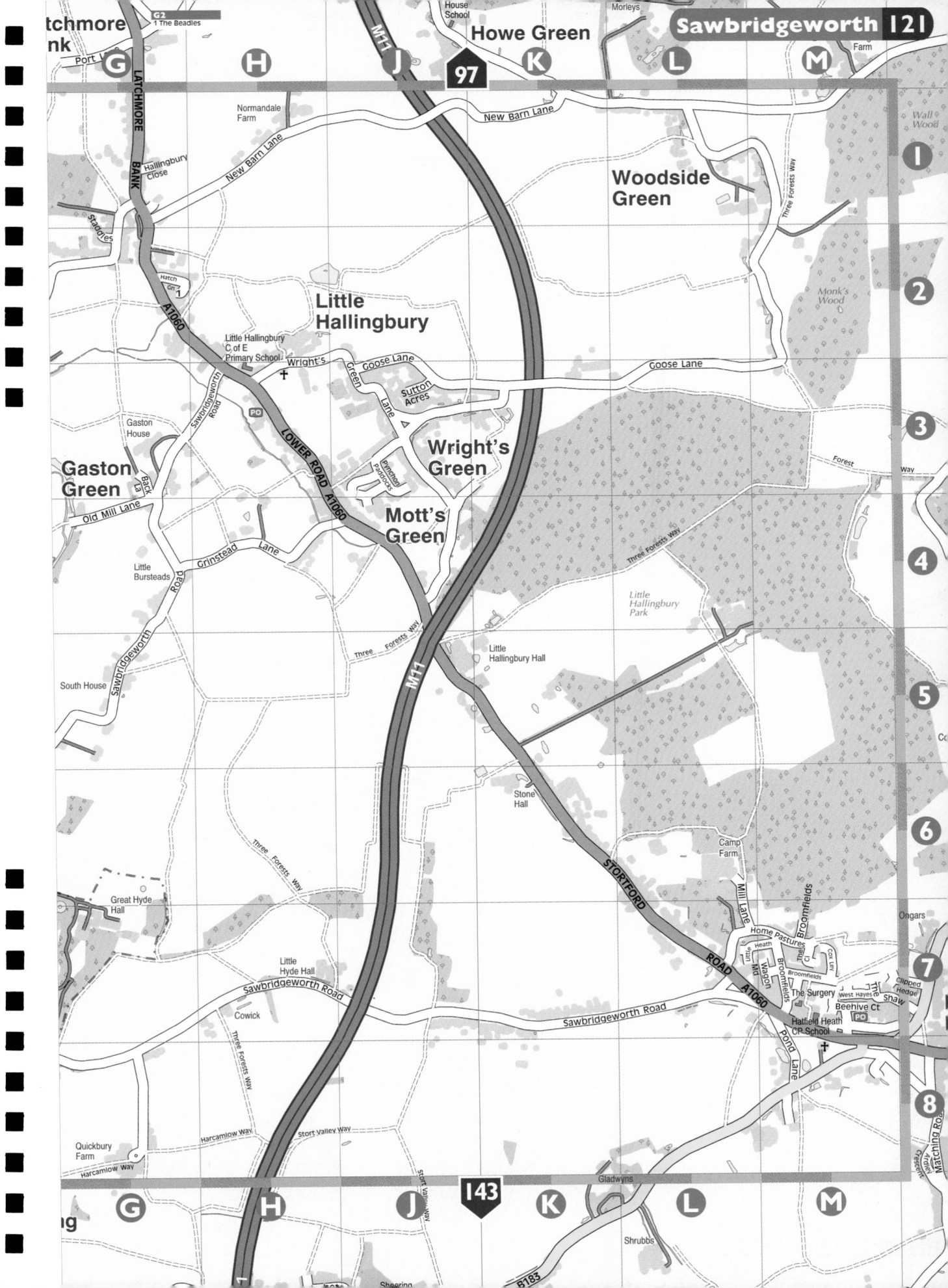
Howe Green
Woodside Green
Little Hallingbury
Wright's Green
Mott's Green
Gaston Green
Little Hallingbury Park
Little Hallingbury Hall
Stone Hall
Camp Farm
Great Hyde Hall
Little Hyde Hall
Cowick
Quickbury Farm
South House
Little Bursteads
Gaston House
Normandale Farm
Monk's Wood
Wall Wood
New Barn Lane
Goose Lane
Wright's Green Lane
Sutton Acres
Pynchon Paddocks
Lower Road
Stortford Road
Sawbridgeworth Road
Grinstead Lane
Old Mill Lane
Back La
Latchmore Bank
Hallingbury Close
Staddles
Hatch Gn
Little Hallingbury C of E Primary School
Three Forests Way
Forest Way
Harcamlow Way
Stort Valley Way
Mill Lane
Broomfields
Home Pastures
The Surgery
Beehive Ct
West Hayes
The Shaw
Clipped Hedge
Hatfield Heath CP School
Pond Lane
Gladwyns
Shrubbs
Ongars
M11
A1060
B183
G H J K L M
97
143
1 2 3 4 5 6 7 8

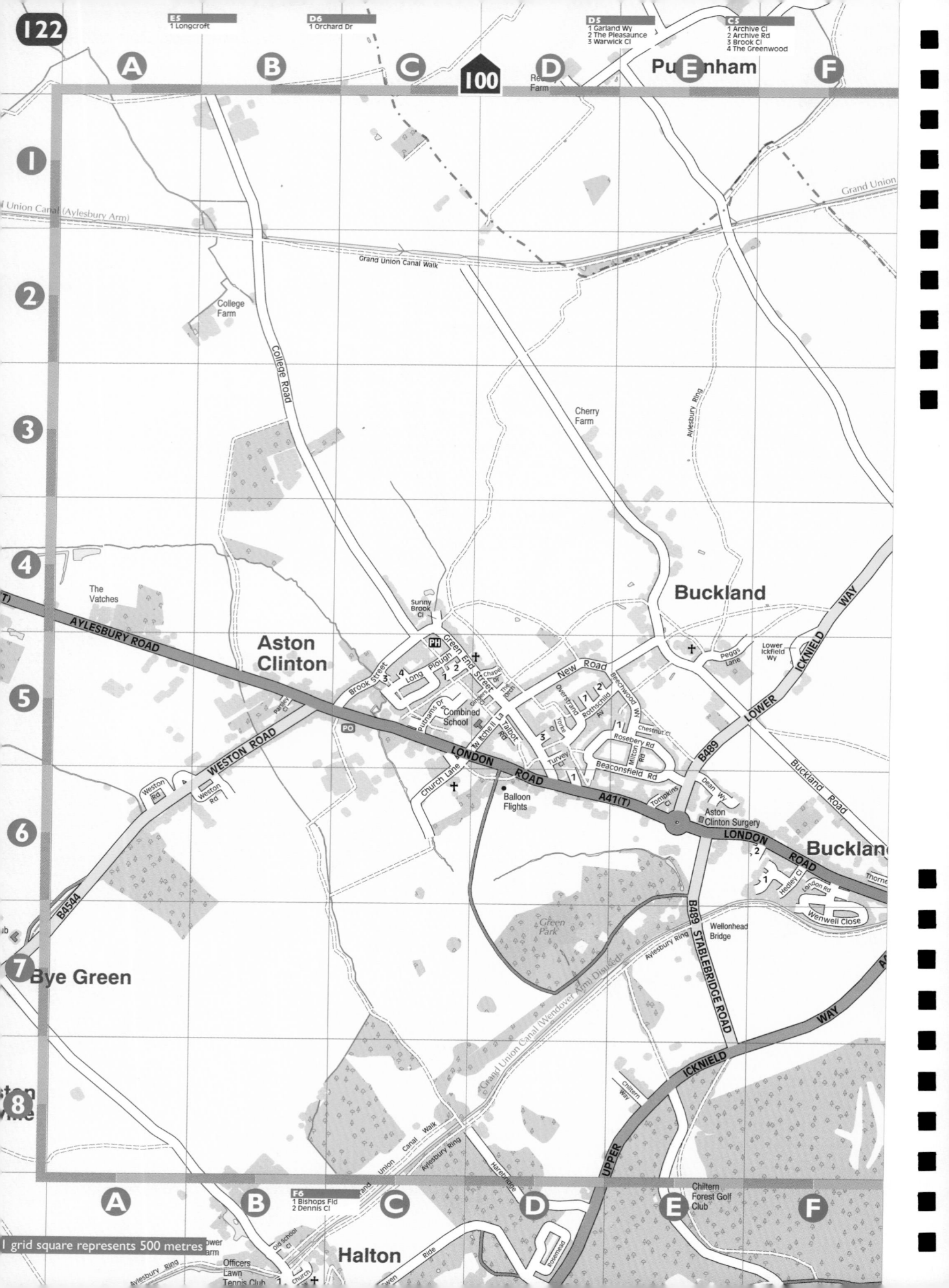

E5
1 Longcroft
D6
1 Orchard Dr
D5
1 Garland Wy
2 The Pleasaunce
3 Warwick Cl
C5
1 Archive Cl
2 Archive Rd
3 Brook Cl
4 The Greenwood
100
Puttenham
Grand Union Canal (Aylesbury Arm)
Grand Union
Grand Union Canal Walk
College Farm
College Road
Cherry Farm
Aylesbury Ring
The Vatches
Buckland
Sunny Brook Cl
Aston Clinton
AYLESBURY ROAD
Green End Street
Brook Street
Long
Plough
New Road
Peggs Lane
Lower Icknield Wy
LOWER ICKNIELD WAY
Beechwood Wy
Overstrand
Rothschild Av
Chestnut Cl
Rosebery Rd
Milton Rd
Combined School
Putnams Dr
Talbot Rd
Turvey Cl
Beaconsfield Rd
WESTON ROAD
Weston Rd
PO
LONDON ROAD
A41(T)
Church Lane
Balloon Flights
Tompkins Cl
Dean Wy
B489
Aston Clinton Surgery
Buckland Road
Bucklan
Hedley Cl
London Rd
Wenwell Close
B4544
Green Park
STABLEBRIDGE ROAD
Wellonhead Bridge
Grand Union Canal (Wendover Arm) Disused
Bye Green
ICKNIELD WAY
UPPER
Chiltern Way
Union Canal Walk
Harebridge
F6
1 Bishops Fld
2 Dennis Cl
Chiltern Forest Golf Club
1 grid square represents 500 metres
Halton
Officers Lawn Tennis Club
Old School Cl
Rosemead
Ride

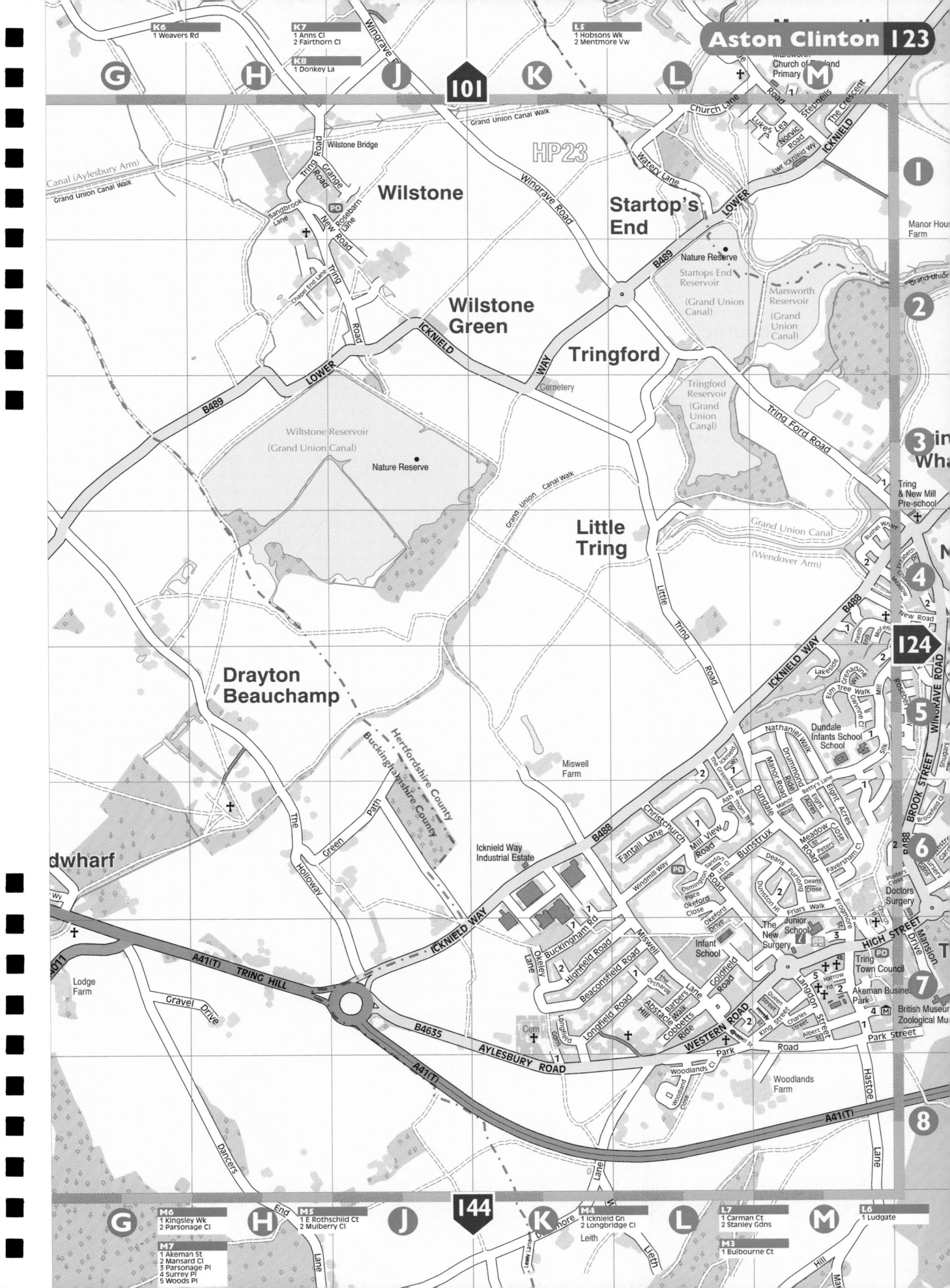

G H J **101** K L M

HP23

Wilstone

Wilstone Bridge

Grand Union Canal Walk

Canal (Aylesbury Arm)
Grand Union Canal Walk

Sandbrook Lane

Chapel End Lane

New Road

Tring Road

Tring Grange Road

Roseban Lane

Wilstone Green

Wilstone Reservoir
(Grand Union Canal)

Nature Reserve

B489

LOWER

ICKNIELD

WAY

Wingrave Road

Startop's End

Startops End Reservoir
(Grand Union Canal)

Nature Reserve

B489

Tringford

Cemetery

Tringford Reservoir
(Grand Union Canal)

Tring Ford Road

Marsworth Reservoir
(Grand Union Canal)

Marsworth Church of England Primary

Church Lane

Water Lane

Lwr Icknield Wy

Lukes Lea

Norvic Road

Stepnells

The Crescent

ICKNIELD

Manor House Farm

I

Grand Union

2

Little
Tring

Grand Union Canal
(Wendover Arm)

Little Tring Road

3
Wha

Tring & New Mill Pre-school

Bushel Wharf

4

124

New Road

B488

ICKNIELD WAY

Lakeside

Elm Tree Walk

Gwynne Cl

Mill

Dundale Infants School

Nathaniel Walk

The Greenway

5

BROOK STREET

WINGRAVE ROAD

Rothschild

Drayton
Beauchamp

Hertfordshire County
Buckinghamshire County

The Green

Holloway

Path

Miswell Farm

Icknield Way Industrial Estate

B488

Christchurch

Fantail Lane

Mill View Road

Ash Rd

Thorn Tree

Dundale Road

Drummond Ride

Manor Road

Betty's Lane

Eight Acres

Peters Hill

Meadow Close

Faversham Cl

Bunstrux

Deans Furlong

Deans Close

Friars Walk

Froxmere

B488

Platter's Close

Doctors Surgery

6

HIGH STREET

dwharf

Wy

Lodge Farm

A4011

A41(T) TRING HILL

Gravel Drive

Dancers

B4635

AYLESBURY ROAD

A41(T)

ICKNIELD WAY

Oxeley

Buckingham Road

Highfield Road

Beaconsfield Road

Longfield Gdns

Cem

Longfield Road

Abstacle Hill

Barbers Walk

Cobbetts Ride

The Orchards

Goldfield Road

Queen St

King Street

Charles Street

Albert St

Park Street

WESTERN ROAD

Woodlands Cl

Woodland Close

Windmill Way

Osmington Sands

Place

Okeford Close

Okeford Drive

PO

Infant School

The New Surgery

Junior School

Tring Town Council

Harrow Yd

Langdon Street

PO

Akeman Business Park

British Museum Zoological Mu

Mansion Drive

Hastoe

7

Woodlands Farm

Lane

A41(T)

8

B5
1 Danvers Cft
2 Hollyfield
3 Sulgrave Crs
A7
1 Dunsley Pl
Church End
A6
1 Evans Wy
2 Mill Gdns
3 Mortimer Rl
4 Treehanger Cl
A4
1 Meadowbrook
2 Pheasant Cl
3 Sutton Cl
College Lake Wildlife Centre
102
Pitstone Hill
Buckinghamshire County
Hertfordshire County
Manor House Farm
Folly Farm
Grand Union Canal Walk
Bulbourne
Parkhill Farm
Tring Wharf
BULBOURNE ROAD
B488
Tring & New Mill Pre-school
New Mill
Marshcroft Lane
Northfield Road
Westland Farm
Ridgeway
123
Grove Road
Grove Road Primary School
WINGRAVE ROAD
BROOK STREET
Tring School
Tring Sports Centre
Tring Health Centre
Station Road
Tring Station
Clarke's Spring
Football Club
Hotel
Cow Lane
Beggars Lane
Doctors Surgery
HIGH STREET
B4635
LONDON ROAD
Upper Dunsley
TRING
Tring Town Council
The Arts Educational School
British Museum (Natural History) Zoological Museum
Park Street
A4251
A41(T)
Oddy Hill
New Ground
Tring Park
The Twist
Park Farm
Wigginton
Bottom House Lane
B6
1 The Beeches
2 Hawkwell Dr
145
Hemp Lane
Vicarage Road
Highfield Road
School
The Firs
grid square represents 500 metres

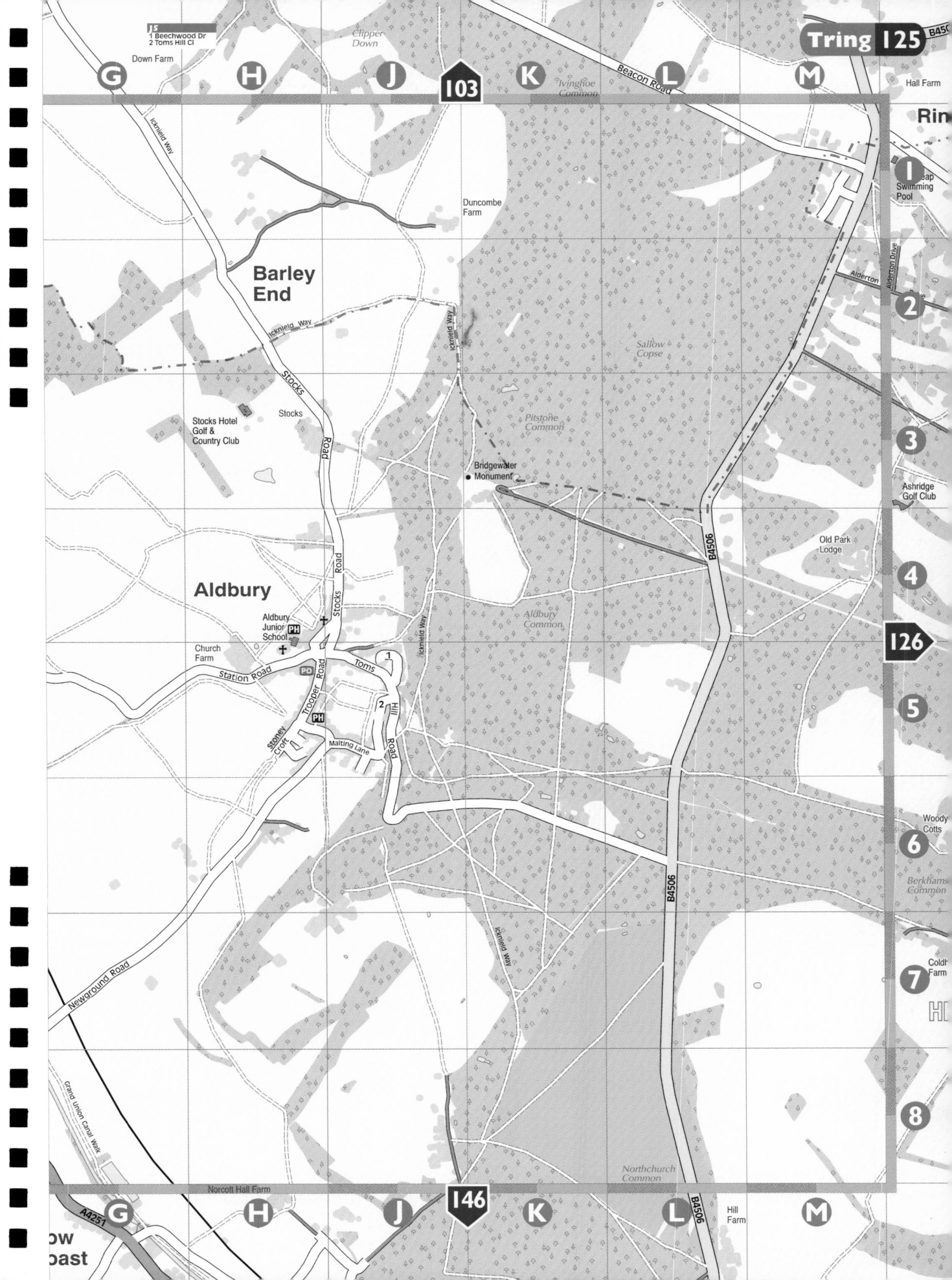

J5
1 Beechwood Dr
2 Toms Hill Cl
Down Farm
Clipper Down
Tring 125
B450
103
Ivinghoe Common
Beacon Road
Hall Farm
Rin
Swimming Pool
Duncombe Farm
Barley End
Alderton
Alderton Drive
Icknield Way
Sallow Copse
Stocks Road
Stocks Hotel Golf & Country Club
Stocks
Pitstone Common
Bridgewater Monument
Ashridge Golf Club
Old Park Lodge
B4506
Aldbury
Aldbury Junior School
PH
Aldbury Common
126
Church Farm
Station Road
PO
Toms Hill Road
Trooper Road
Stoney Croft
Malting Lane
Woody Cotts
Berkhams Common
Newground Road
Grand Union Canal Walk
Norcott Hall Farm
Northchurch Common
146
A4251
Hill Farm
G H J K L M
1 2 3 4 5 6 7 8

126

B4506

Buckinghamshire County

Hertfordshire County

A Hall Farm

B

C

104

D

E

F

Ravensdell Wood

Ringshall

Hoo Wood

Lamsey Farm

Milebarn Farm

A4146

1 Deer Leap Swimming Pool

HEMEL HEMPSTEAD ROAD

Alderton Drive

Drive

Church Farm

2

Ringshall Drive

Gatesdene Close

PO

Church

Road

Nettleden Road

Little Gaddesden JMI School

Hudnall

3

Ashridge Golf Club

Little Gaddesden

Hudnall Lane

Hudnall Corner

ld Park Lodge

Ashridge Park

Hudnall Lane

Chapel Close

The Lye

4

125

Home Farm

5

Ashridge Estate (NT)

6 Woodyard Cotts

Berkhamsted Common

Cromer Cl

Nettleden Road

7 Coldharbour Farm

HP4

8

Nettleden Lodge

A

B Brickkiln Cott

C Frithsden Ditches

147

D Frithsden Gardens

E

F

grid square represents 500 metres

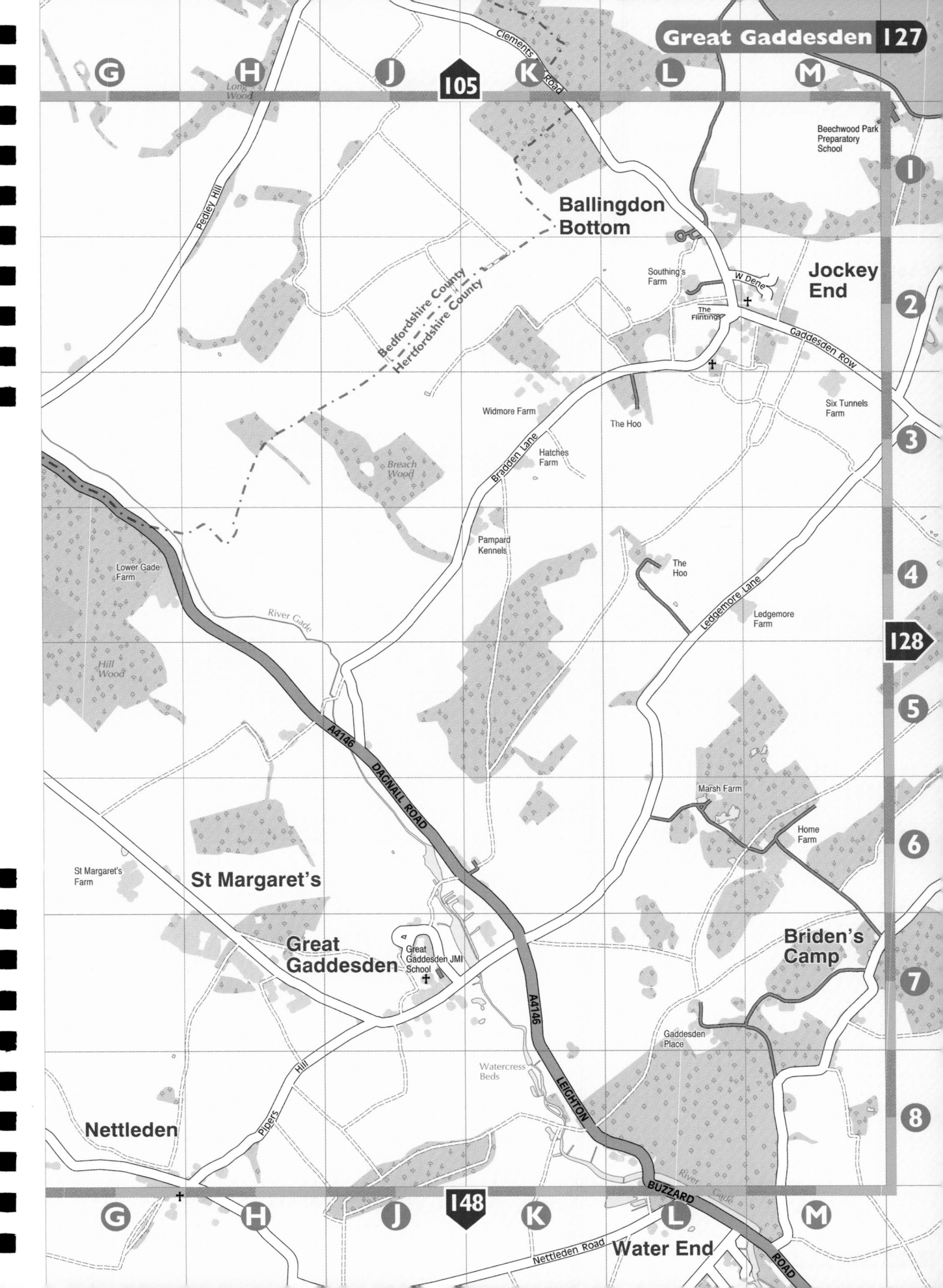
G
H
J
105
K
L
M
Clements Road
Long Wood
Beechwood Park Preparatory School
Pedley Hill
Ballingdon Bottom
Southing's Farm
W Dene
Jockey End
The Flintings
Gaddesden Row
Bedfordshire County
Hertfordshire County
Widmore Farm
The Hoo
Six Tunnels Farm
Breach Wood
Bradden Lane
Hatches Farm
Pampard Kennels
Lower Gade Farm
The Hoo
Ledgemore Lane
Ledgemore Farm
River Gade
128
Hill Wood
A4146
DAGNALL ROAD
Marsh Farm
Home Farm
St Margaret's Farm
St Margaret's
Great Gaddesden
Great Gaddesden JMI School
Briden's Camp
A4146
Gaddesden Place
Watercress Beds
LEIGHTON
Hill
Pipers
Nettleden
BUZZARD
River Gade
148
Nettleden Road
Water End
ROAD
1
2
3
4
5
6
7
8

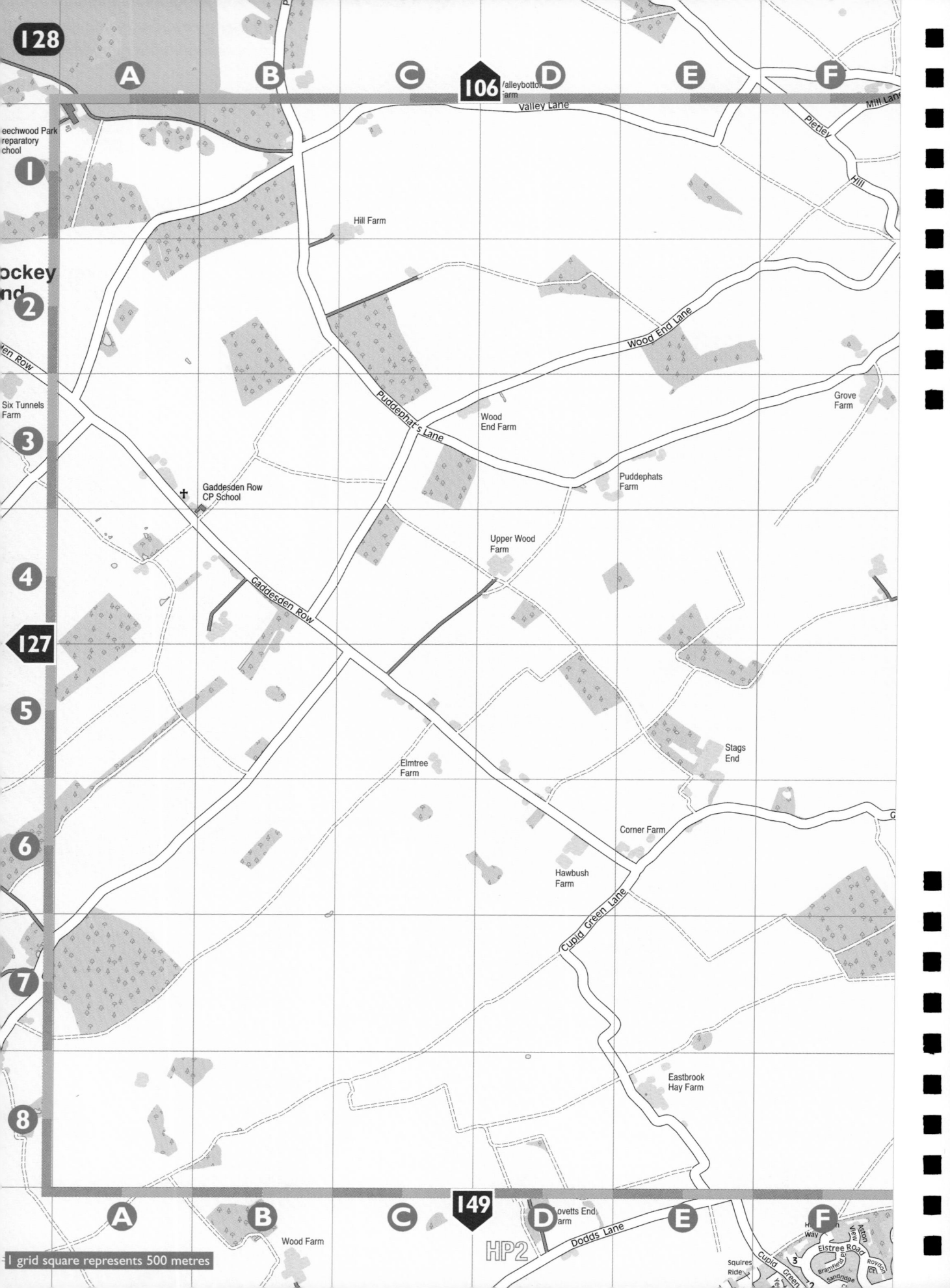

A   B   C   106 D   E   F

Valleybottom Farm

Valley Lane

Mill Lane

Pletley Hill

Beechwood Park Preparatory School

1

Hill Farm

ockey nd

2

Wood End Lane

Grove Farm

en Row

Six Tunnels Farm

Puddephat's Lane

Wood End Farm

3

Gaddesden Row CP School

Puddephats Farm

Upper Wood Farm

4

Gaddesden Row

127

5

Elmtree Farm

Stags End

6

Corner Farm

Hawbush Farm

Cupid Green Lane

7

Eastbrook Hay Farm

8

A   B   149 C   D   E   F

Dovetts End Farm

Dodds Lane

Acton View

Elstree Road

Wood Farm

HP2

Squires Ride

Cupid Green

Bramfield

Sandridge

1 grid square represents 500 metres

Flamstead
M5
1 Ridgedown
M6
1 Vaughan Mead

Singlets Lane
PO
Chec
107

G   H   J   K   L   M

Priory
Orch
High St
Church Rd
Cem
Pie
Church End
Church End
Garden

Vicarage
Gdns
Parson's Close
College
Cl

Flamstead
Junior Middle
& Infant School

Trowley
Bottom
Trowley
Bottom

**Trowley
Bottom**

Delmerend
Farm

Delmerend

Norringtonend
Farm

Redding

Lane

Lane

DUNSTABLE ROAD

A5183

I

Luton

Lane

2

A5183

3

St Agnell's
Farm

M1

Lybury Lane

Redbourn
Recreation
Centre

Dunstable

Rd

Nicholls
Farm

St Luke's
School

Blackhorse La
Linden Rd
Aysgarth
Road

Red

4

Sco
Far

Greenlane
Farm

Tassell Hall
Police
Station

Hilltop

Coopers
Meadow

Long Cutt

Crouch
Hall

Long Cutt

Bettespol
Mdw

Cavan Rd

Crech cots

130

Ridgedown
Holls Cl
Redbourn
Junior &
Infant School

Lords Meadow

The
Me
Practice

5

Snatchup

Lybury

Rickyard
Meadow

Doxey
Edge

Wheatcroft Md

Lane

Church End

Lane

Rd

Flamsteadbury
Farm

St Stephens
Wy

Brache
Cl

North

Common

Hempstead

Hempstead

Silk Mill
House Mus
Silk Mill
Road

Mansdale
Rd

Saberton
Cl

Flamsteadbury La
Ben
Austins

Church
End

Church End

6

Hemel Hempstead Rd
Nicky Line

B487

AL3

Gaddesden Lane

Gaddesden Lane

B487

7

Flowers
Farm

Holtsmere
End

Great Revel
End Farm

HEMPSTEAD

ROAD

Aubrey
Lane

8

Little Revel
End

Nicky Line

Holtsmere

End

HEMEL

Nicky Line

M1

Dane End
Farm

Barnershall Wood
Braemar
Blair Cl
Vall V Green

Road
Glam
1

Woodhall Farm
Surgery

shenley

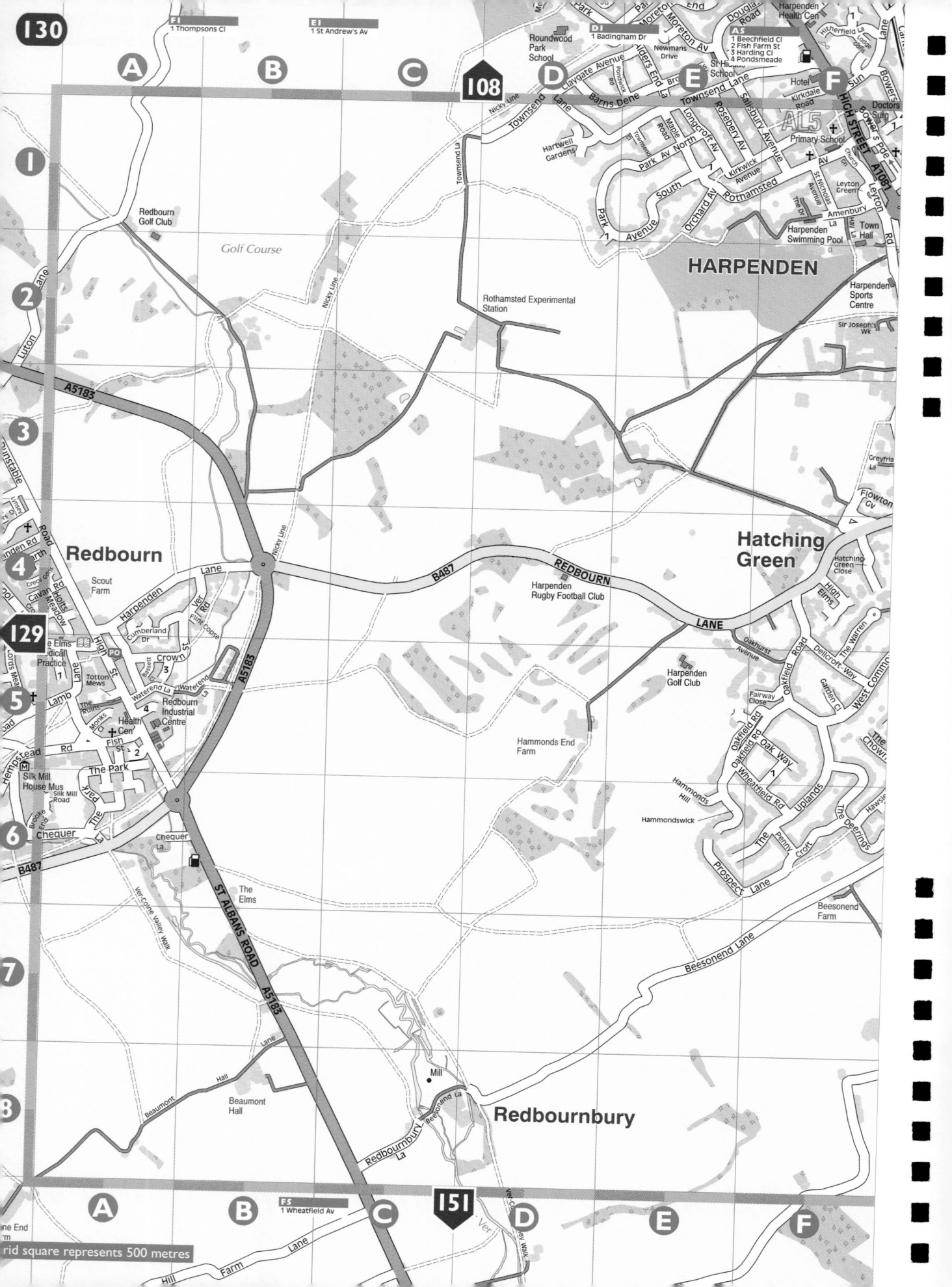

A **B** **C** 108 **D** **E** **F**

F1
1 Thompsons Cl

E1
1 St Andrew's Av

D1
1 Badingham Dr

A5
1 Beechfield Cl
2 Fish Farm St
3 Harding Cl
4 Pondsmead

Hitherfield La
Harpenden Health Cen

Roundwood Park School

Douglas Road
Moreton End
Moreton Av
Bowers Pde

Sun

HIGH STREET A1081

Doctors Surg

POWER'S Pde

Hotel
Kirkdale Road

Primary School
AL5

Newmans Drive
St Hilda's School

Claygate Avenue
Townsend Lane
Barns Dene

Townsend La

Hartwell Gardens

Leyton Green
St Nicholas Avenue
The Dri

Park Av North
Longcroft Av
Roseberry Av
Salisbury Avenue
Kirkwick Avenue

Amenbury La

Leyton Rd
Church Grn
Hay La

Town Hall

1

Redbourn Golf Club

Park Avenue South
Orchard AV
Rothamsted

Harpenden Swimming Pool

Golf Course

HARPENDEN

Luton Lane

2

A5183

Nicky Line

Rothamsted Experimental Station

Harpenden Sports Centre

Sir Joseph's Wk

3

Dunstable Road

Greyfriars La
Flowton Gv

Redbourn

Harpenden Lane
Nicky Line

B487 **REDBOURN**

Hatching Green

Hatching Green Close

4

Scout Farm

Ver Rd
Flint Copse

Harpenden Rugby Football Club

LANE

High Elms

Cumberland Dr

129

The Elms Medical Practice
PO
Crown
3
1

Oakhurst Avenue
Oakfield Road
Dellcroft Way
Garden Cl
The Warren
West Common

5

Bessett
Totton Mews
Waterend La
Waterend La
A5183

Redbourn Industrial Centre

Harpenden Golf Club

Fairway Close

The Chowns

Lamb
Monks
The Ruins
4
Health Cen'

Oakfield Rd
Oak Way
1

Wheatfield Rd

Uplands

Hempstead Rd
Fish St
2

Hammonds End Farm

Hammonds Hill

The Deerings

Silk Mill House Mus
Silk Mill Road

The Park

Hammondswick

The Penny Croft

Hawside

6

Chequer
Chequer La

Prospect Lane

B487

St Elms

7

St Albans Road
A5183

Beesonend Lane

Beesonend Farm

Ver-Colne Valley Walk

The Elms

Lane

8

Beaumont Hall
Beaumont Hall

Mill

Redbournbury

Redbournbury La
Beesonend La

Ver-Colne Valley Walk

Lane End

A **B** C 151 **D** **E** **F**

Leasey Bridge

Harpenden Common

Ayres End

Childwick Green

Aldwickbury Park Golf Club

Harpenden Memorial Hosp

The Elms Practice

Harpenden Station

St Dominic RC School

Southdown Industrial Estate

The Grove JMI School

The Grove Infant School

Cross Farm

West End Farm

Harpenden Common Golf Club

Childwick Hall

Hedge's Farm

Cheapside Farm

Sandridgebury

Wheathampstead Road

Ayres End Lane

Cross Lane

Limbrick Road

West Common

St Albans Road

A1081

Pipers

The Grove

G
G4
1 Hadleigh Ct
2 Tiverton Ct

H
Ch lw Bury
J4
1 Bewdley Cl
2 Camberley Pl
3 Ennis Cl
4 Lilac Wy
5 Newton Cl
6 Ravenscroft
7 Sandhurst Ct

J

K
J3
1 Pendennis Ct

L
1 Dalewood
2 Englehurst
3 Fairfield Cl
4 Wendover Cl

M
H3
1 The Chennies
2 Gorselands
3 Linwood Rd
4 St John's Ct
5 Walkers Cl

G
G1
1 Poets Ct
2 Victoria Rd

H
G5
1 West Common Cl

J
H1
Mar 1 Overstone Rd

K

L
H2
1 Barnfield Ct
2 Gordons Wk

M

109

1 2 3 4 5 6 7 8

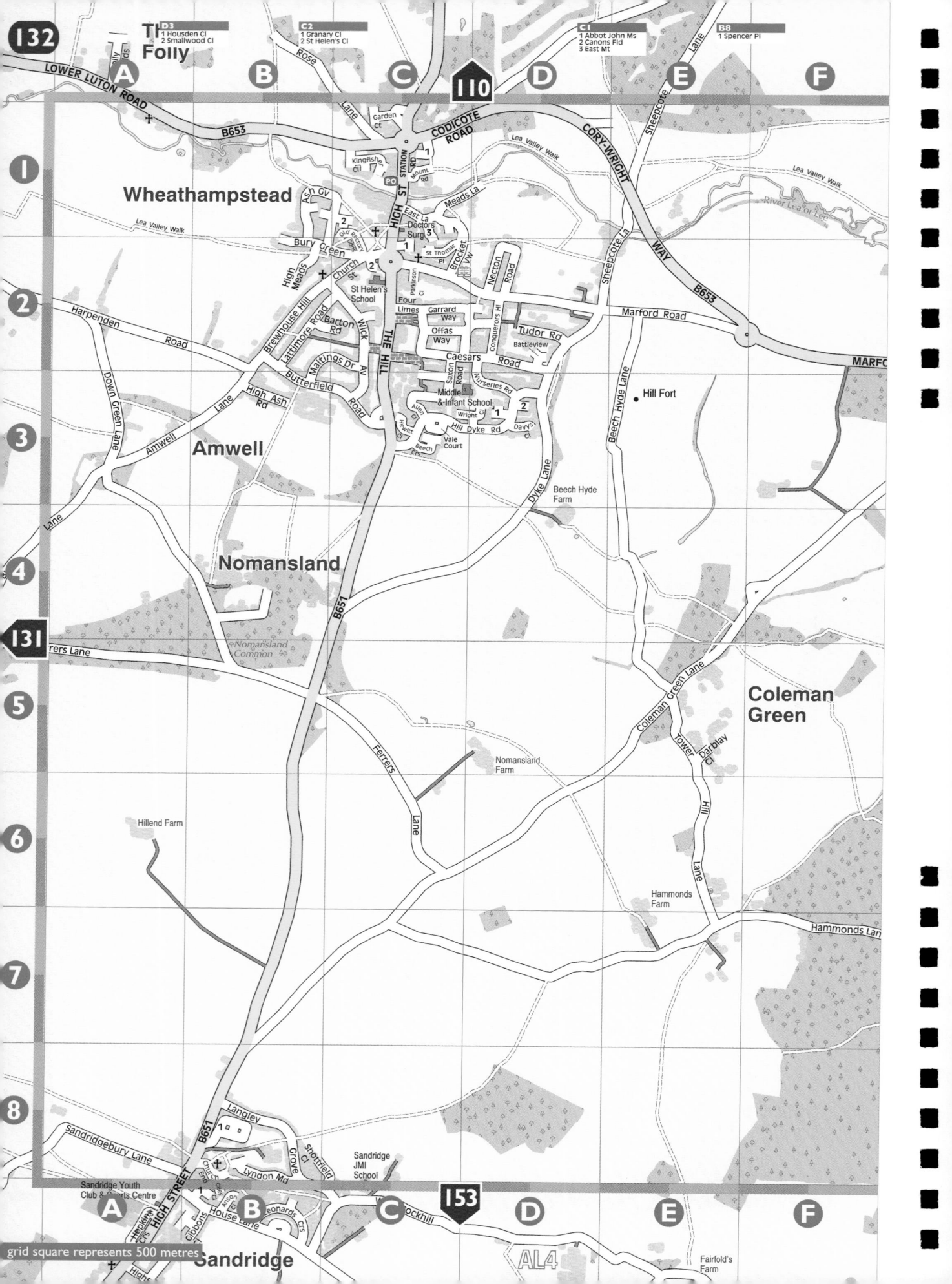
D3
1 Housden Cl
2 Smallwood Cl
C2
1 Granary Cl
2 St Helen's Cl
C1
1 Abbot John Ms
2 Canons Fld
3 East Mt
B8
1 Spencer Pl
110
131
153
Wheathampstead
Amwell
Nomansland
Coleman Green
Sandridge
Lower Luton Road
B653
Codicote Road
Cory-Wright Way
Lea Valley Walk
River Lea or Lee
High St
Station Rd
Mount Rd
Meads La
East La
Doctors Surg
Kingfisher Cl
Ash Gv
Bury Green
Old Rectory Gdns
High Meads
Church St
St Helen's School
Parkinson Cl
Brocket Vw
St Thomas Pl
Necton Road
Four Limes
Garrard Way
Offas Way
Conquerors Hl
Tudor Rd
Battleview
Marford Road
Harpenden Road
Brewhouse Hill
Lattimore Road
Barton Rd
Wick Av
The Hill
Maltings Dr
Caesars Road
Saxon Road
Nurseries Rd
Butterfield Road
High Ash Rd
Middle & Infant School
Allen
Wright Cl
Hewitt
Hill Dyke Rd
Davys Cl
Vale Court
Beech Crs
Down Green Lane
Amwell Lane
Beech Hyde Lane
Hill Fort
Sheepcote La
Sheepcote Lane
Dyke Lane
Beech Hyde Farm
B651
Nomansland Common
Ferrers Lane
Coleman Green Lane
Tower Hill Lane
Darblay Cl
Nomansland Farm
Hillend Farm
Hammonds Farm
Hammonds Lane
Langley Grove
Sandridgebury Lane
Shottfield
Sandridge JMI School
Lyndon Md
Church End
Sandridge Youth Club & Sports Centre
High Street
Anson
House Lane
Leonards Crs
Gibbons
Hopkins Crs
Cockhill
AL4
Fairfold's Farm
grid square represents 500 metres
A B C D E F
1 2 3 4 5 6 7 8

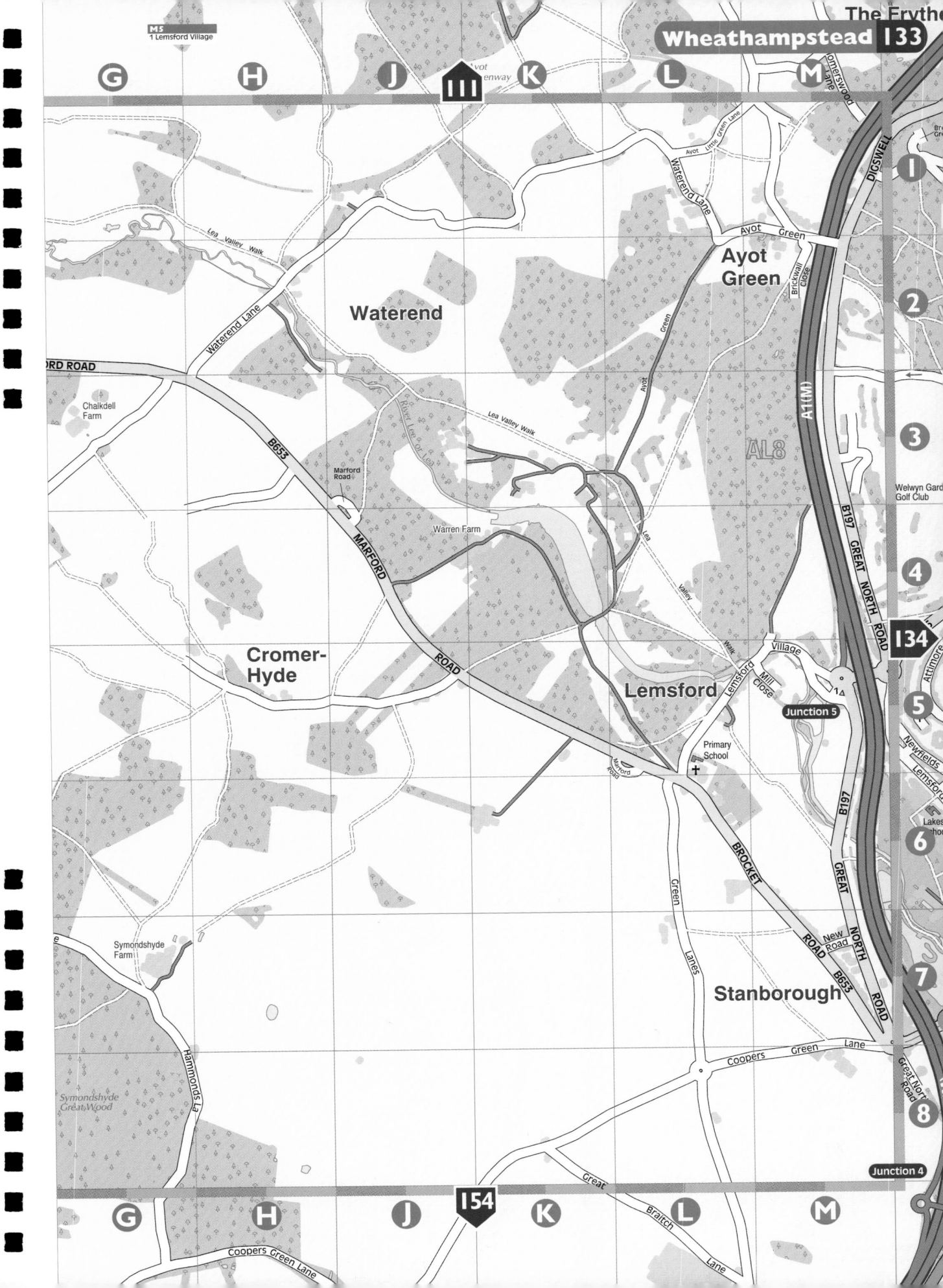

Wheathampstead 133
The Frythe
M5
1 Lemsford Village
111
154
134
Waterend
Ayot Green
Cromer-Hyde
Lemsford
Stanborough
Chalkdell Farm
Marford Road
Warren Farm
Symondshyde Farm
Symondshyde Great Wood
Primary School
Junction 5
Junction 4
Welwyn Garden Golf Club
AL8
Lea Valley Walk
Waterend Lane
Ayot Green
Ayot Little Green Lane
Brickwall Close
DIGSWELL
A1(M)
B653
MARFORD ROAD
BROCKET ROAD
B197 GREAT NORTH ROAD
River Lee or Lea
Lemsford Village
Mill Close
New Road
Green Lanes
Coopers Green Lane
Great Braitch Lane
Hammonds La
Great North Road
Newfields

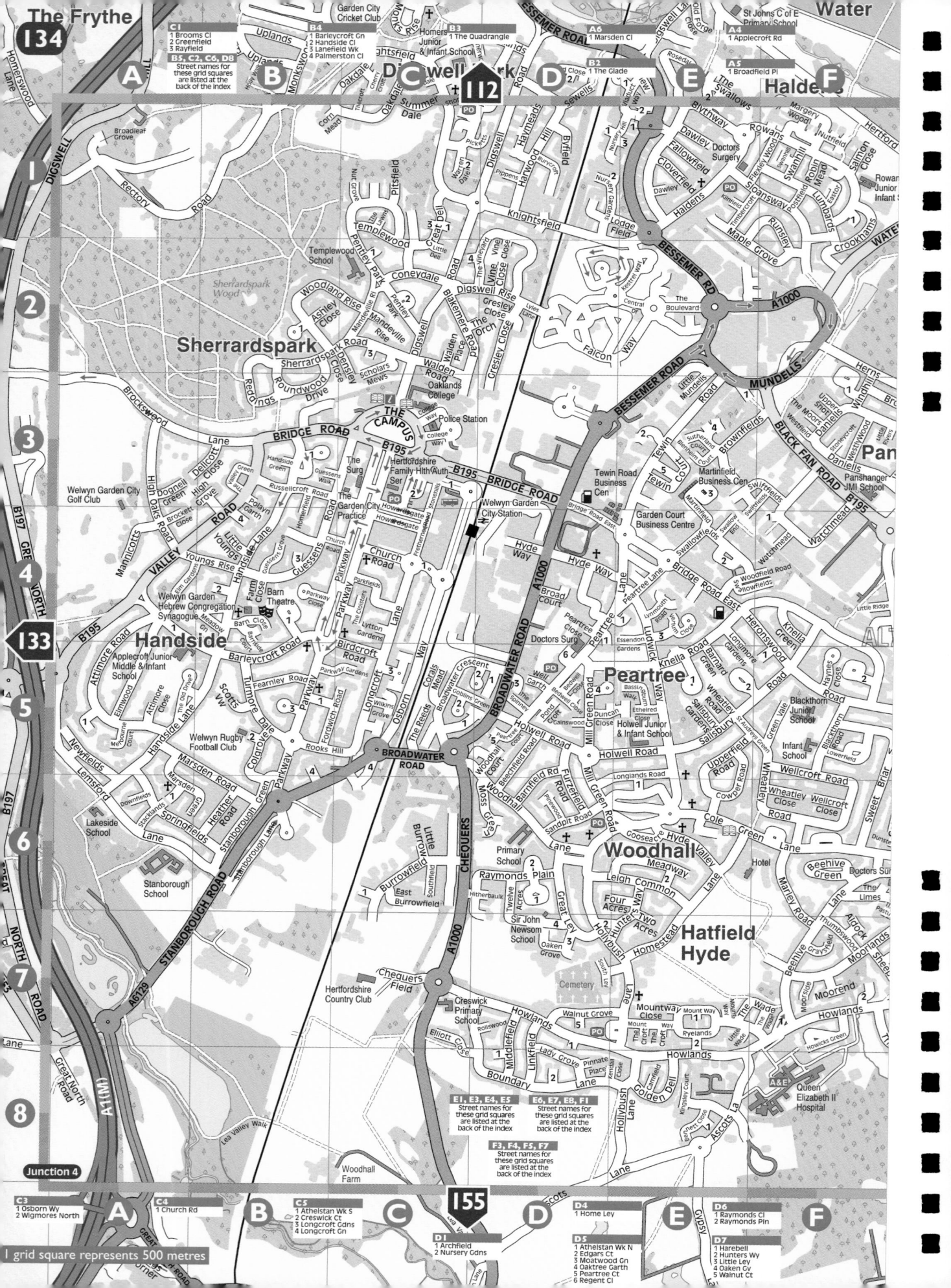

The Frythe
134
C1
1 Brooms Cl
2 Greenfield
3 Rayfield
B5, C2, C6, D8
Street names for these grid squares are listed at the back of the index
B4
1 Barleycroft Gn
2 Handside Cl
3 Lanefield Wk
4 Palmerston Cl
Garden City Cricket Club
B3
1 The Quadrangle
A6
1 Marsden Cl
B2
1 The Glade
St Johns C of E Primary School
A4
1 Applecroft Rd
A5
1 Broadfield Pl
Water
Haldens
112
A
B
C
D
E
F
1
2
3
4
5
6
7
8
133
155
Digswell Park
Sherrardspark Wood
Sherrardspark
Templewood School
Oaklands College
THE CAMPUS
Police Station
Hertfordshire Family Hlth Auth Ser
The Garden City Practice
Welwyn Garden City Station
Welwyn Garden City Golf Club
Welwyn Garden Hebrew Congregation Synagogue
Barn Theatre
Handside
Applecroft Junior Middle & Infant School
Welwyn Rugby Football Club
Lakeside School
Stanborough School
Tewin Road Business Cen
Martinfield Business Cen
Garden Court Business Centre
Panshanger JMI School
Doctors Surgery
Doctors Surg
Peartree
Holwell Junior & Infant School
Blackthorn Junior School
Infant School
Woodhall
Primary School
Sir John Newsom School
Hatfield Hyde
Cemetery
Creswick Primary School
Hertfordshire Country Club
Queen Elizabeth II Hospital
A&E
Hotel
Woodhall Farm
BESSEMER ROAD
BESSEMER RD
BRIDGE ROAD
BROADWATER ROAD
STANBOROUGH ROAD
CHEQUERS
BLACK FAN ROAD
MUNDELLS
VALLEY ROAD
A1000
A6129
B195
B197
A1(M)
GREAT NORTH ROAD
Junction 4
E1, E3, E4, E5
Street names for these grid squares are listed at the back of the index
E6, E7, E8, F1
Street names for these grid squares are listed at the back of the index
F3, F4, F5, F7
Street names for these grid squares are listed at the back of the index
C3
1 Osborn Wy
2 Wigmores North
C4
1 Church Rd
C5
1 Athelstan Wk S
2 Creswick Ct
3 Longcroft Gdns
4 Longcroft Gn
D1
1 Archfield
2 Nursery Gdns
D4
1 Home Ley
D5
1 Athelstan Wk N
2 Edgars Ct
3 Moatwood Gn
4 Oaktree Garth
5 Peartree Ct
6 Regent Cl
D6
1 Raymonds Cl
2 Raymonds Pln
D7
1 Harebell
2 Hunters Wy
3 Little Ley
4 Oaken Gv
5 Walnut Ct
1 grid square represents 500 metres

G3
1 Buddcroft
2 Claycroft
3 Kingscroft
4 Nettlecroft
5 Smallcroft
6 Strawfields
7 Waterfield
8 Wheatbarn
G4
1 Gaddesden Gv
2 The Paddocks
3 Wyddial Gn
G5, G6, H4
Street names for these grid squares are listed at the back of the index
113
Tewin School
Grass Warren
Tewin Bury Farm
Churchfield Road
HERTFORD ROAD
WELWYN GARDEN CITY
Panshanger Golf Club
Old Herns Lane
Archers Green Lane
Doctors Surgery
Tewin Mill House
Warrengate Farm
B1000
Herns Lane
Football & Social Club
Money Hole Lane
Springmead JMI School
Panshanger
Sir Frederic Osborn School
Panshanger Aerodrome
Watchlytes JMI School
Panshanger Drive
BLACK FAN ROAD
Marden Hill
Chain Walk
Hertford Road
136
Birchall
B195
COLE GREEN LANE
BIRCHALL LANE
Birchall Lane
The Old Coach Road
Cole Green
A414
Hall Grove
Commonswood JMI School
Holwell Hyde Lane
Lea Valley Walk
Station Road
Letty Green
156
J4
1 Hunsdon
2 Northwood
3 Oakington
4 Roseacre Gdns
5 Somersham
6 Stapleford
7 Sylvan Wy
8 Tempsford
9 Waterbeach
J3
1 Chedburgh
2 Lysander Wy
H5
1 Aspen Wy
2 Birchall Wd
3 Copperfields
4 Forresters Dr
5 Glenwood
6 High Wickfield
7 Holwell Hyde
8 Pelham Ct
9 Ploughmans End
10 Poppyfields
H3
1 Hedgebrooms
G7
1 Dayemead
HERTFORD ROAD

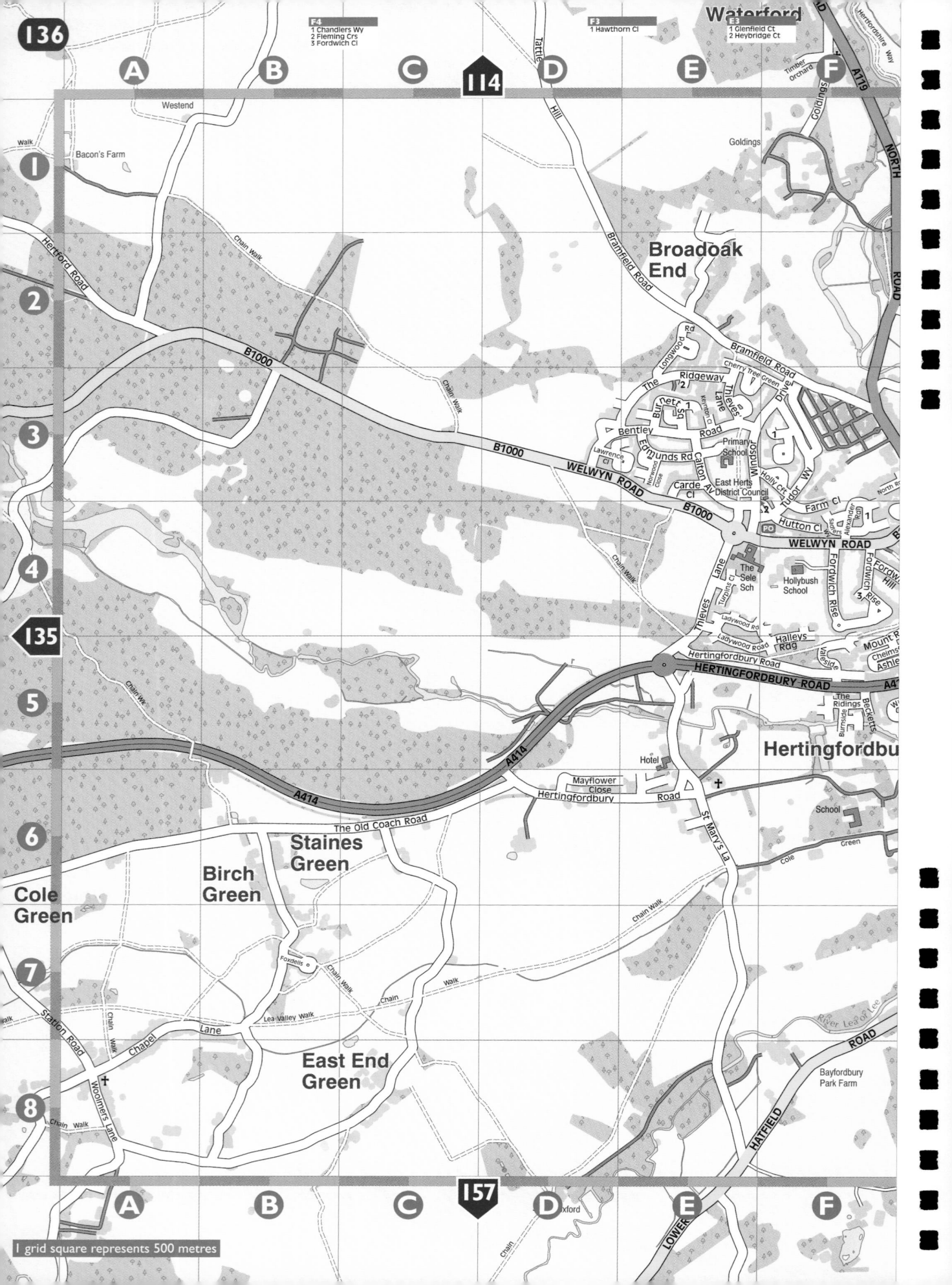
Waterford
F4
1 Chandlers Wy
2 Fleming Crs
3 Fordwich Cl
F3
1 Hawthorn Cl
E3
1 Glenfield Ct
2 Heybridge Ct
114
135
157
Westend
Bacon's Farm
Goldings
Broadoak End
Bramfield Road
Tattle Hill
Hertford Road
Chain Walk
B1000
WELWYN ROAD
A414
HERTINGFORDBURY ROAD
Hertingfordbury Road
The Ridgeway
Thieves Lane
Bentley
Edmunds Rd
Calton Av
Primary School
East Herts District Council
Windsor Drive
Tudor Wy
Holly Cft
Farm Cl
Hutton Cl
The Sele Sch
Hollybush School
Fordwich Rise
Fordwich Hill
Ladywood Road
Halleys Rdg
Hertingfordbury
Hotel
Mayflower Close
St Mary's La
School
Cole Green
Staines Green
Birch Green
The Old Coach Road
Foxdells
Lea Valley Walk
Chapel Lane
Station Road
Woolmers Lane
East End Green
River Lea or Lee
HATFIELD ROAD
Bayfordbury Park Farm
NORTH ROAD
A119
LOWER
1 grid square represents 500 metres

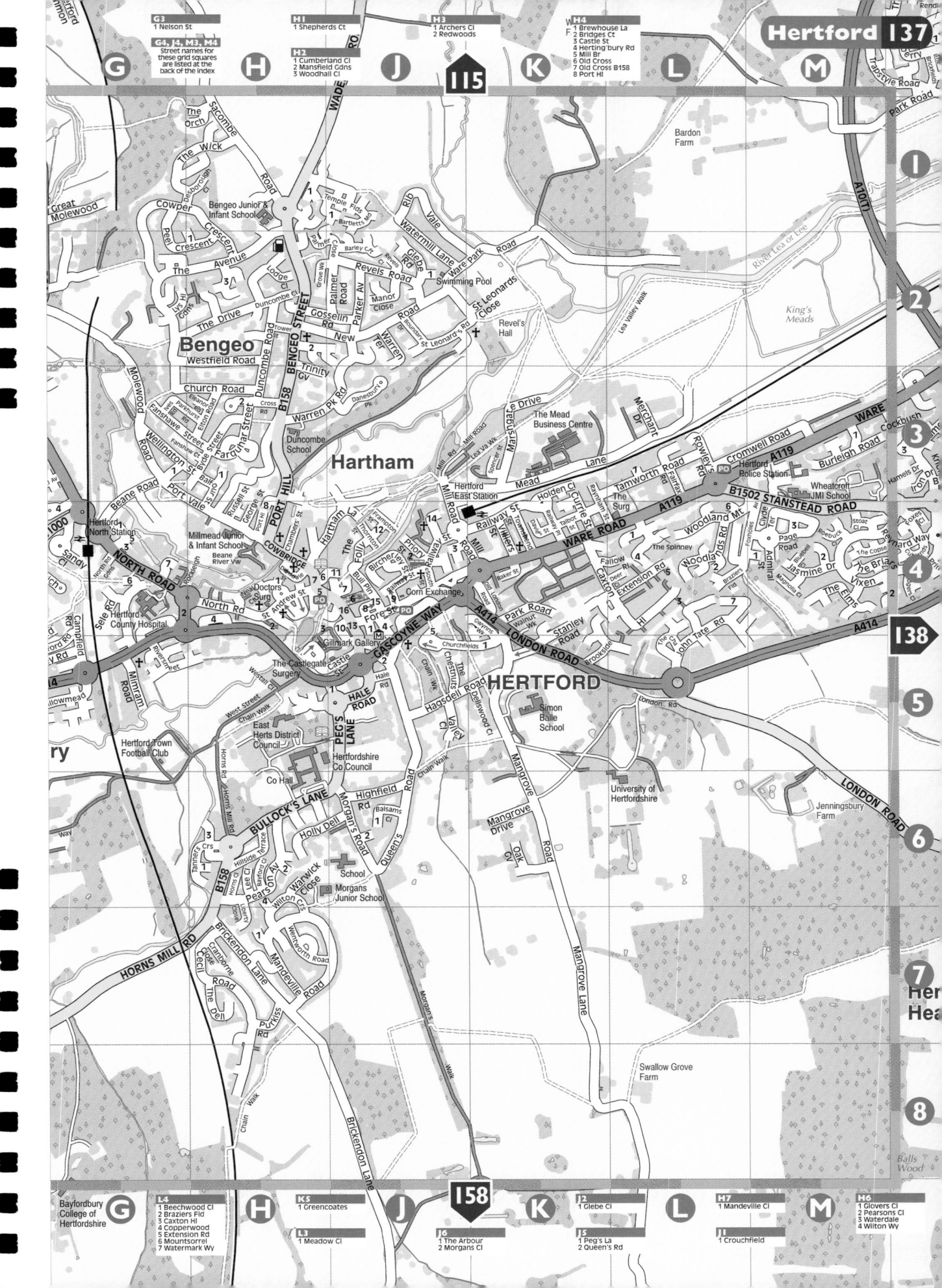

G

H

J

K

L

M

G3
1 Nelson St
G4, J4, M3, M4
Street names for
these grid squares
are listed at the
back of the index

H1
1 Shepherds Ct

H2
1 Cumberland Cl
2 Mansfield Gdns
3 Woodhall Cl

H3
1 Archers Cl
2 Redwoods

H4
F
1 Brewhouse La
2 Bridges Ct
3 Castle St
4 Herting'bury Rd
5 Mill Br
6 Old Cross
7 Old Cross B158
8 Port Hl

115

I

2

3

138

4

5

6

7
Her
Hea

8

The Orch
Sacombe Road
The Wick
Cowper Crescent
Peel Crescent
The Avenue
The Drive
Bengeo
Westfield Road
Church Road
Molewood Road
Fanshawe Street
Wellington St
Beane Road
Port Vale
Bengeo Junior & Infant School
Temple Flds
Bartlett's
Revels Road
Gosselin Rd
New
Warren Ter
Trinity
Warren Pk Rd
Danesbury Pk
Duncombe School
Hartham
Watermill Lane
Rib Vale
Glebe Rd
Ware Park Road
Swimming Pool
St Leonards Close
Revel's Hall
Manor Close
St Leonard's Rd
Mansgate Drive
The Mead Business Centre
Merchant Dr
Lane
Mead
WARE
Cockbush
Cromwell Road
A119
Hertford Police Station
Burleigh Road
Hamels Dr
Tamworth Road
Rowley's Rd
B1502 STANSTEAD ROAD
The Surg
A119
Woodland Mt
Wheatcroft JMI School
The Copse
Reynard Way
Page Road
Jasmine Dr
The Briars
Vixen
The Elms
Hertford North Station
North Rd
NORTH ROAD
Millmead Junior & Infant School
Beane River Vw
Port Hill
Cowbridge
George St
Hartham
Hertford East Station
Mill Road
Railway St
Holden Cl
Currie St
The Surg
Fallow Deer
Extension Rd
Brazier's Fld
Admiral St
The Spinney
Woodland Rd
Magnolia Cl
See Hertford County Hospital
North Rd
St Andrew St
Fore St
Corn Exchange
Gillmark Gallery
CASCOYNE WAY
A414
Park Road
Stanley Rd
Walnut Wk
London Rd
A414
Doctors Surg
The Castlegate Surgery
Castle St
Hale Rd
HALE ROAD
Churchfields
HERTFORD
Simon Balle School
Brookside
London Rd
Jenningsbury Farm
LONDON ROAD
Hertford Town Football Club
West Street
East Herts District Council
Chain Walk
PEG'S LANE
Co Hall
Hertfordshire Co Council
Highfield Rd
Hagsdell Road
Delswood Cl
Valley Road
Chain Walk
Mangrove Road
University of Hertfordshire
Mimram Road
Willowmead
Horns Rd
Horns Mill Rd
BULLOCK'S LANE
Holly Dell
Balsams Cl
Queen's Road
School
Warwick Close
Morgans Junior School
Mangrove Drive
Oak
HORNS MILL RD
B158
Tanners Crs
Bayford Terrace
Hillside
Pearson Av
Brickendon Lane
Mandeville Road
Cecil Road
The Dell
Purkiss Rd
Wentworth Road
Morgans
Mangrove Lane
Swallow Grove Farm
Balls Wood

King's Meads
River Lea or Lee
Park Road
A10(T)
Trapstyle Road
Bardon Farm
Great Molewood

158

Bayfordbury
College of
Hertfordshire
G

L4
1 Beechwood Cl
2 Braziers Fld
3 Caxton Hl
4 Copperwood
5 Extension Rd
6 Mountsorrel
7 Watermark Wy

K5
1 Greencoates

L3
1 Meadow Cl

J6
1 The Arbour
2 Morgans Cl

J2
1 Glebe Cl

J5
1 Peg's La
2 Queen's Rd

J1
1 Crouchfield

H7
1 Mandeville Cl

H6
1 Glovers Cl
2 Pearsons Cl
3 Waterdale
4 Wilton Wy

138
116
137
159
A
B
C
D
E
F
1
2
3
4
5
6
7
8
C2
1 College Cl
2 The Grotto
A7
1 The Paddocks
C1
1 Bluecoat Yd
2 Bridge Foot
3 George Wk
A4
1 The Finches
2 The Squirrels
A6
1 Woodstock Cl
A3
1 Birdie Wy
2 Cotton Dr
3 Divot Pl
4 Ryder Cl
WARE
The Chauncy School
Presdales
Rush Green
Great Amwell
St Margarets
Hertford Heath
Hailey
Golding's Wood
Balls Wood
Brides Farm
Haileybury College
Hailey Hall School
St John Baptist School
Pine Wood School
Middleton School
Presdales School
East Herts Golf Clubhouse
Hertford Regional College
Ware Station
Mill Studio Business Centre
Sacred Heart RC School
Mercers Coll
River Lee Navigation
Lea Valley Walk
HERTFORD ROAD
LONDON ROAD
AMWELL HILL
PEPPER HILL
WARE ROAD
STANSTEAD ROAD
WIDBURY HILL
STAR ST
HIGH ST
VIADUCT RD
A10(T)
A1170
A119
B1004
B7502
B1197
A10
Walnut Tree Walk
Hoe Lane
Downfield Road
Hailey Lane
College Road
Hollycross Road
Lower Road
D1
1 Common Whf
2 Wickhams Whf
E1
1 Barley Ponds Cl
2 Belle Vue Rd
3 Musleigh Manor
4 Widbury Gdns
E5
1 Madgeways Cl
F3
1 Black Smiths Cl
F8
1 Galley Gn
grid square represents 500 metres

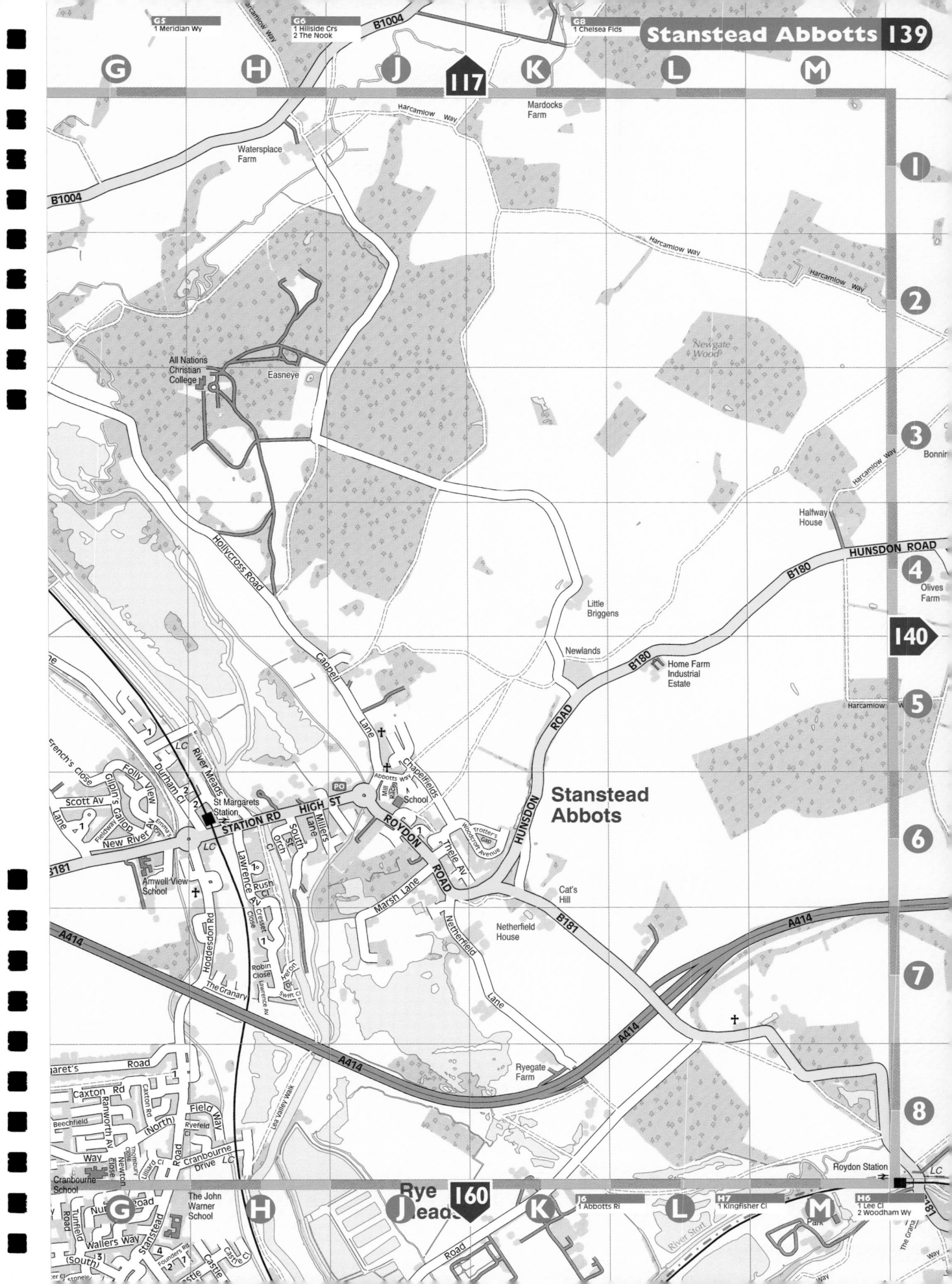

G5
1 Meridian Wy

G6
1 Hillside Crs
2 The Nook

G8
1 Chelsea Flds

B1004

G   H   J   117   K   L   M

Harcamlow Way

Mardocks
Farm

Watersplace
Farm

B1004

Harcamlow Way

I

Harcamlow Way

2

Newgate
Wood

3

Bonnin

All Nations
Christian College

Easneye

Harcamlow Way

Halfway
House

Hollycross Road

HUNSDON ROAD

B180

4

Olives
Farm

Little
Briggens

140

Capdell Lane

Newlands

B180

Home Farm
Industrial
Estate

Harcamlow W

5

LC

River Meads

French's close

Durham Cl

Folly View

Gilpin's Gallop

Scott Av

Emma Cl

Fieldway

New River

St Margarets
Station

PO

Abbots Way

Chapelfields

Mill
Race

School

Stanstead
Abbots

6

B3181

Amwell View
School

STATION RD

HIGH ST

Millers Lane

South St

Orch

Rush Cl

Lawrence Rd

Cresset

LC

ROYDON

Trotters
Gap

Woodcroft Avenue

Thele Av

HUNSDON ROAD

Cat's
Hill

Hoddesdon Rd

Robin
Close

The Granary

Swift Cl

Lawrence Av

Marsh Lane

Netherfield
Lane

Netherfield
House

B3181

A414

7

A414

Ryegate
Farm

A414

St Margaret's Road

Caxton Rd

Beechfield

Ranworth Av

Caxton Rd
(North)

Field Way

Ryefield

Cranbourne
Drive

LC

Lea Valley Walk

Newton Close

Ullard Cl

Thornbury Close

Way

Cranbourne
School

Nut Road

The John
Warner School

Stanstead

Tunfield
Road

Wallers Way

Castle

Founders Rd

Castle

8

Roydon Station

LC

B181

The Gra

G   H   J   160   Rye
Mead   K   L   M

J6
1 Abbotts Ri

H7
1 Kingfisher Cl

H6
1 Lee Cl
2 Woodham Wy

Park

River Stort

140

A B C **118** D E F

1 St Dunstan's Rd

1

Hunsdon Lodge Farm

Fillets Farm

Wheatsheaf Road

Heares Hoppit

Hunsdon

Holland's Croft

Paddock Close

Drury

Hunsdon Lodge Lane

Chestnut Close

HIGH STREET

Drury Lane

PO

Tanners Way

Wicklands Road

Tudor Cl

2

Rectory Close

Acorn Street

Harcamlow Way

3

B180

Spellers

Bonningtons

Copthall

Eastwick Hall Farm

Hunsdonbury

Cockrobin Lane

HUNSDON ROAD

4

Olives Farm

Hunsdon House

Eastwick Hall Lane

139

5

low Way

Lord's Wood

6

Brickhouse Farm

A414

7

Briggen Hotel

Mead Lodge

A414

Stanstead Lodge

Harcamlow Way

Roydon Lea

8

Harcamlow Way

Hertfordshire County

Essex County

ELIZABETH

Canons Gate

Ash Tree

Hobb

don Station

LC

B181

HIGH

LC

A B C **161** D E F

A1169

Canons Brook Golf Club

Roydon

grid square represents 500 metres

Road

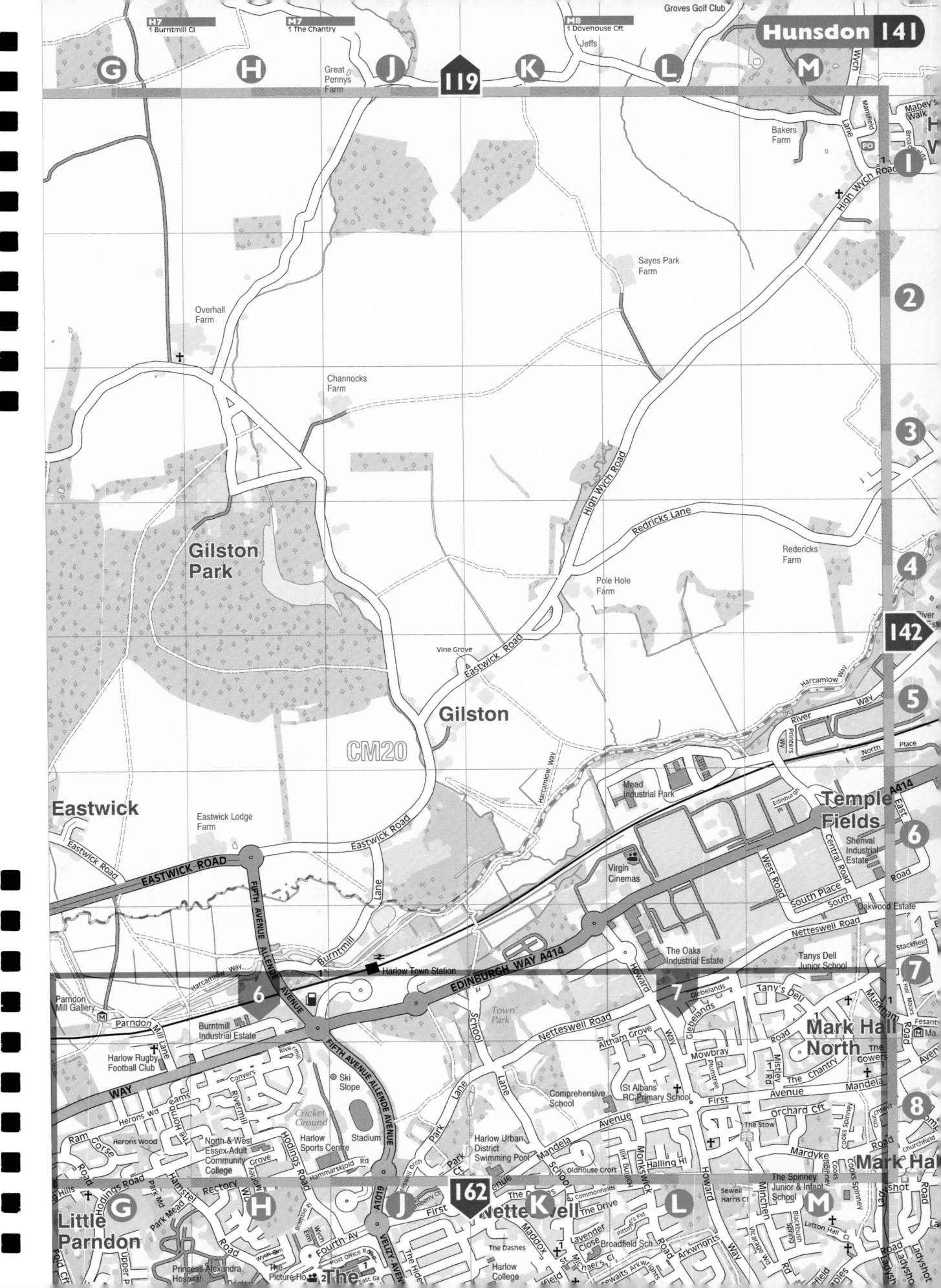

H7 1 Burntmill Cl
M7 1 The Chantry
M8 1 Dovehouse Cft
Groves Golf Club
Jeffs
Great Pennys Farm
119
Bakers Farm
Mabey's Walk
High Wych Road
Sayes Park Farm
Overhall Farm
Channocks Farm
High Wych Road
Redricks Lane
Redericks Farm
Gilston Park
Pole Hole Farm
142
Vine Grove
Eastwick Road
Gilston
Harcamlow Way
River Way
CM20
Mead Industrial Park
Temple Fields
Eastwick
Eastwick Lodge Farm
Eastwick Road
EASTWICK ROAD
FIFTH AVENUE ALLENDE AVENUE
Virgin Cinemas
West Road
Central Road
Shenval Industrial Estate
South Place
Oakwood Estate
Netteswell Road
The Oaks Industrial Estate
Tanys Dell Junior School
Harlow Town Station
EDINBURGH WAY A414
Parndon Mill Gallery
Burntmill Industrial Estate
Harlow Rugby Football Club
Netteswell Road
Town Park
Mark Hall North
Ski Slope
Cricket Ground
Stadium
Harlow Sports Centre
North & West Essex Adult Community College
Comprehensive School
St Albans RC Primary School
Harlow Urban District Swimming Pool
Mandela Avenue
Orchard Cft
Mark Hall
The Spinney Junior & Infant School
162
Little Parndon
Netteswell
Princess Alexandra Hospital
Harlow College

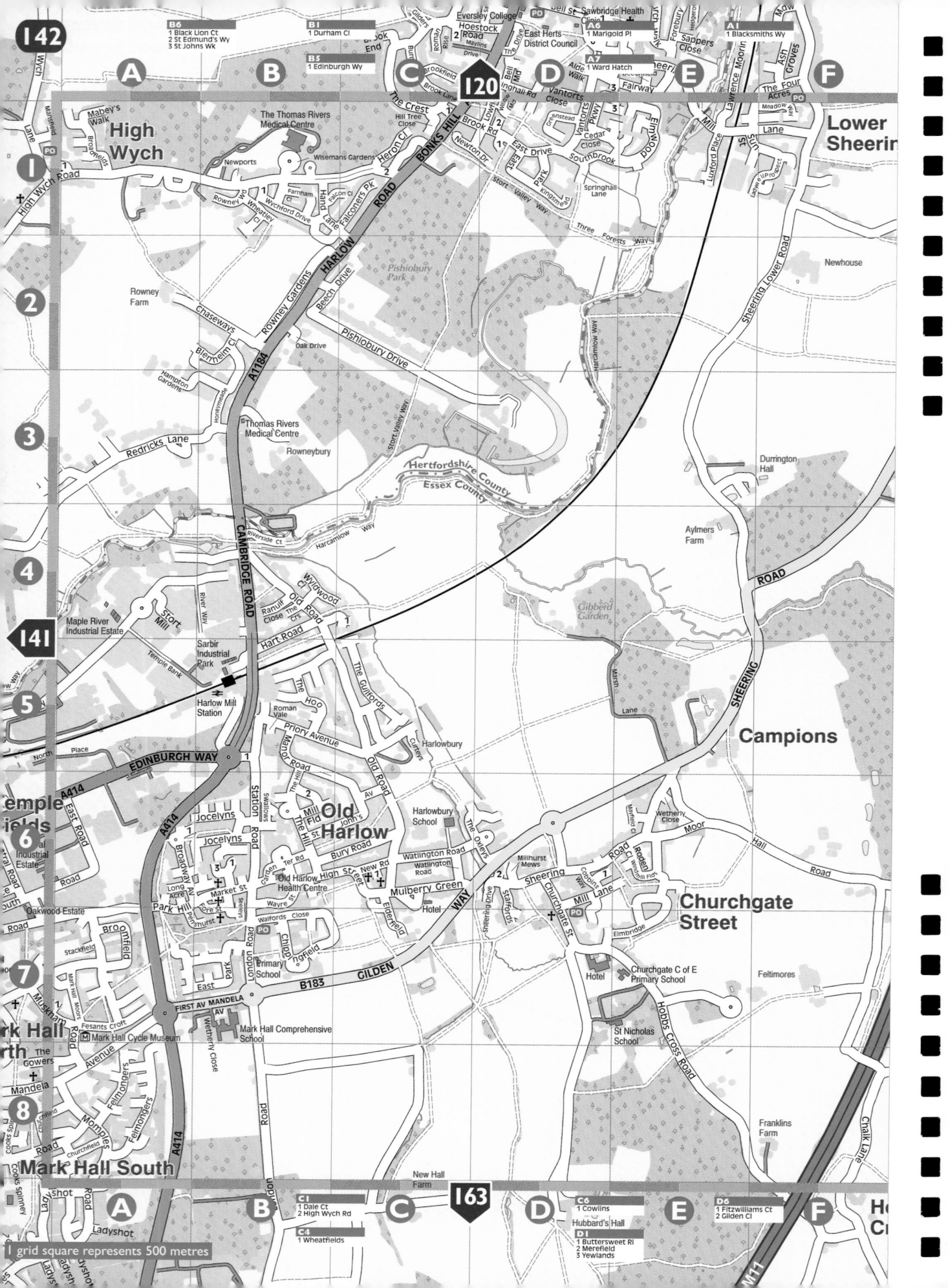
B6
1 Black Lion Ct
2 St Edmund's Wy
3 St Johns Wk
B1
1 Durham Cl
B5
1 Edinburgh Wy
A6
1 Marigold Pl
A7
1 Ward Hatch
A1
1 Blacksmiths Wy
Eversley College
Hoestock Road
Maylins Drive
East Herts District Council
Sawbridge Health Clinic
Sappers Close
Ash Groves
The Four Acres
Meadow Way
120
High Wych
Lower Sheerin
Mabey's Walk
The Thomas Rivers Medical Centre
Wisemans Gardens
Newports
High Wych Road
Rowney Wd
Wheatley Cl
Wychford Drive
Farnham Cl
Hand Lane
Falcon Cl
Falconers Pk
Heron Cl
Bonks Hill
Harlow Road
The Crest
Hill Tree Close
Brook Lane
Brookfield
Brook Rd
Newton Dr
East Drive
Vantorts Close
Vantorts Pkwy
Cedar Close
Elmwood
Southbrook
Kingsmead
Springhall Lane
Stort Valley Way
Three Forests Way
Luxford Place
Lawrence Moorings
Sun St
Lane
Prospect
Sheering Lower Road
Newhouse
Rowney Farm
Rowney Gardens
Beech Drive
Pishiobury Park
Chaseways
Blenheim Cl
Hampton Gardens
Oak Drive
Pishiobury Drive
Harcamlow Way
A1184
Honeymeade
Thomas Rivers Medical Centre
Rowneybury
Redricks Lane
Stort Valley Way
Hertfordshire County
Essex County
Durrington Hall
Riverside Ct
Harcamlow Way
Cambridge Road
Aylmers Farm
Road
Wyldwood Cl
Old Road
Ranulf Close
The Crs
Gibberd Garden
Stort Mill
River Way
Maple River Industrial Estate
141
Hart Road
Sarbir Industrial Park
Temple Bank
Harlow Mill Station
The Hoo
The Gulfords
Marsh Lane
Sheering
Campions
Roman Vale
Priory Avenue
Curteys
Harlowbury
North Place
Edinburgh Way
A414
Manor Road
Old Road
The Hill
Mill Fld
St John's Av
Old Harlow
Temple Fields
East Road
Station Road
Swallows
Jocelyns
Harlowbury School
The Orleys
Wetherly Close
Moor Hall Road
Mayfield Cl
Roden Cl
Windmill Flds
Millhurst Mews
Bury Road
Watlington Road
Ter Rd
Garden Ter Rd
Old Harlow Health Centre
High Street
New Rd
Mulberry Green
Hotel
Sheering Drive
Staffords
Sheering Churchgate St
Cobbins Way
Mill Lane
Churchgate Street
Broadway Av
Market St
Long Acre
Fore St
Seelers
Park Hill
Penshurst
Wayre St
Walfords Close
Elderfield
Elmbridge
Industrial Estate
Oakwood Estate
Broomfield
Stackfield
Chippingfield
London Road
Park
East
Primary School
B183
Gilden Way
Hotel
Churchgate C of E Primary School
Feltimores
Mark Hall Moors
Muskham Road
Fesants Croft
First Av Mandela Av
Wetherly Close
Mark Hall Cycle Museum
Mark Hall Comprehensive School
St Nicholas School
Hobbs Cross Road
The Gowers
Mark Hall North
Avenue
Felmongers
Mandela
Mowbray Road
Momples Road
Churchfield
Cooks Spinney
Mark Hall South
Franklins Farm
Chalk Lane
M11
New Hall Farm
163
Ladyshot
C1
1 Dale Ct
2 High Wych Rd
C4
1 Wheatfields
C6
1 Cowlins
Hubbard's Hall
D1
1 Buttersweet Ri
2 Merefield
3 Yewlands
D6
1 Fitzwilliams Ct
2 Gilden Cl
1 grid square represents 500 metres

121
G
H
J
K
L
M
1
2
3
4
5
6
7
8
Quickbury Farm
Harcamlow Way
Stort Valley Way
Gladwyns
Shrubbs
M11
Plashets
Primley Lane
High Pastures
Crown Cl
Orchard Close
Back Lane
Sheering C of E Primary School
THE STREET
B183
PO
Sheering
Church Lane
B183 HARLOW ROAD
Matching Road
Ardley Crescent
Hotel
Sheering Hall
Wheelers Farm
High Lane
Harlow Road
Newman's End
Housham Hall
Collin's Cross
Matching
Matching Road
Rainbow Road
Matching Tye
Harlow Tye
Carter's Green
Matching Park
Forest Way
Housham Tye
Hobbs Cross
New Way Lane
Faggotters Lane
Loyter's Green

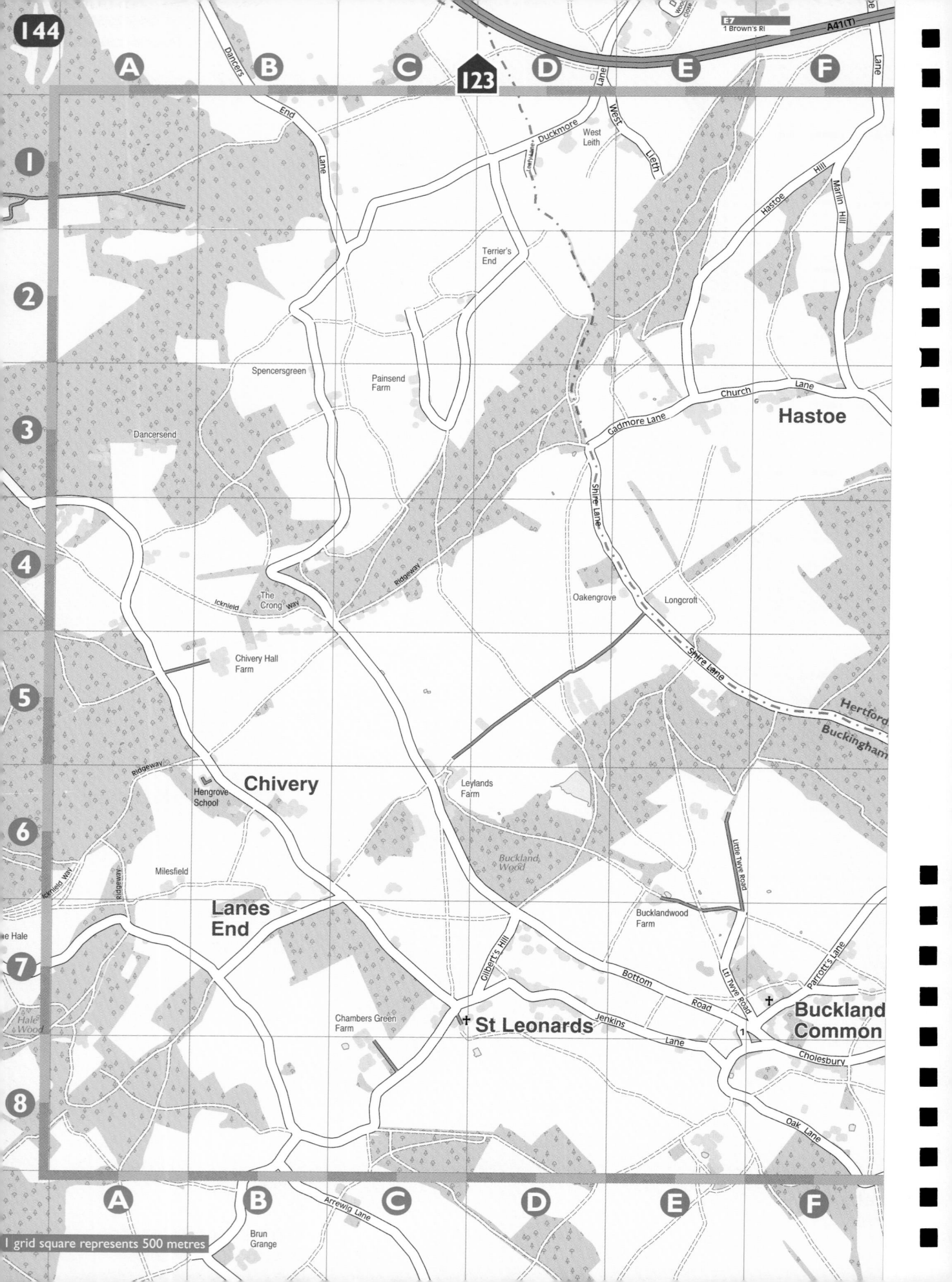

123
A41(T)
E7 1 Brown's Ri
Dancers End Lane
Duckmore Lane
West Lane
West Leith
Leith
Hastoe Hill
Marlin Hill
Terrier's End
Spencersgreen
Painsend Farm
Church Lane
Gadmore Lane
Hastoe
Dancersend
Shire Lane
Ridgeway
The Crong
Icknield Way
Oakengrove
Longcroft
Chivery Hall Farm
Hertford
Buckingham
Ridgeway
Chivery
Hengrove School
Leylands Farm
Buckland Wood
Milesfield
Icknield Way
Ridgeway
Little Twye Road
Lanes End
Bucklandwood Farm
Hale
Gilbert's Hill
Bottom Road
Parrott's Lane
Lt Twye Road
Hale Wood
Chambers Green Farm
St Leonards
Jenkins Lane
Buckland Common
Cholesbury
Oak Lane
Arrewig Lane
Brun Grange
1 grid square represents 500 metres

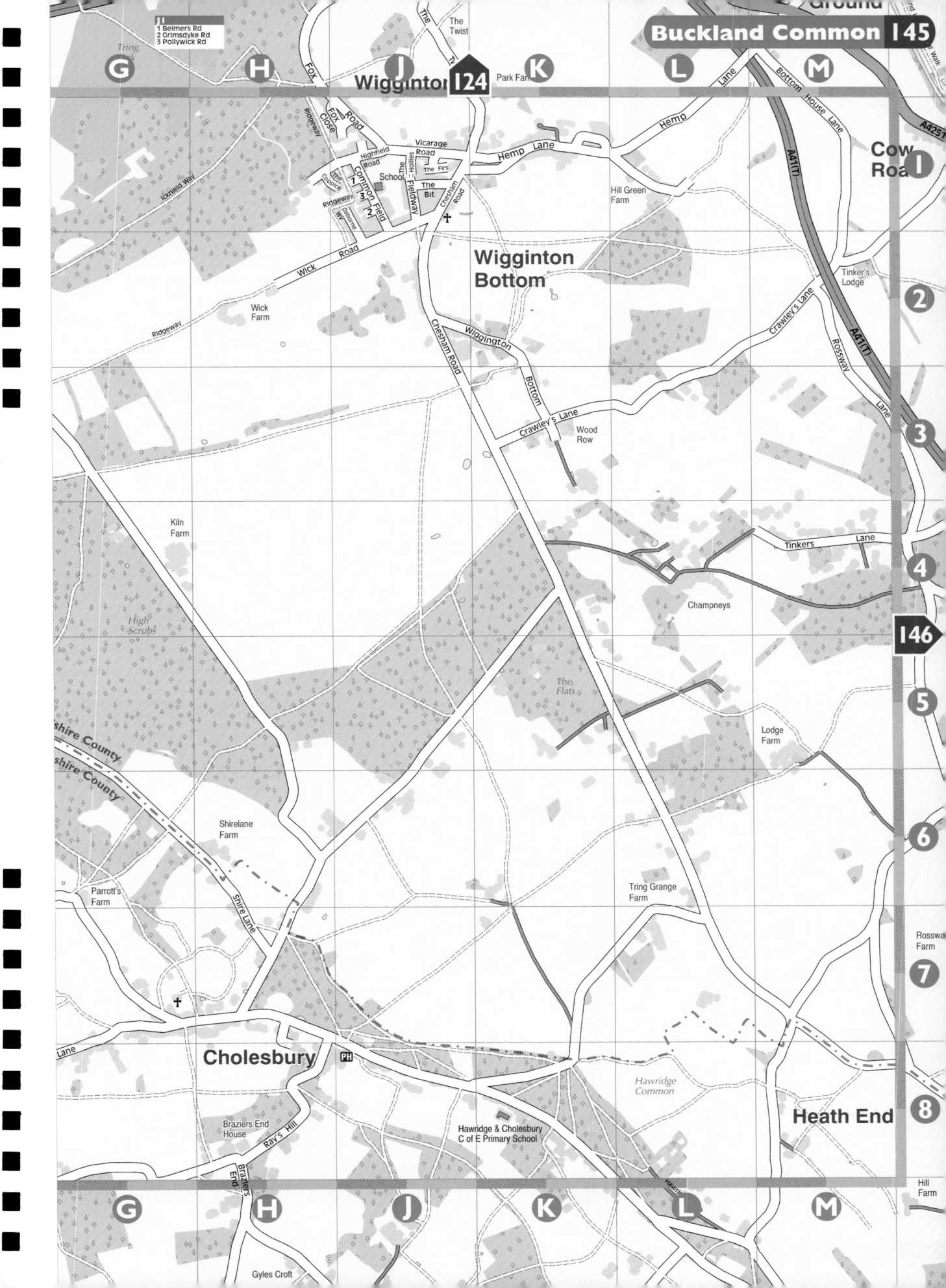

G   H   J   K   L   M

1 Belmers Rd
2 Grimsdyke Rd
3 Pollywick Rd

Tring

Icknield Way

The
The Twist

FOX

Fox
Close

Ridgeway

Highfield
Road

Common Field

The
Coppice

Ridgeway

Osborne
Wy

Wick   Road

School

The
Hollies

Fieldway

The
Bit

Vicarage
Road

The Firs

Chesham
Road

Wigginton **124**

Park Farm

Hemp Lane

Hemp

Bottom House Lane

A4251

**Cow
Roa** **1**

Hill Green
Farm

Tinker's
Lodge

2

Crawley's Lane

Rossway
Lane

A41(T)

A41(T)

**Wigginton
Bottom**

Wick Farm

Ridgeway

Chesham Road

Wigginton
Bottom

Crawley's Lane

Wood
Row

Tinkers   Lane

3

Champneys

146

Kiln
Farm

High
Scrubs

The
Flats

Lodge
Farm

5

...shire County

...shire County

Shirelane
Farm

Tring Grange
Farm

6

Parrott's
Farm

Shire Lane

Rosswa
Farm

7

Lane

Cholesbury

PH

Hawridge
Common

Heath End

8

Braziers End
House

Ray's Hill

Braziers
End

Hawridge & Cholesbury
C of E Primary School

Hawri

Hill
Farm

G   H   J   K   L   M

Gyles Croft

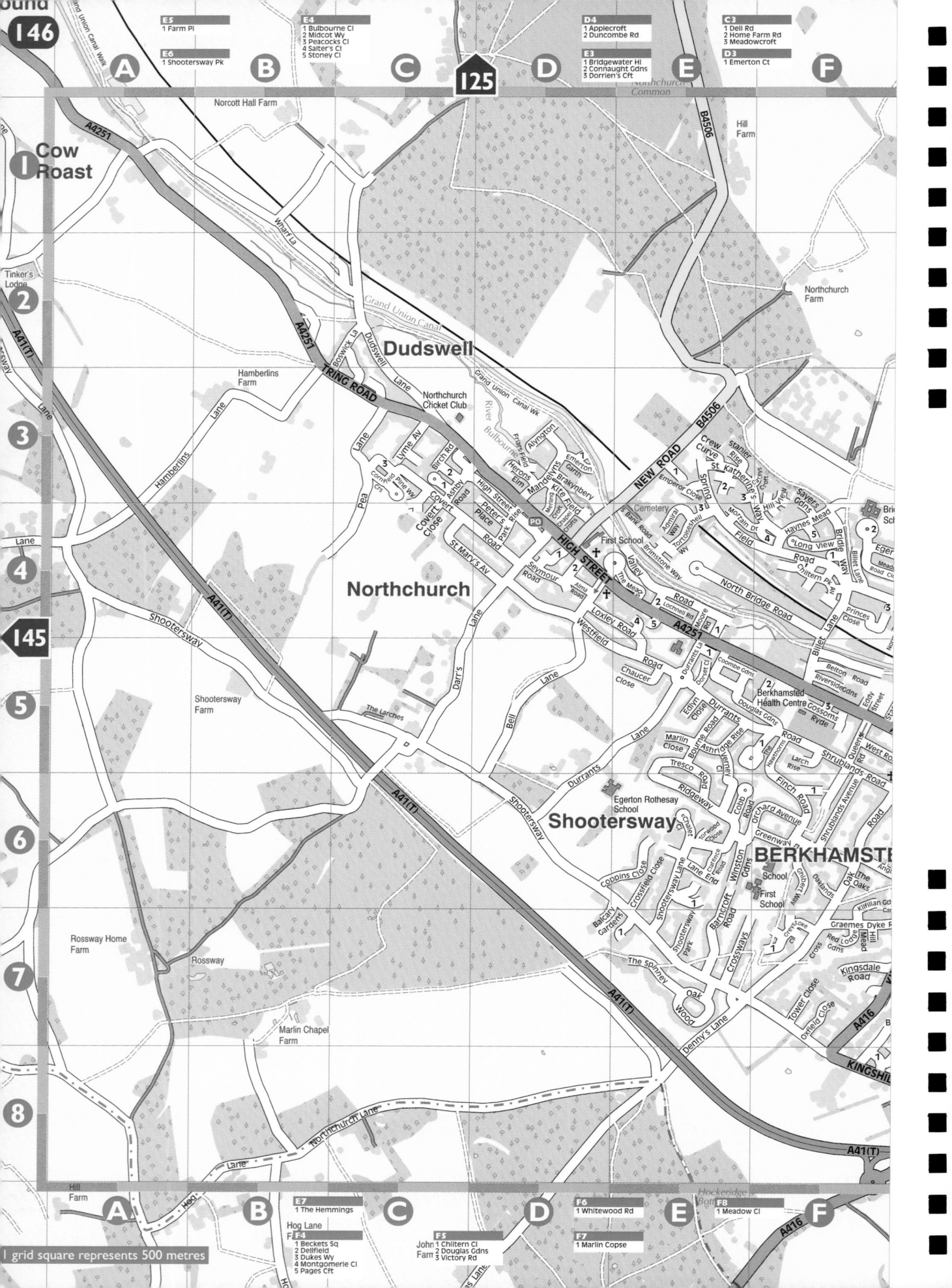

125

E5
1 Farm Pl

E6
1 Shootersway Pk

E4
1 Bulbourne Cl
2 Midcot Wy
3 Peacocks Cl
4 Salter's Cl
5 Stoney Cl

D4
1 Applecroft
2 Duncombe Rd

E3
1 Bridgewater Hl
2 Connaught Gdns
3 Dorrien's Cft

C3
1 Dell Rd
2 Home Farm Rd
3 Meadowcroft

D3
1 Emerton Ct

A   B   C   D   E   F

Cow Roast

Norcott Hall Farm

A4251

Tinker's Lodge

Wharf La

A4251

Dudswell

Grand Union Canal

Hamberlins Farm

TRING ROAD

Boswick La   Dudswell Lane

Northchurch Cricket Club

Grand Union Canal Wk

River Bulbourne

Northchurch Farm

Hill Farm

B4506

Northchurch Common

Hamberlins Lane

Lane

Pea Lane

Lyme Av

Birch Rd

Pine Wy

Corner Cfts

High Street

St Peter's Place

Covert Close

Astby Road

Heron's Elm

Mandeville

Brakynbery

Kite Field

Emerton Garth

Alvington

NEW ROAD

B4506

Crew Curve

Stanier Rise

St Katherine's Wy

Emperor Close

Spring

Savers Gdns

Hill View

Haynes Mead

Long View

Bridle Wy

Northchurch

Cemetery

First School

Admiral Wy

Torcoleshall

Morain Dr

Field

Road

Chiltern Pk

Billet Lane

Road Close

Princes Close

Egerton

Northchurch

St Mary's Av

Seymour Road

Valley

The Mead

The Riding

Road

North Bridge Road

A41(T)

Shootersway

A41(T)

Loxley Road

Westfield Road

Alma Road

Lochnell Rd

Moore

A4251

Durrants La

Coombe Gdns

Dorset Cl

Belton Road

Riverside Gdns

Eddy Street

145

Shootersway Farm

The Larches

Darr's Lane

Bell Lane

Chaucer Close

Edlyn Close

Durrants Road

Douglas Gdns

Berkhamsted Health Centre

Cossoms Ryde

Marlin Close

Bourne Road

Ashridge Rise

Hawthorns

Larch Rise

Shrublands Road

Queens Rd

West Road

Durrants

Tresco Road

Cobb Road

Rideway

Finch Road

Egerton Rothesay School

Shootersway

Greenway

Orchard Avenue

Shrublands Avenue

Road

Graemes Dyke

Shootersway

Coppins Close

Crossfield Close

Shootersway Lane

Lane End

Clarence Road

Winston Gdns

Bancroft Road

First School

School

The Oaks

Kilfillan Gdns

Oaklands

Rossway Home Farm

Rossway

Baileys Gardens

Shootersway Park

Crossways

The Spinney

Oak Wood

Kingsdale Road

Tower Close

Oxfield Close

A416

Marlin Chapel Farm

Denny's Lane

A41(T)

KINGSHILL

Hill Farm

Northchurch Lane

Lane

Hockeridge Bottom

A41(T)

A416

A   B   C   D   E   F

E7
1 The Hemmings

Hog Lane

F4
1 Beckets Sq
2 Dellfield
3 Dukes Wy
4 Montgomerie Cl
5 Pages Cft

F5
John 1 Chiltern Cl
Farm 2 Douglas Gdns
3 Victory Rd

F6
1 Whitewood Rd

F7
1 Marlin Copse

F8
1 Meadow Cl

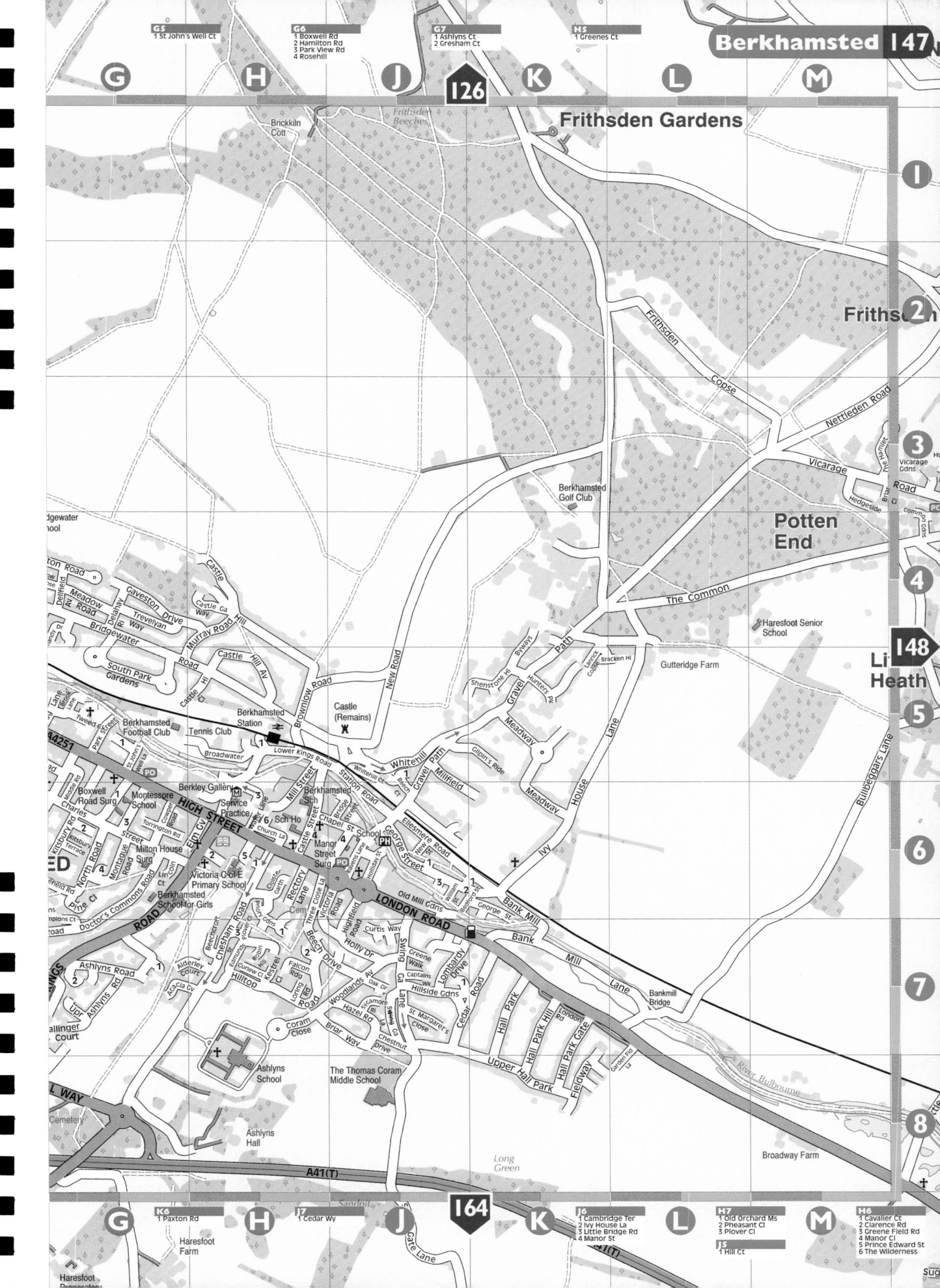

G5 1 St John's Well Ct

G6
1 Boxwell Rd
2 Hamilton Rd
3 Park View Rd
4 Rosehill

G7
1 Ashlyns Ct
2 Gresham Ct

H5 1 Greenes Ct

126

G H J K L M

Frithsden Gardens

Frithsden Beeches

Brickkiln Cott

Frithsden Copse

Frithsden

Nettleden Road

Vicarage Gdns

Berkhamsted Golf Club

Vicarage Road

Hedgeside

Potten End

The Common

Haresfoot Senior School

148

Little Heath

Gutteridge Farm

Bullbeggar's Lane

Bridgewater School

Castle

Meadow Road

Caveston Drive

Trevelyan Way

Murray Road Hill

Castle Hill Av

Brownlow Road

New Road

Castle (Remains)

Bracken Hi

Byways

Shenstone Hi

Hunters Pk

Gravel Path

Meadway

House Lane

Meadway

South Park Gardens

Castle Hi

Berkhamsted Football Club

Tennis Club

Berkhamsted Station

Broadwater

Lower Kings Road

Station Road

Whitehill

Gravel Path

Gilpin's Ride

Millfield

Park Street

A4251

Berkhamsted Sch

Whitehill Ct

PO

Berkley Gallery

HIGH STREET

Montessore School

Service Practice

Sch Ho

Chapel St

Berkhamsted School

George Street

Ellesmere Road

Ivy

Milton House Surg

Victoria C of E Primary School

Berkhamsted School for Girls

Manor Street Surg

PO

Old Mill Cdns

Bank Mill

LONDON ROAD

George St

Bank Mill Lane

Bankmill Bridge

Rectory Lane

Chesham Road

Beech Drive

Holly Dr

Curtis Way

Greene Walk

Captains

Hillside Gdns

Lombardy Drive

Cedar Road

Hall Park

Hall Park Hill

Hall Park Gate

River Bulbourne

Ashlyns Rd

Upr Ashlyns Rd

Coram Close

Briar Way

Hazel Rd

Chestnut Drive

St Margaret's Close

Upper Hall Park

Fieldway

Garden Rd La

Broadway Farm

Ashlyns School

The Thomas Coram Middle School

Cemetery

Ashlyns Hall

Long Green

A41(T)

Sandpit

164

G H J K L M

K6 1 Paxton Rd

Haresfoot Farm

J7 1 Cedar Wy

Gate Lane

A41(T)

J6
1 Cambridge Ter
2 Ivy House La
3 Little Bridge Rd
4 Manor St

H7
1 Old Orchard Ms
2 Pheasant Cl
3 Plover Cl

J5 1 Hill Ct

H6
1 Cavalier Ct
2 Clarence Rd
3 Greene Field Rd
4 Manor Cl
5 Prince Edward St
6 The Wilderness

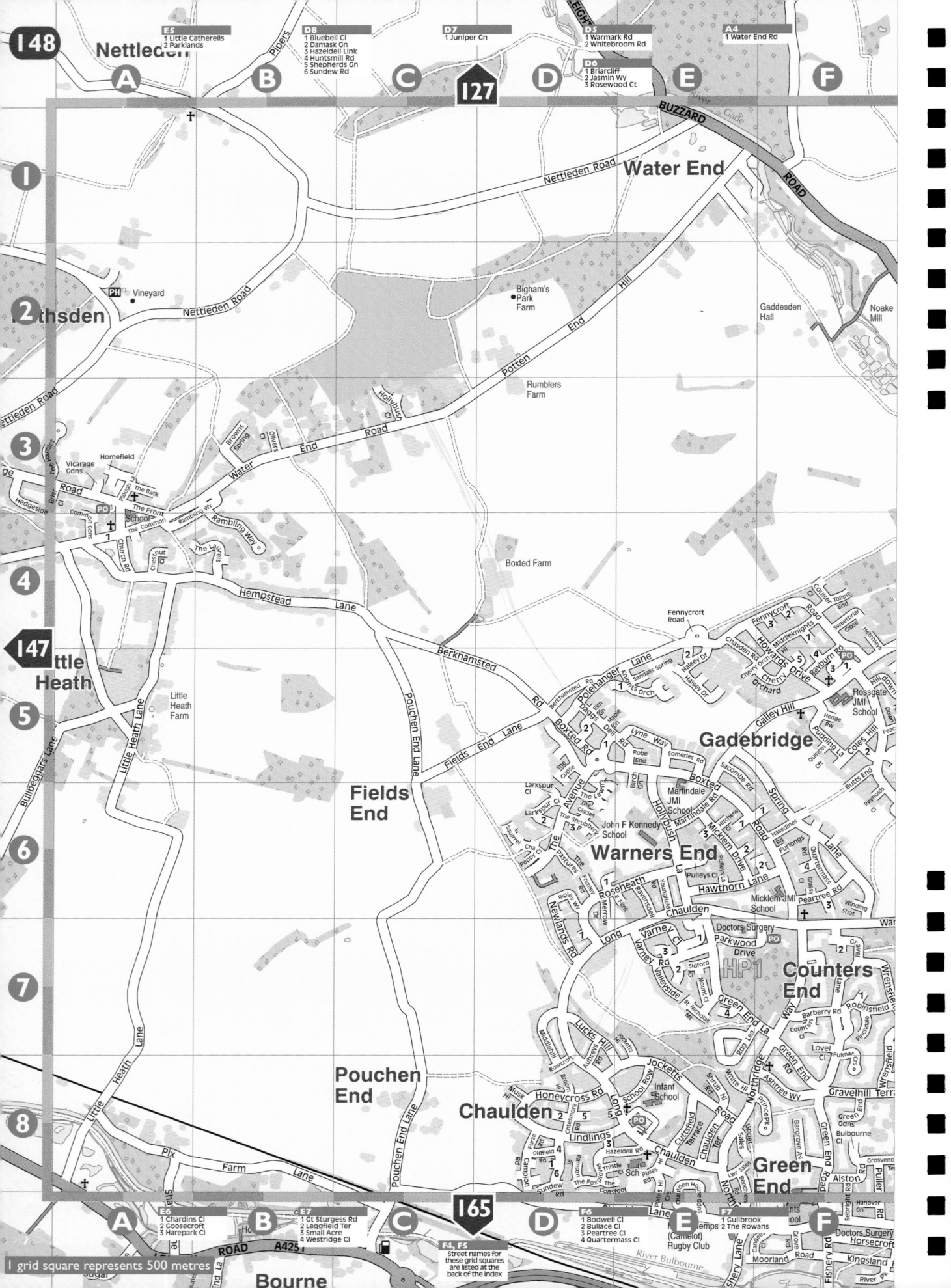

Nettleden

E5
1 Little Catherells
2 Parklands

D8
1 Bluebell Cl
2 Damask Gn
3 Hazeldell Link
4 Huntsmill Rd
5 Shepherds Gn
6 Sundew Rd

D7
1 Juniper Gn

D5
1 Warmark Rd
2 Whitebroom Rd

A4
1 Water End Rd

D6
1 Briarcliff
2 Jasmin Wy
3 Rosewood Ct

127

BUZZARD

Water End

ROAD

River Gade

1

Nettleden Road

2

Nettleden Road

Vineyard

othsden

Nettleden Road

Bigham's
Park
Farm

Gaddesden
Hall

Noake
Mill

Hollybush

Potten   End   Hill

Rumblers
Farm

3

The Hamlet

Homefield

Vicarage
Gdns

Browns
Spring

Olivers

Water   End   Road

Road

Plough   The Back

PO   School   The Front

Common Gdns

Rambling Wy

The Common

Rambling Way

Church Rd   Chestnut Cl

The Laurels

Boxted Farm

147

ttle
Heath

Hempstead   Lane

Little
Heath
Farm

Berkhamsted

Bulbeggars Lane

Little Heath Lane

4

5

Pouchen End Lane

Fields   End   Lane

Fields
End

Rd

Berkhamsted Rd

Polehanger   Lane

Knight's Orch

Sandalls Spring

Elm
Gn

Eagles

Maple
Dell

Boxted   Rd

Lyne   Way

Robe
End

Halsey Dr

Halsey Dr

Chaulden Rd   Cherry Orch

Fennycroft
Road

Middleknights   Hl

Cherry
Orchard

Someries Rd

Fennycroft
Road

Howards   Drive

Rayburn Rd

PO

Galley Hill

Hedge
Rw

Coles   Hill

Coulters   Tollpit

Sweetbriar
Close

Hetchers

Hill down

Rossgate
JMI
School

Pudding   Lane

Quinces   Crt

Butts End

Gadebridge

6

7

Newlands   Rd

Long

Larkspur
Cl

Larkspur Cl

Squirrel

Chapel
Croft

Poppy Cl

The
Copse

The   La

The
Glades

The
Shrubbery

Birch
Gn

Hollybush

Boxted

Sacombe Rd

Martindale
JMI
School

Martindale   Rd

Hasledines

Furlongs

Spring   Road

Reynolds

Quartermass   Rd

Winding
Shot

Grass

John F Kennedy
School

Avenue

The
Pastures

The
Printery

Pulley's La

Pulleys Cl

Micklem   Drive

Micklem JMI
School

Hawthorn   Lane

Peartree   Rd

Roseheath

Merrow

Ravensdene

Varne   Cl

Varney
Rd

Chaulden

Ride   Wy

Sidford   Cl

Mount   Cl

Green   End   La

Doctors Surgery

Parkwood
Drive

PO

HP1

**Counters
End**

Barberry Rd

Robinsfield

Green   End   Way

Countess

Lovel
Cl

Fulmar

8

Little   Heath   Lane

Lucks   Hill

Middleton

Rowcroft

Aubreys Rd

Honeycross   Rd

Cotesmore   Rd

School   Row

Jockerts

Infant
School

Long   Chaulden

Shrub Cl

White Hill

Ashtree   Wy

Northridge   Rd

Prince Pk

Green
Gdns

Bulbourne

**Pouchen
End**

Chaulden

Musk
Hl

Campion
Rd

Oldfield

Lindlings

Ramson

The
Fosse

Thistle

Hazeldell   Rd

Pixies Hl

Cuttsfield
Terrace

Chaulden   Terrace

Chaulden   Rd

Upper   Sales

Lwr Sales   The
Cotsstoot

**Green
End**

Barqrove Av

Gravelhill   Terr

Pix   Farm

Lane

Sundew
Rd

Lwr Bencombe

Chaulden House Gdns Lane

Fishery Rd   Sebright Rd

E6
1 Chardins Cl
2 Goosecroft
3 Harepark Cl

E7
1 Gt Sturgess Rd
2 Leggfield Ter
3 Small Acre
4 Westridge Rd

165

F4, F5
Street names for
these grid squares
are listed at the
back of the index

F6
1 Bodwell Cl
2 Bullace Cl
3 Peartree Cl
4 Quartermass Cl

Temps (Camelot)
Rugby Club

F7
1 Gullbrook
2 The Rowans

Doctors Surgery
Horsecroft

ROAD   A4251

Bourne

River Bulbourne

Moorland

River

Hanover
Cl

Kingsland Rd

Numbered streets
The names of all numbered streets on this page are listed at the back of the index
128
166
150
Hay Farm
Wood Farm
Lovetts End Farm
Piccotts End
Grovehill
Highfield
Hammerfield
HEMEL HEMPSTEAD
Adeyfield
Boxmoor
Barnctoft JMI School
Eastbrook Junior School
Astley Cooper School
Grovehill Medical Cen
Primary School
The Hammond Junior Mixed Infant School
Hemel Hempstead Rugby League Club
Bellgate JMI School
Jupiter Drive JMI School
Highfield Surgery
Blessed Cuthbert Mayne RC School
Gade Valley JMI School
The Cavendish School
The Collett School
Lockers Park School
Community Mental Health Cen
Marlowes Health Cen
Civic Cen & Borough Council
Hertfordshire Co Constabulary
Beta Health Clinic
Fernville Surgery
Bus Station
College
Hobletts Manor Junior School
Everest House Surgery
Adeyfield School
Broadfield Infant School
Junior School
Hemel Hempstead General Hospital
Lincoln Health Surg
County Court
Hot-Shots Ten Pin Bowling
Sports Centre
Odeon Cinema
Dacorum Athletics Track
Ski Centre
Lime Walk JMI School
Dacorum District Sports Centre
South Hill JMI School
Hemel Hempstead School
Cemetery
Jarman Park
LEIGHTON BUZZARD ROAD
QUEENSWAY
ST ALBANS ROAD
REDBOURN ROAD
A4146
A4147
A414
B487

150
B2
1 Birch Leys
2 Half Moon Mdw
3 Lower Emms
4 Rowley Wk
A8
1 Tile Kiln Cl
A6
1 Duxons Turn
2 Wellswood Cl
A2
1 Catherine Cl
2 Chenies Ct
3 Crackley Meadow
4 Medwick Ms
5 The Melings
A1
1 Bronte Crs
2 Dunster Rd
Little Revel End
129
A
B
C
D
E
F
1
2
3
4
5
6
7
8
Holtsmere End Lane
Woodhall Farm Surgery
School
Berkeley Sq
Shenley Road
Coleridge Crs
Holtsmere End Junior & Infant School
Epping Green
Sarratt Av
Botley Rd
Arkley Rd
Latimer Cl
Chalfont Cl
Kimpton Cl
Cleves Rd
Bayford Cl
Cuffley Cl
REDBOURN ROAD
Hunters Oak
HEMEL
B487
Nicky Line
Cherrytree Lane
Woodend Farm
Dane End Farm
M1
Cupid Green
Finway Rd
Brickfields Industrial Est
Three Cherrytrees Lane
9
Lilly La
Eaton Lodge
Punch Bowl Lane
Southend Farm
Eastman Way
Swallowdale Lane
Maxted Road
Boundary Way
Cherry Tree Lane
Buncefield Lane
Old Jeromes
Eaton Road
A4147
MAYLANDS
149
Boundary Wy
Grovelands Business Cen
Green Lane
Hogg End Lane
Maxted Rd
Centro
PO
Hall Road
Cleveland Rd
Mark Road
AMF Bowling
Maxted Cl
Spring
Lane End
Briery Way
AVENUE
Boundary Way
Woodwells Farm
Wood
Crest Pk
Hales Pk
The Coppice
Newford Close
Masons Road
Buncefield La
Cemetery
Junction 8
M1
BREAKSPEAR WAY
A414
Hotel
Buncefield Lane
New Park Drive
The Flags
Green Lane
Hemel Hempstead United Football Club
Maddox Rd
Datchworth Turn
St Margarets Way
Vauxhall Rd
Ranelagh Rd
A414
ALBANS ROAD
Leverstock Gn Rd
Highland Dr
Crossways
Woolmer Dr
Poynders
Mickfield Rd
Clinton End
Leverstock Green JMI School
Lombardy Cl
Westwick Row
Burleigh Rd
Chelsing Ri
Green Lane
Ritcroft Street
Brickmakers Lane
Leverstock Green
Westwick Row
Westwick Hall
Fir Tree Close
Kiln
Tile Kiln Crs
The Wayside
Brickfield Av
The Crofts
Windermere
Curtis Rd
Pancake
Delmar Av
Greenacres
LEVERSTOCK GREEN ROAD
167
Primary School
B5
1 Grovelands
Leverstock Green Lawn Tennis Club
B6
1 Hales Park Cl
2 Romany Ct
3 Welkin Gn
4 Wood End Cl
B7
1 Chartridge Wy
2 Pelham Ct
B8
1 Church Rd
2 Coniston Cl
3 Cumberlow Pl
4 Gravely Ct
5 Hartsbourne Wy
6 Ryecroft Cl
C7
1 St Margarets Wy
C8
1 Badger Cft
2 Trinity Ms
A4147
HEMEL HEMPSTEAD
Woodfield Sch
Corner Farm
Junction 7
1 grid square represents 500 metres

Redbournbury
Beaumont Hall
M8
1 Antonine Ga
130
152
168
G
H
J
K
L
M
1
2
3
4
5
6
7
8
River Ver
Ver-Colne Valley Walk
Hill Farm Lane
Hill Farm
Punch Bowl Lane
New Jerome Cottage
A5183
REDBOURN ROAD
Baker's Farm
Shafford Farm
Hogg End
Hogg End Lane
Beech Hyde
Bow Bridge
Butlers Farm
Batchwood Golf Club
Kettlewells Farm
Maynes Farm
Prince Hotel
REDBOURN ROAD A5183
Gorhambury
Gorhambury (Remains)
Roman Theatre
St Mich
School
VERVLAMIVM Roman Town
HEMEL HEMPSTEAD ROAD
BLUEHOUSE HILL
Prae Wood
Beechtree Lane
Hill End Farm
A4147
Hemel Hempstead Rd
ROAD
Parklands Dr
Lane
Avenue
Augustus
Claudian
Antonine Ga
Ermine Cl
Mayne Av
Prae Wood JMI School
Lindum Pl
Flavian Cl
Westfields
Dubrae Close
Close
King
Cornlium
Beechfield
Mayne Av
HEMPSTE
HEMEL
Cardinal
St Steph

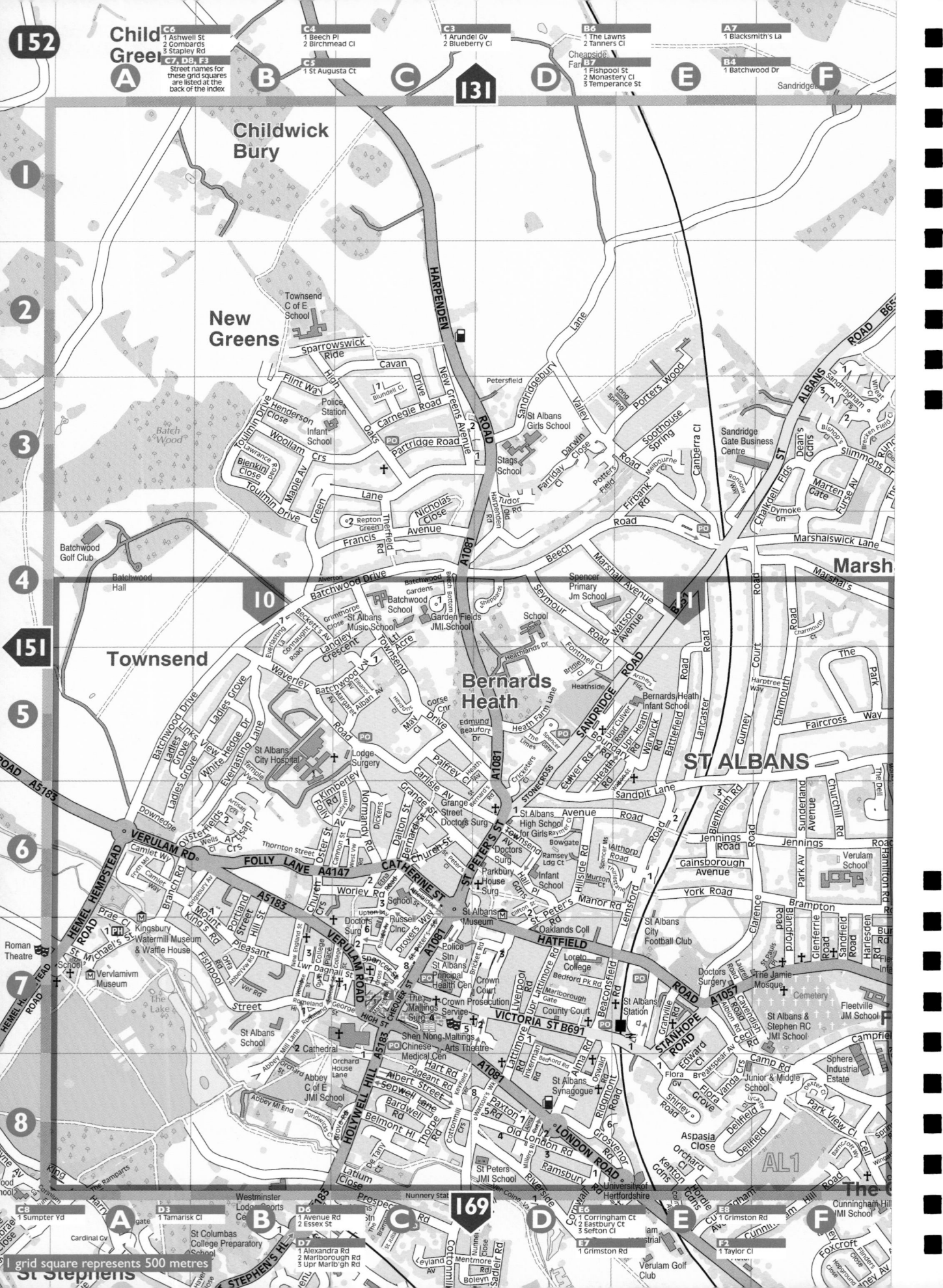

152
C6
1 Ashwell St
2 Combards
3 Stapley Rd
C7, D8, F3
Street names for these grid squares are listed at the back of the index
C4
1 Beech Pl
2 Birchmead Cl
C5
1 St Augusta Ct
C3
1 Arundel Gv
2 Blueberry Cl
B6
1 The Lawns
2 Tanners Cl
B7
1 Fishpool St
2 Monastery Cl
3 Temperance St
A7
1 Blacksmith's La
B4
1 Batchwood Dr
131
Childwick Bury
New Greens
Townsend C of E School
Batch Wood
Batchwood Golf Club
Batchwood Hall
Townsend
Bernards Heath
ST ALBANS
HARPENDEN ROAD
A1081
St Albans Girls School
Stags School
Sandridge Gate Business Centre
Marshalswick Lane
10
11
151
St Albans City Hospital
VERULAM RD
FOLLY LANE A4147
CATHERINE ST
ST PETER'S ST
HATFIELD ROAD A1057
VERULAM ROAD A5183
HEMEL HEMPSTEAD ROAD
St Albans Museum
Kingsbury Watermill Museum & Waffle House
Roman Theatre
Verulamium Museum
The Lake
St Albans School
Cathedral
HOLYWELL HILL A5183
LONDON ROAD A1081
VICTORIA ST B691
St Albans Station
St Albans City Football Club
Loreto College
County Court
Crown Court
Crown Prosecution Service
The Maltings
Shen Nong Maltings Chinese Medical Cen
Arts Theatre
St Albans Synagogue
University of Hertfordshire
St Albans & Stephen RC JMI School
Cemetery
Fleetville JM School
Sphere Industrial Estate
Verulam School
AL1
169
C8
1 Sumpter Yd
D3
1 Tamarisk Cl
D6
1 Avenue Rd
2 Essex St
D7
1 Alexandra Rd
2 Marlborough Rd
3 Upr Marlb'gh Rd
E6
1 Corringham Ct
2 Eastbury Ct
3 Sefton Cl
E7
1 Grimston Rd
E8
1 Grimston Rd
F2
1 Taylor Cl
St Columbas College Preparatory School
Verulam Golf Club
Cunningham Hill JMI School
St Stephens
1 grid square represents 500 metres

132

154

G H J K L M

I

2
Coo
Gree

3

4

5

6

7

8

Symondshyde
Great Wood

Langley

Lyndon Rd

Woodcockhill

AL4

Fairfold's
Farm

Sutton's
Farm

Sandri
JMI
School

Sandridge Youth
Club & Sports Centre

High Street

House Lane

Leonards Crs

Jersey La

Sandridge

Highfield
Rd

Reynolds
Crescent

St Helliers Rd

Wendover Cl

Pirton Cl

Cromwell
Close

Nashe's
Farm

Coopers Green Lane

Beech
Farm

Sandringham Crescent

Wheatfields
Junior &
Infant School

Sandringham
School

Malvern Cl

Chiltern Road

Windmill Av

Windmill

Sandringham Crescent

Chancery
Cl

Craiglands

Beverley Gdns

Beech
Farm Dr

Coopers Green Lane

Oak
Farm

alswick

Ridgeway

Pondfield Crs

Queens Crs

Kingshill Avenue

Sherwood Road

Bentsley
Close

Tewin
Close

Avenue

The Ridgeway

Evans
Grove

Meadow
Close

Ripon Wy

Cheriton Cl

Stanton Cl

House Lane

St John
Fisher RC
JMI School

Skyswood
JMI School

Hazelmere

Woodfield
Road

Briar Road

Springwood
Walk

Elizabeth
Crs

Newgate
Cl

Oaklands Lane

154

Marshalswick Lane

Hughenden Rd

The Ridgeway

Ferny's

Barnfield Road

Arden's Way

Buxton
Cl

Southfield

Sandpit Lane

Jersey La

Rose
Walk

St Albans
Lawn Tennis
Club

Hall Heath
Close

Homewood Road

Sandpit
Lane

Chestnut Dr

Beechwood

Woodland

Hazelwood Drive

Oakwood
JMI
School

North Drive

Oaklands Lane

Woodstock Road N

Gleeve
Cl

St Johns
Cl

Garden
Cl

Beaumont

Farm
Road

Central Dr

Oakwood
Drive

Beaumont
School

Oaklands
College

East Drive

Station

Salisbury Lawn
Tennis Club

Salisbury Avenue

Avenue

Salisbury Av

Elm Drive

South Dr

South Drive

A1057

Hatfield Road

nham

Royal

etville

Woodstock Rd S

Eaton
Rd

Arthur
Rd

Hatfield Rd

A1057

Hatfield

Wynchlands
Crs

Road

Hatfield Road

A1057

Acrewood Way

Lyon Way

leetville

Castle Road

Burleigh Road

Ashley Rd

Willow
Cr

Pinewood Cl

Cedarwood Dr

Cedar
Rd

Bell Vw

Longacres

Gresford
Cl

St Yon
Ct

Hathaway
Court

Sewell
Cl

Charlotte

Cranbrook Rd

Rowan Cl

The Cl'val

Firwood Av

Merryfields

Hedley Road

Guildford Rd

Maxwell Rd

Oakdene Wy

Hill End Lane

Marconi Wy

Grafton
Close

Hobbs
Close

Swans
Close

Boissy Cl

Colney Heath Lane

Cambridge Road

Ely Road

College
Road

Royston
Road

Brick Knoll Park

Diana Dr

Nicholas
Breakspear
RC School

Camp
Road

Wellington Road

Beresford Rd

Oxford Av

Bramley
Wy

Crs

Camp
Rd

Trestle
Theatre Co

Smallford
Farm

Windermere
JMI Primary
School
St Albans
Organ Mus

Camp

G H J K L M

Colney Heath Lane

RD

A4

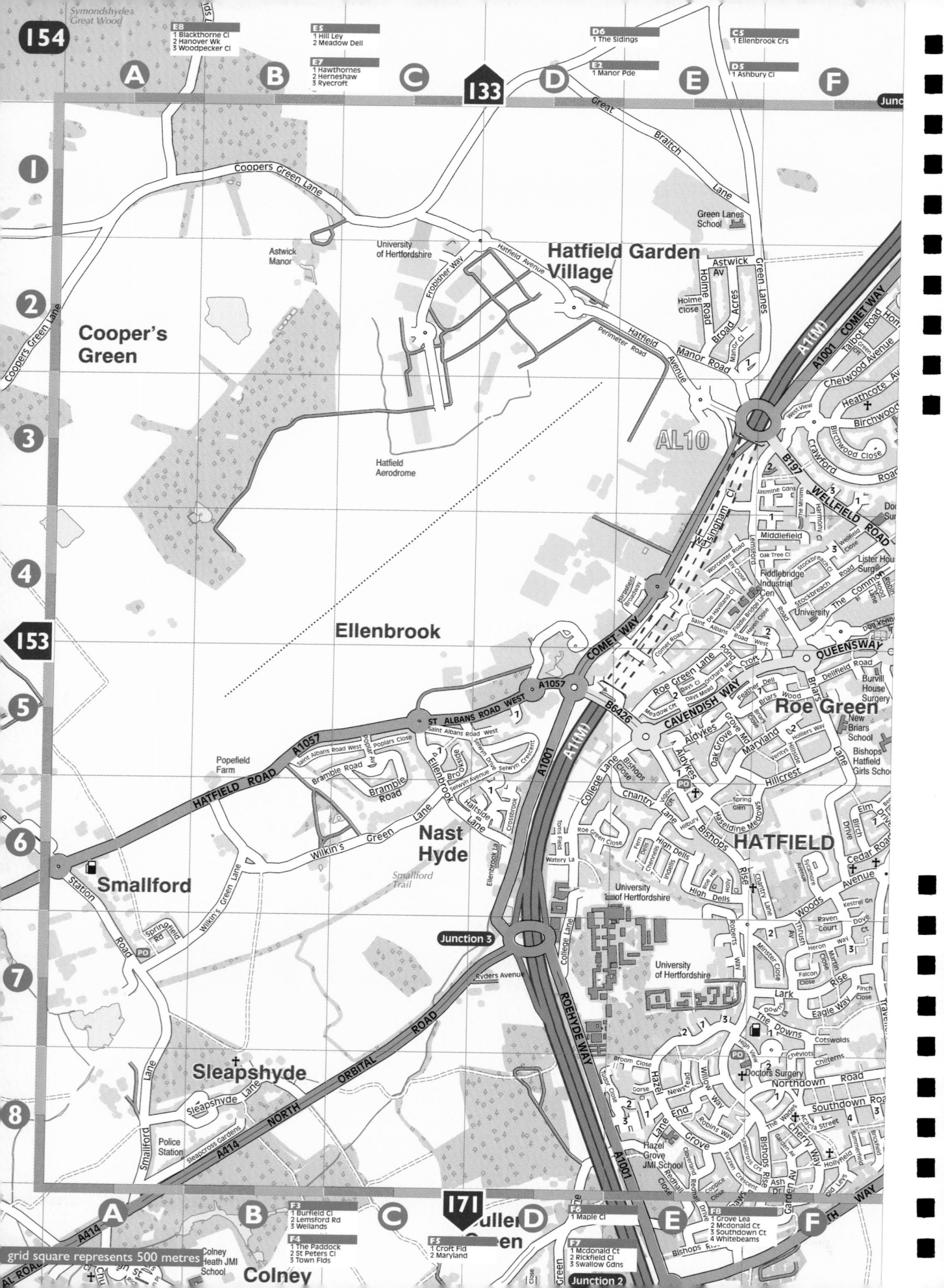

133

171

Junction 3

Junction 2

E8
1 Blackthorne Cl
2 Hanover Wk
3 Woodpecker Cl

E5
1 Hill Ley
2 Meadow Dell

E7
1 Hawthornes
2 Herneshaw
3 Ryecroft

D6
1 The Sidings

E2
1 Manor Pde

C5
1 Ellenbrook Crs

D5
1 Ashbury Cl

F3
1 Burfield Cl
2 Lemsford Rd
3 Wellands

F4
1 The Paddock
2 St Peters Cl
3 Town Flds

F5
1 Croft Fld

D7
1 Maple Cl

E5
1 Mcdonald Ct
2 Rickfield Cl
3 Swallow Gdns

F8
1 Grove Lea
2 Mcdonald Ct
3 Southdown Ct
4 Whitebeams

Symondshyde Great Wood

Coopers Green Lane

Coopers Green Lane

Cooper's Green

Astwick Manor

University of Hertfordshire

Frobisher Way

Hatfield Avenue

Hatfield Garden Village

Green Lanes School

Perimeter Road

Astwick Av

Holme Road

Holme Close

Broad Acres

Green Lanes

Hatfield Aerodrome

Hatfield Manor Road

Manor Cl

AL10

A1(M)

COMET WAY

Talbot Road

Chelwood Ave

Heathcote Ave

Birchwood Ave

Birchwood Close

Crawford Road

B197

WELLFIELD ROAD

Jasmine Gdns

The Minims

Harmony Cl

Middlefield

Oak Tree Cl

Wellfield Close

Lister House Surg

Walsingham

Broadway

Worcester Road

Days Cl

Days Mead

Saint Albans Road West

Fiddlebridge Industrial Cen

Stockbreach Road

Stockbreach Cl

University

The Common

Ellenbrook

QUEENSWAY

Delifield Road

Burvill House Surgery

A1057

ST ALBANS ROAD WEST

Saint Albans Road West

A1057

HATFIELD ROAD

Popefield Farm

Poplar Avenue

Poplars Close

Bramble Road

Bramble Road

Selwyn Drive

Selwyn Avenue

Selwyn Crescent

Crossbrook

Ellenbrook Lane

Haltside Lane

A1057

A1001

A1(M)

B6426

Comet Road

Pond Croft

Roe Green Lane

Meadow Crt

Feather Dell

Briars Wood

CAVENDISH WAY

Aldykes

Oak Grove

Grove Mead

Maryland

Holliers Way

Roe Green

New Briars School

Bishops Hatfield Girls School

Hillcrest

Aldykes

Bishops

Chantry

College Lane

Bishops Close

Toms Field

Roe Green Close

High Dells

High Dells

Haseldine Meadows

Spring Glen

HATFIELD

Elm Drive

Birch Drive

Cedar Road

Sycamore Avenue

Nast Hyde

Wilkin's Green Lane

Smallford Trail

Ellenbrook Lane

Watery La

University of Hertfordshire

Roberts Way

Minster Close

Heron Close

Falcon Close

Lark Rise

Eagle Way

The Downs

Thrush Close

Raven Court

Dove Way

Martin Close

Finch Rise

Kestrel Gn

Smallford

Station Road

Station

Spring Field Rd

Wilkin's Green Lane

Smallford Lane

ROEHYDE WAY

A1001

University of Hertfordshire

Ryders Avenue

Junction 3

The Wales

Broom Close

Willow Way

High Way

Doctors Surgery

Cheviots

Cotswolds

Chilterns

Northdown Road

Sleapshyde

Sleapshyde Lane

Smallford Lane

NORTH

ORBITAL

ROAD

A414

Sleapcross Gardens

Police Station

Hazel Grove

Gorse

Hazel End

Lane End

Robins Way

Tudor Close

News

Shallcross Drive

Surfen Crescent

Coppice

Bishops Rise

Acacia Street

Cherry Way

Southdown Road

Redhall Close

Hazel Grove JMI School

Hollyfield

Whitefield

Ash Cl

Old Ley's

Garden Av

Bishops Close

Colney Heath JMI School

Colney

Smallford Lane

AL ROAD

A414

Sleapshyde

grid square represents 500 metres

134

156

172

AL9

Grid references

G2
1 Little Mead

G3
1 Corncroft
2 Strawmead

G4
1 Brain Cl
2 Breaks Rd
3 French Horn La
4 Kennelwood La
5 Wellfield Rd
6 Wheatfield

G5
1 Old Rectory Dr
2 Rectory Gdns

H5
1 St Eth'reda's Dr

H4
1 Endymion Ct
2 Endymion Ms

H2
1 Highlands
2 Lowlands

G8
1 Bownsfield
2 Richmond Ct

G7
1 Allen Ct
2 Coney Cl
3 Hamilton Ct
4 Kingsmill Ct

G6
1 Foxglove Cl
2 Lamb Cl
3 Primrose Cl

Birchwood

The Ryde

Oxlease

South Hatfield

Old Hatfield

Mill Green

Woodside

Hatfield Station

Welwyn Hatfield Museum Service

Home Park

The Vineyard

Hatfield House

Real Tennis Club

Coombe Wood

Park Dairy

Woodside Place

Millward's Park

Cemetery

Welwyn Hatfield District Council

Police Station

Birchwood Leisure Centre

Woodhall Farm

CHEQUERS

Salisbury Infant School

Avenue Primary School

Howe Dell School

The St Philip Howard Catholic Primary School

Stream Woods School

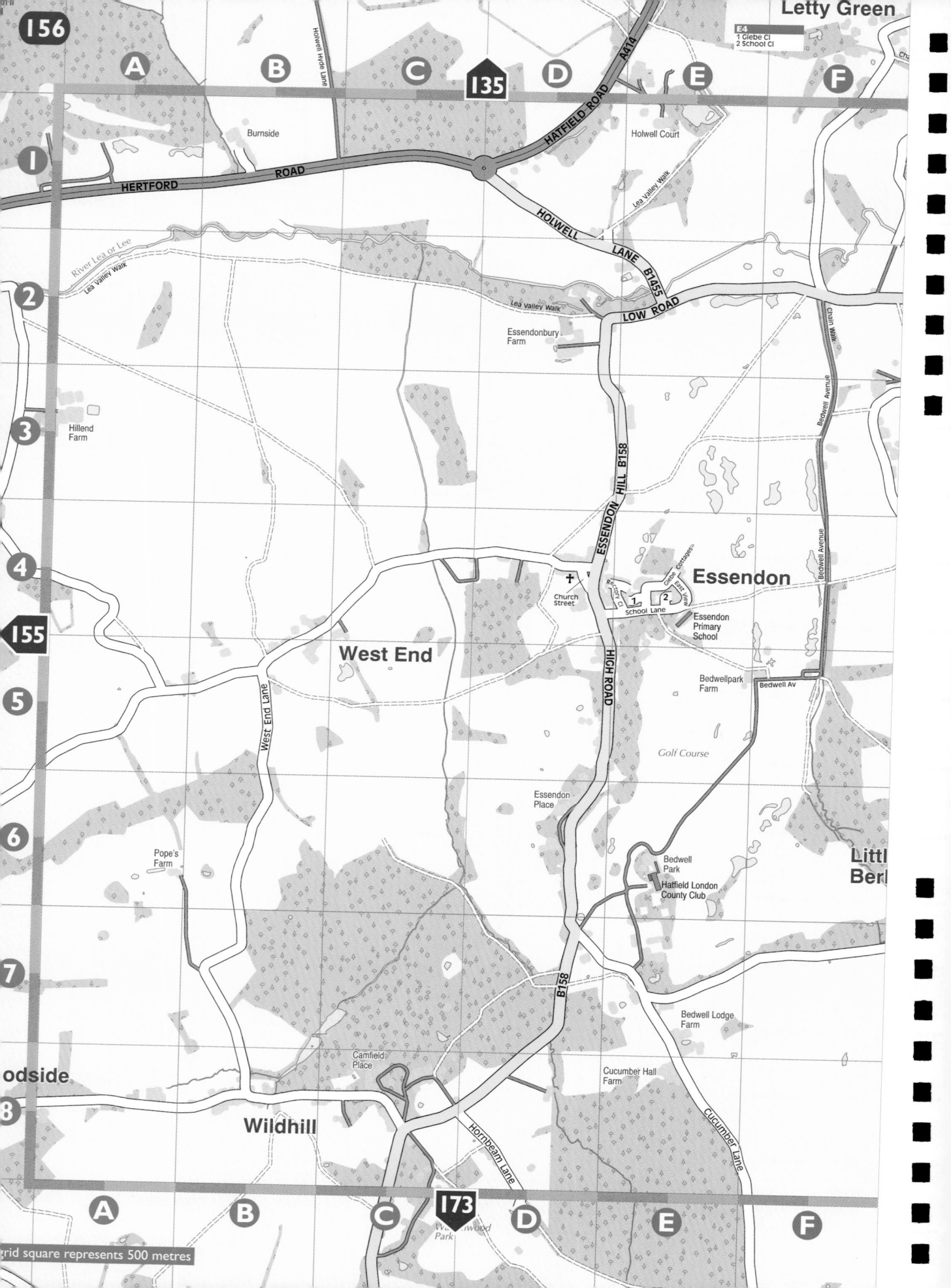

156

A   B   C   **135**   D   E   F

Letty Green

E4
1 Glebe Cl
2 School Cl

1

Burnside

Holwell Court

HERTFORD   ROAD

Holwell Hyde Lane

HOLWELL   LANE   B1455

Holwell Court

Lea Valley Walk

2

River Lea or Lee

Lea Valley Walk

Lea Valley Walk

LOW   ROAD

Essendonbury Farm

Chain Walk

Bedwell Avenue

3

Hillend Farm

ESSENDON HILL B158

4

Church Street

School Lane   1   2   **Essendon**

Rectory   Glebe Cottages   East View

Essendon Primary School

155

West End

West End Lane

HIGH   ROAD

Bedwellpark Farm   Bedwell Av

Bedwell Avenue

5

Golf Course

6

Pope's Farm

Essendon Place

Bedwell Park

Hatfield London County Club

Littl
Berl

7

B158

Bedwell Lodge Farm

odside

Camfield Place

Cucumber Hall Farm

Cucumber Lane

8

Wildhill

Hornbeam Lane

173

A   B   C   **173**   D   E   F

grid square represents 500 metres

Essendon 157
136
158
174
G
H
J
K
L
M
1
2
3
4
5
6
7
8
SG13
Green
Park Farm
Woolmers Lane
Walk
HATFIE
Bayfordbury
College of
Hertfordshire
Roxford
Chain
Walk
LOWER
LOWER HATFIELD ROAD
B158
Water Hall
Farm
Broadgreen
Wood
Broad Green
Broad Green
Wood
Bayford Lane
Howe
Green
Kennel
Hall
Farm
Chain Walk
Bayford
Hall
Warren House
Bayford Green
Culverwood
House
Well Row
Bayford
Wood
Stockings Lane
Bayford
Bayford Junior
Middle &
Infant School
Bayford
Station
Robins Nest Hill
Ashendene Road
Chain Walk
Church
Road
Goddards
Bucks
Alley
e
khamsted
Berkhamsted Lane
Bucks
Farm
Blackfa
Wood
Chain Walk
Bush
Farm
Ashendene
Farm
Woodcock
Lodge
Epping
House
School
Old Claypits
Farm
Chain Walk
Chain Walk
Epping
Green
Woodcock Lodge
Farm
Tylers
Causeway
Ponsbourne Tunnel
Short Valle

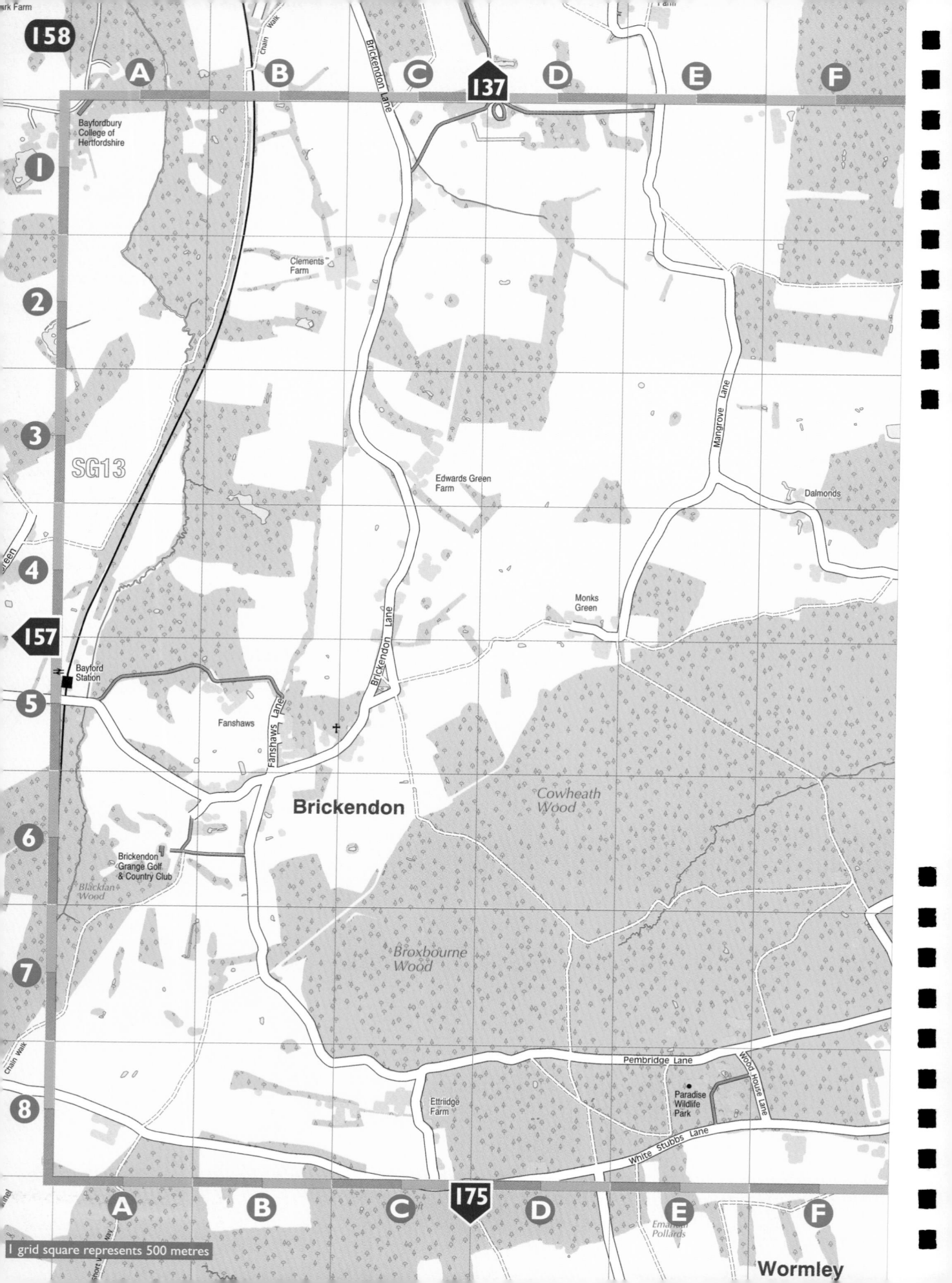

158

A   B   C   137   D   E   F

1

Bayfordbury
College of
Hertfordshire

Clements
Farm

2

3

SG13

Edwards Green
Farm

Dalmonds

Mangrove Lane

4

157

Monks
Green

Bayford
Station

5

Fanshaws

Brickendon Lane

Fanshaws Lane

Brickendon

Cowheath
Wood

6

Brickendon
Grange Golf
& Country Club

Blackfan
Wood

Broxbourne
Wood

7

Pembridge Lane

Wood House Lane

8

Ettridge
Farm

Paradise
Wildlife
Park

White Stubbs Lane

A   B   C   175   D   E   F

Emanuel
Pollards

Wormley

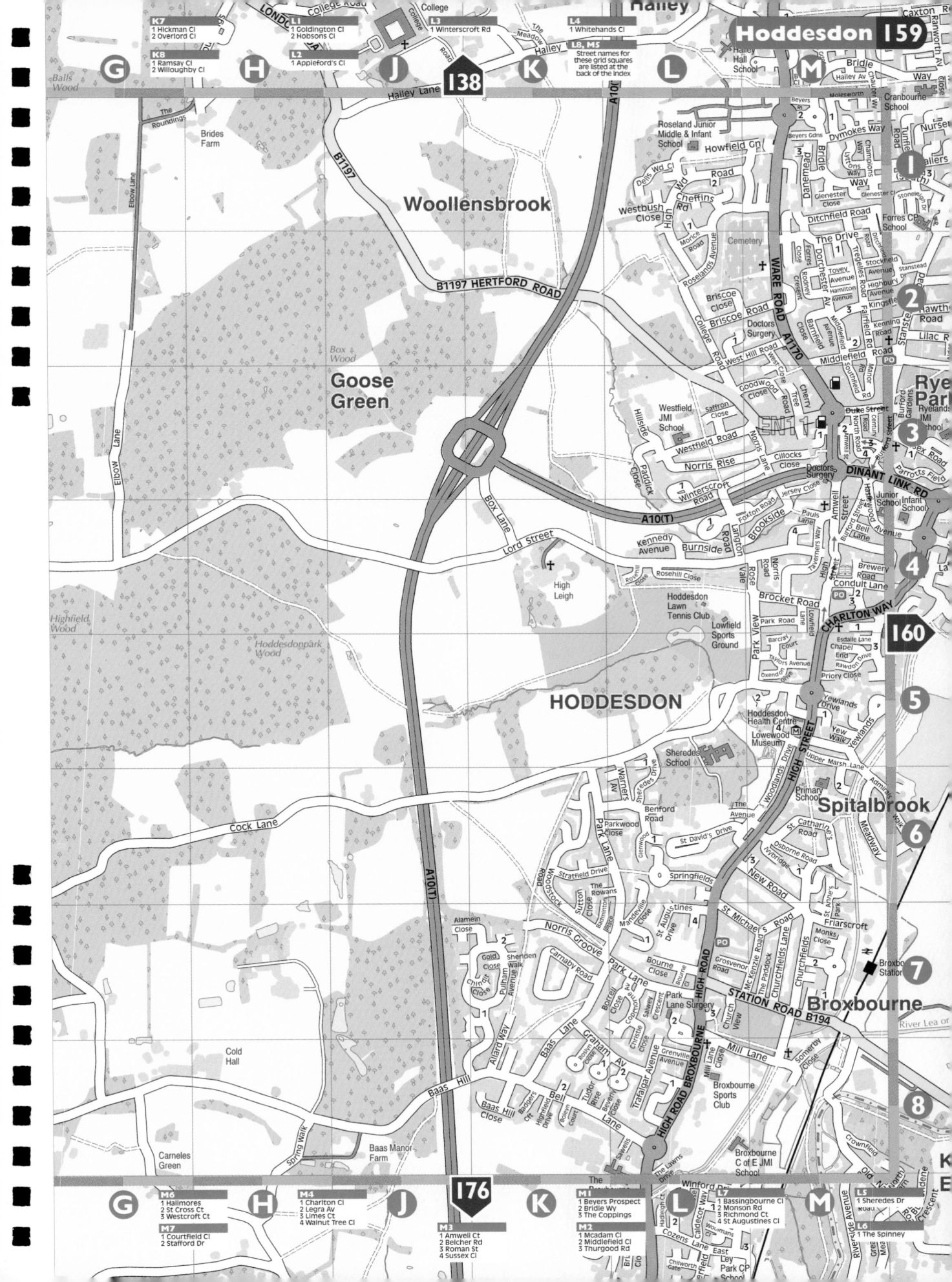

K7
1 Hickman Cl
2 Overlord Cl
K8
1 Ramsay Cl
2 Willoughby Cl
L1
1 Goldington Cl
2 Hobsons Cl
L2
1 Appleford's Cl
L3
1 Winterscroft Rd
L4
1 Whitehands Cl
L8, M5
Street names for these grid squares are listed at the back of the index
138
Hailey Lane
Woollensbrook
B1197 HERTFORD ROAD
Goose Green
Brides Farm
Elbow Lane
Box Wood
Highfield Wood
Hoddesdonpark Wood
HODDESDON
Lord Street
Box Lane
A10(T)
High Leigh
Cock Lane
Cold Hall
Baas Hill
Carneles Green
Baas Manor Farm
Spring Walk
Roseland Junior Middle & Infant School
Howfield Gn
Westbush Close
Cemetery
Briscoe Road
Doctors Surgery
WARE ROAD A1170
West Hill Road
Westfield JMI School
Westfield Road
Norris Rise
Winterscroft Road
DINANT LINK RD
Kennedy Avenue
Burnside
Rosehill Close
Hoddesdon Lawn Tennis Club
Lowfield Sports Ground
Park View
Brocket Road
CHARLTON WAY
160
Yewlands Drive
Hoddesdon Health Centre
Lowewood Museum
Sheredes School
HIGH STREET
Spitalbrook
Primary School
Benford Road
Park Lane
Springfields
New Road
Norris Groove
Carnaby Road
St Augustines Drive
St Michael's Road
Churchfields Lane
Churchfields
Friarscroft
Broxbourne Station
Broxbourne
STATION ROAD B194
River Lea
Park Lane Surgery
Mill Lane
HIGH ROAD BROXBOURNE
Broxbourne Sports Club
Broxbourne C of E JMI School
Baas Lane
Bell Lane
Trafalgar Avenue
Graham Av
Ditchfield Road
Forres CP School
Cranbourne School
Dymokes Way
Middlefield Road
Ryelands JMI School
Junior School
Infant School
Conduit Lane
Priory Close
176
M6
1 Hallmores
2 St Cross Ct
3 Westcroft Ct
M7
1 Courtfield Cl
2 Stafford Dr
M4
1 Charlton Cl
2 Legra Av
3 Limes Ct
4 Walnut Tree Cl
M3
1 Amwell Ct
2 Belcher Rd
3 Roman St
4 Sussex Cl
M1
1 Beyers Prospect
2 Bridle Wy
3 The Coppings
M2
1 Mcadam Cl
2 Middlefield Cl
3 Thurgood Rd
L7
1 Bassingbourne Cl
2 Monson Rd
3 Richmond Ct
4 St Augustines Cl
L5
1 Sheredes Dr
L6
1 The Spinney

160
139
159
177
B2 1 Bosanquet Rd
A3 1 Marston Rd
A2 1 Laburnum Rd
A1 1 Chittenden Cl 2 Estfeld Cl 3 Parkland Cl 4 Theleway Cl
C5 1 S Charlton Md La
Rye Meads
Rye Park
Spitalbrook
Nazeing Mead
Keysers Estate
Roydon Station
Roydon Leisure Park
Rye House Station
Rye House Stadium
Hoddesdon Industrial Estate
New England Industrial Estate
Trident Industrial Estate
Belcon Industrial Estate
Waterside Industrial Estate
The John Warner School
Cranbourne School
Forres CP School
Ryelands JMI School
Junior School
Infant School
Broxbourne Sailing Club
Broxbourne Station
Hillgrove Business Park
The Grove
Dobb's Weir
The Lynch
Downe Hall
Stoneshot
River Stort
River Stort (Navigation)
River Lea or Lee
Stort Valley Way
Three Forests Way
Lea Valley Walk
Hertfordshire County
Essex County
Rye Road
Essex Road
Dobb's Weir Road
Meadgate Road
Sedge Green
Low Hill Road
Glen Faba Road
Netherhall Road
Peck's Hill
Ratty's Lane
Charlton Mead Lane
DINANT LINK RD
Conduit Lane
Stanstead Road
Stortford Road
Pindar Road
Bingley Road
Geddings Road
Plumpton Road
Avenue Road
Blythe Road
Clyde Road
Derby Road
Eldon Road
Shooters Drive
Western Road
Palmers Grove
Hoe Lane
Nursery Road
Lake Road
Maplecroft Lane
Old Nazeing Road
Crownfield
Keysers Road
Buttondene Crescent
1 grid square represents 500 metres

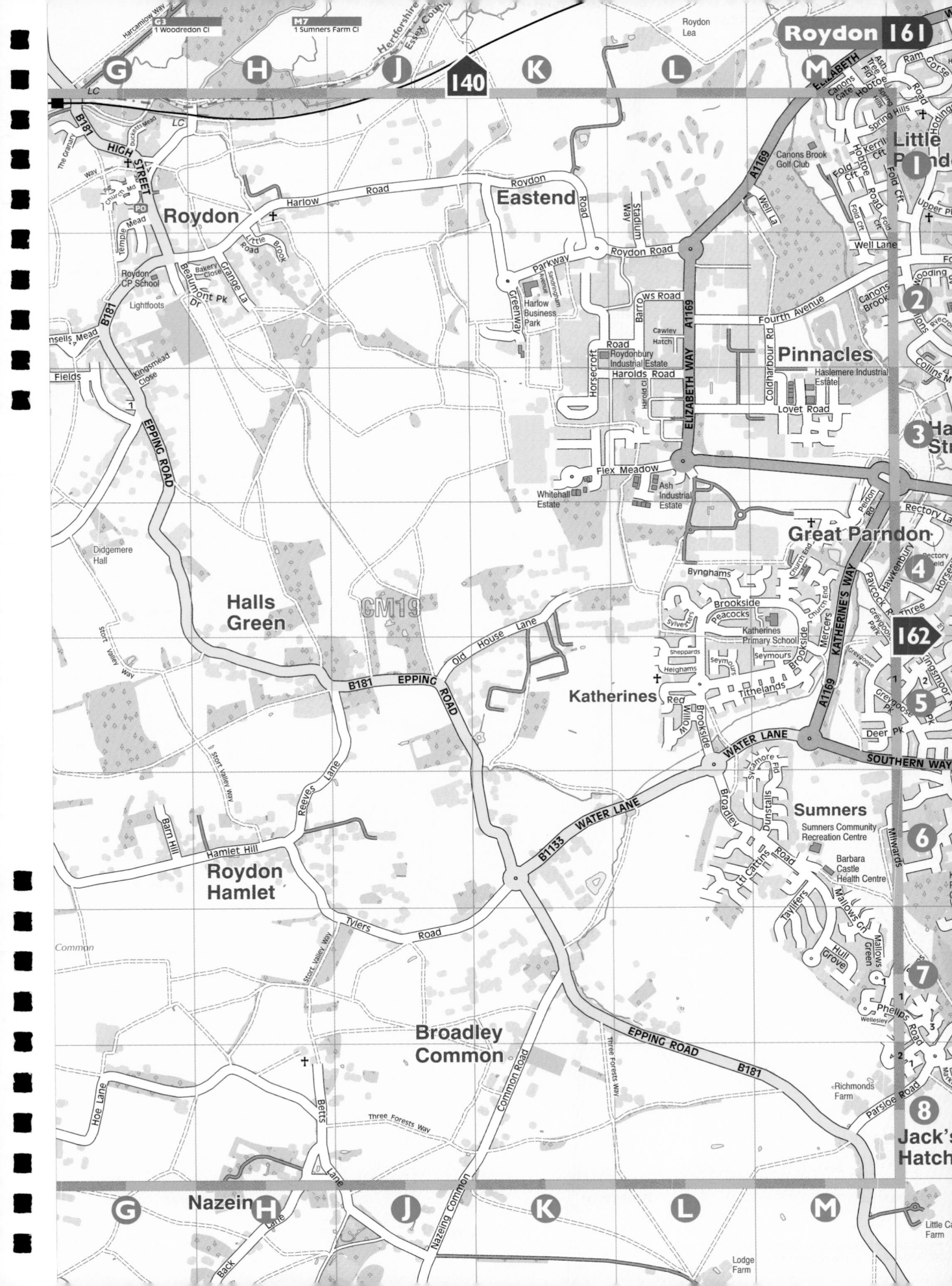

G H J **140** K L M

I
Little Pond

Harcamlow Way
G3 1 Woodredon Cl
M7 1 Sumners Farm Cl

Hertfordshire
Essex Coun...

Roydon Lea

The Granary
LC
LC

B181
HIGH STREET
Way
Church Md
PO

Roydon

Harlow Road
Little Brook
Temple Mead

Roydon CP School
Lightfoots
Bakers Close
Grange La
Beaumont Pk Dr

Kingsmead Close
Fields
Kinsells Mead

B181

EPPING ROAD

Roydon Road
Eastend

Roydon Road

A1169
Canons Brook Golf Club

Canons Gate
Hobtroe
Hobtroe Road
Fold Cft
Kerril Cft
Fold Cft
Spring Hills
Ash Tree Fld
Ram Corse Road
Hoding...

Upper P...

Wooding...

2

Canons Brook
Well Lane
Well La
lions Cft
Rivercro...
Collins M...

Parkway
Greenway
Sandringham Avenue
Harlow Business Park

Stadium Way
ws Road
Barro...

Road
Roydonbury Industrial Estate
Horsecroft
Harolds Road
Harold Cl

Cawley Hatch

A1169
ELIZABETH WAY

Fourth Avenue
Coldharbour Rd
Haslemere Industrial Estate
Lovet Road
Pinnacles

3
Ha...
Str...

Flex Meadow
Whitehall Estate
Ash Industrial Estate

Pardon Rd

Rectory La
Rectory Field

Great Parndon

Hawkenbury
Paycock Rd
Three...
Horse...

4

Bynghams
Brookside
Peacocks
Sylves...ers
Katherines Primary School
Sheppards
Seymours
Seymours
Heighams

Church End
Mercers' Rd
Church End
KATHERINE'S WAY

A1169

Greygoose Park
Greygoose Pk
Greygoose Pk

162
1 2

5

Didgemere Hall

Halls Green

Stort Valley Way

CM19

Old House Lane

B181 EPPING ROAD

Katherines
Red Willow
Brookside
Brookside
Titlelands

WATER LANE
Sycamore Fld
Broadley

Deer Pk

SOUTHERN WAY

Sumners
Sumners Community Recreation Centre
Barbara Castle Health Centre

Millwards

6

Reeves Lane
Stort Valley Way
Barn Hill
Hamlet Hill

Roydon Hamlet

Tylers Road

B1133 WATER LANE

Broadley Road
Dunstalls
Lt Catlins
Mallows Ch

Tavillers
Mallows Green
Hull Grove

7

Common

Common Road
Betts Lane
Three Forests Way

Broadley Common

EPPING ROAD
B181
Three Forests Way

Phelips Road
Wellesley
Wellesley

Richmonds Farm
Parsloe Road

8

Hoe Lane

Back Lane

Nazeing Common

Lodge Farm

Nazein

Jack's Hatch
Little Ca...
Farm

G H J K L M

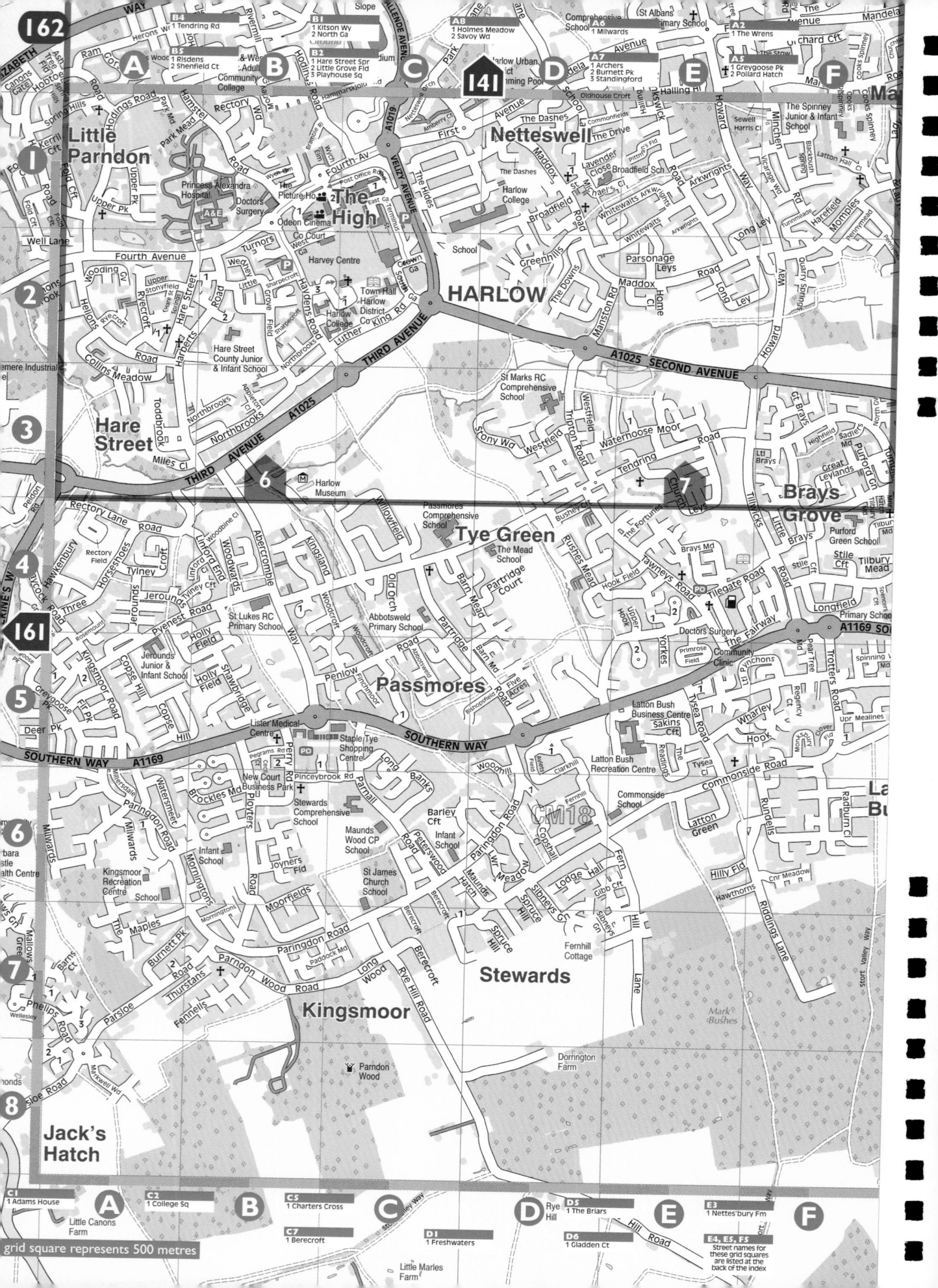

WAY

B4
1 Tendring Rd

B5
1 Risdens
2 Shenfield Ct

B1
1 Kitson Wy
2 North Ga

B2
1 Hare Street Spr
2 Little Grove Fld
3 Playhouse Sq

A8
1 Holmes Meadow
2 Savoy Wd

A6
1 Milwards

St Albans
Primary School

A2
1 The Wrens

A7
1 Archers
2 Burnett Pk
3 Standingford

A5
1 Greygoose Pk
2 Pollard Hatch

Little Parndon

Princess Alexandra Hospital

Doctors Surgery

A&E

The Picture Ho

Odeon Cinema

The High

Co Court

Harvey Centre

Town Hall
Harlow District Co King

Harlow College

HARLOW

Netteswell

Harlow College

Fourth Avenue

Hare Street County Junior & Infant School

Hare Street

Collins Meadow

THIRD AVENUE

A1025

6

Harlow Museum

A1025 SECOND AVENUE

St Marks RC Comprehensive School

Brays Grove

7

Purford Green School

Passmores Comprehensive School

Tye Green

The Mead School

Partridge Court

St Lukes RC Primary School

Abbotsweld Primary School

Jerounds Junior & Infant School

Penlow

Passmores

Five Acres

Doctors Surgery

Community Clinic

A1169 SO

Stewards Comprehensive School

Lister Medical Centre

Staple Tye Shopping Centre

New Court Business Park

Pinceybrook Rd

SOUTHERN WAY

Latton Bush Business Centre

Latton Bush Recreation Centre

Commonside School

Commonside Road

SOUTHERN WAY A1169

Maunds Wood CP School

Barley Cft

Infant School

St James Church School

Kingsmoor Recreation Centre

Infant School

Stewards

Kingsmoor

Fernhill Cottage

Mark Bushes

Jack's Hatch

Dorrington Farm

Parndon Wood

C1
1 Adams House

A
Little Canons Farm

C2
1 College Sq

B
C5
1 Charters Cross

C7
1 Berecroft

C
D1
1 Freshwaters

D
Rye Hill

D5
1 The Briars

D6
1 Gladden Ct

E
E3
1 Nettes'bury Fm

E4, E5, F5
street names for these grid squares are listed at the back of the index

F

grid square represents 500 metres

G3
1 Campbell Cl
H4
1 Florence Cl
2 Jack Stevens Cl
3 Larkswood
142
Hall South
New Hall Farm
Franklin Farm
Hobbs Cross
Hubbard's Hall
Ladyshot
Church Langley
Church Langley Primary School
Florence Nightingale Health Centre
Church Langley Way
Minton Lane
Chamberlain Cl
Aynsley Gdns
Mallards Rise
Ashworth Place
Rushton Grove
Sheldon Cl
Denby Grange
Old Hall Rise
Heathcote Gdns
Ridgeways
Elwood
Doulton Cl
Lane End
Chelsea Gdns
Davenport
Pilkingtons
Wedgewood Drive
Albert Gdns
Westbury Ri
Tickenhall Dr
Bentley Drive
Kiln Lane
Fenton Gra
Hadley Gra
Victoria Ga
Oaklands Dr
Abbey Dale Cl
Bellfield Gdns
Kingsdon Lane
Coalport Cl
Burley Hill
Fullers Mead
Perry Spring
Red Lion Lane
Red Lion Crescent
Potters Fld
Potter Street
Harlow Common
Potter Street Primary School
Brays Grove Comprehensive School
Southern Way
Chapel Flds
Church Rd
Swevne
Forest Way
Latton Street
London Road
Park Av
Carters Mead
Pinewood Cl
Second Av
The Gardiners
A1025
A414
M11
Latton Bush
Nicholls Fld
Manor Hatch Cl
Spencers Cft
Tracyes Rd
Hotel
Priory Ct
Brooklane Fld
Latton House
Foster Street
Threshers Bush
Mill Street
Stort Valley Way
Harlow Park
Hastingwood
Hastingwood Road
Willow Pl
Wynter's Grange
Shonks Brook
Latton Park
Junction 7
PH
Paris Hall
Glovers La
Glovers Farm
Rundells
London Road
Canes Lane
Canes Farm
Horseshoes Farm
G H J K L M
1 2 3 4 5 6 7 8

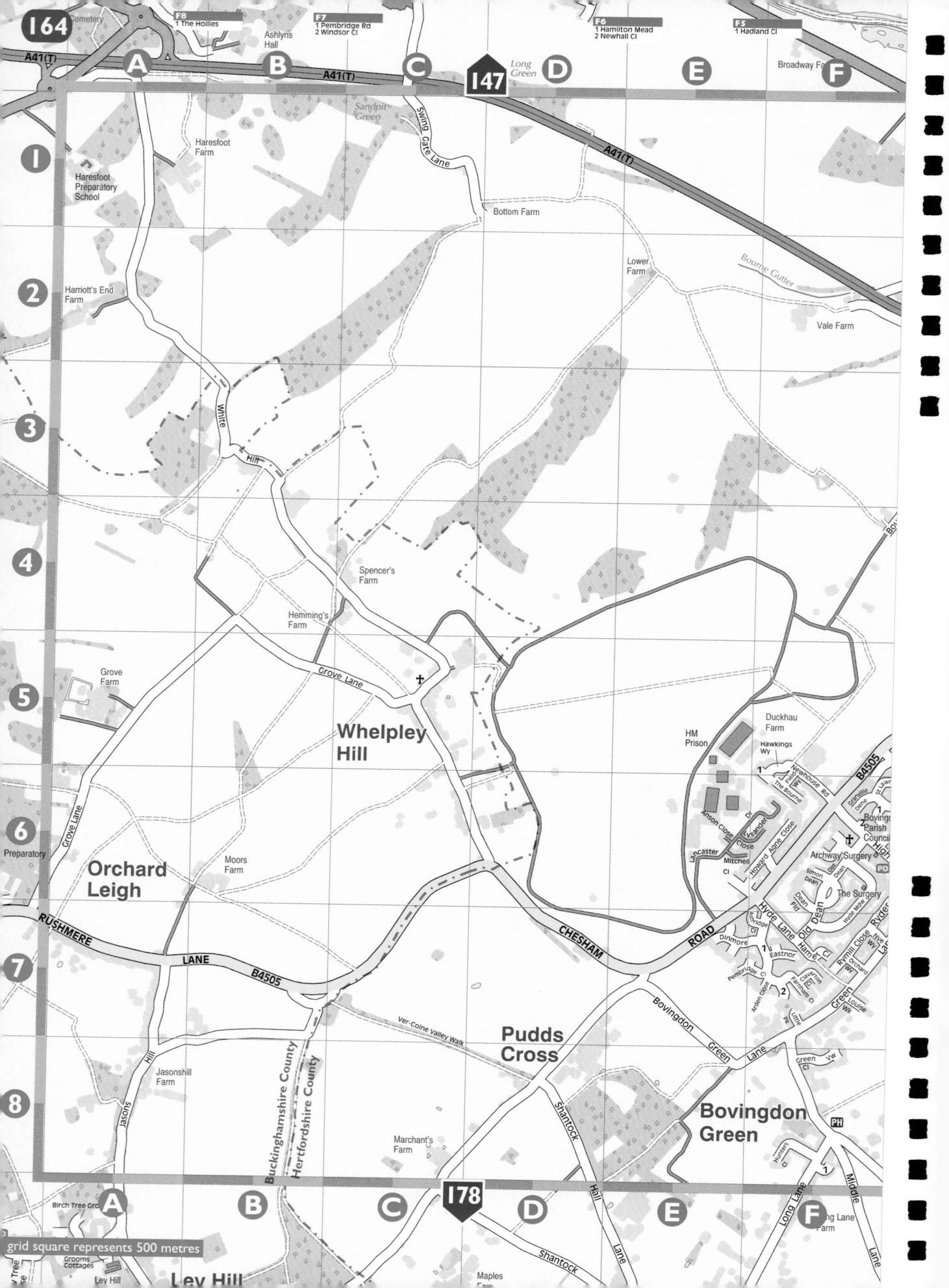
F8
1 The Hollies
F7
1 Pembridge Rd
2 Windsor Cl
F6
1 Hamilton Mead
2 Newhall Cl
F5
1 Hadland Cl
147
178
A41(T)
Cemetery
Ashlyns Hall
Long Green
Broadway Farm
Sandpit Green
Swing Gate Lane
Haresfoot Farm
Haresfoot Preparatory School
Bottom Farm
Lower Farm
Bourne Gutter
Harriott's End Farm
Vale Farm
White Hill
Spencer's Farm
Hemming's Farm
Grove Farm
Grove Lane
Whelpley Hill
Duckhau Farm
HM Prison
Hawkings Wy
Newhouse Rd
The Bourne
B4505
Granville Dene
Bovingdon Parish Council
Anson Close
Lysander Close
Agne Close
Lancaster
Mitchell Cl
Howard
Archway Surgery
PO
Simon Dean
Old Dean
Dean Fld
The Surgery
Preparatory
Grove Lane
Orchard Leigh
Moors Farm
RUSHMERE LANE
B4505
CHESHAM ROAD
Hyde Lane
Old Dean
Hyde Mdw
Ryder
Ashridge Cl
Dinmore
Eastnor
Hamer Cl
Rymill Close
Nye Wy
Orchard Wy
Pembridge Cl
Clayton
Farnham Cl
Arden Close
Little Pk
Green Wk
Louise Wk
Bovingdon Green Lane
Ver-Colne Valley Walk
Pudds Cross
Green Cl
Green Vw
Jasonshill Farm
Jasons Hill
Buckinghamshire County
Hertfordshire County
Shantock Hall Lane
Bovingdon Green
PH
Hunters Cl
Marchant's Farm
Long Lane
Middle Lane
Birch Tree Gro
Long Lane Farm
grid square represents 500 metres
Grooms Cottages
Ley Hill
Shantock
Maples

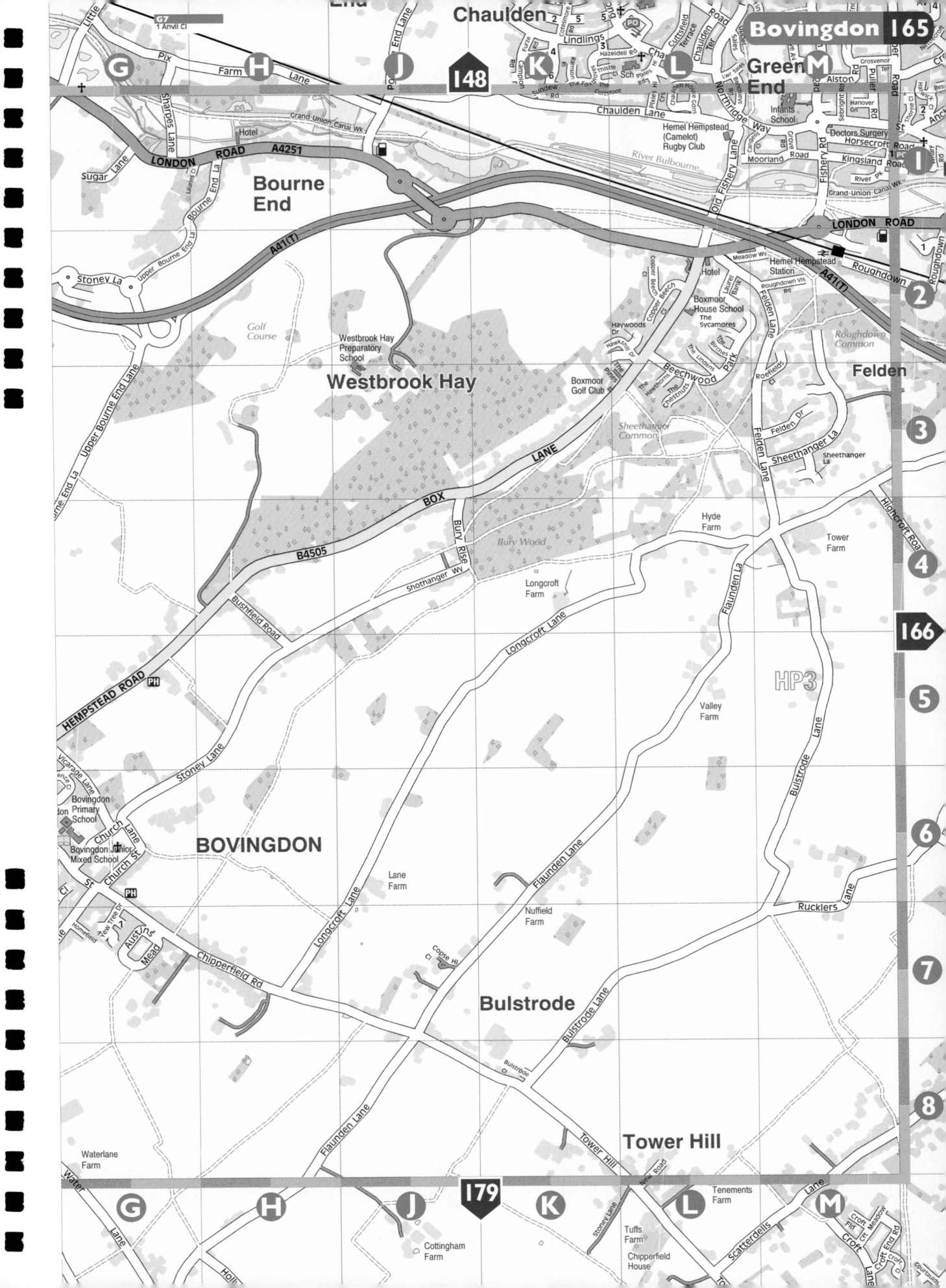
Chaulden
Green End
148
Pix Farm Lane
Sharpes Lane
Grand Union Canal Wk
Hotel
LONDON ROAD A4251
Sugar Lane
Bourne End
A41(T)
Stoney La
Upper Bourne End La
Chaulden Lane
Hemel Hempstead (Camelot) Rugby Club
River Bulbourne
Northridge Way
Old Fishery Lane
Infants School
Doctors Surgery
Horsecroft Road
Moorland Road
Kingsland Road
Fishery Rd
Grand Union Canal Wk
LONDON ROAD
Roughdown
Meadow Wy
Hemel Hempstead Station
Hotel
Roughdown Vis Rd
Boxmoor House School
The Sycamores
Golf Course
Westbrook Hay Preparatory School
Westbrook Hay
Roughdown Common
Felden
Boxmoor Golf Club
Beechwood Park
Sheethanger Common
Felden Lane
Felden Dr
Sheethanger La
Upper Bourne End Lane
BOX LANE
B4505
Bury Rise
Bury Wood
Shothanger Wy
Longcroft Farm
Hyde Farm
Tower Farm
Highcroft Road
Flaunden La
Bushfield Road
Longcroft Lane
166
HEMPSTEAD ROAD
HP3
Valley Farm
Stoney Lane
Bulstrode Lane
Vicarage Lane
Bovingdon Primary School
Church Lane
Bovingdon Junior Mixed School
Church St
BOVINGDON
Flaunden Lane
Lane Farm
Nuffield Farm
Rucklers Lane
Longcroft Lane
Austins Mead
Chipperfield Rd
Copse Hl
Bulstrode
Bulstrode Lane
Bulstrode Cl
Flaunden Lane
Tower Hill
Tower Hill
Waterlane Farm
New Road
179
Water Lane
Tenements Farm
Stoney Lane
Tuffs Farm
Chipperfield House
Cottingham Farm
Scatterdells Lane
Croft Meadow
Croft End Rd
Croft Lane

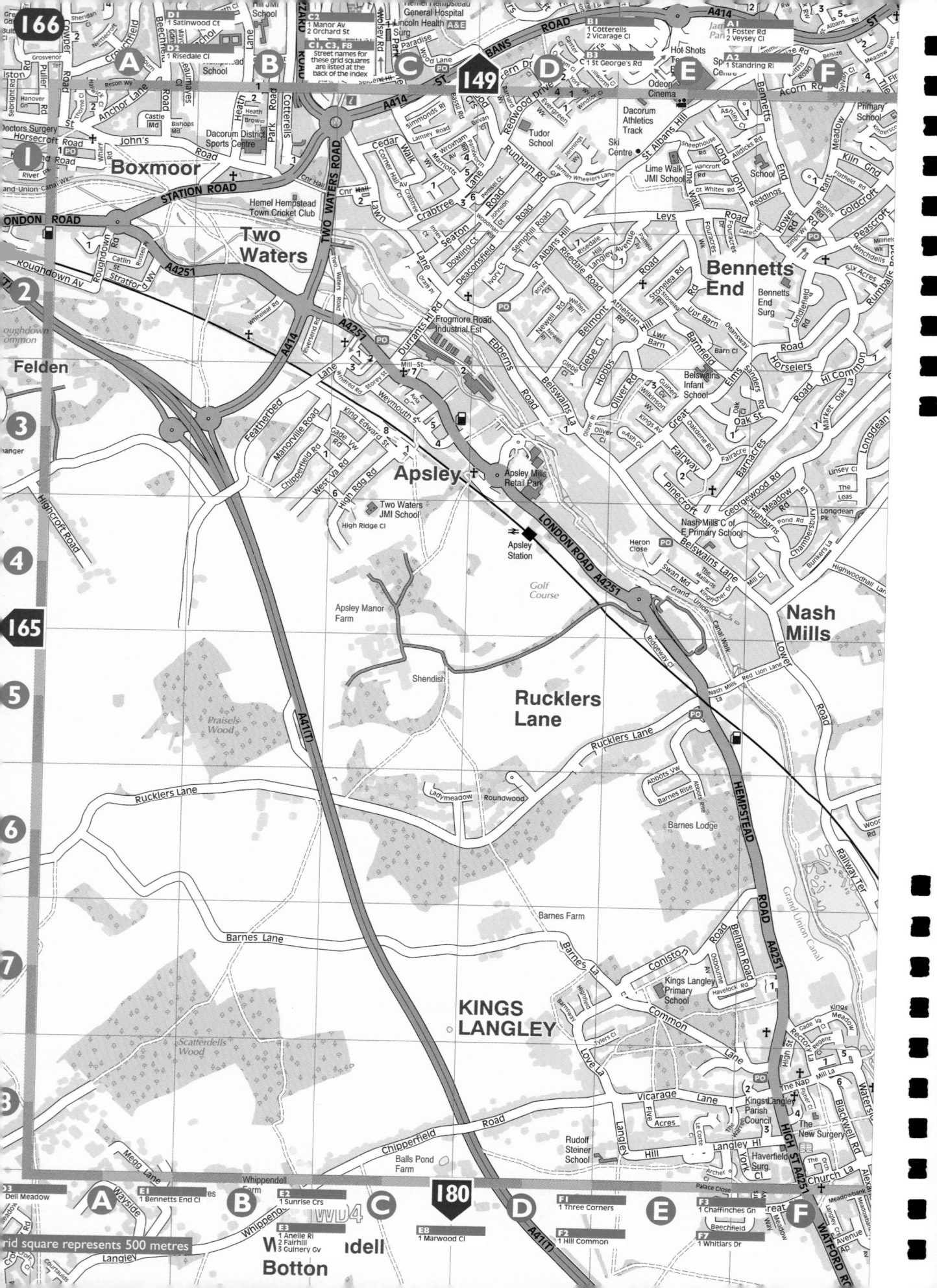

166
165
149
180
A
B
C
D
E
F
1
2
3
4
5
6
7
8
D1 1 Satinwood Ct
D2 1 Risedale Cl
C2 1 Manor Av 2 Orchard St
C1, C3, F8 Street names for these grid squares are listed at the back of the index
B1 1 Cotterells 2 Vicarage Cl
B3 1 St George's Rd
A1 1 Foster Rd 2 Veysey Cl
A2 1 Standring Rl
E1 1 Bennetts End Cl
E2 1 Sunrise Crs
E3 1 Anelle Rl 2 Fairhill 3 Guinery Gv
E8 1 Marwood Cl
F1 1 Three Corners
F2 1 Hill Common
F3 1 Chaffinches Gn
F7 1 Whitlars Dr
Dell Meadow
Grid square represents 500 metres
Hemel Hempstead General Hospital
Lincoln Health Surg
A&E
A414
ST ALBANS ROAD
Boxmoor
Two Waters
Apsley
Felden
Bennetts End
Nash Mills
Rucklers Lane
KINGS LANGLEY
Shendish
Apsley Manor Farm
Praisels Wood
Scatterdells Wood
Barnes Farm
Barnes Lodge
Golf Course
Apsley Station
Apsley Mills Retail Park
Frogmore Road Industrial Est
Two Waters JMI School
High Ridge Cl
Hemel Hempstead Town Cricket Club
Dacorum District Sports Centre
Dacorum Athletics Track
Ski Centre
Tudor School
Lime Walk JMI School
Odeon Cinema
Bennetts End Surg
Belswains Infant School
Nash Mills C of E Primary School
Kings Langley Primary School
Kings Langley Parish Council
Rudolf Steiner School
Haverfield Surg.
The New Surgery
Doctors Surgery
STATION ROAD
LONDON ROAD
TWO WATERS ROAD
A4251
A414
A41(T)
Roughdown Av
Highcroft Road
Featherbed Lane
Rucklers Lane
Barnes Lane
Chipperfield Road
Megg Lane
Vicarage Lane
Langley Hill
Love La
Common Lane
Coniston Road
Belham Road
HEMPSTEAD ROAD
HIGH ST A4251
WATFORD RD
Lower Road
Red Lion Lane
Nash Mills La
Ridgeway Cl
Grand Union Canal
Belswains Lane
Belswains Road
Ebberns Road
Durrants Hl Rd
Weymouth St
King Edward St
Manorville Road
Chipperfield Rd
West Va Rd
High Rdg Rd
Horseclers
Barnfield
Belmont Road
Hobbs Hill
Oliver Rd
Leys Road
St Albans Hill
Long John
Bennetts End Road
Acorn Rd
Redwood Drive
Runham Rd
Crabtree Lane
Cedar Walk
Seaton Road
Deaconsfield Road
Pinecroft
Barnacres
Georgewood Rd
Chambersbury
Highwoodhall La
Abbots Vw
Barnes Rise
Ladymeadow
Roundwood
Whippendell Farm
Botton
Wayside
WD4
Railway Ter

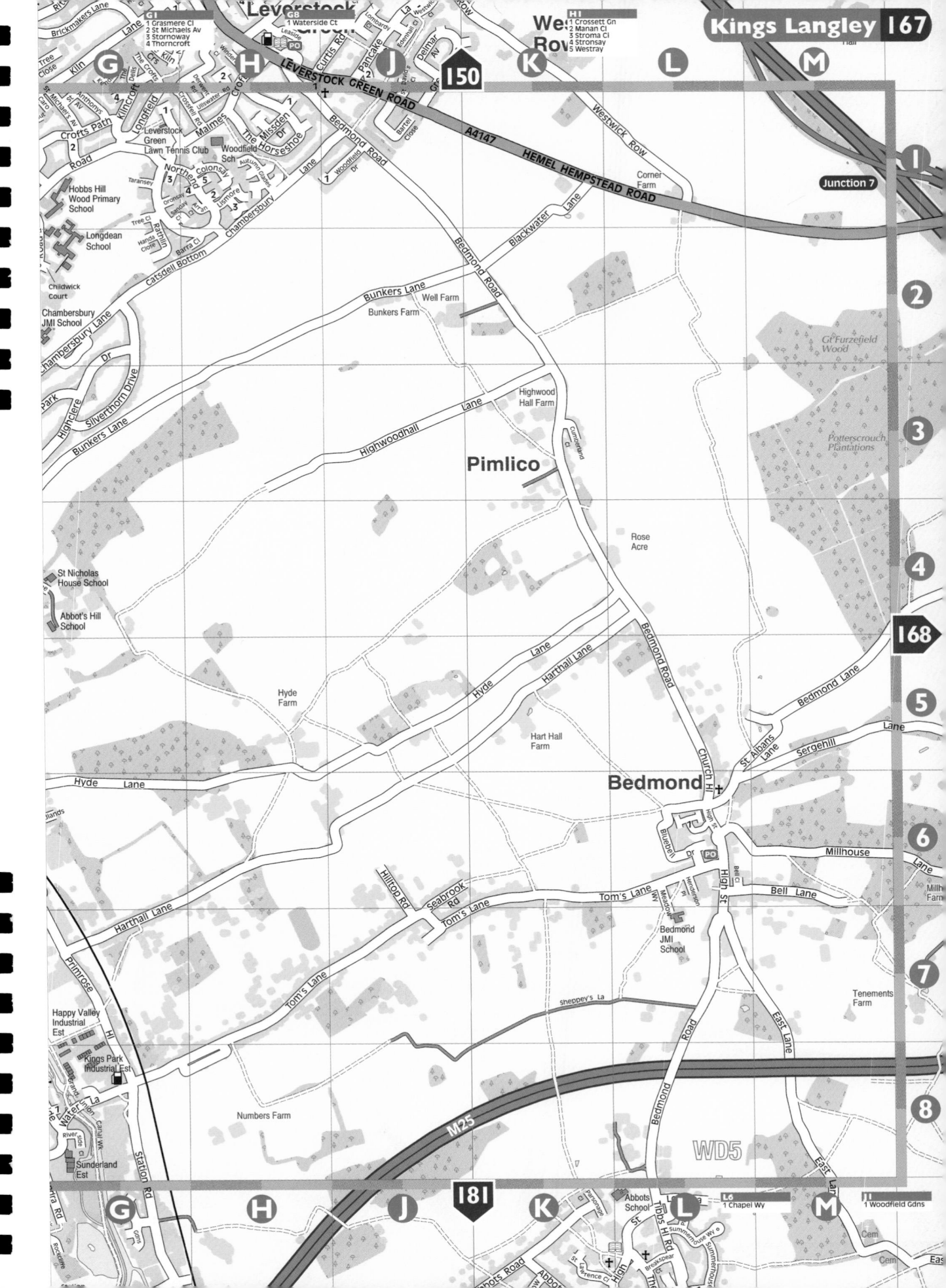

G1
1 Grasmere Cl
2 St Michaels Av
3 Stornoway
4 Thorncroft
G8
1 Waterside Ct
H1
1 Crossett Gn
2 Manan Cl
3 Stroma Cl
4 Stronsay
5 Westray
L6
1 Chapel Wy
J1
1 Woodfield Gdns
150
168
181
Leverstock Green Road
A4147
Hemel Hempstead Road
Junction 7
Westwick Row
Corner Farm
Bedmond Road
Woodfield Dr
Chambersbury Lane
Catsdell Bottom
Blackwater Lane
Bunkers Lane
Well Farm
Bunkers Farm
Hobbs Hill Wood Primary School
Longdean School
Childwick Court
Chambersbury JMI School
Leverstock Green Lawn Tennis Club
Woodfield Sch
Silverthorn Drive
Highclere
Highwood Hall Farm
Highwoodhall Lane
Cumberland Cl
Pimlico
Gt Furzefield Wood
Potterscrouch Plantations
Rose Acre
St Nicholas House School
Abbot's Hill School
Hyde Farm
Hyde Lane
Harthall Lane
Hart Hall Farm
Bedmond Lane
Sergehill Lane
St Albans Lane
Church Hl
Bedmond
High St
Bluebell Dr
Millhouse Lane
Bell Lane
Tom's Lane
Hilltop Rd
Seabrook Rd
Henderson Pl
Meadow Wy
Bedmond JMI School
Sheppey's La
East Lane
Tenements Farm
Primrose Hl
Happy Valley Industrial Est
Kings Park Industrial Est
Numbers Farm
M25
WD5
Riverside Cl
Sunderland Est
Station Rd
Canal Wk
Abbots School
Tibbs Hl Rd
Summerhouse Wy
Parsonage Ct
Breakspear Ct
St Lawrence Cl

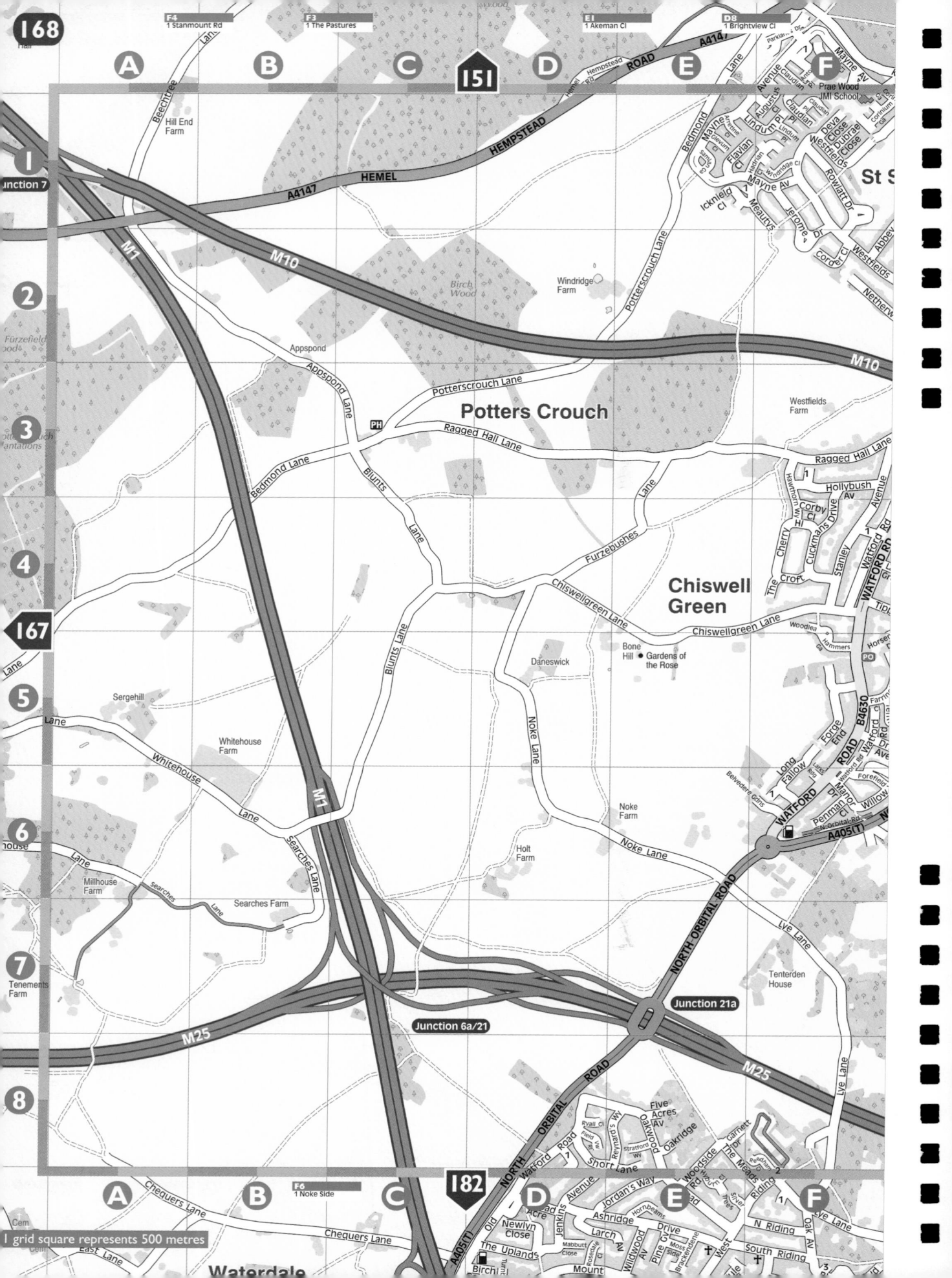
F4 1 Stanmount Rd
F3 1 The Pastures
E1 1 Akeman Cl
D8 1 Brightview Ct
151
182
167
Potters Crouch
Chiswell Green
Junction 7
Junction 6a/21
Junction 21a
M1
M10
M25
A4147
HEMEL HEMPSTEAD ROAD
NORTH ORBITAL ROAD
WATFORD ROAD
A405(T)
B4630
Hill End Farm
Appspond
Birch Wood
Windridge Farm
Westfields Farm
Prae Wood JMI School
Potterscrouch Lane
Appspond Lane
Ragged Hall Lane
Bedmond Lane
Blunts Lane
Furzebushes Lane
Chiswellgreen Lane
Noke Lane
Lye Lane
Whitehouse Lane
Searches Lane
Chequers Lane
Sergehill
Whitehouse Farm
Millhouse Farm
Searches Farm
Tenements Farm
Daneswick
Bone Hill
Gardens of the Rose
Noke Farm
Holt Farm
Tenterden House
Five Acres Av
Short Lane
Newlyn Close
The Uplands
F6 1 Noke Side
1 grid square represents 500 metres
Waterdale

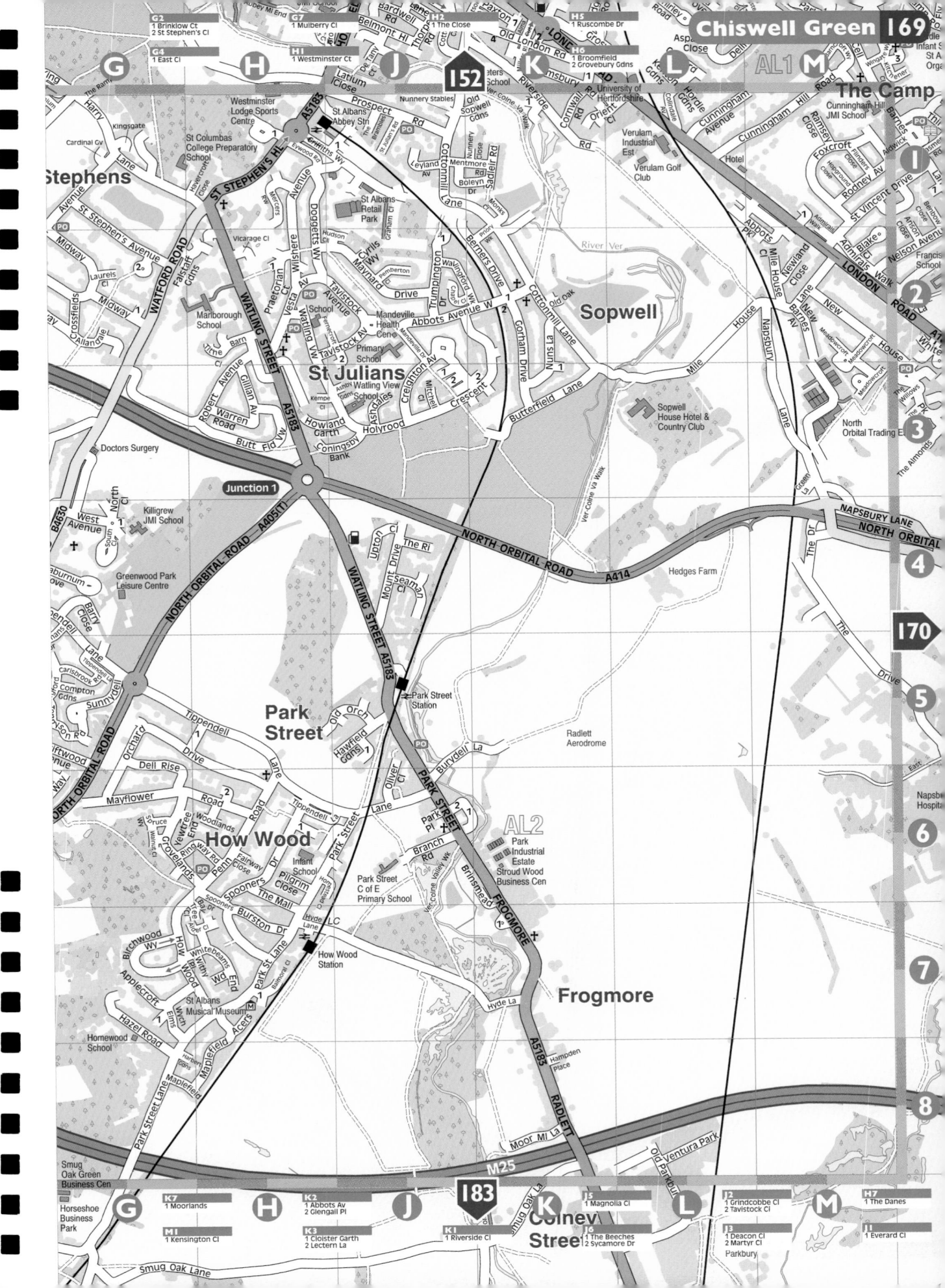
G2
1 Brinklow Ct
2 St Stephen's Cl
G7
1 Mulberry Cl
H2
1 The Close
H5
1 Ruscombe Dr
G4
1 East Cl
H1
1 Westminster Ct
H6
1 Broomfield
2 Grovebury Gdns
152
AL1
The Camp
Cunningham Hill JMI School
Westminster Lodge Sports Centre
St Columbas College Preparatory School
St Albans Abbey Stn
Nunnery Stables
University of Hertfordshire
Verulam Industrial Est
Verulam Golf Club
Stephens
St Albans Retail Park
River Ver
Sopwell
Marlborough School
Mandeville Health Cen
Primary School
St Julians
Watling View School
Sopwell House Hotel & Country Club
North Orbital Trading Est
Doctors Surgery
Junction 1
Killigrew JMI School
Greenwood Park Leisure Centre
NORTH ORBITAL ROAD
WATLING STREET
A5183
A414
A405(T)
Hedges Farm
170
Park Street
Park Street Station
Radlett Aerodrome
AL2
Park Industrial Estate
Stroud Wood Business Cen
How Wood
Infant School
Park Street C of E Primary School
How Wood Station
St Albans Musical Museum
Homewood School
Frogmore
M25
Smug Oak Green Business Cen
Horseshoe Business Park
Napsbury Hospital
183
K7
1 Moorlands
M1
1 Kensington Cl
K2
1 Abbots Av
2 Glengall Pl
K3
1 Cloister Garth
2 Lectern La
K1
1 Riverside Cl
J5
1 Magnolia Cl
J6
1 The Beeches
2 Sycamore Dr
J2
1 Grindcobbe Cl
2 Tavistock Cl
J3
1 Deacon Cl
2 Martyr Cl
H7
1 The Danes
J1
1 Everard Cl
Colney Street
Parkbury
Smug Oak Lane

170
153
169
184
The Camp
Tyttenhanger
LONDON COLNEY
Broad Colney
C4 1 Collingwood Dr
B1 1 Ashbourne Ct
C1 1 Newfield Wy
A2 1 Mountbatten Cl 2 Parkway Ct
A3 1 The Poplars
A1 1 Cell Barnes Cl
Smallford Farm
Colney Heath Lane
Windermere JMI Primary School
Francis Bacon School
Trestle Theatre Co
Highfield Lane
Tyttenhanger Green
Barley Mow Lane
NORTH ORBITAL ROAD
A414
A1081
LONDON ROAD
Nightingale Lane
Highfield Hall
Cemetery
Old Verulamians Rugby Football Club
SHENLEY LANE
B5378
Napsbury Hospital
Hertfordshire Business Cen
Mosquito Aircraft Mus
St Bernadette JMI School
Riverside Industrial Estate
Bowmansgreen Farm
Coursers Road
Lowbell Lane
River Colne
Nature Reserve
THE BELL ROUNDABOUT
Junction 22
M25
B556
BELL LANE
Pastoral Centre
C6 1 Birch Wy 2 Chicken La
D6 1 Armstrong Cl 2 Colnbrook Cl 3 Richardson Cl 4 Riverside 5 Robins Cl
E6 1 Ribbledale 2 Severnvale 3 Thamesdale 4 Tynedale
E7 1 Barnet Rd
rid square represents 500 metres

J2 1 Bennetts Cl
K2 1 Dellsome La
154
Bullen's Green
Colney Heath
Colney Heath JMI School
Police Station
Park Corner
Roestock
Junction 2
Cemetery
Tollgate Farm
Warren Farm
Tyttenhanger Farm
Coursers Farm
Coursers Road
River Colne
Tollgate Road
Walsingham Wood
North Mymms Cricket Club
Cobs Ash
Potwells
Mymmshall Wood
Redwell Wood
Hawkshead Wood
Redwell Wood Farm
Salisbury Hall
Mosquito Aircraft
Lodge School
The Grange
Ridgehill
172
185
A1(M)
A1001
A414
B556
M25
South Hatfi
Well Gree
Fellowes Lane
Dellsome Lane
Roestock Lane
High Street
Bishops Rise
Southdown Road
Bradshaws
Church Lane
Smallford
Sleapcross Gardens
Tollgate
Dixons
Hazel Grove JMI
Meadway
Hall Gardens
Admirals Close
Franklin Close
Roestock Gardens
Heathside
Park La
PO

155

C3
1 Coningsby Cl
2 Sibthorpe Rd

B3
1 Alderman Cl
2 Grove Pl

B2
1 Puttocks Cl
2 Somers Sq

A2
1 Bushwood Cl

A **B** **C** **D** **E** **F**

Woods

Woodside

South
Hatfield

Marshmoor

Lower
Woodside

AL9

I

Pooleys Lane

Travellers Cl
Alpha
Business Park

Welham Green
Station

A1000

GREAT NORTH ROAD

2

Welham
Green

Dixons

Somers Road

Nash Close

Booths Close

Holloways Lane

Welham
Manor

Bulls Lane

Bell
Bar

Bell Lane

3

Dixons Hill Close

Dixons Hill Road

A1(M)

Station Road

Potterells
Medical Centre

Potterells

Golf Club Road

The

Ash Close

4

171

Toligar Road

Peplins Way

Brookmans Park
GM Primary School

Avenue

5

North Mymms
Cricket Club

Bradmore Lane

Peplins Way

Peplins Cl

Green Cl

PO

Bradmore
Green

Brookmans

Lane

Park Close

Moffats Close

Brookmans
Park

Doctors
Surgery

The Grove

Mymr

Water
End

Brookmans Park
Station

Oaklands Avenue

Moffats

Blue Bridge Road

Bluebridge
Avenue

6

Abdale
Lane

Swanland Road

Warrengate Road

Westland Drive

The Gardens

7

Royal Veterinary
College

New
Cottages

Hawkshead Lane

Reeves
Cottages

Boltons Park

8

Mimmshall Brook

Cranborne
Industrial
Estate

A **B** **C** **D** **E** **F**

Cranborne Road

Cranborne
Industrial

Warrengate

Green Meadow

Westwood
Close

Heath Drive

1 grid square represents 500 metres

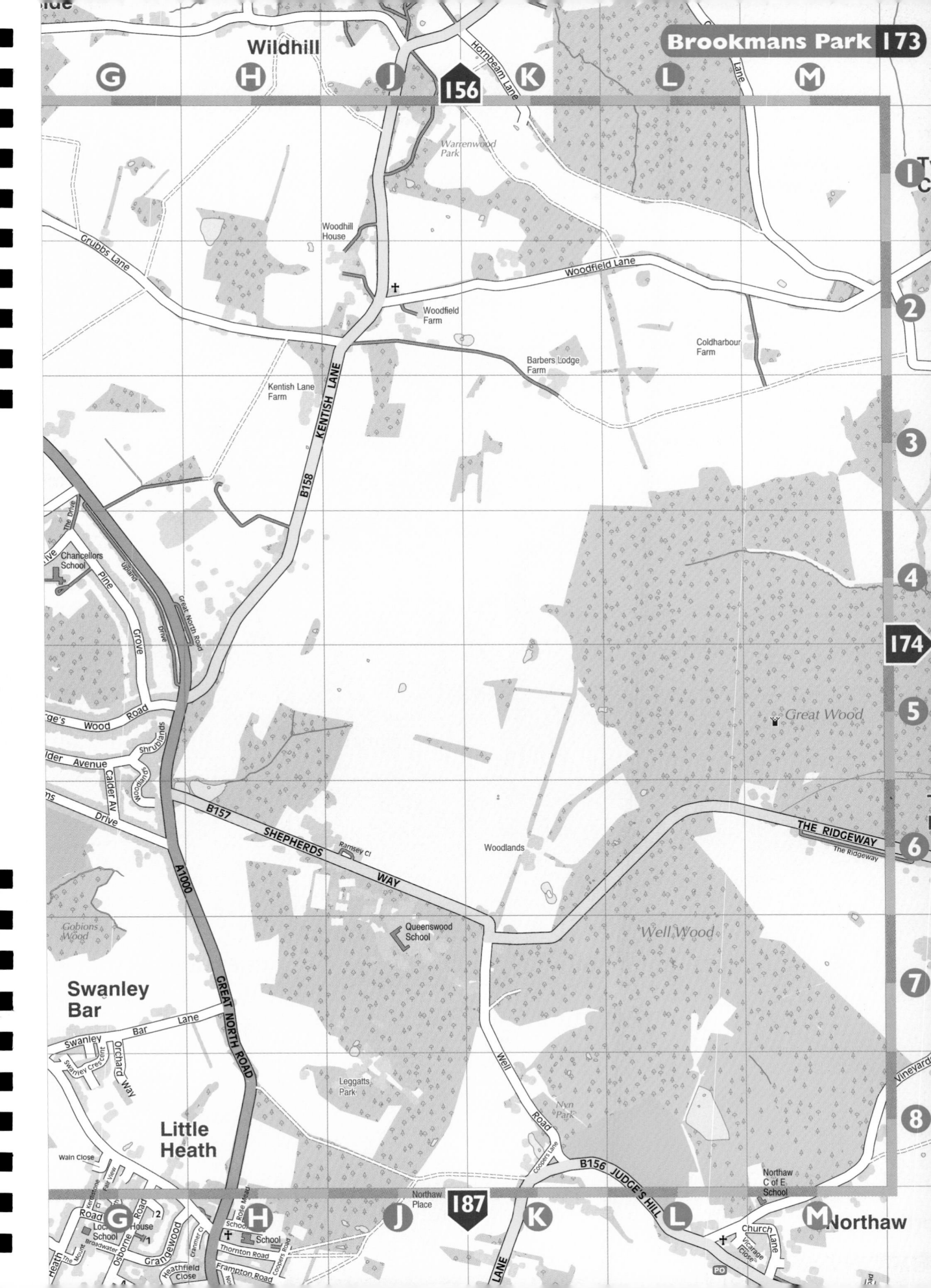

Wildhill

G H J 156 K L M

1 T

Warrenwood Park

2

Woodhill House

Woodfield Lane

Grubbs Lane

† Woodfield Farm

Coldharbour Farm

Barbers Lodge Farm

Kentish Lane Farm

3

KENTISH LANE

B158

The Drive

Chancellors School

Pine

Grove

Great North Road

Drive

4

174

5

Great Wood

St George's Wood

Shrublands

Woodlands

Calder Avenue

Calder Av

Drive

A1000

B157

SHEPHERDS WAY

Ramsey Cl

Woodlands

THE RIGEWAY

The Ridgeway

6

Gobions Wood

Queenswood School

Well Wood

7

Swanley Bar

Bar Lane

GREAT NORTH ROAD

Swanley

Orchard Way

Swanley Cresent

Well

Road

Nyn Park

Leggatts Park

Vineyards

8

Little Heath

Wain Close

Cooper's Lane

B156 JUDGE'S HILL

Northaw C of E. School

Road

Flat View

School

Northaw Place

G 187 H J K L M Northaw

Church

Lock School

House

Grangewood

Broadwater

Thornton Road

Frampton Road

Cooper's Road

LANE

Vicarage Close

PO

Heathfield Close

The Mount

Osborne Road

Cranmer Cl

Heath Road

Herfordshire Cl

174
157
173
188
A
B
C
D
E
F
1
2
3
4
5
6
7
8
House School
Old Claypits Farm
D8
1 Maynard Pl
Epping Green
Tylers Causeway
Woodcock Lodge Farm
Chain Walk
Tylers Causeway
Ponsbourne Tunnel
Ponsbourne Park
Newgate Street
Newgate Street
New Park Farm
New Park Road
PO
Ponsbourne St Marys JMI School
Newgate Street Village
Saint Lawrence Farm
Darnicle Hill
Justice Hill
Burleigh Farm
Grimes Brook
Carbone Hill
Chain Walk
Tolmers
The Ridgeway
Homewood Lane
Home Wood
Brookside
Crescent
Homewood Avenue
Cheshunt Common
B157
Bradgate
Coulter Cl
Warwick Avenue
Warwick Close
Hill Rise
Farm Close
High Ridge
Tolmers Road
Wood Vw
Bradgate Close
Bradgate
Hanyards Lane
High Fields
Robin Way
Hill Leys
Thrush Lane
CUFFLEY
Leefe Way
Sutherland Avenue
Hill Rise
Tolmers Avenue
Orchard Close
Foxes Lane
Starling Lane
The Meadway
Sutherland Way
The Driveway
Kingsmead
B157
EAST RIDGEWAY
Vineyards Road
Oak Lane
Acorn Lane
Cuffley Station
Cranfield Crescent
Bacons Drive
PLOUGH HILL
Health Centre
Tolmers Gardens
CUFFLEY
STATION ROAD
B156
Church Close
PO
Lambs Cl
Sopers Road
King James Avenue
Cuffley Brook
Road
orthaw
Theobald's
Colesdale
Theobald's Close
South Drive
Wells
Cuffley

1 grid square represents 500 metres

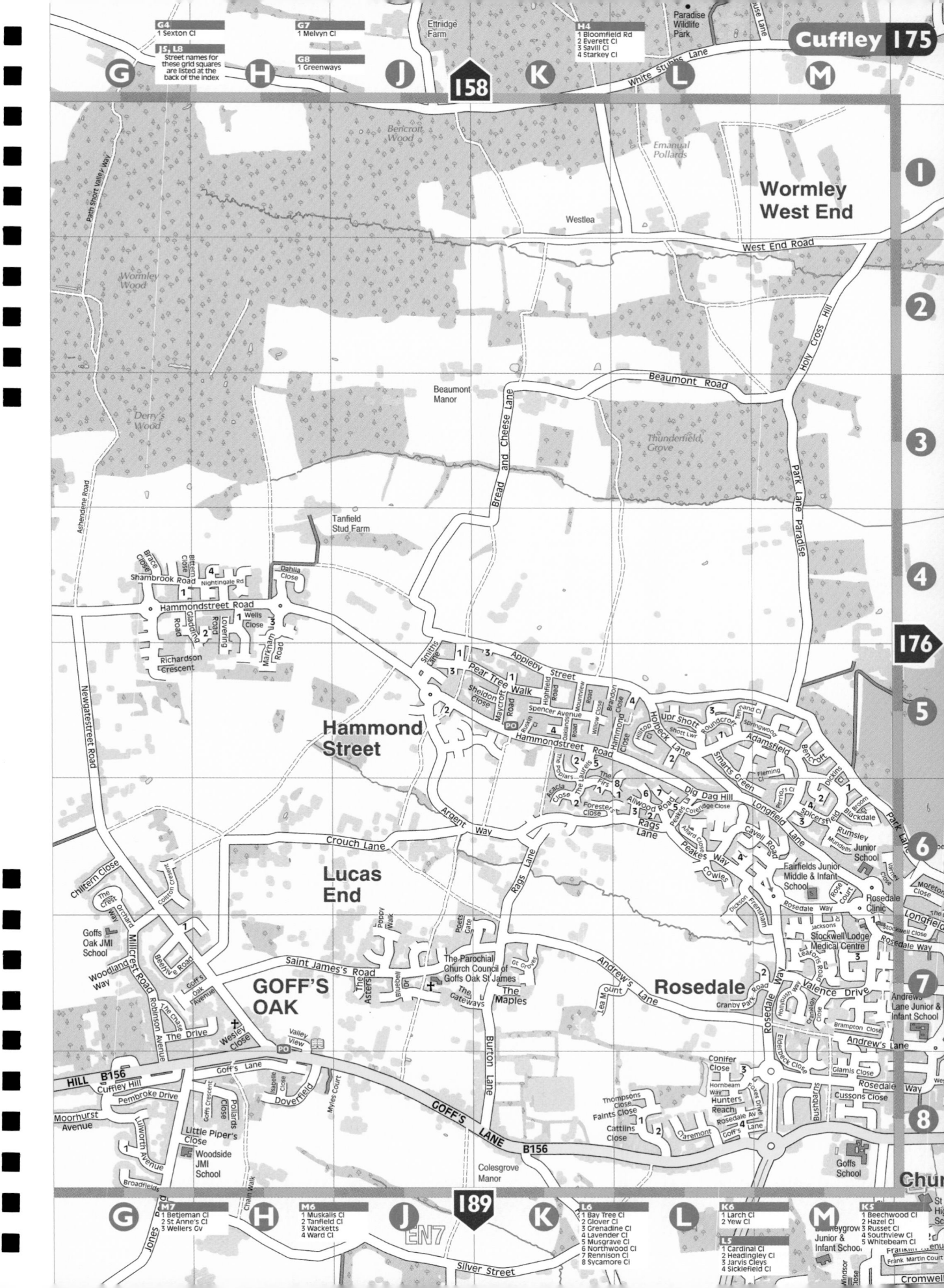

G **H** **J** **158** **K** **L** **M**

I

Paradise
Wildlife
Park

Wormley
West End

Westlea

West End Road

2

Bencroft
Wood

Emanual
Pollards

Holy Cross Hill

Wormley
Wood

Beaumont Road

3

Beaumont
Manor

Thunderfield
Grove

Park Lane Paradise

Derry's
Wood

Bread and Cheese Lane

Ashendene Road

Path short valley Way

Tanfield
Stud Farm

4

Dahlia
Close

Brace
Close

Bittern
Close

4

Shambrook Road

Nightingale Rd

Hammondstreet Road

Gladding
Road

Lovering

Markham
Road

Wells
Close

1

1

Richardson
Crescent

Appleby Street

3

1

Pear Tree Walk

Smiths Lane

Highfield Road

Mountview Road

Willow Close

Brandon Close

176

Maycroft Road

Sheldon
Close

Spencer Avenue

Oakland Road

Hammond Close

Holbeck Lane

Upr shott

Short Lwr

Roundacre

Springwood

Adamsfield

Betycroft

5

Newgatestreet Road

**Hammond
Street**

PO

Hammondstreet Road

Hilltop

The Laurels

The Firs

The Poplars

The Poplars

Acacia
Close

Allwood Road

6

8

Forester
Close

Dig Dag Hill

Aftard Close

Peakes
Way

Coleridge Close

Smarts Green

Longfield

Spicersfield

Rumsley

Blackdale

Broom

Dickins

Perrick

Mundens

Cavell Road

Fleming

Park

6

Argent Way

Rags Lane

Rags Lane

Cowley

Fairfields Junior
Middle & Infant
School

Rosedale
Clinic

Rumsley
Junior
School

Longfield
Close

Morston
Close

Chiltern Close

Crouch Lane

The
Crest

Poppy Walk

Poets
Gate

Andrew's Lane

Dickson

Frensham

Rosedale Way

Jacksons

Valence Drive

Road Court

Stockwell Close

Rosedale Way

7

Goffs
Oak JMI
School

Woodland
Way

Millcrest Road

Colsten Crescent

Orchard
Way

Beehive Road

1

Goff's
Oak
Avenue

**GOFF'S
OAK**

Saint James's Road

The
Asters

Bluebells

The
Gateways

The Parochial
Church Council of
Goffs Oak St James

Gt Groves

The Maples

Lea Mount

Andrew's Lane

Rosedale

Granby Park

Stockwell Lodge
Medical Centre

Leaford's Road

Rosedale Way

Andrews
Lane Junior &
Infant School

Brampton Close

3

The Chase

Robinson Avenue

The Drive

Wesley
Close

PO

Valley
View

Isabelle
Close

Myles Court

Burton Lane

Andrew's Lane

Conifer
Close

3

Glamis Close

HILL **B156**

Moorhurst
Avenue

Cuffley Hill

Pembroke Drive

Goffs Crescent

Pollards
Close

Little Piper's
Close

Woodside
JMI
School

Linworth Avenue

Broadfields

Goff's Lane

Dovectield

Chain Walk

GOFF'S LANE

B156

Colesgrove
Manor

Thompsons
Close

Faints Close

Cattlins
Close

Claremont

Hornbeam
Way

Hunters
Reach

Rosedale Av

Goff's
Lane

Bushbarns

Elderbeck Close

Sykes Drive

Cussons Close

Rosedale
Way

Goffs
School

Chur

8

G **189** **H** **J** **EN7** **K** **L** **M**

Silver Street

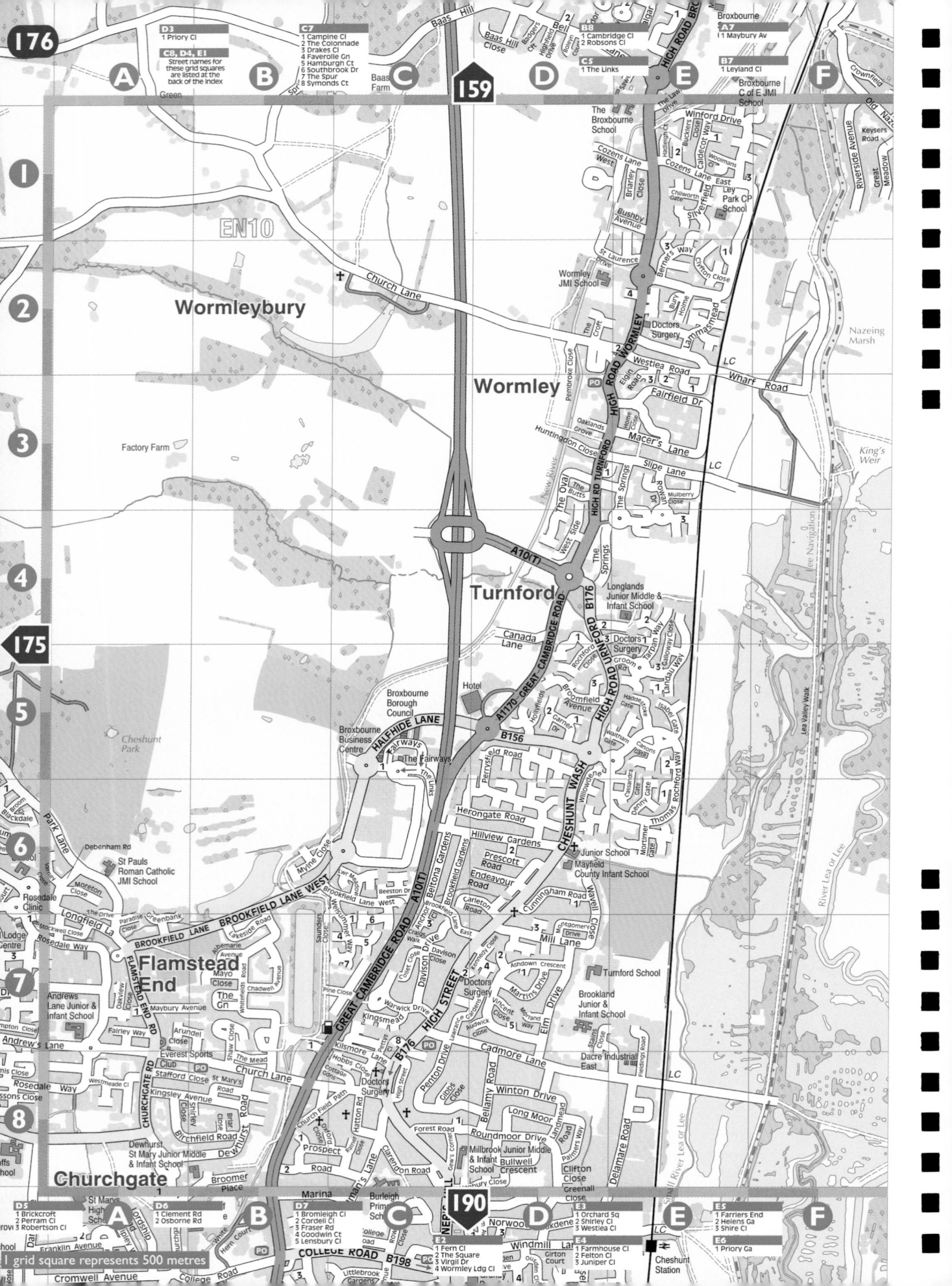

A   B   C   159   D   E   F

EN10

Green

Baas Hill

Baas Hill
Close

Baas
Farm

Broxborne

Crownfield

The
Broxbourne
School

Broxbourne
C of E JMI
School

Winford Drive

Caldecot Way

Woomans

Riverside Avenue

Keysers
Road

Great Meadow

I

Cozens Lane
West

Cozens Lane
East

Chilworth
Gate

Ley
Park CP
School

Silverfield

Nazeing
Marsh

2

Wormleybury

Church Lane

St Laurence
Drive

Wormley
JMI School

Bushby
Avenue

Berners Way

Clifton
Close

Westlea Road

Wharf   Road

LC

3

Factory Farm

Pembroke Close

Wormley

HIGH ROAD WORMLEY

PO

Eigin

Home

Doctors
Surgery

Fairfield Dr

Macer's   Lane

LC

King's
Weir

Oaklands
Grove

Huntingdon Close

The Butts

The Oval

HIGH RD TURNFORD

The Springs

Slipe Lane

Mulberry
Close

LC

Lee Valley Walk

4

175

West Side

A10(T)

Turnford

B176

Longlands
Junior Middle &
Infant School

Canada
Lane

Rochford
Close

Doctors
Surgery

Groom
Rd

Tarpan Way

Galloway Close

Landau Way

Lee Navigation

Cheshunt
Park

Broxbourne
Borough
Council

Hotel

Broxbourne
Business
Centre

HALFHIDE LANE

Fairways

The Fairways

The Links

A117g - GREAT CAMBRIDGE ROAD

B156

HIGH ROAD TURNFORD

Hollyfields

Broomfield
Avenue

Hadley
Gate

Garner
Dr

Waltham
Gate

Isabel Gate

Canons
Gate

5

Perrysfield Road

Herongate Road

Hillview Gardens

CHESHUNT WASH

Chesandra

Denny
Gate

Willowside

Mortimer
Gate

Thomas Rochford Way

Broom
Blackdale

Park Lane

Debenham Rd

St Pauls
Roman Catholic
JMI School

Moreton
Close

The Drive

Paradise Close

Greenbank

Myme Close

Lwr Meadow

Beeston Dr

Brookfield Gardens

Beltona Gardens

Prescott
Road

Endeavour
Road

Junior School

Mayfield
County Infant School

Cunningham Road

6

Rosedale
Clinic

Longfield La

Rosedale Way

Stockwell Close

BROOKFIELD LANE

BROOKFIELD LANE WEST

Albemarie
Avenue

Saunders
Road

Weymouth
Way

Lakeside Road

Archer
Road

BROOKFIELD GARDENS

Davison
Drive

Craigs
Walk

Colvet Close

Davison
Close

Carleton
Road

Kemsley Close

Ashdown Crescent

Montgomery
Drive

Mill Lane

Lodge
Centre

Flamstead
End

FLAMSTEAD END RD

Mayo
Close

Whiterfields Road

Chadwell

The
Gn

Pine Lane

GREAT CAMBRIDGE ROAD

A10(T)

HIGH STREET

Doctors
Surgery

Martins Lane

Vincent
Close

Morand
Way

Elm Drive

Stains
Close

Brookland
Junior &
Infant School

Turnford School

7

Andrews
Lane Junior &
Infant School

Oakview

Fairley Way

Maybury Avenue

Arundel
Close

Shaw Close

The Mead

Everest Sports
Club

Warwick Drive

Kingsmead

B176

PO

Lawrence
Gardens

Aldwick
Close

Cadmore Lane

Dacre Industrial
East

LC

Andrew's Lane

Rosedale
Way

Westmeade Cl

CHURCHGATE RD

Kingsley Avenue

Shirley
Road

St Mary's
Road

Brid
Close

Birchfield Road

Dewhurst Road

Stafford Close

Church Lane

Church Field Path

Kilsmore
Lane

Hobbs Close

Cottage
Close

Doctors
Surgery

Penton Drive

Dobbs
Close

Bellamy Road

Long Moor

Winton Drive

Landmead

Palmers Way

Clifton
Close

Greenall
Close

Delamare Road

LC

Small River Lea or Lee

8

Rosedale   Way

ssons Close

Dewhurst
St Mary Junior Middle &
Infant School

Churchgate

Broomer
Place

Hatton Rd

Oxford
Road

Ravel
Road

Prospect
Road

Forest Road

Roundmoor Drive

Millbrook Junior Middle
& Infant School

Bullwell
Crescent

A   B   C   190   D   E   F

Franklin   Avenue

Cromwell   Avenue

COLLEGE ROAD

Marina

Burleigh
Primary
Sch

B198

NEP

Windmill Lane

Norwood

Girton
Court

Littlebrook
Gardens

Cheshunt
Station

190

G   H   J   **160**   K   L   M

J1
1 Nazeingbury Cl

K1
1 Langfield Cl
2 Whitehall Cl

L1
1 Hoecroft

Keysers Estate

PECK's Hill

North Stream Road

Buttondene Crescent

Green Lane

Old Nazeing Road

Hillgrove Business Park

Nursery Road

Elizabeth Close

Elizabeth Close

PO

Lower Nazeing

North Street

John Clo

Highbridge Road

Short Lane

Banes Down

Shooters Drive

Western Road

1

2

1

Wheelers Close

Palmers Grove

Hoe Lane

Sunnyside

1

Barnfield Close

Mayflower Close

Crooked Way

Hyde Mead

Nazeing CP School

Barnard Acres

Tovey Close

Middle Street

I

Tatsfield Avenue

Perry Hill

Perry Hill

Curtis Farm

Middle

Street

2

3

Bumble's Green

Paynes Lane

SAINT LEONARDS ROAD

St Leonards

Laundry Lane

Waltham Road

Nazeing Long Gree

4

Langridge

Coleman's Lane

Felsteads

5

Lee Valley Park

Holyfield Hall Farm

Marsh Hill House

MARSH HILL B194

Waltham Road

Galleyhill Green

6

C

Galleyhill Wood

7

Hayes Hill Farm

Holyfield

B194

Aimes Green

Claverhambury Road

Claverhambury Road

HOLYFIELD ROAD B194

EN9

Deerpark Wood

8

Monkhams Hall

Fishers Green

Dallam House

Breaches Farm

G   H   **191**   J   K   L   M

CROOKED M

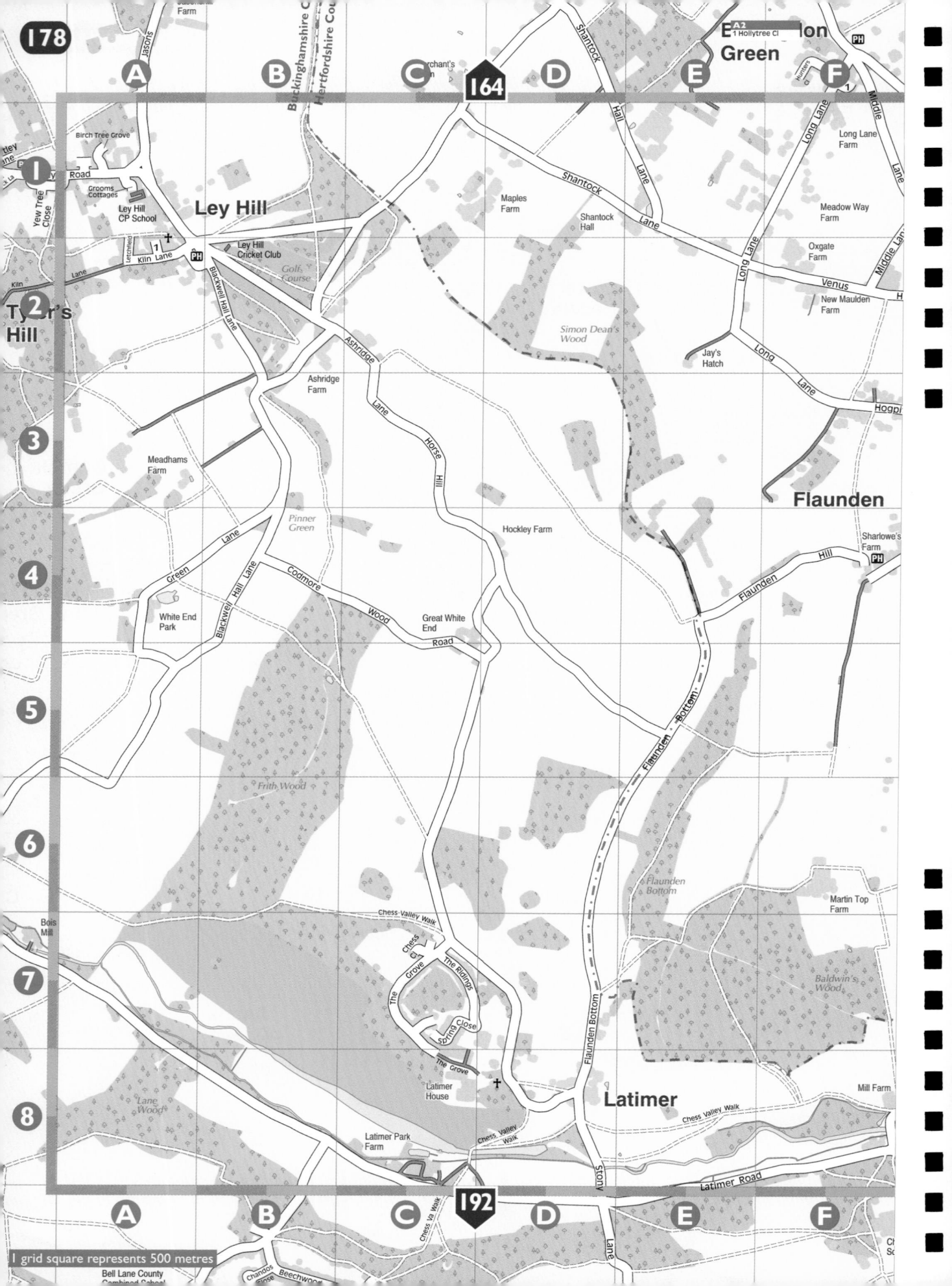

A   B   C   164   D   E   F

Green

E A2
1 Hollytree Cl

PH

Birch Tree Grove

Road

Grooms
Cottages

Ley Hill
CP School

Ley Hill

Ley Hill
Cricket Club

Maples
Farm

Shantock
Hall

Meadow Way
Farm

Oxgate
Farm

1

Yew Tree
Close

Letchfield

1

Kiln Lane

Kiln   Lane

PH

Blackwell Hall Lane

Golf
Course

Shantock   Lane

Long Lane

Long Lane
Farm

2

Ty?er's
Hill

Venus

New Maulden
Farm

Ashridge
Farm

Ashridge

Lane

Simon Dean's
Wood

Jay's
Hatch

Long   Lane

Hogpi

3

Meadhams
Farm

Horse   Hill

Flaunden

Pinner
Green

Hockley Farm

Sharlowe's
Farm

PH

Green   Lane

Blackwell Hall Lane

Codmore

Wood

Great White
End

Hill

Flaunden

4

White End
Park

Road

Flaunden

5

Frith Wood

Flaunden   Bottom

6

Flaunden
Bottom

Martin Top
Farm

Bois
Mill

Chess Valley Walk

Chess   Cl

The Ridings

Baldwin's
Wood

7

The Grove

Springs

Close

Flaunden Bottom

The Grove

Latimer
House

Latimer

Mill Farm

8

Lane
Wood

Latimer Park
Farm

Chess   Valley   Walk

Chess Valley Walk

Stony

Latimer Road

A   B   C   192   D   E   F

Chess va Walk

Bell Lane County
Combined School

Chandos

Beechwood

1 grid square represents 500 metres

L4
1 Dunny La
G
H
J
K
L
M
165
193
180
Tower Hill
Waterlane Farm
Venus Hill
Venus Hill Farm
Hogpits Bottom
Lower Plantation
Holly Hedges Lane
Flaunden Lane
Birch Lane
Cottingham Farm
Woodman's Wood
Cherry Trees Farm
Olleberrie Lane
Hollow Hedge
Belsize
Woodmans Farm
Whitedell Farm
Flaunden Lane
Bragmans Lane
Rose Hall Farm
Rosehall Wood
Poles Hill
Plough Lane
Belsize Farm
Hillmeads Farm
Penman's Green
Windmill Hill
Ltl Windmill Hl
Dunny Lane
Rose Farm
The Common
Chipperfield Common
Queen St
Chipperfield Junior & Infant School
Hotel
The Street
Chapel Croft
Pale Farm
Braziers Farm
Tower Hill
Scatterdells Lane
Tenements Farm
Tuffs Farm
Chipperfield House
Stoney Lane
New Road
Croft Lane
Courtaulds
Commonwood
Hollin's Hall
Moonshine Farm
Great Sarratt Hall
Red Lion Lane
Sarratt
Moor Lane
Dawes Lane
Downer Dr
Alexandra Rd
Sarratt JMI School
The Surgery
Church Lane
Dimmocks Lane
Sarratt Road
Valley Farm
Chess Valley Walk
River Chess
Mount Wood
Sarratt Bottom
Chenies Place
Holloway Lane
Green End Business Centre
Mountwood Farm
Chenies
Church End
Micklefield Green
PH
PO
P

180

A   B   C   **166**   D   E   F

Copperfield Road

Balls Pond Farm

Rudolf Steiner School

Vicarage Lane

Five Acres

Le Corte

The New Surgery

Kingst Langley Parish Council

The Nap

Blackwell Rd

Waters

Langley HI

YORK

Haverfield Surg.

Church La

Palace Close

Great PK

Meadowbank

Beechfield

WALFORD ROAD

Megg Lane

Meggacres Farm

Wayside

Whippendell Farm

WD4

Whippendell Hill

Langley Road

Whippendell Botton

A41(T)

Croft Fld

Meadow

Croft End Rd

I

Crofts

Croft Lane

Courtyards

Alexandra

Chapel Croft

Pale Farm

2

Street

King's Lane

Havenfield

King's Cl

Chipperfield

Hotel

PH

P

Rockery Wood

Langley Ldg La

Langley Lodge Lane

Langley Lodge Lane

Cla Far

Junction 20

Chipperfield Common

3

The Common

Langley Lodge Farm

Callipers Hall

Bucks Hill

4

Jeffery's Farm

Berrybushes Wood

179

PH

Quickmoor Lane

onenwood

Baytree Farm

Model Farm

Bucks Hill

5

P

Bucks Hill

Great Westwood

Old House Lane

Lane

6

arratt

Bottom Lane

Caroon Drive

Ash Lane

Buck's Hill Bottom

Deadman's

Braes

George Wy

7

Dimmocks Lane

Tom's Hill

Junction 19

Lane

Newhall Farm

Templepan Lane

Yew Court Farm

Sarratt Road

Chandler's Lane

M25

White House

8

Centre

Mickleford Green

White Shack Lane

Chandler's Cres

Fir Tree Hill

A   B   C   **194**   D   E   F

1 grid square represents 500 metres

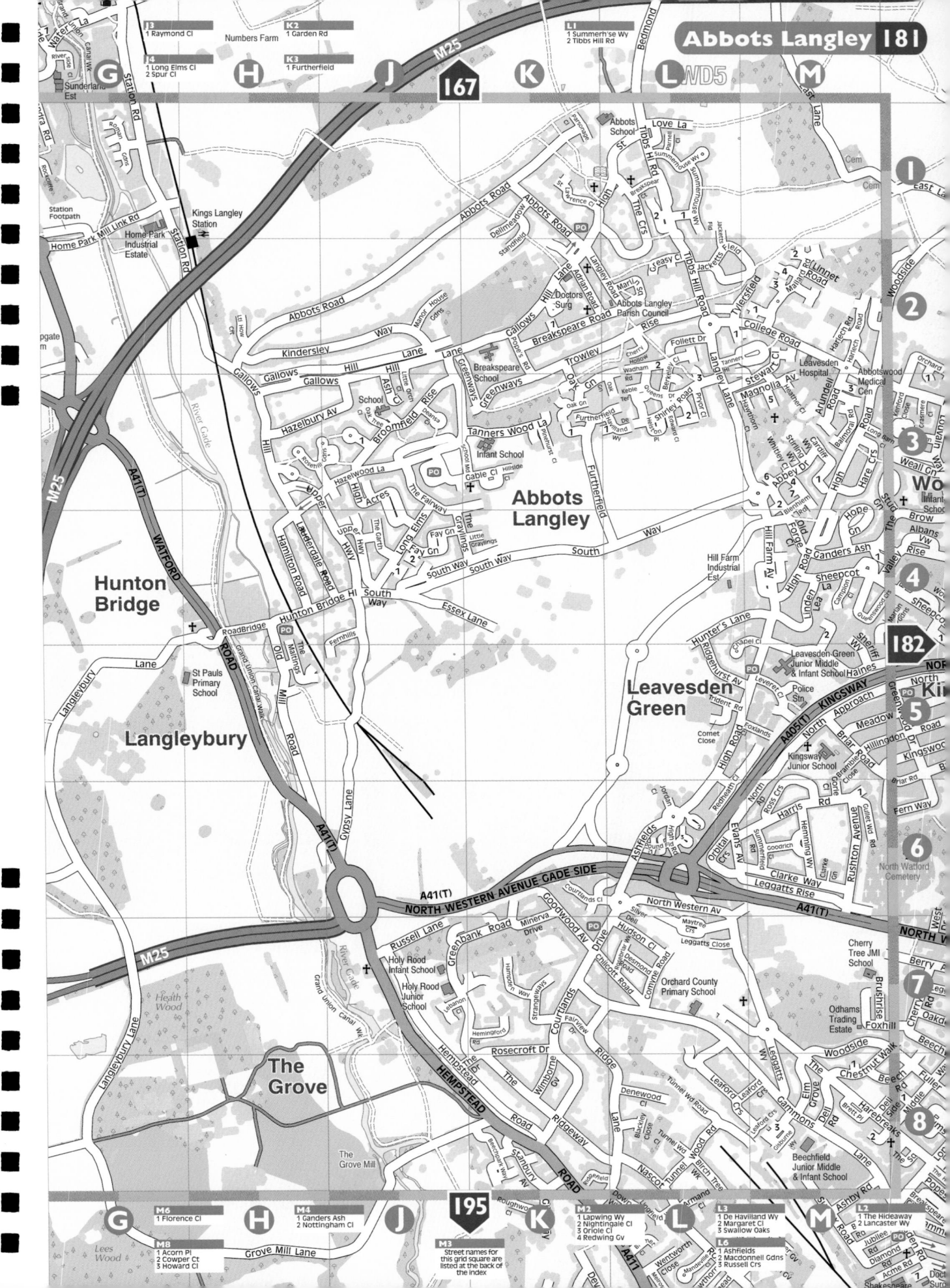

J3
1 Raymond Cl

Numbers Farm

K2
1 Garden Rd

L1
1 Summerh'se Wy
2 Tibbs Hill Rd

J4
1 Long Elms Cl
2 Spur Cl

K3
1 Furtherfield

G   H   J   **167**   K   L   WD5   M

M25

Home Park Mill Link Rd
Kings Langley Station
Station Footpath
Station Rd
Home Park Industrial Estate

Abbots School
Love La
High St
Breakspear

Abbots Road

Abbots Road
Kindersley Way
Gallows Hill Lane
Gallows Gallows Hill
Hazelbury Av
Broomfield Rise
Hazelwood La
The Acres
The Fairway
The Garth
Long Elms
Fay Gn
South Way
South Way
South Way
Essex Lane

Breakspeare School
Greenways
Greenways
Trowley Rise
Tanners Wood La
Infant School

Abbots Langley

College Road
Langley Road
Leavesden Hospital
Abbotswood Medical Cen

Furtherfield
Furtherfield
South Way

Hill Farm Industrial Est

Woodside

I
2
3

Wo

Weall Gn

Wo

Albans Vw
Canders Ash
Sheepcot La

4

182
NOR

Hunter's Lane

Leavesden Green Junior Middle & Infant School Haines
Police Stn.

Leavesden Green

Comet Close

Hunton Bridge

Watford Road
Lane
St Pauls Primary School
Hunton Bridge Hl
The Maltings
Old Mill Road
Ferrhills
A41(T)
Gypsy Lane

Langleybury

Langleybury Lane
Grand Union Canal Walk
River Gade

Heath Wood

M25

The Grove

The Grove Mill

Holy Rood Infant School
Holy Rood Junior School

A41(T)
NORTH WESTERN AVENUE GADE SIDE
North Western Av

Russell Lane
Greenbank Road
Minerva Drive

Hempstead Road

Orchard County Primary School

Cherry Tree JMI School

Odhams Trading Estate

Woodside

KINGSWAY
A405(T)
North Approach
Kingsway Junior School
Harris Rd
Leggatts Rise
Clarke Way

5
6

North Kingswood Road
Kingswood
Fern Way

North Watford Cemetery

7

8

Beechfield Junior Middle & Infant School

G
M6
1 Florence Cl

M8
1 Acorn Pl
2 Cowper Ct
3 Howard Cl

Lees Wood

H
M4
1 Ganders Ash
2 Nottingham Cl

Grove Mill Lane

J
195

M3
street names for this grid square are listed on the back of the index

K

M2
1 Lapwing Wy
2 Nightingale Cl
3 Oriole Cl
4 Redwing Gv

A41(T)

L
L3
1 De Havilland Wy
2 Margaret Cl
3 Swallow Oaks

L6
1 Ashfields
2 Macdonnell Gdns
3 Russell Crs

M
L2
1 The Hideaway
2 Lancaster Wy

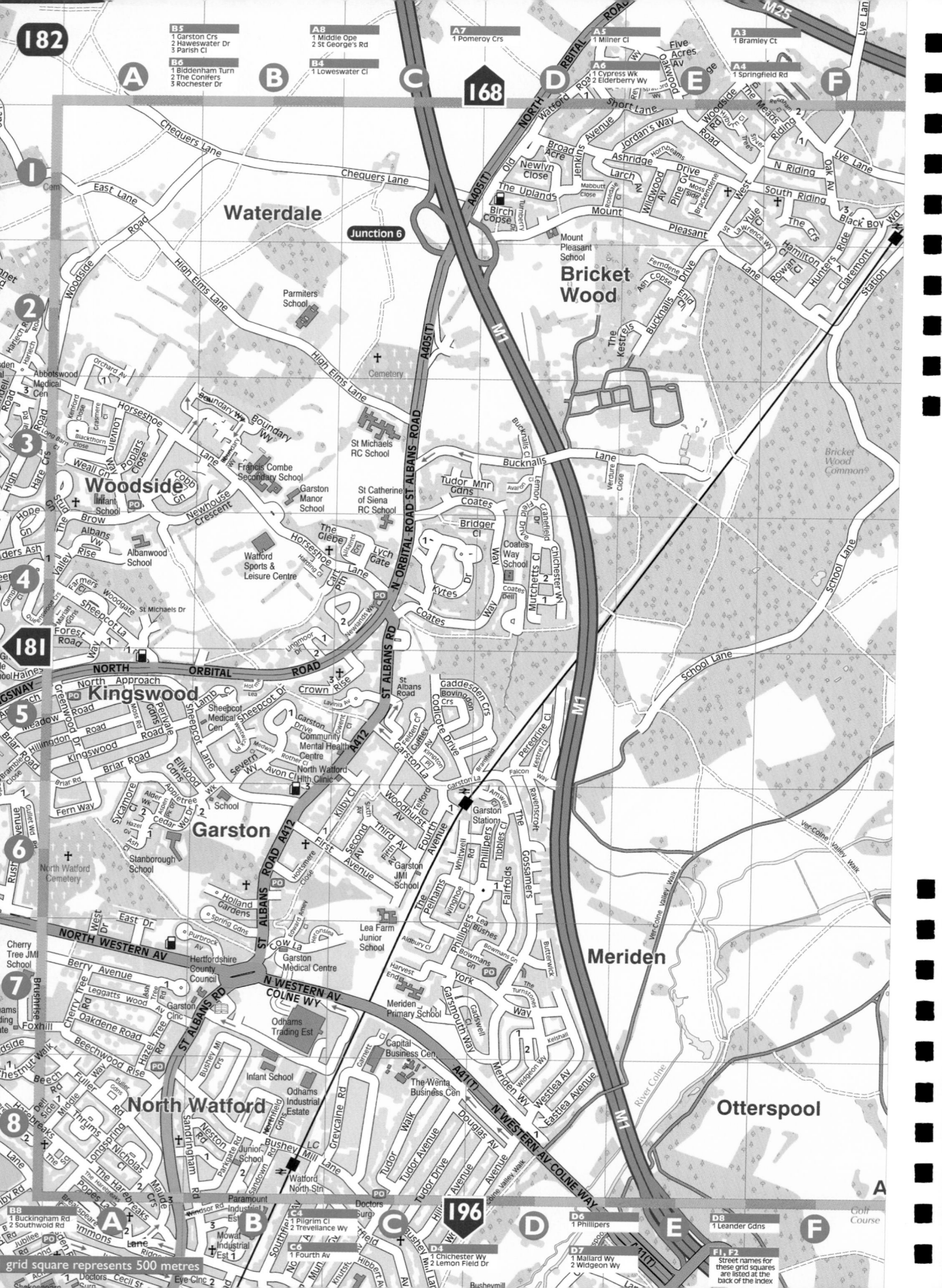

182
B5
1 Garston Crs
2 Haweswater Dr
3 Parish Cl
B6
1 Biddenham Turn
2 The Conifers
3 Rochester Dr
A8
1 Middle Ope
2 St George's Rd
B4
1 Loweswater Cl
A7
1 Pomeroy Crs
A5
1 Milner Cl
A6
1 Cypress Wk
2 Elderberry Wy
A3
1 Bramley Ct
A4
1 Springfield Rd
168
M25
Five Acres Av
Waterdale
Junction 6
Chequers Lane
East Lane
High Elms Lane
Woodside Road
Parmiters School
Cemetery
Bricket Wood
Mount Pleasant School
Mount Pleasant Lane
Birch Copse
The Uplands
Newlyn Close
Broad Acre
Jordan's Way
Ashridge Drive
Short Lane
North Orbital Road
Lye Lane
N Riding
South Riding
Black Boy Wd
Station Road
Bucknalls Lane
Bucknalls Drive
The Kestrels
Ferndene
Ash Copse
Bricket Wood Common
School Lane
St Michaels RC School
Abbotswood Medical Cen
Orchard Av
Horseshoe Lane
Boundary Wy
Francis Combe Secondary School
Garston Manor School
St Catherine of Siena RC School
Woodside
Newhouse Crescent
Infant School
The Brow
Albans Vw
Rise
Albanwood School
Watford Sports & Leisure Centre
The Glebe
Lych Gate
Tudor Mnr Gdns
Coates Way
Bridger Cl
Coates Way School
Kytes Dr
Mutchetts Cl
Chichester Wy
Lemon Field Dr
Cranefield Dr
Farmers Cl
Woodgate
Sheepcot La
St Michaels Dr
Forest Road
181
North Orbital Road
North Approach
Kingswood
Sheepcot Medical Cen
Sheepcot Dr
Crown Rise
St Albans Road
Gaddesden Crs
Bovingdon Crs
Codicote Drive
Greenwood Road
Meadow Road
Hillingdon Rd
Kingswood Road
Briar Road
Perivale Gdns
Sheepcot Lane
Elwood Gdns
Garston Drive
Community Mental Health Centre
North Watford Hlth Clinic
Severn Wy
Avon Cl
Garston La
Peregrine Cl
Falcon Way
Ravenscroft
Garston Station
Fern Way
Sycamore Cl
Appletree Wk
Cedar Wd Dr
School
Garston
Stanborough School
North Watford Cemetery
A412
Kilby Cl
First Avenue
Second Av
Third Av
Fourth Avenue
Fifth Av
Woodhurst Av
Garston JMI School
Holtsmere Close
Holland Gardens
The Pelhams
Whitwell Rd
Phillipers
Tibbles Cl
Fairfolds
The Gossamers
Lea Bushes
M1
Ver-Colne Valley Walk
East Dr
North Western Av
Cherry Tree JMI School
Hertfordshire County Council
Lea Farm Junior School
Garston Medical Centre
Meriden
Berry Avenue
Leggatts Wood Av
Oakdene Road
Cherry Tree Rd
Foxhill
Garston Clinc
Colne Wy
Odhams Trading Est
Meriden Primary School
York Way
Garsmouth Way
Butterwick
Beechwood Rise
Capital Business Cen
The Wenta Business Cen
Odhams Industrial Estate
Infant School
A41(T)
N Western Av
Meriden Wy
Westlea Av
Eastlea Avenue
River Colne
Otterspool
North Watford
Sandringham Rd
Neston Rd
Junior School
Bushey Mill Lane
Greycaine Rd
Tudor Walk
Tudor Avenue
Tudor Drive
Douglas Av
Watford North Stn
Paramount Industrial Est
Doctors Surg
196
Mowat Industrial Est
Golf Course
B8
1 Buckingham Rd
2 Southwold Rd
C4
1 Pilgrim Cl
2 Trevellance Wy
C6
1 Fourth Av
D4
1 Chichester Wy
2 Lemon Field Dr
D6
1 Phillipers
D7
1 Mallard Wy
2 Widgeon Wy
D8
1 Leander Gdns
F1, F2
Street names for these grid squares are listed at the back of the index
grid square represents 500 metres

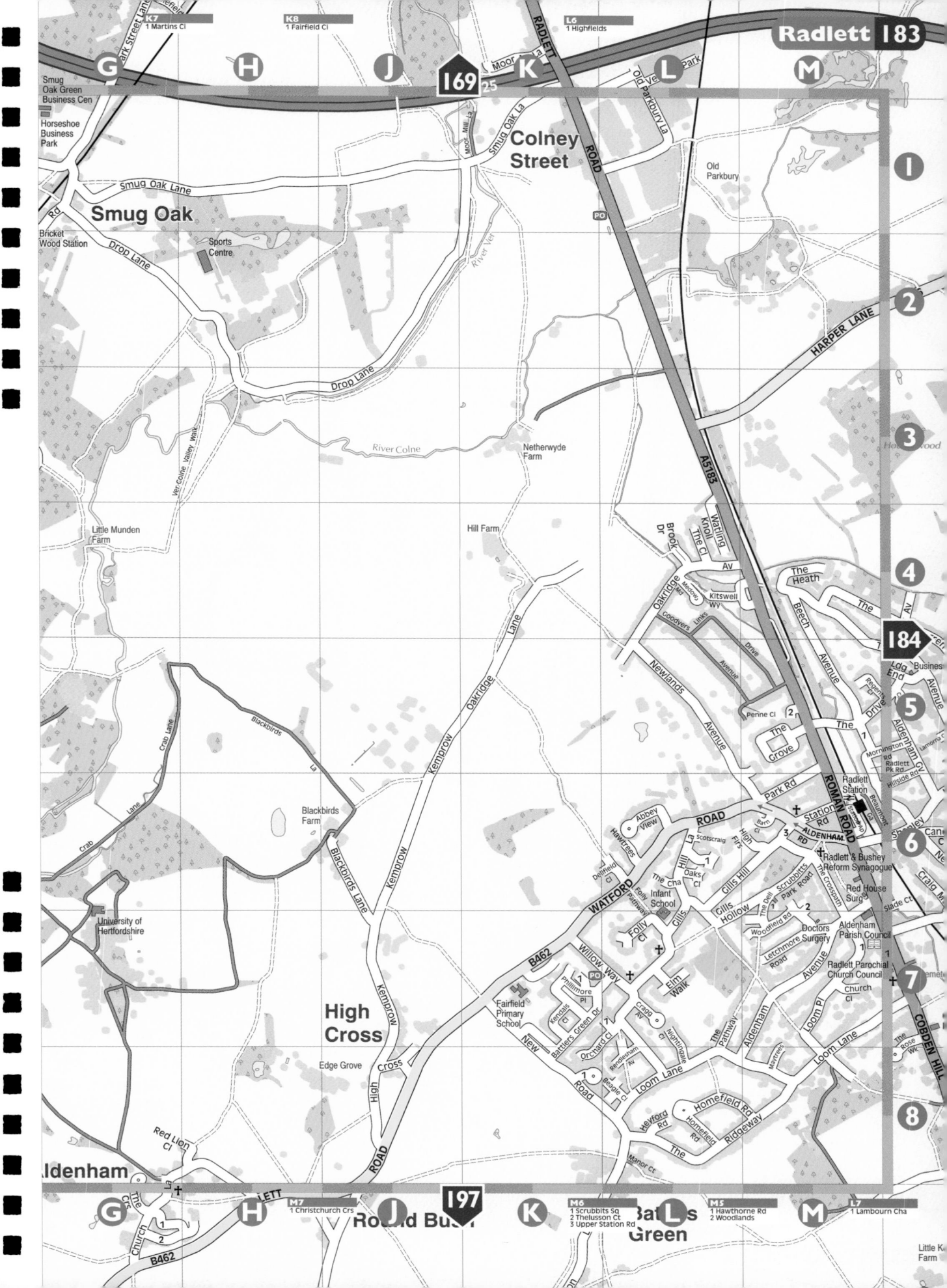

G   H   J   K   L   M

169 25

I

2

3

4

184

5

6

7

8

Smug Oak Green Business Cen

Horseshoe Business Park

Bricket Wood Station

Rd

Smug Oak

Smug Oak Lane

Drop Lane

Sports Centre

Drop Lane

Little Munden Farm

Ver Colne Valley Walk

River Colne

Crab Lane

Blackbirds

La

Blackbirds Farm

Crab Lane

University of Hertfordshire

High Cross

Edge Grove

Red Lion Cl

Aldenham

The La

Church

B462

B462

Blackbirds Lane

Kemprow

Kemprow

New

High

Cross

ROAD

Oakridge Lane

Oakridge Lane

Colney Street

Moor Mill La

Smug Oak La

River Ver

Netherwyde Farm

Hill Farm

RADLETT

ROAD

A5183

Old Parkbury La

Old Parkbury

PO

Brook Dr

Watling Knoll

The Cl

Meadow Rd

Av

Kitswell Wy

Goodyers

Links

Oakridge

Newlands

Avenue

Avenue

Penne Cl 2

The Grove

Park Rd

ROAD

Abbey View

Hawtrees

Delfield

Scotscraig

The Cha

Oaks Cl

The Bell

High Elms

Barn

Gills Hill

Gills Hill La

Gills Hollow

Gills

Park Road

Woodfield Rd

Scrubbits

The Crosspath

Watling

ROAD

Roman Rd

Radlett Station

Station Rd

ALDENHAM

Rd

Radlett & Bushey Reform Synagogue

Red House Surg

Doctors Surgery

Aldenham Parish Council

Radlett Parochial Church Council

Church Cl

Letchmore Road

Nightingale

Aldenham

WATFORD

Infant School

Folly Pathway

Folly Cl

Fairfield Primary School

Willow Way

PO

Phillimore Pl

Kendals Ct

Battlers Green Dr

Orchard Cl

Rendlesham Av

Cragg Cl

Elm Walk

Nightingale

The Pathway

Loom Pl

Avenue

Homefield Rd

Ridgeway

Heyford Rd

Homefield Rd

The

Manor Ct

Loom Lane

Loom Lane

The Rose Wk

COBDEN HILL

Slade Ct

Craig Cl

Canon

Sheeley

Mornington Rd

Radlett Pk Rd

Hillside Rd

Beaufort

Aldenham Ct

Lamorna Cl

Regents Cl

Ldg End

Busines

The Heath

Beech Avenue

Avenue

Drive

The Av

Old Parkbury

HARPER LANE

Hedges Wood

197

Radlett Road Bushey

Batlers Green

Little Ki Farm

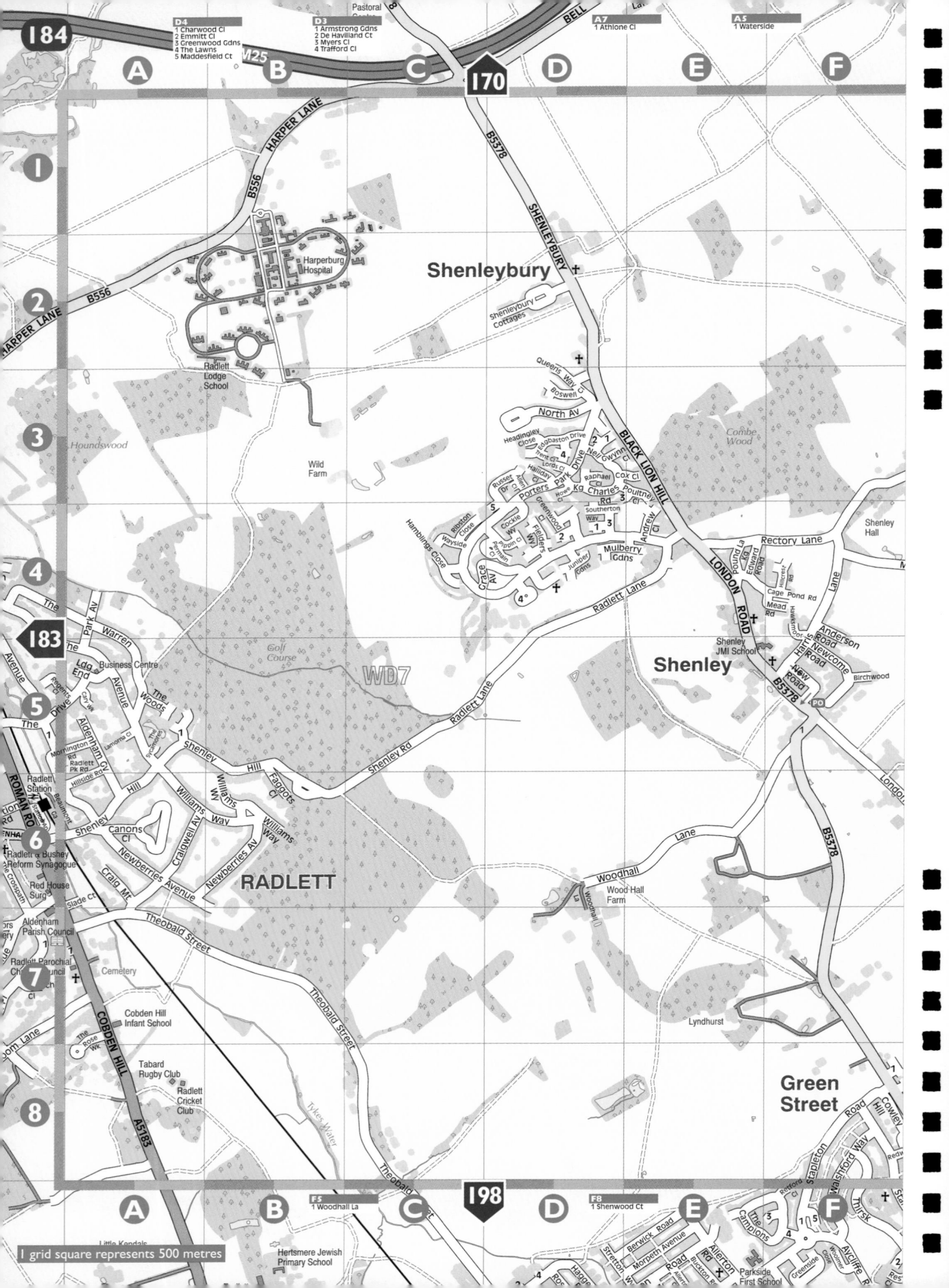

184
D4
1 Charwood Cl
2 Emmitt Cl
3 Greenwood Gdns
4 The Lawns
5 Maddesfield Ct
D3
1 Armstrong Gdns
2 De Havilland Ct
3 Myers Cl
4 Trafford Cl
A7
1 Athlone Cl
A5
1 Waterside
Pastoral
M25
BELL
170
A
B
C
D
E
F
1
2
3
4
5
6
7
8
HARPER LANE
B556
B5378
SHENLEYBURY
Harperburg Hospital
Shenleybury
Shenleybury Cottages
Radlett Lodge School
Queens Way
Boswell Cl
North Av
Houndswood
Wild Farm
Headingley Close
Edgbaston Drive
BLACK LION HILL
Combe Wood
Nelson Gwynn Cl
Trent Cl
Lords Cl
Halliday Cl
Park Drive
Raphael Cl
Cox Cl
Russet Dr
Allen Cl
Porters
Howe Cl
Kg Charles Rd
Poultney Cl
Southerton Way
Andrew Cl
Hamblings Close
Ribston Close
Wayside
Cockle Wy
Greenwood Cl
Fielders Wy
Pippin Cl
Permain Cl
Mulberry Gdns
Juniper Gdns
Crace Av
Rectory Lane
Pound La
Edward Road
LONDON ROAD
Hillcrest Rd
Lane
Shenley Hall
Cage Pond Rd
Mead Rd
Hawksmoor
Radlett Lane
The Warren
Park Av
Golf Course
WD7
Anderson Road
Harris Newcome Road
Shenley JMI School
Shenley
Birchwood
New Road
B5378
PO
183
Avenue
Ldg End
Business Centre
Regents Cl
Cary Wk
Avenue
The Woods
The Drive
Aldenham Gv
Mornington Rd
Radlett Pk Rd
Lamorna Cl
The Sycamores
Shenley Hill
Faggots Cl
Shenley Rd
London
Hillside Rd
Hill
Williams Wy
Williams Way
Radlett Station
ROMAN RD
Beaumont
Station Rd
Shenley
Canons Cl
Craigwell Av
Newberries Av
Lane
Woodhall
B5378
Radlett & Bushey Reform Synagogue
Red House Surg
Crosspath
Craig Mt
Newberries Avenue
RADLETT
Woodhall Lane
Wood Hall Farm
Slade Ct
Aldenham Parish Council
Theobald Street
Radlett Parochial Church Council
Cemetery
Theobald Street
Lyndhurst
Cobden Hill Infant School
COBDEN HILL
The Rose Wk
Tabard Rugby Club
Radlett Cricket Club
A5183
Tykes Water
Green Street
Cowley Hill
Road
Stapleton
Washford Way
Theobald Street
198
F5
1 Woodhall La
F8
1 Shenwood Ct
Retford Cl
The Campions
Thirsk
Berwick Road
Morpeth Avenue
Allerton Rd
Road
Buckton Rd
Parkside First School
Greenside
Woolmer Close
Aycliffe
Little Kendals
Hertsmere Jewish Primary School
1 grid square represents 500 metres

G8
1 Beauchamp Pl
2 Champions Cl
3 Shenwood Ct

Salisbury Hall

Mosquito
Aircraft

G **H** **J** 171 **K** **L** **M**

B556

Redwell Wood
Farm

Redwell
Wood

Hawkshead
Wood

1

2

Manor
Lodge
School

Ridgehill

Shenley
Lodge

Rectory Lane

Packhorse

Southridge

Lane

BLACKHORSE LANE B556

M25

SAINT ALBANS ROAD

Blackhorse Lane

The
Grange

Cover Road

Brookside

CECIL RO

South
Mimm

3

Rabley Park
Farm

Mimms Lane

Catharine

Bourne

B556

Blanche Lane

Frowyke
Crescent

St Giles
Cof E
Primary School

Saint Albans Lane

St Giles'
Avenue

Rectory Lane

Deeves
Hall

Earls

Deeves

Mimms

Lane

Hall

Earl's
Farm

Lane

Hamilton
Close

New Road

Greyhound

Lane

M25

Blanche

Bignell's
Corner

4

186

Mimms
Lane

Hall Lane

Crossoaks

Lane

Lane

Ridge

Blanche Lane

Blanche
Farm

A1(M)

Swanland

5

Pursley
Farm

Crossoaks

Lane

Summerswood

M25

Big

6

Road

Lane

Blanche

A1(M)

7

Silver

Hill

High Canons

Well

Lane

Holmshill

Lane

BARNET BY-PASS

A1(T)

Dyrham

Lane

Trotters Bottom

8

B5378

Wood R

Buckettsland

Lane

Well

End

Road

G **H** **J** 199 **K** **L** **M**

Rowley Lane

Galley Lane

**Well
End**

F2
1 Ritz Ct
2 Wentworth Cl
E3
1 The Ap
2 Weston Cl
3 Wyllyotts Pl
E2
1 Oakfield Cl
D4
1 Elmfield Cl
Boltons Park
A
B
C
D
E
F
172
Cranborne Industrial Estate
Brook
1
2
3
4
5
6
7
8
Warrengate Farm
Warrengate Lane
Mymms Hall
Cranborne Road
Cranborne Industrial Estate
Summit Road
Cranborne Crescent
Cranborne Cl
Bornedene
Cranborne Primary School
Pinewood Dr
Green Meadow
Westwood Close
Heath Drive
The Manor Way
Mountway
Cedar Close
Avenue
Potters Bar Golf Club
Manor Road
Station Close
Lane
Darkes
The Service Road
Strafford Gate
Byng
Ladbrooke
The
Strafford Gate
Birch
B556
Windmore Avenue
PO
Mutton Lane
MUTTON LANE
Deepdene
Wroxham Gardens
Wroxham JMI School
Mimms Hall Road
Cambridge Drive
Suffolk Road
Borough Way
Road
Ormesby Drive
Oulton Crescent
Auckland
Laurel Fields
Neville Cl
Clive Close
Laurel Avenue
Mutton Lane
Allandale Crs
Brooklands Gdns
Berkeley Cl
Elmscroft Gardens
Sherwood Avenue
Drayton Av
Aberdale Gardens
Heather Way
The Drive
Potters Bar Station
Whyllotts Council Offices
The Earl Gallery
The Close
MUTTON LANE
B55
CECIL ROAD
Cowper Field
South Mimms
Saint Giles' Primary School
St Giles' Avenue
A1(M)
Swanland Road
Shillitoe Avenue
Hill
Lane
Elmfield Road
Wellesley Crs
Robert Close
The Shrublands
Santers Lane
Baker Street
Dugdale
Rushfield
Updale Cl
Kimptons Close
Kimptons Mead
Bridgefoot
Daleside Drive
Fairacres Close
The Byway
Brackendale
Sunnybank
Elmroyd Close
Elmroyd Avenue
Field View Road
The Greenway
Road
Oakroyd Avenue
Oakroyd Cl
Great Slades
Primary School
Meadow Way
Greyhound Lane
Albans Road
Bignell's Corner
185
Hotel
Wash
Dame Alice Owens School
Swanland Road
St Albans Road
Bignells Corner
South Mimms Service Area
Junction 1/23
Sawyers Lane
M25
M25
M25
SAINT ALBANS ROAD
A1081
Wash Lane
Dancers Hill
Baker Street
Bentley Heath Lane
Bentley Heath
Dancers Hill Road
Wagon Rd
A1000
Dancers Hill Road
BARNET ROAD
Dyrham Lane
Trotters Bottom
Kitt's End Road
A
B
C
D
E
F
F3
1 Ladbrooke Cl
2 Strafford Cl
200
Kitt's End
F4
1 Winston Wy
A108
1 grid square represents 500 metres

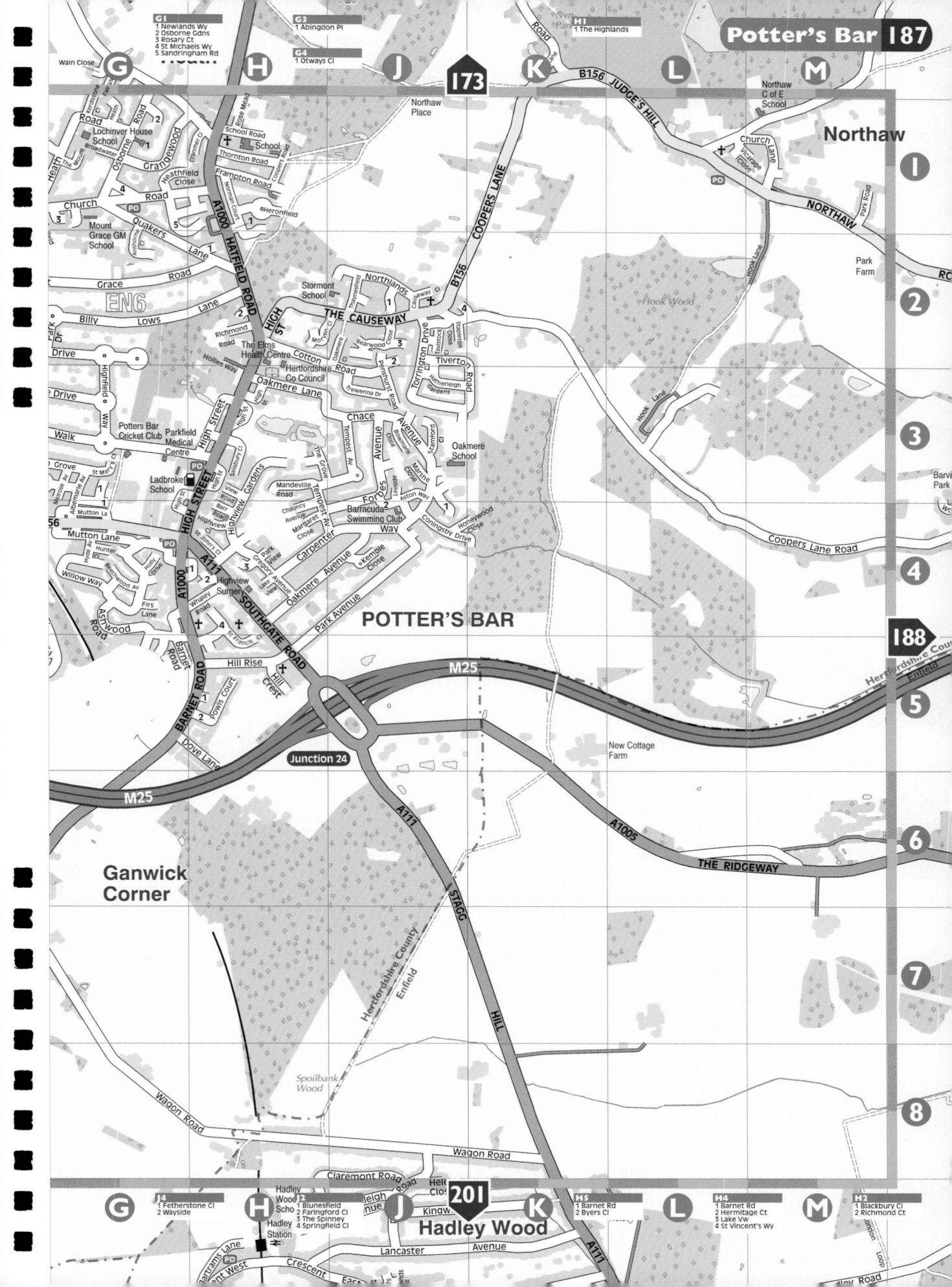

Northaw

POTTER'S BAR

Ganwick Corner

Hadley Wood 201

Junction 24

M25

THE RIDGEWAY

188

173

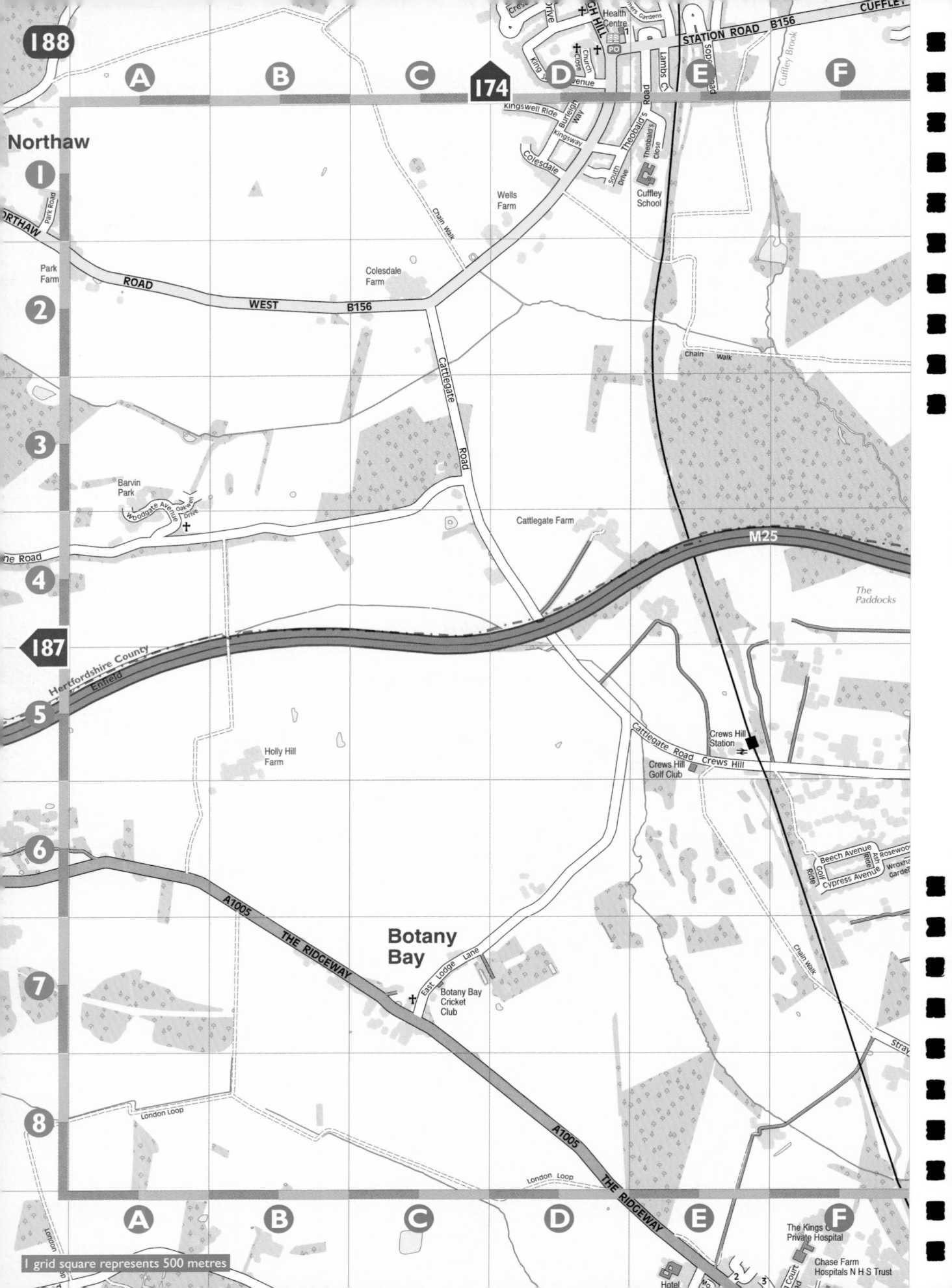

Northaw

CUFFLEY

STATION ROAD B156

Health Centre

174

Kingswell Ride

Burleigh Way

Kingsway

Colesdale

South Drive

King's Avenue

Theobald's Road

Theobald's Close

Church Close

PO

Lambs

Sod...

Cuffley Brook

Wells Farm

Chain Walk

Cuffley School

Park Road

Park Farm

ROAD WEST B156

Colesdale Farm

Colesdale

Cattlegate Road

Chain Walk

Barvin Park

Woodgate Avenue

Oakwell Drive

Cattlegate Farm

M25

187

Hertfordshire County

Enfield

ne Road

The Paddocks

Holly Hill Farm

Cattlegate Road

Crews Hill

Crews Hill Station

Crews Hill Golf Club

Beech Avenue

Ash Ride

Rosewood

Cypress Avenue

Golf Ride

Wroxha Garden

A1005 THE RIDGEWAY

Botany Bay

East Lodge Lane

Botany Bay Cricket Club

Chain Walk

London Loop

A1005 THE RIDGEWAY

London Loop

Stray...

The Kings C Private Hospital

Chase Farm Hospitals N H S Trust

Hotel

Moorhurst Avenue
Lulworth Avenue
Little Piper's Close
Woodside JMI School
Pollards
J8 1 St John's Ter
M2 1 Warrenfield Cl
GOFF'S LANE
Faints Close
Cattlins Close
Claremont
Hunters Reach
Goffs School
175
Broadfields
Jones Road
Chain Walk
EN7
Halstead Hill
Silver Street
Bonneygrove Junior & Infant School
Dark Lane
Cromwell
Cemetery
Grovedale Close
Bonney Grove
Windsor Close
Barrow Lane
Beverley Gardens
Woodgreen Farm
Broadfield Farm
Woodside
Portland Drive
Temple Close
Hargreaves Av
Tudor Avenue
Meux Close
Primrose Path
Bury Green Road
LIEUTENANT ELLIS WAY
Burnt Farm
Burntfarm Ride
Oldpark Ride
Spring Farm
Theobalds Manor
Temple House
Bullscross
190
Hertfordshire County
Enfield
Chain Walk
Cemetery
Bulls Cross Ride
Glasgow Stud
Sloemans Farm
M25
Crews Hill
Whitewebbs Road
The Whitewebbs Museum of Transport & Industry
Theobalds Park Road
Chain Walk
Whitewebbs Lane
Gilmour Close
Capel Manor Primary School
University of London
Bull's Cross
Bulls Cross
Turkey Street
London Loop
St Ignatius College
St Johns C of E Junior & Infant School
Flash Lane
London Loop
Clay Hill
Forty Hill
Forty Hill C of E School
EN2
Clay Hill
Park Nook Gardens
Elm Gardens
Browning Road
Stratton Avenue
London Loop
Cook's Hole Road
Phipps Hatch Lane
Cemetery
Lime Tree Walk
Gloucester Road
Cedar Road
Brodie Road
Morley Hill
Birkbeck Road
Myrtle Grove
Woodbine Grove
Conway Gardens
Burnham Close
Worcesters Infant & Primary School
Goat Lane
St George's Road
Old Forge Road
Worcesters Avenue
Pentrich Avenue
Tynemouth Drive
Meyer Green

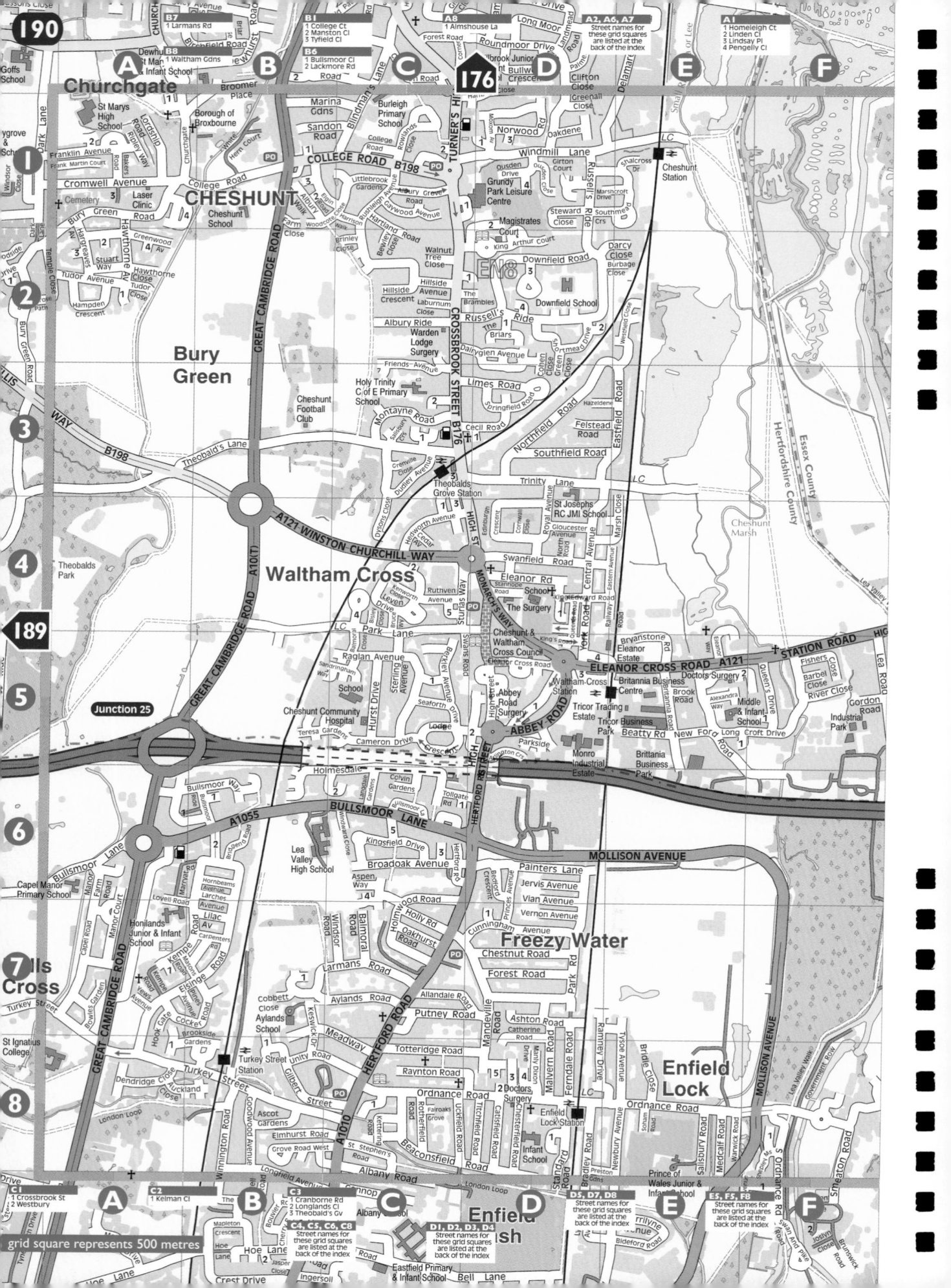

190
176
189
A
B
C
D
E
F
1
2
3
4
5
6
7
8
B7
1 Larmans Rd
B8
1 Waltham Gdns
B1
1 College Ct
2 Manston Cl
3 Tyfield Cl
B6
1 Bullsmoor Cl
2 Lackmore Rd
A8
1 Almshouse La
A2, A6, A7
Street names for these grid squares are listed at the back of the index
A1
1 Homeleigh Ct
2 Linden Cl
3 Lindsay Pl
4 Pengelly Cl
Churchgate
Cheshunt
CHESHUNT
Bury Green
Waltham Cross
Freezy Water
Enfield Lock
Cheshunt Marsh
Theobalds Park
Junction 25
EN8
College Road
B198
Cromwell Avenue
Great Cambridge Road
A10(T)
A121 Winston Churchill Way
Crossbrook Street B176
Monarch's Way
Eleanor Cross Road A121
Station Road
Bullsmoor Lane
A1055
Mollison Avenue
Hertford Road
A1010
Turkey Street
Ordnance Road
Cheshunt Station
Theobalds Grove Station
Waltham Cross Station
Turkey Street Station
Enfield Lock Station
Hertfordshire County
Essex County
Lea Valley Walk
St Marys High School
Burleigh Primary School
Grundy Park Leisure Centre
Magistrates Court
Downfield School
Holy Trinity C of E Primary School
Cheshunt Football Club
St Josephs RC JMI School
Cheshunt & Waltham Cross Council
Cheshunt Community Hospital
Lea Valley High School
Capel Manor Primary School
Honilands Junior & Infant School
St Ignatius College
Aylands School
Infant School
Prince of Wales Junior & Infant School
Eastfield Primary & Infant School
Middle & Infant School
Tricor Trading Estate
Tricor Business Park
Monro Industrial Estate
Brittania Business Park
Britannia Business Centre
Industrial Park
Eleanor Estate
Doctors Surgery
The Surgery
Abbey Road Surgery
Warden Lodge Surgery
C1
1 Crossbrook St
2 Westbury
C2
1 Kelman Cl
C3
1 Cranborne Rd
2 Longlands Cl
3 Theobald's Gv
C4, C5, C6, C8
Street names for these grid squares are listed at the back of the index
D1, D2, D3, D4
Street names for these grid squares are listed at the back of the index
D5, D7, D8
Street names for these grid squares are listed at the back of the index
E5, F5, F8
Street names for these grid squares are listed at the back of the index
Enfield Wash
grid square represents 500 metres

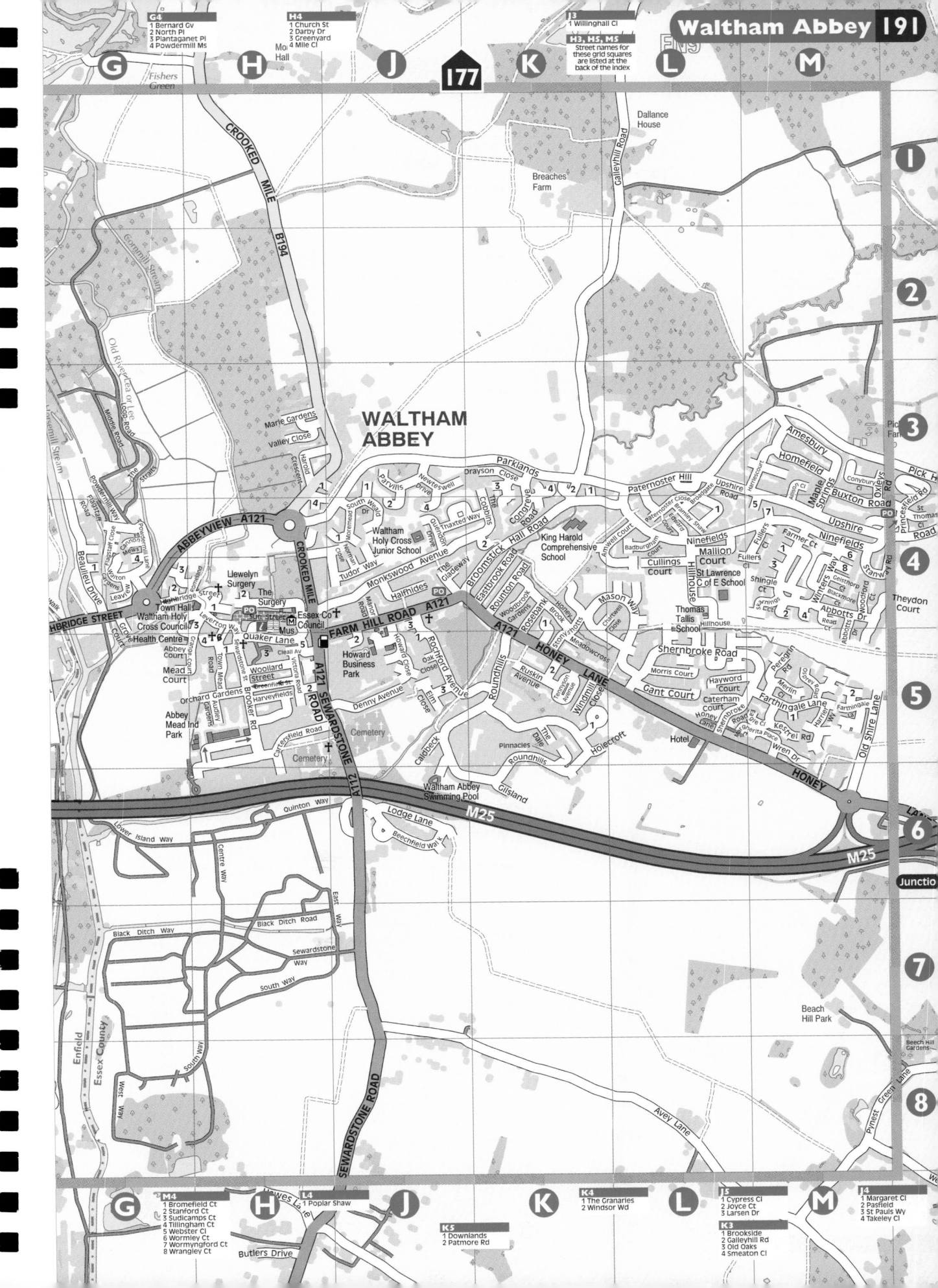

G4
1 Bernard Gv
2 North Pl
3 Plantaganet Pl
4 Powdermill Ms

H4
1 Church St
2 Darby Dr
3 Greenyard
4 Mile Cl

J3
1 Willinghall Cl

H3, H5, M5
Street names for these grid squares are listed at the back of the index

G   H   J   177   K   L   M

I
2
3
4
5
6
Junctio
7
8

CROOKED MILE B194
Fishers Green
Grommill Stream
Old River Lea or Lee Loop Road
Beaumill Stream
The Stratts
Powermill Way
Fasbar Way
Beaulieu Drive
Marie Gardens
Valley Close
Crescent

WALTHAM ABBEY

Breaches Farm
Dallance House
Galleyhill Road
Pick Farm
Amesbury
Homefield
Maple Springs
Buxton Road
Conybury Wy
Oxleys
Princesfield Rd
St Thomas Rd
Pick Lane

Parklands
Parvills
Newtes-well
Drayson Close
The Cobbins
Congreve Road
Paternoster Hill
Upshire Road
Harecourt
Upshire
Ninefields
Farmer Ct
Stanway Rd
Woodford

ABBEYVIEW A121
CROOKED MILE
South Weald Dr
Waremead
Hillman Close
Tudor Way
Thaxted Way
Queendon
Monkswood Avenue
Halfhides
Broomstick Hall Road
Eastbrook Road
Rounton Road
Woodcroft Gardens
Rosebank
King Harold Comprehensive School
Amwell Court
Badburgham
Bramley Shaw
Cullings Court
St Lawrence C of E School
Ninefields
Mallion Court
Fullers Cl
Shingle Ct
Blackmore
Abbotts Rd
Theydon Court

Llewelyn Surgery
The Surgery
Town Hall
Waltham Holy Cross Council
Health Centre
PO
Quaker Lane
Mus
Essex Co Council
Howard Business Park
Manor Road
FARM HILL ROAD A121
Rochford Avenue
Honey Brook
Stony Croft
Mason Way
Charwell Close
Meadowcross
Thomas Tallis School
Hillhouse
Shernbroke Road
Pergarin Rd
Merlin
Kestrel Rd
Farthingale Lane
Caterham Court
Gant Court
Hayward Court
Morris Court

Mead Court
Abbey Court
Orchard Gardens
Woolard Street
Greenfield St
Harveyfields
Abbey Mead Ind Park
Brooker Rd
A121 SEWARDSTONE ROAD
Cartersfield Road
Cemetery
Cemetery
Denny Avenue
Elm Close
Oak Close
Elm Close
HONEY LANE
Ruskin Avenue
Tempylon Avenue
Windmill Close
The Dale
Caldbeck
Pinnacles
Roundhills
Holecroft
Hotel
Wren Dr
Sherborne Road
Sherita Place
Old Shire Lane
HONEY LANE
M25

Quinton Way
Lodge Lane
Beechfield Walk
Waltham Abbey Swimming Pool
Gilsland
M25

Lower Island Way
Centre Way
East Way
Black Ditch Way
Black Ditch Road
Sewardstone Way
South Way

Enfield
Essex County
West Way
South Way
SEWARDSTONE ROAD

Avey Lane
Beach Hill Park
Beech Hill Gardens
Pynest Green Lane

Butlers Drive
Lewes La

G
M4
1 Bromefield Ct
2 Stanford Ct
3 Sudicamps Ct
4 Tillingham Ct
5 Webster Cl
6 Wormley Ct
7 Wormingford Ct
8 Wrangley Ct

H
L4
1 Poplar Shaw

J

K
K4
1 The Granaries
2 Windsor Wd

K5
1 Downlands
2 Patmore Rd

L
J5
1 Cypress Cl
2 Joyce Ct
3 Larsen Dr

K3
1 Brookside
2 Galleyhill Rd
3 Old Oaks
4 Smeaton Cl

M
J4
1 Margaret Cl
2 Pasfield
3 St Pauls Wy
4 Takeley Cl

Latimer
B3 1 Snells Wood Ct
B2 1 Amersham Pl
A2 1 Cumberland Cl
Latimer Park Farm
178
Latimer Road
Stony Lane
Chess Valley Walk
Bell Lane County Combined School
Chandos Close
Beechwood Avenue
Sandycroft Road
Boughton Way
Pavilion Wy
Elizabeth Avenue
Chenies Avenue
Farm Close
Westwood Drive
Westwood Close
Chessfield Park
Chiltern
Cavendish Close
Marygold Walk
Charsley Close
Latimer Close
Beechwood Close
Russell Close
Chalfont Av
Church Grove
Amersham Way
Arbour Vw
Derwent Close
St Nicholas Cl
Bedford Avenue
Chalfont and Latimer Station
AMERSHAM ROAD
CHALFONT STATION ROAD
A404
Beel Close
Clayton Wk
Loudhams Road
Appleyard
Chilcote La
School
Old Fld Cl
Avenue
The Retreat
Oakington
Village Way
PO
Dr Challoners High School for Girls
Little Chalfont Surgery
The Hawthorns
Linfields
Snells Lane
Appleton Close
Yarrowside
COKE'S LANE
Loudhams Wood Lane
Burton's Way
Little Chalfont
Lodge Lane
Lodge Farm
Maplefield Lane
Long Walk
Birkett Way
New Road
B4442
Coke's Farm Lane
Park Gv
Gdn Reach
Coke's Farm
Doggetts Wood Lane
Doggetts Wd Close
Burton's Farm
Burton's Lane
Newhouse Farm
Farm Road
Harewood Down Golf Club
NIGHTINGALES LANE
Pollards Wood
Pollards Park House
Burtons Lane
Chorleywood West
Harewood Downs House
A413
Roughwood Lane
Roughwood Park
Warren Farm
AMERSHAM ROAD
South Bucks Way
HP8
Misbourne Farm
Philipshill Wood
Buckinghamshire County
The Vache
202
Stratton Chase
Headhearn
NIGHTINGALES LANE
grid square represents 500 metres

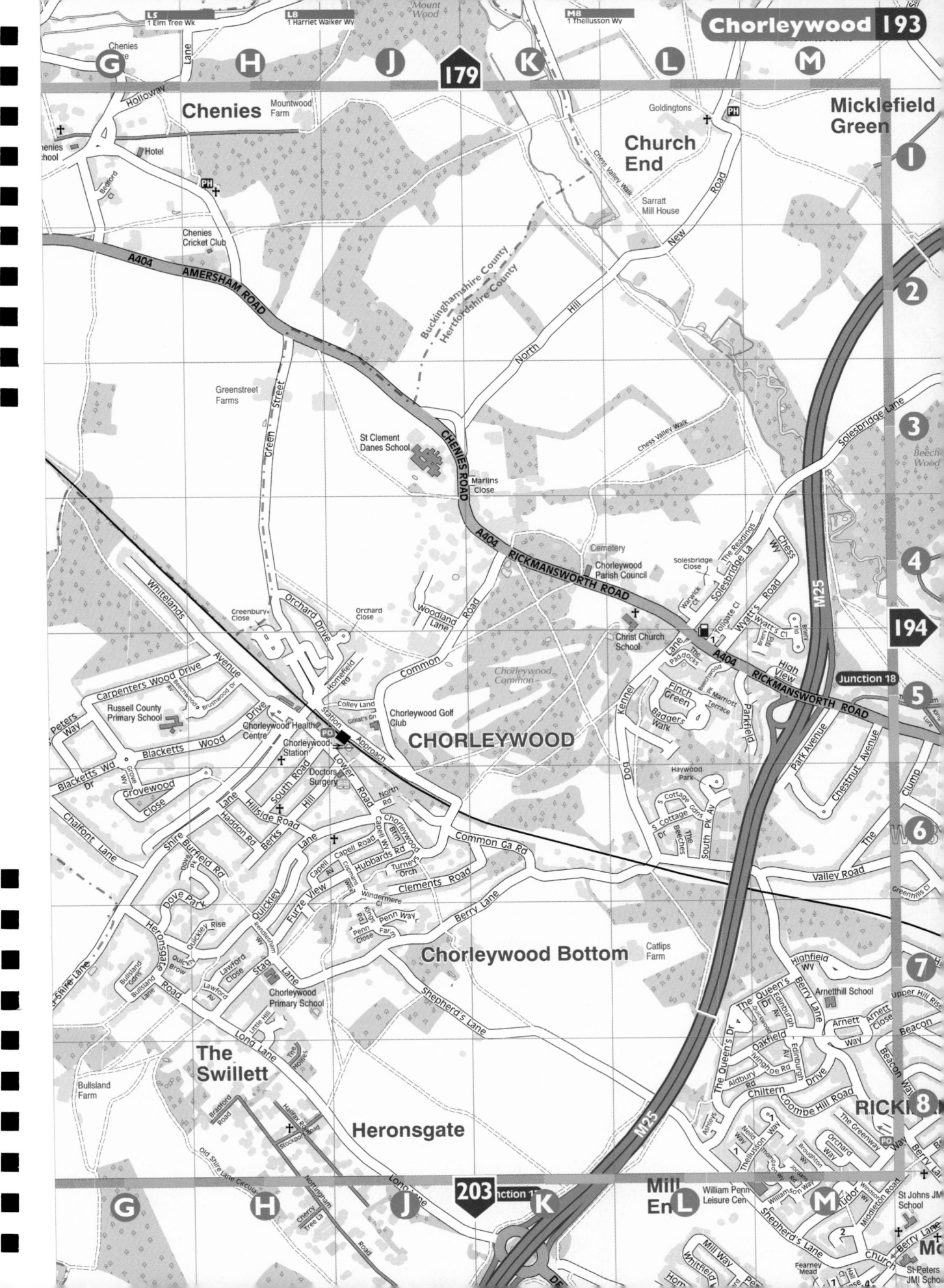

Chenies
Mountwood Farm
Hotel
Chenies Cricket Club
A404 AMERSHAM ROAD
Greenstreet Farms
Green Street
St Clement Danes School
CHENIES ROAD
Marlins Close
Buckinghamshire County
Hertfordshire County
North Hill
New Road
Church End
Goldingtons
Sarratt Mill House
Chess Valley Walk
Micklefield Green
Solesbridge Lane
M25
A404 RICKMANSWORTH ROAD
Cemetery
Chorleywood Parish Council
Christ Church School
Chorleywood Common
CHORLEYWOOD
Chorleywood Golf Club
Common Road
Woodland Lane
Orchard Drive
Orchard Close
Greenbury Close
Whitelands Avenue
Carpenters Wood Drive
Russell County Primary School
Blacketts Wood Drive
Chorleywood Health Centre
Chorleywood Station
Station Approach
Doctors Surgery
Lower Road
South Road
Hillside Road
Haddon Rd
Grovewood Close
Chalfont Lane
Shire Lane
Common Ga Rd
Valley Road
Clements Road
Berry Lane
Chorleywood Bottom
Catlips Farm
Heronsgate Road
Quickley Lane
Furze View
Stag Lane
Chorleywood Primary School
Shepherd's Lane
The Swillett
Long Lane
Bullsland Farm
Heronsgate
Nottingham Road
Old Shire Lane Circular
Mill End
William Penn Leisure Centre
Arnetthill School
The Queen's Drive
Chiltern Drive
Coombe Hill Road
Park Avenue
Chestnut Avenue
Junction 18
Kennel Lane
Dog Kennel Lane
Haywood Park
Finch Green
Badgers Walk
Parkfield
179
194
203
G H J K L M
1 2 3 4 5 6 7 8

E6
1 Copthorne Cl
2 Millthorne Cl
C8
1 Chorleywood Cl
2 Nightingale Pl
3 Solomon's Hl
4 Station Rd
B8
1 Swallow Cl
B5
1 Loudwater Rdg
180
Micklefield Green
Chandler's Cross
M25
White Shack Lane
Fir Tree Hill
Rousebarn Lane
Harrocks Wood
Redhall Lane
Redhall
Sarratt Road
Solesbridge Lane
Sarratt Lane
Cherry Walk
Beechengrove Wood
Redheath
York House School
Waterdell House
Little Green Lane
Thurlwood House
Loudwater
Loudwater Lane
Croxley Green
The Green
Ladywood Close
Whisper Wood
Loudwater Hts
Trout Rise
Cherry Hl
Bridle Lane
Lower Plantation
Wagon Way
Farm La
River Chess
193
Junction 18
Violet Way
Loudwater Drive
Lodge Dr
Timber Rdg
Armitage Close
Rooks Hill
Chess Cl
Chess Hill
Chess Lane
Troutstream
Overstream
Kingfisher Lure
Loudwater Lane
Chess Valley Walk
Harewood
Rasehill Close
Chorleywood Rd
CHORLEYWOOD ROAD
Lime Tree Wk
WD3
The Drive
Lynwood Heights
Spencer Wk
High Close
The Drive
The Climb
Greenhills Cl
Clump
Valley Road
Highfield Way
The Mount
Goosefields
A404
The Royal Masonic School
Upper Hill Rise
Beacon Way
Arnett Close
Shepherds Rise
Ridge Hill
Highfield Way
Winchfield Wy
The Drive
Cemetery
Cedars Av
Nightingale Road
Meadow Way
Beacon Way
CKMANSWORTH
Rickmansworth Station
RECTORY ROAD
Homestead Rd
Northway
Swan Cl
Townfield
Berry Way
Berry Lane
The Highlands
Mead Place
Rectory Lane
High Street
Three Rivers District Council
Cloisters
St Joan of Arc RC School
Caravan La
Wharf La
Waterways Heritage M
Chess Va Wk
Rickmansworth Sports Club
A412 PARK ROAD
SCOTS HILL
Scots Hill Close
Cottage Close
Lavrock Lane
Rickmansworth School
All Saints Lane
Frankland Cl
Bateman Road
WATFORD
Yorke Rd
Dickinson Avenue
New
Evan's Cl
Windmill Drive
Elmcote Way
Chess V Rl
Copthorne Road
Uplands
Green La
On The Gn
The Orch
Old Barn Lane
Owens Way
Parrotts Cl
Cherwell Cl
Dulwich Way
Repton Way
Fuller W
Dugdales
Lovatts
Grove Crs
Baldwins Lane
Whitegates Cl
PO
St Johns JMI School
Middleton Road
West
The Close
Mount View
Money Hill Road
Berkeley Clinic
Wensum Wy
Approach Road
Goral Md
Bury Mdw
Talbot
Skidmore Clinic
Church Street
Norfolk Road
Salters Cl
Skidmore Wy
Doctors Surgery
A404 RIVERSIDE DRIVE
St Peters JMI School
Church
E7
1 Chess Vale Ri
204
grid square represents 500 metres

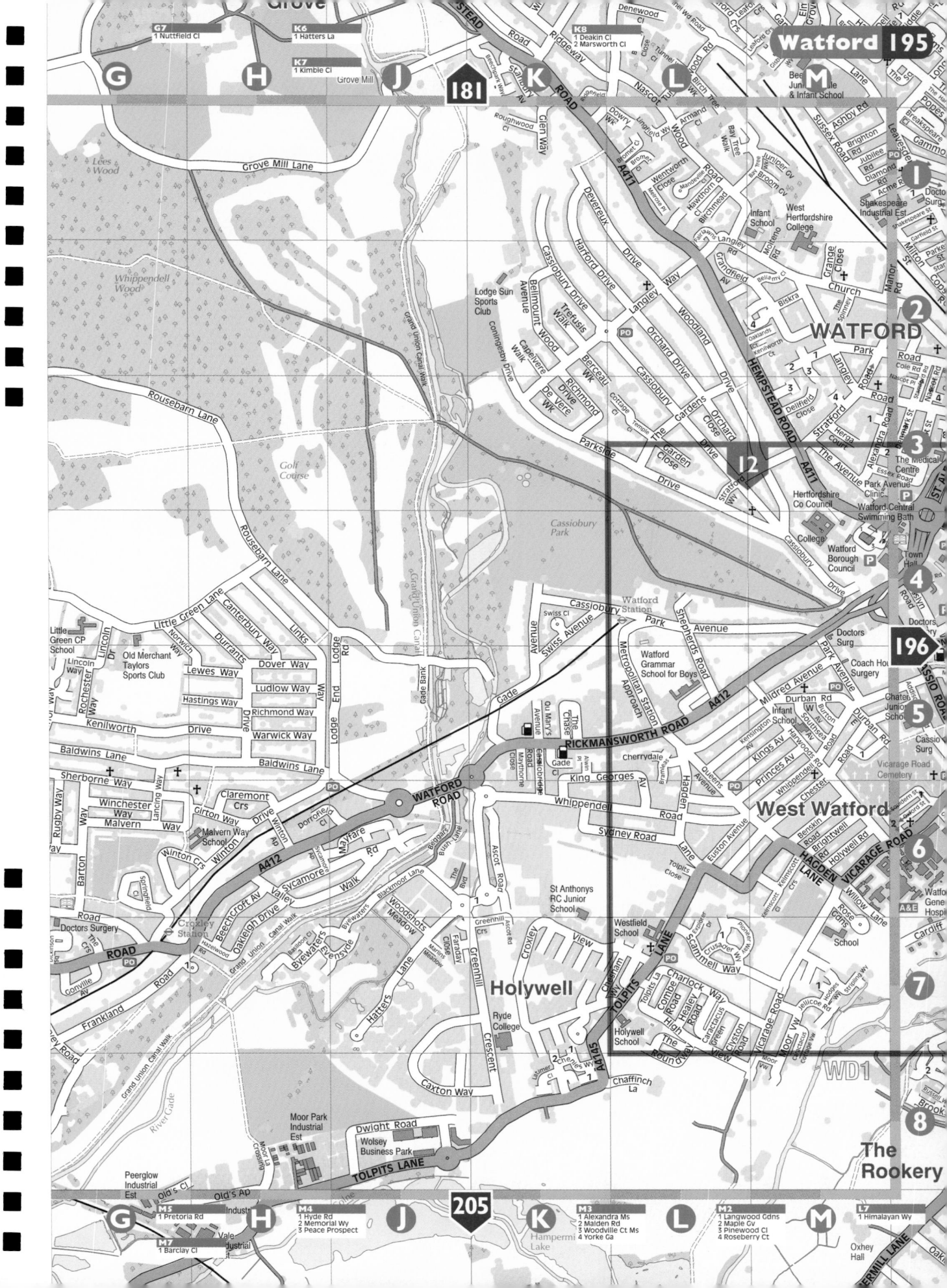

G7 1 Nuttfield Cl
K6 1 Hatters La
K7 1 Kimble Cl
K8 1 Deakin Cl 2 Marsworth Cl
181
12
196
205
WATFORD
West Watford
Holywell
The Rookery
Cassiobury Park
Golf Course
Lees Wood
Whippendell Wood
Grove Mill Lane
Rousebarn Lane
Grand Union Canal
Grand Union Canal Walk
Lodge Sun Sports Club
Watford Station
Watford Grammar School for Boys
Old Merchant Taylors Sports Club
Little Green CP School
Malvern Way School
Croxley Station
Doctors Surgery
St Anthonys RC Junior School
Westfield School
Holywell School
Ryde College
Moor Park Industrial Est
Wolsey Business Park
Peerglow Industrial Est
Hertfordshire Co Council
Watford Borough Council
West Hertfordshire College
Infant School
Shakespeare Industrial Est
Watford Central Swimming Bath
Park Avenue Clinic
The Medical Centre
Coach House Surgery
Vicarage Road Cemetery
HEMPSTEAD ROAD
A411
RICKMANSWORTH ROAD
A412
WATFORD ROAD
TOLPITS LANE
A4145
VICARAGE ROAD
HAGDEN LANE
WD1
M5 1 Pretoria Rd
M7 1 Barclay Cl
M4 1 Hyde Rd 2 Memorial Wy 3 Peace Prospect
M3 1 Alexandra Ms 2 Malden Rd 3 Woodville Ct Ms 4 Yorke Ga
M2 1 Langwood Gdns 2 Maple Gv 3 Pinewood Cl 4 Roseberry Ct
L7 1 Himalayan Wy

196
North Watford
B1
1 Chiswell Ct
2 Cromer Rd
3 Osborne Rd
B2
1 Ellenbrook Cl
2 Federal Wy
A6
1 Aynho St
2 Banbury St
3 Farraline Rd
4 Westbury Rd
A2, A3, A4, A5
Street names for these grid squares are listed at the back of the index
Otterspool
A1
1 Callowland Pl
2 Halsey Pl
3 Lea Rd
4 St George's Rd
182
Odhams Industrial Estate
Business Cen
Watford North Stn
N WESTERN AV COLNE WAY
Golf Course
Paramount Industrial Est
Mowat Industrial Est
Watford Eye Clnc
Shakespeare Industrial Est
Laharna Trading Estate
Knutsford Junior & Infant School
Busheymill Bridge
Junction 5
WD2
M1
A41(T)
STEPHENSON WAY
Holly Industrial Park
Hille Business Centre
ATFORD
Colonial Business Park
United Synagogue
Watford Junction Station
Highwood Primary School
Cp House Business Centre
Hartspring Sports Centre
Hartspring Industrial Park
Watford Co Court
The Medical Centre
Park Avenue Clinic
Police Station
Mag Court
Watford Central Swimming Bath
12
13
Doctors Surgery
The Purcell School
North Lodge Queens School
South Lodge Queens School
ALDENHAM ROAD
Town Hall
Business Cen
West Herts College
Golf Course
195
Pal Theatre
Indoor Market
Telephone Exchange
Harlequin Shopping Cen
Primary School
Chater Junior School
Chinese Medical Cen
Watford High Street Stn
Superstore
International University
Vicarage Road Cemetery
Watford Grammar School for Girls
Watford Springs Pool
Museum
Pump House Theatre
Gazelda Industrial Est
Watford Football Club
Watford General Hospital
A&E
Junior School
Watford Arches Retail Park
Colne Bridge Retail Park
Fisher Industrial Est
Cardiff Road Industrial Est
The Oxhey Infant School
Bushey Manor School
Bushey Hall Swimming Pool
Falconer School
Bushey Hall School
Bushey Mus & Art Gallery
Bushey Health Centre
CHALK HILL A411 LONDON ROAD
Oxhey
Bushey Station
Sacred Heart Junior Middle & Infant School
VD1
Bromet School
Haydon Hill
Golf Course
The Rookery
Watford Heath
D3, D5, D7, D8
Street names for these grid squares are listed at the back of the index
E3, F3, F7, G7
Street names for these grid squares are listed at the back of the index
St Margaret's School
206
A8, B3, B4, B5
Street names for these grid squares are listed at the back of the index
B6
1 Cannon Rd
2 Hamilton St
3 Lammas Rd
4 Local Board Rd
5 Roberts Rd
6 Tucker St
B7
1 The Coppice
2 Rainbow Ct
3 Walverns Cl
B8
1 Hollybush Cl
2 Meadowbank
C3
1 Beasant House
2 Bevan House
3 Gandhi Ct
4 Mandela Pl
5 Orwell Ct
C4
1 Pankhurst Pl
C6, C7, C8
Street names for these grid squares are listed at the back of the index
1 grid square represents 500 metres

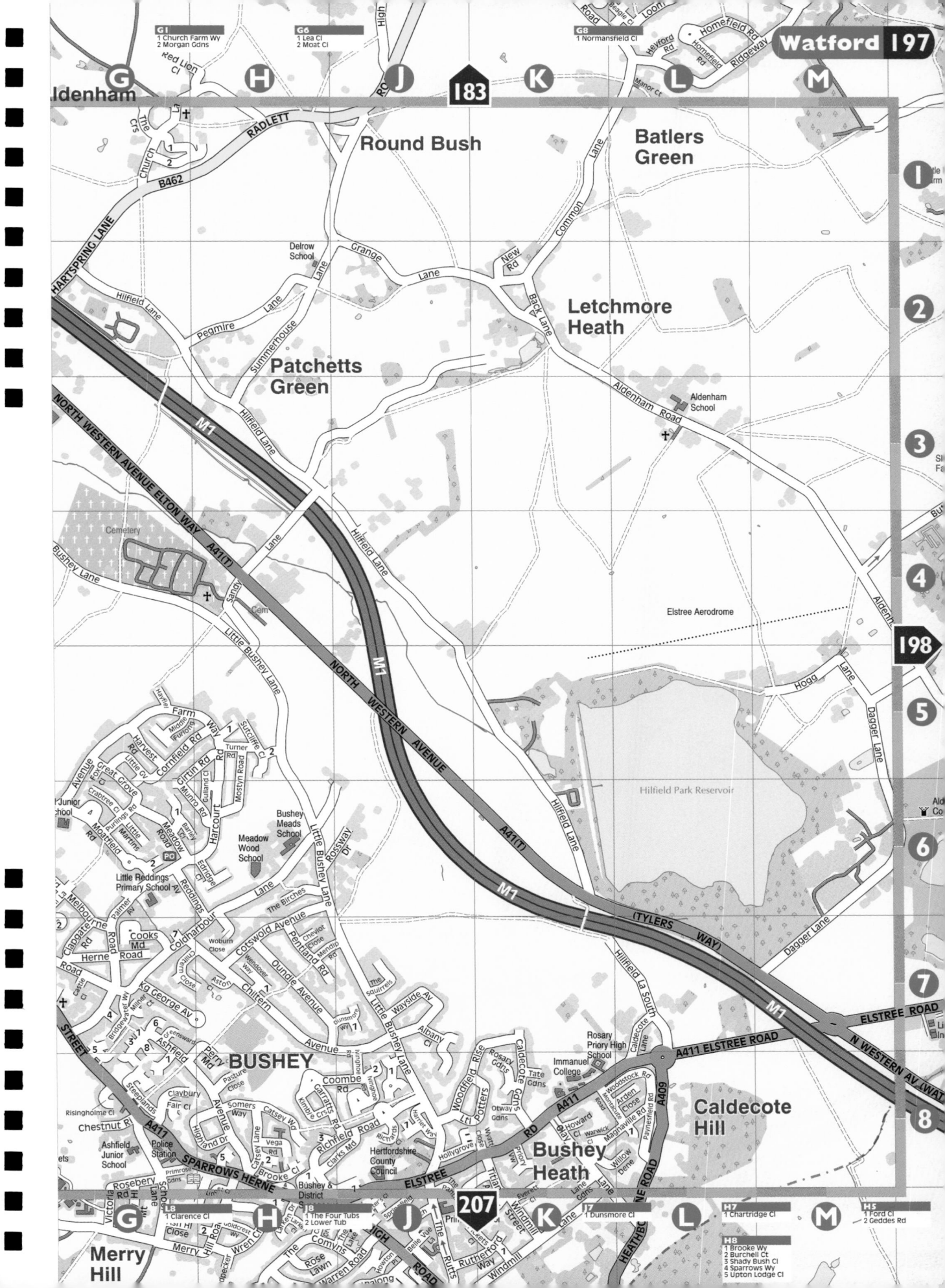
Aldenham
Round Bush
Batlers Green
Letchmore Heath
Patchetts Green
Delrow School
Aldenham School
Cemetery
Elstree Aerodrome
Hilfield Park Reservoir
BUSHEY
Bushey Heath
Caldecote Hill
Merry Hill
Bushey Meads School
Meadow Wood School
Little Reddings Primary School
Rosary Priory High School
Immanuel College
Ashfield Junior School
Police Station
Hertfordshire County Council
G1 1 Church Farm Wy 2 Morgan Gdns
G6 1 Lea Cl 2 Moat Cl
G8 1 Normansfield Cl
L8 1 Clarence Cl
J8 1 The Four Tubs 2 Lower Tub
J7 1 Dunsmore Cl
H7 1 Chartridge Cl
H8 1 Brooke Wy 2 Burchell Ct 3 Shady Bush Cl 4 Sparrows Wy 5 Upton Lodge Cl
H5 1 Ford Cl 2 Geddes Rd
183
198
207

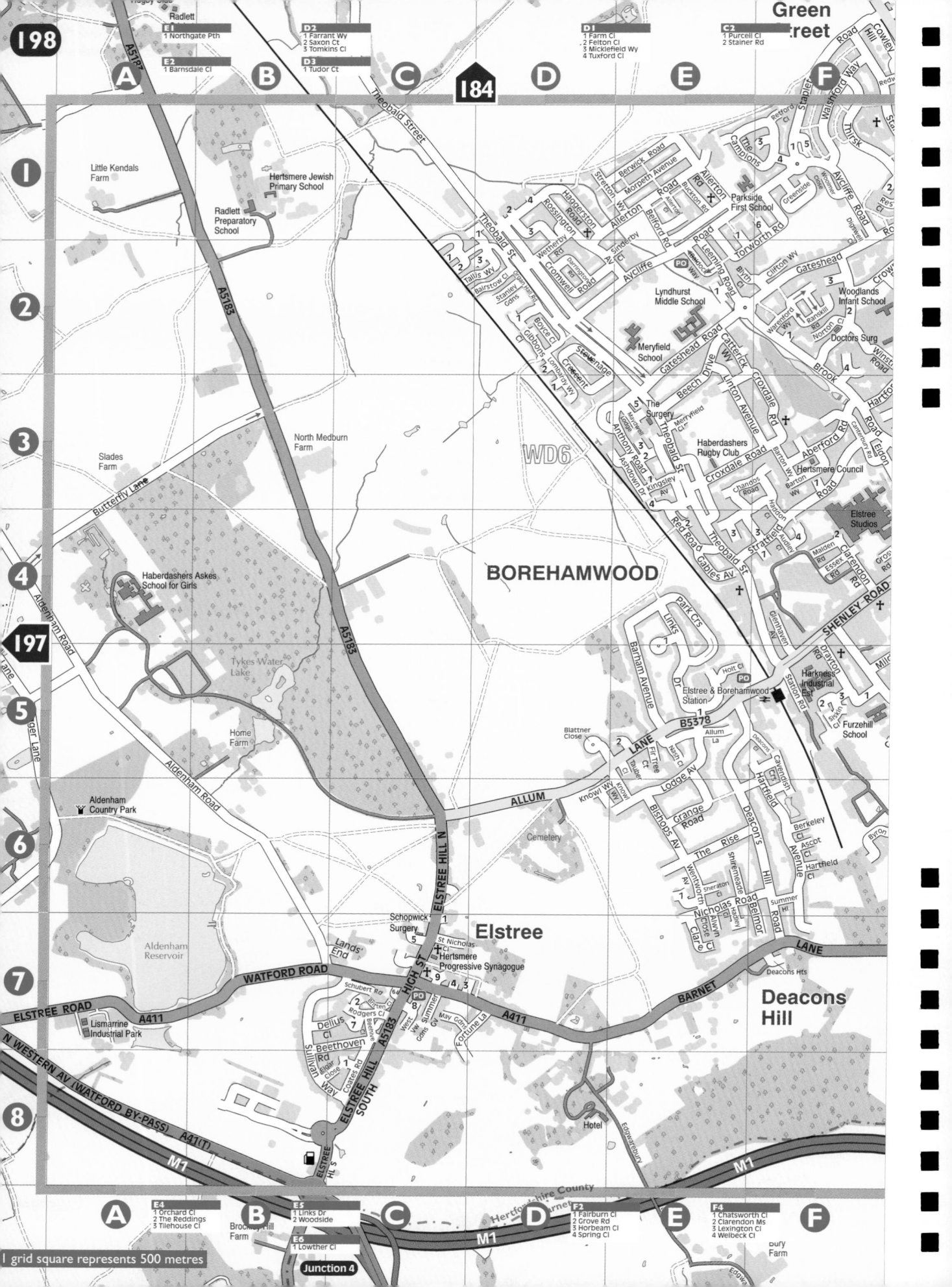
E1
1 Northgate Pth
E2
1 Barnsdale Cl
D2
1 Farrant Wy
2 Saxon Ct
3 Tomkins Cl
D3
1 Tudor Ct
D1
1 Farm Cl
2 Felton Cl
3 Micklefield Wy
4 Tuxford Cl
C2
1 Purcell Cl
2 Stainer Rd
Green Street
184
197
A
B
C
D
E
F
1
2
3
4
5
6
7
8
Radlett
A5183
Little Kendals Farm
Hertsmere Jewish Primary School
Radlett Preparatory School
Theobald Street
Theobald St
North Medburn Farm
Slades Farm
Butterfly Lane
WD6
BOREHAMWOOD
Haberdashers Askes School for Girls
Aldenham Road
Tykes Water Lake
Home Farm
Aldenham Country Park
Aldenham Reservoir
Allum Lane
B5378
Elstree & Borehamwood Station
Cemetery
Elstree Hill N
Elstree Hill South
Elstree Hl S
Schopwick Surgery
St Nicholas Cl
Hertsmere Progressive Synagogue
Lands' End
Watford Road
Elstree Road
A411
Lismarrine Industrial Park
High St
Barnet Lane
Deacons Hill
Deacons Hts
Hotel
Edgwarebury
N Western Av (Watford By-Pass) A41(T)
M1
Hertfordshire County
Lyndhurst Middle School
Meryfield School
Parkside First School
Woodlands Infant School
Doctors Surg
Haberdashers Rugby Club
Hertsmere Council
Elstree Studios
Harkness Industrial Est
Furzehill School
The Surgery
Shenley Road
Gateshead Road
Aycliffe Road
Croxdale Road
Linton Avenue
Beech Drive
Stevenage Crescent
Cromwell Road
Barham Avenue
Park Crs
Links Dr
Lodge Av
Grange Road
Bishops Av
The Rise
Deacon's Hill Road
Hartfield Avenue
Cavendish Crs
Nicholas Road
Belmor
Brockley Hill Farm
Bury Farm
Junction 4
E4
1 Orchard Cl
2 The Reddings
3 Tilehouse Cl
E5
1 Links Dr
2 Woodside
E6
1 Lowther Cl
F2
1 Fairburn Cl
2 Grove Rd
3 Horbeam Cl
4 Spring Cl
F4
1 Chatsworth Cl
2 Clarendon Ms
3 Lexington Cl
4 Welbeck Cl
1 grid square represents 500 metres

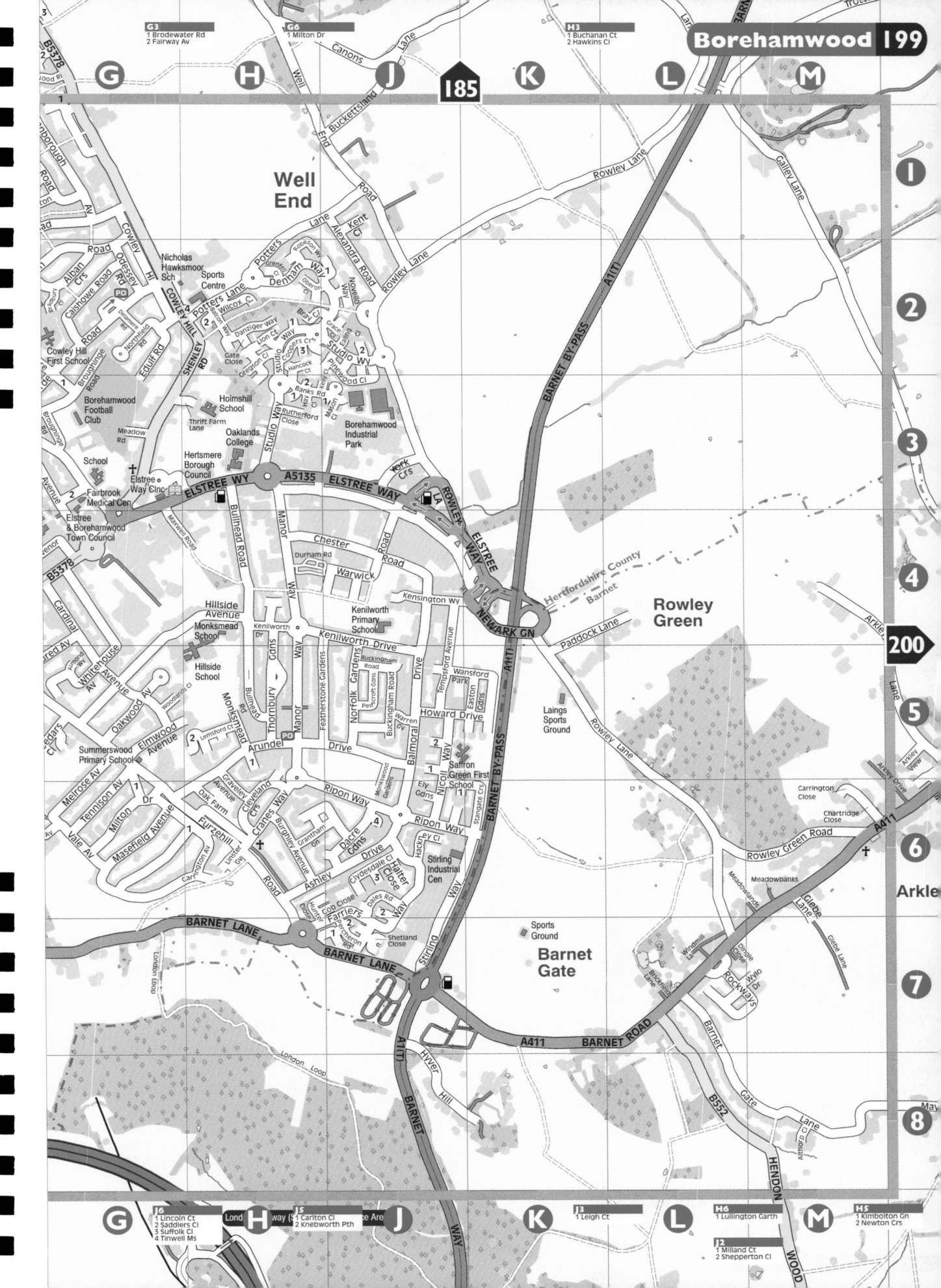
G3
1 Brodewater Rd
2 Fairway Av
G6
1 Milton Dr
H3
1 Buchanan Ct
2 Hawkins Cl
185
200
Well End
Rowley Green
Barnet Gate
Arkle
Nicholas Hawksmoor Sch
Sports Centre
Cowley Hill First School
Borehamwood Football Club
Holmshill School
Oaklands College
Hertsmere Borough Council
Borehamwood Industrial Park
School
Elstree Way Clnc
Fairbrook Medical Cen
Elstree & Borehamwood Town Council
Kenilworth Primary School
Monksmead School
Hillside School
Summerswood Primary School
Saffron Green First School
Stirling Industrial Cen
Laings Sports Ground
Sports Ground
Hertfordshire County
Barnet
BARNET BY-PASS
A1(T)
A5135 ELSTREE WAY
ELSTREE WY
BARNET LANE
A411 BARNET ROAD
NEWARK GN
Rowley Lane
Rowley Green Road
Galley Lane
Canons Lane
Well End Road
Buckettsland Lane
Potters Lane
Cowley Hill
Shenley Rd
B5378
B552
HENDON WOOD
London Loop
Carrington Close
Chartridge Close
Meadowbanks
J6
1 Lincoln Ct
2 Saddlers Cl
3 Suffolk Cl
4 Tinwell Ms
J5
1 Carlton Cl
2 Knebworth Pth
J3
1 Leigh Ct
H6
1 Lullington Garth
J2
1 Milland Ct
2 Shepperton Cl
H5
1 Kimbolton Gn
2 Newton Crs

D7
1 Mayhill Rd
D4
1 Bruce Rd
2 Chipping Cl
C6
1 Eleanor Gdns
2 Palmer Gdns
3 St Anna Rd
C7
1 Southfield
B6
1 Malins Cl
2 Well Ap
186
Kitt's End
Monken Hadley
High Barnet
Hadley
Chipping Barnet
Arkley
Underhill
BARNET
Ducks Island
Totteridge
199
EN5
WOOD STREET
BARNET ROAD
SAINT ALBANS ROAD
HADLEY HIGHSTONE
HADLEY GREEN
HIGH ST
BARNET HILL
TOTTERIDGE COMMON
Barnet General Hospital
The Spires Shopping Centre
The Bull Theatre
Barnet College of Further Education
High Barnet Station
Barnet Football Club
Ravenscroft School
The Print Room Museum
Queen Elizabeths School
Foulds Primary School
Underhill Junior & Infant School
Whittings Hill School
Old Fold Manor Golf Club
St Marthas Convent Senior School
Monken Hadley C of E Primary School
Christ Church C of E Primary School
Mays Lane
London Loop
E2
1 Boundary Cl
2 Old Fold Cl
3 Taylor's La
E4
1 Moon La
2 Tapster St
E5
1 Newlyn Rd
E6
1 Ellesmere Gv
1 grid square represents 500 metres

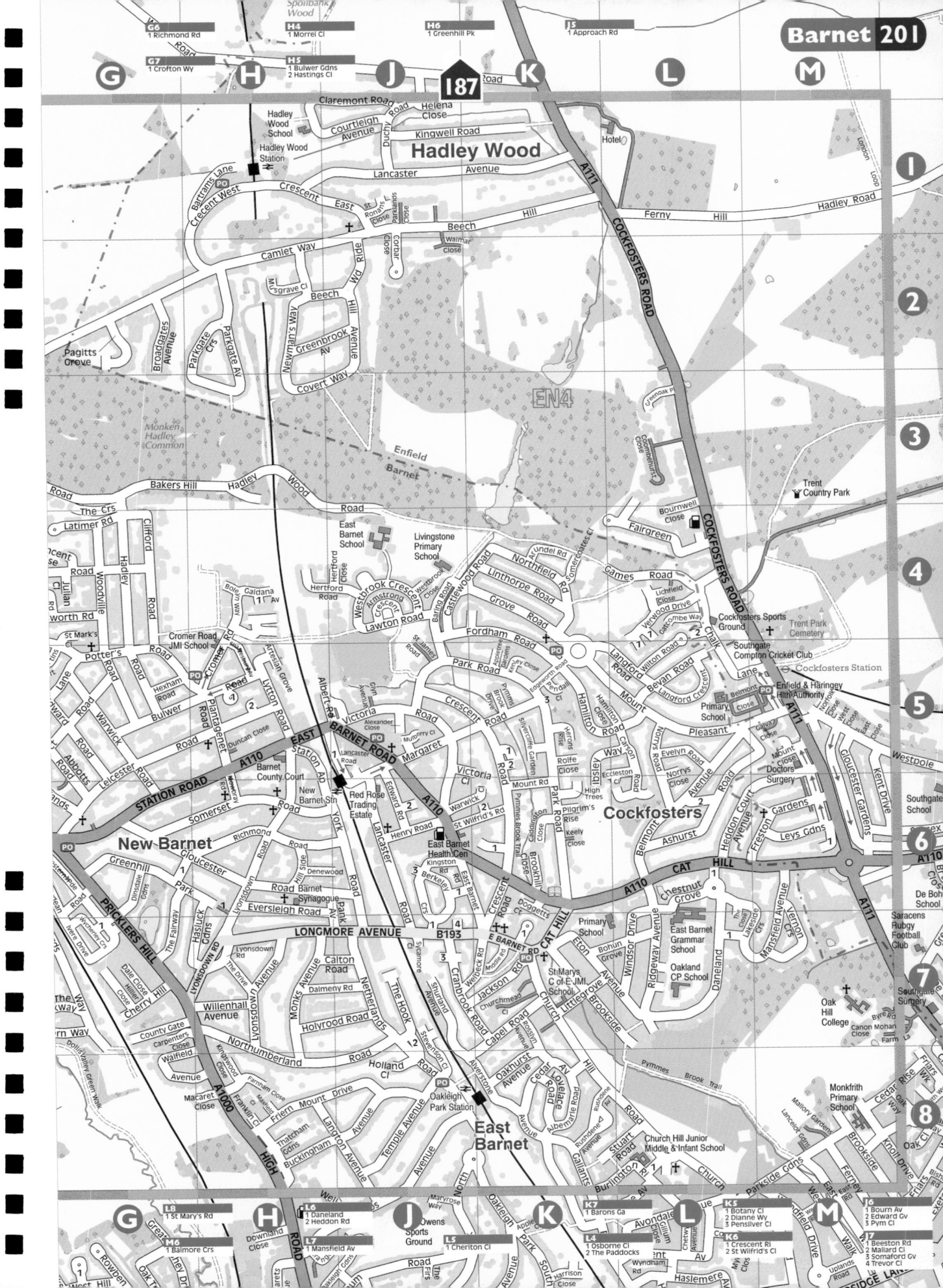
G6
1 Richmond Rd
H4
1 Morrel Cl
H6
1 Greenhill Pk
J5
1 Approach Rd
G7
1 Crofton Wy
H5
1 Bulwer Gdns
2 Hastings Cl
187
Hadley Wood
Hadley Wood School
Hadley Wood Station
Claremont Road
Helena Close
Courtleigh Avenue
Kingwell Road
Lancaster Avenue
Bartrams Lane
Crecent West
Crescent East
Beech Hill
Camlet Way
Ferny Hill
Hadley Road
COCKFOSTERS ROAD
A111
Hotel
Broadgates Avenue
Parkgate Crs
Parkgate Av
Pagitts Grove
Newman's Way
Greenbrook Av
Covert Way
Monken Hadley Common
EN4
Enfield
Barnet
Bakers Hill
Hadley Wood Road
Trent Country Park
Coombehurst Close
Bournwell Close
Fairgreen
East Barnet School
Livingstone Primary School
Westbrook Crescent
Lawton Road
Castlewood Road
Northfield Rd
Linthorpe Road
Grove Road
Games Road
Fordham Road
Cockfosters Sports Ground
Trent Park Cemetery
Southgate Compton Cricket Club
Cockfosters Station
Enfield & Haringey Hlth Authority
Cromer Road JMI School
Potter's Road
Bulwer Road
Plantagenet Road
Lytton Road
Park Road
Crescent Road
Victoria Road
Margaret Road
EAST BARNET ROAD
A110
STATION ROAD
Barnet County Court
New Barnet Stn
Red Rose Trading Estate
Leicester Road
Somerset Road
New Barnet
East Barnet Health Cen
Mount Rd
Park Road
Cockfosters
Pleasant
Belmont Primary School
Westpole
Southgate School
Gloucester Gardens
Kent Drive
Doctors Surgery
Ashurst
CAT HILL
Chestnut Grove
East Barnet Grammar School
Oakland CP School
Primary School
Saracens Rugby Football Club
De Bohun School
Southgate Surgery
Oak Hill College
PRICKLERS HILL
Greenhill
Gloucester Road
Eversleigh Road
Barnet Synagogue
LONGMORE AVENUE
B193
Lyonsdown Road
Calton Road
Dalmeny Rd
Holyrood Road
Netherlands Road
The Hook
Cranbrook Road
Jackson Rd
St Marys C of E JMI School
Church Hill Road
Brookside
Northumberland Road
Holland Cl
Oakleigh Park Station
East Barnet
Friern Mount Drive
Buckingham Road
Langton Avenue
Temple Avenue
HIGH ROAD
A1000
Church Hill Junior Middle & Infant School
Monkfrith Primary School
Pymmes Brook Trail
Parkside Gdns
L8
1 St Mary's Rd
L6
1 Daneland
2 Heddon Rd
K7
1 Barons Ga
K5
1 Botany Cl
2 Dianne Wy
3 Pensilver Cl
J6
1 Bourn Av
2 Edward Gv
3 Pym Cl
M6
1 Balmore Crs
L7
1 Mansfield Av
L5
1 Cheriton Cl
L4
1 Osborne Cl
2 The Paddocks
K6
1 Crescent Ri
2 St Wilfrid's Cl
J7
1 Beeston Rd
2 Mallard Cl
3 Somaford Gv
4 Trevor Cl
Owens Sports Ground
Haslemere

Misbourne Farm

A

D5
1 Hollytree Cl
2 Misbourne Cl
3 Ridgemount End

C7
1 Outfield Rd
2 Topland Rd
3 Windmill Rd

B

C8
1 Churchfield Rd
2 Lansdown Rd
3 Vale Cl

The Vache

C

192

D

A3
1 Hillside Cl
2 Milton Hl

A2
1 Sussex Cl

B8
1 Chipstead

E

Philipshill Wood

F

Buckinghamshire County

Hertfordshire County

1

Stratton Chase

Stratton Mill

2

Dodds Lane

Chase

South Bucks Way

Silver Hill

Albion Road

Albion Crescent

Grayburn Close

Hart Close

Sycamore Road

Cherry Ri

Kings Close

Ashwells Way

High View

Cromwell Cl

Outlook Drive

The Brow

B4442

VACHE LANE

NIGHTINGALES LANE

Deadhearn Lane

Gorelands

Gorelands Lane

Chiltern Open Air Museum M

Shrubs Wood

Buckinghamshire Chilterns University College

Newland Park

Gorelands Lane

3

Dean

Bramble Mead

Narcot Road

Palliser Road

Lightor Close

Parsonage Road

Milton Fields

Infant School

Milton's Cottage

St Giles Surgery

Middle School

Middle Meadow

Woodbank Drive

Turners Dr

LONDON ROAD

Ashwell's Farm

Chesham Lane

Shire Horse Centre

4

Hazel Wood

Chenies Close

Cook Close

Narcot Way

The Lagger

Seymour Rd

Cemetery

Dibden Hill

AMERSHAM ROAD

A413

South Bucks Way

Cherry Rise

Gables Close

Chesham Lane

Brawlings Farm

Brailings

Lane

5

The Lagger

Bowstridge

Pheasant Wy

Fodell Way

Mark Drive

Cherry Rise

Misbourne Av

Podson Drive

Southeote Dr

Avenue

Peterhill

Monument Lane

Micholls Avenue

Nicholls Av

Cross Lanes

Mid Cross Lane

Penn Gaskell Lane

PO

Copper Ridge

Ravensmead

Roberts Wood Drive

Nortoft Road

Rickmansworth Lane

Tate Road

Roberts Lane

Chalfont Common

6

Chalfont Grove

Windmill Farm

The Paddock

Old Mead

Wheatley Way

Danecraft Close

The Dell

Cedars Close

Northdown Rd

Deancroft Road

The Phygtle

Garners Cl

Garners

Denham Lane

Garners Walk

Gravel Hill

Robertswood County Combined School

West Hyde Lane

7

First School

Lovel End

Pinetree Cl

Grove Hill

Pennington Road

Field Way

South Bucks Wy

Chalfont St Peter Football Club

GRAVEL HILL

Wheelers Orch

Rickmansworth Lane

Hillside

Scholars Wk

Hedgerow

Copthall Corner

Copthall Lane

Hillfield Road

Elms Road

Hillfie End

Hill Farm Cl

Glynswood

Highlands Lane

Highlands Close

Amberburn Ho

Amberburn

Cotnall Cl

Ninnings Road

Cemetery

The Drive

Denham Lane

CHALFONT ST PETER

Warren Farm

8

Layters Green

Nicol Road

The Chalfonts Community College

Chalfont Leisure Centre

Weston Rd

Grove

Lovel Lane

Glebe Cl

Laurel Road

Glebe Road

Eleanor Road

Orchard Grove

Pond Lane

Gold Hill

Gold Hill North

Calcot Medical Cen

Middle School

Chalfonts & Gerrards Cross Hlth Clinic

The Misbourne Practice

Market Place

Holy Cross Boarding & Day School

Nucleus Gallery M

Grange Rd

Cem

HIGH STREET

PO

Sandy Rise

Lewis Lane

Joiners Close

Joiners Lane

Uplway

Winkers Lane

Morris Close

Lincoln Road

Chestnut Lane

Chiltern Hill

Haxface

Ellis Avenue

Woodside

A413

LINDEN DRIVE

LOWER ROAD

A

Layters Grn

Layter's Av

B

D6
1 Bramble Cl
2 Fernsleigh Cl
3 Robins Orch

D7
1 Chestnut Wk

Layters End

Criss Grove

Austenwood Close

Cherrytree

Benhurst Cl

C

Croft Rise

Hill Rise

Hill Rise Crs

St Mary's Wy

School La

Croft Road

D

E5
1 Cross Lanes Cl

E7
1 Greenfield End
2 Highlands End
3 Ninnings Wy

E

E8
1 Winkers Cl

Stratrou Wood

F

South Bucks Way

Denham

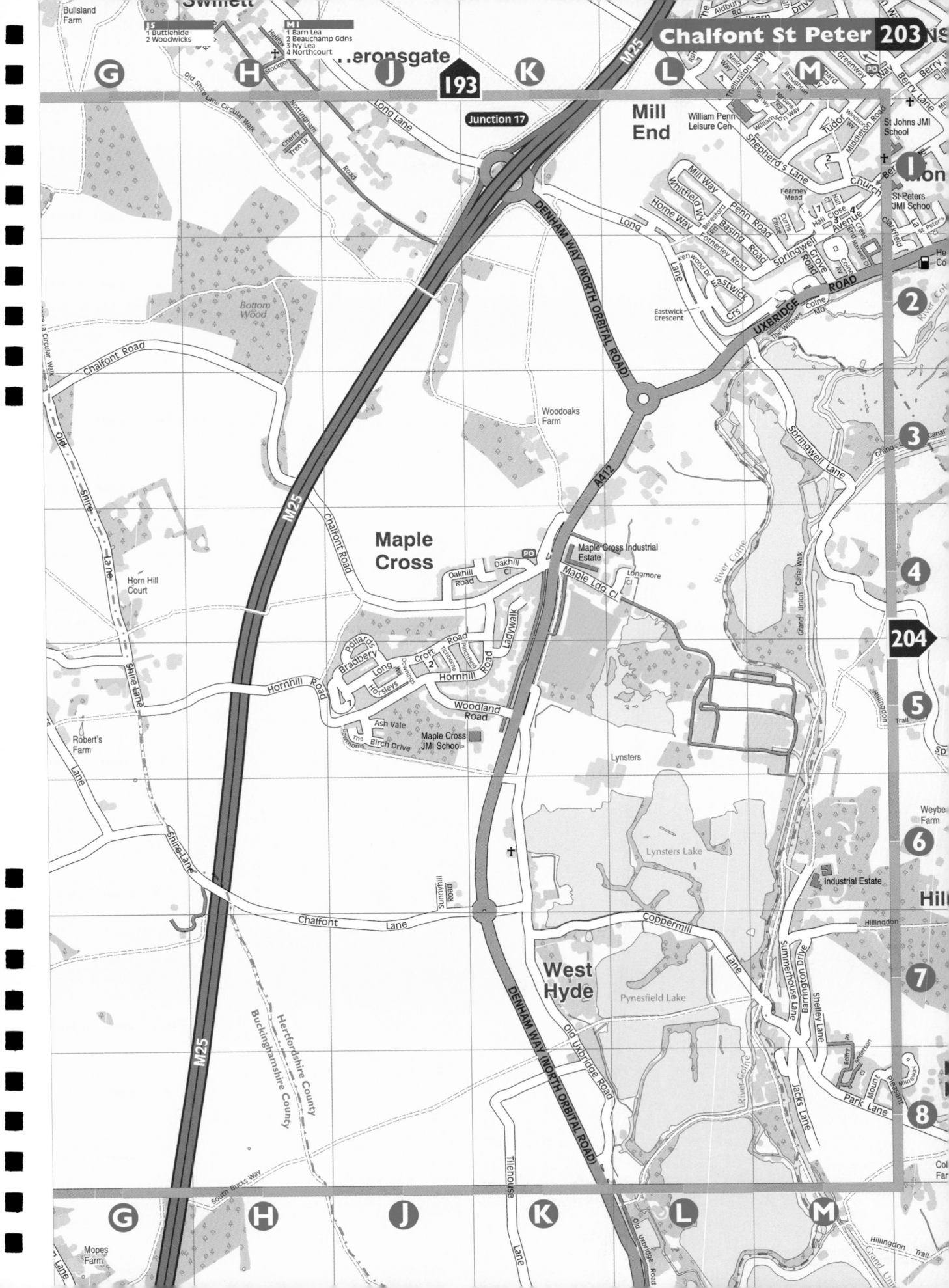

G H J **193** K L M

Junction 17

Mill End

William Penn
Leisure Cen

Bullsland
Farm

Swillett

1 Buttlehide
2 Woodwicks

M1
1 Barn Lea
2 Beauchamp Gdns
3 Ivy Lea
4 Northcourt

eronsgate

St Johns JMI
School

St Peters
JMI School

Old Shire Lane Circular Walk

Cherry
Tree La

Nottingham

Stockport

Long Lane

Halifax

Tudor

Shepherd's Lane

Thellusson Way

Greenway

PO Way

Berry Lane

Mill Way

Whitfield W

Penn Road

Home Way

Long

Eastwick
Crescent

Springwell Rd

Beresford Rd

Basing Road

Rotherley Road

Ken Wood Dr

Eastwick
Crs

Grove Road

Colne

Clarkfield

UXBRIDGE Colne Md ROAD

The Willows

Bottom
Wood

Chalfont Road

Chalfont Road

Woodoaks
Farm

A412

DENHAM WAY (NORTH ORBITAL ROAD)

River Colne

2

Old Shire Lane Circular Walk

Shire La

Maple
Cross

Maple Cross Industrial
Estate

PO

Oakhill
Road

Oakhill
Cl

Maple Lodg Cl

Longmore
Cl

River Colne

Springwell Lane

Grand Union Canal

3

Grand Union Canal Walk

4

204

Horn Hill
Court

Pollards

Bradbery

Long Way

Downings

Horsleys

The

Croft

2

Ladywalk

Trotsworth

Penchard

Hornhill Road

Road

Road

Hornhill Road

Hornhill Road

Woodland
Road

Lynsters

5

Trail

Sp

Robert's
Farm

Shire Lane

Ash Vale

Hawthorns

Birch Drive

Maple Cross
JMI School

1

Industrial Estate

6

Weybeard
Farm

Lynsters Lake

Hillingdon

Hil

Chalfont Lane

Sunnyhill
Road

Coppermill
Lane

Summerhouse Lane

Barrington Drive

Hillingdon

7

West
Hyde

Pynesfield Lake

Shelley Lane

Jacks Lane

Park Lane

Betty Av

Anderson

Mount Pleasant

Wingways

8

Mopes
Farm

M25

Hertfordshire County

Buckinghamshire County

South Bucks Way

Tilehouse

Lane

DENHAM WAY (NORTH ORBITAL ROAD)

Old Uxbridge Road

River Colne

Coppermill Lane

Col
Far

Grand

Hillingdon Trail

G H J K L M

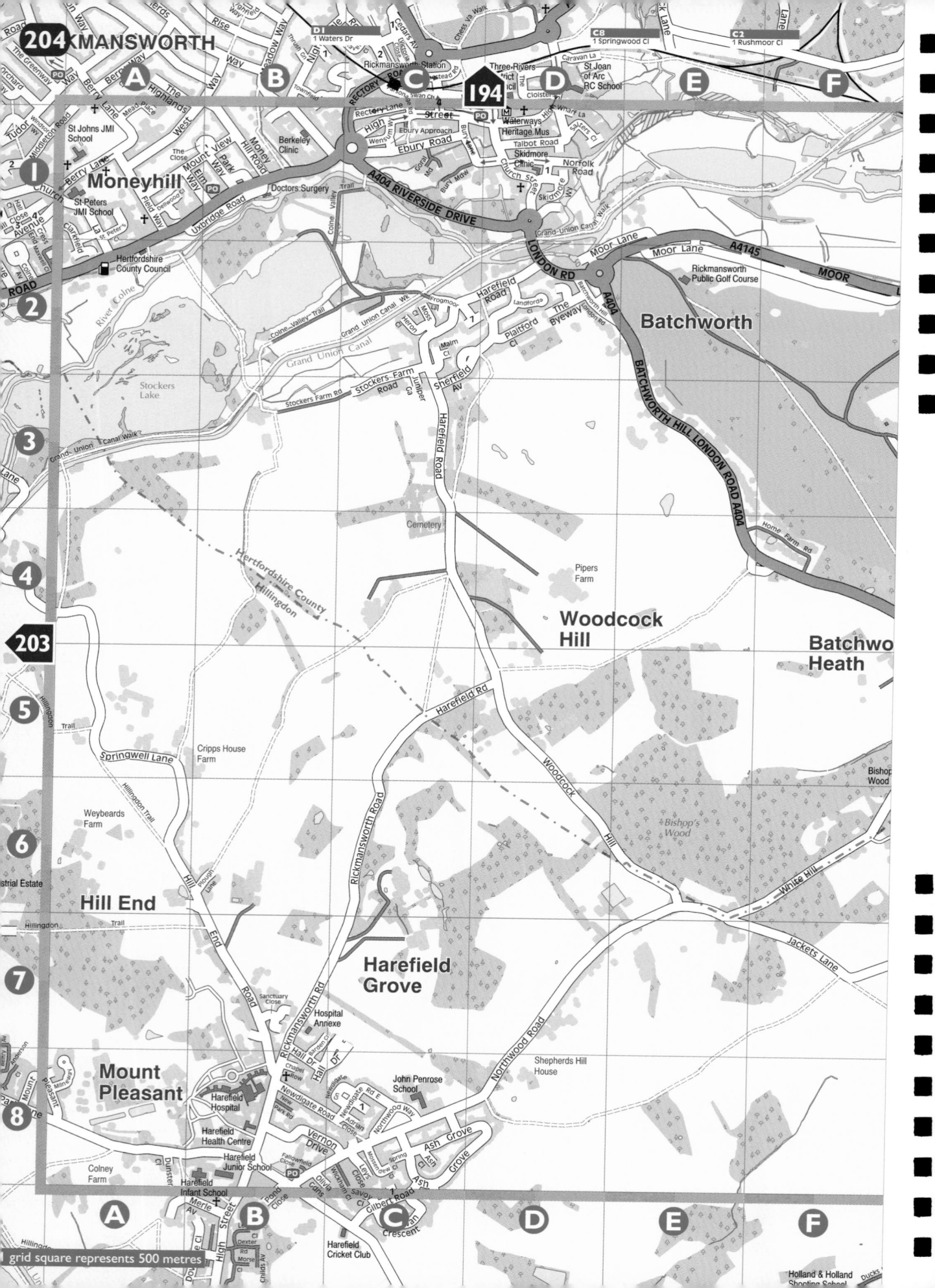

194

203

Moneyhill

St Johns JMI School

St Peters JMI School

Hertfordshire County Council

Berkeley Clinic

Doctors Surgery

Rickmansworth Station

Three Rivers District Council

St Joan of Arc RC School

Waterways Heritage Mus

Skidmore Clinic

Norfolk Road

A404 RIVERSIDE DRIVE

LONDON RD

Grand Union Canal

Moor Lane

Moor Lane A4145

MOOR

Rickmansworth Public Golf Course

Batchworth

BATCHWORTH HILL LONDON ROAD A404

Stockers Lake

River Colne

Grand Union Canal

Grand Union Canal Wk

Stockers Farm Rd

Stockers Farm Road

Sherfield Av

Harefield Road

Harefield Road

Cemetery

Pipers Farm

Woodcock Hill

Batchworth Heath

Hertfordshire County

Hillingdon

Springwell Lane

Cripps House Farm

Harefield Rd

Bishops Wood

Bishop's Wood

White Hill

Woodcock Hill

Weybeards Farm

Hillingdon Trail

Hill End

Trail

Hillingdon

Rickmansworth Road

Harefield Grove

Jackets Lane

Mount Pleasant

Harefield Hospital

Harefield Health Centre

Hospital Annexe

Sanctuary Close

John Penrose School

Shepherds Hill House

Northwood Road

Harefield Junior School

Harefield Infant School

Verion Drive

Gilbert Road

Ash Grove

Ash Grove

Colney Farm

Harefield Cricket Club

Holland & Holland Shooting School

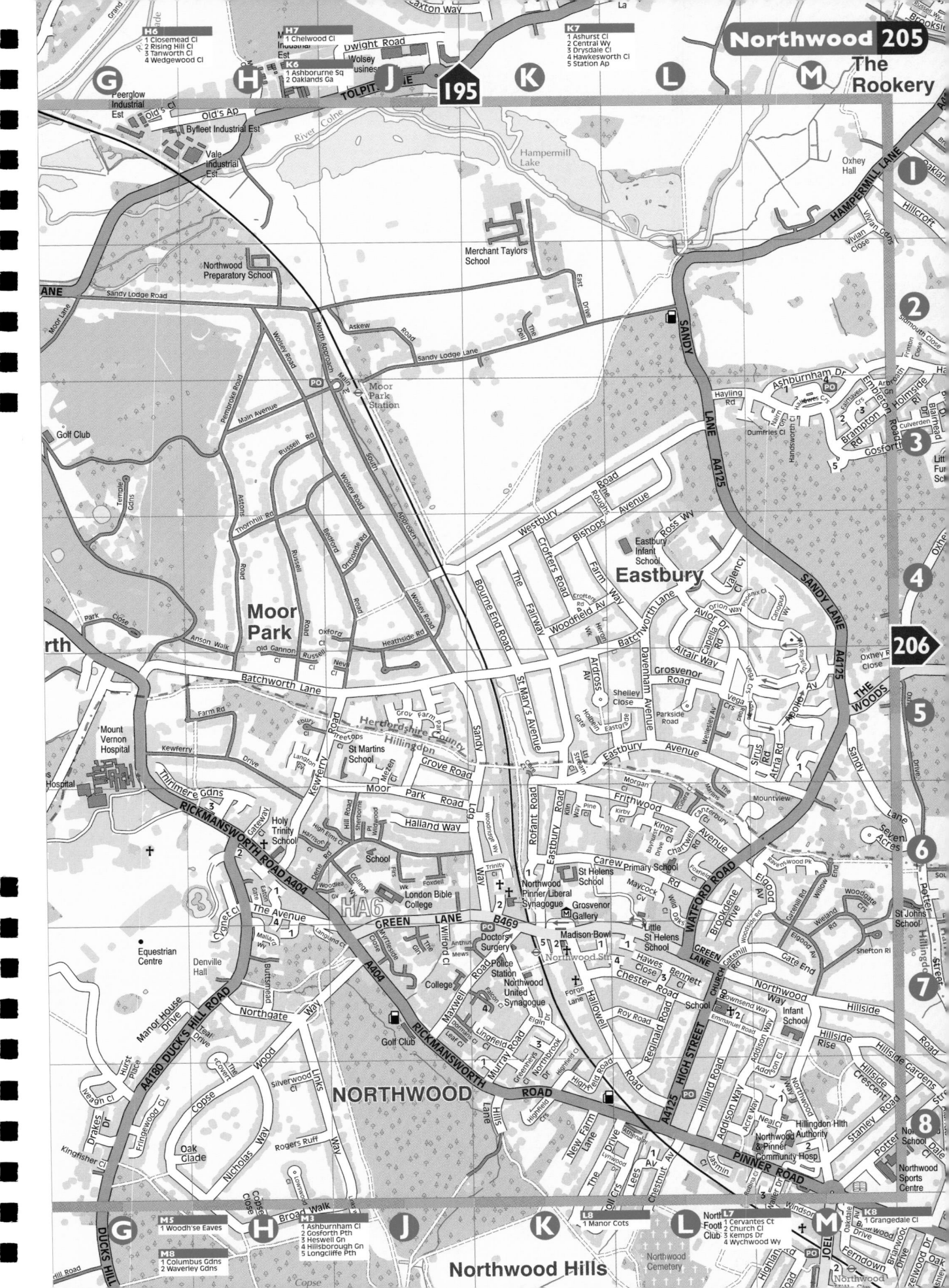

195

206

195

Map labels

G H J K L M I

H6
1 Closemead Cl
2 Rising Hill Cl
3 Tanworth Cl
4 Wedgewood Cl

H7
1 Chelwood Cl
Industrial
Est

K6
1 Ashbourne Sq
2 Oaklands Ga

K7
1 Ashurst Cl
2 Central Wy
3 Drysdale Cl
4 Hawkesworth Cl
5 Station Ap

Dwight Road
Wolsey
Business

TOLPIT ...E

Peerglow
Industrial
Est

Old's Cl
Old's Ap
Old's Ap

River Colne

Byfleet Industrial Est

Vale
Industrial
Est

Hampermill
Lake

Oxhey
Hall

HAMPERMILL LANE

Hillcroft

Oaklan...

Vivian Gdns
Vivian
Close

Sandy Lodge Road

...ANE

Moor Lane

Northwood
Preparatory School

Merchant Taylors
School

East

Drive

The
Del...

Sidmouth Close
Frimton

Askew Road

Sandy Lodge Lane

SANDY

Ashburnham Dr

Hayling
Rd

PO
Hawes
Cl

Emberton
Arbroath
Holmside

Frimton
Blainfield
Culverden

Brampton
Rd

Gosforth

Litt
Fur

Moor Approach

Moor
Park
Station

PO

Main Avenue

Wolsey Road

Dumfries Cl

Handsworth Rd

Main Approach

Pembroke Road

Golf Club

Russell Rd

Russell

South Approach

Wolsey Road

The Roughs

Avenue

Westbury

Crofters Road

Bishops

Farm Way

Eastbury
Infant
School

Eastbury

LANE A4125

Ross Wy

Astons Rd

Thornhill Rd

Bedford Road

Ormonde Rd

Heathside Rd

Temple
Gdns

Park
Close

Anson Walk

Old Gannon
Cl

Oxford Cl

Nevil
Cl

Russell Cl

**Moor
Park**

The Fairway

Woodfield Av

Bourne End Road

Batchworth Lane

Crofters
Gn

Batchworth Lane

Valency

Orion Wy
Phoenix Cl

Oxhey R...
Close

Oxhey

SANDY LANE A4125

THE WOODS

Sandy

Aviar Dr

Altair Way

Capella Rd

Vega
Crs

Grosvenor
Road

Across
Rd

St Mary's Avenue

Davenam Avenue

Shelley
Close

Holbein
Gate
Eastgate

Parkside
Road

Wellesley AV

Sirus
Rd

Atria Rd

Lane

Seven
Acres

Sandy

Farm Rd

Gateway

Eabry
Cl

Treetops

Hertfordshire County

Hillingdon

Kewferry Drive

St Martins
School

Lanston

Mezen Rd

Moor

**Mount
Vernon
Hospital**

Thirlmere Gdns

RICKMANSWORTH ROAD A404

Holy
Trinity
School

Hill Road

High Elms Cl

Sherborne

Grove Road

Park Road

Eastbury

Morgan
Cl

Frithwood

Kiln
Way

Pine
Cl

Kirby
Cl

Kings
Cl

Canterbury
Avenue

Mountview

Ravenswood Pk

Woodcote

... Hospital

Kewferry

Denne
Rd

Woodlea
Rd

College Rd

Widgeon

School

Foxdell

Wk

Halland Way

Woodstock
Rofant Road

Eastbury Road

Trinity
Cl

Carew Primary School

Barristers Cl

Charnwell

Fownlers

Maycock
Gv

St Helens
School

Kings
Cl

Carehill Rd

WATFORD ROAD

St Johns
School

HA6

The Avenue

Cygnet Cl

Mallard
Wy

Langland Cl

GREEN LANE

Wilford Cl

Anthus
Mews

Maxwell Road

B469

PO
Doctors
Surgery

London Bible
College

Little
St Helens
School

Grosvenor
Gallery

Northwood
Pinner Liberal
Synagogue

M

Madison Bowl

Little
St Helens
School

Hawes
Cl

Chester Road

Bennett
Cl

School

Townsend Way

Emmanuel Road

Willow
Rd

Wieland
Rd

Elgood
AV

Gate End

Northwood
Way

Hillside

Shefton Ri

Brookdene
Drive

Elgood Av

Equestrian
Centre

Denville
Hall

Manor House
Drive

A4180 DUCK'S HILL ROAD

Buttsmead

Northgate

Way

A404

Wood

Treat
Drive

Golf Club

Lingfield Rd

Murray Road

Greenhays Cl

Police
Station

Northwood
United
Synagogue

College

Forge
Lane

Hallowell

Roy Road

Reginald Road

CHURCH LANE

HIGH STREET

Infant
School

Hillside Rise

Hillside
Crescent

Hillside
Gardens

Hillside
Road

Stanley Road

No
School

Dale

Hurst
Place

Drakes
Dr

Kingfisher Cl

Neigh Cl

Fringewood Cl

Columbus Way

Silverwood
Cl

Links
Way

Rogers Ruff

NORTHWOOD

RICKMANSWORTH ROAD

Hills
Lane

New Farm
Road

Highfield
Cres

The
Drive

Lynwood
AV

Lees
AV

Chestnut Av

Jasmin

PINNER ROAD

A4125

PO

Hillard Rd

Addison Way

Acre Way

Neal Cl

Northway
Way

Hillingdon Hlth
Northwood
& Pinner
Community Hosp

Northwood
Sports
Centre

Northbrook
Rd

Northbrook
Rd

Dominar
Leaf Cl

Elgin
Cl

JOEL

Oakdale

PO

Ferndown

Oak
Glade

Nicholas Way

Copse
Close

Broad Walk

DUCKS HILL

Northwood Hills

Northwood
Cemetery

M5
1 Woodh'se Eaves

M3
1 Ashburnham Cl
2 Gosforth Pth
3 Heswell Gn
4 Hillsborough Gn
5 Longcliffe Pth

L8
1 Manor Cots

**North
Footb
Club**

L7
1 Cervantes Ct
2 Church Cl
3 Kemps Dr
4 Wychwood Wy

K8
1 Grangedale Cl

M8
1 Columbus Gdns
2 Waverley Gdns

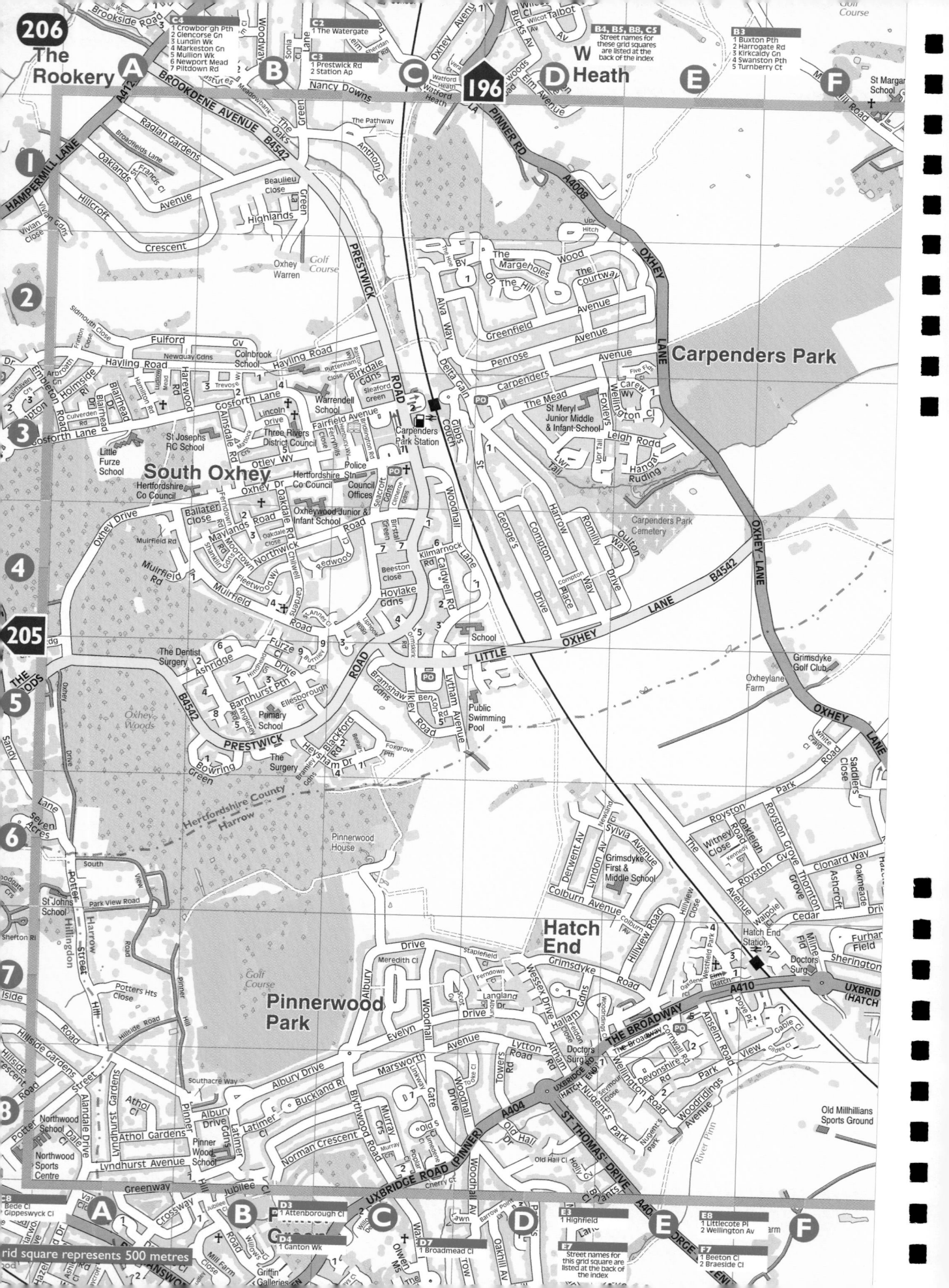

206
The Rookery
C4
1 Crowbor'gh Pth
2 Glencorse Gn
3 Lundin Wk
4 Markeston Gn
5 Mullion Wk
6 Newport Mead
7 Piltdown Rd
C2
1 The Watergate
C3
1 Prestwick Rd
2 Station Ap
196
Heath
B4, B5, B8, C5
Street names for these grid squares are listed at the back of the index
B3
1 Buxton Pth
2 Harrogate Rd
3 Kirkcaldy Gn
4 Swanston Pth
5 Turnberry Ct
St Margaret's School
Nancy Downs
BROOKDENE AVENUE
B4542
HAMPERMILL LANE
A4125
PINNER RD
A4008
Raglan Gardens
Oaklands
Hillcroft
Crescent
Highlands
Beaulieu Close
Golf Course
Oxhey Warren
PRESTWICK
ROAD
OXHEY
LANE
Carpenders Park
Carpenders Park Station
Greenfield
Avenue
Penrose
Fulford
Hayling Road
Colnbrook School
Gosforth Lane
Warrendell School
Fairfield Avenue
St Josephs RC School
Three Rivers District Council
Little Furze School
South Oxhey
Hertfordshire Co Council
Police Stn
Council Offices
St Meryl Junior Middle & Infant School
Carpenders Park Cemetery
Oxhey Drive
Oxheywood Junior & Infant School
Muirfield Rd
Northwick
Woodhall Lane
Compton
George's
Harrow
Drive
205
School
LITTLE
OXHEY
LANE
B4542
Grimsdyke Golf Club
Oxheylane Farm
The Dentist Surgery
Ashridge
Barnhurst Pth
Primary School
Oxhey Woods
Public Swimming Pool
Lytham Avenue
PRESTWICK
The Surgery
Bowring Green
Hertfordshire County
Harrow
Pinnerwood House
Royston Park
Grimsdyke First & Middle School
Colburn Avenue
Hatch End
Hatch End Station
Clonard Way
South View
Park View Road
St Johns School
Potter Street
Hillingdon
Harrow
Golf Course
Pinnerwood Park
Potters Hts Close
Grimsdyke Road
THE BROADWAY
A410
UXBRIDGE RD
Evelyn Drive
Woodhall
Albury Drive
Marsworth Avenue
Buckland Ri
Blythwood Road
Lytton Road
Hallam Gdns
Doctors Surg
Nugent's Park
Devonshire Rd
Woodridings Avenue
Old Millhillians Sports Ground
Northwood School
Northwood Sports Centre
Athol Gardens
Lyndhurst Avenue
Pinner Wood School
Norman Crescent
A404
UXBRIDGE ROAD (PINNER)
ST THOMAS' DRIVE
Greenway
Jubilee
C8
1 Bede Cl
2 Gippeswyck Cl
D3
1 Attenborough Cl
D4
1 Canton Wk
D7
1 Broadmead Cl
E3
1 Highfield
E7
Street names for this grid square are listed at the back of the index
E8
1 Littlecote Pl
2 Wellington Av
F7
1 Beeton Cl
2 Braeside Cl
Grid square represents 500 metres

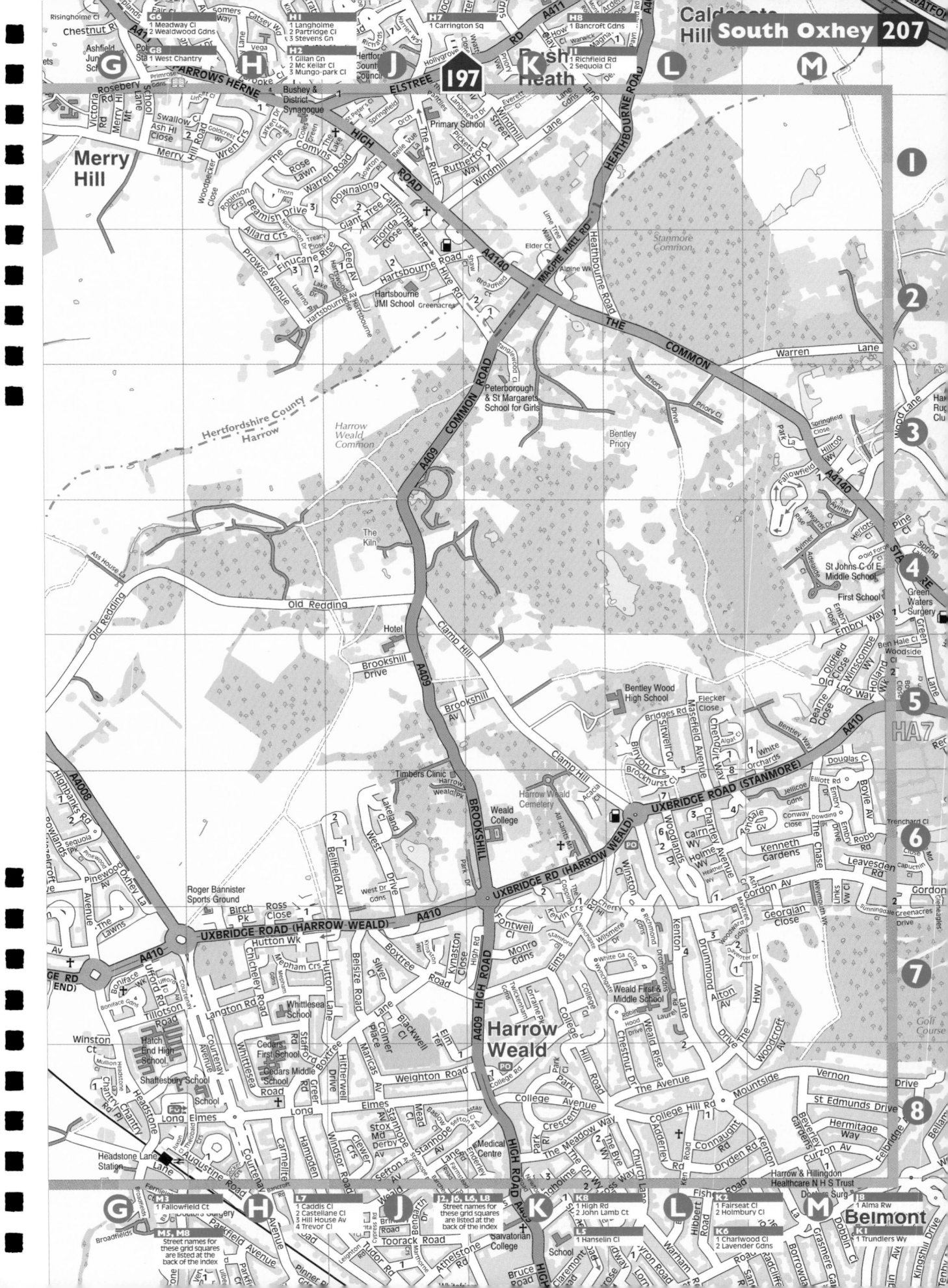
Merry Hill
Bushey Heath
Caldecote Hill
Bushey & District Synagogue
Primary School
Hartsbourne JMI School
Peterborough & St Margarets School for Girls
Hertfordshire County
Harrow
Harrow Weald Common
Stanmore Common
Bentley Priory
The Kiln
Hotel
Bentley Wood High School
Timbers Clinic
Weald College
Harrow Weald Cemetery
Roger Bannister Sports Ground
St Johns C of E Middle School
First School
Green Waters Surgery
Weald First & Middle School
Whittlesea School
Hatch End High School
Cedars First School
Cedars Middle School
Shaftesbury School
School
Headstone Lane Station
Medical Centre
Harrow Weald
Harrow & Hillingdon Healthcare N H S Trust
Salvatorian College
Belmont
Golf Course
HA7
A4140
A409
A410
A4008
A411
COMMON ROAD
BROOKSHILL
HIGH ROAD
UXBRIDGE ROAD (HARROW WEALD)
UXBRIDGE RD (HARROW WEALD)
UXBRIDGE ROAD (STANMORE)
THE COMMON
HEATHBOURNE ROAD
MAGPIE HALL RD
ELSTREE RD
SPARROWS HERNE
Old Redding
Clamp Hill
Warren Lane
Brookshill Drive
Hartsbourne Road
Heathbourne Road
Windmill Lane
Priory Drive
Embry Way
Kenton Lane
College Hill Rd
The Avenue
College Avenue
Weighton Road
Long Elmes
Vernon Drive
St Edmunds Drive
Hermitage Way
Curzon Av
Courtenay Avenue
Whittlesea Road
Langton Rd
Kenneth Gardens
Gordon Av
Georgian Close
Leavesden Rd
Cairn Wy
Woodlands Dr
Chartley Avenue
Masefield Avenue
Drummond Dr
Alton Av
Woodcroft Av
G6 1 Meadway Cl 2 Weatwood Gdns
G8 1 West Chantry
H1 1 Langholme 2 Partridge Cl 3 Stevens Gn
H2 1 Gillan Gn 2 Mc Kellar Cl 3 Mungo-park Cl
H7 1 Carrington Sq
H8 1 Bancroft Gdns
J1 1 Richfield Rd 2 Sequoia Cl
M3 1 Fallowfield Ct
M5, M8 Street names for these grid squares are listed at the back of the index
L7 1 Caddis Cl 2 Castellane Cl 3 Hill House Av 4 Trevor Cl
J2, J6, L6, L8 Street names for these grid squares are listed at the back of the index
K8 1 High Rd 2 John Lamb Ct
L5 1 Hanselin Cl
K2 1 Fairseat Cl 2 Holmbury Cl
K6 1 Charlwood Cl 2 Lavender Gdns
J8 1 Alma Rw
K1 1 Trundlers Wy
197

Abbots Langley 181 K3
Adeyfield 9 G8
Aimes Green 177 L7
Albury 76 F4
Albury End 76 E6
Aldbury 125 H4
Aldenham 182 F8
Aley Green 106 D1
Allen's Green 119 L4
Amwell 132 B3
Ansells End 85 L8
Anstey 46 A4
Apsley 166 C3
Apsley End 36 D3
Ardeley 56 F7
Arkley 200 A6
Arlesey 25 M5
Ashwell 18 D6
Ashwell End 17 M5
Aspenden 58 C5
Aston 71 L8
Aston Clinton 122 B5
Aston End 71 K5
Astrope 101 G7
Astwick 16 E8
Ayot Green 133 L2
Ayot St Lawrence 111 G4
Ayot St Peter 111 L7
Ayres End 131 L5
Babbs Green 117 J6
Bakers End 117 K3
Baldock 40 E2
Ballingdon Bottom 127 K1
Barkway 32 C6
Barley 22 F8
Barleycroft End 61 G6
Barley End 125 H2
Barnet 200 E7
Barnet Gate 199 K7
Barton-le-Clay 35 J7
Barwick 93 H6
Bassus Green 72 D2
Batchworth 204 E2
Batchworth Heath 204 F4
Batford 109 K7
Batlers Green 197 L1
Bayford 157 L5
Bedlar's Green 97 M5
Bedmond 167 K6
Bedwell 5 H4
Beecroft 80 D2
Bell Bar 172 F3
Belsize 179 K3
Bendish 85 M3
Bengeo 137 G2
Benington 72 D6
Bennetts End 166 E2
Bentfield Bury 79 G2
Bentfield Green 79 H2
Bentley Heath 186 E6
Berkhamsted 146 F6
Bernards Heath 11 H2
Bidwell 62 F4
Birchanger 79 K8
Birch Green 136 B6
Birchwood 155 G3
Bird Green 47 K2
Biscot 65 H8
Bishop's Stortford 96 B3
Blackmore End 109 M4
Blue Hill 90 C5
Borehamwood 198 D4
Botany Bay 188 C7
Bourne End 165 H1
Bovingdon 165 G6
Bovingdon Green 164 E8
Bower Heath 109 J4
Boxmoor 166 A1
Bozen Green 59 M7
Bragbury End 89 J3
Bramfield 114 B6
Braughing 75 L4
Braughing Friars 76 C5
Brays Grove 7 L9
Breachwood Green 85 K2
Brent Pelham 46 E8
Brewer's End 99 G3
Brickendon 158 B6
Bricket Wood 182 D2
Briden's Camp 127 M7
Broad Colney 170 C7
Broadgreen Wood 157 M2
Broadley Common 161 J7
Broadoak End 136 E2
Broadwater 88 F1
Broken Green 76 B8
Bromley 94 B2
Brook End 57 H4
Brookmans Park 172 D5
Broxbourne 159 M7
Buckland 44 C2
Buckland 122 E4
Buckland Common 144 F7
Bucklandwharf 122 F6
Bucks Hill 180 B5
Building End 33 M3
Bulbourne 124 A2
Bullen's Green 171 K1
Bulls Cross 189 M7
Bull's Green 113 J3
Bulstrode 165 K7
Bumble's Green 177 M3
Buntingford 58 E3
Burge End 37 J5
Burnham Green 113 H4
Burn's Green 90 E1
Bury Green 95 K3
Bury Green 190 A2
Bury Park 83 G2
Bush End 98 F6
Bushey 197 H8
Bushey Heath 197 K8
Butt's Close 52 D2
Bygrave 28 B5
Caddington 82 E6
Cadwell 38 F5
Caldecote 27 J1
Caldecote Hill 197 L8

Campions 142 E5
The Camp 169 M1
Carpenders Park 206 F1
Carter's Green 143 K8
Chalfont Common 202 E4
Chalfont Grove 202 A6
Chalfont St Peter 202 D7
Chalton 63 J1
Chandler's Green 106 D1
Chapmore End 115 H5
Charlton 52 C5
Chatter End 78 A3
Chaulden 148 C8
Chaul End 82 C3
Cheapside 46 A3
Cheddington 101 L4
Chells 5 M1
Chenies 193 H1
Cherry Green 74 C1
Cheshunt 190 A1
Cheverell's Green 106 D3
Childwick Bury 152 B1
Childwick Green 131 G8
Chiltern Green 84 F7
Chipperfield 180 A2
Chipping 44 C5
Chipping Barnet 200 D5
Chiswell Green 168 E4
Chivery 144 B6
Cholesbury 145 H8
Chorleywood 193 J5
Chorleywood Bottom 193 J7
Chorleywood West 192 F6
Church End 26 A3
Church End 77 J8
Church End 80 B4
Church End 81 J7
Church End 102 D8
Church End 129 M6
Church End 193 L1
Churchgate 176 A8
Churchgate Street 142 E6
Church Langley 163 J2
Clapgate 77 H4
Clay End 72 D3
Clay Hill 189 H8
Clement's End 105 J7
Clothall 41 J6
Clothall Common 41 G2
Cockernhoe 66 C7
Cockfosters 201 K6
Codicote 111 L1
Codicote Bottom 111 J2
Cokenach 32 D5
Cold Christmas 116 F4
Cold Harbour 109 H5
Cole Green 135 M6
Coleman Green 132 F5
Colliers End 92 F4
Colney Heath 171 H1
Colney Street 183 K1
Commonwood 179 M5
Cooper's Green 154 A2
Cottered 57 H2
Counters End 148 F7
Cow Roast 145 M1
Crabbs Green 61 J4
Cradle End 95 L2
Crews Hill 189 G6
Cromer 56 C5
Cromer-Hyde 133 H5
Croxley Green 194 F6
Cuffley 174 E7
Cumberlow Green 42 D8
Cupid Green 150 A3
Dagnall 104 B4
Damask Green 55 G2
Dancers Hill 186 B6
Dane End 91 L3
Danesbury 112 B4
Darleyhall 85 H1
Dassels 59 J7
Datchworth 89 K8
Datchworth Green 113 H1
Deacons Hill 198 F7
Deer's Green 47 M6
Dewes Green 61 L1
Digswell 112 E7
Digswell Park 112 C8
Digswell Water 112 F8
Downside 81 K4
Drayton Beauchamp 123 H5
Driver's End 87 M6
Duck End 97 K1
Ducks Island 200 C8
Dudswell 146 C2
Dunstable 81 J2
Dunton 14 C5
East Barnet 201 J8
Eastbury 205 L4
East End 61 K6
Eastend 161 K1
East End Green 136 B8
Easthall 69 G8
East Hyde 108 E2
Eastwick 141 G6
Edworth 17 G3
Ellenbrook 154 C4
Elstree 198 D7
Enfield Lock 190 E8
Epping Green 174 C1
Essendon 156 E4
Eyeworth 14 E2
Farley Hill 83 G4
Farnham 78 B4
Farnham Green 78 A3
Felden 165 M3
Fields End 148 C6
Fishers Green 69 L2
Flamstead 107 H8
Flamstead End 176 A7
Flaunden 178 F3
The Folly 110 A8
Ford End 47 K6
Foster Street 163 L3
Freezy Water 190 D7
Friar's Wash 107 H7
Frithsden 147 M2

Frithsden Gardens 147 K1
Frogmore 169 K7
The Frythe 111 M8
Furneux Pelham 60 F5
Further Ford End 47 J4
Gadebridge 148 E5
Ganwick Corner 187 G6
Garston 182 B6
Gaston Green 121 G3
Gatley End 19 F3
Gilston 141 J5
Gilston Park 141 H4
Goff's Oak 175 H7
Goose Green 159 J3
Gorhambury 151 H6
Gosmore 52 E7
Graveley 54 B6
Gravel Hill 202 E6
Gravesend 76 F2
Great Amwell 138 D5
Great Chishill 23 K8
Great Gaddesden 127 H7
Greatgap 102 C4
Great Green 15 M5
Great Hallingbury 97 J6
Great Hormead 60 A2
Great Munden 74 C5
Great Offley 51 J8
Great Parndon 161 M4
Great Wymondley 53 K4
Green End 41 H8
Green End 43 J3
Green End 75 J3
Green End 91 K1
Green End 148 E8
Green Street 95 K1
Green Street 184 F8
The Green 104 E2
Green Tye 119 H1
Grovehill 8 C1
The Grove 181 H8
Gubblecote 101 J8
Guilden Morden 15 K5
Gustard Wood 110 B6
Hadham Cross 94 D8
Hadham Ford 95 G2
Hadley 200 F4
Hadley Wood 201 J1
Hailey 138 E8
Haldens 112 F8
Hall Grove 135 G6
Hallingbury Street 98 A6
Halls Green 161 H4
Hall's Green 55 K4
Hammerfield 149 G7
Hammond Street 175 H5
Handside 134 A5
Hanscombe End 36 B2
Harefield Grove 204 C7
Hare Street 6 A9
Hare Street 56 E4
Hare Street 59 J2
Harlow 6 F6
Harmer Green 112 F5
Harpenden 130 E2
Harpenden Common 131 G5
Harrow Weald 207 K7
Hartham 137 J3
Hart Hill 3 J3
Hastingwood 163 L6
Hastoe 144 F3
Hatch End 206 D7
Hatching Green 130 E4
Hatfield 154 E6
Hatfield Garden Village 154 D2
Hatfield Hyde 134 E7
Haultwick 73 L7
Hay Green 30 F4
Hay Street 75 K1
Hazel End 78 F4
Heath End 145 M8
Hebing End 72 F8
Helham Green 117 L6
Hellman's Cross 99 L8
Hemel Hempstead 8 C9
Henlow 25 H1
Heronsgate 193 J8
Hertford 137 K5
Hertford Heath 138 A7
Hertingfordbury 136 F5
Hexton 36 A3
Heydon 23 M5
Higham Gobion 35 M4
High Barnet 200 B4
High Cross 92 E8
High Cross 183 J7
Highfield 8 D4
The High 6 E4
High Town 2 E4
High Wych 142 A1
Hill End 204 A6
Hillfoot End 36 C1
Hinxworth 17 H4
Hitchin 52 E1
Hitchin Hill 52 D5
Hobbs Cross 163 M1
Hockerill 97 G4
Hoddesdon 159 K5
Hogpits Bottom 179 G3
Holwell 38 A3
Holwellbury 25 G8
Holyfield 177 H7
Holywell 105 H3
Holywell 195 K7
Hoo End 86 C6
Hook's Cross 89 M4
Hope End Green 99 K5
Houghton Regis 63 J5
Housham Tye 143 J8
Howe Green 97 K8
How Wood 169 H6
Hudnall 126 D3
Hudnall Corner 126 F3
Hunsdon 140 B1
Hunsdonbury 140 B4
Hunton Bridge 181 G2
Ickleford 38 C6
Ivinghoe 102 E5

Ivinghoe Aston 102 F1
Jack's Hatch 162 A8
Jockey End 127 M2
Katherines 161 K5
Kelshall 30 C4
Kensworth Common 105 K1
Kensworth Lynch 105 M1
Kettle Green 118 B1
Keysers Estate 160 A8
Kimpton 86 C8
Kings Langley 166 D7
Kingsmoor 162 B7
King's Walden 67 L7
Kingswood 182 A5
Kinsbourne Green 108 A5
Kitt's End 200 D1
Knebworth 88 F4
Lanes End 144 B7
Langley 87 L1
Langleybury 181 G5
Latchford 93 L5
Latchmore Bank 96 F8
Latimer 178 D8
Latton Bush 162 F6
Layters Green 202 A8
Leagrave 64 B6
Leasey Bridge 131 L4
Lea Valley 109 L7
Leavesden Green 181 L5
Lemsford 133 L5
Letchmore Heath 197 K2
Letchworth 39 J4
Letty Green 135 M8
Level's Green 78 B5
Levens Green 92 C1
Leverstock Green 150 B4
Lewsey Farm 63 L7
Ley Green 67 L5
Ley Hill 178 A1
Lilley 50 D8
Lilley 64 E5
Limbury 64 E5
Little Almshoe 68 F1
Little Berkamstead 156 F6
Little Chalfont 192 A3
Little Chishill 33 K3
Little Gaddesden 126 C3
Little Green 15 M4
Little Hadham 77 H8
Little Hallingbury 121 H2
Little Heath 147 M5
Little Heath 173 G8
Little Hormead 59 M3
Little Offley 50 F4
Little Parndon 6 A4
Little Tring 123 K4
Little Wymondley 53 J6
London Colney 170 B5
Long Marston 101 G7
Loudwater 194 C4
Lower Green 38 D5
Lower Green 46 D3
Lower Green 47 G1
Lower Nazeing 177 J2
Lower Sheering 142 F1
Lower Stondon 24 E7
Lower Sundon 48 B7
Lower Woodside 172 E1
Lucas End 175 H6
Luffenhall 56 B4
Luton 2 E7
Mackerye End 109 K6
Mangrove Green 66 E6
Maple Cross 203 J4
Mardleybury 89 G8
Mark Hall North 7 L1
Mark Hall South 7 L3
Markyate 106 E5
Marshalls Heath 109 M7
Marshalswick 152 F4
Marsh Farm 64 D3
Marshmoor 172 C1
Marsworth 101 M8
Matching 143 M6
Matching Tye 143 L7
Meesden 46 E5
Meppershall 24 A5
Meriden 182 D7
Merry Hill 207 G1
Micklefield Green 193 M1
Mill End 43 K4
Mill End 203 L1
Mill Green 155 K2
Millow 14 B6
Moneyhill 204 A1
Monken Hadley 200 D3
Moor Green 57 J8
Moor Park 205 H4
Morden Green 19 H1
Mott's Green 121 J4
Mount Pleasant 204 A8
Much Hadham 94 D7
Nash Mills 166 F4
Nast Hyde 154 C6
Nasty 74 C4
Nazeing Long Green 177 M4
Nazeing Mead 160 C6
Nether Street 118 C5
Netteswell 7 H4
Nettleden 127 G6
New Barnet 201 G6
Newgate Street 156 D3
New Greens 152 B2
New Ground 145 L5
Newman's End 143 L5
New Mill 124 A4
New Mill End 108 C2
Newnham 27 L3
Newsells 32 C3
Newton 14 A5
New Town 83 J5
Nobland Green 117 M2
The Node 87 L1
Nomansland 132 B4
Northaw 187 M1
Northchurch 146 C4
North Watford 182 A8
Northwood 205 H8
Norton 40 A1

Norton Green 70 A7
Nup End 88 A6
Nuthampstead 33 G8
Oakfield 53 G4
Oaklands 112 F3
Odsey 29 H1
Old Hall Green 92 E1
Old Harlow 142 B6
Old Hatfield 155 J4
Old Knebworth 88 C4
Old Town 70 B3
Orchard Leigh 164 A6
Otterspool 182 E8
Oxhey 13 H9
Oxlease 155 G6
Painter's Green 89 J8
Panshanger 134 F3
Parkside 63 H5
Park Street 169 H5
Park Town 3 H9
Passmores 162 C5
Patchetts Green 197 H2
Patient End 60 E7
Patmore Heath 77 J2
Peartree 134 D5
Pegsdon 50 B1
Pepperstock 107 H1
Perry Green 119 G2
Peters Green 85 H7
Piccotts End 149 H3
Pimlico 167 K3
Pin Green 70 F2
Pinnacles 161 M2
Pinnerwood Park 206 B7
Pirton 37 H6
Pitstone 102 C7
Pitstone Green 102 D6
Pitstone Hill 124 F1
Poplars 71 J7
Porter's End 109 M3
Potten End 147 M4
Potter's Bar 187 J4
Potters Crouch 168 C3
Pottersheath 112 B1
Potter Street 163 L4
Pouchen End 148 C8
Presdales 138 D3
Preston 68 B4
Puckeridge 75 K7
Pudds Cross 164 D7
Pulloxhill 34 D2
Purwell 53 J2
Puttenham 100 E8
Puttock's End 99 J6
Rableyheath 88 B8
Radlett 183 K5
Radwell 184 B6
Radwell 27 H6
Redbourn 130 A4
Redbournbury 130 D8
Redhill 42 D4
Reed 31 L6
Reed End 31 H4
Rickmansworth 193 M8
Ridge 185 L5
The Ridgeway 174 A6
Ringshall 126 A1
Roast Green 47 L4
Roe End 106 A6
Roe Green 43 G2
Roe Green 154 F5
The Rookery 195 M8
Roestock 171 J2
Rosedale 175 L7
Round Bush 197 J1
Round Green 65 K8
Rowley Green 199 L4
Roydon 161 G1
Roydon Hamlet 161 H6
Royston 21 G3
Rucklers Lane 166 D5
Rushden 42 D6
Rush Green 69 J6
Rush Green 138 B4
Rusling End 87 J3
The Ryde 155 H2
Rye Meads 160 C1
Rye Park 160 A3
Sacombe 91 K7
Sacombe Green 92 A6
St Albans 10 F3
St Ibbs 68 F1
St Ippollitts 52 F8
St Julians 169 H3
St Leonards 144 D7
St Margarets 138 F6
St Margaret's 127 H6
St Nicholas 54 F7
St Paul's Walden 86 F1
St Stephens 168 F1
Sandon 43 G1
Sandridge 153 H1
Sarratt 179 M6
Sarratt Bottom 179 K7
Sawbridgeworth 120 A8
Sewell 62 C8
Shaftenhoe End 33 G2
Sharpenhoe 34 C8
Shaw Green 42 C5
Sheering 143 J2
Shenley 184 E5
Shenleybury 184 C2
Shephall 5 L8
Sherrardspark 134 A2
Shootersway 146 D6
Sleapshyde 154 B8
Slip End 29 G4
Slip End 83 H8
Smallford 154 A6
Smith's End 32 F2
Smith's Green 99 J3
Smug Oak 183 G1
Snailswell 38 C4
Snow End 45 M5
Sopwell 169 G2
South-end 119 G4
Southern Green 42 F6
South Hatfield 155 G8

South Mimms 186 A3
South Oxhey 206 A3
Spellbrook 120 D2
Spitalbrook 159 M6
Staines Green 136 B6
Stanborough 133 L7
Standon 93 K1
Standon Green End 92 D6
Stanstead Abbots 139 K6
Stansted Mountfitchet 79 H3
Stapleford 114 D3
Starling's Green 47 L7
Start Hill 97 M3
Startop's End 123 L1
Steeple Morden 15 M8
Stet 103 K2
Stevenage 4 C2
Stewards 162 D7
Stocking Pelham 61 J3
Stopsley 65 M6
Stotfold 26 F3
Streatley 48 E5
Studham 105 G5
Sumners 161 M6
Sundon Park 64 B3
Swanley Bar 173 G7
The Swillett 193 H8
Symonds Green 69 M3
Takeley 99 G2
Takeley Street 98 E3
Tea Green 67 G7
Temple Fields 141 M6
Tewin 113 K7
Tewin Wood 113 J5
Therfield 30 E3
Thorley 96 B8
Thorley Houses 95 M5
Thorley Street 96 D7
Threshers Bush 163 M3
The Thrift 20 A7
Throcking 57 K1
Thundridge 116 D3
Tilekiln Green 97 L4
Titmore Green 53 K8
Todd's Green 53 M8
Tolmers 174 D5
Tonwell 115 L3
Totteridge 200 D8
Totternhoe 80 A3
Tower Hill 165 L8
Townsend 10 F2
Trims Green 120 B3
Tring 124 A7
Tringford 123 K2
Tring Wharf 124 A3
Trowley Bottom 129 G2
Turnford 176 C4
Two Waters 166 B2
Tye Green 162 C4
Tylers Causeway 174 A1
Tyttenhanger 170 D2
Underhill 200 F7
Uppend 78 A1
Upper Dunsley 124 B7
Upper Stondon 24 D6
Upwick Green 77 K5
Venus Hill 179 G2
Wadesmill 116 C2
Wakeley 57 L8
Walkern 72 A1
Wallington 42 B2
Walsworth 52 F1
Waltham Abbey 191 J3
Waltham Cross 190 B4
Wandon End 85 G1
Ware 116 E8
Wareside 117 L7
Warners End 148 D6
Warren's Green 55 J4
Washall Green 61 G1
Waterdale 182 B1
Waterend 133 J2
Water End 148 E1
Water End 172 B5
Waterford 114 E8
Watford 195 M2
Watford Heath 196 D8
Watton at Stone 90 B6
Welham Green 172 A2
Well End 199 H1
Wellpond Green 94 B1
Welwyn 111 M5
Welwyn Garden City 135 G2
Westbrook Hay 165 H3
West End 156 C5
West Hyde 108 B3
West Hyde 203 K7
Westland Green 94 D2
Westmill 52 B1
Westmill 58 E8
Weston 55 H1
West Watford 12 C6
Westwick Row 150 D8
Wheathampstead 132 A1
Whelpley Hill 164 C5
Whempstead 91 H4
Whippendell Botton 180 B1
Whipsnade 104 F2
Whitehall 43 K6
White Hall 90 A2
Whitwell 86 D4
Widford 118 D6
Wigginton 124 C8
Wigginton Bottom 145 K2
Wildhill 156 B8
Willian 40 A8
Wilstone 123 J1
Wilstone Green 123 J2
Wingfield 62 D1
Winsdon Hill 83 G3
Woodcock Hill 204 D4
Wood End 73 H3
Woodhall 134 D6
Woodside 82 F8
Woodside 155 M8
Woodside 182 A3
Woodside Green 121 L1
Woollensbrook 159 J1
Woolmer Green 89 G8
Wormley 176 D3
Wormleybury 176 A2
Wormley West End 175 M1
Wright's Green 121 J3
Wyddial 44 F6
Wymondley Bury 53 L7
Youngsbury 116 E2

USING THE STREET INDEX

Street names are listed alphabetically. Each street name is followed by its postal town or area locality, the Postcode District, the page number, and the reference to the square in which the name is found.

Example: **Abbey Cl** *FAWY* SO45 .... **155** L5 [1]

Some entries are followed by a number in a blue box. This number indicates the location of the street within the referenced grid square. The full street name is listed at the side of the map page.

GENERAL ABBREVIATIONS

Abbreviation	Meaning
ACC	ACCESS
ALY	ALLEY
AP	APPROACH
AR	ARCADE
ASS	ASSOCIATION
AV	AVENUE
BCH	BEACH
BLDS	BUILDINGS
BND	BEND
BNK	BANK
BR	BRIDGE
BRK	BROOK
BTM	BOTTOM
BUS	BUSINESS
BVD	BOULEVARD
BY	BYPASS
CATH	CATHEDRAL
CEM	CEMETERY
CEN	CENTRE
CFT	CROFT
CH	CHURCH
CHA	CHASE
CHYD	CHURCHYARD
CIR	CIRCLE
CIRC	CIRCUS
CL	CLOSE
CLFS	CLIFFS
CMP	CAMP
CNR	CORNER
CO	COUNTY
COLL	COLLEGE
COM	COMMON
COMM	COMMISSION
CON	CONVENT
COT	COTTAGE
COTS	COTTAGES
CP	CAPE
CPS	COPSE
CR	CREEK
CREM	CREMATORIUM
CRS	CRESCENT
CSWY	CAUSEWAY
CT	COURT
CTRL	CENTRAL
CTS	COURTS
CTYD	COURTYARD
CUTT	CUTTINGS
CV	COVE
CYN	CANYON
DEPT	DEPARTMENT
DL	DALE
DM	DAM
DR	DRIVE
DRO	DROVE
DRY	DRIVEWAY
DWGS	DWELLINGS
E	EAST
EMB	EMBANKMENT
EMBY	EMBASSY
ESP	ESPLANADE
EST	ESTATE
EX	EXCHANGE
EXPY	EXPRESSWAY
EXT	EXTENSION
F/O	FLYOVER
FC	FOOTBALL CLUB
FK	FORK
FLD	FIELD
FLDS	FIELDS
FLS	FALLS
FLS	FLATS
FM	FARM
FT	FORT
FWY	FREEWAY
FY	FERRY
GA	GATE
GAL	GALLERY
GDN	GARDEN
GDNS	GARDENS
GLD	GLADE
GLN	GLEN
GN	GREEN
GND	GROUND
GRA	GRANGE
GRG	GARAGE
GT	GREAT
GTWY	GATEWAY
GV	GROVE
HGR	HIGHER
HL	HILL
HLS	HILLS
HO	HOUSE
HOL	HOLLOW
HOSP	HOSPITAL
HRB	HARBOUR
HTH	HEATH
HTS	HEIGHTS
HVN	HAVEN
HWY	HIGHWAY
IMP	IMPERIAL
IN	INLET
IND EST	INDUSTRIAL ESTATE
INF	INFIRMARY
INFO	INFORMATION
INT	INTERCHANGE
IS	ISLAND
JCT	JUNCTION
JTY	JETTY
KG	KING
KNL	KNOLL
L	LAKE
LA	LANE
LDG	LODGE
LGT	LIGHT
LK	LOCK
LKS	LAKES
LNDG	LANDING
LTL	LITTLE
LWR	LOWER
MAG	MAGISTRATE
MAN	MANSIONS
MD	MEAD
MDW	MEADOWS
MEM	MEMORIAL
MKT	MARKET
MKTS	MARKETS
ML	MALL
ML	MILL
MNR	MANOR
MS	MEWS
MSN	MISSION
MT	MOUNT
MTN	MOUNTAIN
MTS	MOUNTAINS
MUS	MUSEUM
MWY	MOTORWAY
N	NORTH
NE	NORTH EAST
NW	NORTH WEST
O/P	OVERPASS
OFF	OFFICE
ORCH	ORCHARD
OV	OVAL
PAL	PALACE
PAS	PASSAGE
PAV	PAVILION
PDE	PARADE
PH	PUBLIC HOUSE
PK	PARK
PKWY	PARKWAY
PL	PLACE
PLN	PLAIN
PLNS	PLAINS
PLZ	PLAZA
POL	POLICE STATION
PR	PRINCE
PREC	PRECINCT
PREP	PREPARATORY
PRIM	PRIMARY
PROM	PROMENADE
PRS	PRINCESS
PRT	PORT
PT	POINT
PTH	PATH
PZ	PIAZZA
QD	QUADRANT
QU	QUEEN
QY	QUAY
R	RIVER
RBT	ROUNDABOUT
RD	ROAD
RDG	RIDGE
REP	REPUBLIC
RES	RESERVOIR
RFC	RUGBY FOOTBALL CLUB
RI	RISE
RP	RAMP
RW	ROW
S	SOUTH
SCH	SCHOOL
SE	SOUTH EAST
SER	SERVICE AREA
SH	SHORE
SHOP	SHOPPING
SKWY	SKYWAY
SMT	SUMMIT
SOC	SOCIETY
SP	SPUR
SPR	SPRING
SQ	SQUARE
ST	STREET
STN	STATION
STR	STREAM
STRD	STRAND
SW	SOUTH WEST
TDG	TRADING
TER	TERRACE
THWY	THROUGHWAY
TNL	TUNNEL
TOLL	TOLLWAY
TPK	TURNPIKE
TR	TRACK
TRL	TRAIL
TWR	TOWER
U/P	UNDERPASS
UNI	UNIVERSITY
UPR	UPPER
V	VALE
VA	VALLEY
VIAD	VIADUCT
VIL	VILLA
VIS	VISTA
VLG	VILLAGE
VLS	VILLAS
VW	VIEW
W	WEST
WD	WOOD
WHF	WHARF
WK	WALK
WKS	WALKS
WLS	WELLS
WY	WAY
YD	YARD
YHA	YOUTH HOSTEL

POSTCODE TOWNS AND AREA ABBREVIATIONS

Abbreviation	Town / Area
ABLGY	Abbots Langley
AMP/FLIT/BLC	Ampthill/Flitwick/Barton-le-Clay
AMS	Amersham
AMSS	Amersham south
ARL/CHE	Arlesey/Church End
BAR	Barnet
BERK	Berkhamsted
BGSW	Biggleswade
BLDK	Baldock
BORE	Borehamwood
BRKMPK	Brookmans Park
BROX	Broxbourne
BSF	Bishop's Stortford
BUNT	Buntingford
BUSH	Bushey
CFSP/GDCR	Chalfont St Peter/Gerrards Cross
CHES/WCR	Cheshunt/Waltham Cross
CHESW	Cheshunt west
CSHM	Chesham
CSTG	Chalfont St Giles
DEN/HRF	Denham/Harefield
DUN/HR/TOD	Dunstable/Houghton Regis/Toddington
DUN/WHIP	Dunstable/Whipsnade
EBAR	East Barnet
EDGW	Edgware
EN	Enfield
ENC/FH	Enfield Chase/Forty Hill
EPP	Epping
GSTN	Garston
GTDUN	Great Dunmow
GTMIS/PWD	Great Missenden/Prestwood
HARP	Harpenden
HAT	Hatfield
HERT/BAY	Hertford/Bayford
HERT/WAS	Hertford/Watton at Stone
HHNE	Hemel Hempstead northeast
HHS/BOV	Hemel Hempstead south/Bovingdon
HHW	Hemel Hempstead west
HLW	Harlow
HLWE	Harlow east
HLWS	Harlow south
HLWW/ROY	Harlow west/Roydon
HNLW	Henlow
HOD	Hoddesdon
HTCH/STOT	Hitchin/Stotfold
HTCHE/RSTV	Hitchin east/Rural Stevenage
KGLGY	Kings Langley
KNEB	Knebworth
KTN/HRWW/WS	Kenton/Harrow Weald/Wealdstone
LBUZ	Leighton Buzzard
LCOL/BKTW	London Colney/Bricket Wood
LOU	Loughton
LTN	Luton
LTNE	Luton east
LTNN/LIM	Luton north/Limbury
LTNW/LEA	Luton west/Leagrave
LWTH	Letchworth
MHAD	Much Hadham
MLHL	Mill Hill
NTHWD	Northwood
OXHEY	Oxhey
PEND	Ponders End
PIN	Pinner
POTB/CUF	Potters Bar/Cuffley
RAD	Radlett
RAYLNE/WEN	Rural Aylesbury north & east/Wendover
RBSF	Rural Bishop's Stortford
RKW/CH/CXG	Rickmansworth/Chorleywood/Croxley Green
ROY	Royston
RYLN/HDSTN	Rayners Lane/Headstone
SAFWS	Saffron Walden south
SBW	Sawbridgeworth
SDY/GAM/POT	Sandy/Gamlingay/Potton
SHFD	Shefford
STAL	St Albans
STALE/WH	St Albans east/Wheathampstead
STALW/RED	St Albans west/Redbourn
STAN	Stanmore
STDN	Standon
STHGT/OAK	Southgate/Oakwood
STSD	Stansted
STVG	Stevenage
STVGE	Stevenage east
TRDG/WHET	Totteridge/Whetstone
TRING	Tring
WAB	Waltham Abbey
WARE	Ware
WAT	Watford
WATN	Watford north
WATW	Watford west
WGCE	Welwyn Garden City east
WGCW	Welwyn Garden City west
WLYN	Welwyn

Index - streets

A

Abbey Av *STALW/RED* AL3 168 F2
Abbey Ct *WAB* EN9 191 G5
Abbey Dale Cl *HLWE* CM17 163 H3
Abbey Dr *ABLGY* WD5 181 M3
LTNE LU2 3 J3
Abbey Ms *DUN/WHIP* LU6 81 H4
Abbey Mill End *STALW/RED* AL3 10 C8
Abbey Mill La *STALW/RED* AL3 10 C8
Abbey Rd *CHES/WCR* EN8 190 D5 [1]
Abbey Vw *RAD* WD7 183 L6
Abbeyview *WAB* EN9 191 G4
Abbey View Rd *STALW/RED* AL3 10 C6
Abbis Orch *HTCH/STOT* SG5 38 D5
Abbot John Ms
STALE/WH AL4 132 C1 [1]
Abbots Av *STAL* AL1 169 K2 [1]
Abbots Av West *STAL* AL1 169 J2
Abbots Cl *KNEB* SG3 113 J1
Abbots Gv *STVG* SG1 5 G4
Abbots Pk *STAL* AL1 169 L1
Abbots Ri *KGLGY* WD4 166 E6
Abbots Rd *ABLGY* WD5 181 K1
Abbots Vw *KGLGY* WD4 166 E6
Abbotsweld *HLWS* CM18 162 C5
Abbots Wood Rd *LTNE* LU2 3 J3
Abbotts Dr *WAB* EN9 191 M5
Abbotts La *WARE* SG12 118 C6
Abbotts Ri *WARE* SG12 139 J6 [1]
Abbotts Rd *BAR* EN5 201 G5
LWTH SG6 39 J4
Abbotts Wy *BSF* CM23 96 D7
WARE SG12 139 J6
Abdale La *BRKMPK* AL9 172 A6
Abel Cl *HHNE* HP2 9 G9
Abercorn Rd *LTNW/LEA* LU4 63 L7
Abercrombie Wy
HLWW/ROY CM19 6 C9
Aberdale Gdns *POTB/CUF* EN6 186 E4
Aberford Rd *BORE* WD6 198 F3
Abigail Cl *LTNN/LIM* LU3 65 J7
Abingdon Pl *POTB/CUF* EN6 187 G3 [1]
Abingdon Rd *LTNW/LEA* LU4 64 B7
Abridge Cl *CHES/WCR* EN8 190 C6 [1]
Abstacle Hl *TRING* HP23 123 L7
Acacia Cl *CHESW* EN7 175 K6
KTN/HRWW/W HA3 207 K6
Acacia Gv *BERK* HP4 147 G7
Acacia St *HAT* AL10 154 F8
Acacia Wk *HARP* AL5 131 J4
Acers *LCOL/BKTW* AL2 169 H7
Achilles Cl *HHNE* HP2 8 E5
Ackroyd Rd *ROY* SG8 21 K2
Acme Rd *WATN* WD24 195 M1
Acorn Gld *WLYN* AL6 112 E6 [1]
Acorn La *POTB/CUF* EN6 174 D8
Acorn Pl *WATN* WD24 181 M8 [1]

Acorn Rd HHS/BOV HP3 149 M8
Acorn St WARE SG12 140 C3
Acremore St STDN SG11 95 J3
Acre Piece HTCHE/RSTV SG4 52 F4
Acre Wy NTHWD HA6 205 L8
Acre Wd HHNE HP2 149 K8
Acrewood Wy STALE/WH AL4 153 L7
Acton Cl CHES/WCR EN8 190 D2
Acworth Crs LTNW/LEA LU4 64 B5
Adamsfield CHESW EN7 175 L5
Adams House HLW CM20 6 E5
Adams Wy TRING HP23 124 A5
Adderley Rd
KTN/HRWW/W HA3 207 L8
Addington Cl HNLW SG16 25 J1
Addington Wy LTNW/LEA LU4 64 C7
Addiscombe Rd WATW WD18 12 E4
Addison Cl NTHWD HA6 205 M8
Addison Wy NTHWD HA6 205 L8
Adelaide Cl STAN HA7 207 M4
Adelaide St LTN LU1 2 C7
STALW/RED AL3 10 F5
Adele Av WLYN AL6 112 E7
Adeyfield Gdns HHNE HP2 8 F7
Adeyfield Rd HHNE HP2 8 C8
Adhara Rd NTHWD HA6 205 L5
Adinger Cl STVG SG1 4 F7
Admirals Cl STALE/WH AL4 171 K2
Admiral St HERT/BAY SG13 137 M4
Admirals Wk HOD EN11 159 M6
STAL AL1 169 M1
Admiral Wy BERK HP4 146 E4
Adrian Cl DEN/HRF UB9 204 C8
Adrian Rd ABLGY WD5 181 K2
Adstone Rd LTN LU1 82 E7
Aidans Cl DUN/WHIP LU6 80 D1
Ailsworth Rd LTNN/LIM LU3 64 F4
Ainsdale Rd OXHEY WD19 206 B3
Aintree Rd ROY SG8 21 L4
Aintree Wy STVGE SG2 71 H2
Airport Approach Rd LTNE LU2 84 C2
Airport Wy LTN LU1 83 L6
LTNE LU2 84 B4
Aitken Rd BAR EN5 200 B6
Akeman Cl STALW/RED AL3 168 E1
Akeman St TRING HP23 123 M7
Alamein Cl BROX EN10 159 J7
Alandale Dr PIN HA5 206 A8
Alan Dr BAR EN5 200 D7
Alban Av STALW/RED AL3 10 E3
Alban Crs BORE WD6 199 G2
Alban Rd LWTH SG6 40 B7
Albans Vw GSTN WD25 182 A4
Albany Cl BUSH WD23 197 J7
Albany Rd PEND EN3 190 C8
Albemarle Av CHES/WCR EN8 176 B7
POTB/CUF EN6 187 G4
Albemarle Rd EBAR EN4 201 K8
Albermarle Cl LTNW/LEA LU4 63 L7
Albert Ct DUN/WHIP LU6 81 H3
Albert Gdns HLWE CM17 163 J3
Albert Rd ARL/CHE SG15 25 M6
EBAR EN4 201 H5
LTN LU1 83 K5
Albert Rd North WAT WD17 12 F2
Albert Rd South WATW WD18 12 E2
Albert St STAL AL1 10 E8
STALW/RED AL3 106 D5
STVG SG1 70 B3
TRING HP23 123 M7
Albion Crs CSTG HP8 202 A3
Albion Hl HHNE HP2 149 J8
Albion Rd CSTG HP8 202 A2
LBUZ LU7 102 C5
LTNE LU2 2 E5
STAL AL1 11 K7
Albion St DUN/WHIP LU6 81 G2
Albury Cl LTNN/LIM LU3 64 F1
Albury Dr PIN HA5 206 B8
Albury Grove Rd
CHES/WCR EN8 190 C1
Albury Ride CHES/WCR EN8 190 C2
Albury Rd STDN SG11 77 H8
Albury Wk CHES/WCR EN8 190 B1
Alconbury BSF CM23 97 G1
WGCE AL7 135 K4
Aldbanks DUN/WHIP LU6 80 E1
Aldbury Cl GSTN WD25 182 C7
STALE/WH AL4 153 H2
Aldbury Gv WGCE AL7 135 G4
Aldbury Rd RKW/CH/CXG WD3 193 L8
Aldcock Rd STVG SG1 70 D2
Aldeburgh Cl STVG SG1 69 M1
Aldenham Av RAD WD7 183 M8
Aldenham Cl LTNW/LEA LU4 63 L7
Aldenham Gv RAD WD7 184 A5
Aldenham Rd BUSH WD23 196 E5
GSTN WD25 197 L3
OXHEY WD19 13 K8
RAD WD7 183 M6
Alderbury Rd STSD CM24 79 K2
Alder Cl BLDK SG7 40 D3
BSF CM23 96 C6
HOD EN11 160 A2
LCOL/BKTW AL2 169 G7
Alder Crs LTNN/LIM LU3 64 F7
Alderley Ct BERK HP4 147 G7
Alderman Cl BRKMPK AL9 172 B3
Alders End La HARP AL5 108 E8
Alders Wk SBW CM21 120 D8
Alderton Cl LTNE LU2 84 C1
Alderton Dr BERK HP4 125 M2
Alder Wk GSTN WD25 182 A6
Aldhous Cl LTNN/LIM LU3 65 G5
Aldock WGCE AL7 134 F6
Aldridge Ct BLDK SG7 40 D1
Aldwick STAL AL1 169 M1
Aldwickbury Crs HARP AL5 131 J1
Aldwick Rd HARP AL5 131 K2
Aldwyke Ri WARE SG12 116 B7
Aldykes HAT AL10 154 E5
Alesia Rd LTNN/LIM LU3 64 D4
Alexander Cl EBAR EN4 201 J5
Alexander Ga STVGE SG2 71 H2
Alexander Rd HERT/WAS SG14 136 F4
HTCH/STOT SG5 26 E4
LCOL/BKTW AL2 170 B4
Alexandra Av LTNN/LIM LU3 2 B1
Alexandra Ms WAT WD17 195 M3
Alexandra Rd BORE WD6 199 J1
HHNE HP2 8 A7
HTCH/STOT SG5 52 E1
KGLGY WD4 166 F8
KGLGY WD4 179 M1
RKW/CH/CXG WD3 179 M7
STAL AL1 11 H7
WAT WD17 12 D1
Alexandra Wy CHES/WCR EN8 190 E5
Aleyn Wy BLDK SG7 41 G1
Alfred St DUN/HR/TOD LU5 81 H2
Alfriston Cl LTNE LU2 66 B7
Algar Cl STAN HA7 207 L5
Alington La LWTH SG6 39 L7
Allandale HHNE HP2 8 C4
STALW/RED AL3 169 G2
Allandale Crs POTB/CUF EN6 186 D3
Allandale Rd PEND EN3 190 C7
Allard Cl CHESW EN7 175 L6
Allard Crs BUSH WD23 207 H2
Allard Wy BROX EN10 159 K8
Alldicks Rd HHS/BOV HP3 166 E1
Allenby Av DUN/HR/TOD LU5 81 M1
Allen Cl DUN/HR/TOD LU5 81 J2
RAD WD7 184 D3
STALE/WH AL4 132 C3
Allen Ct HAT AL10 155 G7
Allendale LTNN/LIM LU3 64 F2
Allerton Cl BORE WD6 198 E1
Allerton Rd BORE WD6 198 D1
Alleyns Rd STVG SG1 70 C3
Allison Cl WAB EN9 191 M4
All Saints Cl BSF CM23 96 F2
Allsaints Crs GSTN WD25 182 C4
All Saints Rd RKW/CH/CXG WD3 194 F7
All Saints Ms
KTN/HRWW/W HA3 207 K6
All Saints Rd DUN/HR/TOD LU5 63 G5
Allton Rd HNLW SG16 24 F6
Allum La BORE WD6 198 D6
Allwood Rd CHESW EN7 175 L6
Alma Ct STAL AL1 11 G9
Alma Link LTN LU1 2 D6
Alma Rd BERK HP4 146 D4
STAL AL1 11 H8
Alma Rw KTN/HRWW/W HA3 207 J8
Alma St LTN LU1 2 D6
Almonds La STVG SG1 70 D2
The Almonds STAL AL1 170 A3
Almond Wy BORE WD6 199 G5
Almshouse La EN EN1 190 A8
Alms La BLDK SG7 18 C6
Alnwick Dr TRING HP23 100 E3
Alpha Pl BSF CM23 96 E2
Alpine Cl HTCHE/RSTV SG4 52 F5
Alpine Wk BUSH WD23 207 K2
Alpine Wy LTNN/LIM LU3 64 C2
Alsa St STSD CM24 79 L1
Alsop Cl DUN/HR/TOD LU5 63 G4
LCOL/BKTW AL2 170 D7
Alston Rd BAR EN5 200 D4
HHW HP1 148 F8
Altair Wy NTHWD HA6 205 L5
Altham Gv HLW CM20 7 J2
Altham Rd PIN HA5 206 D7
Althorp Cl TRDG/WHET N20 199 M8
Althorp Rd LTNN/LIM LU3 2 A2
STAL AL1 11 H5
Alton Av STAN HA7 207 L7
Alton Rd LTN LU1 83 L5
Altwood HARP AL5 131 J1
Alva Wy OXHEY WD19 206 C2
Alverstone Av EBAR EN4 201 J8
Alverton STALW/RED AL3 10 D1
Alwin Pl WATW WD18 195 K5
Alwyn Cl BORE WD6 198 E7
LTNE LU2 65 K8
Alyngton BERK HP4 146 D3
Alzey Gdns HARP AL5 131 J2
Amberley Cl HARP AL5 109 G8
LTNE LU2 66 C6
Amberley Gn WARE SG12 116 B6
Amberry Ct HLW CM20 6 F4
Ambleside LTNN/LIM LU3 64 E5
Ambrose La HARP AL5 108 F7
Amenbury La HARP AL5 130 F1
Amersham Pl AMSS HP7 192 B2
Amersham Rd AMS HP6 192 C2
CSTG HP8 192 A7
RKW/CH/CXG WD3 193 G2
Amersham Wy AMS HP6 192 D2
Amesbury WAB EN9 191 M3
Ames Cl LTNN/LIM LU3 64 E1
Amhurst Rd LTNW/LEA LU4 63 L7
Amor Wy LWTH SG6 40 A4
Amwell Cl GSTN WD25 182 D6
Amwell Common WGCE AL7 135 G5
Amwell Ct HOD EN11 159 M3
WAB EN9 191 K4
Amwell End WARE SG12 138 C1
Amwell Hl WARE SG12 138 E4
Amwell La STALE/WH AL4 132 A3
WARE SG12 138 F4
Amwell St HOD EN11 159 M4
Anchor Cl CHES/WCR EN8 176 C7
Anchor La HHW HP1 149 G8
WARE SG12 116 A4
Anchor Rd BLDK SG7 40 E3
Anchor St BSF CM23 96 F4
Anderson Cl DEN/HRF UB9 203 M8
Anderson Rd RAD WD7 184 F4
STVGE SG2 71 H4
Anderson's La BUNT SG9 45 M8
Andover Cl LTNW/LEA LU4 64 B4
Andrew Cl RAD WD7 184 E4
Andrews Cl HHNE HP2 8 B5
Andrewsfield WGCE AL7 135 H4
Andrew's La CHESW EN7 175 M7
Anelle Ri HHS/BOV HP3 166 E3
Angell's Meadow BLDK SG7 18 C6
Angels La DUN/HR/TOD LU5 63 G5
Anglefield Rd BERK HP4 146 F6
Anglesey Cl BSF CM23 96 B3
Anglesey Rd OXHEY WD19 206 B5
Angle Ways STVGE SG2 5 J9
Anglian Cl WATN WD24 196 B3
Angotts Md STVG SG1 70 A4
Angus Cl LTNW/LEA LU4 63 M7
Anmer Gdns LTNW/LEA LU4 64 A6
Annables La HARP AL5 107 L6
Anns Cl TRING HP23 123 K7
Anselm Rd PIN HA5 206 E7
Anson Cl HHW HP1 164 E6
STAL AL1 170 A1
STALE/WH AL4 153 H1
Anson Wk NTHWD HA6 205 H4
Anstee Rd LTNW/LEA LU4 64 A4
Anthony Cl OXHEY WD19 206 C1
Anthony Gdns LTN LU1 83 J5
Anthony Rd BORE WD6 198 D3
Anthorne Cl POTB/CUF EN6 187 G2
Anthus Ms NTHWD HA6 205 J7
Antonine Ga
STALW/RED AL3 151 M8
Anvil Av ROY SG8 19 M1
Anvil Cl HHS/BOV HP3 165 G7
Aplins Cl HARP AL5 108 E8
Apollo Av NTHWD HA6 205 M5
Apollo Cl DUN/HR/TOD LU5 81 J3
Apollo Wy HHNE HP2 8 E4
STVG SG1 71 H2
Appleby Gdns DUN/WHIP LU6 81 G3
Appleby St CHESW EN7 175 K5
Applecroft BERK HP4 146 D4
HNLW SG16 24 F7
LCOL/BKTW AL2 169 G7
Applecroft Rd LTNE LU2 66 B6
WGCW AL8 134 A4
Applefield AMSS HP7 192 B2
Appleford's Cl HOD EN11 159 L2
Apple Glebe AMP/FLIT/B MK45 35 H8
The Apple Orch HHNE HP2 8 F5
Appleton Av WARE SG12 117 K5
Appleton Cl AMSS HP7 192 A3
HLWW/ROY CM19 6 C8
Appleton Flds BSF CM23 96 D6
Appletree Gdns EBAR EN4 201 K5
Appletree Wk GSTN WD25 182 A6
Applewood Cl HARP AL5 108 D7
Approach Rd BAR EN5 201 J5
STAL AL1 11 H9
The Approach
POTB/CUF EN6 186 E3
Appspond La LCOL/BKTW AL2 168 B3
Apsley Cl BSF CM23 96 D6
Apsley End Rd HTCH/STOT SG5 36 D5
Apton Ct BSF CM23 96 E3
Apton Flds BSF CM23 96 E4
Apton Rd BSF CM23 96 E3
Aquarius Wy NTHWD HA6 205 M5
Aragon Cl HHNE HP2 150 B2
Aran Cl HARP AL5 131 J4
Arbour Cl LTNN/LIM LU3 64 F1
The Arbour HERT/BAY SG13 137 J6
Arbour Vw AMSS HP7 192 A2
Arbroath Gn OXHEY WD19 205 M3
Arbroath Rd LTNN/LIM LU3 64 C1
Archer Cl KGLGY WD4 166 E8
Archer Rd STVG SG1 5 J1
Archers BUNT SG9 58 E2
EPP CM16 162 A7
Archers Cl HERT/WAS SG14 137 H3
Archers Flds STAL AL1 11 J2
Archers Green La WLYN AL6 135 J2
Archers Ride WGCE AL7 135 G6
Archers Wy LWTH SG6 39 J4
The Arches LWTH SG6 39 M3
Archfield WGCE AL7 134 D1
Archive Cl
RAYLNE/WEN HP22 122 C5
Archive Rd
RAYLNE/WEN HP22 122 C5
Arch Rd HTCHE/RSTV SG4 53 J6
Archway Rd LTNW/LEA LU4 64 D6
Arden Cl BUSH WD23 197 L8
HHS/BOV HP3 164 F7
Arden Gv HARP AL5 131 G1
Arden Pl LTNE LU2 2 F2
Arden Press Wy LWTH SG6 40 A4
Ardens Wy STALE/WH AL4 153 J5
Ardleigh Gn LTNE LU2 84 D1
Ardley Cl DUN/WHIP LU6 81 H5
Ardross Av NTHWD HA6 205 K5
Arenson Wy DUN/HR/TOD LU5 63 H8
Argent Wy CHESW EN7 175 J6
Argyle Rd BAR EN5 200 B5
Argyle Wy STVG SG1 4 A4
Argyll Av LTNN/LIM LU3 65 H8
Argyll Rd HHNE HP2 149 K2
Arkley Dr BAR EN5 199 M5
Arkley La BAR EN5 199 M4
Arkley Rd HHNE HP2 150 A2
Arkley Vw BAR EN5 200 A5
Arkwrights HLW CM20 7 J5
Arlesey New Rd LWTH SG6 39 H3
Arlesey Rd HNLW SG16 25 K2
HTCH/STOT SG5 26 C4
HTCH/STOT SG5 38 D6
Arlington Crs CHES/WCR EN8 190 D5
Armand Cl WAT WD17 195 L1
Armitage Cl RKW/CH/CXG WD3 194 C5
Armitage Gdns LTNW/LEA LU4 82 C1
Armourers Cl BSF CM23 96 A6
Armour Ri HTCHE/RSTV SG4 39 G8
Armstrong Cl LCOL/BKTW AL2 170 D6
Armstrong Crs EBAR EN4 201 J4
Armstrong Gdns RAD WD7 184 D3
Arnald Wy DUN/HR/TOD LU5 62 F6
Arncliffe Crs LTNE LU2 2 E2
Arnett Cl RKW/CH/CXG WD3 193 M7
Arnett Wy RKW/CH/CXG WD3 193 M7
Arnold Cl AMP/FLIT/B MK45 35 H8
HTCHE/RSTV SG4 53 G2
LTNE LU2 65 M7
STVG SG1 70 C1
Arnolds La BLDK SG7 17 J4
Arran Cl HHS/BOV HP3 167 H1
Arretine Cl STALW/RED AL3 168 E1
Arrow Cl LTNN/LIM LU3 64 D4
Artesian Gv BAR EN5 201 H5
Arthur Rd STAL AL1 153 G7
Arthur St BUSH WD23 13 K4
LTN LU1 2 E9
Artisan Crs STALW/RED AL3 10 C4
Arundel Cl CHES/WCR EN8 176 A7
HHNE HP2 9 K7
STVGE SG2 71 K7
Arundel Dr BORE WD6 199 H5
Arundel Gv STALW/RED AL3 152 C3
Arundell Rd ABLGY WD5 181 M3
Arundel Rd EBAR EN4 201 K4
LTNW/LEA LU4 64 F8
Ascot Cl BORE WD6 198 F6
BSF CM23 97 H2
Ascot Crs STVG SG1 71 G1
Ascot Gdns PEND EN3 190 B8
Ascot Rd LTNN/LIM LU3 65 G8
ROY SG8 21 L4
WATW WD18 195 K6
Ascots La BRKMPK AL9 155 K1
Ashanger La BLDK SG7 41 J6
Ashborurne Sq NTHWD HA6 205 K6
Ashbourne Cl LWTH SG6 40 A6
Ashbourne Ct STALE/WH AL4 170 B1
Ashbourne Rd BROX EN10 159 L8
Ashbrook La HTCHE/RSTV SG4 53 H6
Ashburnam Wk STVGE SG2 88 E1
Ashburnham Cl
OXHEY WD19 205 M3
Ashburnham Dr OXHEY WD19 205 M3
Ashburnham Rd LTN LU1 83 G3
Ashbury Cl HAT AL10 154 D5
Ashby Dr AMP/FLIT/B MK45 35 H7
Ashby Gdns STAL AL1 169 J3
Ashby Ri BSF CM23 97 G1
Ashby Rd BERK HP4 146 C3
WATN WD24 195 M1
Ash Cl ABLGY WD5 181 J3
BRKMPK AL9 172 F4
DEN/HRF UB9 204 C8
GSTN WD25 182 A6
STAN HA7 207 M6
Ashcombe WGCW AL8 112 D8
Ash Copse LCOL/BKTW AL2 182 E2
Ashcroft DUN/WHIP LU6 80 E1
PIN HA5 206 F6
Ashcroft Cl HARP AL5 131 K2
Ashcroft Rd LTNE LU2 66 A6
Ashdale BSF CM23 96 C6
Ashdale Gdns LTNN/LIM LU3 64 F1
Ashdale Gv STAN HA7 207 L6
Ashdales STAL AL1 169 J3
Ashdown LWTH SG6 39 K1
Ashdown Crs CHES/WCR EN8 176 D7
Ashdown Dr BORE WD6 198 E3
Ashdown Rd BUSH WD23 13 K3
STVGE SG2 89 G3
Ash Dr HAT AL10 154 F8
HTCHE/RSTV SG4 52 F6
Ashendene Rd CHESW EN7 175 G4
HERT/BAY SG13 157 L5
Ashfield Av BUSH WD23 197 G7
Ashfields GSTN WD25 181 L6
Ashfield Wy LTNN/LIM LU3 64 F4
Ashford Gn OXHEY WD19 206 C5
Ash Gv DEN/HRF UB9 204 C8
DUN/HR/TOD LU5 81 J2
HHS/BOV HP3 166 E3
STALE/WH AL4 132 B1
Ash Groves SBW CM21 120 F8
Ash Hill Cl BUSH WD23 207 G1
Ashleigh STVGE SG2 5 M6
Ashley Cl HHS/BOV HP3 166 E1
WGCW AL8 134 B2
Ashley Dr BORE WD6 199 H6
Ashley Gdns HARP AL5 108 C7
Ashley Rd HERT/WAS SG14 136 F5
STAL AL1 153 H7
Ashleys RKW/CH/CXG WD3 193 L8
Ashlyn Cl BUSH WD23 13 M5
Ashlyns Ct BERK HP4 147 G7
Ashlyns Rd BERK HP4 147 G7
Ash Meadow MHAD SG10 94 E8
Ash Mi ROY SG8 32 B7
Ashmore Gdns HHS/BOV HP3 150 A8
Ash Ride ENC/FH EN2 188 F6
Ashridge Cl HHS/BOV HP3 164 F7
Ashridge Dr LCOL/BKTW AL2 182 D1
OXHEY WD19 206 B5
Ashridge La CSHM HP5 178 C2
Ashridge Ri BERK HP4 146 E5
Ash Rd LTNW/LEA LU4 83 G2
TRING HP23 123 L6
WARE SG12 116 F7
Ashton Rd DUN/WHIP LU6 81 G1
LTN LU1 83 K5
PEND EN3 190 D7
Ashton's La BLDK SG7 40 D4
Ashtree Ct STAL AL1 11 J7
Ash Tree Fld HLW CM20 140 F8
Ash Tree Rd DUN/HR/TOD LU5 63 G4
WATN WD24 182 A7
Ashtree Wy HHW HP1 148 F8
Ashurst Cl NTHWD HA6 205 K7
Ashurst Rd EBAR EN4 201 L6
Ash V RKW/CH/CXG WD3 203 J5
Ashville Wy BLDK SG7 40 F1
Ashwell Av LTNN/LIM LU3 64 B2
Ashwell Cl HTCHE/RSTV SG4 54 A6
Ashwell Common
HTCHE/RSTV SG4 54 A6
Ashwell Pk HARP AL5 131 J1
Ashwell Rd BLDK SG7 17 J5
ROY SG8 18 E1
Ashwell St BLDK SG7 18 C7
STALW/RED AL3 10 E4
Ashwells Wy CSTG HP8 202 B2
Ashwood Rd POTB/CUF EN6 187 G4
Ashworth Pl HLWE CM17 163 J2
Askew Rd NTHWD HA6 205 J2
Aspasia Cl STAL AL1 11 K9
Aspen Cl STVGE SG2 89 G3
Aspenden Rd BUNT SG9 58 D5
Aspen Park Dr GSTN WD25 182 A6
The Aspens BSF CM23 79 G8
HTCHE/RSTV SG4 52 F4
Aspen Wy PEND EN3 190 C6
WGCE AL7 135 H5
Aspfield Rw HHW HP1 149 G5
Aspley Cl LTNW/LEA LU4 63 K7
Ass House La
KTN/HRWW/W HA3 207 G4
Astall Cl KTN/HRWW/W HA3 207 J8
Aster Cl BSF CM23 96 C4
The Asters CHESW EN7 175 J7
Astley Gn LTNE LU2 66 C8
Astley Rd HHW HP1 149 H7
Aston Cl BUSH WD23 197 H7
WATN WD24 13 H1
Aston End Rd STVGE SG2 71 K7
Aston La STVGE SG2 89 K3
Aston Ri HTCHE/RSTV SG4 53 G4
Aston Rd STDN SG11 75 J8
Astons Rd NTHWD HA6 205 H3
Aston Vw HHNE HP2 149 M1
Aston Wy POTB/CUF EN6 187 J3
Astral Cl HNLW SG16 25 G6
Astrope La TRING HP23 100 F7
Astwick Av HAT AL10 154 E2
Astwick Rd HTCH/STOT SG5 16 E8
Athelstan Rd HHS/BOV HP3 166 D2
Athelstan Wk North
WGCE AL7 134 D5
Athelstan Wk South
WGCE AL7 134 C5
Athena Pl NTHWD HA6 205 L8
Atherstone Rd LTNW/LEA LU4 82 C1
Atherton End SBW CM21 120 D7
Athlone Cl RAD WD7 184 A7
Athol Cl PIN HA5 206 A8
Athol Gdns PIN HA5 206 A8
Atholl Cl LTNN/LIM LU3 64 C2
Atria Rd NTHWD HA6 205 M5
Attenborough Cl
OXHEY WD19 206 D3
Attimore Cl WGCW AL8 134 A5
Attimore Rd WGCW AL8 134 A5
Aubrey Av LCOL/BKTW AL2 170 B5
Aubrey La STALW/RED AL3 129 K8
Aubreys LWTH SG6 39 L8
Aubreys Rd HHW HP1 148 D8
Aubries STVGE SG2 72 A2
Auckland Cl EN EN1 190 A8
Auckland Rd POTB/CUF EN6 186 C3
Audley Cl BORE WD6 198 F4
Audley Gdns WAB EN9 191 H5
Audrey Gdns BSF CM23 96 E7
Audwick Cl CHES/WCR EN8 176 C7
Augustine Rd
KTN/HRWW/W HA3 207 G8
Augustus Cl STALW/RED AL3 168 F1
Augustus Ga STVGE SG2 71 H2
Austin Rd LTNN/LIM LU3 65 G6
Austins Md HHS/BOV HP3 165 G7
Austins Pl HHNE HP2 8 A6
Autumn Glades HHS/BOV HP3 167 H1
Autumn Gv WGCE AL7 135 G6
Avalon Cl GSTN WD25 182 D3
Avebury Av LTNE LU2 65 J6
Avenue Ap KGLGY WD4 180 F1
Avenue Ct WLYN AL6 112 D3
Avenue One LWTH SG6 40 B4
Avenue Ri BUSH WD23 196 F6
Avenue Rd BSF CM23 96 F4
HOD EN11 160 C6
STAL AL1 11 H4
Avenue Ter OXHEY WD19 13 L9
The Avenue BAR EN5 200 D4
BUSH WD23 196 E5
DUN/WHIP LU6 80 D3
HERT/WAS SG14 137 G2
HHW HP1 148 D6
HOD EN11 159 L6
HTCH/STOT SG5 26 E4
HTCHE/RSTV SG4 52 F3
KTN/HRWW/W HA3 207 L8
LTNW/LEA LU4 64 C5
NTHWD HA6 205 H6
PIN HA5 206 E6
POTB/CUF EN6 186 E1
RAD WD7 183 M5
STVG SG1 70 B2
WAT WD17 12 D1
WLYN AL6 112 C3
Avey La LOU IG10 191 L8
Avia Cl HHS/BOV HP3 166 C3
Avior Dr NTHWD HA6 205 L4
Avocet LWTH SG6 39 K1
Avon Cl GSTN WD25 182 B5
Avondale Rd LTN LU1 2 A4
Avon Rd HNLW SG16 25 G6
Avon Sq HHNE HP2 149 L2
Axe Cl LTNN/LIM LU3 64 D4
Aycliffe Rd BORE WD6 198 F1
Aydon Rd LTNN/LIM LU3 65 G4
Aylands Rd PEND EN3 190 C7
Aylesbury Rd
RAYLNE/WEN HP22 122 A4
TRING HP23 123 K7
Aylets Fld HLWS CM18 162 D5
Aylmer Cl STAN HA7 207 M4
Aylmer Dr STAN HA7 207 M4
Aylotts Cl BUNT SG9 58 C2
Aylsham Rd HOD EN11 160 B2
Aylward Dr STVGE SG2 5 L5
Aylwards Ri STAN HA7 207 M4
Aynho St WATW WD18 12 E6
Aynscombe Cl DUN/WHIP LU6 80 E2
Aynsley Gdns HLWE CM17 163 H2
Aynsworth Av BSF CM23 78 F8
Ayot Gn WGCW AL8 133 L1
Ayot Little Green La WLYN AL6 133 L1
Ayot St Peter Rd WLYN AL6 111 J6
Ayr Cl STVGE SG2 71 H2
Ayres End La HARP AL5 131 K4
Aysgarth Cl HARP AL5 131 G2
Aysgarth Rd STALW/RED AL3 129 M4

B

Baas Hl BROX EN10 159 J8
Baas Hill Cl BROX EN10 159 K8
Baas La BROX EN10 159 K8
Babbage Rd STVG SG1 70 A5
Back La BUNT SG9 44 C2
GSTN WD25 197 K2
HTCHE/RSTV SG4 68 C4
RBSF CM22 121 G3
RBSF CM22 143 H2

WLYN AL6 113 K8
Back St BLDK SG7 18 B7
LTNE LU2 2 F4
The Back BERK HP4 148 A3
Bacons Dr POTB/CUF EN6 174 D7
Bacon's Yd BLDK SG7 18 C6
Badburgham Ct WAB EN9 191 L4
Baddeley Cl STVGE SG2 5 M9
Bader Cl STVG SG1 70 D1
WGCE AL7 135 H4
Badger Cl KNEB SG3 88 E4
Badger Cft HHNE HP2 150 C8 1
Badgers BSF CM23 96 D5
Badgers Cl BORE WD6 198 E3 1
HERT/BAY SG13 138 A4
STVG SG1 4 F5
Badgers Cft BROX EN10 159 K8
TRDG/WHET N20 200 D8
Badgers Wk RKW/CH/CXG WD3 193 L5
WLYN AL6 113 H5
Badger Wy HAT AL10 155 G7
Badingham Dr HARP AL5 130 D1 1
Badminton Cl BORE WD6 198 F3 1
STVGE SG2 89 G3
Badminton Pl BROX EN10 159 K7
Bagwicks Cl LTNN/LIM LU3 64 D3
Bailey St LTN LU1 3 G9
Baines La KNEB SG3 89 H7
Baird Cl BUSH WD23 197 G7 1
Bairstow Cl BORE WD6 198 D2
Bakers Gv WGCE AL7 135 H3
Bakers Hl BAR EN5 201 G3
Bakers La DUN/WHIP LU6 105 K2
ROY SG8 22 E7
WLYN AL6 111 L1 1
Bakers Rd CHESW EN7 190 A1
Baker St HERT/BAY SG13 137 K4
LTN LU1 83 K5
POTB/CUF EN6 186 E4
Bakery Cl HLWW/ROY CM19 161 H2
Bakewell Cl LTNW/LEA LU4 82 B1
Balcary Gdns BERK HP4 146 D7
Balcombe Cl LTNE LU2 66 B6 1
Balcon Wy BORE WD6 199 H2
Baldock Cl LTNW/LEA LU4 63 L7
Baldock La LWTH SG6 40 A8
Baldock Rd BUNT SG9 58 D3
HTCH/STOT SG5 26 F5
LWTH SG6 40 A5
ROY SG8 20 A7
Baldock St ROY SG8 21 H4
WARE SG12 116 C8
Baldock Wy BORE WD6 198 E2
Baldwins WGCE AL7 135 G4
Baldwins La RKW/CH/CXG WD3 194 F5
Balfour St HERT/WAS SG14 137 H3
Baliol Rd HTCH/STOT SG5 52 E2
Ballater Cl OXHEY WD19 206 A4
Ballinger Ct BERK HP4 146 F7
Ballslough Hl HTCHE/RSTV SG4 110 C1
Balmoral Cl CHES/WCR EN8 190 C5
LCOL/BKTW AL2 169 H7
STVGE SG2 89 H3
Balmoral Dr BORE WD6 199 J5
Balmoral Rd GSTN WD25 181 M3
HTCH/STOT SG5 52 D1
PEND EN3 190 C7
WATN WD24 196 B1
Balmore Crs EBAR EN4 201 M6 1
Balmore Wd LTNN/LIM LU3 65 G1 1
Balsams Cl HERT/BAY SG13 137 J6
Bampton Rd LTNW/LEA LU4 82 A1
Banbury Cl LTNW/LEA LU4 64 E6 1
Banbury St WATW WD18 12 D6
Bancroft HTCH/STOT SG5 52 E3
Bancroft Gdns
KTN/HRWW/W HA3 207 H8 1
Bancroft Rd LTNN/LIM LU3 65 G6
Bandley Ri STVGE SG2 71 H7
Banes Down WAB EN9 177 K1
Bank Cl LTNW/LEA LU4 64 B6
Bank Ml BERK HP4 147 K6
Bankmill Br BERK HP4 147 L7
Bank Mill La BERK HP4 147 K7
Banks Rd BORE WD6 199 H3
Barbel Cl CHES/WCR EN8 190 F5
Barberry Rd HHW HP1 148 F7
Barbers La LTN LU1 2 E6
Barbers Wk TRING HP23 123 L7
Barchester Rd
KTN/HRWW/W HA3 207 J8
Barclay Cl HERT/BAY SG13 138 A6
WATW WD18 12 C8
Barclay Ct HOD EN11 159 M5
Barclay Crs STVG SG1 70 D3
Barden Cl DEN/HRF UB9 204 B8
Bards Cnr HHW HP1 149 G6 1
Bardwell Rd STAL AL1 10 E8
Barford Ri LTNE LU2 84 C1
Bargrove Av HHW HP1 148 F8
Barham Av BORE WD6 198 E4
Barham Rd STVGE SG2 71 H5
Baring Rd EBAR EN4 201 J4
Barkham Cl LBUZ LU7 101 L3
Barking Cl LTNW/LEA LU4 64 A4
Barkway Hl ROY SG8 32 D4
Barkway Rd ROY SG8 21 K5
Barkway St ROY SG8 21 J5
Barley Brow DUN/WHIP LU6 62 D7
Barley Cl BUSH WD23 197 G6
Barleycroft BUNT SG9 58 D4 1
Barley Cft HERT/WAS SG14 114 F7
HERT/WAS SG14 137 J2
HHNE HP2 9 L9
HLWS CM18 162 C6
Barleycroft STVGE SG2 71 J7
WARE SG12 115 L3
Barleycroft Gn WGCW AL8 134 B4 1
Barleycroft Rd WGCW AL8 134 B5
DUN/HR/TOD LU5 62 F5 1
Barleyfield Wy
DUN/HR/TOD LU5 62 F6 1
Barley Hills BSF CM23 96 D6
Barley La LTNW/LEA LU4 64 B5
Barley Mow La STALE/WH AL4 170 D2
Barley Ponds Cl WARE SG12 138 E1 1
Barley Ponds Rd WARE SG12 138 E1
Barley Ri BLDK SG7 41 G2
Barley Rd ROY SG8 22 F4
Barleyvale LTNN/LIM LU3 64 F2 1
Barlings Rd HARP AL5 131 G5
Barnacres Rd HHS/BOV HP3 166 E3
Barnard Acres WAB EN9 177 K2
Barnard Gn WGCE AL7 134 E5
Barnard Rd LTN LU1 82 F3
SBW CM21 120 D7
Barnard Wy HHS/BOV HP3 149 K8
Barn Cl HHS/BOV HP3 166 E2
RAD WD7 183 M6
WGCW AL8 134 B4
Barncroft STDN SG11 77 H3
Barncroft Rd BERK HP4 146 E7
Barncroft Wy STAL AL1 11 M9
Barndell Cl HTCH/STOT SG5 26 E4
Barndicott WGCE AL7 135 H4
Barnes La KGLGY WD4 166 B7
Barnes Ri KGLGY WD4 166 E6
Barnet By-pass BORE WD6 199 K6
Barnet Gate La BAR EN5 199 L7
Barnet Hl BAR EN5 200 E5
Barnet La BORE WD6 198 F8
Barnet Rd EBAR EN4 186 F8
LCOL/BKTW AL2 170 E7 1
MLHL NW7 199 K7
POTB/CUF EN6 187 H4 1
POTB/CUF EN6 187 H5 1
Barnet Wy (Barnet By-pass)
MLHL NW7 199 J8
Barnfield HHS/BOV HP3 166 E2
Barnfield Av LTNE LU2 65 J5
Barnfield Cl HOD EN11 159 M2
WAB EN9 177 L1
Barnfield Ct HARP AL5 131 H2 1
Barnfield Rd HARP AL5 131 H2
STALE/WH AL4 153 H5
WGCE AL7 134 D6
Barn Hl HLWW/ROY CM19 161 G6
Barnhurst Pth OXHEY WD19 206 B5
Barn Lea RKW/CH/CXG WD3 203 M1 1
Barn Md HLWS CM18 162 D5
Barns Ct EPP CM16 162 A7
Barnsdale Cl BORE WD6 198 E2 1
Barns Dene HARP AL5 108 D8
Barnside Ct WGCW AL8 134 B4
Barnston Cl LTNE LU2 84 C1 2
Barnsway KGLGY WD4 166 D7
Barnwell STVGE SG2 5 M9
Baron Ct STVG SG1 70 A1
Barons Ga EBAR EN4 201 K7 1
Barons Rw HARP AL5 131 J3
The Barons BSF CM23 96 C5
Barra Cl HHS/BOV HP3 167 G2
Barrells Down Rd BSF CM23 96 D1
Barrett La BSF CM23 96 E3 1
Barrie Av DUN/WHIP LU6 62 D7
Barrington Dr DEN/HRF UB9 203 M7
Barrington Rd LWTH SG6 39 L7
Barrowby Cl LTNE LU2 84 C1
Barrow La CHESW EN7 189 L2
Barrows Rd HLWW/ROY CM19 161 L2
Barr Rd POTB/CUF EN6 187 H4
Barry Cl LCOL/BKTW AL2 169 G4
Bartel Cl HHS/BOV HP3 167 J1
Bartholomew Rd BSF CM23 96 E4
Bartletts Md HERT/WAS SG14 137 J1
Barton Av DUN/HR/TOD LU5 81 J2
Barton Cl HARP AL5 109 H7
AMP/FLIT/B MK45 34 E8
Barton Rd AMP/FLIT/B MK45 34 F2
HTCH/STOT SG5 49 L1
LTNE LU2 65 H3
LTNN/LIM LU3 49 G7
STALE/WH AL4 132 B2
The Bartons BORE WD6 198 C7 1
Barton Wy BORE WD6 198 F3
RKW/CH/CXG WD3 195 G6
Bartrams La EBAR EN4 201 H1
Barwick La STDN SG11 93 H7
Basbow La BSF CM23 96 E2
Basildon Cl WATW WD18 195 H7
Basildon Sq HHNE HP2 149 L3
Basils Rd STVG SG1 70 B3
Basing Rd RKW/CH/CXG WD3 203 L1
Baslow Cl KTN/HRWW/W HA3 207 J8
Bassett Cl STALW/RED AL3 130 A5
Bassil Rd HHS/BOV HP3 149 J8
Bassingbourne Cl
BROX EN10 159 L7 1
Bassingburn Rbt RBSF CM22 98 E1
Bassingburn Wk WGCE AL7 134 E5
Batchelors STDN SG11 75 J8
Batchwood Dr STALW/RED AL3 10 B4
STALW/RED AL3 10 D1 1
Batchwood Vw STALW/RED AL3 10 E2
Batchworth Hill London Rd
RKW/CH/CXG WD3 204 D2
Batchworth La NTHWD HA6 205 H5
Bateman Rd RKW/CH/CXG WD3 194 F7
Batford Cl WGCE AL7 135 G5 2
Batford Rd HARP AL5 109 J7
Bath Rd LTNN/LIM LU3 65 J8
Bathurst Rd HHNE HP2 8 B3
Batterdale BRKMPK AL9 155 H4
Battlefield Rd STAL AL1 11 J3
Battlers Green Dr RAD WD7 183 K8
Battleview STALE/WH AL4 132 D2
The Baulk LBUZ LU7 101 L3
LBUZ LU7 102 E5
LTNE LU2 50 C8
Bawdsey Cl STVG SG1 70 A2
Bay Cl LTNW/LEA LU4 64 A4
Bayford Cl HERT/BAY SG13 137 H6
HHNE HP2 150 B2
Bayford Gn HERT/BAY SG13 157 M4
Bayford La HERT/BAY SG13 157 L2
Bayhurst Dr NTHWD HA6 205 L6
Baylam Dell LTNE LU2 84 D1 2
Baylie Ct HHNE HP2 8 C6
Baylie La HHNE HP2 8 C6
Bay Tree Cl CHESW EN7 175 L6 1
LCOL/BKTW AL2 169 H6
Bay Tree Wk WAT WD17 195 L1
Bayworth LWTH SG6 40 A5
Beacon Av DUN/WHIP LU6 80 D3
Beacon Cl CFSP/GDCR SL9 202 D7
Beacon Rd BERK HP4 103 L8
WARE SG12 116 F8
Beaconsfield LTNE LU2 3 L5
Beaconsfield Rd HAT AL10 155 H4
PEND EN3 190 C8
RAYLNE/WEN HP22 122 D5
STAL AL1 11 H7
TRING HP23 123 K7
Beacon Wy RKW/CH/CXG WD3 194 A8
TRING HP23 124 B5
The Beadles RBSF CM22 121 G2 1
Beadlow Rd LTNW/LEA LU4 63 L6
Beagle Cl RAD WD7 183 L8
Beale Cl STVGE SG2 71 H4
Beale St DUN/WHIP LU6 62 F8
Beamish Dr BUSH WD23 207 H1
Beane Av STVGE SG2 71 J4
Beane River Vw
HERT/WAS SG14 137 H4
Beane Rd HERT/WAS SG14 90 C6
HERT/WAS SG14 137 G4
The Beaneside
HERT/WAS SG14 90 C6 1
Beane Wk STVGE SG2 71 J4
Beanfield Rd SBW CM21 119 M6
Beanley Cl LTNE LU2 66 D8 1
Bear La BLDK SG7 18 C6
Bearton Av HTCH/STOT SG5 52 D2
Bearton Gn HTCH/STOT SG5 52 C1
Bearton Rd HTCH/STOT SG5 52 D1
Bearwood Cl POTB/CUF EN6 187 J2
Beasant House WATN WD24 13 J1
Beatty Rd CHES/WCR EN8 190 E5
Beauchamp Gdns
RKW/CH/CXG WD3 203 M1 2
Beauchamp Pl BORE WD6 185 G8 1
Beaulieu Cl OXHEY WD19 206 B1
Beaulieu Dr WAB EN9 191 G4
Beaumayes Cl HHW HP1 149 G8
Beaumont Av STAL AL1 153 G6
Beaumont Ga RAD WD7 183 M6
Beaumont Hall La
STALW/RED AL3 130 A8
Beaumont Park Dr
HLWW/ROY CM19 161 G2
Beaumont Pl BAR EN5 200 E2
Beaumont Rd BROX EN10 175 L3
LTNN/LIM LU3 65 C8
Beaumont Vw CHESW EN7 175 J5 1
Beazley Cl WARE SG12 116 D8 1
Becket Gdns WLYN AL6 112 B6
Beckets Sq BERK HP4 146 F4 1
Becketts HERT/WAS SG14 136 F5
Beckett's Av STALW/RED AL3 10 D1
Beckfield La BUNT SG9 43 H3
Beckham Cl LTNE LU2 65 J3 1
Becks Cl STALW/RED AL3 106 C5
Bede Cl PIN HA5 206 C8 1
Bedford Av AMS HP6 192 B2
BAR EN5 200 E6
Bedford Cl RKW/CH/CXG WD3 193 G1
Bedford Crs PEND EN3 190 D6
Bedford Park Rd STAL AL1 11 H6
Bedford Rd AMP/FLIT/B MK45 35 H6
DUN/HR/TOD LU5 62 F4
HTCH/STOT SG5 38 C7
LWTH SG6 39 J3
NTHWD HA6 205 H4
STAL AL1 11 H8
Bedford St BERK HP4 147 J6
WATN WD24 196 A2
Bedmond La ABLGY WD5 167 M5
STALW/RED AL3 168 E1
Bedmond Rd ABLGY WD5 167 L8
HHS/BOV HP3 167 J1
Bedwell Av BRKMPK AL9 156 F5
HERT/BAY SG13 156 F3
Bedwell Cl WGCE AL7 134 D5
Bedwell Crs STVG SG1 4 F3
Bedwell Ri STVG SG1 4 F4
Beech Av ENC/FH EN2 188 F6
RAD WD7 183 M4
Beech Bottom STALW/RED AL3 152 C4
Beech Cl HARP AL5 131 H5
HAT AL10 154 F6
RBSF CM22 99 H2 1
Beech Ct BERK HP4 147 J5
Beech Crs STALE/WH AL4 132 C3
Beechcroft BERK HP4 147 H7
Beechcroft Av
RKW/CH/CXG WD3 195 H7
Beechcroft Rd BUSH WD23 13 L6
Beech Dr BERK HP4 147 H7
BORE WD6 198 E3
SBW CM21 142 B2
STVGE SG2 5 M7
Beechen Gv WAT WD17 12 E2
The Beeches HTCHE/RSTV SG4 52 F4
LCOL/BKTW AL2 169 J6 1
RKW/CH/CXG WD3 193 L6
TRING HP23 124 B6 1
Beech Farm Dr STALE/WH AL4 153 L3
Beechfield HOD EN11 138 F8
KGLGY WD4 180 E1
SBW CM21 120 E8
Beechfield Cl
STALW/RED AL3 130 A5 1
Beechfield Rd HHW HP1 149 G8
WARE SG12 116 E8
WGCE AL7 134 D6
Beechfield Wk WAB EN9 191 J6
Beech Gn DUN/WHIP LU6 80 E1
Beech Gv TRING HP23 124 B6
Beech Hl EBAR EN4 201 J1
LTNE LU2 66 B3
LWTH SG6 39 J3
Beech Hill Av EBAR EN4 201 H2
Beech Hyde La STALE/WH AL4 132 E3
Beeching Cl HARP AL5 109 G6
Beechlands BSF CM23 96 E5
Beech Ms WARE SG12 138 C3
Beechpark Wy WAT WD17 181 K8
Beech Pl STALW/RED AL3 10 F1
Beech Rd DUN/WHIP LU6 81 K6
LTN LU1 2 A4
STALW/RED AL3 152 D4
WATN WD24 181 M8
Beechtree La STALW/RED AL3 168 A1
Beech Tree Wy
DUN/HR/TOD LU5 63 G5 2
Beech Wy STALE/WH AL4 110 A4
Beechwood Av AMS HP6 192 B1
POTB/CUF EN6 187 G4
RKW/CH/CXG WD3 193 G5
STAL AL1 153 G5
Beechwood Cl AMS HP6 192 B2
BLDK SG7 40 E5
CHESW EN7 175 K5 1
HERT/BAY SG13 137 L4 1
HTCH/STOT SG5 38 C8
Beechwood Ct DUN/WHIP LU6 80 E3
Beechwood Dr TRING HP23 125 J5 1
Beechwood Pk HHS/BOV HP3 165 L3
RKW/CH/CXG WD3 193 L5
Beechwood Ri WATN WD24 182 A7
Beechwood Rd LTNW/LEA LU4 64 D6
Beechwood Wy
RAYLNE/WEN HP22 122 D5
Beecroft La STVGE SG2 56 A8
Beecroft Wy DUN/WHIP LU6 80 E2
Beehive Cl BORE WD6 198 C7
Beehive Ct RBSF CM22 121 M7
Beehive Gn WGCE AL7 134 F6
Beehive La WGCE AL7 134 F7 1
Beehive Rd CHESW EN7 175 G7
Beel Cl AMSS HP7 192 B2
Beesonend La HARP AL5 130 E7
STALW/RED AL3 130 G8
Beeston Cl OXHEY WD19 206 C4
Beeston Dr CHES/WCR EN8 176 C6
Beeston Rd EBAR EN4 201 J7 1
Beethoven Rd BORE WD6 198 B8
Beeton Cl PIN HA5 206 F7 1
Beggarman's La STDN SG11 92 C2
Beggars Bush La WATW WD18 195 J6
Beggars La TRING HP23 124 E6
Belcher Rd HOD EN11 159 M3 2
Beldam Av ROY SG8 21 J5
Beldams La BSF CM23 97 G5
Belfairs OXHEY WD19 206 C5
Belford Rd BORE WD6 198 E1
Belfry Av DEN/HRF UB9 203 M8
The Belfry LTNE LU2 65 K4
Belgrave Av WATW WD18 12 B7
Belgrave Cl STALE/WH AL4 153 H3 1
Belgrave Rd LTNW/LEA LU4 64 C5
Belgravia Cl BAR EN5 200 E4
Belham Rd KGLGY WD4 166 E7
Bell Acre LWTH SG6 40 A6
Bell Acre Gdns LWTH SG6 40 A6
Bellamy Cl KNEB SG3 88 E5
WAT WD17 195 M2
Bellamy Rd CHES/WCR EN8 176 D8
Bell Cl ABLGY WD5 167 L6
HTCHE/RSTV SG4 53 G4
KNEB SG3 88 F5
Bellerby Ri LTNW/LEA LU4 64 A4
Belle Vue La BUSH WD23 207 J1
Belle Vue Rd WARE SG12 138 E1 2
Bellfield Av KTN/HRWW/W HA3 207 J6
Bellfield Gdns HLWE CM17 163 H3
Bell La ABLGY WD5 167 M6
BERK HP4 146 D5
BRKMPK AL9 172 F3
BROX EN10 159 K8
HERT/WAS SG14 137 J4 1
HOD EN11 159 M4
LCOL/BKTW AL2 170 D8
ROY SG8 33 G8
STVG SG1 70 B3
WARE SG12 118 C6
Bell Md SBW CM21 120 D8
Bellmount Wood Av WAT WD17 195 K2
The Bell Rbt LCOL/BKTW AL2 170 F6
Bell Rw BLDK SG7 40 D2 1
Bells Cl HTCH/STOT SG5 36 E1
Bells Hl BAR EN5 200 C6
BSF CM23 96 D3
Bells Meadow ROY SG8 15 M5
Bell St SBW CM21 120 D8
Bell Vw STALE/WH AL4 153 J7
Belmers Rd TRING HP23 145 J1 1
Belmont Av EBAR EN4 201 L6
Belmont Cl EBAR EN4 201 L5
Belmont Hl STAL AL1 10 E8
Belmont Rd BUSH WD23 13 L6
HHS/BOV HP3 166 D2
LTN LU1 2 A6
Belmor BORE WD6 198 F6
Belper Rd LTNW/LEA LU4 64 D8
Belsize Cl HHS/BOV HP3 149 M8
STALE/WH AL4 153 H2
Belsize Rd HHS/BOV HP3 149 M8
KTN/HRWW/W HA3 207 J7
LTNW/LEA LU4 63 K7
Belswains La HHS/BOV HP3 166 D3
Beltona Gdns CHES/WCR EN8 176 C6
Belton Rd BERK HP4 146 F5
Belvedere Gdns
LCOL/BKTW AL2 168 E6
Belvedere Rd LTNN/LIM LU3 65 G5 1
Bembridge Gdns LTNN/LIM LU3 64 E3
Ben Austins STALW/RED AL3 129 M6
Benbow Cl STAL AL1 170 A1
Benchley Hl HTCHE/RSTV SG4 53 H2
Benchleys Rd HHW HP1 148 E8
Bencroft CHESW EN7 175 M5
Bencroft Rd HHNE HP2 8 C9
Bendish La HTCHE/RSTV SG4 86 C3
Bendysh Rd BUSH WD23 13 L3
Benford Rd HOD EN11 159 L6
Bengeo St HERT/WAS SG14 137 H3
Ben Hale Cl STAN HA7 207 M5
Benhooks Av BSF CM23 96 D5
Benington Cl LTNE LU2 65 L5
Benington Rd STVGE SG2 71 L8
Bennett Cl BRKMPK AL9 134 E8
NTHWD HA6 205 L7
Bennett Ct LWTH SG6 39 M5
Bennetts Cl DUN/WHIP LU6 81 G3 1
STALE/WH AL4 171 J2 1
Bennetts End Cl
HHS/BOV HP3 166 E1 1
Bennetts End Rd HHS/BOV HP3 149 L8
Benning Av DUN/WHIP LU6 80 E2
Benningfield WARE SG12 118 C5
Benningfield Rd WARE SG12 118 C6
Benskin Rd WATW WD18 12 C6
Benskins Cl BSF CM23 61 M2
Benslow La HTCHE/RSTV SG4 52 F3
Benslow Ri HTCHE/RSTV SG4 52 F3
Benson Cl LTNN/LIM LU3 64 E3
Benstede STVGE SG2 89 H2
Bentfield End Cswy STSD CM24 79 J3
Bentfield Gdns STSD CM24 79 J3
Bentfield Rd STSD CM24 79 J3
Bentick Wy HTCHE/RSTV SG4 87 L8
Bentley Cl BSF CM23 96 E5
Bentley Dr HLWE CM17 163 H3
Bentley Heath La BAR EN5 186 D6
Bentley Rd HERT/WAS SG14 136 D3
Bentley Wy STAN HA7 207 M5
Benton Rd OXHEY WD19 206 C5
Bentsley Cl STALE/WH AL4 153 G3
Berceau Wk WAT WD17 195 K2
Berecroft HLWS CM18 162 C7 1
Berefield HHNE HP2 8 A4
Beresford Rd LTNW/LEA LU4 82 F1
RKW/CH/CXG WD3 203 L1
STAL AL1 153 H8
Bericot Wy WGCE AL7 135 H4 2
Berkeley LWTH SG6 39 M6
Berkeley Cl ABLGY WD5 181 L3
BORE WD6 198 F6
POTB/CUF EN6 186 D3
STVGE SG2 88 F2
WARE SG12 116 B8
Berkeley Crs EBAR EN4 201 J6
Berkeley Sq HHNE HP2 150 B1
Berkhamsted La
HERT/BAY SG13 157 G7
Berkhamsted Rd HHW HP1 148 D5
Berkley Av CHES/WCR EN8 190 C5
Berkley Cl STALE/WH AL4 153 H3
Berks Hl RKW/CH/CXG WD3 193 H6
Bermer Rd WATN WD24 196 B2
Bernard Cl DUN/HR/TOD LU5 81 H1
Bernard Gv WAB EN9 191 G4 1
Bernard St STALW/RED AL3 10 F5
Berners Dr STAL AL1 169 J2
Berners Wy BROX EN10 176 E2
Bernhardt Crs STVGE SG2 71 H4
The Berries STALE/WH AL4 152 F3 1
Berrow Cl LTNE LU2 66 D8 2
Berry Av WATN WD24 182 A7
Berry Cl RKW/CH/CXG WD3 194 A8
Berryfield LBUZ LU7 101 L3 1
Berry Grove La BUSH WD23 196 D1
Berrygrove La GSTN WD25 196 F2
Berry La RKW/CH/CXG WD3 193 J7
RKW/CH/CXG WD3 204 A1
Berry Leys LTNN/LIM LU3 64 D3
Berrymead HHNE HP2 8 E5
Berry Wy RKW/CH/CXG WD3 194 A8
Berwick Cl CHES/WCR EN8 190 F5 1
STAN HA7 207 L6 1
STVG SG1 69 M2
Berwick Rd BORE WD6 198 E1
Besford Cl LTNE LU2 66 C8
Bessemer Cl HTCH/STOT SG5 38 D8
Bessemer Dr STVG SG1 70 A6
Bessemer Rd WGCE AL7 134 E2
WGCW AL8 112 D8
Bethune Cl LTN LU1 83 G4
Betjeman Cl CHESW EN7 175 M7 1
Betjeman Rd ROY SG8 21 J1
Betjeman Wy HHW HP1 149 G5
Betony V ROY SG8 21 K5
Bettespol Mdw
STALW/RED AL3 129 M4
Betts La WAB EN9 161 H8
Betty's La TRING HP23 123 M6
Bevan Cl HHS/BOV HP3 166 C1
Bevan House WATN WD24 13 J1 1
Bevan Rd EBAR EN4 201 L5
Beverley Cl ROY SG8 21 G2
Beverley Gdns CHESW EN7 189 L2
STALE/WH AL4 153 J3
STAN HA7 207 M8
WGCE AL7 135 H4 1
Beverley Rd LTNW/LEA LU4 82 E1
STVG SG1 55 G8
Beverly Cl BROX EN10 159 K8
Bewdley Cl HARP AL5 131 J4 1
Bewley Cl CHES/WCR EN8 190 C2
Bexhill Rd LTNE LU2 66 C8
Beyers Gdns HOD EN11 159 M1
Beyers Prospect HOD EN11 159 M1 1
Beyers Ride HOD EN11 159 M1
Bibbs Hall La HTCHE/RSTV SG4 110 D4
Bibshall Crs DUN/WHIP LU6 81 H4
Biddenham Turn GSTN WD25 182 B6 1
Bideford Gdns LTNN/LIM LU3 65 J6
Bidwell Cl LWTH SG6 40 A5
Bidwell Hl DUN/HR/TOD LU5 62 F5
Biggin Hl BUNT SG9 45 J3
Biggin La HTCH/STOT SG5 52 D3
Bignells Cnr POTB/CUF EN6 186 A5
Bigthan Rd DUN/HR/TOD LU5 81 H2 1
Billet La BERK HP4 146 F5
Billy Lows La POTB/CUF EN6 187 G2
Bilton Rd HTCHE/RSTV SG4 38 E8
Bilton Wy LTN LU1 82 E2
Binder Cl LTNW/LEA LU4 63 K6
Bingen Rd HTCH/STOT SG5 52 B1
Bingley Rd HOD EN11 160 B4
Binham Cl LTNE LU2 65 J3
Binyon Crs STAN HA7 207 L5
Birchall La HERT/WAS SG14 135 L7
Birchalls STSD CM24 79 K2 1
Birchall Wd WGCE AL7 135 H5 2
Birchanger La BSF CM23 79 J8
Birch Copse LCOL/BKTW AL2 182 D1
Birch Dr HAT AL10 154 F6
RKW/CH/CXG WD3 203 J5
Birchen Gv LTNE LU2 65 L7
Bircherley Ct
HERT/WAS SG14 137 J4 2
Bircherley St HERT/WAS SG14 137 J4
The Birches BUSH WD23 197 H6
HHS/BOV HP3 165 L2
LWTH SG6 39 K2
WLYN AL6 111 L2
Birchfield Rd CHES/WCR EN8 176 A8

Birch Gn HHW HP1 148 E6
Birch Gv POTB/CUF EN6 186 F3
WLYN AL6 112 D2
Birch La HHS/BOV HP3 179 G4
Birch Leys HHNE HP2 150 B2
Birch Link LTNW/LEA LU4 2 A3
Birchmead WAT WD17 195 L1
Birchmead Cl
STALW/RED AL3 152 C4
Birch Pk KTN/HRWW/W HA3 207 H7
Birch Rd BERK HP4 146 C3
KNEB SG3 113 G1
Birch Side DUN/WHIP LU6 81 J4
Birch Tree Gv CSHM HP5 178 A1
Birch Tree Wk WAT WD17 181 L8
Birch Wy HARP AL5 131 H2
Birchway HAT AL10 154 F3
Birch Wy LCOL/BKTW AL2 170 C6
Birchwood BSF CM23 79 J8
RAD WD7 184 F5
Birchwood Av HAT AL10 154 F3
Birchwood Cl HAT AL10 154 F3
Birchwood Wy LCOL/BKTW AL2 169 G7
Birdcroft Rd WGCW AL8 134 C5
Birdie Wy HERT/BAY SG13 138 A3
Birds Cl WGCE AL7 135 G6
Birdsfoot La LTNN/LIM LU3 65 G4
Birds Hl LWTH SG6 39 M4
Birkdale Gdns OXHEY WD19 206 C3
Birkett Wy CSTG HP8 192 C4
Birklands La STAL AL1 170 A3
Birling Dr LTNE LU2 66 B5
Birstal Gn OXHEY WD19 206 C4
Birtley Cft LTNE LU2 84 D1
Biscot Rd LTNN/LIM LU3 65 H8
Bishops Av BORE WD6 198 E6
BSF CM23 96 E7
NTHWD HA6 205 K4
Bishops Cl BAR EN5 200 C7
HAT AL10 154 E5
STALE/WH AL4 152 F3
Bishopscote Rd LTNN/LIM LU3 65 G7
Bishopsfield HLWS CM18 162 C5
Bishops Fld
RAYLNE/WEN HP22 122 F6
Bishops Md HHW HP1 166 A1
Bishops Park Wy BSF CM23 96 A3
Bishops Ri HAT AL10 154 E6
Bishops Rd WLYN AL6 113 J4
Biskra WAT WD17 195 M2
Bisley Cl CHES/WCR EN8 190 C4
Bittern Cl CHESW EN7 175 G4
STVGE SG2 71 J8
Bittern Wy LWTH SG6 39 K1
The Bit TRING HP23 145 J1
Blackberry Md STVGE SG2 71 J7
Blackbirds La GSTN WD25 183 H5
Black Boy Wd LCOL/BKTW AL2 182 F1
Blackburn Rd
DUN/HR/TOD LU5 63 G7
Blackbury Cl POTB/CUF EN6 187 H2
Blackbushe BSF CM23 97 H1
Blackbush Spring HLW CM20 7 L4
Blackbush Springs HLW CM20 7 L4
Black Cut STAL AL1 11 H9
Blackdale CHESW EN7 175 M6
Black Ditch Rd WAB EN9 191 H7
Black Ditch Wy WAB EN9 191 G7
Blacketts Wood Dr
RKW/CH/CXG WD3 193 G5
Black Fan Rd WGCE AL7 134 E3
Blackford Rd OXHEY WD19 206 C5
Blackhill La AMP/FLIT/B MK45 34 D2
Blackhorse Cl HTCHE/RSTV SG4 52 F5
Blackhorse La HTCHE/RSTV SG4 52 F6
POTB/CUF EN6 185 K1
STALW/RED AL3 129 M4
Blackhorse Rd LWTH SG6 40 B2
Blackley Cl WAT WD17 181 L8
Black Lion Ct HLWE CM17 142 B6
Black Lion Hl RAD WD7 184 D3
Blackmoor La WATW WD18 195 J6
Blackmore LWTH SG6 40 A7
Blackmore Ct WAB EN9 191 M4
Blackmore Wy STALE/WH AL4 110 A4
Blacksmiths Cl BSF CM23 96 A5
Black Smiths Cl WARE SG12 138 F3
Blacksmiths Hl STVGE SG2 72 D6
Blacksmith's La ROY SG8 31 J5
STALW/RED AL3 10 A6
Blacksmiths Wy SBW CM21 142 A1
Black Swan La LTNN/LIM LU3 64 F5
Blackthorn Cl GSTN WD25 182 A3
STALE/WH AL4 153 H4
Blackthorn Dr LTNE LU2 66 B6
Blackthorne Cl HAT AL10 154 E8
Black Thorn Rd
DUN/HR/TOD LU5 63 H4
Blackthorn Rd WGCE AL7 134 F5
Blackwater La HHS/BOV HP3 167 K2
Blackwell Cl
KTN/HRWW/W HA3 207 J7
Blackwell Dr OXHEY WD19 13 G9
Blackwellhall La CSHM HP5 178 B2
Blackwell Hall La CSHM HP5 178 B4
Blackwell Rd KGLGY WD4 166 F8
Bladon Cl HTCHE/RSTV SG4 53 L7
Blair Cl BSF CM23 96 B3
HHNE HP2 150 A1
STVGE SG2 88 E1
Blairhead Dr OXHEY WD19 206 A3
Blake Cl ROY SG8 21 J1
STAL AL1 169 M2
Blakelands AMP/FLIT/B MK45 35 J8
Blakemere Rd WGCW AL8 134 C2
Blakemore End Rd
HTCHE/RSTV SG4 53 J7
Blakeney Dr LTNE LU2 65 H3
Blakeney Rd STVG SG1 69 M3
Blakes Wy WLYN AL6 112 B4
Blanche La POTB/CUF EN6 185 L5
Blandford Av LTNE LU2 65 J4
Blandford Rd STAL AL1 11 L6
The Blanes WARE SG12 116 B7
Blattner Cl BORE WD6 198 D5
Blaydon Rd LTNE LU2 3 K5
Blenheim Cl OXHEY WD19 196 B8
SBW CM21 142 A2
Blenheim Ct BSF CM23 96 B3
WGCE AL7 134 E3
Blenheim Crs LTNN/LIM LU3 65 H8
Blenheim Rd BAR EN5 200 C4
STAL AL1 11 K4
Blenheim Wy KNEB SG3 89 H3
Blenhiem Rd GSTN WD25 181 M4
Blenkin Cl STALW/RED AL3 152 B3
Blind La STVGE SG2 56 E5
Blindman's La CHES/WCR EN8 190 C1
Bloomfield Av LTNE LU2 3 J2
Bloomfield Rd CHESW EN7 175 H4
HARP AL5 108 E7
Bloomsbury Gdns
DUN/HR/TOD LU5 63 J5
Blows Rd DUN/HR/TOD LU5 81 J3
Bluebell Cl HERT/BAY SG13 137 M4
HHW HP1 148 D8
Bluebell Dr ABLGY WD5 167 L6
CHESW EN7 175 J7
Bluebells WLYN AL6 112 D3
Bluebell Wood Cl LTN LU1 82 E3
Blueberry Cl STALW/RED AL3 152 C3
Bluebridge Av BRKMPK AL9 172 D6
Blue Bridge Rd BRKMPK AL9 172 D6
Bluecoats Av
HERT/WAS SG14 137 J4
Bluecoat Yd WARE SG12 138 C1
Bluehouse Hill
Hemel Hempstead Rd
STALW/RED AL3 151 M8
Bluett Rd LCOL/BKTW AL2 170 C6
Blundell Cl STALW/RED AL3 152 C3
Blundell Rd LTNN/LIM LU3 64 F7
Blunesfield POTB/CUF EN6 187 J2
Blunts La LCOL/BKTW AL2 168 C5
Blyth Cl BORE WD6 198 E2
STVG SG1 69 M3
Blythe Rd HOD EN11 160 C6
Blythway WGCE AL7 134 E1
Blythwood Gdns STSD CM24 79 J4
Blythwood Rd PIN HA5 206 C8
Boardman Cl BAR EN5 200 D6
Bockings STVGE SG2 72 B1
Bodmin Rd LTNW/LEA LU4 64 E6
Bodwell Cl HHW HP1 148 F6
Bogmoor Rd ROY SG8 32 E4
Bognor Gdns OXHEY WD19 206 B5
Bohemia HHNE HP2 8 D6
Bohun Gv EBAR EN4 201 K7
Boissy Cl STALE/WH AL4 153 K8
Boleyn Cl HHNE HP2 150 B2
Boleyn Ct BROX EN10 159 K8
Boleyn Dr STAL AL1 169 J1
Boleyn Wy BAR EN5 201 H4
Bolingbroke Rd LTN LU1 83 G4
Bolingbrook STALE/WH AL4 152 F3
Bolney Gn LTNE LU2 66 C7
Bolton Rd LTN LU1 3 G7
Boniface Gdns
KTN/HRWW/W HA3 207 G7
Boniface Wk
KTN/HRWW/W HA3 207 G7
Bonks Hl SBW CM21 142 C1
Bonney Gv CHESW EN7 189 M1
Bonnick Cl LTN LU1 2 B9
Booths Cl BRKMPK AL9 172 C3
Boot La BGSW SG18 14 C5
Bornedene POTB/CUF EN6 186 D2
Borough Rd DUN/WHIP LU6 81 J3
Borough Wy POTB/CUF EN6 186 D3
Borrell Cl BROX EN10 159 K7
Borrowdale Av DUN/WHIP LU6 81 H4
Borton Av HNLW SG16 25 G6
Bosanquet Rd HOD EN11 160 B2
Boscombe Rd DUN/HR/TOD LU5 63 H8
Bosmore Rd LTNN/LIM LU3 64 E5
Boswell Cl RAD WD7 184 D3
Boswell Dr HTCH/STOT SG5 38 D6
Boswell Gdns STVG SG1 70 C1
Boswick La BERK HP4 146 C2
Bosworth Rd BAR EN5 200 F4
Botany Cl EBAR EN4 201 K5
Botley Rd CSHM HP5 178 A1
HHNE HP2 149 M2
Bottom Dr DUN/WHIP LU6 80 C5
Bottom House La TRING HP23 124 F8
Bottom La KGLGY WD4 180 B6
Bottom Rd TRING HP23 144 E7
Boughton Wy AMS HP6 192 B2
The Boulevard WATW WD18 195 J6
WGCE AL7 134 E2
Boulton Rd STVG SG1 55 H8
The Bounce HHNE HP2 8 A4
Boundary Cl BAR EN5 200 E2
Boundary Dr HERT/WAS SG14 137 J2
Boundary La WGCE AL7 134 D8
Boundary Rd BSF CM23 96 F5
STAL AL1 11 H3
Boundary Wy GSTN WD25 182 B3
HHNE HP2 9 M5
Bourn Av EBAR EN4 201 J6
Bourne Cl BROX EN10 159 L7
WARE SG12 116 C8
Bourne End La HHW HP1 164 F4
Bourne End Rd NTHWD HA6 205 K4
Bournehall Av BUSH WD23 196 F6
Bournehall La BUSH WD23 196 F7
Bournehall Rd BUSH WD23 196 F7
Bourne Honour WARE SG12 115 K3
Bournemouth Rd STVG SG1 70 A2
Bourne Rd BERK HP4 146 E5
BUSH WD23 196 F6
The Bourne BSF CM23 97 G2
HHW HP1 164 F6
WARE SG12 116 C8
Bournwell Cl EBAR EN4 201 L4
Bovingdon Crs GSTN WD25 182 C5
Bovingdon Green La
HHS/BOV HP3 164 E7
Bow Br STALW/RED AL3 151 K4
Bowbrook V LTNE LU2 84 E1
Bowcock Wk STVG SG1 4 F7
Bower Heath La HARP AL5 109 H5
Bowershott LWTH SG6 39 M6
Bower's Pde HARP AL5 130 F1
Bowers Wy HARP AL5 108 F8
Bowes Lyon Ms STALW/RED AL3 10 E7
Bowgate STAL AL1 11 H4
Bowland Crs DUN/WHIP LU6 80 F4
Bowlers Md BUNT SG9 58 C2
Bowles Gn EN EN1 190 A7
Bowling Cl BSF CM23 96 E4
HARP AL5 131 G3
Bowling Gn STVG SG1 70 B2
Bowling Green La BUNT SG9 58 C2
LTNE LU2 65 K8
Bowling Rd WARE SG12 138 D1
Bowmans Av HTCHE/RSTV SG4 53 G3
Bowmans Cl DUN/WHIP LU6 81 H3
POTB/CUF EN6 187 J3
WLYN AL6 112 B3
Bowmans Ct HHNE HP2 8 C4
Bowmans Gn GSTN WD25 182 D7
Bowmans Wy DUN/WHIP LU6 81 H3
Bowring Gn OXHEY WD19 206 B5
Bowyers HHNE HP2 8 B5
Bowyer's Cl HTCH/STOT SG5 52 C1
Boxberry Cl STVG SG1 4 E1
Boxfield WGCE AL7 135 G7
Boxfield Gn STVGE SG2 71 J2
Boxgrove Cl LTNE LU2 66 B5
Boxhill HHNE HP2 8 A4
Box La HHW HP1 165 J4
HOD EN11 159 K3
Boxted Cl LTNW/LEA LU4 64 B5
Boxted Rd HHW HP1 148 E5
Boxtree La KTN/HRWW/W HA3 207 H8
Boxtree Rd KTN/HRWW/W HA3 207 J7
Boxwell Rd BERK HP4 147 G6
Boyce Cl BORE WD6 198 D2
Boyd Cl BSF CM23 97 G2
Boyle Av STAN HA7 207 M6
Boyle Cl LTNE LU2 2 E4
Braceby Cl LTNN/LIM LU3 64 E4
Brace Cl CHESW EN7 175 G4
Brache Cl STALW/RED AL3 129 M5
Brackendale POTB/CUF EN6 186 F4
Brackendale Gv HARP AL5 108 C7
LTNN/LIM LU3 64 F5
Brackendene LCOL/BKTW AL2 182 E1
Bracken Hl BERK HP4 147 K5
Bracken La WLYN AL6 112 E3
Bracklesham Gdns LTNE LU2 66 C7
Bracknell Cl LTNW/LEA LU4 63 L7
Bracknell Pl HHNE HP2 8 F1
Bradbery RKW/CH/CXG WD3 203 J5
Bradbury Cl BORE WD6 199 G2
Bradden La HHNE HP2 127 K3
Bradford Rd RKW/CH/CXG WD3 193 H8
Bradford St HTCH/STOT SG5 52 C3
Bradgate POTB/CUF EN6 174 C6
Bradgate Cl POTB/CUF EN6 174 C7
Bradgers Hill Rd LTNE LU2 65 K6
Bradley Common BSF CM23 79 H7
Bradley Rd LTNW/LEA LU4 82 C1
Bradleys Cnr HTCHE/RSTV SG4 53 H2
Bradman Wy STVG SG1 70 F1
Bradmore Gn BRKMPK AL9 172 D5
Bradmore La BRKMPK AL9 172 C5
Bradmore Wy BRKMPK AL9 172 D5
Bradshaw Rd WATN WD24 196 B2
Bradshaws HAT AL10 171 L1
Bradshaws Cl
AMP/FLIT/B MK45 35 H7
Bradway HTCHE/RSTV SG4 86 D4
Braemar Cl KNEB SG3 89 G3
Braeside Cl PIN HA5 206 F7
Bragbury Cl STVGE SG2 89 J3
Bragbury La KNEB SG3 89 H6
Bragmans La
RKW/CH/CXG WD3 179 J4
Brain Cl HAT AL10 155 G4
Braintree Cl LTNW/LEA LU4 63 L7
Brakynbery BERK HP4 146 D3
Brallings La CFSP/GDCR SL9 202 F4
Bramble Cl CFSP/GDCR SL9 202 D6
GSTN WD25 181 M5
HARP AL5 108 E7
LTNW/LEA LU4 64 B6
Bramble Ri HLW CM20 6 D4
Bramble Rd HAT AL10 154 B6
LTNW/LEA LU4 64 B6
The Brambles BSF CM23 96 B4
CHES/WCR EN8 190 C2
ROY SG8 21 K5
STAL AL1 169 J1
STVG SG1 54 C8
WARE SG12 116 B7
WLYN AL6 112 D2
Brambling Cl BUSH WD23 13 M4
Brambling Ri HHNE HP2 8 D2
Bramfield GSTN WD25 182 D5
HTCHE/RSTV SG4 53 G4
Bramfield La HERT/WAS SG14 114 D7
Bramfield Pl HHNE HP2 149 M1
Bramfield Rd HERT/WAS SG14 136 D2
KNEB SG3 113 J1
Bramhanger Acre LTNN/LIM LU3 64 C3
Bramingham Rd LTNN/LIM LU3 64 F3
Bramleas WATW WD18 12 A6
Bramley Cl BLDK SG7 40 E1
Bramley Ct GSTN WD25 182 A3
Bramley Gdns OXHEY WD19 206 B6
Bramley Shaw WAB EN9 191 L4
Bramley Wy STALE/WH AL4 153 H8
Brampton Cl CHESW EN7 175 M7
HARP AL5 131 J1
Brampton Park Rd
HTCH/STOT SG5 52 D1
Brampton Ri DUN/WHIP LU6 81 H4
Brampton Rd OXHEY WD19 205 M3
ROY SG8 21 L4
STAL AL1 11 L5
Brampton Ter BORE WD6 198 F1
Bramshaw Gdns OXHEY WD19 206 C5
Bramshott Cl HTCHE/RSTV SG4 52 E6
Branch Cl HAT AL10 155 H3
Branch Rd LCOL/BKTW AL2 169 J6
STALW/RED AL3 10 B5
Brandles Rd LWTH SG6 39 M7
Brandon Cl CHESW EN7 175 K5
Brandreth Av DUN/HR/TOD LU5 81 K1
Brand St HTCH/STOT SG5 52 D3
Branksome Cl HHNE HP2 9 G6
Branton Cl LTNE LU2 66 D8
Brantwood Rd LTN LU1 2 B7
Bray Cl BORE WD6 199 H2
Brayes Mnr HTCH/STOT SG5 26 E4
Brays Md HLWS CM18 162 E4
Brays Rd LTNE LU2 66 A7
Brazier Cl AMP/FLIT/B MK45 35 G7
Braziers End CSHM HP5 145 H8
Braziers Fld HERT/BAY SG13 137 L4
Braziers Quay BSF CM23 96 F4
Breachwell Pl LBUZ LU7 101 M1
Bread And Cheese La
BROX EN10 175 K3
Breadcroft La HARP AL5 109 G8
Breakmead WGCE AL7 135 G6
Breakspear STVGE SG2 71 H7
Breakspear Av STAL AL1 11 K8
Breakspear Ct ABLGY WD5 181 L1
Breakspeare Cl WATN WD24 196 A1
Breakspeare Rd ABLGY WD5 181 K2
Breakspear Wy HHNE HP2 9 M8
Breaks Rd HAT AL10 155 G4
Brecken Cl STALE/WH AL4 152 F3
Brecon Cl LTN LU1 2 C9
Brendon Av LTNE LU2 84 B1
Brent Pl BAR EN5 200 F6
Brentwood Cl DUN/HR/TOD LU5 63 J4
Brett Pl WATN WD24 181 M8
Brett Rd BAR EN5 200 B6
Bretts Md LTN LU1 83 H5
Brewers Cl BSF CM23 96 B5
Brewers Hill Rd DUN/WHIP LU6 62 E8
Brewery La BLDK SG7 40 D1
STSD CM24 79 K3
Brewery Rd HOD EN11 159 M4
Brewhouse Hl STALE/WH AL4 132 B2
Brewhouse La
HERT/WAS SG14 137 H4
Briants Cl PIN HA5 206 D8
Briarcliff HHW HP1 148 D6
Briar Cl BERK HP4 147 M3
CHES/WCR EN8 176 B8
LTNE LU2 66 B6
Briardale STVG SG1 4 E6
WARE SG12 116 B7
Briarley Cl BROX EN10 176 E1
Briar Patch La LWTH SG6 39 J7
Briar Rd GSTN WD25 181 M5
STALE/WH AL4 153 H4
Briars Cl HAT AL10 154 F5
Briars La HAT AL10 154 F5
The Briars CHES/WCR EN8 190 D2
HERT/BAY SG13 137 M4
HLWS CM18 162 D5
RKW/CH/CXG WD3 179 M7
Briars Wd HAT AL10 154 F5
Briar Wy BERK HP4 147 H7
Briary La ROY SG8 21 H5
Briary Wood End WLYN AL6 112 E2
Briary Wood La WLYN AL6 112 E2
Brickcroft BROX EN10 176 D5
Brickendon La HERT/BAY SG13 137 H7
HERT/BAY SG13 158 C5
Bricket Rd STAL AL1 10 F7
Brickfield HAT AL10 154 F8
Brickfield Av HHS/BOV HP3 150 A8
Brickfield La BAR EN5 199 L7
The Brickfields WARE SG12 116 A8
Brick Kiln Cl BUSH WD23 13 M8
Brick Kiln La HTCH/STOT SG5 52 D5
Brickkiln Rd STVG SG1 4 A2
Brick Knoll Pk STALE/WH AL4 153 H8
Brickly Rd LTNW/LEA LU4 64 A5
Brickmakers La HHS/BOV HP3 150 A8
Brickwall Cl WGCW AL8 133 M2
Brickyard La ROY SG8 31 K5
Bride Hall La WLYN AL6 110 F6
Bridewell Cl BUNT SG9 58 D2
Bridge End BUNT SG9 58 D2
Bridgefields WGCE AL7 134 E3
Bridgefoot BUNT SG9 58 D3
Bridge Foot WARE SG12 138 C1
Bridgeman Dr DUN/HR/TOD LU5 63 J5
Bridgend Rd EN EN1 190 B6
Bridge Pl WAT WD17 13 J7
Bridger Cl GSTN WD25 182 C4
Bridge Rd KGLGY WD4 181 H4
KNEB SG3 88 F8
LWTH SG6 39 L4
STVG SG1 70 A4
WGCE AL7 134 D3
WGCW AL8 134 B3
Bridge Rd East WGCE AL7 134 E4
Bridges Ct HERT/WAS SG14 137 H4
Bridges Rd STAN HA7 207 L5
Bridge St BERK HP4 147 J6
BSF CM23 96 E3
HHW HP1 149 H8
HTCH/STOT SG5 52 D4
LTN LU1 2 E6
Bridgewater Hl BERK HP4 146 E3
Bridgewater Rd BERK HP4 147 G4
Bridgewater Wy BUSH WD23 197 G7
Bridle Cl HOD EN11 138 F8
PEND EN3 190 E8
STALW/RED AL3 11 H2
Bridle La RKW/CH/CXG WD3 194 B4
Bridle Pth WAT WD17 196 A3
Bridle Wy BERK HP4 146 F4
HOD EN11 159 M1
WARE SG12 138 F4
Bridle Wy (North) HOD EN11 138 F8
Bridle Wy (South) HOD EN11 159 M1
Bridlington Rd OXHEY WD19 206 C3
Brierley Cl DUN/WHIP LU6 81 H5
LTNE LU2 66 C8
Briery Fld RKW/CH/CXG WD3 193 M5
Briery Wy HHNE HP2 9 H5
Brighton Rd WATN WD24 195 M1
Brighton Wy STVG SG1 69 M2
Brightview Cl
LCOL/BKTW AL2 168 D8
Brightwell Av DUN/WHIP LU6 80 B4
Brightwell Rd WATW WD18 12 C7
Brill Cl LTNE LU2 66 C8
Brimfield Cl LTNE LU2 66 C8
Brimstone Wy BERK HP4 146 E4
Brinklow Ct STAL AL1 169 G2
Brinley Cl CHES/WCR EN8 190 C2
Brinsmead LCOL/BKTW AL2 169 J6
Briscoe Cl HOD EN11 159 L2
Briscoe Rd HOD EN11 159 L2
Bristol Rd LTNN/LIM LU3 64 F6
Britain St DUN/WHIP LU6 81 H2
Britannia STDN SG11 75 K8
Britannia Av LTNN/LIM LU3 65 G5
Britannia Rd CHES/WCR EN8 190 E5
Brittains Ri HNLW SG16 24 D8
Brittain Wy STVGE SG2 5 L5
Britten Cl BORE WD6 198 C7
Britton Av STALW/RED AL3 10 E6
Brive Rd DUN/HR/TOD LU5 81 K3
Brixham Cl STVG SG1 70 A3
Brixton Rd WATN WD24 196 A2
Broad Acre LCOL/BKTW AL2 182 D1
Broad Acres HAT AL10 154 E2
Broadacres LTNE LU2 65 J4
Broad Ct WGCE AL7 134 D4
Broadcroft HHNE HP2 8 A4
LWTH SG6 39 L8
Broadfield BSF CM23 78 E8
HLW CM20 7 G5
Broadfield Cl MHAD SG10 118 E1
Broadfield Ct BUSH WD23 207 K2
Broadfield Pl WGCW AL8 134 A5
Broadfield Rd HHNE HP2 8 E8
KNEB SG3 113 G1
RBSF CM22 99 K3
Broadfields CHESW EN7 175 G8
HARP AL5 108 E8
SBW CM21 142 A1
Broadfields La OXHEY WD19 206 A1
Broadfield Wy MHAD SG10 118 E1
Broadgate WAB EN9 191 L4
Broadgates Av EBAR EN4 201 G2
Broad Gn HERT/BAY SG13 157 L2
Broad Green Wd
HERT/BAY SG13 157 L2
Broadhall Wy STVGE SG2 70 F8
Broadlake Cl LCOL/BKTW AL2 170 C6
Broadlawns Ct
KTN/HRWW/W HA3 207 L8
Broadleaf Av BSF CM23 96 B6
Broadleaf Gv WLYN AL6 134 A1
Broadley Rd HLWW/ROY CM19 161 L6
Broadmead HTCHE/RSTV SG4 52 F5
Broad Md LTNN/LIM LU3 64 F7
Broadmead Cl PIN HA5 206 D7
Broadmeadow Ride
HTCHE/RSTV SG4 52 F6
Broadmeads WARE SG12 138 C1
Broadoak Av PEND EN3 190 C6
Broad Oak Wy STVGE SG2 88 E1
Broadstone Rd HARP AL5 131 H4
Broad St HHNE HP2 8 A8
Broadview STVG SG1 4 F2
Broadwater BERK HP4 147 H5
POTB/CUF EN6 187 G1
Broadwater Av LWTH SG6 39 K5
Broadwater Crs STVGE SG2 88 E1
WGCE AL7 134 C5
Broadwater Dl LWTH SG6 39 K5
Broadwater La STVGE SG2 89 J1
Broadwater Rd WGCE AL7 134 D5
WGCW AL8 134 C5
Broadway LWTH SG6 39 K7
Broadway Av HLWE CM17 142 A6
The Broadway BRKMPK AL9 155 H5
PIN HA5 206 E7
STALE/WH AL4 110 A5
WAT WD17 13 H3
Brocket Rd HOD EN11 159 M4
WGCW AL8 133 L6
Brockett Cl WGCW AL8 134 A4
Brocket Vw STALE/WH AL4 132 C2
Brockhurst Cl STAN HA7 207 L6
Brocklesbury Cl WATN WD24 13 H2
Brockles Md HLWW/ROY CM19 162 B6
Brockswood La WGCW AL8 134 A3
Brockwell Shott STVGE SG2 72 A1
Brodewater Rd BORE WD6 199 G3
Bromborough Gn
OXHEY WD19 206 B5
Bromefield Ct WAB EN9 191 M4
Bromet Cl WAT WD17 195 L1
Bromleigh Cl CHES/WCR EN8 176 D7
Bromley TRING HP23 100 F6
Bromley Gdns DUN/HR/TOD LU5 63 J5
Brompton Cl LTNN/LIM LU3 64 E2
Bronte Crs HHNE HP2 150 A1
Brookbridge La KNEB SG3 89 J8
Brook Cl HNLW SG16 25 J1
RAYLNE/WEN HP22 122 C5
Brookdene Av OXHEY WD19 196 A8
Brookdene Dr NTHWD HA6 205 L7
Brook Dr RAD WD7 183 L4
STVGE SG2 89 G2
Brooke Cl BUSH WD23 197 H8
Brooke End STALW/RED AL3 129 M6
Brooke Gdns BSF CM23 97 H3
Brook End SBW CM21 120 C8
Brooke Rd ROY SG8 21 J2
Brooker Rd WAB EN9 191 H5
Brooke Wy BUSH WD23 197 H8
Brook Fld STVGE SG2 71 K8
Brookfield Av DUN/HR/TOD LU5 63 H6
Brookfield Cl TRING HP23 124 A6
Brookfield Gdns
CHES/WCR EN8 176 C6
Brookfield La CHES/WCR EN8 176 A7
STVGE SG2 71 L6
Brookfield La East
CHES/WCR EN8 176 C6
Brookfield La West
CHES/WCR EN8 176 B6
Brookfields SBW CM21 120 C8
Brookhill STVGE SG2 88 E2
Brookhill Cl EBAR EN4 201 K6
Brooklands Cl LTNW/LEA LU4 64 B4
Brooklands Gdns
POTB/CUF EN6 186 D3
Brook La BERK HP4 147 G5
SBW CM21 120 C8
Brooklane Fld HLWS CM18 163 G5
Brookmans Av BRKMPK AL9 172 E5
Brookmead SHFD SG17 24 B4
Brookmill Cl OXHEY WD19 196 A8

Brook Pl BAR EN5 200 F6
Brook Rd BORE WD6 198 F2
CHES/WCR EN8 190 E5
SBW CM21 142 C1
STSD CM24 79 K4
Brooksfield WGCE AL7 135 G3
Brookshill KTN/HRWW/W HA3 207 K6
Brookshill Av
KTN/HRWW/W HA3 207 J5
Brookshill Dr
KTN/HRWW/W HA3 207 J5
Brookside EBAR EN4 201 K7
HAT AL10 154 C5
HERT/BAY SG13 137 K5
HLWW/ROY CM19 161 L5
HOD EN11 159 M4
HTCH/STOT SG5 36 D1
LWTH SG6 39 L5 1
POTB/CUF EN6 185 M3
SHFD SG17 24 B4
WAB EN9 191 K3 1
Brookside Cl BAR EN5 200 C7
Brookside Crs POTB/CUF EN6 174 D6
Brookside Gdns EN EN1 190 A8
Brookside Rd OXHEY WD19 196 A8
Brookside South EBAR EN4 201 M8
Brook St HTCH/STOT SG5 26 D4
LTN LU1 2 C4
RAYLNE/WEN HP22 122 C5
TRING HP23 124 A6
Brook Vw HTCHE/RSTV SG4 53 H4
Broom Cl CHESW EN7 175 M6
HAT AL10 154 E8
Broomer Pl CHES/WCR EN8 176 B8
Broomfield HLW CM20 142 A7
LCOL/BKTW AL2 169 H6 1
Broomfield Av BROX EN10 176 D5
Broomfield Cl WLYN AL6 112 B6 1
Broomfield Ri ABLGY WD5 181 J3
Broomfield Rd WLYN AL6 112 B6
Broomfields RBSF CM22 121 M7
Broom Gv KNEB SG3 88 E6
WAT WD17 195 M1
Broom Hl HHW HP1 148 D8
WLYN AL6 112 F2
Broomhills WGCE AL7 134 F3
Broomleys STALE/WH AL4 153 H4
Brooms Cl WGCW AL8 134 C1 1
Brooms Rd LTNE LU2 3 H4
Broomstick Hall Rd WAB EN9 191 K4
Broom Wk STVG SG1 4 F4
Broughinge Rd BORE WD6 199 G3
Broughton Av LTNN/LIM LU3 65 H5
Broughton Hl LWTH SG6 39 M4
Broughton Wy
RKW/CH/CXG WD3 193 M8
Brownfields WGCE AL7 134 E3
Brownfield Wy STALE/WH AL4 110 A4
Browning Dr HTCHE/RSTV SG4 53 G2
Browning Rd HARP AL5 109 H8
LTNW/LEA LU4 63 M8
Brownlow La LBUZ LU7 101 L3
Brownlow Rd BERK HP4 147 H5
BORE WD6 198 F5 1
Brown's Cl LTNW/LEA LU4 64 C5
Brown's Ri TRING HP23 144 E7 1
Browns Spring BERK HP4 148 B3
The Brow CSTG HP8 202 C3
GSTN WD25 182 A4
Brox Dell STVG SG1 4 F1
Broxley Md LTNW/LEA LU4 64 B5
Bruce Gv WATN WD24 196 A1
Bruce Rd BAR EN5 200 D4 1
Bruce Wy CHES/WCR EN8 190 C4
Brunel Ct LTNW/LEA LU4 63 K7
Brunel Rd LTNW/LEA LU4 63 K7
STVGE SG2 70 F3
Brunswick St LTNE LU2 2 F4
Brushrise WATN WD24 181 M7
Brushwood Dr
RKW/CH/CXG WD3 193 H5
Brussels Wy LTNN/LIM LU3 64 C1
Bryan Rd BSF CM23 96 E2
Bryanstone Rd CHES/WCR EN8 190 E5
Bryant Cl BAR EN5 200 E6
Bryant Ct HARP AL5 108 F7
Bryants Cl HTCH/STOT SG5 36 E1
Bryce Cl WARE SG12 116 C7
Bryony Wy DUN/WHIP LU6 80 D1
Buchanan Ct BORE WD6 199 H3 1
Buchanan Dr LTNE LU2 3 M4
Buckettsland La BORE WD6 199 J1
Buckingham Av
TRDG/WHET N20 201 H8
Buckingham Dr LTNE LU2 66 B8
Buckingham Rd BORE WD6 199 J5
TRING HP23 123 K7
WATN WD24 182 B8 1
Buckland Ri PIN HA5 206 B8
Buckland Rd
RAYLNE/WEN HP22 122 F5
Buckle Cl LTNN/LIM LU3 64 E3
Bucklersbury HTCH/STOT SG5 52 D4
Bucklers Cl BROX EN10 176 E1
Bucknalls Cl GSTN WD25 182 D3
Bucknalls Dr LCOL/BKTW AL2 182 E2
Bucknalls La GSTN WD25 182 D3
Bucks Aly HERT/BAY SG13 157 J6
Bucks Av OXHEY WD19 196 D8
Bucks Hl KGLGY WD4 180 B4
Buckthorn Av STVG SG1 4 E6
Buckton Rd BORE WD6 198 E1
Buckwood Av DUN/HR/TOD LU5 81 K1
Buckwood La DUN/WHIP LU6 105 H3
Buckwood Rd DUN/WHIP LU6 105 M4
Buddcroft WGCE AL7 135 G3 1
Bude Crs STVG SG1 69 M4 1
Bulbourne Cl BERK HP4 146 E4 1
HHW HP1 148 F8
Bulbourne Ct TRING HP23 123 M3 1
Bulbourne Rd TRING HP23 124 A3
Bullace Cl HHW HP1 148 F6 2
Bullbeggars La BERK HP4 147 M6
Bullen's Green La
STALE/WH AL4 171 K2
Bullfields SBW CM21 120 D7
Bullhead Rd BORE WD6 199 H3
Bull La BUNT SG9 44 B2
BUNT SG9 57 H2
STALE/WH AL4 131 M4
Bullock's Hl HTCHE/RSTV SG4 86 F1
Bullock's La HERT/BAY SG13 137 H6
Bull Pln HERT/WAS SG14 137 J4
Bull Pond La DUN/WHIP LU6 81 G3
Bull Rd HARP AL5 131 G2
Bullrush Cl HAT AL10 155 G6
Bull's Cross ENC/FH EN2 189 M7
Bulls Cross Ride CHESW EN7 189 M5
Bullsland Gdns
RKW/CH/CXG WD3 193 G7
Bullsland La RKW/CH/CXG WD3 193 G7
Bulls La BRKMPK AL9 172 D3
Bullsmoor Cl CHES/WCR EN8 190 B6 1
Bullsmoor Gdns
CHES/WCR EN8 190 A6 1
Bullsmoor La EN EN1 190 A6
PEND EN3 190 C6
Bullsmoor Ride CHES/WCR EN8 190 B6
Bullsmoor Wy CHES/WCR EN8 190 A6
Bull Stag Gn BRKMPK AL9 155 H3
Bullwell Crs CHES/WCR EN8 176 D8
Bulstrode Cl KGLGY WD4 165 K8
Bulstrode La KGLGY WD4 165 K8
Bulwer Gdns BAR EN5 201 H5 1
Bulwer Link STVG SG1 4 E7
Bulwer Rd BAR EN5 201 G5
Buncefield La HHNE HP2 9 M6
The Bungalows HARP AL5 109 H7 1
Bunhill Cl DUN/WHIP LU6 80 E2
Bunkers La HHS/BOV HP3 166 F4
Bunnsfield WGCE AL7 135 H3
Bunstrux TRING HP23 123 L6
Buntingford Rd STDN SG11 75 J6
Bunting Rd LTNW/LEA LU4 63 M6
Bunyan Cl HTCH/STOT SG5 37 J6
TRING HP23 124 A5
Bunyan Rd HTCH/STOT SG5 52 E2 1
Bunyans Cl LTNN/LIM LU3 64 F5
Burbage Cl CHES/WCR EN8 190 D2
Burchell Ct BUSH WD23 197 H8 2
Burfield Cl HAT AL10 154 F3 1
Burfield Rd RKW/CH/CXG WD3 193 G6
Burford Cl LTNN/LIM LU3 64 E1
Burford Gdns HOD EN11 160 A3
Burford St HOD EN11 159 M4
Burford Wy HTCH/STOT SG5 38 B8
Burge End La HTCH/STOT SG5 37 H5
Burges Cl DUN/WHIP LU6 81 J5
Burghley Av BORE WD6 199 H6
BSF CM23 96 B3
Burghley Cl STVGE SG2 88 F2
Burgundy Cft WGCE AL7 134 E6 1
Burleigh Md BRKMPK AL9 155 H3
Burleigh Rd CHES/WCR EN8 190 D3 1
HERT/BAY SG13 137 M3
HHS/BOV HP3 150 B8
STAL AL1 153 G7
Burleigh Wy POTB/CUF EN6 188 D1
Burley LWTH SG6 39 L1
Burley Hl HLWE CM17 163 J3
Burley Rd BSF CM23 96 F6
Burnell Ri LWTH SG6 39 J5
Burnells Wy STSD CM24 79 K3
Burnell Wk LWTH SG6 39 K5
Burnet Cl HHS/BOV HP3 149 K8
Burnett Av HNLW SG16 25 G6
Burnett Pk
HLWW/ROY CM19 162 A7 2
Burnett Sq HERT/WAS SG14 136 E3
Burnham Cl WLYN AL6 113 H4
Burnham Green Rd WLYN AL6 113 J4
Burnham Rd LTNE LU2 3 M1
STAL AL1 11 M6
Burnley Cl OXHEY WD19 206 B5
Burnsall Pl HARP AL5 131 H4
Burns Cl HTCHE/RSTV SG4 53 G2 2
STVGE SG2 71 G2
Burns Dr HHNE HP2 150 A2
Burnside HERT/WAS SG14 136 F5
HOD EN11 159 L4
SBW CM21 120 C8
STAL AL1 170 A1
Burnside Cl BAR EN5 200 F4
Burns Rd ROY SG8 21 J2
Burnt Cl LTNN/LIM LU3 64 E3
Burntfarm Ride CHESW EN7 189 G3
Burntmill La HLW CM20 141 H7
Burr Cl AMP/FLIT/B MK45 35 H6
LCOL/BKTW AL2 170 D6
Burrowfield WGCE AL7 134 C6
Burrs La ROY SG8 32 B7
Burr's Pl LTN LU1 2 F8
Burr St DUN/WHIP LU6 81 G2
LTNE LU2 2 F4
Bursland LWTH SG6 39 J4
Burston Dr LCOL/BKTW AL2 169 H7
Burton Av WATW WD18 12 D4
Burton Cl STALE/WH AL4 110 B5
Burton La CHESW EN7 175 K7
Burton's La CSTG HP8 192 D5
RKW/CH/CXG WD3 192 E6
Burton's Wy CSTG HP8 192 B3
Burwell Rd STVGE SG2 5 M6
Burycroft WGCW AL8 134 D1
Burydale STVGE SG2 89 G1
Burydell La LCOL/BKTW AL2 169 J6
Bury End HTCH/STOT SG5 37 J6
Bury Gn HHW HP1 149 H6 1
STALE/WH AL4 132 B2
Bury Green Rd CHESW EN7 189 M2
Bury Hl HHW HP1 149 H6
Bury Hill Cl HHW HP1 149 H6
Bury Holme BROX EN10 176 E2
Bury La HERT/WAS SG14 114 A6
KNEB SG3 89 J7
LTNN/LIM LU3 48 F5
RKW/CH/CXG WD3 204 C1
WLYN AL6 111 L1
Bury Lodge La RBSF CM22 98 B2
STSD CM24 79 M7
Bury Md ARL/CHE SG15 25 M3
Burymead STVG SG1 70 B1
Bury Mdw RKW/CH/CXG WD3 204 C1
Bury Mead Rd HTCH/STOT SG5 38 E8
Bury Park Rd LTN LU1 2 A3
Bury Ri HHS/BOV HP3 165 J4
Bury Rd HAT AL10 155 H4
HHW HP1 149 H6
HLWE CM17 142 B6
Burywick HARP AL5 131 G5
Bushbarns CHESW EN7 175 M8
Bushby Av BROX EN10 176 E1
Bushell Gn BUSH WD23 207 J2 1
Bushel Whf TRING HP23 123 M4
Bushey Cl WGCE AL7 135 G5 3
Bushey Cft HLWS CM18 7 H9
Bushey Gn WGCE AL7 135 G5 4
Bushey Grove Rd BUSH WD23 13 K4
Bushey Hall Dr BUSH WD23 13 M4
Bushey Hall Rd BUSH WD23 13 K4
Bushey Ley WGCE AL7 135 G5
Busheymill Br BUSH WD23 196 D1
Bushey Mill Crs WATN WD24 182 B8
Bushey Mill La BUSH WD23 196 E3
WATN WD24 182 B8
Bushfield Rd HHS/BOV HP3 165 H4
Bush Hall La BRKMPK AL9 155 J2
Bushmead Rd LTNE LU2 65 K5
Bush Spring BLDK SG7 40 F1
Bushwood Cl BRKMPK AL9 172 A2 1
Butchers La HTCHE/RSTV SG4 68 C4
Butely Rd LTNW/LEA LU4 64 A5
Bute Sq LTN LU1 2 E6
Bute St LTN LU1 2 F6
Butlin Rd LTN LU1 83 G3
Buttercup Cl DUN/WHIP LU6 80 F3
Butterfield Green Rd LTNE LU2 65 M4
Butterfield La STAL AL1 169 K3
Butterfield Rd STALE/WH AL4 132 B3
Butterfly La BORE WD6 198 A4
Buttermere Av DUN/WHIP LU6 81 H4
Buttermere Cl STAL AL1 153 G8
Buttersweet Ri SBW CM21 142 D1 1
Butterwick GSTN WD25 182 D7
Butt Field Vw LCOL/BKTW AL2 169 H3
Buttlehide
RKW/CH/CXG WD3 203 J5 1
Buttondene Crs BROX EN10 177 G1
Butts End HHW HP1 148 F6
Buttsmead NTHWD HA6 205 H7
The Butts BROX EN10 176 D3
Buxton Cl SHFD SG17 24 B4
STALE/WH AL4 153 J4
Buxton Pth OXHEY WD19 206 B3 1
Buxton Rd LTN LU1 2 C7
WAB EN9 191 M3
Buxtons La ROY SG8 15 L7
Buzzard Rd LTNW/LEA LU4 63 M5
Byde St HERT/WAS SG14 137 H3
Byers Cl POTB/CUF EN6 187 H5 2
Byewaters WATW WD18 195 J7
The Bye Wy
KTN/HRWW/W HA3 207 K8
The Byeway RKW/CH/CXG WD3 204 D2
Byfield WGCW AL8 134 D1
Byfield Cl LTNW/LEA LU4 82 A1
Bygrave Rd BLDK SG7 40 E1
Bylands Cl BSF CM23 96 C4
Byng Dr POTB/CUF EN6 186 F2
Bynghams HLWW/ROY CM19 161 L4
Byng Rd BAR EN5 200 C4
Byrd Wk BLDK SG7 40 E4
Byre Rd STHGT/OAK N14 201 M7
Byron Av BORE WD6 198 F6
WATN WD24 196 C2
Byron Cl HTCHE/RSTV SG4 53 G2
STVGE SG2 71 H3
Byron Pl HHNE HP2 150 A1
Byron Rd HARP AL5 108 F8
LTNW/LEA LU4 64 A8
ROY SG8 21 J2
Byslips Rd DUN/WHIP LU6 105 J7
By the Wd OXHEY WD19 206 C2
Byways BERK HP4 147 K5
The Byway POTB/CUF EN6 186 F4

C

Cabot Cl STVGE SG2 70 F3
Caddington Cl EBAR EN4 201 K6
Caddington Common
STALW/RED AL3 106 D2
Caddis Cl STAN HA7 207 L7 1
Cade Cl LWTH SG6 40 B1
Cades Cl LTN LU1 82 F4
Cades La LTN LU1 82 F4
Cadmore La CHES/WCR EN8 176 D7
Cadwell La HTCH/STOT SG5 38 E8
Caernarvon Cl HHNE HP2 8 B9
STVGE SG2 89 G3
Caesars Rd STALE/WH AL4 132 C2
Cage Pond Rd RAD WD7 184 F4
Cairn Wy STAN HA7 207 L6
Caishowe Rd BORE WD6 199 G2
Caister Cl HHS/BOV HP3 149 K8
STVG SG1 69 M1
Calbury Cl STAL AL1 153 G8 1
Calcutt Cl DUN/HR/TOD LU5 63 L8
Caldbeck WAB EN9 191 J5
Caldecot Av CHESW EN7 175 L8 1
Caldecote Gdns BUSH WD23 197 K7
Caldecote La BUSH WD23 197 L8
Caldecote Rd BLDK SG7 27 J1
Caldecot Wy BROX EN10 176 E1 1
Calder Av BRKMPK AL9 172 F5
Caldwell Rd OXHEY WD19 206 C4
Caleb Cl LTNW/LEA LU4 64 E8
Caledon Rd LCOL/BKTW AL2 170 B5
California BLDK SG7 40 E1
California La BUSH WD23 207 J1
Callisto Ct HHNE HP2 8 F3
Callowland Pl WATN WD24 196 A1 1
Calnwood Rd LTNW/LEA LU4 64 A8
Calton Av HERT/WAS SG14 136 E3
Calton Rd BAR EN5 201 H7
Calverley Cl BSF CM23 96 D7
Calverton Rd LTNN/LIM LU3 64 E4
Calvert Rd BAR EN5 200 C3
Camberley Pl HARP AL5 131 J4 2
Camborne Dr HHNE HP2 149 K3
Cambrian Wy HHNE HP2 8 D3
Cambridge Cl
CHES/WCR EN8 176 B8 1
Cambridge Dr POTB/CUF EN6 186 D2
Cambridge Rd BGSW SG18 14 C4
HLW CM20 142 B4
HTCHE/RSTV SG4 39 J8
ROY SG8 22 F7
SBW CM21 120 D5
STAL AL1 153 G8
STDN SG11 75 H8
STSD CM24 79 K2
WATW WD18 13 G5 1
Cambridge St LTN LU1 83 L5
Cambridge Ter BERK HP4 147 J6 1
Cameron Dr CHES/WCR EN8 190 C5
Camfield WGCE AL7 134 E8
Camford Wy LTNW/LEA LU4 63 M2
Camlet Wy EBAR EN4 200 F3
STALW/RED AL3 10 B4
Campania Gv LTNN/LIM LU3 64 F2
Campbell Cl BUNT SG9 58 C3
HLWE CM17 163 G3 1
HTCHE/RSTV SG4 53 G2 3
Camp Dr DUN/HR/TOD LU5 63 G5
Campers Av LWTH SG6 39 K5
Campers Rd LWTH SG6 39 J5
Campers Wk LWTH SG6 39 K5
Campfield Rd HERT/WAS SG14 137 G4
STAL AL1 11 M7
Campfield Wy LWTH SG6 39 H5
Campian Cl DUN/WHIP LU6 80 D1
Campine Cl CHES/WCR EN8 176 C7 1
Campion Cl GSTN WD25 181 M4
Campion Rd HHW HP1 148 D8
Campions Ct BERK HP4 146 F7
The Campions BORE WD6 198 E1
STSD CM24 79 K2 2
Campion Wy ROY SG8 21 K5
Campkin Md STVGE SG2 71 J7 1
Camp Rd STAL AL1 11 K7
Campus Five LWTH SG6 40 B3
The Campus WGCW AL8 134 C3
Camp View Rd STAL AL1 153 G8
Canada La BROX EN10 176 D4
The Canadas BROX EN10 176 D4 1
Canberra Cl STALW/RED AL3 152 E3
Canberra Gdns LTNN/LIM LU3 65 G4
Candale Cl DUN/WHIP LU6 81 H4
Candlefield Rd HHS/BOV HP3 166 F2
Canesworde Rd DUN/WHIP LU6 80 F3
Canfield BSF CM23 96 D2
Cangelis Cl HHW HP1 165 M1
Canham Cl HTCHE/RSTV SG4 110 C1
Cannix Cl STVGE SG2 5 J9
Cannon La LTNE LU2 66 A5
Cannon Ms WAB EN9 191 G4
Cannon Rd WATW WD18 13 H7
Cannons Cl BSF CM23 96 F2
ROY SG8 15 L5
Cannons Ct STDN SG11 75 J7
Cannons Md STSD CM24 79 J3
Cannons Meadow WLYN AL6 135 K1
Cannons Mill La BSF CM23 78 F8
Cannon St STALW/RED AL3 10 E5
Canon Mohan Cl EBAR EN4 201 M7
Canons Brook
HLWW/ROY CM19 161 M2
Canons Cl RAD WD7 184 A6
Canons Fld STALE/WH AL4 132 C1 2
WLYN AL6 112 D2
Canonsfield Rd WLYN AL6 112 D2
Canons Ga CHES/WCR EN8 176 E5
HLW CM20 140 F8
Canons Rd WARE SG12 116 B8
Canopus Wy NTHWD HA6 205 M4
Canterbury Cl LTNW/LEA LU4 64 E6
NTHWD HA6 205 L6
Canterbury Rd BORE WD6 198 F3
WAT WD17 196 A3 2
Canterbury Wy
RKW/CH/CXG WD3 195 H4
STVG SG1 54 E8
Capella Rd NTHWD HA6 205 L5
Capell Av RKW/CH/CXG WD3 193 H6
Capell Rd RKW/CH/CXG WD3 193 J6
Capell Wy RKW/CH/CXG WD3 193 J6
Capel Rd EBAR EN4 201 K7
EN EN1 190 A7
OXHEY WD19 13 K8
Capelvere Wk WAT WD17 195 K2
Cape Rd STAL AL1 153 G7
Caponfield WGCE AL7 135 G6
Cappell La WARE SG12 139 H5
Capron Rd DUN/WHIP LU6 62 F8
LTNW/LEA LU4 64 D6
Captains Wk BERK HP4 147 J7
Caractacus Cottage Vw
WATW WD18 195 M8
Caractacus Gn WATW WD18 12 B9
Caravan La RKW/CH/CXG WD3 194 D8
Carbone Hl POTB/CUF EN6 174 C5
Carde Cl HERT/WAS SG14 136 E3
Cardiff Cl STVGE SG2 89 G3
Cardiff Gv LTN LU1 2 C6
Cardiff Rd LTN LU1 2 C7
WATW WD18 12 E8
Cardiff Wy ABLGY WD5 181 M3
Cardigan St LTN LU1 2 C6
Cardinal Av BORE WD6 199 G4
Cardinal Cl CHESW EN7 175 L5 1
Cardinal Gv STALW/RED AL3 169 G1
Cardy Rd HHW HP1 149 G8
Carew Rd NTHWD HA6 205 K6
Carew Wy OXHEY WD19 206 E3
Careys Cft BERK HP4 146 E3
Carfax Cl LTNW/LEA LU4 63 K7
Carisbrooke Av WATN WD24 196 C2
Carisbrooke Rd HARP AL5 109 H8
LTNW/LEA LU4 82 D1
Carisbrook Rd LCOL/BKTW AL2 169 G5
Carleton Ri WLYN AL6 112 A4 1
Carleton Rd CHES/WCR EN8 176 C6
Carlisle Av STALW/RED AL3 10 F3
Carlisle Cl DUN/WHIP LU6 81 G4
Carlton Cl BORE WD6 199 J5 1
LTNN/LIM LU3 65 H8
Carlton Crs LTNN/LIM LU3 65 H7
Carlton Rd HARP AL5 108 F8
Carman Ct TRING HP23 123 L7 1
Carmelite Rd
KTN/HRWW/W HA3 207 H8
LTNW/LEA LU4 63 M7
Carnaby Rd BROX EN10 159 K7
Carnarvon Rd BAR EN5 200 D4
Carnegie Gdns LTNN/LIM LU3 64 F2
Carnegie Rd STALW/RED AL3 152 C3
Caro La HHS/BOV HP3 166 F1
Carol Cl LTNN/LIM LU3 65 G6
Caroline Pl OXHEY WD19 13 K9
Caroon Dr RKW/CH/CXG WD3 180 A7
Carpenders Av OXHEY WD19 206 D3
Carpenders Cl HARP AL5 108 C6 1
Carpenters Cl TRDG/WHET N20 201 G7
Carpenters Rd EN EN1 190 B7
The Carpenters BSF CM23 96 B6 1
Carpenters Wood Dr
RKW/CH/CXG WD3 193 G5
Carpenter Wy POTB/CUF EN6 187 H4
Carrigans BSF CM23 96 D2
Carrington Av BORE WD6 199 G6
Carrington Cl BAR EN5 199 M6
Carrington Pl TRING HP23 124 A5
Carrington Sq
KTN/HRWW/W HA3 207 H7 1
Carsdale Cl LTNN/LIM LU3 64 F4 1
Carson Rd EBAR EN4 201 L5
Carteret Rd LTNE LU2 84 B1
Carters Cl ARL/CHE SG15 25 M3
STVGE SG2 71 J6
Cartersfield Rd WAB EN9 191 H5
Carters Hl BSF CM23 78 F1
Carters Lane
(Wibbly Wobbley Lane)
HTCH/STOT SG5 51 M3
Carters Leys BSF CM23 96 C2
Carters Md HLWE CM17 163 G3
Carters Wy ARL/CHE SG15 25 M3
Carterweys DUN/HR/TOD LU5 63 K8
Cartmel Dr DUN/WHIP LU6 81 G4
Cart Pth GSTN WD25 182 B4
Cartwright Rd ROY SG8 21 J5 1
STVG SG1 55 H8
Carve Ley WGCE AL7 135 G5
Carvers Cft KNEB SG3 113 G1
Cary Wk RAD WD7 184 A5
Cashio La LWTH SG6 39 M1
Caslon Wy LWTH SG6 39 L1
Cassandra Ga CHES/WCR EN8 176 E6
Cassiobridge Rd WATW WD18 195 K5
Cassio Dr WAT WD17 195 L2
Cassiobury Park Av
WATW WD18 195 K4
Cassio Rd WATW WD18 12 E4
Castellane Cl STAN HA7 207 L7 2
Castle Cl BUSH WD23 197 G7
HOD EN11 160 B1
Castle Croft Rd LTN LU1 82 F4
Castle Gate Wy BERK HP4 147 H4
Castle Hl BERK HP4 147 H4
Castle Hill Av BERK HP4 147 H5
Castle Hill Cl BERK HP4 147 G5
Castle Md HHW HP1 166 A1
Castle Ri STALE/WH AL4 109 L8
Castle Rd HOD EN11 160 A1
STAL AL1 153 G7
Castles Cl HTCH/STOT SG5 26 E3
Castle St BERK HP4 147 H6
BSF CM23 96 E4
HERT/BAY SG13 137 J5
HERT/WAS SG14 137 H4 3
LTN LU1 2 E9
Castle Vw BSF CM23 96 F3
Castlewood Rd EBAR EN4 201 J4
Catchacre DUN/WHIP LU6 80 F3
Caterham Ct WAB EN9 191 L5
Catesby Gn LTNN/LIM LU3 64 F1
Catham Cl STAL AL1 170 A1
Catherall Rd LTNN/LIM LU3 65 G4
Catherine Cl HHNE HP2 150 A2 1
Catherine Rd PEND EN3 190 D7
Catherine St STALW/RED AL3 10 F5
Cat Hl EBAR EN4 201 K7
Catisfield Rd PEND EN3 190 D8
Catkin Cl HHW HP1 149 G6
Catlin St HHS/BOV HP3 166 A2
Catsbrook Rd LTNN/LIM LU3 65 G4
Catsdell Bottom HHS/BOV HP3 167 G2
Catsey La BUSH WD23 197 H8
Catsey Wd BUSH WD23 197 H8
Catterick Wy BORE WD6 198 E2
Cattlegate Rd POTB/CUF EN6 188 C2
Cattlegate Road Crews Hl
ENC/FH EN2 188 E5
Cattley Cl BAR EN5 200 D5
Cattlins Cl CHESW EN7 175 K8
Cattsdell HHNE HP2 8 C4
Causeway Cl POTB/CUF EN6 187 J2
The Causeway BSF CM23 96 E3
BUNT SG9 58 D2
BUNT SG9 60 F1
POTB/CUF EN6 187 H2
ROY SG8 30 E2
STDN SG11 75 L3 1
Cautherly La WARE SG12 138 E5
Cavalier Cl LTNN/LIM LU3 64 F4
Cavalier Ct BERK HP4 147 H6 1
Cavan Dr STALW/RED AL3 152 C2
Cavan Rd STALW/RED AL3 129 M4
Cavell Rd CHESW EN7 175 L6
Cavell Wk STVGE SG2 71 H4
Cavendish Cl AMS HP6 192 A2
Cavendish Crs BORE WD6 198 F5
Cavendish Rd BAR EN5 200 B4
LTNN/LIM LU3 65 G8
STAL AL1 11 K7
STALW/RED AL3 106 C4
STVG SG1 69 M4
Cavendish Wy HAT AL10 154 E5
Cawkell Cl STSD CM24 79 J3
Caxton Hl HERT/BAY SG13 137 L4 3
Caxton Rd HOD EN11 139 G8
Caxton Wy STVG SG1 70 A6
WATW WD18 195 J8
Cecil Cl BSF CM23 97 J3
Cecil Ct BAR EN5 200 C4
HLWS CM18 162 B5

Cecil Crs *HAT* AL10 ... 155 G3
Cecil Rd *CHES/WCR* EN8 ... 190 C3
HERT/BAY SG13 ... 137 H7
HOD EN11 ... 160 B2
POTB/CUF EN6 ... 186 A3
STAL AL1 ... 11 K7
Cecil St *WATN* WD24 ... 196 A1
Cedar Av *CHES/WCR* EN8 ... 190 C4
EBAR EN4 ... 201 K8
HTCH/STOT SG5 ... 38 D6
Cedar Cl *HERT/WAS* SG14 ... 137 G4
LTNW/LEA LU4 ... 63 K7
POTB/CUF EN6 ... 186 F1
SBW CM21 ... 142 D1
WARE SG12 ... 138 C2
Cedar Ct *BSF* CM23 ... 96 E1
STALE/WH AL4 ... 153 J7
Cedar Crs *ROY* SG8 ... 21 G4
Cedar Dr *PIN* HA5 ... 206 F6
Cedar Gn *HOD* EN11 ... 159 M5
Cedar Lawn Av *BAR* EN5 ... 200 D6
Cedar Pk *BSF* CM23 ... 96 C6
Cedar Ri *STHGT/OAK* N14 ... 201 M8
Cedar Rd *BERK* HP4 ... 147 J7
HAT AL10 ... 154 F6
OXHEY WD19 ... 13 H9
Cedars Av *RKW/CH/CXG* WD3 ... 194 C8
Cedars Cl *BORE* WD6 ... 198 F5
CFSP/GDCR SL9 ... 202 D5
The Cedars *DUN/WHIP* LU6 ... 81 H3
Cedar Wk *HHS/BOV* HP3 ... 166 C1
Cedar Wy *BERK* HP4 ... 147 J7
Cedar Wood Dr *GSTN* WD25 ... 182 A6
Cedarwood Dr *STALE/WH* AL4 ... 153 J7
Celandine Dr *LTNN/LIM* LU3 ... 64 F2
Cell Barnes Cl *STAL* AL1 ... 170 A1
Cell Barnes La *STAL* AL1 ... 11 M9
Cemetery Hl *HHW* HP1 ... 149 H8
Cemetery Rd *BSF* CM23 ... 96 E5
DUN/HR/TOD LU5 ... 63 G6
Cemmaes Court Rd *HHW* HP1 ... 149 H6
Cemmaes Meadow *HHW* HP1 ... 149 H7
Central Av *CHES/WCR* EN8 ... 190 D4
DUN/WHIP LU6 ... 104 D2
HNLW SG16 ... 25 G7
Central Dr *STAL* AL1 ... 153 H6
WGCE AL7 ... 134 E2
Central Rd *HLW* CM20 ... 141 M6
Central Wy *NTHWD* HA6 ... 205 K7
Centre Wy *WAB* EN9 ... 191 H6
Century Rd *HOD* EN11 ... 159 M3
WARE SG12 ... 116 C8
Cervantes Ct *NTHWD* HA6 ... 205 L7
Chace Av *POTB/CUF* EN6 ... 187 J3
The Chace *STVGE* SG2 ... 88 E1
Chad La *STALW/RED* AL3 ... 107 H5
Chadwell *WARE* SG12 ... 138 B2
Chadwell Av *CHES/WCR* EN8 ... 176 B7
Chadwell Cl *LTNE* LU2 ... 3 H2
Chadwell Ri *WARE* SG12 ... 138 B2
Chadwell Rd *STVG* SG1 ... 70 A6
Chadwick Cl *DUN/WHIP* LU6 ... 80 F1
Chaffinches Gn
HHS/BOV HP3 ... 166 F3
Chaffinch La *WATW* WD18 ... 195 L8
Chagney Cl *LWTH* SG6 ... 39 K4
Chain Wk *BLDK* SG7 ... 19 J8
BUNT SG9 ... 43 G1
BUNT SG9 ... 57 H2
CHESW EN7 ... 189 H1
ENC/FH EN2 ... 188 F7
HERT/BAY SG13 ... 156 F2
HERT/WAS SG14 ... 90 C6
HERT/WAS SG14 ... 113 M8
HERT/WAS SG14 ... 135 M8
ROY SG8 ... 19 L7
ROY SG8 ... 30 D4
STVGE SG2 ... 72 F8
WARE SG12 ... 115 M1
Chalet Cl *BERK* HP4 ... 146 E6
Chalfont Av *AMS* HP6 ... 192 C2
Chalfont Cl *HHNE* HP2 ... 150 A2
Chalfont La *RKW/CH/CXG* WD3 ... 193 J6
RKW/CH/CXG WD3 ... 203 H7
Chalfont Rd *CFSP/GDCR* SL9 ... 203 G3
Chalfont Station Rd *AMSS* HP7 ... 192 B3
Chalfont Wy *LTNE* LU2 ... 66 B8
Chalgrove *WGCE* AL7 ... 135 J3
Chalk Dl *WGCE* AL7 ... 135 G3
Chalkdell Flds *STAL* AL1 ... 152 F4
Chalkdell Hl *HHNE* HP2 ... 8 D8
Chalkdown *LTNE* LU2 ... 65 J3
STVGE SG2 ... 71 J3
Chalk Fld *LWTH* SG6 ... 40 B7
Chalk Hl *LTNE* LU2 ... 66 E6
OXHEY WD19 ... 13 L8
Chalk Hills *BLDK* SG7 ... 40 E5
Chalk La *EBAR* EN4 ... 201 L4
HLWE CM17 ... 142 F8
Chalks Av *SBW* CM21 ... 120 C7
Challinor *HLWE* CM17 ... 163 K2
Challney Cl *LTNW/LEA* LU4 ... 64 C8
Chalton Hts *LTNW/LEA* LU4 ... 63 J1
Chalton Rd *LTNW/LEA* LU4 ... 64 B5
Chamberlain Cl *HLWE* CM17 ... 163 H2
Chamberlaines *HARP* AL5 ... 107 M5
Chambersbury La
HHS/BOV HP3 ... 166 F4
Chambers Ga *STVG* SG1 ... 70 C3
Chambers La *HTCH/STOT* SG5 ... 38 D6
Chambers' St *HERT/WAS* SG14 ... 137 H4
Champions Cl *BORE* WD6 ... 185 G8
Champions Wy *HOD* EN11 ... 159 M1
Chancellors Rd *STVG* SG1 ... 70 B1
Chancery Cl *STALE/WH* AL4 ... 153 J2
Chandlers Cl *BSF* CM23 ... 96 B6
Chandler's La
RKW/CH/CXG WD3 ... 180 D8
Chandlers Rd *STALE/WH* AL4 ... 153 H4
Chandlers Wy
HERT/WAS SG14 ... 136 F4
Chandos Cl *AMS* HP6 ... 192 B1
Chandos Rd *BORE* WD6 ... 198 E3
LTNW/LEA LU4 ... 82 E1
Chantry Cl *BSF* CM23 ... 96 D2
KGLGY WD4 ... 166 F8
Chantry La *HAT* AL10 ... 154 E6
HTCHE/RSTV SG4 ... 53 L8
LCOL/BKTW AL2 ... 170 C5
Chantry Pl *RYLN/HDSTN* HA2 ... 207 G8
Chantry Rd *BSF* CM23 ... 96 D2
KTN/HRWW/W HA3 ... 207 G8
The Chantry *HLW* CM20 ... 7 L2
Chaomans *LWTH* SG6 ... 39 L7
Chapel Cl *BERK* HP4 ... 126 C4
GSTN WD25 ... 181 L5
LTNE LU2 ... 65 H2
STAL AL1 ... 169 J2
Chapel Cottages *HHNE* HP2 ... 8 A5
Chapel Cft *KGLGY* WD4 ... 179 M2
Chapel Crofts *BERK* HP4 ... 146 D4
Chapel Dr *RAYLNE/WEN* HP22 ... 122 D5
Chapel End *BUNT* SG9 ... 58 D3
HOD EN11 ... 159 M5
Chapel End La *TRING* HP23 ... 123 H2
Chapel Flds *HLWE* CM17 ... 163 H4
Chapelfields *WARE* SG12 ... 139 J5
Chapel Hl *STSD* CM24 ... 79 J3
Chapel La *HERT/WAS* SG14 ... 136 A8
HLWE CM17 ... 163 H4
STDN SG11 ... 94 F2
TRING HP23 ... 101 G6
Chapel Pl *HTCH/STOT* SG5 ... 26 E5
Chapel Rd *HTCHE/RSTV* SG4 ... 85 K1
STALW/RED AL3 ... 107 G8
Chapel Rw *DEN/HRF* UB9 ... 204 B8
Chapel St *BERK* HP4 ... 147 H6
BGSW SG18 ... 14 C5
BLDK SG7 ... 17 J4
HHNE HP2 ... 8 A6
LTN LU1 ... 2 E7
TRING HP23 ... 123 L7
Chapel Viad *LTN* LU1 ... 2 D7
Chapel Wy *ABLGY* WD5 ... 167 L6
Chapman Rd *STVG* SG1 ... 70 A1
Chapmans End *STDN* SG11 ... 75 J7
Chapmans Yd *WAT* WD17 ... 13 H5
Chappell Ct *WARE* SG12 ... 115 K3
Chappel Meadow *TRING* HP23 ... 124 A4
Chapter House Rd
LTNW/LEA LU4 ... 63 M8
Chard Dr *LTNN/LIM* LU3 ... 65 G1
Chardins Cl *HHW* HP1 ... 148 E6
Charles St *BERK* HP4 ... 147 G6
HHW HP1 ... 149 H8
LTNE LU2 ... 3 G3
TRING HP23 ... 123 M7
Charlesworth Cl
HHS/BOV HP3 ... 166 C1
Charlock Wy *WATW* WD18 ... 12 B8
Charlotte Cl *STALE/WH* AL4 ... 153 K7
Charlton Cl *HOD* EN11 ... 159 M4
Charlton Mead La *HOD* EN11 ... 160 B5
Charlton Rd *HTCH/STOT* SG5 ... 52 C5
Charlton Wy *HOD* EN11 ... 159 M5
Charlwood Cl
KTN/HRWW/W HA3 ... 207 K6
Charlwood Rd *LTNW/LEA* LU4 ... 82 A1
Charmbury Ri *LTNE* LU2 ... 65 M6
Charmouth Ct *STAL* AL1 ... 11 L1
Charmouth Rd *STAL* AL1 ... 11 L3
Charndon Cl *LTNN/LIM* LU3 ... 65 G1
Charnwood Rd *EN* EN1 ... 190 A7
Charsley Cl *AMS* HP6 ... 192 B2
Charters Cross *HLWS* CM18 ... 162 C5
Chartley Av *STAN* HA7 ... 207 L6
Chartridge Cl *BAR* EN5 ... 199 M6
BUSH WD23 ... 197 H7
Chartridge Wy *HHNE* HP2 ... 9 L9
Chartwell Cl *WAB* EN9 ... 191 K4
Chartwell Dr *LTNE* LU2 ... 65 K7
Chartwell Rd *NTHWD* HA6 ... 205 L6
Charwood Cl *RAD* WD7 ... 184 D4
Chasden Rd *HHW* HP1 ... 148 E4
Chase Cl *ARL/CHE* SG15 ... 25 M2
Chase Hill Rd *ARL/CHE* SG15 ... 25 M3
Chase Side *STHGT/OAK* N14 ... 201 M6
Chaseside Cl *LBUZ* LU7 ... 101 M3
Chase St *LTN* LU1 ... 83 K5
The Chase *BSF* CM23 ... 96 E4
CHESW EN7 ... 175 G7
HERT/BAY SG13 ... 137 L5
HHNE HP2 ... 149 K8
RAD WD7 ... 183 L6
STAN HA7 ... 207 M6
WARE SG12 ... 138 F4
WATW WD18 ... 195 K5
WLYN AL6 ... 112 E3
Chaseways *SBW* CM21 ... 142 A2
Chasten Hl *LWTH* SG6 ... 39 J3
Chatsworth Cl *BORE* WD6 ... 198 F4
BSF CM23 ... 96 B3
Chatsworth Ct *STVGE* SG2 ... 88 E1
Chatsworth Rd *LTNW/LEA* LU4 ... 83 G1
Chatteris Cl *LTNW/LEA* LU4 ... 64 C6
Chatterton *LWTH* SG6 ... 40 A5
Chatton Cl *LTNE* LU2 ... 66 D8
Chaucer Cl *BERK* HP4 ... 146 E5
Chaucer Rd *LTNN/LIM* LU3 ... 2 B1
ROY SG8 ... 21 H2
Chaucer Wk *HHNE* HP2 ... 150 A1
Chaucer Wy *HOD* EN11 ... 138 F8
HTCHE/RSTV SG4 ... 53 H3
Chaulden House Gdns
HHW HP1 ... 165 L1
Chaulden La *HHW* HP1 ... 165 K1
Chaulden Ter *HHW* HP1 ... 148 E8
Chaul End La *LTNW/LEA* LU4 ... 82 D1
Chaul End Rd *LTN* LU1 ... 82 D6
Chauncy Av *POTB/CUF* EN6 ... 187 H4
Chauncy Cl *WARE* SG12 ... 116 B7
Chauncy Gdns *BLDK* SG7 ... 41 G1
Chauncy Rd *STVG* SG1 ... 4 F2
Chaworth Gn *LTNW/LEA* LU4 ... 64 B5
Cheapside *LTN* LU1 ... 2 F6
Cheapside Sq *LTN* LU1 ... 2 E6
Chedburgh *WGCE* AL7 ... 135 J3
Cheddington La *TRING* HP23 ... 101 H5
Cheddington Rd *LBUZ* LU7 ... 102 A5
Cheffins Rd *HOD* EN11 ... 159 L1
Chells La *STVGE* SG2 ... 71 H2
Chells Wy *STVGE* SG2 ... 71 G3
Chelmsford Rd
HERT/WAS SG14 ... 136 F5
Chelsea Flds *HOD* EN11 ... 139 G8
Chelsea Gdns *DUN/HR/TOD* LU5 ... 63 J5
HLWE CM17 ... 163 K3
Chelsing Ri *HHNE* HP2 ... 150 B8
Chelsworth Cl *LTNE* LU2 ... 84 C1
Chelveston *WGCE* AL7 ... 135 J3
Chelwood Av *HAT* AL10 ... 154 F3
Chelwood Cl *NTHWD* HA6 ... 205 H7
Chenduit Wy *STAN* HA7 ... 207 L5
Cheney Rd *LTNW/LEA* LU4 ... 64 B5
Chenies Av *AMS* HP6 ... 192 C2
Chenies Ct *HHNE* HP2 ... 150 A2
Chenies Rd *RKW/CH/CXG* WD3 ... 193 J3
Chenies Wy *WATW* WD18 ... 195 K8
Chennells *HAT* AL10 ... 154 E6
Chennells Cl *HTCHE/RSTV* SG4 ... 39 G8
The Chennies *HARP* AL5 ... 131 H3
Chepstow Cl *STVG* SG1 ... 71 G2
Chequer La *STALW/RED* AL3 ... 129 M6
Chequers *BRKMPK* AL9 ... 155 J2
BSF CM23 ... 96 B2
WGCE AL7 ... 134 C6
Chequers Bridge Rd *STVG* SG1 ... 4 A2
Chequers Cl *BUNT* SG9 ... 58 C2
HTCH/STOT SG5 ... 26 E4
LBUZ LU7 ... 102 B6
Chequers Fld *WGCE* AL7 ... 134 C7
Chequers Hl *STALW/RED* AL3 ... 107 H8
Chequers La *GSTN* WD25 ... 182 A1
HTCHE/RSTV SG4 ... 68 C3
LBUZ LU7 ... 102 B6
Chequer St *LTN* LU1 ... 2 F8
STAL AL1 ... 10 E7
Cheriton Cl *EBAR* EN4 ... 201 L5
STALE/WH AL4 ... 153 J3
Cherry Acre *CFSP/GDCR* SL9 ... 202 C4
Cherry Cl *KNEB* SG3 ... 88 E6
Cherry Cft *WGCW* AL8 ... 112 C8
Cherry Croft Gdns *PIN* HA5 ... 206 E7
Cherrydale *WATW* WD18 ... 12 A5
Cherry Dr *ROY* SG8 ... 21 K3
Cherry Gdns *BSF* CM23 ... 96 F2
SBW CM21 ... 120 D6
Cherry Hl *BAR* EN5 ... 201 G7
KTN/HRWW/W HA3 ... 207 K6
LCOL/BKTW AL2 ... 168 F4
RKW/CH/CXG WD3 ... 194 A4
Cherry Hollow *ABLGY* WD5 ... 181 L2
Cherry Orch *HHW* HP1 ... 148 E5
Cherry Ri *CSTG* HP8 ... 202 C2
Cherry Tree Av *LCOL/BKTW* AL2 ... 170 C5
Cherry Tree Cl *LTNE* LU2 ... 3 J2
ROY SG8 ... 19 M1
Cherry Tree Gn *HERT/WAS* SG14 ... 136 E2
Cherry Tree La *HHNE* HP2 ... 9 M2
Cherrytree La *HHNE* HP2 ... 150 B2
Cherry Tree La
RKW/CH/CXG WD3 ... 203 H1
STALE/WH AL4 ... 109 M8
Cherry Tree Ri *STVGE* SG2 ... 72 A1
Cherry Tree Rd *HOD* EN11 ... 159 M3
WATN WD24 ... 182 A7
Cherry Trees *HNLW* SG16 ... 25 G7
Cherry Wk *RKW/CH/CXG* WD3 ... 194 B3
Cherry Wy *HAT* AL10 ... 154 F8
Chertsey Cl *LTNE* LU2 ... 84 B2
Chertsey Ri *STVGE* SG2 ... 71 H6
Cherwell Cl *RKW/CH/CXG* WD3 ... 194 F6
Chesfield Cl *BSF* CM23 ... 96 E5
Chesford Rd *LTNE* LU2 ... 66 B7
Chesham La *CFSP/GDCR* SL9 ... 202 D4
Chesham Rd *BERK* HP4 ... 147 H7
HHS/BOV HP3 ... 164 D7
TRING HP23 ... 145 J2
Chesham Wy *WATW* WD18 ... 195 K7
Cheshunt Wash
CHES/WCR EN8 ... 176 D6
Cheslyn Cl *LTNE* LU2 ... 66 D8
Chess Cl *CSHM* HP5 ... 178 C7
RKW/CH/CXG WD3 ... 194 C5
Chessfield Pk *AMS* HP6 ... 192 D2
Chess Hl *RKW/CH/CXG* WD3 ... 194 C5
Chess La *RKW/CH/CXG* WD3 ... 194 C5
Chess Vale Ri
RKW/CH/CXG WD3 ... 194 E7
Chess Valley Wk *CSHM* HP5 ... 178 D8
Chess Wy *RKW/CH/CXG* WD3 ... 193 M4
Chester Av *LTNW/LEA* LU4 ... 64 D7
Chester Cl *LTNW/LEA* LU4 ... 64 E8
Chesterfield Rd *BAR* EN5 ... 200 C6
PEND EN3 ... 190 D8
Chester Rd *BORE* WD6 ... 199 H4
NTHWD HA6 ... 205 L7
STVG SG1 ... 70 F1
WATW WD18 ... 12 C6
Chesterton Av *HARP* AL5 ... 131 H1
Chestnut Av *HNLW* SG16 ... 25 G7
LTNN/LIM LU3 ... 64 A1
RKW/CH/CXG WD3 ... 193 M6
WARE SG12 ... 116 E7
Chestnut Cl *BERK* HP4 ... 104 B5
BERK HP4 ... 148 A4
BSF CM23 ... 96 E4
CFSP/GDCR SL9 ... 202 E8
RAYLNE/WEN HP22 ... 122 E5
WARE SG12 ... 140 C1
Chestnut Ct *HTCH/STOT* SG5 ... 52 C2
Chestnut Dr *BERK* HP4 ... 147 J7
KTN/HRWW/W HA3 ... 207 L7
STAL AL1 ... 153 G5
Chestnut Farm *HNLW* SG16 ... 25 J1
Chestnut Gv *EBAR* EN4 ... 201 L6
Chestnut Ri *BUSH* WD23 ... 197 G8
Chestnut Rd *PEND* EN3 ... 190 D7
The Chestnuts *HERT/BAY* SG13 ... 137 J5
HHS/BOV HP3 ... 165 L3
WLYN AL6 ... 87 L8
Chestnut Wk
CFSP/GDCR SL9 ... 202 D7
HTCHE/RSTV SG4 ... 52 F6
STVG SG1 ... 70 C1
WATN WD24 ... 181 M8
WLYN AL6 ... 112 E2
Chestnut Wy *RBSF* CM22 ... 99 H3
The Cheveralls *DUN/WHIP* LU6 ... 81 H4
Cheverells Cl *STALW/RED* AL3 ... 106 C5
Cheviot Cl *BUSH* WD23 ... 197 H7
Cheviot Rd *LTNN/LIM* LU3 ... 64 C3
Cheviots *HAT* AL10 ... 154 F8
HHNE HP2 ... 8 E3
Cheyne Cl *DUN/WHIP* LU6 ... 62 E7
LBUZ LU7 ... 102 C6
WARE SG12 ... 116 C7
Cheyney Cl *ROY* SG8 ... 19 G1
Chicheley Rd
KTN/HRWW/W HA3 ... 207 H7
Chichester Cl *DUN/HR/TOD* LU5 ... 81 J3
Chichester Wy *GSTN* WD25 ... 182 D4
Chicken La *LCOL/BKTW* AL2 ... 170 C6
Chilcote La *AMSS* HP7 ... 192 A2
Chilcott Rd *WATN* WD24 ... 181 K7
Chilcourt *ROY* SG8 ... 21 H4
Childwick Ct *HHS/BOV* HP3 ... 167 G2
Chilham Cl *HHS/BOV* HP3 ... 149 K8
Chiltern Av *BUSH* WD23 ... 197 H7
Chiltern Cl *BERK* HP4 ... 146 F5
BORE WD6 ... 198 E3
BUSH WD23 ... 197 G7
CHESW EN7 ... 175 G6
WARE SG12 ... 116 C7
Chiltern Dr *RKW/CH/CXG* WD3 ... 193 L8
Chiltern Gdns *LTNW/LEA* LU4 ... 64 E7
Chiltern Hl *CFSP/GDCR* SL9 ... 202 D8
Chiltern Pk *DUN/HR/TOD* LU5 ... 63 J8
Chiltern Park Av *BERK* HP4 ... 146 F4
Chiltern Pl *HNLW* SG16 ... 25 H1
Chiltern Ri *LTN* LU1 ... 2 C9
Chiltern Rd *AMP/FLIT/B* MK45 ... 35 H7
BLDK SG7 ... 40 E4
DUN/WHIP LU6 ... 80 F2
HTCHE/RSTV SG4 ... 52 F3
STALE/WH AL4 ... 153 H2
Chilterns *HAT* AL10 ... 154 F8
HHNE HP2 ... 8 D3
The Chilterns *DUN/WHIP* LU6 ... 105 L2
HTCHE/RSTV SG4 ... 52 F4
Chiltern Vw *LWTH* SG6 ... 39 J5
Chiltern Wy *RAYLNE/WEN* HP22 ... 122 E8
TRING HP23 ... 124 B5
Chilton Gn *WGCE* AL7 ... 135 H4
Chilvers Bank *BLDK* SG7 ... 40 D3
Chilwell Gdns *OXHEY* WD19 ... 206 B4
Chilworth Ga *BROX* EN10 ... 176 E1
Chindit Cl *BROX* EN10 ... 159 J7
Chinnery Hl *BSF* CM23 ... 96 E5
Chipperfield Rd *HHS/BOV* HP3 ... 165 G7
KGLGY WD4 ... 166 C8
Chipping Cl *BAR* EN5 ... 200 D4
Chippingfield *HLWE* CM17 ... 142 B7
Chipstead *CFSP/GDCR* SL9 ... 202 B8
Chishill Rd *ROY* SG8 ... 22 F8
ROY SG8 ... 23 L7
Chiswell Ct *WATN* WD24 ... 196 B1
Chiswellgreen La
LCOL/BKTW AL2 ... 168 D4
Chittenden Cl *HOD* EN11 ... 160 A1
Chobham St *LTN* LU1 ... 3 G8
Cholesbury La *TRING* HP23 ... 144 F8
Chorleywood Bottom
RKW/CH/CXG WD3 ... 193 J6
Chorleywood Cl
RKW/CH/CXG WD3 ... 194 C8
Chorleywood Rd
RKW/CH/CXG WD3 ... 194 A6
Chouler Gdns *STVG* SG1 ... 54 C8
The Chowns *HARP* AL5 ... 130 F5
Christchurch Cl *STALW/RED* AL3 ... 10 D6
Christchurch Crs *RAD* WD7 ... 183 M7
Christ Church La *BAR* EN5 ... 200 D3
Christchurch Rd *HHNE* HP2 ... 8 A7
TRING HP23 ... 123 L6
Christie Cl *BROX* EN10 ... 159 L8
Christie Rd *STVGE* SG2 ... 71 H5
Christy's Yd *BLDK* SG7 ... 17 J4
Church Cl *DUN/HR/TOD* LU5 ... 81 H2
NTHWD HA6 ... 205 L7
POTB/CUF EN6 ... 174 D8
RAD WD7 ... 183 M7
WLYN AL6 ... 87 L8
Church Crs *STALW/RED* AL3 ... 10 D5
Church Cft *STALE/WH* AL4 ... 170 B1
Church End *ARL/CHE* SG15 ... 25 M3
DUN/HR/TOD LU5 ... 63 G5
HLWW/ROY CM19 ... 161 M4
ROY SG8 ... 32 F1
STALE/WH AL4 ... 132 B8
STALW/RED AL3 ... 106 C4
STALW/RED AL3 ... 129 H1
STALW/RED AL3 ... 129 M6
STDN SG11 ... 75 L3
STVGE SG2 ... 56 B8
Church Farm La *ROY* SG8 ... 19 G1
TRING HP23 ... 101 L7
Church Farm Wy
GSTN WD25 ... 197 G1
Churchfield *HARP* AL5 ... 131 H2
HLW CM20 ... 7 M3
HLW CM20 ... 142 A8
ROY SG8 ... 32 F1
Church Fld *WARE* SG12 ... 116 A7
Church Field Pth
CHES/WCR EN8 ... 176 B8
Churchfield Rd
CFSP/GDCR SL9 ... 202 C8
DUN/HR/TOD LU5 ... 63 G5
WLYN AL6 ... 135 H1
Churchfields *BROX* EN10 ... 159 M7
HERT/BAY SG13 ... 137 J5
STDN SG11 ... 75 K8
STSD CM24 ... 79 L4
Churchfields La *BROX* EN10 ... 159 M7
Churchgate *CHES/WCR* EN8 ... 190 A1
Churchgate Rd *CHES/WCR* EN8 ... 176 A8
Churchgate St *HLWE* CM17 ... 142 D6
Church Gn *DUN/WHIP* LU6 ... 80 A3
HARP AL5 ... 130 F1
Church Gv *AMS* HP6 ... 192 D2
Church Hl *ABLGY* WD5 ... 167 L5
HERT/BAY SG13 ... 138 A6
LBUZ LU7 ... 101 L2
Church Hill Rd *EBAR* EN4 ... 201 L8
Churchill Cl *LTNN/LIM* LU3 ... 48 E5
Churchill Rd
AMP/FLIT/B MK45 ... 35 H7
DUN/WHIP LU6 ... 81 J5
LTNW/LEA LU4 ... 82 F1
STAL AL1 ... 11 M4
Church La *ARL/CHE* SG15 ... 25 M2
BERK HP4 ... 147 H6
BLDK SG7 ... 18 C6
BRKMPK AL9 ... 155 H5
BROX EN10 ... 176 C2
BSF CM23 ... 96 C8
CFSP/GDCR SL9 ... 202 C8
CHES/WCR EN8 ... 176 B8
GSTN WD25 ... 197 G1
HERT/WAS SG14 ... 114 F4
HHS/BOV HP3 ... 165 G6
HTCHE/RSTV SG4 ... 54 B6
HTCHE/RSTV SG4 ... 55 J1
HTCHE/RSTV SG4 ... 68 C4
HTCHE/RSTV SG4 ... 86 C8
KGLGY WD4 ... 180 F1
KTN/HRWW/W HA3 ... 207 L8
LBUZ LU7 ... 101 M3
LWTH SG6 ... 40 B1
MHAD SG10 ... 94 E7
POTB/CUF EN6 ... 187 L1
RAYLNE/WEN HP22 ... 122 C6
RBSF CM22 ... 99 G3
RBSF CM22 ... 143 J2
RKW/CH/CXG WD3 ... 179 M8
RKW/CH/CXG WD3 ... 203 M1
ROY SG8 ... 15 L5
ROY SG8 ... 30 E3
ROY SG8 ... 31 K5
ROY SG8 ... 32 B6
STALE/WH AL4 ... 171 G1
STVG SG1 ... 70 B3
TRING HP23 ... 123 L1
TRING HP23 ... 144 E3
WARE SG12 ... 91 L2
Church Langley Wy
HLWE CM17 ... 163 H2
Church Leys *HLWS* CM18 ... 7 K9
Church Md *DUN/WHIP* LU6 ... 105 G6
HLWW/ROY CM19 ... 161 G1
Churchmead Cl *EBAR* EN4 ... 201 K7
Church Pth *HTCHE/RSTV* SG4 ... 53 L7
Church Pl *WLYN* AL6 ... 112 B5
Church Rd *AMP/FLIT/B* MK45 ... 34 D2
AMP/FLIT/B MK45 ... 35 H8
BERK HP4 ... 126 B2
BERK HP4 ... 148 A4
DUN/WHIP LU6 ... 80 A4
DUN/WHIP LU6 ... 105 G6
HERT/BAY SG13 ... 157 H6
HERT/WAS SG14 ... 137 G3
HHS/BOV HP3 ... 150 B8
HLWE CM17 ... 163 H5
HTCH/STOT SG5 ... 26 E4
HTCHE/RSTV SG4 ... 67 K7
LBUZ LU7 ... 102 D5
LBUZ LU7 ... 102 D8
LTN LU1 ... 83 H8
LTNN/LIM LU3 ... 48 A7
LTNN/LIM LU3 ... 48 F4
NTHWD HA6 ... 205 L7
POTB/CUF EN6 ... 187 G1
RBSF CM22 ... 97 H8
RBSF CM22 ... 97 M5
STALW/RED AL3 ... 107 G8
STSD CM24 ... 79 L5
WAT WD17 ... 195 M2
WGCW AL8 ... 134 C4
Church St *BGSW* SG18 ... 14 C5
BLDK SG7 ... 40 D2
BRKMPK AL9 ... 155 H4
BRKMPK AL9 ... 156 D4
BSF CM23 ... 96 E3
BUNT SG9 ... 58 D2
DUN/HR/TOD LU5 ... 81 H2
HERT/WAS SG14 ... 137 J4
HHNE HP2 ... 8 A5
HHS/BOV HP3 ... 165 G6
HTCH/STOT SG5 ... 36 D2
LTN LU1 ... 2 F7
RKW/CH/CXG WD3 ... 204 D1
ROY SG8 ... 15 L6
ROY SG8 ... 19 G1
SBW CM21 ... 120 D8
STALE/WH AL4 ... 132 C2
STALW/RED AL3 ... 10 F5
WAB EN9 ... 191 H4
WARE SG12 ... 138 C1
WATW WD18 ... 13 G4
WLYN AL6 ... 112 B5
Church Vw *BROX* EN10 ... 159 L7
TRING HP23 ... 100 F6
Church View Av
HTCH/STOT SG5 ... 36 D1
Church Wk *BUSH* WD23 ... 196 F7
DUN/HR/TOD LU5 ... 81 G2
SBW CM21 ... 120 E8
Church Yd *TRING* HP23 ... 123 M6
Cicero Dr *LTNN/LIM* LU3 ... 64 F2
Cillocks Cl *HOD* EN11 ... 159 M3
Claggy Rd *HTCHE/RSTV* SG4 ... 86 A8
Clamp Hl *KTN/HRWW/W* HA3 ... 207 J4
Clapgate Rd *BUSH* WD23 ... 197 G7
Clare Cl *BORE* WD6 ... 198 E7
Clare Ct *NTHWD* HA6 ... 205 K5
Clare Crs *BLDK* SG7 ... 40 E4
Claremont *CHESW* EN7 ... 175 L8
LCOL/BKTW AL2 ... 182 F2
Claremont Crs
RKW/CH/CXG WD3 ... 195 H6
Claremont Rd *EBAR* EN4 ... 201 H1
LTNW/LEA LU4 ... 83 G1
Clarence Cl *BUSH* WD23 ... 197 L8
Clarence Rd *BERK* HP4 ... 147 H6
HARP AL5 ... 108 F8
STAL AL1 ... 11 K6
STSD CM24 ... 79 K3
Clarendon Cl *HHNE* HP2 ... 8 B6
Clarendon Ms *BORE* WD6 ... 198 F4
Clarendon Rd *BORE* WD6 ... 198 F4
CHES/WCR EN8 ... 176 C8
HARP AL5 ... 109 G7
LTNE LU2 ... 2 D3
RBSF CM22 ... 99 K3
WAT WD17 ... 12 F3
Clarion Cl *HTCH/STOT* SG5 ... 51 H8
Clarke's Rd *HAT* AL10 ... 155 G4
Clarke's Spring *TRING* HP23 ... 124 E5
Clarkes Wy *DUN/HR/TOD* LU5 ... 63 H6

Clarke Wy GSTN WD25 181 M6
Clarkfield RKW/CH/CXG WD3 203 M1
Clarkhill HLWS CM18 162 D6
Clark Rd ROY SG8 21 J3
Clarks Cl WARE SG12 116 C7
Clarks Md BUSH WD23 197 H8
Claudian Pl STALW/RED AL3 168 F1
Claverhambury Rd WAB EN9 177 L8
Claverley Gn LTNE LU2 66 D8
Claverton Cl HHS/BOV HP3 164 F7
Claybury BUSH WD23 197 G8
Claybush Rd BLDK SG7 18 C7
Claycroft WGCE AL7 135 G3 2
Claydon Cl LTNN/LIM LU3 65 H3
Claydown Wy LTN LU1 107 G1
Claygate Av HARP AL5 108 D8
Clay Hall Rd DUN/WHIP LU6 105 L3
Clay Hl ENC/FH EN2 189 H8
Clay La BUSH WD23 197 K8
Claymore HHNE HP2 149 K3
Claymore Dr HTCH/STOT SG5 38 E5
Claymores STVG SG1 4 E2
Clayponds BSF CM23 96 F3
Clayton Wk AMSS HP7 192 B2
Cleall Av WAB EN9 191 H5
The Cleave HARP AL5 131 J1
Clement Rd CHES/WCR EN8 176 D6 1
Clements End Rd
DUN/WHIP LU6 105 K8
Clements Rd
RKW/CH/CXG WD3 193 J6
Clements St WARE SG12 138 D1
Clevedon Rd LTNE LU2 66 A8
Cleveland Crs BORE WD6 199 H6
Cleveland Rd HHNE HP2 9 J5
STALW/RED AL3 106 D5
Cleves Rd HHNE HP2 150 A2
Cleviscroft STVG SG1 4 F5
Clewer Crs KTN/HRWW/W HA3 207 J8
Clifford Crs LTNW/LEA LU4 64 B5
Clifford Rd BAR EN5 201 G4
Clifton Cl CHES/WCR EN8 176 D8
Clifton Hatch HLWS CM18 162 F5 1
Clifton Rd DUN/WHIP LU6 80 F1
HNLW SG16 25 H1
LTN LU1 83 G2
WATW WD18 12 F6
Clifton St STAL AL1 11 G5
Clifton Wy BORE WD6 198 F2
WARE SG12 116 C7
The Climb RKW/CH/CXG WD3 194 A7
Clinton Av LTNE LU2 65 L6
Clinton End HHNE HP2 9 M9
Clipped Hedge RBSF CM22 121 M7
Clitheroe Gdns OXHEY WD19 206 C3
Clive Cl POTB/CUF EN6 186 E2
Clive Wy WATN WD24 196 B2
Cloister Garth BERK HP4 147 H6
STAL AL1 169 K3 1
Cloister Lawns LWTH SG6 39 L6
Cloisters Rd LTNW/LEA LU4 64 A7
LWTH SG6 39 L6
The Cloisters
RKW/CH/CXG WD3 194 D8
WGCW AL8 134 C4
Clonard Wy PIN HA5 206 F6
Closemead Cl NTHWD HA6 205 H6 1
The Close BLDK SG7 40 D3
BRKMPK AL9 172 D5
BUNT SG9 42 C4
BUSH WD23 197 G7 2
EBAR EN4 201 L7
HARP AL5 108 C6
LTNN/LIM LU3 64 F5
POTB/CUF EN6 186 F3
RAD WD7 183 L4
RBSF CM22 121 M7
RKW/CH/CXG WD3 204 A1
ROY SG8 21 L3
STAL AL1 169 H2 1
STALW/RED AL3 106 D5
WARE SG12 138 D1
WLYN AL6 111 L1
Clothall Rd BLDK SG7 40 E2
Clovelly Wy STVG SG1 69 M3
Clover Av BSF CM23 96 A4
Clover Cl LTNW/LEA LU4 63 L7
Clover Fld HLWS CM18 162 F5
Cloverfield WGCE AL7 134 E1
The Clover Fld BUSH WD23 196 E7
Cloverland HAT AL10 154 E8
Clover Wy HHW HP1 149 G6
The Clump RKW/CH/CXG WD3 193 M6
Clusterbolts HERT/WAS SG14 114 F4
Clutterbucks
RKW/CH/CXG WD3 179 M7
Clyde Rd HOD EN11 160 C6
Clydesdale Cl BORE WD6 199 J6
Clydesdale Rd LTNW/LEA LU4 63 M7
ROY SG8 21 K4 1
Clyde Sq HHNE HP2 149 L2 1
Clyde Ter HERT/BAY SG13 137 M4
Clyfton Cl BROX EN10 176 E2
Clyston Rd WATW WD18 12 B9
Coach Dr HTCHE/RSTV SG4 52 E5
The Coach House
AMP/FLIT/B MK45 35 H7
Coachman's La BLDK SG7 40 C2
Coach Rd HNLW SG16 25 J1
Coalport Cl HLWE CM17 163 H3
Coates Dell GSTN WD25 182 D4
Coates Rd BORE WD6 198 C8
Coates Wy GSTN WD25 182 C4
Cobbett Cl PEND EN3 190 B7
Cobbetts Ride TRING HP23 123 L7
Cobb Gn GSTN WD25 182 A3
The Cobbins WAB EN9 191 K3
Cobbins Wy HLWE CM17 142 D6
Cobb Rd BERK HP4 146 E6
Cob Cl BORE WD6 199 H6
Cobden Hl RAD WD7 184 A7
Cobden St LTNE LU2 2 F3
Cobham Rd WARE SG12 116 E8
Cobmead HAT AL10 155 G3
Cockbush Av HERT/BAY SG13 137 M3
Cocker Rd EN EN1 190 A7
Cockfosters Rd EBAR EN4 201 L1
Cockhall Cl ROY SG8 19 M1
Cockhall La ROY SG8 19 M1
Cock La BROX EN10 159 H6
SAFWS CB11 47 L7
Cockle Wy RAD WD7 184 D4
Cockrobin La HLW CM20 140 F3
Codicote Dr GSTN WD25 182 C5
Codicote Rd HTCHE/RSTV SG4 86 E4
STALE/WH AL4 132 C1
WLYN AL6 110 E8
Codicote Rw HHNE HP2 149 M2
Codmore Wood Rd CSHM HP5 178 B4
Cohen Cl CHES/WCR EN8 190 D3
Coke's Farm La CSTG HP8 192 A4
Coke's La CSTG HP8 192 B3
Colburn Av PIN HA5 206 D6
Cold Christmas La WARE SG12 116 C4
Coldham Gv PEND EN3 190 D8 1
Coldharbour La BUSH WD23 197 G7
HARP AL5 109 G6
Coldharbour Rd
HLWW/ROY CM19 161 M3
Colebrook Av LTNN/LIM LU3 64 B3
Cole Green La WGCE AL7 134 E6
Cole Green Wy HERT/WAS SG14 136 F6
Coleman Green La
STALE/WH AL4 132 E5
Coleman's La WAB EN9 177 J5
Colemans Rd HTCHE/RSTV SG4 85 J1
Coleridge Cl CHESW EN7 175 L6
HTCHE/RSTV SG4 53 G2
Coleridge Crs HHNE HP2 150 A1
Cole Rd WAT WD17 196 A2
Colesdale POTB/CUF EN6 188 D1
Coles Gn BUSH WD23 207 H1
Coles Hl HHW HP1 148 F5
Colestrete STVG SG1 5 H5
Colestrete Cl STVG SG1 5 H4
Coleswood Rd HARP AL5 131 H3
Colgrove WGCW AL8 134 B5
Colindale Av STAL AL1 169 L1
Colin Rd LTNE LU2 3 G1
College Av KTN/HRWW/W HA3 207 K8
College Cl BSF CM23 96 C3
KTN/HRWW/W HA3 207 K7
STALW/RED AL3 129 G1
WARE SG12 138 C2 1
College Ct CHES/WCR EN8 190 B1 1
College Hill Rd
KTN/HRWW/W HA3 207 K7
College La HAT AL10 154 D7
College Pl STALW/RED AL3 10 D6
College Rd ABLGY WD5 181 M2
CHES/WCR EN8 190 C1
CHESW EN7 190 A1
HERT/BAY SG13 138 B8
HOD EN11 159 L2
KTN/HRWW/W HA3 207 K8
RAYLNE/WEN HP22 122 B2
STAL AL1 153 G8
College Sq HLW CM20 6 D6
College St STALW/RED AL3 10 E6
College Wy NTHWD HA6 205 J6
WGCW AL8 134 C3
Collens Rd HARP AL5 131 G5
Collenswood Rd STVGE SG2 5 L5
Collet Cl CHES/WCR EN8 176 C7
Collett Rd HHW HP1 149 H7
WARE SG12 116 C8
Colley Land RKW/CH/CXG WD3 193 J5
Collingdon St LTN LU1 2 C5
Collingtree LTNE LU2 66 A6 1
Collingwood Dr
LCOL/BKTW AL2 170 C4 1
Collins Cross BSF CM23 97 G1
Collins Meadow
HLWW/ROY CM19 6 A8
Collison Cl HTCHE/RSTV SG4 39 H8
Collyer Rd LCOL/BKTW AL2 170 C6
Colmer Pl KTN/HRWW/W HA3 207 J7
Colnbrook Cl
LCOL/BKTW AL2 170 D6 2
Colne Av OXHEY WD19 12 F9
RKW/CH/CXG WD3 203 M2
Colne Gdns LCOL/BKTW AL2 170 D6
Colne Md RKW/CH/CXG WD3 203 M2
Colne Valley Trail
RKW/CH/CXG WD3 204 B2
Colne Wy HHNE HP2 149 L2
Colney Heath La STALE/WH AL4 153 K8
Colonial Wy WATN WD24 196 B2
The Colonnade
CHES/WCR EN8 176 C7 2
Colonsay HHS/BOV HP3 167 H1
Colston Crs CHESW EN7 175 G6
Colts Cnr STVGE SG2 5 L6
Colts Cft ROY SG8 23 K8
Coltsfield STSD CM24 79 K3
Coltsfoot WGCE AL7 135 G6
Coltsfoot Dr ROY SG8 21 K4
Coltsfoot Gn LTNW/LEA LU4 63 M5
Coltsfoot La KNEB SG3 113 J3
Coltsfoot Rd WARE SG12 116 D7
The Coltsfoot HHW HP1 148 D8
The Colts BSF CM23 96 D7
Columbus Cl STVG SG1 70 F3
Columbus Gdns NTHWD HA6 205 M8 1
Colvin Gdns CHES/WCR EN8 190 C6
Colwell Ri LTNE LU2 66 D8
Colwell Rd STVGE SG2 71 H7
Colwyn Cl STVG SG1 70 A2
Colyer Cl WLYN AL6 112 E7
Combe Rd WATW WD18 12 A9
Combe St HHW HP1 149 H7 1
Comet Cl GSTN WD25 181 L5
Comet Rd HAT AL10 154 E5
Comet Wy HAT AL10 154 F2
Common Fld TRING HP23 145 J1
Commonfields HLW CM20 7 H3
Common Gdns BERK HP4 148 A4
Common Gate Rd
RKW/CH/CXG WD3 193 J6
Common La BLDK SG7 18 A4
GSTN WD25 197 K1
HARP AL5 109 J5
HTCHE/RSTV SG4 110 A1
KGLGY WD4 166 E7
Common Ri HTCHE/RSTV SG4 52 F1
Common Rd DUN/WHIP LU6 104 F7
HTCH/STOT SG5 26 D2
RKW/CH/CXG WD3 193 J5
STAN HA7 207 J3
WAB EN9 161 K8
Commonside Rd HLWS CM18 162 E6
Commons La HHNE HP2 8 D7
The Commons WGCE AL7 134 F7
The Common BERK HP4 147 L4
BERK HP4 148 A4
HARP AL5 108 A6
HAT AL10 154 F4
KGLGY WD4 179 M3
STAN HA7 207 L2
Common Vw LWTH SG6 39 M2
Common Whf WARE SG12 138 D1 1
Compton Av LTNW/LEA LU4 64 C6
Compton Gdns LCOL/BKTW AL2 169 G5
Compton Pl OXHEY WD19 206 D4
Comyne Rd WATN WD24 181 L7
The Comyns BUSH WD23 207 H1
Concorde Dr HHNE HP2 8 B8
Concorde St LTNE LU2 3 G4
Conduit La BUNT SG9 60 B1
HOD EN11 159 M4
Conduit La East HOD EN11 160 A4
Coney Cl HAT AL10 155 G7 2
Coneydale WGCW AL8 134 C2
Coney Gn SBW CM21 120 C7
Congreve Rd WAB EN9 191 K4
Conifer Cl CHESW EN7 175 L8
The Conifers GSTN WD25 182 B6 2
Conifer Wk STVGE SG2 71 H3
Coningesby Dr WAT WD17 195 K2
Coningsby Bank STAL AL1 169 H3
Coningsby Cl BRKMPK AL9 172 C3 1
Coningsby Dr POTB/CUF EN6 187 J4
Coniston Cl HHS/BOV HP3 150 B8 2
Coniston Rd KGLGY WD4 166 E7
LTNN/LIM LU3 64 E5
Connaught Cl HHNE HP2 9 G5
Connaught Gdns BERK HP4 146 E3 2
Connaught Rd BAR EN5 200 C7
HARP AL5 109 G8 1
KTN/HRWW/W HA3 207 L8
LTNW/LEA LU4 82 E1
STALW/RED AL3 10 D2
Connemara Cl BORE WD6 199 J7 1
Conner's Cl ROY SG8 15 L6
Conquerors Hl STALE/WH AL4 132 D2
Conquest Cl HTCHE/RSTV SG4 52 E5
Conquest Rd DUN/HR/TOD LU5 63 K5
Constable Cl DUN/HR/TOD LU5 63 J5
Constantine Cl STVG SG1 70 E1 1
Constantine Pl BLDK SG7 41 G1 2
Convent Cl HTCH/STOT SG5 52 E2
Conway Cl DUN/HR/TOD LU5 63 K5
STAN HA7 207 M6
Conway Rd LTNW/LEA LU4 83 G1
Conybury Cl WAB EN9 191 M3
Conyers HLW CM20 6 C2
Cookfield Cl DUN/WHIP LU6 80 D2
Cook Rd STVGE SG2 71 G3
Cooks Md BUSH WD23 197 G7
Cooks Spinney HLW CM20 7 L4
Cooks Vennel HHW HP1 149 G5 1
Cooks Wy HAT AL10 155 G7
HTCHE/RSTV SG4 52 F2
Coombe Dr DUN/WHIP LU6 80 D3
Coombe Gdns BERK HP4 146 E5
Coombe Hill Rd
RKW/CH/CXG WD3 193 M8
Coombehurst Cl EBAR EN4 201 L3
Coombelands Rd ROY SG8 21 K2
Coombe Rd BUSH WD23 197 H8
ROY SG8 30 A1
Coombes Rd LCOL/BKTW AL2 170 B5
Cooper Cl HNLW SG16 24 D8 1
Coopers Cl BSF CM23 96 A6
HTCHE/RSTV SG4 110 A2
STVGE SG2 71 J6
Coopers Crs BORE WD6 199 H2
Coopers Green La HAT AL10 154 B1
STALE/WH AL4 153 L4
WGCW AL8 133 L8
Cooper's Hl HTCHE/RSTV SG4 110 A1
Coopers La POTB/CUF EN6 173 K8
Coopers Lane Rd
POTB/CUF EN6 187 M4
Coopers Meadow
STALW/RED AL3 129 M4
Coopers Rd POTB/CUF EN6 187 H1
Coopers Wy DUN/HR/TOD LU5 62 F6
Cooters End La HARP AL5 108 E6
Copenhagen Cl LTNN/LIM LU3 64 C2
Copmans Wick
RKW/CH/CXG WD3 193 J6
The Coppens HTCH/STOT SG5 26 F5
Copper Beech Cl HHW HP1 165 L2
Copper Beeches HARP AL5 131 G1
WLYN AL6 112 C3 1
Copperfields LTNW/LEA LU4 64 A6
ROY SG8 21 H4 1
WGCE AL7 135 H5 3
Copperfields Cl
DUN/HR/TOD LU5 63 J6
Coppermill La
RKW/CH/CXG WD3 203 L7
Copper Rdg CFSP/GDCR SL9 202 E5
Copperwood HERT/BAY SG13 137 L4 4
Coppice Cl HAT AL10 171 L1
KTN/HRWW/W HA3 207 L6 2
Coppice Md HTCH/STOT SG5 26 D5
The Coppice HHNE HP2 9 J6
OXHEY WD19 13 G9
TRING HP23 145 J1
The Coppings HOD EN11 159 M1 3
Coppins Cl BERK HP4 146 D6
The Coppins
KTN/HRWW/W HA3 207 K6
STALW/RED AL3 106 C5
Copse Cl NTHWD HA6 205 H8
Copse Hl HLWW/ROY CM19 162 A5
WLYN AL6 112 F2
Copse Hill Cl HHS/BOV HP3 165 J7
The Copse BSF CM23 97 H2 1
HERT/BAY SG13 137 M4
HHW HP1 148 D5
Copse Wy LTNN/LIM LU3 64 C2
Copsewood Rd WATN WD24 196 A2
Copse Wood Wy NTHWD HA6 205 H8
Copshall Cl HLWS CM18 162 D6
Copthall Cl CFSP/GDCR SL9 202 E7
Copthall Cnr CFSP/GDCR SL9 202 D7
Copthall La CFSP/GDCR SL9 202 D7
Copthorne LTNE LU2 66 C7
Copthorne Av BROX EN10 159 L7
Copthorne Cl
RKW/CH/CXG WD3 194 E6 1
Copthorne Rd
RKW/CH/CXG WD3 194 E7
Coral Gdns HHNE HP2 8 E7
Corals Md WGCE AL7 134 C5
Coram Cl BERK HP4 147 H7
Corbar Cl EBAR EN4 201 J1
Corbridge Dr LTNE LU2 66 D8
Corby Cl LCOL/BKTW AL2 168 F4
Cordell Cl CHES/WCR EN8 176 D7 2
Corder Cl STALW/RED AL3 168 F2
Coreys Mill La STVG SG1 70 A1
Corfe Cl HHS/BOV HP3 149 K8 1
Corinium Gdns LTNN/LIM LU3 64 F2 2
Corinium Ga STALW/RED AL3 168 F1
Corncastle Rd LTN LU1 2 B9
Corncrake Cl LTNE LU2 66 B5
Corncroft HAT AL10 155 G3 1
Cornel Cl LTN LU1 82 F3
Cornerfield HAT AL10 155 G2
Corner Hall HHS/BOV HP3 166 C1 2
Corner Hall Av HHS/BOV HP3 166 C1
Corner Meadow HLWS CM18 162 F6
Corners WGCE AL7 134 F3 1
Corner Wd STALW/RED AL3 106 C5
Cornfield Crs BERK HP4 146 C3
Cornfield Rd BUSH WD23 197 G5
Cornfields HHW HP1 149 G8
STVGE SG2 71 H3 1
Cornhill Dr PEND EN3 190 D8 2
Corn Md WGCW AL8 134 B1
Cornwall Cl CHES/WCR EN8 190 D4
Cornwall Rd HARP AL5 109 G8
PIN HA5 206 E7
STAL AL1 169 K1
Coronation Av ROY SG8 21 H5
Coronation Rd BSF CM23 96 D5
WARE SG12 116 C8
Corringham Ct STAL AL1 11 J5
Corton Cl STVG SG1 70 A2
Cory-wright Wy STALE/WH AL4 132 D1
Cosgrove Wy LTN LU1 82 C2
Cotefield LTNW/LEA LU4 64 B7 1
Cotesmore Rd HHW HP1 148 D8
Cotlandswick LCOL/BKTW AL2 170 B4
Cotney Cft STVGE SG2 71 J7
Cotswold Av BUSH WD23 197 H7
Cotswold Business Pk LTN LU1 82 C8
Cotswold Cl STALE/WH AL4 153 H2 2
Cotswold Gdns LTNN/LIM LU3 64 B3
Cotswolds HAT AL10 154 F7
Cottage Cl RKW/CH/CXG WD3 194 E7
WAT WD17 195 L3
Cottage Gdns CHES/WCR EN8 176 B8
Cottered Rd BUNT SG9 57 L1
Cotterells HHS/BOV HP3 166 B1 1
HHW HP1 166 B1
Cotterells Hl HHW HP1 149 H7
Cotton Dr HERT/BAY SG13 138 A3 2
Cotton Fld HAT AL10 155 G3
Cottonmill Crs STAL AL1 10 F9
Cottonmill La STAL AL1 169 J1
Cotton Rd POTB/CUF EN6 187 H2
Coulser Cl HHW HP1 148 F4
Coulter Cl POTB/CUF EN6 174 C6
Council Rd BSF CM23 97 G3
Counters Cl HHW HP1 148 F7
County Ga TRDG/WHET N20 201 G7
Coursers Rd STALE/WH AL4 170 F6
Courtaulds KGLGY WD4 180 A1
Court Dr DUN/HR/TOD LU5 81 G1
Courtenay Av
KTN/HRWW/W HA3 207 G7
Courtfield Cl BROX EN10 159 M7 1
Courtfields HARP AL5 131 J1
Courtlands Cl WATN WD24 181 K6
Courtlands Dr WAT WD17 181 K7
Courtleigh Av EBAR EN4 201 J1
The Courtway OXHEY WD19 206 D2
The Courtyard STALE/WH AL4 153 L7
Covent Garden Cl LTNW/LEA LU4 64 E7
Coventry Cl STVG SG1 71 G1
Coverdale LTNW/LEA LU4 64 A4
Covert Cl BERK HP4 146 C4
Covert Rd BERK HP4 146 C3
The Covert NTHWD HA6 205 H8
Covert Wy EBAR EN4 201 H3
Cowards La WLYN AL6 111 L2
Cowbridge HERT/WAS SG14 137 H4
Cowdray Cl LTNE LU2 66 B7 1
Cow La BUSH WD23 196 F7 2
GSTN WD25 182 B7
TRING HP23 124 C6
Cowles CHESW EN7 175 L6
Cowley Hl BORE WD6 184 F8
BORE WD6 199 G1
Cowlins HLWE CM17 142 C6 1
Cowper Ct STALW/RED AL3 106 C5
WATN WD24 181 M8 2
Cowper Crs HERT/WAS SG14 137 G1
Cowper Ri STALW/RED AL3 106 C5
Cowper Rd BERK HP4 147 G6
HARP AL5 131 G1
HHW HP1 149 G8
STALW/RED AL3 106 C5
WGCE AL7 134 E6
Cowper St LTN LU1 83 K5
Cowpers Wy WLYN AL6 113 J5
Cowridge Crs LTNE LU2 3 K4
Cowslip Hl LWTH SG6 39 K3
Cox Cl RAD WD7 184 D3
Cox Ley RBSF CM22 121 M7
Cox's Wy ARL/CHE SG15 25 M5
Coyney Gn LTNN/LIM LU3 2 A3
Cozens La East BROX EN10 176 E1
Cozens La West BROX EN10 176 D1
Cozens Rd WARE SG12 116 E8
Crabb's La BUNT SG9 61 K3
Crab La GSTN WD25 183 G5
Crabtree Cl BUSH WD23 197 G6
HHS/BOV HP3 166 C1
Crabtree Dell LWTH SG6 40 B7
Crabtree La HARP AL5 131 H2
HHS/BOV HP3 166 C1
Crab Tree La HTCH/STOT SG5 37 J6
Crab Tree Rd KNEB SG3 88 E7
Crabtree Wy DUN/WHIP LU6 81 G1
Crackle Hill Rd SHFD SG17 24 A4
Crackley Meadow
HHNE HP2 150 A2 3
Cradock Rd LTNW/LEA LU4 82 A1
Cragg Av RAD WD7 183 L7
Cragside KNEB SG3 89 H3 1
Craigavon Rd HHNE HP2 149 L3
Craiglands STALE/WH AL4 153 J3
Craig Mt RAD WD7 184 A6
Craigs Wk CHES/WCR EN8 176 C7
Craigweil Av RAD WD7 184 A6
Cranborne Av HTCH/STOT SG5 52 C4
Cranborne Cl HERT/BAY SG13 137 H7
POTB/CUF EN6 186 D2
Cranborne Crs POTB/CUF EN6 186 D2
Cranborne Gdns WGCE AL7 134 E5 1
Cranborne Rd
CHES/WCR EN8 190 C3 1
HAT AL10 155 G4
HOD EN11 160 A3
POTB/CUF EN6 186 D1
Cranbourne Dr HARP AL5 131 H4
HOD EN11 139 G8
Cranbrook Cl WARE SG12 116 C7 1
Cranbrook Dr LTNN/LIM LU3 64 C2
STALE/WH AL4 153 K7
Cranbrook Rd EBAR EN4 201 J7
Cranefield Dr GSTN WD25 182 D3
Crane Md WARE SG12 138 D2
Cranes Wy BORE WD6 199 H6
Cranfield Crs POTB/CUF EN6 174 D8
Cranleigh Cl CHESW EN7 175 M7
Cranleigh Gdns LTNN/LIM LU3 65 H7
Cranmer Cl POTB/CUF EN6 187 H1
Cranwell Gdns BSF CM23 97 H1
Cravells Rd HARP AL5 131 H4
Crawford Rd HAT AL10 154 F3
Crawley Cl LTN LU1 107 H1
Crawley Dr HHNE HP2 8 E1
Crawley Gn LTNE LU2 3 L3
Crawley Green Rd LTNE LU2 3 J6
Crawley Rd LTN LU1 2 C4
Crawley's La TRING HP23 145 K3
Creamery Ct LWTH SG6 40 B7
Crecy Gdns STALW/RED AL3 129 M4
Creighton Av STAL AL1 169 J3
Crescent East EBAR EN4 201 H1
Crescent Ri EBAR EN4 201 K6 1
LTNE LU2 3 G5
Crescent Rd BSF CM23 96 F4
EBAR EN4 201 J5
HHNE HP2 8 B8
LTNE LU2 3 G5
The Crescent ABLGY WD5 181 L1
BAR EN5 201 G4
BUNT SG9 57 H3
GSTN WD25 197 G1
HLWE CM17 142 B4
HNLW SG16 25 G6
HTCH/STOT SG5 52 C1
HTCHE/RSTV SG4 52 F7
LBUZ LU7 102 B6
LCOL/BKTW AL2 182 F1
LTN LU1 82 D6
LWTH SG6 39 M5
RKW/CH/CXG WD3 195 G7
STVGE SG2 56 E7
TRING HP23 123 M1
WATW WD18 13 G5
WLYN AL6 112 B6
Crescent West EBAR EN4 201 H1
Cress End RKW/CH/CXG WD3 203 M1
Cresset Cl WARE SG12 139 H7
Cresswick HTCHE/RSTV SG4 86 D3
Cresta Cl DUN/HR/TOD LU5 63 M8
Crest Pk HHNE HP2 9 M6
The Crest CHESW EN7 175 G6
DUN/HR/TOD LU5 81 K1
LTNN/LIM LU3 65 G3 1
SBW CM21 120 C8
WARE SG12 116 C6
WLYN AL6 112 C2
Creswick Ct WGCE AL7 134 C5 2
Crew Curve BERK HP4 146 E3
Crib St WARE SG12 116 C8
Cricketers Cl STAL AL1 11 G4
Cricketer's Rd ARL/CHE SG15 25 M5
Cricketfield La BSF CM23 96 C2
Crispin Fld LBUZ LU7 102 B6
Croasdaile Rd STSD CM24 79 K2
Croasdale Cl STSD CM24 79 K2
Crocus Fld BAR EN5 200 E7
Croft Cl KGLGY WD4 179 M1
Croft End Rd KGLGY WD4 179 M1
Crofters SBW CM21 120 D7
Crofters End SBW CM21 120 D6
Crofters Rd NTHWD HA6 205 K4
Croft Fld HAT AL10 154 F5 1
KGLGY WD4 179 M1
Croft Gn DUN/WHIP LU6 80 E2
Croft La KGLGY WD4 179 M1
LWTH SG6 39 M1
Croft Meadow KGLGY WD4 179 M1
Croft Mdw LBUZ LU7 101 M3
Crofton Wy BAR EN5 201 G7 1
Croft Rd LTNE LU2 66 A7 1
WARE SG12 116 B8
Crofts Pth HHS/BOV HP3 167 G1
The Crofts HHS/BOV HP3 150 A8
HTCH/STOT SG5 26 E4
The Croft BAR EN5 200 D5
BROX EN10 176 D2
LCOL/BKTW AL2 168 F4
LTNN/LIM LU3 64 C2
WARE SG12 117 K6
WGCE AL7 134 E7
Croftwell HARP AL5 131 L2
Cromer Cl BERK HP4 126 D6
Cromer Rd BAR EN5 201 H5
WATN WD24 196 B1 2

Cromer Wy *LTNE* LU2 65 J3
Crompton Rd *STVG* SG1 69 M4
Cromwell Av *CHESW* EN7 190 A1
Cromwell Cl *BSF* CM23 96 A3
CSTG HP8 202 B3
STALE/WH AL4 153 J2
Cromwell Gn *LWTH* SG6 40 A2
Cromwell Hl *LTNE* LU2 2 D3
Cromwell Rd *AMP/FLIT/B* MK45 35 H6
BORE WD6 198 D2
HERT/BAY SG13 137 L3
LTNN/LIM LU3 2 C3
LWTH SG6 40 A2
STVGE SG2 71 H5
WARE SG12 138 E1
Cromwell Wy *HTCH/STOT* SG5 37 J6
Crooked Mile *WAB* EN9 191 H1
Crooked Wy *WAB* EN9 177 K1
Crookhams *WGCE* AL7 134 F2
Crop Common *HAT* AL10 155 G3
Crosby Cl *DUN/WHIP* LU6 81 H4 1
LTNW/LEA LU4 64 F8 1
STALE/WH AL4 170 B2
Crossbrook *HAT* AL10 154 D6
Crossbrook St
CHES/WCR EN8 190 C1 1
Crossett Gn *HHS/BOV* HP3 167 H1 1
Crossfell Rd *HHS/BOV* HP3 167 G1
Crossfield Cl *BERK* HP4 146 E6
Crossfield Rd *HOD* EN11 160 A2
Crossfields *STALW/RED* AL3 169 G2
Crossgates *STVG* SG1 4 F3
Crosslands *LTN* LU1 82 D7
Cross La *HARP* AL5 131 H5
HERT/WAS SG14 137 G4 2
CFSP/GDCR SL9 202 E5
Cross Lanes Cl
CFSP/GDCR SL9 202 E5 1
Crossleys *LWTH* SG6 26 E8 1
Crossmead *OXHEY* WD19 12 F9
Cross Oak Rd *BERK* HP4 146 F7
Crossoaks La *BORE* WD6 185 J6
POTB/CUF EN6 185 K5
Crosspaths *HARP* AL5 108 B6
The Crosspath *RAD* WD7 183 M6
Cross Rd *CHES/WCR* EN8 190 D4 1
HERT/WAS SG14 137 H3
OXHEY WD19 13 M8
Cross St *LTNE* LU2 2 F4
LWTH SG6 39 L3
STALW/RED AL3 10 E6
WARE SG12 138 D1
WAT WD17 13 G2
Cross St North *DUN/WHIP* LU6 80 F1 1
Cross Wy *HARP* AL5 109 H7
Crossway *WGCW* AL8 112 A8
Crossways *BERK* HP4 146 E7
DUN/HR/TOD LU5 63 H5
HHS/BOV HP3 9 K9
Crossways Cl *HNLW* SG16 25 J1
The Cross Wy *LTN* LU1 83 H5
Crouchfield *HERT/WAS* SG14 137 J1 1
HHW HP1 149 G8
Crouchfield La *WARE* SG12 115 K6 1
Crouch Hall Gdns
STALW/RED AL3 129 M4
Crouch Hall La *STALW/RED* AL3 129 M4
Crouch La *CHESW* EN7 175 H6
Crowborough Pth
OXHEY WD19 206 C4 1
Crow Furlong *HTCH/STOT* SG5 52 C4
Crowland Rd *LTNE* LU2 66 B5
Crown Cl *RBSF* CM22 143 H2
Crownfield *BROX* EN10 159 M8
Crown Ga *HLW* CM20 6 E6
Crown La *ROY* SG8 31 K5
Crown Ri *GSTN* WD25 182 B5
Crown Rd *BORE* WD6 198 F2
Crown St *STALW/RED* AL3 130 A5
Crown Ter *BSF* CM23 96 F3
Croxdale Rd *BORE* WD6 198 E3
Croxley Vw *WATW* WD18 195 K7
Croxton Cl *LTNN/LIM* LU3 64 F3 1
Crozier Av *BSF* CM23 96 B2
Crusader Wy *WATW* WD18 12 B8
Cubbington Cl *LTNN/LIM* LU3 64 F3 2
Cubitt Cl *HTCHE/RSTV* SG4 53 H3
Cubitts Cl *WLYN* AL6 112 E7
Cublands *HERT/BAY* SG13 138 A4
Cuckmans Dr *LCOL/BKTW* AL2 168 F4
Cuckoos La *GTDUN* CM6 99 L8
Cucumber La *BRKMPK* AL9 156 E8
Cuffley Av *GSTN* WD25 182 C5
Cuffley Cl *LTNN/LIM* LU3 64 E7
Cuffley Ct *HHNE* HP2 150 B2
Cuffley Hl *CHESW* EN7 174 F8
Cullera Cl *NTHWD* HA6 205 L6
Cullings Ct *WAB* EN9 191 L4
Culverden Rd *OXHEY* WD19 206 A3
Culverhouse Rd *LTNN/LIM* LU3 65 H6
Culver Rd *STAL* AL1 11 H4
Culworth Cl *LTN* LU1 82 D7
Cumberland Cl *AMSS* HP7 192 A2 1
HERT/WAS SG14 137 H2 1
HHS/BOV HP3 167 K3
Cumberland Dr
STALW/RED AL3 130 A5
Cumberland St
DUN/HR/TOD LU5 63 G6
LTN LU1 2 F8
Cumberlow Pl *HHS/BOV* HP3 150 B8 3
Cumbria Cl *DUN/HR/TOD* LU5 63 K5
Cundalls Rd *WARE* SG12 116 D8
Cunningham Av *PEND* EN3 190 D7
STAL AL1 169 L1
Cunningham Hill Rd *STAL* AL1 169 L1
Cunningham Rd
CHES/WCR EN8 176 D6
Cupid Green La *HHNE* HP2 128 D7
Curlew Cl *BERK* HP4 147 H7
LWTH SG6 39 K1
Curlew Rd *LTNE* LU2 66 B5
Currie St *HERT/BAY* SG13 137 K3
Curteys *HLWE* CM17 142 C5
Curtis Cl *RKW/CH/CXG* WD3 203 M1
Curtis Rd *HHS/BOV* HP3 150 C8
Curtis Wy *BERK* HP4 147 J7
Curzon Av *STAN* HA7 207 M8
Curzon Rd *LTNN/LIM* LU3 2 B3
Cussons Cl *CHESW* EN7 175 M8
Cusworth Wy *DUN/WHIP* LU6 80 D1
Cutenhoe Rd *LTN* LU1 83 L5
Cutforth Rd *SBW* CM21 120 D7
Cuthbert Cl *CHESW* EN7 175 L8 2
Cutlers Gn *LTNE* LU2 66 E8
Cutmore Dr *STALE/WH* AL4 171 G1
Cut Throat Av *DUN/WHIP* LU6 104 D3
Cuttsfield Ter *HHW* HP1 148 E8
Cutts La *HTCHE/RSTV* SG4 110 C1
Cuttys La *STVG* SG1 4 E4
Cwmbran Ct *HHNE* HP2 8 E1 1
Cygnet Cl *BORE* WD6 199 H2 1
NTHWD HA6 205 H7
Cygnet Ct *BSF* CM23 96 E4
Cylers Thicket *WLYN* AL6 112 B4 1
Cypress Av *ENC/FH* EN2 188 F6
WGCE AL7 135 H5
Cypress Cl *WAB* EN9 191 J5 1
Cypress Wk *GSTN* WD25 182 A6 1
Cyrils Wy *STAL* AL1 169 J2

D

Dacorum Wy *HHW* HP1 149 H7
Dacre Crs *HTCHE/RSTV* SG4 110 B1
Dacre Gdns *BORE* WD6 199 J6
Dacre Gn *ROY* SG8 21 L4
Dacre Rd *HTCH/STOT* SG5 52 F2
Dagger La *BORE* WD6 197 M7
Daggs Dell Rd *HHW* HP1 148 D5
Dagnall Rd *DUN/WHIP* LU6 80 B8
HHW HP1 127 J5
Dagnalls *LWTH* SG6 39 L8 2
Dahlia Cl *CHESW* EN7 175 H4
LTNE LU2 66 A7
Daintrees *WARE* SG12 118 D6
Dairyglen Av *CHES/WCR* EN8 190 C2
Dalby Cl *LTNW/LEA* LU4 64 A6
Dale Av *STALE/WH* AL4 110 A5
Dale Cl *BAR* EN5 201 G7
DUN/HR/TOD LU5 81 L1
HTCHE/RSTV SG4 52 E6
PIN HA5 206 A8
Dale Ct *SBW* CM21 142 C1 1
Dale Rd *DUN/HR/TOD* LU5 81 L1
LTN LU1 2 A6
Daleside Dr *POTB/CUF* EN6 186 E3
Dales Rd *BORE* WD6 199 J6
The Dale *LWTH* SG6 39 K4
WAB EN9 191 K5
Dalewood *HARP* AL5 131 J1 1
WGCE AL7 135 J5
Dalkeith Rd *HARP* AL5 109 H8
Dalling Dr *DUN/HR/TOD* LU5 63 H5
Dallow Rd *LTN* LU1 2 A5
Dalmeny Rd *BAR* EN5 201 H7
Dalton Cl *LTNN/LIM* LU3 65 G1
Dalton Gdns *BSF* CM23 96 D7
Dalton St *STALW/RED* AL3 10 E4
Dalton Wy *HTCHE/RSTV* SG4 86 D4
WAT WD17 13 J8
Daltry Cl *STVG* SG1 54 B8
Daltry Rd *STVG* SG1 54 B8
Damask Cl *HTCHE/RSTV* SG4 55 G2
TRING HP23 124 B6
Damask Gn *HHW* HP1 148 D8 2
Damask Green Rd
HTCHE/RSTV SG4 55 G2
Dammersey Cl *STALW/RED* AL3 106 E6
Damson Wy *STALE/WH* AL4 153 H5
Dancers End La *TRING* HP23 123 H8
Dancers Hill Rd *BAR* EN5 186 C7
Dancote *KNEB* SG3 88 E5
Dane Acres *BSF* CM23 96 C2
Dane Br *MHAD* SG10 95 G7
Dane Bridge La *MHAD* SG10 95 G8
Danebridge Rd *MHAD* SG10 94 F8
Dane Cl *HARP* AL5 109 H6
HTCH/STOT SG5 26 E2
Dane End *ROY* SG8 31 G5
Dane End La *HTCHE/RSTV* SG4 55 K5
Dane End Rd *STDN* SG11 92 C6
Danefield Rd *HTCH/STOT* SG5 37 H6
Daneland *EBAR* EN4 201 L6 1
Danemead *HOD* EN11 159 M1
Dane O'coys Rd *BSF* CM23 96 D1
Dane Pk *BSF* CM23 96 C2
Dane Rd *AMP/FLIT/B* MK45 35 J7
LTNN/LIM LU3 65 G8
Danesbury La *WLYN* AL6 112 B2
Danesbury Pk *HERT/WAS* SG14 137 J3
Danesbury Park Rd *WLYN* AL6 112 B3
Danescroft *LWTH* SG6 39 L1
Danesgate *STVG* SG1 4 C5
The Danes *LCOL/BKTW* AL2 169 H7 1
Dane St *BSF* CM23 96 F4
Danestrete *STVG* SG1 4 C4
Daniells *WGCE* AL7 134 F3
Danvers Cft *TRING* HP23 124 B5 1
Danvers Dr *LTNN/LIM* LU3 65 H1
Danziger Wy *BORE* WD6 199 H2
Darblay Cl *STALE/WH* AL4 132 E5
Darby Dr *WAB* EN9 191 H4 2
WLYN AL6 88 D7
Darcy Cl *CHES/WCR* EN8 190 D2
Darkes La *POTB/CUF* EN6 186 F3
Dark La *BUNT* SG9 43 G1
CHESW EN7 189 M2
HARP AL5 131 J3
WLYN AL6 111 K2
Darley Rd *LTNE* LU2 85 G1
Darnicle Hl *CHESW* EN7 174 F4
Darrington Rd *BORE* WD6 198 D2
Darr's La *BERK* HP4 146 C5
The Dart *HHNE* HP2 149 M2 1
Darwin Cl *HHNE* HP2 150 A1
STALW/RED AL3 152 D3
Darwin Gdns *OXHEY* WD19 206 B5 1
Darwin Rd *STVGE* SG2 5 L1
The Dashes *HLW* CM20 6 B7
Datchet Cl *HHNE* HP2 150 A2
Datchworth Turn *HHNE* HP2 9 M9
Davenham Av *NTHWD* HA6 205 L4
Davenport *HLWE* CM17 163 K3
Daventer Dr *STAN* HA7 207 L7
Davies St *HERT/BAY* SG13 137 K4
Davis Crs *HTCH/STOT* SG5 37 J5
Davison Cl *CHES/WCR* EN8 176 C7
Davison Dr *CHES/WCR* EN8 176 C7
Davis' Rw *ARL/CHE* SG15 25 M6
Davys Cl *STALE/WH* AL4 132 D3
Dawes La *RKW/CH/CXG* WD3 179 L7
Dawley *WGCE* AL7 134 E1
Dawley Ct *HHNE* HP2 149 L3
Dawlish Cl *STVGE* SG2 89 H3
Dawlish Rd *LTNW/LEA* LU4 64 E7
Dawson Cl *HNLW* SG16 25 H5
Dayemead *WGCE* AL7 135 G7 1
Days Cl *HAT* AL10 154 E5
ROY SG8 21 H5
Days Md *HAT* AL10 154 E5
Deacon Cl *STAL* AL1 169 J3 1
Deacons Cl *BORE* WD6 198 F5
Deaconsfield Rd *HHS/BOV* HP3 166 C2
Deacons Hts *BORE* WD6 198 F7
Deacons Hl *OXHEY* WD19 13 G9
Deacon's Hill Rd *BORE* WD6 198 E6
Deacons Wy *HTCH/STOT* SG5 52 C1
Deadhearn La *CSTG* HP8 202 D1
Deadman's Ash La
RKW/CH/CXG WD3 180 A7
Dead Woman's La
HTCHE/RSTV SG4 68 B4
Deakin Cl *WATW* WD18 195 K8 1
Deanacre Cl *CFSP/GDCR* SL9 202 D6
Deancroft Rd *CFSP/GDCR* SL9 202 D6
Dean Fld *HHS/BOV* HP3 164 F6
Deans Cl *ABLGY* WD5 181 J3
TRING HP23 123 M6
Deanscroft *KNEB* SG3 88 E5
Deans Furlong *TRING* HP23 123 M6
Dean's Gdns *STALE/WH* AL4 152 F3
Deans Meadow *BERK* HP4 104 B5
Deansway *HHS/BOV* HP3 166 E2
Dean Wy *RAYLNE/WEN* HP22 122 E6
Deard's End La *KNEB* SG3 88 E5
Deards Wd *KNEB* SG3 88 E5
Dearne Cl *STAN* HA7 207 M5
Debenham Rd *CHESW* EN7 176 A6
Deepdene *POTB/CUF* EN6 186 C2
Deep Denes *LTNE* LU2 65 M8
Deeping Cl *KNEB* SG3 88 E6 1
Deer Cl *HERT/BAY* SG13 137 L4
Deerfield Cl *WARE* SG12 116 C8
The Deerings *HARP* AL5 130 F6
Deer Pk *HLWW/ROY* CM19 161 M5
Deerswood Av *HAT* AL10 155 G7
The Dee *HHNE* HP2 149 L2
Deeves Hall La *POTB/CUF* EN6 185 K4
De Havilland Cl *HAT* AL10 154 E4
De Havilland Ct *RAD* WD7 184 D3 2
De Havilland Wy *ABLGY* WD5 181 L3 1
Deimos Dr *HHNE* HP2 9 G3
Delahay Ri *BERK* HP4 147 G4
Delamare Rd *CHES/WCR* EN8 176 E8
Delamere Rd *BORE* WD6 199 G2
Delfcroft *WARE* SG12 116 B7
Delfield Gdns *LTN* LU1 82 D6
Delius Cl *BORE* WD6 198 B7
Dell Cl *HARP* AL5 109 G7
Dellcot Cl *LTNE* LU2 66 A5
Dellcott Cl *WGCW* AL8 134 A3
Dellcroft Wy *HARP* AL5 130 F4
Dellcut Rd *HHNE* HP2 9 G4
Dellfield *BERK* HP4 146 F4 2
STAL AL1 11 K9
WARE SG12 116 C2
Dellfield Av *BERK* HP4 147 G4
Dellfield Cl *RAD* WD7 183 K6
WAT WD17 195 M3
Dellfield Rd *HAT* AL10 154 F5
Dell La *BSF* CM23 96 F3
RBSF CM22 120 F2
Dellmeadow *ABLGY* WD5 181 K1
Dell Meadow *HHS/BOV* HP3 166 D3 1
Dellmont Rd *DUN/HR/TOD* LU5 63 G5
Dellors Cl *BAR* EN5 200 C6
Dell Ri *LCOL/BKTW* AL2 169 G5
Dell Rd *BERK* HP4 146 C3 1
DUN/HR/TOD LU5 63 G5
WATN WD24 181 M8
Dell Side *WATN* WD24 181 M8
Dellsome La *BRKMPK* AL9 171 L2
STALE/WH AL4 171 K2 1
Dell Springs *BUNT* SG9 58 D2 1
The Dells *HHS/BOV* HP3 150 A8
Dellswood Cl *HERT/BAY* SG13 137 K5
Dells Wood Cl *HOD* EN11 159 L1
The Dell *BLDK* SG7 40 D4
CFSP/GDCR SL9 202 D6
HERT/BAY SG13 137 H7
LTN LU1 82 D7
LTNE LU2 84 E1
NTHWD HA6 205 K2
RAD WD7 183 M7
ROY SG8 21 H5
STAL AL1 11 M3
STVG SG1 4 F3
Dellwood Cl *RKW/CH/CXG* WD3 204 A1
Delmar Av *HHNE* HP2 150 C8
Delmerend La *STALW/RED* AL3 129 H1
Delphine Cl *LTN* LU1 82 F4
Delta Gain *OXHEY* WD19 206 C2
Demontfort Ri *WARE* SG12 116 B7
Denbigh Cl *HHS/BOV* HP3 149 K8 2
Denbigh Rd *LTNN/LIM* LU3 65 G8
Denby *LWTH* SG6 40 A6
Denby Gra *HLWE* CM17 163 K2
Dencora Wy *LTNN/LIM* LU3 64 A2
Dendridge Cl *EN* EN1 190 A8
Dene La *STVGE* SG2 71 K8
Dene Rd *NTHWD* HA6 205 H6
Denewood *BAR* EN5 201 H6
Denewood Cl *WAT* WD17 181 L8
Denham Cl *HHNE* HP2 149 M2 2
LTNN/LIM LU3 64 D2
Denham La *CFSP/GDCR* SL9 202 E6
Denham Wk *CFSP/GDCR* SL9 202 E6
Denham Wy *BORE* WD6 199 H2
Denham Way
(North Orbital Road)
RKW/CH/CXG WD3 203 K7
Denmark Cl *LTNN/LIM* LU3 64 D1
Denmark St *WAT* WD17 12 E1
Dennis Cl *RAYLNE/WEN* HP22 122 F6 2
Denny Av *WAB* EN9 191 J5
Denny Ct *BSF* CM23 79 G8
Denny Ga *CHES/WCR* EN8 176 E6
Denny's La *BERK* HP4 146 E8
Densley Cl *WGCW* AL8 134 B2
Denton Cl *BAR* EN5 200 B6
LTNW/LEA LU4 64 A6
Denton Rd *STVG* SG1 4 F6
Dents Cl *LWTH* SG6 40 B7
Derby Av *KTN/HRWW/W* HA3 207 J8
Derby Rd *HOD* EN11 160 C6
LTNW/LEA LU4 64 B8
WAT WD17 13 H4
Derby Wy *STVG* SG1 71 G2
Derwent Av *LTNN/LIM* LU3 65 G3
PIN HA5 206 D6
Derwent Cl *AMSS* HP7 192 A2
Derwent Dr *DUN/WHIP* LU6 81 H5
Derwent Rd *HARP* AL5 108 B6
HHS/BOV HP3 150 B8
HNLW SG16 25 G6
LTNE LU2 3 J4
Desborough Cl *HERT/WAS* SG14 137 H1
Desborough Dr *WLYN* AL6 113 H5
Desborough Rd
HTCHE/RSTV SG4 53 H2
Desmond Rd *WATN* WD24 181 L7
De Tany Ct *STAL* AL1 10 E9
Deva Cl *STALW/RED* AL3 168 F1
Devereux Dr *WAT* WD17 195 K1
De Vere Wk *WAT* WD17 195 K3
Devoils La *BSF* CM23 96 E3 2
Devon Ct *STAL* AL1 11 H9
Devon Rd *LTNE* LU2 3 L4
WATN WD24 196 C2
Devonshire Cl *STVGE* SG2 88 F2
Devonshire Rd *HARP* AL5 109 G8 2
PIN HA5 206 E8
Dewars Cl *WLYN* AL6 112 B4
Dewes Green Rd *BSF* CM23 61 M2
Dewgrass Gv
CHES/WCR EN8 190 C6 2
Dewhurst Rd *CHES/WCR* EN8 176 B8
Dewpond Cl *STVG* SG1 70 B2
Dewsbury Rd *LTNN/LIM* LU3 65 G4
Dexter Cl *LTNN/LIM* LU3 65 G1
STAL AL1 11 L8
Dexter Rd *BAR* EN5 200 C7
Diamond Rd *WATN* WD24 195 M1
Dianne Wy *EBAR* EN4 201 K5 2
Dickens Cl *STALW/RED* AL3 10 E4
Dickens Ct *HHNE* HP2 150 A1
Dicket Md *WLYN* AL6 112 B5
Dickins Cl *CHESW* EN7 175 M6
Dickinson Av
RKW/CH/CXG WD3 194 F7
Dickinson Sq
RKW/CH/CXG WD3 195 G7
Dickson *CHESW* EN7 175 L6
Dig Dag Hl *CHESW* EN7 175 L6
Digswell Cl *BORE* WD6 198 F1
Digswell Hl *WLYN* AL6 133 M1
Digswell La *WGCE* AL7 112 E8
Digswell Park Rd *WGCW* AL8 112 D7
Digswell Ri *WGCW* AL8 134 C2
Digswell Rd *WGCW* AL8 134 D1
Dimmocks La
RKW/CH/CXG WD3 179 M7
Dimsdale Crs *BSF* CM23 97 G5
Dimsdale St *HERT/WAS* SG14 137 H4
Dinant Link Rd *HOD* EN11 159 M3
Dingle Cl *BAR* EN5 199 L7
Dinmore *HHS/BOV* HP3 164 E7
Dinsdale Gdns *BAR* EN5 201 G6
Ditchfield Rd *HOD* EN11 159 M2
Ditchling Cl *LTNE* LU2 66 B7
Ditchmore La *STVG* SG1 4 B2
Ditton Gn *LTNE* LU2 66 C8
Divot Pl *HERT/BAY* SG13 138 A3 2
Dixies Cl *BLDK* SG7 18 C7
Dixon Pl *BUNT* SG9 58 D3
Dixons Hill Cl *BRKMPK* AL9 172 A4
Dixons Hill Rd *BRKMPK* AL9 172 A4
Dobb's Weir Rd *HOD* EN11 160 C5
Docklands *HTCH/STOT* SG5 37 J6 1
Doctor's Commons Rd
BERK HP4 147 G7
Dodds La *CSTG* HP8 202 A2
HHNE HP2 149 H2
Dodwood *WGCE* AL7 135 G5
Doggetts Ct *EBAR* EN4 201 K6
Doggetts Wy *STAL* AL1 169 H1
Doggetts Wood Cl *CSTG* HP8 192 A5
Doggetts Wood La *CSTG* HP8 192 A4
Dog Kennel La *HAT* AL10 154 F4
RKW/CH/CXG WD3 193 L6
ROY SG8 21 J4
Dognell Gn *WGCW* AL8 134 A3
Dolesbury Dr *WLYN* AL6 112 D1
Dollis Valley Green Wk
TRDG/WHET N20 201 G7
Dollis Valley Wy *BAR* EN5 200 E6
Dolphin Dr *DUN/HR/TOD* LU5 63 J5
Dolphin Wy *BSF* CM23 96 F2
Doncaster Cl *STVG* SG1 71 H2
Doncaster Gn *OXHEY* WD19 206 B5 1
Donkey La *TRING* HP23 123 K8 1
Donne Cl *ROY* SG8 21 H2 1
Dorchester Av *HOD* EN11 159 M2
Dorchester Cl *DUN/HR/TOD* LU5 81 G1
Dordans Rd *LTNW/LEA* LU4 64 D6
Dorel Cl *LTNE* LU2 3 G1
Dormans Cl *NTHWD* HA6 205 J7
Dormer Cl *BAR* EN5 200 C6
Dorrien's Cft *BERK* HP4 146 E3 1
Dorrington Cl *LTNN/LIM* LU3 2 B2 1
Dorrofield Cl
RKW/CH/CXG WD3 195 H6
Dorset Cl *BERK* HP4 146 E5
Douglas Av *WATN* WD24 182 C8
Douglas Cl *STAN* HA7 207 M5
Douglas Crs *DUN/HR/TOD* LU5 62 F7
Douglas Dr *STVG* SG1 70 F2
Douglas Gdns *BERK* HP4 146 F5 2
Douglas Rd *HARP* AL5 108 E8
LTNW/LEA LU4 64 F8
Douglas Wy *WGCE* AL7 135 H4 1
Doulton Cl *HLWE* CM17 163 K3
Dove Cl *BSF* CM23 96 D7
STSD CM24 79 K3
Dove Ct *HAT* AL10 154 F7
Dovedale *LTNE* LU2 65 K4
STVGE SG2 5 M5
WARE SG12 116 B6
Dovehouse Cft *HLW* CM20 7 L2
Dovehouse Hl *LTNE* LU2 3 M1
Dove House La *DUN/WHIP* LU6 105 H3
Dove La *POTB/CUF* EN6 187 G5
Dove Pk *PIN* HA5 206 E7
RKW/CH/CXG WD3 193 G6
Dover Cl *LTNN/LIM* LU3 64 F7
Doverfield *CHESW* EN7 175 H8
Dover Wy *RKW/CH/CXG* WD3 195 H5
Dowding Pl *STAN* HA7 207 M6
Dowling Ct *HHS/BOV* HP3 166 C2
Downalong *BUSH* WD23 207 J1
Downedge *STALW/RED* AL3 10 B4
Down Edge *STALW/RED* AL3 129 L5
Downer Dr *RKW/CH/CXG* WD3 179 L7
Downes Rd *STALE/WH* AL4 153 G3
Downfield Cl *HERT/BAY* SG13 138 B6
Downfield Rd *CHES/WCR* EN8 190 D2
HERT/BAY SG13 138 B6
Downfields *WGCW* AL8 134 A6
Down Green La *STALE/WH* AL4 132 A3
Downhall Ley *BUNT* SG9 58 D4
Downings Wd
RKW/CH/CXG WD3 203 J5
Downlands *BLDK* SG7 40 F1 1
LTNN/LIM LU3 64 B3 1
ROY SG8 21 H4
STVGE SG2 71 J3
WAB EN9 191 K5 1
Downsfield *HAT* AL10 155 G8 1
Downside *HHNE* HP2 8 C7
Downs La *HAT* AL10 154 F7
Downs Rd *DUN/HR/TOD* LU5 81 J2
LTN LU1 2 A7
The Downs *HAT* AL10 154 F7
HLW CM20 7 H6
Dowry Wk *WAT* WD17 195 L1
Drakes Cl *CHES/WCR* EN8 176 C7 3
Drakes Dr *NTHWD* HA6 205 G8
STAL AL1 170 A2
STVGE SG2 71 G3
Drakes Wy *HAT* AL10 155 G7
Drapers Wy *STVG* SG1 70 B3
Drayman's Cl *BSF* CM23 96 A5
Drayson Cl *WAB* EN9 191 J3
Drayton Av *POTB/CUF* EN6 186 D3
Drayton Rd *BORE* WD6 198 F5
LTNW/LEA LU4 63 L7
The Drey *CFSP/GDCR* SL9 202 D5
Driftway *ROY* SG8 31 K6
The Driftway *HHNE* HP2 8 F9
Driftwood Av *LCOL/BKTW* AL2 168 F5
Driver's End La *HTCHE/RSTV* SG4 87 L6
The Drive *BAR* EN5 200 D4
BAR EN5 201 H7
BRKMPK AL9 172 F4
CFSP/GDCR SL9 202 D7
CHESW EN7 175 G7
CHESW EN7 176 A7
HARP AL5 130 F1
HERT/WAS SG14 137 H2
HLW CM20 7 H4
HOD EN11 159 M2
LCOL/BKTW AL2 169 M4
NTHWD HA6 205 K8
POTB/CUF EN6 186 E4
RAD WD7 183 M5
RKW/CH/CXG WD3 194 A6
SBW CM21 120 D8
STALE/WH AL4 110 A3
WAT WD17 181 J8
WLYN AL6 112 F1
The Driveway *POTB/CUF* EN6 174 D7
Dromey Gdns
KTN/HRWW/W HA3 207 L7
Drop La *LCOL/BKTW* AL2 183 G2
Drovers Wy *BSF* CM23 96 B6 3
DUN/WHIP LU6 80 E2
HAT AL10 155 G2
STALW/RED AL3 10 E6
Drummond Dr
KTN/HRWW/W HA3 207 L7
Drummond Ride *TRING* HP23 123 M5
Drury Cl *DUN/HR/TOD* LU5 63 H5 1
Drury La *DUN/HR/TOD* LU5 63 H5
WARE SG12 140 C1
Drycroft *WGCE* AL7 134 D8 1
Dryden Crs *STVGE* SG2 71 H2
Dryden Rd *KTN/HRWW/W* HA3 207 L8
Drysdale Cl *NTHWD* HA6 205 K7 3
Dubbs Knoll Rd *ROY* SG8 15 L5
Dubrae Cl *STALW/RED* AL3 168 F1
Duchess Cl *BSF* CM23 96 A3 1
Duchy Rd *EBAR* EN4 201 J1
Ducketts La *MHAD* SG10 119 J1
Ducketts Md *HLWW/ROY* CM19 161 G1
Ducketts Wd *WARE* SG12 116 C3
Duck La *STVGE* SG2 72 D6
Duckling La *SBW* CM21 120 D8 2
Duckmore La *TRING* HP23 144 D1
Duck's Hill Rd *NTHWD* HA6 205 G7
Dudley Av *CHES/WCR* EN8 190 C3
Dudley Hill Cl *WLYN* AL6 112 D2 2
Dudley St *LTNE* LU2 2 E4
Dudswell La *BERK* HP4 146 C2
Dugdale Hill La *POTB/CUF* EN6 186 D4
Dugdales *RKW/CH/CXG* WD3 194 F5
Dukes Av *DUN/WHIP* LU6 104 D2
Duke's La *HTCH/STOT* SG5 52 D2
Dukes Ride *BSF* CM23 96 B3
Duke St *HOD* EN11 159 M3
LTNE LU2 2 F4
WAT WD17 13 G3
Dukes Wy *BERK* HP4 146 F4 3
Dulwich Wy *RKW/CH/CXG* WD3 194 F6
Dumbarton Av
CHES/WCR EN8 190 C5 1
Dumfries Cl *OXHEY* WD19 205 M3
Dumfries St *LTN* LU1 2 D8

Duncan Cl BAR EN5 201 H5
WGCE AL7 134 D5
Duncan Wy BUSH WD23 196 E3
Duncombe Cl HERT/WAS SG14 137 H2
LTNN/LIM LU3 65 H4 1
Duncombe Dr DUN/HR/TOD LU5 63 K8
Duncombe Rd BERK HP4 146 D4 2
HERT/WAS SG14 137 H3
Duncots Cl HTCH/STOT SG5 38 D7
Dundale Rd TRING HP23 123 M6
Dunhams La LWTH SG6 40 A4
Dunlin LWTH SG6 39 K1
Dunlin Rd HHNE HP2 149 K2
Dunmow Rd BSF CM23 97 G3
RBSF CM22 97 M3
Dunn Cl STVG SG1 4 E7
Dunnock Cl BORE WD6 198 F5 2
Dunny La KGLGY WD4 179 L3
RKW/CH/CXG WD3 179 L4 1
Dunsby Rd LTNN/LIM LU3 64 F4
Dunsley Pl TRING HP23 124 A7 1
Dunsmore Cl BUSH WD23 197 J7 1
Dunsmore Rd LTN LU1 2 A8
Dunsmore Wy BUSH WD23 197 H7
Dunstable Cl LTNW/LEA LU4 82 F1
Dunstable Pl LTN LU1 2 D7
Dunstable Rd DUN/HR/TOD LU5 63 G6
DUN/WHIP LU6 80 B3
LBUZ LU7 62 A4
LTN LU1 2 A4
LTN LU1 82 B7
LTNW/LEA LU4 64 C8 1
STALW/RED AL3 129 L1
Dunstall Rd AMP/FLIT/B MK45 35 H8
Dunstalls HLWW/ROY CM19 161 M6
Dunster Cl BAR EN5 200 C5
DEN/HRF UB9 204 A8
Dunster Rd HHNE HP2 150 A1 2
Dunsters Md WGCE AL7 134 F6
Dunston Hl TRING HP23 123 M6
Durban Rd East WATW WD18 12 D4
Durban Rd West WATW WD18 12 C4
Durbar Rd LTNW/LEA LU4 82 F1
Durham Cl SBW CM21 142 B1 1
WARE SG12 139 G5
Durham Rd LTNE LU2 3 K5
STVG SG1 70 F1
Durley Gdns LTN LU1 83 J5 1
Durrants Dr RKW/CH/CXG WD3 195 H4
Durrants Hill Rd HHS/BOV HP3 166 C2
Durrants La BERK HP4 146 E5
Durrants Rd BERK HP4 146 E5
Dury Rd BAR EN5 200 E2
Duxford Cl LTNN/LIM LU3 65 G3
Duxons Turn HHNE HP2 9 K6
Dwight Rd WATW WD18 195 J8
Dyes La HTCHE/RSTV SG4 69 L7
Dyke La STALE/WH AL4 132 D3
Dylan Cl BORE WD6 198 C8 1
Dymoke Gn STALE/WH AL4 152 F4
Dymokes Wy HOD EN11 159 M1
Dyrham La BAR EN5 185 M7
Dysons Cl CHES/WCR EN8 190 C4

E

Eagle Centre Wy
LTNW/LEA LU4 64 A3 1
Eagle Cl LTNW/LEA LU4 63 M6 1
WAB EN9 191 M5
Eagle Ct HERT/BAY SG13 138 A3
Eagle Wy HAT AL10 154 F7
Ealing Cl BORE WD6 199 J2
Earls Cl BSF CM23 96 C4
Earls Hill Gdns ROY SG8 21 H4
Earls La POTB/CUF EN6 185 K3
Earlsmead LWTH SG6 39 L7
Earls Meade LTNE LU2 2 D2
Earl St WAT WD17 13 G3
Easedale Cl DUN/WHIP LU6 81 H4
Easington Rd WARE SG12 91 K3
Easingwold Gdns LTN LU1 82 E2
East Barnet Rd BAR EN5 201 H5
EBAR EN4 201 K7
Eastbourne Av STVG SG1 69 M4
Eastbrook Rd WAB EN9 191 K4
Eastbrook Wy HHNE HP2 8 D9
East Burrowfield WGCE AL7 134 C6
Eastbury Av NTHWD HA6 205 K5
Eastbury Ct STAL AL1 11 J4
Eastbury Rd NTHWD HA6 205 K6
OXHEY WD19 196 B8
Eastcheap LWTH SG6 39 L5
East Cl EBAR EN4 201 M5
HTCHE/RSTV SG4 53 G1
LCOL/BKTW AL2 169 G4 1
STVG SG1 5 G3
Eastcote Dr HARP AL5 131 J4
Eastcott Cl LTNE LU2 84 B1
East Dr GSTN WD25 182 A7
NTHWD HA6 205 K2
SBW CM21 142 D1
East End DUN/HR/TOD LU5 63 H5
Eastern Av CHES/WCR EN8 190 E4
DUN/HR/TOD LU5 81 J1
HNLW SG16 25 H7
Eastern Wy LWTH SG6 39 M1
Eastfield Av WATN WD24 196 C2
Eastfield Cl LTNE LU2 66 B6
Eastfield Ct STALE/WH AL4 153 J4 1
Eastfield Rd CHES/WCR EN8 190 E3
ROY SG8 21 K3
East Flint HHW HP1 148 D6
East Ga HLW CM20 6 E5 1
Eastgate STVG SG1 4 D5
Eastglade NTHWD HA6 205 K5
Eastham Cl BAR EN5 200 E6
East Hl LTNN/LIM LU3 65 G4
Easthill Rd DUN/HR/TOD LU5 63 H5
Eastholm LWTH SG6 39 M2
Eastholm Gn LWTH SG6 39 M2
East La ABLGY WD5 167 M7
GSTN WD25 182 A1
STALE/WH AL4 132 C1
Eastlea Av GSTN WD25 182 D8
East Lodge La ENC/FH EN2 188 C7
Eastman Wy HHNE HP2 9 H2
East Md WGCE AL7 135 G7
East Mimms HHNE HP2 8 C6
Eastmoor Pk HARP AL5 131 H4
East Mt STALE/WH AL4 132 C1 3
Eastnor HHS/BOV HP3 164 F7
Easton Gdns BORE WD6 199 K5
Eastor WGCE AL7 134 F1
East Pk HLWE CM17 142 B7
SBW CM21 142 D1
East Reach STVGE SG2 5 J9
East Ridgeway POTB/CUF EN6 174 C7
East Riding WLYN AL6 113 J5
East Rd BSF CM23 97 G3
HLW CM20 142 A6
East St HHNE HP2 8 B7
LTNE LU2 50 C8
WARE SG12 138 C1
East Vw BAR EN5 200 E3
BRKMPK AL9 156 E4
HTCHE/RSTV SG4 53 H8
East Wy WAB EN9 191 J6
Eastwick Crs RKW/CH/CXG WD3 203 L2
Eastwick Hall La HLW CM20 140 F4
Eastwick Rd HLW CM20 141 G6
Eastwick Rw HHNE HP2 149 M8
Eaton Ga NTHWD HA6 205 H6
Eaton Green Rd LTNE LU2 84 B2
Eaton Pl LTNE LU2 84 C1
Eaton Rd HHNE HP2 9 K3
STAL AL1 153 G7
Eaton Valley Rd LTNE LU2 3 M3
Ebberns Rd HHS/BOV HP3 166 D2
Ebenezer St LTN LU1 2 D8
Ebury Ap RKW/CH/CXG WD3 204 C1
Ebury Cl NTHWD HA6 205 H5
Ebury Rd RKW/CH/CXG WD3 204 C1
WAT WD17 13 H2
Eccleston Cl EBAR EN4 201 K6
Echo Hl ROY SG8 21 H5
Eddiwick Av DUN/HR/TOD LU5 63 J3
Eddy St BERK HP4 146 F5
Edenhall Cl HHNE HP2 150 C8
Edens Cl BSF CM23 97 G3
Edgars Ct WGCE AL7 134 D5 2
Edgbaston Dr RAD WD7 184 D3
Edgcott Cl LTNN/LIM LU3 65 G1
Edgecote Cl LTN LU1 82 D7
Edgehill Gdns LTNN/LIM LU3 64 B2
Edgewood Dr LTNE LU2 66 B4
Edgeworth Cl STVGE SG2 89 H1 1
Edgeworth Rd EBAR EN4 201 K5
Edgwarebury La BORE WD6 198 E8
Edinburgh Av
RKW/CH/CXG WD3 193 M7
Edinburgh Crs CHES/WCR EN8 190 D4
Edinburgh Dr GSTN WD25 181 M3 1
Edinburgh Pl HLW CM20 141 M6
Edinburgh Wy HLW CM20 6 E1
HLWE CM17 142 B5 1
Edison Cl STALE/WH AL4 153 H8 1
Edison Rd STVGE SG2 5 M1
Edkins Cl LTNE LU2 65 K5 1
Edlyn Cl BERK HP4 146 E5
Edmonds Dr STVGE SG2 71 J6
Edmund Beaufort Dr
STALW/RED AL3 10 F3
Edmunds Rd HERT/WAS SG14 136 E3
Edridge Cl BUSH WD23 197 H6
Edulf Rd BORE WD6 199 G3
Edward Amey Cl GSTN WD25 182 B7
Edward Cl ABLGY WD5 181 L3
STAL AL1 11 J8
Edward Ct HHS/BOV HP3 166 C3 1
WAB EN9 191 L4
Edward Gv EBAR EN4 201 J6 2
Edward Rd EBAR EN4 201 J6
Edward St DUN/WHIP LU6 80 F1
LTNE LU2 3 G3
Edworth Rd BGSW SG18 16 D5
Edwyn Cl BAR EN5 200 B6
Egdon Dr LTNE LU2 65 J4
Egerton Rd BERK HP4 146 F4
Eight Acres TRING HP23 123 M6
Eighth Av LTNN/LIM LU3 64 C3
Eisenberg Cl BLDK SG7 41 G1 3
Eisenhower Rd SHFD SG17 24 B1
Elaine Gdns LTN LU1 106 F1
Elbow La HERT/BAY SG13 159 G3
STVGE SG2 89 G1
Eldefield LWTH SG6 39 J3
Elderbeck Cl CHESW EN7 175 M7
Elderberry Cl LTNE LU2 66 A6 2
Elderberry Dr
HTCHE/RSTV SG4 52 F6 2
Elderberry Wy GSTN WD25 182 A6 2
Elder Ct BUSH WD23 207 K2
Elderfield HLWE CM17 142 C6
Elder Rd WARE SG12 116 E7
Elder Wy STVG SG1 4 D7
Eldon Av BORE WD6 198 F3
Eldon Rd HOD EN11 160 C6
LTNW/LEA LU4 64 B8
Eleanor Av STALW/RED AL3 10 E2
Eleanor Cross Rd
CHES/WCR EN8 190 D5
Eleanor Gdns BAR EN5 200 C6 1
Eleanor Rd CFSP/GDCR SL9 202 B8
CHES/WCR EN8 190 D4
HERT/WAS SG14 137 H3
Eleanor's Cross
DUN/WHIP LU6 81 G2 1
Eleanor Wy CHES/WCR EN8 190 E5
Elfrida Rd WATW WD18 13 G7
Elgar Cl BORE WD6 198 B8
Elgin Dr NTHWD HA6 205 K7
Elgin Rd BROX EN10 176 E3
CHES/WCR EN8 190 B1
Elgood Av NTHWD HA6 205 M7
Eliot Rd ROY SG8 21 J2
STVGE SG2 71 H4
Elizabeth Av AMS HP6 192 B2
Elizabeth Cl BAR EN5 200 C4
WAB EN9 177 J2
WGCE AL7 135 H4 5
Elizabeth Ct STALE/WH AL4 153 J4
Elizabeth Dr TRING HP23 124 A4
Elizabeth Rd BSF CM23 96 D5
Elizabeth St LTN LU1 2 D8
Elizabeth Wy HLW CM20 140 F8
HLWW/ROY CM19 161 L3
Ellenborough Cl BSF CM23 96 C5
Ellenbrook Cl WATN WD24 196 B2 1
Ellenbrook Crs HAT AL10 154 C5 1
Ellenbrook La HAT AL10 154 D6
Ellen Cl HHNE HP2 8 E6
Ellenhall Cl LTNN/LIM LU3 2 B2
Ellerdine Cl LTNN/LIM LU3 65 G6 1
Ellesborough Cl OXHEY WD19 206 B5
Ellesfield WLYN AL6 112 A5
Ellesmere Cl DUN/WHIP LU6 80 B4
Ellesmere Gv BAR EN5 200 E6 1
Ellesmere Rd BERK HP4 147 J6
Ellingham Cl HHNE HP2 9 G5
Ellingham Rd HHNE HP2 8 F6
Elliott Cl WGCE AL7 134 C7
Elliott Rd STAN HA7 207 M6
Ellis Av CFSP/GDCR SL9 202 E8
STVG SG1 70 D2
Elliswick Rd HARP AL5 109 G8
Ellwood Gdns GSTN WD25 182 A5
Elm Av LTN LU1 82 D7
OXHEY WD19 196 D8
Elmbank Av BAR EN5 200 B5
Elmbridge HLWE CM17 142 E7
Elmbrook Dr BSF CM23 96 D6 1
Elm Cl HNLW SG16 25 J1
RBSF CM22 99 H3
WAB EN9 191 J5
Elm Close Extension
RBSF CM22 99 H3 1
Elmcote Wy RKW/CH/CXG WD3 194 E7
Elm Dr CHES/WCR EN8 176 D7
HAT AL10 154 F6
STALE/WH AL4 153 H7
Elmfield Cl POTB/CUF EN6 186 D4 1
Elmfield Rd POTB/CUF EN6 186 D4
Elm Gdns WGCW AL8 134 A4
Elm Gn HHW HP1 148 D5
Elm Gv BERK HP4 147 H6
BSF CM23 97 G3
WATN WD24 181 M8
Elm Hatch PIN HA5 206 E7
Elmhurst Cl BSF CM23 96 D3
Elmhurst Gdns
HTCH/STOT SG5 36 E1 1
Elmhurst Rd PEND EN3 190 B8
Elmoor Av WLYN AL6 112 A5
Elmoor Cl WLYN AL6 112 A6
Elmore Rd LTNE LU2 3 J2
Elm Pk BLDK SG7 40 E2 1
Elm Park Cl DUN/HR/TOD LU5 63 J4
Elm Rd BAR EN5 200 E5
BSF CM23 96 D2
Elmroyd Av POTB/CUF EN6 186 E4
Elmroyd Cl POTB/CUF EN6 186 E4
Elms Cl HTCHE/RSTV SG4 53 K7
Elmscroft Gdns POTB/CUF EN6 186 E3
Elmside DUN/WHIP LU6 105 J2
Elmside Wk HTCH/STOT SG5 52 D3
Elms Rd CFSP/GDCR SL9 202 D7
KTN/HRWW/W HA3 207 K7
WARE SG12 116 F8
The Elms HERT/BAY SG13 137 M4
WLYN AL6 87 L8
Elm Ter KTN/HRWW/W HA3 207 J7
Elmtree Av LTNE LU2 66 D7
Elm Tree Wk
RKW/CH/CXG WD3 193 L5 1
TRING HP23 123 M5
Elm Wk RAD WD7 183 L7
ROY SG8 21 L3
STVGE SG2 5 L7
Elm Wy RKW/CH/CXG WD3 204 A1
Elmwood SBW CM21 142 E1
WGCW AL8 134 A5
Elmwood Av BLDK SG7 40 E3 1
BORE WD6 199 G5
Elmwood Crs LTNE LU2 65 K7
Elsinge Rd EN EN1 190 A7
Elstree Hl North BORE WD6 198 C6
Elstree Hl South BORE WD6 198 C8
Elstree Rd BORE WD6 197 M7
BUSH WD23 207 J1
HHNE HP2 149 M1
STAN HA7 197 L8
Elstree Wy BORE WD6 199 J3
Elton Av BAR EN5 200 E6
Elton Rd HERT/WAS SG14 137 H3
Elveden Cl LTNE LU2 65 K4
Elvington Gdns LTNN/LIM LU3 65 G1
Elwood HLWE CM17 163 K3
Ely Cl HAT AL10 154 E4
STVG SG1 55 G8
Ely Gdns BORE WD6 199 J6
Ely Rd STAL AL1 153 G8
Ely Wy LTNW/LEA LU4 64 C6
Embleton Rd OXHEY WD19 205 M3
Embry Cl STAN HA7 207 M4
Embry Dr STAN HA7 207 M6
Embry Wy STAN HA7 207 M5
Emerald Rd LTNW/LEA LU4 63 L8
Emerton Ct BERK HP4 146 D3 1
Emerton Garth BERK HP4 146 D3
Emmanuel Rd NTHWD HA6 205 L7
Emma Rothschild Ct
TRING HP23 123 M5 1
Emma's Crs WARE SG12 139 G6
Emmer Gn LTNE LU2 66 E8
Emmitt Cl RAD WD7 184 D4 2
Emperor Cl BERK HP4 146 E3
Emperors Ga STVGE SG2 71 H2
Empress Rd LTNN/LIM LU3 64 D6 1
Endeavour Rd CHES/WCR EN8 176 C6
Enderby Rd LTNN/LIM LU3 65 H3
Enderley Rd
KTN/HRWW/W HA3 207 J8
Endersby Rd BAR EN5 200 B6
Endymion Ct HAT AL10 155 H4 1
Endymion Ms HAT AL10 155 H4 2
Endymion Rd HAT AL10 155 H4
Enfield Cl DUN/HR/TOD LU5 63 J4
England Av DUN/WHIP LU6 62 E7 1
Englands La DUN/HR/TOD LU5 81 H2
Englehurst HARP AL5 131 J1 2
Enid Cl LCOL/BKTW AL2 182 E2
Ennerdale Av DUN/WHIP LU6 81 G3
Ennerdale Cl STAL AL1 170 A1
Ennis Cl HARP AL5 131 J4 3
Ennismore Cl LWTH SG6 40 B7 2
Ennismore Gn LTNE LU2 84 E1
Enslow Cl LTN LU1 82 D7
Enterprise Wy LTNN/LIM LU3 65 G2
Epping Gn HHNE HP2 150 A2
Epping Rd WAB EN9 161 L7
Epping Wy LTNN/LIM LU3 64 B1
Ereswell Rd LTNN/LIM LU3 64 F3
Erin Cl LTNW/LEA LU4 64 F8
Ermine Cl CHESW EN7 190 A2 1
ROY SG8 21 J2
STALW/RED AL3 151 M8
Ermine Ct BUNT SG9 58 D2 2
Ermine St BUNT SG9 44 C7
WARE SG12 116 C3
Escarpment Av DUN/WHIP LU6 104 C2
Escot Wy BAR EN5 200 B6
Esdaile La HOD EN11 159 M5
Eskdale LCOL/BKTW AL2 170 E6
LTNW/LEA LU4 64 B5
Essendon Gdns WGCE AL7 134 E4
Essendon Hl BRKMPK AL9 156 D4
Essex Cl LTN LU1 2 F9
Essex La ABLGY WD5 181 J4
Essex Md HHNE HP2 149 L1
Essex Rd BORE WD6 198 F4
HOD EN11 160 A4
STVG SG1 70 A2
WAT WD17 12 D1
Essex St STAL AL1 11 G5
Estcourt Rd WAT WD17 13 G3
Estfeld Cl HOD EN11 160 A1 2
Ethelred Cl WGCE AL7 134 E5
Etna Rd STALW/RED AL3 10 E5
Eton Av EBAR EN4 201 K7
Europa Rd HHNE HP2 8 F3
Euston Av WATW WD18 12 B7
Evans Av GSTN WD25 181 L6
Evans Cl DUN/HR/TOD LU5 63 J6
RKW/CH/CXG WD3 194 F6
Evans Gv STALE/WH AL4 153 H3
Evans Wy TRING HP23 124 A6 1
Evedon Cl LTNN/LIM LU3 64 E4
Evelyn Dr PIN HA5 206 C7
Evelyn Rd DUN/HR/TOD LU5 63 L8
EBAR EN4 201 L5
Evensyde WATW WD18 195 H7
Everard Cl STAL AL1 169 J1 1
Everest Cl ARL/CHE SG15 26 A5
Everest Wy HHNE HP2 9 G8
Everett Cl BUSH WD23 207 K1
CHESW EN7 175 H4 2
Evergreen Cl KNEB SG3 88 F8
Evergreen Rd WARE SG12 116 E7
Evergreen Wk HHS/BOV HP3 166 D1
Evergreen Wy LTNN/LIM LU3 64 F2
Everlasting La STALW/RED AL3 10 D2
Eversleigh Rd BAR EN5 201 H6
Exchange Rd STVG SG1 5 G4
WATW WD18 12 F5
Exeter Cl STVG SG1 55 G8
WATN WD24 196 B3
Explorer Dr WATW WD18 12 B8
Extension Rd
HERT/BAY SG13 137 L4 5
Exton Av LTNE LU2 3 K3
Eyeworth Rd SDY/GAM/PO SG19 15 G1
Eyncourt Rd DUN/HR/TOD LU5 63 H8
Eynsford Ct HTCHE/RSTV SG4 52 E4
Eynsford Rd LTNW/LEA LU4 64 C7 1
Eywood Rd STAL AL1 169 H1

F

Faggots Cl RAD WD7 184 B6
Faints Cl CHESW EN7 175 K8
Fairacre HHS/BOV HP3 166 E3
Fairacres Cl POTB/CUF EN6 186 E4
Fairburn Cl BORE WD6 198 F2 1
Fair Cl BUSH WD23 197 G8
Faircross Wy STAL AL1 11 L3
Fairfax Av LTNN/LIM LU3 64 C3
Fairfax Rd HERT/BAY SG13 137 L3
Fairfield BUNT SG9 58 E4
Fairfield Av OXHEY WD19 206 B3
Fairfield Cl HARP AL5 131 J1 3
RAD WD7 183 K8 1
Fairfield Dr BROX EN10 176 E3
Fairfield Rd DUN/HR/TOD LU5 81 K1
HOD EN11 159 M2
Fairfield Wy BAR EN5 200 F6
HTCHE/RSTV SG4 53 H2
Fairfolds GSTN WD25 182 D6
Fairford Av LTNE LU2 65 K5
Fairgreen EBAR EN4 201 L4
Fairgreen Rd LTN LU1 82 E7
Fairhaven Crs OXHEY WD19 205 M3
Fairhill HHS/BOV HP3 166 E3 2
STVG SG1 4 A3
Fairlands Wy STVG SG1 4 E2
STVGE SG2 71 G2
Fairlawns WAT WD17 195 L2
Fairley Wy CHESW EN7 176 A7
Fairmead Av HARP AL5 131 H2
Fair Oak Dr LTNE LU2 65 L7
Fairoaks Gv PEND EN3 190 C8
Fairseat Cl BUSH WD23 207 K2 1
Fairthorn Cl TRING HP23 123 K7 2
Fair Vw POTB/CUF EN6 187 G1
Fairview Dr WAT WD17 181 K7
Fairview Rd STVG SG1 70 A2
Fairway BSF CM23 97 H4
HHS/BOV HP3 166 E3
SBW CM21 120 E8
WARE SG12 138 B2
Fairway Av BORE WD6 199 G3 2
Fairway Cl HARP AL5 130 F5
LCOL/BKTW AL2 169 H6
Fairways CHES/WCR EN8 176 C5
The Fairway ABLGY WD5 181 J3
BAR EN5 201 G7
HLWS CM18 162 E5
NTHWD HA6 205 K4
Fakeswell La HNLW SG16 24 D8
Falcon Cl DUN/WHIP LU6 80 F1
HAT AL10 154 F7
NTHWD HA6 205 K7
SBW CM21 142 B1
STVGE SG2 71 J8
Falconer Rd BUSH WD23 196 F7
Falconers Fld HARP AL5 108 C7
Falconers Pk SBW CM21 142 C1
Falconers Rd LTNE LU2 3 M3
Falconer St BSF CM23 96 B5
Falcon Rdg BERK HP4 147 H7
Falcon Wy GSTN WD25 182 D5
WGCE AL7 134 D2
Faldo Rd AMP/FLIT/B MK45 34 F6
Falkirk Gdns OXHEY WD19 206 C5 2
Falkland Rd BAR EN5 200 D3
Fallowfield LTNN/LIM LU3 65 G6
STAN HA7 207 M3
STVGE SG2 71 H7
WGCE AL7 134 E1
Fallowfield Cl DEN/HRF UB9 204 B8
Fallowfield Ct STAN HA7 207 M3 1
Fallow Ri HERT/BAY SG13 137 K4
Fallows Gn HARP AL5 109 G7
Falstaff Gdns STAL AL1 169 G2
Falstone Gn LTNE LU2 66 D8
Fanhams Hall Rd WARE SG12 116 D7
Fanhams Rd WARE SG12 116 D8
Fanshaw Ct HERT/WAS SG14 137 G3
Fanshawe Crs WARE SG12 116 A8
Fanshawe St HERT/WAS SG14 137 G3
Fanshaws La HERT/BAY SG13 158 B5
Fantail La TRING HP23 123 L6
Faraday Cl LTNW/LEA LU4 82 B1 1
WATW WD18 195 J7
Faraday Rd STVGE SG2 5 L1
Far End HAT AL10 155 G8
Faringdon Rd LTNW/LEA LU4 64 B7
Faringford Cl POTB/CUF EN6 187 J2 2
Farland Rd HHNE HP2 9 H9
Farley Farm Rd LTN LU1 83 G5
Farley Hl LTN LU1 83 G6
Farm Av HARP AL5 108 C6
Farmbrook LTNE LU2 65 J3
Farm Cl AMS HP6 192 C2
BAR EN5 200 A6
BORE WD6 198 D1 1
CHES/WCR EN8 190 B1
DUN/HR/TOD LU5 63 H5
HERT/WAS SG14 136 F4
LWTH SG6 39 M1
POTB/CUF EN6 174 D6
STVG SG1 4 E6
WGCW AL8 134 B4
Farmer Ct WAB EN9 191 M4
Farmers Cl GSTN WD25 182 A4
Farm Gn LTN LU1 83 H5
Farm Hill Rd WAB EN9 191 J5
Farmhouse Cl BROX EN10 176 E4 1
Farmhouse La HHNE HP2 9 G4
Farm La RKW/CH/CXG WD3 194 A4
STDN SG11 92 F2
STHGT/OAK N14 201 M7
Farm Pl BERK HP4 146 E5 1
Farm Rd LTN LU1 108 A3
NTHWD HA6 205 H5
RKW/CH/CXG WD3 192 F5
STAL AL1 153 G6
Farmstead Rd
KTN/HRWW/W HA3 207 J8
Farm Wy BUSH WD23 197 G5
NTHWD HA6 205 K4
Farnham Cl HHS/BOV HP3 164 F7
SBW CM21 142 B1
TRDG/WHET N20 201 H8
Farquhar St HERT/WAS SG14 137 H3
Farraline Rd WATW WD18 12 F5
Farrant Wy BORE WD6 198 D2 1
Farrer Top STALW/RED AL3 106 D5
Farriday Cl STALW/RED AL3 152 D3
Farriers WARE SG12 138 F4
Farriers Cl BLDK SG7 40 D1 3
WLYN AL6 111 L1 2
Farriers End BROX EN10 176 E5 1
Farriers Wy BORE WD6 199 J7
Farringford Cl LCOL/BKTW AL2 168 F5
Farrow Cl LTNN/LIM LU3 65 G1
Farr's La LTNE LU2 109 G1
Farthingale La WAB EN9 191 M5
Farthing Dr LWTH SG6 40 B7
The Farthings HHW HP1 149 G7 1
Faverolle Gn CHES/WCR EN8 176 C7 4
Faversham Cl TRING HP23 123 M6
Fawcett Rd STVGE SG2 71 G2
Fawn Ct BRKMPK AL9 155 H3
Fay Gn ABLGY WD5 181 J4
Feacey Down HHW HP1 148 F5
Fearney Md RKW/CH/CXG WD3 203 M1
Fearnley Rd WGCW AL8 134 B5
Fearnley St WATW WD18 12 E5
Featherbed La HHS/BOV HP3 166 B3
Feather Dell HAT AL10 154 E5
Featherstone Gdns BORE WD6 199 J5
Featherston Rd STVGE SG2 71 H7
Federal Wy WATN WD24 196 B2 2
Felbridge Av STAN HA7 207 M8
Felbrigg Cl LTNE LU2 66 E8
Felden Cl GSTN WD25 182 C5
Felden Dr HHS/BOV HP3 165 M3
Felden La HHS/BOV HP3 165 M2
Feldon Cl PIN HA5 206 D7
Felix Av LTNE LU2 65 M8
Fellowes La STALE/WH AL4 171 J2
Fellowes Wy STVGE SG2 70 E8
Fells Cl HTCH/STOT SG5 52 E2
Felmersham Ct LTN LU1 83 G3 1
Felmersham Rd LTN LU1 82 F3
Felmongers HLW CM20 142 A8
Felstead Cl LTNE LU2 65 L7 1
Felstead Rd CHES/WCR EN8 190 D3
Felstead Wy LTNE LU2 65 L8
Felton Cl BORE WD6 198 D1 2
BROX EN10 176 E4 2
LTNE LU2 84 C1
Fen End HTCH/STOT SG5 26 E2
Fennells HLWW/ROY CM19 162 A7
Fennycroft Rd HHW HP1 148 E4

Fensome Dr DUN/HR/TOD LU5 63 K5
Fensomes Aly HHNE HP2 8 A7
Fenton Gra HLWE CM17 163 H3
Fenwick Cl LTNN/LIM LU3 65 G5 2
Fenwick Rd DUN/HR/TOD LU5 63 K5
Fermor Crs LTNE LU2 84 B1
Fern Cl BROX EN10 176 E2 1
Ferndale MHAD SG10 94 E8
Ferndale Rd LTN LU1 83 G3
PEND EN3 190 D8
Fern Dells HAT AL10 154 E6
Ferndene LCOL/BKTW AL2 182 E2
Ferndown Cl PIN HA5 206 D7
Ferndown Rd OXHEY WD19 206 B3
Fern Dr HHS/BOV HP3 149 K8
Fernecroft STAL AL1 169 H2
Ferney Rd EBAR EN4 201 M8
Fern Gv WGCW AL8 112 C8
Fernheath LTNN/LIM LU3 64 F1
Fernhill HLWS CM18 162 D6
Fern Hill La HLWS CM18 162 E6
Fernhills ABLGY WD5 181 J5
Fernleys STALE/WH AL4 153 H4
Ferns Cl PEND EN3 190 D7 1
Fernsleigh Cl
CFSP/GDCR SL9 202 D6 2
Fernville La HHNE HP2 8 A8
Fern Wy GSTN WD25 182 A6
Ferny Hl EBAR EN4 201 L1
Ferrars Cl LTNW/LEA LU4 82 A1
Ferrers La STALE/WH AL4 131 M5
STALE/WH AL4 132 C5
Ferrier Rd STVGE SG2 71 H4
Ferryhills Cl OXHEY WD19 206 B3
Fesants Cft HLW CM20 142 A7
Fetherstone Cl
POTB/CUF EN6 187 J4 1
Fiddle Bridge La HAT AL10 154 E4
Fidler Pl BUSH WD23 197 G7 3
Field Cl HARP AL5 131 J3
STALE/WH AL4 152 F3
Field Crs ROY SG8 21 L3
Field End Cl LTNE LU2 66 B6 2
OXHEY WD19 196 D8 1
Fielders Wy RAD WD7 184 D4
Fieldfare LWTH SG6 39 K1
STVGE SG2 71 J7
Field Fare Gn LTNW/LEA LU4 63 M5
Fieldfares LCOL/BKTW AL2 170 C6
Fieldgate Rd LTNW/LEA LU4 64 A7
Fieldings Rd CHES/WCR EN8 176 E8
Field La LWTH SG6 39 L6
Field Rd HHNE HP2 9 H9
OXHEY WD19 13 L9
Fields End TRING HP23 123 M4
Fields End La HHW HP1 148 C5
Fieldside Rd AMP/FLIT/B MK45 34 D1
Field Vw BAR EN5 200 A5
Field View Ri LCOL/BKTW AL2 168 D8
Field View Rd POTB/CUF EN6 186 F4
Fieldway BERK HP4 147 K8
Field Wy CFSP/GDCR SL9 202 C7
HHW HP1 164 F6
HOD EN11 139 G8
RKW/CH/CXG WD3 204 A1
Fieldway TRING HP23 145 J1
WARE SG12 139 G6
Fifth Av GSTN WD25 182 C6
LWTH SG6 40 B4
Fifth Avenue/allende Av
HLW CM20 6 E2
Fifth Avenue Allende Av
HLW CM20 6 E2
Figtree Hl HHNE HP2 8 A6
Fildyke Rd SHFD SG17 24 B4
Filey Cl STVG SG1 69 M3
Filmer Rd LTNW/LEA LU4 64 D6
Finch Cl BAR EN5 200 F6
HAT AL10 154 F7
LTNW/LEA LU4 63 M6
Finchdale HHW HP1 148 F7
Finches End STVGE SG2 72 A2
The Finches HERT/BAY SG13 138 A4 1
HTCHE/RSTV SG4 52 F3
Finch Gn RKW/CH/CXG WD3 193 L5
Finch La BUSH WD23 196 F6
Finchmoor HLWS CM18 162 C5
Finch Rd BERK HP4 146 F6
Finley Rd HARP AL5 109 J7
Finsbury Rd LTNW/LEA LU4 64 C5
Finucane Ri BUSH WD23 207 H2
Finway LTN LU1 82 F2
Finway Rd HHNE HP2 9 J1
Firbank Cl LTNN/LIM LU3 64 B2
Firbank Dr OXHEY WD19 196 D8
Firbank Rd STALW/RED AL3 152 E3
Fir Cl STVGE SG2 88 E1
Firecrest LWTH SG6 39 K1
Firlands BSF CM23 96 D4
Fir Pk HLWW/ROY CM19 162 A5
Firs Cl HAT AL10 155 G6
HTCH/STOT SG5 52 C2 2
Firs Dr STALE/WH AL4 110 B5
Firs La POTB/CUF EN6 187 G4
First Av DUN/WHIP LU6 81 G3
GSTN WD25 182 B6
First Avenue Mandela Av
HLW CM20 6 E4
HLWE CM17 142 A7
The Firs CHESW EN7 175 K5
STAL AL1 170 A3
TRING HP23 145 J1
WGCW AL8 112 B8
Firs Wk NTHWD HA6 205 J6
WLYN AL6 113 J5
Fir Tree Cl HHS/BOV HP3 149 M8
Fir Tree Ct BORE WD6 198 E5
Fir Tree Hl RKW/CH/CXG WD3 180 F8
Firway WLYN AL6 112 E3
Firway Cl WLYN AL6 112 E3
Firwood Av STALE/WH AL4 153 K7
Fisher Cl KGLGY WD4 166 F8
Fishers Cl CHES/WCR EN8 190 F5
STDN SG11 75 J7
Fishers Gn STVG SG1 69 M1
Fisher's Green Rd STVG SG1 70 A2
Fishers Md STDN SG11 75 J7
Fishery Rd HHW HP1 165 M1
Fish Farm St STALW/RED AL3 130 A5 2
Fish Hl ROY SG8 21 J4
Fishponds Rd HTCH/STOT SG5 52 D2
Fishpool St STALW/RED AL3 10 B6
Fish St STALW/RED AL3 130 A5
Fitzjohn Av BAR EN5 200 D6
Fitzroy Av LTNN/LIM LU3 65 G7
Fitzwarin Cl LTNN/LIM LU3 64 D3
Fitzwilliams Ct HLWE CM17 142 D6 1
Five Acres HLWS CM18 162 D5
KGLGY WD4 166 E8
LCOL/BKTW AL2 170 C4
STSD CM24 79 K2
Five Acres Av LCOL/BKTW AL2 168 E8
Five Fields Cl OXHEY WD19 206 E2
Five Oaks LTN LU1 82 E7
Five Springs LTNN/LIM LU3 64 D4
Flagstaff Cl WAB EN9 191 G4
Flagstaff Rd WAB EN9 191 G3
The Flags HHNE HP2 9 K8
Flamsteadbury La
STALW/RED AL3 129 M6
Flamstead End Rd
CHES/WCR EN8 176 A7
Flash La ENC/FH EN2 189 H8
Flatfield Rd HHS/BOV HP3 166 F1
Flaunden Bottom CSHM HP5 178 E5
Flaunden Hl HHS/BOV HP3 178 E4
Flaunden La HHS/BOV HP3 179 G4
RKW/CH/CXG WD3 179 K4
Flavian Cl STALW/RED AL3 168 E1
Flecker Cl STAN HA7 207 L5
The Fleet ROY SG8 21 H4
Fleetwood Crs STVG SG1 70 A3
Fleetwood Wy OXHEY WD19 206 B4
Fleming Cl CHESW EN7 175 M5
Fleming Crs HERT/WAS SG14 136 F4 2
Fletcher Wy HHNE HP2 149 H5
Flexley Wd WGCE AL7 134 E1
Flex Meadow
HLWW/ROY CM19 161 K3
Flinders Cl STAL AL1 169 M1
STVGE SG2 71 H5
Flint Cl LTNN/LIM LU3 64 D3
Flint Copse STALW/RED AL3 130 B4
The Flintings HHNE HP2 127 L2
Flint Rd LWTH SG6 40 B2
Flint Wy STALW/RED AL3 152 B3
Flitch Wy RBSF CM22 98 C3
RBSF CM22 99 L3
Flitton Rd AMP/FLIT/B MK45 34 D1
Flora Gv STAL AL1 11 K8
Floral Dr LCOL/BKTW AL2 170 C5
Florence Av LTNN/LIM LU3 64 C4
Florence Cl GSTN WD25 181 M6 1
HLWE CM17 163 H4 1
Florence St HTCH/STOT SG5 52 E2
Florida Cl BUSH WD23 207 J2
Flowers Wy LTN LU1 2 E7
Flowmere Rd ROY SG8 23 M5
Flowton Gv HARP AL5 130 F3
Fold Cft HLW CM20 6 A5
Foldingshott KNEB SG3 89 J7
Follett Dr ABLGY WD5 181 L2
Folly Av STALW/RED AL3 10 D4
Folly Cl HTCHE/RSTV SG4 52 F5
RAD WD7 183 L7
Folly Flds STALE/WH AL4 110 A8
Folly La LTN LU1 82 D6
STALW/RED AL3 10 C5
Folly Pathway RAD WD7 183 L6
The Folly BUNT SG9 58 C3
HERT/WAS SG14 137 J4
Folly Vw WARE SG12 139 G5
Fontmell Cl STALW/RED AL3 11 H2
Fontwell Cl KTN/HRWW/W HA3 207 K7
Football Cl BLDK SG7 40 D1
Forbes Av POTB/CUF EN6 187 J4
Ford Cl BUSH WD23 197 H5 1
Ford Fld STDN SG11 94 F2
Fordham Cl BLDK SG7 18 C5
Fordham Rd EBAR EN4 201 J4
ROY SG8 21 K5 1
Ford Hl STDN SG11 95 G2
Ford St STDN SG11 75 K4
Fordwich Cl HERT/WAS SG14 136 F4 3
Fordwich Hl HERT/WAS SG14 136 F4
Fordwich Ri HERT/WAS SG14 136 F4
Fordwich Rd WGCW AL8 134 B5 1
Forebury Av SBW CM21 120 E8
The Forebury SBW CM21 120 E8
Forefield LCOL/BKTW AL2 168 F6
Forest Av HHS/BOV HP3 166 C1 1
Foresters Cl CHESW EN7 175 K6
Foresthall Rd STSD CM24 79 J6
Fore St BRKMPK AL9 155 H4
HERT/WAS SG14 137 J4
HLWE CM17 142 B6
HTCHE/RSTV SG4 55 G1
Forest Rd CHES/WCR EN8 176 C8
GSTN WD25 182 A4
PEND EN3 190 D7
Forest Rw STVGE SG2 88 E1
Forest Wy HLWE CM17 143 H8
HLWE CM17 163 G6
RBSF CM22 98 B4
RBSF CM22 121 M3
Forge Cl HTCH/STOT SG5 52 E2 2
KGLGY WD4 179 M2
Forge End LCOL/BKTW AL2 168 F5
Forge La NTHWD HA6 205 K7
WLYN AL6 112 A5
Forres Cl HOD EN11 159 M2
Forrest Crs LTNE LU2 65 M7
Forresters Dr WGCE AL7 135 H5 1
Fortnums Acre STAN HA7 207 L6 3
Fortuna Cl STVGE SG2 71 H2
Fortune La BORE WD6 198 C7
The Fortunes HLWS CM18 162 E4
Forty Hl EN EN1 189 L8
Foster Av DUN/HR/TOD LU5 63 G7
Foster Cl CHES/WCR EN8 190 D1 1
STVG SG1 70 B1
Foster Dr HTCHE/RSTV SG4 52 F5
Foster Rd HHW HP1 166 A1 1
Foster St HLWE CM17 163 L4
Foston Cl LTNN/LIM LU3 64 E5
Fotherley Rd
RKW/CH/CXG WD3 203 L2
Founceley Av WARE SG12 91 L2
Founders Rd HOD EN11 160 A1
Fountain Farm HLWS CM18 162 E4 1
Fountain Pl WAB EN9 191 H5 1
Fountains Rd LTNN/LIM LU3 65 H7
Fouracres LWTH SG6 39 M8
Four Acres STVG SG1 70 C3
WGCE AL7 134 D6
Fouracres Dr HHS/BOV HP3 166 E1
The Four Acres SBW CM21 120 F8
Fouracres Wk HHS/BOV HP3 166 E1
Four Limes STALE/WH AL4 132 C2
Fourth Av GSTN WD25 182 C6 1
HLW CM20 6 E5
HLWW/ROY CM19 161 M2
LTNN/LIM LU3 64 C3
LWTH SG6 40 B3
The Four Tubs BUSH WD23 197 J8 1
BUSH WD23 197 J8 1
Fovant Cl HARP AL5 131 H4
Fowlers Dr SHFD SG17 24 A4
Fowley Cl CHES/WCR EN8 190 E5 1
Foxbury Cl LTNE LU2 65 J4
Fox Cl BGSW SG18 14 C5
BORE WD6 198 C7 2
BUSH WD23 197 G6
TRING HP23 145 H1
Fox Cnr ROY SG8 15 L5
Foxcroft STAL AL1 169 M1
Foxdell NTHWD HA6 205 J6
Fox Dells DUN/WHIP LU6 81 H5
Foxdells HERT/WAS SG14 136 B7
Foxdells La BSF CM23 78 E8
Foxdell Wy CFSP/GDCR SL9 202 D5
Foxes Cl HERT/BAY SG13 138 A4
Foxes Dr CHESW EN7 175 L8
Foxes La POTB/CUF EN6 174 D7
Foxfield STVGE SG2 71 H7
Foxfield Cl NTHWD HA6 205 L6
Foxglove Bank ROY SG8 21 L5 1
Foxglove Cl BSF CM23 96 B4
HAT AL10 155 G6 1
The Foxgloves HHW HP1 148 D8
Foxglove Wy WLYN AL6 112 D2 1
Foxgrove Pth OXHEY WD19 206 C5
Foxhill LTNE LU2 65 K5
Fox Hl ROY SG8 15 L5
Foxhill WATN WD24 181 M7
Fox Hill Rd ROY SG8 15 L5
Foxholes Av HERT/BAY SG13 137 M4 1
Foxhollows HAT AL10 155 G3
Foxlands Cl GSTN WD25 181 L5
Foxley Dr BSF CM23 96 F2
Foxley Gv WLYN AL6 112 D6
Foxleys OXHEY WD19 206 D3
Fox Rd STVG SG1 4 E4
TRING HP23 124 B8
Fox's La BRKMPK AL9 172 D3
Foxton Rd HOD EN11 159 L4
Frampton Rd POTB/CUF EN6 187 H1
Frampton St HERT/WAS SG14 137 J4
Francis Av STALW/RED AL3 152 C4
Francis Cl HTCH/STOT SG5 26 D4
HTCHE/RSTV SG4 52 F5
Francis Rd BLDK SG7 17 H4
WARE SG12 116 C8
WATW WD18 12 E4
Francis St LTN LU1 2 B5
Frankland Cl
RKW/CH/CXG WD3 194 F8
Frankland Rd
RKW/CH/CXG WD3 195 G7
Franklin Av AMP/FLIT/B MK45 35 G7
CHESW EN7 189 M1
Franklin Cl HTCH/STOT SG5 37 J6
STALE/WH AL4 171 K1
TRDG/WHET N20 201 H8
Franklin Gdns HTCHE/RSTV SG4 53 G1
Franklin Rd DUN/WHIP LU6 80 E2
WAT WD17 12 F1
Franklin's Rd STVG SG1 70 B2
Frank Martin Ct CHESW EN7 189 M1
Franks Cl HNLW SG16 25 G5
Fraser Rd CHES/WCR EN8 176 D7 3
Frederick St LTNE LU2 2 E4
Frederick Street Pas LTNE LU2 2 D3
Freeman Av LTNN/LIM LU3 65 G2
Freemans Cl
DUN/HR/TOD LU5 62 F6 2
HTCH/STOT SG5 52 B1
Freewaters Cl HTCH/STOT SG5 38 D6
Freman Dr BUNT SG9 58 C2 3
French Horn La HAT AL10 155 G4 3
French Rw STAL AL1 10 E7
French's Av DUN/WHIP LU6 62 D8
French's Cl WARE SG12 138 F5
Frensham CHESW EN7 175 L6
Frensham Dr HTCHE/RSTV SG4 39 H8
Freshwater Cl LTNN/LIM LU3 64 E3
Freshwaters HLW CM20 7 H4
Freston Gdns EBAR EN4 201 M6
Fretherne Rd WGCW AL8 134 C4
Friars Cl LTN LU1 83 G5
Friarscroft BROX EN10 159 M7
Friars Fld BERK HP4 146 D3
Friars Rd HTCHE/RSTV SG4 55 G1
STDN SG11 75 M3
Friars Wk DUN/WHIP LU6 81 G3
TRING HP23 123 M6
Friars Wy BUSH WD23 196 E2
KGLGY WD4 180 F1
LTN LU1 83 G5
Friars Wd BSF CM23 97 H2
Friary Fld DUN/WHIP LU6 81 G2
Friday Furlong
HTCH/STOT SG5 52 B2 1
Friedberg Av BSF CM23 96 C7
Friendless La STALW/RED AL3 106 D7
Friends Av CHES/WCR EN8 190 C3
Friern Mount Dr
TRDG/WHET N20 201 H8
Friesian Cl LTNW/LEA LU4 63 M7
Frimley Rd HHW HP1 148 D6
Fringewood Cl NTHWD HA6 205 G8
Frinton Cl OXHEY WD19 206 A2
Friston Gn LTNE LU2 84 C1 1
Frithsden Copse BERK HP4 147 L2
Frithwood Av NTHWD HA6 205 L6
Frobisher Cl BUSH WD23 196 F7
Frobisher Dr STVGE SG2 71 G3
Frobisher Rd STAL AL1 170 B1
Frobisher Wy HAT AL10 154 C2
Froghall La STVGE SG2 72 A1
Frogmoor La
RKW/CH/CXG WD3 204 C2
Frogmore LCOL/BKTW AL2 169 K6
Frogmore Hl HERT/WAS SG14 89 M4
Frogmore Rd HHS/BOV HP3 166 C3 2
Frogmore St TRING HP23 123 M6
Frogs Hall La STDN SG11 73 L7
Frome Cl LTNW/LEA LU4 64 D6
Frome Sq HHNE HP2 149 M2 3
Front St LTN LU1 107 H1
The Front BERK HP4 148 A3
Frowick Cl BRKMPK AL9 172 A2
Frowyke Crs POTB/CUF EN6 185 M3
Fry Rd STVGE SG2 71 H5
Fryth Md STALW/RED AL3 10 A5
Fulbourne Cl LTNW/LEA LU4 64 D8
Fulford Gv OXHEY WD19 206 A2
Fuller Ct BSF CM23 96 F3 1
Fuller Gdns WATN WD24 182 A8
Fuller Rd WATN WD24 182 A8
Fullers Cl WAB EN9 191 L4
Fullers Ct LWTH SG6 39 K3
Fullers Md HLWE CM17 163 H3
Fuller Wy RKW/CH/CXG WD3 194 F6
Fulling Mill La WLYN AL6 112 A4
Fulmar Crs HHW HP1 148 F8
Fulmore Cl HARP AL5 109 J6
Fulton Cl STVG SG1 4 A4
Fulton Crs BSF CM23 97 H1
Furham Fld PIN HA5 206 F7
Furlay Cl LWTH SG6 39 J3
Furlong La DUN/WHIP LU6 80 B3
Furlongs HHW HP1 148 F6
Furlong Wy WARE SG12 138 E3
Furness Av DUN/WHIP LU6 81 H3
Furriers Cl BSF CM23 96 B5
The Furrows LTNN/LIM LU3 65 G3
Furse Av STALE/WH AL4 152 F4
Furtherfield ABLGY WD5 181 K3 1
Furtherground HHNE HP2 149 K8 3
Furzebushes La
LCOL/BKTW AL2 168 D4
Furze Cl LTNE LU2 65 J3
OXHEY WD19 206 B5
Furzedown STVGE SG2 5 M5
Furzedown Ct HARP AL5 131 G2
Furzefield Rd WGCE AL7 134 D5
Furze Gv ROY SG8 21 K5 2
Furzehill Rd BORE WD6 199 H6
Furzen Cl DUN/WHIP LU6 81 H5
Furzen Crs HAT AL10 154 E8
Furze Rd HHW HP1 148 D8
Furze Vw RKW/CH/CXG WD3 193 H7

G

Gable Cl ABLGY WD5 181 K3
PIN HA5 206 F7
Gables Av BORE WD6 198 E4
Gables Cl CFSP/GDCR SL9 202 D4
Gaddesden Crs GSTN WD25 182 C5
Gaddesden Gv WGCE AL7 135 G4 1
Gaddesden La STALW/RED AL3 128 F6
Gaddesden Rw HHNE HP2 127 M2
Gade Av WATW WD18 195 K5
Gade Bank RKW/CH/CXG WD3 195 J5
Gadebridge La HHW HP1 149 H5
Gadebridge Rd HHW HP1 149 G6
Gade Cl HHW HP1 149 G4
WATW WD18 195 K5
Gade Valley Cl KGLGY WD4 166 F7
Gade View Rd HHS/BOV HP3 166 B3
Gadmore La TRING HP23 144 D3
Gadswell Cl GSTN WD25 182 D7
Gage Cl ROY SG8 21 J2
Gainsborough Av STAL AL1 11 J5
Gainsborough Dr
DUN/HR/TOD LU5 63 J5 1
Gainsford Crs HTCHE/RSTV SG4 39 H8
Gainswood WGCE AL7 134 D5
Galdana Av BAR EN5 201 H4
Gallants Farm Rd EBAR EN4 201 K8
Gall End La STSD CM24 79 L3
Galley Gn HERT/BAY SG13 138 F8 1
Galley Hl HHW HP1 148 F5 1
Galleyhill Rd WAB EN9 191 K3 2
Galley La BAR EN5 199 M1
Galliard Cl LTNN/LIM LU3 65 G6
Galloway Cl BROX EN10 176 E5
BSF CM23 96 E2
Galloway Rd BSF CM23 96 E2
Gallows Hl KGLGY WD4 181 H2
Gallows Hill La ABLGY WD5 181 H3
Galston Rd LTNN/LIM LU3 64 C2
Galva Cl EBAR EN4 201 M5
Games Rd EBAR EN4 201 K4
Gammon Cl HHS/BOV HP3 149 M8
Gammons La WATN WD24 181 M8
Ganders Ash GSTN WD25 181 M4 1
Gandhi Ct WATN WD24 196 C3 3
Gangies Hl SBW CM21 119 M7
Gant Ct WAB EN9 191 L5
Ganton Wk OXHEY WD19 206 D4 1
Ganymede Pl HHNE HP2 8 F3
Gaping La HTCH/STOT SG5 52 C3
Garden Av HAT AL10 154 F8
Garden Cl BAR EN5 200 B5
HARP AL5 130 F5
ROY SG8 21 K3
STAL AL1 153 G6
WAT WD17 12 A1
Garden Ct STALE/WH AL4 132 C1
Garden Field La BERK HP4 147 L8
Gardenia Av LTNN/LIM LU3 64 F6
Garden La ROY SG8 21 J5
Garden Reach CSTG HP8 192 C4
Garden Rd ABLGY WD5 181 K2 1
BUNT SG9 58 D2
DUN/WHIP LU6 81 H3
KNEB SG3 89 G8
Garden Rw HTCH/STOT SG5 52 E2
The Gardens BLDK SG7 40 D2 2
BRKMPK AL9 172 D6
HNLW SG16 25 J1
HTCH/STOT SG5 26 D4
WAT WD17 195 L3
Garden Terrace Rd HLWE CM17 142 B6
Garden Wk ROY SG8 21 K3
STVG SG1 4 E4
Gardiners La BLDK SG7 18 C6
The Gardiners HLWE CM17 163 G3
Gardner's Cl DUN/WHIP LU6 80 D3
Garfield St WATN WD24 196 A1
Garland Cl CHES/WCR EN8 190 D2 2
HHNE HP2 8 B6
Garland Rd WARE SG12 138 D1
Garland Wy
RAYLNE/WEN HP22 122 D5 1
Garner Dr BROX EN10 176 D5
Garners Cl CFSP/GDCR SL9 202 D6
Garners End CFSP/GDCR SL9 202 D6
Garners Rd CFSP/GDCR SL9 202 D6
Garnett Cl WATN WD24 182 C8
Garnett Dr LCOL/BKTW AL2 168 E8
Garnetts RBSF CM22 99 G2
Garrard Wy STALE/WH AL4 132 C2
Garratts Rd BUSH WD23 197 H8
Garrett Cl DUN/WHIP LU6 81 J5
Garretts Md LTNE LU2 66 A7
Garsmouth Wy GSTN WD25 182 C7
Garston Crs GSTN WD25 182 B5 1
Garston Dr GSTN WD25 182 B5
Garston La GSTN WD25 182 C5
Garthland Dr BAR EN5 200 A6
Garth Rd LWTH SG6 39 K7
The Garth ABLGY WD5 181 J4
Gartlet Rd WAT WD17 12 F2
Gascoyne Wy HERT/BAY SG13 137 J5
Gas La ROY SG8 32 B7
Gatcombe Wy EBAR EN4 201 L4
Gate Cl BORE WD6 199 H2
Gatecroft HHS/BOV HP3 166 E1
Gate End NTHWD HA6 205 M7
Gatehill Gdns LTNN/LIM LU3 65 G1 2
Gatehill Rd NTHWD HA6 205 L7
Gatesbury Wy STDN SG11 75 K7 1
Gatesdene Cl BERK HP4 126 B2
Gateshead Rd BORE WD6 198 E3
Gates Wy STVG SG1 4 B2
Gateway Cl NTHWD HA6 205 H6
The Gateways CHESW EN7 175 J7
Gatwick Cl BSF CM23 97 G1 1
Gauldie Wy STDN SG11 75 J8
Gaumont Ap WATW WD18 12 F2
Gaunts Wy LWTH SG6 26 E8
Gaveston Dr BERK HP4 147 G4
Gayland Av LTNE LU2 3 L5
Gayton Cl LTNN/LIM LU3 64 F6
Gaywood Av CHES/WCR EN8 190 C1
Geddes Rd BUSH WD23 197 H5 2
Geddings Rd HOD EN11 160 A4
Geisthorp Ct WAB EN9 191 M4
Gelding Cl LTNW/LEA LU4 63 L5
The Generals Wk PEND EN3 190 D8 3
Gentlemens Fld WARE SG12 116 A7
George La ROY SG8 21 J4 1
George Leighton Ct STVGE SG2 5 L5
Georges Md BORE WD6 198 C7 3
George St BERK HP4 147 J6
DUN/WHIP LU6 80 F1
HERT/WAS SG14 137 H4
HHNE HP2 8 A6
LTN LU1 2 E7
STALW/RED AL3 10 E7
STALW/RED AL3 106 D5
WATW WD18 13 G5
George St West LTN LU1 2 E7
George's Wood Rd
BRKMPK AL9 172 F5
George V Wy
RKW/CH/CXG WD3 179 M7
George Wk WARE SG12 138 C1 3
Georgewood Rd HHS/BOV HP3 166 E4
Georgian Cl STAN HA7 207 M7
Gerard Av BSF CM23 96 D6
Gernon Rd LWTH SG6 39 L5
Gernon Wk LWTH SG6 39 L5
Gew's Cnr CHES/WCR EN8 176 C8
Ghlbert Wy BERK HP4 146 F6
Giant Tree Hl BUSH WD23 207 J2
Gibb Cft HLWS CM18 162 D6
Gibbons Cl BORE WD6 198 D2
STALE/WH AL4 153 H1
Gibbons Wy KNEB SG3 88 E6
Gibbs Cl CHES/WCR EN8 176 C8
Gibbs Couch OXHEY WD19 206 C3
Gibbs Fld BSF CM23 96 C5
Gibson Cl HTCHE/RSTV SG4 53 G3
Gifford's La STDN SG11 73 M8
Gilbert's Hl TRING HP23 144 D7
Gilbert St PEND EN3 190 B8
Gilbey Av BSF CM23 97 G4
Gilbey Crs STSD CM24 79 K2
Gildea Cl PIN HA5 206 F7
Gilded Acre DUN/WHIP LU6 81 H5 1
Gilden Cl HLWE CM17 142 D6 2
Gilden Wy HLWE CM17 142 C7
Gilder Cl LTNN/LIM LU3 64 F2
Gilderdale LTNW/LEA LU4 64 A4
Gilders SBW CM21 120 C8
Giles Cl STALE/WH AL4 153 H1
Gillam St LTNE LU2 2 F5
Gillan Gn BUSH WD23 207 H2 1
Gillian Av STAL AL1 169 H3
Gilliat's Gn RKW/CH/CXG WD3 193 J5
Gillison Cl LWTH SG6 40 A5
Gills Hl RAD WD7 183 L6
Gills Hill La RAD WD7 183 L7
Gills Hollow RAD WD7 183 L7
Gilmour Cl ENC/FH EN2 189 M6
Gilpin Cl DUN/HR/TOD LU5 63 J5
Gilpin Gn HARP AL5 131 H1
Gilpin Rd WARE SG12 138 D2
Gilpin's Gallop WARE SG12 139 G6
Gilpin's Ride BERK HP4 147 K5
Gilpin St DUN/HR/TOD LU5 62 F8
Gilsland WAB EN9 191 K6

Gingers Cl RAYLNE/WEN HP22 .... 122 D5
Ginns Rd BUNT SG9 .... 61 J4
Gippeswyck Cl PIN HA5 .... 206 C8 2
Gipsy La BSF CM23 .... 79 H6
KNEB SG3 .... 88 D7
LTN LU1 .... 3 J9
Girdle Rd HTCHE/RSTV SG4 .... 38 F8
Girons Cl HTCHE/RSTV SG4 .... 53 G4
Girtin Rd BUSH WD23 .... 197 G6
Girton Ct CHES/WCR EN8 .... 190 D1
Girton Wy RKW/CH/CXG WD3 .... 195 H6
Gisburne Wy WATN WD24 .... 181 M8
Gladden Ct HLWS CM18 .... 162 D6 1
Gladding Rd CHESW EN7 .... 175 G4
Gladeside STALE/WH AL4 .... 153 J4
The Glades HHW HP1 .... 148 D6
The Glade BLDK SG7 .... 40 D3
LWTH SG6 .... 39 L7
WGCW AL8 .... 134 B2 1
The Gladeway WAB EN9 .... 191 J4
Gladsmuir Rd BAR EN5 .... 200 D3
Gladstone Rd HOD EN11 .... 160 A3
WARE SG12 .... 91 L2
WARE SG12 .... 116 B8
WAT WD17 .... 13 H3
Glaisdale LTNW/LEA LU4 .... 64 B5 2
Glamis Cl CHESW EN7 .... 175 M8
HHNE HP2 .... 150 A1
Gleave Cl STAL AL1 .... 153 G6
Glebe Av ARL/CHE SG15 .... 25 M3
Glebe Cl BRKMPK AL9 .... 156 E4 1
CFSP/GDCR SL9 .... 202 C8
HERT/WAS SG14 .... 90 C7
HERT/WAS SG14 .... 137 J2 1
HHS/BOV HP3 .... 166 D2
LBUZ LU7 .... 102 C5
Glebe Cottages BRKMPK AL9 .... 156 E4
Glebe Ct BSF CM23 .... 97 G2
Glebelands HLW CM20 .... 7 K1
Glebe La BAR EN5 .... 199 M7
Glebe Rd CFSP/GDCR SL9 .... 202 B8
HERT/WAS SG14 .... 137 J2
LWTH SG6 .... 39 M3
WLYN AL6 .... 112 A5
The Glebe GSTN WD25 .... 182 B4
KGLGY WD4 .... 166 F8 2
Gleed Av BUSH WD23 .... 207 J2
Glemsford Cl LTNW/LEA LU4 .... 64 A4 1
Glemsford Dr HARP AL5 .... 109 J8
Glencoe Rd BUSH WD23 .... 196 F7
Glencorse Gn OXHEY WD19 .... 206 C4 2
Glendale HHW HP1 .... 149 G7
Gleneagles Cl OXHEY WD19 .... 206 C5 2
Gleneagles Dr LTNE LU2 .... 65 K4
Glenester Cl HOD EN11 .... 159 M1
Glen Faba Rd HLWW/ROY CM19 .... 160 E4
Glenferrie Rd STAL AL1 .... 11 L6
Glenfield Ct HERT/WAS SG14 .... 136 E3 1
Glenfield Rd LTNN/LIM LU3 .... 65 H4
Glengall Pl STAL AL1 .... 169 K2 2
Glenhaven Av BORE WD6 .... 198 F4
Glenlyn Av STAL AL1 .... 153 G8 2
The Glen HHNE HP2 .... 149 M2
LTN LU1 .... 82 D7
NTHWD HA6 .... 205 J7
Glenview Rd HHW HP1 .... 149 G7
Glen Wy WAT WD17 .... 195 K1
Glenwood BROX EN10 .... 159 L6
WGCE AL7 .... 135 H5 5
Glenwood Cl STVGE SG2 .... 71 H8
Glevum Cl STALW/RED AL3 .... 168 E1
Globe Cl HARP AL5 .... 131 H1
Globe Crs BSF CM23 .... 78 C4
Gloucester Av CHES/WCR EN8 .... 190 D4
Gloucester Cl STVG SG1 .... 54 D8 1
Gloucester Gdns EBAR EN4 .... 201 M5
Gloucester Rd BAR EN5 .... 201 G6
LTN LU1 .... 3 G7
Glover Cl CHESW EN7 .... 175 L6 2
Glovers Cl HERT/BAY SG13 .... 137 H6 1
Glovers La HLWE CM17 .... 163 K7
Glyn Av EBAR EN4 .... 201 J5
The Glynde STVGE SG2 .... 89 G2
Glynswood CFSP/GDCR SL9 .... 202 E7
Goblins Gn WGCE AL7 .... 134 C5
Goddard End STVGE SG2 .... 89 H1
Goddards Cl HERT/BAY SG13 .... 157 H6
Godfrey Cl STVGE SG2 .... 5 M7
Godfreys Cl LTN LU1 .... 83 G4
Godfries Cl WLYN AL6 .... 113 K7
Goffs Crs CHESW EN7 .... 175 H8
Goff's La CHESW EN7 .... 175 L8
Goff's Oak Av CHESW EN7 .... 175 G7
Golda Cl BAR EN5 .... 200 C7
Gold Cl BROX EN10 .... 159 K7
Gold Crest Cl LTNW/LEA LU4 .... 63 M5
Goldcrest Wy BUSH WD23 .... 207 H1
Goldcroft HHS/BOV HP3 .... 166 F1
Golden Dell WGCE AL7 .... 134 E8
Goldfield Rd TRING HP23 .... 123 L7
Goldfinch Wy BORE WD6 .... 198 F5 3
Gold Hl North CFSP/GDCR SL9 .... 202 B8
Gold Hl West CFSP/GDCR SL9 .... 202 B8
Goldings BSF CM23 .... 97 G2
Goldings Crs HAT AL10 .... 155 G4
Goldings La HERT/WAS SG14 .... 136 F1
Goldington Cl HOD EN11 .... 159 L1 1
Goldon LWTH SG6 .... 40 A6
Goldstone Cl WARE SG12 .... 116 C8 3
Goldstone Crs DUN/HR/TOD LU5 .... 63 J8
Golf Cl BUSH WD23 .... 13 K2
Golf Club Rd BRKMPK AL9 .... 172 F5
Golf Ride ENC/FH EN2 .... 188 F6
Gombards STALW/RED AL3 .... 10 E5
Gomer Cl HTCHE/RSTV SG4 .... 111 K1
Gonville Av RKW/CH/CXG WD3 .... 195 G7
Gonville Crs STVGE SG2 .... 71 H8
Goodey Meade STVGE SG2 .... 72 E8
Goodliffe Pk BSF CM23 .... 79 G8
Goodrich Cl GSTN WD25 .... 181 M6
Goodwin Ct CHES/WCR EN8 .... 176 D7 1
Goodwins Md LBUZ LU7 .... 101 M3
Goodwin Stile BSF CM23 .... 96 C5
Goodwood Av PEND EN3 .... 190 B8
WATN WD24 .... 181 K6
Goodwood Cl HOD EN11 .... 159 L3
Goodwood Rd ROY SG8 .... 21 L4 1
Goodyers Av RAD WD7 .... 183 L4
Goose Acre LBUZ LU7 .... 101 M3
Gooseacre WGCE AL7 .... 134 E6
Gooseberry Hl LTNN/LIM LU3 .... 65 G3
Goosecroft HHW HP1 .... 148 E6 2
Goosefields RKW/CH/CXG WD3 .... 194 B7
Goose La RBSF CM22 .... 121 J3
Goral Md RKW/CH/CXG WD3 .... 204 C1
Gordian Wy STVG SG1 .... 71 H1
Gordon Av STAN HA7 .... 207 L6
Gordon Cl STAL AL1 .... 11 M9
STAL AL1 .... 153 G8 3
Gordon Rd CHES/WCR EN8 .... 190 F5
Gordon St LTN LU1 .... 2 D6
Gordons Wk HARP AL5 .... 131 H2 2
Gordon Wy BAR EN5 .... 200 E5
Gorelands La CSTG HP8 .... 202 D2
Gore La STDN SG11 .... 93 H7
Gorham Dr STAL AL1 .... 169 K2
Gorham Wy DUN/HR/TOD LU5 .... 63 L8
Gorle Cl GSTN WD25 .... 181 M5
Gorleston Cl STVG SG1 .... 69 M1
Gorse Cl HAT AL10 .... 154 E8
Gorse Cnr STALW/RED AL3 .... 10 F2
Gorselands HARP AL5 .... 131 H3 2
Gorst Cl LWTH SG6 .... 39 K5
Gosforth La OXHEY WD19 .... 205 M3
Gosforth Pth OXHEY WD19 .... 205 M3 2
Goshawk Cl LTNW/LEA LU4 .... 63 M6 2
Gosling Av HTCH/STOT SG5 .... 51 H8
Gosmore Ley Cl
HTCHE/RSTV SG4 .... 52 E7
Gosmore Rd HTCHE/RSTV SG4 .... 52 E5
The Gossamers GSTN WD25 .... 182 D6
Gosselin Rd HERT/WAS SG14 .... 137 H2
Gossoms Ryde BERK HP4 .... 146 F5
Gothic Wy ARL/CHE SG15 .... 25 M5
Gould Cl BRKMPK AL9 .... 172 A3
Government Rw PEND EN3 .... 190 F8
Gowar Fld POTB/CUF EN6 .... 185 M2
Gower Rd ROY SG8 .... 21 H3
The Gowers HLW CM20 .... 7 M2
Grace Av RAD WD7 .... 184 D4
Grace Cl BORE WD6 .... 199 J2
Grace Gdns BSF CM23 .... 96 E6
Grace Wy STVG SG1 .... 5 G1
Graemes Dyke Rd BERK HP4 .... 146 F7
Grafton Cl STALE/WH AL4 .... 153 J8
Graham Av BROX EN10 .... 159 K7
Graham Cl STAL AL1 .... 169 J2
Graham Gdns LTNN/LIM LU3 .... 65 H6
Graham Rd DUN/HR/TOD LU5 .... 81 K3
Grailands BSF CM23 .... 96 C2
Grammar School Wk
HTCH/STOT SG5 .... 52 D3
Grampian Wy LTNN/LIM LU3 .... 64 B2
The Granaries WAB EN9 .... 191 K4 1
Granary Cl STALE/WH AL4 .... 132 C2 1
Granary La HARP AL5 .... 131 G1
The Granary HLWW/ROY CM19 .... 161 G1
WARE SG12 .... 139 H7
Granby Av HARP AL5 .... 109 H8
Granby Park Rd CHESW EN7 .... 175 L7
Granby Rd LTNW/LEA LU4 .... 64 C7
STVG SG1 .... 54 B8
Grandfield Av WAT WD17 .... 195 L2
Grand Union Canal Wk
BERK HP4 .... 146 D3
HHW HP1 .... 165 H1
LBUZ LU7 .... 102 B4
RKW/CH/CXG WD3 .... 203 M4
TRING HP23 .... 101 M8
Grange Av LTNN/LIM LU3 .... 64 D5
LTNW/LEA LU4 .... 64 C6
TRDG/WHET N20 .... 200 D8
Grange Bottom ROY SG8 .... 21 K5
Grange Cl CFSP/GDCR SL9 .... 202 D8
HERT/WAS SG14 .... 137 G4 3
HHNE HP2 .... 149 M8 1
HTCHE/RSTV SG4 .... 52 F6
STALW/RED AL3 .... 106 C4
WAT WD17 .... 195 M2
Grange Ct WAB EN9 .... 191 H5
Grange Court Rd HARP AL5 .... 131 H4
Grangedale Cl NTHWD HA6 .... 205 K8 1
Grange Dr HTCH/STOT SG5 .... 26 E4
Grange Flds CFSP/GDCR SL9 .... 202 D8
Grange Gdns WARE SG12 .... 138 D2
Grange Hl WLYN AL6 .... 112 B4
Grange La GSTN WD25 .... 197 J2
HLWW/ROY CM19 .... 161 H2
Grange Pk BSF CM23 .... 96 E1
Grange Ri WLYN AL6 .... 111 L1
Grange Rd AMP/FLIT/B MK45 .... 35 G7
BORE WD6 .... 198 E6
BSF CM23 .... 96 F3
CFSP/GDCR SL9 .... 202 C8
LBUZ LU7 .... 102 C6
LWTH SG6 .... 39 L2
TRING HP23 .... 123 H1
TRING HP23 .... 124 B6
Grangeside BSF CM23 .... 78 E8
Grange St STALW/RED AL3 .... 10 F4
Grange Wk BSF CM23 .... 96 F3
Grangewood POTB/CUF EN6 .... 187 G1
Gransden Cl LTNN/LIM LU3 .... 64 F3
Grant Gdns HARP AL5 .... 109 G8
Grantham Cl ROY SG8 .... 21 G2
Grantham Gdns WARE SG12 .... 116 D8
Grantham Gn BORE WD6 .... 199 H6
Grantham Rd LTNW/LEA LU4 .... 82 F1
Granville Dene HHS/BOV HP3 .... 164 F6
Granville Gdns HOD EN11 .... 138 F8
Granville Rd BAR EN5 .... 200 B5
HTCHE/RSTV SG4 .... 53 H1
LTN LU1 .... 83 G2
STAL AL1 .... 11 J7
WATW WD18 .... 13 G5
Graphic Cl DUN/WHIP LU6 .... 81 J4
Grasmere Av HARP AL5 .... 109 H8
LTNN/LIM LU3 .... 65 G3
Grasmere Cl DUN/WHIP LU6 .... 81 G3
GSTN WD25 .... 182 A3
HHS/BOV HP3 .... 167 G1 1
Grasmere Rd LTNN/LIM LU3 .... 65 G3
STAL AL1 .... 170 A1
WARE SG12 .... 116 D7 1
Grassingham End
CFSP/GDCR SL9 .... 202 D7
Grassingham Rd
CFSP/GDCR SL9 .... 202 D7
Grassington Cl
LCOL/BKTW AL2 .... 182 F1 1
Grass Mdw STVGE SG2 .... 71 J3
Grass Warren WLYN AL6 .... 135 K1
Grassy Cl HHW HP1 .... 148 F6
Grasvenor Av BAR EN5 .... 200 F7
Gravel Dr TRING HP23 .... 123 H7
Graveley Av BORE WD6 .... 199 H5
Graveley Dell WGCE AL7 .... 135 G5 3
Graveley La HTCHE/RSTV SG4 .... 53 L5
Graveley Rd HTCHE/RSTV SG4 .... 53 K4
STVG SG1 .... 54 A7
Gravel Hl CFSP/GDCR SL9 .... 202 C6
Gravelhill Ter HHW HP1 .... 148 F8
Gravel La HHW HP1 .... 148 F7
Gravelly La STDN SG11 .... 75 K3
Gravel Pth BERK HP4 .... 147 J6
Gravely Ct HHS/BOV HP3 .... 150 B8 1
The Graylings ABLGY WD5 .... 181 K4
Grays Cl AMP/FLIT/B MK45 .... 35 H7
ROY SG8 .... 21 H2
Grays Ct BSF CM23 .... 96 D2
Graysfield WGCE AL7 .... 134 F7
Gray's La HTCH/STOT SG5 .... 52 C3
The Grazings HHNE HP2 .... 8 F5
Greasy Cl ABLGY WD5 .... 181 L2
Great Ashby Wy STVG SG1 .... 54 F7
Great Braitch La HAT AL10 .... 133 K8
Great Brays HLWS CM18 .... 7 L8
Great Break WGCE AL7 .... 135 G5
Great Cambridge Rd
BROX EN10 .... 176 D5
CHES/WCR EN8 .... 190 B5
Great Canfield Rd RBSF CM22 .... 99 J6
Great Conduit WGCE AL7 .... 135 H3
Great Dell WGCW AL8 .... 134 C2
Great Eastern Cl BSF CM23 .... 96 F4 1
Great Elms Rd HHS/BOV HP3 .... 166 E3
Greatfield Cl HARP AL5 .... 108 B6
Great Ganett WGCE AL7 .... 135 G6
Great Gn HTCH/STOT SG5 .... 37 J6
Great Gv BUSH WD23 .... 197 G5
Great Groves CHESW EN7 .... 175 K7
Great Hadham Rd BSF CM23 .... 95 L5
Greatham Rd BUSH WD23 .... 13 K3
Great Heart HHNE HP2 .... 8 C5
Great Heath HAT AL10 .... 155 G2
Great Innings North
HERT/WAS SG14 .... 90 C7
Great Innings South
HERT/WAS SG14 .... 90 C7 1
Great Lawne KNEB SG3 .... 89 J8
Great Ley WGCE AL7 .... 134 D6
Great Leylands HLWS CM18 .... 7 M9
Great Meadow BROX EN10 .... 176 F1
Great Molewood
HERT/WAS SG14 .... 137 G1
Great Northern Rd
DUN/WHIP LU6 .... 81 H3
Great North Rd BRKMPK AL9 .... 155 H8
WGCW AL8 .... 133 M6
WLYN AL6 .... 112 C4
Great Palmers HHNE HP2 .... 149 L2 2
Great Pk KGLGY WD4 .... 180 F1
Great Plumtree HLW CM20 .... 7 K2
Great Rd HHNE HP2 .... 8 E6
Great Slades POTB/CUF EN6 .... 186 E4
Great Sturgess Rd HHW HP1 .... 148 E7 1
Great Whites Rd HHS/BOV HP3 .... 166 E1
Greenacre Cl BAR EN5 .... 200 E1
Greenacres BUSH WD23 .... 207 J2
HHS/BOV HP3 .... 167 J1
LBUZ LU7 .... 102 B6 1
Green Acres LTNE LU2 .... 50 C8
STVGE SG2 .... 89 H1
WGCE AL7 .... 134 E7 1
Greenall Cl CHES/WCR EN8 .... 190 D1
Greenbank CHESW EN7 .... 176 A7
Greenbank Rd WAT WD17 .... 181 J7
Greenbrook Av EBAR EN4 .... 201 H2
Greenbury Cl
RKW/CH/CXG WD3 .... 193 H4
ROY SG8 .... 32 E1 1
Green Cl BRKMPK AL9 .... 172 D5
CHES/WCR EN8 .... 190 D3
LTNW/LEA LU4 .... 64 A5
STVGE SG2 .... 88 E1
Greencoates HERT/BAY SG13 .... 137 K5 1
Green Cft HAT AL10 .... 154 F2
Green Dell Wy HHS/BOV HP3 .... 9 K9
Green Drift ROY SG8 .... 21 G4
Greene Field Rd BERK HP4 .... 147 H6 3
Green End WLYN AL6 .... 112 A6 1
Green End Gdns HHW HP1 .... 148 F8
Green End La HHW HP1 .... 148 E7
Green End Rd HHW HP1 .... 148 F8
Green End St
RAYLNE/WEN HP22 .... 122 C5
Greenes Ct BERK HP4 .... 147 H5 1
Greene Wk BERK HP4 .... 147 J7
Greenfield BRKMPK AL9 .... 155 J2
ROY SG8 .... 21 G3
WGCW AL8 .... 134 C1 2
Greenfield Av HTCH/STOT SG5 .... 38 C6
OXHEY WD19 .... 206 D2
Greenfield Cl DUN/WHIP LU6 .... 80 D1
Greenfield End
CFSP/GDCR SL9 .... 202 E7 1
Greenfield La HTCH/STOT SG5 .... 38 D6 1
Greenfield Rd
AMP/FLIT/B MK45 .... 34 C1
STVG SG1 .... 70 D3
Greenfields HTCH/STOT SG5 .... 36 D1
STSD CM24 .... 79 K3
Greenfield St WAB EN9 .... 191 H5
Greenfield Wy BGSW SG18 .... 14 C5
Greengate LTNN/LIM LU3 .... 64 B2
Greenheys Cl NTHWD HA6 .... 205 K8
Greenhill Av LTNE LU2 .... 65 J7
Green Hill Cl STDN SG11 .... 75 L4 1
Greenhill Crs WATW WD18 .... 195 K7
Greenhill Pk BAR EN5 .... 201 H6 1
BSF CM23 .... 96 C5
Greenhills HLW CM20 .... 7 H6
WARE SG12 .... 116 B7
Greenhills Cl RKW/CH/CXG WD3 .... 194 A6
Greenland Rd BAR EN5 .... 200 B7
Green La BLDK SG7 .... 18 D5
BROX EN10 .... 177 G2
CSHM HP5 .... 178 A4
DUN/WHIP LU6 .... 105 K2
HHNE HP2 .... 150 C5
HHS/BOV HP3 .... 164 F7
HTCHE/RSTV SG4 .... 53 G1
LBUZ LU7 .... 102 D5 1
LCOL/BKTW AL2 .... 169 M3
LTNE LU2 .... 66 A6
LWTH SG6 .... 40 A1
NTHWD HA6 .... 205 J7
OXHEY WD19 .... 206 B1
RKW/CH/CXG WD3 .... 194 E6
STALW/RED AL3 .... 106 E6
STALW/RED AL3 .... 152 B4
STDN SG11 .... 75 L3
WGCE AL7 .... 135 H6
Green Lane Cl HARP AL5 .... 131 K2
Green La HAT AL10 .... 154 E2
WGCW AL8 .... 133 L6
Green Meadow POTB/CUF EN6 .... 186 F1
Green Milverton
LTNN/LIM LU3 .... 64 F3 3
Greenoak Pl EBAR EN4 .... 201 L3
Green Oaks LTNE LU2 .... 65 L7
Green Pth TRING HP23 .... 123 H6
Green Poets LTNW/LEA LU4 .... 63 M8
Greenriggs LTNE LU2 .... 66 E8 1
Greenside BORE WD6 .... 198 F1
Greenside Dr HTCH/STOT SG5 .... 52 C2
Greenside Pk LTNE LU2 .... 65 K7
Greensleeves Cl
STALE/WH AL4 .... 153 H8 2
Greenstead SBW CM21 .... 142 D1
Green St GTDUN CM6 .... 99 K7
RAD WD7 .... 184 F6
RKW/CH/CXG WD3 .... 193 H3
ROY SG8 .... 21 J2
STVG SG1 .... 70 B3
Greensward BUSH WD23 .... 197 G7
The Green BSF CM23 .... 96 E7 1
CHES/WCR EN8 .... 176 B7
DUN/HR/TOD LU5 .... 63 H6
HTCH/STOT SG5 .... 26 E3
KNEB SG3 .... 88 A5
LTNE LU2 .... 85 H7
LTNW/LEA LU4 .... 64 B5
RKW/CH/CXG WD3 .... 194 E5
RKW/CH/CXG WD3 .... 194 E7
ROY SG8 .... 19 H1
ROY SG8 .... 21 J4 2
WARE SG12 .... 116 C7
WLYN AL6 .... 111 K1
WLYN AL6 .... 112 A5
STVG SG1 .... 4 E2
Green V WGCE AL7 .... 134 F5
Green View Cl HHS/BOV HP3 .... 164 F8
Greenway BERK HP4 .... 146 F6
BSF CM23 .... 97 H4
HARP AL5 .... 131 J2
HLWW/ROY CM19 .... 161 K2
LWTH SG6 .... 39 M8
STVGE SG2 .... 72 A2
Greenways ABLGY WD5 .... 181 J2
BUNT SG9 .... 58 C2
CHESW EN7 .... 175 G8 1
HERT/WAS SG14 .... 137 G4 3
LTNE LU2 .... 66 A5
STVG SG1 .... 4 E2
The Green Wy
KTN/HRWW/W HA3 .... 207 K8
The Greenway PEND EN3 .... 190 C6 3
POTB/CUF EN6 .... 186 F4
RKW/CH/CXG WD3 .... 193 M8
TRING HP23 .... 123 L5
Greenwood Av CHESW EN7 .... 190 A2
Greenwood Cl CHESW EN7 .... 190 A2 2
RAD WD7 .... 184 D3
Greenwood Dr GSTN WD25 .... 182 A5
Greenwood Gdns RAD WD7 .... 184 D4 3
The Greenwood
RAYLNE/WEN HP22 .... 122 C5 2
Greenyard WAB EN9 .... 191 H4 3
Greer Rd KTN/HRWW/W HA3 .... 207 H8
Gregories Cl LTNE LU2 .... 2 D3
Gregory Av POTB/CUF EN6 .... 187 H4
Gregson Cl BORE WD6 .... 199 H3
Grenadier Cl STALE/WH AL4 .... 153 H8 3
Grenadine Cl CHESW EN7 .... 175 L6 3
Grenadine Wy TRING HP23 .... 123 M5
Grenfell Cl BORE WD6 .... 199 H2
Grenville Av BROX EN10 .... 159 L8
Grenville Cl CHES/WCR EN8 .... 190 C3
Grenville Wy STVGE SG2 .... 88 F1
Gresford Cl STALE/WH AL4 .... 153 J7
Gresham Cl LTNE LU2 .... 84 C1
Gresham Ct BERK HP4 .... 147 G7 2
Gresley Cl WGCW AL8 .... 134 D3
Gresley Wy STVGE SG2 .... 71 J1
Greville Cl BRKMPK AL9 .... 172 A3
Greycaine Rd WATN WD24 .... 182 C8
Greydells Rd STVG SG1 .... 4 E1
Greyfriars WARE SG12 .... 116 A7
Greyfriars La HARP AL5 .... 130 F3
Greygoose Pk
HLWW/ROY CM19 .... 162 A5 1
Greyhound La POTB/CUF EN6 .... 185 M4
Greystoke Cl BERK HP4 .... 146 F7
Griffiths Wy STAL AL1 .... 169 H1
Grimaldi Av LTNN/LIM LU3 .... 64 F7
Grimsdyke Crs BAR EN5 .... 200 B4
Grimsdyke Rd PIN HA5 .... 206 D7
TRING HP23 .... 145 J1 2
Grimstone Rd HTCHE/RSTV SG4 .... 53 K6
Grimston Rd STAL AL1 .... 11 J8
Grimthorpe Cl STALW/RED AL3 .... 10 E1
Grindcobbe Cl STAL AL1 .... 169 J2 1
Grinstead La RBSF CM22 .... 121 H4
Groom Rd BROX EN10 .... 176 E5
Groomsby Dr LBUZ LU7 .... 102 D5
Grooms Cottages CSHM HP5 .... 178 A1
Grosvenor Cl BSF CM23 .... 96 C7
Grosvenor Rd BLDK SG7 .... 40 E1
BORE WD6 .... 198 F4
BROX EN10 .... 159 L7
LTNN/LIM LU3 .... 65 G5
NTHWD HA6 .... 205 L5
STAL AL1 .... 11 H8
WAT WD17 .... 13 H3
Grosvenor Rd West BLDK SG7 .... 40 E1 2
Grosvenor Ter HHW HP1 .... 148 F8
The Grotto WARE SG12 .... 138 C2 2
Ground La HAT AL10 .... 155 G3
Grove Av HARP AL5 .... 131 J3
Grovebury Cl DUN/WHIP LU6 .... 81 J4 1
Grovebury Gdns
LCOL/BKTW AL2 .... 169 H6 2
Grove Ct WAB EN9 .... 191 G4
Grove Crs RKW/CH/CXG WD3 .... 194 F5
Grovedale Cl CHESW EN7 .... 189 L1
Grove End LTN LU1 .... 83 G5
Grove Farm Pk NTHWD HA6 .... 205 J5
Grove Gdns TRING HP23 .... 124 A5
Grove Hall Rd BUSH WD23 .... 13 L5
Grove Hl CFSP/GDCR SL9 .... 202 B7
STSD CM24 .... 79 K3
Grovelands LCOL/BKTW AL2 .... 169 G6
Grovelands Av HTCHE/RSTV SG4 .... 39 H8
Groveland Wy HTCH/STOT SG5 .... 26 F5
Grove La CFSP/GDCR SL9 .... 202 A8
CSHM HP5 .... 164 A6
Grove Lea HAT AL10 .... 154 F8 1
Grove Md HAT AL10 .... 154 E5
Grove Meadow WGCE AL7 .... 135 H4
Grove Mill La
RKW/CH/CXG WD3 .... 195 H1
Grove Pk TRING HP23 .... 124 B5
Grove Park Rd LTN LU1 .... 82 F7
Grove Pl BRKMPK AL9 .... 172 B3 2
Grover Cl HHNE HP2 .... 8 B6
Grove Rd BORE WD6 .... 198 F2 2
DUN/HR/TOD LU5 .... 63 H3
DUN/HR/TOD LU5 .... 81 J3
EBAR EN4 .... 201 K4
HARP AL5 .... 131 J3
HHW HP1 .... 165 M1
HTCH/STOT SG5 .... 52 E2
LTN LU1 .... 2 C6
LTN LU1 .... 83 G8
NTHWD HA6 .... 205 J5
RKW/CH/CXG WD3 .... 203 M2
STAL AL1 .... 10 E9
STVG SG1 .... 70 B3
TRING HP23 .... 124 A5
WARE SG12 .... 116 E8
Grove Rd West PEND EN3 .... 190 B8
Grover Rd OXHEY WD19 .... 13 K9
The Grove BRKMPK AL9 .... 172 F6
CSHM HP5 .... 178 C7
LTN LU1 .... 83 G5
POTB/CUF EN6 .... 187 H3
RAD WD7 .... 183 M5
RBSF CM22 .... 97 L6
STDN SG11 .... 95 K3
Grove Wk HERT/WAS SG14 .... 137 H2
Grove Wy RKW/CH/CXG WD3 .... 193 G5
Grovewood Cl
RKW/CH/CXG WD3 .... 193 G6
Grubbs La BRKMPK AL9 .... 173 G1
Guernsey Cl LTNW/LEA LU4 .... 63 L7
Guessens Gv WGCW AL8 .... 134 B4
Guessens Rd WGCW AL8 .... 134 B4
Guessens Wk WGCW AL8 .... 134 B3
Guildford Cl STVG SG1 .... 54 D8
Guildford Rd STAL AL1 .... 153 G8
Guildford St LTN LU1 .... 2 E6
The Guilfords HLWE CM17 .... 142 C5
Guinery Gv HHS/BOV HP3 .... 166 E3 3
Guinevere Gdns
CHES/WCR EN8 .... 190 D1 2
Gulland Cl BUSH WD23 .... 197 H6
Gullbrook HHW HP1 .... 148 F7 1
Gullet Wood Rd GSTN WD25 .... 181 M6
The Gulphs HERT/BAY SG13 .... 137 J4 3
Gun La KNEB SG3 .... 88 E6
Gun Meadow Av KNEB SG3 .... 88 F6 1
Gunnels Wood Rd STVG SG1 .... 4 B7
Gun Rd KNEB SG3 .... 88 F6
Gun Road Gdns KNEB SG3 .... 88 E6
Gurney Court Rd STAL AL1 .... 11 K2
Gurney's La HTCH/STOT SG5 .... 38 A3
Gwent Cl GSTN WD25 .... 182 C5
Gwynfa Cl WLYN AL6 .... 112 C3
Gwynne Cl TRING HP23 .... 123 M5
Gwynns Wk HERT/BAY SG13 .... 137 K4
Gypsy Cl WARE SG12 .... 138 E6
Gypsy La BRKMPK AL9 .... 155 L1
GSTN WD25 .... 181 J6
WARE SG12 .... 138 E6

H

Hackforth Cl BAR EN5 .... 200 A6
Hackney Cl BORE WD6 .... 199 J6
Haddestoke Ga BROX EN10 .... 176 E5
Haddon Cl BORE WD6 .... 198 F3
HHS/BOV HP3 .... 149 M8 2
STVGE SG2 .... 89 H3
Haddon Rd LTNE LU2 .... 3 H5
RKW/CH/CXG WD3 .... 193 H6
Hadham Ct BSF CM23 .... 96 C2
Hadham Gv BSF CM23 .... 96 B2
Hadham Rd BSF CM23 .... 95 L1
STDN SG11 .... 93 L1
Hadland Cl HHW HP1 .... 164 F5 1
Hadleigh Ct BROX EN10 .... 176 E1
HARP AL5 .... 131 K4 1
Hadley Cl BORE WD6 .... 198 E6
Hadley Gra HLWE CM17 .... 163 H3
Hadley Gn BAR EN5 .... 200 E4
Hadley Green Rd BAR EN5 .... 200 E3
Hadley Gn West BAR EN5 .... 200 D3
Hadley Gv BAR EN5 .... 200 D3
Hadley Highstone BAR EN5 .... 200 E2
Hadley Rdg BAR EN5 .... 200 E4
Hadley Rd BAR EN5 .... 201 G4
EBAR EN4 .... 201 M1
Hadley Wood Rd BAR EN5 .... 200 F3
Hadlow Down Cl LTNN/LIM LU3 .... 64 F5
Hadrian Av DUN/HR/TOD LU5 .... 63 K8
Hadrian Cl STALW/RED AL3 .... 168 E1
Hadrians Wk STVGE SG2 .... 71 H2 3
Hadrian Wy LWTH SG6 .... 40 C3

Hadwell Cl STVGE SG2 5 K7
Hagdell Rd LTN LU1 83 H5
Hagden La WATW WD18 12 A5
Haggerston Rd BORE WD6 198 D1
Hagsdell Rd HERT/BAY SG13 137 J5
Haig Cl STAL AL1 153 G8 4
Hailey Av HOD EN11 138 F8
Hailey La HOD EN11 159 J1
Haines Wy GSTN WD25 181 M5
Haldens WGCE AL7 134 E1
Hale Rd HERT/BAY SG13 137 J5
Hales Meadow HARP AL5 108 F8 1
Hales Pk HHNE HP2 9 L6
Hales Park Cl HHNE HP2 9 L6
Haleswood Rd HHNE HP2 9 H7
Half Acre HTCH/STOT SG5 52 C4
Halfacre Hl CFSP/GDCR SL9 202 E8
Halfacre La BUNT SG9 59 M1
Half Acres BSF CM23 96 E2
Halfhide La CHES/WCR EN8 176 C5
Halfhides WAB EN9 191 J4
Half Moon La DUN/HR/TOD LU5 81 J3
LTN LU1 107 H2
Half Moon Meadow
HHNE HP2 150 B2 2
Halfway Av LTNW/LEA LU4 82 C1
Halifax Rd RKW/CH/CXG WD3 193 H8
Halifax Wy WGCE AL7 135 K4
Hallam Cl WATN WD24 196 B3
Hallam Gdns PIN HA5 206 D7
Halland Wy NTHWD HA6 205 J6
Hall Cl RKW/CH/CXG WD3 203 M1
Hall Dr DEN/HRF UB9 204 B8
Halleys Rdg HERT/WAS SG14 136 F5
Halley's Wy DUN/HR/TOD LU5 63 J6
Hall Gdns STALE/WH AL4 171 J2
Hall Gv WGCE AL7 135 G6
Hall Heath Cl STAL AL1 153 G5
Halliday Cl RAD WD7 184 D3
Hallingbury Cl RBSF CM22 121 G1
Hallingbury Rd BSF CM23 97 G6
SBW CM21 120 F6
Halling Hl HLW CM20 7 H3
Hall La BUNT SG9 59 M1
HTCHE/RSTV SG4 110 B2
KNEB SG3 88 F8
ROY SG8 23 L8
Hall Md LWTH SG6 39 H4
Hallmores BROX EN10 159 M6 1
Hallowell Rd NTHWD HA6 205 K7
Hallowes Crs OXHEY WD19 205 M3
Hall Pk BERK HP4 147 K7
Hall Park Ga BERK HP4 147 K8
Hall Park Hl BERK HP4 147 K8
Hall Place Gdns STAL AL1 11 G5
Halls Cl WLYN AL6 112 B6
Hallside BGSW SG18 14 B5
Hallwicks Rd LTNE LU2 66 A7
Hallworth Dr HTCH/STOT SG5 26 D4 1
Halsey Dr HHW HP1 148 E5
HTCHE/RSTV SG4 53 H4
Halsey Pk LCOL/BKTW AL2 170 E6
Halsey Pl WATN WD24 196 A1 2
Halsey Rd WATW WD18 12 E3
Halstead Hl CHESW EN7 189 K1
Halter Cl BORE WD6 199 J6
Haltside HAT AL10 154 C6
Halwick Cl HHW HP1 149 G8
Halyard Cl LTNN/LIM LU3 65 G4
Hamberlins La BERK HP4 146 A3
Hambling Pl DUN/WHIP LU6 80 E2
Hamblings Cl RAD WD7 184 C4
Hambridge Wy HTCH/STOT SG5 37 J6
Hambro Cl LTNE LU2 108 E3
Hamburgh Ct
CHES/WCR EN8 176 C7 5
Hamels Dr HERT/BAY SG13 138 A3
Hamels La BUNT SG9 74 E3
Hamer Cl HHS/BOV HP3 164 F7
Hamilton Av HOD EN11 159 M2
Hamilton Cl EBAR EN4 201 K5
LCOL/BKTW AL2 182 F1
POTB/CUF EN6 185 M4
Hamilton Ct HAT AL10 155 G7 3
Hamilton Md HHS/BOV HP3 164 F6 1
Hamilton Rd BERK HP4 147 G6 2
EBAR EN4 201 K5
KGLGY WD4 181 H4
OXHEY WD19 206 A3
RBSF CM22 99 L2
STAL AL1 11 M5
Hamilton St WATW WD18 13 H7
Hamlet Hl HLWW/ROY CM19 161 H6
The Hamlet BERK HP4 147 M3
Hammarskjold Rd HLW CM20 6 D4
Hammers Ga LCOL/BKTW AL2 168 F5
Hammersmith Cl
DUN/HR/TOD LU5 63 H5 2
Hammersmith Gdns
DUN/HR/TOD LU5 63 H5
Hammond Cl CHESW EN7 175 L5
STVG SG1 4 C1
Hammonds Hl HARP AL5 130 E5
Hammonds La HAT AL10 133 G7
STALE/WH AL4 132 F7
Hammondstreet Rd
CHESW EN7 175 K5
Hammondswick HARP AL5 130 E6
Hampden HTCHE/RSTV SG4 110 B1
Hampden Cl LWTH SG6 40 A2
Hampden Crs CHESW EN7 190 A2
Hampden Hl WARE SG12 138 E1
Hampden Hill Cl WARE SG12 116 E8 1
Hampden Pl LCOL/BKTW AL2 169 K8
Hampden Rd HTCHE/RSTV SG4 53 H1
KTN/HRWW/W HA3 207 H8
Hampden Wy WAT WD17 181 K7
Hampermill La OXHEY WD19 205 M1
Hampshire Wy LTNN/LIM LU3 64 C1
Hampton Cl STVGE SG2 89 H3
Hampton Gdns SBW CM21 142 A3
Hampton Rd LTNW/LEA LU4 83 G1
Hamstel Rd HLW CM20 6 B4
Hanaper Dr ROY SG8 32 E1
Hanbury Cl CHES/WCR EN8 190 C1
WARE SG12 116 C8
Hanbury Dr WARE SG12 116 B4
Hancock Ct BORE WD6 199 H2
Hancock Dr LTNE LU2 65 K4
Hancroft Rd HHS/BOV HP3 166 E1
Handa Cl HHS/BOV HP3 167 G2
Handcross Rd LTNE LU2 66 C7
Hand La SBW CM21 142 B1
Handside Cl WGCW AL8 134 B4 2
Handside Gn WGCW AL8 134 B3
Handside La WGCW AL8 134 A5
Handsworth Cl OXHEY WD19 205 M3
Hangar Ruding OXHEY WD19 206 E3
Hanger Cl HHW HP1 149 G8
Hangmans La WLYN AL6 112 E2
Hanover Cl STVGE SG2 88 E1
Hanover Gn HHW HP1 165 M1
Hanover Pl AMP/FLIT/B MK45 35 H6
Hanover Wk HAT AL10 154 E8 2
Hanscombe End Rd
HTCH/STOT SG5 36 C2
Hanselin Cl STAN HA7 207 L5 1
Hansells Md HLWW/ROY CM19 160 F2
Hanswick Cl LTNE LU2 66 A8
Hanworth Cl LTNE LU2 65 J3 2
Hanyards La POTB/CUF EN6 174 C7
Harbert Gdns LCOL/BKTW AL2 169 G8
Harberts Rd HLWW/ROY CM19 6 B8
Harborne Cl OXHEY WD19 206 B5 5
Harbury Dell LTNN/LIM LU3 65 G3
Harcamlow Wy RBSF CM22 98 A6
STDN SG11 75 M8
WARE SG12 139 M2
Harcourt Rd BUSH WD23 197 H6
TRING HP23 124 B6
Harcourt St LTN LU1 83 K5
Harding Cl GSTN WD25 182 B4
LTNN/LIM LU3 64 D3 1
STALW/RED AL3 130 A5 3
Hardings WGCE AL7 135 H3
Hardwick Cl STVGE SG2 89 H3
Hardwicke Pl LCOL/BKTW AL2 170 C6
Hardwick Gn LTNN/LIM LU3 64 F3
Hardy Cl BAR EN5 200 D6
HTCHE/RSTV SG4 53 H3
Hardy Dr ROY SG8 21 J2
Hardy Rd HHNE HP2 8 E7
Harebell WGCE AL7 134 D7 1
Harebell Cl HERT/BAY SG13 138 A4
The Harebreaks WATN WD24 181 M8
Harebridge La
RAYLNE/WEN HP22 122 D8
Hare Crs GSTN WD25 181 M3
Harefield HLW CM20 7 L5
STVGE SG2 71 H7
Harefield Pl STALE/WH AL4 153 J4
Harefield Rd LTN LU1 82 E2
RKW/CH/CXG WD3 204 C2
Hare La HAT AL10 155 G7
Harepark Cl HHW HP1 148 E6 3
Hare St HLWW/ROY CM19 6 B7
Hare Street Rd BUNT SG9 58 E3
Hare Street Springs
HLWW/ROY CM19 6 B7
Harewood RKW/CH/CXG WD3 194 B6
Harewood Rd OXHEY WD19 206 A2
Harford Dr WAT WD17 195 K1
Hargrave Cl STSD CM24 79 K2
Hargreaves Av CHESW EN7 190 A2
Hargreaves Cl CHESW EN7 190 A2 3
Hargreaves Rd ROY SG8 21 J5 2
Harkness Wy HTCHE/RSTV SG4 39 H8
Harlech Rd ABLGY WD5 181 M2
Harlesden Rd STAL AL1 11 M6
Harlestone Cl LTNN/LIM LU3 64 F1
Harley Ct STALE/WH AL4 153 J3 1
The Harlings HERT/BAY SG13 138 B8
Harlington Rd DUN/HR/TOD LU5 34 A8
LTNN/LIM LU3 48 A6
Harlow Common HLWE CM17 163 J5
Harlow Ct HHNE HP2 149 L3
Harlow Rd HLWE CM17 143 G3
HLWW/ROY CM19 161 H1
SBW CM21 142 B2
Harmer Dell WLYN AL6 112 F6
Harmer Green La WLYN AL6 112 E6
Harmony Cl HAT AL10 154 F3
Harness Wy STALE/WH AL4 153 J4
Harold Crs WAB EN9 191 H3
Harold Rd AMP/FLIT/B MK45 35 H7
Harolds Rd HLWW/ROY CM19 161 L3
Harpenden La STALW/RED AL3 130 A4
Harpenden Ri HARP AL5 108 D7
Harpenden Rd HARP AL5 131 G3
STALE/WH AL4 132 A2
STALW/RED AL3 131 H6
STALW/RED AL3 152 C2
Harper La RAD WD7 183 M2
Harpsfield Broadway HAT AL10 154 E4
Harptree Wy STAL AL1 11 L2
Harrier Wy WAB EN9 191 M5
Harriescourt WAB EN9 191 M3
Harriet Walker Wy
RKW/CH/CXG WD3 193 L8 1
Harriet Wy BUSH WD23 197 J8
Harrington Hts
DUN/HR/TOD LU5 63 G5 4
Harris Ct AMP/FLIT/B MK45 35 G6
Harris La HTCH/STOT SG5 51 J8
RAD WD7 184 F5
Harrison Cl HTCHE/RSTV SG4 52 E3 1
NTHWD HA6 205 H6
Harrisons BSF CM23 79 J8
Harrison Wk CHES/WCR EN8 190 C1
Harris Rd GSTN WD25 181 M6
Harris's La WARE SG12 138 B1
Harrogate Rd OXHEY WD19 206 B3 2
Harrowdene STVGE SG2 71 H6
Harrowden Rd LTNE LU2 3 M5
Harrow Wy OXHEY WD19 206 D3
Harrow Weald Pk
KTN/HRWW/W HA3 207 J6
Harrow Yd TRING HP23 123 M7
Harry Scott Ct LTNW/LEA LU4 64 B4
Hartfield Av BORE WD6 198 F5
Hartfield Cl BORE WD6 198 F6
Hartforde Rd BORE WD6 198 F3
Harthall La KGLGY WD4 167 G7
Hartham La HERT/WAS SG14 137 H4
Hart Hill Dr LTNE LU2 3 H5
Hart Hill La LTNE LU2 3 J6 1
Hartland Rd CHES/WCR EN8 190 C1
Hart La LTNE LU2 3 J3
Hartley Rd LTNE LU2 3 G5
Hartmoor Ms PEND EN3 190 C8 1
Hart Rd HLWE CM17 142 B5
STAL AL1 10 F8
Hartsbourne Av BUSH WD23 207 H2
Hartsbourne Rd BUSH WD23 207 J2
Hartsbourne Wy HHNE HP2 150 B8 5
Harts Cl BUSH WD23 196 F3 1
Hartsfield Rd LTNE LU2 3 K1
Hartspring La GSTN WD25 196 F3
Hartswood Gn BUSH WD23 207 J2
Hart Wk LTNE LU2 3 J3
Hartwell Gdns HARP AL5 130 D1
Harvest Cl LTNW/LEA LU4 63 M7 1
Harvest Ct STALE/WH AL4 153 H3
WLYN AL6 112 D3
Harvest End GSTN WD25 182 C7
Harvest La STVGE SG2 71 J3
Harvest Md HAT AL10 155 G4
Harvest Rd BUSH WD23 197 G5
Harveyfields WAB EN9 191 H5
Harvey Rd DUN/WHIP LU6 80 C3
LCOL/BKTW AL2 170 B5
RKW/CH/CXG WD3 194 F7
STVGE SG2 5 M2
Harvey's Hl LTNE LU2 65 L5
Harwood Cl WGCW AL8 112 D8 2
WLYN AL6 113 K8
Harwood Hl WGCW AL8 134 D1
Harwoods Rd WATW WD18 12 C4
Hasedines Rd HHW HP1 148 F6
Haseldine Mdw HAT AL10 154 E6
Haseldine Rd LCOL/BKTW AL2 170 C5
Haselfoot LWTH SG6 39 K4
Hasketon Dr LTNW/LEA LU4 64 A4
Haslemere BSF CM23 96 F6
Haslewood Av HOD EN11 159 M3
Haslingden Cl HARP AL5 108 C7
Hasluck Gdns BAR EN5 201 H7
Hastings Cl BAR EN5 201 H5 2
STVG SG1 69 M2
Hastings Rd AMP/FLIT/B MK45 35 H7
Hastings St LTN LU1 2 D7 1
Hastings Wy BUSH WD23 13 L5 1
RKW/CH/CXG WD3 195 G5
Hastingwood Rd HLWE CM17 163 K7
Hastoe Hl TRING HP23 144 F1
Hastoe La TRING HP23 123 M8
Hatch Gn RBSF CM22 121 G2
Hatching Green Cl HARP AL5 130 F4
Hatch La BLDK SG7 40 E5
Hatfield Av HAT AL10 154 E2
Hatfield Crs HHNE HP2 8 E1
Hatfield Rd BRKMPK AL9 155 M1
POTB/CUF EN6 187 H2
STAL AL1 11 G6
STALE/WH AL4 153 H7
WATN WD24 196 A2
Hathaway Cl LTNW/LEA LU4 64 A8 1
STAN HA7 207 M5 1
Hathaway Ct STALE/WH AL4 153 K7
Hatherleigh Gdns
POTB/CUF EN6 187 J3
Hatters La WATW WD18 195 K6 1
Hatters Wy LTN LU1 82 E1
Hatton Rd CHES/WCR EN8 176 C8
Havelock Ri LTNE LU2 2 E2
Havelock Rd KGLGY WD4 166 E7
LTNE LU2 2 F2
Haven Cl HAT AL10 154 E4
Havenfield KGLGY WD4 180 A2
Havercroft Cl STAL AL1 169 H1
Haverdale LTNW/LEA LU4 64 B6 1
Havers La BSF CM23 96 E5
Haward Rd HOD EN11 160 B2
Hawbush Cl WLYN AL6 112 A6 2
Hawbush Ri WLYN AL6 112 A5
Hawes Cl NTHWD HA6 205 L7
Haweswater Dr GSTN WD25 182 B5 2
Hawfield Gdns LCOL/BKTW AL2 169 J5
Hawk Cl WAB EN9 191 M5 1
Hawkenbury HLWW/ROY CM19 161 M4
Hawkesworth Cl
NTHWD HA6 205 K7 4
Hawkfields LTNE LU2 65 K4
Hawkings Wy HHW HP1 164 F5
Hawkins Cl BORE WD6 199 H3 2
Hawkins Hall La KNEB SG3 89 K8
Hawkshead La BRKMPK AL9 172 D7
Hawkshill Dr HHW HP1 165 K2
Hawksmead Cl PEND EN3 190 C6 4
Hawksmoor RAD WD7 184 F4
Hawkwell Dr TRING HP23 124 B6 2
Hawsley Rd HARP AL5 130 F6
Hawthorn Av LTNE LU2 66 A6
Hawthorn Cl ABLGY WD5 181 L3
DUN/WHIP LU6 81 H3
HARP AL5 131 J3
HERT/WAS SG14 136 F3 1
HTCH/STOT SG5 52 C4
RBSF CM22 99 H3
ROY SG8 21 L3 1
WAT WD17 195 L1
Hawthorn Crs LTN LU1 82 D7
Hawthorne Av CHESW EN7 190 A1
Hawthorne Cl CHESW EN7 190 A2
Hawthorne Rd RAD WD7 183 M5 1
Hawthornes HAT AL10 154 E7 1
Hawthorn Hl LWTH SG6 39 K3
Hawthorn La HHW HP1 148 E6
Hawthorn Ri BSF CM23 96 E7
Hawthorn Rd HOD EN11 160 A2
Hawthorns HLWS CM18 162 E6
WGCW AL8 134 C2 1
The Hawthorns BERK HP4 146 F5
CSTG HP8 192 B3
HHS/BOV HP3 165 L3
RKW/CH/CXG WD3 203 J5
STVG SG1 5 H5
WARE SG12 116 A7
Hawthorn Wy HNLW SG16 37 K1
LCOL/BKTW AL2 168 F3
ROY SG8 21 L3
Hawtrees RAD WD7 183 L6
Haybourn Md HHW HP1 149 G8
Hay Cl BORE WD6 199 H3
Haycroft BSF CM23 97 H4
LTNE LU2 65 K4 1
Haycroft Rd STVG SG1 70 C3
Haydens Rd HLWW/ROY CM19 6 D7
Haydock Rd ROY SG8 21 L4 2
Haydon Rd OXHEY WD19 13 M8
Hayes Cl LTNE LU2 66 A5
Hayfield STVGE SG2 71 J3
Hayfield Cl BUSH WD23 197 G5
Haygarth KNEB SG3 88 F6
Hayhurst Rd LTNW/LEA LU4 64 A8
Hay La HARP AL5 130 F1
Hayley Bell Gdns BSF CM23 96 E7
Hayley Common STVGE SG2 71 H6
Hayley Ct DUN/HR/TOD LU5 63 H4 1
Hayling Dr LTNE LU2 66 B7
Hayling Rd OXHEY WD19 205 L3
Haymarket Rd LTNW/LEA LU4 63 K6
Haymeads WGCW AL8 134 D1
Haymeads La BSF CM23 97 H4
Haymoor LWTH SG6 39 K3
Haynes Cl WGCE AL7 134 F5
Haynes Md BERK HP4 146 F4
Haysman Cl LWTH SG6 39 M3
Hayton Cl LTNN/LIM LU3 49 G8
Haywood La ROY SG8 30 F4
Haywood Pk
RKW/CH/CXG WD3 193 L6
Haywoods Dr HHW HP1 165 L2
Haywoods La ROY SG8 21 K3
Hayword Ct WAB EN9 191 L5
Hazelbury Av ABLGY WD5 181 H3
Hazelbury Crs LTN LU1 2 A5
Hazel Cl CHESW EN7 175 K5 2
WLYN AL6 112 D7
Hazelcroft PIN HA5 206 F6
Hazeldell HERT/WAS SG14 90 C7
Hazeldell Link HHW HP1 148 D8 3
Hazeldell Rd HHW HP1 148 D8
Hazeldene CHES/WCR EN8 190 D3
Hazelend Rd BSF CM23 79 G7
Hazel Gv GSTN WD25 182 A6
HAT AL10 154 E8
HTCH/STOT SG5 26 D5
WGCE AL7 135 G3
Hazel Md BAR EN5 200 A6
Hazelmere Rd STALE/WH AL4 153 H4
STVGE SG2 88 F2
Hazel Rd BERK HP4 147 J7
LCOL/BKTW AL2 169 G7
The Hazels WLYN AL6 113 K8 1
Hazel Tree Rd WATN WD24 182 A8
Hazelwood Cl HTCH/STOT SG5 52 E2 3
LTNE LU2 66 A6
Hazelwood Dr STALE/WH AL4 153 H6
Hazelwood La ABLGY WD5 181 J3
Hazelwood Rd
RKW/CH/CXG WD3 195 H7
Hazely TRING HP23 124 B6
Heacham Cl LTNW/LEA LU4 64 A6
Headingley Cl CHESW EN7 175 L5 2
RAD WD7 184 D3
STVG SG1 70 D2
Headstone La
KTN/HRWW/W HA3 207 G8
Healey Rd WATW WD18 12 B9
Heath Av ROY SG8 21 H4
STALW/RED AL3 10 F3
Heathbourne Rd BUSH WD23 207 L1
STAN HA7 207 K2
Heath Brow HHW HP1 166 B1
Heathbrow Rd WLYN AL6 112 D2
Heath Cl HARP AL5 131 G3
HHW HP1 149 H8
LTN LU1 83 G3
POTB/CUF EN6 187 G1
Heathcote Av HAT AL10 154 F3
Heathcote Gdns HLWE CM17 163 K2
Heath Dr POTB/CUF EN6 186 F1
WARE SG12 116 C7
Heather Cl ABLGY WD5 181 M3
BSF CM23 96 C4
Heathermere LWTH SG6 39 L1
Heather Ri BUSH WD23 196 E3
Heather Rd WGCW AL8 134 B6
Heather Wy HHNE HP2 8 A6
POTB/CUF EN6 186 E3
STAN HA7 207 L6
Heath Farm La STALW/RED AL3 11 G3
Heathfield ROY SG8 21 G4
Heathfield Cl LTN LU1 82 E6 1
POTB/CUF EN6 187 G1
Heathfield Rd BUSH WD23 13 M5
HTCH/STOT SG5 38 E8
LTNN/LIM LU3 65 H6
Heathgate HERT/BAY SG13 138 A7
Heathlands WLYN AL6 112 E1
Heathlands Dr STALW/RED AL3 11 G2
Heath La HERT/BAY SG13 138 B8
HHW HP1 166 B1
HTCHE/RSTV SG4 111 K1
WLYN AL6 111 L1 3
Heath Rd HTCHE/RSTV SG4 85 J1
OXHEY WD19 196 C8
POTB/CUF EN6 187 G1
STAL AL1 11 H4
WLYN AL6 112 E1
Heath Rw BSF CM23 97 G1
Heathside STALE/WH AL4 171 G2
STALW/RED AL3 11 H2
Heathside Rd NTHWD HA6 205 J4
The Heath HTCHE/RSTV SG4 67 J8
RAD WD7 183 M4
Heaton Dell LTNE LU2 84 D1
Heay Flds WGCE AL7 135 H3
Hebden Cl LTNW/LEA LU4 64 A6
Heddon Court Av EBAR EN4 201 L6
Heddon Rd EBAR EN4 201 L6 2
Hedgebrooms WGCE AL7 135 H3 1
Hedgerow CFSP/GDCR SL9 202 D6
Hedge Rw HHW HP1 148 F5
Hedgerow Cl STVGE SG2 71 J2 1
Hedgerows SBW CM21 120 E8
The Hedgerows STVGE SG2 71 J2
The Hedgerow LTNW/LEA LU4 64 B5
Hedges Cl HAT AL10 155 G4
Hedgeside BERK HP4 147 M3
Hedley Cl RAYLNE/WEN HP22 122 F6
Hedley Ri LTNE LU2 66 D8
Hedley Rd STAL AL1 153 G7
Hedworth Av CHES/WCR EN8 190 C4
Heighams HLWW/ROY CM19 161 L5
Helena Cl EBAR EN4 201 J1
Helens Ga CHES/WCR EN8 176 E5 2
Helions Rd HLWW/ROY CM19 6 A7
Hellards Rd STVG SG1 70 C3
Helmsley Cl LTNW/LEA LU4 64 A5
Helston Cl PIN HA5 206 E7 2
Helston Gv HHNE HP2 149 K2 1
Helston Pl ABLGY WD5 181 L3
Hemel Hempstead Rd
BERK HP4 126 E1
HHS/BOV HP3 167 K1
STALW/RED AL3 10 A6
STALW/RED AL3 129 L7
Hemingford Dr LTNE LU2 65 J5
Hemingford Rd WAT WD17 181 K7
The Hemmings BERK HP4 146 E7 1
Hemming Wy GSTN WD25 181 M6
Hemp La TRING HP23 145 K1
Hempstall WGCE AL7 135 G6 3
Hempstead La BERK HP4 148 B4
Hempstead Rd HHS/BOV HP3 165 G5
KGLGY WD4 166 E6
WAT WD17 12 C1
Henbury Wy OXHEY WD19 206 C3
Henderson Cl STALW/RED AL3 152 B3
Henderson Pl ABLGY WD5 167 L6
Hendon Wood La MLHL NW7 199 M8
Henge Wy LTNN/LIM LU3 64 C3
Henley Cl DUN/HR/TOD LU5 63 K5
Henry Rd EBAR EN4 201 J6
Henrys Grant STAL AL1 11 G9
Henry St HHS/BOV HP3 166 C3 3
TRING HP23 123 M7
Hensley Cl HTCHE/RSTV SG4 53 G4 2
WLYN AL6 112 B4 2
Henstead Pl LTNE LU2 84 C1
Herald Cl BSF CM23 96 C4
Herbert St HHNE HP2 8 A6
Hereford Rd LTNW/LEA LU4 63 M7
Hereward Cl WAB EN9 191 H3 1
Herga Ct WAT WD17 195 M3
Heriots Cl STAN HA7 207 M4
Herkomer Cl BUSH WD23 197 G7 4
Herkomer Rd BUSH WD23 196 F6
Hermitage Ct
POTB/CUF EN6 187 H4 2
Hermitage Rd HTCH/STOT SG5 52 E3
Hermitage Wy STAN HA7 207 M8
Herne Rd BUSH WD23 197 G7
STVG SG1 70 A1
Herneshaw HAT AL10 154 E7 2
Herns La WGCE AL7 135 G4
Herns Wy WGCE AL7 134 F2
Heron Cl HHS/BOV HP3 166 E4
RKW/CH/CXG WD3 204 C2
SBW CM21 142 C1
Heron Ct BSF CM23 96 F3
Heron Dr LTNE LU2 65 K4
WARE SG12 139 H7
Heronfield POTB/CUF EN6 187 H1
Herongate Rd CHES/WCR EN8 176 C6
Herons Elm BERK HP4 146 D3
Heronsgate Rd
RKW/CH/CXG WD3 193 G7
Heronslea GSTN WD25 182 B7
Herons Ri EBAR EN4 201 K5
Herons Wd HLW CM20 6 B3
Heronswood Pl WGCE AL7 134 F5 1
Heronswood Rd WGCE AL7 134 E4
Heron Wk NTHWD HA6 205 K4
Heron Wy HAT AL10 154 F7
HTCH/STOT SG5 26 D4
Hertford Cl EBAR EN4 201 J4
Hertford Rd BRKMPK AL9 155 J3
EBAR EN4 201 H4
HOD EN11 159 K2
PEND EN3 190 C6
STVGE SG2 88 E2
WARE SG12 138 E6
WGCE AL7 134 F1
WGCW AL8 112 D7
WLYN AL6 112 B6 2
Hertfordshire Wy BLDK SG7 41 L6
BUNT SG9 59 K3
Hertfordshire way BUNT SG9 59 M2
Hertfordshire Wy BUNT SG9 59 M4
HERT/WAS SG14 114 F8
HTCHE/RSTV SG4 54 A3
HTCHE/RSTV SG4 86 D4
MHAD SG10 118 E4
ROY SG8 31 L1
Hertfordshire way ROY SG8 32 F8
Hertfordshire Wy STDN SG11 77 K6
WARE SG12 117 J3
Hertingfordbury Rd
HERT/WAS SG14 136 D6
HERT/WAS SG14 137 H4 4
Heswell Gn OXHEY WD19 205 M3 3
Hetchleys HHW HP1 148 F4
Hewitt Cl STALE/WH AL4 132 C3
Hewlett Rd LTNW/LEA LU4 64 D6
Hexham Rd BAR EN5 201 G5
Hexton Rd AMP/FLIT/B MK45 35 H8
HTCH/STOT SG5 51 K2
LTNE LU2 50 A6
Heybridge Ct
HERT/WAS SG14 136 E3 2
Heydon Rd ROY SG8 23 K8
Heydons Cl STALW/RED AL3 10 E2
Heyford Rd RAD WD7 183 L8
Heyford Wy HAT AL10 155 H3
Heysham Dr OXHEY WD19 206 B5
Heywood Dr LTNE LU2 65 L7
Hibbert Av WATN WD24 196 C1
Hibbert St LTN LU1 2 E9
Hickling Cl LTNE LU2 84 C1 5
Hickling Wy HARP AL5 109 H7
Hickman Cl BROX EN10 159 K7 1
Hicks Rd STALW/RED AL3 106 D5
Hidalgo Ct HHNE HP2 8 E4
The Hideaway ABLGY WD5 181 L2 1
The Hides HLW CM20 6 F5
High Acres ABLGY WD5 181 J3
Higham Dr LTNE LU2 84 C1

Higham Rd *AMP/FLIT/B* MK45 ...... 35 H6
High Ash Rd *STALE/WH* AL4 .... 132 B3
High Av *LWTH* SG6 .... 39 J5
Highbanks Rd *PIN* HA5 .... 207 G6
Highbarns *HHS/BOV* HP3 .... 166 F4
High Beech Rd *LTNN/LIM* LU3......... 64 C3
Highbridge St *WAB* EN9 .... 190 F5
Highbury Av *HOD* EN11 .... 159 M2
Highbury Rd *HTCHE/RSTV* SG4 ...... 52 F3
LTN LU1 .... 2 B3
Highbush Rd *HTCH/STOT* SG5 .... 26 D5
High Canons *BORE* WD6 .... 185 H8
Highclere Dr *HHS/BOV* HP3 .... 167 G3
High Cl *RKW/CH/CXG* WD3 .... 194 B6
ROY SG8 .... 23 M5
Highcroft Rd *HHS/BOV* HP3 .... 165 M4
High Cross *GSTN* WD25 .... 183 J8
High Dane *HTCHE/RSTV* SG4 .... 38 F8
High Dells *HAT* AL10 .... 154 E6
High Elms *HARP* AL5 .... 130 F4
High Elms Cl *NTHWD* HA6 .... 205 H6
High Elms La *GSTN* WD25 .... 182 A2
STVGE SG2 .... 90 D2
Highfield *HLWS* CM18 .... 7 L8
KGLGY WD4 .... 166 D7
LWTH SG6 .... 39 J6
OXHEY WD19 .... 206 E3 1
Highfield Av *BSF* CM23 .... 97 H4
HARP AL5 .... 131 H2
Highfield Cl *NTHWD* HA6 .... 205 K8
Highfield Crs *NTHWD* HA6 .... 205 K8
Highfield Dr *BROX* EN10 .... 159 K8
Highfield La *HHNE* HP2 .... 8 F5
STALE/WH AL4 .... 170 B1
Highfield Ov *HARP* AL5 .... 108 F7
Highfield Rd *BERK* HP4 .... 147 J7
BUSH WD23 .... 13 L7
CHESW EN7 .... 175 K5
HERT/BAY SG13 .... 137 J6
LTNW/LEA LU4 .... 83 G1
NTHWD HA6 .... 205 K8
STALE/WH AL4 .... 153 G1
TRING HP23 .... 123 K7
Highfields *POTB/CUF* EN6............ 174 D7
RAD WD7 .... 183 L6 1
Highfields Cl *DUN/HR/TOD* LU5 .... 63 M8
Highfield Wy *POTB/CUF* EN6 .... 187 G2
RKW/CH/CXG WD3 .... 193 M7
High Firs *RAD* WD7 .... 183 L6
High Firs Crs *HARP* AL5 .... 131 J2
Highgate Gv *SBW* CM21 .... 120 C8 1
High Gv *WGCW* AL8 .... 134 A3
Highland Dr *BUSH* WD23 .... 197 G8
HHS/BOV HP3 .... 9 K9
Highland Rd *BSF* CM23 .... 96 E7
WAB EN9 .... 177 K1
Highlands *BRKMPK* AL9 .... 155 H2 1
OXHEY WD19 .... 206 B1
ROY SG8 .... 21 K4
Highlands Cl *CFSP/GDCR* SL9 ...... 202 E7
Highlands End
CFSP/GDCR SL9 .... 202 E7 2
Highlands La *CFSP/GDCR* SL9 ...... 202 E6
Highlands Rd *BAR* EN5 .... 200 F5
The Highlands
POTB/CUF EN6 .... 187 H1 1
RKW/CH/CXG WD3 .... 194 A8
High La *RBSF* CM22 .... 143 K4
STSD CM24 .... 79 K2
High Md *LTNN/LIM* LU3 .... 64 F7
Highmead *STSD* CM24 .... 79 K2 3
High Meads *STALE/WH* AL4 .... 132 B2
Highmoor *HARP* AL5 .... 108 F6 1
High Oak Rd *WARE* SG12 .... 116 C8
High Oaks *STALW/RED* AL3 .... 152 B2
High Oaks Rd *WGCW* AL8 .... 134 A3
Highover Cl *LTNE* LU2 .... 3 L3
Highover Rd *LWTH* SG6 .... 39 J5
Highover Wy *HTCHE/RSTV* SG4 ...... 53 G1
High Pastures *RBSF* CM22 .... 143 H2
High Rdg *HARP* AL5 .... 108 D7
LTNE LU2 .... 84 B1
POTB/CUF EN6 .... 174 D6
High Ridge Cl *HHS/BOV* HP3 .... 166 C4
High Ridge Rd *HHS/BOV* HP3 .... 166 C4
High Rd *BRKMPK* AL9 .... 156 D5
BROX EN10 .... 159 L7
BUSH WD23 .... 207 J1
GSTN WD25 .... 181 L5
HERT/WAS SG14 .... 114 E4
HERT/WAS SG14 .... 114 F7
HTCH/STOT SG5 .... 36 D3
KTN/HRWW/W HA3 .... 207 K8 1
TRDG/WHET N20 .... 201 H8
High Road Broxbourne
BROX EN10 .... 159 L8
High Road Turnford
BROX EN10 .... 176 D5
High Road Wormley
BROX EN10 .... 176 E3
High St *ABLGY* WD5 .... 167 L6
AMP/FLIT/B MK45 .... 34 D2
ARL/CHE SG15 .... 25 M4
BAR EN5 .... 200 E5
BERK HP4 .... 146 D3
BGSW SG18 .... 14 C5
BLDK SG7 .... 17 H4
BLDK SG7 .... 18 C6
BLDK SG7 .... 40 E2
BORE WD6 .... 198 C7
BROX EN10 .... 176 D4
BSF CM23 .... 96 E3
BUNT SG9 .... 58 D2
BUSH WD23 .... 196 F7
CFSP/GDCR SL9 .... 202 D8
CHES/WCR EN8 .... 176 C8
CHES/WCR EN8 .... 190 D5
DUN/HR/TOD LU5 .... 63 G6
HARP AL5 .... 108 F8
HERT/WAS SG14 .... 90 C6
HHNE HP2 .... 149 H6
HHS/BOV HP3 .... 164 F6
HLWE CM17 .... 142 B6
HLWW/ROY CM19 .... 161 G1
HOD EN11 .... 159 M4
HTCH/STOT SG5 .... 26 E4
HTCH/STOT SG5 .... 37 J6
HTCH/STOT SG5 .... 51 H7
HTCHE/RSTV SG4 .... 52 E7
HTCHE/RSTV SG4 .... 54 B6
HTCHE/RSTV SG4 .... 86 E3
HTCHE/RSTV SG4 .... 110 B1
HTCHE/RSTV SG4 .... 110 D1
KGLGY WD4 .... 166 F8
LBUZ LU7 .... 101 M3
LBUZ LU7 .... 102 D5
LCOL/BKTW AL2 .... 170 B4
LTNW/LEA LU4 .... 64 B6
MHAD SG10 .... 94 E7
NTHWD HA6 .... 205 L8
POTB/CUF EN6 .... 187 H3
RKW/CH/CXG WD3 .... 204 C1
ROY SG8 .... 15 L6
ROY SG8 .... 21 J4
ROY SG8 .... 22 E8
ROY SG8 .... 31 K5
ROY SG8 .... 32 B7
SDY/GAM/PO SG19 .... 14 E2
SHFD SG17 .... 24 A5
STAL AL1 .... 10 E7
STALE/WH AL4 .... 132 C1
STALE/WH AL4 .... 153 G1
STALE/WH AL4 .... 171 G1
STALW/RED AL3 .... 106 D4
STALW/RED AL3 .... 107 G8
STALW/RED AL3 .... 130 A5
STDN SG11 .... 75 J7
STDN SG11 .... 93 L1
STVG SG1 .... 70 B3
STVGE SG2 .... 72 A2
TRING HP23 .... 123 M7
WARE SG12 .... 118 D6
WARE SG12 .... 138 C1
WARE SG12 .... 139 H6
WARE SG12 .... 140 C1
WAT WD17 .... 12 F3
WATW WD18 .... 12 E3
WLYN AL6 .... 111 L1
WLYN AL6 .... 112 B5
High Street Gn *HHNE* HP2 .... 9 G5
High St North *DUN/WHIP* LU6 .... 62 F8 1
High St South *DUN/WHIP* LU6 .... 81 H2
High Town Rd *LTNE* LU2 .... 2 F5
High Trees *EBAR* EN4 .... 201 K6
High Vw *BSF* CM23 .... 79 H7
CSTG HP8 .... 202 C2
HAT AL10 .... 154 E7
HTCH/STOT SG5 .... 52 C4
RKW/CH/CXG WD3 .... 193 M5
STALW/RED AL3 .... 106 D6
WATW WD18 .... 12 A9
Highview Cl *POTB/CUF* EN6 .... 187 H4
Highview Gdns *POTB/CUF* EN6 ...... 187 H4
STALE/WH AL4 .... 153 H2
The Highway *STAN* HA7 .... 207 L8
High Wickfield *WGCE* AL7 .... 135 H5 6
Highwood Av *BUSH* WD23 .... 196 E2
High Wood Cl *LTN* LU1 .... 82 E3
Highwoodhall La
HHS/BOV HP3 .... 166 F4
High Wood Rd *HOD* EN11 .... 159 L1
High Wych La *SBW* CM21 .... 119 M8
High Wych Rd *HLW* CM20 .... 141 K4
SBW CM21 .... 142 C1 2
High Wych Wy *HHNE* HP2 .... 149 M1
Hilbury *HAT* AL10 .... 154 E6
Hilfield La *GSTN* WD25 .... 197 G2
Hiljon Crs *CFSP/GDCR* SL9 .... 202 D8
Hillary Cl *LTNN/LIM* LU3 .... 64 C3
Hillary Crs *LTN* LU1 .... 2 A8
Hillary Ri *ARL/CHE* SG15 .... 26 A5
BAR EN5 .... 200 F5
Hillary Rd *HHNE* HP2 .... 9 G7
Hillborough Crs
DUN/HR/TOD LU5 .... 63 H3
Hillborough Rd *LTN* LU1 .... 2 C9
Hillbrow *LWTH* SG6 .... 39 J5
Hill Cl *BAR* EN5 .... 200 B6
HARP AL5 .... 109 H6
LBUZ LU7 .... 62 C1
LTNN/LIM LU3 .... 65 H3
Hill Common *HHS/BOV* HP3 ...... 166 F2 1
Hill Ct *BERK* HP4 .... 147 J5 1
Hillcrest *BLDK* SG7 .... 40 E3
HAT AL10 .... 154 F6
Hill Crest *HTCHE/RSTV* SG4 .... 86 D4
POTB/CUF EN6 .... 187 H5
Hillcrest *STVG* SG1 .... 4 F3
Hillcrest Av *LTNE* LU2 .... 65 H2
Hillcrest Rd *RAD* WD7 .... 184 F4
Hillcroft *DUN/WHIP* LU6 .... 80 D1
Hill Croft Cl *LTNW/LEA* LU4 .... 64 A4
Hillcroft Crs *OXHEY* WD19 .... 206 A1
Hilldown Rd *HHW* HP1 .... 148 F5
Hill Dyke Rd *STALE/WH* AL4 .... 132 C3
Hill End La *STAL* AL1 .... 170 A2
STALE/WH AL4 .... 170 B2
Hill End Rd *DEN/HRF* UB9 .... 204 A6
Hill Farm Av *GSTN* WD25 .... 181 M4
Hill Farm La *STALW/RED* AL3 .... 151 G1
WLYN AL6 .... 111 H5
Hill Farm Rd *CFSP/GDCR* SL9 .... 202 D7
Hillfield *HAT* AL10 .... 155 G2
Hillfield Av *HTCHE/RSTV* SG4 .... 38 F8
Hillfield Ct *HHNE* HP2 .... 8 C9
Hillfield La South *BUSH* WD23 .... 197 K7
Hillfield Rd *CFSP/GDCR* SL9 .... 202 D7
HHNE HP2 .... 8 B9
Hillfield Sq *CFSP/GDCR* SL9 .... 202 D7
Hillfoot Rd *HTCH/STOT* SG5 .... 36 D1
Hillgate *HTCHE/RSTV* SG4 .... 38 F7
Hillhouse *WAB* EN9 .... 191 L4
Hill House Av *STAN* HA7 .... 207 L7 3
Hilliard Rd *NTHWD* HA6 .... 205 L8
Hillier Cl *BAR* EN5 .... 201 G7
Hillingdon Rd *GSTN* WD25 .... 181 M5
Hillingdon Trail *DEN/HRF* UB9 .... 203 M7
Hill Ley *HAT* AL10 .... 154 E5 1
Hill Leys *POTB/CUF* EN6 .... 174 D7
Hill Md *BERK* HP4 .... 146 F7
Hillmead *STVG* SG1 .... 5 J2
Hill Milford *HARP* AL5 .... 109 J7
Hill Pickford *HARP* AL5 .... 109 J6
Hill Ri *LTNN/LIM* LU3 .... 64 B3
POTB/CUF EN6 .... 174 C6
POTB/CUF EN6 .... 187 H5
RKW/CH/CXG WD3 .... 194 A8
Hillrise Av *WATN* WD24 .... 196 C1
Hill Rd *HTCHE/RSTV* SG4 .... 111 K1
NTHWD HA6 .... 205 J6
Hillsborough Gn
OXHEY WD19 .... 205 M3 4
Hillshott *LWTH* SG6 .... 39 M4
Hill Side *LBUZ* LU7 .... 101 L4
BAR EN5 .... 201 H6
DUN/HR/TOD LU5 .... 63 G5
Hillside *HAT* AL10 .... 154 F5
HLWE CM17 .... 163 H4
HOD EN11 .... 159 L3
ROY SG8 .... 21 J5
STVG SG1 .... 5 H3
WARE SG12 .... 138 C2
WGCE AL7 .... 135 G7
WLYN AL6 .... 111 L1
Hillside Av *BORE* WD6 .... 199 H4
BSF CM23 .... 96 F3
CHES/WCR EN8 .... 190 C2
Hillside Cl *ABLGY* WD5 .... 181 K3
CFSP/GDCR SL9 .... 202 D6
CSTG HP8 .... 202 A3 1
HTCH/STOT SG5 .... 36 D1
Hillside Crs *CHES/WCR* EN8 .... 190 C2
NTHWD HA6 .... 205 M8
OXHEY WD19 .... 13 K9
WARE SG12 .... 139 G6 1
Hillside Gdns *BAR* EN5 .... 200 D5
BERK HP4 .... 147 J7
NTHWD HA6 .... 205 M7
Hillside La *WARE* SG12 .... 138 F5
Hillside Ri *NTHWD* HA6 .... 205 M7
Hillside Rd *BUSH* WD23 .... 13 L7
DUN/HR/TOD LU5 .... 81 J3 1
HARP AL5 .... 108 E7
HNLW SG16 .... 24 D7
HTCH/STOT SG5 .... 36 D1
LTNN/LIM LU3 .... 2 C3
NTHWD HA6 .... 205 M7
PIN HA5 .... 206 A7
RAD WD7 .... 184 A6
RKW/CH/CXG WD3 .... 193 H6
STAL AL1 .... 11 H5
Hillside Ter *HERT/BAY* SG13 .... 137 H6
Hillside Wy *WLYN* AL6 .... 112 F2
Hills La *NTHWD* HA6 .... 205 K8
Hill St *STALW/RED* AL3 .... 10 C6
Hills Vw *LTNN/LIM* LU3 .... 48 A6
The Hill *HLWE* CM17 .... 142 B6
STALE/WH AL4 .... 132 C2
Hill Top *BLDK* SG7 .... 40 D3
Hilltop *STALW/RED* AL3 .... 129 L4
Hilltop Cl *CHESW* EN7 .... 175 L5
Hilltop Rd *BERK* HP4 .... 147 H7
KGLGY WD4 .... 167 J6
Hilltop Vw *SHFD* SG17 .... 24 A4
Hilltop Wy *STAN* HA7 .... 207 M3
Hill Tree Cl *SBW* CM21 .... 142 C1
Hill Vw *BERK* HP4 .... 146 F4
BUNT SG9 .... 44 C2
HTCHE/RSTV SG4 .... 86 D4
Hillview Cl *PIN* HA5 .... 206 E6
Hillview Crs *LTNE* LU2 .... 65 H3
Hillview Gdns *CHES/WCR* EN8 .... 176 D6
Hillview Rd *PIN* HA5 .... 206 E7
Hilly Fld *HLWS* CM18 .... 162 E6
Hillyfields *DUN/WHIP* LU6 .... 81 H4
Hilly Flds *WGCE* AL7 .... 135 H3
Hilmay Dr *HHW* HP1 .... 149 G8
Hilton Av *DUN/WHIP* LU6 .... 81 G4
Hilton Cl *STVG* SG1 .... 70 A3
Himalayan Wy *WATW* WD18 .... 12 B8 1
Hindhead Gn *OXHEY* WD19 .... 206 B5
Hine Wy *HTCH/STOT* SG5 .... 52 B1
BLDK SG7 .... 17 G8
Hinxworth Rd *BLDK* SG7 .... 17 L6
Hipkins *BSF* CM23 .... 96 D6
Hitchens Cl *HHW* HP1 .... 148 E6
Hitchin Hl *HTCHE/RSTV* SG4 .... 52 D4
Hitchin La *SHFD* SG17 .... 25 G1
Hitchin Rd *ARL/CHE* SG15 .... 25 M7
HNLW SG16 .... 25 G5
HTCH/STOT SG5 .... 26 C7
HTCH/STOT SG5 .... 50 C1
HTCHE/RSTV SG4 .... 52 E6
HTCHE/RSTV SG4 .... 55 G1
HTCHE/RSTV SG4 .... 86 C8
LTNE LU2 .... 3 G4
LWTH SG6 .... 39 K7
SHFD SG17 .... 24 D1
STVG SG1 .... 54 A8
Hitchin St *BLDK* SG7 .... 40 D2
Hitherbaulk *WGCE* AL7 .... 134 C6
Hither Fld *WARE* SG12 .... 116 D7
Hitherfield La *HARP* AL5 .... 108 F8
Hitherway *WGCW* AL8 .... 112 C8
Hitherwell Dr
KTN/HRWW/W HA3 .... 207 J8
Hive Rd *BUSH* WD23 .... 207 J2
Hobbs Cl *CHES/WCR* EN8 .... 176 C8
STALE/WH AL4 .... 153 K8
Hobbs Cross Rd *HLWE* CM17 .... 142 E7
Hobbs Hill Rd *HHS/BOV* HP3 .... 166 D3
Hobbs Wy *WGCW* AL8 .... 134 B5 2
Hobletts Rd *HHNE* HP2 .... 8 F6
Hobsons Cl *HOD* EN11 .... 159 L1 2
Hobsons Wk *TRING* HP23 .... 123 L5 1
Hobtoe Rd *HLW* CM20 .... 161 M1
Hockerill *HERT/WAS* SG14 .... 90 D7
Hockerill St *BSF* CM23 .... 96 F3
Hocklands *WGCE* AL7 .... 135 H3
Hockliffe Rd *LBUZ* LU7 .... 62 A1
Hockwell Ring *LTNW/LEA* LU4 .... 64 A5
Hoddesdon Rd *WARE* SG12 .... 139 H7
Hodges Wy *WATW* WD18 .... 12 D9
Hodings Rd *HLW* CM20 .... 6 A5
Hodwell *BLDK* SG7 .... 18 C6
Hoecroft *WAB* EN9 .... 177 L1 1
Hoe La *WAB* EN9 .... 161 G8
WARE SG12 .... 138 C4
Hoestock Rd *SBW* CM21 .... 120 C8
The Hoe *OXHEY* WD19 .... 206 C2
Hogg End La *STALW/RED* AL3 .... 150 F5
Hogg La *BORE* WD6 .... 197 M5
Hog Hall La *BERK* HP4 .... 103 M5
Hogpits Bottom *HHS/BOV* HP3 .. 178 F3
Hogsdell La *HERT/BAY* SG13 .... 138 A6
Holbeck La *CHESW* EN7 .... 175 L5
Holbein Ga *NTHWD* HA6 .... 205 K5
Holborn Cl *STALE/WH* AL4 .... 153 J2
Holcroft Rd *HARP* AL5 .... 109 J7
Holdbrook *HTCHE/RSTV* SG4 .... 53 G3
Holden Cl *HERT/BAY* SG13 .... 137 K3
HTCHE/RSTV SG4 .... 53 H3 1
Holders La *STVGE* SG2 .... 71 K5
The Holdings *BRKMPK* AL9 .... 155 J3
Holecroft *WAB* EN9 .... 191 K5
Holford Wy *LTNN/LIM* LU3 .... 65 G1
Holgate Dr *LTNW/LEA* LU4 .... 64 A7
Holkham Cl *LTNW/LEA* LU4 .... 63 M6
Holland Cl *BAR* EN5 .... 201 J8
Holland Gdns *GSTN* WD25 .... 182 B6
Holland Rd *LTNN/LIM* LU3 .... 65 G8
Holland's Cft *WARE* SG12 .... 140 C1
Holland Wk *STAN* HA7 .... 207 M5
Hollick's La *DUN/WHIP* LU6 .... 81 J8
Holliday St *BERK* HP4 .... 147 J6
Holliers Wy *HAT* AL10 .... 154 F5
Hollies Cl *ROY* SG8 .... 21 G4
The Hollies *HHS/BOV* HP3 .... 164 F8 1
RKW/CH/CXG WD3 .... 193 H8
TRING HP23 .... 145 J1
Hollies Wy *POTB/CUF* EN6 .... 187 H2
Holliwick Rd *DUN/HR/TOD* LU5 .... 63 K8
Holloway La *RKW/CH/CXG* WD3 .... 193 G1
Holloways La *BRKMPK* AL9 .... 172 C2
The Holloway
RAYLNE/WEN HP22 .... 123 H6
Hollow La *HTCHE/RSTV* SG4 .... 52 E3
Hollybush Av *LCOL/BKTW* AL2 .... 168 F3
Hollybush Cl *BERK* HP4 .... 148 C3
OXHEY WD19 .... 196 B8 1
WLYN AL6 .... 112 D2 1
Hollybush Hl *LTNE* LU2 .... 66 E1
Hollybush La *BRKMPK* AL9 .... 134 E8
HARP AL5 .... 108 E7
HHW HP1 .... 148 E6
HTCHE/RSTV SG4 .... 86 A2
KNEB SG3 .... 89 H7
STALW/RED AL3 .... 106 F7
WGCE AL7 .... 134 D7
Hollybush Rd *LTNE* LU2 .... 84 B1
Hollybush Wy *CHESW* EN7 .... 175 M7
Holly Cl *HAT* AL10 .... 154 E6
Holly Copse *STVG* SG1 .... 5 G5
Holly Cft *HERT/WAS* SG14 .... 136 E3
Hollycross Rd *WARE* SG12 .... 138 E2
Holly Dell *HERT/BAY* SG13 .... 137 H6
Holly Dr *BERK* HP4 .... 147 J7
POTB/CUF EN6 .... 187 G4
Holly Farm Cl *LTN* LU1 .... 82 D6
Hollyfield *HAT* AL10 .... 154 F8
Holly Fld *HLWW/ROY* CM19 .... 162 B5
Hollyfield *TRING* HP23 .... 124 B5 2
Hollyfield Cl *TRING* HP23 .... 124 B5
Hollyfields *BROX* EN10 .... 176 D5
Hollygrove *BUSH* WD23 .... 197 J8
Holly Gv *PIN* HA5 .... 206 D8
Holly Grove Rd *HERT/WAS* SG14 .... 114 B7
Holly Hall Ct *WLYN* AL6 .... 112 B5 2
Holly Hedges La *HHS/BOV* HP3 .... 179 H1
Holly La *HARP* AL5 .... 109 K3
Holly Leys *STVGE* SG2 .... 89 G2
Holly Rd *KNEB* SG3 .... 112 F1
PEND EN3 .... 190 C7
Holly Shaws *STVGE* SG2 .... 71 G8
Holly St *LTN* LU1 .... 2 E8
Hollytree Cl *CFSP/GDCR* SL9 .... 202 D5 1
CSHM HP5 .... 178 A2 1
Holly Tree Ct *HHNE* HP2 .... 9 J9
Holly Wk *HARP* AL5 .... 131 J1
WGCW AL8 .... 112 B8
Holmbrook Av *LTNN/LIM* LU3 .... 65 H5
Holmbury Cl *BUSH* WD23 .... 207 K2 2
Holmdale *LWTH* SG6 .... 39 M5
Holmdale Cl *BORE* WD6 .... 198 E3 1
Holme Cl *CHES/WCR* EN8 .... 190 D2 1
HAT AL10 .... 154 E2
Holme Lea *GSTN* WD25 .... 182 B5
Holme Pk *BORE* WD6 .... 198 E3 4
Holme Rd *HAT* AL10 .... 154 E2
Holmesdale *CHES/WCR* EN8 .... 190 B6
Holmes Meadow *EPP* CM16 .... 162 A8 1
Holme Wy *STAN* HA7 .... 207 L6
Holmfield Cl *LTN* LU1 .... 83 J5 2
Holmscroft Rd *LTNN/LIM* LU3 .... 64 E4
Holmshill La *BORE* WD6 .... 185 L8
Holmside Ri *OXHEY* WD19 .... 206 A3
Holmwood Rd *PEND* EN3 .... 190 C7
Holroyd Crs *BLDK* SG7 .... 40 D3
Holt Cl *BORE* WD6 .... 198 E5
Holts Meadow *STALW/RED* AL3 .... 130 A4
Holtsmere Cl *GSTN* WD25 .... 182 B6
LTNE LU2 .... 84 C1
Holtsmere End La *HHNE* HP2 .... 129 G8
The Holt *HHNE* HP2 .... 149 K8
WGCE AL7 .... 135 J5
Holwell Hyde *WGCE* AL7 .... 135 H5 2
Holwell Hyde La *BRKMPK* AL9 .... 135 H8
Holwell La *BRKMPK* AL9 .... 156 D2
Holwell Rd *HTCH/STOT* SG5 .... 37 L4
WGCE AL7 .... 134 D5
Holy Cross Hl *BROX* EN10 .... 175 M2
Holyfield Rd *WAB* EN9 .... 177 H8
Holyrood Crs *STAL* AL1 .... 169 J3
Holyrood Rd *BAR* EN5 .... 201 H7
Holywell Cl *DUN/WHIP* LU6 .... 105 G4
Holywell Hl *STAL* AL1 .... 10 E9
Holywell Rd *DUN/WHIP* LU6 .... 105 G3
WATW WD18 .... 12 D7
Home Cl *BROX* EN10 .... 176 E3
HLW CM20 .... 7 J6
HTCH/STOT SG5 .... 26 E4
LTNW/LEA LU4 .... 64 B6
Homedale Dr *LTNW/LEA* LU4 .... 64 D6
Home Farm Rd *BERK* HP4 .... 146 C3 2
RKW/CH/CXG WD3 .... 204 F4
Homefield *BERK* HP4 .... 148 A3
BLDK SG7 .... 17 J4
HHS/BOV HP3 .... 165 G7
WAB EN9 .... 191 M3
Homefield La *HTCHE/RSTV* SG4 .... 69 L8
Homefield Rd *BUSH* WD23 .... 196 F6
HHNE HP2 .... 9 G9
RAD WD7 .... 183 L8
RKW/CH/CXG WD3 .... 193 J5
WARE SG12 .... 116 D8
Homeleigh Ct
CHES/WCR EN8 .... 190 A1 1
Home Ley *WGCE* AL7 .... 134 D4 1
Home Meadow *WGCE* AL7 .... 134 E4 1
Home Park Mill Link Rd
KGLGY WD4 .... 181 G2
Home Pastures *RBSF* CM22 .... 121 L7
Homerfield *WGCW* AL8 .... 134 B4
Homerswood La *WLYN* AL6 .... 111 M8
Homerton Rd *LTNN/LIM* LU3 .... 64 F4
Homestead Cl *LCOL/BKTW* AL2 .... 169 H6
Homestead La *WGCE* AL7 .... 134 E7
Homestead Moat *STVG* SG1 .... 4 F5
Homestead Rd *HAT* AL10 .... 154 F2
RKW/CH/CXG WD3 .... 194 C8
Homestead Wy *LTN* LU1 .... 83 H5
Home Wy *RKW/CH/CXG* WD3 .... 203 L1
Homewood Av *POTB/CUF* EN6 .... 174 D6
Homewood La *POTB/CUF* EN6 .... 174 B6
Homewood Rd *STAL* AL1 .... 153 G4
Honeybourne *BSF* CM23 .... 96 D6
Honey Brook *WAB* EN9 .... 191 K4
Honeycroft *WGCW* AL8 .... 134 B5 3
Honeycroft Dr *STALE/WH* AL4 .... 170 B2
Honeycross Rd *HHW* HP1 .... 148 D8
Honeygate *LTNE* LU2 .... 65 K6
Honey La *BUNT* SG9 .... 58 D2
CHES/WCR EN8 .... 190 E5
SAFWS CB11 .... 47 L7
WAB EN9 .... 191 L5
Honeymeade *HLW* CM20 .... 142 B3
Honeysuckle Cl *BSF* CM23 .... 96 B4
HERT/BAY SG13 .... 137 M4 2
Honeysuckle Gdns *HAT* AL10 .... 155 G6
Honeyway *ROY* SG8 .... 21 K3
Honeywood Cl *POTB/CUF* EN6 .... 187 J4
Hook Fld *HLWS* CM18 .... 162 D4
Hook Ga *EN* EN1 .... 190 A8
Hook La *POTB/CUF* EN6 .... 187 L3
The Hook *BAR* EN5 .... 201 J7
Hoops La *ROY* SG8 .... 30 E4
Hoo Rd *SHFD* SG17 .... 24 C3
Hoo St *LTN* LU1 .... 83 K5 1
The Hoo *HLWE* CM17 .... 142 B5
Hope Gn *GSTN* WD25 .... 181 M4
Hopewell Rd *BLDK* SG7 .... 40 C2
Hopground Cl *STAL* AL1 .... 169 M1
Hopkins Crs *STALE/WH* AL4 .... 153 G1
Hopkins Yd *STAL* AL1 .... 11 G8
Hopton Rd *STVG* SG1 .... 69 M3
Horace Gay Gdns *LWTH* SG6 .... 39 K5 1
Horbeam Cl *BORE* WD6 .... 198 F2 3
Hordle Gdns *STAL* AL1 .... 11 K9
Hornbeam La *BRKMPK* AL9 .... 156 D8
Hornbeams *LCOL/BKTW* AL2 .... 182 E1
Hornbeams Av *EN* EN1 .... 190 B6
Hornbeam Spring *KNEB* SG3 .... 88 E6
The Hornbeams *HLW* CM20 .... 6 C3
STVGE SG2 .... 5 M6
Hornbeam Wy *CHESW* EN7 .... 175 L8
Horn Hl *HTCHE/RSTV* SG4 .... 86 D4
Hornhill Rd *RKW/CH/CXG* WD3 .... 203 H5
Hornsby Cl *LTNE* LU2 .... 84 B1
Horns Cl *HERT/BAY* SG13 .... 137 H6
Hornsfield *WGCE* AL7 .... 135 H3
Horns Mill Rd *HERT/BAY* SG13 .... 137 G7
Horns Rd *HERT/BAY* SG13 .... 137 H5
Horrocks Cl *WARE* SG12 .... 116 C7
Horsecroft Rd *HHW* HP1 .... 165 M1
HLWW/ROY CM19 .... 161 K3
Horse Hl *CSHM* HP5 .... 178 C3
Horselers *HHS/BOV* HP3 .... 166 F2
Horsemans Dr *LCOL/BKTW* AL2 .... 168 F5
Horseshoe Cl *BGSW* SG18 .... 14 C5
Horseshoe Hl *BUNT* SG9 .... 59 M2
Horseshoe La *BUNT* SG9 .... 59 L3
GSTN WD25 .... 182 A3
Horseshoes Cl *LBUZ* LU7 .... 101 L3 2
The Horseshoe *HHS/BOV* HP3 .... 167 H1
Horsham Cl *LTNE* LU2 .... 66 C7
Horsler Cl *AMP/FLIT/B* MK45 .... 35 H8
Horsleys *RKW/CH/CXG* WD3 .... 203 J5
Horton Gdns *HHNE* HP2 .... 149 M1 1
Hospital Rd *ARL/CHE* SG15 .... 25 L7
Houghton Park Rd
DUN/HR/TOD LU5 .... 63 K4
Houghton Rd *DUN/HR/TOD* LU5 .... 62 F7
Housden Cl *STALE/WH* AL4 .... 132 D3 1
Housefield Wy *STALE/WH* AL4 .... 170 B2
House La *ARL/CHE* SG15 .... 25 M3
STALE/WH AL4 .... 153 J2
Housewood End *HHW* HP1 .... 149 G4
Housman Av *ROY* SG8 .... 21 H1
Howard Agne Cl *HHW* HP1 .... 164 F6
Howard Cl *BUSH* WD23 .... 197 K8
HTCH/STOT SG5 .... 26 D5 1
LTNN/LIM LU3 .... 64 F6 1
STALE/WH AL4 .... 170 B2
WAB EN9 .... 191 J5
WATN WD24 .... 181 M8 3
Howard Dr *BORE* WD6 .... 199 J5
LWTH SG6 .... 40 A7
Howard Ga *LWTH* SG6 .... 40 A6 1
Howard Pl *DUN/WHIP* LU6 .... 81 J3
Howards Dr *HHW* HP1 .... 148 E4
Howardsgate *WGCW* AL8 .... 134 C4
Howards Wd *LWTH* SG6 .... 40 A7
Howard Wy *BAR* EN5 .... 200 C6
HLW CM20 .... 7 J1
Howe Cl *RAD* WD7 .... 184 D3
Howe Dell *HAT* AL10 .... 155 G5
Howe Rd *HHS/BOV* HP3 .... 166 F1
How Fld *HARP* AL5 .... 108 D7
Howfield Gn *HOD* EN11 .... 159 L1
Howicks Gn *WGCE* AL7 .... 134 F7
Howland Garth *STAL* AL1 .... 169 H3
Howlands *WGCE* AL7 .... 134 F7 2
Howton Pl *BUSH* WD23 .... 207 J1
How Wd *LCOL/BKTW* AL2 .... 169 G7
Hoylake Gdns *OXHEY* WD19 .... 206 C4
Hubbards Rd *RKW/CH/CXG* WD3 .... 193 J6
Huckleberry Cl *LTNN/LIM* LU3 .... 64 F2 3
Hudnall La *BERK* HP4 .... 126 C4
Hudson Cl *STAL* AL1 .... 169 H2
WATN WD24 .... 181 L7

Hudson Rd STVGE SG2 ... 71 G3
Huggins La BRKMPK AL9 ... 172 A2
Hughenden Rd
STALE/WH AL4 ... 153 G4
Hull Gv HLWW/ROY CM19 ... 161 M7
Hull La STDN SG11 ... 75 K3
Humberstone Cl LTNW/LEA LU4 ... 64 D8
Humberstone Rd LTNW/LEA LU4 .. 64 D8
Humphrey Talbot Av
DUN/WHIP LU6 ... 104 E3
Humphrys Rd DUN/HR/TOD LU5 .. 63 J7
Hunsdon WGCE AL7 ... 135 J4 1
Hunsdon Rd WARE SG12 ... 118 C6
WARE SG12 ... 139 K6
Hunston Cl LTNW/LEA LU4 ... 64 A5
Hunt Cl STALE/WH AL4 ... 153 J4 2
Hunter Cl BORE WD6 ... 199 H6
POTB/CUF EN6 ... 187 G4
Huntercrombe Gdns
OXHEY WD19 ... 206 B5 6
Hunters Cl HHS/BOV HP3 ... 164 F8
HTCH/STOT SG5 ... 26 D4 2
STVGE SG2 ... 71 J3
TRING HP23 ... 124 A5
Hunter's La GSTN WD25 ... 181 L5
Hunters Oak HHNE HP2 ... 150 A2
Hunters Pk BERK HP4 ... 147 K5
Hunters Reach CHESW EN7 ... 175 L8
Hunters Ride LCOL/BKTW AL2 ... 182 F2
Hunters Wy ROY SG8 ... 21 K4
WGCE AL7 ... 134 D7 2
Huntingdon Cl BROX EN10 ... 176 D3
Huntingdon Rd STVG SG1 ... 70 A2
Hunting Ga HHNE HP2 ... 8 D1
HTCHE/RSTV SG4 ... 38 F7
Hunton Bridge Hl KGLGY WD4 ... 181 H4
Hunts Cl LTN LU1 ... 2 B9
Huntsman Cl STDN SG11 ... 75 J7
Huntsmans Cl BERK HP4 ... 104 B5 2
Huntsmill Rd HHW HP1 ... 148 D8 1
Hurlock Cl DUN/WHIP LU6 ... 80 F4
Hurlock Wy LTNW/LEA LU4 ... 64 B5
Hurricane Wy GSTN WD25 ... 181 M3 2
Hurst Cl BLDK SG7 ... 40 F1
WGCE AL7 ... 135 H5
Hurst Dr CHES/WCR EN8 ... 190 C5
Hurstlings WGCE AL7 ... 135 G6
Hurst Pl NTHWD HA6 ... 205 G8
Hurst Ri BAR EN5 ... 200 F4
Hurst Wy LTNN/LIM LU3 ... 64 D5
Hutton Cl HERT/WAS SG14 ... 136 F4
Hutton La KTN/HRWW/W HA3 ... 207 H7
Hutton Wk KTN/HRWW/W HA3 .. 207 H7
Hyburn Cl HHS/BOV HP3 ... 150 A8
LCOL/BKTW AL2 ... 182 E1
Hydean Wy STVGE SG2 ... 5 J9
Hyde Av HTCH/STOT SG5 ... 26 D5
POTB/CUF EN6 ... 187 G4
Hyde Cl BAR EN5 ... 200 E4
HARP AL5 ... 109 G6
Hyde Gn East STVGE SG2 ... 5 M8
Hyde Gn North STVGE SG2 ... 5 L8
Hyde Gn South STVGE SG2 ... 5 L8
Hyde La HHS/BOV HP3 ... 164 F6
KGLGY WD4 ... 167 G6
LCOL/BKTW AL2 ... 169 K7
LTNE LU2 ... 85 G8
Hyde Md WAB EN9 ... 177 K2
Hyde Mdw HHS/BOV HP3 ... 164 F7
Hyde Rd LTN LU1 ... 82 E6
WAT WD17 ... 12 D2 1
The Hyde WARE SG12 ... 116 A8
Hyde Va WGCE AL7 ... 134 E6
Hyde View Rd HARP AL5 ... 109 G6
Hyde Wy WGCE AL7 ... 134 D4
Hyperion Ct HHNE HP2 ... 8 F2
Hyver Hl MLHL NW7 ... 199 J7

I

Ibberson Wy HTCHE/RSTV SG4 ... 52 F3
Ibsley Wy EBAR EN4 ... 201 K6
Iceni Ct LWTH SG6 ... 40 A3
Ickleford Rd HTCH/STOT SG5 ... 52 E2
Ickley Cl LTNW/LEA LU4 ... 64 A5 1
Icknield Cl HTCH/STOT SG5 ... 38 D6
STALW/RED AL3 ... 168 E1
Icknield Gn LWTH SG6 ... 39 K4
TRING HP23 ... 123 M4 1
Icknield Rd LTNN/LIM LU3 ... 64 E6
Icknield St DUN/WHIP LU6 ... 81 G2
Icknield Wk ROY SG8 ... 21 K3
Icknield Wy BERK HP4 ... 104 D5
BLDK SG7 ... 40 D1
BUNT SG9 ... 30 B8
DUN/WHIP LU6 ... 80 C5
LTNN/LIM LU3 ... 65 G2
LWTH SG6 ... 39 L4
ROY SG8 ... 30 F7
TRING HP23 ... 123 L5
TRING HP23 ... 125 G1
TRING HP23 ... 144 B4
Icknield Wy East BLDK SG7 ... 40 E1 3
Icknield Way Pth
AMP/FLIT/B MK45 ... 48 F2
BLDK SG7 ... 27 K7
DUN/HR/TOD LU5 ... 48 A4
DUN/WHIP LU6 ... 62 C6
HTCH/STOT SG5 ... 37 H7
HTCH/STOT SG5 ... 50 C4
LTNN/LIM LU3 ... 48 D3
LTNN/LIM LU3 ... 64 E5
LTNW/LEA LU4 ... 64 B7
ROY SG8 ... 19 G4
ROY SG8 ... 22 E3
Ilford Cl LTNE LU2 ... 66 B7
Ilkley Rd OXHEY WD19 ... 206 C5
Imberfield LTNW/LEA LU4 ... 64 B7 2
Imperial Wy WATN WD24 ... 196 B2
Indells HAT AL10 ... 154 E6
Index Dr DUN/WHIP LU6 ... 81 J3
Ingelheim Ct STVG SG1 ... 70 C3 1
Inglefield POTB/CUF EN6 ... 186 F1
Ingles WGCW AL8 ... 134 D1
Ingleside Dr STVG SG1 ... 70 A1
Ingram Gdns LTNE LU2 ... 65 J4
Inkerman Rd STAL AL1 ... 11 G8
Inkerman St LTN LU1 ... 2 D6
Innes Ct HHS/BOV HP3 ... 166 C1
Inn's Cl STVG SG1 ... 4 C1
Inskip Crs STVG SG1 ... 4 F3
Iona Cl STVG SG1 ... 54 E8
Iredale Vw BLDK SG7 ... 40 F1
Iron Dr HERT/BAY SG13 ... 138 A3
Irving Cl BSF CM23 ... 96 C6 1
Irving Crs LBUZ LU7 ... 101 M2
Isabel Ga CHES/WCR EN8 ... 176 E5
Isabelle Cl CHESW EN7 ... 175 H8
Isenburg Wy HHNE HP2 ... 149 J2
Isherwood Cl ROY SG8 ... 21 H2 2
Isle of Wight La DUN/WHIP LU6 ... 81 G7
Islington Wy STVG SG1 ... 54 E8
Iveagh Cl NTHWD HA6 ... 205 G8
Ivel Cl AMP/FLIT/B MK45 ... 35 J7 1
Ivel Rd STVG SG1 ... 70 B3
Ivel Wy BLDK SG7 ... 40 F4
HTCH/STOT SG5 ... 26 E2
Ivere Dr BAR EN5 ... 201 G7
Ives Rd HERT/WAS SG14 ... 137 G3
Ivinghoe Br LBUZ LU7 ... 102 B2
Ivinghoe Cl GSTN WD25 ... 182 C6
STALE/WH AL4 ... 153 H2 3
Ivinghoe Rd BUSH WD23 ... 197 J7
RKW/CH/CXG WD3 ... 193 L8
Ivinghoe Wy DUN/WHIP LU6 ... 103 K1
Ivory Cl STALE/WH AL4 ... 170 B1
Ivory Ct HHS/BOV HP3 ... 166 D2
Ivybridge BROX EN10 ... 159 M6
Ivy Cl DUN/WHIP LU6 ... 80 D1
Ivy House La BERK HP4 ... 147 J6 2
Ivy Lea RKW/CH/CXG WD3 ... 203 M1 3
Ivy Rd LTN LU1 ... 2 A4
Ivy Ter HOD EN11 ... 160 B2

J

Jackdaw Cl STVGE SG2 ... 71 J6
Jackdaws WGCE AL7 ... 135 H4 6
Jackets La DEN/HRF UB9 ... 204 F7
Jacketts Fld ABLGY WD5 ... 181 L2
Jackman's Pl LWTH SG6 ... 40 A4
Jacks La DEN/HRF UB9 ... 203 M8
RBSF CM22 ... 99 J3
Jackson Rd EBAR EN4 ... 201 K7
Jacksons Dr CHESW EN7 ... 175 M7
Jackson's La ROY SG8 ... 31 K5
Jackson St BLDK SG7 ... 40 D1 6
Jack Stevens Cl HLWE CM17 ... 163 H4 3
James Cl BUSH WD23 ... 13 M6
James Ct LTN LU1 ... 2 E9
Jameson Rd HARP AL5 ... 109 G7
James Wy STVG SG1 ... 70 B3
Jane Cl HHNE HP2 ... 150 A2
Jarden LWTH SG6 ... 40 B6
Jardine Wy DUN/HR/TOD LU5 ... 81 K3
Jarman Cl HHS/BOV HP3 ... 166 D1
Jarman Wy ROY SG8 ... 21 G3
Jarvis Cleys CHESW EN7 ... 175 L5 3
Jarvis Cl BAR EN5 ... 200 C6
Jasmin Cl BSF CM23 ... 96 B4
NTHWD HA6 ... 205 L8
Jasmine Dr HERT/BAY SG13 ... 137 M4
Jasmine Gdns HAT AL10 ... 154 E3
Jasmin Wy HHW HP1 ... 148 D6 2
Jasons Hl CSHM HP5 ... 164 A8
Jay Cl LWTH SG6 ... 39 K2
Jaywood LTNE LU2 ... 66 B5
Jeans La BSF CM23 ... 96 D3
Jeans Wy DUN/HR/TOD LU5 ... 81 K2
Jeffrey Cl ROY SG8 ... 21 H2
Jellicoe Gdns STAN HA7 ... 207 L6 4
Jellicoe Rd WATW WD18 ... 12 C9
Jenkins Av LCOL/BKTW AL2 ... 182 D1
Jenkins La BSF CM23 ... 97 G6
TRING HP23 ... 144 D7
Jennings Cl STVG SG1 ... 4 E7
Jennings Rd STAL AL1 ... 11 L4
Jennings Wy BAR EN5 ... 200 B4
HHS/BOV HP3 ... 166 D1
Jenning Wd WLYN AL6 ... 112 E3
Jepps La ROY SG8 ... 21 J4 3
Jerome Dr STALW/RED AL3 ... 168 F1
Jerounds HLWW/ROY CM19 ... 162 A4
Jersey Cl HOD EN11 ... 159 M3
Jersey La STAL AL1 ... 153 G5
STALE/WH AL4 ... 153 H1
Jersey Rd LTNW/LEA LU4 ... 63 M7
Jervis Av PEND EN3 ... 190 D6
Jervis Rd BSF CM23 ... 96 E4
Jessop Rd STVG SG1 ... 70 F1
Jeve Cl BLDK SG7 ... 40 F1
Jill Grey Pl HTCH/STOT SG5 ... 52 E4
Jillifer Rd LTNW/LEA LU4 ... 63 M7
The Jinnings WGCE AL7 ... 135 G7
Jocelyns HLWE CM17 ... 142 B6
Jocketts Hl HHW HP1 ... 148 E7
Jocketts Rd HHW HP1 ... 148 E8
John Barker Pl HTCH/STOT SG5 ... 52 B1
John Bunyan Trail
AMP/FLIT/B MK45 ... 48 E2
HTCH/STOT SG5 ... 35 M7
LTNE LU2 ... 50 B8
LTNN/LIM LU3 ... 49 G8
SHFD SG17 ... 24 A2
Johnby Cl PEND EN3 ... 190 D8 4
John Eliot Cl WAB EN9 ... 177 K1
John Howland Cl HNLW SG16 ... 25 J2
John Lamb Ct
KTN/HRWW/W HA3 ... 207 K8 2
Johnson Ct HHS/BOV HP3 ... 166 D1
Johns Rd BSF CM23 ... 96 F1
John St LTN LU1 ... 2 F6
ROY SG8 ... 21 J4 8
John Tate Rd HERT/BAY SG13 ... 137 L5
Joiner's Cl CFSP/GDCR SL9 ... 202 E7
Joiners La CFSP/GDCR SL9 ... 202 D8
Joiners Wy CFSP/GDCR SL9 ... 202 D7
The Joint ROY SG8 ... 31 M4
Jones Rd CHESW EN7 ... 189 G1
Jonquil Cl WGCE AL7 ... 135 G6
Jordan Cl GSTN WD25 ... 181 L6
Jordans Rd RKW/CH/CXG WD3 ... 193 M8
Jordan's Wy LCOL/BKTW AL2 ... 182 D1
Joyce Ct WAB EN9 ... 191 J5 2
Joyners Fld HLWS CM18 ... 162 B6
Jubilee Av LCOL/BKTW AL2 ... 170 C5
WARE SG12 ... 116 E8 2
Jubilee Crs ARL/CHE SG15 ... 25 L8
Jubilee Rd LWTH SG6 ... 40 B3
STVG SG1 ... 70 A2
WATN WD24 ... 195 M1
Jubilee St LTNE LU2 ... 3 G3
Judge's Hl POTB/CUF EN6 ... 173 L8
Judge St WATN WD24 ... 196 A1
Julia Ga STVG SG1 ... 71 H2
Julian Cl BAR EN5 ... 201 G4
Julian's Ct STVG SG1 ... 70 B2
Julian's Rd STVG SG1 ... 70 A2
Julius Gdns LTNN/LIM LU3 ... 64 E3
Juniper Av LCOL/BKTW AL2 ... 182 F2 1
Juniper Cl BAR EN5 ... 200 C6
BROX EN10 ... 176 E4 3
LTNW/LEA LU4 ... 64 D8
Juniper Gdns RAD WD7 ... 184 D4
Juniper Ga RKW/CH/CXG WD3 ... 204 C2
Juniper Gn HHW HP1 ... 148 D7 1
Juniper Gv WAT WD17 ... 195 M1
Jupiter Dr HHNE HP2 ... 8 E4
Juxon Cl RYLN/HDSTN HA2 ... 207 G8

K

Kardwell Cl HTCHE/RSTV SG4 ... 52 F4 1
Katescroft WGCE AL7 ... 134 D8 2
Katherine Dr DUN/HR/TOD LU5 ... 63 K8
Katherine Pl ABLGY WD5 ... 181 M3 3
Katherine's Wy
HLWW/ROY CM19 ... 161 M5
Keaton Cl DUN/HR/TOD LU5 ... 63 J5 2
Keats Cl HHNE HP2 ... 150 A1
ROY SG8 ... 21 H2 3
STVGE SG2 ... 71 G2
Keats Wy HTCHE/RSTV SG4 ... 53 H3
Keble Ter ABLGY WD5 ... 181 L3
Kecksy's SBW CM21 ... 120 E6
Keeble Cl LTNE LU2 ... 84 D1
Keele Cl WATN WD24 ... 13 G1
Keely Cl EBAR EN4 ... 201 K6
Keepers Cl LBUZ LU7 ... 101 M3 2
LTNE LU2 ... 66 B8
Keiths Rd HHS/BOV HP3 ... 149 M8
Keiths Wd KNEB SG3 ... 88 E5
Kelbys WGCE AL7 ... 135 H3
Keller Cl STVGE SG2 ... 5 L5
Kelling Cl LTNE LU2 ... 65 H2
Kelly Cl BORE WD6 ... 199 J3
Kelman Cl CHES/WCR EN8 ... 190 C2 1
Kelmscott Crs WATW WD18 ... 12 C7
Kelshall GSTN WD25 ... 182 D7
Kelshall St ROY SG8 ... 30 D6
Kelvin Cl LTN LU1 ... 2 E9
Kelvin Crs KTN/HRWW/W HA3 ... 207 K7
Kemble Cl POTB/CUF EN6 ... 187 J4
Kempe Cl STAL AL1 ... 169 H3
Kempe Rd EN EN1 ... 190 A7
Kemp Pl BUSH WD23 ... 196 F7
Kemprow GSTN WD25 ... 183 J6
Kemps Dr NTHWD HA6 ... 205 L7 3
Kempsey Cl LTNE LU2 ... 66 C8
Kendal Cl LTNN/LIM LU3 ... 64 C3
Kendale HHS/BOV HP3 ... 150 A8
Kendale Rd HTCHE/RSTV SG4 ... 52 E4
LTNW/LEA LU4 ... 64 A8
Kendall Cl WGCE AL7 ... 134 E8
Kendals Cl RAD WD7 ... 183 K7
Kenerne Dr BAR EN5 ... 200 D6
Kenford Cl GSTN WD25 ... 182 A3
Kenilworth Cl HHS/BOV HP3 ... 149 K8
STVGE SG2 ... 89 H3
Kenilworth Ct WAT WD17 ... 195 M2
Kenilworth Dr BORE WD6 ... 199 H4
RKW/CH/CXG WD3 ... 195 C5
Kenilworth Gdns
OXHEY WD19 ... 206 B5 7
Kenilworth Rd LTN LU1 ... 2 A5
Kenley Cl EBAR EN4 ... 201 K5
Kennedy Av HOD EN11 ... 159 L4
Kennedy Cl CHES/WCR EN8 ... 176 D7
PIN HA5 ... 206 E6
Kennedy Rd WARE SG12 ... 91 K3
Kennel La HARP AL5 ... 107 M5
Kennelwood La HAT AL10 ... 155 G4 4
Kenneth Gdns STAN HA7 ... 207 M6
Kenneth Rd LTNE LU2 ... 3 J2
Kenning Rd HOD EN11 ... 159 M2
Kennington Rd LTNN/LIM LU3 ... 65 G8
Kensington Av WATW WD18 ... 12 B5
Kensington Ct DUN/HR/TOD LU5 .. 63 K6
STAL AL1 ... 169 M1 1
Kensington Wy BORE WD6 ... 199 J4
Kensworth Rd DUN/WHIP LU6 ... 105 H6
Kent Cl BORE WD6 ... 199 J1
Kent Crs BSF CM23 ... 96 D6
Kent Dr EBAR EN4 ... 201 M5
Kentish La BRKMPK AL9 ... 173 H3
Kenton Gdns STAL AL1 ... 11 J9
Kenton La KTN/HRWW/W HA3 ... 207 M8
Kent Rd DUN/HR/TOD LU5 ... 63 J4
LTN LU1 ... 82 E2
Kents Av HHS/BOV HP3 ... 166 C3 1
Kent's La STDN SG11 ... 75 K8
Kenway Dr AMSS HP7 ... 192 A2
Kenwood Dr
RKW/CH/CXG WD3 ... 203 L2
Kenworth Cl CHES/WCR EN8 ... 190 C4
Kerdistone Cl POTB/CUF EN6 ... 187 G1
Kerr Cl KNEB SG3 ... 88 E5
Kerri Cl BAR EN5 ... 200 B5
Kerril Cft HLW CM20 ... 161 M1
Kershaw Cl LTNN/LIM LU3 ... 64 F2
Kershaw's Hl HTCHE/RSTV SG4 ... 52 E4
Kessingland Av STVG SG1 ... 69 M1
Keston Ms WAT WD17 ... 196 A3 3
Kestrel Cl BERK HP4 ... 147 H7
GSTN WD25 ... 182 D5
STVGE SG2 ... 71 J8
Kestrel Gdns BSF CM23 ... 96 D4
Kestrel Gn HAT AL10 ... 154 F6
Kestrel Rd WAB EN9 ... 191 M5
The Kestrels LCOL/BKTW AL2 ... 182 D2
Kestrel Wk LWTH SG6 ... 40 A7
Kestrel Wy LTNW/LEA LU4 ... 63 M5
WGCE AL7 ... 134 E2
Keswick Cl DUN/WHIP LU6 ... 81 G3
STAL AL1 ... 153 G8
Keswick Dr PEND EN3 ... 190 B7
Kettering Rd PEND EN3 ... 190 C8
Kettle Green Rd MHAD SG10 ... 94 D8
Ketton Cl LTNE LU2 ... 3 K7
Kewferry Dr NTHWD HA6 ... 205 G5
Kewferry Rd NTHWD HA6 ... 205 H6
Keyfield Ter STAL AL1 ... 10 F8
Keymer Cl LTNE LU2 ... 66 B7 2
Keynton Cl HERT/WAS SG14 ... 136 E3
Keysers Rd BROX EN10 ... 176 F1
Kibes La WARE SG12 ... 138 C1
Kidner Cl LTNE LU2 ... 65 K5
Kilbride Ct HHNE HP2 ... 149 L3 2
Kilby Cl GSTN WD25 ... 182 C6
Kilfillan Gdns BERK HP4 ... 146 F7
Kilmarnock Dr LTNE LU2 ... 65 K5
Kilmarnock Rd OXHEY WD19 ... 206 C4
Kiln Av AMS HP6 ... 192 B1
Kilncroft HHS/BOV HP3 ... 167 G1
Kilnfield WGCE AL7 ... 134 E1
Kiln Gnd HHS/BOV HP3 ... 166 F1
Kiln House Cl WARE SG12 ... 116 D8
Kiln La CSHM HP5 ... 178 A2
HLWE CM17 ... 163 J3
Kiln Wy NTHWD HA6 ... 205 K6
Kilsmore La CHES/WCR EN8 ... 176 C7
Kilworth Cl WGCE AL7 ... 135 G6
Kimberley LWTH SG6 ... 26 E8
Kimberley Cl BSF CM23 ... 96 F5 1
LTNW/LEA LU4 ... 63 K7
Kimberley Rd STALW/RED AL3 ... 10 D4
Kimble Cl WATW WD18 ... 195 K7 1
Kimble Crs BUSH WD23 ... 197 H8
Kimbolton Crs KNEB SG3 ... 88 F2
Kimbolton Gn BORE WD6 ... 199 H5 1
Kimps Wy HHS/BOV HP3 ... 166 F2
Kimpton Bottom HARP AL5 ... 109 K3
Kimpton Cl HHNE HP2 ... 150 A2
Kimpton Pl GSTN WD25 ... 182 C5
Kimpton Rd HTCHE/RSTV SG4 ... 111 H1
LTNE LU2 ... 3 L9
STALE/WH AL4 ... 110 B4
WLYN AL6 ... 111 K4
Kimptons Cl POTB/CUF EN6 ... 186 C4
Kimptons Md POTB/CUF EN6 ... 186 C4
Kinderscout HHS/BOV HP3 ... 166 F1
Kindersley Cl WLYN AL6 ... 112 B4 3
Kindersley Wy ABLGY WD5 ... 181 H2
King Arthur Ct CHES/WCR EN8 .. 190 D2
King Charles Rd RAD WD7 ... 184 D3
King Croft Rd HARP AL5 ... 131 J3
King Edward Rd BAR EN5 ... 200 F5
CHES/WCR EN8 ... 190 D4
OXHEY WD19 ... 13 L8
RAD WD7 ... 184 E4
King Edward's Rd WARE SG12 ... 116 D8
King Edward St HHS/BOV HP3 ... 166 C3
Kingfisher Cl NTHWD HA6 ... 205 G8
STALE/WH AL4 ... 132 C1
WARE SG12 ... 139 H7 1
Kingfisher Ct
HTCHE/RSTV SG4 ... 52 F4 2
Kingfisher Dr HHS/BOV HP3 ... 166 E4
Kingfisher Lure
RKW/CH/CXG WD3 ... 194 A5
Kingfisher Ri STVGE SG2 ... 71 J8
Kingfisher Wy BSF CM23 ... 96 F3
King George Av BUSH WD23 ... 197 G7
King George Cl STVG SG1 ... 4 E2
King George Rd WAB EN9 ... 191 H5 2
WARE SG12 ... 116 D8
King Georges Av WATW WD18 ... 195 K6
King Georges Cl HTCH/STOT SG5 .. 38 C8
King George's Wy
HTCHE/RSTV SG4 ... 86 D4
Kingham Rd WARE SG12 ... 117 K5
Kinghamway LTNE LU2 ... 2 E3
King Harry La STALW/RED AL3 ... 151 M8
King Harry St HHNE HP2 ... 8 A9
King Henry's Ms PEND EN3 ... 190 F8 1
King James Av POTB/CUF EN6 ... 174 D8
King James Wy ROY SG8 ... 21 J4
Kings Av HHS/BOV HP3 ... 166 E3
WATW WD18 ... 12 B5
Kingsbridge Rd BSF CM23 ... 96 F2
Kingsbury Av DUN/HR/TOD LU5 .. 81 K1
STALW/RED AL3 ... 10 C5
Kingsbury Ct
DUN/HR/TOD LU5 ... 81 H2 2
Kingsbury Gdns
DUN/HR/TOD LU5 ... 81 L1
Kings Cl CSTG HP8 ... 202 C2
KGLGY WD4 ... 180 A2
NTHWD HA6 ... 205 L6
WATW WD18 ... 13 G5 2
Kings Ct BSF CM23 ... 96 F2
Kingscroft WGCE AL7 ... 135 G3 3
Kingscroft Av DUN/HR/TOD LU5 .. 81 G1
Kingsdale Rd BERK HP4 ... 146 F7
Kingsdon La HLWE CM17 ... 163 H3
Kingsdown HTCHE/RSTV SG4 ... 53 G3
Kingsdown Av LTNE LU2 ... 65 J6
Kings Farm Rd
RKW/CH/CXG WD3 ... 193 J7
Kingsfield HOD EN11 ... 159 M2
Kingsfield Ct OXHEY WD19 ... 13 J9
Kingsfield Dr PEND EN3 ... 190 C6
Kingsfield Rd OXHEY WD19 ... 196 C8
WARE SG12 ... 91 K3
Kingsfield Wy PEND EN3 ... 190 C6 3
Kingsgate STALW/RED AL3 ... 169 G1
Kingshill Av STALE/WH AL4 ... 153 G4
Kingshill Wy BERK HP4 ... 146 F8
Kingsland HLWS CM18 ... 162 B4
Kingsland Cl DUN/HR/TOD LU5 ... 63 K6
Kingsland Rd HHW HP1 ... 165 M1
LTN LU1 ... 3 G9
Kingsland Wy BLDK SG7 ... 18 D7
King's La KGLGY WD4 ... 179 M2
Kingsley Av BORE WD6 ... 198 E3
CHES/WCR EN8 ... 176 A8
Kingsley Ct BRKMPK AL9 ... 134 E8
Kingsley Rd LTNN/LIM LU3 ... 64 F5
Kingsley Wk TRING HP23 ... 123 M6 1
Kingsmead BAR EN5 ... 200 F5
CHES/WCR EN8 ... 176 C7
POTB/CUF EN6 ... 174 D7
SBW CM21 ... 142 D1
STALE/WH AL4 ... 153 J4
Kingsmead Cl
HLWW/ROY CM19 ... 161 G3
Kings Meadow KGLGY WD4 ... 166 F7
Kingsmill Ct HAT AL10 ... 155 G7 4
Kingsmoor Rd
HLWW/ROY CM19 ... 162 A5
Kings Pond Cl BGSW SG18 ... 14 C5
Kings Rd BAR EN5 ... 200 B4
BERK HP4 ... 147 G7
CHES/WCR EN8 ... 190 D5
HERT/BAY SG13 ... 137 M3 1
HTCH/STOT SG5 ... 52 E2
LCOL/BKTW AL2 ... 170 B5
STALW/RED AL3 ... 10 B6
STVG SG1 ... 4 C6
Kingston Rd EBAR EN4 ... 201 J6
LTNE LU2 ... 3 G2
Kingston V ROY SG8 ... 21 K5 3
King St BSF CM23 ... 96 E3
DUN/HR/TOD LU5 ... 63 G6
DUN/WHIP LU6 ... 81 H3
LTN LU1 ... 2 E7
STALW/RED AL3 ... 106 D5
TRING HP23 ... 123 M7
WATW WD18 ... 13 G5
Kings Walden Ri STVGE SG2 ... 71 H3
King's Walden Rd
HTCH/STOT SG5 ... 51 H8
Kingsway DUN/HR/TOD LU5 ... 81 H1
HTCH/STOT SG5 ... 26 D3
LTN LU1 ... 82 F2
LTNW/LEA LU4 ... 82 F1
POTB/CUF EN6 ... 188 D1
ROY SG8 ... 21 H2
WARE SG12 ... 116 C7
Kingsway North Orbital Rd
GSTN WD25 ... 181 M5
Kingswell Ride POTB/CUF EN6 ... 188 D1
Kingswood Av HTCHE/RSTV SG4 .. 53 J2
Kingswood Cl TRDG/WHET N20 .. 201 H7
Kingswood Rd GSTN WD25 ... 182 A5
Kingwell Rd EBAR EN4 ... 201 J1
King William Cl
AMP/FLIT/B MK45 ... 35 J6
Kinmoor Cl LTNN/LIM LU3 ... 64 C2
Kinross Crs LTNN/LIM LU3 ... 64 C2
Kinsbourne Cl HARP AL5 ... 108 B6
Kinsbourne Crs HARP AL5 ... 108 C6 2
Kinsbourne Green La HARP AL5 .. 108 A7
Kipling Cl HTCHE/RSTV SG4 ... 53 H3
Kipling Gv HHNE HP2 ... 150 A1
Kipling Rd ROY SG8 ... 21 K1
The Kipling LTNN/LIM LU3 ... 65 G4 1
Kipling Wy HARP AL5 ... 131 G1
Kirby Cl NTHWD HA6 ... 205 L6
Kirby Dr LTNN/LIM LU3 ... 64 E1
Kirby Rd DUN/WHIP LU6 ... 80 F2
Kirkcaldy Gn OXHEY WD19 ... 206 B3 3
Kirkdale Rd HARP AL5 ... 108 F8
Kirklands WGCW AL8 ... 112 D8
Kirkstone Dr DUN/WHIP LU6 ... 81 G4
Kirkwick Av HARP AL5 ... 130 E1
Kirkwood Rd LTNW/LEA LU4 ... 63 L7
Kitcheners La STVGE SG2 ... 72 A1
Kitching La STVG SG1 ... 69 L5
Kite Fld BERK HP4 ... 146 D3
Kite Wy LWTH SG6 ... 39 K2
Kitsbury Rd BERK HP4 ... 147 G6
Kitsbury Ter BERK HP4 ... 147 G6
Kit's La BLDK SG7 ... 42 B2
Kitson Wy HLW CM20 ... 6 D5
Kitswell Wy RAD WD7 ... 183 L4
Kitt's End Rd BAR EN5 ... 186 D8
Knap Cl LWTH SG6 ... 40 B2
Knebworth Pth BORE WD6 ... 199 J5 2
Kneesworth St ROY SG8 ... 21 H3
Knella Gn WGCE AL7 ... 134 F4
Knella Rd WGCE AL7 ... 134 E5
Knights Cl BSF CM23 ... 96 A2
BUNT SG9 ... 58 D4
Knights Fld LTNE LU2 ... 2 D2
Knightsfield WGCW AL8 ... 112 C8
Knights Orch HHW HP1 ... 148 E5
STALW/RED AL3 ... 10 D6
Knights Templars Gn STVGE SG2 .. 71 H2
Knight St SBW CM21 ... 120 D8
Knoll Dr STHGT/OAK N14 ... 201 M8
Knolles Crs BRKMPK AL9 ... 172 A3
Knoll Ri LTNE LU2 ... 65 K6
The Knoll HERT/BAY SG13 ... 138 A3
Knotts Cl DUN/WHIP LU6 ... 81 H5
Knowle Dr HARP AL5 ... 131 J3
The Knowle HOD EN11 ... 159 M5 2
Knowl Piece HTCHE/RSTV SG4 ... 38 F7
Knowl Wy BORE WD6 ... 198 E6
Knutsford Av WATN WD24 ... 196 C1
Koh-i-noor Av BUSH WD23 ... 196 F7
Kristiansand Wy LWTH SG6 ... 40 B2
Kymswell Rd STVGE SG2 ... 71 H6
Kynance Cl LTNE LU2 ... 65 M7
Kynaston Cl
KTN/HRWW/W HA3 ... 207 J7
Kynaston Wd
KTN/HRWW/W HA3 ... 207 J7
Kyrkeby LWTH SG6 ... 40 B6
Kytes Dr GSTN WD25 ... 182 C4

L

Laburnum Cl CHES/WCR EN8 ... 190 C2
LTNN/LIM LU3 ... 65 H3
Laburnum Gv LCOL/BKTW AL2 ... 168 F4
LTNN/LIM LU3 ... 65 G3
Laburnum Rd HOD EN11 ... 160 A2 1
Lachbury Cl LTN LU1 ... 82 F4
Lackmore Rd EN EN1 ... 190 B6 2
Lacre Wy LWTH SG6 ... 40 B3
Ladbrooke Cl POTB/CUF EN6 ... 186 F3 1

Ladbrooke Dr POTB/CUF EN6 186 F3
Ladies Gv STALW/RED AL3 10 B4
Lady Gv WGCE AL7 134 D8
Ladyhill LTNW/LEA LU4 64 A4
Ladymeadow HHS/BOV HP3 166 C6
Lady's Cl WATW WD18 12 F5
Ladyshot HLW CM20 7 M5
Ladysmith Rd LBUZ LU7 102 D5
STALW/RED AL3 10 E4
Ladywalk RKW/CH/CXG WD3 203 K5
Ladywell Prospect SBW CM21 142 E1
Ladywood Cl
RKW/CH/CXG WD3 194 A4
Ladywood Rd HERT/WAS SG14 136 E4
Lagger Cl CSTG HP8 202 A3
The Lagger CSTG HP8 202 A3
Laidon Sq HHNE HP2 149 J3
Lake Dr BUSH WD23 207 H2
Lakeland Cl KTN/HRWW/W HA3 207 J6
Laker Ct LTNE LU2 2 D2
Lake Rd WAB EN9 160 D8
Lakeside TRING HP23 123 M5
Lakeside Crs EBAR EN4 201 L7
Lakeside Pl LCOL/BKTW AL2 170 C7
Lakeside Rd CHES/WCR EN8 176 B7
The Lake BUSH WD23 207 J1
Lake Vw POTB/CUF EN6 187 H4 2
Lalleford Rd LTNE LU2 84 B1
Lamb Cl GSTN WD25 182 B5
HAT AL10 155 G6 2
Lambert Ct BUSH WD23 13 K5
Lamb La STALW/RED AL3 130 A5
Lamb Meadow ARL/CHE SG15 25 L7
Lambourn Cha RAD WD7 183 L7 1
Lambourn Dr LTNE LU2 65 K4
Lambourn Gdns HARP AL5 108 E7 2
Lambs Cl DUN/HR/TOD LU5 81 L1
POTB/CUF EN6 174 E8
Lambton Av CHES/WCR EN8 190 C4 1
Lamer La STALE/WH AL4 110 C6
Lamers Rd LTNE LU2 66 A8
Lammasmead BROX EN10 176 E2
Lammas Md HTCH/STOT SG5 38 D8
Lammas Rd HERT/WAS SG14 90 C6
LBUZ LU7 101 M3
WATW WD18 13 G7
Lammas Wy LWTH SG6 39 L2
Lamorna Cl LTNN/LIM LU3 64 E4 1
RAD WD7 184 A5
Lampits HOD EN11 160 A4
Lampitts Cross LTNN/LIM LU3 64 F5 1
Lamplighters Cl WAB EN9 191 M5 2
Lamsey Rd HHS/BOV HP3 166 C1
Lancaster Av EBAR EN4 201 J1
LTNE LU2 65 H2 1
Lancaster Cl
AMP/FLIT/B MK45 35 J6 1
STVG SG1 54 D8
Lancaster Dr HHW HP1 164 E6
Lancaster Pl SHFD SG17 24 B1 1
Lancaster Rd EBAR EN4 201 J6
HTCH/STOT SG5 52 D2
STAL AL1 11 K3
Lancaster Wy ABLGY WD5 181 L2 2
BSF CM23 96 A2
Lancelot Gdns EBAR EN4 201 M8
Lancing Rd LTNE LU2 66 C7
Lancing Wy RKW/CH/CXG WD3 195 G6
Lancot Av DUN/WHIP LU6 80 D3
Lancotbury Cl DUN/WHIP LU6 80 B3
Lancot Dr DUN/WHIP LU6 80 D2
Landau Wy BROX EN10 176 E5
Landford Cl RKW/CH/CXG WD3 204 D2
Landmead Rd CHES/WCR EN8 176 D8
Landrace Rd LTNW/LEA LU4 63 K6
Lands' End BORE WD6 198 C7
Lane End BERK HP4 146 E6
HAT AL10 154 E8
HLWE CM17 163 K3
Lanefield Wk WGCW AL8 134 B4 3
Lane Gdns BUSH WD23 207 K1
Lanercost Cl WLYN AL6 112 E3
The Lane LTNW/LEA LU4 63 K1
Langbridge Cl HTCHE/RSTV SG4 52 F5
Langdale Av HARP AL5 109 J8
Langdale Cl DUN/WHIP LU6 81 H3
Langdale Gdns PEND EN3 190 C6
Langdale Rd DUN/WHIP LU6 81 G3
Langdon St TRING HP23 123 M7
Langfield Cl WAB EN9 177 K1 1
Langford Crs EBAR EN4 201 L5
Langford Dr LTNE LU2 65 M7
Langford Rd EBAR EN4 201 L5
Langham Cl LTNE LU2 65 J3
STALE/WH AL4 153 H2
Langholme BUSH WD23 207 H1 1
Langland Ct NTHWD HA6 205 H7
Langland Dr PIN HA5 206 D7
Langley Av HHS/BOV HP3 166 D2
Langleybury La KGLGY WD4 181 G5
WAT WD17 181 G8
Langley Crs KGLGY WD4 180 F1
STALW/RED AL3 10 D2
Langley Gv STALE/WH AL4 132 B8
Langley Hl KGLGY WD4 166 E8
Langley Hill Cl KGLGY WD4 166 F8 3
Langley La ABLGY WD5 181 L2
HTCHE/RSTV SG4 69 J8
Langley Lodge La KGLGY WD4 180 D2
Langley Rd ABLGY WD5 181 K2
KGLGY WD4 180 A1
WAT WD17 195 L2
Langley Rw BAR EN5 200 E2
Langley St LTN LU1 2 F8
Langley Wy WAT WD17 195 L2
Langmead Dr BUSH WD23 207 J1
Langthorne Av STVG SG1 4 E1
Langton Av TRDG/WHET N20 201 H8
Langton Gv NTHWD HA6 205 H5
Langton Rd HOD EN11 159 L4
KTN/HRWW/W HA3 207 H7
Langwood Gdns WAT WD17 195 M2 1
Lankester Rd ROY SG8 21 H5
Lannock LWTH SG6 40 B6
Lannock Hl HTCHE/RSTV SG4 40 C8
Lanrick Copse BERK HP4 147 K5
Lansdowne Rd LTNN/LIM LU3 2 B2
Lansdown Rd
CFSP/GDCR SL9 202 C8 2
Lanterns La STVGE SG2 71 J4
Laporte Wy LTNW/LEA LU4 82 E1
Lapwing Cl HHNE HP2 8 D1
Lapwing Dell LWTH SG6 40 A8
Lapwing Ri STVGE SG2 71 J8
Lapwing Rd LTNW/LEA LU4 63 M6
Lapwing Wy ABLGY WD5 181 M2 1
Larch Av HTCHE/RSTV SG4 52 F6
LCOL/BKTW AL2 182 D1
Larch Cl CHESW EN7 175 K6 1
Larches Av EN EN1 190 B6
The Larches BERK HP4 146 C5
BUSH WD23 13 L7
LTNE LU2 2 D3
STALE/WH AL4 153 J3
WARE SG12 116 B6
Larch Ri BERK HP4 146 F5
Larchwood BSF CM23 96 C5
Larchwood Rd HHNE HP2 8 F4
Larken Cl BUSH WD23 207 H1
Larken Dr BUSH WD23 207 H1
Larkens Cl STDN SG11 75 J7
Larkin Cl ROY SG8 21 J1 1
Larkins Cl BLDK SG7 40 E1
Larkinson STVG SG1 70 B3
Lark Ri HAT AL10 154 F7
Larksfield WARE SG12 116 D7
Larkspur Cl BSF CM23 96 C4
HHW HP1 148 D6
Larkspur Gdns LTNW/LEA LU4 64 E8
Larks Rdg LCOL/BKTW AL2 168 F5
Larksway BSF CM23 96 B4
Larkswood HLWE CM17 163 H4 3
Larkswood Ri STALE/WH AL4 153 H2
Larmans Rd PEND EN3 190 B7 1
Larsen Dr WAB EN9 191 J5 3
Larwood Gv STVG SG1 70 F2
Latchmore Bank RBSF CM22 97 G8
Latchmore Cl HTCHE/RSTV SG4 52 E5
Latimer Cl AMS HP6 192 B2
HHNE HP2 150 A2
PIN HA5 206 B8
WATW WD18 195 K8
Latimer Gdns PIN HA5 206 B8
WGCE AL7 135 G4
Latimer Rd AMS HP6 192 E1
BAR EN5 201 G4
LTN LU1 2 F9
Latium Cl STAL AL1 10 E9
Lattimore Rd STAL AL1 11 G8
STALE/WH AL4 132 B2
Latton Gn HLWS CM18 162 E6
Latton Hall Cl HLW CM20 7 M4
Latton House HLWS CM18 163 G5
Latton St HLW CM20 163 G2
HLWE CM17 163 G3
Lauderdale Rd ABLGY WD5 181 H4
Laundry La WAB EN9 177 L4
Launton Cl LTNN/LIM LU3 65 G1
Laureate Wy HHW HP1 149 G5
Laurel Av POTB/CUF EN6 186 E3
Laurel Bank HHS/BOV HP3 165 L2
Laurel Cl HHNE HP2 8 E7
Laureldene MHAD SG10 118 E1 1
Laurel Flds POTB/CUF EN6 186 E2
Laurel Pk KTN/HRWW/W HA3 207 L7
Laurel Rd CFSP/GDCR SL9 202 C8
STAL AL1 11 K6
Laurels Cl STALW/RED AL3 169 G2
The Laurels BERK HP4 148 A4
CHESW EN7 175 K6
Laurel Wy HTCH/STOT SG5 38 D7
Lauries Cl HHW HP1 165 G1
Laurino Pl BUSH WD23 207 H2
Lavender Cl BSF CM23 96 C4
CHESW EN7 175 L6 3
HLW CM20 7 H4
LTNE LU2 65 K3
Lavender Ct BLDK SG7 40 D1 3
Lavender Gdns
KTN/HRWW/W HA3 207 K6 2
Lavender Wy HTCH/STOT SG5 52 C3
Lavinia Av GSTN WD25 182 B5
Lavrock La RKW/CH/CXG WD3 194 E8
Lawford Av RKW/CH/CXG WD3 193 H7
Lawford Cl LTN LU1 2 B8
RKW/CH/CXG WD3 193 H7
Law Hall La HTCHE/RSTV SG4 85 M2
Lawn Av HTCHE/RSTV SG4 110 B1
Lawn La HHS/BOV HP3 166 C1
Lawns Cl HTCH/STOT SG5 51 H8
The Lawns Dr BROX EN10 176 E1
The Lawns HHW HP1 148 D6
PIN HA5 207 G7
RAD WD7 184 D4 4
STVGE SG2 71 J6
WGCW AL8 134 C1
Lawrance Gdns CHES/WCR EN8 176 C7
Lawrance Rd STALW/RED AL3 152 B3
Lawrence Av LWTH SG6 39 M6
SBW CM21 120 D6
STVG SG1 70 D3
WARE SG12 139 H6
Lawrence Cl HERT/WAS SG14 136 D3
Lawrence End Rd LTNE LU2 85 H7
Lawrence Moorings SBW CM21 142 E1
Lawrence Wy DUN/WHIP LU6 62 E8 1
Lawton Rd EBAR EN4 201 J4
Laxton Cl LTNE LU2 84 D1
Laxton Gdns BLDK SG7 40 F3
Lay Brook STALE/WH AL4 152 F3 3
Layham Dr LTNE LU2 84 C1
Layhill HHNE HP2 8 A5
Layston Meadow BUNT SG9 58 E4
Layston Pk ROY SG8 21 J5
Lea Bushes GSTN WD25 182 D6
Lea Cl BSF CM23 97 G1
BUSH WD23 197 G6 1
Leaf Cl NTHWD HA6 205 J7
Leafield LTNN/LIM LU3 64 E6
Leafields DUN/HR/TOD LU5 63 H4
Leaford Crs WATN WD24 181 L8
Leaforis Rd CHESW EN7 175 M7
Leaf Rd DUN/HR/TOD LU5 63 G4
Leafy La TRING HP23 144 D1
Leagrave High St LTNW/LEA LU4 63 L7
Leagrave Rd LTNN/LIM LU3 64 F7
Lea Gv BSF CM23 97 G1
Leamington Rd LTNN/LIM LU3 64 F3
Lea Mt CHESW EN7 175 K7
Leander Gdns GSTN WD25 182 D8 1
Lea Rd HARP AL5 109 G7
HOD EN11 160 B2
LTN LU1 3 G7
WAB EN9 190 F5
WATN WD24 196 A1 3
Leasey Bridge La
STALE/WH AL4 131 L1
Leasey Dell Dr STALE/WH AL4 109 M8
Leaside HHNE HP2 150 B8
The Leas BLDK SG7 40 D3
BUSH WD23 196 E3
HHS/BOV HP3 166 F3
Leat Cl SBW CM21 120 E7
Leathwaite Cl LTNN/LIM LU3 64 E5
Lea Valley Wk BRKMPK AL9 134 B8
HERT/BAY SG13 137 K3
HERT/WAS SG14 136 B7
LTNE LU2 84 C8
WAB EN9 176 F5
WAB EN9 190 F4
WARE SG12 138 F4
WGCW AL8 133 L4
Leavesden Rd STAN HA7 207 M6
WATN WD24 196 A1
Leaves Spring STVGE SG2 70 E8
Leaview WAB EN9 191 G4
Lea Wk HARP AL5 109 H6
Lebanon Cl WAT WD17 181 J7
Le Corte Cl KGLGY WD4 166 E8
Lectern La STAL AL1 169 K3 2
Ledgemore La HHNE HP2 127 L4
Ledwell Rd LTN LU1 82 E7
Leeches Wy LBUZ LU7 101 M3
Lee Cl HERT/BAY SG13 137 H6
WARE SG12 139 H6 1
Leecroft Rd BAR EN5 200 D6
Leefe Wy POTB/CUF EN6 174 C7
Leeming Rd BORE WD6 198 E2
Lees Av NTHWD HA6 205 L8
Lees Cl BGSW SG18 14 C5
Leeside BAR EN5 200 D7
POTB/CUF EN6 187 J3
Leete Pl ROY SG8 21 H3
Leggatts Cl WATN WD24 181 L7
Leggatts Ri GSTN WD25 181 M6
Leggatts Wy WATN WD24 181 M7
Leggatts Wood Av WATN WD24 182 A7
Leggett Gv STVG SG1 70 D2
Leggfield Ter HHW HP1 148 E7 2
Leghorn Crs LTNW/LEA LU4 63 M7
Legions Wy BSF CM23 96 F2
Legra Av HOD EN11 159 M4 2
Leicester Rd BAR EN5 201 G6
LTNW/LEA LU4 82 D1
Leigh Common WGCE AL7 134 D6
Leigh Ct BORE WD6 199 J3 1
Leigh Rodd OXHEY WD19 206 D3
Leighton Buzzard Rd HHW HP1 127 K8
Leighton Ct DUN/WHIP LU6 80 F2
Lemon Field Dr GSTN WD25 182 D4 2
Lemsford Ct BORE WD6 199 H5
Lemsford La WGCW AL8 134 A5
Lemsford Rd HAT AL10 154 F3 2
STAL AL1 11 J5
Lemsford Village WGCW AL8 133 M5 1
Lennox Gn LTNE LU2 66 E8 2
Lensbury Cl CHES/WCR EN8 176 D7 3
Leonard's Cl WLYN AL6 112 D2
Lesbury Cl LTNE LU2 84 D1
Leslie Cl STVGE SG2 71 H8
Leston Cl DUN/WHIP LU6 81 J5
Letchfield CSHM HP5 178 A2
Letchmore Cl STVG SG1 4 C1
Letchmore Rd RAD WD7 183 M7
STVG SG1 4 B1
Letchworth Cl OXHEY WD19 206 C5 4
Letchworth Ga LWTH SG6 40 A7
Letchworth La LWTH SG6 39 L7
Letchworth Rd BLDK SG7 40 C3
LTNN/LIM LU3 64 E6
LWTH SG6 40 C3
Levenage La WARE SG12 118 D7
Leven Cl CHES/WCR EN8 190 C4 2
OXHEY WD19 206 C5 5
Levendale LTNW/LEA LU4 64 B5 3
Leven Dr CHES/WCR EN8 190 C4
Leven Wy HHNE HP2 149 J3 1
Leveret Cl GSTN WD25 181 M5
Leverstock Green Rd HHNE HP2 9 J8
HHS/BOV HP3 9 K9
Leverstock Green Wy HHNE HP2 9 L9
Leverton Wy WAB EN9 191 H4
Lewes Wy RKW/CH/CXG WD3 195 G5
Lewis La ARL/CHE SG15 25 M4
CFSP/GDCR SL9 202 D8
Lewsey Rd LTNW/LEA LU4 64 A7
Lexington Cl BORE WD6 198 F4 3
Lexington Wy BAR EN5 200 C5
Leyburne Rd LTNN/LIM LU3 65 G4
Leycroft Wy HARP AL5 131 K3
Leyden Rd STVG SG1 4 C9
Ley Fld RBSF CM22 99 H3
Leygreen Cl LTNE LU2 3 K4
Leyhill Dr LTN LU1 83 G6
Leyland Av STAL AL1 169 J1
Leyland Cl CHES/WCR EN8 176 B7 1
Leys Av LWTH SG6 39 L4
Leys Cl DEN/HRF UB9 204 C8
Leysdown WGCE AL7 135 J4
Leys Gdns EBAR EN4 201 M6
Leys Rd HHS/BOV HP3 166 E1
The Leys STALE/WH AL4 153 J4
TRING HP23 124 B6
Leyton Gn HARP AL5 130 F1
Leyton Rd HARP AL5 130 F1
Ley Wk WGCE AL7 135 H4
Liberty Cl HERT/BAY SG13 137 H6
Library Rd LTN LU1 2 E6
Lichfield Cl EBAR EN4 201 L4
Lichfield Wy BROX EN10 176 E1 2
Liddel Cl LTNN/LIM LU3 64 F7
Lidgate Cl LTNW/LEA LU4 64 A4
Lieutenant Ellis Wy
CHESW EN7 189 L2
Lighthorne Ri LTNN/LIM LU3 64 F3
Lilac Av EN EN1 190 B7
Lilac Cl CHESW EN7 190 A2 3
Lilac Gv LTNN/LIM LU3 64 B1
Lilac Rd HOD EN11 160 A2
Lilac Wy HARP AL5 131 J4 3
Lilley Bottom LTNE LU2 66 D1
Lilley Bottom Rd
HTCHE/RSTV SG4 67 K8
Lilleyhoo La LTNE LU2 50 E8
Lilliard Cl HOD EN11 139 G8
Lilly La HHNE HP2 150 C3
The Limberlost WLYN AL6 112 A3
Limbrick Rd HARP AL5 131 G4
Limbury Rd LTNN/LIM LU3 64 E6
Lime Av LTNW/LEA LU4 64 A7
STALE/WH AL4 110 A4
Lime Cl AMP/FLIT/B MK45 35 H7
OXHEY WD19 196 C8 1
STVGE SG2 71 J6
WARE SG12 116 D8
Limedene Cl PIN HA5 206 C8
Lime Gv ROY SG8 21 K2
Limekiln La BLDK SG7 40 E3
STSD CM24 79 H4
Limes Ct HOD EN11 159 M4 3
Limes Crs BSF CM23 96 F3
Limes Rd CHES/WCR EN8 190 C3
The Limes ARL/CHE SG15 25 M2
HTCH/STOT SG5 52 C4
STALW/RED AL3 11 G3
WGCE AL7 134 F6
Limetree Av LTN LU1 107 M3
Lime Tree Cl LTNN/LIM LU3 64 B1
Lime Tree Pl STAL AL1 11 H9
Lime Tree Wk BUSH WD23 207 K1
RKW/CH/CXG WD3 194 A6
Lime Wk HHS/BOV HP3 166 E1
Linacres LTNW/LEA LU4 64 C6
Linbridge Wy LTNE LU2 66 D8
Linces Wy WGCE AL7 135 G6
Lincoln Cl BSF CM23 96 C5
DUN/HR/TOD LU5 81 L4 1
WGCE AL7 135 H3
Lincoln Ct BERK HP4 147 G6
BORE WD6 199 J6 1
Lincoln Dr OXHEY WD19 206 B3
RKW/CH/CXG WD3 195 G5
Lincoln Rd CFSP/GDCR SL9 202 D8
LTNW/LEA LU4 83 G1
STVG SG1 55 G8
Lincoln's Cl STALE/WH AL4 153 H2
Lincoln Wy RKW/CH/CXG WD3 195 G5
Lincot La HTCHE/RSTV SG4 87 H3
Lindbergh WGCE AL7 135 H4 2
Linden Cl CHESW EN7 190 A1 2
DUN/HR/TOD LU5 81 L1
Linden Ct HARP AL5 131 G2
Linden Crs STAL AL1 153 H7
Lindencroft LWTH SG6 39 M1
Linden Dr CFSP/GDCR SL9 202 D8
Linden Gld HHW HP1 149 G8 1
Linden Lea GSTN WD25 181 M4
Linden Rd DUN/HR/TOD LU5 63 L8
LTNW/LEA LU4 64 D6
STALW/RED AL3 129 M4
The Lindens BSF CM23 96 E4
DUN/HR/TOD LU5 63 G6
HHS/BOV HP3 165 L2
STVG SG1 4 F5
Lindley Cl HARP AL5 108 F6
Lindlings HHW HP1 148 D8
Lindsay Av HTCHE/RSTV SG4 53 G5
Lindsay Cl ROY SG8 21 H1
Lindsay Pl CHESW EN7 190 A1 2
Lindsey Cl BSF CM23 96 E1
Lindsey Rd BSF CM23 96 E1
LTNE LU2 84 C1
Lindum Pl STALW/RED AL3 168 E1
Linfields AMSS HP7 192 B3
Linford Cl HLWW/ROY CM19 162 B4
Linford End HLWW/ROY CM19 162 B4
Lingfield Cl NTHWD HA6 205 K7
Lingfield Rd ROY SG8 21 K4 2
STVG SG1 71 H1
Lingfield Wy WAT WD17 195 L1
Lingholm Wy BAR EN5 200 C6
Lingmoor Dr GSTN WD25 182 B5
Link Cl HAT AL10 155 G5
Link Dr HAT AL10 155 G5
Linkfield WGCE AL7 134 D8
Link Rd BSF CM23 96 E2
BUSH WD23 13 J1
WLYN AL6 112 E3 1
Links Av HERT/BAY SG13 138 A3
Links Dr BORE WD6 198 E5 1
RAD WD7 183 L4
The Links CHES/WCR EN8 176 C5 1
Links Vw STALW/RED AL3 10 B3
Links View Cl STAN HA7 207 M6
Links Wy RKW/CH/CXG WD3 195 H4
LTNE LU2 65 J2
NTHWD HA6 205 H8
Linksway NTHWD HA6 205 J8
Link Wy BSF CM23 96 D4
Linkway PIN HA5 206 C8
Linkways East STVG SG1 5 G3
Linkways West STVG SG1 5 G3
The Linkway BAR EN5 200 F7
Linnet Cl BUSH WD23 207 H1
LTNW/LEA LU4 63 M6
LWTH SG6 39 K2
Linnet Rd ABLGY WD5 181 M2
Linsey Cl HHS/BOV HP3 166 F3
Linster Gv BORE WD6 199 H6
Linten Cl HTCHE/RSTV SG4 53 H4
Linthorpe Rd EBAR EN4 201 K4
Linton Av BORE WD6 198 E3
Lintott Cl STVG SG1 4 C1
Linwood SBW CM21 120 D8 3
Linwood Rd HARP AL5 131 H3 3
WARE SG12 116 E7
Lion Ct BORE WD6 199 H2
Liphook Rd OXHEY WD19 206 C4
Lippitts Hl LTNE LU2 65 K5
Liscombe Rd DUN/HR/TOD LU5 81 K1
Lismore HHS/BOV HP3 167 H1
STVGE SG2 89 H1
Lister Av HTCHE/RSTV SG4 52 E5
Liston Cl LTNW/LEA LU4 64 A5
Litlington Rd ROY SG8 19 H1
Little Acre STALW/RED AL3 10 E2
Little Acres WARE SG12 138 C2
Little Berries LTNN/LIM LU3 64 D3
Little Brays HLWS CM18 7 L9
Little Bridge Rd BERK HP4 147 J6 3
Littlebrook Gdns
CHES/WCR EN8 190 C1
Little Brook Rd
HLWW/ROY CM19 161 H2
Little Burrow WGCE AL7 134 C6
Little Bushey La BUSH WD23 196 F4
Little Catherells HHW HP1 148 E5 1
Little Cattins HLWW/ROY CM19 161 L6
Little Chishill Rd ROY SG8 33 H2
Little Church Rd LTNE LU2 66 A7
Littlecote Pl PIN HA5 206 E8 1
Little Dell WGCW AL8 134 C2
Littlefield Rd LTNE LU2 66 A7
Little Ganett WGCE AL7 135 G6
Little Graylings ABLGY WD5 181 K4
Littlegreen La LTN LU1 82 D8
Little Green La
RKW/CH/CXG WD3 194 E4
Little Gv BUSH WD23 197 G5
Littlegrove EBAR EN4 201 K7
Little Grove Fld HLWW/ROY CM19 6 C7
Little Hardings WGCE AL7 135 H3
Little Hayes KGLGY WD4 166 F8 3
Little Heath RBSF CM22 121 L7
Little Heath La BERK HP4 148 A8
Little Hl RKW/CH/CXG WD3 193 H7
Little Hoo TRING HP23 123 L6
Little How Cft ABLGY WD5 181 H2
Little Lake WGCE AL7 135 G7
Little La HARP AL5 131 H4
HTCH/STOT SG5 37 J5
Little Ley WGCE AL7 134 D7 3
Little Martins BUSH WD23 197 G6
Little Md HAT AL10 155 G2 1
Little Mimms HHNE HP2 8 C6
Little Mundells WGCE AL7 134 E3
Little Orchard Cl ABLGY WD5 181 J2
Little Oxhey La OXHEY WD19 206 D5
Little Pk HHS/BOV HP3 164 F7
Little Piper's Cl CHESW EN7 175 G8
Little Potters BUSH WD23 197 J8
Little Pynchons HLWS CM18 162 E5
Little Rdg WGCE AL7 134 F4
Little Rivers WGCE AL7 134 F3
Little Rd HHNE HP2 8 D6
Little Stream Cl NTHWD HA6 205 K5
Little Thistle WGCE AL7 135 H6
Little Tring Rd TRING HP23 123 L4
Little Twye Rd TRING HP23 144 E7
Little Wade WGCE AL7 134 E7
Little Widbury WARE SG12 138 E1
Little Widbury La WARE SG12 138 E1
Little Windmill Hl KGLGY WD4 179 K3
Little Wood Cft LTNN/LIM LU3 64 D3
Little Youngs WGCW AL8 134 B4
Liverpool Rd LTN LU1 2 C6
STAL AL1 11 G7
WATW WD18 12 F6
Livingstone Link STVGE SG2 71 G2
Llanbury Cl CFSP/GDCR SL9 202 D7
Lloyd-taylor Cl STDN SG11 77 G8
Lloyd Wy HTCHE/RSTV SG4 110 B1
Loates La WAT WD17 13 G3
Local Board Rd WATW WD18 13 H7
Locarno Av LTNW/LEA LU4 64 B4
Lochnell Rd BERK HP4 146 E4
Lockers Park La HHW HP1 149 G6 2
Lockhart Cl DUN/WHIP LU6 81 J4
Lockington Crs
DUN/HR/TOD LU5 63 K8
Lockley Crs HAT AL10 155 G3
Lockleys Dr WLYN AL6 112 B5
Lodge Av BORE WD6 198 E6
Lodge Cl HERT/WAS SG14 137 H2
Lodge Ct HTCH/STOT SG5 38 D7
Lodge Crs CHES/WCR EN8 190 D5 2
Lodge Dr BRKMPK AL9 155 J2
RKW/CH/CXG WD3 194 B5
Lodge End RAD WD7 184 A5
RKW/CH/CXG WD3 195 J5
Lodge Fld WGCE AL7 134 D1
Lodge Gdns HARP AL5 108 F8
Lodge Hall HLWS CM18 162 D6
Lodge La CSTG HP8 192 E6
WAB EN9 191 J6
Lodge Rd RKW/CH/CXG WD3 195 J5
Lodge Wy STVGE SG2 88 F1
Loftus Cl LTNW/LEA LU4 64 A6
Lollard Cl LTNW/LEA LU4 63 K7 1
Lombardy Cl HHNE HP2 150 C8
Lombardy Dr BERK HP4 147 J7
Lombardy Wy BORE WD6 198 D2
Lomond Rd HHNE HP2 149 J3
Lomond Wy STVG SG1 55 H7
London Loop BORE WD6 199 G7
ENC/FH EN2 188 D8
MLHL NW7 199 H8
London Rd BERK HP4 147 J6
BGSW SG18 16 C1
BLDK SG7 40 E4
BSF CM23 96 F6
BUNT SG9 58 E4
CSTG HP8 202 B2
DUN/WHIP LU6 81 K4
HARP AL5 107 M4
HERT/BAY SG13 137 M6
HHS/BOV HP3 166 C2
HHW HP1 165 G1
HLWE CM17 142 B7
HTCHE/RSTV SG4 52 E5
KNEB SG3 88 F7
LTN LU1 83 K6
RAD WD7 184 E4
RAYLNE/WEN HP22 122 C5
RKW/CH/CXG WD3 204 D1
ROY SG8 21 J5
SBW CM21 120 D8
STAL AL1 169 M2

STALW/RED AL3 ... 106 D5
STVG SG1 ... 4 D7
TRING HP23 ... 124 A7
WARE SG12 ... 138 C2
WLYN AL6 ... 112 B6
London Rw *ARL/CHE* SG15 ... 25 M7
Long Acre *HLWE* CM17 ... 142 A6
Longacres *STALE/WH* AL4 ... 153 J7
Long Arrotts *HHW* HP1 ... 149 G5
Long Banks *HLWS* CM18 ... 162 C5
Long Barn Cl *GSTN* WD25 ... 181 M3
Long Border Rd *RBSF* CM22 ... 98 D1
Longbridge Cl *TRING* HP23 ... 123 M4 2
Longbrooke *DUN/HR/TOD* LU5 ... 63 J6
Long Buftlers *HARP* AL5 ... 131 L2
Long Chaulden *HHW* HP1 ... 148 D8
Longcliffe Pth *OXHEY* WD19 ... 205 M3 5
Long Cl *HNLW* SG16 ... 24 D8
LTNE LU2 ... 66 B7
Long Cft *OXHEY* WD19 ... 196 A8
Longcroft
RAYLNE/WEN HP22 ... 122 E5 1
RBSF CM22 ... 99 H3
Long Cft *STSD* CM24 ... 79 J2
Longcroft Av *HARP* AL5 ... 130 E1
Long Croft Dr *CHES/WCR* EN8 ... 190 E5
Longcroft Gdns *WGCW* AL8 ... 134 C5 3
Longcroft Gn *WGCW* AL8 ... 134 C5 4
Longcroft La *HHS/BOV* HP3 ... 165 H7
WGCW AL8 ... 134 C5
Longcroft Rd *AMP/FLIT/B* MK45 ... 35 G8
Long Croft Rd *LTN* LU1 ... 82 F3
RKW/CH/CXG WD3 ... 203 J5
Longcroft Rd *STVG* SG1 ... 70 D3
Long Cutt *STALW/RED* AL3 ... 129 M4
Longdean Pk *HHS/BOV* HP3 ... 166 F4
Long Elmes *KTN/HRWW/W* HA3 ... 207 H8
Long Elms *ABLGY* WD5 ... 181 J4
Long Elms Cl *ABLGY* WD5 ... 181 J4 1
Long Fallow *LCOL/BKTW* AL2 ... 168 F6
Longfield *HHS/BOV* HP3 ... 167 G1
HLWS CM18 ... 162 F4
Longfield Av *PEND* EN3 ... 190 B8
Longfield Dr *LTNW/LEA* LU4 ... 82 C1
Longfield Gdns *TRING* HP23 ... 123 K7
Longfield La *CHESW* EN7 ... 175 L6
Longfield Rd *HARP* AL5 ... 131 H3
TRING HP23 ... 123 K7
Longfields *STVGE* SG2 ... 89 H1
Long Hedge *DUN/HR/TOD* LU5 ... 81 J2 1
Long John *HHS/BOV* HP3 ... 166 E1
Longlands *HHNE* HP2 ... 8 F7
Longlands Cl *CHES/WCR* EN8 ... 190 C3 2
Longlands Rd *WGCE* AL7 ... 134 E6
Long La *HHS/BOV* HP3 ... 178 E2
HTCHE/RSTV SG4 ... 85 M3
RKW/CH/CXG WD3 ... 193 H7
STVGE SG2 ... 71 K5
Long Ley *HLW* CM20 ... 7 K6
LBUZ LU7 ... 101 M3
WGCE AL7 ... 135 H4
Long Marston La *LBUZ* LU7 ... 101 K4
Long Marston Rd *TRING* HP23 ... 101 K8
Longmead *BUNT* SG9 ... 58 C3
Long Md *DUN/HR/TOD* LU5 ... 63 G4
Longmead *HAT* AL10 ... 155 G2
KNEB SG3 ... 88 F8 1
LWTH SG6 ... 39 K3
Long Meadow *BSF* CM23 ... 96 C4
DUN/WHIP LU6 ... 80 F2
STALW/RED AL3 ... 106 D5
Longmeadow Dr
HTCH/STOT SG5 ... 38 D5
Long Mimms *HHNE* HP2 ... 8 C6
Long Moor *CHES/WCR* EN8 ... 176 D8
Longmore Av *BAR* EN5 ... 201 H7
Longmore Cl
RKW/CH/CXG WD3 ... 203 L4
Longmore Gdns *WGCE* AL7 ... 134 E4
Long Plough
RAYLNE/WEN HP22 ... 122 C5
Long Rdg *STVGE* SG2 ... 89 J1
Long Spring *STALW/RED* AL3 ... 152 E3
Longspring *WATN* WD24 ... 182 A8
Long Vw *BERK* HP4 ... 146 F4
Long Wk *CSTG* HP8 ... 192 D4
Long Wd *HLWS* CM18 ... 162 C7
Longwood Rd *HERT/WAS* SG14 ... 136 E3
Lonsdale *HHNE* HP2 ... 8 D3
Lonsdale Cl *LTNN/LIM* LU3 ... 64 F5
Lonsdale Rd *STVG* SG1 ... 5 C1
Loom La *RAD* WD7 ... 183 L8
Loom Pl *RAD* WD7 ... 183 M7
Loop Rd *WAB* EN9 ... 191 G3
Lord Mead La *WLYN* AL6 ... 111 H3
Lords Av *BSF* CM23 ... 96 A3
Lords Cl *RAD* WD7 ... 184 D3
Lord's Hl *DUN/HR/TOD* LU5 ... 62 E1
Lordship La *LWTH* SG6 ... 40 A6
Lordship Rd *CHESW* EN7 ... 190 A1
Lords Meadow *STALW/RED* AL3 ... 129 M5
Lord St *HOD* EN11 ... 159 K4
WAT WD17 ... 13 G3
Lords Wd *WGCE* AL7 ... 135 H4
Loring Rd *BERK* HP4 ... 147 H7
DUN/WHIP LU6 ... 80 E2
Lorraine Pk *KTN/HRWW/W* HA3 ... 207 K7
Lorrimer Cl *LTNE* LU2 ... 65 K4
Lothair Rd *LTNE* LU2 ... 65 M6
Loudhams Rd *AMSS* HP7 ... 192 B2
Loudhams Wood La *CSTG* HP8 ... 192 C3
Loudwater Dr
RKW/CH/CXG WD3 ... 194 B5
Loudwater Hts
RKW/CH/CXG WD3 ... 194 A4
Loudwater La
RKW/CH/CXG WD3 ... 194 B6
Loudwater Rdg
RKW/CH/CXG WD3 ... 194 B5 1
Louise Wk *HHS/BOV* HP3 ... 164 F7
Louvain Wy *GSTN* WD25 ... 182 A3
Lovatts *RKW/CH/CXG* WD3 ... 194 F5
Lovelace Rd *EBAR* EN4 ... 201 K8
Love La *ABLGY* WD5 ... 181 L1
BLDK SG7 ... 17 M5
KGLGY WD4 ... 166 D8
Lovel Cl *HHW* HP1 ... 148 F7
Lovel End *CFSP/GDCR* SL9 ... 202 B7
Lovell Cl *HTCHE/RSTV* SG4 ... 52 F4 5
Lovell Rd *EN* EN1 ... 190 A6
Lovel Rd *CFSP/GDCR* SL9 ... 202 B7
Lovering Rd *CHESW* EN7 ... 175 H4
Lovers' Wk *DUN/WHIP* LU6 ... 81 H2
Lovet Rd *HLWW/ROY* CM19 ... 161 M3
Lovett Wy *DUN/HR/TOD* LU5 ... 63 J7
Lowbell La *LCOL/BKTW* AL2 ... 170 E6
Lower Adeyfield Rd *HHNE* HP2 ... 8 B7
Lower Barn *HHS/BOV* HP3 ... 166 E2
Lower Bourne Gdns
WARE SG12 ... 116 B7
Lower Clabdens *WARE* SG12 ... 138 E1
Lower Dagnall St
STALW/RED AL3 ... 10 D6
Lower Derby Rd *WAT* WD17 ... 13 H5
Lower Emms *HHNE* HP2 ... 150 B2 3
Lowerfield *WGCE* AL7 ... 134 F5
Lower Gower Rd *ROY* SG8 ... 21 J2
Lower Harpenden Rd *LTN* LU1 ... 84 A5
LTN LU1 ... 108 D2
Lower Hatfield Rd
HERT/BAY SG13 ... 157 K2
Lower High St *WAT* WD17 ... 13 H5
Lower Ickfield Wy
RAYLNE/WEN HP22 ... 122 F5
Lower Icknield Wy
RAYLNE/WEN HP22 ... 122 E5
TRING HP23 ... 123 H3
Lower Innings *HTCH/STOT* SG5 ... 52 B2
Lower Island Wy *WAB* EN9 ... 191 G6
Lower Kings Rd *BERK* HP4 ... 147 H5
Lower King St *ROY* SG8 ... 21 J4
Lower Luton Rd *HARP* AL5 ... 109 H6
HARP AL5 ... 109 H7 2
HARP AL5 ... 109 J7 1
LTNE LU2 ... 109 G4
STALE/WH AL4 ... 109 L8
Lower Mardley Hl *WLYN* AL6 ... 112 E2
Lower Meadow
CHES/WCR EN8 ... 176 C6
HLWS CM18 ... 162 D6
Lower Paddock Rd
OXHEY WD19 ... 13 L8
Lower Park Crs *BSF* CM23 ... 96 E5
Lower Paxton Rd *STAL* AL1 ... 11 G9
Lower Plantation
RKW/CH/CXG WD3 ... 194 B4
Lower Rd *CFSP/GDCR* SL9 ... 202 D8
HHS/BOV HP3 ... 166 F5
HTCHE/RSTV SG4 ... 85 L1
RBSF CM22 ... 121 H3
RKW/CH/CXG WD3 ... 193 J5
WARE SG12 ... 138 E4
Lower Sales *HHW* HP1 ... 148 E8
Lower Sean *STVGE* SG2 ... 5 K8
Lower St *STSD* CM24 ... 79 L3 1
Lower Tail *OXHEY* WD19 ... 206 D3
Lower Tub *BUSH* WD23 ... 197 J8 2
Lower Yott *HHNE* HP2 ... 149 K8
Lowestoft Rd *WATN* WD24 ... 196 A2 1
Loweswater Cl *GSTN* WD25 ... 182 B4 1
Lowfield *SBW* CM21 ... 142 D1
Lowfield La *HOD* EN11 ... 159 M4
Lowgate La *WARE* SG12 ... 91 M6
Low Hill Rd *HLWW/ROY* CM19 ... 160 E4
Lowlands *BRKMPK* AL9 ... 155 H2 2
Low Rd *BRKMPK* AL9 ... 156 E2
Lowry Dr *DUN/HR/TOD* LU5 ... 63 J5
Lowson Gv *OXHEY* WD19 ... 196 D8
Lowswood Cl *NTHWD* HA6 ... 205 H8
Lowther Cl *BORE* WD6 ... 198 E6 1
Lowther Rd *DUN/WHIP* LU6 ... 81 H4
Loxley Rd *BERK* HP4 ... 146 D4
Lucan Rd *BAR* EN5 ... 200 D4
Lucas Gdns *LTNN/LIM* LU3 ... 65 G2
Lucas La *BLDK* SG7 ... 18 D6
HTCH/STOT SG5 ... 52 C3
Lucerne Wy *LTNN/LIM* LU3 ... 65 H6
Lucks Hl *HHW* HP1 ... 148 D7
Ludgate *TRING* HP23 ... 123 L6 1
Ludlow Av *LTN* LU1 ... 83 K6
Ludlow Md *OXHEY* WD19 ... 206 A3
Ludlow Wy *RKW/CH/CXG* WD3 ... 195 H5
Ludun Cl *DUN/HR/TOD* LU5 ... 81 K2
Ludwick Wy *WGCE* AL7 ... 134 E4
Lukes La *TRING* HP23 ... 101 J7
Lukes Lea *TRING* HP23 ... 123 M1
Lullington Cl *LTNE* LU2 ... 66 B7
Lullington Garth *BORE* WD6 ... 199 H6 1
Lulworth Av *CHESW* EN7 ... 175 G8
Lumbards *WGCE* AL7 ... 134 F1
Lumen Rd *ROY* SG8 ... 21 J3
Lunardi Ct *STDN* SG11 ... 75 H7
Lundin Wk *OXHEY* WD19 ... 206 C4 3
Luther King Rd *HLW* CM20 ... 6 E7
The Luton Dr *LTN* LU1 ... 83 M5
Luton La *STALW/RED* AL3 ... 129 M2
Luton Rd *AMP/FLIT/B* MK45 ... 49 G1
DUN/HR/TOD LU5 ... 81 J2
HARP AL5 ... 108 D6
HTCHE/RSTV SG4 ... 85 M8
LTN LU1 ... 82 E6
LTNE LU2 ... 50 F8
LTNN/LIM LU3 ... 49 G5
STALW/RED AL3 ... 106 D3
Luton White Hl *LTNE* LU2 ... 66 F2
Luxembourg Cl *LTNN/LIM* LU3 ... 64 C2
Luxford Pl *SBW* CM21 ... 142 E1
Luynes Ri *BUNT* SG9 ... 58 D4
Lybury La *STALW/RED* AL3 ... 129 K3
Lycaste Cl *STAL* AL1 ... 11 K8
Lych Ga *GSTN* WD25 ... 182 C4
Lydia Ms *BRKMPK* AL9 ... 172 B3
Lye Hl *HTCHE/RSTV* SG4 ... 85 J3
Lye La *LCOL/BKTW* AL2 ... 168 F7
The Lye *BERK* HP4 ... 126 C4
Lygean Av *WARE* SG12 ... 138 D1
Lygetun Dr *LTNN/LIM* LU3 ... 64 E3
Lygrave *STVGE* SG2 ... 89 H2
Lyles La *WGCW* AL8 ... 134 D2
Lyle's Rw *HTCHE/RSTV* SG4 ... 52 E4
Lymans Rd *ARL/CHE* SG15 ... 25 M4
Lyme Av *BERK* HP4 ... 146 C3
Lymington Rd *STVG* SG1 ... 70 A2
Lynch Hl *DUN/WHIP* LU6 ... 105 M2
The Lynch *HOD* EN11 ... 160 A4
Lyndale *STVG* SG1 ... 4 E5
Lyndhurst Av *PIN* HA5 ... 206 A8
Lyndhurst Cl *HARP* AL5 ... 109 H8 1
Lyndhurst Dr *HARP* AL5 ... 109 H8
Lyndhurst Gdns *PIN* HA5 ... 206 A8
Lyndhurst Rd *LTN* LU1 ... 2 B6
Lyndon Av *PIN* HA5 ... 206 D6
Lyndon Md *STALE/WH* AL4 ... 132 B8
Lyneham Rd *LTNE* LU2 ... 84 B1
Lyne Wy *HHW* HP1 ... 148 E5
Lynmouth Rd *WGCE* AL7 ... 134 E4
Lynsey Cl *STALW/RED* AL3 ... 129 M3
Lynton Av *ARL/CHE* SG15 ... 25 M5
STAL AL1 ... 170 B1
Lynwood Av *LTNE* LU2 ... 65 M7
Lynwood Dr *NTHWD* HA6 ... 205 K8
Lynwood Hts
RKW/CH/CXG WD3 ... 194 A6
Lyonsdown Av *BAR* EN5 ... 201 H7
Lyonsdown Rd *BAR* EN5 ... 201 H7
Lyon Wy *STALE/WH* AL4 ... 153 M7
Lyrical Wy *HHW* HP1 ... 149 G5
Lysander Cl *HHW* HP1 ... 164 E6
Lysander Wy *ABLGY* WD5 ... 181 M3 4
WGCE AL7 ... 135 J3 2
Lys Hill Gdns *HERT/WAS* SG14 ... 137 G2
Lytham Av *OXHEY* WD19 ... 206 C5
Lytton Av *LWTH* SG6 ... 39 L5
Lytton Flds *KNEB* SG3 ... 88 E6 2
Lytton Gdns *WGCW* AL8 ... 134 C4
Lytton Rd *BAR* EN5 ... 201 H5
PIN HA5 ... 206 D7
Lyttons Wy *HOD* EN11 ... 159 M1
Lytton Wy *STVG* SG1 ... 4 B4

M

Mabbutt Cl *LCOL/BKTW* AL2 ... 182 D1
Mabey's Wk *SBW* CM21 ... 142 A1
Macaret Cl *TRDG/WHET* N20 ... 201 G8
Macaulay Rd *LTNW/LEA* LU4 ... 63 M8
Macdonnell Gdns
GSTN WD25 ... 181 L6 2
Macer's La *BROX* EN10 ... 176 E3
Macintosh Cl *CHESW* EN7 ... 175 J5 2
Mackenzie Sq *STVGE* SG2 ... 5 M7
Mackerel Hall *ROY* SG8 ... 21 G4
Maddesfield Ct *RAD* WD7 ... 184 D4 5
Maddles *LWTH* SG6 ... 40 C6
Maddox Rd *HHNE* HP2 ... 9 K9
HLW CM20 ... 7 G4
Made Feld *STVG* SG1 ... 5 G3
Madgeways Cl *WARE* SG12 ... 138 E5 1
Madgeways La *WARE* SG12 ... 138 E5
Magdalene Cl *BGSW* SG18 ... 14 C5
Magellan Cl *STVGE* SG2 ... 71 J5 1
Magna Cl *HARP* AL5 ... 131 J4
Magnaville Rd *BSF* CM23 ... 96 D6
BUSH WD23 ... 197 K8
Magnolia Av *ABLGY* WD5 ... 181 L3
Magnolia Cl *HERT/BAY* SG13 ... 137 M4
LCOL/BKTW AL2 ... 169 J5 1
Magpie Crs *STVGE* SG2 ... 71 J6
Magpie Hall Rd *BUSH* WD23 ... 207 K2
The Magpies *LTNE* LU2 ... 65 J4
Maidenbower Av
DUN/WHIP LU6 ... 80 E1
Maidenhall Rd *LTNW/LEA* LU4 ... 64 F8
Maidenhead St
HERT/WAS SG14 ... 137 J4 6
Maidenhead Yd
HERT/WAS SG14 ... 137 J4 7
Maiden St *HTCHE/RSTV* SG4 ... 55 H1
Main Av *NTHWD* HA6 ... 205 H3
Main Rd *HERT/WAS* SG14 ... 114 B7
Main Rd North *BERK* HP4 ... 103 M3
Main Rd South *BERK* HP4 ... 104 B5
Maitland Rd *STSD* CM24 ... 79 K4
Malborough Rd *WATW* WD18 ... 12 E4
Malden Flds *BUSH* WD23 ... 13 K6
Malden Rd *BORE* WD6 ... 198 F4
WAT WD17 ... 12 D1
Maldon Ct *HARP* AL5 ... 109 G8 3
Malham Cl *LTNW/LEA* LU4 ... 64 E7
Malins Cl *BAR* EN5 ... 200 B6 1
Mallard Cl *BAR* EN5 ... 201 J7 2
Mallard Gdns *LTNN/LIM* LU3 ... 64 F5
Mallard Rd *ABLGY* WD5 ... 181 M2
ROY SG8 ... 21 H4
STVGE SG2 ... 71 J8
Mallards Ri *HLWE* CM17 ... 163 H2
The Mallards *HHS/BOV* HP3 ... 166 E4
Mallard Wy *GSTN* WD25 ... 182 D7 1
NTHWD HA6 ... 205 H7
Mallion Ct *WAB* EN9 ... 191 L4
Mallory Gdns *EBAR* EN4 ... 201 M8
Mallows Gn *HLWW/ROY* CM19 ... 161 M7
Mallow Wk *ROY* SG8 ... 21 K5 4
The Mall *DUN/HR/TOD* LU5 ... 81 H1
LCOL/BKTW AL2 ... 169 H6
Malm Cl *RKW/CH/CXG* WD3 ... 204 C2
Malmes Cft *HHS/BOV* HP3 ... 167 H1
Malms Cl *DUN/WHIP* LU6 ... 105 J1
Malmsdale *WGCW* AL8 ... 112 C8
Malthouse Gn *LTNE* LU2 ... 84 E1
Malthouse La *HTCH/STOT* SG5 ... 26 F3
Malting La *MHAD* SG10 ... 94 E8
STDN SG11 ... 75 K3
TRING HP23 ... 125 J5
Maltings Cl *BLDK* SG7 ... 41 G1 4
ROY SG8 ... 21 H3 1
Maltings Dr *STALE/WH* AL4 ... 132 B3
Maltings La *ROY* SG8 ... 23 K8
Maltings Orch *HTCH/STOT* SG5 ... 37 J7
The Maltings *KGLGY* WD4 ... 181 H4
STAL AL1 ... 10 F7
STVGE SG2 ... 72 A2
Malus Cl *HHNE* HP2 ... 9 H8
Malvern Cl *STALE/WH* AL4 ... 153 G3
Malvern Rd *LTN* LU1 ... 83 G3
PEND EN3 ... 190 D8
Malvern Wy *HHNE* HP2 ... 8 E4
RKW/CH/CXG WD3 ... 195 G6
Malzeard Rd *LTNN/LIM* LU3 ... 2 B3
Manan Cl *HHS/BOV* HP3 ... 167 H1 2
Manchester Cl *STVG* SG1 ... 54 E7
Manchester Pl *DUN/WHIP* LU6 ... 81 G1
Manchester St *LTN* LU1 ... 2 E6 1
Mancroft Rd *LTN* LU1 ... 82 C7
Mandela Pl *WATN* WD24 ... 13 J1 2
Mandelyns *BERK* HP4 ... 146 D3
Mandeville *STVGE* SG2 ... 89 H1
Mandeville Cl *BROX* EN10 ... 159 L7
HERT/BAY SG13 ... 137 H7 1
WAT WD17 ... 195 L1
Mandeville Dr *STAL* AL1 ... 169 J2
Mandeville Ri *WGCW* AL8 ... 134 C2
Mandeville Rd *HERT/BAY* SG13 ... 137 H7
PEND EN3 ... 190 D8
POTB/CUF EN6 ... 187 H3
Mangrove Dr *HERT/BAY* SG13 ... 137 K6
Mangrove La *HERT/BAY* SG13 ... 137 K7
Mangrove Rd *HERT/BAY* SG13 ... 137 K5
LTNE LU2 ... 66 B7
Manland Av *HARP* AL5 ... 109 H8
Manland Wy *HARP* AL5 ... 109 H8
Manley Hwy *HTCH/STOT* SG5 ... 52 A3
Manley Rd *HHNE* HP2 ... 8 D7
Manly Dixon Dr *PEND* EN3 ... 190 D8
Mannicotts *WGCW* AL8 ... 134 A4
Manning Pl *LTNE* LU2 ... 66 D8 1
Manor Av *HHS/BOV* HP3 ... 166 C2 1
Manor Cl *BAR* EN5 ... 200 D5
BERK HP4 ... 147 H6 4
HAT AL10 ... 154 E2
HERT/WAS SG14 ... 137 J2
HTCH/STOT SG5 ... 38 D7
LWTH SG6 ... 39 L7
Manor Cottages *NTHWD* HA6 ... 205 L8 1
Manor Ct *EN* EN1 ... 190 A7
RAD WD7 ... 183 L8
Manor Crs *HTCHE/RSTV* SG4 ... 53 G4
Manor Dr *LCOL/BKTW* AL2 ... 168 F6
Manor Farm Cl *LTNW/LEA* LU4 ... 64 B7
Manor Farm Rd *EN* EN1 ... 190 A6
Manor Hatch *HLWS* CM18 ... 7 M9
Manor Hatch Cl *HLWS* CM18 ... 163 G3
Manor House Dr *NTHWD* HA6 ... 205 G7
Manor House Gdns *ABLGY* WD5 ... 181 J2
Manor Links *BSF* CM23 ... 97 H3
Manor Pde *HAT* AL10 ... 154 E2 1
Manor Pk *DUN/HR/TOD* LU5 ... 63 G6
Manor Pound Rd *LBUZ* LU7 ... 101 M3 3
Manor Rd *AMP/FLIT/B* MK45 ... 35 J8
BAR EN5 ... 200 D5
BSF CM23 ... 96 F3
HAT AL10 ... 154 E2
HLWE CM17 ... 142 B5
HNLW SG16 ... 25 H1
HOD EN11 ... 159 M2
LBUZ LU7 ... 101 L3
LCOL/BKTW AL2 ... 170 B5
LTN LU1 ... 3 G8
LTNN/LIM LU3 ... 48 A7
POTB/CUF EN6 ... 186 E2
STAL AL1 ... 11 H5
STALE/WH AL4 ... 109 L8
STSD CM24 ... 79 K5
TRING HP23 ... 123 M6
WAB EN9 ... 191 J4
WAT WD17 ... 196 A2
Manorside *BAR* EN5 ... 200 D5
Manor St *BERK* HP4 ... 147 J6 5
Manor Vw *STVGE* SG2 ... 89 G1
Manorville Rd *HHS/BOV* HP3 ... 166 B3
Manor Wy *BORE* WD6 ... 199 H5
KNEB SG3 ... 88 B4
LWTH SG6 ... 39 L7
POTB/CUF EN6 ... 186 F1
RKW/CH/CXG WD3 ... 194 F5
Mansard Cl *TRING* HP23 ... 123 M7 2
Manscroft Rd *HHW* HP1 ... 149 G5
Mansdale Rd *STALW/RED* AL3 ... 129 L6
Mansfield *SBW* CM21 ... 141 M1
Mansfield Av *EBAR* EN4 ... 201 L7 1
Mansfield Gdns
HERT/WAS SG14 ... 137 H2 2
Mansfield Rd *BLDK* SG7 ... 40 D3
LTNW/LEA LU4 ... 83 G1
Mansion Dr *TRING* HP23 ... 124 A7
Manston Cl *CHES/WCR* EN8 ... 190 B1 2
Manston Dr *BSF* CM23 ... 97 G1
Manston Rd *HLW* CM20 ... 7 H7
Manton Dr *LTNE* LU2 ... 65 J6
Manton Rd *DUN/WHIP* LU6 ... 80 C5
HTCHE/RSTV SG4 ... 53 H4
Manx Cl *LTNW/LEA* LU4 ... 64 F8
Maple Av *BSF* CM23 ... 96 C2
STALW/RED AL3 ... 152 B3
Maple Cl *BSF* CM23 ... 96 C2
BUSH WD23 ... 13 M1
HAT AL10 ... 154 F6 1
HNLW SG16 ... 24 D8
Maplecroft La *WAB* EN9 ... 160 D8
Maplefield *LCOL/BKTW* AL2 ... 169 H8
Maplefield La *CSTG* HP8 ... 192 A4
Maple Gn *HHW* HP1 ... 148 D5
Maple Gv *BSF* CM23 ... 96 C2
WAT WD17 ... 195 M2 2
WGCE AL7 ... 134 E1
Maple Leaf Cl *ABLGY* WD5 ... 181 M3 5
Maple Lodge Cl
RKW/CH/CXG WD3 ... 203 K4
Maple Rd *HARP* AL5 ... 130 E1
Maple Rd East *LTN* LU1 ... 83 G2
Maple Rd West *LTNW/LEA* LU4 ... 83 G2
Maple Spring *BSF* CM23 ... 96 B2
Maple Springs *WAB* EN9 ... 191 M4
The Maples *CHESW* EN7 ... 175 K7
HLWW/ROY CM19 ... 162 A7
HTCHE/RSTV SG4 ... 52 E5
Maple Wy *DUN/WHIP* LU6 ... 105 K2
ROY SG8 ... 21 K2
Maplewood *WARE* SG12 ... 116 B7 4
Maran Av *WLYN* AL6 ... 112 B6 3
Marconi Wy *STALE/WH* AL4 ... 153 J7
Mardale Av *DUN/WHIP* LU6 ... 81 H4
Mardlebury Rd *KNEB* SG3 ... 112 F1
Mardley Av *WLYN* AL6 ... 112 E2
Mardleybury *KNEB* SG3 ... 88 F8 2
Mardley Dell *WLYN* AL6 ... 112 E1
Mardley Hts *WLYN* AL6 ... 112 F2
Mardley Hl *WLYN* AL6 ... 112 E2
Mardley Wd *WLYN* AL6 ... 112 E2 1
Mardyke Rd *HLW* CM20 ... 7 L3
Marford Rd *STALE/WH* AL4 ... 132 E2
WGCW AL8 ... 133 L5
Margaret Av *STALW/RED* AL3 ... 10 E2
Margaret Cl *ABLGY* WD5 ... 181 L3 2
POTB/CUF EN6 ... 187 H4
WAB EN9 ... 191 J4 1
Margaret Rd *EBAR* EN4 ... 201 J5
Margeholes *OXHEY* WD19 ... 206 D2
Margery Wd *WGCE* AL7 ... 112 F8
Margherita Pl *WAB* EN9 ... 191 L5
Marguerite Wy *BSF* CM23 ... 96 B4
Marian Gdns *GSTN* WD25 ... 182 A4
Maricas Av *KTN/HRWW/W* HA3 ... 207 J8
Marigold Pl *HLWE* CM17 ... 142 A6 1
Marina Dr *DUN/WHIP* LU6 ... 80 D3
Marina Gdns *CHES/WCR* EN8 ... 190 B1
Mariner Wy *HHNE* HP2 ... 149 M8 3
Marion Cl *BUSH* WD23 ... 196 E2
Mark Dr *CFSP/GDCR* SL9 ... 202 C4
Markeston Gn *OXHEY* WD19 ... 206 C4 1
Market Hl *BUNT* SG9 ... 58 D3 2
ROY SG8 ... 21 J4
Market Oak La *HHS/BOV* HP3 ... 166 F3
Market Pl *CFSP/GDCR* SL9 ... 202 C8
HERT/WAS SG14 ... 137 J4 8
STAL AL1 ... 10 E7
WAT WD17 ... 13 G4
Market Sq *BSF* CM23 ... 96 E3
STVG SG1 ... 4 D4
Market St *BSF* CM23 ... 96 E3 5
HERT/WAS SG14 ... 137 J4 9
HLWE CM17 ... 142 B6
WATW WD18 ... 12 F5
Markfield Cl *LTNN/LIM* LU3 ... 65 H4 2
Mark Hall Moors *HLW* CM20 ... 7 M1
Markham Crs *DUN/HR/TOD* LU5 ... 63 K8
Markham Rd *CHESW* EN7 ... 175 H5
LTNN/LIM LU3 ... 65 H2
Mark Rd *HHNE* HP2 ... 9 H4
Markwell Wd *EPP* CM16 ... 162 A8
Markyate Rd *LTN* LU1 ... 107 G1
Marlborough Cl *BSF* CM23 ... 96 E5
HTCHE/RSTV SG4 ... 55 G2
WLYN AL6 ... 112 E2 2
Marlborough Ga *STAL* AL1 ... 11 G7
Marlborough Ri *HHNE* HP2 ... 8 C2
Marlborough Rd *LTNN/LIM* LU3 ... 2 B2
STAL AL1 ... 11 G7
STVGE SG2 ... 71 H5
Marle Gdns *WAB* EN9 ... 191 H3
Marley Rd *WGCE* AL7 ... 134 F6
Marlin Cl *BERK* HP4 ... 146 E5
Marlin Copse *BERK* HP4 ... 146 F7 1
Marlin Ct *LTNW/LEA* LU4 ... 63 K6
Marlin Hl *TRING* HP23 ... 144 F1
Marlin Rd *LTNW/LEA* LU4 ... 63 K7
Marlins Cl *RKW/CH/CXG* WD3 ... 193 K3
Marlins Meadow *WATW* WD18 ... 195 J7
Marlin Sq *ABLGY* WD5 ... 181 L2
The Marlins *NTHWD* HA6 ... 205 L6
Marlins Turn *HHW* HP1 ... 149 G4
Marlowe Cl *STVGE* SG2 ... 71 H2
Marlowes *HHNE* HP2 ... 8 A9
Marnham Ri *HHW* HP1 ... 148 F5 1
Marquis Cl *BSF* CM23 ... 96 A3
HARP AL5 ... 109 J8
Marquis Hl *HTCH/STOT* SG5 ... 36 F1
Marquis La *HARP* AL5 ... 109 J8
Marriott Rd *BAR* EN5 ... 200 C4
LTNN/LIM LU3 ... 65 G4
Marriotts Wy *HHS/BOV* HP3 ... 166 C1
Marriott Ter *RKW/CH/CXG* WD3 ... 193 L5
Marryat Rd *EN* EN1 ... 190 A6
Marschefield *HTCH/STOT* SG5 ... 26 D4
Marsden Cl *WGCW* AL8 ... 134 A6 1
Marsden Gn *WGCW* AL8 ... 134 A5
Marsden Rd *WGCW* AL8 ... 134 A5
Marshall Av *STALW/RED* AL3 ... 152 D4
Marshall Rd *LTNE* LU2 ... 66 B8
Marshalls Av *HTCH/STOT* SG5 ... 36 E1
Marshalls Heath La *HARP* AL5 ... 109 M5
Marshall's La *WARE* SG12 ... 91 M6
Marshalls Wy *STALE/WH* AL4 ... 109 L8
Marshal's Dr *STAL* AL1 ... 152 F4
Marshalswick La *STAL* AL1 ... 152 F4
Marshbarns *BSF* CM23 ... 96 B2
Marsh Cl *CHES/WCR* EN8 ... 190 E4
Marshcroft Dr *CHES/WCR* EN8 ... 190 D1
Marshcroft La *TRING* HP23 ... 124 C4
Marshe Cl *POTB/CUF* EN6 ... 187 J3
Marshgate *STVG* SG1 ... 4 D3
Marshgate Dr *HERT/BAY* SG13 ... 137 K3
Marsh Hl *WAB* EN9 ... 177 K6
Marsh La *HLWE* CM17 ... 142 D5
WARE SG12 ... 138 D2
WARE SG12 ... 139 J7
Marshmoor Crs *BRKMPK* AL9 ... 172 C1
Marshmoor La *BRKMPK* AL9 ... 172 B1
Marsh Rd *LTNN/LIM* LU3 ... 64 D5
Marsom Gv *LTNN/LIM* LU3 ... 65 G2
Marston Cl *HHS/BOV* HP3 ... 149 M8 4
Marston Gdns *LTNE* LU2 ... 65 J6
Marston Rd *HOD* EN11 ... 160 A3 1
Marsworth Av *PIN* HA5 ... 206 C8
Marsworth Cl *WATW* WD18 ... 195 K8 2
Marsworth Rd *LBUZ* LU7 ... 102 C6
Marten Ga *STALE/WH* AL4 ... 152 F3
Martian Av *HHNE* HP2 ... 8 F3
Martin Cl *HAT* AL10 ... 154 F7
Martindale Rd *HHW* HP1 ... 148 E6
Martinfield *WGCE* AL7 ... 134 E3 3
Martingale Rd *ROY* SG8 ... 21 K4 3
Martins Cl *RAD* WD7 ... 183 K7 1
Martins Dr *CHES/WCR* EN8 ... 176 D7
HERT/BAY SG13 ... 138 A4
Martins Mt *BAR* EN5 ... 200 F5
Martins Wy *STVG* SG1 ... 70 B2
Martin Wy *LWTH* SG6 ... 39 J5
Martlesham *WGCE* AL7 ... 135 K4
Martyr Cl *STAL* AL1 ... 169 J3 2
Marwood Cl *KGLGY* WD4 ... 166 E8 1
Marygold Wk *AMS* HP6 ... 192 B2
Maryland *HAT* AL10 ... 154 F5 2
Mary McArthur Pl *STSD* CM24 ... 79 K2 1
Marymead Ct *STVGE* SG2 ... 88 F2
Marymead Dr *STVGE* SG2 ... 88 F2
Mary Park Gdns *BSF* CM23 ... 96 E6
Maryport Rd *LTNW/LEA* LU4 ... 64 F8

Mary Proud Ct WLYN AL6 .... 112 D3 2
Marywells SHFD SG17 .... 24 A6
Masefield HTCHE/RSTV SG4 .... 53 H3
Masefield Av BORE WD6 .... 199 G6
STAN HA7 .... 207 L5
Masefield Ct HARP AL5 .... 109 G6 1
Masefield Rd HARP AL5 .... 109 G7
Masefield Wy ROY SG8 .... 21 J1
Mason Cl BORE WD6 .... 199 J3
Masons Ct BSF CM23 .... 96 D3
Masons Rd EN EN1 .... 190 A7
HHNE HP2 .... 9 J7
Mason Wy WAB EN9 .... 191 K4
Masters Cl LTN LU1 .... 83 G5
Matching La BSF CM23 .... 96 C2
Matching Rd HLWE CM17 .... 143 G6
Mathams Dr BSF CM23 .... 96 C5
Mathews Cl STVG SG1 .... 70 C1
Matlock Cl BAR EN5 .... 200 C6
Matlock Crs LTNW/LEA LU4 .... 82 B1
OXHEY WD19 .... 206 B3
Matthew Ga HTCHE/RSTV SG4 .... 52 F5
Matthew St DUN/WHIP LU6 .... 81 G2
Mattocke Rd HTCH/STOT SG5 .... 52 B1
Maude Crs WATN WD24 .... 182 A8
Maud Jane's Cl LBUZ LU7 .... 102 D5
Maulden Cl LTNE LU2 .... 84 B1
Maundsey Cl DUN/WHIP LU6 .... 81 H5
Maunds Hatch HLWS CM18 .... 162 C6
Maxfield Cl TRDG/WHET N20 .... 201 H8
Maxted Rd HHNE HP2 .... 9 K4
Maxwell Cl RKW/CH/CXG WD3 .... 203 M2
Maxwell Ri OXHEY WD19 .... 196 D8 2
Maxwell Rd BORE WD6 .... 199 G4
NTHWD HA6 .... 205 J7
STAL AL1 .... 153 G8
STVG SG1 .... 70 A5
Maybury Av CHES/WCR EN8 .... 176 A7
CHESW EN7 .... 176 A7 1
May Cl STALW/RED AL3 .... 10 F3
Maycock Gv NTHWD HA6 .... 205 L6
Maycroft LWTH SG6 .... 39 M1
Maycroft Rd CHESW EN7 .... 175 K5
Maydencroft La HTCH/STOT SG5 .... 52 C6
Maydwell Ldg BORE WD6 .... 198 E3
Mayer Wy DUN/HR/TOD LU5 .... 62 F7
Mayes Cl BSF CM23 .... 97 J2
Mayfair Cl STALE/WH AL4 .... 153 H2
Mayfare RKW/CH/CXG WD3 .... 195 J6
Mayfield WGCW AL8 .... 112 B8
Mayfield Cl HARP AL5 .... 108 D7
HLWE CM17 .... 142 E6
Mayfield Crs HNLW SG16 .... 24 D8
Mayfield Pk BSF CM23 .... 96 C7 1
Mayfield Rd DUN/HR/TOD LU5 .... 81 J3
DUN/WHIP LU6 .... 81 J4
LTNE LU2 .... 66 A6
Mayflower Av HHNE HP2 .... 8 B8
Mayflower Cl HERT/WAS SG14 .... 136 D6
WAB EN9 .... 177 K2
WLYN AL6 .... 111 L1 5
Mayflower Gdns BSF CM23 .... 96 A4
Mayflower Rd LCOL/BKTW AL2 .... 169 G6
May Gdns BORE WD6 .... 198 C7
Mayhill Rd BAR EN5 .... 200 D7 1
Maylands Av HHNE HP2 .... 9 K4
Maylands Rd OXHEY WD19 .... 206 B4
Maylin Cl HTCHE/RSTV SG4 .... 53 H2
Maylins Dr SBW CM21 .... 120 C8
Maynard Dr STAL AL1 .... 169 J2
Maynard Pl POTB/CUF EN6 .... 174 D8 1
Maynard Rd HHNE HP2 .... 149 J8
Mayne Av LTNW/LEA LU4 .... 64 B6
STALW/RED AL3 .... 151 M8
Mayo Cl CHES/WCR EN8 .... 176 B7
Mayo Gdns HHW HP1 .... 149 G8
Mayshades Cl KNEB SG3 .... 88 F8
Mays La BAR EN5 .... 200 A8
May St ROY SG8 .... 23 K8
Maythorne Cl WATW WD18 .... 195 K5
Maytree Crs WATN WD24 .... 181 L7
Maytree La STAN HA7 .... 207 L6
Maytrees HTCHE/RSTV SG4 .... 52 F4
RAD WD7 .... 183 M8
May Wk STSD CM24 .... 79 M1
Maze Green Hts BSF CM23 .... 96 B3
Maze Green Rd BSF CM23 .... 96 C3
Mazoe Cl BSF CM23 .... 96 E5
Mazoe Rd BSF CM23 .... 96 E5
Mcadam Cl HOD EN11 .... 159 M2 1
Mcdonald Ct HAT AL10 .... 154 F7 1
HAT AL10 .... 154 F8 2
Mc Kellar Cl BUSH WD23 .... 207 H2 2
Mc Kenzie Rd BROX EN10 .... 159 M7
Mead Cl KTN/HRWW/W HA3 .... 207 J8
STVG SG1 .... 5 H2
Mead Ct WAB EN9 .... 191 G5
Meadgate Rd HOD EN11 .... 160 C7
Mead La HERT/BAY SG13 .... 137 K3
Meadowbank HTCHE/RSTV SG4 .... 53 G1
KGLGY WD4 .... 180 F1
OXHEY WD19 .... 196 B8 2
Meadowbanks BAR EN5 .... 199 M6
Meadowbrook TRING HP23 .... 124 A4 1
BAR EN5 .... 200 E7
Meadow Cl BAR EN5 .... 200 F4
BERK HP4 .... 146 F8 1
BRKMPK AL9 .... 172 C3
HERT/BAY SG13 .... 137 L3 1
KNEB SG3 .... 89 J8
LCOL/BKTW AL2 .... 170 C6
LCOL/BKTW AL2 .... 182 F1 2
STALE/WH AL4 .... 153 H4
TRING HP23 .... 123 M6
Meadowcroft BERK HP4 .... 146 C3 3
BUSH WD23 .... 197 G7 3
Meadow Cft HAT AL10 .... 154 E5
Meadowcroft STAL AL1 .... 169 M3
STSD CM24 .... 79 K3 2
Meadowcross WAB EN9 .... 191 K5
Meadow Dell HAT AL10 .... 154 E5 2
Meadow Gn WGCW AL8 .... 134 B4
Meadowlands BAR EN5 .... 199 L6
BSF CM23 .... 96 F1
Meadow La DUN/HR/TOD LU5 .... 63 G5
LBUZ LU7 .... 102 D7
Meadow Rd BERK HP4 .... 147 G4
BORE WD6 .... 199 G3
BUSH WD23 .... 197 G6
GSTN WD25 .... 181 M5
HHS/BOV HP3 .... 166 F4
LTNN/LIM LU3 .... 65 G6
Meadow Road Cl BERK HP4 .... 146 F4
The Meadows BSF CM23 .... 96 D5
HTCHE/RSTV SG4 .... 85 K1
SBW CM21 .... 120 F8
Meadowsweet HNLW SG16 .... 24 E8
Meadowsweet Cl BSF CM23 .... 96 B4 1
The Meadow HERT/BAY SG13 .... 138 D8
WGCE AL7 .... 135 H4
Meadow Vw BUNT SG9 .... 58 C4
Meadow Wk HARP AL5 .... 131 H2
STDN SG11 .... 75 K8
Meadow Wy ABLGY WD5 .... 167 L6
HHS/BOV HP3 .... 165 L2
HTCH/STOT SG5 .... 26 D4
HTCH/STOT SG5 .... 51 H7
HTCH/STOT SG5 .... 52 C4
HTCHE/RSTV SG4 .... 111 K1
KGLGY WD4 .... 180 F1
LTN LU1 .... 82 D6
LWTH SG6 .... 39 L5
POTB/CUF EN6 .... 186 F5
RKW/CH/CXG WD3 .... 194 B8
ROY SG8 .... 30 F4
SBW CM21 .... 142 F1
STVG SG1 .... 5 H3
The Meadow Wy
KTN/HRWW/W HA3 .... 207 K8
Mead Pl RKW/CH/CXG WD3 .... 204 A1
Mead Rd RAD WD7 .... 184 F4
Meads Cl DUN/HR/TOD LU5 .... 63 G5
Meads La STALE/WH AL4 .... 132 C1
The Meads BERK HP4 .... 146 E4
LCOL/BKTW AL2 .... 168 E8
LTNN/LIM LU3 .... 64 F7
LWTH SG6 .... 39 K4
Mead Temple HHNE HP2 .... 8 B5 2
The Mead CHES/WCR EN8 .... 176 B8
HTCH/STOT SG5 .... 38 D8
OXHEY WD19 .... 206 D3
Mead Vw BUNT SG9 .... 61 K4
Meadview Rd WARE SG12 .... 138 B2
Meadway BAR EN5 .... 200 F5
BERK HP4 .... 147 K6
Mead Wy BUSH WD23 .... 13 L1
Meadway DUN/WHIP LU6 .... 80 F3
HARP AL5 .... 131 K3
HOD EN11 .... 159 M6
KNEB SG3 .... 88 E6
PEND EN3 .... 190 C7
STALE/WH AL4 .... 171 J2
STVG SG1 .... 69 M4
WGCE AL7 .... 134 E6 2
Meadway Cl PIN HA5 .... 207 G6 1
The Meadway POTB/CUF EN6 .... 174 E7
Meautys STALW/RED AL3 .... 168 E1
Medalls Link STVGE SG2 .... 5 K7
Medalls Pth STVGE SG2 .... 5 K7
Medcalf Rd PEND EN3 .... 190 E8
Medina Rd LTNW/LEA LU4 .... 82 F1
Medlows HARP AL5 .... 108 D8
Medow Md RAD WD7 .... 183 L4
Medway Cl GSTN WD25 .... 182 B5
Medway Rd HHNE HP2 .... 149 L2
Medwick Ms HHNE HP2 .... 150 A2 2
Mees Cl LTNN/LIM LU3 .... 64 E1
Meeting House La BLDK SG7 .... 40 D1 2
Megg La KGLGY WD4 .... 166 A8
Melbourn Cl HTCH/STOT SG5 .... 26 E5
Melbourne Cl STALW/RED AL3 .... 152 E3
Melbourne Ct WGCW AL8 .... 134 A5
Melbourne Rd BUSH WD23 .... 197 G6
Melbourn Rd ROY SG8 .... 21 K3
Melbourn St ROY SG8 .... 21 J4
Melford Cl LTNE LU2 .... 84 C1 3
The Melings HHNE HP2 .... 150 A2 2
Melne Rd STVGE SG2 .... 89 G2
Melrose Av BORE WD6 .... 199 G6
POTB/CUF EN6 .... 187 G4
Melrose Pl WAT WD17 .... 195 L1
Melson St LTN LU1 .... 2 F7
Melsted Rd HHW HP1 .... 149 G7
Melvern Cl STVGE SG2 .... 89 G3
Melvyn Cl CHESW EN7 .... 175 G7 1
Memorial Rd LTNN/LIM LU3 .... 64 E6
Memorial Wy WATW WD18 .... 12 D3
Mendip Cl STALE/WH AL4 .... 153 H2 4
Mendip Rd BUSH WD23 .... 197 H7
Mendip Wy HHNE HP2 .... 8 D3
LTNN/LIM LU3 .... 64 B2
Mendlesham WGCE AL7 .... 135 K4
Mentley La STDN SG11 .... 74 D6
Mentley La East STDN SG11 .... 75 J6 1
Mentley La West STDN SG11 .... 75 G6
Mentmore Crs DUN/WHIP LU6 .... 81 H5
Mentmore Rd LBUZ LU7 .... 101 L2
STAL AL1 .... 169 J1
Mentmore Vw TRING HP23 .... 123 L5 2
Mepham Crs
KTN/HRWW/W HA3 .... 207 H7
Mepham Gdns
KTN/HRWW/W HA3 .... 207 H7
Meppershall Rd HNLW SG16 .... 24 C6
Mercers HHNE HP2 .... 8 C5
HLWW/ROY CM19 .... 161 M5
Mercers Av BSF CM23 .... 96 A6
Mercers Rw STAL AL1 .... 169 H1
Merchant Dr HERT/BAY SG13 .... 137 L3
Merchants Wk BLDK SG7 .... 41 G1 5
Mercia Rd BLDK SG7 .... 40 F2
Meredith Cl PIN HA5 .... 206 C7
Meredith Rd STVG SG1 .... 70 F3
Merefield SBW CM21 .... 142 D1 2
Meriden Wy GSTN WD25 .... 182 D8
Meridian Wy WARE SG12 .... 139 G5 1
Merlin Cl WAB EN9 .... 191 M5
Merling Cft BERK HP4 .... 146 D4
Mermaid Cl HTCHE/RSTV SG4 .... 53 G3 1
Merritt Wk BRKMPK AL9 .... 172 A3
Merrow Dr HHW HP1 .... 148 D6
Merryfield Cl BORE WD6 .... 198 E3
Merryfields STALE/WH AL4 .... 153 K7
Merry Hill Mt BUSH WD23 .... 207 G1
Merry Hill Rd BUSH WD23 .... 196 F8
Mersey Pl HHNE HP2 .... 149 L2 3
LTN LU1 .... 2 C6 1
Merton Rd WATW WD18 .... 12 E5
Metropolitan Station Ap
WATW WD18 .... 12 A4
Meux Cl CHESW EN7 .... 189 M2
The Mews SBW CM21 .... 120 D7 1
Meyrick Av LTN LU1 .... 2 A8
Mezen Cl NTHWD HA6 .... 205 J5
Michaels Rd BSF CM23 .... 78 F8
Micholls Av CFSP/GDCR SL9 .... 202 D5
Micklefield Rd HHNE HP2 .... 9 M9
Micklefield Wy BORE WD6 .... 198 D1 3
Micklem Dr HHW HP1 .... 148 E6
Midcot Wy BERK HP4 .... 146 E4 2
Mid Cross La CFSP/GDCR SL9 .... 202 E5
Middle Drift ROY SG8 .... 21 H4
Middlefield HAT AL10 .... 154 F4
WGCE AL7 .... 134 D8
Middlefield Av HOD EN11 .... 159 M2
Middlefield Cl HOD EN11 .... 159 M2 2
STALE/WH AL4 .... 153 H4
Middlefield Rd HOD EN11 .... 159 M2
Middlefields LWTH SG6 .... 39 L2
Middle Furlong BUSH WD23 .... 197 G5
Middlehill HHW HP1 .... 148 D7
Middleknights Hl HHW HP1 .... 148 F5
Middle La HHS/BOV HP3 .... 164 F8
Middle Meadow CSTG HP8 .... 202 A3
Middle Ope WATN WD24 .... 182 A8 1
Middle Rd BERK HP4 .... 147 G6
EBAR EN4 .... 201 K7
WAB EN9 .... 191 G3
Middle Rw BSF CM23 .... 96 E4
Middlesborough Cl STVG SG1 .... 54 E8 1
Middle St WAB EN9 .... 177 L2
Middleton Rd LTNE LU2 .... 66 C6 2
RKW/CH/CXG WD3 .... 203 M1
Middle Wy WATN WD24 .... 182 A8
Midhurst LWTH SG6 .... 39 K2
Midhurst Gdns LTNN/LIM LU3 .... 65 H5
Midland Rd HHNE HP2 .... 8 A8
LTNE LU2 .... 2 E5
Midway STALW/RED AL3 .... 169 G2
Milburn Cl LTNN/LIM LU3 .... 65 G1
Mildmay Rd STVG SG1 .... 71 G2
Mildred Av BORE WD6 .... 198 F5
WATW WD18 .... 12 B5
Mile Cl WAB EN9 .... 191 H4 1
Mile House Cl STAL AL1 .... 169 M2
Mile House La STAL AL1 .... 169 L3
Miles Cl HLWW/ROY CM19 .... 6 B9
Milestone Cl STVGE SG2 .... 71 J6
Milestone Rd HTCH/STOT SG5 .... 52 C1
KNEB SG3 .... 88 F5
Miletree Crs DUN/WHIP LU6 .... 81 J4
Milford Cl STALE/WH AL4 .... 153 J3
Milford Hl HARP AL5 .... 109 J6
Milksey La HTCHE/RSTV SG4 .... 54 A5
Milland Ct BORE WD6 .... 199 J2 1
Millard Wy HTCHE/RSTV SG4 .... 39 H8
Millbank HHS/BOV HP3 .... 166 C3 5
Mill Br HERT/WAS SG14 .... 137 H4 5
Millbrook Rd BUSH WD23 .... 196 E2
Mill Cl BUNT SG9 .... 58 D3
HHS/BOV HP3 .... 166 F4
HHW HP1 .... 149 G3
HTCH/STOT SG5 .... 26 F4
WARE SG12 .... 138 C1
WGCW AL8 .... 133 M5
Mill Cnr BAR EN5 .... 200 E2
Millcrest Rd CHESW EN7 .... 175 G7
Millcroft BSF CM23 .... 96 F1
Mill End STDN SG11 .... 75 L8
Millers Cl BSF CM23 .... 96 B5
Millersdale HLWW/ROY CM19 .... 162 A6
Millers La WARE SG12 .... 139 H6
Millers Lay DUN/HR/TOD LU5 .... 63 L8
Millers Ri STAL AL1 .... 11 G9
Millers Vw MHAD SG10 .... 118 D1
Millers Wy DUN/HR/TOD LU5 .... 62 F6
Millers Yd HERT/WAS SG14 .... 137 J4 10
Mill Fld HLWE CM17 .... 142 B6
Millfield BERK HP4 .... 147 J5
WARE SG12 .... 116 D2
WGCE AL7 .... 135 H3
Millfield La HTCHE/RSTV SG4 .... 52 E6
LTN LU1 .... 82 B7
STDN SG11 .... 95 J2
Millfield Rd LTNN/LIM LU3 .... 65 G7
Millfields SBW CM21 .... 120 E7
STSD CM24 .... 79 K4 1
Millfield Wk HHS/BOV HP3 .... 166 F2
Millfield Wy LTN LU1 .... 82 C7
Mill Gdns TRING HP23 .... 124 A6 2
Mill Green La BRKMPK AL9 .... 155 K1
Mill Green Rd WGCE AL7 .... 134 D5
Mill Hl BSF CM23 .... 78 D5
ROY SG8 .... 21 K6
STSD CM24 .... 79 J4
Millhouse La ABLGY WD5 .... 167 M6
Millhurst Ms HLWE CM17 .... 142 D6
Milliners Wy BSF CM23 .... 96 B6
LTNN/LIM LU3 .... 2 A2
Mill La AMP/FLIT/B MK45 .... 35 G7
ARL/CHE SG15 .... 25 L6
BROX EN10 .... 159 L8
BUNT SG9 .... 46 F5
CHES/WCR EN8 .... 176 D7
HERT/WAS SG14 .... 90 E5
HLWE CM17 .... 142 D6
HTCH/STOT SG5 .... 26 E1
HTCH/STOT SG5 .... 26 F4
HTCH/STOT SG5 .... 36 A7
HTCHE/RSTV SG4 .... 52 E7
HTCHE/RSTV SG4 .... 55 H1
KGLGY WD4 .... 166 F8
RBSF CM22 .... 121 L6
ROY SG8 .... 30 E2
SBW CM21 .... 120 E7
STALW/RED AL3 .... 128 F1
STDN SG11 .... 77 J4
WLYN AL6 .... 112 B5
Mill Lane Cl BROX EN10 .... 159 L8
Mill Race WARE SG12 .... 139 J6
Mill Rd DUN/HR/TOD LU5 .... 62 F6
HERT/BAY SG13 .... 137 J3
HERT/WAS SG14 .... 137 J3
HTCHE/RSTV SG4 .... 52 E7
ROY SG8 .... 21 J3
Mill Side STSD CM24 .... 79 J4
Millstream Cl
HERT/WAS SG14 .... 137 G4 5
HTCHE/RSTV SG4 .... 38 F8
Mill St BERK HP4 .... 147 H6
BLDK SG7 .... 18 C6
BSF CM23 .... 96 F5
HHS/BOV HP3 .... 166 C3
HLWE CM17 .... 163 K5
LTN LU1 .... 2 D5
Millthorne Cl
RKW/CH/CXG WD3 .... 194 E6 2
Mill View Rd TRING HP23 .... 123 L6
Millwards HAT AL10 .... 155 G8
Mill Wy BUSH WD23 .... 196 D3
Millway HTCHE/RSTV SG4 .... 67 J8
Mill Wy RKW/CH/CXG WD3 .... 203 L1
Milne Cl LWTH SG6 .... 40 A7
Milne Fld PIN HA5 .... 206 F7
Milner Cl GSTN WD25 .... 182 A5 1
Milner Ct BUSH WD23 .... 197 G7
Milneway DEN/HRF UB9 .... 204 A8
Milton Av BAR EN5 .... 200 E6
Milton Cl ROY SG8 .... 21 H1 1
Milton Ct WAB EN9 .... 191 H5 3
Milton Dene HHNE HP2 .... 150 A2
Milton Dr BORE WD6 .... 199 G6 1
Milton Flds CSTG HP8 .... 202 A3
Milton Hl CSTG HP8 .... 202 A3 2
Milton Rd HARP AL5 .... 131 G1
LTN LU1 .... 2 A8
RAYLNE/WEN HP22 .... 122 E5
WARE SG12 .... 116 C8
Milton St WATN WD24 .... 196 A2
Milton Vw HTCHE/RSTV SG4 .... 53 H3
Milton Wy DUN/HR/TOD LU5 .... 63 J6
Milverton Gn LTNN/LIM LU3 .... 64 F3
Milwards HLWW/ROY CM19 .... 162 A6 1
Mimms Hall Rd POTB/CUF EN6 .... 186 C2
Mimms La BORE WD6 .... 185 J4
RAD WD7 .... 184 F4
Mimram Cl HTCHE/RSTV SG4 .... 86 D3
Mimram Rd HERT/WAS SG14 .... 137 G5
WLYN AL6 .... 112 B5 3
Minchen Rd HLW CM20 .... 7 K3
Minehead Wy STVG SG1 .... 69 M3
Minerva Cl STVG SG1 .... 71 H1
Minerva Dr WAT WD17 .... 181 K7
The Minims HAT AL10 .... 154 F4
Minorca Wy LTNW/LEA LU4 .... 63 M7
Minsden Rd STVGE SG2 .... 71 J7
Minster Cl HAT AL10 .... 154 F7
Minster Rd ROY SG8 .... 21 H2
Minstrel Cl HHW HP1 .... 149 G6 3
Minton La HLWE CM17 .... 163 H2
Misbourne Av CFSP/GDCR SL9 .... 202 D5
Misbourne Cl
CFSP/GDCR SL9 .... 202 D5 2
Missden Dr HHS/BOV HP3 .... 167 H1
Miss Joans Ride DUN/WHIP LU6 .... 104 D3
Mistletoe Hl LTNE LU2 .... 84 B2
Mistley Rd HLW CM20 .... 7 L2
Miswell La TRING HP23 .... 123 L7
Mitchell Cl ABLGY WD5 .... 181 M3 6
HHW HP1 .... 164 E6
STAL AL1 .... 169 J3
WGCE AL7 .... 135 H4 8
Mitre Gdns BSF CM23 .... 96 F6 1
Mixes Hill Rd LTNE LU2 .... 65 L7
The Mixies HTCH/STOT SG5 .... 26 D4
The Moakes LTNN/LIM LU3 .... 64 D3
Moat Cl BUSH WD23 .... 197 G6 2
Moatfield Rd BUSH WD23 .... 197 G6
Moat La LTNN/LIM LU3 .... 65 G6
Moatside BUNT SG9 .... 45 M3
The Moat STDN SG11 .... 75 J7
Moatwood Gn WGCE AL7 .... 134 D5 3
Mobbsbury Wy STVGE SG2 .... 71 G3
Mobley Gn LTNE LU2 .... 66 A7
Moffats Cl BRKMPK AL9 .... 172 F5
Moffats La BRKMPK AL9 .... 172 D6
Moira Cl LTNN/LIM LU3 .... 64 B4
Molescroft HARP AL5 .... 108 C6
Moles La BUNT SG9 .... 44 F7
Molesworth HOD EN11 .... 138 F8
Molewood Rd HERT/WAS SG14 .... 137 G3
Mollison Av PEND EN3 .... 190 F8
Molteno Rd WAT WD17 .... 195 M2
Momples Rd HLW CM20 .... 7 M5
Monarch's Wy
CHES/WCR EN8 .... 190 C4 3
Monastery Cl STALW/RED AL3 .... 10 D7
Money Hill Rd
RKW/CH/CXG WD3 .... 204 B1
Money Hole La WLYN AL6 .... 135 K3
Monica Cl WATN WD24 .... 13 J1
Monklands LWTH SG6 .... 39 J4
Monks Av BAR EN5 .... 201 H7
Monksbury HLWS CM18 .... 162 F5
Monks Cl BROX EN10 .... 159 M7
DUN/HR/TOD LU5 .... 81 K1
LWTH SG6 .... 39 H4
STAL AL1 .... 169 K1
STALW/RED AL3 .... 130 A5
Monks Horton Wy STAL AL1 .... 11 M3
Monksmead BORE WD6 .... 199 H5
Monks Ri WGCW AL8 .... 112 C8
Monks Vw STVGE SG2 .... 5 H9
Monks Wk BUNT SG9 .... 58 D3
Monkswick Rd HLW CM20 .... 7 J3
Monkswood WGCW AL8 .... 112 B8
Monkswood Av WAB EN9 .... 191 J4
Monkswood Dr BSF CM23 .... 96 C4
Monkswood Gdns BORE WD6 .... 199 J6
Monkswood Wy STVG SG1 .... 4 E6
STVGE SG2 .... 70 D8
Monmouth Rd WAT WD17 .... 12 F2
Monro Gdns
KTN/HRWW/W HA3 .... 207 K7
Mons Av BLDK SG7 .... 40 E4
Mons Cl HARP AL5 .... 131 J4
Monson Rd BROX EN10 .... 159 L7 2
Montacute Rd BUSH WD23 .... 197 K8
Montague Av LTNW/LEA LU4 .... 64 B4
Montague Hall Pl
BUSH WD23 .... 196 F7 3
Montague Rd BERK HP4 .... 147 G6
Montayne Rd CHES/WCR EN8 .... 190 C3
Montfitchet Wk STVGE SG2 .... 71 J3
Montgomerie Cl BERK HP4 .... 146 F4 5
Montgomery Av HHNE HP2 .... 9 H8
SHFD SG17 .... 24 B1
Montgomery Dr
CHES/WCR EN8 .... 176 D7
Monton Cl LTNN/LIM LU3 .... 64 E4
Montrose Av LTNN/LIM LU3 .... 65 H7
Monument La CFSP/GDCR SL9 .... 202 D6
Moon La BAR EN5 .... 200 E4 1
Moorend WGCE AL7 .... 134 F7
Moor End Rd HHW HP1 .... 149 H8
Moore Rd BERK HP4 .... 146 E4
Moorfields HLWS CM18 .... 162 B7
Moor Hall Rd HLWE CM17 .... 142 E6
Moorhead Cl HTCH/STOT SG5 .... 52 C4
Moorhurst Av CHESW EN7 .... 175 G8
The Moorings BSF CM23 .... 96 F4
Moorland Gdns LTNE LU2 .... 2 D4
Moorland Rd HARP AL5 .... 109 G6
HHW HP1 .... 165 L1
Moorlands LCOL/BKTW AL2 .... 169 K7 1
WGCE AL7 .... 134 F7
Moor La RKW/CH/CXG WD3 .... 179 K7
RKW/CH/CXG WD3 .... 204 D2
Moor Lane Crossing
WATW WD18 .... 195 H8
Moormead Hl HTCH/STOT SG5 .... 52 B4
Moor Mill La LCOL/BKTW AL2 .... 169 K8
Moor Park Rd NTHWD HA6 .... 205 J6
Moorside WGCE AL7 .... 134 F7
Moors Ley STVGE SG2 .... 71 M1
The Moors WGCE AL7 .... 134 F3
Moor St LTN LU1 .... 2 B5
Moors Wk WGCE AL7 .... 135 H4
Moortown Rd OXHEY WD19 .... 206 B4
Moor Vw WATW WD18 .... 195 M8
Moorymead Cl HERT/WAS SG14 .... 90 C7
Morcom Rd DUN/HR/TOD LU5 .... 81 K4
Morecambe Cl STVG SG1 .... 70 A3
Morefields TRING HP23 .... 123 M4
Moremead WAB EN9 .... 191 J4
Moreton Av HARP AL5 .... 108 E8
Moreton Cl CHESW EN7 .... 176 A6
Moreton End Cl HARP AL5 .... 108 E8 1
Moreton End La HARP AL5 .... 108 E8
Moreton Pl HARP AL5 .... 108 E7 3
Moreton Rd LTNE LU2 .... 3 J1
Morgan Cl NTHWD HA6 .... 205 L5
STVG SG1 .... 70 C1
Morgan Gdns GSTN WD25 .... 197 G1 2
Morgans Cl HERT/BAY SG13 .... 137 J6 2
Morgan's Rd HERT/BAY SG13 .... 137 J6
Morgan's Wk HERT/BAY SG13 .... 137 J7
Morice Rd HOD EN11 .... 159 L2
Morland Cl DUN/WHIP LU6 .... 80 F4 1
Morland Wy CHES/WCR EN8 .... 176 D7
Morley Gv HLW CM20 .... 6 D4
Mornington WLYN AL6 .... 112 F6
Mornington Rd RAD WD7 .... 183 M5
Morningtons HLWW/ROY CM19 .... 162 A6
Morpeth Av BORE WD6 .... 198 E1
Morrel Cl BAR EN5 .... 201 H4 1
Morrell Cl LTNN/LIM LU3 .... 64 F3
Morris Cl CFSP/GDCR SL9 .... 202 E8
HNLW SG16 .... 25 H5
LTNN/LIM LU3 .... 64 D2
Morris Ct WAB EN9 .... 191 L5
Morriston Cl OXHEY WD19 .... 206 B5 3
Morris Wy LCOL/BKTW AL2 .... 170 C5
Mortain Dr BERK HP4 .... 146 E4
Mortimer Cl BUSH WD23 .... 197 G7 3
LTN LU1 .... 82 E4
Mortimer Ga CHES/WCR EN8 .... 176 E6
Mortimer Hl TRING HP23 .... 124 A6
Mortimer Ri TRING HP23 .... 124 A6 3
Mortimer Rd ROY SG8 .... 21 K4
Morton Cl LBUZ LU7 .... 102 B6
Morton St ROY SG8 .... 21 J2
Morven Cl POTB/CUF EN6 .... 187 H2
Mossbank Av LTNE LU2 .... 84 B2
Moss Cl RKW/CH/CXG WD3 .... 204 C2
Mossendew Cl DEN/HRF UB9 .... 204 C8
Moss Gn WGCE AL7 .... 134 D6
Mossman Dr LTN LU1 .... 82 D6
Moss Rd GSTN WD25 .... 182 A5
Moss Side LCOL/BKTW AL2 .... 182 E1
Moss Wy HTCH/STOT SG5 .... 52 B1
Mostyn Rd BUSH WD23 .... 197 H6
LTNW/LEA LU4 .... 64 D6
Motts Cl HERT/WAS SG14 .... 90 B6
Moulton Ri LTNE LU2 .... 3 G5
Mountbatten Cl STAL AL1 .... 170 A2 1
Mountbel Rd STAN HA7 .... 207 M8 1
Mount Cl EBAR EN4 .... 201 M5
HHW HP1 .... 148 E7
Mount Dr LCOL/BKTW AL2 .... 169 J4
STSD CM24 .... 79 K5
Mounteagle ROY SG8 .... 21 J5
Mountfield Rd HHNE HP2 .... 8 C8
LTNE LU2 .... 2 F1
Mountfitchet Rd STSD CM24 .... 79 K5
Mount Garrison
HTCHE/RSTV SG4 .... 52 E3
Mount Grace Rd LTNE LU2 .... 66 B4
POTB/CUF EN6 .... 186 F2
Mountjoy HTCHE/RSTV SG4 .... 53 H1
Mount Pleasant DEN/HRF UB9 .... 203 M8
EBAR EN4 .... 201 L5
HTCH/STOT SG5 .... 52 C4
STALW/RED AL3 .... 10 C6
Mount Pleasant Cl
BRKMPK AL9 .... 155 H2
Mount Pleasant La
BRKMPK AL9 .... 155 H2
LCOL/BKTW AL2 .... 182 C1 1
Mount Pleasant Rd
LTNN/LIM LU3 .... 64 D5
Mount Rd EBAR EN4 .... 201 K6
HERT/WAS SG14 .... 136 F5
STALE/WH AL4 .... 132 C1
Mountside KTN/HRWW/W HA3 .... 207 L8
Mountsorrel HERT/BAY SG13 .... 137 L4 5
The Mount CHESW EN7 .... 175 J5 3
POTB/CUF EN6 .... 187 G1
RKW/CH/CXG WD3 .... 194 B7
ROY SG8 .... 32 D1

Mount Vw LCOL/BKTW AL2 170 D6
Mountview NTHWD HA6 205 M6
Mount Vw RKW/CH/CXG WD3 204 A1
Mountview Av
DUN/HR/TOD LU5 81 J4
Mountview Rd CHESW EN7 175 K5
Mountway POTB/CUF EN6 186 F1
Mount Wy WGCE AL7 134 E7
Mountway Cl WGCE AL7 134 E7
Mowbray Crs HTCH/STOT SG5 26 E4
Mowbray Gdns
HTCHE/RSTV SG4 52 F5
Mowbray Rd BAR EN5 201 H5
HLW CM20 7 K2
Moxes Wd LTNN/LIM LU3 64 D3
Moxom Av CHES/WCR EN8 190 D1
Moxon St BAR EN5 200 E4
Mozart Ct STVG SG1 4 A3
Muddy La LWTH SG6 39 L7
Muirfield LTNE LU2 65 K4
Muirfield Cl OXHEY WD19 206 B5 5
OXHEY WD19 206 B5 6
Muirfield Gn OXHEY WD19 206 B4 1
Muirfield Rd OXHEY WD19 206 A4
Muirhead Wy KNEB SG3 88 E5 1
Mulberry Cl BROX EN10 176 E3
EBAR EN4 201 J5
LCOL/BKTW AL2 169 G7 1
LTN LU1 83 G3
TRING HP23 123 M5 2
Mulberry Ct BSF CM23 96 F5
Mulberry Gdns RAD WD7 184 D4
Mulberry Gn HLWE CM17 142 C6
Mulberry Wy HTCH/STOT SG5 38 C8
Mullion Cl KTN/HRWW/W HA3 207 G8
LTNE LU2 66 A6
Mullion Wk OXHEY WD19 206 C4 5
Mullway LWTH SG6 39 H4
Mundells CHESW EN7 175 M6
WGCE AL7 134 E3
Munden Gv WATN WD24 196 B1
Munden Rd WARE SG12 91 K3
Mundesley Cl STVG SG1 70 A1
Mundesly Cl OXHEY WD19 206 B4 2
Mungo-park Cl BUSH WD23 207 H2 3
Munro Rd BUSH WD23 197 G6
The Muntings STVGE SG2 5 J7
Munts Meadow
HTCHE/RSTV SG4 55 H1
Murchison Rd HOD EN11 160 A2
Muriel Av WATW WD18 13 H7
Murray Crs PIN HA5 206 C8
Murray Rd BERK HP4 147 H5
NTHWD HA6 205 K8
Murrell La HTCH/STOT SG5 26 F5
Murton Ct STAL AL1 11 H5
Musgrave Cl CHESW EN7 175 L6 3
EBAR EN4 201 H2
Muskalls Cl CHESW EN7 175 M6 1
Muskham Rd HLW CM20 7 M1
Musk Hl HHW HP1 148 D8
Musleigh Mnr WARE SG12 138 E1 3
Musley Hl WARE SG12 116 D8
Musley La WARE SG12 116 D8
Mussons Pth LTNE LU2 2 E4
Muswell Cl LTNN/LIM LU3 65 G4
Mutchetts Cl GSTN WD25 182 D4
Mutford Cft LTNE LU2 84 C1 2
Mutton La POTB/CUF EN6 186 C2
Myddleton Rd WARE SG12 138 C2
Myers Cl RAD WD7 184 D3 3
Myles Ct CHESW EN7 175 H8
Mylne Cl CHES/WCR EN8 176 B6
Mymms Dr BRKMPK AL9 172 F6
Myrtleside Cl NTHWD HA6 205 J7

N

Nails La BSF CM23 96 E3 4
Nairn Cl HARP AL5 131 J4
Nairn Gn OXHEY WD19 205 M3
Nancy Downs OXHEY WD19 196 B8
Napier Cl LCOL/BKTW AL2 170 C4
Napier Dr BUSH WD23 13 L5
Napier Rd LTN LU1 2 C7
Nappsbury Rd LTNW/LEA LU4 64 C5
Napsbury Av LCOL/BKTW AL2 170 B5
Napsbury La LCOL/BKTW AL2 169 M4
STAL AL1 169 M2
The Nap KGLGY WD4 166 F8
Nascot Pl WAT WD17 196 A3
Nascot Rd WAT WD17 196 A3
Nascot St WAT WD17 12 E1
Nascot Wood Rd WAT WD17 181 L8
Naseby Rd LTN LU1 83 G3
Nash Cl BORE WD6 198 E5
BRKMPK AL9 172 C2
DUN/HR/TOD LU5 63 J5
STVGE SG2 5 L2
Nash Mills La HHS/BOV HP3 166 E5
Nash Rd ROY SG8 21 J5 3
Nathaniel Wk TRING HP23 123 M5
Nathans Cl WLYN AL6 112 B3
Nayland Cl LTNE LU2 84 D1 3
Nazeingbury Cl WAB EN9 177 J1 1
Neal Cl NTHWD HA6 205 M8
Neal Ct HERT/WAS SG14 137 H4
Neal St WATW WD18 13 G6
Neaole Cl BORE WD6 199 H2 2
Necton Rd STALE/WH AL4 132 D2
Needham Rd LTNW/LEA LU4 64 A4
Neild Wy RKW/CH/CXG WD3 193 L8
Nell Gwynn Cl RAD WD7 184 D3
Nelson Av STAL AL1 170 A2
Nelson Rd BERK HP4 104 B5
BSF CM23 96 F5
Nelson St HERT/WAS SG14 137 G3 1
Nene Rd HNLW SG16 25 G6
Neptune Dr HHNE HP2 8 D5
Neptune Ga STVGE SG2 71 J1
Neston Rd WATN WD24 182 B8
Netherby Cl TRING HP23 124 A4
Nethercott Cl LTNE LU2 84 B1 1
Netherfield La WARE SG12 139 J7
Netherfield Rd HARP AL5 131 G6
Netherhall Rd
HLWW/ROY CM19 160 E4
Netherlands Rd BAR EN5 201 J7
Netherstones HTCH/STOT SG5 26 E3 1
Nether St WARE SG12 118 D5
Netherway STALW/RED AL3 168 F2
Netley Dell LWTH SG6 40 A7
Netteswellbury Farm
HLWS CM18 7 J8
Netteswell Orch HLW CM20 6 E4
Netteswell Rd HLW CM20 7 G2
Nettle Cl LTNW/LEA LU4 63 K7 2
Nettlecroft HHW HP1 149 G8
WGCE AL7 135 G3 4
Nettleden Rd BERK HP4 126 B3
Nevell's Gn LWTH SG6 39 L3
Nevells Rd LWTH SG6 39 L4
Nevil Cl NTHWD HA6 205 J5
Neville Cl POTB/CUF EN6 186 E2
Neville Rd LTNN/LIM LU3 64 F5
Nevill Gv WATN WD24 196 A2
Newark Cl ROY SG8 21 H2
Newark Gn BORE WD6 199 K4
Newark Rd LTNW/LEA LU4 64 F8
New Barnes Av STAL AL1 169 M2
New Barn La RBSF CM22 121 H1
New Barns La MHAD SG10 94 D6
New Bedford Rd LTN LU1 2 D6
LTNE LU2 2 D4 1
Newberries Av RAD WD7 184 B6
Newbiggin Pth OXHEY WD19 206 B4 3
Newbold Rd LTNN/LIM LU3 65 G3
Newbolt Rd STAN HA7 207 L6 5
Newbury Av PEND EN3 190 E8
Newbury Cl BSF CM23 96 D2
LTNW/LEA LU4 64 D8
STVG SG1 70 C1 1
Newbury Rd DUN/HR/TOD LU5 63 K4
Newcastle Cl STVG SG1 54 E8 2
New Cl KNEB SG3 88 E4
Newcombe Rd LTN LU1 2 A6
Newcome Rd RAD WD7 184 F5
New Cottages BRKMPK AL9 172 C7
New Ct KNEB SG3 88 F8 3
Newdigate Gn DEN/HRF UB9 204 C8
Newdigate Rd DEN/HRF UB9 204 B8
Newdigate Rd East
DEN/HRF UB9 204 C8
Newell La STVGE SG2 56 B3
Newell Ri HHS/BOV HP3 166 D2
Newell Rd HHS/BOV HP3 166 D2
Newells LWTH SG6 40 C6
Newells Hedge LBUZ LU7 102 C5 1
New England Cl
HTCHE/RSTV SG4 52 E6 1
New England St STALW/RED AL3 10 B6
New Farm La NTHWD HA6 205 K8
Newfield La HHNE HP2 8 E9
Newfields WGCW AL8 134 A5
Newfield Wy STALE/WH AL4 170 C1 1
Newford Cl HHNE HP2 9 J6
New Ford Rd CHES/WCR EN8 190 E5
Newgate STVGE SG2 5 K7
Newgate Cl STALE/WH AL4 153 J4
Newgate St HERT/BAY SG13 174 C2
Newgatestreet Rd CHESW EN7 175 G5
Newgate Street Village
HERT/BAY SG13 174 D4
New Greens Av STALW/RED AL3 152 C2
Newground Rd TRING HP23 125 G7
Newhall Cl HHS/BOV HP3 164 F6 2
Newhouse Crs GSTN WD25 182 A4
New House Pk STAL AL1 169 M2
Newhouse Rd HHW HP1 164 F5
New Inn Rd BLDK SG7 17 J6
New Kent Rd STAL AL1 10 F7
Newland Cl PIN HA5 206 D6
STAL AL1 169 M2
Newlands LWTH SG6 39 M7
Newlands Av RAD WD7 183 L5
Newlands Cl East
HTCHE/RSTV SG4 52 E6 2
Newlands Cl West
HTCHE/RSTV SG4 52 E6 3
Newlands La HTCHE/RSTV SG4 52 E6
Newlands Pl BAR EN5 200 C6
Newlands Rd HHW HP1 148 D6
LTN LU1 83 H7
Newlands Wk GSTN WD25 182 C4
Newlands Wy
POTB/CUF EN6 187 G1 1
Newlyn Cl LCOL/BKTW AL2 182 D1
STVG SG1 69 M4
Newlyn Rd BAR EN5 200 E5 1
Newman Av ROY SG8 21 L4
Newmans Dr HARP AL5 108 E8
Newman's Wy EBAR EN4 201 H3
Newmarket Rd ROY SG8 21 K4
Newnham Cl LTNE LU2 84 C1
Newnham Rd BLDK SG7 27 L3
Newnham Wy BLDK SG7 27 M1
New Park Dr HHNE HP2 9 J7
New Park La STVGE SG2 71 K8
New Park Rd DEN/HRF UB9 204 B8
HERT/BAY SG13 174 B3
New Pl WLYN AL6 112 A6 3
Newport Cl PEND EN3 190 D8 5
Newport Md OXHEY WD19 206 C4 6
Newports SBW CM21 142 B1
Newquay Gdns OXHEY WD19 206 A2
New River Av WARE SG12 139 G6
New River Cl HOD EN11 160 A3
New Rd BERK HP4 146 E3
BERK HP4 147 J5
BROX EN10 159 L6
CSTG HP8 192 D4
GSTN WD25 197 K2
HERT/WAS SG14 137 J2
HLWE CM17 142 C6
KGLGY WD4 179 L1
KNEB SG3 89 G7
POTB/CUF EN6 185 M4
RAD WD7 183 K7
RAD WD7 184 F5
RAYLNE/WEN HP22 122 D5
RKW/CH/CXG WD3 193 L2
RKW/CH/CXG WD3 194 F6
ROY SG8 15 M5
ROY SG8 23 G1
ROY SG8 23 K6
SHFD SG17 24 F1
STDN SG11 94 F3
TRING HP23 123 H1
TRING HP23 124 A4
WARE SG12 138 D1
WAT WD17 13 H5
WGCW AL8 133 M7
WLYN AL6 112 M7
Newstead HAT AL10 154 E8
New St BERK HP4 147 J6
LBUZ LU7 101 L3
LTN LU1 2 D8
LTN LU1 107 H1
SBW CM21 120 D7
WATW WD18 13 G4
Newteswell Dr WAB EN9 191 J3
Newton Cl HARP AL5 131 J4 5
HOD EN11 139 G8
Newton Crs BORE WD6 199 H5 2
Newtondale LTNW/LEA LU4 64 B5 4
Newton Dr SBW CM21 142 C1
Newton Rd KTN/HRWW/W HA3 207 K8
STVGE SG2 5 L1
Newtons Wy HTCHE/RSTV SG4 52 E4
New Town WLYN AL6 111 L1
Newtown Rd BSF CM23 96 E4
New Town Rd LTN LU1 2 F9
New Town St LTN LU1 2 F9
New Wk HTCH/STOT SG5 36 E1
New Wd WGCE AL7 135 H3
New Woodfield Gn
DUN/HR/TOD LU5 81 K4
Niagara Cl CHES/WCR EN8 176 C8 1
Nicholas Cl STALW/RED AL3 152 C4
WATN WD24 182 A8
Nicholas La HERT/WAS SG14 137 J4 11
Nicholas Pl STVG SG1 70 C1
Nicholas Rd BORE WD6 198 E7
Nicholas Wy HHNE HP2 8 F5
NTHWD HA6 205 H8
Nicholls Cl AMP/FLIT/B MK45 35 G7
STALW/RED AL3 129 L5
Nicholls Fld HLWS CM18 163 G3
Nichols Cl LTNE LU2 66 A8
Nicholson Dr BUSH WD23 207 H1
Nicky Line HHNE HP2 8 C7
STALW/RED AL3 129 M6
Nicoll Wy BORE WD6 199 J6
Nicol Rd CFSP/GDCR SL9 202 B8
Nightingale Cl ABLGY WD5 181 M2 2
LTNE LU2 66 B4
RAD WD7 183 L7
Nightingale La STAL AL1 170 B3
STALE/WH AL4 170 B2
Nightingale Pl
RKW/CH/CXG WD3 194 C8 2
Nightingale Rd BUSH WD23 196 F6
CHESW EN7 175 H4
HTCH/STOT SG5 52 E2
RKW/CH/CXG WD3 194 B8
Nightingales La CSTG HP8 192 C6
Nightingale Wk STVGE SG2 71 H5
Nightingale Wy BLDK SG7 40 D4
Nimbus Wy HTCHE/RSTV SG4 53 H3 2
Nimrod Cl STALE/WH AL4 153 H5
Ninefields WAB EN9 191 L4
Ninesprings Wy
HTCHE/RSTV SG4 53 H4
Ninian Rd HHNE HP2 149 K2
Ninning's La WLYN AL6 88 C8
Ninnings Rd CFSP/GDCR SL9 202 E7
Ninnings Wy CFSP/GDCR SL9 202 E7 3
Ninth Av LTNN/LIM LU3 64 C3
Niton Cl BAR EN5 200 C7
Niven Cl BORE WD6 199 H2 3
The Nobles BSF CM23 96 C4 1
Nodes Dr STVGE SG2 88 F1
Noke La LCOL/BKTW AL2 168 D5
Noke Shot HARP AL5 109 H6
Noke Side LCOL/BKTW AL2 168 F6 1
Nokeside STVGE SG2 89 G2
The Nokes HHW HP1 148 F5 3
The Noke STVGE SG2 89 G2
The Nook WARE SG12 139 G6 2
Norbury Av WATN WD24 196 B2
Norcott Cl DUN/HR/TOD LU5 81 J3
Norfolk Av WATN WD24 196 B1
Norfolk Cl EBAR EN4 201 M5
Norfolk Gdns BORE WD6 199 J5
Norfolk Rd BAR EN5 200 F4
BUNT SG9 58 C2
DUN/HR/TOD LU5 81 K4
LTNE LU2 3 K6
RKW/CH/CXG WD3 204 D1
Norfolk Wy BSF CM23 96 E5
Norman Av BSF CM23 96 C4
Norman Cl WAB EN9 191 J4
Norman Ct POTB/CUF EN6 187 H1
Norman Crs PIN HA5 206 B8
Normandy Av BAR EN5 200 E6
Normandy Ct HHNE HP2 8 B7
Normandy Dr BERK HP4 146 F5
Normandy Rd STALW/RED AL3 10 E4
Norman Rd AMP/FLIT/B MK45 35 H7
LTNN/LIM LU3 65 G8
WLYN AL6 112 A7 1
Normans Cl LWTH SG6 39 L1
Normansfield Cl BUSH WD23 197 G8 1
Normans La WLYN AL6 88 D8
Norman's Wy STSD CM24 79 K3
Norman Wy DUN/WHIP LU6 80 D2
Norris Cl BSF CM23 97 H3
Norris Gv BROX EN10 159 K7
Norris La HOD EN11 159 M3
Norris Ri HOD EN11 159 L3
Norris Rd HOD EN11 159 M4
Norrys Cl EBAR EN4 201 L6
Norrys Rd EBAR EN4 201 L5
North Ap GSTN WD25 181 M5
RKW/CH/CXG WD3 205 H2
North Av LWTH SG6 40 A2
RAD WD7 184 D3
Northaw Cl HHNE HP2 150 A2
Northaw Rd West
POTB/CUF EN6 187 M1
North Barn BROX EN10 177 G1
North Bridge Rd BERK HP4 146 E4
Northbrook Dr NTHWD HA6 205 K8
Northbrook Rd BAR EN5 200 D7
Northbrooks HLWW/ROY CM19 6 C9
Northchurch La CSHM HP5 146 B8
North Cl BAR EN5 200 B6
LCOL/BKTW AL2 169 G4
ROY SG8 21 H3
North Common Rd
STALW/RED AL3 129 M6
Northcourt
RKW/CH/CXG WD3 203 M1 4
Northdown Rd CFSP/GDCR SL9 202 D6
HAT AL10 154 F8
North Drift Wy LTN LU1 83 G4
North Dr STDN SG11 116 E1
Northend HHS/BOV HP3 167 G1
Northern Av HNLW SG16 25 G7
Northfield STDN SG11 75 L3 2
Northfield Gdns WATN WD24 182 B8
Northfield Rd BLDK SG7 18 B2
BORE WD6 199 G2
CHES/WCR EN8 190 D3
EBAR EN4 201 K4
HARP AL5 109 H6
SBW CM21 120 D6
TRING HP23 124 D2
Northfields DUN/HR/TOD LU5 62 E7
LWTH SG6 39 L1
North Ga HLW CM20 6 D5
Northgate NTHWD HA6 205 H7
Northgate End BSF CM23 96 E2
Northgate Pth BORE WD6 198 E1 1
North Gv HLWS CM18 7 M8
North Hl RKW/CH/CXG WD3 193 K3
Northlands POTB/CUF EN6 187 J2
Northolt Av BSF CM23 97 G1
North Orbital Rd
LCOL/BKTW AL2 168 E7
STALE/WH AL4 154 B8
North Orbital Road St Albans Rd
GSTN WD25 182 C4
North Pl HLW CM20 141 M5
WAB EN9 191 G4 2
North Ride WLYN AL6 112 B4
Northridge Wy HHW HP1 148 E8
North Riding LCOL/BKTW AL2 182 F1
North Rd BERK HP4 147 G6
BLDK SG7 27 K8
CHES/WCR EN8 190 D4
HERT/WAS SG14 137 H4
HOD EN11 159 M3
RBSF CM22 99 H2
RKW/CH/CXG WD3 193 J6
STVG SG1 54 B8
North Road Av HERT/WAS SG14 136 F3
North Road Gdns
HERT/WAS SG14 137 G4
North Station Wy
DUN/WHIP LU6 80 E1
North St BSF CM23 96 E2
LTNE LU2 2 F3
WAB EN9 177 K1
North Ter BSF CM23 96 E2
Northumberland Rd BAR EN5 201 H7
Northview Rd DUN/HR/TOD LU5 62 F8
LTNE LU2 65 L8
Northway RKW/CH/CXG WD3 194 C8
WGCE AL7 134 E1 2
Northwell Dr LTNN/LIM LU3 64 D1
North Western Av GSTN WD25 181 M6
WATN WD24 181 L6
North Western Av Colne Wy
WATN WD24 182 B7
North Western Av Elton Wy
GSTN WD25 197 G3
North Western Av Gade Side
KGLGY WD4 181 H6
WAT WD17 181 J6
North Western Av Otterspool Wy
GSTN WD25 196 E1
North Western Av
(Tylers Way) BUSH WD23 197 H5
North Western Av
(Watford By-pass) STAN HA7 197 M7
Northwick Rd OXHEY WD19 206 B4
Northwood WGCE AL7 135 J4 2
Northwood Cl CHESW EN7 175 L6 6
Northwood Rd DEN/HRF UB9 204 D8
Northwood Wy DEN/HRF UB9 204 C8
NTHWD HA6 205 M8
Nortoft Rd CFSP/GDCR SL9 202 E6
Norton Bury La LWTH SG6 27 H8
Norton Cl BORE WD6 198 F2
Norton Crs BLDK SG7 40 D2
Norton Green Rd STVG SG1 4 B7
Norton Mill La LWTH SG6 27 J7
Norton Rd HTCH/STOT SG5 26 F5
LTNN/LIM LU3 64 E6
LWTH SG6 39 M2
STVG SG1 4 B6
Nortonstreet La
HTCHE/RSTV SG4 87 H3
Norton Wy North LWTH SG6 39 M2
Norton Wy South LWTH SG6 39 M4
Norvic Rd TRING HP23 123 M1
Norwich Cl STVG SG1 71 G1
Norwich Wy RKW/CH/CXG WD3 195 G4
Norwood Cl HERT/WAS SG14 136 E3
Norwood Rd CHES/WCR EN8 190 D1
Nottingham Cl GSTN WD25 181 M4 2
Nottingham Rd
RKW/CH/CXG WD3 203 H1
Novello Wy BORE WD6 199 J2
Nugent's Pk PIN HA5 206 E8
Nunnery Cl STAL AL1 169 K1
Nunnery La LTNN/LIM LU3 65 G5
Nunnery Stables STAL AL1 169 J1
Nunsbury Dr BROX EN10 176 D4 2
Nun's Cl HTCH/STOT SG5 52 D3
Nuns La STAL AL1 169 K3
Nupton Dr BAR EN5 200 B7
Nurseries Rd STALE/WH AL4 132 D3
Nursery Cl DUN/WHIP LU6 80 F2 1
STVGE SG2 88 F2
Nursery Flds SBW CM21 120 C8
Nursery Gdns TRING HP23 124 A6
WGCE AL7 134 D1 2
Nursery Hl WGCE AL7 134 E1 3
Nursery Rd BROX EN10 176 D4 3
BSF CM23 96 E4
HOD EN11 160 A1
LTNN/LIM LU3 64 E5
WAB EN9 177 J1
Nutcroft KNEB SG3 89 J8
Nutfield WGCE AL7 134 F1
Nut Gv WGCW AL8 134 C1
Nuthampstead Rd ROY SG8 32 C8
Nutleigh Gv HTCH/STOT SG5 52 C1
Nut Slip BUNT SG9 58 D4 2
Nuttfield Cl
RKW/CH/CXG WD3 195 G7 1
Nye Wy HHS/BOV HP3 164 F7
Nymans Cl LTNE LU2 66 C7

O

Oak Av LCOL/BKTW AL2 182 F1
Oak Cl DUN/HR/TOD LU5 81 J2 2
HHS/BOV HP3 166 E3
WAB EN9 191 J5
Oakdale WGCW AL8 134 C1
Oakdale Cl OXHEY WD19 206 B4
Oakdale Rd OXHEY WD19 206 B3
Oakdene CHES/WCR EN8 190 D1
Oakdene Cl PIN HA5 206 E7
Oakdene Rd HHS/BOV HP3 166 E3
WATN WD24 182 A7
Oakdene Wy STAL AL1 153 H7
Oak Dr BERK HP4 147 J7
HNLW SG16 25 J1
SBW CM21 142 B2
Oak End BUNT SG9 58 C4
HLWS CM18 162 E4 2
Oaken Gv WGCE AL7 134 D7 4
Oak Farm BORE WD6 199 H6
Oakfield RKW/CH/CXG WD3 193 M8
Oakfield Av HTCHE/RSTV SG4 53 G5
Oakfield Cl POTB/CUF EN6 186 E2 1
Oakfield Rd HARP AL5 130 F5
Oakfields STVGE SG2 89 G1
Oakfields Av KNEB SG3 88 F4
Oakfields Cl STVGE SG2 89 H1
Oakfields Rd KNEB SG3 88 F4
Oak Gld NTHWD HA6 205 G8
Oak Gn ABLGY WD5 181 K3
Oak Gv HAT AL10 154 E5
HERT/BAY SG13 137 K6
Oakhill LWTH SG6 40 C6
Oakhill Cl RKW/CH/CXG WD3 203 K4
Oakhill Dr WLYN AL6 111 M4
Oakhill Rd RKW/CH/CXG WD3 203 J4
Oakhurst Av EBAR EN4 201 K8
HARP AL5 130 E4
Oakhurst Rd PEND EN3 190 C7
Oakington WGCE AL7 135 J4 3
Oakington Av AMS HP6 192 D2
Oaklands BERK HP4 146 F6
Oaklands Av BRKMPK AL9 172 D6
OXHEY WD19 206 A1
Oaklands Cl BSF CM23 79 G8
Oaklands Ct WAT WD17 195 M2
Oaklands Dr BSF CM23 97 G1
HLWE CM17 163 H3
Oaklands Ga NTHWD HA6 205 K6 2
Oaklands Gv BROX EN10 176 D3
Oaklands La BAR EN5 200 A5
STALE/WH AL4 153 L5
Oaklands Pk BSF CM23 79 G8
Oaklands Ri WLYN AL6 112 E3
Oaklands Rd CHESW EN7 175 K5
TRDG/WHET N20 200 E8
Oak La HTCHE/RSTV SG4 54 A6
POTB/CUF EN6 174 E7
TRING HP23 144 F8
Oaklea WLYN AL6 112 D3
Oaklea Cl WLYN AL6 112 D2
Oaklea Wd WLYN AL6 112 D3
Oakleigh Dr RKW/CH/CXG WD3 195 H7
Oakleigh Rd PIN HA5 206 E6
Oakley Cl LTNW/LEA LU4 64 C6
Oakley Rd HARP AL5 131 J3
LTNW/LEA LU4 64 C6
Oakmeade PIN HA5 206 F6
Oakmere Av POTB/CUF EN6 187 H4
Oakmere Cl POTB/CUF EN6 187 J2
Oakmere La POTB/CUF EN6 187 H3
Oak Piece WLYN AL6 112 C3
Oakridge LCOL/BKTW AL2 168 E8
Oakridge Av RAD WD7 183 L4
Oakridge La GSTN WD25 183 K5
Oak Rd KNEB SG3 113 G1
Oakroyd Av POTB/CUF EN6 186 E4
Oakroyd Cl POTB/CUF EN6 186 E5
Oaks Cl HTCHE/RSTV SG4 52 E5
RAD WD7 183 L6
Oaks Cross STVGE SG2 89 G2
The Oaks BERK HP4 146 F6
LTN LU1 107 H1
OXHEY WD19 206 B1
Oak St BSF CM23 96 E4
HHS/BOV HP3 166 E3
Oak Tree Cl ABLGY WD5 181 J3
Oaktree Cl BSF CM23 96 E3
Oak Tree Cl HAT AL10 154 F4
HERT/BAY SG13 138 B7
STVGE SG2 72 E6 1
Oak Tree Ct BORE WD6 198 C7 4
Oaktree Garth WGCE AL7 134 D5 3
Oakview Cl CHESW EN7 176 A7
Oakway DUN/WHIP LU6 105 G3
Oak Wy HARP AL5 130 F5
STHGT/OAK N14 201 M8
Oakwell Cl DUN/WHIP LU6 80 E3
STVGE SG2 89 J3
Oakwell Dr POTB/CUF EN6 188 A4
Oak Wd BERK HP4 146 E7
Oakwood Av BORE WD6 199 G5
DUN/HR/TOD LU5 81 K3
Oakwood Cl STVGE SG2 71 H8
Oakwood Dr LTNN/LIM LU3 64 B2
STALE/WH AL4 153 H6
Oakwood Rd LCOL/BKTW AL2 168 E8
Oatfield Cl LTNW/LEA LU4 63 L6

Oberon Cl BORE WD6 199 H2
Obrey Wy BSF CM23 96 D7
Occupation Rd WATW WD18 12 E6
Octavia Ct WATN WD24 13 H1
Oddy Hl TRING HP23 124 B7
Odessey Rd BORE WD6 199 G2
Offa Rd STALW/RED AL3 10 C6
Offas Wy STALE/WH AL4 132 C2
Offley Hl HTCH/STOT SG5 51 H7
Offley Rd HTCH/STOT SG5 52 C4
Ogard Rd HOD EN11 160 B2
Okeford Cl TRING HP23 123 L6
Okeford Dr TRING HP23 123 L7
Okeley La TRING HP23 123 K7
Old Barn La RKW/CH/CXG WD3 194 E6
Old Bedford Rd LTN LU1 2 E6
LTNE LU2 2 D3
Old Bell Cl STSD CM24 79 J4
Old Bourne Wy STVG SG1 54 F7
Old Brewery Cl HTCH/STOT SG5 26 E3 2
Old Burylodge La STSD CM24 79 M6
Old Chantry La STVG SG1 53 M8
Old Charlton Rd HTCH/STOT SG5 52 D4
Old Church La WARE SG12 116 D3
The Old Coach Rd
HERT/WAS SG14 135 L7
Old Crabtree La HHS/BOV HP3 149 K8
Old Cross HERT/WAS SG14 137 H4 6
Old Cross B158
HERT/WAS SG14 137 H4 7
Old Dean HHS/BOV HP3 164 F7
The Old Dr WGCW AL8 134 A5
Olden Md LWTH SG6 40 A7
Old Farm LBUZ LU7 102 C6
Old Field Cl AMS HP6 192 D2
Oldfield Cl STAN HA7 207 M5
Oldfield Farm Rd HNLW SG16 25 G6
Oldfield Ri HTCHE/RSTV SG4 86 D3
Oldfield Rd HHW HP1 148 D8
LCOL/BKTW AL2 170 C4
Old Fishery La HHW HP1 165 L1
Old Fold Cl BAR EN5 200 E2 2
Old Fold La BAR EN5 200 E2
Old Fold Vw BAR EN5 200 B4
Old Forge Cl GSTN WD25 181 M4
STAN HA7 207 M4
WGCE AL7 112 E8
Old French Horn La HAT AL10 155 G4
Old Gannon Cl NTHWD HA6 205 H4
Old Hale Wy HTCH/STOT SG5 52 D1
Old Hall Cl PIN HA5 206 D8
Old Hall Dr PIN HA5 206 D8
Old Hall Ri HLWE CM17 163 K2
Oldhall St HERT/WAS SG14 137 J4 12
Old Harpenden Rd
STALW/RED AL3 152 D3
Old Herns La WGCE AL7 135 H2
Old Hertford Rd BRKMPK AL9 155 H3
Old Hwy HOD EN11 160 A2
Oldhill DUN/WHIP LU6 81 H4
Oldhouse Cft HLW CM20 7 H3
Old House La HLWW/ROY CM19 161 J5
KGLGY WD4 180 F6
Old House Rd HHNE HP2 8 E8
Oldings Cnr HAT AL10 155 G1
Old Knebworth La KNEB SG3 88 B4
Old La KNEB SG3 89 G5
Old Leys HAT AL10 171 M1
Old Lodge Wy STAN HA7 207 M5
Old London Rd HERT/BAY SG13 137 K4
STAL AL1 10 F8
The Old Maltings BSF CM23 96 F3 2
Old Maple HHNE HP2 149 L1
Old Md CFSP/GDCR SL9 202 D6
Old Mill Gdns BERK HP4 147 J6
Old Mill La RBSF CM22 121 G4
Old Mill Rd KGLGY WD4 181 H5
Old Nazeing Rd BROX EN10 159 M8
WAB EN9 177 H1
Old North Rd ROY SG8 21 H2
Old Oak STAL AL1 169 K2
Old Oak Cl ARL/CHE SG15 25 M2
Old Oaks WAB EN9 191 K3 3
Old Orch HLWS CM18 162 C4
LCOL/BKTW AL2 169 J5
LTN LU1 83 J5
Old Orchard Ms BERK HP4 147 H7 1
Old Parkbury La
LCOL/BKTW AL2 169 L8
Oldpark Ride CHESW EN7 189 J3
Old Park Rd HTCH/STOT SG5 52 D3
Old Rectory Cl HARP AL5 108 F8 2
Old Rectory Dr HAT AL10 155 G5 1
Old Rectory Gdns
STALE/WH AL4 132 C1
Old Redding
KTN/HRWW/W HA3 207 G5
Old River La BSF CM23 96 E3 3
Old Rd AMP/FLIT/B MK45 49 H1
HLWE CM17 142 B4
Old's Ap WATW WD18 205 H1
Old School Cl HTCHE/RSTV SG4 111 L1
Old School Gdns
AMP/FLIT/B MK45 35 H8 1
Old School Gn STVGE SG2 72 D5
Old School Wk ARL/CHE SG15 25 M6
Old's Cl WATW WD18 205 G1
Old Shire La CFSP/GDCR SL9 203 G3
RKW/CH/CXG WD3 192 F7
WAB EN9 191 M5
Old Shire Lane Circular Wk
RKW/CH/CXG WD3 193 H8
Old Sopwell Gdns STAL AL1 169 K1
Old South Cl PIN HA5 206 C8
Old Uxbridge Rd
RKW/CH/CXG WD3 203 K7
Old Vicarage Gdns
STALW/RED AL3 106 C4 1
The Old Walled Gdn STVG SG1 70 B1
Old Watford Rd
LCOL/BKTW AL2 182 D1
Old Watling St STALW/RED AL3 107 G6
Oldwood WLYN AL6 112 D3
Oliver Cl HHS/BOV HP3 166 D3
LCOL/BKTW AL2 169 J6
Oliver Ri HHS/BOV HP3 166 D3
Oliver Rd HHS/BOV HP3 166 E3
Olivers Cl BERK HP4 148 B3
Oliver's La HTCH/STOT SG5 26 E3
Olivia Gdns DEN/HRF UB9 204 B8
Olleberrie La
RKW/CH/CXG WD3 179 K3
Olma Rd DUN/HR/TOD LU5 62 F8
Olympic Cl LTNN/LIM LU3 64 D1
Olympus Rd HNLW SG16 25 G6
Onslow Cl HAT AL10 155 G5
Onslow Rd LTNW/LEA LU4 64 C5
On the Hl OXHEY WD19 206 D2
The Opening WLYN AL6 111 L2 1
Openshaw Wy LWTH SG6 39 M4
Oram Pl HHS/BOV HP3 166 C2
Orbital Crs GSTN WD25 181 L6
Orchard BUSH WD23 207 J1
Orchard Av BERK HP4 146 F6
GSTN WD25 182 A2
HARP AL5 130 E1
Orchard Cl AMP/FLIT/B MK45 49 H1
BORE WD6 198 E4 1
DUN/HR/TOD LU5 63 G7
HHNE HP2 8 F5
HTCHE/RSTV SG4 52 E7
LWTH SG6 39 L2
POTB/CUF EN6 174 D7
RAD WD7 183 K8
RBSF CM22 143 H2
RKW/CH/CXG WD3 193 J4
SHFD SG17 24 B4
STAL AL1 11 K9
WARE SG12 116 C8 3
WARE SG12 139 H6
WAT WD17 195 L3
Orchard Crs STVG SG1 70 B3
Orchard Cft HLW CM20 7 L3
Orchard Dr LCOL/BKTW AL2 169 G5
RAYLNE/WEN HP22 122 D6 1
RKW/CH/CXG WD3 193 H4
WAT WD17 195 L2
Orchard Gdns WAB EN9 191 G5
Orchard Gv CFSP/GDCR SL9 202 B8
Orchard House La STAL AL1 10 E8
Orchard Md HAT AL10 154 E5
The Orchard on the Gn
RKW/CH/CXG WD3 194 E6
Orchard Rd AMP/FLIT/B MK45 34 D2
BAR EN5 200 D5
BLDK SG7 40 D2
BSF CM23 97 G1
HTCHE/RSTV SG4 53 G1
ROY SG8 21 G3
STVG SG1 70 A2
WLYN AL6 112 B5 4
Orchard Sq BROX EN10 176 E3 1
The Orchards LTN LU1 83 H8
SBW CM21 120 D8 1
TRING HP23 123 L7
Orchard St HHS/BOV HP3 166 C2 2
STALW/RED AL3 10 D8
The Orchard BLDK SG7 40 E2
HERT/WAS SG14 137 G1
KGLGY WD4 166 F8
RAYLNE/WEN HP22 122 D5
WARE SG12 115 K3
WGCW AL8 134 C2
WLYN AL6 111 K1
Orchard Wy CHESW EN7 175 G6
HHS/BOV HP3 164 F7
HNLW SG16 24 F7
HTCHE/RSTV SG4 85 K1
KNEB SG3 88 D5
LBUZ LU7 102 D5
LTNW/LEA LU4 64 B6
LWTH SG6 39 L2
POTB/CUF EN6 173 G7
RKW/CH/CXG WD3 193 M8
ROY SG8 21 H2
Orchid Cl DUN/WHIP LU6 80 D1
Ordelmere LWTH SG6 39 L1
Ordnance Rd PEND EN3 190 C8
Oregon Wy LTNN/LIM LU3 64 F2
Organ Hall Rd BORE WD6 198 D2
Orient Cl STAL AL1 169 K1
Oriole Cl ABLGY WD5 181 M2 3
Oriole Wy BSF CM23 96 B4
Orion Wy NTHWD HA6 205 L4
Orlando Cl HTCHE/RSTV SG4 52 F4 4
Ormesby Dr POTB/CUF EN6 186 C3
Ormonde Rd NTHWD HA6 205 J4
Ormsby Cl LTN LU1 83 K5
Ormskirk Rd OXHEY WD19 206 C4
Oronsay HHS/BOV HP3 167 G1
Orphanage Rd WAT WD17 13 G1 1
Orpington Cl LTNW/LEA LU4 63 M7 2
Orton Cl STALE/WH AL4 152 F3
Orwell Ct WATN WD24 13 J2
Orwell Vw BLDK SG7 41 G1
Osborne Cl EBAR EN4 201 L4 1
Osborne Gdns
POTB/CUF EN6 187 G1 2
Osborne Rd BROX EN10 159 M6
CHES/WCR EN8 176 D6 2
DUN/WHIP LU6 81 G3
LTN LU1 3 H9
POTB/CUF EN6 187 G1
WATN WD24 196 B1 3
Osborne Wy TRING HP23 145 J1
Osborn Rd AMP/FLIT/B MK45 35 J7
Osborn Wy WGCW AL8 134 C3 1
Osbourne Av KGLGY WD4 166 E7
Osmington Pl TRING HP23 123 L6
Osprey Gdns STVGE SG2 71 J8
Osprey Rd WAB EN9 191 M5
Osterley Cl STVGE SG2 89 H3
Oster St STALW/RED AL3 10 D5
Ostler Cl BSF CM23 96 B6 4
Oswald Rd STAL AL1 11 H8
Otley Wy OXHEY WD19 206 B3
Otter Gdns HAT AL10 155 G6
Otterspool La GSTN WD25 196 D1
Otterspool Wy GSTN WD25 196 E2
Otterton Cl HARP AL5 108 E7 1
Ottoman Ter WAT WD17 13 H2 1
Ottway Wk WLYN AL6 112 A6
Otway Gdns BUSH WD23 197 K8
Otways Cl POTB/CUF EN6 187 G4 1
Oudle La MHAD SG10 94 E7
Oughtonhead La
HTCH/STOT SG5 52 A2
Oughton Head Wy
HTCH/STOT SG5 52 C2
Oulton Crs POTB/CUF EN6 186 C3
Oulton Ri HARP AL5 109 H7
Oulton Wy OXHEY WD19 206 E4
Oundle Av BUSH WD23 197 H7
Oundle Ct STVGE SG2 89 H2
Oundle Pth STVGE SG2 89 H2
The Oundle STVGE SG2 89 H1
Ousden Cl CHES/WCR EN8 190 D1
Ousden Dr CHES/WCR EN8 190 D1
Ouseley Cl LTNW/LEA LU4 64 C7
Outfield Rd CFSP/GDCR SL9 202 C7 1
Outlook Dr CSTG HP8 202 C3
The Oval BROX EN10 176 D4
HNLW SG16 25 H7
Overfield Rd LTNE LU2 84 B1
Overlord Cl BROX EN10 159 K7 2
SHFD SG17 24 B1 2
Overstone Rd HARP AL5 131 H1 1
LTNW/LEA LU4 82 C1
Overstrand RAYLNE/WEN HP22 122 D5
Overstream RKW/CH/CXG WD3 194 A5
Oving Cl LTNE LU2 66 C8
Owen Dr ROY SG8 21 J1 2
Owen Jones Cl HNLW SG16 25 H5
Owens Wy RKW/CH/CXG WD3 194 F6
Owles La BUNT SG9 58 F4
Oxcroft BSF CM23 96 E7
Oxendon Dr HOD EN11 159 M5
Oxen Rd LTNE LU2 3 H3
Oxfield Cl BERK HP4 146 F7
Oxford Av STAL AL1 153 H8
Oxford Cl CHES/WCR EN8 176 B8
NTHWD HA6 205 H4
Oxford Rd HTCHE/RSTV SG4 85 K1
LTN LU1 2 F8
Oxford St WATW WD18 12 E6
Oxhey Av OXHEY WD19 196 C8
Oxhey Dr OXHEY WD19 206 A4
Oxhey La OXHEY WD19 196 C8
PIN HA5 206 F5
Oxhey Ridge Cl OXHEY WD19 205 M5
Oxhey Rd OXHEY WD19 196 B8
Ox La HARP AL5 109 G7
Oxlease Dr HAT AL10 155 G6
Oxleys Rd STVGE SG2 5 M8
WAB EN9 191 M4
The Oxleys HLWE CM17 142 C6
Oysterfields STALW/RED AL3 10 C4

P

Pacatian Wy STVGE SG2 71 H2
Packhorse Cl STALE/WH AL4 153 H4
Packhorse La RAD WD7 185 J2
Paddick Cl HOD EN11 159 L3
Paddock Cl LTNW/LEA LU4 63 L6
LWTH SG6 39 L5
OXHEY WD19 13 M9
WARE SG12 140 C1
Paddock La BAR EN5 199 K5
Paddock Md HLWS CM18 162 B7
Paddock Rd BUNT SG9 58 D2
Paddocks Cl STVGE SG2 5 L6
The Paddocks EBAR EN4 201 L4 2
HERT/BAY SG13 138 A7 1
RKW/CH/CXG WD3 193 L5
STALE/WH AL4 110 A4
STVGE SG2 5 L6
WGCE AL7 135 G4 2
WLYN AL6 111 L1 3
The Paddock BROX EN10 159 M7
BSF CM23 96 C7 2
CFSP/GDCR SL9 202 D5
HAT AL10 154 F4 1
HTCHE/RSTV SG4 52 F5 1
Paddock Wd HARP AL5 131 K3
Pageant Rd STAL AL1 10 F8
Page Cl BLDK SG7 40 E4
Page Hl WARE SG12 116 A8
Page Rd HERT/BAY SG13 137 M4
Pages Cl BSF CM23 96 E5 1
Pages Cft BERK HP4 146 F4 3
Pagitts Gv EBAR EN4 201 G2
Paignton Cl LTNW/LEA LU4 64 C6 2
Paines Orch LBUZ LU7 101 M2
Painters La PEND EN3 190 D6
Palace Cl KGLGY WD4 180 E1
Palace Gdns BSF CM23 96 D5 1
ROY SG8 21 H4
Palfrey Cl STALW/RED AL3 10 F3
Pallas Rd HHNE HP2 8 E4
Palma Cl DUN/HR/TOD LU5 62 E7
Palmer Av BUSH WD23 197 G7
Palmer Cl HERT/WAS SG14 137 H2
Palmer Gdns BAR EN5 200 C6 2
Palmer Rd HERT/WAS SG14 137 J2
Palmers Gv WAB EN9 177 L1
Palmers Rd BORE WD6 199 H2 4
Palmerston Cl WGCW AL8 134 B4 4
Palmers Wy CHES/WCR EN8 176 D8
Pamela Av HHS/BOV HP3 166 E2
Pamela Gdns BSF CM23 96 E7
Pams La HTCHE/RSTV SG4 110 C1
Pancake La HHS/BOV HP3 150 C8
Pank Av BAR EN5 201 J6
Pankhurst Crs STVGE SG2 5 M3
Pankhurst Pl WATN WD24 13 H2 2
Panshanger Dr WGCE AL7 135 G4
The Pantiles BUSH WD23 197 J8
Panxworth Rd HHS/BOV HP3 166 C1
Paper Mill La STDN SG11 93 K1
Paradise HHNE HP2 149 J8
Paradise Cl CHESW EN7 176 A7
Paradise Rd WAB EN9 191 H5 4
Paringdon Rd
HLWW/ROY CM19 162 A6
Parish Cl GSTN WD25 182 B5 3
Parishes Md STVGE SG2 71 J6
Park Av BSF CM23 96 E7
BUSH WD23 13 K2
DUN/HR/TOD LU5 63 H5
DUN/WHIP LU6 80 A3
HLWE CM17 163 H5
LTNN/LIM LU3 64 B3
POTB/CUF EN6 187 H4
RAD WD7 184 A4
RKW/CH/CXG WD3 193 M6
STAL AL1 11 L5
WATW WD18 12 D4
Park Av North HARP AL5 130 E1
Park Av South HARP AL5 130 D1
Park Cl BLDK SG7 40 D3
BRKMPK AL9 155 H4
BRKMPK AL9 172 E5
BUSH WD23 13 K2
KTN/HRWW/W HA3 207 K8
RKW/CH/CXG WD3 205 G4
STALW/RED AL3 106 C5
STVGE SG2 89 G1
Park Ct HLW CM20 6 F4
Park Crs BLDK SG7 40 D3 1
BORE WD6 198 E4
KTN/HRWW/W HA3 207 K8
Park Dr BLDK SG7 40 D3
KTN/HRWW/W HA3 207 J6
POTB/CUF EN6 187 G2
STDN SG11 75 J7
Parker Av HERT/WAS SG14 137 J2
Parker Cl LWTH SG6 39 K6
Parker's Fld STVGE SG2 71 H6
Parker St WATN WD24 196 A2
Park Farm Cl HNLW SG16 25 J2
Park Farm La ROY SG8 33 H8
Parkfield LWTH SG6 40 C6
RKW/CH/CXG WD3 193 L5
Parkfield Crs HTCHE/RSTV SG4 110 C1
Parkfield Rd STALW/RED AL3 106 C5
Park Flds HLWW/ROY CM19 160 F2
Parkfields WGCW AL8 134 C4
Park Gdns BLDK SG7 40 D3 2
Park Ga HTCHE/RSTV SG4 52 E4
Parkgate Av EBAR EN4 201 H2
Parkgate Crs EBAR EN4 201 H2
Parkgate Rd WATN WD24 182 B8
Park Gv CSTG HP8 192 C4
Park Hl HARP AL5 108 E8
HLWE CM17 142 A7
Park Hill Rd HHW HP1 149 G7 2
Parkhurst Rd HERT/WAS SG14 137 G3
Parkins Cl STDN SG11 92 F4 1
Parkinson Cl STALE/WH AL4 132 C2
Parkland Cl HOD EN11 160 A1 3
Parkland Dr LTN LU1 83 J5
Parklands HHW HP1 148 E5 2
ROY SG8 21 K4
WAB EN9 191 K3
Parklands Cl EBAR EN4 201 J1
Parklands Dr STALW/RED AL3 151 M8
Park La BROX EN10 159 K6
BSF CM23 96 E6
CHES/WCR EN8 190 C4
CHESW EN7 175 M6
DEN/HRF UB9 203 M8
HHNE HP2 149 J8
HLW CM20 6 F3
HNLW SG16 25 J1
HTCHE/RSTV SG4 86 B8
KNEB SG3 88 A6
SAFWS CB11 33 M6
STALE/WH AL4 171 H2
STAN HA7 207 M3
STDN SG11 75 J7
Park Lane Paradise
BROX EN10 175 M3
Park Md HLW CM20 6 B4
Park Meadow BRKMPK AL9 155 H4
Park Mt HARP AL5 108 D8
Park Nook Gdns ENC/FH EN2 189 J8
Park Pl LCOL/BKTW AL2 169 J6
Park Ri BERK HP4 146 D4
HARP AL5 108 D7
KTN/HRWW/W HA3 207 K8
Park Rise Cl HARP AL5 108 D7
Park Rd BAR EN5 200 E5
BUSH WD23 196 F7
CHES/WCR EN8 190 C4 4
DUN/HR/TOD LU5 81 H3
EBAR EN4 201 J5
HERT/BAY SG13 137 K4
HHW HP1 166 B1
HOD EN11 159 M4
PEND EN3 190 D7
POTB/CUF EN6 187 M1
RAD WD7 183 M6
RKW/CH/CXG WD3 194 D8
STSD CM24 79 K4
TRING HP23 123 L8
WARE SG12 138 A1
WAT WD17 195 M2
Park Rd North
DUN/HR/TOD LU5 63 H5 3
Parkside BUNT SG9 44 B7
CHES/WCR EN8 190 D5
Parkside Cl DUN/HR/TOD LU5 63 J5
Parkside Dr DUN/HR/TOD LU5 63 J4
WAT WD17 195 K3
Parkside Rd NTHWD HA6 205 L5
Park St BERK HP4 147 G5
BLDK SG7 40 D2
BRKMPK AL9 155 H4
DUN/WHIP LU6 80 F1
HTCHE/RSTV SG4 52 D4
LCOL/BKTW AL2 169 J6
LTN LU1 2 F7
TRING HP23 123 M7
Park Street La LCOL/BKTW AL2 169 G8
Park St West LTN LU1 2 F8
Park Ter LTN LU1 3 G8
The Park STAL AL1 11 M2
STALW/RED AL3 130 A6
Park Viad LTN LU1 3 G8
Park Vw BRKMPK AL9 155 H3
HOD EN11 159 M5
PIN HA5 206 E8
POTB/CUF EN6 187 H4
STVGE SG2 89 G1
Park View Cl LTNN/LIM LU3 64 C4
STAL AL1 11 M8
Park View Dr STALW/RED AL3 106 C4
Park View Rd BERK HP4 147 G6 3
PIN HA5 206 A6
Park Wy HTCH/STOT SG5 52 D4
RKW/CH/CXG WD3 204 B1
Parkway HLWW/ROY CM19 161 K2
SBW CM21 142 D1
STVGE SG2 88 F1
WGCW AL8 134 C4
Parkway Cl WGCW AL8 134 B4
Parkway Ct STAL AL1 170 A2 2
Parkway Gdns WGCW AL8 134 B5
Parkwood Cl HOD EN11 159 K6
Parkwood Dr HHW HP1 148 E7
Parliament Sq
HERT/WAS SG14 137 J4 13
Parnall Rd HLWS CM18 162 C6
Parndon Mill La HLW CM20 6 B1
Parndon Wood Rd
HLWW/ROY CM19 162 B7
Parnell Cl ABLGY WD5 181 L1
Parnel Rd WARE SG12 116 E8
Parr Crs HHNE HP2 150 A2
Parrot Cl DUN/HR/TOD LU5 81 K1
Parrotts Cl RKW/CH/CXG WD3 194 F5
Parrotts Fld HOD EN11 160 A3
Parrott's La TRING HP23 144 F7
Parsley Cl RAYLNE/WEN HP22 122 B5
Parsloe Rd EPP CM16 161 M8
Parsonage Cl ABLGY WD5 181 K1
TRING HP23 123 M6 2
Parsonage La BRKMPK AL9 172 A2
BSF CM23 97 G2
STDN SG11 76 E4
STSD CM24 79 L6
Parsonage Leys HLW CM20 7 J5
Parsonage Pl TRING HP23 123 M7 3
Parsonage Rd BRKMPK AL9 172 A2
CSTG HP8 202 A3
RBSF CM22 99 G2
RKW/CH/CXG WD3 194 C8
Parson's Cl STALW/RED AL3 129 G1
Parthia Cl ROY SG8 21 K4
Partridge Cl BAR EN5 200 B7
BUSH WD23 207 H1 2
LTNW/LEA LU4 63 M5 1
Partridge Ct HLWS CM18 162 D4
Partridge Hl BLDK SG7 18 B7
Partridge Rd HLWS CM18 162 C4
STALW/RED AL3 152 C3
Parva Cl HARP AL5 131 J4
Parvills WAB EN9 191 J3
Parys Rd LTNN/LIM LU3 65 G4
Pascal Wy LWTH SG6 40 A3
Pascomb Rd DUN/WHIP LU6 80 E2
Pasfield WAB EN9 191 J4 2
Passingham Av
HTCHE/RSTV SG4 52 F4
Paston Rd HHNE HP2 8 B4
Pasture Cl BUSH WD23 197 H8
Pasture La HTCHE/RSTV SG4 85 K2
Pasture Loates STSD CM24 79 J2
Pasture Rd LWTH SG6 39 K7
The Pastures HAT AL10 155 G6
HHW HP1 148 D6
LCOL/BKTW AL2 168 F3 1
OXHEY WD19 196 B8
STVGE SG2 71 J2
WARE SG12 116 B7
WGCE AL7 134 F6
Pastures Wy LTNW/LEA LU4 63 L5
Paternoster Cl WAB EN9 191 L4
Paternoster Hl WAB EN9 191 L3
Path Stort Valley Wy
HERT/BAY SG13 175 G1
The Pathway OXHEY WD19 206 C1
RAD WD7 183 L7
Patmore Cl BSF CM23 96 B2
Patmore Link Rd HHNE HP2 9 M9
Patmore Rd WAB EN9 191 K5 2
Patricia Gdns BSF CM23 96 D5
Patterdale Cl DUN/WHIP LU6 81 G3
Pauls La HOD EN11 159 M4
Pavilion Wy AMS HP6 192 B2
Paxton Rd BERK HP4 147 K6 1
STAL AL1 11 G8
Paycock Rd HLWW/ROY CM19 161 M4
Payne End BUNT SG9 43 G1
Paynes Cl LWTH SG6 39 M1 1
Paynesfield Rd BUSH WD23 197 L8
Paynes La WAB EN9 177 H3
Payne's Pk HTCH/STOT SG5 52 D3
Peace Gv WLYN AL6 112 F3
Peace Prospect WAT WD17 12 D2 2
Peacocks HLWW/ROY CM19 161 L4
Peacocks Cl BERK HP4 146 E4 3
Peakes La CHESW EN7 175 L6
Peakes Wy CHESW EN7 175 L6
Pea La BERK HP4 146 C4
Pearman Dr WARE SG12 91 K3
Pearsall Cl LWTH SG6 40 A5
Pearson Av HERT/BAY SG13 137 H6
Pearsons Cl HERT/BAY SG13 137 H6 2
Peartree Cl HHW HP1 148 F6 3
Pear Tree Cl HNLW SG16 25 G7 1
Peartree Cl WGCE AL7 134 D4
Peartree Ct WGCE AL7 134 D5 3
Pear Tree Dell LWTH SG6 40 A8
Peartree La WGCE AL7 134 D5
Pear Tree Md HLWS CM18 162 F4
Peartree Rd HHW HP1 148 F6
LTNE LU2 66 B6
Pear Tree Wk CHESW EN7 175 J5
Peartree Wy STVGE SG2 5 K7
Peascroft Rd HHS/BOV HP3 166 F2
Peasmead BUNT SG9 58 D4 3
Peck Ct AMP/FLIT/B MK45 35 G6
Peck's Hl WAB EN9 160 D8
Pedlars La ROY SG8 30 D3
Pedley Hl DUN/WHIP LU6 127 H1
Peel Crs HERT/WAS SG14 137 G1
Peel Pl LTN LU1 2 D7
Peel St DUN/HR/TOD LU5 63 G5 3
LTN LU1 2 D6
Peggs La RAYLNE/WEN HP22 122 E5
Pegmire La GSTN WD25 197 H2
Pegrams Rd HLWS CM18 162 B5
Pegsdon Cl LTNN/LIM LU3 65 G3
Pegsdon Wy HTCH/STOT SG5 50 C1
Peg's La HERT/BAY SG13 137 J5 1

WARE SG12 .... 118 C5
Peldon Rd HLWW/ROY CM19 .... 161 M4
Pelham Ct HHNE HP2 .... 9 L9
   WCCE AL7 .... 135 H5
Pelham Rd STDN SG11 ...... 75 J3
The Pelhams GSTN WD25 .... 182 C6
Pelican Wy LWTH SG6 .... 39 L1
Pemberton CI STAL AL1 ...... 169 J2
Pembridge CI HHS/BOV HP3.. 164 E7
Pembridge La BROX EN10 .... 158 E8
Pembridge Rd HHS/BOV HP3 . 164 F7
Pembroke Av LTNW/LEA LU4 .. 64 D7
Pembroke CI BROX EN10 ...... 176 D3
Pembroke Dr CHESW EN7 .... 175 G4
Pembroke Rd BLDK SG7 ...... 40 E2
   NTHWD HA6 .... 205 H3
Pemsel CI HHS/BOV HP3 ...... 166 D1
Penda CI LTNN/LIM LU3 ...... 64 E4
Pendall CI EBAR EN4 .... 201 K5
Pendennis Ct HARP AL5 ...... 131 J5
Penfold CI BLDK SG7 .... 40 F3
Pengelly CI CHESW EN7 ...... 190 A1
Penhill LTNN/LIM LU3 .... 64 D3
Penlow Rd HLWS CM18 ...... 162 B5
Penman CI LCOL/BKTW AL2 .. 168 F6
Penn CI RKW/CH/CXG WD3 .. 193 J7
Penne CI RAD WD7 .... 183 M5
Penn Gaskell La
   CFSP/GDCR SL9 .... 202 E5
Pennine Av LTNN/LIM LU3 .... 64 B2
Pennine Wy HHNE HP2 ...... 8 F2
Pennington La STSD CM24 .... 79 J2
Pennington Rd CFSP/GDCR SL9.. 202 C7
Penningtons BSF CM23 ...... 96 B5
Penn Rd LCOL/BKTW AL2 .... 169 H6
   RKW/CH/CXG WD3 ...... 203 L1
   STVG SG1 .... 4 E5
Penn Wy LWTH SG6 .... 40 A7
   RKW/CH/CXG WD3 ...... 193 J7
Penny Cft HARP AL5 .... 130 F6
Pennyfather CI KNEB SG3 .... 89 K8
Pennyfathers La WLYN AL6 .. 112 F6
Pennymead HLW CM20 ...... 7 M6
Penrith Av DUN/WHIP LU6 .... 81 G3
Penrose Av OXHEY WD19 .... 206 D2
Penrose Ct HHNE HP2 .... 149 K3
Penscroft Gdns BORE WD6 .. 199 J5
Penshurst HLWE CM17 ...... 142 A7
Penshurst Rd HARP AL5 ...... 108 C6
Penshurst Rd POTB/CUF EN6.. 187 J2
Pensilver CI EBAR EN4 ...... 201 K5
Pentland Rd BUSH WD23 .... 197 H7
Pentley Pk WGCW AL8 ...... 134 C2
Penton Dr CHES/WCR EN8 .. 176 C6
Peplins CI BRKMPK AL9 ...... 172 D5
Peplins Wy BRKMPK AL9 .... 172 D4
Peppercorn Wk
   HTCHE/RSTV SG4 ...... 53 G3
Pepper HI WARE SG12 ...... 138 E5
Pepsal End STVGE SG2 ...... 89 G1
Pepsal End Rd LTN LU1 ...... 107 H4
Pepys Crs BAR EN5 .... 200 B6
Pepys Wy BLDK SG7 .... 40 C2
Percheron Dr LTNW/LEA LU4 .. 63 M7
Percheron Rd BORE WD6 .... 199 J7
Percival Wy LTNE LU2 .... 84 B3
Percy Rd WATW WD18 .... 12 F4
Peregrine CI BSF CM23 ...... 96 C4
   GSTN WD25 .... 182 D5
Peregrine Rd LTNW/LEA LU4 .. 63 M7
Peregrin Rd WAB EN9 .... 191 M5
Perham Wy LCOL/BKTW AL2 .. 170 C5
Perimeter Rd HAT AL10 ...... 154 D2
Perivale Gdns GSTN WD25 .. 182 A5
Periwinkle CI ROY SG8 ...... 32 B5
Periwinkle La DUN/WHIP LU6.. 81 H1
   HTCH/STOT SG5 .... 52 E1
Permain CI RAD WD7 .... 184 D4
Perowne Wy STDN SG11 .... 75 K7
Perram CI BROX EN10 ...... 176 D5
Perriors CI CHESW EN7 ...... 175 M6
Perry Dr ROY SG8 .... 21 K3
Perry Gn HHNE HP2 .... 149 M1
Perry HI WAB EN9 .... 177 L2
Perry Md BUSH WD23 ...... 197 H7
Perrymead LTNE LU2 .... 66 E8
Perry Rd HLWS CM18 .... 162 B5
Perrysfield Rd CHES/WCR EN8.. 176 D6
Perry Spring HLWE CM17 .... 163 H4
Perrywood La HERT/WAS SG14 .. 113 M4
Pescot HI HHW HP1 .... 149 G5
Petard CI LTNW/LEA LU4 .... 63 M8
Peterhill CI CFSP/GDCR SL9 .. 202 D5
Peterlee Ct HHNE HP2 ...... 8 E1
Peters Av LCOL/BKTW AL2 .. 170 D5
Petersfield STALW/RED AL3 .. 152 D3
Petersfield Gdns LTNW/LEA LU3.. 64 D1
Peter's PI BERK HP4 .... 146 D4
Peters Wy KNEB SG3 .... 88 E4
Peterswood HLWS CM18 .... 162 C6
Peters Wood HI WARE SG12 .. 138 C3
Pettys CI CHES/WCR EN8 .... 176 C8
Petunia CI LTNW/LEA LU4 .... 2 A2
Petworth CI STVGE SG2 ...... 89 H3
Pevensey CI LTNE LU2 ...... 66 C6
Pewterers Av BSF CM23 .... 96 B6
Pheasant CI BERK HP4 ...... 147 H7
   TRING HP23 .... 124 F4
Pheasant HI CSTG HP8 ...... 202 B2
Pheasant Wk CFSP/GDCR SL9.. 202 C4
Phelips Rd EPP CM16 .... 161 M7
Phillimore PI RAD WD7 ...... 183 K7
Phillipers GSTN WD25 ...... 182 D6
Phillips Av ROY SG8 .... 21 H2
Phoenix CI NTHWD HA6 .... 205 L4
The Phygtle CFSP/GDCR SL9.. 202 D6
Piccotts End La HHW HP1 .. 149 H5
Piccotts End La HHNE HP2 .. 8 A1
Piccotts End Rd HHW HP1 .. 149 G3
Pickets CI BUSH WD23 ...... 207 J1
Picketts WGCE AL8 .... 134 C1
Pickford HI HARP AL5 .... 109 H7
Pickford Rd STALW/RED AL3.. 106 B3
Picknage Rd ROY SG8 ...... 22 F8
Pie Cnr STALW/RED AL3 .... 129 G1
Pierian Spring HHW HP1 .... 149 G5
Pietley HI STALW/RED AL3.. 128 F1

Pigeonwick HARP AL5 ...... 108 F7
Piggottshill La HARP AL5 .. 131 H3
Piggotts La LTNW/LEA LU4 .. 64 C6
Piggotts Wy BSF CM23 ...... 96 D5
Pightle CI ROY SG8 .... 21 H3
Pig La BSF CM23 .... 96 F7
Pike End STVG SG1 .... 4 D1
Pilgrim CI GSTN WD25 ...... 182 C4
   LCOL/BKTW AL2 .... 169 H6
Pilgrim's Ri EBAR EN4 ...... 201 K6
Pilgrims Wy STVG SG1 ...... 55 G8
Pilkingtons HLWE CM17 .... 163 J2
Piltdown Rd OXHEY WD19 .. 206 C4
   OXHEY WD19 .... 206 C4
Pinceybrook Rd HLWS CM18.. 162 B6
Pinchfield RKW/CH/CXG WD3.. 203 J5
Pindar Rd HOD EN11 .... 160 B3
Pine CI BERK HP4 .... 147 G6
   CHES/WCR EN8 .... 176 B7
   NTHWD HA6 .... 205 K6
Pine Crest WLYN AL6 ...... 112 D2
Pinecrest HHS/BOV HP3 .... 166 E3
Pinecroft Crs BAR EN5 ...... 200 D5
Pine Gv BRKMPK AL9 ...... 173 G4
   BSF CM23 .... 97 G4
   BUSH WD23 .... 196 E2
   LCOL/BKTW AL2 .... 182 C1
Pinehurst CI ABLGY WD5 .. 181 K3
Pinelands BSF CM23 .... 96 E1
Pine Rd DUN/WHIP LU6 .... 103 L2
Pines HI EN EN1 .... 190 B7
Pines HI STSD CM24 .... 79 J5
The Pines BORE WD6 ...... 198 E3
   HHW HP1 .... 165 L3
Pinetree CI CFSP/GDCR SL9.. 202 B7
Pine Wk BERK HP4 .... 146 C2
Pinewood Av PIN HA5 ...... 207 G6
Pinewood CI BORE WD6 .... 199 J2
   HLWE CM17 .... 163 H4
   LTNN/LIM LU3 .... 64 B1
   PIN HA5 .... 207 G6
   STAL AL1 .... 153 H7
   WAT WD17 .... 195 M2
Pinewood Dr POTB/CUF EN6.. 186 E2
Pinewood Gdns
   HHS/BOV HP3 .... 149 K8
   HHW HP1 .... 149 G7
Pinfold Rd BUSH WD23 .... 196 E3
Pinford Dell LTNE LU2 ...... 84 C1
Pinnacles WAB EN9 .... 191 K5
Pinnate PI WGCE AL7 ...... 134 D8
Pinner HI PIN HA5 .... 206 A7
Pinner Hill Rd PIN HA5 .... 206 B8
Pinner Rd NTHWD HA6 .... 205 L8
   OXHEY WD19 .... 13 K8
Pinnocks La BLDK SG7 .... 40 E3
Pinto CI BORE WD6 .... 199 J7
Pioneer Wy WATW WD18 .. 12 B8
Pipers Av HARP AL5 .... 131 J3
Pipers CI STALW/RED AL3 .. 129 M4
Pipers CI DUN/WHIP LU6 .. 80 E3
Pipers HI HHW HP1 .... 127 H8
Pipers La HARP AL5 .... 131 K3
   STALW/RED AL3 .... 106 D2
Pippens WGCW AL8 .... 134 D1
Pippin CI RAD WD7 .... 184 D4
Pirton CI HTCH/STOT SG5 .. 52 C3
   STALE/WH AL4 .... 153 H2
Pirton Rd HTCH/STOT SG5 .. 37 M4
   HTCH/STOT SG5 .... 52 A3
   LTNW/LEA LU4 .... 64 B5
Pishiobury Dr SBW CM21 .. 142 C2
Pitsfield WGCW AL8 .... 134 C1
Pitstone CI STALE/WH AL4 .. 153 H1
Pitt Dr STALE/WH AL4 ...... 170 B2
Pittman's Fld HLW CM20 .... 7 H4
Pix Ct ARL/CHE SG15 ...... 25 M2
Pix Farm La HHW HP1 ...... 148 A5
Pixies Hill Crs HHW HP1 .. 165 L1
Pixies Hill Rd HHW HP1 .. 148 E8
Pixmore Av LWTH SG6 ...... 40 A4
Pixmore Wy LWTH SG6 .... 39 L5
Pix Rd HTCH/STOT SG5 .... 26 D5
   LWTH SG6 .... 39 M4
Plaistow Wy ROY SG8 ...... 23 K8
Plaiters CI TRING HP23 .... 123 M6
Plaiters Wy DUN/HR/TOD LU5 .. 62 F5
Plaitford CI RKW/CH/CXG WD3.. 204 D2
Plantaganet PI WAB EN9 .. 191 G4
Plantagenet Rd BAR EN5 .. 201 H5
Plantation Rd LTNN/LIM LU3.. 64 C3
Plantation Wk HHW HP1 .. 148 F4
   HHW HP1 .... 148 F5
Plash Dr STVG SG1 .... 4 E3
Plashes CI STDN SG11 .... 75 J8
Plashets RBSF CM22 ...... 143 H1
Platt CI LTNW/LEA LU4 .... 64 C6
Plaw Hatch CI BSF CM23 .. 97 G2
Playhouse Sq HLW CM20 .. 6 D6
The Pleasance HARP AL5 .. 108 C6
Pleasant Mt HERT/BAY SG13.. 138 B6
Pleasant Ri BRKMPK AL9 .. 155 H2
Pleasant Rd BSF CM23 .... 96 D2
The Pleasance
   RAYLNE/WEN HP22 .... 122 D5
Plewes CI DUN/WHIP LU6 .. 105 K2
Plough CI LTNW/LEA LU4 .. 63 K6
Plough HI POTB/CUF EN6 .. 174 D8
Plough La BSF CM23 .... 148 A3
   DEN/HRF UB9 .... 204 B6
   HTCHE/RSTV SG4 ...... 67 M5
   RKW/CH/CXG WD3 .... 179 L4
Ploughmans CI BSF CM23 .. 96 B5
Ploughmans End WGCE AL7.. 135 H5
Plover CI BERK HP4 .... 147 H7
Ployters Rd HLWS CM18 .. 162 B6
Plummers La LTNE LU2 .... 109 J1
Plumpton CI LTNE LU2 .... 66 C7
Plumpton Rd HOD EN11 .. 160 B2
Plum Tree Rd HNLW SG16 .. 25 G7
Pluto Ri HHW HP1 .... 8 D5
Poets Cha HHW HP1 ...... 149 G5
Poets CI HHW HP1 .... 149 G5
Poets Ct HARP AL5 .... 131 G1
Poets Ga CHESW EN7 ...... 175 J7
Poets Gn LTNW/LEA LU4 .. 63 M8
Polayn Garth WGCW AL8 .. 134 B3

Polegate LTNE LU2 .... 66 C8
Polehanger La HHW HP1 .. 148 D5
Poles HI RKW/CH/CXG WD3.. 179 K4
Poles La WARE SG12 ...... 116 B7
Police Rw ROY SG8 .... 30 E3
Pollard Gdns STVG SG1 .. 70 E2
Pollard Hatch
   HLWW/ROY CM19 .... 162 A5
Pollards RKW/CH/CXG WD3 .. 203 J5
Pollards CI CHESW EN7 .... 175 H8
Pollards Wy HTCH/STOT SG5.. 37 H6
Pollywick Rd TRING HP23 .. 145 J3
Polzeath CI LTNE LU2 ...... 84 B2
Pomeroy Crs WATN WD24 .. 182 A7
Pomeroy Gv LTNE LU2 .... 65 K5
Pomfret Av LTNW/LEA LU4 .. 64 A5
Pond CI LTNW/LEA LU4 .... 64 A5
   WCCE AL7 .... 134 D5
Pondcroft Rd KNEB SG3 .. 88 F5
Pondfield Crs STALE/WH AL4 .. 153 G4
Pond La BLDK SG7 .... 40 D2
   CFSP/GDCR SL9 .... 202 A8
   RBSF CM22 .... 121 M7
Pond Rd HHS/BOV HP3 .... 166 F4
Pondside HTCHE/RSTV SG4 .. 54 B6
Pondsmeade
   STALW/RED AL3 .... 130 A5
Pondwick Rd HARP AL5 .. 108 D8
Pondwicks CI STALW/RED AL3.. 10 D8
Pondwicks Rd LTN LU1 .... 3 H6
Pooleys La BRKMPK AL9 .. 172 A2
Popes La WATN WD24 ...... 182 A8
Pope's Rd ABLGY WD5 .... 181 K2
Popes Rw WARE SG12 .... 116 C7
Popis Gdns WARE SG12 .. 116 C6
Poplar Av HAT AL10 ...... 154 C5
   LTNN/LIM LU3 .... 65 H2
Poplar CI HTCHE/RSTV SG4 .. 52 F5
   PIN HA5 .... 206 C8
   ROY SG8 .... 21 K3
   STDN SG11 .... 116 E1
Poplar Dr ROY SG8 .... 21 K3
Poplar Rd DUN/WHIP LU6 .. 105 K2
Poplars WGCE AL7 .... 135 G3
Poplars CI GSTN WD25 .... 182 A3
   HAT AL10 .... 154 C5
Poplar Shaw WAB EN9 .... 191 L4
The Poplars ARL/CHE SG15 .. 25 M2
   CHESW EN7 .... 175 K5
   HHW HP1 .... 149 G8
   HTCH/STOT SG5 .... 38 E5
   STAN HA7 .... 170 A3
Popple Wy STVG SG1 ...... 4 E2
Poppy CI HHW HP1 .... 148 D6
Poppyfields WGCE AL7 .... 135 H5
Poppy Md STVG SG1 ...... 5 H5
Poppy Wk CHESW EN7 .... 189 M2
Porlock Dr LTNE LU2 ...... 84 B1
Porters CI BUNT SG9 ...... 58 D2
Porters HI HARP AL5 ...... 109 H6
Porters Park Dr RAD WD7 .. 184 D3
Porters Wd STALW/RED AL3 .. 152 E3
Port HI HERT/WAS SG14 .. 137 H4
Portland CI DUN/HR/TOD LU5.. 62 F5
Portland Dr CHESW EN7 .. 189 M2
Portland PI BSF CM23 .... 96 E3
   HERT/BAY SG13 .... 138 B6
Portland Rd BSF CM23 .... 96 E3
Portland St STALW/RED AL3.. 10 C6
Port La RBSF CM22 .... 97 G8
Portman CI HTCH/STOT SG5 .. 38 C8
   STALE/WH AL4 .... 153 H2
Portmill La HTCH/STOT SG5.. 52 E3
Port V HERT/WAS SG14 .. 137 G5
Porz Av DUN/HR/TOD LU5 .. 63 J7
Postfield WGCE AL7 .... 134 F1
Post Office Rd HLW CM20 .. 6 E5
Post Office Rw
   HTCHE/RSTV SG4 ...... 55 G1
Postwood Gn HERT/BAY SG13.. 138 D3
Post Wood Rd WARE SG12 .. 138 D3
Potash La TRING HP23 .... 100 E6
Potten End HI HHW HP1 .. 148 D2
Potterscrouch La
   LCOL/BKTW AL2 .... 168 C3
Potters Fld HLWE CM17 .. 163 J4
   STALW/RED AL3 .... 152 D3
Pottersheath Rd WLYN AL6 .. 112 C1
Potters Heights CI PIN HA5.. 206 A7
Potter's La BAR EN5 ...... 200 F5
   BORE WD6 .... 199 H2
   STVG SG1 .... 70 A6
Potter's Rd BAR EN5 ...... 201 G5
Potter St BSF CM23 .... 96 E3
   HLWE CM17 .... 163 H3
   NTHWD HA6 .... 205 M8
Potter Street HI NTHWD HA6.. 206 A6
Pottery CI LTNN/LIM LU3 .. 64 E3
Potton Rd ROY SG8 .... 15 K4
Pouchen End La HHW HP1 .. 148 C8
Poultney Rd STSD CM24 .. 79 K2
Poultney CI RAD WD7 ...... 184 D3
Pound Av STVG SG1 ...... 4 C1
Pound CI WAB EN9 .... 177 K2
Pound Fld GSTN WD25 .... 181 L6
Pound Gn ROY SG8 .... 15 L5
Pound La RAD WD7 .... 184 E4
Poundwell WGCE AL7 .... 134 F5
Powdermill La WAB EN9 .. 191 G4
Powdermill Ms WAB EN9 .. 191 G4
Powdermill Wy WAB EN9 .. 191 G3
Power Ct LTN LU1 .... 3 C6
Powis St POTB/CUF EN6 .. 187 H5
Poynders Av LTNW/LEA LU4 .. 64 D2
Poynders Meadow
   WLYN AL6 .... 111 L2
Poynings CI HARP AL5 .... 131 G1
Poynters Rd DUN/HR/TOD LU5.. 63 K7
Prae CI STALW/RED AL3 .. 10 A5
Praetorian Ct STAL AL1 .. 169 H2
Prebendal Dr LTN LU1 .... 83 G8
Prentice Wy LTNE LU2 .... 84 C1
Prescott Rd CHES/WCR EN8.. 176 D6
Presdales Dr WARE SG12 .. 138 C2
President Wy LTNE LU2 .. 84 C2

Preslent CI HTCH/STOT SG5.. 36 E1
Prestatyn CI STVG SG1 .... 70 A3
Preston Gdns LTNE LU2 .. 3 H1
   PEND EN3 .... 190 D8
Preston Rd HTCHE/RSTV SG4.. 68 D3
Prestwick CI LTNE LU2 .... 65 K5
Prestwick Dr BSF CM23 .. 97 G1
Pretoria Rd WATW WD18 .. 12 B5
Pretwick Rd OXHEY WD19 .. 206 C3
Prickent La LTNE LU2 ...... 82 F3
Pricklers HI BAR EN5 ...... 201 G6
Priestleys LTN LU1 .... 82 F3
Primary Wy ARL/CHE SG15 .. 25 M6
Primett Rd STVG SG1 ...... 4 B1
Primley La RBSF CM22 .... 143 H1
Primrose CI ARL/CHE SG15 .. 25 M6
   BSF CM23 .... 96 B4
   HAT AL10 .... 155 G6
Primrose Dr HERT/BAY SG13.. 138 A4
Primrose Fld HLWS CM18 .. 162 E5
Primrose Gdns BUSH WD23.. 197 G8
Primrose HI KGLGY WD4 .. 167 G7
Primrose Hill Rd STVG SG1 .. 70 C3
Primrose Pth CHESW EN7 .. 189 M2
Primrose Vw ROY SG8 .... 21 L5
Prince Andrew's CI ROY SG8.. 21 J5
Prince Edward St BERK HP4.. 147 H6
Prince Pk HHW HP1 .... 148 F3
Princes Av PEND EN3 ...... 190 D7
   WATW WD18 .... 12 B6
Princes CI BERK HP4 ...... 146 F4
   BSF CM23 .... 96 B3
Princes Ga BSF CM23 .... 96 B3
Princes Ms ROY SG8 ...... 21 H5
Princess Diana Dr
   STALE/WH AL4 .... 153 H8
Princess St LTN LU1 ...... 2 D8
Princes St DUN/WHIP LU6.. 80 F2
   HTCH/STOT SG5 .... 26 E3
   WARE SG12 .... 116 C8
Prince St WAT WD17 ...... 13 G2
Prince Wy LTNE LU2 ...... 84 C2
Printers Wy DUN/WHIP LU6.. 63 G8
   HLW CM20 .... 141 M5
Priors CI HERT/BAY SG13 .. 138 B7
Priors HI HTCH/STOT SG5 .. 37 H6
Priors Wood Rd
   HERT/BAY SG13 .... 138 B7
   RBSF CM22 .... 99 H3
Priory Av HLWE CM17 .... 142 B5
Priory CI BROX EN10 ...... 176 D3
   HOD EN11 .... 159 M5
   ROY SG8 .... 21 K4
   STAN HA7 .... 207 L3
   TRDG/WHET N20 ...... 200 E8
Priory Ct BSF CM23 .... 96 D3
   HLWS CM18 .... 163 G5
Priory Dell STVG SG1 ...... 4 F4
Priory Dr STAN HA7 ...... 207 L3
   STSD CM24 .... 79 K5
Priory End HTCHE/RSTV SG4.. 52 E5
Priory Gdns BERK HP4 .... 147 H6
   LTNE LU2 .... 65 J7
Priory Ga CHES/WCR EN8 .. 176 E6
   ROY SG8 .... 21 J5
Priory La HTCHE/RSTV SG4 .. 53 L6
   ROY SG8 .... 21 J5
Priory Orch STALW/RED AL3.. 107 G8
Priory Rd DUN/HR/TOD LU5.. 81 H2
Priory St HERT/WAS SG14 .. 137 J4
   WARE SG12 .... 138 B1
Priory Vw BUSH WD23 .... 197 K8
   HTCHE/RSTV SG4 ...... 53 K6
Priory Wk STAL AL1 .... 169 K2
Priory Wy HTCHE/RSTV SG4.. 52 D6
Priory Wood Rbt RBSF CM22.. 97 M2
Proctors Wy BSF CM23 .... 96 F6
Proctor Wy LTNE LU2 ...... 84 B3
Progress Wy LTNW/LEA LU4.. 64 A4
Prospect La HARP AL5 .... 130 E6
Prospect Rd BAR EN5 .... 200 F5
   CHES/WCR EN8 .... 176 B8
   STAL AL1 .... 169 J1
Prospect PI LTNE LU2 .... 84 B3
Protea Wy LTN LU1 .... 84 A4
Providence Gv STVG SG1 .. 70 D2
Providence Wy BLDK SG7 .. 40 E3
Provost Wy LTNE LU2 .... 84 B2
Prowse Av BUSH WD23 .. 207 H2
Pryor CI ABLGY WD5 ...... 181 L3
Pryor Rd BLDK SG7 .... 40 E3
Pryors CI BSF CM23 ...... 96 F4
Pryor Wy LTNW/LEA LU4 .. 40 C5
Puddephat's La
   STALW/RED AL3 .... 128 C3
Pudding La HHW HP1 .... 148 F5
   ROY SG8 .... 32 F1
The Pudgell ROY SG8 .... 23 K8
Pulham Av BROX EN10 .. 159 K7
Puller Rd BAR EN5 .... 200 C3
   HHW HP1 .... 148 F8
Pulleys CI HHW HP1 ...... 148 E6
Pulleys La HHW HP1 ...... 148 E6
Pullman Dr HTCHE/RSTV SG4.. 53 G3
Pulter's Wy HTCHE/RSTV SG4.. 52 F4
Pump HI BUNT SG9 .... 46 F8
Punch Bowl La HHNE HP2 .. 150 C4
   STALW/RED AL3 .... 150 F3
Purbrock Av GSTN WD25 .. 182 B7
Purcell CI BORE WD6 .... 198 C2
   WLYN AL6 .... 113 J4
Purcell Rd LTNW/LEA LU4 .. 63 L6
Purford Gn HLWS CM18 .. 7 M9
Purkiss Rd HERT/BAY SG13.. 137 H7
Purlings Rd BUSH WD23 .. 197 G6
Pursley Gdns BORE WD6 .. 198 F1
Purway CI LTNN/LIM LU3 .. 64 D2
Purwell La HTCHE/RSTV SG4.. 53 H2
Putnams Dr
   RAYLNE/WEN HP22 .... 122 C5
Putney PI PEND EN3 ...... 190 C7
Puttenham CI OXHEY WD19.. 206 B3
Putteridge Rd LTNE LU2 .. 66 C5
Putters Cft HHNE HP2 .... 149 K3
Puttocks CI BRKMPK AL9 .. 172 B2
Puttocks Dr BRKMPK AL9 .. 172 B2
Pyenest Rd HLWW/ROY CM19.. 162 A5
The Pyghtle BUNT SG9 .... 58 C2

LTN LU1 .... 82 F3
Pym CI EBAR EN4 .... 201 J6
   EBAR EN4 .... 201 K6
Pymmes Brook Trail EBAR EN4.. 201 L8
Pymms Brook Dr EBAR EN4.. 201 K5
Pyms CI LWTH SG6 .... 40 A2
Pynchbek BSF CM23 ...... 97 G3
Pynchon Paddocks RBSF CM22.. 121 J3
Pynders La DUN/HR/TOD LU5.. 63 K8
Pynest Green La WAB EN9.. 191 M8
Pytchley CI LTNE LU2 .... 65 K5
Pytt Fld HLWE CM17 ...... 163 G3

Q

The Quadrangle WGCW AL8.. 134 B3
The Quadrant DUN/HR/TOD LU5.. 63 H5
   LWTH SG6 .... 39 L4
   ROY SG8 .... 21 H2
   STALE/WH AL4 .... 153 G4
   STVG SG1 .... 4 D4
Quaker La WAB EN9 ...... 191 H5
Quaker Rd WARE SG12 .. 116 D7
Quakers La POTB/CUF EN6.. 187 G1
Quantock CI LTNN/LIM LU3 .. 65 G2
   STALE/WH AL4 .... 153 H3
Quantock Ri LTNN/LIM LU3.. 65 G2
Quantocks HHNE HP2 .... 8 E3
Quarry Springs HLW CM20.. 7 L6
Quartermass CI HHW HP1 .. 148 F6
Quartermass Rd HHW HP1.. 148 F6
Queen Anne's CI HTCH/STOT SG5.. 26 E5
Queen Hoo La WLYN AL6 .. 113 L4
Queen Mary's Av WATW WD18.. 195 K5
Queens Av WATW WD18 .. 12 B5
Queens CI LTN LU1 .... 3 G8
   SBW CM21 .... 120 E6
   STSD CM24 .... 79 K2
Queens Crs BSF CM23 .... 96 D5
   STALE/WH AL4 .... 153 G4
Queens Dr ABLGY WD5 .. 181 L3
   CHES/WCR EN8 .... 190 F5
The Queen's Dr
   RKW/CH/CXG WD3 .... 193 L7
Queen's PI WAT WD17 .... 13 H3
Queens Rd BAR EN5 ...... 200 C4
   BERK HP4 .... 146 F5
   CHES/WCR EN8 .... 190 D5
   HARP AL5 .... 131 G3
   HERT/BAY SG13 .... 137 J5
   ROY SG8 .... 21 J3
   WARE SG12 .... 116 E8
   WAT WD17 .... 13 H3
Queen St DUN/HR/TOD LU5.. 63 G6
   HTCH/STOT SG5 .... 26 E5
   HTCHE/RSTV SG4 ...... 52 E4
   KGLGY WD4 .... 179 M2
   LBUZ LU7 .... 102 C6
   STALW/RED AL3 .... 10 D7
   TRING HP23 .... 123 M7
Queens Wy RAD WD7 .... 184 D2
   CHES/WCR EN8 .... 190 E5
Queensway DUN/WHIP LU6.. 81 G1
   HAT AL10 .... 154 F5
   HHNE HP2 .... 8 D8
   HHW HP1 .... 149 H6
   ROY SG8 .... 21 J3
Queenswood Crs GSTN WD25.. 181 M4
Queenswood Dr
   HTCHE/RSTV SG4 ...... 53 H1
Quendell Wk HHNE HP2 .. 8 D8
Quendon Dr WAB EN9 .... 191 J4
Quickbeams WGCE AL7 .. 134 F1
Quickley La RKW/CH/CXG WD3.. 193 H7
Quickley Ri RKW/CH/CXG WD3.. 193 G7
Quickly Brow
   RKW/CH/CXG WD3 .... 193 G7
Quickmoor La KGLGY WD4.. 180 A4
Quickswood LTNN/LIM LU3.. 64 F3
Quickwood CI
   RKW/CH/CXG WD3 .... 193 L7
Quills LWTH SG6 .... 40 C6
Quilter CI LTNN/LIM LU3 .. 64 E6
Quinces Cft HHW HP1 .... 148 F5
Quincey Rd WARE SG12 .. 116 B7
Quin Ct STDN SG11 ...... 75 L3
Quinn Wy LWTH SG6 .... 40 B5
Quinta Dr BAR EN5 .... 200 A6
Quinton Wy WAB EN9 .... 191 H6

R

Raban CI STVGE SG2 ...... 89 H1
Rabley Heath Rd WLYN AL6.. 111 M1
Rackman Dr LTNN/LIM LU3.. 65 H5
Radburn CI HLWS CM18 .. 163 G5
Radburn Ct DUN/WHIP LU6.. 80 F1
Radburn Wy LWTH SG6 .. 40 B5
Radcliffe Rd HTCH/STOT SG5.. 52 F2
Radlett La RAD WD7 ...... 184 C5
Radlett Park Rd RAD WD7 .. 184 A5
Radlett Rd GSTN WD25 .. 197 H1
   LCOL/BKTW AL2 .... 169 K8
   WATN WD24 .... 13 H2
Radnor Rd LTNW/LEA LU4 .. 63 L6
Radstone PI LTNE LU2 .... 84 D1
Radwell La BLDK SG7 .... 27 H6
Raebarn Gdns BAR EN5 .. 200 A6
Raffin CI KNEB SG3 ...... 89 J7
Raffin Green La HERT/WAS SG14.. 89 L5
   KNEB SG3 .... 89 K7
Raffin Pk KNEB SG3 ...... 89 K7
Ragged Hall La LCOL/BKTW AL2.. 168 C3
Raglan Av CHES/WCR EN8.. 190 C5
Raglan CI LTNW/LEA LU4 .. 63 L7
Raglan Gdns OXHEY WD19.. 206 A3
Rags La CHESW EN7 ...... 175 L6
Railway PI HERT/BAY SG13 .. 137 K6
Railway Rd CHES/WCR EN8.. 190 E4
Railway St HERT/WAS SG14.. 137 K4
Railway Ter KGLGY WD4 .. 166 F4
Rainbow CI STALW/RED AL3.. 129 L5
Rainbow Ct OXHEY WD19 .. 13 H9
Rainbow Rd HLWE CM17 .. 143 K7

Rainer Cl CHES/WCR EN8 176 C8
Rainsford Rd STSD CM24 79 J2
Raleigh Crs STVGE SG2 70 F3
Raleigh Gv LTNW/LEA LU4 82 C1
The Rally ARL/CHE SG15 25 M3
Ralston Wy OXHEY WD19 206 C2
Ramblers Wy WGCE AL7 135 G5
Rambling Wy BERK HP4 148 B4
Ramerick Gdns ARL/CHE SG15 25 L8
Ram Gorse HLW CM20 6 B3
Ramney Dr PEND EN3 190 D7
The Ramparts STALW/RED AL3 169 G1
Ramridge Rd LTNE LU2 3 J1
Ramsay Cl BROX EN10 159 K8 1
Ramsbury Rd STAL AL1 11 C9
Ramsdell STVG SG1 5 H5
Ramsey Cl BRKMPK AL9 173 J6
LTNW/LEA LU4 63 L7
STAL AL1 169 M1
Ramsey Lodge Ct STAL AL1 11 H5 1
Ramsey Rd AMP/FLIT/B MK45 35 H7
Ramson Ri HHW HP1 148 D8
Randalls Ride HHNE HP2 8 B5
Randals Hl STVGE SG2 5 M8
Rand's Meadow HTCH/STOT SG5 38 A3
Ranelagh Rd HHNE HP2 9 J9
Ranleigh Wk HARP AL5 131 J4
Ranock Cl LTNN/LIM LU3 64 C2
Ranskill Rd BORE WD6 198 F2
Ransom Cl HTCHE/RSTV SG4 52 E6 4
OXHEY WD19 196 B8
Rant Meadow HHS/BOV HP3 149 M8
Ranulf Cl HLWE CM17 142 B4
Ranworth Av HOD EN11 139 G8
STVGE SG2 89 H3
Ranworth Cl HHS/BOV HP3 166 C1 4
Raphael Cl RAD WD7 184 D3
Raphael Dr WATN WD24 13 J1
Rasehill Cl RKW/CH/CXG WD3 194 B6
Rathlin HHS/BOV HP3 167 G1
Ratty's La HOD EN11 160 C4
Ravenbank Rd LTNE LU2 66 B5
Raven Cl RKW/CH/CXG WD3 194 B8
Raven Ct HAT AL10 154 F7
Ravenhill Wy LTNW/LEA LU4 63 M6
Ravensburgh Cl
AMP/FLIT/B MK45 35 G7 1
Ravenscourt DUN/WHIP LU6 62 E7 2
Ravenscroft GSTN WD25 182 D6
HARP AL5 131 J4 1
Ravenscroft Pk BAR EN5 200 C5
Ravensdell HHW HP1 148 E6
Ravens La BERK HP4 147 J6
Ravensmead CFSP/GDCR SL9 202 E5
Ravensthorpe LTNE LU2 66 A6
Ravenswood Pk NTHWD HA6 205 M6
Rawdon Dr HOD EN11 159 M5
Rayburn Rd HHW HP1 148 F5
Raydean Rd BAR EN5 200 F6
Rayfield WGCW AL8 134 C1 1
Raymer Cl STAL AL1 11 H4
Raymond Cl ABLGY WD5 181 J3 1
Raymonds Cl WGCE AL7 134 D6 1
Raymonds Pln WGCE AL7 134 D6 2
Raynham Cl BSF CM23 97 H3
Raynham Rd BSF CM23 97 G2
Raynham St HERT/BAY SG13 137 K3
Raynham Wy LTNE LU2 84 C1
Raynsford Rd WARE SG12 138 D1
Raynton Rd PEND EN3 190 C8
Ray's Hl CSHM HP5 145 H8
Read Ct WAB EN9 191 M4
Readers Cl DUN/WHIP LU6 62 F8
The Readings HLWS CM18 162 E5
RKW/CH/CXG WD3 193 L4
Reaper Cl LTNW/LEA LU4 63 K6
Recreation Gnd STSD CM24 79 J4
Recreation Rd
DUN/HR/TOD LU5 63 H4
Rectory Cl BRKMPK AL9 156 D4
WARE SG12 140 C2
Rectory Fld HLWW/ROY CM19 162 A4
Rectory Gdns HAT AL10 155 G5 2
Rectory La BERK HP4 147 H6
BSF CM23 78 B4
HERT/WAS SG14 90 C7
HLWW/ROY CM19 162 A4
KGLGY WD4 166 F7
KNEB SG3 89 H8
LTNE LU2 50 C8
RAD WD7 184 E4
RAD WD7 185 H2
RKW/CH/CXG WD3 204 C1
STVG SG1 70 B1
Rectory Rd RKW/CH/CXG WD3 194 C8
SHFD SG17 24 A5
WGCW AL8 134 A1
Rectory Wd HLW CM20 6 C4
Redan Rd WARE SG12 116 D7
Redbournbury La
STALW/RED AL3 130 C8
Redbourn La HARP AL5 130 D4
Redbourn Rd HHNE HP2 9 G2
STALW/RED AL3 151 K3
Redcar Dr STVG SG1 69 M4
Redding La STALW/RED AL3 129 K1
Reddings HHS/BOV HP3 166 E1
WGCW AL8 134 B3
Reddings Av BUSH WD23 197 G6
The Reddings BORE WD6 198 E4 2
Redferns Cl LTN LU1 82 F4
Redfield Cl DUN/WHIP LU6 80 D1
Redgrave Gdns LTNN/LIM LU3 64 E2
Redhall Cl HAT AL10 154 E8
Redhall Dr HAT AL10 154 E8
Redhall La RKW/CH/CXG WD3 194 D2
Redheath Cl GSTN WD25 181 L6
Redhill Rd HTCH/STOT SG5 52 B2
Redhoods Wy East LWTH SG6 39 K4
Redhoods Wy West LWTH SG6 39 K4
Red House Cl WARE SG12 138 D3
Red Lion Cl GSTN WD25 183 G8
Red Lion Crs HLWE CM17 163 H4
Red Lion La HHS/BOV HP3 166 E5
HLWE CM17 163 H4
RKW/CH/CXG WD3 179 M6
Red Lodge Gdns BERK HP4 146 F7
Redmire Cl LTNW/LEA LU4 64 A4 2
Red Rails LTN LU1 83 H5
Redricks La HLW CM20 141 L4
Red Rd BORE WD6 198 E4
Redvers Cl BSF CM23 78 F8
Red White And Blue Rd
BSF CM23 79 G8
Red Willow HLWW/ROY CM19 161 L5
Redwing Cl STVGE SG2 71 H6
Redwing Gv ABLGY WD5 181 M2 4
Redwood Cl OXHEY WD19 206 B4
Redwood Dr HHS/BOV HP3 166 D1
LTNN/LIM LU3 64 B2
Redwood Ri BORE WD6 184 F8
Redwoods HERT/WAS SG14 137 H3 2
WGCW AL8 112 C7 1
Redwood Wy BAR EN5 200 C6
Reed Cl LCOL/BKTW AL2 170 C6
Reedham Cl LCOL/BKTW AL2 168 F8
Reedings Wy SBW CM21 120 E6
Reeds Crs WATN WD24 196 B3
Reedsdale LTNE LU2 66 E8 3
The Reeds WGCE AL7 134 C5
Reeves Av LTNN/LIM LU3 65 G6
Reeves La HLWW/ROY CM19 161 H6
Reeves Pightle ROY SG8 23 L7
Regal Cl STDN SG11 75 K8
Regal Wy WATN WD24 196 B1
Regency Cl BSF CM23 96 D3
Regency Ct DUN/WHIP LU6 81 H3
HLWS CM18 162 F5
Regent Cl KGLGY WD4 166 F8
STALE/WH AL4 153 H3
WGCE AL7 134 D5 6
Regent Ct HTCH/STOT SG5 26 E3
Regents Cl RAD WD7 183 M5
Regent St DUN/WHIP LU6 81 G1
HTCH/STOT SG5 26 E4
LTN LU1 2 D7
WATN WD24 196 A1
Reginald Rd NTHWD HA6 205 L8
Reginald St LTNE LU2 2 E3
Regis Rd LTNW/LEA LU4 63 K6
Rendlesham Av RAD WD7 183 L8
Rendlesham Cl WARE SG12 116 A8
Rendlesham Wy
RKW/CH/CXG WD3 193 H7
Rennison Cl CHESW EN7 175 L6 7
Renshaw Cl LTNE LU2 66 D8 3
Repton Cl LTNN/LIM LU3 64 E4
Repton Gn STALW/RED AL3 152 C4
Repton Wy RKW/CH/CXG WD3 194 F6
Reson Wy HHW HP1 149 G8
Reston Cl BORE WD6 198 F1
Retford Cl BORE WD6 198 F1
The Retreat AMS HP6 192 D2
DUN/HR/TOD LU5 81 L1
Revels Cl HERT/WAS SG14 137 J2
Revels Rd HERT/WAS SG14 137 J2
Reynard Copse BSF CM23 96 E1
Reynards Rd WLYN AL6 112 A3
Reynard's Wy LCOL/BKTW AL2 168 E8
Reynard Wy HERT/BAY SG13 137 M4
Reynolds Cl HHW HP1 148 F6
Reynolds Crs STALE/WH AL4 153 G2
Rhee Spring BLDK SG7 41 G1
Rhodes Av BSF CM23 96 E5
Rhodes Wy WATN WD24 196 C3
Rhymes HHW HP1 149 G5
Ribbledale LCOL/BKTW AL2 170 E6 1
Ribblesdale HHNE HP2 8 D3
Rib Cl STDN SG11 75 K8
Ribocon Wy LTNW/LEA LU4 64 A3
Ribston Cl RAD WD7 184 C4
Rib V HERT/WAS SG14 137 J1
Rice Cl HHNE HP2 8 F6
Richards Cl BUSH WD23 197 J8
LTN LU1 83 G4
Richardson Cl
LCOL/BKTW AL2 170 D6 3
Richardson Crs CHESW EN7 175 G5
Richardson Pl STALE/WH AL4 171 G1
Richard Stagg Cl STAL AL1 170 A1
Richard St DUN/HR/TOD LU5 81 H2
Richfield Rd BUSH WD23 207 J1 1
Richmond Cl BSF CM23 96 B3 2
WARE SG12 116 A7
Richmond Ct BROX EN10 159 L7 3
HAT AL10 155 G8 2
POTB/CUF EN6 187 H2 2
Richmond Dr WAT WD17 195 K3
Richmond Gdns
KTN/HRWW/W HA3 207 L7
Richmond Hl LTNE LU2 3 G2
Richmond Rd BAR EN5 201 G6 1
POTB/CUF EN6 187 H2
Richmond Wy
RKW/CH/CXG WD3 195 H5
Rickfield Cl HAT AL10 154 F7 2
Rickmansworth La
CFSP/GDCR SL9 202 E5
Rickmansworth Rd
DEN/HRF UB9 204 B8
NTHWD HA6 205 J7
RKW/CH/CXG WD3 193 K4
WATW WD18 195 K5
Rickyard Cl LTNE LU2 66 A7 2
Rickyard Meadow
STALW/RED AL3 129 M5
The Rickyard BLDK SG7 18 C7 1
Riddell Gdns BLDK SG7 40 E2 2
Riddings La HLWS CM18 162 F6
Riddy Hill Cl HTCHE/RSTV SG4 52 F4 3
Riddy La LTNN/LIM LU3 65 G5
The Riddy WLYN AL6 111 L2
The Ride DUN/WHIP LU6 80 A4
Ridge Av HARP AL5 108 D6
LWTH SG6 39 M4
Ridgedown STALW/RED AL3 129 M5 1
Ridgefield WAT WD17 181 K8
Ridgehurst Av GSTN WD25 181 L4
Ridge La WAT WD17 181 K7
Ridge Lea HHW HP1 148 E8
Ridgemount End
CFSP/GDCR SL9 202 D5 3
Ridge Rd LWTH SG6 39 M4
Ridge St WATN WD24 196 A1
Ridgeview LCOL/BKTW AL2 170 E7
Ridge Vw TRING HP23 124 B5
Ridgeview Cl BAR EN5 200 C7
Ridge Wy RKW/CH/CXG WD3 194 A8
Ridgeway BERK HP4 146 E6
DUN/WHIP LU6 105 K2
HARP AL5 108 D6 1
LBUZ LU7 103 H4
STDN SG11 95 G1
STVG SG1 5 H3
TRING HP23 102 F8
TRING HP23 124 C8
TRING HP23 144 A7
WGCE AL7 135 G5
Ridgeway Av DUN/HR/TOD LU5 63 J8
EBAR EN4 201 L7
Ridgeway Cl HHS/BOV HP3 166 E4
Ridgeway Dr DUN/HR/TOD LU5 81 K1
Ridgeways HLWE CM17 163 K2
The Ridgeway ENC/FH EN2 188 B7
HERT/WAS SG14 136 E3
HTCH/STOT SG5 52 C4
POTB/CUF EN6 173 M6
POTB/CUF EN6 187 L6
RAD WD7 183 L8
STALE/WH AL4 152 F3
WARE SG12 116 B7
WAT WD17 181 K8
WLYN AL6 111 L1
Ridgewood Dr HARP AL5 108 D7
Ridgewood Gdns HARP AL5 108 D6 2
Ridgmont Rd STAL AL1 11 H9
Ridgway Rd LTNE LU2 3 G3
The Ridings BSF CM23 96 C6
CSHM HP5 178 C7
HERT/WAS SG14 136 F5
LTNW/LEA LU4 2 A2
STALW/RED AL3 106 D4
STVGE SG2 5 L7
Ridlins End STVGE SG2 71 H8
Rigery La STDN SG11 92 E4
Ringshall Dr BERK HP4 126 A2
Ringshall Rd BERK HP4 104 A7
Ringtale Pl BLDK SG7 41 G1 1
Ringway Rd LCOL/BKTW AL2 169 G6
Ringwood Rd LTNE LU2 65 J4
Ripley Rd LTNW/LEA LU4 82 B1
Ripley Wy CHESW EN7 190 A1
HHW HP1 148 D6
Ripon Rd STVG SG1 54 E8
Ripon Wy BORE WD6 199 H6
STALE/WH AL4 153 J3
Risdens HLWS CM18 162 B5 1
Risedale Cl HHS/BOV HP3 166 D2 1
Risedale Hl HHS/BOV HP3 166 D2
Risedale Rd HHS/BOV HP3 166 D2
The Rise BLDK SG7 40 D3
BORE WD6 198 E6
LCOL/BKTW AL2 169 J4
Rising Hill Cl NTHWD HA6 205 H6 2
Risingholme Cl BUSH WD23 197 G8
Ritcroft Cl HHS/BOV HP3 150 A8
Ritcroft Dr HHS/BOV HP3 150 A8
Ritcroft St HHS/BOV HP3 150 A8
Ritz Ct POTB/CUF EN6 186 F2 1
Rivenhall End WGCE AL7 135 H4
River Av HOD EN11 160 A3
River Cl CHES/WCR EN8 190 F5
River Ct HTCH/STOT SG5 38 E6
Riverfield La SBW CM21 120 D7 2
Riverford Cl HARP AL5 109 G6
River Hl STALW/RED AL3 107 G8
River Md HTCH/STOT SG5 38 B8
River Meads WARE SG12 139 H5
Rivermill HLW CM20 6 C3
River Pk HHW HP1 165 M1
Riversend Rd HHS/BOV HP3 166 B2
Rivershill HERT/WAS SG14 90 D7
Riverside BSF CM23 96 E3
BUNT SG9 58 D3
LCOL/BKTW AL2 170 D6 4
WLYN AL6 112 A5
Riverside Av BROX EN10 176 F1
Riverside Cl KGLGY WD4 167 G8
STAL AL1 169 K1 1
Riverside Ct HLW CM20 142 B4
Riverside Dr RKW/CH/CXG WD3 204 C1
Riverside Gdns BERK HP4 146 F5
Riverside Rd LTNN/LIM LU3 64 F5
OXHEY WD19 12 F9
STAL AL1 11 G9
Riversmead HOD EN11 159 M5 3
Riversmeet HERT/WAS SG14 137 G5
River St WARE SG12 138 D1
River Vw WGCE AL7 112 D8
River Wy HLW CM20 141 M5
LTNN/LIM LU3 64 D5
Rivett Cl BLDK SG7 40 F1
Robbery Bottom La WLYN AL6 112 E2
Robb Rd STAN HA7 207 M6
Robbs Cl HHW HP1 148 F5 5
Robe End HHW HP1 148 E5
Robert Av LCOL/BKTW AL2 169 H3
Robert Cl POTB/CUF EN6 186 D4
Roberts Cl CHES/WCR EN8 190 D1 3
Roberts La CFSP/GDCR SL9 202 F5
Robertson Cl BROX EN10 176 D5 3
Roberts Rd WATW WD18 13 G6 1
Roberts Wy HAT AL10 154 E7
Roberts Wood Dr
CFSP/GDCR SL9 202 F5
Robert Wallace Cl BSF CM23 96 E1
Robeson Wy BORE WD6 199 H2
Robin Cl WARE SG12 139 H7
Robin Hl BERK HP4 147 H7
Robin Hood Dr BUSH WD23 196 E2
KTN/HRWW/W HA3 207 L7
Robin Hood La HAT AL10 154 F4
Robin Hood Meadow
HHNE HP2 149 L2 4
Robin Md WGCE AL7 134 F1
Robins Cl LCOL/BKTW AL2 170 D6 5
Robinsfield HHW HP1 148 F7
Robins Nest Hl HERT/BAY SG13 157 H5
Robinson Av CHESW EN7 175 G7
Robinson Cl BSF CM23 96 E5
Robinson Crs BUSH WD23 207 H1
Robins Orch CFSP/GDCR SL9 202 D6 3
Robins Rd HHS/BOV HP3 166 F1
Robins Wy HAT AL10 154 E8
Robinswood LTNE LU2 65 K5
Robin Wy POTB/CUF EN6 174 D7
Robson Cl CFSP/GDCR SL9 202 D5
Robsons Cl CHES/WCR EN8 176 B8 2
Rochester Av LTNE LU2 66 B6
Rochester Dr GSTN WD25 182 B6 3
Rochester Wy
RKW/CH/CXG WD3 195 G5
ROY SG8 21 J2 1
Rochford Av WAB EN9 191 J5
Rochford Cl BROX EN10 176 D5
Rochford Dr LTNE LU2 66 D8
Rochford Rd BSF CM23 97 G1
Rockcliffe Av KGLGY WD4 181 G1
Rockfield Av WARE SG12 116 C7
Rockingham Wy STVG SG1 4 F7
Rockleigh HERT/WAS SG14 137 G4
Rockley Rd LTN LU1 82 F4
Rock Rd ROY SG8 21 H2
Rockways BAR EN5 199 L7
Rodeheath LTNW/LEA LU4 64 C7
Roden Cl HLWE CM17 142 E6
Rodgers Cl BORE WD6 198 C7
Rodney Av STAL AL1 169 M1
Rodney Cl LTNW/LEA LU4 63 L7
Rodney Crs HOD EN11 159 M2
Roebuck Cl HERT/BAY SG13 137 M4
LTN LU1 82 F4
Roebuck Ga STVGE SG2 88 E1
Roe Cl HTCH/STOT SG5 26 D5
Roedean Cl LTNE LU2 66 C7
Roe End La STALW/RED AL3 105 M6
Roefields Cl HHS/BOV HP3 165 M3
Roe Green Cl HAT AL10 154 D6
Roe Green La HAT AL10 154 E5
Roe Hill Cl HAT AL10 154 E6
Roehyde Wy HAT AL10 154 D7
Roestock Gdns STALE/WH AL4 171 K1
Roestock La STALE/WH AL4 171 J2
Rofant Rd NTHWD HA6 205 K6
Rogate Rd LTNE LU2 66 B5
Rogers Ruff NTHWD HA6 205 H8
Roland St STAL AL1 11 M7
Rolfe Cl EBAR EN4 201 K5
Rolleston Cl WARE SG12 116 B7 6
Rollswood WGCE AL7 134 D7
Rollswood Rd WLYN AL6 111 M3
Rollys La BLDK SG7 18 C6
Roman Gdns DUN/HR/TOD LU5 63 G6
KGLGY WD4 181 G1
LWTH SG6 39 K4
Roman La BLDK SG7 40 E2
Roman Ri SBW CM21 120 C8
Roman Rd AMP/FLIT/B MK45 35 J7
LTNW/LEA LU4 64 D7
RAD WD7 183 M6
Roman St HOD EN11 159 M3 3
Roman V HLWE CM17 142 B5
Roman Wy STALW/RED AL3 106 D4
STDN SG11 75 J7 1
WLYN AL6 112 B5
Romany Cl LWTH SG6 39 H4
Romany Ct HHNE HP2 9 L6 1
Romeland BORE WD6 198 C7 5
STALW/RED AL3 10 D7
WAB EN9 191 H4
Romeland Hl STALW/RED AL3 10 D7
Romilly Dr OXHEY WD19 206 D4
Rondini Av LTNN/LIM LU3 65 G8
Ronsons Wy STALW/RED AL3 152 E3
Rookery Dr LTNE LU2 65 K4
The Rookery STSD CM24 79 K2 6
Rookery Yd STVG SG1 70 B3 1
Rookes Cl LWTH SG6 40 A7
Rooks Hl RKW/CH/CXG WD3 194 B5
WGCW AL8 134 B5
Rooks Nest La ROY SG8 30 E3
Rook Tree Cl HTCH/STOT SG5 26 F4 1
Rook Tree La HTCH/STOT SG5 26 E3
Rookwood Dr STVGE SG2 89 G1
Roosevelt Av SHFD SG17 24 B1
Rosary Ct POTB/CUF EN6 187 G1 3
Rosary Gdns BUSH WD23 197 K8
Roseacre Gdns WGCE AL7 135 J4 1
Roseacres RBSF CM22 99 H3
SBW CM21 120 C7
Rosebank WAB EN9 191 K5
Rosebarn La TRING HP23 123 J1
Roseberry Ct WAT WD17 195 M2 4
Rosebery BSF CM23 97 H4
Rosebery Av HARP AL5 108 E8
Rosebery Rd BUSH WD23 207 G1
RAYLNE/WEN HP22 122 E5
Rosebery Wy TRING HP23 124 A5
Rosebriar Wk WATN WD24 181 L7
Rose Ct CHESW EN7 175 M6
Rosecroft Dr WAT WD17 181 K8
Rosecroft La WLYN AL6 112 F2
Rosedale DUN/HR/TOD LU5 63 K5
WGCE AL7 112 E8
Rosedale Av CHESW EN7 175 L8
Rosedale Cl LCOL/BKTW AL2 182 D1
LTNW/LEA LU4 64 B3
Rosedale Wy CHESW EN7 175 M8
Rose Gdns WATW WD18 12 D7
Roseheath HHW HP1 148 D6
Rosehill BERK HP4 147 G6 6
Rosehill Cl HOD EN11 159 L4
Rosehill Gdns ABLGY WD5 181 H3
Roselands Av HOD EN11 159 L2
Rose La STALE/WH AL4 110 B8
Rose Lawn BUSH WD23 207 H1
Rose Md POTB/CUF EN6 187 H1
Rose Meadow STDN SG11 59 K6
Rosemont Cl LWTH SG6 39 K4 1
Rosemount HLWW/ROY CM19 162 A5
Rose V HOD EN11 159 M4
Rose Wk ROY SG8 21 H3 2
STALE/WH AL4 153 G5
The Rose Wk RAD WD7 184 A7
Rose Wood Cl LTNE LU2 65 L8
Rosewood Ct HHW HP1 148 D6 3
Rosewood Dr ENC/FH EN2 188 F6
Roslyn Cl BROX EN10 159 K8
Roslyn Wy DUN/HR/TOD LU5 62 F5
Ross Cl KTN/HRWW/W HA3 207 H7
LTN LU1 83 G4
Ross Crs GSTN WD25 181 M6
Rossfold Rd LTNN/LIM LU3 64 C2
Rossington Av BORE WD6 198 D1
Rossiter Flds BAR EN5 200 D7
Rosslyn Av EBAR EN4 201 K7
Rosslyn Crs LTNN/LIM LU3 65 H5
Rosslyn Rd WATW WD18 12 E3
Rossway LTN LU1 107 G1
Ross Wy NTHWD HA6 205 L4
Rossway Dr BUSH WD23 197 H6
Rossway La TRING HP23 145 M2
Roswell Cl CHES/WCR EN8 190 D1 4
Rothamsted Av HARP AL5 130 E1
Rotheram Av LTN LU1 83 G5
Rother Cl GSTN WD25 182 B5
Rother Fld LTNE LU2 66 C7
Rotherfield Rd PEND EN3 190 C8
Rotherwood Cl
DUN/WHIP LU6 80 D1 1
Rothesay Rd LTN LU1 2 C7
Rothschild Av
RAYLNE/WEN HP22 122 D5
Roughdown Av HHS/BOV HP3 165 M2
Roughdown Rd HHS/BOV HP3 166 A2
Roughdown Villas Rd
HHS/BOV HP3 165 M2
The Roughs NTHWD HA6 205 K3
Roughwood Cl WAT WD17 195 K1
Roughwood La CSTG HP8 192 D7
Roundabout La WLYN AL6 112 E2
Round Coppice Rd RBSF CM22 97 M2
Roundcroft CHESW EN7 175 L5
Roundfield Av HARP AL5 109 J6
Roundhaye STDN SG11 75 J7
Roundhills WAB EN9 191 K5
The Roundings HERT/BAY SG13 138 B8
Roundmoor Dr CHES/WCR EN8 176 D8
The Roundway WATW WD18 12 A9
Roundwood HHS/BOV HP3 166 D6
Roundwood Cl HTCHE/RSTV SG4 39 H8
WLYN AL6 112 C2
Roundwood Dr WGCW AL8 134 B3
Roundwood Gdns HARP AL5 108 D8
Roundwood La HARP AL5 108 A7
Roundwood Pk HARP AL5 108 D7
Rounton Rd WAB EN9 191 K4
Rousebarn La
RKW/CH/CXG WD3 194 E1
Rowan Cl HTCHE/RSTV SG4 55 G2
KTN/HRWW/W HA3 207 L6 3
LCOL/BKTW AL2 182 F2
LTN LU1 83 G3
STALE/WH AL4 153 K7
Rowan Crs LWTH SG6 39 K4
STVG SG1 70 C3
Rowan Dr BROX EN10 176 E3
Rowan Gv HTCHE/RSTV SG4 52 F6
Rowans WGCE AL7 134 E1
The Rowans BLDK SG7 40 D3
BROX EN10 159 K6
HHW HP1 148 F7 2
Rowan Wk SBW CM21 120 D8
Rowan Wy HARP AL5 131 H2
Rowcroft HHW HP1 148 D8
Rowelfield LTNE LU2 84 B1
Rowington Cl LTNE LU2 66 D8
Rowland Rd STVG SG1 4 F6
Rowlands Av PIN HA5 206 F6
Rowlands Cl CHES/WCR EN8 190 C1
Rowland Wy LWTH SG6 39 L4 1
Rowlatt Dr STALW/RED AL3 168 F1
Rowley Cl OXHEY WD19 13 L8
Rowley Green Rd BAR EN5 199 M6
Rowley La BAR EN5 199 K5
BORE WD6 199 J2
Rowley's Rd HERT/BAY SG13 137 L3
Rowley Wk HHNE HP2 150 B2 1
Rowney Gdns SBW CM21 142 B2
Rowney La WARE SG12 92 A5
Rowney Wd SBW CM21 142 B1
Royal Av CHES/WCR EN8 190 D4
Royal Ct HHS/BOV HP3 166 D2
Royal Oak Cl BUNT SG9 44 C5
Royal Oak Gdns BSF CM23 96 D4
Royal Oak La HTCH/STOT SG5 37 J6
Royal Rd STAL AL1 153 G7
Royal Wk DUN/WHIP LU6 81 H3
Royce Cl BROX EN10 159 L8 2
DUN/WHIP LU6 80 E3
Roydon Cl LTNW/LEA LU4 63 M6
Roydon Ct HHNE HP2 149 M1
Roydon Rd HLWW/ROY CM19 161 L2
WARE SG12 139 J6
Royle Cl CFSP/GDCR SL9 202 E7
Roy Rd NTHWD HA6 205 L7
Royse Gv ROY SG8 21 J6
Royston Cl HERT/WAS SG14 137 G4 6
Royston Gv PIN HA5 206 E6
Royston Park Rd PIN HA5 206 E6
Royston Rd BLDK SG7 40 F1
ROY SG8 19 M1
ROY SG8 22 E7
ROY SG8 32 B5
STAL AL1 153 G8
Rucklers La KGLGY WD4 165 M7
Ruckles Cl STVG SG1 4 F3
Rudd Cl STVGE SG2 5 M9
Rudham Gv LWTH SG6 40 B7 5
Rudolph Rd BUSH WD23 196 F7
Rudyard Cl LTNW/LEA LU4 64 C7
Rue De St Lawrence
WAB EN9 191 H5 5
Rueley Dell Rd LTNE LU2 50 C8
Rugby Wy RKW/CH/CXG WD3 195 G6
The Ruins STALW/RED AL3 130 A5
Rumballs Rd HHS/BOV HP3 166 F2
Rumbold Rd HOD EN11 160 B2
Rumsley CHESW EN7 175 M6
Runcie Cl STALE/WH AL4 152 F3
Runcorn Crs HHNE HP2 8 D1
Rundells HLWS CM18 162 F6
LWTH SG6 40 C6
Runfold Av LTNN/LIM LU3 64 F5
Runham Cl LTNW/LEA LU4 64 A6
Runham Rd HHS/BOV HP3 166 D1
Runley Rd LTN LU1 82 E3
Runnalow LWTH SG6 39 J3
Runsley WGCE AL7 134 F1

Ruscombe Dr
LCOL/BKTW AL2 169 H5 1
Rushall Cn LTNE LU2 66 C8
Rushby Md LWTH SG6 39 M4
Rushby Pl LWTH SG6 39 M5
Rushby Wk LWTH SG6 39 M4
Rush Cl WARE SG12 139 H6
Rushdene Av EBAR EN4 201 K8
Rushden Rd BUNT SG9 43 C2
Rushendon Furlong
LBUZ LU7 102 D5 2
Rushen Dr HERT/BAY SG13 138 B7
Rushes Md HLWS CM18 162 D4
Rushfield POTB/CUF EN6 186 C4
SBW CM21 120 D8 1
Rushfield Rd WARE SG12 116 E7 1
Rushleigh Av CHES/WCR EN8 190 C1
Rushleigh Gn BSF CM23 96 C7
Rushmoor Cl
RKW/CH/CXG WD3 204 C2 1
Rushton Av GSTN WD25 181 M6
Rushton Gv HLWE CM17 163 J2
Ruskin Av WAB EN9 191 K5
Ruskin Cl CHESW EN7 175 K5
Ruskin La HTCHE/RSTV SG4 53 H3
Rusper Gn LTNE LU2 66 C7
Russell Av STALW/RED AL3 10 E6
Russell Cl AMS HP6 192 C2
DUN/WHIP LU6 105 K2
NTHWD HA6 205 H5
STVGE SG2 71 G8
Russell Ct LCOL/BKTW AL2 182 F1 1
Russell Crs GSTN WD25 181 L6 3
Russellcroft Rd WGCW AL8 134 B3
Russell La WAT WD17 181 J7
Russell Pl HHS/BOV HP3 166 A2
Russell Ri LTN LU1 2 C9
Russell Rd NTHWD HA6 205 H3
Russell's Dr CHES/WCR EN8 190 D2 2
Russell's Ride CHES/WCR EN8 190 C2
Russell St HERT/WAS SG14 137 H4
LTN LU1 2 C8
Russell Wy OXHEY WD19 196 A8
Russet Cl CHESW EN7 175 K5 3
Russet Dr RAD WD7 184 D3
STALE/WH AL4 153 H8
Russett Wd WGCE AL7 135 J5
Rutherford Cl BORE WD6 199 H3
STVG SG1 69 M4
Rutherford Wy BUSH WD23 207 J1
Ruthin Cl LTN LU1 83 J5
Ruthven Av CHES/WCR EN8 190 C4
Rutland Crs LTNE LU2 3 K6
The Rutts BUSH WD23 207 J1
Ryall Cl LCOL/BKTW AL2 168 D8
Ryan Wy WATN WD24 196 B2
Rydal Wy LTNN/LIM LU3 64 E5
Ryder Av HTCH/STOT SG5 38 C7
Ryder Cl BUSH WD23 197 G7 7
HERT/BAY SG13 138 A3 4
HHS/BOV HP3 164 F7
Ryders Av STALE/WH AL4 154 D7
The Ryde BRKMPK AL9 155 H3
Rye Cl HARP AL5 109 G6 2
Ryecroft HAT AL10 154 E7 3
HLWW/ROY CM19 6 A7
STVG SG1 70 D3
Ryecroft Cl HHNE HP2 150 B8 6
Ryecroft Crs BAR EN5 200 A6
Ryecroft Wy LTNE LU2 65 M7
Ryefeld Cl HOD EN11 139 G8
Ryefield LTNN/LIM LU3 64 F1 2
Rye Gdns BLDK SG7 41 G1 7
Rye Hl HARP AL5 109 G6
Rye Hill Rd HLWS CM18 162 C7
Ryelands WGCE AL7 134 E7 2
Rye Rd HOD EN11 160 A3
Rye St BSF CM23 96 E1
Rylands Heath LTNE LU2 66 E8
Ryley Cl HNLW SG16 25 G5
Rymill Cl HHS/BOV HP3 164 F7
Ryton Cl LTN LU1 83 G3

S

Saberton Cl STALW/RED AL3 129 L6
Sacombe Gn LTNN/LIM LU3 65 G1
Sacombe Green Rd WARE SG12 91 K6
Sacombe Pound WARE SG12 91 J8
Sacombe Rd HERT/WAS SG14 115 G6
HHW HP1 148 E5
Sacombs Ash La SBW CM21 119 K3
Saddlers Cl BLDK SG7 40 D2 3
BORE WD6 199 J6 2
PIN HA5 206 F5
Saddlers Pl ROY SG8 21 H3 3
Sadleir Rd STAL AL1 169 K1
Sadlers Md HLWS CM18 7 M8
Sadlers Wy HERT/WAS SG14 136 F4
Sadlier Rd STDN SG11 75 J8 2
Saffron Cl ARL/CHE SG15 25 M3
HOD EN11 159 L3
LTNE LU2 65 J3 3
LTNE LU2 65 J4 2
Saffron Hl LWTH SG6 39 K4
Saffron La HHW HP1 149 G6 4
Saffron Mdw STDN SG11 75 K8
Saffron St ROY SG8 21 L5
Sainfoin End HHNE HP2 9 G4
St Agnells Ct HHNE HP2 149 M3
St Agnells La HHNE HP2 149 M2
St Albans Dr STVG SG1 70 D1
St Albans Hl HHS/BOV HP3 166 D2
St Albans La ABLGY WD5 167 M5
St Albans Link STVG SG1 70 D1 1
St Albans Rd BAR EN5 200 D2
GSTN WD25 182 C5
HARP AL5 131 G4
HHNE HP2 149 L8 1
HHS/BOV HP3 149 M8
POTB/CUF EN6 185 M3
STALE/WH AL4 152 F3
STALW/RED AL3 130 B6
WAT WD17 12 E1
WATN WD24 196 A1
WLYN AL6 111 K4
St Albans Rd East HAT AL10 155 G4
St Albans Rd West HAT AL10 154 E4
St Andrew's Av HARP AL5 130 E1 1
St Andrew's Cl LTN LU1 107 H1
St Andrews Dr STVG SG1 54 E7
St Andrews La
DUN/HR/TOD LU5 63 H5 4
St Andrew's Meadow
HLWS CM18 7 J8
St Andrew's Pl
HTCHE/RSTV SG4 52 E4 1
St Andrew's Rd
HHS/BOV HP3 166 C3 6
St Andrew St HERT/WAS SG14 137 H4
St Anna Rd BAR EN5 200 C6 3
St Anne's Cl CHESW EN7 175 M7 2
OXHEY WD19 206 B4
St Anne's Pk BROX EN10 159 M7
St Anne's Rd HTCH/STOT SG5 52 E2 4
LCOL/BKTW AL2 170 C6
St Ann's Rd LTN LU1 2 F7
St Anthonys Av HHS/BOV HP3 167 G1
St Audreys Cl HAT AL10 155 G8
St Audreys Gn WGCE AL7 134 E5
St Augusta Ct STALW/RED AL3 10 E2
St Augustine Av LTNN/LIM LU3 65 G7
St Augustine Cl
HTCH/STOT SG5 52 E2 5
St Augustines Cl BROX EN10 159 L7 4
St Augustines Dr BROX EN10 159 L7
St Bernard's Cl LTNN/LIM LU3 65 H7
St Bernard's Rd STALW/RED AL3 11 G4
St Catharine's Rd BROX EN10 159 M6
St Catherines Av LTNN/LIM LU3 65 G6
St Christopher's Cl
DUN/HR/TOD LU5 81 L1
St Cross Ct HOD EN11 159 M6 2
St Cuthberts Gdns PIN HA5 206 E7 3
St Cuthberts Rd HOD EN11 160 B1
St David's Cl HHS/BOV HP3 167 J1
STVG SG1 54 E7
St David's Dr BROX EN10 159 L6
St Dunstan's Rd WARE SG12 140 C2 1
St Edmunds BERK HP4 147 H7
St Edmunds Dr STAN HA7 207 M8
St Edmunds Wk
STALE/WH AL4 153 J8 1
St Edmund's Wy HLWE CM17 142 B6 2
St Elmo Ct HTCHE/RSTV SG4 52 E5 1
St Ethelbert Av LTNN/LIM LU3 65 G6
St Etheldreda's Dr HAT AL10 155 H5 1
St Faiths Cl HTCHE/RSTV SG4 53 G1
St Francis Cl BUNT SG9 58 E4
OXHEY WD19 206 A1
POTB/CUF EN6 187 H4
St George's Dr OXHEY WD19 206 D3
St George's Rd HHS/BOV HP3 166 B3 1
WATN WD24 182 A8 2
WATN WD24 196 A1 4
St George's Wy STVG SG1 4 D3
St Giles' Av POTB/CUF EN6 185 M4
St Giles Rd HTCHE/RSTV SG4 87 L8
St Helen's Cl STALE/WH AL4 132 C2 2
St Heliers Rd STALE/WH AL4 153 G2
St Ives Cl LTNN/LIM LU3 65 G7
WLYN AL6 112 E7
St James Cl AMP/FLIT/B MK45 34 D2
DUN/HR/TOD LU5 63 K6 1
St James Rd EBAR EN4 201 J4
HARP AL5 109 G7
LTNN/LIM LU3 65 G7
WATW WD18 12 F6
St James's Rd CHESW EN7 175 H7
BSF CM23 96 A5
St James Wy BSF CM23 96 D8
St John Cl LTN LU1 83 G5
St Johns STDN SG11 75 K7
St John's Av HLWE CM17 142 B6
St John's Cl POTB/CUF EN6 187 H4
WLYN AL6 112 B4
St John's Ct HARP AL5 131 H3 4
STAL AL1 153 G6
St John's Crs STSD CM24 79 K3
St John's La STSD CM24 79 K3 3
WARE SG12 138 F4
St John's Rd ARL/CHE SG15 25 M6
HARP AL5 131 H3
HHW HP1 166 A1
HTCHE/RSTV SG4 52 E5 2
STSD CM24 79 K3
WAT WD17 12 F1
St John's St HERT/WAS SG14 137 J4 14
St John's Ter ENC/FH EN2 189 J8 1
St Johns Wk HLWE CM17 142 B6 3
St John's Well Ct BERK HP4 147 G5 1
St John's Well La BERK HP4 147 G5
St Joseph's Cl LTNN/LIM LU3 64 F6
St Julian's Rd STAL AL1 169 J1
St Katharines Cl HTCH/STOT SG5 38 C7
St Katherine's Wy BERK HP4 146 E3
St Kilda Rd LTNW/LEA LU4 63 L6
St Laurence Dr BROX EN10 176 D2
St Lawrence Cl ABLGY WD5 181 K1
HHS/BOV HP3 164 F6
St Lawrences Av LTNN/LIM LU3 65 H6
St Lawrence Wy
LCOL/BKTW AL2 182 E1
St Leonards Cl BUSH WD23 13 L4
HERT/WAS SG14 137 K2
St Leonard's Ct
STALE/WH AL4 153 H1 1
St Leonards Crs STALE/WH AL4 153 H1
St Leonard's Rd
HERT/WAS SG14 137 J2
WAB EN9 177 J3
St Luke's Cl LTNW/LEA LU4 64 D8
St Margarets STVGE SG2 70 E8
St Margarets Av LTNN/LIM LU3 65 G6
St Margaret's Cl BERK HP4 147 J7
LTNN/LIM LU3 48 E4
St Margaret's Rd WARE SG12 138 F8
St Margaret's Wy HHNE HP2 9 M9
HHNE HP2 150 C7 1
St Mark's Cl BAR EN5 201 G4
STALE/WH AL4 171 G1
St Martin's Av LTNE LU2 65 L8
St Martins Cl HARP AL5 109 H6 1
OXHEY WD19 206 B4 4
St Martin's Rd KNEB SG3 88 F5
St Mary's Av BERK HP4 146 C4
HTCH/STOT SG5 26 E4
NTHWD HA6 205 K5
St Mary's Cl HTCH/STOT SG5 37 J6 2
LWTH SG6 39 L8
STALW/RED AL3 129 M5
STVGE SG2 71 K8
WLYN AL6 112 B5 6
St Mary's Ct POTB/CUF EN6 187 G3
St Mary's Dr STSD CM24 79 L4
St Mary's Ga DUN/WHIP LU6 81 G2 2
St Mary's La HERT/WAS SG14 136 E6
St Mary's Pl SHFD SG17 24 A5
St Mary's Ri HTCHE/RSTV SG4 85 J1
St Mary's Rd CHES/WCR EN8 176 B8
EBAR EN4 201 L8 1
HHNE HP2 8 A6
LTN LU1 2 F6
STDN SG11 75 J8 3
WATW WD18 12 F5
St Marys Wk STALE/WH AL4 153 G3
St Mary's Wy BLDK SG7 40 D4
St Matthews Cl LTNE LU2 2 F4
OXHEY WD19 13 J8
St Michaels Av
DUN/HR/TOD LU5 62 F6
HHS/BOV HP3 150 A8
HHS/BOV HP3 167 G1 2
St Michael's Crs LTNN/LIM LU3 65 H7
St Michaels Dr GSTN WD25 182 A4
St Michael's Mt HTCHE/RSTV SG4 52 F2
St Michael's Rd BROX EN10 159 L7
HTCHE/RSTV SG4 53 G2
St Michael's St STALW/RED AL3 10 A6
St Michaels Wy
POTB/CUF EN6 187 G1 4
St Mildreds Av LTNN/LIM LU3 65 G6
St Monicas Av LTNN/LIM LU3 65 G7
St Neots Cl BORE WD6 198 F1 3
St Nicholas Av HARP AL5 130 F1
St Nicholas Cl AMSS HP7 192 A2
BORE WD6 198 C7
St Nicholas Mt HHW HP1 148 E7
St Olam's Cl LTNN/LIM LU3 65 G4 2
St Olives HTCH/STOT SG5 26 D4
St Pauls Pl STAL AL1 11 L6
St Paul's Rd HHNE HP2 8 B7
LTN LU1 83 K5
St Pauls Wy WAB EN9 191 J4 3
WATN WD24 13 H1
St Peter's Av ARL/CHE SG15 25 M3
St Peter's Cl BAR EN5 200 A6
BUSH WD23 207 J1
HAT AL10 154 F4 2
RKW/CH/CXG WD3 204 A2
STALW/RED AL3 10 F5
St Peters Hl TRING HP23 123 M6
St Peter's Rd DUN/HR/TOD LU5 81 H2
LTN LU1 83 G3
STAL AL1 11 G6
St Peter's St STAL AL1 10 F6
St Peters Wy
RKW/CH/CXG WD3 193 G5
St Ronans Cl EBAR EN4 201 J1
St Saviours Crs LTN LU1 2 C8
St Stephen's Av
STALW/RED AL3 169 G1
St Stephen's Cl
STALW/RED AL3 169 G2 2
St Stephen's Hl STAL AL1 169 H1
St Stephens Rd BAR EN5 200 C6
PEND EN3 190 C8
St Thomas' Dr PIN HA5 206 D8
St Thomas Pl STALE/WH AL4 132 C2
St Valery RBSF CM22 99 H3
St Vincent Dr STAL AL1 169 M1
St Vincent's Wy
POTB/CUF EN6 187 H4 4
St Wilfrid's Cl EBAR EN4 201 K6 2
St Wilfrid's Rd EBAR EN4 201 J6
St Winifreds Av LTNN/LIM LU3 65 H6
St Yon Ct STALE/WH AL4 153 J7
Sakins Cft HLWS CM18 162 E5
Sale Dr BLDK SG7 40 E1
Salisbury Av HARP AL5 108 E8
STAL AL1 153 G7
Salisbury Cl BSF CM23 96 E5
POTB/CUF EN6 187 H3
Salisbury Crs CHES/WCR EN8 190 C3
Salisbury Gdns WGCE AL7 134 E5
Salisbury Rd BAR EN5 200 D4
BLDK SG7 40 D1
HARP AL5 109 J7
HOD EN11 160 B3
LTN LU1 2 C8
PEND EN3 190 E8
STVG SG1 54 F8
WATN WD24 196 A1
WGCE AL7 134 E5
Salisbury Sq
HERT/WAS SG14 137 J4 15
Sallowsprings DUN/WHIP LU6 104 E1
Sally Deards La WLYN AL6 88 A6
Salmon Cl WGCE AL7 134 F1
Salmons Cl WARE SG12 116 C7
Saltdean Cl LTNE LU2 66 C6
Salters BSF CM23 96 B6
Salter's Cl BERK HP4 146 E4 4
RKW/CH/CXG WD3 204 D1
Salters Wy DUN/WHIP LU6 62 E7
Saltfield Cresent LTNW/LEA LU4 64 B6
Salusbury La HTCH/STOT SG5 51 H8
Salwey Crs BROX EN10 159 L7
Samian Ga STALW/RED AL3 168 E1
Sampson Av BAR EN5 200 C6
Sanctuary Cl DEN/HRF UB9 204 B7
Sandalls Spring HHW HP1 148 E5
Sandalwood Cl LTNN/LIM LU3 65 G3 2
Sanday Cl HHS/BOV HP3 167 G1
Sandbrook La TRING HP23 123 H1
Sandell Cl LTNE LU2 65 L8
Sanderling Cl LWTH SG6 39 K2
Sanders Cl LCOL/BKTW AL2 170 C6
Sanders Rd HHS/BOV HP3 166 E2
Sandfield Rd STAL AL1 11 M6
Sandgate Rd LTNW/LEA LU4 64 C8
Sandhurst Ct HARP AL5 131 J4 7
Sandifield HAT AL10 155 G8
Sandland Cl DUN/WHIP LU6 80 F1
Sand La AMP/FLIT/B MK45 35 G3
Sandle Rd BSF CM23 96 F3
Sandmere Cl HHNE HP2 149 M8 2
Sandon Cl TRING HP23 123 L6
Sandon Rd CHES/WCR EN8 190 B1
Sandover Cl HTCHE/RSTV SG4 53 G4
Sandown Rd STVG SG1 71 H1
WATN WD24 196 B1
Sandpit La STAL AL1 11 H4
Sandpit Rd WGCE AL7 134 D6
Sandridgebury La
STALW/RED AL3 132 A8
Sandridge Cl HHNE HP2 149 M1
Sandridge Rd STAL AL1 11 H3
Sandringham Av
HLWW/ROY CM19 161 K2
Sandringham Crs
STALE/WH AL4 152 F3
Sandringham Dr
DUN/HR/TOD LU5 63 K6
Sandringham Rd
POTB/CUF EN6 187 G1 5
WATN WD24 182 A8
Sandringham Wy
CHES/WCR EN8 190 B5
Sandy Cl HERT/WAS SG14 137 G4
Sandycroft Rd AMS HP6 192 A2
Sandy Gv HTCHE/RSTV SG4 52 E4
Sandy La BUSH WD23 197 H4
NTHWD HA6 205 L2
NTHWD HA6 205 M5
Sandy Lodge La NTHWD HA6 205 J2
Sandy Lodge Rd
RKW/CH/CXG WD3 205 G2
Sandy Lodge Wy NTHWD HA6 205 K5
Sandy Ri CFSP/GDCR SL9 202 D8
Sanfoine Cl HTCHE/RSTV SG4 53 H2
Sanfoin Rd LTNW/LEA LU4 63 M6
Santers La POTB/CUF EN6 186 D4
Santingfield North LTN LU1 83 G4
Santingfield South LTN LU1 83 G5
Sappers Cl SBW CM21 120 E8
Saracens Head HHNE HP2 9 H7 1
Sarratt Av HHNE HP2 149 M2
Sarratt La RKW/CH/CXG WD3 194 A3
Sarratt Rd RKW/CH/CXG WD3 180 A8
Sarum Pl HHNE HP2 8 D1
Sarum Rd LTNN/LIM LU3 64 D6
Satinwood Ct HHS/BOV HP3 166 D1 1
Saturn Wy HHNE HP2 8 F3
Sauncey Av HARP AL5 109 G7
Sauncey Wd HARP AL5 109 J6
Sauncey Wood La HARP AL5 109 K5
Saunders Cl CHES/WCR EN8 176 B7
LWTH SG6 40 A3
Savill Cl CHESW EN7 175 H4 5
Savoy Wd EPP CM16 162 A8 2
Sawbridgeworth Rd
RBSF CM22 121 G5
SBW CM21 121 H7
Sawells BROX EN10 159 L8
Sawtry Cl LTNN/LIM LU3 64 F4
Sawtry Wy BORE WD6 198 F1 4
Sawyers La POTB/CUF EN6 186 C5
Sawyers Wy HHNE HP2 8 F9
Saxon Av HTCH/STOT SG5 26 E2
Saxon Cl DUN/WHIP LU6 80 D2
HARP AL5 109 H6
LWTH SG6 39 L1
Saxon Ct BORE WD6 198 D2 2
Saxon Crs AMP/FLIT/B MK45 35 H6
Saxon Rd LTNN/LIM LU3 2 A1
STALE/WH AL4 132 C3
WLYN AL6 112 A7
Saxon Wy BLDK SG7 41 G1
Saxtead Cl LTNE LU2 84 C1
Sayers Gdns BERK HP4 146 F3
Sayer Wy KNEB SG3 88 E6
Sayesbury Av SBW CM21 120 C7
Sayesbury Rd SBW CM21 120 D8
Sayes Gdns SBW CM21 120 E8
Saywell Rd LTNE LU2 3 L1
Scammell Wy WATW WD18 12 B8
Scarborough Av STVG SG1 69 M3
Scatterdells La KGLGY WD4 179 L1
Scawsby Cl DUN/WHIP LU6 80 D1
Scholar's Hl WARE SG12 117 L6
Scholars Ms WGCW AL8 134 C3
Scholars Wk CFSP/GDCR SL9 202 D6
School Cl BRKMPK AL9 156 E4 2
STVGE SG2 5 L7
Schoolfields LWTH SG6 40 B5
School La BRKMPK AL9 156 E4
BUSH WD23 197 G8
HAT AL10 155 G4
HERT/WAS SG14 90 D7
HLW CM20 7 G1
HTCH/STOT SG5 51 H7
HTCHE/RSTV SG4 55 H1
HTCHE/RSTV SG4 68 D4
LCOL/BKTW AL2 182 E5
LTNW/LEA LU4 64 C6
ROY SG8 32 F1
STVGE SG2 56 E7
STVGE SG2 71 K8
WLYN AL6 112 A6
WLYN AL6 135 K1
School Md ABLGY WD5 181 J3
School Rd POTB/CUF EN6 187 H1
School Rw HHW HP1 148 E8
School Wk LWTH SG6 40 A4
Schubert Rd BORE WD6 198 C7
Scot Gv PIN HA5 206 C7
Scotscraig RAD WD7 183 L6
Scots Hl RKW/CH/CXG WD3 194 E7
Scots Hill Cl RKW/CH/CXG WD3 194 E7
Scots Mill La RKW/CH/CXG WD3 194 E7
Scott Av WARE SG12 139 G6
Scott Cl ROY SG8 21 J1 3
Scott Rd BSF CM23 96 D4
LTNN/LIM LU3 64 B3
STVGE SG2 5 L1
Scotts Cl WARE SG12 138 C2
Scott's Rd WARE SG12 138 C2
Scotts Vw WGCW AL8 134 B5
Scottswood Cl BUSH WD23 196 D3 1
Scottswood Rd BUSH WD23 196 D3
Scriveners Cl HHNE HP2 8 C9
Scrubbits Sq RAD WD7 183 M6 1
Scrubbitts Park Rd RAD WD7 183 M6
Seabrook LTNW/LEA LU4 64 A7
Seabrook Rd KGLGY WD4 167 J7
Seacroft Gdns OXHEY WD19 206 C3
Seaford Cl LTNE LU2 66 B7
Seaforth Dr CHES/WCR EN8 190 C5
Seal Cl LTNW/LEA LU4 64 C7
Seaman Cl LCOL/BKTW AL2 169 J4
Seamons Cl DUN/WHIP LU6 81 J4
Searches La ABLGY WD5 168 A6
HHS/BOV HP3 168 B6
Seaton Rd HHS/BOV HP3 166 C2
LCOL/BKTW AL2 170 C6
LTNW/LEA LU4 64 E7
Sebright Rd BAR EN5 200 C3
HHW HP1 165 M1
STALW/RED AL3 106 D5
Secker Crs KTN/HRWW/W HA3 207 H8
Second Av GSTN WD25 182 C6
HLWE CM17 163 G3
HLWS CM18 7 L8
LWTH SG6 40 B4
Sedbury Cl LTNN/LIM LU3 64 F4
Sedge Gn HLWW/ROY CM19 160 E6
WAB EN9 160 D7
Sedgwick Rd LTNW/LEA LU4 64 A3
Seebohm Cl HTCH/STOT SG5 52 B1
Seeleys HLWE CM17 142 B6
Sefton Av KTN/HRWW/W HA3 207 J8
Sefton Cl STAL AL1 11 K4
Sefton Rd STVG SG1 71 G1
Selbourne Rd LTNW/LEA LU4 64 E7
Selby Av STALW/RED AL3 10 E6
Selden Hl HHNE HP2 149 J8
Sele Ml HERT/WAS SG14 137 G4 7
Sele Rd HERT/WAS SG14 137 G4
Selina Cl LTNN/LIM LU3 64 B3
Sells Rd WARE SG12 116 E8
Sellwood Dr BAR EN5 200 C6
Selsey Dr LTNE LU2 66 C5
Selwyn Av HAT AL10 154 C6
Selwyn Crs HAT AL10 154 D5
Selwyn Dr HAT AL10 154 D5
Semphill Rd HHS/BOV HP3 166 D2
Senate Pl STVG SG1 55 G8
Sequoia Cl BUSH WD23 207 J1 2
Sequoia Pk PIN HA5 207 G6
Serby Av ROY SG8 21 H2
Sergehill La ABLGY WD5 167 M5
Serpentine Cl STVG SG1 55 H8
The Service Rd POTB/CUF EN6 186 F3
Seven Acres NTHWD HA6 205 M6
The Severalls LTNE LU2 66 A7 3
Severnmead HHNE HP2 8 C2
Severnvale LCOL/BKTW AL2 170 E6 2
Severn Wy GSTN WD25 182 B5
Sewardstone Rd WAB EN9 191 H5
Sewardstone St WAB EN9 191 H5
Sewardstone Wy WAB EN9 191 H7
Sewell Cl STALE/WH AL4 153 K7
Sewell Harris Cl HLW CM20 7 K4
Sewell La DUN/WHIP LU6 62 C8
Sewells WGCW AL8 134 D1
Sexton Cl CHESW EN7 175 G4 1
Seymour Av LTN LU1 3 G9
Seymour Cl PIN HA5 206 E8
Seymour Crs HHNE HP2 8 C8
Seymour Rd BERK HP4 146 D4
CSTG HP8 202 B4
LTN LU1 83 L5
STALW/RED AL3 11 H1
Seymours HLWW/ROY CM19 161 L5
Shackledell STVGE SG2 5 H9
Shacklegate La
HTCHE/RSTV SG4 86 E4
Shackleton Spring STVGE SG2 5 J8
Shackleton Wy ABLGY WD5 181 M3 2
WGCE AL7 135 J4
Shady Bush Cl BUSH WD23 197 H8 3
Shady La WAT WD17 12 F1
Shaftenhoe End Rd ROY SG8 32 F1
Shaftesbury Av BAR EN5 201 H5
Shaftesbury Rd LTNW/LEA LU4 83 G2
WAT WD17 13 H3
Shaftesbury Wy ROY SG8 21 K5
Shakespeare ROY SG8 21 J2
Shakespeare Rd HARP AL5 131 G1
LTNW/LEA LU4 64 A7
Shakespeare St WATN WD24 196 A1
Shalcross Dr CHES/WCR EN8 190 E1
Shallcross Crs HAT AL10 154 E8
Shambrook Rd CHESW EN7 175 G4
Shangani Rd BSF CM23 96 E5
Shanklin Cl CHESW EN7 175 L8 3
LTNN/LIM LU3 64 F3
Shanklin Gdns OXHEY WD19 206 B4
Shannon Cl HNLW SG16 24 D8
Shantock Hall La HHS/BOV HP3 164 D8
Shantock La HHS/BOV HP3 178 D1
Sharmans Cl WLYN AL6 112 E6
Sharose Ct STALW/RED AL3 106 D5
Sharpcroft HHNE HP2 8 A4
Sharpecroft HLWW/ROY CM19 6 D7
Sharpenhoe Rd
AMP/FLIT/B MK45 34 F8
LTNN/LIM LU3 49 G6
Sharpes La HHW HP1 148 A8
Sharples Gn LTNN/LIM LU3 65 G2
Sharps Wy HTCHE/RSTV SG4 52 F2
Shawbridge HLWW/ROY CM19 162 B5
Shaw Cl BUSH WD23 207 K2
CHES/WCR EN8 176 B8
The Shaws WGCE AL7 135 H5
The Shaw RBSF CM22 121 M7
The Shearers BSF CM23 96 A6
Sheares Hoppit WARE SG12 118 C8
Shearwater Cl STVGE SG2 71 J6
Sheepcot Dr GSTN WD25 182 B5
Sheepcote WGCE AL7 134 F7
Sheepcote La STALE/WH AL4 132 D2
Sheepcot La GSTN WD25 181 M4
Sheepcroft Hl STVGE SG2 71 J7
Sheephouse Rd HHS/BOV HP3 166 E1
Sheering Dr HLWE CM17 142 D7
Sheering Lower Rd SBW CM21 142 E2

Sheering Mill La *SBW* CM21 ...... 120 E8
Sheering Rd *HLWE* CM17 ...... 142 D6
Sheethanger La *HHS/BOV* HP3 ...... 165 M3
Shefford Rd *SHFD* SG17 ...... 24 C1
Shefton Ri *NTHWD* HA6 ...... 205 M7
  HLWE CM17 ...... 163 K2
Sheldon Cl *CHESW* EN7 ...... 175 J5
Shelford Rd *BAR* EN5 ...... 200 B7
Shelley Cl *HTCHE/RSTV* SG4 ...... 53 H3
  NTHWD HA6 ...... 205 L5
  ROY SG8 ...... 21 J1
Shelley La *DEN/HRF* UB9 ...... 203 M7
Shelley Rd *LTNW/LEA* LU4 ...... 63 M8
Shelton Wy *LTNE* LU2 ...... 65 M7
Shenfield Ct *HLWS* CM18 ...... 162 B5
Shenleybury *RAD* WD7 ...... 184 D1
Shenleybury Cottages
  RAD WD7 ...... 184 D2
Shenley HI *RAD* WD7 ...... 184 A5
Shenley La *LCOL/BKTW* AL2 ...... 170 A4
Shenley Rd *BORE* WD6 ...... 198 F4
  HHNE HP2 ...... 150 A4
  RAD WD7 ...... 184 C6
Shenstone HI *BERK* HP4 ...... 147 K5
Shenwood Ct *BORE* WD6 ...... 184 F8
  BORE WD6 ...... 185 G8
Shephall Gn *STVGE* SG2 ...... 5 L9
Shephall La *STVGE* SG2 ...... 88 E1
Shephall Vw *STVGE* SG1 ...... 5 M3
Shephall Wy *STVGE* SG2 ...... 5 M6
Shepherd Cl *STVG* SG1 ...... 21 K5
Shepherd Rd *LTNW/LEA* LU4 ...... 63 K6
Shepherds Ct *BSF* CM23 ...... 96 B6
Shepherds Ct
  HERT/WAS SG14 ...... 137 H1
Shepherds Gn *HHW* HP1 ...... 148 D8
  HHW HP1 ...... 148 D8
Shepherd's La
  RKW/CH/CXG WD3 ...... 193 J7
  STVG SG1 ...... 69 L4
Shepherds Md *HTCH/STOT* SG5 ...... 38 D8
Shepherds Rd *WATW* WD18 ...... 12 B3
Shepherds Wk *BUSH* WD23 ...... 207 J2
Shepherds Wy *BRKMPK* AL9 ...... 173 H6
  HARP AL5 ...... 108 C6
  RKW/CH/CXG WD3 ...... 194 A8
Sheppards *HLWW/ROY* CM19 ...... 161 L5
Sheppards Cl *STALW/RED* AL3 ...... 11 G1
Shepperton Cl *BORE* WD6 ...... 199 J2
Sheppey's La *KGLGY* WD4 ...... 167 K7
Sheraton Cl *BORE* WD6 ...... 198 E6
Sherborne Av *LTNE* LU2 ...... 65 J4
Sherborne Wy
  RKW/CH/CXG WD3 ...... 195 G5
Sherbourne Cl *HHS/BOV* HP3 ...... 165 K8
Sheredes Dr *HOD* EN11 ...... 159 L5
Sherfield Av *RKW/CH/CXG* WD3 ...... 204 C3
Sheridan Cl *HHW* HP1 ...... 149 G8
Sheridan Rd *LTNN/LIM* LU3 ...... 65 H8
  OXHEY WD19 ...... 196 C6
Sheriden Cl *DUN/WHIP* LU6 ...... 81 G1
Sheriden Wk *BROX* EN10 ...... 159 K7
Sheriff Wy *GSTN* WD25 ...... 181 M4
Sheringham Av *STVG* SG2 ...... 70 A1
Sheringham Cl *LTNE* LU2 ...... 65 H3
Sherington Av *PIN* HA5 ...... 206 F7
Shernbroke Rd *WAB* EN9 ...... 191 L5
Sherrardspark Rd
  WGCW AL8 ...... 134 C2
Sherrards Wy *BAR* EN5 ...... 200 F6
Sherwood *LWTH* SG6 ...... 39 L2
Sherwood Av *POTB/CUF* EN6 ...... 186 D3
  STALW/RED AL3 ...... 153 G4
Sherwood Pl *HHNE* HP2 ...... 149 L3
Sherwood Rd *LTNW/LEA* LU4 ...... 64 F8
Sherwoods Ri *HARP* AL5 ...... 131 J2
Sherwoods Rd *OXHEY* WD19 ...... 196 D8
Shetland Cl *BORE* WD6 ...... 199 J7
Shillington Rd *HTCH/STOT* SG5 ...... 24 A8
  HTCH/STOT SG5 ...... 36 D4
  SHFD SG17 ...... 24 A6
Shingle Cl *LTNN/LIM* LU3 ...... 64 F2
Shingle Ct *WAB* EN9 ...... 191 M4
Shire Cl *BROX* EN10 ...... 176 E5
Shire La *CFSP/GDCR* SL9 ...... 203 G5
  RKW/CH/CXG WD3 ...... 193 G6
  TRING HP23 ...... 144 D3
Shiremeade *BORE* WD6 ...... 198 E6
The Shires *LTNE* LU2 ...... 2 D3
  ROY SG8 ...... 21 K4
Shirley Cl *BROX* EN10 ...... 176 E8
  CHES/WCR EN8 ...... 176 B8
  STVGE SG2 ...... 71 G2
Shirley Rd *ABLGY* WD5 ...... 181 L3
  LTN LU1 ...... 2 A5
  STAL AL1 ...... 11 J8
Shooters Dr *WAB* EN9 ...... 177 K1
Shootersway *BERK* HP4 ...... 146 D6
Shootersway La *BERK* HP4 ...... 146 C7
Shootersway Pk *BERK* HP4 ...... 146 E6
Shoplands *WGCW* AL8 ...... 134 C1
Shoreham Cl *STVG* SG1 ...... 69 M2
Shortcroft Cl *BSF* CM23 ...... 97 J2
Shortcroft Ct
  AMP/FLIT/B MK45 ...... 35 G8
Shortlands Gn *WGCE* AL7 ...... 134 E5
Shortlands Pl *BSF* CM23 ...... 96 E2
Short La *LCOL/BKTW* AL2 ...... 168 D8
  STVGE SG2 ...... 71 K6
Shortmead Dr *CHES/WCR* EN8 ...... 190 D2
Shothanger Wy *HHS/BOV* HP3 ...... 165 J4
Shottfield Cl *STALW/RED* AL3 ...... 132 B8
Shott La *LWTH* SG6 ...... 39 M4
Shott Lower *CHESW* EN7 ...... 175 L5
Shrubbery Gv *ROY* SG8 ...... 21 J6
The Shrubbery *HHW* HP1 ...... 148 D6
Shrub Hill Rd *HHW* HP1 ...... 148 E8
Shrublands *BRKMPK* AL9 ...... 173 G5
Shrublands Av *BERK* HP4 ...... 146 F6
Shrublands Rd *BERK* HP4 ...... 146 F5
The Shrublands *POTB/CUF* EN6 ...... 186 D4
Shugars Gn *TRING* HP23 ...... 124 A5
Shurland Av *EBAR* EN4 ...... 201 J7
Sibley Av *HARP* AL5 ...... 131 J3
Sibley Cl *LTNE* LU2 ...... 66 A7

Sibneys Gn *HLWS* CM18 ...... 162 D7
Sibthorpe Rd *BRKMPK* AL9 ...... 172 C3
Siccut Rd *HTCHE/RSTV* SG4 ...... 53 K6
Sicklefield Cl *CHESW* EN7 ...... 175 L5
Siddons Rd *LTNE* LU2 ...... 71 H4
Sidford Rd *HHW* HP1 ...... 148 E7
The Sidings *BROX* EN10 ...... 176 E1
  HAT AL10 ...... 154 D6
  HHNE HP2 ...... 8 B9
Sidmouth Cl *OXHEY* WD19 ...... 206 A2
Sidney Ter *BSF* CM23 ...... 96 E4
Silam Rd *STVG* SG1 ...... 4 E4
Silecroft Rd *LTNE* LU2 ...... 3 K5
  STALW/RED AL3 ...... 130 A6
Silk Mill Rd *OXHEY* WD19 ...... 196 A8
Silk Mill Wy *TRING* HP23 ...... 123 M5
Silverbirch Av *HTCH/STOT* SG5 ...... 26 E2
Silvercliffe Gdns *EBAR* EN4 ...... 201 K5
Silver Cl *RKW/HRWW/W* HA3 ...... 207 J7
Silverdale Rd *BUSH* WD23 ...... 13 M6
Silver Dell *WATN* WD24 ...... 181 L6
Silverfield *BROX* EN10 ...... 176 E1
Silver HI *BORE* WD6 ...... 185 H7
  CSTG HP8 ...... 202 A2
Silver St *BLDK* SG7 ...... 18 C6
  CHESW EN7 ...... 189 J1
  LTN LU1 ...... 2 E6
  ROY SG8 ...... 15 L7
  STSD CM24 ...... 79 J4
  WAB EN9 ...... 191 H5
Silverthorn Dr *HHS/BOV* HP3 ...... 167 G3
Silver Trees *LCOL/BKTW* AL2 ...... 182 E1
Silverwood Cl *NTHWD* HA6 ...... 205 H8
Simmonds Ri *HHS/BOV* HP3 ...... 166 C1
Simon Dean *HHS/BOV* HP3 ...... 164 F6
Simpkins Dr *AMP/FLIT/B* MK45 ...... 35 H6
Simpson Cl *LTNW/LEA* LU4 ...... 64 C8
Simpson Dr *BLDK* SG7 ...... 40 E2
Sinderby Cl *BORE* WD6 ...... 198 D2
Sinfield Cl *STVG* SG1 ...... 5 J3
Singlets La *STALW/RED* AL3 ...... 107 H3
Sir Joseph's Wk *HARP* AL5 ...... 130 F2
Sir Peter's Wy *DUN/WHIP* LU6 ...... 104 D4
Sirus Rd *NTHWD* HA6 ...... 205 M5
Sish Cl *STVG* SG1 ...... 4 D1
Sish La *STVG* SG1 ...... 4 C1
Siskin Cl *BORE* WD6 ...... 198 F5
  BUSH WD23 ...... 13 M4
Sisson Cl *STVGE* SG2 ...... 71 H8
Six Acres *HHS/BOV* HP3 ...... 166 F2
Six Hills Wy *STVG* SG1 ...... 4 A7
Sixth Av *GSTN* WD25 ...... 182 C6
  LWTH SG6 ...... 40 B4
Skarnings Ct *WAB* EN9 ...... 191 M4
Skegness Rd *STVG* SG1 ...... 69 M2
Skegsbury La *HTCHE/RSTV* SG4 ...... 109 L1
Skelton Cl *LTNN/LIM* LU3 ...... 65 G1
Skidmore Wy
  RKW/CH/CXG WD3 ...... 204 D1
Skimpans Cl *BRKMPK* AL9 ...... 172 C3
Skimpot Rd *LTNW/LEA* LU4 ...... 81 M1
Skinners St *BSF* CM23 ...... 96 B6
Skipton Cl *STVGE* SG2 ...... 88 E2
Skua Cl *LTNW/LEA* LU4 ...... 63 M5
Skylark Cnr *STVG* SG2 ...... 71 J7
Skys Wood Rd *STALW/RED* AL4 ...... 153 C5
Slade Ct *RAD* WD7 ...... 184 A7
Sleaford Gn *OXHEY* WD19 ...... 206 C3
Sleapcross Gdns *STALW/RED* AL4 ...... 154 B8
Sleaps Hyde *STVGE* SG2 ...... 89 H1
Sleapshyde La *STALW/RED* AL4 ...... 154 B8
Sleddale *HHNE* HP2 ...... 8 D2
Sleets End *HHW* HP1 ...... 149 G5
Slimmons Dr *STALW/RED* AL4 ...... 152 F3
Slipe La *BROX* EN10 ...... 176 E5
The Slipe *LBUZ* LU7 ...... 101 M3
Slip La *KNEB* SG3 ...... 88 B4
Slippers HI *HHNE* HP2 ...... 8 B6
Sloansway *WGCE* AL7 ...... 134 E1
The Slype *STALW/RED* AL4 ...... 109 M5
Small Acre *HHW* HP1 ...... 148 E7
Smallcroft *WGCE* AL7 ...... 135 G3
Smallford La *STALW/RED* AL4 ...... 154 A4
Smallwood Cl *STALW/RED* AL4 ...... 132 D3
Smarts Gn *CHESW* EN7 ...... 175 L5
Smeaton Cl *WAB* EN9 ...... 191 K3
Smithfield *HHNE* HP2 ...... 8 B5
Smith's End La *ROY* SG8 ...... 32 E1
Smiths La *CHESW* EN7 ...... 175 J5
Smith St *WATW* WD18 ...... 13 G5
The Smithy *STDN* SG11 ...... 77 G8
Smug Oak La *LCOL/BKTW* AL2 ...... 183 G1
Snailswell La *HTCH/STOT* SG5 ...... 38 D5
Snatchup *STALW/RED* AL3 ...... 129 M5
Snells La *AMSS* HP7 ...... 192 A3
Snells Md *BLDK* SG7 ...... 18 B4
Snells Wood Ct *CSTG* HP8 ...... 192 B3
The Snipe *HTCHE/RSTV* SG4 ...... 54 F1
Snowdrop Cl *BSF* CM23 ...... 96 B4
Snowford Cl *LTNN/LIM* LU3 ...... 64 F3
Soham Rd *PEND* EN3 ...... 190 E8
Solesbridge Cl
  RKW/CH/CXG WD3 ...... 193 L6
Solesbridge La
  RKW/CH/CXG WD3 ...... 193 L4
Sollershott East *LWTH* SG6 ...... 39 K6
Sollershott West *LWTH* SG6 ...... 39 K6
Solomon's HI
  RKW/CH/CXG WD3 ...... 194 C8
Solway *HHNE* HP2 ...... 8 E4
Solway Rd North *LTNN/LIM* LU3 ...... 64 F1
Solway Rd South *LTNN/LIM* LU3 ...... 64 F2
Somaford Gv *EBAR* EN4 ...... 201 J3
Somerby Cl *BROX* EN10 ...... 159 M8
Somercoates Cl *EBAR* EN4 ...... 201 K4
Someries Rd *HARP* AL5 ...... 109 H6
  HHW HP1 ...... 148 E5
Somersby Cl *LTN* LU1 ...... 83 K5
Somerset Av *LTNE* LU2 ...... 3 K2
Somerset Rd *BAR* EN5 ...... 201 L6
Somersham *WGCE* AL7 ...... 135 J4
Somers Rd *BRKMPK* AL9 ...... 172 B3
Somers Sq *BRKMPK* AL9 ...... 172 B2
Somers Wy *BUSH* WD23 ...... 197 H5
Sonia Cl *OXHEY* WD19 ...... 196 B8
Soothouse Spring
  STALW/RED AL3 ...... 152 E3

Sopers Rd *POTB/CUF* EN6 ...... 174 E8
Sopwell La *STAL* AL1 ...... 10 E8
Sorrel Cl *LTNN/LIM* LU3 ...... 64 F2
  ROY SG8 ...... 21 L5
Sorrel Garth *HTCHE/RSTV* SG4 ...... 52 F4
Sotheron Rd *WAT* WD17 ...... 13 G1
Souberie Av *LWTH* SG6 ...... 39 L5
Southacre Wy *PIN* HA5 ...... 206 B8
Southall Cl *WARE* SG12 ...... 116 C8
Southampton Gdns
  LTNN/LIM LU3 ...... 64 C1
South Bank Rd *BERK* HP4 ...... 146 E4
Southbrook *SBW* CM21 ...... 142 D1
Southbrook Dr
  CHES/WCR EN8 ...... 176 C7
South Charlton Mead La
  HOD EN11 ...... 160 C5
Southcliffe Dr *CFSP/GDCR* SL9 ...... 202 D5
South Dr *BAR* EN5 ...... 200 E4
  BLDK SG7 ...... 40 E3
  LCOL/BKTW AL2 ...... 169 G4
  ROY SG8 ...... 21 G3
South Cottage Dr
  RKW/CH/CXG WD3 ...... 193 L6
South Cottage Gdns
  RKW/CH/CXG WD3 ...... 193 L6
Southdown Ct *HAT* AL10 ...... 154 F8
Southdown Rd *HARP* AL5 ...... 131 G2
  HAT AL10 ...... 154 F8
South Drift Wy *LTN* LU1 ...... 83 G4
South Dr *POTB/CUF* EN6 ...... 188 D1
  STALE/WH AL4 ...... 153 K6
Southend Cl *STVG* SG1 ...... 70 B3
Southern Av *HNLW* SG16 ...... 25 C7
Southern Ri *LTNE* LU2 ...... 108 E3
Southern Wy *DUN/WHIP* LU6 ...... 105 H6
  HLWE CM17 ...... 163 H4
  HLWS CM18 ...... 162 F4
  HLWW/ROY CM19 ...... 161 M5
  LWTH SG6 ...... 39 K2
Southernwood Cl *HHNE* HP2 ...... 9 G7
Southern Rd *WAD* WD7 ...... 184 D4
Southfield *BAR* EN5 ...... 200 C7
  STDN SG11 ...... 75 J3
  WGCE AL7 ...... 134 C6
Southfield Av *WATN* WD24 ...... 196 B1
Southfield Rd *CHES/WCR* EN8 ...... 190 D3
  HOD EN11 ...... 159 L5
Southfields *LWTH* SG6 ...... 39 L1
  STDN SG11 ...... 75 K8
Southfields Rd *DUN/WHIP* LU6 ...... 81 J4
Southfield Wy *STALE/WH* AL4 ...... 153 J4
South Ga *HLW* CM20 ...... 6 E6
Southgate *LWTH* SG6 ...... 39 L5
Southgate Rd *POTB/CUF* EN6 ...... 187 H4
South Hill Cl *HTCHE/RSTV* SG4 ...... 52 F4
South Hill Rd *HHW* HP1 ...... 149 H7
South Ley *WGCE* AL7 ...... 134 D7
Southmead Crs *CHES/WCR* EN8 ...... 190 D1
Southmill Rd *BSF* CM23 ...... 96 F4
South Ordnance Rd *PEND* EN3 ...... 190 F8
South Park Av
  RKW/CH/CXG WD3 ...... 193 L6
South Park Gdns *BERK* HP4 ...... 147 G5
South Pl *HLW* CM20 ...... 141 M7
  HTCH/STOT SG5 ...... 52 C2
South Riding *LCOL/BKTW* AL2 ...... 182 F1
South Rd *BLDK* SG7 ...... 40 E3
  BSF CM23 ...... 96 F5
  HLW CM20 ...... 141 M7
  LTN LU1 ...... 2 E9
  RBSF CM22 ...... 99 H2
  RKW/CH/CXG WD3 ...... 193 H6
  STDN SG11 ...... 75 J8
Southsea Av *WATW* WD18 ...... 12 C4
Southsea Rd *STVG* SG1 ...... 70 A2
South St *BSF* CM23 ...... 96 E4
  HERT/WAS SG14 ...... 137 J4
  WARE SG12 ...... 116 C7
South Vw *LWTH* SG6 ...... 39 L5
Southview Cl *CHESW* EN7 ...... 175 K5
South View Rd *PIN* HA5 ...... 206 A4
Southview Rd *HARP* AL5 ...... 109 H7
Southwark Cl *STVG* SG1 ...... 71 G1
South Wy *ABLGY* WD5 ...... 181 K4
  GSTN WD25 ...... 181 K4
  HAT AL10 ...... 171 M1
  WAB EN9 ...... 191 J8
South Weald Dr *WAB* EN9 ...... 191 J4
Southwold Rd *WATN* WD24 ...... 182 B8
Southwood Rd
  DUN/HR/TOD LU5 ...... 81 L4
Sowerby Av *LTNE* LU2 ...... 66 B7
Sparhawke *LWTH* SG6 ...... 39 M1
Sparrow Cl *LTNW/LEA* LU4 ...... 63 M6
Sparrow Dr *STVGE* SG2 ...... 71 H6
Sparrows Herne *BUSH* WD23 ...... 197 G8
Sparrows Wy *BUSH* WD23 ...... 197 H8
Sparrowswick Ride
  STALW/RED AL3 ...... 152 B2
Spayne Cl *LTNN/LIM* LU3 ...... 65 G2
Spear Cl *LTNN/LIM* LU3 ...... 64 D4
Speedwell Cl *LTNN/LIM* LU3 ...... 64 F2
Speke Cl *STVGE* SG2 ...... 71 J7
Spellbrooke *HTCH/STOT* SG5 ...... 52 C2
Spellbrook La East *BSF* CM23 ...... 120 E2
Spellbrook La West *SBW* CM21 ...... 120 C3
Spencer Av *CHESW* EN7 ...... 175 K5
  STSD CM24 ...... 79 K4
Spencer Ga *STAL* AL1 ...... 11 H3
Spencer Ms *STAL* AL1 ...... 11 H5
Spencer Rd *LTNW/LEA* LU4 ...... 132 B8
  LTNN/LIM LU3 ...... 2 A2
Spencers Cft *HLWS* CM18 ...... 162 F4
Spencer St *HERT/BAY* SG13 ...... 137 K3
  STALW/RED AL3 ...... 10 E6
Spencer Wk *RKW/CH/CXG* WD3 ...... 194 B6
Spencer Wy *HHW* HP1 ...... 148 F4
Spenser Cl *ROY* SG8 ...... 21 J1
Spenser Rd *HARP* AL5 ...... 131 H1
Sperberry HI *HTCHE/RSTV* SG4 ...... 53 C8
Spicersfield *CHESW* EN7 ...... 175 M6
Spicer St *STALW/RED* AL3 ...... 10 D7
Spindle Berry Cl *WLYN* AL6 ...... 112 F3
Spinney Crs *DUN/WHIP* LU6 ...... 80 E2
Spinney La *WLYN* AL6 ...... 88 C3

Spinney Rd *LTNN/LIM* LU3 ...... 64 C3
Spinney St *HERT/BAY* SG13 ...... 137 M4
The Spinney *BERK* HP4 ...... 146 E7
  BLDK SG7 ...... 40 D3
  BROX EN10 ...... 159 L6
  HARP AL5 ...... 108 D7
  HERT/BAY SG13 ...... 137 L4
  POTB/CUF EN6 ...... 187 J2
  STSD CM24 ...... 79 K5
  STVGE SG2 ...... 71 J3
  WAT WD17 ...... 195 M2
  WGCE AL7 ...... 134 D5
Spitfire Rd *SHFD* SG17 ...... 24 B1
Spoondell *DUN/WHIP* LU6 ...... 80 E3
Spooners Dr *LCOL/BKTW* AL2 ...... 169 H6
Spratts La *DUN/WHIP* LU6 ...... 105 L1
Spreckley Cl *HNLW* SG16 ...... 25 C5
Spring Cl *BAR* EN5 ...... 200 C6
  BORE WD6 ...... 198 F2
  CSHM HP5 ...... 178 C7
  DEN/HRF UB9 ...... 204 C8
Spring Crofts *BUSH* WD23 ...... 196 F6
Spring Dr *STVGE* SG2 ...... 88 F2
Springfield *BCSW* SG18 ...... 14 B6
  BUSH WD23 ...... 207 J1
Springfield Cl *POTB/CUF* EN6 ...... 187 J2
  RKW/CH/CXG WD3 ...... 195 C6
  STAN HA7 ...... 207 M3
Springfield Crs *HARP* AL5 ...... 108 F6
Spring Field Rd *BERK* HP4 ...... 146 E4
Springfield Rd *CHES/WCR* EN8 ...... 190 D5
  DUN/WHIP LU6 ...... 80 B5
  GSTN WD25 ...... 182 A4
  HHNE HP2 ...... 8 E6
  LTNN/LIM LU3 ...... 65 H4
  STAL AL1 ...... 11 M9
  STALE/WH AL4 ...... 154 A7
Springfields *BROX* EN10 ...... 159 L6
  WGCW AL8 ...... 134 A6
Spring Gdns *GSTN* WD25 ...... 182 A6
  HAT AL10 ...... 154 B6
Spring Gln *HAT* AL10 ...... 154 B6
Springhall La *SBW* CM21 ...... 142 D1
Springhall Rd *SBW* CM21 ...... 120 D8
Springhead *BLDK* SG7 ...... 18 C6
Spring Hills *HLW* CM20 ...... 6 A4
  HLW CM20 ...... 161 M1
Spring La *BUNT* SG9 ...... 57 H5
  HHW HP1 ...... 148 F6
Springle La *HERT/BAY* SG13 ...... 138 E7
Spring Pl *LTN* LU1 ...... 4 D4
Spring Rd *HARP* AL5 ...... 107 M6
  LWTH SG6 ...... 39 K5
Springshott *LWTH* SG6 ...... 39 K5
The Springs *BROX* EN10 ...... 176 D4
Spring View Rd *WARE* SG12 ...... 138 B2
Spring Wk *BROX* EN10 ...... 159 H8
Springwell Av
  RKW/CH/CXG WD3 ...... 203 M2
Springwell La
  RKW/CH/CXG WD3 ...... 203 M3
Springwood *CHESW* EN7 ...... 175 L5
Springwood Cl
  DEN/HRF UB9 ...... 204 C8
Springwood Wk *STALE/WH* AL4 ...... 153 H4
Spruce HI *HLWS* CM18 ...... 162 D7
Spruce Wy *LCOL/BKTW* AL2 ...... 169 G6
Spur Cl *ABLGY* WD5 ...... 181 J4
Spurcroft *LTNN/LIM* LU3 ...... 65 H1
Spurrs Cl *HTCHE/RSTV* SG4 ...... 53 C5
The Spur *CHES/WCR* EN8 ...... 176 C7
  STVG SG1 ...... 4 F5
The Square *BROX* EN10 ...... 176 E2
  BUNT SG9 ...... 44 B5
  DUN/WHIP LU6 ...... 81 G2
  SBW CM21 ...... 120 D8
  STALW/RED AL3 ...... 129 L4
  WATN WD24 ...... 182 A8
Squires Cl *BSF* CM23 ...... 96 B2
Squires Ride *HHNE* HP2 ...... 149 L1
Squirrel Cha *HHW* HP1 ...... 148 D6
Squirrels Cl *BSF* CM23 ...... 96 E2
The Squirrels *BUSH* WD23 ...... 197 J7
  HERT/BAY SG13 ...... 138 A4
Stablebridge Rd
  RAYLNE/WEN HP22 ...... 122 E7
Stackfield *HLW* CM20 ...... 142 A7
Stacklands *WGCW* AL8 ...... 134 A6
Staddles *RBSF* CM22 ...... 121 G1
Stadium Wy *HLWW/ROY* CM19 ...... 161 L1
Stafford Cl *CHES/WCR* EN8 ...... 176 A8
Stafford Dr *BROX* EN10 ...... 159 M7
Stafford Rd *KTN/HRWW/W* HA3 ...... 207 H4
Staffords *HLWE* CM17 ...... 142 D6
Stagg HI *POTB/CUF* EN6 ...... 187 J6
Stag Green Av *BRKMPK* AL9 ...... 155 H3
Stag La *BERK* HP4 ...... 146 F5
  RKW/CH/CXG WD3 ...... 193 H7
Stainer Rd *BORE* WD6 ...... 198 C2
Stainers *BSF* CM23 ...... 96 B5
Staines Sq *DUN/WHIP* LU6 ...... 81 H3
Stains Cl *CHES/WCR* EN8 ...... 176 D7
Stake Piece Rd *ROY* SG8 ...... 21 H5
Stakers Ct *HARP* AL5 ...... 131 G1
Stamford Av *ROY* SG8 ...... 21 J3
Stamford Cl
  KTN/HRWW/W HA3 ...... 207 K7
  POTB/CUF EN6 ...... 187 J2
Stamford Rd *WAT* WD17 ...... 196 A3
Stanborough Av *BORE* WD6 ...... 198 F1
Stanborough Cl *WGCW* AL8 ...... 134 B5
Stanborough Ga *WGCW* AL8 ...... 134 A6
Stanborough La *WGCW* AL8 ...... 134 A6
Stanborough Rd *WGCW* AL8 ...... 134 A7
Stanbury Av *WAT* WD17 ...... 181 K8
Standfield *ABLGY* WD5 ...... 181 K2
Standhill Cl *HTCHE/RSTV* SG4 ...... 52 E4
Standhill Rd *HTCHE/RSTV* SG4 ...... 52 E4
Standingford *EPP* CM16 ...... 162 A7
Standon Hl *STDN* SG11 ...... 75 H8
Standon Gdns *STDN* SG11 ...... 76 D7
Standring Ri *HHS/BOV* HP3 ...... 166 A2
Stane Cl *BSF* CM23 ...... 96 E2
Stane Fld *LWTH* SG6 ...... 40 A7
Stane St *BLDK* SG7 ...... 40 F1
Stanford Ct *WAB* EN9 ...... 191 M4

Stanford Rd *LTNE* LU2 ...... 3 K2
Stangate Crs *BORE* WD6 ...... 199 K6
Stanhope Av
  KTN/HRWW/W HA3 ...... 207 J8
Stanhope Rd *BAR* EN5 ...... 200 C7
  CHES/WCR EN8 ...... 190 D4
  STAL AL1 ...... 11 J7
Stanier Ri *BERK* HP4 ...... 146 E3
Stanley Av *LCOL/BKTW* AL2 ...... 168 F4
Stanley Cl *AMP/FLIT/B* MK45 ...... 34 C3
Stanley Dr *HAT* AL10 ...... 155 G7
Stanley Gdns *BORE* WD6 ...... 198 D2
  TRING HP23 ...... 123 J7
Stanley Rd *HERT/BAY* SG13 ...... 137 K5
  LTNN/LIM LU3 ...... 48 F5
  NTHWD HA6 ...... 205 M8
  STVGE SG2 ...... 71 G3
  WAT WD17 ...... 13 H3
Stanley St *LTN* LU1 ...... 2 C8
Stanmore Crs *LTNN/LIM* LU3 ...... 64 C6
Stanmore Rd *STVG* SG1 ...... 70 B3
  WATN WD24 ...... 196 A2
Stanmount Rd
  LCOL/BKTW AL2 ...... 168 F4
Stansted Dr *HOD* EN11 ...... 160 A2
Stanstead Rd *HERT/BAY* SG13 ...... 137 M3
  HOD EN11 ...... 160 A2
  WARE SG12 ...... 138 C5
Stansted Hl *MHAD* SG10 ...... 118 F1
Stansted Rd *BSF* CM23 ...... 79 H7
Stanton Cl *STALE/WH* AL4 ...... 153 J3
Stanton Rd *LTNW/LEA* LU4 ...... 64 D8
Stanway Rd *WAB* EN9 ...... 191 M4
Staplefield Cl *PIN* HA5 ...... 206 D7
Stapleford *WGCE* AL7 ...... 135 J4
Stapleford Rd *LTNE* LU2 ...... 66 A6
Stapleton Cl *POTB/CUF* EN6 ...... 187 J2
Stapleton Rd *BORE* WD6 ...... 198 F1
Stapley Rd *STALW/RED* AL3 ...... 10 E5
Staplyton Rd *BAR* EN5 ...... 200 D4
Star Holme Ct *WARE* SG12 ...... 138 D1
Starkey Cl *CHESW* EN7 ...... 175 H4
Starling La *POTB/CUF* EN6 ...... 174 E2
Star St *WARE* SG12 ...... 138 D1
Statham Cl *LTNN/LIM* LU3 ...... 65 G1
Station Ap *BAR* EN5 ...... 201 H5
  CHES/WCR EN8 ...... 190 D5
  HARP AL5 ...... 131 G1
  HTCHE/RSTV SG4 ...... 52 F2
  KNEB SG3 ...... 88 B6
  NTHWD HA6 ...... 205 K7
  OXHEY WD19 ...... 13 H1
  RAD WD7 ...... 183 M6
  RKW/CH/CXG WD3 ...... 193 H5
Station Cl *BRKMPK* AL9 ...... 172 D5
  POTB/CUF EN6 ...... 186 E2
Station Footpath *KGLGY* WD4 ...... 181 G1
Station Pl *LWTH* SG6 ...... 39 L4
Station Rd *ARL/CHE* SG15 ...... 25 C4
  BAR EN5 ...... 201 G6
  BERK HP4 ...... 147 J5
  BLDK SG7 ...... 18 E6
  BLDK SG7 ...... 19 J8
  BLDK SG7 ...... 40 E1
  BORE WD6 ...... 198 F5
  BRKMPK AL9 ...... 172 C4
  BROX EN10 ...... 159 L7
  BSF CM23 ...... 96 F4
  BUNT SG9 ...... 58 D3
  CHES/WCR EN8 ...... 190 F5
  DUN/HR/TOD LU5 ...... 81 J2
  HARP AL5 ...... 131 G1
  HERT/WAS SG14 ...... 90 C7
  HERT/WAS SG14 ...... 135 M7
  HHS/BOV HP3 ...... 166 A1
  HLWE CM17 ...... 142 E6
  HNLW SG16 ...... 24 E6
  KGLGY WD4 ...... 167 G8
  KNEB SG3 ...... 88 E5
  LBUZ LU7 ...... 101 M1
  LBUZ LU7 ...... 102 D5
  LCOL/BKTW AL2 ...... 182 F2
  LTN LU1 ...... 2 E5
  LTNW/LEA LU4 ...... 64 D5
  LWTH SG6 ...... 39 L4
  MHAD SG10 ...... 118 D1
  POTB/CUF EN6 ...... 174 E8
  RAD WD7 ...... 183 M6
  RBSF CM22 ...... 99 H3
  RKW/CH/CXG WD3 ...... 194 C8
  ROY SG8 ...... 19 G2
  SBW CM21 ...... 120 E7
  STALE/WH AL4 ...... 132 C1
  STALE/WH AL4 ...... 154 A6
  STDN SG11 ...... 75 J7
  STSD CM24 ...... 79 K4
  TRING HP23 ...... 100 F6
  TRING HP23 ...... 124 A6
  WAB EN9 ...... 177 K6
  WARE SG12 ...... 138 C1
  WARE SG12 ...... 139 H6
  WAT WD17 ...... 196 A3
  WCGW AL8 ...... 112 D7
Station Wy *LWTH* SG6 ...... 39 K4
Staveley Rd *DUN/WHIP* LU6 ...... 81 G4
  LTNW/LEA LU4 ...... 82 B1
Steeplands *BUSH* WD23 ...... 197 G8
Steeple Vw *BSF* CM23 ...... 96 E2
Stephens Cl *LTNE* LU2 ...... 65 M7
Stephenson Cr *ROY* SG8 ...... 21 G3
Stephenson Wy *BUSH* WD23 ...... 196 C3
Stephens Wy *STALW/RED* AL3 ...... 129 L5
Stepnells *TRING* HP23 ...... 123 M1
Sterling Av *CHES/WCR* EN8 ...... 190 C5
Stevenage Crs *BORE* WD6 ...... 198 D2
Stevenage Ri *HHNE* HP2 ...... 7 M8
Stevenage Rd *HTCHE/RSTV* SG4 ...... 52 E2
  KNEB SG3 ...... 88 E3
  STVGE SG2 ...... 71 L2
Stevens Gn *BUSH* WD23 ...... 207 H1
Stevenson Cl *BAR* EN5 ...... 201 L4
Steward Cl *CHES/WCR* EN8 ...... 190 D1
Stewart Clark Ct
  DUN/WHIP LU6 ...... 80 F1
Stewart Cl *ABLGY* WD5 ...... 181 M4
Stewart Rd *HARP* AL5 ...... 109 G8
The Stewarts *BSF* CM23 ...... 96 D3
Stile Cft *HLWS* CM18 ...... 162 F4

Stilton Pth BORE WD6 198 F1 5
Stirling Cl HTCHE/RSTV SG4 53 H3 5
STVGE SG2 89 H3
Stirling Wy ABLGY WD5 181 M3
BORE WD6 199 J7
WGCE AL7 135 K4
Stoat Cl HERT/BAY SG13 137 M4
Stobarts Cl KNEB SG3 88 E4
Stockbreach Cl HAT AL10 154 F4
Stockbreach Rd HAT AL10 154 F4
Stockens Dell KNEB SG3 88 E6
Stockens Gn KNEB SG3 88 E6 3
Stockers Farm Rd
RKW/CH/CXG WD3 204 B3
Stockfield Av HOD EN11 159 M2
Stockholm Wy LTNN/LIM LU3 64 D2
Stocking La ROY SG8 46 B1
Stockings La HERT/BAY SG13 157 J5
Stockingstone Rd LTNE LU2 65 K7
Stockmen Fld BSF CM23 96 B5
Stockport Rd
RKW/CH/CXG WD3 193 H8
Stocks Meadow HHNE HP2 9 H6
Stocks Rd TRING HP23 125 J4
Stockwell Cl CHESW EN7 175 M7
Stockwood Crs LTN LU1 2 D9
Stondon Rd SHFD SG17 24 B6
Stonecroft KNEB SG3 88 E5
Stonecroft Cl BAR EN5 200 A5
Stonecross STAL AL1 11 G4
Stonecross Rd HAT AL10 155 G3
Stonehills WGCW AL8 134 C4
Stonelea Rd HHS/BOV HP3 166 E2
Stoneleigh SBW CM21 120 C7 1
Stoneleigh Cl
CHES/WCR EN8 190 C4 5
LTNN/LIM LU3 65 G3
Stoneleigh Dr HOD EN11 160 A1
Stoneley LWTH SG6 39 L1
Stonemason Cl HARP AL5 108 F7 2
Stonemead WGCW AL8 112 C7
Stonesdale LTNW/LEA LU4 64 B6 2
Stoneways Cl LTNW/LEA LU4 64 C4 1
Stoney Cl BERK HP4 146 E4 5
Stoney Common STSD CM24 79 K5
Stoney Common Rd STSD CM24 79 J5
Stoney Cft TRING HP23 125 H5
Stoneycroft WGCE AL7 134 F3
Stoneyfield Dr STSD CM24 79 K5
Stoneygate Rd LTNW/LEA LU4 64 C8
Stoney La HHS/BOV HP3 165 G6
HHW HP1 165 G7
KGLGY WD4 179 K1
Stonnells Cl LWTH SG6 39 L2
Stony Cft STVG SG1 4 E2
Stony Hills WARE SG12 115 H4
Stony La CSHM HP5 178 D8
LTNE LU2 67 G7
Stonyshotts WAB EN9 191 K5
Stony Wd HLWS CM18 7 G9
Stopsley Wy LTNE LU2 65 M7
Storehouse La
HTCHE/RSTV SG4 52 E3 2
Storey St HHS/BOV HP3 166 C3
Stormont Rd HTCH/STOT SG5 52 E1
Stornoway HHS/BOV HP3 167 G1 3
Stortford Hall Pk BSF CM23 97 G2
Stortford Hall Rd BSF CM23 97 G2
Stortford Rd GTDUN CM6 99 M3
HOD EN11 160 A3
RBSF CM22 121 K6
STDN SG11 77 H8
STDN SG11 93 L1
Stort Ldg BSF CM23 96 C2 1
Stort Ml HLW CM20 142 A4
Stort Rd BSF CM23 96 E4 3
Stort Valley Wy HLW CM20 142 C3
HLWE CM17 143 K8
HLWW/ROY CM19 160 E2
SBW CM21 121 H8
Stotfold Rd ARL/CHE SG15 25 M2
BLDK SG7 27 H2
HTCHE/RSTV SG4 39 H6
LWTH SG6 39 H3
The Stow HLW CM20 7 K3
Stox Md KTN/HRWW/W HA3 207 J8
Strafford Cl POTB/CUF EN6 186 F3 2
Strafford Ct KNEB SG3 88 F5 1
Strafford Ga POTB/CUF EN6 186 F3
Strafford Rd BAR EN5 200 D4
The Straits WAB EN9 191 G3
Strangers Wy LTNW/LEA LU4 64 B6
Strangeways WAT WD17 181 K7
Stratfield Dr BROX EN10 159 K6
Stratfield Rd BORE WD6 198 E4
Stratford Rd LTNW/LEA LU4 83 G1
WAT WD17 195 M3
Stratford Wy HHS/BOV HP3 166 A2
LCOL/BKTW AL2 168 E8
WAT WD17 12 B1
Strathmore Av HTCH/STOT SG5 52 D1
LTN LU1 83 K5
Strathmore Rd HTCHE/RSTV SG4 86 D4
Strathmore Wk LTN LU1 3 G9
Stratton Av ENC/FH EN2 189 J8
Stratton Gdns LTNE LU2 65 J6
Strawberry Fields WARE SG12 116 A8
Strawberry Fld LTNN/LIM LU3 64 D3 2
Strawfields WGCE AL7 135 G3 6
Strawmead HAT AL10 155 G3 2
Straw Plait ARL/CHE SG15 25 L6
Strayfield Rd ENC/FH EN2 188 F7
Streatley Rd LTNN/LIM LU3 48 B6
The Street BLDK SG7 42 B2
BUNT SG9 59 M4
BUNT SG9 60 F6
KGLGY WD4 179 M2
RBSF CM22 97 M5
RBSF CM22 143 J2
STDN SG11 73 L7
STDN SG11 75 L3
Stretton Wy BORE WD6 198 D1
Stringers La STVGE SG2 89 K1
Stripling Wy WATW WD18 12 D9
Stroma Cl HHS/BOV HP3 167 H1 5
Stronnell Cl LTNE LU2 65 M7
Stronsay HHS/BOV HP3 167 H1 4
Stuart Ct BORE WD6 198 C7 6
Stuart Dr HTCHE/RSTV SG4 53 G3
ROY SG8 21 J2
Stuart Rd AMP/FLIT/B MK45 35 H7
EBAR EN4 201 K8
WLYN AL6 112 A6
Stuarts Cl HHS/BOV HP3 166 C1 5
Stuart St DUN/WHIP LU6 80 F1
LTN LU1 2 E7
Stuart Wy CHESW EN7 190 A2
Stubbs Cl DUN/HR/TOD LU5 63 J5
Stud Gn GSTN WD25 181 M3
Studham La BERK HP4 104 D6
The Studios BUSH WD23 196 F7 4
Studio Wy BORE WD6 199 H2
Studlands Ri ROY SG8 21 K4
Studley Rd LTNN/LIM LU3 2 C3
Sturgeon's Rd HTCHE/RSTV SG4 39 G8
Sturlas Wy CHES/WCR EN8 190 C4
Sturmer Cl STALE/WH AL4 153 H8 4
Sturrock Wy HTCHE/RSTV SG4 53 H4
Styles Cl LTNE LU2 66 B8
Such Cl LWTH SG6 40 A3
Sudbury Rd LTNW/LEA LU4 64 A4
Sudicamps Ct WAB EN9 191 M4 5
Suffolk Cl BORE WD6 199 J6 3
LCOL/BKTW AL2 170 B4
LTNW/LEA LU4 63 M7
Suffolk Rd LTN LU1 81 L4
POTB/CUF EN6 186 D3
ROY SG8 21 K4
Sugar La HHW HP1 165 G1
Sugden Ct DUN/WHIP LU6 80 F2
Sulgrave Crs TRING HP23 124 B5 3
Sullivan Wy BORE WD6 198 B7
Summer Dl WGCW AL8 112 C8
Summerfield HAT AL10 154 F8
Summerfield Cl
LCOL/BKTW AL2 170 B5
Summerfield Rd GSTN WD25 181 M6
LTN LU1 82 E2
Summer Gv BORE WD6 198 C7
Summer Hl BORE WD6 198 F6
Summerhouse La
DEN/HRF UB9 203 M7
GSTN WD25 197 H2
Summerhouse Wy
ABLGY WD5 181 L1 1
Summersland Rd
STALE/WH AL4 153 H3 3
Summers Rd LTNE LU2 84 B1
Summer St LTN LU1 83 H8
Summerswood La BORE WD6 185 K6
Summer Wk STALW/RED AL3 106 D5 1
Summit Rd POTB/CUF EN6 186 D1
Sumners Farm Cl EPP CM16 161 M7 1
Sumpter Yd STAL AL1 10 E7
Sunbower Av DUN/WHIP LU6 62 D7
Suncote Av DUN/WHIP LU6 62 D7
Suncote Cl DUN/WHIP LU6 62 D8
Sunderland Av STAL AL1 11 L4
Sundew Rd HHW HP1 148 D8 3
Sundon Park Rd LTNN/LIM LU3 64 B2
Sundon Rd DUN/HR/TOD LU5 63 H5
LTNN/LIM LU3 48 E5
LTNW/LEA LU4 63 M1
Sundown Av DUN/WHIP LU6 81 J3
Sun Hl ROY SG8 21 H5
Sun La HARP AL5 108 F8
Sunmead Rd HHNE HP2 8 A5
Sunningdale BSF CM23 96 D4
LTNE LU2 65 L7
Sunningdale Cl STAN HA7 207 M7
Sunningdale Ms WGCE AL7 112 E8 1
Sunny Bank LBUZ LU7 101 L3 3
Sunnybank Rd POTB/CUF EN6 186 F4
Sunny Brook Cl
RAYLNE/WEN HP22 122 C4
Sunny Cft HLWS CM18 162 E5 1
Sunnydell LCOL/BKTW AL2 169 G5
Sunnyfield BRKMPK AL9 155 J2
Sunny Hl BUNT SG9 58 D3
Sunnyhill Rd HHW HP1 149 G7
RKW/CH/CXG WD3 203 J6
Sunnyside STSD CM24 79 K4
WAB EN9 177 L1
Sunnyside Rd HTCHE/RSTV SG4 52 F4
Sunridge Av LTNE LU2 2 F1
Sunrise Crs HHS/BOV HP3 166 E2 1
Sunset Dr LTNE LU2 65 L7
Sunset Vw BAR EN5 200 D3
Sun St BLDK SG7 40 D2 2
HTCH/STOT SG5 52 D4
SBW CM21 142 E1
WAB EN9 191 H4
Surrey Pl TRING HP23 123 M7 4
Surrey St LTN LU1 2 F9
Sursham Ct STALW/RED AL3 106 D5 2
Sussex Cl CSTG HP8 202 A2 1
HOD EN11 159 M3 4
LTNW/LEA LU4 63 L6
Sussex Pl LTNE LU2 66 C8 3
Sussex Rd WATN WD24 195 M1
Sutcliffe Cl BUSH WD23 197 H5
STVG SG1 70 F2
Sutherland Av POTB/CUF EN6 174 C7
Sutherland Cl BAR EN5 200 D5
Sutherland Ct WGCE AL7 134 E3 3
Sutherland Pl LTN LU1 83 J5
Sutherland Wy POTB/CUF EN6 174 C7
Sutton Acres RBSF CM22 121 J3
Sutton Cl BROX EN10 159 K7
TRING HP23 124 A4 3
Sutton Crs BAR EN5 200 C6
Sutton Gdns LTNN/LIM LU3 64 C4
Sutton Rd BGSW SG18 14 A1
SDY/GAM/PO SG19 14 E2
STAL AL1 153 G8
WAT WD17 13 G3
Swallow Cl BUSH WD23 207 G1
LTNW/LEA LU4 63 M6
RKW/CH/CXG WD3 194 B8 1
Swallowdale La HHNE HP2 9 J2
Swallow End WGCE AL7 134 E4
Swallowfields WGCE AL7 134 E4 2
Swallow Gdns HAT AL10 154 F7 3
Swallow La STAL AL1 170 A2
Swallow Oaks ABLGY WD5 181 L3 3
Swallows HLWE CM17 142 B6
The Swallows WGCE AL7 112 E8 2
Swan Cl LBUZ LU7 102 F1
RKW/CH/CXG WD3 194 C8
Swan Ct BSF CM23 96 E4 2
Swanells Wd DUN/WHIP LU6 105 G6
Swanfield Rd CHES/WCR EN8 190 D4
Swangley's La KNEB SG3 88 F6
Swanhill WGCE AL7 134 F1
Swanland Rd BRKMPK AL9 172 A6
POTB/CUF EN6 186 A5
Swan La ROY SG8 15 L6
Swanley Bar La POTB/CUF EN6 173 G7
Swanley Crs POTB/CUF EN6 173 G8
Swan Md HHS/BOV HP3 166 E4
LTNW/LEA LU4 63 M6
Swans Cl STALE/WH AL4 153 K8
Swans Rd CHES/WCR EN8 190 C5
Swanstand LWTH SG6 40 C6
Swanston Pth OXHEY WD19 206 B3 6
Swan St BLDK SG7 18 C6
Swasedale Rd LTNN/LIM LU3 64 F4
Sweet Briar BSF CM23 96 A4
WGCE AL7 134 F6
Sweetbriar Cl HHW HP1 148 F4
Sweyne HLWE CM17 163 H5
Sweyns Md STVGE SG2 71 H2
Swift Cl LWTH SG6 39 K2
ROY SG8 21 J1 6
WARE SG12 139 H7
Swiftfields WGCE AL7 134 E3
Swifts Green Cl LTNE LU2 66 A5
Swifts Green Rd LTNE LU2 66 A5
Swinburne Av HTCH/STOT SG5 52 B1
Swinburne Cl ROY SG8 21 J1 7
Swingate STVG SG1 4 C4
Swing Br LBUZ LU7 102 A5
Swing Gate La BERK HP4 147 J7
Swiss Av WATW WD18 195 K5
Swiss Cl WATW WD18 195 K4
Sworder Cl LTNN/LIM LU3 64 E1
Sworders Yd BSF CM23 96 E3 7
Sycamore Ap
RKW/CH/CXG WD3 195 H6
Sycamore Av HAT AL10 154 F6
Sycamore Cl CHESW EN7 175 L6 3
EBAR EN4 201 J7
GSTN WD25 182 A6
HTCHE/RSTV SG4 52 F6
LTNN/LIM LU3 64 B1 1
RBSF CM22 99 H3
Sycamore Dr LCOL/BKTW AL2 169 J6 2
TRING HP23 124 A6
Sycamore Fld
HLWW/ROY CM19 161 M6
Sycamore Ri BERK HP4 147 J7
Sycamore Rd DUN/HR/TOD LU5 63 H4
RKW/CH/CXG WD3 195 H6
The Sycamores BLDK SG7 40 D1
BSF CM23 97 G4
HHS/BOV HP3 165 L2
RAD WD7 184 A5
Sydney Rd WATW WD18 195 K6
Sylam Cl LTNN/LIM LU3 64 D3
Sylvan Cl HHS/BOV HP3 149 M8
Sylvandale WGCE AL7 135 H5
Sylvan Wy WGCE AL7 135 J4 2
Sylvesters HLWW/ROY CM19 161 L4
Sylvia Av PIN HA5 206 E6
Symonds Ct CHES/WCR EN8 176 C7 3
Symonds Green La STVG SG1 69 M3
Symonds Green Rd STVG SG1 69 M3
Symonds Rd HTCH/STOT SG5 52 C2

T

Tabbs Cl LWTH SG6 40 A2
Tacitus Cl STVGE SG2 71 H2
Tailors BSF CM23 96 A5
Takeley Cl WAB EN9 191 J4 3
Talbot Av OXHEY WD19 196 D8
Talbot Ct HHS/BOV HP3 166 C1 6
Talbot Rd HAT AL10 154 F2
LTNE LU2 3 H2
RAYLNE/WEN HP22 122 D5
RKW/CH/CXG WD3 204 D1
Talbot St HERT/BAY SG13 137 K4
HTCH/STOT SG5 52 C2
Talbot Wy LWTH SG6 40 A2
Talisman St HTCHE/RSTV SG4 53 H3
Tallents Crs HARP AL5 109 J7
Tallis Wy BORE WD6 198 C2
Tall Trees HTCHE/RSTV SG4 52 F6
ROY SG8 21 K4
Tamar Cl STVG SG1 54 F7
Tamar Gn HHNE HP2 149 L2
Tamarisk Cl STALW/RED AL3 152 D3 1
Tameton Cl LTNE LU2 66 D8
Tamworth Rd HERT/BAY SG13 137 L3
Tancred Rd LTNE LU2 65 M6
Tanfield Cl CHESW EN7 175 M6 2
Tanfield Gn LTNE LU2 84 D1 5
Tanglewood WLYN AL6 112 F3 2
Tanglewood Cl STAN HA7 207 K2
Tankerfield Pl STALW/RED AL3 10 D7
Tanners Cl STALW/RED AL3 10 C4
Tanners Crs HERT/BAY SG13 137 H6
Tanners Hl ABLGY WD5 181 L2
Tanners Wy WARE SG12 140 B1
Tanners Wood La ABLGY WD5 181 K3
Tannery Cl ROY SG8 21 H4
Tannery Drift ROY SG8 21 H3
The Tannery BUNT SG9 58 D3
Tannsfield Dr HHNE HP2 8 E5
Tannsmore Cl HHNE HP2 8 F5
Tansycroft WGCE AL7 135 G3
Tanworth Cl NTHWD HA6 205 H6 3
Tanyard La HTCHE/RSTV SG4 111 H2
Tany's Dell HLW CM20 7 L1
Tapster St BAR EN5 200 E4 2
Taransey HHS/BOV HP3 167 G1
Tarnside Cl DUN/WHIP LU6 81 G4
Tarpan Wy BROX EN10 176 E5
Tarrant Dr HARP AL5 131 H3
Tassell Hall STALW/RED AL3 129 L4
Tate Gdns BUSH WD23 197 K8
Tate Rd CFSP/GDCR SL9 202 E5
Tatlers La STVGE SG2 71 J5
Tatsfield Av WAB EN9 177 J2
Tattershall Dr HHNE HP2 149 M1
Tattle Hl HERT/WAS SG14 114 D8
Tauber Cl BORE WD6 198 E5
Taunton Rd LTNE LU2 3 L3
Taverners HHNE HP2 8 C5
Taverners Wy HOD EN11 159 M4
Tavistock Av STAL AL1 169 H2
Tavistock Cl POTB/CUF EN6 187 J2
STAL AL1 169 J2 3
Tavistock Crs LTN LU1 83 K5
Tavistock Rd WATN WD24 196 C2
Tavistock St DUN/WHIP LU6 62 F8
LTN LU1 2 E9
Tawneys Rd HLWS CM18 162 E4
Taylifers HLWW/ROY CM19 161 M7
Taylor Cl STALE/WH AL4 152 F2 1
Taylors Av HOD EN11 159 M5
Taylors Cl SHFD SG17 24 A5
Taylors End Rd STSD CM24 98 D1
Taylor's La BAR EN5 200 E2 3
Taylor's Rd HTCH/STOT SG5 26 E2
Taylor St LTNE LU2 3 G4
Taywood Cl STVGE SG2 71 G8
Teal Dr NTHWD HA6 205 H7
Teasdale Cl ROY SG8 21 J1 8
Teasel Cl ROY SG8 21 K5
Tedder Av HNLW SG16 25 G5
Tedder Rd HHNE HP2 9 G7
Teesdale HHNE HP2 8 D3
LTNW/LEA LU4 64 B5
Tee Side HERT/BAY SG13 138 A3
Telford Av STVGE SG2 5 L3
Telford Cl GSTN WD25 182 C6
Telford Rd LCOL/BKTW AL2 170 B6
Telford Wy LTN LU1 2 C5
Telscombe Wy LTNE LU2 66 B7
Temperance St STALW/RED AL3 10 D6
Tempest Av POTB/CUF EN6 187 H3
Templar Av BLDK SG7 40 E4 2
Templars Dr
KTN/HRWW/W HA3 207 J6 1
Templars La HTCHE/RSTV SG4 68 C4
Temple Av TRDG/WHET N20 201 J8
Temple Bank HLW CM20 142 A5
Temple Cl CHESW EN7 189 M2
HTCHE/RSTV SG4 52 A6
LTNE LU2 65 K5 3
WAT WD17 195 L3
Temple Flds HERT/WAS SG14 137 H1
Temple Gdns
RKW/CH/CXG WD3 205 G3
Temple La WARE SG12 115 K3
Temple Md HLWW/ROY CM19 161 G2
Templepan La
RKW/CH/CXG WD3 180 D8
Temple Vw STALW/RED AL3 10 C3
Templewood WGCW AL8 134 C1
Tempsford WGCE AL7 135 J4 3
Tempsford Av BORE WD6 199 J5
Tenby Dr LTNW/LEA LU4 64 E7
Tenby Ms LTNW/LEA LU4 64 D7
Tendring Rd HLWS CM18 7 J9
HLWS CM18 162 B4 1
The Tene BLDK SG7 40 E2
Tennand Cl CHESW EN7 175 L5
Tennison Av BORE WD6 199 G6
Tennyson Av DUN/HR/TOD LU5 63 J6
HTCHE/RSTV SG4 53 H4
WAB EN9 191 K5
Tennyson Cl ROY SG8 21 J1 9
Tennyson Rd HARP AL5 108 F7
LCOL/BKTW AL2 168 F5
LTN LU1 83 K5
Tenth Av LTNN/LIM LU3 64 B3
Tenzing Gv LTN LU1 2 B9
Tenzing Rd HHNE HP2 9 H8
Teresa Gdns CHES/WCR EN8 190 B5
Terminus St HLW CM20 6 E5 2
Terrace Gdns WAT WD17 196 A3
Tethys Rd HHNE HP2 8 F3
Tewin Cl STALE/WH AL4 153 H3
WLYN AL6 113 H5
Tewin Ct WGCE AL7 134 E3 5
Tewin Hl WLYN AL6 113 K7
Tewin Rd HHNE HP2 9 M9
WGCE AL7 134 E3
Thackeray Cl ROY SG8 21 J1 10
Thames Av HHNE HP2 149 L2
Thamesdale LCOL/BKTW AL2 170 E6 3
Thatcham Gdns
TRDG/WHET N20 201 H8
Thatch Cl LTNW/LEA LU4 63 L6
Thatchers End HTCHE/RSTV SG4 53 J2
The Thatchers BSF CM23 96 B6
Thaxted Cl LTNE LU2 66 E8 4
Thaxted Wy WAB EN9 191 J4
Thaynesfield POTB/CUF EN6 187 J2
Thelby Cl LTNN/LIM LU3 64 E4
Thele Av WARE SG12 139 J6
Theleway Cl HOD EN11 160 A1 4
Thellusson Wy
RKW/CH/CXG WD3 193 M8 1
Thelusson Ct RAD WD7 183 M6 2
Theobald Crs
KTN/HRWW/W HA3 207 G8
Theobald's Cl POTB/CUF EN6 188 E1
Theobald's Gv
CHES/WCR EN8 190 C3 3
Theobald's La CHES/WCR EN8 190 A3
Theobalds Park Rd
ENC/FH EN2 189 G6
Theobald's Rd POTB/CUF EN6 188 D1
Theobald St RAD WD7 184 A7
Therfield Rd STALW/RED AL3 152 C4
Thetford Gdns LTNE LU2 65 J4 3
HERT/WAS SG14 136 E3
Thieves La HERT/WAS SG14 136 E4
Third Av GSTN WD25 182 C6
HLWS CM18 6 E7
HLWW/ROY CM19 6 B9
LTNN/LIM LU3 64 C3
LWTH SG6 40 B3
Thirlestane STAL AL1 11 H5
Thirlestone Rd LTNW/LEA LU4 82 C1
Thirlmere STVG SG1 55 H8
Thirlmere Dr STAL AL1 170 A1
Thirlmere Gdns NTHWD HA6 205 G5
Thirsk Rd BORE WD6 198 F1
Thistle Cl HHW HP1 148 D8
Thistlecroft HHW HP1 149 G8 3
Thistle Gv WGCE AL7 135 H7
Thistle Rd LTN LU1 3 H7
The Thistles HHW HP1 149 G6
Thistley La HTCHE/RSTV SG4 52 E8
Thomas Rochford Wy
CHES/WCR EN8 176 E6
Thomas Wy ROY SG8 21 J1 11
Thompsons Cl CHESW EN7 175 K8
HARP AL5 130 F1 1
Thompsons Meadow ROY SG8 15 M6
Thompson Wy
RKW/CH/CXG WD3 193 M8
Thorley Hl BSF CM23 96 E5
Thorley La BSF CM23 96 E7
Thorley Park Rd BSF CM23 96 E6
Thornage Cl LTNE LU2 65 J3
Thorn Av BUSH WD23 207 H1
Thornbera Cl BSF CM23 96 E6
Thornbera Gdns BSF CM23 96 D6
Thornbera Rd BSF CM23 96 E6
Thornbury DUN/HR/TOD LU5 63 L8 1
HARP AL5 131 J1
Thornbury Cl HOD EN11 139 G8
STVGE SG2 88 F2
Thornbury Ct DUN/HR/TOD LU5 63 H3
Thornbury Gdns BORE WD6 199 H5
Thorncroft HHS/BOV HP3 167 G1 4
Thorndyke Ct PIN HA5 206 E7 4
Thorne Cl HHW HP1 166 A1
Thorne Wy RAYLNE/WEN HP22 122 F6
Thornfield Rd BSF CM23 96 D2
Thorn Gv BSF CM23 97 G4
Thornhill Cl DUN/HR/TOD LU5 63 J3
Thornhill Rd LTNW/LEA LU4 82 E1
NTHWD HA6 205 H4
Thorn Rd DUN/HR/TOD LU5 62 D4
Thorntondale LTNW/LEA LU4 64 B5 5
Thornton Gv PIN HA5 206 F6
Thornton Rd BAR EN5 200 D4
POTB/CUF EN6 187 H1
RBSF CM22 99 L2
Thornton St HERT/WAS SG14 137 J4
STALW/RED AL3 10 D5
Thorn Tree Dr TRING HP23 123 L6
Thorn View Rd
DUN/HR/TOD LU5 63 G5 6
Thorpe Crs OXHEY WD19 196 A8
Thorpefield Cl STALE/WH AL4 153 J4 3
Thorpe Rd STAL AL1 10 F9
Thrales Cl LTNN/LIM LU3 64 D3
Three Cherrytrees La HHNE HP2 9 L1
Three Close La BERK HP4 147 H7
Three Closes HTCH/STOT SG5 37 H6
Three Corners HHS/BOV HP3 166 F1 1
Three Forests Wy
HLWW/ROY CM19 160 E2
RBSF CM22 98 C6
RBSF CM22 121 M1
SBW CM21 142 D1
WAB EN9 161 J8
Three Forest Wy RBSF CM22 98 A5
Three Horseshoes Rd
HLWW/ROY CM19 162 A4
Three Houses La
HTCHE/RSTV SG4 87 H7
Three Stiles STVGE SG2 72 D6
Three Valleys Wy BUSH WD23 13 K6
Thremhall Av RBSF CM22 98 E1
Thresher Cl BSF CM23 96 B5
LTNW/LEA LU4 63 L5
Thricknells Cl LTNN/LIM LU3 64 D3 3
Thrift Farm La BORE WD6 199 G3
Thristers Cl LWTH SG6 40 A7 1
Throcking La BUNT SG9 58 B1
Throcking Rd BUNT SG9 57 J2
Thrums WATN WD24 182 A8
Thrush Av HAT AL10 154 F7
Thrush Gn RKW/CH/CXG WD3 194 B8
Thrush La POTB/CUF EN6 174 D7
Thumbswood WGCE AL7 134 F7
Thumpers HHNE HP2 8 D5
Thundercourt WARE SG12 116 C8
Thundridge Cl WGCE AL7 135 G5 6
Thurgood Rd HOD EN11 159 M2 3
Thurlow Cl LTNW/LEA LU4 63 L7
STVG SG1 70 C1
Thurnall Av ROY SG8 21 J5
Thurnall Cl BLDK SG7 40 E2
Thurstans HLWW/ROY CM19 162 A7
Tibbett Cl DUN/WHIP LU6 81 J4 2
Tibbles Cl GSTN WD25 182 D6
Tibbs Hill Rd ABLGY WD5 181 L1 2
Tiberius Rd LTNN/LIM LU3 64 E4
Tichborne RKW/CH/CXG WD3 203 J5
Tickenhall Dr HLWE CM17 163 J2
Tilbury Md HLWS CM18 7 M9
Tilecroft WGCW AL8 134 C1
Tilegate Rd HLWS CM18 162 E4
Tilehouse Cl BORE WD6 198 E4 3
Tilehouse La RKW/CH/CXG WD3 203 K8
Tilehouse St HTCH/STOT SG5 52 D3
Tile Kiln Cl HHS/BOV HP3 150 A8 1
Tile Kiln Crs HHS/BOV HP3 150 A8
Tile Kiln La HHS/BOV HP3 149 M8
Tilgate LTNE LU2 66 C7
Tillers Link STVGE SG2 5 J9
Tillingham Ct WAB EN9 191 M4 5
Tillotson Rd
KTN/HRWW/W HA3 207 G7
Tilsworth Wk STALE/WH AL4 153 H2 6
Timbercroft WGCE AL7 134 E1
Timber Orch HERT/WAS SG14 114 F8
Timber Rdg RKW/CH/CXG WD3 194 B5
Timbers Ct HARP AL5 108 E8 3
Times Cl HTCH/STOT SG5 38 C8
Timplings Rw HHW HP1 149 G5 3
Timworth Cl LTNE LU2 84 C1
Tingeys Cl STALW/RED AL3 129 M5
Tinkers La TRING HP23 145 M4
Tinsley Cl LTN LU1 83 G5
Tintagel Cl HHNE HP2 149 J2 1
LTNN/LIM LU3 65 G6
Tintern Cl HARP AL5 108 B6
KNEB SG3 88 F3

Tinwell Ms BORE WD6 ... 199 J6 4
Tippendell La LCOL/BKTW AL2 ... 168 F4
Tippet Ct STVG SG1 ... 4 D7
Titan Ct LTNW/LEA LU4 ... 82 E1
Titan Rd HHNE HP2 ... 8 F3
Titchfield Rd PEND EN3 ... 190 D8
Tithe Barn Cl STAL AL1 ... 169 H2
Tithe Cl WLYN AL6 ... 111 L1
Tithe Farm Rd DUN/HR/TOD LU5 .. 63 G4
Tithelands HLWW/ROY CM19 ... 161 L5
Titian Av BUSH WD23 ... 197 K8
Titmus Cl STVG SG1 ... 4 F1
Tiverton Ct HARP AL5 ... 131 K4 2
Tiverton Rd POTB/CUF EN6 ... 187 J2
Toddbrook HLWW/ROY CM19 ... 6 B8
Toddington Rd LTNW/LEA LU4 ... 64 C5
Toland Cl LTNW/LEA LU4 ... 82 B1
Tollgate Cl RKW/CH/CXG WD3 ... 193 L5
Tollgate Rd BRKMPK AL9 ... 171 M4
CHES/WCR EN8 ... 190 C6
STALE/WH AL4 ... 171 K3
Tollpit End HHW HP1 ... 148 F4
Tollsworth Wy STDN SG11 ... 75 H7
Tolmers Av POTB/CUF EN6 ... 174 D7
Tolmers Gdns POTB/CUF EN6 ... 174 D8
Tolmers Rd POTB/CUF EN6 ... 174 D6
Tolpits Cl WATW WD18 ... 12 A7
Tolpits La WATW WD18 ... 12 A9
Tomkins Cl BORE WD6 ... 198 D2 3
Tomlinson Av LTNW/LEA LU4 ... 63 L6
Tompkins Cl
RAYLNE/WEN HP22 ... 122 E6
Toms Cft HHNE HP2 ... 149 K8
Toms Fld HAT AL10 ... 154 D6
Tom's Hl KGLGY WD4 ... 180 D7
Toms Hill Cl TRING HP23 ... 125 J5 2
Toms Hill Rd TRING HP23 ... 125 J5
Tom's La KGLGY WD4 ... 167 H7
Tooke Cl PIN HA5 ... 206 D8
Tooveys Mill Cl KGLGY WD4 ... 166 F8 5
Topland Rd CFSP/GDCR SL9 ... 202 C7 2
Topstreet Wy HARP AL5 ... 131 H2
Torquay Crs STVG SG1 ... 70 A3
Torquay Dr LTNW/LEA LU4 ... 64 C6
Torrington Dr POTB/CUF EN6 ... 187 J3
Torrington Rd BERK HP4 ... 147 G6
Tortoiseshell Wy BERK HP4 ... 146 E4
Torwood Cl BERK HP4 ... 146 E6
Torworth Rd BORE WD6 ... 198 E2
Tot La BSF CM23 ... 79 J7
Totteridge Rd PEND EN3 ... 190 C8
Totternhoe Rd DUN/WHIP LU6 ... 80 D3
Totton Ms STALW/RED AL3 ... 130 A5
Totts La STVGE SG2 ... 72 B1
Toulmin Dr STALW/RED AL3 ... 152 B3
Tovey Av HOD EN11 ... 159 M2
Tovey Cl LCOL/BKTW AL2 ... 170 C5
WAB EN9 ... 177 K2
Tower Cl BERK HP4 ... 146 F7
HTCHE/RSTV SG4 ... 53 L7
Tower Hl KGLGY WD4 ... 165 K8
MHAD SG10 ... 94 E8
Tower Hill La STALE/WH AL4 ... 132 E5
Tower Rd HTCHE/RSTV SG4 ... 87 K8
LTNE LU2 ... 3 J4
WARE SG12 ... 116 D8
Towers Rd HHNE HP2 ... 8 D6
PIN HA5 ... 206 B8
Tower St HERT/WAS SG14 ... 137 H2
Tower Vw HTCHE/RSTV SG4 ... 86 C4
Tower Wy LTNE LU2 ... 3 J4
Towne Rd ROY SG8 ... 21 J5
Town Farm LBUZ LU7 ... 101 M3 5
Town Farm Crs STDN SG11 ... 75 L8
Townfield RKW/CH/CXG WD3 ... 194 B8
Town Flds HAT AL10 ... 154 F4 3
Town La STVGE SG2 ... 72 D6
Townley LWTH SG6 ... 40 B6
Town Mead Rd WAB EN9 ... 191 H5
Townsend HHNE HP2 ... 8 A4
Townsend Av STAL AL1 ... 11 G4
Townsend Cl HARP AL5 ... 130 E1
ROY SG8 ... 32 B7
Townsend Dr STALW/RED AL3 ... 10 E1
Townsend Farm Rd
DUN/HR/TOD LU5 ... 63 G7
Townsend La HARP AL5 ... 130 D1
Townsend Rd HARP AL5 ... 108 F8
Townsend Wy NTHWD HA6 ... 205 L7
Townshend St HERT/WAS SG14 ... 137 K4
Townsley Cl LTN LU1 ... 2 E9
Tracyes Rd HLWS CM18 ... 163 G4
Trafalgar Av BROX EN10 ... 159 L8
Trafford Cl RAD WD7 ... 184 D3 4
STVG SG1 ... 70 D1
Traherne Cl HTCHE/RSTV SG4 ... 52 E5 3
Trajan Ga STVG SG1 ... 71 J1
Trap Rd ROY SG8 ... 15 M6
Trapstyle Rd WARE SG12 ... 115 M8
Travellers Cl BRKMPK AL9 ... 172 B2
Travellers La BRKMPK AL9 ... 155 G8
HAT AL10 ... 154 F7
Treacle La BUNT SG9 ... 42 E7
Treacy Cl BUSH WD23 ... 207 H2
Trebellan Dr HHNE HP2 ... 8 E7
Tree Cl HHS/BOV HP3 ... 167 G1
Treehanger Cl TRING HP23 ... 124 A6 2
Treetops Cl NTHWD HA6 ... 205 J5
Trefoil Cl LTNW/LEA LU4 ... 63 L6
Trefusis Wk WAT WD17 ... 195 K2
Tregelles Rd HOD EN11 ... 159 M2
Tremaine Gv HHNE HP2 ... 149 K3
Trent Cl RAD WD7 ... 184 D3
STVG SG1 ... 70 D1
Trent Rd LTNN/LIM LU3 ... 65 G7
Tresco Rd BERK HP4 ... 146 E5
Trescott Cl LTNE LU2 ... 66 D8 3
Trevalga Wy HHNE HP2 ... 149 J2
Trevellance Wy GSTN WD25 ... 182 C4 2
Trevelyan Wy BERK HP4 ... 147 G4
Trevor Cl EBAR EN4 ... 201 J7 2
KTN/HRWW/W HA3 ... 207 L7 4
Trevor Rd HTCHE/RSTV SG4 ... 52 F2
Trevose Wy OXHEY WD19 ... 206 B3
Trewenna Dr POTB/CUF EN6 ... 187 J3
Trident Dr DUN/HR/TOD LU5 ... 63 J4
Trident Rd GSTN WD25 ... 181 L5
Triggs Wy LTNE LU2 ... 66 D7
Trimley Cl LTNW/LEA LU4 ... 64 A5
Trinder Rd BAR EN5 ... 200 B6
Tring Ford Rd TRING HP23 ... 123 M3
Tring Hl TRING HP23 ... 123 H7
Tring Rd BERK HP4 ... 146 B3
DUN/WHIP LU6 ... 80 D4
DUN/WHIP LU6 ... 103 K3
RAYLNE/WEN HP22 ... 100 B1
TRING HP23 ... 101 H7
Trinity Cl BSF CM23 ... 96 E4
NTHWD HA6 ... 205 K6
Trinity Gv HERT/WAS SG14 ... 137 H3
Trinity Hall Cl WATN WD24 ... 13 H2
Trinity La CHES/WCR EN8 ... 190 D3
Trinity Ms HHS/BOV HP3 ... 150 C8 2
Trinity Rd HERT/BAY SG13 ... 138 B7
HTCH/STOT SG5 ... 26 D3
LTNN/LIM LU3 ... 64 F6
STVG SG1 ... 4 A2
WARE SG12 ... 116 D8
Trinity St BSF CM23 ... 96 E4 5
Trinity Wk HERT/BAY SG13 ... 138 B7
Trinity Wy BSF CM23 ... 96 E4
Tripton Rd HLWS CM18 ... 7 H8
Tristram Rd HTCHE/RSTV SG4 ... 38 F8
Triton Wy HHNE HP2 ... 8 E4
Troon Gdns LTNE LU2 ... 65 K4
Trooper Rd TRING HP23 ... 125 H5
Trotters Bottom BAR EN5 ... 185 M8
Trotter's Gap WARE SG12 ... 139 K6
Trotters Rd HLWS CM18 ... 162 F5
Trout Ri RKW/CH/CXG WD3 ... 194 A4
Troutstream Wy
RKW/CH/CXG WD3 ... 194 A5
Trouvere Pk HHW HP1 ... 149 G5
Trowbridge Gdns LTNE LU2 ... 65 K7
Trowley Bottom
STALW/RED AL3 ... 129 G2
Trowley Hill Rd STALW/RED AL3 .. 107 G8
Trowley Ri ABLGY WD5 ... 181 K2
Truemans Rd HTCH/STOT SG5 ... 38 C8
Trumper Rd STVG SG1 ... 70 E2
Trumpington Dr STAL AL1 ... 169 J2
Trundlers Wy BUSH WD23 ... 207 K1 1
Truro Gdns LTNN/LIM LU3 ... 65 G5
Trust Rd CHES/WCR EN8 ... 190 D5 1
Tucker's Rw BSF CM23 ... 96 E4
Tucker St WATW WD18 ... 13 G6
Tudor Av CHESW EN7 ... 190 A2
WATN WD24 ... 182 C8
Tudor Cl AMP/FLIT/B MK45 ... 35 H6 1
CHESW EN7 ... 190 A2
HAT AL10 ... 154 D8
STVG SG1 ... 70 B1
WARE SG12 ... 140 C2
Tudor Ct BORE WD6 ... 198 D3 1
HTCH/STOT SG5 ... 52 C4 1
Tudor Dr DUN/HR/TOD LU5 ... 63 K6
WATN WD24 ... 196 C1
Tudor Manor Gdns GSTN WD25 .. 182 C3
Tudor Ri BROX EN10 ... 159 K8
Tudor Rd BAR EN5 ... 200 F4
LTNN/LIM LU3 ... 65 G8
STALE/WH AL4 ... 132 D2
STALW/RED AL3 ... 152 D3
WLYN AL6 ... 112 A7
Tudor Wk WATN WD24 ... 182 C8
Tudor Wy HERT/WAS SG14 ... 136 F4
RKW/CH/CXG WD3 ... 203 M1
WAB EN9 ... 191 J4
Tuffnells Wy HARP AL5 ... 108 C6
Tumbler Rd HLWS CM18 ... 7 L8
Tunfield Rd HOD EN11 ... 160 A1
Tunnel Wood Cl WAT WD17 ... 181 L8
Tunnel Wood Rd WAT WD17 ... 181 L8
WATN WD24 ... 181 L8
Tunnmeade HLW CM20 ... 7 L5
Turf La HTCHE/RSTV SG4 ... 54 A6
Turkey St EN EN1 ... 189 M7
Turmore Dl WGCW AL8 ... 134 B5
Turnberry Ct OXHEY WD19 ... 206 B3 5
Turnberry Dr LCOL/BKTW AL2 ... 182 D1
Turn Braemar HHNE HP2 ... 150 A1
Turner Cl DUN/HR/TOD LU5 ... 63 J5
STVG SG1 ... 54 B8
Turner Rd BUSH WD23 ... 197 H5
Turners Cl HARP AL5 ... 109 H6
HERT/WAS SG14 ... 114 B6
Turners Crs BSF CM23 ... 96 B6
Turner's Hl CHES/WCR EN8 ... 190 C1
HHNE HP2 ... 149 K8
Turners Rd North LTNE LU2 ... 65 M8
Turners Rd South LTNE LU2 ... 3 K1 1
Turners Wood Dr CSTG HP8 ... 202 C3
Turneys Orch
RKW/CH/CXG WD3 ... 193 J6
Turnors HLWW/ROY CM19 ... 6 C6
Turnpike Cl DUN/WHIP LU6 ... 81 H4 2
Turnpike Dr LTNN/LIM LU3 ... 65 H1
Turnpike Gn HHNE HP2 ... 149 L3
Turnpike La HTCH/STOT SG5 ... 38 C7
The Turnstones GSTN WD25 ... 182 D7
Turpins Cha WLYN AL6 ... 112 E3
Turpins Cl HERT/WAS SG14 ... 136 E4
Turpin's Ride ROY SG8 ... 21 J5
WLYN AL6 ... 112 D3
Turpin's Ri STVGE SG2 ... 88 D1
Turpin's Wy BLDK SG7 ... 40 E3
Turvey Cl RAYLNE/WEN HP22 ... 122 D5
Tuxford Cl BORE WD6 ... 198 D1 4
Tweed Cl BERK HP4 ... 147 G5
Twelve Acres WGCE AL7 ... 134 D6
Twickenham Gdns
KTN/HRWW/W HA3 ... 207 K7
Twin Foxes KNEB SG3 ... 112 F1
Twinwoods STVG SG1 ... 5 H5
The Twist TRING HP23 ... 124 C8
Twitchell La RAYLNE/WEN HP22 .. 122 D5
The Twitchell BLDK SG7 ... 40 E2 3
Two Acres WGCE AL7 ... 134 E7
Two Oaks Dr WLYN AL6 ... 113 H4
Two Waters Rd HHS/BOV HP3 ... 166 B2
Twyford Bury La BSF CM23 ... 96 F6
Twyford Cl BSF CM23 ... 96 F5
Twyford Dr LTNE LU2 ... 84 C1
Twyford Gdns BSF CM23 ... 96 E6
Twyford Rd BSF CM23 ... 96 F5
STALE/WH AL4 ... 153 H3
Tyburn La AMP/FLIT/B MK45 ... 34 C2
Tye End STVGE SG2 ... 89 G2
Tye Green Village
HLWS CM18 ... 162 E5 2
Tyfield Cl CHES/WCR EN8 ... 190 B1 3
Tylers HARP AL5 ... 131 J1
Tylers Cswy HERT/BAY SG13 ... 174 B1
Tylers Cl BUNT SG9 ... 58 C3 1
KGLGY WD4 ... 166 E8
Tylersfield ABLGY WD5 ... 181 L2
Tylers Md LTNE LU2 ... 65 K5
Tylers Rd HLWW/ROY CM19 ... 161 J7
Tylers Wd WLYN AL6 ... 113 H5
Tylney Cft HLWW/ROY CM19 ... 162 A4
Tynedale LCOL/BKTW AL2 ... 170 E6 4
Typleden Cl HHNE HP2 ... 8 B4
Tysea Cl HLWS CM18 ... 162 E5
Tysea Rd HLWS CM18 ... 162 E5
Tysoe Av PEND EN3 ... 190 E7
Tythe Rd LTNW/LEA LU4 ... 64 B4
Tyttenhanger Gn
STALE/WH AL4 ... 170 C2

U

Uckfield Rd PEND EN3 ... 190 C8
Ufford Cl KTN/HRWW/W HA3 ... 207 G7
Ufford Rd KTN/HRWW/W HA3 ... 207 G7
Ullswater Cl STVG SG1 ... 55 H8
Ullswater Rd DUN/WHIP LU6 ... 81 G4
HHS/BOV HP3 ... 167 H1
Ulverston Rd DUN/WHIP LU6 ... 80 F4
Underacres Cl HHNE HP2 ... 9 H6
Underhill BAR EN5 ... 200 F6
Underwood Cl LTNN/LIM LU3 ... 64 D1
Underwood Rd STVG SG1 ... 54 B8
Union Gn HHNE HP2 ... 8 B6
Union St BAR EN5 ... 200 D5
DUN/WHIP LU6 ... 80 F2
LTN LU1 ... 2 E8
Union Ter BUNT SG9 ... 58 D3
Unity Rd PEND EN3 ... 190 B8
Unwin Cl LWTH SG6 ... 39 K6
Unwin Rd STVGE SG2 ... 71 H7
Updale Cl POTB/CUF EN6 ... 186 D4
Upland Dr BRKMPK AL9 ... 173 G4
Uplands LTNN/LIM LU3 ... 64 C2
RKW/CH/CXG WD3 ... 194 E7
STDN SG11 ... 75 L4
STVGE SG2 ... 71 J2
WARE SG12 ... 116 E8
WGCW AL8 ... 112 B8
Uplands Av HTCHE/RSTV SG4 ... 53 G4
The Uplands HARP AL5 ... 130 F6
LCOL/BKTW AL2 ... 182 D1
Upper Ashlyns Rd BERK HP4 ... 147 G7
Upper Barn HHS/BOV HP3 ... 166 E2
Upper Bourne End La
HHW HP1 ... 165 G3
Upper Clabdens WARE SG12 ... 138 E1
Upper Culver Rd STAL AL1 ... 11 H3
Upper Dagnall St
STALW/RED AL3 ... 10 E6
Upperfield Rd WGCE AL7 ... 134 E5
Upper George St LTN LU1 ... 2 D6
Upper Gn WLYN AL6 ... 113 J6
Upper Green Rd WLYN AL6 ... 113 K7
Upper Hall Pk BERK HP4 ... 147 K8
Upper Heath Rd STAL AL1 ... 11 J3
Upper Hwy ABLGY WD5 ... 181 H3
Upper Hill Ri RKW/CH/CXG WD3 .. 194 A7
Upper Hitch OXHEY WD19 ... 206 D1
Upper Hook HLWS CM18 ... 162 E4
Upper Icknield Wy TRING HP23 .. 124 C2
Upper King St ROY SG8 ... 21 J4
Upper Lattimore Rd STAL AL1 ... 11 G7
Upper Lea Valley Wk LTNE LU2 ... 65 J7
LTNE LU2 ... 84 B5
Upper Marlborough Rd
STAL AL1 ... 11 G7
Upper Marsh La HOD EN11 ... 159 M5
Upper Maylins LWTH SG6 ... 40 B6
Upper Mealines HLWS CM18 ... 162 F5
Upper Paddock Rd
OXHEY WD19 ... 13 L9
Upper Pk HLW CM20 ... 6 A5
Upper Sales HHW HP1 ... 148 E8
Upper Sean STVGE SG2 ... 5 K8
Upper Shot WGCE AL7 ... 134 F3
Upper Shott CHESW EN7 ... 175 L5
Upper Station Rd RAD WD7 ... 183 M6 5
Upperstone Cl
HTCH/STOT SG5 ... 26 E4 1
Upper Stonyfield
HLWW/ROY CM19 ... 6 B6
Upper Tail OXHEY WD19 ... 206 D3
Upper Tilehouse St
HTCH/STOT SG5 ... 52 C4
Upshire Rd WAB EN9 ... 191 L3
Upton Av STALW/RED AL3 ... 10 E5
Upton Cl LCOL/BKTW AL2 ... 169 J4
LTNE LU2 ... 65 J4
Upton Lodge Cl BUSH WD23 ... 197 H8 5
Upton Rd WATW WD18 ... 12 E4
Upway CFSP/GDCR SL9 ... 202 E8
Upwell Rd LTNE LU2 ... 66 A8
Uranus Rd HHNE HP2 ... 8 D5
Urban Rd BSF CM23 ... 97 G3
Uxbridge Rd
RKW/CH/CXG WD3 ... 203 M2
Uxbridge Rd (Harrow Weald)
KTN/HRWW/W HA3 ... 207 K6
Uxbridge Rd (Hatch End)
PIN HA5 ... 206 E7 5
Uxbridge Rd (Stanmore)
STAN HA7 ... 207 L6 7

V

Vache La CSTG HP8 ... 202 B2
Vadis Cl LTNN/LIM LU3 ... 64 D3 5
Valance Rd SAFWS CB11 ... 47 M3
Vale Av BORE WD6 ... 199 G6
Vale Cl CFSP/GDCR SL9 ... 202 C8 5
HARP AL5 ... 108 C6
Vale Ct STALE/WH AL4 ... 132 C3
Vale Dr BAR EN5 ... 200 E5
Valence Dr CHESW EN7 ... 175 M7
Valence End DUN/WHIP LU6 ... 81 J5
Valency Cl NTHWD HA6 ... 205 L4
Valerian Wy STVGE SG2 ... 71 J2
Valerie Cl STAL AL1 ... 153 G7
Vale Rd BUSH WD23 ... 13 L7
Valeside HERT/WAS SG14 ... 136 F5
The Vale CFSP/GDCR SL9 ... 202 C8
Vallans Cl WARE SG12 ... 116 C7
Vallansgate STVGE SG2 ... 89 G1
Valley Cl DUN/WHIP LU6 ... 104 D3
DUN/WHIP LU6 ... 105 G6
HERT/BAY SG13 ... 137 J5
WAB EN9 ... 191 H3
WARE SG12 ... 116 A8 1
Valley Gn HHNE HP2 ... 150 A1
The Valley Gn WGCW AL8 ... 134 B3
Valley La STALW/RED AL3 ... 128 D1
Valley Ri GSTN WD25 ... 182 A4
ROY SG8 ... 21 K5
STALE/WH AL4 ... 109 L8
Valley Rd BERK HP4 ... 146 E4
DUN/WHIP LU6 ... 105 G6
LWTH SG6 ... 39 J3
RKW/CH/CXG WD3 ... 193 M6
STALW/RED AL3 ... 152 D3
WGCW AL8 ... 134 A4
WLYN AL6 ... 111 L1
Valley Rd South WLYN AL6 ... 111 L2 5
Valleyside HHW HP1 ... 148 E7
The Valley HTCHE/RSTV SG4 ... 86 D3
Valley Vw BAR EN5 ... 200 D7
CHESW EN7 ... 175 H7
Valley Wk RKW/CH/CXG WD3 ... 195 H6
Valley Wy STVGE SG2 ... 5 H9
Vanbrugh Dr DUN/HR/TOD LU5 ... 63 J5
Vanda Crs STAL AL1 ... 11 K8
Vantorts Cl SBW CM21 ... 120 D8
Vantorts Rd SBW CM21 ... 142 D1
Vardon Rd STVG SG1 ... 70 E2
Varna Cl LTNN/LIM LU3 ... 64 F7
Varney Cl CHESW EN7 ... 175 M6
HHW HP1 ... 148 E7
Varney Rd HHW HP1 ... 148 E7
Vaughan Md
STALW/RED AL3 ... 129 M6 1
Vaughan Rd HARP AL5 ... 131 G1
HTCH/STOT SG5 ... 26 D4
Vauxhall Rd HHNE HP2 ... 9 H9
LTNE LU2 ... 84 A5
Vauxhall Wy LTNE LU2 ... 3 M3
Vega Crs NTHWD HA6 ... 205 L5
Vega Rd BUSH WD23 ... 197 H8
Velizy Av HLW CM20 ... 6 E4
Venetia Rd LTNE LU2 ... 65 M6
Ventnor Gdns LTNN/LIM LU3 ... 64 F3
Ventura Pk LCOL/BKTW AL2 ... 169 L8
Venus Hl HHS/BOV HP3 ... 178 F2
Vera Ct OXHEY WD19 ... 196 C8
Ver-colne Valley Wk BUSH WD23 .. 13 J3
HHS/BOV HP3 ... 164 C7
STALW/RED AL3 ... 10 A6
STALW/RED AL3 ... 130 A6
Verdure Cl GSTN WD25 ... 182 D3
Verey Rd DUN/HR/TOD LU5 ... 63 H8
Veritys HAT AL10 ... 154 F5
Verity Wy STVG SG1 ... 70 F1
Verlum Cl WGCE AL7 ... 134 E4 3
Verney Cl BERK HP4 ... 146 E5
TRING HP23 ... 124 B5
Vernon Av PEND EN3 ... 190 D7
Vernon Crs EBAR EN4 ... 201 M6
Vernon Dr DEN/HRF UB9 ... 204 B8
STAN HA7 ... 207 M8
Vernon Pl DUN/HR/TOD LU5 ... 81 G1
Vernon Rd BUSH WD23 ... 13 L6
LTN LU1 ... 2 A5
Vernon's Cl STAL AL1 ... 11 G8 1
Ver Rd STALW/RED AL3 ... 10 C6
STALW/RED AL3 ... 130 B4
Verulam Gdns LTNN/LIM LU3 ... 64 E4
Verulam Rd HTCH/STOT SG5 ... 52 E2
STALW/RED AL3 ... 10 B4
Verwood Dr EBAR EN4 ... 201 L4
Vespers Cl LTNW/LEA LU4 ... 63 M8 2
Vesta Av STAL AL1 ... 169 H2
Vestry Cl LTN LU1 ... 2 C6
Veysey Cl HHW HP1 ... 166 A1 2
Viaduct Rd WARE SG12 ... 138 D2
Viaduct Wy WGCE AL7 ... 134 E1
Vian Av PEND EN3 ... 190 D6
Vicarage Cswy HERT/BAY SG13 .. 138 A6
Vicarage Cl ARL/CHE SG15 ... 25 M2
HHW HP1 ... 149 H8 1
HHW HP1 ... 166 B1 2
HTCH/STOT SG5 ... 36 E2
POTB/CUF EN6 ... 187 L1
STAL AL1 ... 169 H2
STDN SG11 ... 75 K8
Vicarage Gdns BERK HP4 ... 148 A3
STALW/RED AL3 ... 129 G1
TRING HP23 ... 101 M8 1
Vicarage La HERT/WAS SG14 ... 114 F7
HHS/BOV HP3 ... 165 G5
KGLGY WD4 ... 166 E8
LBUZ LU7 ... 102 E5
Vicarage Rd BERK HP4 ... 147 M3
BUNT SG9 ... 58 D2
DUN/HR/TOD LU5 ... 63 G5
LBUZ LU7 ... 102 C7
TRING HP23 ... 101 L8
TRING HP23 ... 145 J1
WARE SG12 ... 138 D1
WATW WD18 ... 12 C8
Vicarage St LTN LU1 ... 3 G7
Vicarage Wd HLW CM20 ... 7 L4
Vicerons Pl BSF CM23 ... 96 C6
Victoria Cl EBAR EN4 ... 201 J5
RKW/CH/CXG WD3 ... 194 C8
STVG SG1 ... 70 C3
Victoria Crs ROY SG8 ... 21 J3
Victoria Ga HLWE CM17 ... 163 G2
Victoria Rd BERK HP4 ... 147 H7
BUSH WD23 ... 207 G1
EBAR EN4 ... 201 J5
HARP AL5 ... 131 G1 2
WAB EN9 ... 191 H5
WATN WD24 ... 196 A1
Victoria St DUN/WHIP LU6 ... 80 F1
LTN LU1 ... 2 E8
STAL AL1 ... 11 G7
Victoria Wy HTCH/STOT SG5 ... 52 C2
Victors Wy BAR EN5 ... 200 E4
Victory Rd BERK HP4 ... 146 F5 3
View Rd POTB/CUF EN6 ... 187 H3
Vigors Cft HAT AL10 ... 154 E6
Village St HTCHE/RSTV SG4 ... 87 L1
Village Wy AMSS HP7 ... 192 C3
Villa Rd LTNE LU2 ... 2 D4
Villiers Crs STALE/WH AL4 ... 153 J4
Villiers Rd OXHEY WD19 ... 13 L9
Villiers St HERT/WAS SG14 ... 137 K4
Villiers-sur-marne Av BSF CM23 .. 96 C6
Vincent LWTH SG6 ... 40 B6
Vincent Cl BAR EN5 ... 200 F4
CHES/WCR EN8 ... 176 D7
Vincent Rd LTNW/LEA LU4 ... 64 C5
Vincenzo Cl BRKMPK AL9 ... 172 B2
Vine Cl WGCW AL8 ... 134 D2
Vine Gv HLW CM20 ... 141 J5
Vineyards Rd POTB/CUF EN6 ... 174 A8
The Vineyard WARE SG12 ... 116 E8
WGCW AL8 ... 134 C2 4
Vinters Av STVG SG1 ... 5 G4
Violets La BUNT SG9 ... 61 G6
Violet Wy RKW/CH/CXG WD3 ... 194 B5
Virgil Dr BROX EN10 ... 176 E2 5
Virginia Cl LTNE LU2 ... 65 L7
Viscount Cl LTNN/LIM LU3 ... 64 F5
Vivian Cl OXHEY WD19 ... 205 M2
Vivian Gdns OXHEY WD19 ... 205 M1
Vixen Dr HERT/BAY SG13 ... 137 M4
Vyse Cl BAR EN5 ... 200 B5

W

Wacketts CHESW EN7 ... 175 M6 5
Waddesdon Cl LTNE LU2 ... 66 C8 4
Waddington Rd
STALW/RED AL3 ... 10 E6 1
Wadesmill Rd HERT/WAS SG14 ... 137 J1
WARE SG12 ... 116 B7
The Wades HAT AL10 ... 154 F8
The Wade WGCE AL7 ... 134 E7
Wadham Rd ABLGY WD5 ... 181 L2
Wadhurst Av LTNN/LIM LU3 ... 65 H6
Wadley Cl HHNE HP2 ... 149 L8 5
Wadnall Wy KNEB SG3 ... 88 E6
Wagon Md RBSF CM22 ... 121 M7
Wagon Rd BAR EN5 ... 186 F6
EBAR EN4 ... 187 G8
Wagon Wy RKW/CH/CXG WD3 ... 194 B4
Wain Cl POTB/CUF EN6 ... 173 G8
Walcot Av LTNE LU2 ... 3 K1
Waldeck Rd LTN LU1 ... 2 B4
Waldegrave Pk HARP AL5 ... 131 J1
Walden End STVG SG1 ... 4 E5
Walden Pl WGCW AL8 ... 134 C2
Walden Rd WGCW AL8 ... 134 C2
Waleran Cl STAN HA7 ... 207 L6 5
Waleys Cl LTNN/LIM LU3 ... 64 D2
Walfield Av TRDG/WHET N20 ... 201 G8
Walfords Cl HLWE CM17 ... 142 B7
Walgrave Rd DUN/HR/TOD LU5 ... 63 L8
Walkern Rd HERT/WAS SG14 ... 90 C6
STVG SG1 ... 70 C2
STVGE SG2 ... 71 M6
Walkers Cl HARP AL5 ... 131 H3 5
Walkers Rd HARP AL5 ... 131 G3
Walkley Rd DUN/HR/TOD LU5 ... 63 G6
The Walk POTB/CUF EN6 ... 186 F3
Wallace Wy HTCHE/RSTV SG4 ... 38 F7
Waller Av LTNW/LEA LU4 ... 64 E7
Waller's Cl ROY SG8 ... 33 L1
Wallers Wy HOD EN11 ... 160 A1
Wallingford Wk STAL AL1 ... 169 J2
Wallington Rd BLDK SG7 ... 40 F2
Walmar Cl EBAR EN4 ... 201 J2
Walnut Av BLDK SG7 ... 40 F3
Walnut Cl HTCH/STOT SG5 ... 26 E4 2
HTCHE/RSTV SG4 ... 52 F4
LCOL/BKTW AL2 ... 169 G6
LTNE LU2 ... 66 A7
MHAD SG10 ... 94 E8
Walnut Ct WGCE AL7 ... 134 D7 5
Walnut Dr BSF CM23 ... 96 C7
Walnut Gn BUSH WD23 ... 196 E3 1
Walnut Gv HHNE HP2 ... 8 B9
WGCE AL7 ... 134 D7
Walnut Tree Av SBW CM21 ... 120 D6
Walnut Tree Cl CHES/WCR EN8 .. 190 C2
HOD EN11 ... 159 M4 4
STVGE SG2 ... 71 J6
Walnut Tree Crs SBW CM21 ... 120 D7 3
Walnut Tree Rd HTCH/STOT SG5 .. 37 J7
Walnut Tree Wk WARE SG12 ... 138 C4
Walnut Wy HTCH/STOT SG5 ... 38 D6
Walpole Cl PIN HA5 ... 206 F7
Walsham Cl STVGE SG2 ... 89 H3
Walsh Cl HTCH/STOT SG5 ... 52 C3
Walshford Wy BORE WD6 ... 198 F1
Walsingham Cl HAT AL10 ... 154 E4
LTNE LU2 ... 65 J3 4
Walsingham Wy
LCOL/BKTW AL2 ... 170 B6
Walsworth Rd HTCHE/RSTV SG4 .. 52 F3
Waltham Gdns PEND EN3 ... 190 B8 1
Waltham Ga CHES/WCR EN8 ... 176 D5
Waltham Rd HTCHE/RSTV SG4 ... 52 E4
WAB EN9 ... 177 K5
Walton Gdns WAB EN9 ... 191 G4
Walton Rd BUSH WD23 ... 13 K4
HOD EN11 ... 160 A2
WARE SG12 ... 138 C2
Walton St STAL AL1 ... 11 J4
Walverns Cl OXHEY WD19 ... 13 H9
Wandon Cl LTNE LU2 ... 66 B6
Wansbeck Cl HTCHE/RSTV SG4 ... 54 F7
Wansford Pk BORE WD6 ... 199 J5
Warburton Cl
KTN/HRWW/W HA3 ... 207 J6 2

234 War - Wil

Ward Cl *CHESW* EN7 175 M6 4
WARE SG12 116 B8
Ward Crs *BSF* CM23 96 D4
Warden Hill Cl *LTNE* LU2 65 H2 2
Warden Hill Gdns *LTNE* LU2 65 H2
Warden Hill Rd *LTNE* LU2 65 H2
Ward Hatch *HLW* CM20 7 M1
HLW CM20 142 A7 1
Wardown Crs *LTNE* LU2 2 E1
Warenford Wy *BORE* WD6 198 F2
Ware Park Rd *HERT/WAS* SG14 137 J2
Ware Rd *HERT/BAY* SG13 137 M3
HERT/WAS SG14 90 D8
HOD EN11 159 M2
WARE SG12 115 K3
WARE SG12 118 B6
WARE SG12 138 F7
Wareside *HHNE* HP2 149 M1 2
Wareside Cl *WGCE* AL7 135 G5 7
Warmark Rd *HHW* HP1 148 D5 1
Warminster Cl *LTNE* LU2 84 E1
Warneford Pl *OXHEY* WD19 13 L8
Warner Rd *WARE* SG12 138 C2
Warners Av *HOD* EN11 159 L6
Warners Cl *STVGE* SG2 5 M7
Warners End Rd *HHW* HP1 148 F7
Warren Cl *HAT* AL10 155 G2
LWTH SG6 39 J3
RBSF CM22 99 J3
Warren Dl *WGCW* AL8 134 C1
The Warren Dr *LTN* LU1 108 A1
Warrenfield Cl *CHESW* EN7 189 M2 1
Warrengate La *POTB/CUF* EN6 186 B2
Warrengate Rd *BRKMPK* AL9 172 B7
Warren Gn *HAT* AL10 155 G2
Warren Gv *BORE* WD6 199 J5
Warren La *BLDK* SG7 41 K5
BUNT SG9 57 G4
STAN HA7 207 M2
Warren Park Rd
HERT/WAS SG14 137 H3
Warren Rd *BUSH* WD23 207 H1
LCOL/BKTW AL2 169 H3
LTN LU1 82 E2
Warrensgreen La
HTCHE/RSTV SG4 55 J5
Warren Ter *HERT/WAS* SG14 137 J2
The Warren *CFSP/GDCR* SL9 202 E7
HARP AL5 130 F5
KGLGY WD4 166 E8
RAD WD7 183 M4
ROY SG8 21 J5
Warren Wy *WLYN* AL6 112 D7
Warton Gn *LTNE* LU2 66 D8
Warwick Av *POTB/CUF* EN6 174 C6
Warwick Cl *BUSH* WD23 197 K8
EBAR EN4 201 J6
HERT/BAY SG13 137 H6
POTB/CUF EN6 174 C6
RAYLNE/WEN HP22 122 D5 3
Warwick Ct *RKW/CH/CXG* WD3 193 L4
Warwick Dr *CHES/WCR* EN8 176 C7
Warwick Rd *BAR* EN5 201 G5
BORE WD6 199 J4
BSF CM23 97 G4
PEND EN3 190 E8
RBSF CM22 99 K2
STAL AL1 11 J3
STVGE SG2 5 M2
Warwick Rd East
LTNW/LEA LU4 83 G2 1
Warwick Rd West
LTNW/LEA LU4 83 G1
Warwick Wy
RKW/CH/CXG WD3 195 H5
Washbrook Cl *AMP/FLIT/B* MK45 49 H1
Washington Av *HHNE* HP2 149 K2
Wash La *BAR* EN5 186 B6
POTB/CUF EN6 186 B4
The Wash *BUNT* SG9 61 J5
HERT/WAS SG14 137 J4 16
Watchlytes *WGCE* AL7 135 H4
Watchmead *WGCE* AL7 134 F4 1
Waterbeach *WGCE* AL7 135 J4 9
Watercress Cl *STVGE* SG2 71 J5
Waterdale *HERT/BAY* SG13 137 H6 3
Waterdell La *HTCHE/RSTV* SG4 52 E8
Waterend La *STALE/WH* AL4 133 H2
STALW/RED AL3 130 A5
Water End Rd *BERK* HP4 148 A4 1
Waterfield *WGCE* AL7 135 G3 7
Waterfields Wy *WAT* WD17 13 K4
Waterford Common
HERT/WAS SG14 115 G8
Waterford Gn *WGCE* AL7 135 G4
The Watergate *OXHEY* WD19 206 C2 1
Waterhoose Moor *HLWS* CM18 7 J9
Waterhouse St *HHW* HP1 149 H7
Water La *BERK* HP4 147 H6
BSF CM23 96 E2
HHS/BOV HP3 165 G8
HLWW/ROY CM19 161 K6
HTCH/STOT SG5 52 E2 6
KGLGY WD4 167 G8
STSD CM24 79 K4
WAT WD17 13 H5
Waterloo La *HTCH/STOT* SG5 37 M4
Waterlow Rd *DUN/WHIP* LU6 80 F1
Waterman Cl *OXHEY* WD19 12 E9
Watermark Wy
HERT/BAY SG13 137 L4 7
Watermead Rd *LTNN/LIM* LU3 64 E4
Watermill La *HERT/WAS* SG14 137 J1
Waters Dr
RKW/CH/CXG WD3 204 D1 1
Waters End *HTCH/STOT* SG5 26 D4
Waterside *KGLGY* WD4 166 F8
LCOL/BKTW AL2 170 D6
RAD WD7 184 A5 1
STSD CM24 79 K4 4
WGCE AL7 134 F2
Waterside Ct *KGLGY* WD4 167 G8 1
Waterslade Gn *LTNN/LIM* LU3 65 G4 3
Watersmeet *HLWW/ROY* CM19 162 A6
Waterwick Hl *SAFWS* CB11 47 G1
Watery La *BSF* CM23 78 B1
HAT AL10 154 D6
STALW/RED AL3 107 K7
TRING HP23 123 L1
Watford Field Rd *WAT* WD17 13 J6
WATW WD18 13 H6
Watford Heath *OXHEY* WD19 196 C8
Watford Rd *BORE* WD6 198 B7
KGLGY WD4 180 F1
LCOL/BKTW AL2 168 F6
NTHWD HA6 205 L7
RAD WD7 183 K7
RKW/CH/CXG WD3 194 F7
STAL AL1 169 G2
Watling Cl *HHNE* HP2 8 D2
Watling Knoll *RAD* WD7 183 L4
Watling Pl *DUN/HR/TOD* LU5 63 G6
Watling St *DUN/WHIP* LU6 62 D6
LCOL/BKTW AL2 169 J4
STAL AL1 169 H2
Watlington Rd *HLWE* CM17 142 C6
Watling Vw *STAL* AL1 169 H2
Watson Av *STALW/RED* AL3 11 H1
Watson's Wk *STAL* AL1 11 G8
Watton Rd *KNEB* SG3 88 F5
WARE SG12 116 B8
Watts Cl *STDN* SG11 77 G8
Waulud s Bank Dr *LTNN/LIM* LU3 64 D4
Wavell Cl *CHES/WCR* EN8 176 D6
Waveney *HHNE* HP2 149 L2
Waveney Rd *HARP* AL5 109 H7
Waverley Cl *STVGE* SG2 88 F2
Waverley Gdns *NTHWD* HA6 205 M8 2
Waverley Rd *STALW/RED* AL3 10 D2
Wayre St *HLWE* CM17 142 B6
Waysbrook *LWTH* SG6 40 A6
Wayside *DUN/WHIP* LU6 81 J5
KGLGY WD4 180 A1
POTB/CUF EN6 187 J4 2
RAD WD7 184 C4
Wayside Av *BUSH* WD23 197 J7
The Wayside *HHS/BOV* HP3 150 B8
Waysmeet *LWTH* SG6 39 M6
Waytemore Rd *BSF* CM23 96 D5
Weald Ri *KTN/HRWW/W* HA3 207 L7
Wealdwood Gdns *PIN* HA5 207 G6 2
Weall Gn *GSTN* WD25 182 A3
Weatherby *DUN/WHIP* LU6 80 D2
Weatherby Rd *LTNW/LEA* LU4 64 C8
Weavers Rd *TRING* HP23 123 K6 1
Weaver St *BSF* CM23 96 B6
Weavers Wy *BLDK* SG7 40 F2 1
Webb Cl *LWTH* SG6 40 B5
Webber Cl *BORE* WD6 198 C7 7
Webb Ri *STVG* SG1 70 E3
Webster Cl *WAB* EN9 191 M4 5
Wedgewood Cl
HTCHE/RSTV SG4 53 H3
NTHWD HA6 205 H6 4
Wedgewood Dr *HLWE* CM17 163 J3
Wedgewood Pk *STVG* SG1 55 H8
Wedgewood Rd
HTCHE/RSTV SG4 53 G3
LTNW/LEA LU4 63 L6
Wedgwood Ct *STVG* SG1 55 H8
Wedgwood Ga *STVG* SG1 55 G8
Wedgwood Wy *STVG* SG1 55 G8
Wedhey *HLWW/ROY* CM19 6 C6
Wedmore Rd *HTCHE/RSTV* SG4 52 F4
Wedon Wy *BLDK* SG7 28 B6
Weedon Cl *CFSP/GDCR* SL9 202 A8
HNLW SG16 25 H5
Weighton Rd
KTN/HRWW/W HA3 207 J8
Welbeck Cl *BORE* WD6 198 F4 4
Welbeck Ri *HARP* AL5 131 J4
Welbeck Rd *EBAR* EN4 201 J7
LTNE LU2 3 G4 1
Welbury Av *LTNN/LIM* LU3 65 H3
Welch Pl *PIN* HA5 206 B8 1
Welclose St *STALW/RED* AL3 10 D7
Weldon Cl *LTNE* LU2 84 D1
Welham Cl *BRKMPK* AL9 172 B3
Welham Mnr *BRKMPK* AL9 172 B3
Welkin Gn *HHNE* HP2 9 L6
Wellands *HAT* AL10 154 F3 3
Well Ap *BAR* EN5 200 B6 2
Well Cft *HHW* HP1 149 G6
Wellcroft *LBUZ* LU7 102 E5
Wellcroft Cl *WGCE* AL7 134 F6
Wellcroft Rd *WGCE* AL7 134 F5
Well End Rd *BORE* WD6 185 H8
Wellen Ri *HHS/BOV* HP3 166 D2
Wellers Gv *CHESW* EN7 175 M7 3
Wellesley *EPP* CM16 161 M7
Wellesley Av *NTHWD* HA6 205 L5
Wellesley Crs *POTB/CUF* EN6 186 D4
Wellfield Av *LTNN/LIM* LU3 64 B2
Wellfield Cl *HAT* AL10 154 F4
Wellfield Rd *HAT* AL10 155 G4 5
Well Garth *WGCE* AL7 134 D5
Wellgate Rd *LTNW/LEA* LU4 64 C8
Well Gn *HERT/WAS* SG14 114 B6
Well Head Rd *DUN/WHIP* LU6 80 B4
Wellhouse Cl *LTN* LU1 82 F3
Wellhouse La *BAR* EN5 200 B5
Wellingham Av *HTCH/STOT* SG5 52 C1
Wellington Av *PIN* HA5 206 E8 2
Wellington Cl *OXHEY* WD19 206 D3
Wellington Dr *WGCE* AL7 135 H4
Wellington Rd *LCOL/BKTW* AL2 170 C5
PIN HA5 206 E8
STAL AL1 153 G8
STVGE SG2 71 H5
WAT WD17 12 F1
Wellington St *HERT/WAS* SG14 137 G3
LTN LU1 2 D8
Wellington Ter
DUN/WHIP LU6 81 H2 3
Well La *HLW* CM20 161 M2
HLWW/ROY CM19 161 M1
Wellonhead Br
RAYLNE/WEN HP22 122 E7
Well Rd *BAR* EN5 200 B6
POTB/CUF EN6 173 K8
Well-row *HERT/BAY* SG13 157 L4
Wells Cl *CHESW* EN7 175 H4
HARP AL5 108 D6
STALW/RED AL3 10 C4
Wellside Cl *BAR* EN5 200 B5
Wellstones *WAT* WD17 12 F4 1
Wellswood Cl *HHNE* HP2 9 J7
Welsummer Wy
CHES/WCR EN8 176 C6
Weltmore Rd *LTNN/LIM* LU3 64 E4
Welwyn by Pass Rd *WLYN* AL6 112 B7
Welwyn Ct *HHNE* HP2 8 E1
Welwyn Hall *WLYN* AL6 112 B5 7
Welwyn Rd *HERT/WAS* SG14 136 D3
Wendover Cl *HARP* AL5 131 J1 4
STALE/WH AL4 153 H2
Wendover Ct *WLYN* AL6 112 B5 8
Wendover Dr *WLYN* AL6 112 B5
Wendover Wy *BUSH* WD23 197 H7
LTNE LU2 65 L7
Wengeo La *WARE* SG12 116 A8
Wenlock St *LTNE* LU2 2 E4
Wensley Cl *HARP* AL5 131 J4
Wensley Dl *LTNE* LU2 2 E2
Wensum Wy
RKW/CH/CXG WD3 204 C1
Wentbridge Pth *BORE* WD6 198 F1 6
Wentworth Av *BORE* WD6 198 E6
LTNW/LEA LU4 64 B5
Wentworth Cl
POTB/CUF EN6 186 F2 2
WAT WD17 195 L1
Wentworth Dr *BSF* CM23 96 C4
Wentworth Rd *BAR* EN5 200 C3
HERT/BAY SG13 137 H7
Wenwell Cl *RAYLNE/WEN* HP22 122 F7
Wesley Cl *ARL/CHE* SG15 25 M6
CHESW EN7 175 H7
Wesley Rd *STALW/RED* AL3 106 D5
Wessex Dr *PIN* HA5 206 D7
Westall Cl *HERT/WAS* SG14 137 H5
West Aly *HTCH/STOT* SG5 52 D3 1
West Av *BLDK* SG7 40 D2
LCOL/BKTW AL2 169 G4
Westbourne Rd *LTNW/LEA* LU4 83 G1
Westbrook Cl *EBAR* EN4 201 J4
ROY SG8 18 F2
Westbrook Crs *EBAR* EN4 201 J4
West Burrowfield *WGCE* AL7 134 C6 1
Westbury *CHES/WCR* EN8 190 C1 2
Westbury Cl *DUN/HR/TOD* LU5 63 G7
HTCH/STOT SG5 52 B2
Westbury Gdns *LTNE* LU2 65 J7
Westbury Pl *LWTH* SG6 39 K5
Westbury Ri *HLWE* CM17 163 J3
Westbury Rd *NTHWD* HA6 205 K4
WATW WD18 12 F6
Westbush Cl *HOD* EN11 159 L1
West Chantry
RYLN/HDSTN HA2 207 G8 1
West Cl *BAR* EN5 200 A6
EBAR EN4 201 M5
HOD EN11 159 M2
HTCHE/RSTV SG4 39 G8
STVG SG1 5 G3
Westcombe Dr *BAR* EN5 200 F6
West Common *HARP* AL5 131 G4
West Common Cl *HARP* AL5 131 G5 1
West Common Gv *HARP* AL5 131 G4
West Common Wy *HARP* AL5 130 F5
Westcott *WGCE* AL7 135 J3
Westcroft Ct *BROX* EN10 159 M6 3
West Dene *DUN/WHIP* LU6 127 L2
Westdown Gdns *DUN/WHIP* LU6 80 E3
West Dr *ARL/CHE* SG15 25 M6
GSTN WD25 182 A7
HTCH/STOT SG5 26 A7
KTN/HRWW/W HA3 207 J6
West Drive Gdns
KTN/HRWW/W HA3 207 J6
Westell Cl *BLDK* SG7 40 F2
West End *BLDK* SG7 18 B7
West End La *BAR* EN5 200 C5
BRKMPK AL9 156 B5
West End Rd *BROX* EN10 175 L2
LBUZ LU7 101 L3
Westerdale *LTNW/LEA* LU4 64 A5
Western Av *HNLW* SG16 25 G7
Western Cl *LWTH* SG6 39 K1
Western Pde *BAR* EN5 200 F6
Western Rd *LTN* LU1 2 C8
TRING HP23 123 L7
WAB EN9 177 K1
Western Wy *BAR* EN5 200 F7
DUN/HR/TOD LU5 81 K1
LWTH SG6 39 K2
Westfield *BRKMPK* AL9 172 F2
HLWS CM18 7 H9
WGCE AL7 134 F3
Westfield Av *HARP* AL5 108 F7
WATN WD24 196 C1
Westfield Cl *BSF* CM23 96 D2
CHES/WCR EN8 190 E2
HTCH/STOT SG5 52 C3
Westfield Ct *STALE/WH* AL4 153 J4 4
Westfield Dr *HARP* AL5 109 G6
Westfield La *HTCH/STOT* SG5 52 C3
Westfield Pk *PIN* HA5 206 E7
Westfield Pl *HARP* AL5 109 G6
Westfield Rd *BERK* HP4 146 D4
BSF CM23 96 D2
DUN/WHIP LU6 80 E1
HARP AL5 109 G6
HERT/WAS SG14 137 H2
HNLW SG16 25 H1
HOD EN11 159 L3
Westfields *STALW/RED* AL3 168 F1
West Ga *HLW* CM20 6 D6
West Hayes *RBSF* CM22 121 M7
West Hl *DUN/WHIP* LU6 81 H5
HTCH/STOT SG5 52 C3
West Hill Rd *HOD* EN11 159 L2
LTN LU1 83 K5
Westholme *LWTH* SG6 39 L2
West Hyde La *CFSP/GDCR* SL9 202 E7
Westland Dr *BRKMPK* AL9 172 D6
Westland Rd *KNEB* SG3 88 F5
WAT WD17 12 F1
West La *HTCH/STOT* SG5 37 J5
HTCH/STOT SG5 51 H8
Westlea Av *GSTN* WD25 182 D8
Westlea Cl *BROX* EN10 176 E3 3
Westlea Rd *BROX* EN10 176 E2
Westlecote Gdns *LTNE* LU2 65 J6
West Lieth *TRING* HP23 144 D1
Westly Wd *WGCE* AL7 134 F3
West Md *WGCE* AL7 135 G7
Westmeade Cl *CHESW* EN7 176 A8
Westmill La *HTCH/STOT* SG5 38 B8
Westmill Lawns
HTCH/STOT SG5 52 C1 1
Westmill Rd *HTCH/STOT* SG5 38 B8
WARE SG12 115 L5
Westminster Ct
STALW/RED AL3 169 H1 1
Westminster Gdns
DUN/HR/TOD LU5 63 J4
Westmorland Av *LTNN/LIM* LU3 64 E5
Weston Av *ROY* SG8 21 H3
Weston Cl *POTB/CUF* EN6 186 E3 2
Weston Rd *RAYLNE/WEN* HP22 122 B6
STVG SG1 54 F7
Weston Wy *BLDK* SG7 40 D2
West Pde *DUN/WHIP* LU6 80 F2
Westray *HHS/BOV* HP3 167 H1 5
West Reach *STVGE* SG2 5 H9
Westridge Cl *HHW* HP1 148 E7 4
West Riding *LCOL/BKTW* AL2 182 E1
WLYN AL6 113 J5
West Rd *BERK* HP4 146 F5
BSF CM23 96 D4
HLW CM20 141 M6
SBW CM21 120 A7
STSD CM24 79 K5
Westron Gdns *TRING* HP23 124 A6
West Side *BROX* EN10 176 D4
West St *DUN/WHIP* LU6 80 F2
HERT/BAY SG13 137 H5
LTNE LU2 66 C1
WARE SG12 138 C1
WAT WD17 196 A3 8
West Valley Rd *HHS/BOV* HP3 166 B3
West Vw *HAT* AL10 154 F3
LWTH SG6 39 K5
Westview Ct *BORE* WD6 198 C7 8
West View Gdns *BORE* WD6 198 C7
Westview Ri *HHNE* HP2 8 B7
West View Rd *STALW/RED* AL3 10 E5
West Wy *HARP* AL5 109 H8
Westway *LTNE* LU2 66 B6
West Wy *RKW/CH/CXG* WD3 204 A1
WAB EN9 191 G8
Westwick Cl *HHNE* HP2 150 C8
Westwick Pl *GSTN* WD25 182 B5
Westwick Rw *HHNE* HP2 150 C8
Westwood Av *HTCHE/RSTV* SG4 52 F4
Westwood Cl *AMS* HP6 192 C2
POTB/CUF EN6 186 F1
Westwood Dr *AMS* HP6 192 C2
Wetherby Cl *STVG* SG1 71 H2
Wetherby Rd *BORE* WD6 198 D2
Wetherfield *STSD* CM24 79 J3
HLWE CM17 142 B7
Wetherly Cl *HLWE* CM17 142 E6
Wetherne Link *LTNW/LEA* LU4 64 B5
Wexham Cl *LTNN/LIM* LU3 64 D2
Weybourne Cl *HARP* AL5 109 J8
Weybourne Dr *LTNE* LU2 65 H3
Weymouth St *HHS/BOV* HP3 166 C3
Weymouth Wk *STAN* HA7 207 M6
Whaley Rd *POTB/CUF* EN6 187 H4
Wharfdale *LTNW/LEA* LU4 64 B5 6
Wharfedale *HHNE* HP2 8 D2
Wharf La *BERK* HP4 146 B1
RKW/CH/CXG WD3 194 D8
Wharf Rd *BROX* EN10 176 E3
BSF CM23 96 E4
HHW HP1 166 A1
Wharley Hook *HLWS* CM18 162 E5
Wheatbarn *WGCE* AL7 135 G3 8
Wheat Cl *STALE/WH* AL4 152 F3
Wheatcotes *KNEB* SG3 113 H1
Wheat Cft *BSF* CM23 96 D6 2
Wheatfield *HAT* AL10 155 G4 6
HHNE HP2 8 A4
Wheatfield Av *HARP* AL5 130 F5 1
Wheatfield Crs *ROY* SG8 21 K4 4
Wheatfield Rd *HARP* AL5 130 E5
LTNW/LEA LU4 63 K6
Wheatfields *HLWE* CM17 142 C4 1
Wheathampstead Rd
HARP AL5 131 J2
Wheat Hl *LWTH* SG6 39 K3
Wheatlands *STVGE* SG2 71 H3
Wheatley Cl *SBW* CM21 142 B1
WGCE AL7 134 F6
Wheatley Rd *WGCE* AL7 134 E5
Wheatleys *STALE/WH* AL4 153 H5 1
Wheatley Wy *CFSP/GDCR* SL9 202 D6
Wheatlock Md *STALW/RED* AL3 129 M5
Wheatsheaf Dr *WARE* SG12 116 A7
Wheatsheaf Rd *WARE* SG12 118 C8
Wheelers Cl *WAB* EN9 177 K1
Wheelers La *HHS/BOV* HP3 166 D1
Wheelers Orch *CFSP/GDCR* SL9 202 D6
Wheelright Cl *BUSH* WD23 197 G7 8
Wheel Wright Cl
HTCH/STOT SG5 36 E1 2
Wheelwrights Cl *BSF* CM23 96 B6 6
Whempstead La *WARE* SG12 91 G4
Whempstead Rd *STVGE* SG2 72 E7
Whetstone Cl *WLYN* AL6 112 D2 5
Whinbush Gv *HTCH/STOT* SG5 52 E2 7
Whinbush Rd *HTCH/STOT* SG5 52 E3
Whinnett's Wy
AMP/FLIT/B MK45 34 C1
Whippendell Hl *KGLGY* WD4 180 B1
Whippendell Rd *WATW* WD18 12 D5
Whipperley Ring *LTN* LU1 82 F4
Whipperley Wy *LTN* LU1 83 G4
Whipsnade Rd *DUN/WHIP* LU6 80 E3
Whisper Wd *RKW/CH/CXG* WD3 194 A4
Whitby Rd *LTNN/LIM* LU3 2 B3
Whitebarns La *BUNT* SG9 60 F5
Whitebeam Cl *CHESW* EN7 175 K5 5
Whitebeams *HAT* AL10 154 F8 4
LCOL/BKTW AL2 169 G7
White Bear *STSD* CM24 79 K2 7
Whitebroom Rd *HHW* HP1 148 D5 2
Whitechurch Cl *LTNE* LU2 66 C8 5
Whitechurch Gdns *LWTH* SG6 40 B7
White Craig Cl *PIN* HA5 206 F5
Whitecroft *STAL* AL1 170 A2
Whitecroft Rd *LTNE* LU2 3 J5
White Crofts *HTCH/STOT* SG5 26 D3
Whitefield Av *LTNN/LIM* LU3 64 B3
Whitefields Rd *CHES/WCR* EN8 176 B7
Whitegale Cl *HTCHE/RSTV* SG4 52 F4 7
White Gate Gdns
KTN/HRWW/W HA3 207 K7
Whitegates Cl
RKW/CH/CXG WD3 194 F5
Whitehall Cl *WAB* EN9 177 K1 2
Whitehall La *BSF* CM23 96 E1
Whitehall Rd *BSF* CM23 96 D1
Whitehands Cl *HOD* EN11 159 L4 1
White Hart Cl *BUNT* SG9 58 C2
White Hart Dr *HHNE* HP2 149 L8
White Hart Rd *HHNE* HP2 149 M8
Whitehaven *LTNN/LIM* LU3 64 E1
White Hedge Dr *STALW/RED* AL3 10 C3
Whitehicks *LWTH* SG6 39 M1
Whitehill *BERK* HP4 147 J5
White Hl *BERK* HP4 164 B3
HHW HP1 148 E8
NTHWD HA6 204 F6
STALW/RED AL3 129 G2
STVGE SG2 56 B7
WLYN AL6 111 M8
Whitehill Av *LTN* LU1 83 J5
Whitehill Ct *BERK* HP4 147 J5
White Hill Rd *AMP/FLIT/B* MK45 35 H7
Whitehill Rd *HTCHE/RSTV* SG4 52 F4
White Horse La *KNEB* SG3 113 G1
LCOL/BKTW AL2 170 D5
Whitehorse St *BLDK* SG7 40 E2
Whitehorse V *LTNN/LIM* LU3 64 E1
Whitehouse Av *BORE* WD6 199 G5
White House Cl *CFSP/GDCR* SL9 202 D7
Whitehouse Cl
DUN/HR/TOD LU5 63 G6
Whitehouse La *ABLGY* WD5 168 A5
Whitehurst Av *HTCH/STOT* SG5 52 E1
Whitelands Av
RKW/CH/CXG WD3 193 G4
White La *HTCHE/RSTV* SG4 69 H4
Whiteleaf Rd *HHS/BOV* HP3 166 B2
Whiteley Cl *WARE* SG12 91 K3 1
Whiteley La *BUNT* SG9 44 B3
White Lion St *HHS/BOV* HP3 166 C3 7
White Orchards *STAN* HA7 207 M5
TRDG/WHET N20 200 E8
White Post Fld *SBW* CM21 120 C8
White Shack La
RKW/CH/CXG WD3 180 E8
Whitesmead Rd *STVG* SG1 70 D3
Whitestone Wk *HHW* HP1 148 F4 3
White Stubbs La *BROX* EN10 158 E8
Whitethorn *WGCE* AL7 134 F5
Whitethorn La *LWTH* SG6 39 M7
Whitethorn Wy *LTN* LU1 82 F4
Whitewaits *HLW* CM20 7 H6
Whitewaybottom La *LTNE* LU2 85 M6
The White Wy *STVGE* SG2 71 H3
Whitewebbs La *ENC/FH* EN2 189 L6
Whitewebbs Rd *ENC/FH* EN2 189 G6
Whitewood Rd *BERK* HP4 146 F6 1
Whitfield Wy
RKW/CH/CXG WD3 203 L1
Whit Hern Ct *CHES/WCR* EN8 190 B1
Whitings Cl *HARP* AL5 109 J6
Whitings Rd *BAR* EN5 200 B6
Whitlars Dr *KGLGY* WD4 166 F7 1
Whitley Cl *ABLGY* WD5 181 M3
Whitley Rd *HOD* EN11 160 A2
Whitmores Wd *HHNE* HP2 9 J6
Whitney Dr *STVG* SG1 70 B1
Whittingham Cl *LTNE* LU2 84 E1 1
Whittingstall Rd *HOD* EN11 160 A2
Whittington La *STVG* SG1 4 F6
Whittington Wy *BSF* CM23 96 D7
Whittle Cl *HNLW* SG16 25 G6 1
Whittlesea Rd
KTN/HRWW/W HA3 207 H7
Whitwell Cl *LTNN/LIM* LU3 65 G2
Whitwell Rd *GSTN* WD25 182 C6
Whitworth Jones Av *HNLW* SG16 25 H5
Whitworth Rd *STVG* SG1 55 G7
Whomerley Rd *STVG* SG1 4 F6
Whydale Rd *ROY* SG8 21 K5 5
Whytingham Rd *TRING* HP23 124 B6
Wick Av *STALE/WH* AL4 132 C2
Wicken Flds *WARE* SG12 116 B7
The Wickets *LTNE* LU2 2 D2
Wickfield Cl *KNEB* SG3 88 F8 4
Wickham Cl *DEN/HRF* UB9 204 C8
Wickhams Whf *WARE* SG12 138 D1 2
Wickham Wy *STDN* SG11 75 K7 2
Wick Hl *DUN/WHIP* LU6 105 L2
Wicklands Rd *WARE* SG12 140 C2
Wickmere Cl *LTNE* LU2 65 H3 2
Wick Rd *TRING* HP23 145 H2
Wickstead Av *LTNW/LEA* LU4 64 D7
The Wick *HERT/WAS* SG14 137 G1
Widbury Gdns *WARE* SG12 138 E1 4
Widbury Hl *WARE* SG12 138 F1
Widford Rd *MHAD* SG10 118 D3
WARE SG12 118 C8
WGCE AL7 135 G4
Widford Ter *HHNE* HP2 149 M1 3
Widgeon Wy *GSTN* WD25 182 D7 2
Widmore Dr *HHNE* HP2 9 G5
Wieland Rd *NTHWD* HA6 205 M7
Wiggenhall Rd *WATW* WD18 12 F6
Wiggington Bottom
TRING HP23 145 J2
Wigmore La *LTNE* LU2 66 C8
Wigmore Pl *LTNE* LU2 84 D1
Wigmores North *WGCW* AL8 134 C3 2
Wigram Wy *STVGE* SG2 5 L6
Wilbury Cl *LWTH* SG6 39 H3
Wilbury Dr *DUN/HR/TOD* LU5 63 K8
Wilbury Hills Rd *LWTH* SG6 39 H4
Wilbury Rd *LWTH* SG6 39 J3
Wilbury Wy *HTCHE/RSTV* SG4 38 F7
Wilcot Av *OXHEY* WD19 196 D8
Wilcot Cl *OXHEY* WD19 196 D8
Wilcox Cl *BORE* WD6 199 H2
Wild Cherry Dr *LTN* LU1 83 J5 3
The Wilderness *BERK* HP4 147 H6 6

Wildhill Rd BRKMPK AL9 .... 155 L8
Wild Oaks Cl NTHWD HA6 .... 205 L6
Wildwood NTHWD HA6 .... 205 J6
Wildwood Av LCOL/BKTW AL2 ... 182 E1
Wildwood La STVGE SG1 .... 4 F6
Wilford Cl NTHWD HA6 .... 205 J7
Wilga Rd WLYN AL6 .... 112 A5
Wilkin's Green La HAT AL10 ...... 154 B6
  STALE/WH AL4 .... 154 B7
Wilkins Gv WGCW AL8 .... 134 C5
Wilkinson Wy HHS/BOV HP3 ..... 166 E3
Willenhall Av BAR EN5 .... 201 H7
Willenhall Cl LTNN/LIM LU2 .... 64 F3
William Ct HHS/BOV HP3 .... 166 C3
William Pl STVGE SG2 .... 5 J8
Williamson Wy
  RKW/CH/CXG WD3 .... 203 M1
William St BERK HP4 .... 147 J6
  BUSH WD23 .... 13 K3
  LTNE LU2 .... 2 E3
  STALW/RED AL3 .... 106 C5
Williams Wy RAD WD7 .... 184 B6
Willian Church Rd LWTH SG6 ..... 39 M8
Willian Rd HTCHE/RSTV SG4 ...... 53 G1
Willian Wy BLDK SG7 .... 40 D4
  LWTH SG6 .... 39 M6
Willinghall Cl WAB EN9 .... 191 J5
Williton Rd LTNE LU2 .... 3 M1
Willoughby Cl BROX EN10 .... 159 K8
Willoughby Rd HARP AL5 .... 109 C6
Willoughby Wy
  HTCHE/RSTV SG4 .... 52 F4
Willowby Ct LCOL/BKTW AL2 ... 170 D6
Willow Cl BSF CM23 .... 96 D2
  BUNT SG9 .... 59 M2
  CHESW EN7 .... 175 K5
  ROY SG8 .... 31 J5
Willow Crs STAL AL1 .... 153 H7
Willow Dene BUSH WD23 .... 197 K6
Willowdene CHES/WCR EN8 ..... 176 D6
Willow Dr BAR EN5 .... 200 D5
Willow Edge KGLGY WD4 .... 166 F8
Willow End NTHWD HA6 .... 205 M6
Willow Gv WGCW AL8 .... 112 C7
Willow La HTCH/STOT SG5 .... 52 C4
  WATW WD18 .... 12 D7
Willowmead HERT/WAS SG14 ... 136 F5
Willow Md SBW CM21 .... 142 D1
Willow Pl HLWE CM17 .... 163 L6
Willowside LCOL/BKTW AL2 .... 170 D6
Willowside Wy ROY SG8 .... 21 H2
Willows Link STVGE SG2 .... 88 F1
Willow Springs BSF CM23 .... 96 C2
The Willows HTCHE/RSTV SG4 ... 52 F5
  OXHEY WD19 .... 196 A8
  RKW/CH/CXG WD3 .... 203 M2
  STAL AL1 .... 170 A3
  STVGE SG2 .... 88 F2
Willow Tree Wy HTCH/STOT SG5 .. 38 D8
Willow Wk WLYN AL6 .... 112 B2
Willow Wy HARP AL5 .... 109 H6
  HAT AL10 .... 154 E8
  HHW HP1 .... 149 G5
  LCOL/BKTW AL2 .... 168 F6
  LTNN/LIM LU3 .... 64 D5
  POTB/CUF EN6 .... 187 C4
  RAD WD7 .... 183 K7
Wilsden Av LTN LU1 .... 2 A9
Wilshere Av STAL AL1 .... 169 H2
Wilshere Crs HTCHE/RSTV SG4 .. 53 J2
Wilshere Rd WLYN AL6 .... 111 M5
Wilsmere Dr
  KTN/HRWW/W HA3 .... 207 K7
Wilson Cl BSF CM23 .... 96 E5
  STVG SG1 .... 70 C1
Wilsons La BLDK SG7 .... 18 B6
Wilstone Br TRING HP23 .... 123 J1
Wilstone Dr STALE/WH AL4 ...... 153 H2
Wilton Cl BSF CM23 .... 97 C3
Wilton Crs HERT/BAY SG13 ...... 137 H7
Wilton Rd EBAR EN4 .... 201 L5
  HTCH/STOT SG5 .... 52 D1
Wilton Wy HERT/BAY SG13 ...... 137 H6
Wiltshire Rd STVGE SG2 .... 5 K6
Wimborne Cl SBW CM21 .... 120 C8
Wimborne Gv WAT WD17 .... 181 M3
Wimborne Rd LTN LU1 .... 83 G2
Wimple Rd LTNW/LEA LU4 ...... 63 M8
Winch Cl WLYN AL6 .... 111 L2
Winchdells HHS/BOV HP3 .... 166 F2
Winchester Cl BSF CM23 .... 96 C6
  STVG SG1 .... 54 F8
Winchester Gdns LTNN/LIM LU3 .. 64 D1
Winchester Wy
  RKW/CH/CXG WD3 .... 195 G6
Winchfield Wy
  RKW/CH/CXG WD3 .... 194 B8
Winch St LTNE LU2 .... 3 H2
Windermere Av STAL AL1 .... 170 A1
Windermere Cl DUN/WHIP LU6 .. 80 F3
  HHS/BOV HP3 .... 150 B8
  RKW/CH/CXG WD3 .... 193 J6
Windermere Crs LTNN/LIM LU3 .. 64 E5
Windhill BSF CM23 .... 96 D4
  WGCE AL7 .... 134 F3
Windhill Old Rd BSF CM23 .... 96 D3
Winding Hl MHAD SG10 .... 94 F6

Winding Shot HHW HP1 .... 148 F6
Winding Shott HERT/WAS SG14 .. 114 B6
Windmill Av STALE/WH AL4 ...... 153 H3
Windmill Cl LBUZ LU7 .... 102 E5
  ROY SG8 .... 32 B5
  WAB EN9 .... 191 K5
Windmill Dr RKW/CH/CXG WD3 .. 194 E7
Windmill Fld WARE SG12 .... 138 C2
Windmill Flds HLWE CM17 ...... 142 E6
Windmill Hl BUNT SG9 .... 58 E4
  HTCHE/RSTV SG4 .... 52 E3
  KGLGY WD4 .... 179 L3
Windmill La BAR EN5 .... 199 L7
  BUSH WD23 .... 207 K1
  CHES/WCR EN8 .... 190 D1
Windmill Rd CFSP/GDCR SL9 ... 202 C7
  HHNE HP2 .... 8 F9
  HTCHE/RSTV SG4 .... 67 J8
  LTN LU1 .... 3 H8
  LTN LU1 .... 106 F4
Windmills WARE SG12 .... 91 K2
Windmill St BUSH WD23 .... 207 K1
Windmill Wy MHAD SG10 .... 118 D1
  TRING HP23 .... 123 L6
Windmore Av POTB/CUF EN6 .. 186 B2
Windridge Cl STALW/RED AL3 .. 168 F1
Winds End Cl HHNE HP2 .... 9 G5
Windsor Cl CHESW EN7 .... 189 M1
  HHS/BOV HP3 .... 164 F7
  HHS/BOV HP3 .... 166 D1
  STVGE SG2 .... 89 G3
  WLYN AL6 .... 112 A7
Windsor Dr DUN/HR/TOD LU5 .. 63 J6
  EBAR EN4 .... 201 L7
  HERT/WAS SG14 .... 136 E3
Windsor Gdns BSF CM23 .... 96 B3
Windsor Rd AMP/FLIT/B MK45 .. 35 H6
  BAR EN5 .... 200 C7
  KTN/HRWW/W HA3 .... 207 H8
  PEND EN3 .... 190 C7
  ROY SG8 .... 21 L4
  WATN WD24 .... 196 B1
  WLYN AL6 .... 112 A7
Windsor St LTN LU1 .... 2 D8
Windsor Wk LTN LU1 .... 2 D8
Windsor Wy RKW/CH/CXG WD3 .. 203 M1
Windward Cl PEND EN3 .... 190 C6
Windy Ri WARE SG12 .... 91 L3
Winfield St DUN/WHIP LU6 .... 81 G1
Winford Dr BROX EN10 .... 176 E1
Wingate Gdns WLYN AL6 .... 112 A5
Wingate Rd DUN/HR/TOD LU5 .. 81 K1
  LTNW/LEA LU4 .... 64 E8
Wingate Wy STAL AL1 .... 11 M9
Wingrave Rd TRING HP23 .... 101 J8
Winifred Rd HHS/BOV HP3 ...... 166 C3
Winkers Cl CFSP/GDCR SL9 .... 202 E8
Winkers La CFSP/GDCR SL9 .... 202 E8
Winkfield Cl LTNW/LEA LU4 ...... 82 A1
Winscombe Wy STAN HA7 ...... 207 M5
Winsdon Rd LTN LU1 .... 2 C8
Winslow Cl LTNN/LIM LU3 .... 65 H6
Winston Churchill Wy
  CHES/WCR EN8 .... 190 B4
Winston Cl HTCH/STOT SG5 ...... 52 C3
  KTN/HRWW/W HA3 .... 207 L6
Winston Crs PIN HA5 .... 207 G7
Winston Gdns BERK HP4 .... 146 E6
Winston Wy POTB/CUF EN6 .... 186 F4
Winstre Rd BORE WD6 .... 198 F2
Wintercroft Rd HOD EN11 .... 159 L3
Winters La STVGE SG2 .... 72 A1
Winters Wy WAB EN9 .... 191 M4
Winton Ap RKW/CH/CXG WD3 .. 195 H6
Winton Cl LTNE LU2 .... 65 J4
  LWTH SG6 .... 40 B2
Winton Crs RKW/CH/CXG WD3 .. 195 G6
Winton Dr CHES/WCR EN8 ...... 176 D8
  RKW/CH/CXG WD3 .... 195 H6
Winton Rd WARE SG12 .... 138 E1
Wisden Rd STVG SG1 .... 70 E2
Wiseman Cl LTNE LU2 .... 65 K3
Wisemans Gdns SBW CM21 .... 142 B1
Wistlea Crs STALE/WH AL4 ...... 171 G1
Wistow Rd LTNN/LIM LU3 .... 64 F1
Witchford WGCE AL7 .... 135 J4
Withy Cl LTNW/LEA LU4 .... 64 A5
Withy Pl LCOL/BKTW AL2 .... 169 H7
Witney Cl PIN HA5 .... 206 E6
Witter Av HTCH/STOT SG5 .... 38 D6
Wiveton Cl LTNE LU2 .... 65 J3
Woburn Av BSF CM23 .... 96 B3
Woburn Cl BUSH WD23 .... 197 H7
  STVGE SG2 .... 89 H3
Wodecroft Rd LTNN/LIM LU3 .... 65 G4
Wolsey Av CHESW EN7 .... 175 L8
Wolsey Rd HHNE HP2 .... 149 J8
  RKW/CH/CXG WD3 .... 205 H2
Wolston Cl LTN LU1 .... 2 A7
Wolvescroft KNEB SG3 .... 88 F8
Wolves Mere KNEB SG3 .... 88 F8
Woodacre Dr WLYN AL6 .... 112 F2
Woodbank Dr CSTG HP8 .... 202 C3
Woodbine Cl HLWW/ROY CM19 .. 162 B4
Woodbridge Cl LTNW/LEA LU4 .. 64 D6
Woodbrook Gdns WAB EN9 .... 191 K4

Woodbury Hl LTNE LU2 .... 2 F1
Wood Cl DUN/WHIP LU6 .... 105 K1
  HAT AL10 .... 155 G5
Woodcock Hl
  RKW/CH/CXG WD3 .... 204 D5
Woodcockhill STALE/WH AL4 .. 153 J1
Woodcock Rd LTN LU1 .... 82 F3
  STVGE SG2 .... 71 J8
Wood Common HAT AL10 .... 155 G5
Woodcote Cl CHES/WCR EN8 .. 190 B1
Woodcroft HHS/BOV HP3 .... 149 J8
  HLWS CM18 .... 162 B4
Woodcroft Av STAN HA7 .... 207 M8
  WARE SG12 .... 139 A6
Wood Dr STVGE SG2 .... 71 G8
Wood End LCOL/BKTW AL2 .... 169 H7
Wood End Hl HHNE HP2 .... 9 L6
Wood End Hl HARP AL5 .... 108 C7
Wood End La STALW/RED AL3 .. 128 C2
Wood End Rd HARP AL5 .... 108 C7
Woodfall Av BAR EN5 .... 200 E6
Woodfield Av NTHWD HA6 ...... 205 J4
Woodfield Cl STSD CM24 .... 79 K4
Woodfield Dr HHS/BOV HP3 .... 167 J1
Woodfield Gdns
  HHS/BOV HP3 .... 167 J1
Woodfield Ga
  DUN/HR/TOD LU5 .... 81 K4
Woodfield La BRKMPK AL9 ...... 173 K2
Woodfield Ri BUSH WD23 .... 197 J8
Woodfield Rd RAD WD7 .... 183 M7
  STVG SG1 .... 70 B1
  WGCE AL7 .... 134 E4
Woodfields STSD CM24 .... 79 K4
Woodfields Ter STSD CM24 ...... 79 K4
Woodfield Wy STALE/WH AL4 .. 153 H4
Woodford Cl WAB EN9 .... 191 M4
Woodforde Cl BLDK SG7 .... 18 D6
Woodford Rd DUN/HR/TOD LU5 .. 63 K8
  WAT WD17 .... 13 G1
Woodgate GSTN WD25 .... 182 A4
Woodgate Av POTB/CUF EN6 .. 188 A4
Woodgate Crs NTHWD HA6 .... 205 M6
Wood Green Cl LTNE LU2 .... 66 A5
Wood Green Rd LTNE LU2 .... 66 A5
Woodhall Av PIN HA5 .... 206 D8
Woodhall Cl HERT/WAS SG14 .. 137 H2
Woodhall Dr PIN HA5 .... 206 C8
Woodhall Ga PIN HA5 .... 206 C7
Woodhall Gv BSF CM23 .... 96 C4
Woodhall La HHNE HP2 .... 8 D6
  OXHEY WD19 .... 206 C3
  RAD WD7 .... 184 F5
  WGCE AL7 .... 134 D6
Woodham Wy WARE SG12 ...... 139 H6
Woodhill HLWS CM18 .... 162 D5
Woodhouse Eaves
  NTHWD HA6 .... 205 M5
Wood House La BROX EN10 .... 158 E8
Woodhurst LWTH SG6 .... 39 L2
Woodhurst Av GSTN WD25 .... 182 C6
Wooding Gv HLWW/ROY CM19 .. 6 A6
Woodland Cl HHW HP1 .... 149 G8
  LTNN/LIM LU3 .... 64 D5
  TRING HP23 .... 123 L8
Woodland Dr STALE/WH AL4 .. 153 H6
  WAT WD17 .... 12 C1
Woodland La
  RKW/CH/CXG WD3 .... 193 J4
Woodland Mt HERT/BAY SG13 .. 137 J4
Woodland Pl HHW HP1 .... 149 G8
Woodland Ri DUN/WHIP LU6 .. 105 G3
  WGCW AL8 .... 134 B2
Woodland Rd HERT/BAY SG13 .. 138 B7
  RKW/CH/CXG WD3 .... 203 J5
Woodlands BRKMPK AL9 .... 173 G6
  BSF CM23 .... 97 H2
  HARP AL5 .... 108 D7
  LCOL/BKTW AL2 .... 169 H6
  LTN LU1 .... 82 D8
  RAD WD7 .... 183 M5
  ROY SG8 .... 21 K4
Woodlands Av BERK HP4 .... 147 J7
  DUN/HR/TOD LU5 .... 63 H6
Woodlands Cl BORE WD6 .... 199 G5
  HOD EN11 .... 159 M5
  TRING HP23 .... 123 L8
Woodlands Dr HOD EN11 .... 159 M6
  STAN HA7 .... 207 L6
Woodlands Meade
  HTCHE/RSTV SG4 .... 55 G2
Woodlands Rd BUSH WD23 ...... 13 M6
  HERT/BAY SG13 .... 137 L4
  KGLGY WD4 .... 166 F6
  WARE SG12 .... 116 C4
Woodland Wy BLDK SG7 .... 40 E4
  CHESW EN7 .... 175 G7
  STVGE SG2 .... 5 M9
  WLYN AL6 .... 112 E3
Wood La BSF CM23 .... 79 K8
  BUNT SG9 .... 46 F4
  HHNE HP2 .... 149 J8
Wood Lane End HHNE HP2 .... 9 H7
Woodlea LCOL/BKTW AL2 ...... 168 F4

Woodlea Gv NTHWD HA6 .... 205 H6
Woodley Rd WARE SG12 .... 116 E8
Woodman Rd HHS/BOV HP3 .... 166 D1
Woodmans Yd WAT WD17 .... 13 H5
Woodmere LTNN/LIM LU3 .... 64 F1
Woodmere Av WATN WD24 .... 196 C1
Woodpecker Cl BSF CM23 .... 96 B4
  BUSH WD23 .... 207 H1
  HAT AL10 .... 154 E8
  KTN/HRWW/W HA3 .... 207 L8
Woodredon Cl
  HLWW/ROY CM19 .... 161 G3
Wood Ride EBAR EN4 .... 201 J2
Woodridge Wy PIN HA5 .... 206 E8
Woodridings Cl PIN HA5 .... 206 F7
Woods Av HAT AL10 .... 154 F6
Woodshots Meadow
  WATW WD18 .... 195 J6
Woodside BORE WD6 .... 198 E5
  BSF CM23 .... 97 J2
  CHESW EN7 .... 189 M2
  HERT/BAY SG13 .... 138 B7
  WATN WD24 .... 181 M8
Woodside Cl STAN HA7 .... 207 M5
Woodside La BRKMPK AL9 ...... 172 F1
Woodside Rd GSTN WD25 .... 182 A2
  LCOL/BKTW AL2 .... 182 E1
  LTN LU1 .... 83 G6
  NTHWD HA6 .... 205 L7
  WLYN AL6 .... 112 E7
Woods Pl TRING HP23 .... 123 M7
The Woods NTHWD HA6 .... 205 M5
  RAD WD7 .... 184 A5
Woodstock KNEB SG3 .... 88 E7
Woodstock Cl
  HERT/BAY SG13 .... 138 A6
Woodstock Rd BROX EN10 ...... 159 K6
  BUSH WD23 .... 197 K8
Woodstock Rd North STAL AL1 .. 153 G5
Woodstock Rd South STAL AL1 .. 153 G7
Wood St BAR EN5 .... 200 B5
  DUN/WHIP LU6 .... 81 H2
  LTN LU1 .... 3 G9
Wood V HAT AL10 .... 155 G5
Wood Vw HHW HP1 .... 149 G5
  POTB/CUF EN6 .... 174 D6
Woodville Court Ms
  WAT WD17 .... 195 M3
Woodville Rd BERK HP4 .... 201 G4
Woodward Gdns STAN HA7 .... 207 J4
Woodwards HLWW/ROY CM19 .. 162 B4
Woodwaye OXHEY WD19 .... 196 B8
Woodwicks
  RKW/CH/CXG WD3 .... 203 J5
Woolgrove Rd HTCHE/RSTV SG4 .. 52 F1
Woollam Crs STALW/RED AL3 .. 152 B3
Woollard St WAB EN9 .... 191 H5
Woolmans Cl BROX EN10 .... 176 E1
Woolmer Cl BORE WD6 .... 198 F1
Woolmerdine Ct BUSH WD23 .. 13 K3
Woolmer Dr HHNE HP2 .... 9 L9
Woolmers La HERT/WAS SG14 .. 136 A8
Woolners Wy STVG SG1 .... 4 A1
Woolpack Cl DUN/WHIP LU6 .. 81 H5
Woolston Av LWTH SG6 .... 39 M6
Wootton Cl LTNN/LIM LU3 .... 65 G3
Wootton Dr HHNE HP2 .... 149 L2
Worboys Ct ROY SG8 .... 15 L5
Worcester Rd HAT AL10 .... 154 E4
Wordsworth Cl ROY SG8 .... 21 J1
Wordsworth Rd HARP AL5 ...... 108 F7
  LTNW/LEA LU4 .... 63 M8
Works Rd LWTH SG6 .... 40 A3
Worley Rd STALW/RED AL3 ...... 10 E5
Wormley Cl WAB EN9 .... 191 M4
Wormley Lodge Cl
  BROX EN10 .... 176 E2
Wormyngford Ct WAB EN9 .... 191 M4
Worsdell Wy HTCHE/RSTV SG4 .. 53 G3
Worsted La BUNT SG9 .... 59 K3
Wortham Rd ROY SG8 .... 21 K6
Wortham Wy STVGE SG2 .... 5 M9
Worthington Rd DUN/WHIP LU6 .. 80 E2
The Wraglins BSF CM23 .... 97 G5
Wrangley Ct WAB EN9 .... 191 M4
Wratten Cl HTCH/STOT SG5 ...... 52 D4
Wratten Rd East
  HTCH/STOT SG5 .... 52 D4
Wratten Rd West
  HTCH/STOT SG5 .... 52 C4
Wrayfields HTCH/STOT SG5 ...... 27 G3
Wraysbury Cl LTNW/LEA LU4 .. 64 C7
Wrenbrook Rd BSF CM23 .... 96 C5
Wren Cl HTCHE/RSTV SG4 ...... 110 A1
  LTNE LU2 .... 66 B4
  STVGE SG2 .... 5 L2
Wren Crs BUSH WD23 .... 207 H1
Wren Dr WAB EN9 .... 191 M5
Wrensfield HHW HP1 .... 148 F7
The Wrens HLWW/ROY CM19 .... 6 B7
Wren Wd WGCE AL7 .... 135 G5
Wright Cl STALE/WH AL4 .... 132 C3
Wright's Green La RBSF CM22 .. 121 H3
Wrights Meadow STVGE SG2 .. 72 A2
Wrights Orch STVGE SG2 .... 71 K8
Wrotham Rd BAR EN5 .... 200 D3

Wroxham Av HHS/BOV HP3 .... 166 C1
Wroxham Gdns ENC/FH EN2 .. 188 F6
  POTB/CUF EN6 .... 186 C2
Wroxham Wy HARP AL5 .... 109 H7
Wulfrath Wy HARP AL5 .... 116 B7
Wulwards Cl LTN LU1 .... 83 G4
Wyatt Cl BUSH WD23 .... 197 K8
  HTCH/STOT SG5 .... 38 C6
Wyatt's Cl RKW/CH/CXG WD3 .. 193 M4
Wyatt's Rd RKW/CH/CXG WD3 .. 193 L5
Wyburn Av BAR EN5 .... 200 E4
Wychdell STVGE SG2 .... 89 H2
Wych Elm HLW CM20 .... 6 C5
Wych Elm La KNEB SG3 .... 88 D7
Wych Elms LCOL/BKTW AL2 .. 169 G7
Wycherley Crs BAR EN5 .... 201 G7
Wychford Dr SBW CM21 .... 142 B1
Wychwood Av LTNE LU2 .... 65 K6
Wychwood Wy NTHWD HA6 .. 205 L7
Wycklond Cl HTCH/STOT SG5 .. 26 D4
Wycliffe Cl LTNN/LIM LU3 .... 65 H4
Wycombe Wy LTNN/LIM LU3 .. 65 H2
  STALE/WH AL4 .... 153 G4
Wyddial Gn WGCE AL7 .... 135 G4
Wyddial Rd BUNT SG9 .... 58 D2
Wyedale LCOL/BKTW AL2 ...... 170 E6
Wyken Cl LTNN/LIM LU3 .... 64 F3
Wyldwood Cl HLWE CM17 ...... 142 B4
Wyllyotts Pl POTB/CUF EN6 .. 186 E5
Wylo Dr BAR EN5 .... 199 M7
Wymondley Cl HTCHE/RSTV SG4 .. 52 F4
Wymondley Rd
  HTCHE/RSTV SG4 .... 52 F4
Wynches Farm Dr
  STALE/WH AL4 .... 153 J7
Wynchgate KTN/HRWW/W HA3 .. 207 K7
Wynchlands Crs STALE/WH AL4 .. 153 J7
Wyndham Rd LTNW/LEA LU4 .. 64 B8
Wyndhams End
  BRKMPK AL9 .... 134 E8
Wynn Cl BLDK SG7 .... 40 F1
Wyrley Dell LWTH SG6 .... 39 M7
Wyton WGCE AL7 .... 135 J4
Wyvern Cl LTNW/LEA LU4 .... 64 D7

Y

Yardley LWTH SG6 .... 40 A6
Yardley Av LBUZ LU7 .... 102 B6
Yarmouth Rd STVG SG1 .... 69 M3
  WATN WD24 .... 196 A1
Yarrowside AMSS HP7 .... 192 A3
Yately Cl LTNE LU2 .... 65 J3
Yearling Cl WARE SG12 .... 138 E3
Yeats Cl ROY SG8 .... 21 J1
Yeomanry Dr BLDK SG7 .... 40 F1
Yeomans Av HARP AL5 .... 108 C7
Yeomans Cl BSF CM23 .... 96 C5
Yeomans Dr STVGE SG2 .... 71 K8
Yeomans Ride HHNE HP2 .... 149 M1
Yeovil Rd LTNE LU2 .... 3 M1
Yew Cl CHESW EN7 .... 175 K6
Yew Gv WGCE AL7 .... 135 H5
Yewlands HOD EN11 .... 159 M5
  SBW CM21 .... 142 D1
Yewlands Dr HOD EN11 .... 159 M5
Yews Av EN EN1 .... 190 A1
Yew Tree Cl LBUZ LU7 .... 102 D6
Yew Tree Ct BORE WD6 .... 198 C2
Yew Tree Dr HHS/BOV HP3 ...... 165 G7
Yewtree End LCOL/BKTW AL2 .. 169 G6
Yew Tree Pl BSF CM23 .... 96 E2
Yew Wk HOD EN11 .... 159 M5
York Cl AMP/FLIT/B MK45 .... 35 H6
  KGLGY WD4 .... 166 F8
York Crs BORE WD6 .... 199 J3
Yorke Cl RAYLNE/WEN HP22 .. 122 D5
Yorke Ga WAT WD17 .... 195 M3
Yorke Rd RKW/CH/CXG WD3 .. 194 F7
Yorkes HLWS CM18 .... 162 E4
York Rd BAR EN5 .... 201 H6
  CHES/WCR EN8 .... 190 D5
  HTCH/STOT SG5 .... 52 D2
  STAL AL1 .... 11 J5
  STVG SG1 .... 70 E1
  WATW WD18 .... 13 H7
York St LTNE LU2 .... 3 G4
York Wy GSTN WD25 .... 182 C7
  HHS/BOV HP3 .... 149 K8
  ROY SG8 .... 21 G2
  WLYN AL6 .... 112 A7
Youngfield Rd HHW HP1 .... 148 E6
Youngsbury La WARE SG12 .... 116 C2
Youngs Ri WGCW AL8 .... 134 A4
Yule Cl LCOL/BKTW AL2 .... 182 E1

Z

Zambesi Rd BSF CM23 .... 96 E5

Index - featured places

Abbey C of E JMI School
  STALW/RED AL3 .... 10 D8
Abbeygate Business Centre
  LTNE LU2 .... 3 G5
Abbey Mead Industrial Park
  WAB EN9 .... 191 G5
Abbey Road Surgery
  CHES/WCR EN8 .... 190 D5
Abbot's Hill School
  HHS/BOV HP3 .... 167 G4

Abbots Langley Parish Council
  ABLGY WD5 .... 181 L2
Abbots School
  ABLGY WD5 .... 181 L1
Abbotsweld Primary School
  HLWS CM18 .... 162 C4
Abbotswood Medical Centre
  ABLGY WD5 .... 181 M3
Aboyne Lodge School
  STALW/RED AL3 .... 10 E5

Adeyfield School
  HHNE HP2 .... 9 G9
Akeman Business Park
  TRING HP23 .... 123 M7
Alban Wood Infant School
  GSTN WD25 .... 182 A3
Albanwood School
  GSTN WD25 .... 182 A4
Albury School
  STDN SG11 .... 76 F4

Aldbury Junior School
  TRING HP23 .... 125 H4
Aldenham Parish Council
  RAD WD7 .... 183 M7
Aldenham School
  BORE WD6 .... 197 L3
Aldwickbury Park Golf Club
  HARP AL5 .... 131 K1
Algrey Trading Estate
  HTCHE/RSTV SG4 .... 52 F1

Allied Business Centre
  HARP AL5 .... 109 H7
All Nations Christian College
  WARE SG12 .... 139 G2
All Saints C of E Junior Middle
  & Infant School
  BSF CM23 .... 97 G2
Almonds Hill Junior Mixed School
  STVG SG1 .... 70 C2
Alpha Business Park
  BRKMPK AL9 .... 172 B2

Alsa Business Park STSD CM24 79 L1
A M F Bowling HHNE HP2 9 J5
Amwell View School WARE SG12 139 G6
Andrews Lane Junior & Infant School CHESW EN7 175 M7
Anglian Business Park ROY SG8 21 G3
Anstey School BUNT SG9 45 M4
Apex Business Centre DUN/HR/TOD LU5 63 H8
Applecroft Junior Middle & Infant School WGCW AL8 134 A5
Apsley Mills Retail Park HHS/BOV HP3 166 D3
Archway Surgery HHS/BOV HP3 164 F6
Ardeley School STVGE SG2 56 E7
Ardley Hill Lower School DUN/WHIP LU6 81 H4
Arndale Shopping Centre LTN LU1 2 E6
Arnetthill School RKW/CH/CXG WD3 193 M7
Arnold Middle School AMP/FLIT/B MK45 35 J8
Arseley Football Club ARL/CHE SG15 25 M7
The Arthur Findlay College STSD CM24 79 M5
The Arts Educational School TRING HP23 124 A7
Ascot Business Centre LTN LU1 2 C7
Ascot Industrial Estate LWTH SG6 40 A3
Ashcroft High School LTNE LU2 66 B8
Ashfield Junior School BUSH WD23 197 G8
Ash Industrial Estate HLWW/ROY CM19 161 L3
Ashley Business Centre HTCH/STOT SG5 52 E2
Ashlyns School BERK HP4 147 H8
Ashridge Golf Club BERK HP4 126 A3
Ashton C of E Middle School DUN/WHIP LU6 81 G1
Ashton C of E School DUN/HR/TOD LU5 81 G2
Ashville Trading Estate BLDK SG7 40 E1
Asquith Court School HARP AL5 108 E7
Astley Cooper School HHNE HP2 149 M2
Aston Clinton County Combined School RAYLNE/WEN HP22 122 C5
Aston Clinton Surgery RAYLNE/WEN HP22 122 E6
Aycliffe Drive Primary School HHNE HP2 8 D1
Aylands School PEND EN3 190 B7
Baldock Health Centre BLDK SG7 40 E3
Baldock Industrial Estate BLDK SG7 40 E3
Bancroft Business Centre HTCH/STOT SG5 52 E2
Barbara Castle Health Centre HLWW/ROY CM19 161 M6
The Barclay School STVG SG1 70 C2
The Barking Dog Theatre Co BSF CM23 96 E5
Barkway Park Golf Club ROY SG8 32 D8
Barkway Va First School ROY SG8 32 B6
Barley Vp School ROY SG8 32 F1
Barncroft JMI School HHNE HP2 149 J2
Barnet College of Further Education BAR EN5 200 E5
Barnet County Court BAR EN5 201 H5
Barnet Football Club BAR EN5 200 F6
Barnet General Hospital BAR EN5 200 C5
Barnet Health Centre BAR EN5 200 F6
Barnet Hill Primary School BAR EN5 200 E6
Barnet Hospital Chest Clinic BAR EN5 200 C5
Barnet Magistrates Court BAR EN5 200 E5
Barnet Synagogue BAR EN5 201 H6
Barnfield College LTN LU1 83 G5
Barnfield College LTNE LU2 65 J5
Barnfield College LTNN/LIM LU3 65 G2
The Barn School MHAD SG10 94 E8
Barn Theatre WGCW AL8 134 B4
Barnwell School STVGE SG2 5 M9
Barracuda Swimming Club POTB/CUF EN6 187 J4
Barratt Industrial Park LTNE LU2 84 B4
Barton Industrial Estate AMP/FLIT/B MK45 34 F6
Barton Rovers Football Club AMP/FLIT/B MK45 35 H8
Batchwood Golf Club STALW/RED AL3 152 A4
Batchwood School STALW/RED AL3 10 E1
Batford JMI School HARP AL5 109 J6
Bayfordbury College of Hertfordshire HERT/BAY SG13 158 A1
Bayford Junior Middle & Infant School HERT/BAY SG13 157 L5
Beaumont School STALE/WH AL4 153 J6
Bedmond JMI School ABLGY WD5 167 L7
Bedwell Junior & Infant School STVG SG1 5 J2
Bedwell Medical Centre STVG SG1 5 J3
Beechfield Junior Middle & Infant School WATN WD24 181 M8
Beech Hill Community School LTNW/LEA LU4 83 G1
Beech Hyde Junior Middle & Infant School STALE/WH AL4 132 C3
Beechwood Infant School LTNW/LEA LU4 64 D7
Beechwood Infants & Junior School LTNW/LEA LU4 64 D6
Beechwood Park Preparatory School STALW/RED AL3 127 M1
Beecroft School DUN/WHIP LU6 80 E1
Belcon Industrial Estate HOD EN11 160 B4
Bellgate JMI School HHNE HP2 8 D4
Bell Lane County Combined School AMS HP6 192 A1
Bells House Gallery LWTH SG6 39 L4
Belswains Infant School HHS/BOV HP3 166 E3
Bengeo Junior & Infant School HERT/WAS SG14 137 H1
Benington Primary School STVGE SG2 72 C5
Bennetts End Surgery HHS/BOV HP3 166 F2
Bentfield County Primary School STSD CM24 79 J2
Bentley Wood High School STAN HA7 207 L5
Berkeley Clinic RKW/CH/CXG WD3 204 B1
Berkhamsted Football Club BERK HP4 147 G5
Berkhamsted Golf Club BERK HP4 147 K3
Berkhamsted Health Centre BERK HP4 146 F5
Berkhamsted School BERK HP4 147 H6
Berkhamsted School for Girls BERK HP4 147 G6
Berkhamsted School House BERK HP4 147 H6
Berkhamsted Tennis Club BERK HP4 147 H5
Berkley Gallery BERK HP4 147 G6
Bernards Heath Infant School STAL AL1 11 J2
Beta Health Clinic HHNE HP2 8 A8
Birchwood High School BSF CM23 97 H2
Birchwood Leisure Centre HAT AL10 155 G2
Bishops Hatfield Girls School HAT AL10 154 F5
Bishop's Park Health Centre BSF CM23 96 E2
Bishops Stortford College BSF CM23 96 D3
The Bishops Stortford High School BSF CM23 96 E6
Bishops Stortford Town Council BSF CM23 96 E3
Bishops Wood Hospital RKW/CH/CXG WD3 204 F5
Bishop Wood Junior School TRING HP23 123 M7
Blackthorn Junior School WGCE AL7 134 F5
Blessed Cuthbert Mayne RC School HHW HP1 149 G6
Blue Gold Trading Estate ARL/CHE SG15 25 M5
Bondor Business Centre BLDK SG7 40 D3
Bonneygrove Junior & Infant School CHESW EN7 189 M1
Borehamwood Football Club BORE WD6 199 G3
Borehamwood Industrial Park BORE WD6 199 J3
The Borough Industrial Estate LTNN/LIM LU3 64 F7
Borough of Broxbourne CHES/WCR EN8 190 A1
Botany Bay Cricket Club ENC/FH EN2 188 C7
Bournehall Junior & Infant School BUSH WD23 196 F6
Bovingdon Junior Mixed School HHS/BOV HP3 165 G6
Bovingdon Parish Council HHS/BOV HP3 164 F6
Bovingdon Primary School HHS/BOV HP3 165 G6
Bowmans Trading Estate STVG SG1 70 A5
Boxmoor Golf Club HHW HP1 165 K3
Boxmoor House School HHS/BOV HP3 165 L2
Boxwell Road Surgery BERK HP4 147 G6
Bramingham Business Park LTNN/LIM LU3 65 G2
Bramingham Medical Centre LTNN/LIM LU3 65 G2
Bramingham Park Medical Centre LTNN/LIM LU3 64 F2
Bramingham Primary School LTNN/LIM LU3 65 G2
Brandles Close School BLDK SG7 40 D3
Brays Grove Comprehensive School HLWS CM18 163 G4
Breakspeare School ABLGY WD5 181 K2
Brewers Hill Middle School DUN/WHIP LU6 80 D1
Brickendon Grange Golf & Country Club HERT/BAY SG13 158 A6
Brickfields Industrial Estate HHNE HP2 9 J1
Bridge Cottage Surgery WLYN AL6 112 A5
Bridger Packaging Football Club LWTH SG6 39 L7
Bridgewater School BERK HP4 146 F4
Britannia Business Centre CHES/WCR EN8 190 E5
British Museum Zoological Museum TRING HP23 124 A7
Brittania Business Park CHES/WCR EN8 190 E5
Broadfield Infant School HHNE HP2 8 E8
Broadfield Junior School HHNE HP2 8 E9
Broadfield School HLW CM20 7 H5
Broadmead School LTN LU1 83 K5
Brockswood JMI School HHNE HP2 150 A1
Bromet School OXHEY WD19 196 C8
Brookland Junior & Infant School CHES/WCR EN8 176 D7
Brookmans Park Gm Primary School BRKMPK AL9 172 D5
Brookmead School LBUZ LU7 102 D5
Brookside Business Centre RBSF CM22 120 E1
Broom Barns Infant School STVG SG1 4 F5
Broxbourne Borough Council CHES/WCR EN8 176 C5
Broxbourne Business Centre CHES/WCR EN8 176 C5
Broxbourne C of E JMI School BROX EN10 159 L8
Broxbourne Sailing Club HOD EN11 160 C7
The Broxbourne School BROX EN10 176 D1
Broxbourne Sports Club BROX EN10 159 L8
Buckinghamshire Chilterns University College CSTG HP8 202 F2
The Bull Theatre BAR EN5 200 E5
Burleigh Primary School CHES/WCR EN8 190 C1
Burnt Mill Comprehensive School HLW CM20 7 H2
Burnt Mill Industrial Estate HLW CM20 6 C1
Burvill House Surgery HAT AL10 154 F5
Burydale Junior Mixed School STVGE SG2 89 G1
Bus Garage LTN LU1 2 E8
Bushey & District Synagogue BUSH WD23 197 H8
Bushey Hall School BUSH WD23 196 E7
Bushey Hall Swimming Pool BUSH WD23 196 E6
Bushey Health Centre BUSH WD23 196 E7
Bushey Heath Primary School BUSH WD23 207 J1
Bushey Manor School BUSH WD23 13 M7
Bushey Meads School BUSH WD23 197 H6
Bushey Museum & Art Gallery BUSH WD23 196 F7
Bushmead Infant School LTNE LU2 65 J5
Business Centre RAD WD7 184 A5
The Business Centre LTNE LU2 3 H2
Byfleet Industrial Estate WATW WD18 205 H1
Caddington Sports Club LTN LU1 82 E7
Caddington Surgery LTN LU1 82 D6
Calcot Medical Centre CFSP/GDCR SL9 202 C8
Camp Junior Middle & Infant School STAL AL1 153 G8
Canary Club Football Club HTCH/STOT SG5 52 D2
Canons Brook Golf Club HLW CM20 161 M1
Canterbury Way Surgery STVG SG1 54 F8
Capel Manor Primary School EN EN1 189 M6
Capital Business Centre WATN WD24 182 C7
Cardiff Road Industrial Estate WATW WD18 12 F8
Cardinal Newman RC School LTNE LU2 65 H1
Cassio Surgery WATW WD18 12 E5
Castle BERK HP4 147 J5
The Castlegate Surgery HERT/BAY SG13 137 H5
Castle Montessore School BERK HP4 147 J6
Castle Walk Clinic STSD CM24 79 L4
The Causeway Business Centre BSF CM23 96 E3
The Cavendish School HHW HP1 149 G6
Cedars First School KTN/HRWW/W HA3 207 H8
Cedars Middle School KTN/HRWW/W HA3 207 H8
Central Primary School WAT WD17 13 H4
Central Surgery SBW CM21 120 D8
Chalfont Leisure Centre CFSP/GDCR SL9 202 B8
Chalfont St Giles County Middle School CSTG HP8 202 A3
Chalfont St Giles Infant School CSTG HP8 202 A3
Chalfont St Peter C of E Middle School CFSP/GDCR SL9 202 C8
Chalfont St Peter Football Club CFSP/GDCR SL9 202 C7
The Chalfonts Community College CFSP/GDCR SL9 202 B7
Chalfonts & Gerrards Cross Health Clinic CFSP/GDCR SL9 202 C8
Challney High School for Boys LTNW/LEA LU4 64 B7
Chalton Primary School LTNW/LEA LU4 63 K1
Chambersbury JMI School HHS/BOV HP3 167 G2
Chancellors School BRKMPK AL9 173 G4
Chantry Junior & Infant School LTNW/LEA LU4 63 L6
Chater Infant School WATW WD18 12 C5
Chater Junior School WATW WD18 12 D5
Chaulden Junior & Infant School HHW HP1 148 E8
The Chauncy School WARE SG12 116 A8
Cheddington Lower School LBUZ LU7 101 M3
Chenies Cricket Club RKW/CH/CXG WD3 193 H2
Chenies School RKW/CH/CXG WD3 192 F1
Cherry Tree JMI School WATN WD24 181 M7
Cheshunt Community Hospital CHES/WCR EN8 190 B5
Cheshunt Football Club CHES/WCR EN8 190 B3
Cheshunt School CHES/WCR EN8 190 B1
Cheshunt & Waltham Cross Council CHES/WCR EN8 190 D5
Chesterfield Junior & Infant School PEND EN3 190 D8
Chiltern Open Air Museum CSTG HP8 202 E2
Chiltern Park Industrial Estate DUN/HR/TOD LU5 63 J8
Chiltern Park Industrial Estate DUN/HR/TOD LU5 81 J1
Chinese Medical Centre BAR EN5 200 D4
Chinese Medical Centre Watford WAT WD17 13 H5
Chipperfield Junior & Infant School KGLGY WD4 179 M2
Chorleywood Golf Club RKW/CH/CXG WD3 193 J5
Chorleywood Health Centre RKW/CH/CXG WD3 193 H5
Chorleywood Parish Council RKW/CH/CXG WD3 193 K4
Chorleywood Primary RKW/CH/CXG WD3 193 H7
Christ Church C of E Primary School BAR EN5 200 C3
Christ Church Junior Middle & Infant School WARE SG12 138 D1
Christ Church School RKW/CH/CXG WD3 193 L5
Churchgate C of E Primary School HLWE CM17 142 E7
Church Hill Junior Middle & Infant School EBAR EN4 201 L8
Church Langley Primary School HLWE CM17 163 H2
Church Street Surgery WARE SG12 116 C8
Cinema LTN LU1 2 E7
Civic Centre WLYN AL6 112 B5
Civic Centre & Dacorum Borough Council HHW HP1 149 H7
Clarklands Industrial Estate SBW CM21 120 D5
Club House LBUZ LU7 102 A5
The Club House HERT/WAS SG14 90 D7
Coach House Surgery WATW WD18 12 D4
Coates Way School GSTN WD25 182 D4
Cobden Hill Infant School RAD WD7 184 A7
Cockfosters Sports Ground EBAR EN4 201 L4
Codicote Junior & Infant School WLYN AL6 111 K1
Coleman Business Centre HTCHE/RSTV SG4 86 B8
Collenswood School STVGE SG2 71 H6
The Collett School HHW HP1 149 G6
Colnbrook School OXHEY WD19 206 B2
Colne Bridge Retail Park WAT WD17 13 K7
Colney Heath JMI School STALE/WH AL4 171 H1
Colonial Business Park WATN WD24 196 B2
Commonside School HLWS CM18 162 E6
Commonswood JMI School WGCE AL7 135 G7
Community Clinic HLWS CM18 162 E5
Community Mental Health Centre GSTN WD25 182 B5
Community Mental Health Centre HHNE HP2 8 A6
Corn Exchange HERT/WAS SG14 137 J4
Cotswold Business Park LTN LU1 82 C8
Council Offices OXHEY WD19 206 C3
Countess Anne C of E Primary School HAT AL10 155 H4
County Hall HERT/BAY SG13 137 H6
Cowley Hill First School BORE WD6 199 G2
CP House Business Centre GSTN WD25 196 E2
Crabtree Junior Mixed School HARP AL5 131 J1
Crabtree Lane Infant School HARP AL5 131 H1
Cranborne Industrial Estate POTB/CUF EN6 172 D8
Cranborne Industrial Estate POTB/CUF EN6 186 D1
Cranborne Primary School POTB/CUF EN6 186 D2
Cranbourne School HOD EN11 160 A1
Crawley Green Primary School LTNE LU2 3 L5
Creswick Primary School WGCE AL7 134 C7
Crews Hill Golf Club ENC/FH EN2 188 E5
Cricket Squash Tennis & Hockey Club BSF CM23 96 B2
Cromer Road JMI School BAR EN5 201 G4
Crown Court STAL AL1 10 F7
Crown Prosecution Service LTN LU1 2 F7
Crown Prosecution Service STAL AL1 10 F7
Cuffley School POTB/CUF EN6 188 E1
Cunningham Hill Junior Middle & Infant School STAL AL1 169 M1
Dacorum Athletics Track HHS/BOV HP3 166 E1
Dacorum District Sports Centre HHW HP1 166 B1
Dacre Industrial Estate CHES/WCR EN8 176 D8
Dagnall CP School BERK HP4 104 B5

Dallow Junior School
LTN LU1 ... 2 B5
Dalroad Industrial Estate
LTN LU1 ... 83 G2
Dame Alice Owens School
POTB/CUF EN6 ... 186 D4
Danegrove Primary School
EBAR EN4 ... 201 K7
Danesbury Park Golf Club
WLYN AL6 ... 112 B3
Datchworth School
KNEB SG3 ... 89 J7
Deer Leap Swimming Pool
BERK HP4 ... 126 A1
Delrow School
GSTN WD25 ... 197 H2
Denbigh High School
LTNN/LIM LU3 ... 2 B1
Denbigh Infant School
LTNN/LIM LU3 ... 65 G8
The Dentist Surgery
OXHEY WD19 ... 206 A5
Denture Clinic
HARP AL5 ... 108 B6
Derwent Lower School
HNLW SG16 ... 25 G5
Dewhurst St Mary Junior Middle & Infant School
CHESW EN7 ... 176 A8
Diamond Industrial Centre
LWTH SG6 ... 40 B3
Discover Bible School
GSTN WD25 ... 182 B6
Divine Saviour RC JMI School
ABLGY WD5 ... 181 J3
The Downs CP School
HLW CM20 ... 6 F6
Downside Junior & Infant School
LTNW/LEA LU4 ... 82 D1
Downside Lower School
DUN/HR/TOD LU5 ... 81 K3
Dr Challoners High School for Girls
AMSS HP7 ... 192 A3
Dr P J Walkers Surgery
HTCHE/RSTV SG4 ... 86 D3
Duncombe School
HERT/WAS SG14 ... 137 H3
Dundale Infants School
TRING HP23 ... 123 M5
Dundale J M School
TRING HP23 ... 123 M5
Dunstable College
DUN/HR/TOD LU5 ... 81 H1
Dunstable Downs Golf Club
DUN/WHIP LU6 ... 80 E5
Dunstable Football Club
DUN/WHIP LU6 ... 62 E8
Dunstable Health Centre
DUN/WHIP LU6 ... 81 G2
Dunstable Icknield Lower School
DUN/WHIP LU6 ... 80 F2
Dunstable Leisure Centre
DUN/HR/TOD LU5 ... 81 G1
Dunstable Road Infant School
LTN LU1 ... 2 B5
Dunstable Town Cricket Club
DUN/WHIP LU6 ... 80 B3
Dunstablians Rugby Union Football Club
DUN/HR/TOD LU5 ... 62 F4
Dunton Primary School
BGSW SG18 ... 14 C5
The Earl Gallery
POTB/CUF EN6 ... 186 E3
East Barnet Grammar School
EBAR EN4 ... 201 L7
East Barnet Health Centre
EBAR EN4 ... 201 J6
East Barnet School
EBAR EN4 ... 201 J4
Eastbrook Junior School
HHNE HP2 ... 149 L2
Eastbury Infant School
NTHWD HA6 ... 205 L4
Eastern Avenue Industrial Estate
DUN/HR/TOD LU5 ... 81 J2
East Herts District Council
BSF CM23 ... 96 E2
East Herts District Council
HERT/BAY SG13 ... 137 H5
East Herts District Council
HERT/WAS SG14 ... 136 E3
East Herts District Council
SBW CM21 ... 120 D8
East Herts Golf Club
BUNT SG9 ... 75 G5
East Herts Golf Clubhouse
WARE SG12 ... 138 B2
Edwinstree Middle School
BUNT SG9 ... 58 C2
Egerton Rothesay School
BERK HP4 ... 146 E6
Eleanor Estate
CHES/WCR EN8 ... 190 E5
Elliswick Lawn Tennis Club
HARP AL5 ... 109 G8
The Elms Health Centre
POTB/CUF EN6 ... 187 H2
The Elms Medical Practice
HARP AL5 ... 109 G8
The Elms Medical Practice
STALW/RED AL3 ... 129 M5
Elstree & Borehamwood Town Council
BORE WD6 ... 199 G4
Elstree Studios
BORE WD6 ... 198 F4
Elstree Way Clinic
BORE WD6 ... 199 G3
Emmanuel C of E School
NTHWD HA6 ... 205 L7
Enfield & Haringey Health Authority
EBAR EN4 ... 201 M5
Epping House School
HERT/BAY SG13 ... 157 H8
Essendon Primary School
BRKMPK AL9 ... 156 E4
Essex County Council
WAB EN9 ... 191 H4
Everest House Surgery
HHNE HP2 ... 9 G8
Everest Sports Club
CHES/WCR EN8 ... 176 A8
Eversley College
SBW CM21 ... 120 C8
Factory
STVG SG1 ... 4 B8
Fairbrook Medical Centre
BORE WD6 ... 199 G3
Fairfield Primary School
RAD WD7 ... 183 K7
Fairfields Junior Middle & Infant School
CHESW EN7 ... 175 M6
The Fairways
CHES/WCR EN8 ... 176 C5
Falconer School
BUSH WD23 ... 196 E6
Farley Hill Primary School
LTN LU1 ... 83 H5
Farnham School
BSF CM23 ... 78 C4
Fawbert & Barnards Primary School
HLWE CM17 ... 142 B7
Fearnhill School
LWTH SG6 ... 39 H5
Fearnhill Sports Centre
LWTH SG6 ... 39 H5
Featherstone Wood Primary School
STVGE SG2 ... 71 H7
Fernville Surgery
HHNE HP2 ... 8 A8
Ferrars Infant School
LTNW/LEA LU4 ... 64 A7
Fiddlebridge Industrial Centre
HAT AL10 ... 154 F4
Field Junior School
WATW WD18 ... 13 H6
Firbank Industrial Estate
LTN LU1 ... 82 F2
The Firs Junior School
BSF CM23 ... 96 D4
First School
CFSP/GDCR SL9 ... 202 B7
Fisher Industrial Estate
WATW WD18 ... 13 G7
Five Oaks School
LTN LU1 ... 82 E7
Five Springs School
LTNN/LIM LU3 ... 64 E3
Flamstead End Junior School
CHESW EN7 ... 175 M6
Flamstead Junior Middle & Infant School
STALW/RED AL3 ... 129 G1
Fleetville J M School
STAL AL1 ... 11 M7
Florance Nightingale Health Centre
HLWE CM17 ... 163 H2
Flowers Industrial Estate
LTN LU1 ... 2 F8
Football Club
TRING HP23 ... 124 C6
Football & Social Club
WGCE AL7 ... 135 G2
Forres CP School
HOD EN11 ... 160 A1
Forty Hill C of E School
EN EN1 ... 189 M8
Foulds Primary School
BAR EN5 ... 200 C4
The Four Swanns JMI School
CHES/WCR EN8 ... 190 D4
Foxdell Infant School
LTN LU1 ... 82 F2
Foxdell Junior School
LTN LU1 ... 82 D2
Foye Gallery
LTN LU1 ... 2 C8
Francis Bacon School
STAL AL1 ... 170 A2
Francis Combe Secondary School
GSTN WD25 ... 182 B3
Frithwood Primary School
NTHWD HA6 ... 205 L6
Frogmore Road Industrial Estate
HHS/BOV HP3 ... 166 C2
Furneux Pelham C of E School
BUNT SG9 ... 60 F6
Furzehill School
BORE WD6 ... 198 F5
Gaddesden Row CP School
HHNE HP2 ... 128 B3
Gade Valley JMI School
HHW HP1 ... 149 G6
The Gallery
DUN/WHIP LU6 ... 81 G2
The Garden City Practice
WGCW AL8 ... 134 C3
Garden City Surgery
LWTH SG6 ... 39 L4
Garden Court Business Centre
WGCE AL7 ... 134 E4
Garden Fields Junior Middle & Infant School
STALW/RED AL3 ... 10 E1
Garston Clinic
WATN WD24 ... 182 A7
Garston JMI School
GSTN WD25 ... 182 C6
Garston Manor School
GSTN WD25 ... 182 B3
Garston Medical Centre
GSTN WD25 ... 182 B7
Gascoyne Cecil Primary School
HAT AL10 ... 155 G3
Gazelda Industrial Estate
WAT WD17 ... 13 J6
The Giles Infant & Junior School
STVG SG1 ... 70 E1
Gillmark Gallery
HERT/BAY SG13 ... 137 H5
Glenwood School
DUN/WHIP LU6 ... 81 K5
Goffs Oak JMI School
CHESW EN7 ... 175 G7
Goffs School
CHESW EN7 ... 175 M8
Goldfield Infant School
TRING HP23 ... 123 L7
Golf Club Flat
NTHWD HA6 ... 205 J7
Gooseberry Hill Health Centre
LTNN/LIM LU3 ... 65 G3
Gorhambury
STALW/RED AL3 ... 151 G6
Gothic Mede Lower School
ARL/CHE SG15 ... 25 M5
The Gowan Gallery
SBW CM21 ... 120 D8
Grange Junior Mixed School
LWTH SG6 ... 26 E8
Grange Paddock Swimming Pool
BSF CM23 ... 96 E1
Grange Street Doctors Surgery
STALW/RED AL3 ... 10 F4
Grasvenor Avenue Infant School
BAR EN5 ... 200 F7
Graveley Junior Mixed School
HTCHE/RSTV SG4 ... 54 A6
Great Gaddesden JMI School
HHW HP1 ... 127 J7
Great Hormead C of E School
BUNT SG9 ... 59 L2
Green End Business Centre
RKW/CH/CXG WD3 ... 179 M8
Greenfield Primary School
OXHEY WD19 ... 206 B5
The Greenhouse Health Centre
LTN LU1 ... 2 C5
Green Lane Industrial Estate
LWTH SG6 ... 40 A3
Green Lanes School
HAT AL10 ... 154 E1
Green Side School
STVGE SG2 ... 70 F8
Greenway County First School
BERK HP4 ... 146 F6
Greenwood Park Leisure Centre
LCOL/BKTW AL2 ... 169 G4
The Greneway School
ROY SG8 ... 21 K3
Griffin Golf Club
LTN LU1 ... 82 C4
Grimsdyke First & Middle School
PIN HA5 ... 206 E6
Grimsdyke Golf Club
PIN HA5 ... 206 F5
Grosvenor Gallery
NTHWD HA6 ... 205 K6
Grovehill Medical Centre
HHNE HP2 ... 149 L3
The Grove Infant School
HARP AL5 ... 131 J2
The Grove JMI School
HARP AL5 ... 131 J2
Grovelands Business Centre
HHNE HP2 ... 9 L4
Grove Road Primary School
TRING HP23 ... 124 A5
Grundy Park Leisure Centre
CHES/WCR EN8 ... 190 D1
Guardian Industrial Estate
LTN LU1 ... 2 A5
Guilden Morden School
ROY SG8 ... 15 L5
G X Superbowl
DUN/HR/TOD LU5 ... 63 G8
Haberdashers Askes School for Girls
BORE WD6 ... 198 A4
Haberdashers Rugby Club
BORE WD6 ... 198 E3
Hadley Wood School
EBAR EN4 ... 201 H1
Hadrian Lower School
DUN/HR/TOD LU5 ... 63 K8
Haileybury College
HERT/BAY SG13 ... 138 C8
Hailey Hall School
HOD EN11 ... 138 E8
Halyard High School
LTNW/LEA LU4 ... 63 L7
The Hammond Junior Mixed Infant School
HHNE HP2 ... 8 E2
Happy Valley Industrial Estate
KGLGY WD4 ... 167 G7
Harefield Health Centre
DEN/HRF UB9 ... 204 B8
Harefield Hospital
DEN/HRF UB9 ... 204 B8
Harefield Infant School
DEN/HRF UB9 ... 204 A8
Harefield Junior School
DEN/HRF UB9 ... 204 B8
Haresfoot Prep School
BERK HP4 ... 164 A1
Haresfoot Senior School
BERK HP4 ... 147 M4
Hare Street County Junior & Infant School
HLWW/ROY CM19 ... 6 C7
Harewood Down Golf Club
CSTG HP8 ... 192 A5
Harkness Industrial Estate
BORE WD6 ... 198 F5
Harlequin Shopping Centre
WAT WD17 ... 13 G4
Harlowbury School
HLWE CM17 ... 142 C6
Harlow Business Park
HLWW/ROY CM19 ... 161 K2
Harlow College
HLW CM20 ... 6 E7
Harlow College
HLW CM20 ... 7 G5
Harlow Museum
HLWS CM18 ... 6 D9
Harlow Rugby Football Club
HLW CM20 ... 6 B2
Harlow Sports Centre
HLW CM20 ... 6 D3
Harlow Sports Centre
HLW CM20 ... 6 E2
Harlow Urban District Swimming Pool
HLW CM20 ... 7 G3
Harpenden Common Golf Club
HARP AL5 ... 131 G4
Harpenden Golf Club
HARP AL5 ... 130 E5
Harpenden Health Centre
HARP AL5 ... 108 F8
Harpenden Hospital
HARP AL5 ... 108 F6
Harpenden Memorial Hospital
HARP AL5 ... 109 G8
Harpenden Preparatory School
HARP AL5 ... 108 E8
Harpenden Rugby Football Club
HARP AL5 ... 130 D4
Harpenden Sports Centre
HARP AL5 ... 130 F2
Harpenden Swimming Pool
HARP AL5 ... 130 F1
Harperburg Hospital
RAD WD7 ... 184 B2
Harrow & Hillingdon Healthcare NHS Trust
KTN/HRWW/W HA3 ... 207 M8
Hart Hill Junior School
LTNE LU2 ... 3 H4
Hartsbourne JMI School
BUSH WD23 ... 207 J2
Hartsfield Junior Middle & Infant School
BLDK SG7 ... 40 E2
Hartspring Industrial Park
GSTN WD25 ... 196 F3
Hartspring Sports Centre
BUSH WD23 ... 196 F3
Harvey Centre
HLW CM20 ... 6 E6
Haselmere Industrial Estate
BSF CM23 ... 96 F6
Haslemere Industrial Estate
HLWW/ROY CM19 ... 161 M3
Haslewood Junior School
HOD EN11 ... 159 M3
Hatch End High School
KTN/HRWW/W HA3 ... 207 G7
Hatfield Heath CP School
RBSF CM22 ... 121 M7
Hatfield House
BRKMPK AL9 ... 155 J5
Hatfield London County Club
BRKMPK AL9 ... 156 E6
Haverfield Surgery
KGLGY WD4 ... 166 F8
Havers Infant School
BSF CM23 ... 96 D5
Hawridge & Cholesbury C of E Primary School
CSHM HP5 ... 145 J8
Hawthorn Park Lower School
DUN/HR/TOD LU5 ... 63 J4
Hazel Grove JMI School
HAT AL10 ... 154 E8
Heathcote School
STVGE SG2 ... 5 K9
Heathfield Lower School
LTN LU1 ... 82 D6
Heathlands School for Deaf Children
STALW/RED AL3 ... 11 G1
Heath Mount School
HERT/WAS SG14 ... 91 G8
Heath Sports Club
ROY SG8 ... 21 H4
Hemel Hempstead Rugby Club
HHW HP1 ... 165 L1
Hemel Hempstead General Hospital
HHNE HP2 ... 149 J8
Hemel Hempstead Rugby League Club
HHNE HP2 ... 8 F2
Hemel Hempstead School
HHW HP1 ... 149 H8
Hemel Hempstead Town Cricket Club
HHS/BOV HP3 ... 166 B1
Hemel Hempstead United Football Club
HHNE HP2 ... 9 H8
Hengrove School
TRING HP23 ... 144 B6
Henlow Middle School
HNLW SG16 ... 25 K1
Heron Trading Estate
LTNN/LIM LU3 ... 64 B3
Hertford County Hospital
HERT/WAS SG14 ... 137 G4
Hertford Police Station
HERT/BAY SG13 ... 137 L3
Hertford Regional College
WARE SG12 ... 138 C2
Hertfordshire Business Centre
LCOL/BKTW AL2 ... 170 C5
Hertfordshire Country Club
WGCE AL7 ... 134 B7
Hertfordshire County Constabulary
HHW HP1 ... 149 H7
Hertfordshire County Council
BUSH WD23 ... 197 J8
Hertfordshire County Council
GSTN WD25 ... 182 B7
Hertfordshire County Council
HERT/BAY SG13 ... 137 J5
Hertfordshire County Council
OXHEY WD19 ... 206 A3
Hertfordshire County Council
OXHEY WD19 ... 206 B3
Hertfordshire County Council
POTB/CUF EN6 ... 187 H3
Hertfordshire County Council
RKW/CH/CXG WD3 ... 204 A2
Hertfordshire County Council
WAT WD17 ... 12 D1
Hertfordshire County Council
WAT WD17 ... 12 E1
Hertfordshire & Essex General Hospital
BSF CM23 ... 97 H4
Hertfordshire & Essex High School
BSF CM23 ... 97 G3
Hertfordshire Family Health Authority Services
WGCW AL8 ... 134 C3
Hertford Town Football Club
HERT/WAS SG14 ... 137 G5
Hertsmere Borough Council
BORE WD6 ... 199 H3
Hertsmere Council
BORE WD6 ... 198 F3
Hertsmere Jewish Primary School
RAD WD7 ... 198 B1
Hertsmere Progressive Synagogue
BORE WD6 ... 198 C7
Hexton Junior Middle & Infant School
HTCH/STOT SG5 ... 49 M1
Heydon Grange Golf Club
ROY SG8 ... 23 J1
High Beeches JMI School
HARP AL5 ... 131 J2
Highbury Infant School
HTCHE/RSTV SG4 ... 52 E4
High Cross Puller Memorial Junior & Infant School
STDN SG11 ... 92 D8
Highfield School
LWTH SG6 ... 39 J7
Highfield Surgery
HHNE HP2 ... 8 F4
Highover JMI School
HTCHE/RSTV SG4 ... 53 H1
Hightown Recreation Centre
LTNE LU2 ... 2 E4
Highview Surgery
POTB/CUF EN6 ... 187 H4
Highwood Primary School
BUSH WD23 ... 196 D2
Hillborough Junior School
LTN LU1 ... 2 B9
Hillcrest School
DUN/HR/TOD LU5 ... 81 K1
Hille Business Centre
WATN WD24 ... 196 A2
Hill Farm Industrial Estate
GSTN WD25 ... 181 L4
Hillgrove Business Park
WAB EN9 ... 177 H1
Hillingdon Health Authority
NTHWD HA6 ... 205 M8
Hillmead JMI School
BSF CM23 ... 97 H1
Hillshott Infant School
LWTH SG6 ... 39 M4
Hillside Junior & Infant School
NTHWD HA6 ... 205 M7
Hillside School
BORE WD6 ... 199 H5
Hitchin Boys School
HTCH/STOT SG5 ... 52 D2
Hitchin Cricket Club
HTCH/STOT SG5 ... 52 B3
Hitchin Girls School
HTCHE/RSTV SG4 ... 52 E3
Hitchin Swimming Pool
HTCH/STOT SG5 ... 52 D2
HM Prison
CSHM HP5 ... 164 E5
Hobbs Hill Wood Primary School
HHS/BOV HP3 ... 167 G1
Hobletts Manor Junior School
HHNE HP2 ... 9 G6
Hockerill Anglo European Gm School
BSF CM23 ... 97 G3
Hockerill Sports Club
BSF CM23 ... 97 G5
Hockwell Surgery
LTNW/LEA LU4 ... 64 B5
Hoddesdon Health Centre
HOD EN11 ... 159 M5
Hoddesdon Industrial Estate
HOD EN11 ... 160 B3
Hoddesdon Lawn Tennis Club
HOD EN11 ... 159 L4
Hoddesdon St Pauls Infant School
HOD EN11 ... 160 A4
Holdbrook Junior Middle & Infant School
CHES/WCR EN8 ... 190 E5
Hollybush School
HERT/WAS SG14 ... 136 F4
Holly Industrial Park
WATN WD24 ... 196 B2
Holly Street Trading Estate
LTN LU1 ... 2 E8
Hollywood Bowl
STVG SG1 ... 4 A5
Holmshill School
BORE WD6 ... 199 H3

Holtsmere End Junior &
Infant School
HHNE HP2 .... 150 A2
Holwell Junior & Infant School
WCCE AL7 .... 134 E5
Holy Cross Boarding &
Day School
CFSP/GDCR SL9 .... 202 C8
Holy Cross RC Primary School
HLWS CM18 .... 162 F4
Holyrood Infant School
WAT WD17 .... 181 J7
Holy Rood Junior School
WAT WD17 .... 181 J7
Holy Trinity C of E
Primary School
CHES/WCR EN8 .... 190 C3
Holy Trinity School
NTHWD HA6 .... 205 H6
Holywell School
WATW WD18 .... 12 A9
Home Farm Industrial Estate
WARE SG12 .... 139 L5
Home Park Industrial Estate
KGLGY WD4 .... 181 G1
Homerswood Junior &
Infant School
WGCW AL8 .... 112 C8
Homewood School
LCOL/BKTW AL2 .... 169 G7
Honilands Junior &
Infant School
EN EN1 .... 190 A7
Horseshoe Business Park
LCOL/BKTW AL2 .... 183 G1
Hospital
LTN LU1 .... 2 B6
Hospital Annexe
DEN/HRF UB9 .... 204 B7
Hot Shots Ten Pin Bowling
HHS/BOV HP3 .... 149 L8
Houghton Regis Health Centre
DUN/HR/TOD LU5 .... 63 G5
Houghton Regis Lower School
DUN/HR/TOD LU5 .... 62 F6
Houghton Regis Medical Centre
DUN/HR/TOD LU5 .... 63 G5
Howard Business Park
WAB EN9 .... 191 J5
Howe Dell School
HAT AL10 .... 155 G5
Howe Green House School
RBSF CM22 .... 97 J8
How Wood Junior &
Infant School
LCOL/BKTW AL2 .... 169 H6
Hurst Drive JMI School
CHES/WCR EN8 .... 190 C5
Hyatt Trading Estate
STVG SG1 .... 69 M5
Icknield High School
LTNN/LIM LU3 .... 65 H5
Icknield Infant School
LWTH SG6 .... 39 J4
Icknield Walk First School
ROY SG8 .... 21 K3
Icknield Way Industrial Estate
TRING HP23 .... 123 K6
Immanuel College
BUSH WD23 .... 197 K8
Indoor Market
WAT WD17 .... 13 G3
Industrial Estate
DEN/HRF UB9 .... 203 M6
Industrial Park
CHES/WCR EN8 .... 190 F5
International University
BUSH WD23 .... 196 E5
Ivinghoe Business Centre
DUN/HR/TOD LU5 .... 63 G7
Ivinghoe Golf Club
LBUZ LU7 .... 102 E4
The Jamie Mosque
STAL AL1 .... 11 K6
Jerounds Junior &
Infant School
HLWW/ROY CM19 .... 162 A5
John F Kennedy School
HHW HP1 .... 148 D6
John Henry Newman RC School
STVG SG1 .... 70 A1
John Penrose School
DEN/HRF UB9 .... 204 C8
The John Warner School
HOD EN11 .... 160 A1
Jubilee Trading Estate
LWTH SG6 .... 40 B3
Junior & Infant School
STVG SG1 .... 70 C3
Jupiter Drive JMI School
HHNE HP2 .... 8 F4
Katherines Primary School
HLWW/ROY CM19 .... 161 L4
Kenilworth Primary School
BORE WD6 .... 199 J4
Kensworth Lower School
DUN/WHIP LU6 .... 105 L2
Kevin Hinds Practice
WARE SG12 .... 138 C1
Killigrew Junior Middle & Infant
School
LCOL/BKTW AL2 .... 169 G4
Kimpton Junior Middle & Infant
School
HTCHE/RSTV SG4 .... 110 B1
King George Surgery
STVG SG1 .... 4 C2
King Harold
Comprehensive School
WAB EN9 .... 191 K4
Kingsbury Watermill Museum
& Waffle House
STALW/RED AL3 .... 10 A5
Kingshott School
HTCHE/RSTV SG4 .... 53 G5
Kings Houghton Middle School
DUN/HR/TOD LU5 .... 63 J3

Kingsland Community College
DUN/HR/TOD LU5 .... 63 K4
Kings Langley Parish Council
KGLGY WD4 .... 166 F8
Kings Langley Primary School
KGLGY WD4 .... 166 E7
Kingsmoor Junior &
Infant School
HLWW/ROY CM19 .... 162 B6
Kingsmoor Recreation Centre
HLWW/ROY CM19 .... 162 A6
Kings Park Industrial Estate
KGLGY WD4 .... 167 G8
Kingsway Industrial Estate
LTN LU1 .... 82 F2
Kingsway Junior School
GSTN WD25 .... 181 M5
Knebworth Golf Club
KNEB SG3 .... 88 E4
Knebworth Ho
KNEB SG3 .... 88 B4
Knebworth
Physiotherapy Clinic
STVGE SG2 .... 89 H3
Knights Templar School
BLDK SG7 .... 40 D2
Knowl Piece
HTCHE/RSTV SG4 .... 38 F7
Knutsford Junior &
Infant School
WATN WD24 .... 196 C1
Ladbroke School
POTB/CUF EN6 .... 187 G3
Lady Zia Wernher School
LTNE LU2 .... 66 A7
Laharna Trading Estate
WATN WD24 .... 196 B1
Laings Sports Ground
BAR EN5 .... 199 K5
Lakeside School
WGCW AL8 .... 134 A6
Lakeside School
HTCH/STOT SG5 .... 26 D4
Lancot Lower School
DUN/WHIP LU6 .... 80 D2
Langley Terrace
Industrial Park
LTN LU1 .... 2 F9
Lannock JMI School
LWTH SG6 .... 40 B6
Lark Rise Lower School
DUN/WHIP LU6 .... 81 G4
Larwood School
STVG SG1 .... 70 E3
Laser Clinic
CHESW EN7 .... 190 A1
Latton Bush Business Centre
HLWS CM18 .... 162 E5
Latton Bush Recreation Centre
HLWS CM18 .... 162 D5
Laurence Haines School
WATW WD18 .... 12 D8
Lawrence Industrial Estate
DUN/WHIP LU6 .... 62 E8
Layston First School
BUNT SG9 .... 58 E2
Lea Farm Junior School
GSTN WD25 .... 182 C7
Leagrave Health Centre
LTNW/LEA LU4 .... 64 B6
Leagrave Junior & Infant School
LTNW/LEA LU4 .... 64 B6
Lea Industrial Estate
HARP AL5 .... 109 F4
Lealands High School
LTNN/LIM LU3 .... 64 B2
Lea Manor High School &
Community College
LTNN/LIM LU3 .... 64 C2
The Leas Junior & Infant School
HARP AL5 .... 108 F6
Lea Valley High School
PEND EN3 .... 190 B6
Leavesden Green Junior
Middle & Infant School
GSTN WD25 .... 181 M5
Leavesden Hospital
ABLGY WD5 .... 181 M2
Lensey Farm Clinic
LTNW/LEA LU4 .... 63 L6
Letchworth Business Centre
LWTH SG6 .... 40 B4
Letchworth Garden City
Football Club
LWTH SG6 .... 40 B5
Letchworth Golf Club
LWTH SG6 .... 39 L8
Letchworth Museum
LWTH SG6 .... 39 L5
Letchworth Swimming Pool
LWTH SG6 .... 39 M3
The Leventhorpe School
SBW CM21 .... 120 D6
Leverstock Green JMI School
HHNE HP2 .... 150 C8
Leverstock Green Lawn
Tennis Club
HHS/BOV HP3 .... 167 G1
Ley Hill CP School
CSHM HP5 .... 178 A1
Ley Hill Cricket Club
CSHM HP5 .... 178 B2
Ley Park CP School
BROX EN10 .... 176 E1
Leys Primary School
STVG SG1 .... 54 F8
Lime Walk JMI School
HHS/BOV HP3 .... 166 E1
Lincoln Health Surgery
HHNE HP2 .... 149 J8
Links Business Centre
BSF CM23 .... 97 H3
Lismarrine Industrial Park
BORE WD6 .... 198 A7
Lister Hospital
STVG SG1 .... 54 A8
Lister House Surgery
HAT AL10 .... 154 F4

Lister House Surgery
LTNW/LEA LU4 .... 64 E8
Lister Medical Centre
HLWS CM18 .... 162 B5
Little Chalfont CP School
AMS HP6 .... 192 D2
Little Chalfont Surgery
AMSS HP7 .... 192 B3
Little Furze School
OXHEY WD19 .... 206 A3
Little Gaddesden JMI School
BERK HP4 .... 126 B3
Little Green CP School
RKW/CH/CXG WD3 ...... 195 G4
Little Hallingbury C of E Primary
School
RBSF CM22 .... 121 H2
Little Heath Junior Mixed School
POTB/CUF EN6 .... 187 H1
Little Munden JMI School
WARE SG12 .... 91 K2
Little Reddings Primary School
BUSH WD23 .... 197 G6
Little St Helens School
NTHWD HA6 .... 205 L7
The Little Theatre
DUN/WHIP LU6 .... 81 H2
Liverpool Road Health Centre
LTN LU1 .... 2 C5
Livingstone Primary School
EBAR EN4 .... 201 H4
Llewelyn Surgery
WAB EN9 .... 191 H4
Lochinver House School
POTB/CUF EN6 .... 187 G1
Lockers Park School
HHW HP1 .... 149 G7
Lodge Clinic
LTN LU1 .... 2 E7
Lodge Farm Infant School
STVGE SG2 .... 71 G1
Lodge Farm Junior School
STVGE SG2 .... 71 H3
Lodge Sun Sports Club
WAT WD17 .... 195 K2
Lodge Surgery
STALW/RED AL3 .... 10 E3
London Bible College
NTHWD HA6 .... 205 J6
London Colney JMI School
LCOL/BKTW AL2 .... 170 C4
London Luton Airport
LTNE LU2 .... 84 B3
London Luton Airport
LTNE LU2 .... 84 C3
Longdean School
HHS/BOV HP3 .... 167 G2
Longlands Junior Middle &
Infant School
BROX EN10 .... 176 D4
Long Marston JMI School
TRING HP23 .... 101 G6
Long Meadow Infant &
Junior School
STVGE SG2 .... 89 G1
Longrove Surgery
BAR EN5 .... 200 D4
Loreto College
STAL AL1 .... 11 H6
Lowewood Museum
HOD EN11 .... 159 M5
Lowfield Sports Ground
HOD EN11 .... 159 L4
Luton Co-operative Sports Club
LTNE LU2 .... 65 L8
Luton County Court
LTN LU1 .... 2 D6
Luton Crown Court
LTN LU1 .... 2 F7
Luton & Dunstable
Hospital NHS Trust
LTNW/LEA LU4 .... 64 B8
Luton Hoo
LTN LU1 .... 83 M8
Luton Leisure Park
LTN LU1 .... 2 D5
Luton Police Station
LTN LU1 .... 2 D7
Luton Sixth Form College
LTNE LU2 .... 65 K6
Luton Town Football Club
LTN LU1 .... 83 G2
Lyndhurst Middle School
BORE WD6 .... 198 E2
Madison Bowl
NTHWD HA6 .... 205 K7
Maidenhall Junior School
LTNW/LEA LU4 .... 64 F8
Maltings Arts Theatre
STAL AL1 .... 10 F7
The Maltings Industrial Estate
SBW CM21 .... 120 E8
The Maltings Surgery
STAL AL1 .... 10 F6
Malvern Way School
RKW/CH/CXG WD3 ...... 195 H6
The Management Practice
STVG SG1 .... 70 A6
Mandeville Health Centre
STAL AL1 .... 169 J2
Mandeville Primary School
STAL AL1 .... 169 J2
Manland Primary School
HARP AL5 .... 109 G7
Manor Fields JMI School
BSF CM23 .... 96 C5
Manor Lodge School
RAD WD7 .... 185 H1
The Manor of Groves
SBW CM21 .... 119 L8
Manor Street Surgery
BERK HP4 .... 147 H6
Manshead C of E School
LTN LU1 .... 81 L5
Maple Cross Industrial Estate
RKW/CH/CXG WD3 ...... 203 K4

Maple Cross Junior Middle &
Infant School
RKW/CH/CXG WD3 ...... 203 J5
Maple Junior & Infant School
STAL AL1 .... 11 H5
Maple River Industrial Estate
HLW CM20 .... 142 A4
Margaret Wix Junior &
Infant School
STALW/RED AL3 .... 152 B3
Mark Hall Comprehensive
School
HLWE CM17 .... 142 B7
Mark Hall Cycle Museum
HLW CM20 .... 142 A7
Markyate Primary School
STALW/RED AL3 .... 106 C4
Marlborough School
STAL AL1 .... 169 H2
Marlowes Health Centre
HHW HP1 .... 149 H7
Marquis Business Centre
BLDK SG7 .... 40 F1
Marriotts School
STVGE SG2 .... 5 K2
Marsworth C of E
Primary School
TRING HP23 .... 101 M8
Martindale JMI School
HHW HP1 .... 148 E6
Martinfield Business Centre
WGCE AL7 .... 134 E3
Martins Wood JMI School
STVG SG1 .... 71 G1
Mary Exton JMI School
HTCHE/RSTV SG4 .... 53 H3
Maunds Wood CP School
HLWS CM18 .... 162 C6
Mayfield County Infant School
CHES/WCR EN8 .... 176 D6
The Mead Business Centre
HERT/BAY SG13 .... 137 K3
Mead Industrial Park
HLW CM20 .... 141 L6
Meadow Wood School
BUSH WD23 .... 197 H6
The Mead School
HLWS CM18 .... 162 D4
The Meads Primary School
LTNN/LIM LU3 .... 64 E4
Megabowl
STVG SG1 .... 4 D8
Mercers College
WARE SG12 .... 138 C1
Merchant Taylors School
NTHWD HA6 .... 205 K2
Meriden Primary School
GSTN WD25 .... 182 C7
Meridian School
ROY SG8 .... 21 L2
Meryfield School
BORE WD6 .... 198 E2
Micklem JMI School
HHW HP1 .... 148 E6
Middleton School
WARE SG12 .... 138 C3
Mid Herts Golf Club
STALE/WH AL4 .... 110 C6
Millbrook Junior Middle & Infant
School
CHES/WCR EN8 .... 176 D8
Millfield First School
BUNT SG9 .... 58 D3
Millmead Junior & Infant School
HERT/WAS SG14 .... 137 H4
Mill Studio Business Centre
WARE SG12 .... 138 D1
Mill Vale School
DUN/HR/TOD LU5 .... 63 K8
Millwards CP School
HLWW/ROY CM19 .... 162 A6
Milton House Surgery
BERK HP4 .... 147 G6
The Misbourne Practice
CFSP/GDCR SL9 .... 202 C8
Monken Hadley C of E
Primary School
EBAR EN4 .... 200 F2
Monkfrith Primary School
EBAR EN4 .... 201 M8
Monksmead School
BORE WD6 .... 199 H4
Monks Walk School
WGCW AL8 .... 112 B7
Monkswood Retail Park
STVG SG1 .... 4 D7
Monro Industrial Estate
CHES/WCR EN8 .... 190 D5
Montessore School
BERK HP4 .... 147 G6
Moorlands School
LTNW/LEA LU4 .... 64 B7
Moor Park Industrial Estate
WATW WD18 .... 195 H8
Moreton Park
Industrial Estate
LTNE LU2 .... 3 K1
Moreton Park
Industrial Estate
LTNE LU2 .... 65 M8
Morgans Junior School
HERT/BAY SG13 .... 137 J6
Morgans Walk Junior
Mixed School
HERT/BAY SG13 .... 137 J6
Morgans Walk Junior
Mixed School
HERT/WAS SG14 .... 136 F6
Mosquito Aircraft
LCOL/BKTW AL2 .... 171 G8
Mosquito Aircraft Museum
LCOL/BKTW AL2 .... 170 C5
The Mountfitchet School
STSD CM24 .... 79 L6
Mount Grace Gm School
POTB/CUF EN6 .... 187 G1
Mount Pleasant School
LCOL/BKTW AL2 .... 182 D1

Mount Vernon Hospital
RKW/CH/CXG WD3 ...... 205 G5
Mowat Industrial Estate
WATN WD24 .... 196 B1
M S F Whitehall College
BSF CM23 .... 96 D1
Museum
WAB EN9 .... 191 H5
Musley Infant School
WARE SG12 .... 116 D8
Napsbury Hospital
LCOL/BKTW AL2 .... 170 A6
Nascot Wood Junior &
Infant School
WAT WD17 .... 195 M1
Nash Mills C of E Primary
School
HHS/BOV HP3 .... 166 E4
Natural Art Gallery &
Science Pictures
HTCH/STOT SG5 .... 52 D4
Nazeing CP School
WAB EN9 .... 177 K2
Neville Road Surgery
LTNN/LIM LU3 .... 64 F5
New Briars School
HAT AL10 .... 154 F5
New Court Business Park
HLWW/ROY CM19 .... 162 B6
New England Industrial Estate
HOD EN11 .... 160 B3
The New Surgery
KGLGY WD4 .... 166 F8
The New Surgery
TRING HP23 .... 123 M7
New Town Trading Estate
LTN LU1 .... 83 K5
Nicholas Breakspear RC School
STALE/WH AL4 .... 153 K8
Nicholas Hawksmoor School
BORE WD6 .... 199 G2
Nobel Secondary School
STVGE SG2 .... 71 H3
Northaw C of E School
POTB/CUF EN6 .... 173 M8
Northchurch Cricket Club
BERK HP4 .... 146 C3
Northchurch St Marys C of E
First School
BERK HP4 .... 146 D4
Northfields Infant School
LWTH SG6 .... 39 L1
Northfields Upper School
DUN/HR/TOD LU5 .... 62 F7
Northgate JMI School
BSF CM23 .... 96 D2
North Hertfordshire College
HTCHE/RSTV SG4 .... 53 G2
North Hertfordshire College
LWTH SG6 .... 39 L4
North Hertfordshire College
STVG SG1 .... 4 D6
North Hertfordshire
Leisure Centre
LWTH SG6 .... 40 B4
North Hertfordshire Secondary
Centre
LWTH SG6 .... 39 J7
North Lodge Queens School
BUSH WD23 .... 196 E4
North Luton Industrial Estate
LTNW/LEA LU4 .... 64 A3
North Mymms Cricket Club
BRKMPK AL9 .... 171 M5
North Orbital Trading Estate
STAL AL1 .... 169 M3
North Watford Health Clinic
GSTN WD25 .... 182 B5
North & West Essex
Adult Community College
HLW CM20 .... 6 C3
Northwood College Educational
Foundation
NTHWD HA6 .... 205 J7
Northwood & Pinner
Community Hospital
NTHWD HA6 .... 205 M8
Northwood Pinner
Liberal Synagogue
NTHWD HA6 .... 205 K6
Northwood
Preparatory School
RKW/CH/CXG WD3 ...... 205 H2
Northwood School
NTHWD HA6 .... 206 A8
Northwood Sports Centre
PIN HA5 .... 206 A8
Northwood United Synagogue
NTHWD HA6 .... 205 K7
Norton Road Primary School
LTNN/LIM LU3 .... 64 E6
Norton School
LWTH SG6 .... 39 M2
Nucleus Gallery
CFSP/GDCR SL9 .... 202 C8
Nup End Industrial Estate
WLYN AL6 .... 88 A6
Oak Hill College
EBAR EN4 .... 201 M7
Oakland CP School
EBAR EN4 .... 201 L7
Oaklands College
BORE WD6 .... 199 H3
Oaklands College
HARP AL5 .... 131 G1
Oaklands College
STAL AL1 .... 11 G6
Oaklands College
STALE/WH AL4 .... 153 K6
Oaklands College
WGCW AL8 .... 134 C3
Oaklands JMI School
WLYN AL6 .... 112 D2
The Oakley Surgery
LTNW/LEA LU4 .... 64 C6
Oakmere School
POTB/CUF EN6 .... 187 J3

The Oaks Industrial Estate
  HLW CM20 .... 141 L7
Oakwood Estate
  HLW CM20 .... 141 M7
Oakwood JMI School
  STALE/WH AL4 .... 153 H6
Odeon Cinema
  BAR EN5 .... 200 F6
Odeon Cinema
  HHS/BOV HP3 .... 149 L8
Odeon Cinema
  HLW CM20 .... 6 D5
Odhams Industrial Estate
  WATN WD24 .... 182 B8
Odhams Trading Estate
  WATN WD24 .... 181 M7
Odhams Trading Estate
  WATN WD24 .... 182 B7
Old Airfield Industrial Estate
  LBUZ LU7 .... 101 J4
Old Airfield Industrial Estate
  LBUZ LU7 .... 101 L5
Old Boys School
  STDN SG11 .... 75 L3
Old Fold Manor Golf Club
  BAR EN5 .... 200 D2
Old Harlow Health Centre
  HLWE CM17 .... 142 B6
Old Merchant Taylors
  Sports Club
  RKW/CH/CXG WD3 ...... 195 G5
Old Millhillians Sports Ground
  PIN HA5 .... 206 F8
Old Oak Close Industrial Estate
  ARL/CHE SG15 .... 25 M2
Old Verulamians Rugby
  Football Club
  LCOL/BKTW AL2 .... 170 B4
Orchard County Primary School
  WATN WD24 .... 181 L7
Oughtonhead Junior &
  Infant School
  HTCH/STOT SG5 .... 52 B1
Our Ladys Catholic
  Primary School
  WGCE AL7 .... 134 D6
Oxen Industrial Estate
  LTNE LU2 .... 3 H3
Oxhey Infant School
  BUSH WD23 .... 13 L7
Oxheywood Junior &
  Infant School
  OXHEY WD19 .... 206 B4
Palace Theatre
  WAT WD17 .... 12 F1
Panshanger Golf Club
  WGCE AL7 .... 135 H2
Panshanger JMI School
  WGCE AL7 .... 134 F7
Paramount Industrial Estate
  WATN WD24 .... 196 B1
Pardon Mill Gallery
  HLW CM20 .... 6 A1
Park Avenue Clinic
  WAT WD17 .... 12 D1
Park Avenue Industrial Estate
  LTNN/LIM LU3 .... 64 A3
Parkbury House Surgery
  STAL AL1 .... 11 G5
Park Farm Industrial Estate
  BUNT SG9 .... 58 C1
Parkfield Medical Centre
  POTB/CUF EN6 .... 187 G4
Parkgate Infant School
  WATN WD24 .... 182 B8
Parkgate Junior School
  WATN WD24 .... 182 B8
Park Industrial Estate
  LCOL/BKTW AL2 .... 169 K6
Park Lane Surgery
  BROX EN10 .... 159 L7
Parkside First School
  BORE WD6 .... 198 E1
Park Street C of E
  Primary School
  LCOL/BKTW AL2 .... 169 J6
Parmiters School
  GSTN WD25 .... 182 G7
The Parochial Church
  Council of Goffs Oak St James
  CHESW EN7 .... 175 J7
Parsonage Farm
  Industrial Estate
  STSD CM24 .... 79 J2
Passmores
  Comprehensive School
  HLWS CM18 .... 162 C4
Peckworth Industrial Estate
  HNLW SG16 .... 24 F6
Peerglow Industrial Estate
  WATW WD18 .... 195 G8
Peterborough & St
  Margarets School for Girls
  STAN HA7 .... 207 K3
Peterswood Junior &
  Infant School
  HLWS CM18 .... 162 C6
The Picture House
  HLW CM20 .... 6 D5
Pilgrim Christian School
  DUN/WHIP LU6 .... 81 G2
Pinehill Hospital
  HTCHE/RSTV SG4 .... 53 G3
Pine Wood School
  WARE SG12 .... 138 C3
Pin Green JMI School
  STVG SG1 .... 5 G1
Pinner Wood School
  PIN HA5 .... 206 B8
Pirton Hill Infant School
  LTNW/LEA LU4 .... 64 A4
Pirton JMI School
  HTCH/STOT SG5 .... 37 H6
Pitstone Surgery
  LBUZ LU7 .... 102 C5
Pixies Hill JMI School
  HHW HP1 .... 148 E8

Pixmore Junior School
  LWTH SG6 .... 39 M5
Ponsbourne St Marys JMI School
  HERT/BAY SG13 .... 174 D3
Pope Paul RC Primary School
  POTB/CUF EN6 .... 186 E4
Portland Industrial Estate
  ARL/CHE SG15 .... 25 L8
Potten End School
  BERK HP4 .... 148 A4
Potterells Medical Centre
  BRKMPK AL9 .... 172 C4
Potters Bar Cricket Club
  POTB/CUF EN6 .... 187 G3
Potters Bar Golf Club
  POTB/CUF EN6 .... 186 F2
Potter Street Primary School
  HLWE CM17 .... 163 G4
Prae Wood JMI School
  STALW/RED AL3 .... 151 M8
Presdales School
  WARE SG12 .... 138 C2
Prince Hotel
  STALW/RED AL3 .... 151 M5
Princess Alexandra Hospital
  HLW CM20 .... 6 C5
The Princess Helena College
  HTCHE/RSTV SG4 .... 68 D4
The Print Room/Museum Books
  & Prints
  BAR EN5 .... 200 D6
Priors Wood JMI School
  WARE SG12 .... 116 F7
Priory Middle School
  DUN/HR/TOD LU5 .... 81 H2
Priory School
  HTCH/STOT SG5 .... 38 D8
Public Swimming Pool
  OXHEY WD19 .... 206 D5
Pump House Theatre
  WAT WD17 .... 13 H6
The Purcell School
  BUSH WD23 .... 196 E3
Purford Green School
  HLWS CM18 .... 162 F4
Purwell JMI School
  HTCHE/RSTV SG4 .... 53 H2
Putteridge High School &
  Community College
  LTNE LU2 .... 66 B5
Putteridge Junior &
  Infant School
  LTNE LU2 .... 66 B5
Pyghtle School
  AMP/FLIT/B MK45 .... 48 D1
Queen Elizabeth II Hospital
  BRKMPK AL9 .... 134 F8
Queen Elizabeths Girls School
  BAR EN5 .... 200 E5
Queen Elizabeths School
  BAR EN5 .... 200 C4
Queen Mother Theatre
  HTCH/STOT SG5 .... 52 E3
Queensbury School
  DUN/WHIP LU6 .... 80 F4
Queensway Health Centre
  HAT AL10 .... 155 G4
Queenswood School
  BRKMPK AL9 .... 173 J7
Queen Victoria
  Memorial Hospital
  WLYN AL6 .... 111 M6
Radburn JMI School
  LWTH SG6 .... 40 B5
Radlett & Bushey
  Reform Synagogue
  RAD WD7 .... 183 M6
Radlett Cricket Club
  RAD WD7 .... 184 A8
Radlett Lodge School
  RAD WD7 .... 184 A3
Radlett Parochial
  Church Council
  RAD WD7 .... 183 M7
Radlett Preparatory School
  RAD WD7 .... 198 B1
R A F Edlesborough
  DUN/WHIP LU6 .... 103 L3
Ramridge Infant School
  LTNE LU2 .... 66 A8
Ramridge Junior School
  LTNE LU2 .... 65 M8
Ramsey Manor Lower School
  AMP/FLIT/B MK45 .... 35 J8
Ravenscroft School
  TRDG/WHET N20 .... 200 E8
Raynham Road
  Industrial Estate
  BSF CM23 .... 97 G2
Real Tennis Club
  BRKMPK AL9 .... 155 J5
Recreation Centre
  LTNE LU2 .... 66 B5
Redbourn Golf Club
  STALW/RED AL3 .... 130 A1
Redbourn Industrial Centre
  STALW/RED AL3 .... 130 A5
Redbourn Junior &
  Infant School
  STALW/RED AL3 .... 129 M4
Redbourn Recreation Centre
  STALW/RED AL3 .... 129 M3
Reddings JMI School
  HHS/BOV HP3 .... 166 E1
Red House Surgery
  RAD WD7 .... 183 M6
Red Rose Trading Estate
  BAR EN5 .... 201 J6
Reed First School
  ROY SG8 .... 31 K5
Regal Chambers Surgery
  HTCH/STOT SG5 .... 52 D2
Rhodes Museum &
  Commonwealth Centre
  BSF CM23 .... 96 F5
Richard Whittington JMI
  School
  BSF CM23 .... 96 D6

Richmond Hill School
  LTNE LU2 .... 2 F1
Rickmansworth Public
  Golf Course
  RKW/CH/CXG WD3 .... 204 F2
Rickmansworth School
  RKW/CH/CXG WD3 .... 194 F7
Rickmansworth Sports Club
  RKW/CH/CXG WD3 .... 194 D7
Riverside Business Park
  STSD CM24 .... 79 J4
Riverside Estate
  HARP AL5 .... 109 H6
Riverside Industrial Estate
  LCOL/BKTW AL2 .... 170 D6
R N I B Sunshine House School
  NTHWD HA6 .... 205 M6
Roaring Meg Retail Park
  STVG SG2 .... 4 E8
Roaring Meg Retail Park
  STVG SG2 .... 4 E9
Robertswood County Combined
  School
  CFSP/GDCR SL9 .... 202 E7
Roebuck JMI School
  STVGE SG2 .... 70 E8
Roecroft School
  HTCH/STOT SG5 .... 26 F4
Roger Bannister Sports Ground
  KTN/HRWW/W HA3 ...... 207 H6
Roger De Clare School
  STDN SG11 .... 75 K7
Roman Theatre
  STALW/RED AL3 .... 151 M7
Roman Way First School
  ROY SG8 .... 21 H1
Rosary Priory High School
  BUSH WD23 .... 197 K7
Rosedale Clinic
  CHESW EN7 .... 175 M6
Roseland Junior Middle & Infant
  School
  HOD EN11 .... 159 L1
Rossgate JMI School
  HHW HP1 .... 148 F5
Round Diamond School
  STVG SG1 .... 71 G2
Roundwood Park School
  HARP AL5 .... 108 D8
Rowans Junior Mixed
  Infant School
  WGCE AL7 .... 134 F1
The Royal Masonic School
  RKW/CH/CXG WD3 .... 194 C7
Royal Veterinary College
  BRKMPK AL9 .... 172 C7
Roydonbury Industrial Estate
  HLWW/ROY CM19 .... 161 L2
Roydon CP School
  HLWW/ROY CM19 .... 161 G2
Roydon Leisure Park
  HLWW/ROY CM19 .... 160 F1
Roysia Middle School
  ROY SG8 .... 21 H2
Roysia Surgery
  ROY SG8 .... 21 J2
Royston & District Hospital
  ROY SG8 .... 21 J6
Royston Golf Club
  ROY SG8 .... 21 H4
Royston Health Centre
  ROY SG8 .... 21 J4
Royston Museum
  ROY SG8 .... 21 H4
Royston Swimming Pool
  ROY SG8 .... 21 J4
Royston Town Football Club
  ROY SG8 .... 21 J3
Rudolf Steiner School
  KGLGY WD4 .... 166 D8
Rugby Club
  BSF CM23 .... 96 C1
Russell Clinic
  STALW/RED AL3 .... 10 E6
Russell County Primary School
  RKW/CH/CXG WD3 .... 193 G5
Ryde College
  WATW WD18 .... 195 K7
Ryde Junior Mixed
  Infant School
  BRKMPK AL9 .... 155 H2
Rye House Stadium
  HOD EN11 .... 160 C2
Ryelands JMI School
  HOD EN11 .... 160 A3
Sacred Heart Junior
  Middle & Infant School
  OXHEY WD19 .... 196 E7
Sacred Heart RC Junior & Infant
  School
  LTNE LU2 .... 65 M7
Sacred Heart RC School
  WARE SG12 .... 138 C1
Saffron Green First School
  BORE WD6 .... 199 J5
St Adrians RC JMI School
  STAL AL1 .... 169 H2
St Albans City Football Club
  STAL AL1 .... 11 J6
St Albans City Hospital
  STALW/RED AL3 .... 10 D3
St Albans Girls School
  STALW/RED AL3 .... 152 D3
St Albans High School for Girls
  STAL AL1 .... 11 G4
St Albans Lawn Tennis Club
  STALE/WH AL4 .... 153 H5
St Albans Museum
  STAL AL1 .... 11 G5
St Albans Musical Museum
  LCOL/BKTW AL2 .... 169 G7
St Albans Music School
  STALW/RED AL3 .... 10 E1
St Albans Organ Museum
  STAL AL1 .... 153 G8
St Albans Principal
  Health Centre
  STAL AL1 .... 10 F6

St Albans RC Primary School
  HLW CM20 .... 7 J2
St Albans Retail Park
  STAL AL1 .... 169 J1
St Albans School
  STALW/RED AL3 .... 10 D7
St Albans & Stephen RC
  JMI School
  STAL AL1 .... 11 L7
St Albans Synagogue
  STAL AL1 .... 10 E7
St Albans Synagogue
  STAL AL1 .... 11 H8
St Alban & Stephen Junior &
  Middle School
  STAL AL1 .... 11 K8
St Albert the Great RC
  Primary School
  HHS/BOV HP3 .... 166 F1
St Andrews C of E
  Primary School
  HERT/WAS SG14 .... 136 E3
St Andrews JMI School
  HTCHE/RSTV SG4 .... 52 F3
St Andrews School
  WARE SG12 .... 139 J6
St Anthonys RC Junior School
  WATN WD18 .... 195 K6
St Bernadette JMI School
  LCOL/BKTW AL2 .... 170 B6
St Catherine of Siena RC School
  GSTN WD25 .... 182 C3
St Christopher School
  LWTH SG6 .... 39 L7
St Christophers Lower School
  DUN/HR/TOD LU5 .... 63 L8
St Clement Danes School
  RKW/CH/CXG WD3 .... 193 J3
St Clements Mixed
  Junior School
  CHES/WCR EN8 .... 176 D6
St Columbas College
  Preparatory School
  STALW/RED AL3 .... 169 H1
St Cross RC Primary School
  HOD EN11 .... 159 M6
St Dominic RC School
  HARP AL5 .... 131 G2
St Edmunds College
  STDN SG11 .... 92 F7
St Elizabeths School & Home
  MHAD SG10 .... 119 G4
St Francis College
  LWTH SG6 .... 39 K6
St Georges School
  DUN/HR/TOD LU5 .... 81 J4
St Giles C of E Primary School
  POTB/CUF EN6 .... 185 M3
St Giles C of E Primary School
  POTB/CUF EN6 .... 186 A4
St Giles Surgery
  CSTG HP8 .... 202 B3
St Helens School
  NTHWD HA6 .... 205 K6
St Helens School
  STALE/WH AL4 .... 132 C2
St Hildas School
  HARP AL5 .... 108 E8
St Ignatius College
  EN EN1 .... 189 M8
St Ippolyts School
  HTCHE/RSTV SG4 .... 53 G7
St James Church School
  HLWS CM18 .... 162 C6
St Joan of Arc RC School
  RKW/CH/CXG WD3 .... 194 D8
St John Baptist School
  WARE SG12 .... 138 F5
St John Fisher RC JMI School
  STALE/WH AL4 .... 153 H4
St Johns C of E First School
  STAN HA7 .... 207 M4
St Johns C of E Junior &
  Infant School
  ENC/FH EN2 .... 189 G7
St Johns C of E Middle School
  STAN HA7 .... 207 M4
St Johns C of E Primary School
  WGCW AL8 .... 133 L5
St Johns C of E Primary School
  WLYN AL6 .... 112 E8
St Johns Industrial Estate
  RBSF CM22 .... 99 K3
St Johns Infant School
  RAD WD7 .... 183 L6
St Johns RC JMI School
  BLDK SG7 .... 40 E3
St Johns RC Junior Middle &
  Infant School
  RKW/CH/CXG WD3 .... 204 A1
St Johns School
  NTHWD HA6 .... 206 A6
St Josephs Junior &
  Infant School
  LTNN/LIM LU3 .... 64 F6
St Josephs RC JMI School
  CHES/WCR EN8 .... 190 D4
St Josephs RC Junior Middle &
  Infant School
  BSF CM23 .... 96 C4
St Josephs RC School
  OXHEY WD19 .... 206 A3
St Lawrence C of E School
  WAB EN9 .... 191 L4
St Lukes RC Primary School
  HLWW/ROY CM19 .... 162 B4
St Luke's School
  STALW/RED AL3 .... 129 M4
St Margarets of Scotland Junior
  School
  LTN LU1 .... 82 F5
St Margarets of Scotland RC Va
  Infant School
  LTN LU1 .... 82 F5
St Margarets School
  BUSH WD23 .... 196 H3

St Marks RC Comprehensive
  School
  HLWS CM18 .... 7 G8
St Marthas Convent Senior School
  EBAR EN4 .... 200 F2
St Martin De Porres Junior School
  LTNW/LEA LU4 .... 63 M6
St Martins School
  NTHWD HA6 .... 205 J5
St Marys Catholic School
  BSF CM23 .... 96 D3
St Marys Catholic School
  LTN LU1 .... 81 L4
St Marys C of E JMI School
  EBAR EN4 .... 201 K7
St Marys C of E
  Primary School
  STSD CM24 .... 79 K3
St Marys High School
  CHESW EN7 .... 190 F4
St Marys Infant School
  WLYN AL6 .... 112 A6
St Marys Junior & Infant School
  BLDK SG7 .... 40 D4
St Marys Junior Mixed School
  WARE SG12 .... 116 C7
St Marys RC JMI School
  ROY SG8 .... 21 J3
St Marys School
  STVGE SG2 .... 71 K7
St Marys Voluntary
  Lower School
  HTCH/STOT SG5 .... 26 F4
St Matthews Infant School
  LTNE LU2 .... 3 G3
St Meryl Junior Middle &
  Infant School
  OXHEY WD19 .... 206 D3
St Michaels C of E JMI School
  STALW/RED AL3 .... 10 A6
St Michaels Primary School
  BSF CM23 .... 96 D3
St Michaels RC School
  GSTN WD25 .... 182 C3
St Nichaols Recreation Centre
  STVG SG1 .... 55 G7
St Nicholas C of E
  Primary School
  STVG SG1 .... 5 H6
St Nicholas Health Centre
  STVG SG1 .... 54 E8
St Nicholas House School
  HHS/BOV HP3 .... 167 G4
St Nicholas Junior & Infant School
  LWTH SG6 .... 40 B1
St Nicholas School
  HLWE CM17 .... 142 E7
St Nicholas Voluntary
  Primary School
  HARP AL5 .... 130 F1
St Pauls Primary School
  KGLGY WD4 .... 181 H5
St Pauls Roman Catholic
  JMI School
  CHESW EN7 .... 176 A6
St Pauls Walden Junior School
  HTCHE/RSTV SG4 .... 86 C3
St Peters JMI School
  STAL AL1 .... 11 G9
St Peters Junior Middle & Infant
  School
  RKW/CH/CXG WD3 .... 204 A1
The St Philip Howard
  Catholic Primary School
  HAT AL10 .... 155 G5
St Roses Infants School
  HHW HP1 .... 165 M1
St Teresas RC School
  KTN/HRWW/W HA3 ...... 207 H8
St Thomas Moore RC
  JMI School
  BERK HP4 .... 146 F4
St Thomas More RC
  Junior & Infant School
  LWTH SG6 .... 39 J6
St Thomas of Canterbury
  Catholic School
  STDN SG11 .... 75 H7
St Vincents RC Lower School
  DUN/HR/TOD LU5 .... 63 H5
Salisbury Hall
  LCOL/BKTW AL2 .... 171 G8
Salisbury Infant School
  HAT AL10 .... 155 G3
Salisbury Lawn Tennis Club
  STAL AL1 .... 153 G6
Sandon Junior & Infant School
  BUNT SG9 .... 43 G1
Sandridge Gate
  Business Centre
  STALW/RED AL3 .... 152 E3
Sandridge JMI School
  STALE/WH AL4 .... 132 C8
Sandridge Youth Club &
  Sports Centre
  STALW/RED AL3 .... 153 G1
Sandringham School
  STALE/WH AL4 .... 153 G3
Saracens Rugby Football Club
  STHGT/OAK N14 .... 201 M7
Sarbir Industrial Park
  HLW CM20 .... 142 B5
Sarratt Junior Middle &
  Infant School
  RKW/CH/CXG WD3 .... 179 M7
Sawbridge Health Clinic
  SBW CM21 .... 120 D8
Schidegger Mis College
  LTN LU1 .... 2 C5
Schopwick Surgery
  BORE WD6 .... 198 C7
Sebright School
  STALW/RED AL3 .... 106 C6
The Sele School
  HERT/WAS SG14 .... 136 E4
Service Practice
  BERK HP4 .... 147 H6

Shaftesbury Industrial Centre *LWTH* SG6 40 A3
Shaftesbury School *KTN/HRWW/W* HA3 207 G8
Shakespeare Industrial Estate *WATN* WD24 195 M1
Sheepcot Medical Centre *GSTN* WD25 182 B5
Sheering C of E Primary School *RBSF* CM22 143 J1
Shenley JMI School *RAD* WD7 184 E5
Shen Nong Chinese Medical Centre *STAL* AL1 10 E7
Shenval Industrial Estate *HLW* CM20 141 M6
Shephall Infant School *STVGE* SG2 5 L9
Shephall Way Surgery *STVGE* SG2 5 M9
Shephall Way Surgery *STVGE* SG2 71 G8
Sheredes School *HOD* EN11 159 L5
Sherrardswood School *WLYN* AL6 112 C5
Shillington Lower School *HTCH/STOT* SG5 36 D1
Shirley's Temple *LTN* LU1 2 D5
Silk Mill House Museum *STALW/RED* AL3 129 M6
Simon Balle School *HERT/BAY* SG13 137 K5
Sir Frederic Osborn School *WGCE* AL7 135 G3
Sir John Lawes School *HARP* AL5 109 H7
Sir John Newsom School *WGCE* AL7 134 D7
Ski Centre *HHS/BOV* HP3 166 D1
Skidmore Clinic *RKW/CH/CXG* WD3 204 D1
Skyswood JMI School *STALE/WH* AL4 153 H4
Slip End Lower School *LTN* LU1 107 G1
Smug Oak Green Business Centre *LCOL/BKTW* AL2 169 G8
Snap Theatre *BSF* CM23 96 F3
Someries Castle *LTNE* LU2 84 D5
Someries Junior School *LTNE* LU2 66 B7
Sopwell House Hotel & Country Club *STAL* AL1 169 L3
South Bedfordshire Golf Club *LTNE* LU2 49 J8
South Bedfordshire Magistrates Court *LTN* LU1 2 D7
Southdown Industrial Estate *HARP* AL5 131 H2
Southfield Junior & Infant School *LTNW/LEA* LU4 63 L6
Southgate Compton Cricket Club *EBAR* EN4 201 L5
Southgate Health Centre *STVG* SG1 4 D5
South Hill JMI School *HHW* HP1 149 H8
South Lodge Queens School *BUSH* WD23 196 F4
South Street Surgery *BSF* CM23 96 E4
Spellbrook JMI School *BSF* CM23 120 E3
Spencer Primary Jm School *STALW/RED* AL3 11 H1
Sphere Industrial Estate *STAL* AL1 11 M8
The Spinney Junior & Infant Schools *HLW* CM20 7 L4
The Spires Shopping Centre *BAR* EN5 200 D4
Sports Centre *BORE* WD6 199 H2
Sports Centre *HHS/BOV* HP3 149 L8
Sports Centre *LCOL/BKTW* AL2 183 H2
Sports Ground *BAR* EN5 199 K7
Springmead JMI School *WGCE* AL7 135 H3
Stadium Industrial Estate *LTNW/LEA* LU4 64 A8
Stags School *STALW/RED* AL3 152 D3
Stanborough School *GSTN* WD25 182 A6
Stanborough School *WGCW* AL8 134 A6
Standon Health Centre *STDN* SG11 75 K8
Stanmore Road Health Centre *STVG* SG1 70 B3
Stansted Clinic *STSD* CM24 79 K3
Staple Tye Shopping Centre *HLWS* CM18 162 C5
Steeple Morden School *ROY* SG8 15 M8
Stevenage Borough Football Club *STVG* SG1 4 D4
Stevenage Borough Football Club *STVGE* SG2 4 F9
Stevenage Borough Football Club *STVGE* SG2 70 D8
Stevenage Business Park *STVG* SG1 55 H8
Stevenage Cricket Club *STVG* SG1 4 C2
Stevenage Leisure Centre *STVG* SG1 4 C4
Stevenage Mosque *STVG* SG1 70 C3
Stevenage Museum *STVG* SG1 4 E4
Stewards Comprehensive School *HLWS* CM18 162 B6
Stirling Industrial Centre *BORE* WD6 199 J6
Stocks Hotel Golf & Country Club *TRING* HP23 125 H3
Stockwell Lodge Medical Centre *CHESW* EN7 175 M7
Stockwood Park Museum *LTN* LU1 83 J6
Stockwood Park Rugby Club *LTN* LU1 83 J6
Stondon Lower School *HNLW* SG16 24 D7
Stondon Museum & Garden Centre *HNLW* SG16 24 E7
Stonehill JMI School *LWTH* SG6 39 K1
Stopsley High School & Community College *LTNE* LU2 65 L6
Stopsley Infant School *LTNE* LU2 65 M6
Stormont School *POTB/CUF* EN6 187 H2
Stortford Hall Industrial Park *BSF* CM23 97 G3
Stort Valley Industrial Estate *BSF* CM23 79 G8
Stotfold Health Centre *HTCH/STOT* SG5 26 D4
Strathmore Infant School *HTCH/STOT* SG5 38 D8
Stream Woods School *HAT* AL10 155 G6
Streetfield Middle School *DUN/HR/TOD* LU5 81 K4
Stroud Wood Business Centre *LCOL/BKTW* AL2 169 K6
Studham Vc Lower School *DUN/WHIP* LU6 105 G6
Studlands Rise First School *ROY* SG8 21 K5
Summercroft Junior & Infant School *BSF* CM23 97 H2
Summerswood Primary School *BORE* WD6 199 G5
Sumners Community Recreation Centre *HLWW/ROY* CM19 161 M6
Sunderland Estate *KGLGY* WD4 167 G8
Sundon Business Park *LTNN/LIM* LU3 64 A2
Sundon Industrial Estate *LTNN/LIM* LU3 64 A2
Sundon Lower School *LTNN/LIM* LU3 48 A6
Sundon Medical Centre *LTNN/LIM* LU3 64 B3
Sundon Park Junior School *LTNN/LIM* LU3 64 B2
Sunshine Riding School *LTNE* LU2 65 J2
Surrey Street School *LTN* LU1 3 G9
Swimming Pool *HERT/WAS* SG14 137 J2
Swimming Pool *STVG* SG1 4 D3
The Symonds Green Health Centre *STVG* SG1 69 M3
Tabard Rugby Club *RAD* WD7 184 A8
Takeley Business Centre *RBSF* CM22 99 H3
Takeley Gm Primary School *RBSF* CM22 99 H2
Tanners Wood Junior & Infant School *ABLGY* WD5 181 K3
Tannery Drift School *ROY* SG8 21 H4
Tanys Dell Junior School *HLW* CM20 141 M7
Telephone Exchange *WATW* WD18 12 F4
Telmere Industrial Estate *LTN* LU1 2 F9
Templewood School *WGCW* AL8 134 B2
Tennyson Road Primary School *LTN* LU1 83 K5
Tewin Road Business Centre *WGCE* AL7 134 D3
Tewin School *WLYN* AL6 113 K8
Tewin Water School *WLYN* AL6 113 G8
Thames Industrial Estate *DUN/WHIP* LU6 81 H2
Therfield First School *ROY* SG8 30 E3
Thomas Alleyne School *STVG* SG1 70 B2
The Thomas Coram Middle School *BERK* HP4 147 J8
Thomas Rivers Medical Centre *HLW* CM20 142 B3
The Thomas Rivers Medical Centre *SBW* CM21 142 B1
Thomas Tallis School *WAB* EN9 191 L4
Thorley Hill JMI School *BSF* CM23 96 E6
Thorn Grove Primary School *BSF* CM23 97 G4
Thornhill Lower School *DUN/HR/TOD* LU5 63 J3
Three Rivers District Council *OXHEY* WD19 206 B3
Three Rivers District Council *RKW/CH/CXG* WD3 194 D8
Thumbswood Infant School *WGCE* AL7 134 F5
Thundridge JMI School *WARE* SG12 116 C3
Timbers Clinic *KTN/HRWW/W* HA3 207 J6
Tithe Farm Lower School *DUN/HR/TOD* LU5 63 G4
Tonwell School *WARE* SG12 115 K3
Totternhoe Football Club *DUN/WHIP* LU6 80 B3
Totternhoe Lower School *DUN/WHIP* LU6 80 A3
Town Council *HAT* AL10 154 F4
Town Hall & Council Offices *LTN* LU1 2 E6
Townsend C of E School *STALW/RED* AL3 152 B2
Trent C of E Primary School *EBAR* EN4 201 L5
Trestle Theatre Co *STALE/WH* AL4 153 H8
Tricor Business Park *CHES/WCR* EN8 190 D5
Tricor Trading Estate *CHES/WCR* EN8 190 D5
Trident Industrial Estate *HOD* EN11 160 B4
Tring Health Centre *TRING* HP23 124 A6
Tring & New Mill Pre-school *TRING* HP23 124 A3
Tring School *TRING* HP23 124 A6
Tring Sports Centre *TRING* HP23 124 A6
Tring Town Council *TRING* HP23 123 M7
Trotts Hill JMI School *STVG* SG1 70 E1
Tudor School *HHS/BOV* HP3 166 D1
Turnford School *CHES/WCR* EN8 176 D7
Two Waters JMI School *HHS/BOV* HP3 166 C4
Twyford Business Centre *BSF* CM23 96 F5
Underhill Junior & Infant School *BAR* EN5 200 D6
University of Hertfordshire *GSTN* WD25 183 G7
University of Hertfordshire *HAT* AL10 154 C2
University of Hertfordshire *HAT* AL10 154 E6
University of Hertfordshire *HERT/BAY* SG13 137 L6
University of Hertfordshire *STAL* AL1 11 J9
University of London *ENC/FH* EN2 189 M7
University of Luton *LTN* LU1 2 E7
University of Luton *LTN* LU1 2 E8
University of Luton *LTN* LU1 3 G8
University of Luton *LTNE* LU2 66 C4
Vale Industrial Estate *WATW* WD18 205 H1
The Van Straten Clinic *LBUZ* LU7 101 M1
Verulam Golf Club *STAL* AL1 169 L1
Verulam Industrial Estate *STAL* AL1 169 L1
Verulamium Museum *STALW/RED* AL3 10 A6
Verulam School *STAL* AL1 11 M5
Victoria C of E Primary School *BERK* HP4 147 H6
Virgin Cinemas *HLW* CM20 141 L6
Waltham Abbey Swimming Pool *WAB* EN9 191 J6
Waltham Holy Cross Council *WAB* EN9 191 G4
Waltham Holy Cross Junior School *WAB* EN9 191 J4
Warden Hill Infant School *LTNN/LIM* LU3 65 H3
Warden Hill Junior School *LTNN/LIM* LU3 65 H3
Warden Lodge Surgery *CHES/WCR* EN8 190 C2
Ward Freman School *BUNT* SG9 58 C2
Wardown Park Museum *LTNE* LU2 65 H2
Wardown Swimming & Leisure Centre *LTNN/LIM* LU3 65 J8
Warrendell School *OXHEY* WD19 206 B3
Watchlytes JMI School *WGCE* AL7 135 G4
Waterside Industrial Estate *HOD* EN11 160 C5
Waterside (School) *BSF* CM23 78 D3
Waterways Heritage Museum *RKW/CH/CXG* WD3 204 D1
Watford Arches Retail Park *WAT* WD17 13 J7
Watford Borough Council *WAT* WD17 12 D2
Watford Business Centre *WAT* WD17 12 E2
Watford Central Swimming Baths *WAT* WD17 12 D2
Watford County Court *WAT* WD17 196 A3
Watford Eye Clinic *WATN* WD24 196 A1
Watford Football Club *WATW* WD18 12 E6
Watford General Hospital *WATW* WD18 12 E7
Watford Grammar School for Boys *WATW* WD18 12 A4
Watford Grammar School for Girls *WATW* WD18 13 G6
Watford Museum *WAT* WD17 13 H6
Watford Sports & Leisure Centre *GSTN* WD25 182 B4
Watford Springs Pool *WAT* WD17 13 H6
Watford United Synagogue *WAT* WD17 196 A2
Watling Lower School *DUN/WHIP* LU6 81 G3
Watling View School *STAL* AL1 169 J3
Wauluds Bank Junior & Infant School *LTNN/LIM* LU3 64 D3
Weald College *KTN/HRWW/W* HA3 207 K6
Weald First & Middle School *KTN/HRWW/W* HA3 207 L7
Weatherfield School *DUN/WHIP* LU6 80 D1
Wedgewood Gate Industrial Estate *STVG* SG1 55 G8
Welwyn Garden City Cricket Club *WGCW* AL8 112 B8
Welwyn Garden City Golf Club *WGCW* AL8 134 A3
Welwyn Garden Hebrew Congregation Synagogue *WGCW* AL8 134 A4
Welwyn Hatfield District Council *HAT* AL10 155 G4
Welwyn Hatfield Museum Service *BRKMPK* AL9 155 K2
Welwyn Rugby Football Club *WGCW* AL8 134 A5
Welwyn Tennis Club *WLYN* AL6 112 A6
Wenlock C of E School *LTNE* LU2 3 L5
The Wenta Business Centre *WATN* WD24 182 C8
Westbrook Hay Preparatory School *HHW* HP1 165 J2
Western House Hospital *WARE* SG12 116 C8
Westfield JMI School *HOD* EN11 159 L3
Westfield School *WATW* WD18 12 A8
West Hertfordshire College *WAT* WD17 12 C1
West Hertfordshire College *WAT* WD17 195 M1
West Herts College *BUSH* WD23 13 K3
West Herts College *HHW* HP1 149 H6
Westminster Lodge Sports Centre *STALW/RED* AL3 10 D9
Westminster Lodge Sports Centre *STALW/RED* AL3 169 H1
Wheatcroft JMI School *HERT/BAY* SG13 137 M3
Wheatfields Junior & Infant School *STALE/WH* AL4 153 G3
Whipperley Infant School *LTN* LU1 82 F4
Whipsnade Park Golf Club *BERK* HP4 104 D5
Whitefield Infant School *LTNN/LIM* LU3 64 D2
Whitehall Estate *HLWW/ROY* CM19 161 K3
Whitehead C of E Primary School *DUN/HR/TOD* LU5 63 G5
Whitehill Junior School *HTCHE/RSTV* SG4 52 F5
The Whitewebbs Museum of Transport & Industry *ENC/FH* EN2 189 G6
Whittings Hill School *BAR* EN5 200 B6
Whittlesea School *KTN/HRWW/W* HA3 207 H7
Whyllotts Council Offices *POTB/CUF* EN6 186 E3
Widford Junior & Infant School *WARE* SG12 118 C6
Wigginton JMI School *TRING* HP23 145 J1
Wigmore Primary School *LTNE* LU2 66 D8
Wilbury Junior Mixed School *LWTH* SG6 39 K4
William Austin Infant School *LTNN/LIM* LU3 65 H6
William Austin Junior School *LTNN/LIM* LU3 65 H6
William Penn Leisure Centre *RKW/CH/CXG* WD3 203 L1
William Ransom JMI School *HTCHE/RSTV* SG4 53 G3
Willow Field School *LTN* LU1 82 E6
Windermere JMI Primary School *STAL* AL1 170 A1
Windmill Trading Estate *LTN* LU1 3 J7
Wisteria House Clinic *WLYN* AL6 112 A4
Wodson Park Leisure Centre *WARE* SG12 116 B6
Wolsey Business Park *WATW* WD18 195 J8
Wood End JMI School *HARP* AL5 108 C7
Woodfield School *HHS/BOV* HP3 167 H1
Woodgreen Animal Shelter *ROY* SG8 23 M7
Woodhall Farm Surgery *HHNE* HP2 150 A1
Woodlands Infant School *BORE* WD6 198 F2
Woodside Clinic *DUN/HR/TOD* LU5 81 J2
Woodside Industrial Park *LWTH* SG6 40 A4
Woodside JMI School *CHESW* EN7 175 H8
Woolenwick Junior & Infant School *STVG* SG1 70 A4
Woolgrove School *LWTH* SG6 40 C5
Wormley JMI School *BROX* EN10 176 D2
Wroxham JMI School *POTB/CUF* EN6 186 C2
Wymondley Junior & Infant School *HTCHE/RSTV* SG4 53 J6
York House School *RKW/CH/CXG* WD3 194 E3

Page 21

J1
1 Larkin Cl
2 Owen Dr
3 Scott Cl
4 Shelley Cl
5 Spenser Cl
6 Swift Cl
7 Swinburne Cl
8 Teasdale Cl
9 Tennyson Cl
10 Thackeray Cl
11 Thomas Wy
12 Wordsworth Cl

L4
1 Goodwood Rd
2 Haydock Rd

Page 40

D1
1 Aldridge Ct
2 Brewery La
3 Farriers Cl
4 Jackson St
5 Lavender Ct
6 Meeting House La

Page 52

F4
1 Kardwell Cl
2 Kingfisher Ct
3 Lovell Cl
4 Orlando Cl
5 Riddy Hill Cl
6 South Hill Cl
7 Whitegale Cl

Page 64

B5
1 Chaworth Gn
2 Glaisdale
3 Levendale
4 Newtondale
5 Thorntondale
6 Wharfdale

C7
1 Eynsford Rd

D3
1 Harding Cl
2 Strawberry Fld
3 Thricknells Cl
4 Vadis Cl

D7
1 Wyvern Cl

E4
1 Lamorna Cl

E6
1 Banbury Cl

F1
1 Ashdale Gdns
2 Ryefield

F2
1 Barleyvale
2 Corinium Gdns
3 Huckleberry Cl

F3
1 Croxton Cl
2 Cubbington Cl
3 Green Milverton
4 Quickswood

F4
1 Carsdale Cl

F5
1 Lampitts Cross

F6
1 Howard Cl

F8
1 Crosby Cl

Page 65

J3
1 Beckham Cl
2 Hanworth Cl
3 Saffron Cl
4 Walsingham Cl

J4
1 Broadacres
2 Saffron Cl
3 Thetford Gdns

Page 83

J3
1 Alma Link
2 Buxton Rd
3 Gordon St
4 Hastings St
5 King St
6 Mersey St
7 Napier Rd
8 Regent St
9 Rothesay Rd

J4
1 Brecon Cl
2 Ebenezer St
3 Elizabeth St
4 Spring Pl
5 Western Rd
6 Windsor Wk

K3
1 Barbers La
2 Bute Sq
3 Castle St
4 Chapel St
5 Cheapside
6 Cheapside Sq
7 Flowers Wy
8 George St West
9 Library Rd
10 Park St
11 Stuart St

K5
1 Hoo St
2 Somersby Cl

Page 96

C2
1 Stort Lodge

E3
1 Barrett La
2 Devoils La
3 Market St
4 Nails La
5 Old River La
6 Portland Pl
7 Sworders Yd

E4
1 Bowling Cl
2 Chestnut Cl
3 Stort Rd
4 Swan Ct
5 Trinity St

F3
1 Fuller Ct
2 The Old Maltings

F4
1 Great Eastern Cl
2 Station Rd

F5
1 Kimberley Cl

F6
1 Mitre Gdns

Page 112

B5
1 Church Pl
2 Holly Hall Cl
3 Mimram Rd
4 Orchard Rd
5 Prospect Pl
6 St Marys Cl
7 Welwyn Hall
8 Wendover Ct

B6
1 Broomfield Cl
2 Hertford Rd
3 Maran Av

Page 134

B5
1 Fordwich Rd
2 Hobbs Wy
3 Honeycroft
4 Stanborough Rd

C2
1 Hawthorns
2 Pentley Pk
3 Sherrardspark Rd
4 The Vineyard

C6
1 West Burrowfield

D8
1 Drycroft
2 Katescroft

E1
1 Blythway
2 Northway
3 Nursery Hl

E3
1 Black Fan Rd
2 Bridgefields
3 Martinfield
4 Sutherland Ct
5 Tewin Ct

E4
1 Home Meadow
2 Swallowfields
3 Verlum Cl

E5
1 Cranborne Gdns
2 Shortlands Gn

E6
1 Burgundy Cft
2 Meadway

E7
1 Green Acres
2 Ryelands

E8
1 Wyndhams End

F1
1 Quickbeams

F5
1 Corners

F4
1 Watchmead

F5
1 Heronswood Pl
2 Poundwell

F7
1 Beehive La
2 Howlands

Page 135

G5
1 Amwell Common
2 Batford Cl
3 Bushey Cl
4 Bushey Gn
5 Graveley Dell
6 Thundridge Cl
7 Wareside Cl

G6
1 Autumn Gv
2 Breakmead
3 Hempstall

H4
1 Andrewsfield
2 Bericot Wy
3 Beverley Gdns
4 Douglas Wy
5 Elizabeth Cl
6 Jackdaws
7 Lindbergh
8 Mitchell Cl

Page 137

G4
1 Cedar Cl
2 Cross La
3 Grange Cl
4 Greenways
5 Millstream Cl
6 Royston Cl
7 Sele Ml

J4
1 Bell La
2 Bircherley Ct
3 Bluecoats Av
4 Church St
5 The Gulphs
6 Maidenhead St
7 Maidenhead Yd
8 Market Pl
9 Market St
10 Millers Yd
11 Nicholas La
12 Oldhall St
13 Parliament Sq
14 St John's St
15 Salisbury Sq
16 The Wash

M3
1 King's Rd

M4
1 Foxholes Av
2 Honeysuckle Cl
3 Spinney St

Page 148

F4
1 Plantation Wk
2 Spencer Wy
3 Whitestone Wk

F5
1 Galley Hl
2 Marnham Ri
3 The Nokes
4 Plantation Wk
5 Robbs Cl

Page 149

G5
1 Cooks Vennel
2 Pierian Spring
3 Timplings Rw
4 Willow Wy

G6
1 Bards Cnr
2 Lockers Park La
3 Minstrel Cl
4 Saffron La

G7
1 The Farthings
2 Park Hill Rd

G8
1 Linden Gld
2 The Poplars
3 Thistlecroft
4 Woodland Cl
5 Woodland Pl

H6
1 Bury Gn

H7
1 Combe St

H8
1 Vicarage Cl

J2
1 Tintagel Cl

J3
1 Leven Wy

J5
1 Andrews Cl
2 The Bounce
3 Boxhill
4 Broadcroft
5 Mead Temple
6 Sharpcroft
7 Typleden Cl

J6
1 The Brackens
2 Chapel Cottages
3 Fensoms Alley
4 Fensom's Cl
5 Garland Cl
6 Normandy Ct
7 Pine Tree Cl
8 Union Cl

J7
1 Caernarvon Cl
2 Concorde Dr

J8
1 Albion Hl

K2
1 Helston Gv

K3
1 Thatchers Cft

K4
1 Watling Cl

K6
1 Clarendon Cl
2 East Mimms
3 Long Mimms
4 Manley Rd

K7
1 Chalkdell Hl
2 Quendell Wk

K8
1 Corfe Cl
2 Denbigh Cl
3 Furtherground
4 Pinewood Gdns
5 Sherbourne Cl

L2
1 Clyde Sq
2 Great Palmers
3 Mersey Pl
4 Robin Hood Meadow

L3
1 Cwmbran Ct
2 Kilbride Ct
3 Peterlee Ct
4 Sherwood Pl
5 Welwyn Ct

L4
1 Callisto Ct
2 Ganymede Pl
3 Pentland

L5
1 Nicholas Wy
2 Tannsmore Cl
3 Triton Wy

L6
1 Coral Gdns
2 Hammer La
3 Rice Cl

L7
1 The Queen's Sq
2 Sawyers Wy
3 Sheepcote Rd

L8
1 St Albans Rd
2 Wadley Cl

M1
1 Horton Gdns
2 Wareside
3 Widford Ter

M2
1 The Dart
2 Denham Cl
3 Frome Sq

M5
1 Sainfoin End
2 Winds End Cl

M6
1 Saracens Head
2 Southernwood Cl

M8
1 Grange Cl
2 Haddon Cl
3 Mariner Wy
4 Marston Cl
5 Sandmere Cl

Page 152

C7
1 Bowes Lyon Ms
2 Britton Av
3 French Rw
4 The Maltings
5 New Kent Rd
6 Selby Av
7 Upper Dagnall St
8 Waddington Rd

D8
1 Approach Rd
2 Black Cut
3 Devon Ct
4 Henrys Grant
5 Hopkins Yd
6 Lime Tree Pl
7 Lower Paxton Rd
8 Vernon's Cl

F3
1 The Berries
2 Bolingbrook
3 Lay Brook

Page 153

G8
1 Calbury Cl
2 Clenlyn Av
3 Gordon Cl
4 Haig Cl

H1
1 St Leonard's Ct

Page 159

L8
1 Ashbourne Rd
2 Royce Cl

M5
1 Cedar Gn
2 The Knowle
3 Riversmead
4 Woodlands Cl

Page 162

E4
1 Fountain Farm
2 Oak End

E5
1 Sunny Cft
2 Tye Green Village

F5
1 Clifton Hatch

Page 166

C1
1 Charlesworth Cl
2 Corner Hall
3 Forest Av
4 Ranworth Cl
5 Stuarts Cl
6 Talbot Ct

C3
1 Edward Ct
2 Frogmore Rd
3 Henry St
4 Kents Av
5 Millbank
6 St Andrew's Rd
7 White Lion St
8 William St

F8
1 Chantry Cl
2 The Glebe
3 Langley Hill Cl
4 Little Hayes
5 Tooveys Mill Cl
6 Willow Edge

Page 175

J5
1 Beaumont Vw
2 Macintosh Cl
3 The Mount

L8
1 Caldecot Av
2 Cuthbert Cl
3 Shanklin Cl
4 Wolsey Av

Page 176

C8
1 Niagara Cl

D4
1 The Canadas
2 Nunsbury Dr
3 Nursery Rd

E1
1 Caldecot Wy
2 Lichfield Wy
3 The Sidings

Page 181

M3
1 Edinburgh Dr
2 Hurricane Wy
3 Katherine Pl
4 Lysander Wy
5 Maple Leaf Cl
6 Mitchell Cl
7 Shackleton Wy

Page 182

F1
1 Grassington Cl
2 Meadow Cl
3 Russell Ct

F2
1 Juniper Av

Page 190

A2
1 Ermine Cl
2 Greenwood Cl
3 Hargreaves Cl
4 Lilac Cl

A6
1 Bullsmoor Gdns

A7
1 Charnwood Rd

C4
1 Lambton Cl
2 Leven Cl
3 Monarch's Wy
4 Park Rd
5 Stoneleigh Cl

C5
1 Dumbarton Av

C6
1 Abridge Gv
2 Dewgrass Gv
3 The Greenway
4 Hawksmead Cl
5 Kingsfield Wy

C8
1 Hartmoor Ms

D1
1 Foster Cl
2 Guinevere Gdns
3 Roberts Cl
4 Roswell Cl

D2
1 Acton Cl
2 Garland Cl
3 Holme Cl
4 Russell's Dr

D3
1 Burleigh Rd

D4
1 Cross Rd

D5
1 Abbey Rd
2 Lodge Crs
3 Station Ap
4 Trust Rd

D7
1 Ferns Cl

D8
1 Coldham Gv
2 Cornhill Dr
3 The Generals Wk
4 Johnby Cl
5 Newport Cl

E5
1 Fowley Cl
2 Queens Wy

F5
1 Berwick Cl

F8
1 King Henry's Ms

Page 191

H3
1 Hereward Cl

H5
1 Fountain Pl
2 King George Rd
3 Milton Ct
4 Paradise Rd
5 Rue De St Lawrence
6 Silver St

M5
1 Hawk Cl
2 Lamplighters Cl

Page 196

A2
1 Lowestoft Rd

A3
1 Albert Rd North
2 Canterbury Rd
3 Franklin Rd
4 Keston Ms
5 Shady La
6 Wellington Rd
7 Westland Rd
8 West St

A4
1 Albert Rd South
2 Clarendon Rd
3 Monmouth Rd

A5
1 Fearnley St
2 The Hornets
3 Percy Rd
4 Wellstones

A8
1 Brookmill Cl
2 Silk Mill Rd
3 The Willows

B3
1 Anglian Cl
2 Aston Cl
3 Keele Cl
4 Octavia Ct
5 Orphanage Rd
6 St Pauls Wy

B4
1 The Broadway
2 Earl St
3 Lord St
4 Ottoman Ter
5 Queen's Pl
6 Queen's Rd
7 Shaftesbury Rd
8 Stanley Rd
9 Trinity Hall Cl

B5
1 Cambridge Rd
2 Chapmans Yd
3 Church St
4 The Crescent
5 Derby Rd
6 Granville Rd
7 Kings Cl
8 Lower Derby Rd
9 Market Pl
10 New St
11 Smith St
12 Water La
13 Watford Field Rd
14 Woodmans Yd

C6
1 Bridge Pl

C7
1 St Matthews Cl

C8
1 Lime Cl

D3
1 Scottswood Cl
2 Sycamore Cl

D5
1 Brambling Cl
2 Hastings Wy
3 Siskin Cl

D7
1 Avenue Ter
2 Brick Kiln Cl
3 Caroline Pl
4 Hillside Cl
5 Rowley Cl
6 Warneford Pl

D8
1 Field End Cl
2 Maxwell Ri

E3
1 Walnut Gn

F3
1 Harts Cl

F7
1 Church Wk
2 Cow La
3 Montague Hall Pl
4 The Studios

Page 197

G7
1 Baird Cl
2 The Close
3 Fidler Pl
4 Herkomer Cl
5 Meadowcroft
6 Mortimer Cl
7 Ryder Cl
8 Wheelright Cl

Page 198

C2
2 Stainer Rd

C7
1 The Bartons
2 Fox Cl
3 Georges Mead
4 Oak Tree Ct
5 Romeland
6 Stuart Ct
7 Webber Cl
8 Westview Cl
9 Yew Tree Ct

C8
1 Dylan Cl

E3
1 Badgers Cl
2 Chiltern Cl
3 Holmdale Cl
4 Holme Pk
5 The Pines

F1
1 Brampton Ter
2 Pursley Gdns
3 St Neots Cl
4 Sawtry Wy
5 Stilton Pth
6 Wentbridge Pth

F3
1 Badminton Cl

F5
1 Brownlow Rd
2 Dunnock Cl
3 Goldfinch Wy

Page 199

H2
1 Cygnet Cl
2 Neagle Cl
3 Niven Cl
4 Palmers Rd

J7
1 Connemara Cl
2 Pinto Cl

Page 206

B4
1 Muirfield Gn
2 Mundesley Cl
3 Newbiggin Pth
4 St Martins Cl

B5
1 Bognor Gdns
2 Bromborough Gn
3 Darwin Gdns
4 Doncaster Gn
5 Harborne Cl
6 Huntercombe Gdns
7 Kenilworth Gdns
8 Morriston Cl
9 Muirfield Cl

B8
1 Welch Cl

C5
1 Ashford Gn
2 Falkirk Gdns
3 Gleneagles Cl
4 Letchworth Cl
5 Leven Cl

E7
1 Cherry Croft Gdns
2 Helston Cl
3 St Cuthberts Gdns
4 Thorndyke Cl
5 Uxbridge Rd (Hatch End)

Page 207

J2
1 Bushell Gn
2 Shepherds Wk

J3
1 Templars Dr
2 Warburton Cl

L6
1 Berwick Cl
2 Coppice Cl
3 Fortnums Acre
4 Jellicoe Gdns
5 Newbolt Rd
6 Rowan Cl
7 Uxbridge Rd (Stanmore)
8 Waleran Cl

L8
1 Broadlawns Ct
2 Woodpecker Cl

M5
1 Hathaway Cl

M8
1 Mountbel Rd

Notes